Moody's® Handbook of Dividend Achievers

1994

SUZANNE WITTEBORT, *Associate Director*

DANNY A. ZOTTOLI, JR., *Publisher*

HOWARD G. KIEDAISCH, *Managing Director*

Editors

MONICA D. GARRETT   SAMUEL A. YOUNG

Business Analysts

BRAD A. ARMBRUSTER   THOMAS J. MALLIS
D. WOODROW BIRD III   RICHARD V. McPHAIL III
MICHAEL A. GOLDEN   STACY K. MUNN
ANDREW HERRNSTEIN   SEAN POLLAND

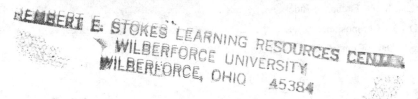

REMBERT E. STOKES LEARNING RESOURCES CENTER
WILBERFORCE UNIVERSITY
WILBERFORCE, OHIO 45384

Moody's Investors Service

a company of
The Dun & Bradstreet Corporation

TABLE OF CONTENTS

REF
HG   Moody's handbook of
4050   dividend achievers.
.M66

Page

HOW TO USE THIS BOOK 3a

SPECIAL FEATURES

Moody's Dividend Achievers 7a
Ranking By Selected Investment Criteria 11a
Classification of Companies by Industry...................................... 12a

CHARTS

Dow-Jones Industrial Average 16a
New York Stock Exchange Index 17a
American Stock Exchange Index 18a
NASDAQ - Composite 19a
Moody's Daily Commodity Price Index 20a

COMPANY REPORTS   Arranged Alphabetically

Moody's Handbook of Dividend Achievers is a compact, easy-to-use reference for people who recognize that investing wisely in stocks with increasing annual dividend payments can be a profitable endeavor. This valuable investment tool provides basic financial and business information on 332 companies that have increased their dividends consistently over the past 10 years. The presentation of background information plus current and historical data provides the answers to three basic questions:

1. What does the company do?
   (See H)
2. How has it done in the past?
   (See B, D, E, G, J, K)
3. How is it doing now?
   (See D, E, F, G, I)

The following common terms are used throughout the *Moody's Handbook of Dividend Achievers:*

A. CAPSULE STOCK INFORMATION – The stock symbol, plus the approximate yield afforded by the indicated dividend, based on a recent price, and the price/earnings ratio are shown. Also included is an indication whether a company's stock can be purhased on margin.

B. LONG-TERM PRICE CHART – The chart illustrates the pattern of monthly stock price movements, fully adjusted for stock dividends and splits. Monthly stock trading volume is also included.

C. PRICE SCORES – Below each company's price/volume chart are *Moody's Price Scores*. These are two basic measures of the stock's performance. Each stock is measured against the New York Stock Exchange Composite Index. A score of 100 indicates that the stock did as well as the New York Stock Exchange Composite Index during the time period. A score of less than 100 means that the stock did not do as well; a score of more than 100 means that the stock outperformed the NYSE Composite Index.

Thus, *Moody's Price Scores* allow the user to make easy, across-the-board comparisons of various stocks' historical price performance. All stocks, regardless of exchange, are measured against the NYSE Composite Index so that their scores may be compared with any other stock.

The *7 YEAR PRICE SCORE* mirrors the common stock's price growth over the previous 7 years. The higher the price score, the better the relative performance. It is based on the ratio of the latest 12-month average price to the current 7-year average. This ratio is then put on an index basis in which the same ratio for the market as a whole (the New York Stock Exchange Composite Index) is taken as 100.

The *12 MONTH PRICE SCORE* is a similar measurement but for a shorter period of time. It indicates the recent vigor or sluggishness of a stock's price movement. It is based on the ratio of the latest 2-month average price to the current 12-month average. As was done for the Long-Term Price Score, this ratio is also indexed to the same ratio for the market as a whole.

In both cases, all prices are adjusted for all stock dividends and splits.

D. INTERIM EARNINGS (Per Share) – This figure essentially is what has been reported by the company. Figures are reported before extraordinary items, discontinued operations and cummulative effects of accounting changes (unless otherwise noted).

E. INTERIM DIVIDENDS (Per Share) – The cash dividends are the actual dollar amounts declared by the company. No adjustments have been made for stock dividends and splits. **Ex-Dividend Date:** a stockholder must purchase the stock prior to this date in order to be entitled to the dividend. The **Record Date** indicates the date on which the shareholder had to have been a holder of record in order to have qualified for the dividend. The **Payable Date** indicates the date the company paid or intends to pay the dividend. The cash amount shown in the first column is followed by a letter (example ''Q'' for quarterly) to indicate the frequency of the dividend.

Indicated Dividend is the annualized rate (fully adjusted) of the latest regular cash dividend.

F. CAPITALIZATION – These are certain items in the company's capital account. Both the dollar amounts and their respective percentages are given.

ILLUSTRATIVE INC.

YIELD 2.2%
P/E RATIO 16.1

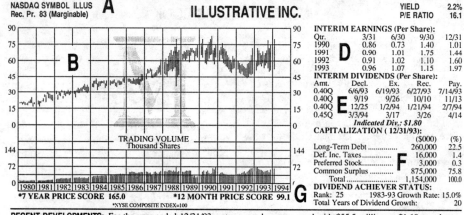

B

C *7 YEAR PRICE SCORE 165.0   *12 MONTH PRICE SCORE 99.1
*NYSE COMPOSITE INDEX=100

TRADING VOLUME
Thousand Shares

INTERIM EARNINGS (Per Share): **D**

Qtr.	3/31	6/30	9/30	12/31
1990	0.86	0.73	1.40	1.01
1991	0.90	1.01	1.75	1.44
1992	0.91	1.02	1.10	1.60
1993	0.96	1.07	1.15	1.97

INTERIM DIVIDENDS (Per Share):

Amt.	Decl.	Ex.	Rec.	Pay.
0.40Q	6/6/93	6/19/93	6/27/93	7/14/93
0.40Q	9/19	9/26	10/10	11/13
0.40Q	12/25	1/2/94	1/21/94	2/7/94
0.45Q	3/3/94	3/17	3/26	4/14

E

Indicated Div.: $1.80

CAPITALIZATION (12/31/93):

	($000)	(%)
Long-Term Debt	260,000	22.5
Def. Inc. Taxes	16,000	1.4
Preferred Stock	3,000	0.3
Common Surplus	875,000	75.8
Total	1,154,000	100.0

F

DIVIDEND ACHIEVER STATUS: **G**
Rank: 25   1983-93 Growth Rate: 15.0%
Total Years of Dividend Growth: 20

RECENT DEVELOPMENTS: For the year ended 12/31/93, net sales were $3.68 billion compared with $3.40 billion last year. Net income was $185.4 million or $5.15 per share versus $178.0 million or $4.63 per share a year ago. Increased sales were due in part to an overall acceptance of Company's new products. The start-up costs of these new products limited net income growth. For the fourth quarter ended 12/31/92, net income rose to $58.0 million or $1.97 **I** per share compared with $55.5 million or $1.60 per share a year ago. Sales totaled $860.0 million, up 4% from $825.0 million a year ago. Sales and earnings in foreign markets advanced 17% and 20%, respectively over the year earlier results. During the fourth quarter, the Company introduced a new drug product for hypertension, called PresLoe, which has had a favorable market impact.

BUSINESS **H**

ILLUSTRATIVE INC. is engaged in the research, manufacture and marketing of ethical pharmaceuticals, proprietary drugs and other products used in human and animal health care. It also provides medical services and manufactures medical instruments. Products are distributed in the U.S. and most free-world countries. Major products include tranquilizers, amphetamines, specialty antibiotics and vaccines; animals health products include vaccines and feed additives; medical services include a full range of pathology services. Sales (operating income) in 1993 were as follows: pharmaceutical products, 55% (48%); medical services and instruments 20% (18%); industrial products, 7% (8%); and others, 18% (26%).

ANNUAL EARNINGS AND DIVIDENDS PER SHARE **J**

	1993	1992	1991	1990	1989	1988	1987
Earnings Per Share	5.15	4.63	5.10	4.00	4.16	4.10	3.70
Dividends Per Share	1.55	1.36	1.32	1.23	1.16	1.06	0.96
Dividend Payout%	30.1	29.4	25.9	30.7	27.9	25.6	25.9

ANNUAL FINANCIAL DATA

RECORD OF EARNINGS (IN MILLIONS): **K**

	1993	1992	1991	1990	1989	1988	1987
Net Sales	3,675.0	3,400.0	3,214.2	2,526.3	2,500.6	2,234.8	2,116.5
Costs and Expenses	3,200.2	3,100.0	2,900.1	2,399.1	2,210.4	2,074.3	1,937.4
Depreciation	20.0	18.0	19.0	17.4	15.3	16.4	12.3
Operating Profit	455.0	282.0	295.1	109.4	274.9	144.1	166.8
Income Before Taxes	242.4	230.0	220.1	123.6	251.3	133.6	118.7
Income Taxes	57.0	52.0	75.1	70.2	84.0	41.1	38.1
Net Income	185.4	178.0	145.5	53.3	167.3	92.5	80.6
Aver. Com. Shs. (000)	36,000	17,500	17,000	15,250	15,200	14,530	14,500

BALANCE SHEET (IN MILLIONS):

Cash, Securities, Etc.	380.0	350.0	310.6	270.3	290.4	282.0	279.5
Receivables	140.0	120.0	125.0	120.9	130.3	126.3	120.3
Inventories	250.0	230.0	220.2	206.5	200.6	202.4	190.6
Gross Property	1,600.0	1,500.9	1,000.7	1,100.0	1,004.5	980.6	902.5
Depreciation Reserve	513.1	510.1	500.1	510.1	475.0	450.3	470.1
Long-Term Debt	260.0	249.0	229.4	300.5	296.1	301.6	322.3
Net Stockholders' Equity	875.0	540.0	530.1	523.7	518.2	504.6	501.4
Total Assets	2,800.0	2,700.0	2,432.0	2,031.6	1,963.4	1,825.4	1,612.0
Total Current Assets	1,960.0	1,400.0	1,021.4	926.2	700.1	626.3	650.0
Total Current Liabs.	973.0	470.0	426.5	400.1	296.4	251.4	225.3
Net Working Capital	987.0	930.0	594.9	526.1	403.7	374.9	424.7
Yr.-End Com. Shs. (000)	35,000	16,500	16,000	15,063	15,047	14,490	14,500

STATISTICAL RECORD:

Operating Profit Margin %	12.4	8.3	9.2	4.3	11.0	6.4	7.0
Book Value Per Share	25.00	32.73	33.13	34.53	34.31	34.80	37.12
Return on Equity %	21.2	33.0	27.4	10.2	32.3	18.3	16.1
Return on Assets %	6.6	6.6	5.9	2.6	8.5	5.1	5.0
Average Yield %	2.3	2.3	2.1	1.7	1.7	2.1	1.8
P/E Ratio	16.5-9.5	15.6-9.5	15.2-9.4	21.1-14.9	18.0-14.4	19.8-9.3	16.6-11.7
Price Range	85-49	72-44	77½-48	84½-59½	75-59¾		81-38 61½-43¼

Statistics are as originally reported.

OFFICERS:
V. Martinez, Chmn.
S.R. Fogle, Vice Chmn.
S.D. Johnson, Pres. & C.E.O.
S.S. Stephens, V.P.-Fin
Y. Cohen, Secretary
S. Mankovich, Treas.

INCORPORATED: DE, June, 1929

PRINCIPAL OFFICE: 99 Church St., New York, NY 10007

TELEPHONE NUMBER: (212) 885-2160

NO. OF EMPLOYEES: 24,000 (approx.)

ANNUAL MEETING: In July

SHAREHOLDERS: 15,500

INSTITUTIONAL HOLDINGS: **L**
No. of Institutions: 15
Shares Held: 5,700,675

REGISTRAR(S): First National Bank of N.Y.

TRANSFER AGENT(S): First National Bank of N.Y.

HOW TO USE THIS BOOK (Continued)

Long-term Debt is the total amount of debt owed by the company due beyond one year.

Capital Lease Obligations is shown as a separate caption when displayed on the balance sheet as such.

Deferred Income Taxes represents the company's tax liability arising from accelerated depreciation and investment tax credit.

Preferred Stock and/or Preference Stock is the sum of equity issues, exclusive of common stock, whose holders have a prior claim, ahead of the common shareholders, to the income of the company while it continues to operate and to its assets in the event of dissolution.

Minority Interest in this instance is a capital item reflecting the share of ownership by an outside party in a consolidated subsidiary of the company.

Common and Surplus is the sum of the stated or par value of the common stock, plus additional paid-in capital and retained earnings less the dollar amount of treasury shares.

G. DIVIDEND ACHIEVER STATUS – The company's rank among the dividend achievers is given. Also included is the company's average annual compound dividend growth rate for the latest 10 year period and the number of consecutive calendar years the cash payment increased.

H. COMPANY BUSINESS – This is what a company does: its products or services, its markets and production facilities.

I. RECENT DEVELOPMENTS – This paragraph focuses on the current position of an individual company. In addition to analysis of recently released sales and earnings figures, items covered include, where applicable (if available), new product introductions, capital expenditures, expanded operations, acquisitions, labor developments, equity or debt financing, the rate of incoming orders, the level of backlog and other operating statistics.

J. ANNUAL EARNINGS AND DIVIDENDS PER SHARE – These figures are fully adjusted for all stock dividends and stock splits.

Earnings Per Share are as reported by the company except for adjustment for certain items as footnoted.

Dividends Per Share represent the sum of all cash payments on a calendar year basis. Any fiscal year ending prior to June 30, for example, is shown with dividends for the prior calendar year.

Dividend Payout % is the percentage of cash paid out of **Earnings Per Share**.

K. ANNUAL FINANCIAL DATA – Here is pertinent earnings and balance sheet information essential to analyzing a Company's performance. The comparisons, each year shown as originally reported, provide the necessary historical perspective to intelligently review the various operating and financial trends.

RECORD OF EARNINGS:

Net Sales is the total income from operations; non-operating revenues are excluded.

Revenues is the total income from operations including non-operating revenues.

Costs and Expenses are the total of all costs related to the operation of the business – including cost of sales, selling, and general and administrative expenses. Excluded items are depreciation, interest and non-operating expenses.

Depreciation includes all non-cash charges such as depletion and amortization as well as depreciation.

Operating Profit is the profit remaining after deducting depreciation as well as all operating costs and expenses from the company's net sales and revenues. The figure is *before* interest expenses, extraordinary gains and charges, and income and expense items of a non-operating nature.

Income Before Taxes is the remaining income *after* deducting all costs, expenses, property charges, interest, etc. but *before* deducting income taxes.

Income Taxes are as reported by the company and include both the amount of current taxes actually paid out and the amount deferred.

Minority Interest in the income statement is that portion of *profits* of a consolidated subsidiary that is allocated to a minority owner of that subsidiary who shares in the results of its operations.

Net Income is as reported by the company, before extraordinary gains and losses.

Average Common Shares is the weighted average number of shares including common equivalent shares outstanding during the year, as reported by the company.

BALANCE SHEET:

Cash and Securities comprise unrestricted cash and temporary investments in marketable securities, such as U.S. Government securities, certificates of deposit and short-term investments.

Receivables are all accounts due from customers, etc., shown as current assets.

Inventories are the sum of the raw materials, work-in-process and finished goods as valued by the company.

Gross Property is total fixed assets, including all property, land, plants, buildings, equipment, fixtures, etc.

Depreciation Reserve is the accumulation of annual charges to income representing a computed decline in the value of an asset due to wear and tear or obsolescence.

Long-term Debt is the total long-term debt (due beyond one year) reported by the company, including bonds, capital lease obligations, notes, mortgages, debentures, etc.

Stockholders' Equity is the sum of all capital stock accounts – stated values of preferred and common stock, paid-in capital, earned surplus (retained earnings), etc., net of all treasury stock.

Total Assets represent the sum of all tangible and intangible assets as reported.

Total Current Assets are all of the company's short-term assets such as cash, marketable securities, inventories, etc., as reported.

Total Current Liabilities are all of the obligations of the company due within one year, as reported.

Net Working Capital is derived by subtracting Current Liabilities from Current Assets.

Year-end Common Shares are the number of shares outstanding as of the date of the company's annual report, exclusive of treasury stock and adjusted for subsequent stock dividends and splits.

STATISTICAL RECORD:

Operating Profit Margin is the amount of operating profit derived from net sales or revenues.

Book Value Per Share is calculated by taking the aggregate dollar value of tangible assets as carried on the Company's books and dividing it by the outstanding shares of common stock at year end. This figure is fully adjusted for all stock dividends and splits. Book value for Banks and Public Utilities is as reported by the company.

Return on Equity, a measure of profitability, is the ratio of net income to net stockholders' equity, expressed as a percentage.

Return on Assets is the ratio of net income to total assets, expressed as a percentage.

Average Yield is the ratio (expressed as a percentage) of the annual dividend to the mean price of the common stock (average of the high and low for the year). Both prices and dividends are for calendar years.

Price/Earnings Ratio is shown as a range. The figures are calculated by dividing the stock's highest price for the year and its lowest price by the year's earnings per share. Prices are for calendar years.

L. ADDITIONAL INFORMATION on each stock includes the officers of the company, date of incorporation, its address, telephone number, annual meeting date, the number of employees, the number of stockholders, institutional holdings, registrar and transfer agent.

INSTITUTIONAL HOLDINGS – indicates the number of investment companies, insurance companies, bank trust and college endowment funds holding the stock and the total number of shares held as last reported.

ABBREVIATIONS AND SYMBOLS

d	Deficit
E	Extra
M	Monthly
N.M.	Not Meaningful
OTC	Over-The-Counter Market
P.F.	Pro Forma
Q	Quarterly
r	Revised
S	Semi-annual
Sp	Special Dividend

Moody's
DIVIDEND ACHIEVERS

In 1979, Moody's introduced a study of companies that have increased their payment of cash dividends annually for at least ten consecutive calendar years. Moody's has dubbed these distinctive companies Dividend Achievers.

Each year, Moody's compiles its list of Dividend Achievers from more than 10,000 companies in its equity data base, which includes firms listed on the New York and American Stock Exchanges and those actively traded on the NASDAQ over-the-counter market.

Moody's Dividend Achievers list is based on the concept that an investment in a fixed-income security with a high current yield does not necessarily provide the most income over the long run. Not only can investors enjoy a high cash return from a stock that pays consistently increasing dividends, but they can also receive a higher total return when adding in the appreciation in the price of the stock. Rising dividends are generally linked to increasing earnings, which, of course, directly influence stock prices. Moreover, managements of many companies use dividend increases as signals to investors about the future. They're saying, in effect, that they believe that future earnings will be able to sustain the higher payouts.

A solid investment not only offers a certain degree of stability but also grows in overall value. Thus dividend achiever companies are attractive not only compared with other stocks, but also when measured against such currently low-yielding investments as bank certificates of deposit and money-market mutual funds.

Moody's 1994 survey has identified 332 companies that have increased their payment of cash dividends annually for at least the past ten consecutive calendar years. A list of Dividend Achievers follows, ranked by average annual compound dividend growth rate over the ten-year period of 1983-93. The list includes the exchange on which each stock is traded, its ten-year dividend growth rate, and the number of consecutive calendar years in which the company has paid out a higher per share cash dividend.

For the second consecutive year Cintas Corp., with an average annual dividend growth rate of 39.5%, topped our list of companies with the highest rate. Cintas designs and manufactures rental uniforms for businesses of all sizes. Wal-Mart Stores, Inc., one of the nation's largest retailers, boasted a dividend growth rate of 31.5%. Golden West Financial Corp., a newcomer to our list, had a growth rate of 29.7%. The savings and loan holding company operates branch offices in California and 7 other states. Progressive Corp., which specializes in auto insurance for those cancelled or rejected by other insurers, accumulated a growth rate of 29.6%. The fifth highest rate, 26.9%, belonged to TCA Cable TV, Inc., an owner and operator of cable tv systems serving 455,000 customers in a seven-state region. Legg Mason, a securities brokerage firm and another new addition to our list, posted a rate of 26.7%. Rounding out our list of highest achievers was Circuit City Stores, Inc. with a growth rate of 25.5%. Circuit City is the nation's leading specialty retailer of brand-name electronics.

Winn-Dixie Stores, Inc. has posted dividend increases for 50 consecutive years and once again the Sunbelt's largest food retailer heads our list of companies with the most consecutive dividend increases. Ohio Casualty Corp., a property and casualty insurance concern, follows with 48 continuous years of growth. Both FPL Group, a provider of electricity to coastal Florida, and Texas Utilities have reported 47 consecutive years of rising dividends. Central & South West Corp., providing electric service to customers in Texas, Oklahoma, Louisiana and Arkansas, ranks fifth with 43 years. Aon Corp., Dun and Bradstreet Corp., SCANA Corp., Tambrands Inc. and Torchmark Corp. have all achieved dividend growth for 42 consecutive years.

Company	Div. Growth Rate %	No. of Yrs.	Company	Div. Growth Rate %	No. of Yrs.
1. ②Cintas Corp. (O)	39.5	11	62. ①Walgreen Co. (N)	14.7	18
2. ①Wal-Mart Stores, Inc. (N)	31.5	12	63. ①AFLAC Inc. (N)	14.6	12
3. ①Golden West Financial Corp. (N)	29.7	10	64. ②Kelly Services, Inc. (O)	14.6	22
4. ①Progressive Corp. (N)	29.6	24	65. ①National Service Ind., Inc. (N)	14.6	32
5. ②TCA Cable TV, Inc. (O)	26.9	11	66. ②Sigma-Aldrich Corp. (O)	14.6	12
6. ①Legg Mason, Inc. (N)	26.7	10	67. ①Avery Dennison Corp. (N)	14.4	18
7. ①Circuit City Stores, Inc. (N)	25.2	13	68. ①Quaker Oats Co. (N)	14.4	27
8. ①Ennis Business Forms, Inc. (N)	24.4	17	69. ②RPM Inc. (O)	14.4	20
9. ①Hasbro Inc. (A)	23.4	12	70. First Empire State Corp. (A)	14.3	13
10. ①Philip Morris Cos., Inc. (N)	22.3	25	71. ①Flowers Industries, Inc. (N)	14.3	21
11. ①WMX Technologies, Inc. (N)	22.3	17	72. ①Hannaford Brothers Co. (N)	14.3	22
12. Citizens Banking (MI) (O)	22.2	10	73. ①Johnson & Johnson (N)	14.2	31
13. ①Sysco Corporation (N)	21.5	17	74. ②Cincinnati Financial Corp. (O)	14.1	33
14. ①Merck & Co. (N)	20.8	10	75. ①Rite Aid Corp. (N)	14.1	25
15. ①UST, Inc. (N)	20.8	23	76. Strawbridge & Clothier (O)	14.1	10
16. ①Family Dollar Stores, Inc. (N)	20.0	17	77. ①Automatic Data Process.. Inc. (N)	14.0	18
17. ①Syntex Corp. (N)	19.5	18	78. Bowl America, Inc. (A)	13.9	21
18. ①Hartford Stm. Boiler Insp. (N)	19.1	28	79. Compass Bancshares, Inc. (O)	13.9	10
19. ①Abbott Laboratories (N)	18.6	20	80. ①Firstar Corp. (N)	13.9	15
20. ①Bard (C.R.) Inc. (N)	18.6	22	81. ①General Mills, Inc. (N)	13.9	29
21. ②Dibrell Brothers, Inc. (O)	18.6	19	82. ①Banc One Corp. (N)	13.8	23
22. National Penn Bancshares (O)	18.6	10	83. ①Medtronic, Inc. (N)	13.8	16
23. ②Eaton Vance Corp. (O)	18.5	12	84. ①Nucor Corp. (N)	13.8	21
24. ①Crompton & Knowles Corp. (N)	18.4	17	85. ①Stanhome, Inc. (N)	13.8	10
25. ①Wrigley (Wm.) Jr. Co. (N)	18.4	13	86. ①Teleflex, Inc. (A)	13.8	16
26. ①Valspar Corp. (A)	18.2	15	87. ①Baxter International Inc. (N)	13.7	37
27. Glatfelter (P.H.) Co. (A)	18.0	10	88. ①Wachovia Corp. (N)	13.7	16
28. ①Pall Corp. (N)	17.9	13	89. ②Apogee Enterprises, Inc. (O)	13.6	19
29. ①Anheuser-Busch Cos., Inc. (N)	17.5	19	90. ②First Hawaiian Inc. (O)	13.5	11
30. ①Bemis Co., Inc. (N)	17.5	10	91. ②Golden Enterprises, Inc. (O)	13.5	16
31. Wilmington Trust Corp. (O)	17.5	12	92. ①Campbell Soup (N)	13.4	11
32. ①Bristol-Myers Squibb Co. (N)	17.3	21	93. ①Clorox Co. (N)	13.4	17
33. ①Harland (John H.) Co. (N)	17.3	41	94. ①Hormel (Geo. A.) & Co. (N)	13.4	26
34. ①Albertson's Inc. (N)	17.1	22	95. ①Lilly (Eli) & Co. (N)	13.4	26
35. ①Flightsafety Intl., Inc. (N)	17.1	17	96. ①Tootsie Roll Industries, Inc. (N)	13.4	30
36. ②Nordstrom, Inc. (O)	17.1	20	97. Central Fidelity Banks, Inc. (O)	13.3	13
37. ②Liqui-Box Corp. (O)	16.9	15	98. Old Kent Financial Corp. (O)	13.1	13
38. ①Cooper Tire & Rubber Co. (N)	16.8	14	99. ①PPG Industries, Inc. (N)	13.0	22
39. ①GEICO Corp. (N)	16.8	16	100. ①First Union Corp. (N)	12.9	16
40. ①Dean Foods Co. (N)	16.7	21	101. ①Fleetwood Enterprises Inc. (N)	12.9	11
41. ①Rubbermaid, Inc. (N)	16.6	39	102. ①Illinois Tool Works, Inc. (N)	12.9	31
42. ①Smucker (J.M.) Co. (N)	16.6	18	103. ①NBD Bancorp, Inc. (N)	12.9	27
43. ①Deluxe Corp. (N)	16.4	33	104. ①Sherwin Williams Co. (N)	12.8	14
44. ①Great Lakes Chemical Corp. (A)	16.3	20	105. American Recreation Cts., Inc. (O)	12.6	26
45. ②State Street Boston Corp. (O)	16.3	13	106. ①Crawford & Co. (N)	12.6	13
46. ①Giant Food Inc. (A)	16.2	13	107. ①First of America Corp. (N)	12.6	10
47. Superior Surgical Mfg. Co. (A)	16.1	10	108. Hubbell Inc. (N)	12.6	33
48. ①Great Western Financial Corp. (N)	15.9	10	109. ①Interpublic Group of Cos.. Inc. (N)	12.6	12
49. ①Conagra Inc. (N)	15.5	16	110. ①Kimberly-Clark Corp. (N)	12.6	20
50. ②General Binding Corp. (O)	15.5	18	111. ②Lilly Industries, Inc. (O)	12.6	10
51. ①Premier Industrial Corp. (N)	15.5	19	112. ①Luby's Cafeterias Inc. (N)	12.6	20
52. ①Block (H&R) Inc. (N)	15.4	30	113. American Precision Ind. Inc. (N)	12.5	13
53. ②Bruno's Inc. (O)	15.4	19	114. ①Kellogg Co. (N)	12.5	37
54. ②Fifth Third Bancorp (O)	15.4	21	115. ①Pepsico, Inc. (N)	12.4	22
55. ①Harcourt General Corp (N)	15.3	26	116. ①Wallace Computer Serv., Inc. (N)	12.4	22
56. ①Hillenbrand Industries Inc. (N)	15.1	23	117. ①Warner-Lambert Co. (N)	12.4	41
57. Sonoco Products Co. (O)	15.1	10	118. AVEMCO Corp. (N)	12.3	18
58. ①Torchmark Corp. (N)	15.0	42	119. ①NationsBank Corp. (N)	12.3	16
59. ①Heinz (H.J.) Co. (N)	14.9	30	120. CCB Financial Corp. (O)	12.1	29
60. ①Pitney Bowes Inc. (N)	14.9	10	121. ①Pep Boys-Manny, Moe & Jack (N)	12.1	16
61. ①Sara Lee Corp. (N)	14.9	17	122. ①American Business Products (N)	12.0	36

Company	Div. Growth Rate %	No. of Yrs.	Company	Div. Growth Rate %	No. of Yrs.
123. ☐Dun & Bradstreet Corp. (N)	12.0	42	186. ☐Weyco Group, Inc. (O)	9.7	13
124. ☐Hershey Foods Corp. (N)	12.0	20	187. Comerica Inc. (N)	9.6	10
125. ☐Hunt Manufacturing Co. (N)	12.0	26	188. ☐Dover Corp. (N)	9.6	38
126. ☐Coca-Cola Co. (N)	11.8	31	189. ☐Marshall & Ilsley Corp. (O)	9.6	20
127. ☐AMP Inc. (N)	11.6	41	190. ☐Mark Twain Bancshares, Inc. (O)	9.5	23
128. Betz Laboratories, Inc. (N)	11.4	28	191. ☐Marsh & McLennan Cos., Inc. (N)	9.4	32
129. ☐Fuller (H.B.) Co. (O)	11.4	26	192. New Plan Realty Trust (N)	9.4	12
130. ☐General RE Corp. (N)	11.4	17	193. ☐Lance, Inc. (O)	9.3	19
131. ☐Masco Corp. (N)	11.4	35	194. ☐Servicemaster L.P. (N)	9.3	23
132. ☐McDonalds's Corp. (N)	11.4	17	195. Washington R.E.I.T. (A)	9.3	32
133. Black Hills Corp. (N)	11.3	13	196. ☐General Host Corp. (N)	9.2	15
134. ☐Jefferson Pilot Corp. (N)	11.3	26	197. ☐American Home Prods. Corp. (N)	9.1	41
135. ☐Quaker Chemical Corp. (O)	11.3	22	198. American National Ins. Co. (N)	9.1	20
136. ☐U.S. Bancorp (Portland, OR) (O)	11.3	34	199. ☐Southern National Corp. (N)	9.0	22
137. ☐EG & G, Inc. (N)	11.2	20	200. ☐Grainger (W.W.) Inc. (N)	8.9	22
138. ☐Intl. Flavors & Frag., Inc. (N)	11.2	32	201. ☐Becton, Dickinson & Co. (N)	8.7	21
139. ☐Leggett & Platt, Inc. (N)	11.2	24	202. ☐First Virginia Banks, Inc. (N)	8.7	17
140. Oshawa Group Ltd. (O)	11.2	15	203. ☐Rockwell International Corp.(N)	8.6	17
141. ☐Pfizer Inc. (N)	11.2	26	204. ☐Ball Corp. (N)	8.5	22
142. Southtrust Corp. (O)	11.2	24	205. ☐Ohio Casualty Corp. (O)	8.5	48
143. ☐American Water Wks Co., Inc.(N)	11.1	18	206. ☐Pentair, Inc. (O)	8.5	17
144. ☐SAFECO Corp. (O)	11.1	18	207. NACCO Industries Inc. (N)	8.4	10
145. ☐Super Valu Stores, Inc. (N)	11.1	21	208. ☐Witco Corp. (N)	8.4	21
146. ☐VF Corp. (N)	11.1	21	209. ☐American Brands, Inc. (N)	8.3	26
147. ☐Huntington Bancshares, Inc. (O)	11.0	27	210. ☐AmSouth Bancorporation (N)	8.3	23
148. ☐Millipore Corp. (N)	11.0	23	211. Regions Financial Corp. (O)	8.3	22
149. ☐Weis Markets Inc. (N)	11.0	19	212. First Bancorp of Ohio (O)	8.3	11
150. ☐KeyCorp (N)	10.9	13	213. ☐Monsanto Co. (N)	8.3	21
151. Bancorp Hawaii, Inc. (N)	10.8	16	214. ☐Haverty Furniture Cos., Inc. (O)	8.2	19
152. ☐General Electric Co. (N)	10.8	18	215. Telephone & Data Sys. Inc. (A)	8.2	19
153. ☐La-Z-Boy Chair Co. (N)	10.8	12	216. Home Beneficial Corp. (O)	8.1	30
154. Stepan Co. (A)	10.8	27	217. ☐Tambrands, Inc. (N)	8.1	42
155. ☐Anthony Industries, Inc. (N)	10.7	15	218. Valley Resources Inc. (A)	8.1	13
156. ☐Bankers Trust New York (N)	10.7	15	219. ☐Gannett Co., Inc. (N)	8.0	22
157. ☐Gillette Co. (N)	10.7	16	220. ☐Atlanta Gas Light Co. (N)	7.8	22
158. ☐May Department Stores Co. (N)	10.7	18	221. ☐Colgate-Palmolive Co. (N)	7.8	31
159. ☐Melville Corp. (N)	10.7	30	222. ☐McGraw-Hill Inc. (N)	7.8	20
160. Selective Insurance Grp, Inc. (O)	10.6	15	223. NWNL Companies, Inc. (N)	7.7	22
161. ☐Nordson Corp. (O)	10.5	12	224. ☐ALLTEL Corp. (N)	7.6	33
162. ☐Rohm & Haas Co. (N)	10.5	16	225. ☐Providian Corp. (N)	7.6	24
163. ☐Diebold, Inc. (N)	10.4	40	226. ☐Longs Drug Stores Corp. (N)	7.6	12
164. ☐Jostens, Inc. (N)	10.4	29	227. ☐Consolid. Edison Co. of NY (N)	7.5	19
165. ☐K Mart Corp. (N)	10.4	29	228. Federal Realty Invest. Trust (N)	7.5	26
166. ☐Utilicorp United Inc. (N)	10.4	36	229. ☐Emerson Electric Co. (N)	7.4	37
167. ☐Bandag Inc. (N)	10.3	17	230. ☐Kenan Transport Co. (O)	7.4	10
168. Mercantile Bankshares Corp. (O)	10.3	17	231. North Carolina Natural Gas (N)	7.4	15
169. ☐Mine Safety Appliances Co. (O)	10.3	23	232. ☐Potlatch Corp. (N)	7.4	10
170. Myers Industries (A)	10.3	17	233. ☐Universal Corp. (N)	7.4	23
171.† Valley Bancorporation (O)	10.3	26	234. ☐Honeywell, Inc. (N)	7.3	18
172. ☐Donnelly (R.R.) & Sons Co. (N)	10.2	24	235. ☐Houghton Mifflin Co. (N)	7.3	11
173. RLI Corp. (N)	10.2	17	236. ☐Lincoln National Corp. (N)	7.3	10
174. ☐Block Drug Co., Inc. (O)	10.1	22	237. ☐National Fuel Gas Co. (N)	7.3	22
175. ☐Dayton Hudson Corp. (N)	10.1	22	238. ☐USLIFE Corp. (N)	7.3	20
176. ☐Keystone International, Inc. (N)	10.1	22	239. ☐Angelica Corp. (N)	7.2	15
177. ☐Archer Daniels Midland Co. (N)	10.0	19	240. Labatt (John) Ltd. (O)	7.2	21
178. ☐Morgan (J.P.) & Co., Inc. (N)	10.0	17	241. ☐Lowe's Cos., Inc. (N)	7.2	16
179. ☐Lee Enterprises, Inc. (N)	9.9	33	242. ☐Martin Marietta Corp. (N)	7.2	22
180. ☐Stanley Works (N)	9.9	26	243. ☐Minnesota Mining & Mfg. Co.(N)	7.2	35
181. American Heritage L.I. Corp. (N)	9.8	24	244. ☐Piedmont Natural Gas Co. (N)	7.2	14
182. ☐Chubb Corp. (N)	9.7	29	245. Pratt & Lambert, Inc. (A)	7.0	15
183. ☐Church & Dwight Co., Inc. (N)	9.7	20	246. Trustmark Corp. (O)	7.0	20
184. First Tennessee National Corp. (O)	9.7	16	247. ☐Consumers Water Co. (O)	6.9	36
185. ☐Loral Corp. (N)	9.7	17	248. ☐Procter & Gamble Co. (N)	6.9	40

9a

Company	Div. Growth Rate %	No. of Yrs.	Company	Div. Growth Rate %	No. of Yrs.
249. United Carolina Bancshares (O)	6.9	13	291. ①Engelhard Corp. (N)	4.6	12
250. ①Wisconsin Energy Corp. (N)	6.9	32	292. ①SCEcorp (N)	4.6	17
251. ②Boatmen's Bancshares, Inc. (O)	6.7	13	293. ①Central Louisiana Electric Co. (N)	4.5	12
252. ①Consolidated Natural Gas Co.(N)	6.7	29	294. ①San Diego Gas & Electric Co. (N)	4.5	17
253. ①Star Banc Corp. (N)	6.7	22	295. ②Nash-Finch Co. (O)	4.4	24
254. ①Indiana Energy, Inc (N)	6.6	18	296. ①Western Resources, Inc. (N)	4.4	19
255. ①Louisiana-Pacific Corp (N)	6.6	17	297. ①Dominion Resources Inc. (N)	4.3	18
256. ①TECO Energy, Inc. (N)	6.6	34	298. ②Middlesex Water Co. (O)	4.3	21
257. ①GTE Corp. (N)	6.5	23	299. ①Washington Gas Light Co. (N)	4.3	17
258. ①Southern Indiana Gas & Elec.(N)	6.5	34	300. ①Hawaiian Electric Industries (N)	4.2	30
259. ①Central & South West Corp. (N)	6.4	43	301. ②Southern California Water Co. (O)	4.2	40
260. ①Exxon Corp. (N)	6.4	11	302. ②Tennant Co. (O)	4.2	21
261. ①Potomac Electric Power Co. (N)	6.3	17	303. ②United Cities Gas Co. (O)	4.2	12
262. Commerce Bancshares Inc. (O)	6.2	25	304. ①Carlisle Companies, Inc. (N)	4.1	17
263. ②Pacific Telecom, Inc. (O)	6.2	17	305. ①Florida Progress Corp. (N)	4.1	41
264. ①St. Joseph Light & Power Co. (N)	6.2	13	306. Gorman-Rupp Co. (A)	4.1	21
265. ①Winn-Dixie Stores, Inc. (N)	6.2	50	307. ①Chemed Corp. (N)	4.0	23
266. BB&T Financial Corp. (O)	6.1	17	308. ①Helmerich & Payne, Inc. (N)	4.0	17
267. ①Northern States Power Co. (N)	6.0	18	309. ①Rochester Telephone Corp. (N)	3.9	34
268. ①Aon Corp. (N)	5.9	42	310. ①WICOR Inc. (N)	3.7	10
269. ①Johnson Controls, Inc. (N)	5.9	18	311. ①Texas Utilities Co. (N)	3.6	47
270. ①Old Republic Intl. Corp. (N)	5.9	12	312. ②TRW, Inc. (N)	3.6	22
271. ①Peoples Energy Corp. (N)	5.9	10	313. ①FPL Group (N)	3.5	47
272. Clarcor Inc. (N)	5.7	13	314. ①Household International Inc. (N)	3.5	41
273. Wesco Financial Corp. (A)	5.7	22	315. ①Union Electric Co. (N)	3.5	18
274. ①Alco Standard Corp. (N)	5.6	29	316. ①KU Energy Corp. (N)	3.4	12
275. ②American Filtrona Corp. (O)	5.5	23	317. Century Tel. Ent., Inc. (N)	3.3	20
276. ②California Water Service Co.(O)	5.5	26	318. ②Madison Gas & Electric Co. (O)	3.3	18
277. MacNeal Schwendler Corp. (A)	5.5	10	319. ②Otter Tail Power Co. (O)	3.3	18
278. Mobile Gas Service Corp. (O)	5.4	16	320. ①Brooklyn Union Gas Co. (N)	3.2	17
279. SJW Corp. (A)	5.4	27	321. ①Penn. Pwr. & Lgt. Co. (N)	3.2	17
280. ①Minnesota Power & Light Co. (N)	5.1	23	322. ABM Industries, Inc. (N)	3.1	29
281. Frisch's Restaurants, Inc. (A)	5.0	10	323. ②Northwest Natural Gas Co. (O)	3.0	37
282. Northwestern Public Serv. Co. (N)	5.0	10	324. ②Orange & Rockland Utilities (N)	3.0	18
283. ①Questar Corp. (N)	5.0	14	325. ①Atlantic Energy, Inc. (N)	2.9	41
284. Empire District Electric (N)	4.9	12	326. ①Green Mountain Power Corp. (N)	2.8	19
285. ②Public Serv. Co. of N.C., Inc. (O)	4.9	25	327. ①LG&E Energy Corp. (N)	2.8	39
286. ①WPL Holdings (N)	4.9	21	328. ①Allegheny Power System, Inc. (N)	2.7	33
287. ①CSX Corp. (N)	4.8	13	329. ①SCANA Corp. (N)	2.5	42
288. ①Republic New York Corp. (N)	4.8	18	330. ①BCE, Inc. (N)	2.4	22
289. ①Duke Power Co. (N)	4.7	18	331. Colonial Gas. Co. (O)	2.4	13
290. ①Wisconsin Public Service (N)	4.7	35	332. ②Connecticut Water Serv., Inc.(O)	1.9	18

① Moody's Handbook of Common Stocks. ② Moody's Handbook of Nasdaq Stocks. †Acquired

Company	No. of Years	Company	No. of Years
Winn-Dixie Stores, Inc.	50	Household International	41
Ohio Casualty Corp.	48	Warner-Lambert Co.	41
FPL Group, Inc.	47	Diebold, Inc.	40
Texas Utilities Co.	47	Procter & Gamble Co.	40
Central & South West Corp.	43	Southern California Water Co.	40
Aon Corp.	42	LG&E Energy Corp.	39
The Dun & Bradstreet Corp.	42	Rubbermaid, Inc.	39
SCANA Corp.	42	Dover Corp.	38
Tambrands, Inc.	42	Baxter Int'l Inc.	37
Torchmark Corp.	42	Emerson Electric Co.	37
American Home Prods. Corp.	41	Kellogg Co.	37
AMP, Incorporated	41	Northwest Natural Gas Co.	37
Atlantic Energy, Inc.	41	American Business Prods. Inc.	36
Florida Progress Co.	41	Consumers Water Co.	36
Harland (John H.) Co.	41	UtiliCorp United Inc.	36

10a

RANKING BY SELECTED INVESTMENT CRITERIA

Rank	Company	Ten Year Dividend Growth Rate	Return On Equity	Average Annual Yield
1.	Cintas Corp.	39.5%	16.9%	0.4%
2.	Wal-Mart Stores, Inc.	31.5	22.8	0.3
3.	Golden West Financial Corp.	29.7	13.3	0.6
4.	Progressive Corp.	29.6	26.8	0.5
5.	TCA Cable TV, Inc.	26.9	22.7	1.6
6.	Legg Mason, Inc.	26.7	17.1	1.6
7.	Circuit City Stores, Inc.	25.2	19.2	0.3
8.	Ennis Business Forms, Inc.	24.4	34.2	2.9
9.	Hasbro, Inc.	23.4	15.7	0.7
10.	Philip Morris Cos., Inc.	22.3	30.7	4.2
11.	WMX Technologies, Inc.	22.3	10.9	1.8
12.	Citizens Banking	22.2	10.1	3.2
13.	Sysco Corporation	21.5	17.7	1.1
14.	Merck & Co.	20.8	21.6	2.8
15.	UST, Inc.	20.8	79.7	3.4
16.	Family Dollar Stores, Inc.	20.0	19.9	1.5
17.	Syntex Corp.	19.5	23.9	4.0
18.	Hartford Steam Boiler Inspection & Insurance Co.	19.1	4.0	4.1
19.	Abbott Laboratories	18.6	38.1	2.5
20.	Bard (C.R.) Inc.	18.6	16.2	1.9
21.	Dibrell Brothers, Inc.	18.6	25.1	2.1
22.	National Penn Bancshares, Inc.	18.6	15.6	2.1

Rank	Company	Average Annual Yield	Ten Year Dividend Growth Rate	Return On Equity
1.	BCE Inc.	7.5%	2.4%	1.6%
2.	Rochester Telephone Corp.	7.4	3.9	12.3
3.	TECO Energy, Inc.	7.2	6.6	13.9
4.	Chemed Corp.	7.2	4.0	12.5
5.	Atlantic Energy, Inc.	6.7	2.9	10.9
6.	Texas Utilities Co.	6.7	3.6	4.8
7.	Hawaiian Electric Industries, Inc.	6.6	4.2	8.9
8.	FPL Group, Inc.	6.5	3.5	9.4
9.	Allegheny Power System, Inc.	6.3	2.7	9.8
10.	Green Mountain Power Corp.	6.3	2.8	10.9
11.	Minnesota Mining & Manufacturing Co.	6.2	7.2	19.4
12.	SCEcorp	6.1	4.6	10.1
13.	Minnesota Power & Light Co.	6.0	5.1	10.6
14.	SCANA Corp.	5.9	2.5	12.4
15.	Consumers Water Co.	5.9	6.9	12.4
16.	Union Electric Co.	5.8	3.5	12.3
17.	Northern States Power Co.	5.8	6.0	10.2
18.	Florida Progress Corp.	5.8	4.1	10.1
19.	San Diego Gas & Electric Co.	5.8	4.5	13.6
20.	Empire District Electric Co.	5.8	4.9	9.1
21.	Orange & Rockland Utilities, Inc.	5.8	3.0	10.7

Rank	Company	Return On Equity [1]	Average Annual Yield	Ten Year Dividend Growth Rate
1.	UST, Inc.	79.7%	3.4%	20.8%
2.	Tambrands, Inc.	64.1	3.0	8.1
3.	ServiceMaster L.P.	50.5	3.7	9.3
4.	Coca-Cola Co.	47.7	1.6	11.8
5.	Quaker Oats Co.	44.2	2.9	14.4
6.	General Mills, Inc.	41.5	2.3	13.9
7.	Kellogg Co.	39.7	2.3	12.5
8.	Dun & Bradstreet Corp.	38.6	3.9	12.0
9.	Abbott Laboratories	38.1	2.5	18.6
10.	American Home Products Corp.	37.9	4.6	9.1
11.	Syntex Corp.	36.8	4.0	19.5
12.	Ennis Business Forms, Inc.	33.0	2.9	24.4
13.	Bristol-Myers Squibb Co.	33.0	4.9	17.3
14.	Johnson & Johnson	32.1	2.3	14.2
15.	Philip Morris Cos., Inc.	30.7	4.2	22.3
16.	Wrigley (Wm.) Jr. Co.	30.4	2.0	18.4
17.	Colgate Palmolive Co.	29.2	2.4	7.8
18.	Gillette Co.,(The)	28.9	1.5	10.7

[1] Based on most recent available data.

ADVERTISING
Interpublic Group of Companies, Inc.

AIRCRAFT & AEROSPACE
Rockwell International Corp.

AMUSEMENTS
Bowl America Inc.
Hasbro, Inc.
Stanhome, Inc.

APPAREL
Angelica Corp.
Superior Surgical Manufacturing. Co.
VF Corp.

AUTOMOBILE PARTS
Clarcor Inc.
Myers Industries, Inc.

BANKS - MAJOR
Bankers Trust New York Corp.
Morgan (J.P.) & Co., Inc.

BANKS - MID-ATLANTIC
Central Fidelity Banks, Inc.
First Virginia Banks, Inc.
Marshall & Ilsley Corp.
Mercantile Bankshares Corp.
National Penn Bancshares, Co.

BANKS - MIDWEST
Banc One Corp.
Boatmen's Bancshares, Inc.
Citizens Banking
Comerica, Inc.
Commerce Bancshares, Inc.
Fifth Third Bancorp
First Bancorporation of Ohio
First of America Corp.
Firstar Corp.
Mark Twain Bancshares, Inc.
NBD Bancorp, Inc.
Old Kent Financial Corp.
Star Banc Corp.
Valley Bancorporation

BANKS - NORTHEAST
First Empire State Corp.
Huntington Bancshares, Inc.
KeyCorp
Republic New York Corp.
State Street Boston Corp.
Wilmington Trust Corporation

BANKS - SOUTH
AmSouth Bancorporation
BB&T Financial Corp.
CCB Financial Corp.
Compass Bancshares, Inc.
First Tennessee National Corp.
First Union Corp.
NationsBank Corporation
Regions Financial Corp.
Southern National Corp.

Southtrust Corp.
Trustmark Corp.
United Carolina Bancshares Corporation
Wachovia Corp.

BANKS - WEST
Bancorp Hawaii, Inc.
First Hawaiian, Inc.
U.S. Bancorp (Portland, Ore.)

BREWING
Anheuser-Busch Companies, Inc.
Labatt (John) Ltd.

BUILDING MATERIALS & EQUIPMENT
Apogee Enterprises, Inc.

CANDY & GUM
Hershey Foods Corporation
Tootsie Roll Industries, Inc.
Wrigley (Wm.) Jr. Co.

CHEMICALS
Betz Laboratories Inc.
Chemed Corp.
Crompton & Knowles Corp.
Engelhard Corporation
Fuller (H.B.) Co.
Great Lakes Chemical Corp.
Monsanto Company
PPG Industries, Inc.
Quaker Chemical Corp.
Rohm & Haas. Co.
Sigma-Aldrich Corporation
Stepan Co.
Witco Corp.

COAL
NACCO Industries Inc.

COMPUTERS-COMPONENTS & PERIPHERAL EQUIPMENT
MacNeal-Schwendler Corp.

COMPUTERS - MAJOR
Honeywell Inc.

COMPUTERS - SERVICES
Automatic Data Processing, Inc.

CONGLOMERATES
Carlisle Companies, Inc.
Hillenbrand Industries, Inc.
Martin Marietta Corp.
Minnesota Mining & Manufacturing Co.
TRW Inc.

CONTAINERS
Ball Corp.

COSMETICS & TOILETRIES
Gillette Co.
International Flavors & Fragrances, Inc.
Tambrands, Inc.

DEFENSE SYSTEMS & EQUIPMENT
Loral Corporation

DRUGS
American Home Products Corp.
Block Drug Co. Inc.
Bristol-Myers Squibb Co.
Lilly (Eli) & Co.
Merck & Co., Inc.
Pfizer Inc.
Syntex Corp.
Warner-Lambert Co.

ELECTRIC POWER - CENTRAL & SOUTHEASTERN REGIONS
Central Louisiana Electric Company, Inc.
Duke Power Co.
Florida Progress Corp.
FPL Group, Inc.
KU Energy Corporation
LG&E Energy Corp.
Madison Gas & Electric Co.
Pennsylvania Power & Light Co.
SCANA Corp.
Southern Indiana Gas & Electric Co.
TECO Energy, Inc.
Wisconsin Energy Corp.
Wisconsin Public Service Corp.
WPL Holdings, Inc

ELECTRIC POWER - NORTHEASTERN REGION
Allegheny Power System, Inc.
Consolidated Edison Co. of New York, Inc.
Dominion Resources, Inc.
Green Mountain Power Corp.
Orange & Rockland Utilities, Inc.
Potomac Electric Power Co.

ELECTRIC POWER - WESTERN REGION
Black Hills Corp.
Central & South West Corp.
Empire District Electric Company
Hawaiian Electric Industries, Inc.
Minnesota Power & Light Co.
Northern States Power Co. (Minn.)
Northwestern Public Service Co.
Otter Tail Power Co.
San Diego Gas & Electric Co.
SCECorp
St. Joseph Light & Power Co.
Texas Utilities Co.
Union Electric Co.
UtiliCorp United Inc.

ELECTRICAL EQUIPMENT
AMP, Inc.
Emerson Electric Co.
General Electric Co.
Hubbell Inc.

ELECTRIC COMPONENTS
American Precision Industries, Inc.
EG&G, Inc.
Premier Industrial Corp.

ENGINEERING & CONSTRUCTION
Masco Corp.

FINANCE
Household International, Inc.

FINANCIAL SERVICES
Eaton Vance Corp.

FOOD - GRAIN & AGRICULTURE
Archer Daniels Midland Co.
ConAgra, Inc.

FOOD PROCESSING
Campbell Soup Company
Dean Foods Co.
Flowers Industries, Inc.
General Mills, Inc.
Golden Enterprises, Inc.
Heinz (H.J.) Co.
Kellogg Co.
Lance, Inc.
Quaker Oats Co.
Sara Lee Corp.
The Smucker (J.M.) Co.

FOOD WHOLESALERS
Nash Finch Company
Super Valu Stores, Inc.
Sysco Corporation

FOREST PRODUCTS
General Host Corp.
Louisiana-Pacific Corp.
Potlatch Corp.

FURNITURE & FIXTURES
La-Z-Boy Chair Co.
Leggett & Platt, Inc.

GROCERY CHAINS
Albertson's Inc.
Bruno's, Inc.
Giant Food Inc.
Weis Markets, Inc.
Winn-Dixie Stores, Inc.

HARDWARE & TOOLS
Illinois Tool Works Inc.
The Stanley Works

INSURANCE - BROKERAGE
Marsh & McLennan Companies, Inc.
Torchmark Corp.

INSURANCE - COMBINED
Aon Corp.
Cincinnati Financial Corp.
Crawford & Co.
Jefferson-Pilot Corp.
Lincoln National Corp.
Old Republic International Corp.
The Progressive Corp.
SAFECO Corp.

INSURANCE - LIFE
AFLAC Inc.
American Heritage Life Investment Corp.
American National Insurance Co.
Home Beneficial Corp.

NWNL Companies, Inc.
Providian Corp.
USLIFE Corp.

INSURANCE - PROPERTY & CASUALTY
Avemco Corp.
The Chubb Corp.
GEICO Corp.
General Re Corp.
Hartford Steam Boiler Inspection & Insurance Co.
Ohio Casualty Corp.
RLI Corp.
Selective Insurance Group Inc.

JEWELRY
Jostens, Inc.

MACHINERY & EQUIPMENT
Dover Corp.
Nordson Corporation
Tennant Co.

MAINTENANCE & SECURITY SERVICES
ABM Industries, Inc.

MEASURING & CONTROL INSTRUMENTS
Gorman-Rupp Co.
Johnson Controls, Inc.
Keystone International, Inc.
Millipore Corp.
Teleflex, Inc.

MEAT PACKING & PROCESSING
Hormel (George A.) & Co.

MEDICAL & DENTAL EQUIPMENT & SUPPLIES
Abbott Laboratories
Bard (C.R.), Inc.
Baxter International Inc.
Becton, Dickinson & Co.
Johnson & Johnson
Medtronic, Inc.
Mine Safety Appliances Co.

MOBILE HOMES
Fleetwood Enterprises

NATURAL GAS
Consolidated Natural Gas Co.
National Fuel Gas Co.
North Carolina Natural Gas Corp.
Peoples Energy Corp.
Questar Corp.
Valley Resources, Inc.

NATURAL GAS - DISTRIBUTORS
Atlanta Gas Light Co.
Brooklyn Union Gas Co.
Colonial Gas Co.
Indiana Energy, Inc.
Mobile Gas Service Corp.
Northwest Natural Gas Co.
Piedmont Natural Gas Co., Inc.
Public Service Co. of North Carolina, Inc.
United Cities Gas Company
The Washington Gas Light Co.
WICOR, Inc.

NEWSPAPERS
Lee Enterprises, Inc.

OFFICE EQUIPMENT & SUPPLIES
American Business Products, Inc.
Avery Dennison Corp.
Diebold, Inc.
Ennis Business Forms, Inc.
General Binding Corp.
Hunt Manufacturing Co.
Pitney Bowes Inc.
Wallace Computer Services, Inc.

OIL
Atlantic Energy, Inc.
Exxon Corp.

OIL SERVICE & EQUIPMENT
Helmerich & Payne, Inc.

PAINTS & RELATED PRODUCTS
Lilly Industries, Inc.
Pratt & Lambert, Inc.
RPM Inc.
Sherwin-Williams Co.
The Valspar Corp.

PAPER
Bemis Co., Inc.
Kimberly-Clark Corp.
Pentair, Inc.
Sonoco Products Co.

PLASTICS & PLASTIC PRODUCTS
American Filtrona Corp.
Liqui-Box Corp.
Rubbermaid, Inc.

POLLUTION CONTROL
Pall Corp.
WMX Technologies Inc.

PRINTING & ENGRAVING
Alco Standard Corp.
Deluxe Corp.
Donnelley (R. R.) & Sons Co.
Glatfelter (P.H.) Co.
Harland (John H.) Co.

PUBLISHING
Houghton Mifflin Co.
McGraw-Hill, Inc.

RAILROADS
CSX Corporation

REAL ESTATE
Federal Realty Investment Trust

REAL ESTATE INVESTMENT TRUSTS
New Plan Realty Trust
Washington Real Estate Investment Trust

RECREATION
American Recreation Centers, Inc.
Anthony Industries, inc.

RESTAURANTS
Frisch's Restaurants, Inc.
Luby's Cafeterias, Inc.
McDonald's Corp.

RETAIL DEPARTMENT STORES
Dayton Hudson Corp.
May Department Stores Co.
Strawbridge & Clothier

RETAIL - DISCOUNT & VARIETY STORES
Family Dollar Stores, Inc.
K Mart Corp.
Wal-Mart Stores, Inc.

RETAIL - DRUG STORES
Longs Drug Stores, Inc.
Rite Aid Corp.
Walgreen Co.

RETAIL - SPECIALTY STORES
Circuit City Stores, Inc.
Hannaford Bros. Co.
Harcourt General, Inc.
Haverty Furniture Companies, Inc.
Lowe's Companies, Inc.
Melville Corp.
Nordstrom, Inc.
Pep Boys-Manny, Moe & Jack

SAVINGS & LOAN
Golden West Financial Corp.
Great Western Financial Corp.
Wesco Financial Corp.

SECURITIES BROKERAGE
Legg Mason, Inc.

SERVICES
Block (H & R), Inc.
Cintas Corporation
The Dun & Bradstreet Corp.
FlightSafety International, Inc.
Kelly Services, Inc.
National Service Industries, Inc.
Servicemaster Limited Partnership

SHOE MANUFACTURING
Weyco Group, Inc.

SOAPS & CLEANERS
Church & Dwight Co., Inc.
Clorox Co.
Colgate-Palmolive Co.
Procter & Gamble Co.

SOFT DRINKS
The Coca-Cola Co.
Pepsico, Inc.

STEEL
Nucor Corp.

TELECOMMUNICATIONS
ALLTEL Corp.
BCE Inc.
Century Telephone Enterprises, Inc.
GTE Corp.
Pacific Telecom, Inc.
Rochester Telephone Corp.
Telephone & Data Systems, Inc.

TELEVISION & RADIO BROADCASTING
Gannett Co., Inc.
TCA Cable TV, Inc.

TIRES & RUBBER GOODS
Bandag, Inc.
Cooper Tire & Rubber Co.

TOBACCO
American Brands, Inc.
Dibrell Brothers, Inc.
Philip Morris Companies, Inc.
Universal Corp.
UST, Inc.

TRUCKING
Kenan Transport Co.

WATER COMPANIES
American Water Works Company, Inc.
California Water Service Co.
Connecticut Water Service, Inc.
Consumers Water Co.
Middlesex Water Company
SJW Corp.
Southern California Water Co.

WHOLESALERS - DISTRIBUTORS - JOBBERS
Grainger (W.W.), Inc.
Oshawa Group Ltd.

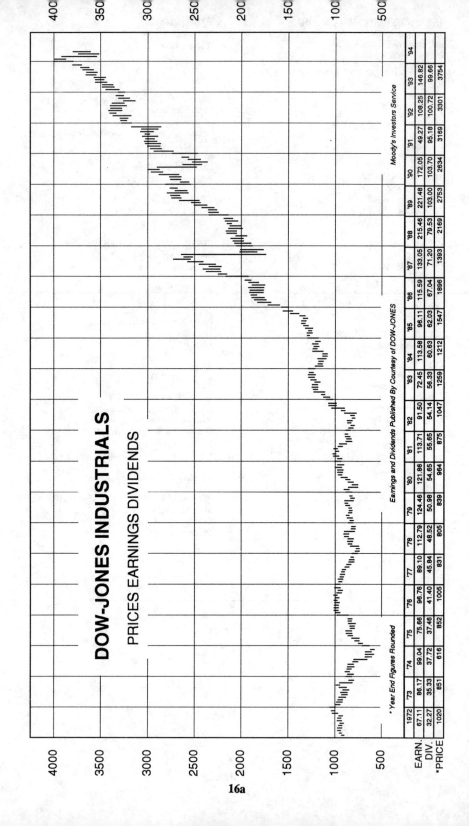

DOW-JONES INDUSTRIALS
PRICES EARNINGS DIVIDENDS

* Year End Figures Rounded

Earnings and Dividends Published By Courtesy of DOW-JONES

Moody's Investors Service

	1972	'73	'74	'75	'76	'77	'78	'79	'80	'81	'82	'83	'84	'85	'86	'87	'88	'89	'90	'91	'92	'93	'94
EARN.	67.11	86.17	99.04	75.66	96.76	89.10	112.79	124.46	121.86	113.71	91.50	72.45	113.58	96.11	115.59	133.05	215.46	221.48	172.05	49.27	108.25	146.82	
DIV.	32.27	35.33	37.72	37.46	41.40	45.84	48.52	50.98	54.65	55.65	54.14	56.33	60.63	62.03	67.04	71.20	79.53	103.00	103.70	95.18	100.72	99.66	
*PRICE	1020	851	616	852	1005	831	805	839	964	875	1047	1259	1212	1547	1896	1393	2169	2753	2634	3169	3301	3754	

16a

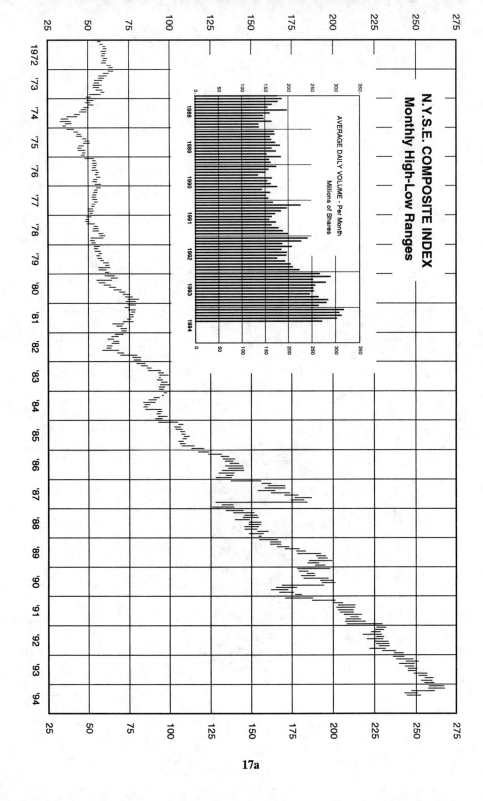

N.Y.S.E. COMPOSITE INDEX
Monthly High-Low Ranges

AVERAGE DAILY VOLUME - Per Month
Millions of Shares

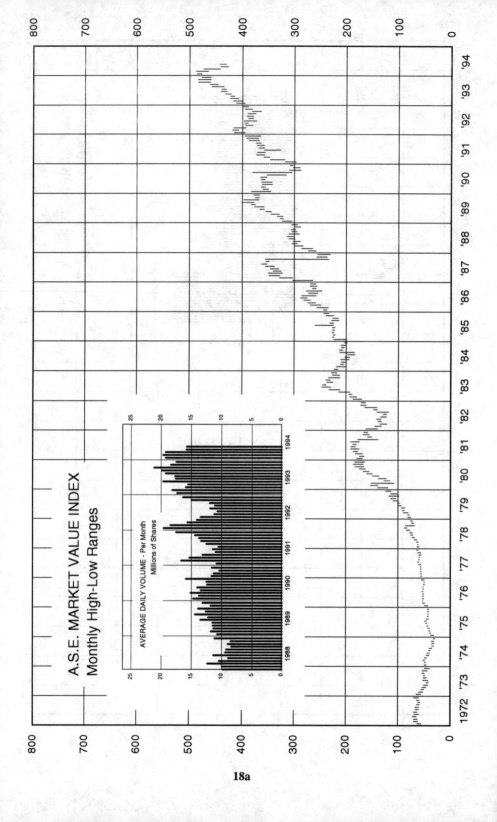

A.S.E. MARKET VALUE INDEX
Monthly High-Low Ranges

AVERAGE DAILY VOLUME - Per Month
Millions of Shares

18a

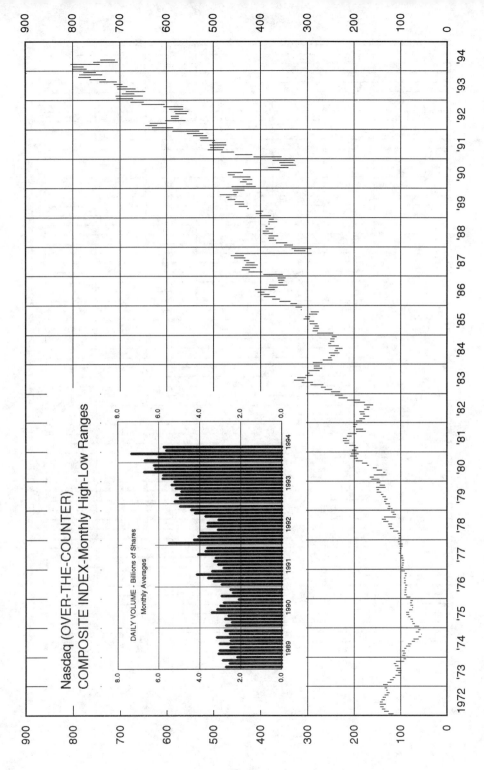

Nasdaq (OVER-THE-COUNTER)
COMPOSITE INDEX-Monthly High-Low Ranges

DAILY VOLUME - Billions of Shares
Monthly Averages

19a

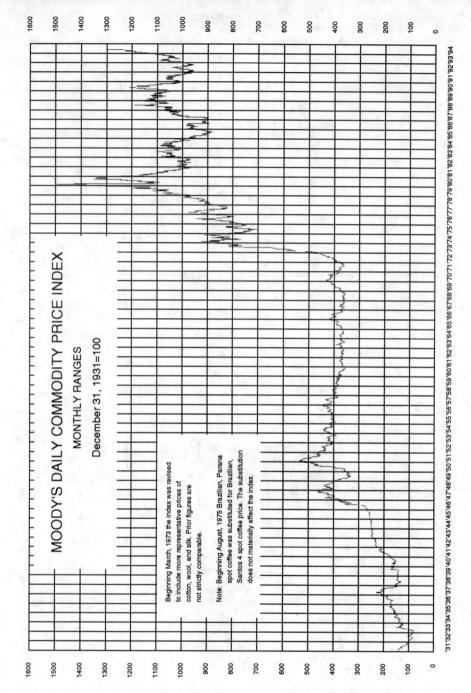

MOODY'S DAILY COMMODITY PRICE INDEX

MONTHLY RANGES

December 31, 1931=100

Beginning March, 1973 the index was revised
to include more representative prices of
cotton, wool, and silk. Prior figures are
not strictly comparable.

Note: Beginning August, 1975 Brazilian, Parana
spot coffee was substituted for Brazilian,
Santos 4 spot coffee price. The substitution
does not materially affect the index.

20a

ABBOTT LABORATORIES

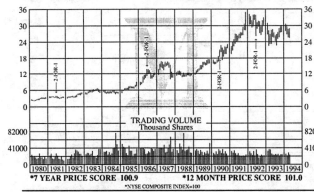

TRADING VOLUME
Thousand Shares

*7 YEAR PRICE SCORE 100.9   *12 MONTH PRICE SCORE 101.0
*NYSE COMPOSITE INDEX=100

INTERIM EARNINGS (Per Share):

Qtr.	Mar.	June	Sept.	Dec.
1990	0.26	0.27	0.26	0.32
1991	0.30	0.31	0.29	0.37
1992	0.35	0.37	0.33	0.42
1993	0.41	0.42	0.38	0.48

INTERIM DIVIDENDS (Per Share):

Amt.	Decl.	Ex.	Rec.	Pay.
0.17Q	2/12/93	4/8/93	4/15/93	5/15/93
0.17Q	6/11	7/9	7/15	8/15
0.17Q	9/10	10/8	10/15	11/15
0.17Q	12/10	1/10/94	1/15/94	2/15/94
0.19Q	2/11/94	4/11	4/15	5/15

Indicated div.: $0.76

CAPITALIZATION (12/31/93):

	($000)	(%)
Long-Term Debt	306,840	7.6
Deferred Income Tax	51,383	1.3
Common & Surplus	3,674,929	91.1
Total	4,033,152	100.0

DIVIDEND ACHIEVER STATUS:
Rank: 19   1983-93 Growth Rate: 18.6%
Total Years of Dividend Growth: 20

RECENT DEVELOPMENTS: For the year ended 12/31/93, net income increased 12.9% to $1.40 billion compared with $1.24 billion a year ago. Net sales were up 7.1% to $8.41 billion from $7.85 billion. Worldwide sales of pharmaceutical and nutritional products rose 9.0% to $4.39 billion led by Biaxin, a broad spectrum anti-infective, and Hytrin, an alpha blocker used in treating benign prostatic hyperplasia, an enlargement of the prostate.

PROSPECTS: Earnings should grow despite a competitive and changing health care industry. Abbott will proceed with efforts to shift its hospital-focused product mix to technology-based products. The drug Hytrin continues to gain momentum in international markets with recent launches in several European countries, including the U.K. and Germany. Operating results will benefit from the Ross Products division's introduction of Advera, a nutritional food product designed specifically for people with HIV (patent pending).

BUSINESS

ABBOTT LABORATORIES principal business is the discovery, development, manufacture, and sale of a broad and diversified line of human health care products and services. Pharmaceutical and nutritional products include a broad line of adult and pediatric pharmaceuticals, nutritional vitamins, and hematinics; personal care products, agricultural and chemical products, and bulk pharmaceuticals. Hospital and laboratory products include diagnostic systems; intravenous and irrigating fluids and related administration equipment; venipuncture products, anesthetics, critical care equipment; and other specialty products.

BUSINESS LINE ANALYSIS

(12/31/93)	Rev(%)	Inc(%)
Pharmac &		
Nutritional	52.2	60.4
Hospital &		
Laboratory	47.8	39.6
Total	100.0	100.0

ANNUAL EARNINGS AND DIVIDENDS PER SHARE

	1993	1992	1991	1990	1989	1988	1987
Earnings Per Share	1.69	1.47	② 1.27	1.11	0.97	0.84	0.70
Dividends Per Share	0.66	① 0.577	0.48	③ 0.403	0.338	0.29	0.24
Dividend Payout %	39.1	39.3	37.6	36.3	35.1	34.5	34.5

① 2-for-1 stk split, 6/1/92 ② Before extraord. item & acctg. chg. ③ 2-for-1 stk split, 5/31/90

ANNUAL FINANCIAL DATA

RECORD OF EARNINGS (IN MILLIONS):

Total Revenues	8,407.8	7,851.9	6,876.6	6,158.7	5,379.8	4,937.0	4,387.9
Costs and Expenses	5,999.8	5,898.1	4,940.5	4,396.8	3,851.3	3,564.1	3,138.5
Depreciation & Amort	484.1	427.8	379.0	355.9	307.3	270.9	243.7
Operating Earnings	1,924.0	1,526.0	1,557.0	1,406.0	1,221.1	1,102.0	1,005.7
Earnings Before Taxes	1,943.2	1,738.8	1,544.2	1,350.7	1,194.2	1,055.5	937.1
Taxes on Earnings	544.1	499.7	455.5	385.0	334.4	303.4	304.6
Net Income	1,399.1	1,239.1	① 1,088.7	965.8	859.8	752.0	632.6
Aver. Shs. Outstg. (000)	828,988	844,122	854,062	870,098	893,288	903,052	910,824

① Before extra. item cr$128,182,000; and acctg. chg dr$128,114,000.

BALANCE SHEET (IN MILLIONS):

Cash and Cash Equivalents	378.8	258.2	146.2	53.2	48.7	582.6	519.9
Receivables, Net	1,336.2	1,244.4	1,150.9	1,070.2	892.7	781.8	728.0
Total Inventories	940.5	863.8	815.4	777.6	696.0	611.3	612.2
Gross Property	6,221.1	5,497.1	4,785.2	4,257.6	3,626.8	3,289.7	2,859.6
Accumulated Depreciation	2,710.2	2,397.9	2,123.1	1,881.8	1,536.6	1,337.1	1,118.0
Long-Term Debt	306.8	110.0	125.1	134.8	146.7	349.3	271.0
Net Stockholders' Equity	3,674.9	3,347.6	3,203.0	2,833.6	2,726.4	2,464.6	2,093.5
Total Assets	7,688.6	6,941.2	6,255.3	5,563.2	4,851.6	4,825.1	4,385.7
Total Current Assets	3,585.5	3,231.7	2,891.1	2,461.2	2,102.8	2,353.0	2,155.5
Total Current Liabilities	3,094.9	2,782.5	2,229.3	2,001.2	1,383.6	1,439.7	1,486.8
Net Working Capital	490.6	449.2	661.7	460.1	719.2	913.3	668.7
Year End Shs Outstg (000)	821,130	836,052	850,529	858,281	884,959	899,382	906,924

STATISTICAL RECORD:

Operating Profit Margin %	22.9	19.4	22.6	22.8	22.7	22.3	22.9
Book Value Per Share	4.48	4.00	3.77	3.30	3.08	2.74	2.31
Return on Equity %	38.1	37.0	34.0	34.1	31.5	30.5	30.2
Return on Assets %	18.2	17.9	17.4	17.4	17.7	15.6	14.4
Average Yield %	2.5	1.9	1.8	2.1	2.3	2.4	1.8
P/E Ratio	18.3-13.4	23.3-17.8	27.5-15.5	20.9-14.1	18.2-12.0	15.6-12.8	24.3-14.5
Price Range	30⅞-22⅝	34¼-26⅛	34⅞-19⅝	23¼-15⅜	17⅝-11⅝	13⅛-10¾	16¾-10

Statistics are as originally reported.

OFFICERS:
D.L. Burnham, Chmn. & C.E.O.
T.R. Hodgson, Pres. & C.O.O.
G.P. Coughlan, Sr. V.P.-Finance & C.F.O.

INCORPORATED: IL, Mar., 1900

PRINCIPAL OFFICE: One Abbott Park Road, Abbott Park, IL 60064-3500

TELEPHONE NUMBER: (708) 937-6100
FAX: (708) 937-1511
NO. OF EMPLOYEES: 2,081
ANNUAL MEETING: In April
SHAREHOLDERS: 24,550
INSTITUTIONAL HOLDINGS:
No. of Institutions: 910
Shares Held: 416,437,759

REGISTRAR(S): First National Bank of Boston, Shareholder Services Division, Boston, MA

TRANSFER AGENT(S): First National Bank of Boston, Shareholder Services Division, Boston, MA

NYS SYMBOL ABM
Rec. Pr. 21¾

ABM INDUSTRIES, INC.

YIELD 2.4%
P/E RATIO 14.7

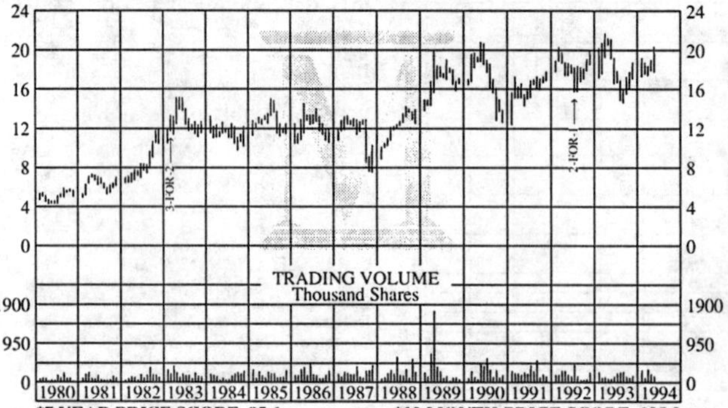

***7 YEAR PRICE SCORE 85.6** ***12 MONTH PRICE SCORE 105.0**

*NYSE COMPOSITE INDEX=100

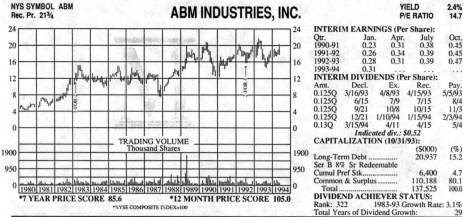

INTERIM EARNINGS (Per Share):

Qtr.	Jan.	Apr.	July	Oct.
1990-91	0.23	0.31	0.38	0.45
1991-92	0.26	0.34	0.39	0.45
1992-93	0.28	0.31	0.39	0.47
1993-94	0.31	...	...	...

INTERIM DIVIDENDS (Per Share):

Amt.	Decl.	Ex.	Rec.	Pay.
0.125Q	3/16/93	4/8/93	4/15/93	5/5/93
0.125Q	6/15	7/9	7/15	8/4
0.125Q	9/21	10/8	10/15	11/3
0.125Q	12/21	1/10/94	1/15/94	2/3/94
0.13Q	3/15/94	4/11	4/15	5/4

Indicated div.: $0.52

CAPITALIZATION (10/31/93):

	($000)	(%)
Long-Term Debt	20,937	15.2
Ser B 8% Sr Redeemable Cumul Pref Stk................	6,400	4.7
Common & Surplus	110,188	80.1
Total	137,525	100.0

DIVIDEND ACHIEVER STATUS:
Rank: 322 1983-93 Growth Rate: 3.1%
Total Years of Dividend Growth: 29

RECENT DEVELOPMENTS: For the quarter ended 1/31/94, net income fell to $2.4 million, or $0.28 per share, compared with $2.8 million, or $0.31 per share, for the corresponding period a year earlier. Revenues totaled $187.2 million, down 11.2% from revenues of $210.8 million a year ago. For the year ended 10/31/93, net income increased slightly from $12.0 million in 1992. Revenue was up 1.7% to $773.3 million compared with $760.1 million the previous year. Earnings per share increased by two cents for both the fourth quarter and the year-end to $0.47 and $1.45, respectively. Operating income fell to $20.2 million from $20.4 million.

BUSINESS

ABM INDUSTRIES, INCORPORATED provides janitorial and building maintenance services to commercial and industrial users. The Janitorial Services Group includes various basic janitorial services to all types of organizations. The Amtech group offers a wide range of mechanical, electrical and elevator services to retail and commercial businesses. Other services group provides parking facility management services and business security and investigative services. ABM operates over 160 offices in 38 states, District of Columbia and three provinces of Canada.

BUSINESS LINE ANALYSIS

(10/31/93)	Rev(%)	Inc(%)
Janitorial Services	57.4	57.9
Amtech Services........	26.8	27.1
Other Services	15.8	15.0
Total	100.0	100.0

ANNUAL EARNINGS AND DIVIDENDS PER SHARE

	10/31/93	10/31/92	10/31/91	10/31/90	10/31/89	10/31/88	10/31/87
Earnings Per Share	**1.45**	**1.43**	**1.37**	**[2] 1.24**	**1.13**	**0.93**	**0.65**
Dividends Per Share	**0.50**	**[1] 0.49**	**0.473**	**0.47**	**0.463**	**0.458**	**0.45**
Dividend Payout %	**34.5**	**34.3**	**34.6**	**37.9**	**41.1**	**49.5**	**69.2**

[1] 2-for-1 stk split, 7/31/92 [2] Before extraord. item

ANNUAL FINANCIAL DATA

	10/31/93	10/31/92	10/31/91	10/31/90	10/31/89	10/31/88	10/31/87
RECORD OF EARNINGS (IN THOUSANDS):							
Revenues & Other Income	773,312	760,097	745,721	679,128	638,362	581,667	528,442
Costs and Expenses	743,748	730,985	717,052	658,903	614,265	560,427	509,931
Depreciation & Amort	7,158	6,634	6,970	7,019	6,778	7,348	7,749
Operating Income	22,406	22,478	21,699	13,206	17,319	13,892	10,762
Inc Fr Cont Opers Bef Income Taxes	20,242	20,417	18,578	10,539	14,592	12,679	9,300
Income Taxes	7,596	8,425	7,478	4,237	5,864	5,579	4,378
Net Income	12,646	11,992	11,100	[1] 6,302	8,728	7,100	4,922
Aver. Shs. Outstg.	8,646	8,397	8,146	7,950	8	7,688	7,582
[1] Before extra. item cr$1,387,000.							
BALANCE SHEET (IN THOUSANDS):							
Cash and Cash Equivalents	1,688	2,365	2,484	1,608	2,504	3,455	618
Receivables, Net	138,868	130,469	119,869	110,377	103,652	92,514	83,451
Inventories & Supplies	16,288	13,802	13,343	12,590	10,534	10,190	10,621
Gross Property	50,838	47,275	46,488	47,760	45,260	43,014	48,590
Accumulated Depreciation	33,795	32,266	30,893	31,545	29,648	26,425	26,257
Long-Term Debt	20,937	15,435	9,477	20,005	20,032	14,036	9,182
Net Stockholders' Equity	116,588	100,825	89,554	79,558	69,389	61,918	71,241
Total Assets	268,140	226,340	211,652	201,696	189,983	172,018	152,174
Total Current Assets	166,933	153,721	141,598	132,383	121,977	111,341	99,173
Total Current Liabilities	90,320	78,535	80,119	66,453	63,625	66,054	68,275
Net Working Capital	76,613	75,186	61,479	65,930	58,352	45,287	30,898
Year End Shares Outstg	8,778	8,514	8,260	8,040	7,854	7,654	7,682
STATISTICAL RECORD:							
Operating Profit Margin %	2.9	3.0	2.9	1.9	2.7	2.4	2.0
Book Value Per Share	5.97	8.02	7.11	5.89	5.13	4.82	6.29
Return on Equity %	11.5	11.9	12.4	7.9	12.6	11.5	6.9
Return on Assets %	4.7	5.3	5.2	3.1	4.6	4.1	3.2
Average Yield %	2.7	2.7	3.1	2.8	2.8	4.0	4.3
P/E Ratio	15.0-10.1	14.2-11.0	13.1-9.1	26.1-15.8	17.7-12.3	15.5-9.6	20.6-11.5
Price Range	21¾-14⅝	20⅜-15¾	17⅞-12⅜	20⅞-12⅝	19⅞-13¾	14¼-8⅞	13⅜-7½

Statistics are as originally reported.

OFFICERS:
S.J. Rosenberg, Chmn. & C.E.O.
W.W. Steele, Pres. & C.O.O.
D.H. Hebble, Corp. V.P. & C.F.O.

INCORPORATED: CA, Apr., 1955; reincorp., DE, Mar., 1985

PRINCIPAL OFFICE: 50 Fremont Street, Suite 2600, San Francisco, CA 94105-2230

TELEPHONE NUMBER: (415) 597-4500

FAX: (415) 597-7160

NO. OF EMPLOYEES: 40,000 (approx.)

ANNUAL MEETING: In February

SHAREHOLDERS: 3,300 (approx.)

INSTITUTIONAL HOLDINGS:
No. of Institutions: 47
Shares Held: 2,114,632

REGISTRAR(S):

TRANSFER AGENT(S):

NYS SYMBOL AFL
Rec. Pr. 33⅜

AFLAC INC.

YIELD 1.4%
P/E RATIO 14.4

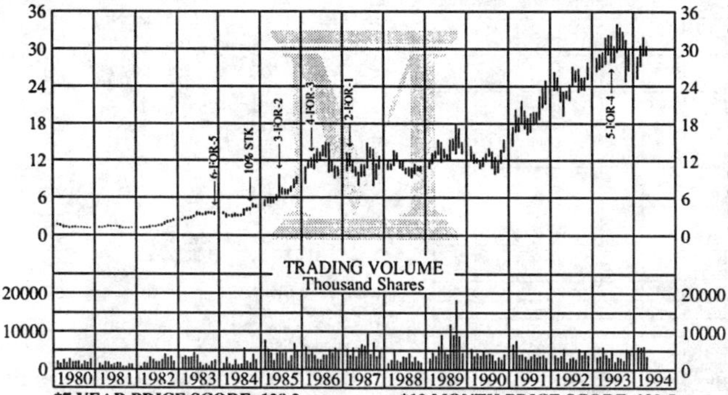

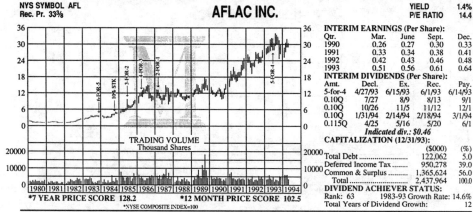

***7 YEAR PRICE SCORE 128.2** ***12 MONTH PRICE SCORE 102.5**

*NYSE COMPOSITE INDEX=100

INTERIM EARNINGS (Per Share):

Qtr.	Mar.	June	Sept.	Dec.
1990	0.26	0.27	0.30	0.33
1991	0.33	0.34	0.38	0.41
1992	0.42	0.43	0.46	0.48
1993	0.51	0.56	0.61	0.64

INTERIM DIVIDENDS (Per Share):

Amt.	Decl.	Ex.	Rec.	Pay.
5-for-4	4/27/93	6/15/93	6/1/93	6/14/93
0.10Q	7/27	8/9	8/13	9/1
0.10Q	10/26	11/5	11/12	12/1
0.10Q	1/31/94	2/14/94	2/18/94	3/1/94
0.115Q	4/25	5/16	5/20	6/1

Indicated div.: $0.46

CAPITALIZATION (12/31/93):

	($000)	(%)
Total Debt	122,062	5.0
Deferred Income Tax	950,278	39.0
Common & Surplus	1,365,624	56.0
Total	2,437,964	100.0

DIVIDEND ACHIEVER STATUS:
Rank: 63 1983-93 Growth Rate: 14.6%
Total Years of Dividend Growth: 12

RECENT DEVELOPMENTS: Net income for the three months ended 12/31/93 jumped 37% from the corresponding 1992 period to $66.9 million. Strong contributions from the supplemental insurance business in both the US and Japan were cited as the primary reason for improved results. Results also benefited from the strong yen into dollar translation. Revenues increased 24.5% to $1.33 billion. For the twelve months ended 12/31/93, income before accounting adjustments was up 33% to $243.9 million. Revenues were $5.00 billion versus $3.99 billion in the prior year.

PROSPECTS: The Company's insurance operations are well-positioned to obtain future growth opportunities in the United States and Japan. All Japanese citizens are covered by either government-provided or employee-sponsored health plans. Fallout from these plans produces large coverage gaps and AFL fills those gaps with supplemental health insurance. AFLAC anticipates business will grow once health care reform is instituted in the US. Demand for the Company's products has risen steadily over the past few years.

BUSINESS

AFLAC INC. is an international insurance organization whose principal subsidiary is American Family Life Assurance Company of Columbus. In addition to life, and health & accident insurance, AFL has pioneered cancer-expense and intensive-care insurance coverage. AFLAC's subsidiary Communicorp specializes in printing, advertising, audio-visuals, sales incentives, business meetings and mailings.

BUSINESS LINE ANALYSIS

(12/31/93)	Rev(%)	Inc(%)
Insurance	98.3	98.0
Broadcast	1.7	2.0
Total	100.0	100.0

ANNUAL EARNINGS AND DIVIDENDS PER SHARE

	1993	1992	1991	1990	1989	1988	1987
Earnings Per Share	**2.32**	**1.79**	**1.46**	**1.15**	**0.80**	**1.08**	**0.93**
Dividends Per Share	**1 0.388**	**0.344**	**0.296**	**0.264**	**0.232**	**0.20**	**0.18**
Dividend Payout %	**16.7**	**19.2**	**20.3**	**22.9**	**29.0**	**18.5**	**19.4**

1 5-for-4 stk split,06/15/93

ANNUAL FINANCIAL DATA

	1993	1992	1991	1990	1989	1988	1987
RECORD OF EARNINGS (IN MILLIONS):							
Tot Prem, Princip Suppl Health Insuranc	4,225.4	3,369.2	2,765.3	2,259.1	2,033.2	1,959.7	1,606.1
Net Investment Income	689.3	533.2	431.3	341.0	295.7	262.0	192.8
Total Revenues	5,000.6	3,986.5	3,282.7	2,678.4	2,438.2	2,324.6	1,876.1
Benefits & Claims	3,423.3	2,692.4	2,188.8	1,759.2	1,561.1	1,518.0	1,223.5
Earn Bef Income Taxes	428.4	324.5	264.7	216.4	178.0	199.1	163.1
Total Income Taxes	184.5	141.2	116.0	99.2	97.2	90.2	69.9
Gain on Sale Of Securities	...	...	...	...	...	2 0.0	8.8
Net Income	1 243.9	183.4	148.7	117.2	80.8	108.9	102.1
Aver. Shs. Outstg. (000)	105,201	102,544	101,980	101,719	101,420	101,219	100,899
1 Before acctg. change cr$11,438,000. 2 Equal to $1,000.							
BALANCE SHEET (IN MILLIONS):							
Cash	23.4	36.1	46.3	26.4	24.0	20.1	18.5
Fixed Matur Held to Maturity, Amort Cost	2,082.3	1,084.4	7,678.2	5,922.4	4,632.4	4,207.5	3,483.1
Eq Secur Available for Sale	82.1	68.3	61.2	55.1	49.4	112.6	117.3
Mtge Loans on Real Estate	57.5	85.3	85.4	80.0	35.1	...	...
Total Assets	15,442.7	11,901.4	10,144.5	8,034.8	6,515.4	6,073.8	5,030.5
Benefits and Claims	11,947.1	9,263.0	7,799.3	6,149.2	4,865.6	4,523.6	3,719.3
Net Stockholders' Equity	1,365.6	1,081.9	923.5	791.0	702.2	642.4	549.1
Year End Shs Outstg (000)	103,471	82,412	81,735	101,814	101,578	101,319	101,195
STATISTICAL RECORD:							
Book Value Per Share	13.20	13.13	11.30	7.77	6.91	6.34	5.43
Return on Equity %	17.9	16.9	16.1	14.8	11.5	17.0	18.6
Return on Assets %	1.6	1.5	1.5	1.5	1.2	1.8	2.0
Average Yield %	1.3	1.5	1.5	2.1	1.6	1.7	1.6
P/E Ratio	14.7-10.7	15.6-10.8	17.0-9.8	13.4-8.5	22.5-13.4	12.6-8.6	15.9-8.5
Price Range	34-24¾	27⅞-19¼	24⅞-14¼	15⅜-9¾	18-10¾	13⅝-9¼	14¾-7⅞

Statistics are as originally reported.

OFFICERS:
P.S. Amos, Chairman
D.P. Amos, Pres. & C.E.O.
K. Cloninger, III, Exec. V.P., C.F.O. & Treas.

PRINCIPAL OFFICE: 1932 Wynnton Road, Columbus, GA 31999

TELEPHONE NUMBER: (706) 323-3431
FAX: (706) 324-6330
NO. OF EMPLOYEES: 3,618
ANNUAL MEETING: In May
SHAREHOLDERS: 43,781
INSTITUTIONAL HOLDINGS:
No. of Institutions: 248
Shares Held: 56,245,932

REGISTRAR(S):

TRANSFER AGENT(S):

NYS SYMBOL ABS
Rec. Pr. 27⅝

ALBERTSON'S INC.

YIELD 1.6%
P/E RATIO 20.6

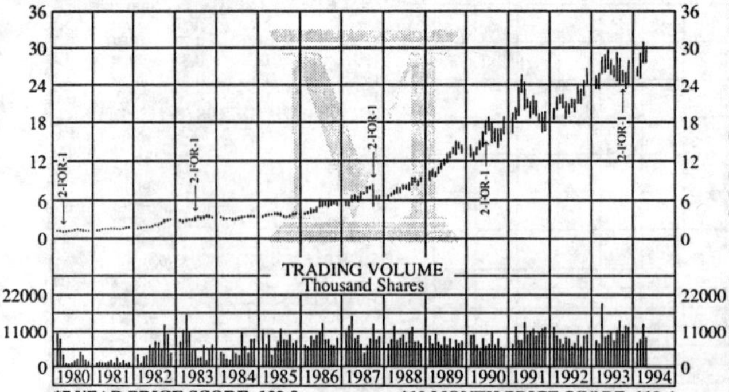

***7 YEAR PRICE SCORE 132.0** ***12 MONTH PRICE SCORE 112.4**

*NYSE COMPOSITE INDEX=100

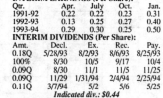

INTERIM EARNINGS (Per Share):

Qtr.	Apr.	July	Oct.	Jan.
1991-92	0.22	0.22	0.23	0.31
1992-93	0.13	0.25	0.27	0.40
1993-94	0.29	0.30	0.25	0.50

INTERIM DIVIDENDS (Per Share):

Amt.	Decl.	Ex.	Rec.	Pay.
0.18Q	5/28/93	8/2/93	8/6/93	8/25/93
100%	8/30	10/5	9/17	10/4
0.09Q	8/30	11/1	11/5	11/25
0.09Q	11/29	1/31/94	2/4/94	2/25/94
0.11Q	3/7/94	5/2	5/6	5/25

Indicated div.: $0.44

CAPITALIZATION (1/28/93):

	($000)	(%)
Long-Term Debt	404,476	21.1
Cap. Lease Oblig.	103,764	5.4
Deferred Income Tax	20,763	1.1
Common & Surplus	1,388,428	72.4
Total	1,917,431	100.0

DIVIDEND ACHIEVER STATUS:
Rank: 34 1983-93 Growth Rate: 17.1%
Total Years of Dividend Growth: 22

RECENT DEVELOPMENTS: For the year ended 2/3/94, earnings were $339.7 million, or $1.34 per share, compared with earnings of $276.1 million, or $1.04 per share, before accounting changes, last year. The results included adjustments for a norecurring charge to cover the settlement of an employment discrimination lawsuit filed in 1992. Sales totaled $11.28 billion, up from $10.17 billion a year earlier. Operating profit increased 31.8% compared with 1992. For the quarter, sales increased 13.9% to $3.06 billion. Net earnings for the quarter were $127.0 million compared with $105.7 million last year. During the quarter, 22 stores were opened for a total of 39 store openings for the year. Remodeling was completed on 11 stores for a total of 42 remodels completed for the year. Nineteen stores were closed during the year.

BUSINESS

ALBERTSON'S is the fourth largest retail food-drug chain in the United States. As of 5/5/94, the Company operated 678 stores in 19 western, midwestern, and southern states. ABS operates conventional supermarkets, superstores, combination food-drug units and warehouse stores. Superstores, averaging 42,000 square feet, have in addition to regular supermarket items, service departments such as a pharmacy, fish and meat counter, salad bar, and delicatessen. Combination food-drug units, averaging 55,000 square feet, offer prescription and proprietary drugs together with non-food merchandise. The grocery warehouse stores are full-line, mass-merchandise markets.

QUARTERLY DATA

(1/30/93)($000)	Rev	Inc
1st Quarter	2,296,848	26,053
2nd Quarter	2,604,203	65,962
3rd Quarter	2,585,137	71,495
4th Quarter	2,687,488	105,707

ANNUAL EARNINGS AND DIVIDENDS PER SHARE

	1/28/93	1/30/92	1/31/91	2/1/90	2/2/89	1/28/88	1/29/87
Earnings Per Share	**[1] 1.05**	**0.97**	**0.88**	**0.74**	**0.61**	**0.47**	**0.38**
Dividends Per Share	**0.31**	**0.27**	**0.23**	**0.185**	**0.135**	**[2] 0.117**	**0.103**
Dividend Payout %	**29.7**	**27.8**	**26.3**	**25.3**	**22.1**	**24.7**	**27.3**

Note: 100%stk.div.10/4/93. [1] Before acctg. chg. [2] 100% stk. div., 10/87.

ANNUAL FINANCIAL DATA

	1/28/93	1/30/92	1/31/91	2/1/90	2/2/89	1/28/88	1/29/87
RECORD OF EARNINGS (IN MILLIONS):							
Total Revenues	10,173.7	8,680.5	8,218.6	7,422.7	6,773.1	5,869.4	5,379.6
Costs and Expenses	9,524.2	8,133.5	7,720.8	6,997.1	6,426.8	5,579.5	5,124.6
Depreciation & Amort	171.7	132.8	122.2	105.9	85.7	73.1	66.4
Operating Profit	477.8	414.2	375.6	319.6	260.6	216.8	188.6
Earn Bef Income Taxes	443.7	406.4	366.0	309.8	257.0	211.9	184.8
Income Taxes	167.6	148.6	132.2	113.2	94.4	86.5	84.6
Net Income	269.2	257.8	233.8	196.6	162.5	125.4	100.2
Aver. Shs. Outstg. (000)	264,418	266,338	267,554	268,272	266,424	267,480	266,668
BALANCE SHEET (IN MILLIONS):							
Cash & Cash Equivalents	39.5	34.4	23.4	43.7	81.6	201.4	245.8
Receivables, Net	130.9	93.0	79.7	69.2	69.2	62.8	55.5
Inventories	830.1	613.2	562.7	544.7	432.3	361.6	316.5
Gross Property	2,727.3	2,166.2	1,959.4	1,745.2	1,477.9	1,175.4	997.9
Accumulated Depreciation	882.3	773.5	691.0	598.5	518.2	449.9	388.8
Long-Term Debt	404.5	52.5	56.1	111.5	64.0	69.7	75.0
Obligs Under Cap Lses	103.8	99.2	103.0	106.9	113.0	113.5	112.2
Net Stockholders' Equity	1,388.4	1,199.5	1,087.9	929.5	800.5	665.2	594.4
Total Assets	2,945.6	2,216.2	2,013.5	1,862.7	1,591.0	1,402.1	1,264.7
Total Current Assets	1,013.5	751.3	677.4	668.1	592.0	635.0	625.3
Total Current Liabilities	815.8	652.2	585.6	555.0	488.4	440.0	380.0
Net Working Capital	197.6	99.0	91.8	113.1	103.6	195.0	245.2
Year End Shs Outstg (000)	264,659	264,261	267,640	267,840	267,716	265,444	267,260
STATISTICAL RECORD:							
Operating Profit Margin %	4.7	4.8	4.6	4.3	3.8	3.7	3.5
Book Value Per Share	5.25	4.54	4.06	3.47	2.99	2.51	2.22
Return on Equity %	19.9	21.5	21.5	21.1	20.3	18.8	16.8
Return on Assets %	9.4	11.6	11.6	10.6	10.2	8.9	7.9
Average Yield %	1.4	1.3	1.5	1.5	1.7	1.7	2.0
P/E Ratio	25.7-17.7	26.5-16.9	21.4-13.9	20.4-12.3	16.0-9.8	18.1-10.9	16.4-10.2
Price Range	26¾-18⅜	25¾-16⅜	18⅞-12¼	15⅛-9⅛	9¾-6	8½-5⅛	6¼-3⅞

Statistics are as originally reported.

OFFICERS:
G.G. Michael, Chmn. & C.E.O.
J.B. Carley, Pres. & C.O.O.
A.C. Olson, Sr. V.P.-Fin. & C.F.O.

INCORPORATED: DE, Apr., 1969

PRINCIPAL OFFICE: 250 Parkcenter Blvd., P.O. Box 20, Boise, ID 83726

TELEPHONE NUMBER: (208) 385-6200

FAX: (208) 385-6539

NO. OF EMPLOYEES: 37,630 approx.

ANNUAL MEETING: In May

SHAREHOLDERS: 6,909 approx.

INSTITUTIONAL HOLDINGS:
No. of Institutions: 450
Shares Held: 57,720,954

REGISTRAR(S): Pittsburgh National Bank, Pittsburgh, PA 15230
First Security Bank, Boise, ID

TRANSFER AGENT(S): Pittsburgh National Bank, Pittsburgh, PA 15265
West One Bank, Boise, ID 83701

NYS SYMBOL ASN
Rec. Pr. 55½

ALCO STANDARD CORP.

YIELD 1.8%
P/E RATIO N.M

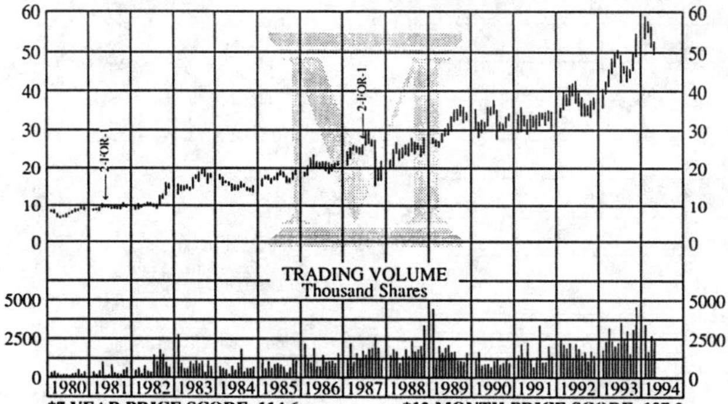

*7 YEAR PRICE SCORE 114.6 *12 MONTH PRICE SCORE 107.3

*NYSE COMPOSITE INDEX=100

INTERIM EARNINGS (Per Share):

Qtr.	Dec.	Mar.	June	Sept.
1990-91	0.38	0.45	0.52	0.60
1991-92	0.43	0.52	0.58	0.69
1992-93	0.52	0.57	0.58	d1.71
1993-94	0.60	0.64	...	...

INTERIM DIVIDENDS (Per Share):

Amt.	Decl.	Ex.	Rec.	Pay.
0.24Q	5/5/93	5/18/93	5/24/93	6/10/93
0.24Q	8/10	8/17	8/23	9/10
0.25Q	11/12	11/16	11/22	12/10
0.25Q	2/4/94	2/15/94	2/22/94	3/10/94
0.25Q	5/3	5/17	5/23	6/10

Indicated div.: $1.00

CAPITALIZATION (9/30/93):

	($000)	(%)
Long-Term Debt	590,154	36.1
Preferred Stock	222,900	13.6
Common & Surplus	822,716	50.3
Total	1,635,770	100.0

DIVIDEND ACHIEVER STATUS:
Rank: 274 1983-93 Growth Rate: 5.6%
Total Years of Dividend Growth: 29

RECENT DEVELOPMENTS: For the quarter ended 3/31/94, revenues increased 32.1% to $1.97 billion from $1.49 billion a year ago. Operating income was $84.9 million versus $66.7 million for the same period last year. Net income from continuing operations rose to $38.0 million from $29.5 million last year. Alco Office Products posted a 46.6% gain in revenues to $544.3 million while operating income rose 42.8% to $47.8 million. Unisource revenues increased 27.2% to $1.4 billion with operating income up 11.8% to $37.0 million.

PROSPECTS: Alco Office Products has been strengthened by several acquisitions and is now in a dominant position in the North American market. Its nationwide expansion of its on-site copier and fax machine management business should help future earnings. Latest acquisitions include Weiss Bros Miyuon, Inc. a distributor of paper, plastics and related products, and Copy Draft Inc. which sells, leases and services Canon copiers and facsimile machines.

BUSINESS

ALCO STANDARD is a distribution and service company with operations in paper distributing and converting, office products distribution and aviation and industrial services. The Company has three business groups. Paper Corporation of America markets and distributes paper, plastic and disposable products for office, industrial and food service use. Alco Office Products sells, leases and rents photocopiers, facsimile machines, micrographic equipment, typewriters and other automated office equipment and provides equipment service and supplies. Alco Diversified Services (formerly The Triumph Group) provides services and component distribution to the aviation industry and provides industrial services including steel processing, distribution and fabrication.

BUSINESS LINE ANALYSIS

(09/30/93)	Rev(%)	Inc(%)
Unisource	75.4	50.3
Alco Office Products	24.6	49.7
Total	100.0	100.0

ANNUAL EARNINGS AND DIVIDENDS PER SHARE

	9/30/93	9/30/92	9/30/91	9/30/90	9/30/89	9/30/88	9/30/87
Earnings Per Share	[1] d0.04	[1] 2.22	[1] 1.95	[1] 2.19	[1] 2.68	[1] 2.12	[1] 1.81
Dividends Per Share	0.97	0.93	0.89	0.85	0.78	0.70	[2] 0.65
Dividend Payout %	...	41.9	45.6	38.8	29.1	33.0	35.9

[1] Before disc. oper. [2] 2-for-1 stk. split, 6/87.

ANNUAL FINANCIAL DATA

RECORD OF EARNINGS (IN MILLIONS):

Total Revenues	6,444.6	4,925.1	4,758.2	4,320.4	4,145.9	3,816.9	3,633.2
Costs and Expenses	[1] 6,178.6	4,644.0	4,492.2	4,075.4	3,918.4	3,618.8	3,449.0
Depreciation & Amort	...	64.1	68.5	54.6	50.6	47.5	42.3
Operating Income	266.0	217.0	197.5	190.4	177.0	150.6	141.8
Inc Fr Contin Opers Bef Taxes	24.6	172.5	144.2	145.2	148.8	131.9	131.1
Taxes on Income	17.0	68.3	56.3	54.3	32.6	30.7	52.9
Net Income	[2] 7.6	[3] 104.2	[4] 87.9	[5] 90.9	[6] 116.2	[7] 100.0	[8] 75.5
Aver. Shs. Outstg. (000)	47,396	46,876	44,574	41,523	43,309	47,195	44,393

[1] Incl. Dep. [2] Before disc. op. dr$7,515,000. [3] Before disc. op. dr$8,455,000. [4] Before disc. op. cr$29,715,000. [5] Before disc. op. cr$15,268,000. [6] Before disc. op. cr$54,550,000. [7] Before disc. op. cr$10,006,000. [8] Before disc. op. cr$4,758,000.

BALANCE SHEET (IN MILLIONS):

Cash and Cash Equivalents	36.5	24.4	120.1	27.5	37.8	37.0	49.7
Accounts Receivable, Net	855.7	659.2	559.2	547.0	482.5	468.0	452.4
Inventories	592.0	460.2	365.9	361.2	324.0	315.9	339.7
Gross Property	596.9	545.0	460.7	521.6	463.9	421.4	436.9
Accumulated Depreciation	260.6	250.6	216.8	230.3	194.1	171.2	174.5
Long-Term Debt	590.2	472.0	291.0	237.6	165.6	170.5	177.9
Net Stockholders' Equity	1,045.6	860.4	821.2	685.7	594.4	658.8	604.3
Total Assets	3,348.9	2,444.8	2,020.6	1,738.1	1,478.7	1,399.0	1,324.3
Total Current Assets	1,576.7	1,183.5	1,078.9	957.9	865.7	838.6	861.3
Total Current Liabilities	1,020.2	687.5	562.9	570.1	535.7	443.2	408.9
Net Working Capital	556.6	496.0	516.0	387.8	330.0	395.4	452.3
Year End Shs Outstg (000)	46,964	45,949	44,638	40,887	40,280	48,640	47,300

STATISTICAL RECORD:

Operating Profit Margin %	4.1	4.4	4.2	4.4	4.3	3.9	3.9
Book Value Per Share	2.72	7.69	10.19	9.96	9.21	10.54	11.44
Return on Equity %	0.7	12.1	10.7	13.3	19.6	15.2	12.5
Return on Assets %	0.2	4.3	4.3	5.2	7.9	7.1	5.7
Average Yield %	2.1	2.5	2.7	2.6	2.5	2.9	2.9
P/E Ratio	...	19.2-14.9	18.4-14.9	17.3-12.6	13.7-9.5	13.2-9.6	17.6-9.0
Price Range	54¾-35¾	42⅝-33⅛	35⅞-29	37⅞-27⅝	36⅝-25⅜	28-20¼	30-15¼

Statistics are as originally reported.

OFFICERS:
R.B. Mundt, Chmn.
W.F. Drake, Jr., Vice-Chmn.
J.E. Stuart, Pres. & C.E.O.
K.E. Dinkelacker, Exec. V.P. & C.F.O.

INCORPORATED: OH, Nov., 1952

PRINCIPAL OFFICE: 825 Duportail Rd., Wayne, PA 19087-5589

TELEPHONE NUMBER: (215) 296-8000
FAX: (215) 296-8419
NO. OF EMPLOYEES: 28,500 (approx.)
ANNUAL MEETING: In February
SHAREHOLDERS: 13,973
INSTITUTIONAL HOLDINGS:
No. of Institutions: 228
Shares Held: 23,941,688

REGISTRAR(S): National City Bank, Cleveland, OH 44114

TRANSFER AGENT(S): National City Bank, Cleveland, OH 44114

NYS SYMBOL AYP
Rec. Pr. 20⅝

ALLEGHENY POWER SYSTEM, INC.

YIELD 8.0%
P/E RATIO 11.0

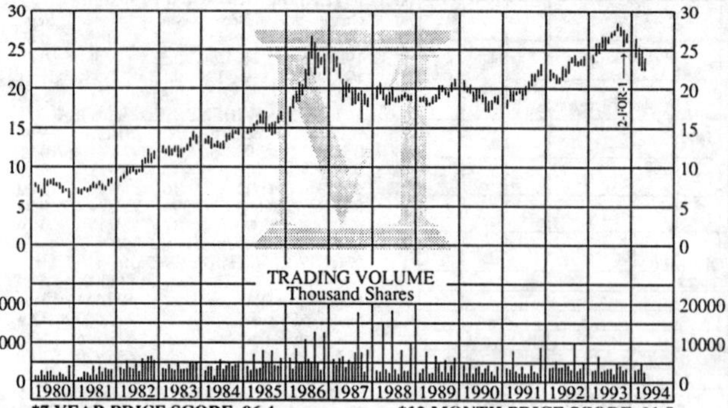

2-FOR-1
TRADING VOLUME
Thousand Shares
1980 1981 1982 1983 1984 1985 1986 1987 1988 1989 1990 1991 1992 1993 1994

*7 YEAR PRICE SCORE 96.4 *12 MONTH PRICE SCORE 91.5

*NYSE COMPOSITE INDEX=100

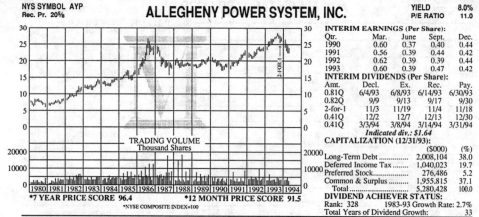

INTERIM EARNINGS (Per Share):

Qtr.	Mar.	June	Sept.	Dec.
1990	0.60	0.37	0.40	0.44
1991	0.56	0.39	0.44	0.42
1992	0.62	0.39	0.39	0.44
1993	0.60	0.39	0.47	0.42

INTERIM DIVIDENDS (Per Share):

Amt.	Decl.	Ex.	Rec.	Pay.
0.81Q	6/4/93	6/8/93	6/14/93	6/30/93
0.82Q	9/9	9/13	9/17	9/30
2-for-1	11/3	11/19	11/4	11/18
0.41Q	12/2	12/7	12/13	12/30
0.41Q	3/3/94	3/8/94	3/14/94	3/31/94

Indicated div.: $1.64

CAPITALIZATION (12/31/93):

	($000)	(%)
Long-Term Debt	2,008,104	38.0
Deferred Income Tax	1,040,023	19.7
Preferred Stock	276,486	5.2
Common & Surplus	1,955,815	37.1
Total	5,280,428	100.0

DIVIDEND ACHIEVER STATUS:

Rank: 328 1983-93 Growth Rate: 2.7%

Total Years of Dividend Growth: 33

RECENT DEVELOPMENTS: For the quarter ended 3/31/94, net income advanced 16.7% to $78.9 million from $67.6 million in 1993. Revenues were $704.3 million, up 14.6%. The improved results are due to greater kilowatthour sales to retail customers and rate increases, primarily in Maryland and Pennsylvania. Retail sales were favorably affected by record-setting cold temperatures in January. These increases in retail revenues were offset in part by continued increases in maintenance, depreciation, and other expenses.

PROSPECTS: The Company has reported that compliance with Phase I of the Clean Air Act of 1990 will cost it $669 million, down from a 1991 estimate of $806 million. The costs savings are mostly due to regulators allowing the Company to include certain construction costs in its rates during construction. Other savings came from favorable constuction contracts and planning. The full cost of Phase II of the Clean Air Act cannot be estimated at this time, but is expected to be significant.

BUSINESS

ALLEGHENY POWER SYSTEM, INC. furnishes electricity in western Pennsylvania, northern West Virginia, western Maryland and small adjoining sections of Ohio and Virginia. Monongahela Power Co., Potomac Edison Co., and West Penn Power Co., its subsidiaries, serve 1.3 million customers in an area of 29,100 square miles with a population of 2.9 million. The service areas contains heavy industry, particularly iron and steel operations and bituminous coal mining. In 1993, about 90% of generating capacity was fueled by coal.

REVENUES

(12/31/93)	($000)	(%)
Residential	818,400	35.1
Commercial	430,202	18.5
Industrial	673,418	28.8
Nonaffiliated Utilities	346,705	14.9
Other	62,801	2.7
Total	2,331,526	100.0

ANNUAL EARNINGS AND DIVIDENDS PER SHARE

	1993	1992	1991	1990	1989	1988	1987
Earnings Per Share	**1.88**	**1.83**	**1.81**	**1.81**	**1.86**	**1.98**	**2.03**
Dividends Per Share	**[1] 1.63**	**1.605**	**1.585**	**1.58**	**1.55**	**1.51**	**1.47**
Dividend Payout %	**86.7**	**87.7**	**87.8**	**87.5**	**83.3**	**76.3**	**72.6**

[1] Adj for 2-for-1 stk split, 11/19/93

ANNUAL FINANCIAL DATA

	1993	1992	1991	1990	1989	1988	1987
RECORD OF EARNINGS (IN MILLIONS):							
Total Operating Revenues	2,331.5	2,306.7	2,282.2	2,301.9	2,260.7	2,170.5	1,981.2
Depreciation	210.4	197.8	189.7	180.9	172.3	165.7	158.8
Maintenance	231.2	210.9	204.2	182.0	185.5	166.6	180.8
Operating Income	374.6	356.1	349.5	341.5	337.3	350.6	354.6
Interest Expense	154.3	145.8	142.3	138.2	134.3	134.9	132.0
Net Income	215.8	203.5	194.0	191.4	194.9	205.1	207.0
Aver. Shs. Outstg. (000)	114,937	111,226	107,548	106,102	104,786	103,460	102,184
BALANCE SHEET (IN MILLIONS):							
Gross Plant	7,176.8	6,679.9	6,255.7	5,986.2	5,721.5	5,493.0	5,320.2
Accumulated Depreciation	2,388.8	2,240.0	2,093.7	1,946.1	1,807.1	1,680.2	1,539.3
Prop, Plant & Equip-net	4,788.1	4,439.9	4,162.0	4,040.1	3,914.4	3,812.9	3,781.0
Long-term Debt	2,008.1	1,951.6	1,747.6	1,642.2	1,578.4	1,586.1	1,604.3
Net Stockholders' Equity	2,232.3	2,105.9	1,950.0	1,897.9	1,848.2	1,790.7	1,717.5
Total Assets	5,949.2	5,039.3	4,855.0	4,561.3	4,433.3	4,334.4	4,304.3
Year End Shs Outstg (000)	117,664	113,898	108,452	106,984	105,578	104,268	102,982
STATISTICAL RECORD:							
Book Value Per Share	16.49	15.92	15.40	15.12	14.85	14.48	13.95
Op. Inc/Net Pl %	7.8	8.0	8.4	8.5	8.6	9.2	9.4
Dep/Gr. Pl %	2.9	3.0	3.0	3.0	3.0	3.0	3.0
Accum. Dep/Gr. Pl %	33.3	33.5	33.5	32.5	31.6	30.6	28.9
Return on Equity %	9.8	9.8	10.1	10.2	10.7	11.7	12.3
Average Yield %	6.3	7.1	7.8	8.3	7.9	7.8	7.3
P/E Ratio	15.2-12.5	13.3-11.3	12.9-9.7	11.7-9.4	11.4-9.6	10.5-9.1	12.1-7.8
Price Range	28½-23½	24⅜-20¾	23¼-17½	21⅛-17	21¼-17⅞	20¾-18	24½-15¾

Statistics are as originally reported.

OFFICERS:
K. Bergman, Chmn., Pres. & C.E.O.
S.I. Garnett, II, V.P.-Fin.
N.L. Campbell, V.P. & Treas.

INCORPORATED: MD, Dec., 1925

PRINCIPAL OFFICE: 12 East 49th Street, New York, NY 10017-1028

TELEPHONE NUMBER: (212) 752-2121
FAX: (212) 836-4340
NO. OF EMPLOYEES: 819
ANNUAL MEETING: In May
SHAREHOLDERS: 43,743
INSTITUTIONAL HOLDINGS:
No. of Institutions: 265
Shares Held: 22,594,402

REGISTRAR(S): Manufacturers Hanover Trust Co., New York, NY
Manufacturers Hanover Trust Co. of CA, Los Angeles, CA

TRANSFER AGENT(S): Manufacturers Hanover Trust Co., New York, NY
Manufacturers Hanover Trust Co. of CA, Los Angeles, CA

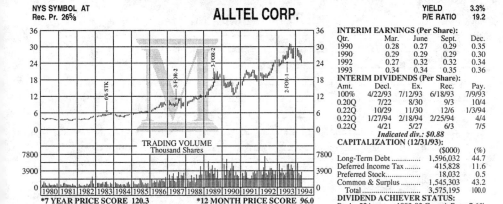

ALLTEL CORP.

YIELD 3.3%
P/E RATIO 19.2

INTERIM EARNINGS (Per Share):

Qtr.	Mar.	June	Sept.	Dec.
1990	0.28	0.27	0.29	0.35
1990	0.29	0.29	0.29	0.30
1992	0.27	0.32	0.32	0.34
1993	0.34	0.34	0.35	0.36

INTERIM DIVIDENDS (Per Share):

Amt.	Decl.	Ex.	Rec.	Pay.
100%	4/22/93	7/12/93	6/18/93	7/9/93
0.20Q	7/22	8/30	9/3	10/4
0.22Q	10/29	11/30	12/6	1/3/94
0.22Q	1/27/94	2/18/94	2/25/94	4/4
0.22Q	4/21	5/27	6/3	7/5

Indicated div.: $0.88

CAPITALIZATION (12/31/93):

	($000)	(%)
Long-Term Debt	1,596,032	44.7
Deferred Income Tax	415,828	11.6
Preferred Stock	18,032	0.5
Common & Surplus	1,545,303	43.2
Total	3,575,195	100.0

DIVIDEND ACHIEVER STATUS:
Rank: 224   1983-93 Growth Rate: 7.6%
Total Years of Dividend Growth: 33

*7 YEAR PRICE SCORE 120.3   *12 MONTH PRICE SCORE 96.0
*NYSE COMPOSITE INDEX=100

RECENT DEVELOPMENTS: For the year ended 12/31/93, net income increased 14.6% to $262.0 million from $228.6 million last year. Revenues were $2.34 billion, up 12.5%. Telephone Operations reported a 12% increase in operating income to $353.2 million. Telephone Operation's results reflect solid internal growth, as well as expansion in Georgia in connection with repositioning efforts. Information Services had a 23% increase in operating income to $116.6 million.

PROSPECTS: ALLTEL's data processing segment should be able to maintain strong profit growth due to the addition of new customers. Telephone operation's earnings growth will hinge on continued control of expense levels. AT is aggressively pursuing new subscribers to its cellular service and should continue to demonstrate double-digit growth rate potential. Cellular operations are making larger contributions to the Company's financial performance.

BUSINESS

ALLTEL CORPORATION provides telephone service to nearly 1.2 million customers in twenty-five states and has subsidiaries or investments in companies that provide cellular telephone service, information services, communications products and other related services. The Company's cellular operations serve 6.8 million "pops" (one gauge of potential customers) in twenty-one states. ALLTEL distributes equipment nationwide through two subsidiaries: ALLTEL Supply Inc., a supplier of telecommunications equipment, and HWC Distributing Corp., one of the nation's largest master distributors of special wire and cable products. Systematics, Inc., is a provider of data processing management, applications software and consulting services for banks and other financial institutions.

BUSINESS LINE ANALYSIS

(12/31/93)	Rev(%)	Inc(%)
Telephone	43.4	65.4
Information Services	28.9	21.6
Product Distribution	15.8	3.1
Cellular	8.6	8.2
Other Operations	3.3	1.7
Total	100.0	100.0

ANNUAL EARNINGS AND DIVIDENDS PER SHARE

	1993	1992	1991	1990	1989	1988	1987
Earnings Per Share	1.39	1.22	1.17	1.17	1.16	0.97	1.03
Dividends Per Share	① 1.40	0.74	0.70	0.64	② 0.575	0.506	③ 0.467
Dividend Payout %	N.M.	60.7	59.8	54.5	49.6	52.2	45.5

① 2-for-1 stk split,07/12/93 ② 3-for-2 stk split, 7/14/89 ③ 3-for-2 stk split, 5/87

ANNUAL FINANCIAL DATA

RECORD OF EARNINGS (IN MILLIONS):

	1993	1992	1991	1990	1989	1988	1987
Revenues & Sales	2,342.1	2,092.1	1,747.8	1,573.8	1,225.6	1,068.5	735.6
Costs and Expenses	1,550.6	①1,404.8	①1,181.9	①1,031.2	①772.7	①663.9	①421.6
Depreciation & Amort	272.4	...	...	...	...	...	...
Operating Income	519.0	442.7	348.9	350.5	287.7	250.0	188.7
Income Bef Income Taxes	449.9	357.3	282.3	283.7	220.2	191.8	158.3
Fed & State Income Taxes	187.9	128.7	93.3	90.9	66.3	66.8	54.0
Net Income	262.0	228.6	189.0	192.8	153.9	125.0	104.4
Aver. Shs. Outstg. (000)	187,665	185,672	160,096	162,446	130,816	126,082	148,582

① Incl. Dep.

BALANCE SHEET (IN MILLIONS):

Cash & Short-term Invests	7.9	30.4	50.4	42.4	29.1	36.1	41.8
Accounts Receivable	379.7	257.3	219.1	222.0	189.3	171.1	92.5
Inventories	91.0	78.1	82.2	88.6	89.7	58.4	45.2
Gross Property	4,234.8	3,297.4	2,913.5	2,759.4	2,485.7	2,394.8	1,991.2
Accumulated Depreciation	1,558.4	1,235.4	1,088.1	1,004.6	871.2	842.3	680.1
Long-Term Debt	1,596.0	1,018.2	992.3	905.2	799.0	675.1	554.1
Net Stockholders' Equity	1,563.3	1,314.0	1,093.0	1,028.8	920.2	817.3	612.9
Total Assets	4,270.5	3,126.0	2,787.5	2,623.8	2,379.1	2,153.1	1,681.7
Total Current Assets	494.1	378.4	361.7	363.0	317.7	273.5	188.2
Total Current Liabilities	608.6	451.5	360.5	343.3	321.6	314.3	224.3
Net Working Capital	d114.4	d73.0	1.2	19.6	d4.0	d40.8	d36.2
Year End Shs Outstg (000)	187,458	184,678	158,438	158,438	132,542	126,934	148,914

STATISTICAL RECORD:

Book Value Per Share	5.53	4.86	4.58	4.60	4.85	5.14	3.30
Return on Equity %	16.9	17.5	17.5	19.0	17.2	15.8	17.9
Average Yield %	5.2	3.5	3.7	4.0	3.5	4.8	4.9
P/E Ratio	22.5-16.5	20.5-14.4	18.5-13.6	16.8-10.6	18.1-10.0	13.0-8.9	11.2-7.5
Price Range	31¼-22⅞	25-17⅝	21⅝-15⅞	19⅝-12⅜	21-11⅝	12⅝-8⅝	11⅜-7⅝

Statistics are as originally reported.

OFFICERS:
J.T. Ford, Chmn. & C.E.O.
M.E. Bobbitt, President
J.M. Green, Treasurer

INCORPORATED: OH, Jun., 1960

PRINCIPAL OFFICE: One Allied Drive, Little Rock, AR 72202

TELEPHONE NUMBER: (501) 661-8000
FAX: (501) 664-3469
NO. OF EMPLOYEES: 14,864
ANNUAL MEETING: In April
SHAREHOLDERS: 61,141
INSTITUTIONAL HOLDINGS:
No. of Institutions: 282
Shares Held: 71,035,064

REGISTRAR(S): Society National Bank, Cleveland, OH

TRANSFER AGENT(S): Society National Bank, Cleveland, OH

NYS SYMBOL AMB
Rec. Pr. 30⅝

AMERICAN BRANDS INC.

YIELD 6.5%
P/E RATIO 9.3

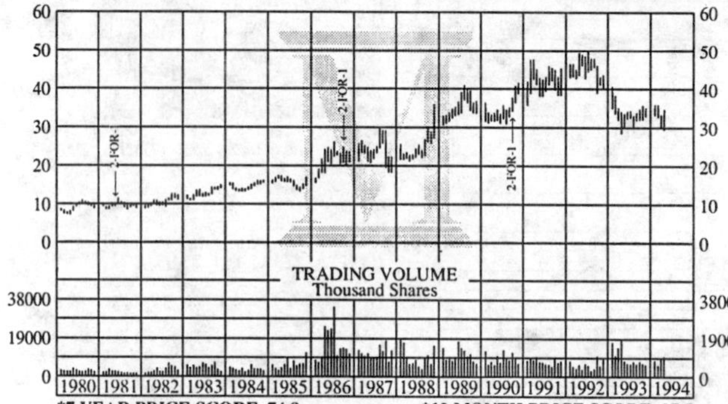

60
50
40
30
20
10
0
2-FOR-1
2-FOR-1
2-FOR-1
TRADING VOLUME
Thousand Shares
38000
19000
0
1980 1981 1982 1983 1984 1985 1986 1987 1988 1989 1990 1991 1992 1993 1994

*7 YEAR PRICE SCORE 74.8 *12 MONTH PRICE SCORE 97.5

*NYSE COMPOSITE INDEX=100

INTERIM EARNINGS (Per Share):

Qtr.	Mar.	June	Sept.	Dec.
1990	1.00	0.81	1.16	0.04
1991	1.06	0.90	0.91	1.04
1992	1.18	0.98	0.98	1.15
1993	1.22	0.75	0.42	0.91

INTERIM DIVIDENDS (Per Share):

Amt.	Decl.	Ex.	Rec.	Pay.
0.4925Q	4/27/93	5/5/93	5/11/93	6/1/93
0.4925Q	7/27	8/2	8/6	9/1
0.4925Q	10/27	11/1	11/5	12/1
0.4925Q	1/25/94	1/28/94	2/3/94	3/1/94
0.50Q	4/26	5/4	5/10	6/1

Indicated div.: $2.00

CAPITALIZATION (12/31/93):

	($000)	(%)
Long-Term Debt	2,492,400	36.2
Deferred Income Tax	124,700	1.8
Preferred Stock	17,100	0.2
Common & Surplus	4,254,300	61.8
Total	6,888,500	100.0

DIVIDEND ACHIEVER STATUS:
Rank: 209 1983-93 Growth Rate: 8.3%
Total Years of Dividend Growth: 26

RECENT DEVELOPMENTS: Net income for the year ended 12/31/93 was $668.2 million compared with $883.8 million a year ago. Results were before an accounting change of $198.4 million. The decline in profit was attributed to exchange rate fluctuations and fierce competition within the tobacco industry. Revenues decreased 6.3% to $13.70 billion. The American Tobacco unit reported a profit of $169.2 million, down 68% from 1992. Jim Beam's profit increased 13%.

PROSPECTS: Fierce competition and major price reductions in the U.S. cigarette market have negatively affected contributions from the domestic tobacco segment. In response, American Tobacco will move aggressively to reduce overhead through employment and promotional expense reductions. Internationally, Gallaher will move to capitalize on the growing mid-price segment, while Jim Beam is positioned for future growth with low cost production and a broad brand portfolio.

BUSINESS

AMERICAN BRANDS INC. is a global consumer products holding company. Tobacco Products include American Tobacco, one of the largest cigarette producers in the U.S. and Gallaher Ltd., the leading cigarette producer in the U.K. Major brands are Carlton, Pall Mall and Benson & Hedges. Distilled Spirits include Jim Beam Brands Co. and the U.K.-based Whyte & Mackay Distillers Ltd. Life insurance is marketed through the Franklin group of companies. ACCO World Corporation manufactures and markets office supplies. Hardware and Home Improvement operates through MasterBrand Industries. Specialty Businesses include golf and leisure equipment and optical goods.

BUSINESS LINE ANALYSIS

(12/31/93)	Rev(%)	Inc(%)
Tobacco Products	54.3	47.0
Distilled Spirits	8.7	15.4
Hardware & Home Improvement Products	7.8	11.1
Life Insurance	8.2	15.5
Office Products	7.1	4.5
Specialty Businesses	13.9	6.5
Total	100.0	100.0

ANNUAL EARNINGS AND DIVIDENDS PER SHARE

	1993	1992	1991	1990	1989	1988	1987
Earnings Per Share	**3.30**	**4.29**	**3.91**	**[1] 2.99**	**3.26**	**[3] 2.72**	**[3] 2.21**
Dividends Per Share	**1.97**	**1.805**	**1.593**	**[2] 1.405**	**1.255**	**1.13**	**1.055**
Dividend Payout %	**59.7**	**42.1**	**40.7**	**47.0**	**38.6**	**41.5**	**47.7**

[1] Per primary shrare [2] 2-for-1 stk split, 10/25/90 [3] Before disc. oper.

ANNUAL FINANCIAL DATA

RECORD OF EARNINGS (IN MILLIONS):

	1993	1992	1991	1990	1989	1988	1987
Total Revenues	13,701.4	14,623.6	14,063.8	13,780.9	11,921.4	11,980.0	9,152.9
Costs and Expenses	2,544.2	2,523.1	2,408.2	2,125.4	1,778.8	1,702.1	8,109.7
Depreciation & Amort	308.9	304.1	281.2	250.5	206.0	211.9	141.0
Operating Income	1,397.9	1,755.0	1,630.8	1,607.2	1,397.8	1,313.9	1,070.8
Income Bef Income Taxes	1,076.1	1,398.1	1,238.0	1,047.5	1,062.4	984.2	854.7
Income Taxes	407.9	514.3	431.9	451.5	431.6	443.4	351.9
Net Income	[1] 668.2	883.8	806.1	596.0	630.8	[2] 540.8	[3] 502.7
Aver. Shs. Outstg. (000)	201,800	204,000	202,600	194,451	189,153	193,400	220,308

[1] Before acctg. change dr$198,400,000. [2] Before disc. op. cr$39,200,000. [3] Before disc. op. cr$19,944,000.

BALANCE SHEET (IN MILLIONS):

	1993	1992	1991	1990	1989	1988	1987
Cash and Cash Equivalents	141.6	140.2	128.5	154.0	149.3	115.7	55.0
Receivables, Net	1,342.7	1,354.2	1,434.6	1,493.1	1,175.6	1,217.8	1,089.1
Inventories	2,043.2	1,810.2	2,141.0	2,032.6	1,675.0	1,815.9	1,693.4
Gross Property	[1] 1,472.1	[1] 1,406.4	[1] 1,472.4	2,430.5	1,991.1	1,933.4	1,839.7
Accumulated Depreciation	...	1,107.8	1,070.0	959.0	803.0	768.0	774.6
Long-Term Debt	2,492.4	2,406.8	2,555.1	2,433.8	1,717.4	2,359.2	1,631.5
Net Stockholders' Equity	4,271.4	4,301.6	4,316.0	3,790.0	3,101.5	2,660.7	3,103.9
Total Assets	16,339.0	14,963.0	15,115.5	13,835.2	11,394.2	12,200.6	7,343.1
Total Current Assets	...	3,680.7	4,060.9	3,963.9	3,095.3	3,235.0	3,393.2
Year End Shs Outstg (000)	201,744	202,577	203,918	200,357	189,412	186,800	220,178

[1] Net

STATISTICAL RECORD:

	1993	1992	1991	1990	1989	1988	1987
Operating Profit Margin %	10.2	12.0	11.6	11.7	11.7	11.0	11.7
Book Value Per Share	2.64	5.39	3.87	2.83	5.34	2.14	7.06
Return on Equity %	15.6	20.5	19.3	16.3	21.3	21.4	16.9
Return on Assets %	4.1	5.9	5.3	4.3	5.5	4.4	6.8
Average Yield %	5.7	4.1	3.8	3.9	3.5	4.0	4.4
P/E Ratio	12.3-8.6	11.6-9.1	12.2-9.1	13.9-10.3	12.6-9.4	13.2-7.8	13.6-8.3
Price Range	40⅝-28½	49⅞-39	47⅝-35⅝	41⅝-30⅞	41-30⅝	35⅞-21⅛	30-18¼

Statistics are as originally reported.

OFFICERS:
W.J. Alley, Chmn. & C.E.O.
T.C. Hays, Pres. & C.O.O.
A. Henson, Exec. V.P. & C.F.O.

INCORPORATED: DE, 1985

PRINCIPAL OFFICE: 1700 East Putnam Ave. P.O. Box 811, Old Greenwich, CT 06870-0811

TELEPHONE NUMBER: (203) 698-5000
FAX: (203) 637-2580
NO. OF EMPLOYEES: 5,766
ANNUAL MEETING: In May
SHAREHOLDERS: 43,951 common
INSTITUTIONAL HOLDINGS:
No. of Institutions: 560
Shares Held: 107,756,454

REGISTRAR(S): First Chicago Trust Co. of New York, New York, NY 10008

TRANSFER AGENT(S): First Chicago Trust Co. of New York, New York, NY 10008

AMERICAN BUSINESS PRODUCTS, INC.

YIELD	3.6%
P/E RATIO	14.0

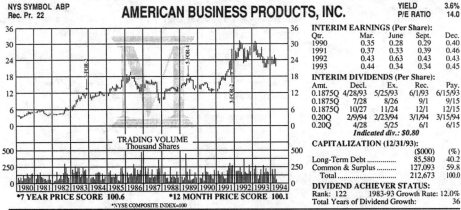

TRADING VOLUME
Thousand Shares

| 1980|1981|1982|1983|1984|1985|1986|1987|1988|1989|1990|1991|1992|1993|1994 |

*7 YEAR PRICE SCORE 100.6   *12 MONTH PRICE SCORE 100.1

*NYSE COMPOSITE INDEX=100

INTERIM EARNINGS (Per Share):

Qtr.	Mar.	June	Sept.	Dec.
1990	0.35	0.28	0.29	0.40
1991	0.37	0.33	0.39	0.46
1992	0.43	0.63	0.43	0.43
1993	0.44	0.34	0.34	0.45

INTERIM DIVIDENDS (Per Share):

Amt.	Decl.	Ex.	Rec.	Pay.
0.1875Q	4/28/93	5/25/93	6/1/93	6/15/93
0.1875Q	7/28	8/26	9/1	9/15
0.1875Q	10/27	11/24	12/1	12/15
0.20Q	2/9/94	2/23/94	3/1/94	3/15/94
0.20Q	4/28	5/25	6/1	6/15

Indicated div.: $0.80

CAPITALIZATION (12/31/93):

	($000)	(%)
Long-Term Debt	85,580	40.2
Common & Surplus	127,093	59.8
Total	212,673	100.0

DIVIDEND ACHIEVER STATUS:

Rank: 122   1983-93 Growth Rate: 12.0%
Total Years of Dividend Growth: 36

RECENT DEVELOPMENTS: For the year ended 12/31/93, net income declined 14.8% to $16.7 million compared with $19.6 million, before an accounting adjustment, a year ago. Sales rose 4.9% to $486.1 million from $463.5 million. Earnings were adversely affected by an increase in the federal tax rate and costs associated with two acquisitions. Sales and earnings included the results of Discount Labels and International Envelope Company, both acquired in 1993.

PROSPECTS: Competitive conditions in the industry are expected to adversely affect operating results. The growth trend in revenues should continue into 1994. The Jen-Coat subsidiary's polyethylene coated paper and non-woven fabrics will contribute significantly to results. Revenues will be enhanced by the acquisition of International Envelope Company of Exton, PA. International Envelope will operate as a division of American Fiber-Velope Manufacturing Company.

BUSINESS

AMERICAN BUSINESS PRODUCTS, INC. is a leading manufacturer and distributor of business forms, envelopes and supplies used to manage information more efficiently. ABP's product line consists of three segments: business supplies printing, book manufacturing, and specialty extrusion coating and laminating. Business supplies and products consist primarily of business forms and specialty mailers and envelopes. Book manufacturing includes production of hard and soft covered books, catalogs, and brochures. Specialty extrusion coating and laminating applies plastic coatings to rolls of paper, film, or fabric.

ANNUAL EARNINGS AND DIVIDENDS PER SHARE

	1993	1992	1991	1990	1989	1988	1987
Earnings Per Share	1.56	1.83	1.55	1.33	1.27	1.21	④ 1.04
Dividends Per Share	0.75	① 0.70	② 0.627	0.587	③ 0.523	0.469	0.427
Dividend Payout %	48.1	38.3	40.3	44.0	41.3	38.7	41.0

① Bef acctg chge ② 3-for-2 stk split,12/17/91 ③ 5-for-4 stk split, 6/89 ④ Before disc. oper.

ANNUAL FINANCIAL DATA

RECORD OF EARNINGS (IN THOUSANDS):

	1993	1992	1991	1990	1989	1988	1987
Total Revenues	486,139	463,470	446,533	398,794	387,140	358,242	325,768
Costs and Expenses	439,348	419,760	403,060	363,366	354,068	327,537	297,768
Depreciation & Amort	14,661	11,809	10,953	9,650	8,806	7,632	6,701
Operating Profit	32,130	31,901	32,520	25,778	24,266	23,073	21,299
Income Bef Income Taxes	26,643	30,487	26,736	22,465	22,101	21,510	19,864
Total Prov for Inc Taxes	9,960	10,905	10,248	8,197	8,484	8,500	8,708
Net Income	16,683	① 19,582	16,488	14,268	13,617	13,010	② 11,156
Aver. Shs. Outstg.	10,683	10,691	10,671	10,718	10,728	10,712	10,701

① Before acctg. change dr$12,449,000. ② Before disc. op. dr$1,785,000.

BALANCE SHEET (IN THOUSANDS):

	1993	1992	1991	1990	1989	1988	1987
Cash & Cash Equivalents	30,151	30,025	25,256	20,092	13,522	7,421	13,909
Receivables, Net	65,000	53,671	52,871	51,789	49,546	49,158	43,380
Inventories	45,687	37,272	37,384	35,147	31,713	34,205	26,999
Gross Property	176,220	149,466	135,922	130,058	115,739	105,758	96,247
Accumulated Depreciation	81,772	71,540	62,572	58,018	52,912	47,561	42,170
Long-Term Debt	85,580	40,005	41,673	43,339	11,277	8,858	10,088
Net Stockholders' Equity	127,093	118,819	119,783	109,875	103,264	95,145	87,117
Total Assets	302,192	237,238	218,086	207,003	164,140	152,257	141,036
Total Current Assets	141,768	121,938	115,735	107,418	95,088	90,987	84,415
Total Current Liabilities	55,330	44,509	42,809	39,825	36,451	35,983	32,563
Net Working Capital	86,438	77,429	72,926	67,593	58,637	55,004	51,852
Year End Shares Outstg	10,682	10,686	10,683	10,656	10,740	10,715	10,704

STATISTICAL RECORD:

	1993	1992	1991	1990	1989	1988	1987
Operating Profit Margin %	6.6	6.9	7.3	6.5	6.3	6.4	6.5
Book Value Per Share	8.63	9.50	9.49	8.49	9.37	8.82	8.07
Return on Equity %	13.1	16.5	13.8	13.0	13.2	13.7	12.8
Return on Assets %	5.5	8.3	7.6	6.9	8.3	8.5	7.9
Average Yield %	2.9	2.6	3.1	4.2	3.4	3.9	3.4
P/E Ratio	19.9-13.5	17.1-12.4	18.1-8.1	11.9-9.1	14.2-10.2	11.8-8.0	16.1-7.9
Price Range	31-21⅛	31¼-22¾	28-12½	15⅞-12⅛		18-13	14¼-9⅝	16¾-8¼

Statistics are as originally reported.

OFFICERS:
T.R. Carmody, Pres. & C.E.O.
W.C. Downer, V.P.-Fin., C.F.O. & Chief Accounting Off.
D.M. Gray, Sec.

INCORPORATED: GA, Apr., 1986

PRINCIPAL OFFICE: 2100 RiverEdge Pkwy., Suite 1200, Atlanta, GA 30328

TELEPHONE NUMBER: (404) 953-8300
FAX: (404) 952-2343
NO. OF EMPLOYEES: 269
ANNUAL MEETING: In April
SHAREHOLDERS: 713 (approx.)
INSTITUTIONAL HOLDINGS:
No. of Institutions: 50
Shares Held: 2,702,961

REGISTRAR(S): C & S Investor Services, Atlanta, GA 30348

TRANSFER AGENT(S): C & S Investor Services, Atlanta, GA 30348

AMERICAN FILTRONA CORP.

YIELD 3.3%
P/E RATIO 14.7

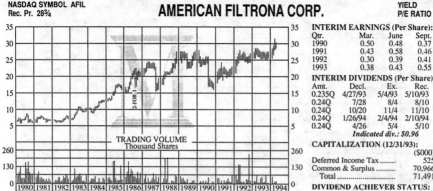

*7 YEAR PRICE SCORE 89.5   *12 MONTH PRICE SCORE 110.6

*NYSE COMPOSITE INDEX=100

INTERIM EARNINGS (Per Share):

Qtr.	Mar.	June	Sept.	Dec.
1990	0.50	0.48	0.37	0.52
1991	0.43	0.58	0.46	0.49
1992	0.30	0.39	0.41	d0.77
1993	0.38	0.43	0.55	0.60

INTERIM DIVIDENDS (Per Share):

Amt.	Decl.	Ex.	Rec.	Pay.
0.235Q	4/27/93	5/4/93	5/10/93	5/25/93
0.24Q	7/28	8/4	8/10	8/25
0.24Q	10/20	11/4	11/10	11/24
0.24Q	1/26/94	2/4/94	2/10/94	2/25/94
0.24Q	4/26	5/4	5/10	5/25

Indicated div.: $0.96

CAPITALIZATION (12/31/93):

	($000)	(%)
Deferred Income Tax	525	0.7
Common & Surplus	70,966	99.3
Total	71,491	100.0

DIVIDEND ACHIEVER STATUS:
Rank: 275   1983-93 Growth Rate: 5.5%
Total Years of Dividend Growth: 23

RECENT DEVELOPMENTS: For the year ended 12/31/93, income from continuing operations increased 4.4% to $6.7 million, or $1.80 per share, from $6.4, or $1.73 per share, million in 1992. Total revenues rose 7.1% to $131.5 million from $122.9 million a year ago. Net sales were up 7.1% to $130.9 million, or 99.5% of total revenues, from $122.3 million, or 99.5% of total revenues, in 1992. Bonded fibers segment sales decreased marginally as higher sales of writing instrument and other fiber products did not offset a decrease in tobacco filter sales. Plastic products segment sales increased 12% and investment income increased 2% for the year. For the quarter, income from continuing operations increased 2% to $1.94 million, or $0.52 per share, from $1.90 million, or $0.51 per share, for the comparable 1992 quarter. Net sales rose 12.6% to $32.4 million from $28.8 million for the same period last year.

BUSINESS

AMERICAN FILTRONA CORPORATION develops and manufactures various fiber products in the United States and Canada and industrial filtration products in the United States and Ireland. The Company's principal products are: fiber filters for cigarettes and cigars, fiber ink reservoirs, tips and wicks for writing instruments; a variety of plastic products, converted from plastic resins and films and used in food packaging, lighting fixtures, signs and displays and many other applications; and filters and filtration systems primarily for protecting industrial equipment from contaminents.

BUSINESS LINE ANALYSIS

(12/31/93)	Rev(%)	Inc(%)
Bonded Fibers	38.9	43.4
Plastic Products	61.1	56.6
Total	100.0	100.0

ANNUAL EARNINGS AND DIVIDENDS PER SHARE

	1993	1992	1991	1990	1989	1988	1987
Earnings Per Share	1.96	0.33	1.96	1.87	2.08	1.68	1.50
Dividends Per Share	0.95	0.94	0.92	0.88	0.83	0.78	0.74
Dividend Payout %	48.5	N.M.	46.9	47.1	39.9	46.4	49.3

ANNUAL FINANCIAL DATA

RECORD OF EARNINGS (IN THOUSANDS):

	1993	1992	1991	1990	1989	1988	1987
Total Revenues	131,532	145,423	145,861	145,414	148,236	135,859	123,830
Costs and Expenses	117,141	131,912	130,423	129,985	131,924	122,821	110,218
Depreciation & Amort	3,910	4,549	4,032	4,306	3,715	3,310	2,895
Operating Profit	26,112	32,388	33,685	32,792	32,639	29,329	26,712
Income Bef Income Taxes	10,480	2,462	11,406	11,124	12,597	9,727	9,517
Income Taxes	3,775	1,250	4,100	4,175	4,900	3,600	4,000
Net Income	⊡ 6,705	1,212	7,306	6,949	7,697	6,127	5,517
Aver. Shs. Outstg.	3,728	3,716	3,719	3,716	3,695	3,658	3,680

⊡ Before disc. op. cr$611,288.

BALANCE SHEET (IN THOUSANDS):

	1993	1992	1991	1990	1989	1988	1987
Cash and Cash Equivalents	24,276	18,211	18,977	14,083	7,677	14,655	16,955
Receivables, Net	14,139	14,406	14,751	15,301	17,165	13,430	12,857
Inventories	11,475	15,366	13,614	15,310	15,084	15,664	13,129
Gross Property	47,208	54,095	51,193	48,577	46,414	46,377	39,835
Accumulated Depreciation	28,688	30,676	27,755	25,567	22,122	26,367	23,582
Long-Term Debt	...	...	...	...	...	1,000	...
Net Stockholders' Equity	70,966	67,421	70,159	66,397	62,511	57,130	53,254
Total Assets	87,094	83,069	86,070	82,869	80,199	73,994	67,039
Total Current Assets	51,160	49,730	49,360	46,056	41,483	45,233	43,875
Total Current Liabilities	13,182	11,351	12,700	13,647	14,206	13,237	11,680
Net Working Capital	37,978	38,380	36,660	32,409	27,276	31,995	32,195
Year End Shares Outstg	3,739	3,718	3,707	3,714	3,709	3,671	3,650

STATISTICAL RECORD:

	1993	1992	1991	1990	1989	1988	1987
Operating Profit Margin %	8.0	6.2	7.8	7.6	8.5	7.2	8.7
Book Value Per Share	17.82	16.35	16.59	15.42	14.26	13.48	12.85
Return on Equity %	9.4	1.8	10.4	10.5	12.3	10.7	10.4
Return on Assets %	7.7	1.5	8.5	8.4	9.6	8.3	8.2
Average Yield %	3.6	3.8	4.4	4.0	3.3	3.5	3.7
P/E Ratio	15.8-13.9	84.8-63.6	12.4-9.2	15.0-8.6	13.3-10.7	16.4-10.4	16.3-10.3
Price Range	28½-25	28-21	24¼-18	28-16	27¾-22¼	27½-17½	24½-15½

Statistics are as originally reported.

OFFICERS:
R.H. Bunzl, Chmn.
J.L. Morgan, Pres. & C.E.O.
J.D. Barlow, Jr., V.P.-Fin. & Treas.
A.B. Gibbs, Sec.

INCORPORATED: NY, 1954; reincorp., VA, 1971

PRINCIPAL OFFICE: 3951 Westerre Parkway Suite 300, Richmond, VA 23233

TELEPHONE NUMBER: (804) 346-2400

FAX: (804) 346-0164

NO. OF EMPLOYEES: 1,200 (approx.)

ANNUAL MEETING: In April

SHAREHOLDERS: 1,200 (approx.)

INSTITUTIONAL HOLDINGS:
No. of Institutions: 24
Shares Held: 926,600

REGISTRAR(S): Wachovia Bank of North Carolina, N.A., P.O. Box 3001, Winston-Salem, NC 27102

TRANSFER AGENT(S): Wachovia Bank of North Carolina, N.A., P.O. Box 3001, Winston-Salem, NC 27102

AMERICAN HERITAGE LIFE INVESTMENT CORP.

YIELD 3.3%
P/E RATIO 11.9

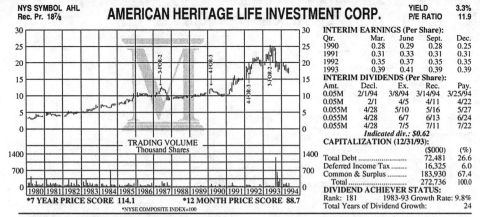

TRADING VOLUME
Thousand Shares

*7 YEAR PRICE SCORE 114.1   *12 MONTH PRICE SCORE 88.7
*NYSE COMPOSITE INDEX=100

INTERIM EARNINGS (Per Share):

Qtr.	Mar.	June	Sept.	Dec.
1990	0.28	0.29	0.28	0.25
1991	0.31	0.33	0.31	0.31
1992	0.35	0.37	0.35	0.35
1993	0.39	0.41	0.39	0.39

INTERIM DIVIDENDS (Per Share):

Amt.	Decl.	Ex.	Rec.	Pay.
0.05M	2/1/94	3/8/94	3/14/94	3/25/94
0.05M	2/1	4/5	4/11	4/22
0.055M	4/28	5/10	5/16	5/27
0.055M	4/28	6/7	6/13	6/24
0.055M	4/28	7/5	7/11	7/22

Indicated div.: $0.62

CAPITALIZATION (12/31/93):

	($000)	(%)
Total Debt	72,481	26.6
Deferred Income Tax	16,325	6.0
Common & Surplus	183,930	67.4
Total	272,736	100.0

DIVIDEND ACHIEVER STATUS:

Rank: 181   1983-93 Growth Rate: 9.8%
Total Years of Dividend Growth: 24

RECENT DEVELOPMENTS: For the quarter ended 3/31/94, net earnings rose to $5.8 million, or $0.42 per share, compared with $4.7 million, or $0.39 per share, a year earlier. Insurance revenues were $54.1 million, a decrease of 0.3% from the $54.3 million for the same period in 1993. Insurance revenues do not include group and credit premium equivalents and cash deposits from interest-sensitive products. Net investment income was $16.3 million, an increase of 9.0% over the $15.0 million reported last a year ago. The increase was due primarily to an increase in invested assets, additional income on the net proceeds of AHL's secondary public offering, and certain changes made in the equity security and fixed maturity portfolios during 1994 and 1993 to improve investment results.

BUSINESS

AMERICAN HERITAGE LIFE INVESTMENT CORPORATION is a holding company whose principal subsidiary is American Heritage Life Insurance Company. The insurance company is licensed in 49 states, Puerto Rico, The District of Columbia and the U.S. Virgin Islands and markets ordinary life, individual accident and health and annuities, group life and group accident and health, and credit life and credit accident and health insurance, through licensed agents and brokers. In addition, First Colonial Insurance Company, a subsidiary of American Heritage Life Insurance Company, markets credit property insurance and is currently licensed in twelve states.

BUSINESS LINE ANALYSIS

(12/31/93)	(Rev %)	(Inc %)
Ordinary	47.9	56.5
Group	23.2	19.8
Credit	28.9	23.7
Total	100.0	100.0

ANNUAL EARNINGS AND DIVIDENDS PER SHARE

	1993	1992	1991	1990	1989	1988	1987
Earnings Per Share	1.59	1.42	1.27	1.10	④ 0.97	0.91	0.81
Dividends Per Share	① 0.587	② 0.558	0.53	③ 0.50	0.436	0.421	⑤ 0.349
Dividend Payout %	36.9	39.3	41.7	45.5	44.9	46.5	43.3

① 3-for-2 stk split,05/21/93 ② 33.3% stk div, 3/2/92 ③ 33% stk div, 2/26/90 ④ Before extraord. item ⑤ 50% stk. div., 5/87.

ANNUAL FINANCIAL DATA

RECORD OF EARNINGS (IN MILLIONS):

	1993	1992	1991	1990	1989	1988	1987
Insurance Revenues	227.4	212.1	195.9	178.0	163.2	197.7	181.7
Net Investment Income	63.9	59.7	54.5	43.4	38.9	33.1	25.0
Total Income	292.4	272.0	250.5	220.8	201.6	...	...
Benefits & Claims	159.3	155.7	147.7	128.1	121.2	160.7	142.0
Earn Bef Income Taxes	28.9	24.2	22.0	18.7	16.6	...	...
Total Income Taxes	9.2	7.3	6.9	5.7	4.9	4.1	2.3
Net Income	19.7	16.9	15.1	13.1	① 11.6	11.0	10.6
Aver. Shs. Outstg. (000)	12,399	11,903	11,860	11,898	11,975	12,044	12,313

① Before extra. item cr$3,316,000.

BALANCE SHEET (IN MILLIONS):

	1993	1992	1991	1990	1989	1988	1987
Cash	19.0	18.1	15.2	13.2	8.3	6.4	6.2
Fixed Matur Held for Sale	443.3	365.4	332.3	297.8	266.6	224.3	189.1
Equity Securities	54.9	87.6	54.4	33.7	36.4	30.9	17.5
Policy Loans	334.7	292.5	247.9	207.3	111.8	72.7	61.2
Mtge Loans on Real Estate	17.9	14.0	15.1	16.8	17.0	16.2	17.1
Total Assets	1,138.6	1,017.0	892.6	780.6	610.9	510.8	440.3
Benefits and Claims	818.9	745.6	684.9	615.4	446.5	344.6	286.6
Net Stockholders' Equity	183.9	148.0	131.1	114.1	109.3	101.8	95.5
Year End Shs Outstg (000)	13,834	7,927	11,835	11,855	11,985	11,977	12,106

STATISTICAL RECORD:

	1993	1992	1991	1990	1989	1988	1987
Book Value Per Share	13.30	18.67	11.08	9.63	9.12	8.50	7.89
Return on Equity %	10.7	11.4	11.5	11.5	10.6	10.8	11.1
Return on Assets %	1.7	1.7	1.7	1.7	1.9	2.2	2.4
Average Yield %	2.8	3.0	4.1	4.5	4.3	4.4	3.3
P/E Ratio	16.0-10.8	15.2-10.7	12.7-7.9	11.1-8.9	11.3-9.7	11.1-9.9	15.7-10.6
Price Range	25⅜-17¼	21⅝-15¼	16⅛-10	12¼-9¾	11-9⅜	10⅛-9	12¾-8⅝

Statistics are as originally reported.

OFFICERS:
W.A. Verlander, Chairman
T.O. Douglas, Pres. & C.E.O.
C.A. Verlander, Exec. V.P. & Corp. Sec.
C.R. Morehead, Sr. V.P., Treas. & C.F.O.

INCORPORATED: FL, Sep., 1968

PRINCIPAL OFFICE: 76 South Laura Street, Jacksonville, FL 32202

TELEPHONE NUMBER: (904) 354-1776

NO. OF EMPLOYEES: 481

ANNUAL MEETING: In April

SHAREHOLDERS: 7,200 (approx.)

INSTITUTIONAL HOLDINGS:
No. of Institutions: 35
Shares Held: 1,344,369

REGISTRAR(S): Barnett Bank Trust Co., Jacksonville, FL

TRANSFER AGENT(S): Barnett Banks Trust Co., Jacksonville, FL

NYS SYMBOL AHP
Rec. Pr. 57⅜

AMERICAN HOME PRODUCTS CORP.

YIELD 5.1%
P/E RATIO 12.1

***7 YEAR PRICE SCORE 89.0** ***12 MONTH PRICE SCORE 94.7**

*NYSE COMPOSITE INDEX=100

INTERIM EARNINGS (Per Share):

Qtr.	Mar.	June	Sept.	Dec.
1990	1.00	0.86	1.01	1.04
1991	1.12	0.84	1.22	1.18
1992	1.29	0.94	1.37	1.16
1993	1.29	0.93	1.28	1.23

INTERIM DIVIDENDS (Per Share):

Amt.	Decl.	Ex.	Rec.	Pay.
0.71Q	4/21/93	5/7/93	5/13/93	6/1/93
0.71Q	7/29	8/9	8/13	9/1
0.73Q	10/28	11/5	11/12	12/1
0.73Q	1/27/94	2/7/94	2/11/94	3/1/94
0.73Q	4/20	5/9	5/13	6/1

Indicated div.: $2.92

CAPITALIZATION (12/31/93):

	($000)	(%)
Long-Term Debt	859,278	17.4
Minority Interests	198,630	4.0
Preferred Stock	100	0.0
Common & Surplus	3,876,388	78.6
Total	4,934,396	100.0

DIVIDEND ACHIEVER STATUS:

Rank: 197 1983-93 Growth Rate: 9.1%

Total Years of Dividend Growth: 41

RECENT DEVELOPMENTS: For the year ended 12/31/93, net income increased 27.7% to $1.47 billion compared with $1.15 billion, before an accounting adjustment a year ago. Sales rose 5.5% to $8.30 billion. Pharmaceutical sales were up 4% to $4.77 billion. The improved pharmaceutical sales were achieved despite increasingly competitive conditions in the U.S. market, soft economies, and the negative impact of a strong U.S. dollar on foreign exchange rates.

PROSPECTS: Operating results will benefit from the introduction of Effexor, an antidepressant which according to AHP has fewer side-effects than similar products. U.S. pharmaceutical sales should continue to rise as a result of growth in female health care, anti-inflammatory, rAHF and veterinary product sales. Consumer Health Care sales growth will be driven by the cough/cold product line and oral health care product lines in Latin America.

BUSINESS

AMERICAN HOME PRODUCTS CORPORATION is a leading manufacturer of health care products such as prescription drugs, medical devices, supplies and instrumentation, and over-the-counter medications. The Company also markets food and consumer products in the U.S. and Canada. Prescription drug subsidiaries include: Wyeth-Ayerst Labs, A.H. Robins Company, Sherwood Medical, Corometrics Medical Systems, Fort Dodge Laboratories and Whitehall Labs. Food Products include: American Home Foods producing Chef Boy-ar-dee, Gulden's mustard, Dennison's chili, Luck's beans and peas, Pam cooking spray, and Polaner All Fruit products.

BUSINESS LINE ANALYSIS

(12/31/93)	Rev(%)	Inc(%)
Healthcare Products	88.7	92.3
Food Products	11.3	7.7
Total	100.0	100.0

ANNUAL EARNINGS AND DIVIDENDS PER SHARE

	1993	1992	1991	1990	1989	1988	1987
Earnings Per Share	**4.73**	**[1] 3.66**	**4.36**	**3.92**	**3.54**	**3.19**	**2.87**
Dividends Per Share	**2.86**	**2.66**	**2.375**	**2.15**	**1.95**	**1.80**	**1.67**
Dividend Payout %	**60.5**	**72.7**	**54.5**	**54.8**	**55.2**	**56.4**	**58.3**

[1] Before acctg. chg.

ANNUAL FINANCIAL DATA

	1993	1992	1991	1990	1989	1988	1987
RECORD OF EARNINGS (IN MILLIONS):							
Total Revenues	8,304,9	7,873.7	7,079.4	6,775.2	6,747.0	5,530.6	5,072.5
Costs and Expenses	6,068.1	5,757.3	5,195.2	5,079.8	5,037.9	4,040.5	3,675.0
Depreciation & Amort	241.1	210.2	167.2	179.8	168.2	141.7	112.6
Operating Profit	1,995.7	1,906.2	1,717.0	1,515.7	1,541.0	1,348.5	1,284.9
Inc Bef Fed & Fgn Tax on Income	1,992.7	1,724.1	1,759.8	1,828.3	1,414.3	1,348.5	1,284.9
Tot Prov for Taxes on Inc	523.4	573.3	384.5	597.7	312.2	416.3	439.8
Net Income	1,469.3	[1] 1,150.7	1,375.3	1,230.6	1,102.2	932.2	845.1
Aver. Shs. Outstg. (000)	310,668	314,201	315.726	314,066	311,644	298.358	294,938

[1] Before acctg. change cr$310,104,000.

	1993	1992	1991	1990	1989	1988	1987
BALANCE SHEET (IN MILLIONS):							
Cash and Cash Equivalents	2,220.3	1,982.4	2,064.6	1,788.5	1,207.8	758.7	1,060.1
Accounts Receivable, Net	1,389.6	1,250.5	1,024.2	1,021.4	1,197.6	957.2	852.8
Inventories	958.9	944.6	842.0	795.9	892.1	735.1	698.8
Gross Property	3,460.4	3,056.9	2,659.2	2,532.8	2,453.2	2,061.6	1,806.2
Accumulated Depreciation	1,400.6	1,279.1	1,182.4	1,095.4	971.5	752.3	653.2
Long-Term Debt	859.3	601.9	104.7	...	...	...	...
Net Stockholders' Equity	3,876.5	3,562.6	3,300.5	2,675.2	1,970.0	2,975.7	2,529.7
Total Assets	7,687.4	7,141.4	5,938.8	5,637.1	5,681.5	4,610.7	4,608.4
Total Current Assets	4,807.7	4,552.1	4,119.1	3,826.1	3,532.8	2,576.2	2,714.9
Total Current Liabilities	1,584.4	1,492.7	1,270.1	1,028.7	1,108.9	866.0	1,291.0
Net Working Capital	3,223.3	3,059.4	2,848.9	2,797.4	2,423.9	1,710.2	1,423.9
Year End Shs Outstg (000)	310,326	313,048	315,623	314,028	312,532	292,236	290,440
STATISTICAL RECORD:							
Operating Profit Margin %	24.0	24.2	24.3	22.4	22.8	24.4	25.3
Book Value Per Share	12.49	11.38	10.46	8.52	6.30	7.98	6.47
Return on Equity %	37.9	32.3	41.7	46.0	55.9	31.3	33.4
Return on Assets %	19.1	16.1	23.2	21.8	19.4	20.2	18.3
Average Yield %	4.6	3.6	3.6	4.4	4.1	4.6	4.2
P/E Ratio	14.6-11.7	23.0-17.0	19.8-10.7	14.1-11.0	15.5-11.3	13.3-11.1	16.9-10.8
Price Range	69-55½	84¼-62¼	86¼-46½	55⅛-43	54¾-39⅞	42½-35¼	48⅜-31

Statistics are as originally reported.

OFFICERS:
J.R. Stafford, Chmn., C.E.O. & Pres.
J.R. Considine, V.P.-Fin.
R.E. Parker, Treas.
C.G. Emerling, Sec.

INCORPORATED: DE, Feb., 1926

PRINCIPAL OFFICE: Five Giralda Farms, Madison, NJ 07940

TELEPHONE NUMBER: (201) 660-5000

FAX: (201) 660-5771

NO. OF EMPLOYEES: 51,399

ANNUAL MEETING: In April

SHAREHOLDERS: 726 pfd.; 72,664 com.

INSTITUTIONAL HOLDINGS:
No. of Institutions: 959
Shares Held: 197,401,271

REGISTRAR(S): Continental Bank, N.A., Chicago, IL 60697
Manufacturers Hanover Trust Co., New York, NY

TRANSFER AGENT(S): Continental Bank, N.A., Chicago, IL 60697
Manufacturers Hanover Trust Co., New York, NY

NASDAQ SYMBOL ANAT
Rec. Pr. 49 (Marginable)

AMERICAN NATIONAL INSURANCE CO.

YIELD 4.5%
P/E RATIO 7.0

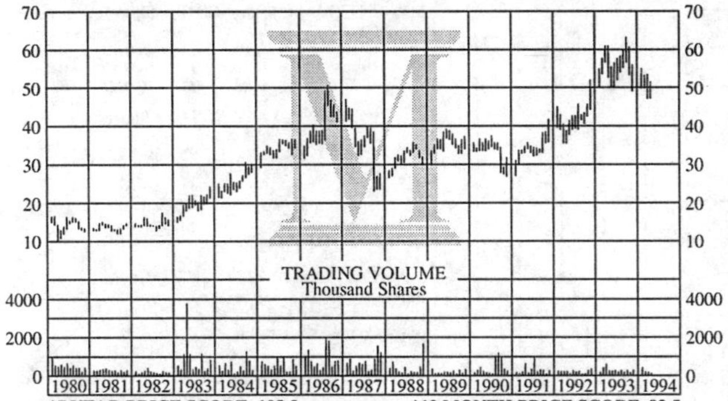

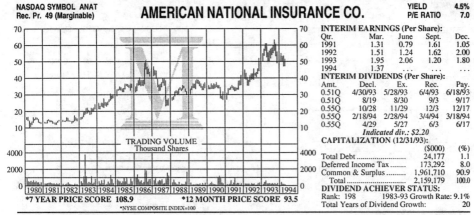

*7 YEAR PRICE SCORE 108.9 *12 MONTH PRICE SCORE 93.5

*NYSE COMPOSITE INDEX=100

INTERIM EARNINGS (Per Share):

Qtr.	Mar.	June	Sept.	Dec.
1991	1.31	0.79	1.61	1.05
1992	1.51	1.24	1.62	2.00
1993	1.95	2.06	1.20	1.80
1994	1.37	...	...	...

INTERIM DIVIDENDS (Per Share):

Amt.	Decl.	Ex.	Rec.	Pay.
0.51Q	4/30/93	5/28/93	6/4/93	6/18/93
0.51Q	8/19	8/30	9/3	9/17
0.55Q	10/28	11/29	12/3	12/17
0.55Q	2/18/94	2/28/94	3/4/94	3/18/94
0.55Q	4/29	5/27	6/3	6/17

Indicated div.: $2.20

CAPITALIZATION (12/31/93):

	($000)	(%)
Total Debt	24,177	1.1
Deferred Income Tax	173,292	8.0
Common & Surplus	1,961,710	90.9
Total	2,159,179	100.0

DIVIDEND ACHIEVER STATUS:

Rank: 198 1983-93 Growth Rate: 9.1%

Total Years of Dividend Growth: 20

RECENT DEVELOPMENTS: For the quarter ended 3/31/94, net income declined 29.7% to $36.3 million, or $1.37 per share, from $51.5 million, or $1.95 per share, for the same period last year. Gain from operations, excluding gain or loss from the sale of investments, increased 12.6% to $37.5 million from $33.3 million for the corresponding 1993 quarter. ANAT reported a loss from the sale of investments, net of tax, of $1.3 million, or $0.05 per share, for the current quarter, compared with a gain of $18.2 million, or $0.69 per share, for the 1993 quarter. Gross revenues for the quarter declined 6.3% to $320.6 million from $341.9 million for the same quarter last year. Gross revenues for the 1994 quarter include a $1.7 million pre-tax realized loss from the sale of investments, compared with a $27.4 million gain for the 1993 quarter.

BUSINESS

AMERICAN NATIONAL INSURANCE COMPANY is licensed to do business in 49 states, the District of Columbia, Puerto Rico, Guam, American Samoa and Western Europe. The Company offers a broad line of insurance coverages including: life, health, disability and annuities; group life and health; personal lines property and casualty and credit insurance. The Company also offers a variety of mutual funds for sale through its licensed representatives. In addition to ANAT, the family of companies includes: Standard Life and Accident Insurance Co., American National Life Insurance Co. of Texas, American National Property and Casualty Co., Garden State Life Insurance Co. and Securities Management and Research, Inc., manager and distributor for the American National group of funds.

BUSINESS LINE ANALYSIS

(12/31/93)	Rev(%)	Inc(%)
Individual Life	38.9	32.2
Indiv Accident & Health	19.2	6.4
Group Insurance	14.9	5.0
Credit Insurance	2.5	0.4
Prop & Casualty Insurance	14.6	8.4
Capital & Surplus	8.2	47.5
Non-Insurance	1.7	0.1
Total	100.0	100.0

ANNUAL EARNINGS AND DIVIDENDS PER SHARE

	1993	1992	1991	1990	1989	1988	1987
Earnings Per Share	**7.00**	**[1] 6.68**	**4.76**	**3.96**	**3.59**	**3.33**	**3.17**
Dividends Per Share	**2.08**	**1.92**	**1.76**	**1.63**	**1.51**	**1.42**	**1.34**
Dividend Payout %	**29.7**	**28.7**	**37.0**	**41.2**	**42.1**	**42.6**	**42.3**

[1] Before acctg. chg.

ANNUAL FINANCIAL DATA

	1993	1992	1991	1990	1989	1988	1987
RECORD OF EARNINGS (IN MILLIONS):							
Insurance Premiums	863.9	843.5	779.9	697.6	646.3	581.8	615.2
Net Investment Income	312.2	313.2	312.3	303.8	291.9	279.1	265.6
Total Prem & Other Rev	1,329.0	1,318.1	1,197.4	1,100.3	1,031.9	933.7	901.7
Life and Annuity Benefits	265.5	260.2	259.6	257.1	242.9	247.6	260.5
Gain Fr Opers Bef Fed Inc Taxes	289.1	253.6	184.9	158.9	148.6	135.5	147.6
Income Taxes	103.6	85.0	58.9	50.1	47.2	41.2	55.1
Gain on Sale Of Securities	...	...	...	...	...	...	0.8
Net Income	185.5	168.6	126.0	108.7	101.4	94.2	92.1
Aver. Shs. Outstg. (000)	26,479	26,479	26,481	27,477	28,258	...	28,841
BALANCE SHEET (IN MILLIONS):							
Cash	16.7	14.3	13.4	18.6	15.5	10.9	6.9
Bonds, At Amortized Cost	2,022.9	1,887.8	1,828.0	1,842.7	1,735.1	1,724.9	1,614.6
Com Stocks, At Market	673.0	602.0	733.0	534.0	615.8	468.6	468.9
Policy Loans	301.1	304.3	309.6	309.8	285.5	287.8	291.0
Mtge Loans on Real Estate	915.7	850.1	856.1	769.5	703.4	673.6	685.4
Total Assets	5,450.9	5,164.5	5,076.7	4,754.2	4,516.1	4,303.3	4,144.6
Benefits and Claims	3,068.9	2,911.1	2,876.0	2,794.0	2,547.2	2,486.9	2,359.9
Net Stockholders' Equity	1,961.7	1,856.7	1,777.5	1,607.0	1,617.0	1,522.8	1,481.3
Year End Shs Outstg (000)	26,479	26,479	26,479	26,504	28,162	28,267	28,267
STATISTICAL RECORD:							
Book Value Per Share	74.09	70.12	67.13	60.63	57.42	53.87	52.40
Return on Equity %	9.5	9.1	7.1	6.8	6.3	6.2	6.2
Return on Assets %	3.4	3.3	2.5	2.3	2.2	2.2	2.2
Average Yield %	3.7	4.4	5.1	5.1	4.4	4.6	3.8
P/E Ratio	9.0-7.0	8.2-5.6	8.8-5.7	9.5-6.8	10.9-8.3	10.7-8.0	14.8-7.3
Price Range	63¼-49	52-35½	41¾-27	37½-26¾	39¼-29¾	35¾-26½	47-23

Statistics are as originally reported.

OFFICERS:
R.L. Moody, Chmn. & C.E.O.
O.C. Clay, President
C.D. Thompson, Sec. & Treas.

INCORPORATED: TX, Mar., 1905

PRINCIPAL OFFICE: One Moody Plaza, Galveston, TX 77550

TELEPHONE NUMBER: (409) 763-4661

FAX: (409) 766-6502

NO. OF EMPLOYEES: 1,272

ANNUAL MEETING: In April

SHAREHOLDERS: 2,230

INSTITUTIONAL HOLDINGS:
No. of Institutions: 85
Shares Held: 20,915,780

REGISTRAR(S): Boatmen's Trust Co., St.Louis, MO 63101

TRANSFER AGENT(S): Boatmen's Trust Co., St. Louis, MO 63101

AMERICAN PRECISION INDUSTRIES INC.

YIELD 3.5%
P/E RATIO 24.6

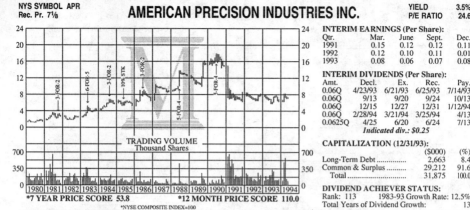

*7 YEAR PRICE SCORE 53.8   *12 MONTH PRICE SCORE 110.0
*NYSE COMPOSITE INDEX=100

TRADING VOLUME
Thousand Shares

INTERIM EARNINGS (Per Share):

Qtr.	Mar.	June	Sept.	Dec.
1991	0.15	0.12	0.12	0.11
1992	0.12	0.10	0.11	0.01
1993	0.08	0.06	0.07	0.08

INTERIM DIVIDENDS (Per Share):

Amt.	Decl.	Ex.	Rec.	Pay.
0.06Q	4/23/93	6/21/93	6/25/93	7/14/93
0.06Q	9/13	9/20	9/24	10/13
0.06Q	12/15	12/27	12/31	1/12/94
0.06Q	2/28/94	3/21/94	3/25/94	4/13
0.0625Q	4/25	6/20	6/24	7/13

Indicated div.: $0.25

CAPITALIZATION (12/31/93):

	($000)	(%)
Long-Term Debt	2,663	8.4
Common & Surplus	29,212	91.6
Total	31,875	100.0

DIVIDEND ACHIEVER STATUS:
Rank: 113   1983-93 Growth Rate: 12.5%
Total Years of Dividend Growth: 13

RECENT DEVELOPMENTS: For the year ended 12/31/93, net earnings totaled $2.1 million, or $0.29 per share, compared with $2.4 million, or $0.34 per share, last year. Consolidated sales for the year were $50.9 million, up slightly from $50.6 million for 1992. The decline in earnings was primarily attributable to losses in the Rapidsyn Division, totaling almost $560,000 after tax, relating to the division's aerospace business. Also, APR spent $600,000 on product develop-

ment, significantly higher than in previous years. Bookings for 1993 were up 6.8% to $54.8 million, the highest level in the Company's history. Backlog at year-end 1993 was a record $17.3 million, up 25.7% from last year. For the quarter, consolidated sales were $12.4 million versus 1992 fourth quarter sales of $12.9 million. Net earnings were $549,000, or $0.08 per share, compared with $58,000, or $0.01 per share, for the same period last year.

BUSINESS

AMERICAN PRECISION INDUS-TRIES, INC. and its subsidiaries conduct operations in two major industrial classifications, namely Industrial Process Equipment which includes the Heat Transfer Group, and Electronics Products, which is comprised of the Electronic Components and Motion Control Groups. The Industrial Process Equipment segment produces and sells heat transfer products for cooling oil, air, and other gases; steam condensing; vapor recovery; and many other processing requirements. The Electronics Products produces and sells an extensive line of quality inductors used in electronic circuits to satisfy various filtering requirements used in telecommunications, aerospace, avionics, industrial, computer, diagnostic medical equipment and military/defense applications; and electro-magnetic components used in the continous starting, stopping and cycling of equipment.

BUSINESS LINE ANALYSIS

(12/31/93)	Rev(%)	Inc(%)
Industrial Process		
Equip	53.3	79.0
Electronic Products	46.7	21.0
Total	100.0	100.0

ANNUAL EARNINGS AND DIVIDENDS PER SHARE

	12/31/93	1/1/93	1/3/92	12/28/90	12/29/89	12/30/88	1/1/88
Earnings Per Share	0.29	0.34	0.50	0.46	0.62	0.49	0.22
Dividends Per Share	0.23	0.21	0.19	0.17	0.148	0.132	0.123
Dividend Payout %	79.3	61.8	38.0	37.0	23.9	26.9	55.9

ANNUAL FINANCIAL DATA

RECORD OF EARNINGS (IN THOUSANDS):

	12/31/93	1/1/93	1/3/92	12/28/90	12/29/89	12/30/88	1/1/88
Revenues	51,334	51,295	51,453	48,640	52,379	49,731	37,609
Costs and Expenses	46,230	45,760	44,150	42,165	44,327	42,338	33,142
Deprec & Amortzation	1,712	1,531	1,382	1,358	1,050	1,167	1,066
Operating Profit	3,994	4,097	5,921	5,663	7,002	6,226	3,401
Earn Bef Income Taxes	3,148	3,711	5,522	4,852	6,905	5,464	2,831
Fed & State Income Taxes	1,098	1,324	1,887	1,506	2,406	1,893	1,220
Net Income	2,050	2,387	3,635	3,346	4,499	3,571	1,611
Aver. Shs. Outstg.	7,057	7,104	7,251	7,344	7,304	7,281	7,245

BALANCE SHEET (IN THOUSANDS):

Cash and Cash Equivalents	6,508	5,457	5,011	3,987	4,863	3,905	2,803
Accounts Receivable, Net	7,082	7,814	6,712	7,350	8,267	7,585	6,069
Inventories	6,369	5,808	6,140	5,881	5,670	5,647	5,315
Gross Property	23,438	21,736	20,235	19,136	17,631	14,513	14,427
Accumulated Depreciation	15,085	13,536	12,246	10,960	9,889	9,544	9,033
Long-Term Debt	2,663	3,039	4,110	4,683	5,559	4,135	1,489
Net Stockholders' Equity	29,212	28,712	28,068	27,695	25,713	22,071	19,519
Total Assets	37,332	36,725	36,280	36,801	37,060	30,862	24,827
Total Current Assets	20,598	19,803	19,381	18,939	20,377	18,863	15,724
Total Current Liabilities	5,457	4,974	4,102	4,423	5,088	4,656	3,819
Net Working Capital	15,141	14,829	15,279	14,516	15,289	14,207	11,905
Year End Shares Outstg	7,058	7,055	7,117	7,362	7,317	7,306	7,257

STATISTICAL RECORD:

Operating Profit Margin %	6.6	7.8	11.5	10.5	13.4	12.5	9.0
Book Value Per Share	4.14	4.07	3.94	3.76	3.51	3.02	2.69
Return on Equity %	7.0	8.3	13.0	12.1	17.5	16.2	8.3
Return on Assets %	5.5	6.5	10.0	9.1	12.1	11.6	6.5
Average Yield %	3.3	2.8	1.8	1.1	1.1	1.2	1.5
P/E Ratio	27.6-19.8	25.0-19.1	30.0-12.5	39.1-31.3	26.2-15.9	28.1-17.9	47.2-29.5
Price Range	8-5¾	8½-6½	15-6¼	18-14⅜	16¼-9⅞	13¾-8¾	10⅜-6½

Statistics are as originally reported.

OFFICERS:
K. Wiedenhaupt, Pres.
J.M. Murray, V.P.-Fin. & Treas.
L.A. Marotto, Sec.

INCORPORATED: DE, Dec., 1986

PRINCIPAL OFFICE: 2777 Walden Ave., Buffalo, NY 14225

TELEPHONE NUMBER: (716) 684-9700

NO. OF EMPLOYEES: 30

ANNUAL MEETING: In April

SHAREHOLDERS: 333

INSTITUTIONAL HOLDINGS:
No. of Institutions: 21
Shares Held: 931,090

REGISTRAR(S): Manufacturers Hanover Trust Co., New York, NY

TRANSFER AGENT(S): Manufacturers Hanover Trust Co., New York, NY

AMERICAN RECREATION CENTERS, INC.

YIELD 3.8%
P/E RATIO 18.2

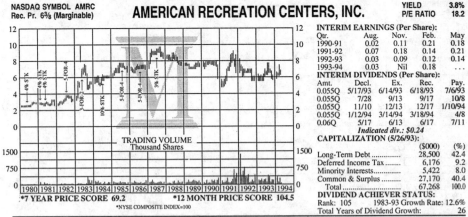

INTERIM EARNINGS (Per Share):

Qtr.	Aug.	Nov.	Feb.	May
1990-91	0.02	0.11	0.21	0.18
1991-92	0.07	0.18	0.14	0.21
1992-93	0.03	0.09	0.12	0.14
1993-94	0.03	Nil	0.18	...

INTERIM DIVIDENDS (Per Share):

Amt.	Decl.	Ex.	Rec.	Pay.
0.055Q	5/17/93	6/14/93	6/18/93	7/6/93
0.055Q	7/28	9/13	9/17	10/8
0.055Q	11/10	12/13	12/17	1/10/94
0.055Q	1/12/94	3/14/94	3/18/94	4/8
0.06Q	5/17	6/13	6/17	7/11

Indicated div.: $0.24

CAPITALIZATION (5/26/93):

	($000)	(%)
Long-Term Debt	28,500	42.4
Deferred Income Tax	6,176	9.2
Minority Interests	5,422	8.0
Common & Surplus	27,170	40.4
Total	67,268	100.0

TRADING VOLUME
Thousand Shares

DIVIDEND ACHIEVER STATUS:
Rank: 105   1983-93 Growth Rate: 12.6%
Total Years of Dividend Growth: 26

*7 YEAR PRICE SCORE 69.2   *12 MONTH PRICE SCORE 104.5
*NYSE COMPOSITE INDEX=100

RECENT DEVELOPMENTS: For the quarter ended 2/23/94, net income rose 54% to $889,000, or $0.18 per share, from $578,000, or $0.12 per share, for the corresponding period last year. Last year's third quarter included an after-tax charge of $237,000, or $0.05 per share, related to the restructuring of the California bowling division and one time expenses associated with refinancing of high interest debt on two centers in the Company's Texas partnership. Operating income increased to $2.4 million compared with $1.8 million a year ago. Operating revenues for the bowling division advanced 14% to $11 million, while operating income increased 33% to $2.3 million. Operating revenues for the direct marketing division, which comprises the operations of The Right Start, Inc., rose 27% to $10.9 million. Operating income was $248,000 versus $217,000 for the same period last year.

BUSINESS

AMERICAN RECREATION CENTERS, INC. is an industry leader in both bowling and specialty direct marketing industries. The Company's bowling division operates 31 bowling centers, 21 in California and 7 in Texas and one each in Kentucky, Missouri and Oklahoma. The Company's non-California bowls are operated by two 85% company-owned joint ventures, Triangle Bowl Associates and Mid-America Associates. The Company owns majority-interest in The Right Start, Inc., a dire ct marketer of products for infants and children through age 5.

REVENUE

(5/26/93)	($000)	(%)
Bowling	35,482	43.8
Direct Marketing	42,347	52.2
Other	3,281	4.0
Total	81,110	100.0

ANNUAL EARNINGS AND DIVIDENDS PER SHARE

	5/26/93	5/27/92	5/29/91	5/30/90	5/31/89	5/25/88	5/27/87
Earnings Per Share	0.38	0.60	0.52	0.31	0.17	① 0.24	0.16
Dividends Per Share	0.19	0.17	0.148	0.13	0.125	② 0.117	③ 0.111
Dividend Payout %	50.0	28.3	28.5	41.9	73.5	48.8	69.4

① Before acctg. chg. ② 3% stk div, 7/87 ③ 5-for-4 stk split, 7/86

ANNUAL FINANCIAL DATA

RECORD OF EARNINGS (IN THOUSANDS):

Total Operating Revenues	81,110	65,258	57,025	47,114	38,356	24,071	23,932
Costs and Expenses	71,780	57,509	48,886	40,819	34,302	20,030	20,157
Depreciation & Amort	3,226	2,427	2,638	2,078	1,652	1,486	1,465
Operating Income	6,104	5,322	5,501	4,217	2,402	2,555	2,310
Inc Bef Income Taxes & Minor Interst	3,695	5,091	4,160	2,281	1,411	1,857	1,138
Income Taxes	1,314	1,767	1,616	779	600	800	437
Minority Interests	540	338	...	...	...	...	...
Net Income	1,841	2,986	2,544	1,502	811	① 1,057	701
Aver. Shs. Outstg.	4,889	4,920	...	...	...	...	...

① Before acctg. change cr$923,000.

BALANCE SHEET (IN THOUSANDS):

Cash and Cash Equivalents	7,907	14,347	3,495	2,216	1,080	2,498	4,406
Receivables, Net	938	976	644	550	882	803	316
Inventories	5,574	2,480	2,361	2,217	1,014	...	...
Gross Property	71,949	62,057	58,865	54,022	51,593	45,825	43,576
Accumulated Depreciation	21,681	19,037	19,127	16,798	15,208	14,139	13,467
Long-Term Debt	28,500	24,899	22,847	20,480	17,261	15,136	15,687
Net Stockholders' Equity	27,170	26,377	23,727	22,990	22,175	21,160	19,720
Total Assets	80,029	72,866	61,208	56,605	51,893	45,969	44,906
Total Current Assets	17,803	19,893	9,017	6,638	4,309	4,762	5,924
Total Current Liabilities	12,761	10,774	8,750	8,263	7,092	5,393	5,283
Net Working Capital	5,042	9,119	267	d1,625	d2,783	d631	641
Year End Shares Outstg	4,886	4,924	4,920	4,907	4,907	4,341	4,342

STATISTICAL RECORD:

Operating Profit Margin %	7.5	8.2	9.6	9.0	6.3	10.6	9.7
Book Value Per Share	5.56	5.36	4.82	4.68	4.52	4.87	4.54
Return on Equity %	6.8	11.3	10.7	6.5	3.7	5.0	3.6
Return on Assets %	2.3	4.1	4.2	2.7	1.6	2.3	1.6
Average Yield %	2.8	2.4	2.2	1.7	1.5	1.4	1.6
P/E Ratio	21.7-14.5	15.4-7.9	15.4-11.1	25.8-22.6	52.9-43.4	40.6-29.2	...
Price Range	8¼-5½	9¼-4¾	8-5¾	8-7	9-7⅜	9¾-7	7⅝-6½

Statistics are as originally reported.

OFFICERS:
R. Feuchter, Chmn.
R.A. Crist, Pres. & C.E.O.
K.B. Wagner, V.P., Treas. & Asst. Sec.
G.G. Davis, III, V.P.-Legal & Sec.

INCORPORATED: CA, Apr., 1959

PRINCIPAL OFFICE: 11171 Sun Center Dr. Suite 120, Rancho Cordova, CA 95670

TELEPHONE NUMBER: (916) 852-8005

FAX: (916) 852-8004

NO. OF EMPLOYEES: 1400

ANNUAL MEETING: In September

SHAREHOLDERS: 2,829 (approx.)

INSTITUTIONAL HOLDINGS:
No. of Institutions: 12
Shares Held: 544,084

REGISTRAR(S):

TRANSFER AGENT(S): First Interstate Bank of California, Los Angeles, CA

AMERICAN WATER WORKS COMPANY, INC.

YIELD 3.9%
P/E RATIO 12.1

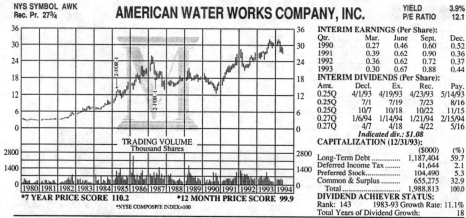

7 YEAR PRICE SCORE 110.2   **12 MONTH PRICE SCORE 99.9**
NYSE COMPOSITE INDEX=100

INTERIM EARNINGS (Per Share):

Qtr.	Mar.	June	Sept.	Dec.
1990	0.27	0.46	0.60	0.52
1991	0.39	0.62	0.90	0.36
1992	0.36	0.62	0.72	0.37
1993	0.30	0.67	0.88	0.44

INTERIM DIVIDENDS (Per Share):

Amt.	Decl.	Ex.	Rec.	Pay.
0.25Q	4/1/93	4/19/93	4/23/93	5/14/93
0.25Q	7/1	7/19	7/23	8/16
0.25Q	10/7	10/18	10/22	11/15
0.27Q	1/6/94	1/14/94	1/21/94	2/15/94
0.27Q	4/7	4/18	4/22	5/16

Indicated div.: $1.08

CAPITALIZATION (12/31/93):

	($000)	(%)
Long-Term Debt	1,187,404	59.7
Deferred Income Tax	41,644	2.1
Preferred Stock	104,490	5.3
Common & Surplus	655,275	32.9
Total	1,988,813	100.0

DIVIDEND ACHIEVER STATUS:

Rank: 143   1983-93 Growth Rate: 11.1%
Total Years of Dividend Growth: 18

RECENT DEVELOPMENTS: For the year ended 12/31/93, AWK reported record net income of $75.4 million, up 10.6% from $68.2 million a year ago. Revenues were up 9.2% to $717.5 million from $657.4 million in 1992. Benefiting from the impact of summer weather patterns and the Company's acquisition of four midwestern water supply companies, water sales volume increased 5% during the year. For the quarter ended 12/31/93, net income advanced 16.5% to $14.7 million on a sales increase of 13.3% to $182 million.

PROSPECTS: Results for the Company will continue to be affected by varied weather conditions. Consistent monitoring of water quality in areas served will help it meet and overcome these challenges. AWK's day-to-day commitment to controlling costs by conserving energy will help it achieve operating efficiencies. Revenues will continue to benefit from rate adjustments in certain areas.

BUSINESS

AMERICAN WATER WORKS COMPANY is engaged in the ownership of companies providing water supply service. The Company's 25 utility subsidiaries provide water service to about six million people in 717 communities in 21 states. American Water Works Service Company, a subsidiary, provides professional and staff services to affiliated companies. Another subsidiary, American Commonwealth Management Services Company, provides services under contract to publicly-owned water and sewer systems that serve about 350,000 people in Pennsylvania, Massachusetts, and Florida.

REVENUES

(12/31/93)	($000)	(%)
Residential	400,230	55.8
Commercial	159,359	22.2
Industrial	50,490	7.0
Public & Other Service	84,865	11.8
Other Water	5,579	0.8
Sewer Service	11,801	1.6
Authority Management Fees..	5,213	0.8
Total	717,537	100.0

ANNUAL EARNINGS AND DIVIDENDS PER SHARE

	1993	1992	1991	1990	1989	1988	1987
Earnings Per Share	2.29	2.07	2.27	1.85	1.56	1.84	1.82
Dividends Per Share	1.00	0.925	0.86	0.80	0.74	0.68	Ⓤ 0.64
Dividend Payout %	43.7	44.7	37.9	43.2	47.4	37.0	35.2

Ⓤ 2-for-1 stk. split, 5/87.

ANNUAL FINANCIAL DATA

RECORD OF EARNINGS (IN MILLIONS):

	1993	1992	1991	1990	1989	1988	1987
Operating Revenues	717.5	657.4	633.0	570.7	527.5	511.9	483.4
Depreciation & Amort	66.8	58.4	52.1	47.0	39.7	35.5	30.7
Prov for Fed Inc Taxes	40.5	31.4	32.1	25.1	22.7	26.7	36.2
Operating Income	172.5	164.5	166.1	147.2	128.7	128.9	118.7
Interest Expense	95.7	93.7	91.8	89.6	80.7	70.3	63.3
Net Income	75.4	68.2	73.6	57.1	48.3	56.9	56.0
Aver. Shs. Outstg. (000)	31,139	30,943	30,731	30,535	30,462	30,462	30,279

BALANCE SHEET (IN MILLIONS):

Gross Plant	2,990.7	2,590.1	2,408.7	2,241.0	2,051.3	1,852.4	1,452.3
Accumulated Depreciation	484.2	406.2	371.5	338.5	309.0	283.1	...
Prop, Plant & Equip, Net	2,506.4	2,183.9	2,037.1	1,902.6	1,742.3	1,569.3	1,452.3
Long-term Debt	1,187.4	944.1	948.0	799.7	775.3	684.3	623.5
Net Stockholders' Equity	759.8	719.1	675.5	569.8	537.9	521.6	489.0
Total Assets	2,994.0	2,415.8	2,240.5	2,092.6	1,916.3	1,737.1	1,615.6
Year End Shs Outstg (000)	31,244	31,035	30,794	30,618	30,462	30,462	30,462

STATISTICAL RECORD:

Book Value Per Share	20.25	18.91	17.74	16.31	15.27	14.45	13.29
Op. Inc/Net Pl %	6.9	7.5	8.2	7.7	7.4	8.2	8.2
Dep/Gr. Pl %	2.2	2.3	2.2	2.1	1.9	1.9	2.1
Accum. Dep/Gr. Pl %	16.2	15.7	15.4	15.1	15.1	15.3	...
Return on Equity %	11.2	10.9	12.5	10.6	9.5	11.8	12.6
Average Yield %	3.5	3.8	4.1	5.0	3.9	4.0	3.2
P/E Ratio	14.1-10.8	13.8-10.0	11.8-6.8	10.6-6.8	13.8-10.7	10.2-8.1	14.2-7.6
Price Range	32¼-24⅝	28½-20⅝	26¾-15½	19⅝-12½	21½-16¾	18¾-14⅞	25⅞-13⅞

Statistics are as originally reported.

OFFICERS:
M.W. Lewis, Chairman
N.G. Harris, Vice-Chmn.
G.W. Johnstone, Pres. & C.E.O.

INCORPORATED: DE, Aug., 1936

PRINCIPAL OFFICE: 1025 Laurel Oak Road, Voorhees, NJ 08043

TELEPHONE NUMBER: (609) 346-8200
NO. OF EMPLOYEES: 3,982
ANNUAL MEETING: In May
SHAREHOLDERS: 9,571 com.; 318 5% pfd; 1,069 5% pref.
INSTITUTIONAL HOLDINGS:
No. of Institutions: 124
Shares Held: 14,952,546

REGISTRAR(S): First National Bank of Boston, Shareholder Services Division, Boston, MA

TRANSFER AGENT(S): First National Bank of Boston, Shareholder Services Division, Boston, MA

AMP, INC.

YIELD **2.6%**
P/E RATIO **22.9**

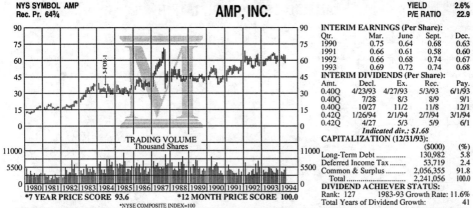

7 YEAR PRICE SCORE 93.6   **12 MONTH PRICE SCORE 100.0**
*NYSE COMPOSITE INDEX=100

INTERIM EARNINGS (Per Share):

Qtr.	Mar.	June	Sept.	Dec.
1990	0.75	0.64	0.68	0.63
1991	0.66	0.61	0.58	0.60
1992	0.66	0.68	0.74	0.67
1993	0.69	0.72	0.74	0.68

INTERIM DIVIDENDS (Per Share):

Amt.	Decl.	Ex.	Rec.	Pay.
0.40Q	4/23/93	4/27/93	5/3/93	6/1/93
0.40Q	7/28	8/3	8/9	9/1
0.40Q	10/27	11/2	11/8	12/1
0.42Q	1/26/94	2/1/94	2/7/94	3/1/94
0.42Q	4/27	5/3	5/9	6/1

Indicated div.: $1.68

CAPITALIZATION (12/31/93):

	($000)	(%)
Long-Term Debt	130,982	5.8
Deferred Income Tax	53,719	2.4
Common & Surplus	2,056,355	91.8
Total	2,241,056	100.0

DIVIDEND ACHIEVER STATUS:

Rank: 127   1983-93 Growth Rate: 11.6%
Total Years of Dividend Growth: 41

RECENT DEVELOPMENTS: For the quarter ended 12/31/93, net income rose 1% to $71.0 million compared with $70.3 million for the same period in 1992. Meanwhile, net sales rose 3% to $873.0 million. Growth in profits was attributed to positive results for all product categories, with strong sales of automotive and networking/premise wiring markets. European sales were cut sharply by the inflation of the U.S. dollar in spite of improving volumes for computer products. Meanwhile, Asia/Pacific sales grew by 11% as local currencies inflated against the dollar.

PROSPECTS: The steady recovery of AMP's international markets should provide a good foundation for continued revenue growth. In addition, the formation of many new business units and subsidiaries should create new markets. Plants in China, India, the Phillippines, and Eastern Europe should provide a good return on investment in an international market which already accounts for 60% of sales. Furthermore, AMP's low debt and strong balance sheet position make it possible to continue to expand internationally.

BUSINESS

AMP INCORPORATED is the world's leading producer of electrical and electronic connection devices and switching and programming devices which are sold throughout many diverse markets. Over 100,000 types and sizes of terminals, splices, connectors, cable assemblies, switches, touch screen data entry systems and related applications tooling (53,000 machines and many millions of tools) are supplied to more than 200,000 electrical and electronic equipment manufacturers, and tens of thousands of customers who install and maintain that equipment. The Company has over 160 facilities in the U.S. and 32 other countries.

ANNUAL EARNINGS AND DIVIDENDS PER SHARE

	1993	1992	1991	1990	1989	1988	1987
Earnings Per Share	2.83	2.75	2.45	2.70	2.63	2.96	2.31
Dividends Per Share	1.60	1.52	1.44	1.36	1.20	1.00	0.85
Dividend Payout %	56.5	55.3	58.8	50.4	45.6	33.8	36.8

ANNUAL FINANCIAL DATA

RECORD OF EARNINGS (IN MILLIONS):

	1993	1992	1991	1990	1989	1988	1987
Total Revenues	3,450.6	3,337.1	3,095.0	3,043.6	2,796.6	2,669.7	2,317.8
Costs and Expenses	2,643.6	2,515.8	2,370.0	2,338.1	2,141.7	1,981.3	1,741.4
Depreciation & Amort	282.2	288.0	255.2	217.7	180.3	158.5	140.6
Income From Operations	524.8	533.3	469.8	487.8	474.6	529.9	435.8
Income Bef Income Taxes	485.9	479.1	423.6	462.0	455.3	529.2	430.5
Income Taxes	189.3	188.8	163.9	174.9	174.4	210.1	180.8
Net Income	296.7	290.3	259.7	287.1	280.9	319.1	249.7
Aver. Shs. Outstg. (000)	104,898	105,496	105,883	106,312	106,716	107,869	108,007

BALANCE SHEET (IN MILLIONS):

	1993	1992	1991	1990	1989	1988	1987
Cash and Cash Equivalents	407.0	478.0	451.0	460.2	334.2	331.6	212.9
Receivables	625.2	561.0	589.2	557.5	520.0	472.0	475.6
Inventories	459.3	435.1	440.6	481.7	494.8	481.6	410.1
Gross Property	2,954.9	2,715.2	2,550.4	2,303.3	1,927.5	1,749.5	1,630.5
Accumulated Depreciation	1,709.8	1,536.5	1,370.2	1,181.8	973.8	855.0	765.1
Long-Term Debt	131.0	42.9	53.0	61.1	69.5	82.8	71.4
Net Stockholders' Equity	2,056.4	1,943.3	1,913.0	1,792.8	1,625.4	1,521.3	1,348.6
Total Assets	3,117.9	3,005.1	3,006.9	2,928.6	2,529.8	2,375.5	2,082.1
Total Current Assets	1,644.4	1,614.1	1,616.4	1,618.4	1,437.2	1,363.1	1,162.9
Total Current Liabilities	752.4	845.5	888.4	953.2	725.5	662.2	537.7
Net Working Capital	892.0	768.7	728.0	665.2	711.7	700.9	625.3
Year End Shs Outstg (000)	104,906	104,930	106,034	105,951	106,490	107,445	107,500

STATISTICAL RECORD:

	1993	1992	1991	1990	1989	1988	1987
Operating Profit Margin %	15.2	16.0	15.2	16.0	17.0	19.8	18.8
Book Value Per Share	19.60	18.52	18.04	16.92	15.26	14.16	12.55
Return on Equity %	14.4	14.9	13.6	16.0	17.3	21.0	18.5
Return on Assets %	9.5	9.7	8.6	9.8	11.1	13.4	12.0
Average Yield %	2.6	2.5	2.9	2.9	2.7	2.1	1.6
P/E Ratio	23.8-19.3	25.0-19.1	24.5-16.7	20.5-14.0	18.8-15.2	18.3-13.7	31.0-14.8
Price Range	67¼-54⅝	68¾-52⅝	60-40⅞	55¼-37⅞	49⅜-40	54¼-40½	71½-34⅛

Statistics are as originally reported.

OFFICERS:

J.E. Marley, Chmn.
W.J. Hudson, Pres. & C.E.O.
B. Savidge, Exec. V.P. & C.F.O.
J.C. Overbaugh, Treas.
INCORPORATED: PA, Apr., 1989
PRINCIPAL OFFICE: P.O. Box 3608, Harrisburg, PA 17105-3608

TELEPHONE NUMBER: (717) 564-0100
FAX: (717) 780-6348
NO. OF EMPLOYEES: 13,303
ANNUAL MEETING: In April
SHAREHOLDERS: 5,405
INSTITUTIONAL HOLDINGS:
No. of Institutions: 576
Shares Held: 84,922,275

REGISTRAR(S): Manufacturers Hanover Trust Co., New York, NY

TRANSFER AGENT(S): Manufacturers Hanover Trust Co., New York, NY
Continental Stock Transfer & Trust Co., New York, NY

AMSOUTH BANCORPORATION

YIELD 4.5%
P/E RATIO 9.8

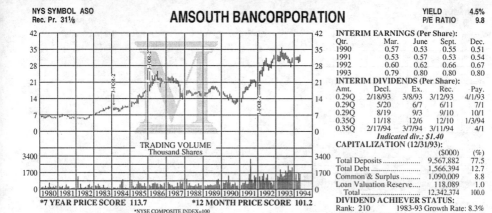

INTERIM EARNINGS (Per Share):

Qtr.	Mar.	June	Sept.	Dec.
1990	0.57	0.53	0.55	0.51
1991	0.53	0.57	0.53	0.54
1992	0.60	0.62	0.66	0.67
1993	0.79	0.80	0.80	0.80

INTERIM DIVIDENDS (Per Share):

Amt.	Decl.	Ex.	Rec.	Pay.
0.29Q	2/18/93	3/8/93	3/12/93	4/1/93
0.29Q	5/20	6/7	6/11	7/1
0.29Q	8/19	9/3	9/10	10/1
0.35Q	11/18	12/6	12/10	1/3/94
0.35Q	2/17/94	3/7/94	3/11/94	4/1

Indicated div.: $1.40

CAPITALIZATION (12/31/93):

	($000)	(%)
Total Deposits	9,567,882	77.5
Total Debt	1,566,394	12.7
Common & Surplus	1,090,009	8.8
Loan Valuation Reserve	118,089	1.0
Total	12,342,374	100.0

DIVIDEND ACHIEVER STATUS:
Rank: 210   1983-93 Growth Rate: 8.3%
Total Years of Dividend Growth: 23

TRADING VOLUME
Thousand Shares

*7 YEAR PRICE SCORE 113.7   *12 MONTH PRICE SCORE 101.2
*NYSE COMPOSITE INDEX=100

RECENT DEVELOPMENTS: For the quarter and year ended 12/31/93, net income totaled $38.1 million and $146.2 million respectively. For both the quarter and year end, net income was up 35% from the prior-year periods. All major lines of business posted increased results. Credit quality improved and the Company's capital position was strengthened. The consumer loan portfolio surged 51% paced by a 113% jump in first residential mortgage lending.

PROSPECTS: The Company is acquiring Fortune Bancorp, Inc., the largest independent financial institution on the west coast of Florida. To lessen the effect of narrowing interest margins and to enhance long-term performance, AmSouth has instituted Productivity Improvement Project. The Company has taken a one-time charge of $11 million in association with early retirement benefits as plans are underway to reduce the workforce by 750 this year. ASO expects to realize cost savings of $20 million per year once this phase of the project is complete.

BUSINESS

AMSOUTH BANCORPORATION is headquartered in Birmingham, Alabama and as of 12/31/93, had assets of $12.5 billion. The Company operates 233 banking offices in four states and 44 mortgage banking offices in nine southeastern states. Bank affiliates are AmSouth Bank N.A., AmSouth Bank of Florida, AmSouth Bank of Tennessee, AmSouth Bank of Georgia and AmSouth Bank of Walker, Alabama. Bank-related affiliates include: AmSouth Mortgage Company, Inc., AmSouth Investment Services, and AmSouth Leasing Corp.

LOAN DISTRIBUTION

(12/31/93)	($000)	(%)
Commercial	2,373,517	29.7
Commercial Real Est Mtges	1,056,752	13.2
Real Estate Construction	342,534	4.3
Residential First Mtges	2,262,669	28.3
Other Residential Mtges	487,984	6.1
Dealer Indirect	599,031	7.4
Other Consumer	877,438	11.0
Total	7,999,925	100.0

ANNUAL EARNINGS AND DIVIDENDS PER SHARE

	1993	1992	1991	1990	1989	1988	1987
Earnings Per Share	3.10	2.55	2.17	2.17	1.73	2.20	1.75
Dividends Per Share	1.16	☐ 1.04	0.96	0.933	0.88	0.827	0.773
Dividend Payout %	37.4	40.8	44.2	42.9	50.8	37.6	44.1

☐ 3-for-2 stk split, 1/16/92

ANNUAL FINANCIAL DATA

RECORD OF EARNINGS (IN MILLIONS):

	1993	1992	1991	1990	1989	1988	1987
Tot Rev Fr Earning Assets	777.0	673.7	745.3	773.3	771.4	679.2	530.1
Total Interest Expense	314.9	297.7	426.5	491.9	509.5	428.6	307.1
Net Interest Income	462.1	376.0	318.9	281.4	261.9	250.6	223.0
Provision for Loan Losses	19.0	36.6	41.5	31.1	43.3	18.8	41.9
Net Income	146.2	102.0	80.4	76.7	63.2	79.8	60.2
Aver. Shs. Outstg. (000)	47,153	40,006	36,970	35,274	36,413	36,320	34,398

BALANCE SHEET (IN MILLIONS):

	1993	1992	1991	1990	1989	1988	1987
Cash & Due From Banks	577.0	528.9	502.1	563.4	450.8	467.0	423.6
Net Loans	7,812.1	5,902.8	5,478.7	5,561.9	5,536.9	5,241.7	4,843.6
Total Domestic Deposits	9,567.9	7,428.6	7,372.7	7,066.9	6,672.4	6,510.9	5,718.4
Long-term Debt	163.1	136.2	139.0	128.7	130.6	131.3	132.8
Net Stockholders' Equity	1,090.0	782.8	715.7	588.5	560.7	533.4	483.2
Total Assets	12,547.9	9,750.7	9,459.3	8,706.1	8,565.4	8,312.9	7,527.1
Year End Shs Outstg (000)	49,516	40,192	39,791	35,130	36,174	36,347	35,475

STATISTICAL RECORD:

	1993	1992	1991	1990	1989	1988	1987
Return on Assets %	1.17	1.05	0.85	0.88	0.74	0.96	0.80
Return on Equity %	13.40	13.00	11.20	13.00	11.30	15.00	12.50
Book Value Per Share	22.01	19.48	17.99	16.75	15.50	14.68	13.62
Average Yield %	3.7	3.9	5.6	6.5	5.1	5.1	4.2
P/E Ratio	11.6-8.8	12.8-8.4	10.2-5.7	7.9-5.3	11.2-8.7	8.0-6.8	13.5-7.8
Price Range	35⅞-27⅜	32⅝-21⅜	22⅛-12⅜	17⅛-11½	19⅜-15⅛	17⅝-14⅞	23⅝-13⅝

Statistics are as originally reported.

OFFICERS:
J.W. Woods, Chmn., C.E.O. & Pres.
C.S. Bailey, Vice-Chmn.
C.D. Ritter, Vice-Chmn.
INCORPORATED: DE, Nov., 1970
PRINCIPAL OFFICE: 1400 Amsouth-Sonat Tower, Birmingham, AL 35203

TELEPHONE NUMBER: (205) 320-7151
NO. OF EMPLOYEES: 5,177
ANNUAL MEETING: In April
SHAREHOLDERS: 14,000 (approx.)
INSTITUTIONAL HOLDINGS:
No. of Institutions: 156
Shares Held: 20,340,822

REGISTRAR(S): Registrar & Transfer Co., Cranford, NJ 07016

TRANSFER AGENT(S): Registrar & Transfer Co., Cranford, NJ 07016
AmSouth Bank, N.A., Birmingham, AL 35202

ANGELICA CORP.

YIELD 3.6%
P/E RATIO 21.4

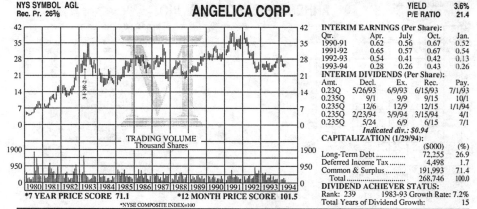

INTERIM EARNINGS (Per Share):

Qtr.	Apr.	July	Oct.	Jan.
1990-91	0.62	0.56	0.67	0.52
1991-92	0.65	0.57	0.67	0.54
1992-93	0.54	0.41	0.42	0.13
1993-94	0.28	0.26	0.43	0.26

INTERIM DIVIDENDS (Per Share):

Amt.	Decl.	Ex.	Rec.	Pay.
0.23Q	5/26/93	6/9/93	6/15/93	7/1/93
0.235Q	9/1	9/9	9/15	10/1
0.235Q	12/6	12/9	12/15	1/1/94
0.235Q	2/23/94	3/9/94	3/15/94	4/1
0.235Q	5/24	6/9	6/15	7/1

Indicated div.: $0.94

CAPITALIZATION (1/29/94):

	($000)	(%)
Long-Term Debt	72,255	26.9
Deferred Income Tax	4,498	1.7
Common & Surplus	191,993	71.4
Total	268,746	100.0

DIVIDEND ACHIEVER STATUS:
Rank: 239   1983-93 Growth Rate: 7.2%
Total Years of Dividend Growth: 15

TRADING VOLUME
Thousand Shares

***7 YEAR PRICE SCORE 71.1**   ***12 MONTH PRICE SCORE 101.5**
*NYSE COMPOSITE INDEX=100

RECENT DEVELOPMENTS: For the quarter ended 10/31/93, net income increased 1.5% to $3.9 million from $3.8 million in the comparable period last year. Sales increased a slight 1.1% to $110.5 million from $109.3 million in 1992. Improved earnings overall were in part due to higher earnings in the Rental Services segment, which prospered as a result of good cost control efforts. The Manufacturing and Marketing segments also contributed to increased earnings by producing sales volume increases. Life Retail stores posted higher sales due to an increase in same-store sales.

PROSPECTS: Angelica's outlook for future profitability is promising. The Rental Services segment will help earnings as it continues to have good success in adding new accounts and controlling operating costs. Manufacturing and Marketing will continue to be affected by a weak health care industry caused by apprehension about potential federal actions to control health care costs. Angelica has acquired two health care and general linen and laundry businesses in Nevada and Ohio which will operate as part of the Company's Health-Care Services Group.

BUSINESS

ANGELICA CORPORATION provides rental and laundry services of textiles and garments primarily to health care institutions; manufactures and markets uniforms for institutions and businesses; and operates a national chain of 244 retail uniform and shoe stores. Principal markets are: health services including hospital, nurses and other health care professionals; hospitality, including hotels and restaurants; commerce, including retailers and transportation companies; industry, including manufacturers, food processors and high technology companies.

BUSINESS LINE ANALYSIS

(1/29/94)	Rev(%)	Inc(%)
Rental services	48.2	63.2
Manufacturing & marketing	39.1	23.1
Retail Sales	12.7	13.7
Total	100.0	100.0

ANNUAL EARNINGS AND DIVIDENDS PER SHARE

	1/29/94	1/30/93	2/1/92	1/26/91	1/27/90	1/28/89	1/30/88
Earnings Per Share	1.23	ⓘ 1.50	2.43	2.37	2.06	1.79	1.85
Dividends Per Share	0.925	0.92	0.88	0.82	0.76	0.72	0.68
Dividend Payout %	75.6	64.7	36.2	34.6	36.9	40.2	36.9

ⓘ Before acctg. chg.

ANNUAL FINANCIAL DATA

RECORD OF EARNINGS (IN THOUSANDS):

Total Revenues	427,128	430,797	434,471	413,635	368,752	328,134	306,669
Costs and Expenses	385,237	385,770	377,300	360,213	323,029	290,153	267,233
Depreciation	12,872	12,578	11,743	10,313	9,502	8,612	7,683
Income From Operations	29,019	32,449	45,428	43,109	36,221	29,369	31,753
Income Bef Income Taxes	18,060	22,253	36,518	35,910	31,236	27,062	30,236
Income Taxes	6,909	8,450	13,848	13,814	12,022	10,420	13,001
Net Income	11,151	ⓘ 13,803	22,670	22,096	19,214	16,642	17,235
Aver. Shs. Outstg.	9,089	9,217	9,345	9,330	9,327	9,299	9,335

ⓘ Before acctg. change cr$1,984,000.

BALANCE SHEET (IN THOUSANDS):

Cash & Short-term Invests	2,020	2,746	6,121	2,038	6,887	2,457	3,242
Receivables, Net	68,247	66,507	67,311	68,118	61,821	53,510	48,918
Inventories	104,570	102,596	100,217	97,509	83,625	73,447	63,348
Gross Property	189,905	181,587	173,203	153,684	135,201	115,502	110,613
Accumulated Depreciation	95,937	86,709	76,387	67,882	61,072	54,827	47,906
Long-Term Debt	72,255	78,175	80,506	57,782	50,588	19,013	21,588
Net Stockholders' Equity	191,993	189,209	190,303	175,684	161,134	149,712	138,760
Total Assets	332,861	326,657	335,173	316,439	279,168	232,883	216,441
Total Current Assets	210,255	204,878	210,762	205,339	183,796	156,058	140,579
Total Current Liabilities	53,067	43,749	50,383	70,375	53,724	51,840	45,340
Net Working Capital	157,188	161,129	160,379	134,964	130,072	104,218	95,239
Year End Shares Outstg	9,086	9,064	9,316	9,286	9,284	9,306	9,284

STATISTICAL RECORD:

Operating Profit Margin %	6.8	7.5	10.5	10.4	9.8	9.0	10.4
Book Value Per Share	20.49	20.19	19.85	18.45	17.01	15.73	14.63
Return on Equity %	5.8	7.3	11.9	12.6	11.9	11.1	12.4
Return on Assets %	3.4	4.2	6.8	7.0	6.9	7.1	8.0
Average Yield %	3.6	3.0	2.5	2.7	2.9	3.1	2.6
P/E Ratio	23.1-18.3	26.7-14.8	16.6-12.2	14.3-11.4	14.7-10.7	15.3-11.0	18.6-10.0
Price Range	28⅜-22½	40-22¼	40¼-29⅝	33⅞-27	30⅜-22	27⅜-19⅝	34⅜-18½

Statistics are as originally reported.

OFFICERS:
L.J. Young, Chmn. & Pres.
T.M. Armstrong, Sr. V.P. & C.F.O.
J. Witter, V.P., Gen. Counsel & Sec.
T.M. Degnan, Treas.

INCORPORATED: MO, Mar., 1968

PRINCIPAL OFFICE: 10176 Corporate Square Drive, Saint Louis, MO 63132

TELEPHONE NUMBER: (314) 854-3800

NO. OF EMPLOYEES: 1,224 approx.

ANNUAL MEETING: In May

SHAREHOLDERS: 1,386

INSTITUTIONAL HOLDINGS:
No. of Institutions: 98
Shares Held: 7,612,102

REGISTRAR(S): Boatmen's Trust Co., St.Louis, MO 63101

TRANSFER AGENT(S): Boatmen's Trust Co., St. Louis, MO 63101

NYS SYMBOL BUD
Rec. Pr. 54¼

ANHEUSER-BUSCH COS., INC.

YIELD 2.7%
P/E RATIO 25.2

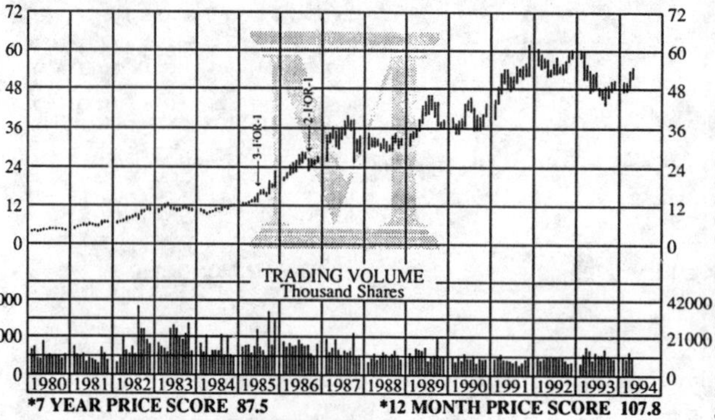

*7 YEAR PRICE SCORE 87.5 *12 MONTH PRICE SCORE 107.8

*NYSE COMPOSITE INDEX=100

INTERIM EARNINGS (Per Share):

Qtr.	Mar.	June	Sept.	Dec.
1990	0.64	0.90	0.92	0.50
1991	0.70	1.00	1.01	0.55
1992	0.77	1.10	1.12	0.61
1993	0.69	1.12	d0.28	0.62

INTERIM DIVIDENDS (Per Share):

Amt.	Decl.	Ex.	Rec.	Pay.
0.32Q	4/28/93	5/4/93	5/10/93	6/9/93
0.36Q	7/28	8/3	8/9	9/9
0.36Q	10/27	11/3	11/9	12/9
0.36Q	12/15	2/3/94	2/9/94	3/9/94
0.36Q	4/27/94	5/3	5/9	6/9

Indicated div.: $1.44

CAPITALIZATION (12/31/93):

	($000)	(%)
Long-Term Debt	3,031,700	35.9
Deferred Income Tax	1,170,400	13.8
Common & Surplus	4,255,500	50.3
Total	8,457,600	100.0

DIVIDEND ACHIEVER STATUS:
Rank: 29 1983-93 Growth Rate: 17.5%
Total Years of Dividend Growth: 19

RECENT DEVELOPMENTS: For the year ended 12/31/93, net income was $594.5 million compared with $994.2 million in 1992. The 1992 results were before an accounting change of $76.7 million. Sales increased 1.0% to $11.51 billion from $11.39 billion last year. Beer sales and volume growth were affected by competitive price discounting and higher than normal price spreads between premium and sub-premium brands; however, beer sales volume represented 44.3% of total industry sales. Additionally, Busch Entertainment Corp. posted record sales and earnings as a result of higher attendance at its theme parks. The Company plans to enhance premium brand volume growth through increased marketing initiatives, the introduction of a new premium products called Ice Draft, and selective price increases. In December 1993, BUD acquired the remaining 50% of International Label Company for $19.2 million.

BUSINESS

ANHEUSER-BUSCH COMPANIES, INC. is a diversified corporation whose chief subsidiary is Anheuser-Busch, Inc., the world's largest brewer. Brands include Budweiser, Bud Light, Bud Dry, Michelob, Michelob Light, Michelob Dry, Michelob Classic Dark, Mich, Busch, Busch Light, Natural Light. BUD is also the country's second-largest producer of fresh baked goods and the second largest theme park operator. BUD also engages in container manufacturing and recycling, malt and rice production, international beer marketing, non-beer beverages, snack foods, family entertainment, real estate development, major league baseball, stadium ownership, creative services, railcar repair and transportation services.

BUSINESS LINE ANALYSIS

(12/31/93)	Rev(%)	Inc(%)
Beer & Beer Related	75.2	110.5
Food Products	18.4	(7.0)
Entertainment	6.4	(3.5)
Total	100.0	100.0

ANNUAL EARNINGS AND DIVIDENDS PER SHARE

	1993	1992	1991	1990	1989	1988	1987
Earnings Per Share	**2.17**	**[1]3.48**	**3.26**	**2.96**	**2.68**	**2.45**	**2.04**
Dividends Per Share	**1.36**	**1.20**	**1.06**	**0.94**	**0.80**	**0.66**	**0.54**
Dividend Payout %	**62.7**	**34.5**	**32.5**	**31.8**	**29.9**	**26.9**	**26.5**

[1] Before acctg. chg.

ANNUAL FINANCIAL DATA

	1993	1992	1991	1990	1989	1988	1987
RECORD OF EARNINGS (IN MILLIONS):							
Total Revenues	11,505.3	11,393.7	10,996.3	10,743.6	9,481.3	8,924.1	8,258.4
Costs and Expenses	9,685.1	9,051.0	8,740.7	8,648.9	7,742.3	7,301.0	6.813.8
Depreciation & Amort	608.3	567.0	534.1	495.7	410.3	359.0	315.5
Operating Income	1,211.9	1,775.7	1,721.5	1,599.0	1,328.7	1,264.1	1,129.1
Income Bef Income Taxes	1,050.4	1,615.2	1,520.6	1,352.1	1,226.7	1,160.1	1,056.1
Provision for Inc Taxes	455.9	621.0	580.8	509.7	459.5	444.2	441.4
Net Income	594.5	[1]994.2	939.8	842.4	767.2	715.9	614.7
Aver. Shs. Outstg. (000)	274,300	285,800	287,900	284,600	286,200	292,200	301,500
[1] Before acctg. change dr$76,700,000.							
BALANCE SHEET (IN MILLIONS):							
Cash & Mktable Securities	127.4	215.0	97.3	95.3	36.4	63.9	111.3
Accts & Notes Receiv, Net	751.1	649.8	654.8	562.6	527.8	463.1	382.5
Total Inventories	626.7	660.7	635.6	567.2	531.7	512.2	451.9
Gross Property	11,727.1	11,385.1	10,589.6	10,016.7	9,187.9	7,643.0	6,816.6
Accumulated Depreciation	4,230.0	3,861.4	3,393.1	2,952.9	2,516.6	2,175.3	1,902.5
Long-Term Debt	3,031.7	2,642.5	2,644.9	3,147.1	3,307.3	1,615.3	1,396.5
Net Stockholders' Equity	4,255.5	4,620.4	4,438.1	3,679.1	3,099.9	3,102.9	2,892.2
Total Assets	10,880.3	10,537.9	9,986.5	9,634.3	9,025.7	7,109.8	6,491.6
Total Current Assets	1,795.2	1,815.8	1,627.7	1,426.3	1,276.9	1,194.3	1,125.3
Total Current Liabilities	1,815.6	1,459.8	1,402.8	1,411.9	1,302.6	1,179.1	1,042.4
Net Working Capital	d20.4	356.0	224.9	14.4	d25.7	15.2	82.9
Year End Shs Outstg (000)	267,037	278,402	285,052	282,306	282,988	283,406	283,406
STATISTICAL RECORD:							
Operating Profit Margin %	10.5	15.6	15.7	14.9	14.0	14.2	13.7
Book Value Per Share	14.08	14.78	13.75	11.14	9.06	10.58	9.78
Return on Equity %	14.0	21.5	21.2	22.9	24.7	23.1	21.3
Return on Assets %	5.5	9.4	9.4	8.7	8.5	10.1	9.5
Average Yield %	2.6	2.1	2.1	2.4	2.1	2.1	1.6
P/E Ratio	27.8-19.8	17.5-14.9	19.0-12.0	15.3-11.5	17.2-11.4	14.0-11.8	19.7-12.6
Price Range	60¼-43	60¾-51¾	62-39¼	45¼-34	46-30⅝	34⅜-29	40⅛-25¾

Statistics are as originally reported.

OFFICERS:
A.A. Busch, III, Chmn. & Pres.
J.E. Ritter, Exec. V.P. & C.F.O.
W.J. Kimmins, Treasurer

INCORPORATED: DE, Apr., 1979

PRINCIPAL OFFICE: One Busch Place, Saint Louis, MO 63118

TELEPHONE NUMBER: (314) 577-2000

NO. OF EMPLOYEES: 5,895

ANNUAL MEETING: In April

SHAREHOLDERS: 46,652

INSTITUTIONAL HOLDINGS:
No. of Institutions: 679
Shares Held: 157,016,195

REGISTRAR(S): Boatmen's Trust Co., St.Louis, MO 63101

TRANSFER AGENT(S): Boatmen's Trust Co., St. Louis, MO 63101

ANTHONY INDUSTRIES, INC.

YIELD 3.0%
P/E RATIO 14.8

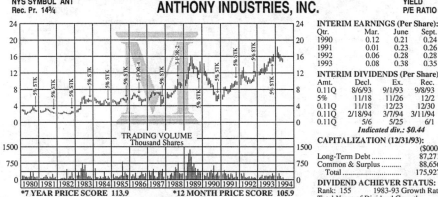

INTERIM EARNINGS (Per Share):

Qtr.	Mar.	June	Sept.	Dec.
1990	0.12	0.21	0.24	d0.29
1991	0.01	0.23	0.26	0.14
1992	0.06	0.28	0.28	0.19
1993	0.08	0.38	0.35	0.18

INTERIM DIVIDENDS (Per Share):

Amt.	Decl.	Ex.	Rec.	Pay.
0.11Q	8/6/93	9/1/93	9/8/93	10/1/93
5%	11/18	11/26	12/2	12/30
0.11Q	11/18	12/23	12/30	1/4/94
0.11Q	2/18/94	3/7/94	3/11/94	4/1
0.11Q	5/6	5/25	6/1	7/1

Indicated div.: $0.44

CAPITALIZATION (12/31/93):

	($000)	(%)
Long-Term Debt	87,271	49.6
Common & Surplus	88,656	50.4
Total	175,927	100.0

DIVIDEND ACHIEVER STATUS:
Rank: 155   1983-93 Growth Rate: 10.7%
Total Years of Dividend Growth: 15

TRADING VOLUME
Thousand Shares

*7 YEAR PRICE SCORE 113.9   *12 MONTH PRICE SCORE 105.9

*NYSE COMPOSITE INDEX=100

RECENT DEVELOPMENTS: For the year ended 12/31/93, net income was $11.1 million, or $0.99 per share, compared with $8.5 million, or $0.77 per share. Sales increased 7.4% to $431.6 million from $402.0 million a year earlier. Both the recreational and industrial products segments contributed to the sales and profit growth. The recreational products group increased sales 7% to $286 million, or 66% of ANT's total sales. Operating profit for this cement was $12.2 million, up 5% from last year, and represented 47% of total operating profit in 1993. The industrial products group increased sales 8% to $146 million, from $135 million last year. Operating profit climbed to $14.0 million, up from $11.0 million a year ago.

BUSINESS

ANTHONY INDUSTRIES, INC. is organized into two industry segments. The recreational products segment includes alpine and nordic skis and ski apparel; athletic jackets, imprintable shirts and bowling shirts; personal floatation devices; construction of residential concrete swimming pools, swimming pool equipment, pool covers; and the manufacture and sale of rods, reels and other fishing tackle items. The industrial products segment consists of the manufacture and sale of extruded monofilament used by the paperweaving industry and for cutting line, fishing line and sewing thread; fiberglass marine antennas and light poles; and laminated and coated paperboard products.

BUSINESS LINE ANALYSIS

(12/31/93)

	Rev(%)	Inc(%)
Recreational Products	66.2	46.6
Industrial Products	33.8	53.4
Total	100.0	100.0

ANNUAL EARNINGS AND DIVIDENDS PER SHARE

	1993	1992	1991	1990	1989	1988	1987
Earnings Per Share	0.99	0.77	0.60	③0.26	1.30	1.16	0.85
Dividends Per Share	①0.425	②0.399	③0.38	④0.362	⑤0.365	⑥0.207	0.219
Dividend Payout %	42.9	51.8	63.3	N.M.	28.1	17.8	25.8

① 5% stk div,4th qtr. ② 5% stk div,11/24/92 ③ 5% stk div,11/25/91 ④ Before extraord. item ⑤ 5% stk div, 11/27/90 ⑥ 5% stk div, 12/89 ⑦ 3-for-2 stk split, 9/88

ANNUAL FINANCIAL DATA

RECORD OF EARNINGS (IN THOUSANDS):

Total Revenues	432,945	403,206	371,596	377,958	382,999	309,077	264,959
Costs and Expenses	401,142	373,865	344,224	355,216	345,827	281,745	241,726
Depreciation & Amort	9,083	9,653	9,786	9,508	7,997	5,757	5,549
Operating Profit	22,720	19,688	17,586	13,234	29,175	21,575	17,684
Income Bef Income Taxes	16,961	12,911	10,680	4,468	21,309	16,136	12,711
Provision for Inc Taxes	5,840	4,390	4,075	1,745	7,885	5,810	5,210
Net Income	11,121	8,521	6,605	①2,723	13,424	...	7,501
Aver. Shs. Outstg.	11,236	11,081	11,026	10,828	10,395	...	8,883

① Before extra. item dr$988,000.

BALANCE SHEET (IN THOUSANDS):

Cash & Cash Equivalents	5,860	2,123	3,069	2,599	2,765	3,696	2,993
Receivables, Net	96,448	85,470	75,919	73,262	66,899	60,374	46,542
Inventories	82,375	77,448	70,610	68,371	70,188	55,282	36,710
Gross Property	122,085	113,755	108,510	105,356	97,519	83,765	72,885
Accumulated Depreciation	71,991	65,446	58,491	50,988	49,048	42,377	39,195
Long-Term Debt	87,271	68,525	43,451	53,750	36,816	26,066	12,711
Net Stockholders' Equity	88,656	83,598	80,663	78,137	78,134	62,937	48,753
Total Assets	257,274	236,200	221,650	220,551	209,809	179,927	129,396
Total Current Assets	187,756	168,916	152,439	147,017	143,663	124,102	93,016
Total Current Liabilities	69,976	73,095	87,197	78,754	...	70,234	44,792
Net Working Capital	117,780	95,821	65,242	68,263	143,663	53,868	48,224
Year End Shares Outstg	11,212	11,110	11,021	11,086	10,508	...	8,328

STATISTICAL RECORD:

Operating Profit Margin %	5.2	4.9	4.7	3.5	7.6	7.0	6.7
Book Value Per Share	6.50	6.14	5.90	5.59	6.08	...	5.85
Return on Equity %	12.5	10.2	8.2	3.5	17.2	16.4	15.4
Return on Assets %	4.3	3.6	3.0	1.2	6.4	5.7	5.8
Average Yield %	3.0	3.5	4.8	3.7	2.9	2.5	3.8
P/E Ratio	16.7-11.5	17.4-11.9	16.9-9.2	57.0-20.5	12.5-6.9		9.0-4.6
Price Range	16½-11⅜	13⅜-9⅛	10⅛-5½	14¼-5⅛	16⅛-8⅞	10½-5¾	7⅝-3⅞

Statistics are as originally reported.

OFFICERS:
B.I. Forester, Chairman & C.E.O.
R.M. Rodstein, President & C.O.O.
J.J. Rangel, Sr. V.P.-Finance
M.E. Lane, V.P. & Treas.
S.E. McConnell, Secretary

INCORPORATED: DE, Sep., 1959

PRINCIPAL OFFICE: 4900 South Eastern Ave., Suite 200, Los Angeles, CA 90040

TELEPHONE NUMBER: (213) 724-2800

NO. OF EMPLOYEES: 1,113 approx.

ANNUAL MEETING: In May

SHAREHOLDERS: 923

INSTITUTIONAL HOLDINGS:
No. of Institutions: 44
Shares Held: 3,059,366 (Adj.)

REGISTRAR(S): Harris Trust Co. of N.Y., New York, NY 10005

TRANSFER AGENT(S): Harris Trust Co. of N.Y., New York, NY 10005

AON CORP.

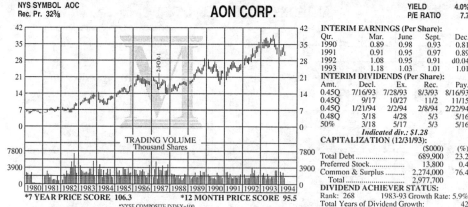

*7 YEAR PRICE SCORE 106.3   *12 MONTH PRICE SCORE 95.5
*NYSE COMPOSITE INDEX=100

INTERIM EARNINGS (Per Share):

Qtr.	Mar.	June	Sept.	Dec.
1990	0.89	0.98	0.93	0.81
1991	0.91	0.95	0.97	0.89
1992	1.08	0.95	0.91	d0.04
1993	1.18	1.03	1.01	1.01

INTERIM DIVIDENDS (Per Share):

Amt.	Decl.	Ex.	Rec.	Pay.
0.45Q	7/16/93	7/28/93	8/3/93	8/16/93
0.45Q	9/17	10/27	11/2	11/15
0.45Q	1/21/94	2/2/94	2/8/94	2/22/94
0.48Q	3/18	4/28	5/3	5/16
50%	3/18	5/17	5/3	5/16

Indicated div.: $1.28

CAPITALIZATION (12/31/93):

	($000)	(%)
Total Debt	689,900	23.2
Preferred Stock	13,800	0.4
Common & Surplus	2,274,000	76.4
Total	2,977,700	

DIVIDEND ACHIEVER STATUS:

Rank: 268   1983-93 Growth Rate: 5.9%
Total Years of Dividend Growth: 42

RECENT DEVELOPMENTS: For the three months ended 12/31/93, net income totaled $77.9 million, up significantly from $1.2 million in the corresponding 1992 period. Total revenues advanced to $977.3 million from $901.1 million. For 1993, net income was up 57% from 1992 totaling $323.8 million. Consumer businesses reported solid results led by strong demand for extended warranties. Revenues totaled $3.84 billion up 15% from the prior year. Brokerage revenue jumped 51% to $765.5 million and benefit consulting operations produced revenue of $168.5 million.

PROSPECTS: Specialty property and casualty operations continue to post reduced revenues as a result of AOC's strategy to exit certain underwriting programs. The extended warranty product line continues to offer excellent growth opportunities. Although direct sales in the international business are impressive, the effect of foreign currency translation is negative and offsetting. Brokerage and consulting businesses are providing a solid boost to revenues. All of AOC's business lines are contibuting favorably to the bottom line.

BUSINESS

AON COPRORATION is an international insurance and financial services company serving individuals and corporate clients with a broad range of specialized insurance products marketed through a wide variety of distribution channels. Brokerage and consulting services are directed toward small and large companies, financial institutions, municipalities and associates. The Company acquired K&K Insurance Specialties, Inc. in 1993.

BUSINESS LINE ANALYSIS

(12/31/93)	Rev(%)	Inc(%)
Insur Brokerage &		
Consult	31.6	26.7
Life	24.3	22.2
Accident & Health	31.2	34.8
Specialty Prop &		
Casualty	8.5	9.1
Corporate & Other	4.4	7.2
Total	100.0	100.0

ANNUAL EARNINGS AND DIVIDENDS PER SHARE

	1993	1992	1991	1990	1989	1988	1987
Earnings Per Share	4.22	① 2.89	3.71	3.61	3.54	3.18	2.80
Dividends Per Share	1.77	1.66	1.58	1.49	1.37	1.26	② 1.18
Dividend Payout %	41.9	57.4	42.6	41.3	38.7	39.6	42.1

Note: 50%stk.div.5/16/94. ① Before acctg. chg. ② 2-for-1 stk. split, 5/87.

ANNUAL FINANCIAL DATA

RECORD OF EARNINGS (IN MILLIONS):

	1993	1992	1991	1990	1989	1988	1987
Premiums & Policy Fees	1,823.0	1,826.3	1,734.0	1,558.7	1,396.5	1,939.2	1,812.7
Net Investment Income	745.2	737.0	712.8	660.6	589.8	503.4	405.0
Total Revenue Earned	3,844.8	3,336.5	2,930.9	2,626.4	2,324.7	2,732.4	2,469.0
Benefits to Policyholders	1,267.3	1,305.6	1,247.0	1,104.5	957.6	1,444.4	1,279.8
Income Before Income Tax	479.1	290.5	331.5	325.2	314.1	278.4	259.8
Income Taxes	155.3	84.3	89.5	86.2	81.7	74.0	74.7
Realized Inv Gains(losses), Net Of Tax	...	...	...	...	...	d24.8	d28.9
Net Income	323.8	① 206.2	242.0	239.0	232.4	179.5	156.2
Aver. Shs. Outstg. (000)	106,368	104,885	97,878	99,206	98,453	96,494	99,023

① Before acctg. change dr$79,600,000.

BALANCE SHEET (IN MILLIONS):

	1993	1992	1991	1990	1989	1988	1987
Cash	163.8	87.7	38.1	74.1	31.9	18.0	32.5
Fixed Matur Held to Maturity	5,021.1	5,089.8	6,253.5	5,367.7	4,343.5	3,920.2	3,109.5
Com Stock At Fair Value	349.2	268.8	228.0	365.9	552.3	446.3	379.1
Policy Loans	207.3	204.5	193.9	178.3	162.7	146.7	134.8
Mtge Loans on Real Estate	557.1	592.3	657.7	715.6	721.0	677.4	614.4
Total Assets	16,279.1	14,289.8	11,633.2	10,432.2	9,156.4	8,266.0	7,084.2
Benefits and Claims	8,776.3	7,759.2	7,341.8	6,832.5	5,566.9	5,186.7	4,347.3
Net Stockholders' Equity	2,287.8	2,103.9	1,775.0	1,457.6	1,422.4	1,284.8	1,133.4
Year End Shs Outstg (000)	100,055	99,986	97,908	97,664	97,605	98,871	96,975

STATISTICAL RECORD:

	1993	1992	1991	1990	1989	1988	1987
Book Value Per Share	22.73	20.89	18.09	14.91	14.56	12.68	11.65
Return on Equity %	14.2	9.8	13.6	16.4	16.3	14.3	13.8
Return on Assets %	2.0	1.4	2.1	2.3	2.5	2.2	2.2
Average Yield %	3.4	3.6	4.4	4.3	3.9	5.0	4.5
P/E Ratio	20.8-16.4	28.0-20.3	16.9-12.0	17.7-11.1	18.3-11.4	13.6-10.3	16.9-11.0
Price Range	58½-46¼	54-39⅛	41¾-29¾	42⅝-26¾	43¼-27	28¾-21⅞	31½-20½

Statistics are as originally reported.

OFFICERS:

P.G. Ryan, Chmn., Pres. & C.E.O.
H.N. Medvin, Exec. V.P., C.F.O. & Treas.
A.F. Quern, Sr. V.P. & Sec.

INCORPORATED: IL, Oct., 1949

PRINCIPAL OFFICE: 123 North Wacker Drive, Chicago, IL 60606

TELEPHONE NUMBER: (312) 701-3000

NO. OF EMPLOYEES: 22,000 approx., U.S.

ANNUAL MEETING: In April

SHAREHOLDERS: 14,746

INSTITUTIONAL HOLDINGS:
No. of Institutions: 275
Shares Held: 32,458,566

REGISTRAR(S): First Chicago Trust Co. of New York, New York, NY 10008

TRANSFER AGENT(S): First Chicago Trust Co. of New York, New York, NY 10008

APOGEE ENTERPRISES, INC.

YIELD 2.4%
P/E RATIO 26.1

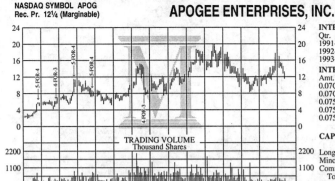

*7 YEAR PRICE SCORE 79.6 *12 MONTH PRICE SCORE 105.9
*NYSE COMPOSITE INDEX=100

INTERIM EARNINGS (Per Share):

Qtr.	May	Aug.	Nov.	Feb.
1991-92	0.20	0.29	0.02	0.12
1992-93	0.02	0.15	0.15	0.02
1993-94	0.07	0.18	0.22	d0.22

INTERIM DIVIDENDS (Per Share):

Amt.	Decl.	Ex.	Rec.	Pay.
0.07Q	4/26/93	5/4/93	5/10/93	5/26/93
0.07Q	7/26	8/3	8/9	8/25
0.075Q	10/19	10/27	11/2	11/18
0.075Q	1/14/94	1/26/94	2/1/94	2/17/94
0.075Q	4/26	5/4	5/10	5/26

Indicated div.: $0.30

CAPITALIZATION (2/26/94):

	($000)	(%)
Long-Term Debt	35,688	23.6
Minority Interest	1,331	0.9
Common & Surplus	114,063	75.5
Total	151,082	100.0

DIVIDEND ACHIEVER STATUS:
Rank: 89   1983-93 Growth Rate: 13.6%
Total Years of Dividend Growth: 19

RECENT DEVELOPMENTS: For the year ended 2/26/94, earnings before accounting changes were $3.3 million, or $0.25 per share, compared with earnings of $4.5 million, or $0.34 per share, a year earlier. Sales rose 20% to $688.2 million from $572.5 million. The results include a restructuring charge of $4.5 million, or $0.34 per share, related to its construction oriented businesses. APOG's commercial construction division recorded an operating loss of $19.0 million compared with a year-earlier loss of $5.1 million, due to low margins and international marketing costs. Operating profits at the glass fabrication division improved to $13.6 million, an increase of 73% over last year's $7.8 million. In a move designed to restore profitability to its underperforming units, APOG closed unprofitable units and reorganized management in key operations. At year end, backlog was up 26% to $405 million.

BUSINESS

APOGEE ENTERPRISES INC. is an industry leader in the fabrication, installation and distribution of glass and aluminum. Its products and services include glass, windows and curtainwall for commercial and institutional construction and remodeling markets; curtainwall installation at major high-rise construction sites; design, manufacture and installation of institutional and government security systems; metal and glass coating services; fabrication, sale and installation of automotive glass; and such consumer-oriented products as venetian blinds, shutters, picture frame glass and computer anti-glare screens.

BUSINESS LINE ANALYSIS

(2/26/94)	Rev(%)	Inc($000)
Commercial		
Construction	42.5	(18,959)
Window Fabrication	11.5	(3,484)
Glass Fabrication	18.7	13,560
Installation & Distrib.	27.3	13,918
Total	100.0	5,035

ANNUAL EARNINGS AND DIVIDENDS PER SHARE

	2/26/94	2/27/93	2/29/92	3/2/91	3/3/90	2/25/89	2/27/88
Earnings Per Share	[1] 0.25	0.34	0.63	1.25	1.04	1.00	0.87
Dividends Per Share	0.29	0.265	0.255	0.23	0.19	0.155	0.13
Dividend Payout %	N.M.	77.9	40.5	18.4	18.3	15.5	14.9

ANNUAL FINANCIAL DATA

RECORD OF EARNINGS (IN THOUSANDS):

Total Revenues	688,233	572,450	596,281	599,525	589,657	433,740	312,051
Costs and Expenses	665,451	550,971	560,727	552,949	545,483	400,619	285,254
Depreciation & Amort	15,724	15,110	16,305	13,309	12,141	8,987	6,586
Operating Income	9,352	8,244	16,720	30,232	30,399	24,269	20,211
Income Bef Income Taxes	6,617	6,450	15,750	28,842	23,375	21,634	19,687
Income Taxes	2,634	1,936	7,245	11,825	9,280	8,213	8,072
Minority Interest	675	...	...	...	...	...	...
Net Income	[1] 3,308	4,514	8,505	17,017	14,095	13,421	11,615
Aver. Shs. Outstg.	13,289	13,293	13,512	13,630	13,566	13,447	13,398

[1] Before acctg. change cr$525,000.

BALANCE SHEET (IN THOUSANDS):

Cash & Cash Equivalents	10,824	8,908	18,742	20,468	...	...	3,020
Receivables, Net	153,051	114,902	102,703	98,402	102,744	88,093	58,825
Inventories	52,732	40,189	39,489	39,531	37,010	34,127	23,166
Gross Property	141,410	132,261	126,922	117,961	107,289	93,284	68,915
Accumulated Depreciation	76,493	66,133	56,341	46,469	37,434	28,598	21,287
Long-Term Debt	35,688	28,419	25,267	29,398	41,366	46,277	17,899
Net Stockholders' Equity	114,063	112,335	113,781	109,050	95,754	83,871	72,062
Total Assets	306,188	251,456	249,509	250,343	244,103	207,686	143,487
Total Current Assets	221,286	169,029	166,376	162,676	154,845	126,881	86,026
Total Current Liabilities	140,846	99,787	101,011	102,492	94,948	71,767	49,133
Net Working Capital	80,440	69,242	65,365	60,184	59,897	55,114	36,893
Year End Shares Outstg	13,312	13,177	13,461	13,477	13,467	13,414	13,349

STATISTICAL RECORD:

Operating Profit Margin %	1.4	1.4	2.8	5.0	5.2	5.6	6.5
Book Value Per Share	8.42	8.15	8.04	7.72	6.72	5.80	5.06
Return on Equity %	2.9	4.0	7.5	15.6	14.7	16.0	16.1
Return on Assets %	1.1	1.8	3.4	6.8	5.8	6.5	8.1
Average Yield %	2.1	2.4	1.9	1.4	1.2	1.3	1.3
P/E Ratio	71.0-39.0	41.2-24.3	28.6-15.1	16.1-10.9	18.0-11.4	14.1-9.0	14.1-8.6
Price Range	17¾-9¾	14-8¼	18-9½	20⅛-13⅝	18¾-11⅞	14⅛-9	12¼-7½

Statistics are as originally reported.

OFFICERS:
D.W. Goldfus, Chmn. & C.E.O.
G.K. Anderson, Pres.
W.G. Gardner, C.F.O., Treas. & Sec.

INCORPORATED: MN, Jul., 1949

PRINCIPAL OFFICE: 7900 Xerxes Ave S.
Suite 1800, Minneapolis, MN 55431-1159

TELEPHONE NUMBER: (612) 835-1874

FAX: (612) 835-3196

NO. OF EMPLOYEES: 5,863

ANNUAL MEETING: In June

SHAREHOLDERS: 2,322 (approx.)

INSTITUTIONAL HOLDINGS:
No. of Institutions: 48
Shares Held: 4,040,456

REGISTRAR(S): American Stock Transfer
Co., 40 Wall St., 46th Floor, New York, NY
10005

TRANSFER AGENT(S): American Stock
Transfer Co., 40 Wall St., 46th Floor, New
York, NY 10005

ARCHER DANIELS MIDLAND CO.

YIELD 0.4%
P/E RATIO 17.2

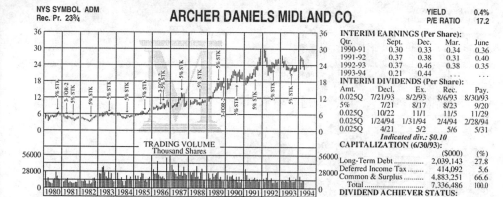

7 YEAR PRICE SCORE 98.5   **12 MONTH PRICE SCORE 104.3**
*NYSE COMPOSITE INDEX=100

INTERIM EARNINGS (Per Share):

Qtr.	Sept.	Dec.	Mar.	June
1990-91	0.30	0.33	0.34	0.36
1991-92	0.37	0.38	0.31	0.40
1992-93	0.37	0.46	0.38	0.35
1993-94	0.21	0.44	...	...

INTERIM DIVIDENDS (Per Share):

Amt.	Decl.	Ex.	Rec.	Pay.
0.025Q	7/21/93	8/2/93	8/6/93	8/30/93
5%	7/21	8/17	8/23	9/20
0.025Q	10/22	11/1	11/5	11/29
0.025Q	1/24/94	1/31/94	2/4/94	2/28/94
0.025Q	4/21	5/2	5/6	5/31

Indicated div.: $0.10

CAPITALIZATION (6/30/93):

	($000)	(%)
Long-Term Debt	2,039,143	27.8
Deferred Income Tax	414,092	5.6
Common & Surplus	4,883,251	66.6
Total	7,336,486	100.0

DIVIDEND ACHIEVER STATUS:

Rank: 177   1983-93 Growth Rate: 10.0%
Total Years of Dividend Growth: 19

RECENT DEVELOPMENTS: Net income for the quarter ended 12/31/93 was $146.1 million compared with $155.4 million last year. Earnings per share declined slightly to $0.44 from $0.45 on 330,400,000 shares outstanding. Net income for the six-month period was $215.1 million compared with $281.0 million last year. Prior year's results were before an accounting credit of $33.0 million, or $0.10 a share. Earnings per share declined to $0.65 from $0.82. Earnings were adversely affected by crop damage caused by flooding in the Midwest during the first quarter.

PROSPECTS: Near-term earnings should improve gradually once the Company fully recovers from operations damaged by earlier floods in the Midwest. ADM should benefit from strong demand for soy protein products, including an all-vegetable protein food, Harvest Burger. The rapid rise in global wheat consumption should also help results. ADM will seek to expand its existing processing, transportation and merchandising base. For the long term, ADM is focusing on a strategy that will emphasize more value-added product lines.

BUSINESS

ARCHER DANIELS MIDLAND COMPANY is engaged in the business of processing and merchandising agricultural commodities. It is one of the largest domestic processors of oil seeds and of vegetable oil. ADM is one of the largest flour millers and corn refiners in the U.S. Corn syrups, high fructose syrups, glucose, corn starches and ethyl alcohol (ethanol) are products of the corn wet milling operations. Other operations include storage of grain, shelling of peanuts, production of consumer food products and formula feeds, production of malt products and refining of sugar. ADM Investor Services provides ADM and other commercial firms with commodity hedging services and is a futures commission merchant.

ANNUAL EARNINGS AND DIVIDENDS PER SHARE

	6/30/93	6/30/92	6/30/91	6/30/90	6/30/89	6/30/88	6/30/87
Earnings Per Share	[3] 1.56	1.47	1.35	1.41	1.25	1.02	0.77
Dividends Per Share	[2] 0.10	[3] 0.091	[4] 0.087	[5] 0.083	0.061	[6] 0.05	[7] 0.048
Dividend Payout %	6.4	6.2	6.4	5.9	4.8	4.9	5.9

Note: 5%stk.div.9/20/93. [1] Before acctg. chg. [2] 5% stk div, 8/11/92 [3] 5% stk div 8/13/91 [4] 5% stk div, 9/17/90 [5] 50% stk div, 12/4/89 [6] 5% stk div, 9/87 [7] 5% stk div, 9/86

ANNUAL FINANCIAL DATA

RECORD OF EARNINGS (IN MILLIONS):

Net Sales & Other Oper Inc	9,811.4	9,231.5	8,468.2	7,751.3	7,928.8	6,798.4	5,774.6
Costs and Expenses	8,744.7	8,189.5	7,589.8	6,828.8	7,086.0	6,073.5	5,237.9
Depreciation & Amort	328.5	293.7	261.4	248.1	220.5	184.0	155.9
Operating Income	738.2	748.3	617.0	674.4	622.3	540.9	380.8
Earn Bef Income Taxes	746.0	759.6	718.0	753.2	667.7	571.9	477.8
Income Taxes	211.5	255.8	251.3	269.6	243.1	218.9	212.5
Net Income	[1] 534.5	503.8	466.7	483.5	424.7	353.1	265.4
Aver. Shs. Outstg. (000)	342,775	343,692	344,883	343,676	340,472	346,397	345,959

[1] Before acctg. change cr$33,018,000.

BALANCE SHEET (IN MILLIONS):

Cash and Cash Equivalents	1,868.3	1,403.5	890.5	829.5	841.9	644.4	465.1
Receivables	824.9	696.8	639.0	632.9	510.9	637.8	450.7
Inventories	1,131.8	1,025.0	917.5	771.2	695.0	773.7	784.3
Gross Property	6,001.7	5,548.1	4,831.9	3,977.7	3,281.6	2,851.9	2,467.8
Accumulated Depreciation	2,786.8	2,488.0	2,136.3	1,845.9	1,449.3	1,190.7	989.3
Long-Term Debt	2,039.1	1,562.5	980.3	750.9	690.1	692.9	657.5
Net Stockholders' Equity	4,883.3	4,492.4	3,922.3	3,573.2	3,033.5	2,630.5	2,367.7
Total Assets	8,404.1	7,524.5	6,260.6	5,450.0	4,728.3	4,397.6	3,862.1
Total Current Assets	3,921.7	3,213.4	2,531.6	2,303.8	2,105.7	2,118.8	1,749.7
Total Current Liabilities	960.2	936.8	856.9	676.3	618.5	710.1	497.3
Net Working Capital	2,961.5	2,276.6	1,674.7	1,627.5	1,487.2	1,408.7	1,252.4
Year End Shs Outstg (000)	342,299	342,804	342,794	328,481	328,481	339,739	347,079

STATISTICAL RECORD:

Operating Profit Margin %	7.5	8.1	7.3	8.7	7.8	8.0	6.6
Book Value Per Share	14.27	13.10	11.44	10.88	9.23	7.74	6.82
Return on Equity %	10.9	11.2	11.9	13.5	14.0	13.4	11.2
Return on Assets %	6.4	6.7	7.5	8.9	9.0	8.0	6.9
Average Yield %	0.4	0.4	0.4	0.4	0.4	0.5	0.4
P/E Ratio	16.6-12.7	20.2-13.8	22.3-12.4	15.9-10.6	15.5-8.6	11.4-9.1	17.9-10.7
Price Range	27⅝-21	29¾-20¼	30⅛-16¾	22⅜-15	19⅜-10¾	11⅝-9¼	13¾-8¼

Statistics are as originally reported.

OFFICERS:
D.O. Andreas, Chmn. & C.E.O.
M.D. Andreas, Vice-Chmn. & Exec. V.P.
J.R. Randall, Pres.
D.J. Schmalz, V.P., Contr. & C.F.O.
INCORPORATED: DE, May, 1923
PRINCIPAL OFFICE: 4666 Faries Pkwy. Box 1470, Decatur, IL 62525

TELEPHONE NUMBER: (217) 424-5200
NO. OF EMPLOYEES: 585
ANNUAL MEETING: In October
SHAREHOLDERS: 10,500
INSTITUTIONAL HOLDINGS:
No. of Institutions: 568
Shares Held: 174,152,227

REGISTRAR(S): Harris Trust & Savings Bank, Chicago, IL

TRANSFER AGENT(S): Harris Trust & Savings Bank, Chicago, IL

NYS SYMBOL ATG
Rec. Pr. 34⅞

ATLANTA GAS LIGHT CO.

YIELD 6.0%
P/E RATIO 15.0

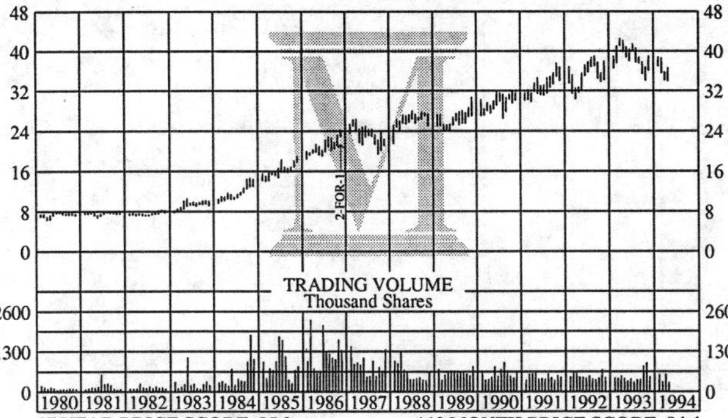

***7 YEAR PRICE SCORE 95.2** ***12 MONTH PRICE SCORE 94.4**

*NYSE COMPOSITE INDEX=100

INTERIM EARNINGS (Per Share):

Qtr.	Dec.	Mar.	June	Sept.
1990-91	1.05	1.47	d0.11	d0.30
1991-92	0.88	1.79	d0.08	d0.31
1992-93	0.87	1.79	d0.14	d0.34
1993-94	1.01	...	...	...

INTERIM DIVIDENDS (Per Share):

Amt.	Decl.	Ex.	Rec.	Pay.
0.52Q	5/7/93	5/17/93	5/21/93	6/1/93
0.52Q	8/6	8/16	8/20	9/1
0.52Q	11/5	11/15	11/19	12/1
0.52Q	2/4/94	2/14/94	2/18/94	3/1/94
0.52Q	5/6	5/16	5/20	6/1

Indicated div.: $2.08

CAPITALIZATION (9/30/93):

	($000)	(%)
Long-Term Debt	375,000	33.9
Deferred Income Tax	181,500	16.4
Preferred Stock	58,700	5.3
Common & Surplus	492,000	44.4
Total	1,107,200	100.0

DIVIDEND ACHIEVER STATUS:
Rank: 220 1983-93 Growth Rate: 7.8%
Total Years of Dividend Growth: 22

RECENT DEVELOPMENTS: For the year ended 12/31/93, net income was $61.7 million, up 9.8% from $56.2 million last year. Revenues were $1.16 billion, up 12.6%. The increase in net income was primarily due to growth in the number of customers served, rate increases granted by the Georgia Public Service Commission and increased other income. Gas costs are recovered from customers under purchased gas provisions and have no direct effect on net income.

PROSPECTS: Earnings will stabilize due to a weather-normalization clause. Growth in ATG's service area has slowed. However, growth for ATG will likely outpace most comparable sized distributors. Capital expenditures will continue to be significant. The Georgia Public Service Commission (GPSC) awarded ATG an increase in annual revenue of $11.2 million, effective October 1, 1993, far below ATG's requested $62.5 million.

BUSINESS

ATLANTA GAS LIGHT COMPANY is the largest natural gas distribution company in the southeast and serves more than 1.2 million customers in Georgia. In parts of Georgia, the Company distributes gas under the trade names of Georgia Natural Gas Company and Savannah Gas Company. Through its subsidiary, Chattanooga Gas Company, ATG serves more than 40,000 customers in Chattanooga and Cleveland, Tennessee. ATG has gas exploration and production interests in Texas, Louisiana and Alabama. Making a small contribution to earnings are non-utility operations: gas appliance merchandising, rental property, liquified petroleum, engine sales and service, and real estate.

REVENUES

(9/30/93)	($000)	(%)
Residential Gas	658,200	58.2
Commercial Gas	268,100	23.7
Industrial Gas	157,900	14.0
Transportation	33,800	3.0
Miscellaneous	12,300	1.1
Total	1,130,300	100.0

ANNUAL EARNINGS AND DIVIDENDS PER SHARE

	9/30/93	9/30/92	9/30/91	9/30/90	9/30/89	9/30/88	9/30/87
Earnings Per Share	**2.16**	**2.26**	**2.07**	**2.02**	**1.90**	**[1] 2.25**	**2.04**
eDividends Per Share	**2.08**	**2.07**	**2.04**	**1.98**	**1.90**	**1.79**	**1.64**
Dividend Payout %	**96.3**	**91.6**	**98.5**	**98.0**	**100.0**	**79.6**	**80.4**

[1] Before acctg. chg.

ANNUAL FINANCIAL DATA

	9/30/93	9/30/92	9/30/91	9/30/90	9/30/89	9/30/88	9/30/87
RECORD OF EARNINGS (IN MILLIONS):							
Operating Revenues	1,130.3	994.6	963.9	1,000.9	938.6	975.6	983.5
Maintenance	30.9	29.5	28.6	28.1	25.3	24.0	22.4
Income Taxes	28.2	25.6	26.2	23.4	13.1	19.9	34.8
Operating Income	99.9	100.2	94.5	93.1	78.3	73.3	66.3
Total Interest Charges	46.7	47.4	46.9	44.8	41.9	32.7	30.3
Net Income	57.5	55.4	49.4	45.6	42.1	[1] 46.0	39.4
Aver. Shs. Outstg. (000)	24,600	24,100	23,330	21,927	21,469	19,778	18,507
[1] Before acctg. change cr$2,908,000.							
BALANCE SHEET (IN MILLIONS):							
Gross Plant	1,786.2	1,678.9	1,559.0	1,432.7	1,330.7	1,156.1	1,036.4
Accumulated Depreciation	522.7	477.4	435.6	399.6	369.0	310.6	278.7
Utility Plant-net	1,263.5	1,201.5	1,123.4	1,033.0	961.7	845.4	757.7
Long-term Debt	375.0	326.4	455.5	417.8	368.8	378.7	271.4
Net Stockholders' Equity	550.7	486.3	462.8	414.1	401.2	389.7	316.3
Total Assets	1,578.6	1,472.1	1,392.3	1,322.2	1,267.8	1,220.6	948.3
Year End Shs Outstg (000)	24,800	24,300	23,787	22,160	21,699	21,236	18,708
STATISTICAL RECORD:							
Book Value Per Share	19.84	19.43	18.84	17.93	17.66	17.44	15.81
Op. Inc/Net Pl %	7.9	8.3	8.4	9.0	8.1	8.7	8.7
Dep/Gr. Pl %	3.3	3.3	3.2	3.2	3.2	3.1	3.0
Accum. Dep/Gr. Pl %	29.3	28.4	27.9	27.9	27.7	26.9	26.9
Return on Equity %	11.6	11.7	11.0	11.4	10.9	12.3	13.2
Average Yield %	5.4	6.0	6.1	6.8	7.0	7.2	7.2
P/E Ratio	19.7-15.7	17.3-13.4	18.2-14.4	15.9-13.1	16.2-12.6	12.4-9.6	12.9-9.5
Price Range	42½-34	39-30¼	37⅝-29¾	32⅛-26½	30¾-23⅞	28-21½	26⅜-19⅜

Statistics are as originally reported.

OFFICERS:
D.R. Jones, Pres. & C.E.O.
K.A. Royse, Pres.-Chattanooga Gas Co.
R.L. Goocher, Sr. V.P. & C.F.O.
C.C. Moore, Jr., Treasurer

INCORPORATED: GA, Feb., 1856

PRINCIPAL OFFICE: 303 Peachtree Street NE
P.O. Box 4569, Atlanta, GA 30302

TELEPHONE NUMBER: (404) 584-4000

NO. OF EMPLOYEES: 512

ANNUAL MEETING: In February

SHAREHOLDERS: 12,675

INSTITUTIONAL HOLDINGS:
No. of Institutions: 130
Shares Held: 4,833,641

REGISTRAR(S): Wachovia Bank & Trust Co., N.A., Atlanta, GA

TRANSFER AGENT(S): Wachovia Bank & Trust Co., N.A., Atlanta, GA

ATLANTIC ENERGY, INC.

YIELD	8.5%
P/E RATIO	22.4

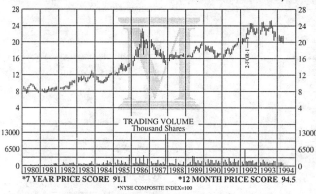

*7 YEAR PRICE SCORE 91.1   *12 MONTH PRICE SCORE 94.5

*NYSE COMPOSITE INDEX=100

TRADING VOLUME
Thousand Shares

INTERIM EARNINGS (Per Share):

Qtr.	Mar.	June	Sept.	Dec.
1989	0.34	0.27	0.84	0.08
1991	0.19	0.22	1.09	0.23
1992	0.55	0.21	0.76	0.15
1993	0.38	0.21	0.99	0.22

INTERIM DIVIDENDS (Per Share):

Amt.	Decl.	Ex.	Rec.	Pay.
0.385Q	6/10/93	6/15/93	6/21/93	7/15/93
0.385Q	9/9	9/14	9/20	10/15
0.385Q	12/9	12/14	12/20	1/17/94
0.385Q	3/10/94	3/15/94	3/21/94	4/15

Indicated div.: $1.54

CAPITALIZATION (12/31/93):

	($000)	(%)
Long-Term Debt	766,101	33.3
Cap. Lease Oblig.	44,407	1.9
Deferred Income Tax	437,527	19.1
Preferred Stock	213,750	9.3
Common & Surplus	835,992	36.4
Total	2,297,777	100.0

DIVIDEND ACHIEVER STATUS:

Rank: 325	1983-93 Growth Rate: 2.9%
Total Years of Dividend Growth:	41

RECENT DEVELOPMENTS: For the year ended 12/31/93, net income advanced 10.6% to $95.3 million. Revenues were $865.7 million, up 6.0%. Net income reflects charges of $5.3 million related to restructuring. Sales to residential and commercial customers increased 6.7% and 5.1%, respectively. Sales to industrial and other customers increased approximately 2.5%.

PROSPECTS: ATE is facing stiff competition from nonutility electric generators. Atlantic City Electric's rates are high by national and regional norms. The Company's financial flexibility may be negatively affected as it becomes increasingly reliant on purchased power from neighboring investor-owned utilities and from independent power producers. ATE's construction program will increase as a result of compliance with the Clean Air Act.

BUSINESS

ATLANTIC ENERGY, INC. provides electric service to the southern third of New Jersey. Tourism plays a major part in the eastern shore economy, while commercial and light industrial customers are situated in the western section of the service area. Farming and agriculture is significant in the south and west. Other subsidiaries include Atlantic Southern Properties, Inc. which owns, develops and manages commercial real estate; Atlantic Generation, Inc.; ATE Investment, Inc.; Atlantic Energy Technology, Inc. and Deepwater Operating Company.

REVENUES

(12/31/93)	($000)	(%)
Residential	393,866	48.0
Commercial	315,089	38.4
Industrial	100,812	12.3
All others	10,575	1.3
Total	820,342	100.0

ANNUAL EARNINGS AND DIVIDENDS PER SHARE

	1993	1992	1991	1990	1989	1988	1987
Earnings Per Share	1.80	1.67	1.75	1.51	1.87	1.84	2.02
Dividends Per Share	1.53	①1.51	1.49	1.46	1.41	1.385	1.325
Dividend Payout %	85.0	90.4	85.4	96.7	75.4	75.3	66.0

① 2-for-1 stk split, 5/15/92

ANNUAL FINANCIAL DATA

RECORD OF EARNINGS (IN MILLIONS):

	1993	1992	1991	1990	1989	1988	1987
Total Revenues	865.7	816.8	778.0	716.8	705.0	675.9	648.2
Depreciation & Amort	68.0	69.4	66.0	62.1	58.5	54.8	51.1
Maintenance	45.4	49.8	52.0	52.4	55.2	59.6	51.9
Prov for Fed Inc Taxes	45.3	37.1	36.2	26.9	22.9	26.5	48.9
Operating Income	159.6	137.2	144.9	124.6	134.7	122.8	114.7
Net Interest on Charges	59.6	54.5	51.7	54.2	50.5	49.4	46.1
Net Income	95.3	86.2	85.6	68.9	81.0	72.2	73.8
Aver. Shs. Outstg. (000)	52,888	51,592	49,000	45,590	43,268	39,186	36,622

BALANCE SHEET (IN MILLIONS):

	1993	1992	1991	1990	1989	1988	1987
Gross Plant	2,417.0	2,296.6	2,190.6	2,042.1	1,861.5	1,725.3	1,611.0
Accumulated Depreciation	668.8	599.1	545.8	504.2	459.2	419.2	388.3
Prop, Plant & Equip, Net	1,748.1	1,697.5	1,644.8	1,537.9	1,402.2	1,306.1	1,222.7
Long-term Debt	810.5	680.1	617.9	632.9	638.9	545.5	526.3
Net Stockholders' Equity	1,049.7	1,022.2	986.5	822.4	756.8	658.0	530.2
Total Assets	2,487.5	2,220.2	2,151.4	2,006.0	1,864.5	1,660.3	1,499.4
Year End Shs Outstg (000)	53,507	52,199	50,896	45,952	45,092	40,024	36,694

STATISTICAL RECORD:

	1993	1992	1991	1990	1989	1988	1987
Book Value Per Share	15.62	15.17	14.84	14.36	14.27	13.58	12.86
Op. Inc/Net Pl %	9.1	8.1	8.8	8.1	9.6	9.4	9.4
Dep/Gr. Pl %	2.8	3.0	3.0	3.1	3.2	3.2	3.2
Accum. Dep/Gr. Pl %	27.9	26.3	25.1	24.9	25.0	24.6	24.3
Return on Equity %	10.9	10.4	10.8	9.8	11.8	12.4	14.4
Average Yield %	6.7	6.8	8.1	8.3	7.8	8.4	7.5
P/E Ratio	14.1-11.3	14.7-11.7	12.1-9.2	12.7-10.6	10.6-8.7	9.5-8.4	10.3-7.1
Price Range	25⅜-20⅜	24⅝-19½	21-16	19¼-16	19⅞-16¼	17½-15⅜	20¾-14⅜

Statistics are as originally reported.

OFFICERS:
E.D. Huggard, Chmn. & C.E.O.
J.L. Jacobs, pres.
J.G. Salomone, V.P. & Treas.

INCORPORATED: NJ, Aug., 1986

PRINCIPAL OFFICE: 6801 Black Horse Pike, Pleasantville, NJ 08232

TELEPHONE NUMBER: (609) 645-4500
FAX: (609) 645-4100
NO. OF EMPLOYEES: 2,023 (Atlantic Electric)
ANNUAL MEETING: In April
SHAREHOLDERS: 46,524
INSTITUTIONAL HOLDINGS:
No. of Institutions: 117
Shares Held: 10,199,095

REGISTRAR(S): At Company's Office

TRANSFER AGENT(S): At Company's Office

AUTOMATIC DATA PROCESSING INC.

YIELD 1.0%
P/E RATIO 23.1

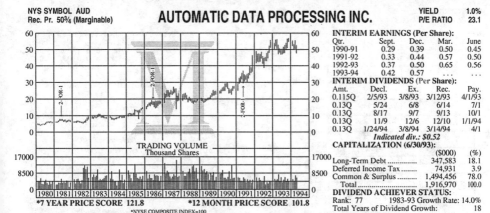

*7 YEAR PRICE SCORE 121.8   *12 MONTH PRICE SCORE 101.8
*NYSE COMPOSITE INDEX=100

INTERIM EARNINGS (Per Share):

Qtr.	Sept.	Dec.	Mar.	June
1990-91	0.29	0.39	0.50	0.45
1991-92	0.33	0.44	0.57	0.50
1992-93	0.37	0.50	0.65	0.56
1993-94	0.42	0.57	...	...

INTERIM DIVIDENDS (Per Share):

Amt.	Decl.	Ex.	Rec.	Pay.
0.115Q	2/5/93	3/8/93	3/12/93	4/1/93
0.13Q	5/24	6/8	6/14	7/1
0.13Q	8/17	9/7	9/13	10/1
0.13Q	11/9	12/6	12/10	1/1/94
0.13Q	1/24/94	3/8/94	3/14/94	4/1

Indicated div.: $0.52

CAPITALIZATION (6/30/93):

	($000)	(%)
Long-Term Debt	347,583	18.1
Deferred Income Tax	74,931	3.9
Common & Surplus	1,494,456	78.0
Total	1,916,970	100.0

DIVIDEND ACHIEVER STATUS:
Rank: 77   1983-93 Growth Rate: 14.0%
Total Years of Dividend Growth: 18

RECENT DEVELOPMENTS: For the quarter ended 12/31/93, net income climbed 14% to $80.2 million from $70.1 million for the same period last year. Revenues rose 11% to $577.7 million versus $518.5 million a year ago. Growth in revenues was boosted by a 28% increase in Brokerage Services revenues, aided by a prior acquisition and by high brokerage trading volume. Meanwhile, earnings were additionally boosted by a 24% jump in revenues for Dealer Services. Margins improved in each business unit in spite of increased marketing and development expenses.

PROSPECTS: The Company's Brokerage services unit should enjoy steady earnings gains due to robust demand for stock quotation systems and proxy services. In addition, the acquisition of Quotron's foreign equities business will fuel growth in the near term. The introduction of a new family of advanced products will contribute to earnings in the Automotive Claims division. Earnings from the Employer Services group will benefit from improved client retention rates and increased payroll processing services.

BUSINESS

AUTOMATIC DATA PROCESSING, INC. is the largest independent company in the United States dedicated exclusively to providing computerized transaction processing, recordkeeping, data communications, and information services. The Company services about 250,000 clients in nearly every segment of business, industry, and government for the collection of data, data processing and data dissemination. The Company primarily operates out of nine business services that include: Employer, Brokerage, Dealer, Automotive, Claims, Interactive Business, ADP Credit Corp. Network Services and International operations.

REVENUES

(06/30/93)	($000)	(%)
Employer Services	1,311,000	60.0
Brokerage Services	502,000	22.0
Dealer Services	274,000	12.0
Other	133,000	6.0
Total	2,223,000	100.0

ANNUAL EARNINGS AND DIVIDENDS PER SHARE

	6/30/93	6/30/92	6/30/91	6/30/90	6/30/89	6/30/88	6/30/87
Earnings Per Share	2.08	1.84	1.63	1.44	1.27	1.10	0.88
Dividends Per Share	0.49	0.43	① 0.375	0.325	0.28	0.24	0.205
Dividend Payout %	23.6	23.4	23.0	22.6	22.1	21.8	23.3

① Adj for 2-for-1 stk split, 5/01/91

ANNUAL FINANCIAL DATA

RECORD OF EARNINGS (IN MILLIONS):

Revenues	2,223.4	1,940.6	1,771.8	1,714.0	1,677.7	1,549.2	1,384.2
Costs and Expenses	1,676.8	1,470.6	1,349.5	1,303.2	1,266.1	1,171.5	1,039.9
Depreciation & Amort	140.2	116.1	114.5	113.5	123.6	107.0	102.2
Operating Income	406.4	353.8	307.8	297.4	291.5	272.1	242.1
Earn Bef Income Taxes	386.6	341.6	299.6	285.3	271.8	255.0	221.9
Income Taxes	92.4	85.4	71.9	73.6	84.2	84.7	89.9
Net Income	294.2	256.2	227.7	211.7	187.6	170.3	132.0
Aver. Shs. Outstg. (000)	141,327	139,045	139,936	147,168	148,448	155,118	149,922

BALANCE SHEET (IN MILLIONS):

Cash and Cash Equivalents	368.2	413.5	320.2	396.3	372.8	390.8	480.9
Accounts Receivable	294.3	243.6	225.4	262.0	240.7	206.7	182.3
Inventories	...	...	...	35.7	38.6	29.6	29.6
Gross Property	911.9	943.3	909.9	914.5	915.1	882.3	749.6
Accumulated Depreciation	550.7	586.7	537.6	514.2	482.3	460.0	399.6
Long-Term Debt	347.6	333.2	49.1	82.1	259.9	244.7	205.7
Net Stockholders' Equity	1,494.5	1,296.7	1,052.6	1,127.0	949.5	982.3	875.1
Total Assets	2,439.4	2,169.3	1,564.9	1,692.3	1,679.3	1,653.5	1,444.9
Total Current Assets	771.3	733.7	621.8	735.1	728.4	688.3	754.9
Total Current Liabilities	416.3	367.0	322.3	382.2	376.6	338.7	284.8
Net Working Capital	355.0	366.8	299.5	352.9	351.8	349.6	470.1
Yr End Com Shs Outstg (000)	141,119	140,151	138,227	147,652	145,504	154,512	155,034

STATISTICAL RECORD:

Operating Profit Margin %	18.3	18.2	17.4	17.4	17.4	17.6	17.5
Book Value Per Share	6.51	5.29	5.75	6.27	5.05	4.96	4.34
Return on Equity %	19.7	19.8	21.6	18.8	19.8	17.3	15.1
Return on Assets %	12.1	11.8	14.5	12.5	11.2	10.3	9.1
Average Yield %	0.9	0.9	1.1	1.2	1.3	1.2	1.0
P/E Ratio	27.3-22.5	30.2-21.1	28.5-15.3	20.9-15.7	20.1-14.2	21.5-15.8	31.0-15.8
Price Range	56⅞-46⅞	55⅝-38¾	46⅜-25	30⅛-22⅝	25⅜-17⅞	23⅝-17⅜	27¼-13⅞

Statistics are as originally reported.

OFFICERS:
J.S. Weston, Chmn. & C.E.O.
A.F. Weinbach, Pres. & C.O.O.
F.D. Anderson, Jr., V.P. & C.F.O.

INCORPORATED: DE, Jun., 1961

PRINCIPAL OFFICE: One ADP Blvd.,
Roseland, NJ 07068-1728

TELEPHONE NUMBER: (201) 994-5000
NO. OF EMPLOYEES: 2,856 approx.
ANNUAL MEETING: In November
SHAREHOLDERS: 14,576
INSTITUTIONAL HOLDINGS:
No. of Institutions: 540
Shares Held: 98,543,171

REGISTRAR(S): Manufacturers Hanover Trust Co., New York, NY

TRANSFER AGENT(S): Manufacturers Hanover Trust Co., New York, NY

NYS SYMBOL AVE
Rec. Pr. 15⅝ (Marginable)

AVEMCO CORP.

YIELD 2.8%
P/E RATIO 11.8

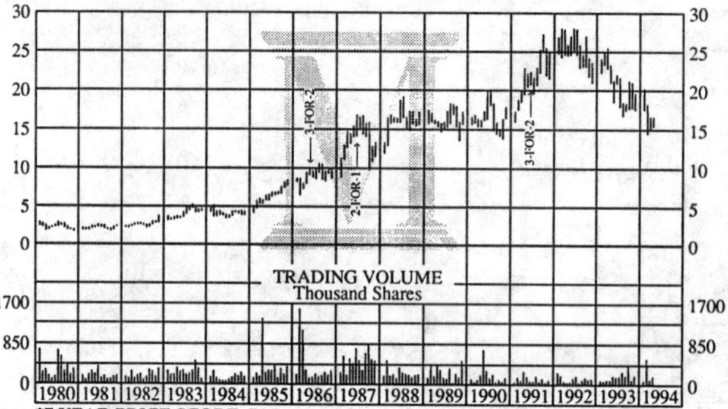

30
25
20
15
10
5
0
3-FOR-2
2-FOR-1
3-FOR-2
TRADING VOLUME
Thousand Shares
1700
850
0
1980 1981 1982 1983 1984 1985 1986 1987 1988 1989 1990 1991 1992 1993 1994

*7 YEAR PRICE SCORE 76.9 *12 MONTH PRICE SCORE 87.5

*NYSE COMPOSITE INDEX=100

INTERIM EARNINGS (Per Share):

Qtr.	Mar.	June	Sept.	Dec.
1990	0.31	0.24	0.24	0.28
1991	0.52	0.30	0.25	0.27
1992	0.32	0.20	0.13	0.17
1993	0.35	0.24	0.43	0.30

INTERIM DIVIDENDS (Per Share):

Amt.	Decl.	Ex.	Rec.	Pay.
0.10Q	5/12/93	6/21/93	6/25/93	7/22/93
0.11Q	7/29	10/6	10/13	10/21
0.11Q	11/5	12/17	12/23	1/20/94
0.11Q	1/26/94	3/21/94	3/25/94	4/22
0.11Q	5/6	6/27	7/1	7/26

Indicated div.: $0.44

CAPITALIZATION (12/31/93):

	($000)	(%)
Total Debt	54,500	50.3
Common & Surplus	53,930	49.7
Total	108,430	100.0

DIVIDEND ACHIEVER STATUS:
Rank: 118 1983-93 Growth Rate: 12.3%
Total Years of Dividend Growth: 18

RECENT DEVELOPMENTS: For the year ended 12/31/93, earnings before an accounting change were $14.6 million, or $1.33 per share, compared with earnings of $9.6 million, or $0.82 per share, in 1992. Total revenues increased 19.5% to $103.9 million from $86.9 million last year. AIC's gross premiums written during 1993 for general aviation business were $58.2 million, up slightly from the $57.9 million written in 1992. Non-aviation premiums amounted to $24.1 million, up from the $21.6 million in 1992. For the year, AVE's loss ratio for all lines of business was 66.2% versus 64.1% a year earlier. On 10/1/93, the company announced the sale by GEICO Corporation of 3.29 million of its 3.89 million shares of AVEMCO common stock. AVE repurchased 2.3 million of these shares at $17.50 per share for $40.2 million. Also, the company repurchased 110,000 additional shares during the course of 1993 at an average cost of $20.41 per share.

BUSINESS

AVEMCO CORPORATION, a Delaware Corporation, is an insurance holding company organized in 1959, that coordinates the activities of its subsidiaries and provides them with management, business planning, human resource, marketing and financial services. The subsidiaries of the the Company are engaged in the business of providing specialty property and casualty insurance products and services, principally involving general aviation. Insurance products are distributed on a direct basis, through exclusive agents and through independent agents and brokers. AVEMCO Insurance Company (AIC), the largest of the AVEMCO Group subsidiaries, is the hub of the Group's insurance activities. AIC serves both as a direct writer of insurance and as the reinsurer for the major portion of the business produced and managed by other members of the AVEMCO Group. Other subsidiaries include National Aviation Underwriters, Inc., Eastern Aviation and Marine Underwriters, Inc., Matterhorn Bank Programs, Inc., Loss Management Services, Inc., Brooks-Shettle Company, MEDEX Assistance Corporaiton, and The Wheatley Group, Ltd.

ANNUAL EARNINGS AND DIVIDENDS PER SHARE

	1993	1992	1991	1990	1989	1988	1987
Earnings Per Share	**1.33**	**0.82**	**1.34**	**1.06**	**1.03**	**1.36**	**1.29**
Dividends Per Share	**0.41**	**0.40**	**1 0.347**	**0.273**	**0.257**	**0.207**	**2 0.177**
Dividend Payout %	**30.8**	**48.8**	**25.9**	**25.8**	**24.8**	**15.2**	**13.7**

1 3-for-2 stk split,06/17/91 2 2-for-1 stk. slit, 6/87.

ANNUAL FINANCIAL DATA

	1993	1992	1991	1990	1989	1988	1987
RECORD OF EARNINGS (IN THOUSANDS):							
Premiums Earned	62,702	57,385	51,874	53,792	66,028	85,561	96,278
Net Investment Income	9,004	9,218	9,332	9,774	10,780	9,381	8,684
Total Revenues	103,901	86,923	84,540	79,257	93,299	106,405	116,183
Earn Bef Income Taxes	18,853	10,787	18,777	14,851	16,645	24,781	25,491
Total Income Taxes	4,224	1,184	3,367	2,396	3,014	6,259	7,050
Realized Gain on Sale Of Invest	...	...	...	...	...	d111	1,220
Net Income	1 14,629	9,603	15,410	12,455	13,631	18,411	19,661
Aver. Shs. Outstg.	11,041	11,734	11,511	11,726	13,197	13,628	14,348

1 Before acctg. change cr$943,000.

	1993	1992	1991	1990	1989	1988	1987
BALANCE SHEET (IN THOUSANDS):							
Cash	2,918	2,358	983	346	366	1,006	536
Fixed Matur, At Amortized Cost	113,887	121,723	120,383	108,331	103,358	95,001	94,006
Equity Securities, At Mkt	16,721	21,971	22,816	28,835	36,667	31,877	28,676
Total Assets	210,693	203,158	194,065	184,543	191,213	202,918	194,510
Benefits and Claims	76,517	51,117	49,279	55,672	62,202	71,207	82,856
Net Stockholders' Equity	53,930	89,215	84,065	68,720	75,922	84,019	68,422
Year End Shares Outstg	9,082	11,493	11,417	11,098	11,927	13,238	13,256
STATISTICAL RECORD:							
Return on Equity %	27.1	10.8	18.3	18.1	18.0	21.9	28.7
Book Value Per Share	5.94	7.76	7.36	6.19	6.37	6.35	5.16
Average Yield %	1.9	1.6	1.6	1.6	1.6	1.3	1.4
P/E Ratio	19.2-12.6	34.1-25.6	20.3-11.9	19.0-13.1	17.8-13.2	14.1-8.7	13.1-6.9
Price Range	25½-16¾	28-21	27¼-16	20⅛-13⅞	18⅜-13⅝	19⅛-11⅞	16⅞-8⅞

Statistics are as originally reported.

OFFICERS:
W.P. Condon, Chmn., Pres. & C.E.O.
J.R. Yuska, Sr. V.P. & C.F.O.
T.H. Chero, Sr. V.P. & Sec.
T.E. Lentz, Treasurer

INCORPORATED: DE, 1959

PRINCIPAL OFFICE: 411 Aviation Way, Frederick, MD 21701

TELEPHONE NUMBER: (301) 694-5700

FAX: (301) 694-4242

NO. OF EMPLOYEES: 409

ANNUAL MEETING: In May

SHAREHOLDERS: 3,550 (approx.)

INSTITUTIONAL HOLDINGS:
No. of Institutions: 51
Shares Held: 8,166,020

REGISTRAR(S): Chemical Bank, New York, NY

TRANSFER AGENT(S): Chemical Bank, New York, NY

AVERY DENNISON CORP.

YIELD 3.3%
P/E RATIO 20.3

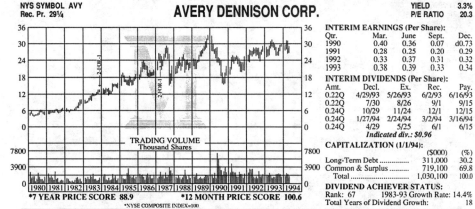

*7 YEAR PRICE SCORE 88.9   *12 MONTH PRICE SCORE 100.6
*NYSE COMPOSITE INDEX=100

INTERIM EARNINGS (Per Share):

Qtr.	Mar.	June	Sept.	Dec.
1990	0.40	0.36	0.07	d0.73
1991	0.28	0.25	0.20	0.29
1992	0.33	0.37	0.31	0.32
1993	0.38	0.39	0.33	0.34

INTERIM DIVIDENDS (Per Share):

Amt.	Decl.	Ex.	Rec.	Pay.
0.22Q	4/29/93	5/26/93	6/2/93	6/16/93
0.22Q	7/30	8/26	9/1	9/15
0.24Q	10/29	11/24	12/1	12/15
0.24Q	1/27/94	2/24/94	3/2/94	3/16/94
0.24Q	4/29	5/25	6/1	6/15

Indicated div.: $0.96

CAPITALIZATION (1/1/94):

	($000)	(%)
Long-Term Debt	311,000	30.2
Common & Surplus	719,100	69.8
Total	1,030,100	100.0

DIVIDEND ACHIEVER STATUS:
Rank: 67   1983-93 Growth Rate: 14.4%
Total Years of Dividend Growth: 18

RECENT DEVELOPMENTS: For the year ended 1/1/94, income before accounting adjustments was $83.3 million or 4% above last year. Sales declined slightly from $2.62 billion to $2.61 billion. Impressive sales and profit growth was achieved in the domestic market. The office products unit was adversely affected by the continued weak economic conditions in Europe and increased promotional expenses at home.

PROSPECTS: Company efforts to minimize production and administrative costs will increase future earnings potential. AVY is reducing inventory, improving the speed and accuracy of customer service, and consolidating and closing European facilities. A major investment made in the Fasson roll materials business will commence with the construction of a $30 million plant in Greenfield, Indiana to focus on the information-processing market.

BUSINESS

AVERY DENNISON CORPORATION was formed through the merger of Avery International Corp. (a California-based manufacturer of self-adhesive base materials, labels, tapes, office products and specialty chemicals) and Dennison Manufacturing Co. (a Massachusetts-based manufacturer serving worldwide markets for stationery and office products, systems for identification and control and package decoration systems). Businesses from both companies continue to operate separately. The Company's operating groups are as follows: Materials North America, Materials Europe, Automotive & Graphic Systems Divisions, Specialty Tape Divisions, Chemical Divisions, Converting Europe, Label Divisions N.A., Soabar Products and Fastener Divisions and Office Products Group.

BUSINESS LINE ANALYSIS

(01/01/94)	Rev(%)	Inc(%)
Adhesives &		
Materials..............	49.7	59.7
Office Products..........	28.8	26.0
Product ID & Control		
Sys.........................	21.5	14.3
Total	100.0	100.0

ANNUAL EARNINGS AND DIVIDENDS PER SHARE

	1/1/94	1/2/93	1/4/92	12/31/90	11/30/89	11/30/88	11/30/87
Earnings Per Share	①1.44	1.33	1.02	0.10	1.96	1.77	0.81
Dividends Per Share	0.90	0.82	0.76	0.64	0.54	0.515	②0.41
Dividend Payout %	62.5	61.7	74.5	N.M.	27.6	29.1	50.6

① Bef. acct. chge. ② 2-for-1 stk split, 3/87

ANNUAL FINANCIAL DATA

RECORD OF EARNINGS (IN MILLIONS):

	1/1/94	1/2/93	1/4/92	12/31/90	11/30/89	11/30/88	11/30/87
Total Revenues	2,608.7	2,622.9	2,545.1	2,590.2	1,732.4	1,582.0	1,465.5
Costs and Expenses	2,337.9	2,356.5	2,319.7	2,453.8	1,520.5	1,385.2	1,320.7
Depreciation & Amort	95.4	93.9	83.1	80.8	50.3	45.1	45.4
Operating Profit	175.4	172.5	142.3	55.6	161.6	151.7	99.4
Inc Bef Taxes on Income	132.2	130.2	104.8	15.6	139.1	127.8	77.9
Taxes on Income	48.9	50.1	41.8	9.7	52.6	50.1	43.2
Net Income	①83.3	80.1	63.0	5.9	86.5	77.7	34.7
Aver. Shs. Outstg. (000)	58,000	60,400	61,900	62,000	44,200	44,000	42,665

① Before acctg. change cr$1,100,000.

BALANCE SHEET (IN MILLIONS):

Cash and Cash Equivalents	5.8	3.9	5.3	6.5	3.1	5.9	8.0
Receivables, Net	411.2	415.4	423.8	491.5	298.6	281.4	257.8
Inventories	184.1	225.1	253.1	325.0	193.8	202.2	195.1
Gross Property	1,412.7	1,399.2	1,420.7	1,395.7	758.3	711.9	624.3
Accumulated Depreciation	654.2	619.3	606.5	574.0	279.3	249.3	223.0
Long-Term Debt	311.0	334.8	329.5	376.0	213.2	214.7	203.9
Net Stockholders' Equity	719.1	802.6	825.0	846.3	538.6	509.4	465.9
Total Assets	1,639.0	1,684.0	1,740.4	1,890.3	1,142.1	1,119.1	1,050.8
Total Current Assets	614.6	661.3	700.5	846.8	505.7	502.5	489.4
Total Current Liabilities	473.0	438.7	474.5	548.0	324.1	329.6	323.6
Net Working Capital	141.6	222.6	226.0	298.8	181.6	172.9	165.8
Year End Shs Outstg (000)	56,194	58,875	61,253	61,980	44,232	44,081	43,932

STATISTICAL RECORD:

Operating Profit Margin %	6.7	6.6	5.6	2.1	9.3	9.6	6.8
Book Value Per Share	10.50	11.29	11.07	11.21	9.10	8.45	7.89
Return on Equity %	11.6	10.0	7.6	0.7	16.1	15.3	7.5
Return on Assets %	5.1	4.8	3.6	0.3	7.6	6.9	3.3
Average Yield %	3.2	3.1	3.4	2.6	2.0	2.3	1.8
P/E Ratio	21.9-17.4	21.9-17.5	25.2-18.6	N.M	17.0-10.7	14.7-10.9	36.1-18.7
Price Range	31½-25⅛	29⅛-23¼	25¾-19	33-15½	33¼-21	26-19¼	29¼-15⅛

Statistics are as originally reported.

OFFICERS:
C.D. Miller, Chmn. & C.E.O.
P.M. Neal, Pres. & C.O.O.
R.G. Jenkins, Sr. V.P.-Finance & C.F.O.
W.H. Smith, V.P. & Treas.

INCORPORATED: DE, Sep., 1946

PRINCIPAL OFFICE: 150 N. Orange Grove Blvd., Pasadena, CA 91103-7090

TELEPHONE NUMBER: (818) 304-2000

NO. OF EMPLOYEES: 2,142

ANNUAL MEETING: In April

SHAREHOLDERS: 6,618

INSTITUTIONAL HOLDINGS:
No. of Institutions: 305
Shares Held: 36,484,468

REGISTRAR(S): Security Pacific National Bank, Los Angeles, CA 90060

TRANSFER AGENT(S): Security Pacific National Bank, Los Angeles, CA 90060

BALL CORP.

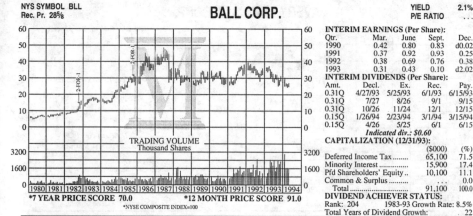

INTERIM EARNINGS (Per Share):

Qtr.	Mar.	June	Sept.	Dec.
1990	0.42	0.80	0.83	d0.02
1991	0.37	0.92	0.93	0.25
1992	0.38	0.69	0.76	0.38
1993	0.31	0.43	0.10	d2.02

INTERIM DIVIDENDS (Per Share):

Amt.	Decl.	Ex.	Rec.	Pay.
0.31Q	4/27/93	5/25/93	6/1/93	6/15/93
0.31Q	7/27	8/26	9/1	9/15
0.31Q	10/26	11/24	12/1	12/15
0.15Q	1/26/94	2/23/94	3/1/94	3/15/94
0.15Q	4/26	5/25	6/1	6/15

Indicated div.: $0.60

CAPITALIZATION (12/31/93):

	($000)	(%)
Deferred Income Tax........	65,100	71.5
Minority Interest	15,900	17.4
Pfd Shareholders' Equity ..	10,100	11.1
Common & Surplus	...	0.0
Total	91,100	100.0

DIVIDEND ACHIEVER STATUS:
Rank: 204   1983-93 Growth Rate: 8.5%
Total Years of Dividend Growth: 22

TRADING VOLUME
Thousand Shares

*7 YEAR PRICE SCORE 70.0   ***12 MONTH PRICE SCORE 91.0**
*NYSE COMPOSITE INDEX=100

RECENT DEVELOPMENTS: For the year ended 12/31/93, loss from continuing operations totaled $32.5 million compared with net income of $60.9 million in 1992. Sales increased 12.1% to $2.44 billion. Sales were positively affected by operating results at Heekin Can, which is now fully integrated into Ball's North American metal packaging organization. Ball's glass facility in Asheville, N.C. will close by mid-1994, cutting 300 jobs.

PROSPECTS: Earnings have been suppressed due to various restructuring costs. Ongoing plant consolidations have kept BLL from operating efficiently and at full capacity. Operating results will take a turn for the better now that Heekin is completely integrated and start-up costs at BLL's Ruston, La. facility are out of the way. Overcapacity is hurting the metal and glass packaging industries.

BUSINESS

BALL CORPORATION manufactures and markets packaging products for the food and beverage industries and provides aerospace and communications systems and services to government and commercial customers. Packaging Products include operations which manufacture aluminum and steel beverage containers and ends, steel food containers, and glass containers. Aerospace and Communications include electro-optics/cryogenics, telecommunication systems, space systems, time/frequency standards and systems engineering markets. In 1992, Ball spun off its home canning supplies, zinc products, metal printing, plastic products, and x-ray and video inspection equipment businesses into Alltrista Corporation.

ANNUAL EARNINGS AND DIVIDENDS PER SHARE

	1993	1992	1991	1990	1989	1988	1987
Earnings Per Share	d1.24	① 2.21	2.42	2.03	1.44	③ 1.40	2.80
Dividends Per Share	1.24	② 1.22	1.18	1.14	1.10	1.02	0.89
Dividend Payout %	...	55.2	48.8	56.2	76.4	72.9	31.8

① Before disc. oper. ② Bef discont opers ③ Before acctg. chg.

ANNUAL FINANCIAL DATA

RECORD OF EARNINGS (IN MILLIONS):

	1993	1992	1991	1990	1989	1988	1987
Total Revenues	2,440.9	2,177.8	2,267.4	1,357.2	1,222.4	1,073.0	1,054.1
Costs and Expenses	2,330.1	1,932.8	2,008.4	1,204.4	1,112.6	954.6	893.9
Depreciation & Amort	116.3	105.5	108.0	58.2	50.1	43.9	41.3
Operating Profit	103.2	139.5	151.0	94.6	59.7	74.5	118.9
Inc Bef Taxes on Income	d51.4	102.3	109.9	63.3	48.6	48.1	113.5
Provision for Inc Taxes	cr21.2	...	...	...	12.8	15.4	47.2
Eq In Earn (losses) Of Affils	1.3	0.6	dr0.8	6.6	9.2	8.4	1.0
Minority Interest	3.6	3.8	2.7	...	...	...	...
Net Income	① d32.5	② 62.9	66.2	50.2	35.8	③ 32.7	66.3
Aver. Shs. Outstg. (000)	28,712	26,039	23,125	21,886	22,959	23,299	23,633

① Before disc. op. cr$2,100,000; and acctg. chg dr$34,700,000. ② Before disc. op. cr$6,200,000. ③ Before acctg. change cr$17,800,000.

BALANCE SHEET (IN MILLIONS):

	1993	1992	1991	1990	1989	1988	1987
Cash & Temporary Invests	8.2	14.5	20.8	30.0	10.4	15.7	16.6
Receivables, Net	244.4	200.9	246.1	217.9	176.2	133.9	114.6
Inventories	409.3	375.2	336.9	272.5	165.3	155.5	...
Gross Property	1,449.3	1,242.2	1,325.2	1,051.9	715.4	683.8	629.6
Accumulated Depreciation	626.6	532.3	564.7	441.8	280.7	250.8	227.7
Long-Term Debt	...	...	333.9	404.8	262.8	196.3	100.7
Net Stockholders' Equity	...	...	...	...	...	...	397.4
Total Assets	1,795.6	1,563.9	1,558.6	1,307.6	938.0	876.5	794.9
Total Current Assets	692.1	619.2	634.0	542.2	374.0	331.7	315.7
Total Current Liabilities	451.2	359.1	441.7	323.0	219.3	183.0	203.4
Net Working Capital	240.9	260.1	192.3	219.2	154.7	148.7	112.3
Year End Shs Outstg (000)	29,447	26,429	25,768	23,806	23,806	23,516	23,328

STATISTICAL RECORD:

	1993	1992	1991	1990	1989	1988	1987
Operating Profit Margin %	...	6.4	6.7	7.0	4.9	6.9	11.3
Book Value Per Share	...	...	21.39	16.97	16.09	17.92	17.04
Return on Equity %	...	...	10.9	11.0	9.3	7.8	16.7
Return on Assets %	...	4.0	4.2	3.8	3.8	3.7	8.3
Average Yield %	4.0	3.6	3.7	3.8	3.7	3.3	2.3
P/E Ratio	...	17.9-12.7	15.8-10.6	17.0-12.8	23.9-17.5	25.6-18.3	17.3-9.7
Price Range	37¼-25⅛	39½-28	38¼-25⅝	34½-26	34⅜-25¼	35⅞-25⅝	48½-27¼

Statistics are as originally reported.

OFFICERS:
D.A. Davis, Pres. & C.E.O.
R.D. Hoover, Sr. V.P. & C.F.O.
R.J. Seabrook, V.P. & Treas.

INCORPORATED: IN, 1922

PRINCIPAL OFFICE: 345 South High Street
P.O. Box 2407, Muncie, IN 47307-0407

TELEPHONE NUMBER: (317) 747-6100
FAX: (317) 747-6203
NO. OF EMPLOYEES: 13,954
ANNUAL MEETING: In April
SHAREHOLDERS: 9,359
INSTITUTIONAL HOLDINGS:
No. of Institutions: 208
Shares Held: 16,176,788

REGISTRAR(S): First Chicago Trust Co. of
New York, New York, NY 10008

TRANSFER AGENT(S): First Chicago Trust
Co. of New York, New York, NY 10008

BANC ONE CORP.

YIELD 3.8%
P/E RATIO 10.4

TRADING VOLUME
Thousand Shares

*7 YEAR PRICE SCORE 117.2   *12 MONTH PRICE SCORE 93.3
*NYSE COMPOSITE INDEX=100

INTERIM EARNINGS (Per Share):

Qtr.	Mar.	June	Sept.	Dec.
1991	0.50	0.53	0.53	0.56
1992	0.61	0.61	0.58	0.59
1993	0.75	0.74	0.75	0.69

INTERIM DIVIDENDS (Per Share):

Amt.	Decl.	Ex.	Rec.	Pay.
0.31Q	10/19/93	12/9/93	12/15/93	1/2/94
10%	1/25/94	2/10/94	2/16/94	3/4
0.31Q	1/25	3/9	3/15	3/31
0.31Q	4/19	6/9	6/15	6/30

Indicated div.: $1.24

CAPITALIZATION (12/31/93):

	($000)	(%)
Total Deposits	60,943,181	76.8
Total Debt	10,466,275	13.2
Preferred Stock	249,900	0.3
Common & Surplus	6,783,738	8.5
Loan Valuation Reserve	918,153	1.2
Total	79,361,247	100.0

DIVIDEND ACHIEVER STATUS:
Rank: 82   1983-93 Growth Rate: 13.8%
Total Years of Dividend Growth: 23

RECENT DEVELOPMENTS: For the fiscal year ended 12/31/93, income was up 28% to $1.12 billion from the prior year. The provision for loan losses was reduced 39% to $368.5 million and nonperforming assets as a percentage of total loans reached an eleven-year low. Consumer lending increased 24% and credit card outstandings were 20% above last year's level. Commercial loans were 4% above 1992. The net interest margin was 6.29% versus 5.98% last year.

PROSPECTS: The Company has withdrawn its offer to acquire FirsTier Financial Inc., headquartered in Omaha, Nebraska. The acquisition was thwarted because ONE declined to increase its offer. However, the acquisition of Liberty National Bancorp is still pending. Upon completion, ONE will obtain the top market share position in Kentucky. Liberty National has assets of $4.7 billion and will account from 6% of ONE's total assets.

BUSINESS

BANC ONE CORPORATION is a $79.9 billion bank holding company. The Corporation operates 81 affiliate banking organizations in Arizona, California, Colorado, Illinois, Indiana, Kentucky, Michigan, Ohio, Oklahoma, Texas, Utah, West Virginia and Wisconsin. It also operates several additional corporations that engage in data processing, venture capital, investment and merchant banking, trust brokerage, investment management, equipment leasing, mortgage banking, consumer finance and insurance.

LOAN DISTRIBUTION

(12/31/93)	($000)	(%)
Comm, Finl & Agricultural	14,000,724	26.0
Commercial Real Estate	4,432,848	8.2
Construction Real Estate	1,632,137	3.1
Residential Real Estate	10,705,172	19.9
Consumer	15,961,028	29.6
Credit Card	6,050,750	11.2
Leases	1,062,961	2.0
Total	53,845,620	100.0

ANNUAL EARNINGS AND DIVIDENDS PER SHARE

	1993	1992	1991	1990	1989	1988	1987
Earnings Per Share	① 2.93	2.38	2.12	1.83	1.66	1.56	1.19
Dividends Per Share	② 1.03	③ 0.82	0.74	④ 0.67	0.61	⑤ 0.56	0.53
Dividend Payout %	35.2	34.5	34.9	36.6	36.7	35.9	44.5

Note: 10%stk.div.3/4/94. ① Before acct chge. ② 5-for-4 split,09/01/93 ③ 10% stk div, 2/10/92 ④ 10% stk div, 3/2/90 ⑤ 10% stk div, 3/88

ANNUAL FINANCIAL DATA

RECORD OF EARNINGS (IN MILLIONS):

	1993	1992	1991	1990	1989	1988	1987
Total Interest Income	5,735.1	4,829.1	3,309.6	2,801.6	2,651.1	2,271.5	1,669.4
Total Interest Expense	1,645.0	1,664.2	1,538.9	1,560.6	1,534.7	1,211.0	856.6
Net Interest Income	4,090.1	3,165.0	1,770.7	1,240.9	1,116.3	1,060.5	812.9
Prov for Loan & Lse Losses	368.5	510.5	424.4	300.3	197.5	183.4	177.9
Net Income	① 1,120.6	781.3	529.5	423.4	② 348.2	340.2	208.9
Aver. Shs. Outstg. (000)	376,828	290,204	220,823	209,356	196,804	195,733	158,826

① Before acctg. change cr$19,391,000. ② Before acctg. change cr$14,626,000.

BALANCE SHEET (IN MILLIONS):

	1993	1992	1991	1990	1989	1988	1987
Cash & Due From Banks	4,757.5	4,095.0	2,924.7	1,881.3	1,687.8	1,610.4	...
US Government Securities	...	7,713.4	4,446.0	3,094.4	2,937.6	1,258.9	...
Tax-exempt Securities	...	1,495.3	1,385.4	1,310.3	1,249.2	1,364.8	...
Net Loans & Leases	52,927.5	37,995.4	29,658.7	20,043.1	17,658.3	17,087.4	12,752.5
Total Domestic Deposits	60,943.2	48,464.7	37,057.0	22,316.0	20,952.2	19,501.8	14,478.3
Long-term Borrowings	1,701.7	1,197.5	703.1	581.0	371.6	378.9	266.2
Net Stockholders' Equity	7,033.6	5,213.5	3,814.1	2,899.5	2,279.2	2,040.8	1,489.5
Total Assets	79,918.6	61,417.4	46,293.1	30,336.0	26,552.2	25,273.7	18,730.0
Year End Shs Outstg (000)	380,687	290,102	230,750	218,398	198,014	195,482	163,606

STATISTICAL RECORD:

	1993	1992	1991	1990	1989	1988	1987
Return on Assets %	1.40	1.27	1.14	1.40	1.31	1.35	1.12
Return on Equity %	15.90	15.00	13.90	14.60	15.30	16.70	14.00
Book Value Per Share	17.82	17.08	15.36	13.17	11.39	10.31	9.10
Average Yield %	2.7	2.7	3.3	4.3	3.8	3.7	4.1
P/E Ratio	15.3-11.0	14.8-11.7	15.0-7.1	10.9-6.2	12.6-7.6	9.7-7.5	12.3-7.4
Price Range	44¾-32¼	38⅞-30⅝	34⅞-16½	21⅞-12½	22¼-13⅜	16⅝-12⅞	16⅛-9¾

Statistics are as originally reported.

OFFICERS:
J.B. McCoy, Chmn. & C.E.O.
D.L. McWhorter, Pres. & C.O.O.
G.R. Meiling, Treasurer

INCORPORATED: DE, Oct., 1967

PRINCIPAL OFFICE: 100 East Broad St., Columbus, OH 43271

TELEPHONE NUMBER: (614) 248-5944

NO. OF EMPLOYEES: 45,300

ANNUAL MEETING: In April

SHAREHOLDERS: 71,384

INSTITUTIONAL HOLDINGS:
No. of Institutions: 668
Shares Held: 181,426,942 (adj.)

REGISTRAR(S): Bank One, Indianapolis, N.A., Bank One Center/ Tower, Indianapolis, IN 46204

TRANSFER AGENT(S): Bank One, Indianapolis, N.A., Bank One Center/Tower, Indianapolis, IN 46204

BANCORP HAWAII, INC.

YIELD 3.3%
P/E RATIO 6.8

*7 YEAR PRICE SCORE 98.6   *12 MONTH PRICE SCORE 105.9
*NYSE COMPOSITE INDEX=100

INTERIM EARNINGS (Per Share):

Qtr.	Mar.	June	Sept.	Dec.
1990	0.91	0.92	0.92	0.92
1991	0.96	1.01	1.02	1.07
1992	1.08	1.13	1.12	0.79
1993	1.15	1.18	1.05	1.24

INTERIM DIVIDENDS (Per Share):

Amt.	Decl.	Ex.	Rec.	Pay.
0.345Q	7/16/93	8/18/93	8/24/93	9/15/93
0.345Q	10/29	11/12	11/18	12/14
0.39Q	1/27/94	2/11/94	2/17/94	3/15/94
50%	1/27	3/16	2/17	3/15
0.26Q	4/28	5/16	5/20	6/14

Indicated div.: $1.04

CAPITALIZATION (12/31/93):

	($000)	(%)
Total Deposits	7,004,975	57.1
Total Debt	4,211,601	34.3
Common & Surplus	938,104	7.6
Loan Valuation Reserve	125,284	1.0
Total	12,279,964	100.0

DIVIDEND ACHIEVER STATUS:
Rank: 151   1983-93 Growth Rate: 10.8%
Total Years of Dividend Growth: 16

RECENT DEVELOPMENTS: For the quarter ended 3/31/94, earnings were $34.4 million, up 4.3% from the corresponding period in 1993. Earnings per share were $0.80 compared with $0.77 reported for the first quarter of 1993. Return on average assets was 1.11% and return on average equity was 14.63%. As of 3/31/94, total assets were $12.9 billion versus $12.7 billion at the same time in 1993. Asset quality improved modestly relative to the fourth quarter of 1993. Nonperforming assets declined to $66.8 million, representing a 26.4% drop from $90.8 million in the first quarter of 1993, and a 2.9% decrease from $68.8 million at year-end 1993. BOH's reserve for loan losses was 194.8% of total nonperforming assets.

BUSINESS

BANCORP HAWAII, INC. has more than 115 offices throughout Hawaii, Asia and the Pacific. Its principal subsidiaries are the state's largest commercial bank, Bank of Hawaii; thrift holding company, Bancorp Pacific, Inc.; Arizona commercial bank, First National Bank of Arizona; and securities brokerage firm, Bancorp Investment Group, Ltd. The state's largest trust company, Hawaiian Trust Company, Ltd., along with leasing subsidiary Bancorp Leasing of Hawaii are subsidiaries of Bank of Hawaii. Bank of Hawaii has locations in Hawaii, the West and South Pacific, Taipei, Tokyo, Hong Kong, Singapore, Seoul, Manila, Cebu, Davao, New York and Nassau.

LOANS DISTRIBUTION

(12/31/93)	($000)	(%)
Commercial & Industrial	1,709,194	23.5
Construction loans	171,303	2.4
Mortgage loans	3,706,529	51.1
Installment	676,170	9.3
Foreign loans	593,497	8.2
Lease financing	401,675	5.5
Total	7,258,368	100.0

ANNUAL EARNINGS AND DIVIDENDS PER SHARE

	1993	1992	1991	1990	1989	1988	1987
Earnings Per Share	4.63	4.12	4.04	3.67	3.28	3.18	2.31
Dividends Per Share	1.358	1 1.267	2 1.173	3 1.057	0.887	4 1.168	0.68
Dividend Payout %	29.3	30.8	29.0	28.8	27.0	36.7	29.3

Note: 50%stk.div.3/15/94. 1 Bef acctg chge 2 3-for-2 stk split,09/16/91 3 10% stk div, 5/4/90 4 50% stk div, 11/88

ANNUAL FINANCIAL DATA

RECORD OF EARNINGS (IN MILLIONS):

	1993	1992	1991	1990	1989	1988	1987
Total Interest Income	808.8	827.2	929.0	871.0	685.4	519.7	432.5
Total Interest Expense	335.4	386.5	521.1	521.0	399.1	278.1	231.7
Net Interest Income	473.4	440.7	407.9	350.1	286.3	241.6	200.8
Prov for Possible Loan Losses	54.2	50.1	29.6	28.0	20.9	30.9	17.2
Net Income	132.6	1 116.8	112.7	95.7	79.9	74.9	53.9
Aver. Shs. Outstg. (000)	42,968	42,528	41,846	39,504	37,076	35,310	34,943

1 Before acctg. change cr$10,762,000.

BALANCE SHEET (IN MILLIONS):

	1993	1992	1991	1990	1989	1988	1987
Cash & Non-int Bearing Deps	395.3	393.6	485.9	488.9	409.7	381.6	296.5
Net Loans	6,983.1	6,691.7	6,517.2	6,286.1	4,806.3	4,014.1	3,326.6
Total Domestic Deposits	6,170.8	6,726.3	7,882.7	7,692.7	5,950.1	4,981.8	4,752.1
Foreign Deposits	834.2	1,164.2	783.5	1,092.3	1,074.1	679.7	165.5
Long-term Debt	357.9	84.1	75.5	117.1	47.6	36.7	56.5
Net Stockholders' Equity	938.1	828.3	724.0	630.3	482.7	400.0	347.0
Total Assets	12,462.1	12,713.1	11,409.3	10,698.5	8,317.1	6,634.7	5,826.3
Year End Shs Outstg (000)	42,638	42,084	41,504	27,314	22,544	32,709	34,104

STATISTICAL RECORD:

	1993	1992	1991	1990	1989	1988	1987
Return on Assets %	1.06	0.92	0.99	0.89	0.96	1.13	0.93
Return on Equity %	14.10	14.10	15.60	15.20	16.50	18.70	15.50
Book Value Per Share	22.00	19.68	17.44	23.07	21.41	12.23	10.17
Average Yield %	4.3	4.1	4.6	5.5	4.4	7.9	5.0
P/E Ratio	11.6-8.6	12.6-9.8	11.8-7.0	10.1-5.8	11.7-7.2	8.0-5.9	10.4-7.4
Price Range	35⅞-26⅝	34⅝-26⅞	31⅞-18⅞	24½-14	25¼-15½	17-12½	16-11⅜

Statistics are as originally reported.

OFFICERS:
H.H. Stephenson, Chmn. & C.E.O.
L.M. Johnson, President
D.A. Houle, Sr. V.P., Treas. & C.F.O.
R.E. Miyashiro, V.P. & Sec.

INCORPORATED: HI, Aug., 1971

PRINCIPAL OFFICE: Financial Plaza of The Pacific 130 Merchants Street, Honolulu, HI 96813

TELEPHONE NUMBER: (808) 537-8111
FAX: (808) 521-7602
NO. OF EMPLOYEES: 4,424
ANNUAL MEETING: In April
SHAREHOLDERS: 8,315
INSTITUTIONAL HOLDINGS:
No. of Institutions: 191
Shares Held: 17,580,635

REGISTRAR(S): Hawaiian Trust Co. Ltd., Honolulu, HI 96802
The Bank of New York, New York, NY

TRANSFER AGENT(S): Hawaiian Trust Co., Ltd., Honolulu, HI 96802
The Bank of New York, New York, NY

BANDAG, INC.

YIELD 1.4%
P/E RATIO 17.8

*7 YEAR PRICE SCORE 93.0   *12 MONTH PRICE SCORE 99.6
*NYSE COMPOSITE INDEX=100

INTERIM EARNINGS (Per Share):

Qtr.	Mar.	June	Sept.	Dec.
1990	0.54	0.64	0.74	0.83
1991	0.47	0.66	0.81	0.92
1992	0.59	0.77	0.81	0.81
1993	0.51	0.70	0.83	0.84

INTERIM DIVIDENDS (Per Share):

Amt.	Decl.	Ex.	Rec.	Pay.
0.1625Q	5/7/93	6/15/93	6/21/93	7/22/93
0.1625Q	8/11	9/14	9/20	10/21
0.175Q	11/16	12/14	12/20	1/20/94
0.175Q	2/28/94	3/15/94	3/21/94	4/20
0.175Q	5/5	6/15	6/21	7/21

Indicated div.: $0.70

CAPITALIZATION (12/31/93):

	($000)	(%)
Deferred Income Tax	24,058	5.5
Common & Surplus	413,092	94.5
Total	437,150	100.0

DIVIDEND ACHIEVER STATUS:
Rank: 167   1983-93 Growth Rate: 10.3%
Total Years of Dividend Growth: 17

RECENT DEVELOPMENTS: For the quarter ended 12/31/93, net income rose 3% to $23.0 million compared with $22.4 million for the same period in 1992. Sales remained flat at $160.4 million. Earnings per share of $0.84 were 4% higher than last year's total of $0.81. For the fiscal year ended 12/31/93, net income fell 5% to $78.7 million compared with net income before accounting changes of $83.0 million for the fiscal year 1992. Sales remained flat at $590.2 million, while yearly earnings per share fell 4% to $2.88.

PROSPECTS: Sales of the new Eclipse tire have not met expectations due to declining demand, constraining growth in revenues. Due to temporarily satisfied demand for retread tires, earnings will remain under pressure. However, governmental sales are expected to increase. Also, government legislation promoting the use of retread tires should supply a foundation for long term earnings growth. Setbacks in the European trucking industry will most likely limit near-term foreign earnings.

BUSINESS

BANDAG, INC. is engaged in the production and sale of precured tread rubber and equipment used by franchised dealers for the retreading of tires for trucks, buses, light commerical trucks, industrial equipment, off-the-road equipment and passenger cars. The Company specializes in a patented cold-bonding retreading process which it introduced to the United States in 1957. The Bandag Method, as it is called, separates the process of vulcanizing the tread rubber from the process of bonding the tread rubber to the tire casing, allowing for optimization of temperature and pressure levels at each stage of the retreading process.

BUSINESS LINE ANALYSIS

(12/31/93)	Rev(%)	Inc(%)
United States	64.3	86.4
Western Europe	16.7	1.5
Other	19.0	12.1
Total	100.0	100.0

ANNUAL EARNINGS AND DIVIDENDS PER SHARE

	1993	1992	1991	1990	1989	1988	1987
Earnings Per Share	2.88	2.99	2.86	2.75	2.61	2.34	1.95
Dividends Per Share	① 0.65	0.60	0.55	0.50	0.45	0.40	② 0.438
Dividend Payout %	22.6	20.1	19.2	18.2	17.2	17.1	22.4

① 2-for-1 stk split,06/10/92 ② 100% stk div, 1/87

ANNUAL FINANCIAL DATA

RECORD OF EARNINGS (IN THOUSANDS):

	1993	1992	1991	1990	1989	1988	1987
Total Income	601,059	602,388	593,917	595,853	535,159	498,109	431,169
Costs and Expenses	440,979	441,894	440,807	445,288	390,425	365,907	307,673
Prov for Deprec & Amort	32,939	27,550	21,813	18,964	15,515	14,178	12,068
Operating Profit	127,141	132,944	131,297	131,601	129,219	118,024	111,428
Earn Bef Income Taxes	124,975	130,746	128,385	128,102	123,322	112,851	107,711
Income Taxes	46,241	47,723	48,786	49,319	47,395	43,096	45,158
Net Income	78,734	① 83,023	79,599	78,783	75,927	69,755	62,553
Aver. Shs. Outstg.	27,337	27,743	27,842	28,632	29,076	29,830	32,080

① Before acctg. change dr$220,000.

BALANCE SHEET (IN THOUSANDS):

	1993	1992	1991	1990	1989	1988	1987
Cash and Cash Equivalents	83,047	36,767	37,183	11,321	4,869	7,018	20,042
Receivables, Net	181,716	187,286	199,663	186,376	162,564	158,461	135,696
Total Inventories	43,133	53,471	51,460	57,815	57,422	42,819	36,810
Gross Property	320,142	291,917	237,510	211,163	177,860	152,290	138,628
Accumulated Depreciation	173,521	149,622	126,410	113,168	92,739	80,082	70,181
Capital Lease Obligations	...	...	...	...	...	2,111	2,196
Net Stockholders' Equity	413,092	334,610	297,052	235,953	212,793	158,121	133,900
Total Assets	550,731	469,239	442,157	392,166	347,247	314,761	291,070
Total Current Assets	316,141	284,593	293,746	260,160	228,749	212,238	197,413
Total Current Liabilities	102,542	115,633	117,617	126,241	107,355	128,198	121,610
Net Working Capital	213,599	168,960	176,129	133,919	121,394	84,040	75,803
Year End Shares Outstg	27,152	27,292	27,737	27,732	28,960	29,277	30,294

STATISTICAL RECORD:

	1993	1992	1991	1990	1989	1988	1987
Operating Profit Margin %	21.2	22.1	22.1	22.1	24.1	23.7	25.8
Book Value Per Share	15.21	12.26	10.71	8.51	7.35	5.40	4.42
Return on Equity %	19.1	24.8	26.8	33.4	35.7	44.1	46.7
Return on Assets %	14.3	17.7	18.0	20.1	21.9	22.2	21.5
Average Yield %	1.2	0.9	1.1	1.3	1.2	1.3	1.6
P/E Ratio	20.9-15.5	24.5-18.7	21.0-14.2	16.5-12.0	17.1-12.3	14.4-11.3	17.7-10.8
Price Range	60¼-44¾	73¼-56	60-40¾	45½-33	44⅝-32⅛	33⅝-26⅜	34½-21

Statistics are as originally reported.

OFFICERS:
M.G. Carver, Chmn., C.E.O. & Pres.
T.E. Dvorchak, Sr. V.P. & C.F.O.
L.A. Carver, Treasurer

INCORPORATED: IA, Dec., 1957

PRINCIPAL OFFICE: 2905 North Highway 61, Muscatine, IA 52761-5886

TELEPHONE NUMBER: (319) 262-1400
FAX: (319) 262-1386
NO. OF EMPLOYEES: 2,334
ANNUAL MEETING: In May
SHAREHOLDERS: 4,467
INSTITUTIONAL HOLDINGS:
No. of Institutions: 160
Shares Held: 6,498,019

REGISTRAR(S):

TRANSFER AGENT(S): First National Bank of Boston, Shareholder Services Division, Boston, MA

BANKERS TRUST NEW YORK CORP.

	YIELD	5.4%
	P/E RATIO	5.3

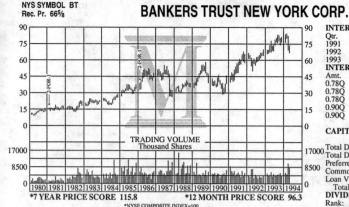

*7 YEAR PRICE SCORE 115.8   *12 MONTH PRICE SCORE 96.3
•NYSE COMPOSITE INDEX=100

INTERIM EARNINGS (Per Share):

Qtr.	Mar.	June	Sept.	Dec.
1991	1.85	2.16	2.17	1.57
1992	2.02	2.39	2.45	1.97
1993	2.69	2.97	3.71	3.26

INTERIM DIVIDENDS (Per Share):

Amt.	Decl.	Ex.	Rec.	Pay.
0.78Q	3/16/93	3/25/93	3/31/93	4/25/93
0.78Q	6/15	6/24	6/30	7/25
0.78Q	9/21	9/30	10/6	10/25
0.90Q	12/21	12/31	1/6/94	1/25/94
0.90Q	3/15/94	3/24/94	3/30	4/25

Indicated div.: $3.60

CAPITALIZATION (12/31/93):

	($000)	(%)
Total Deposits	22,776,000	26.4
Total Debt	57,772,000	66.9
Preferred Stock	250,000	0.3
Common & Surplus	4,284,000	4.9
Loan Valuation Reserve	1,324,000	1.5
Total	86,406,000	100.0

DIVIDEND ACHIEVER STATUS:

Rank: 156   1983-93 Growth Rate: 10.7%
Total Years of Dividend Growth: 15

RECENT DEVELOPMENTS: For the quarter ended 12/31/93, net income soared 110% from the comparable quarter of 1992 to $279 million. Results benefited from an 87% increase in noninterest revenue which totaled $869 million. Trading revenue of $449 million rose by $348 million from a year earlier while fiduciary and funds management revenue and fees and commissions revenue was up 27% and 48% respectively. For the year ended 12/31/93, income before accounting adjustments totaled $1.07 billion, up 67%.

PROSPECTS: In terms of igniting earnings growth the Company's loan portfolio takes a back seat to the strong demand for and performance of its client-risk management service and proprietary trading activities. The strength of the interest rate and currency derivative products will drive earnings well into 1994. Equity derivative and sovereign bond trading is also turning in impressive results. Fee income is receiving a boost from securities underwriting and loan and lease syndication.

BUSINESS

BANKERS TRUST NEW YORK CORP. is a bank holding company whose principal subsidiary is Bankers Trust Company. As of 12/31/93, BT had consolidated assets of $92.1 billion making it the seventh largest bank holding company in the United States. Bankers Trust is a commercial bank, providing banking and trust services to financial institutions, governments, and individuals of high net worth.

LOAN DISTRIBUTION

(12/31/93)	($000)	(%)
Commercial &		
Industrial	2,794,000	18.3
Financial Institutions	3,210,000	21.0
Real Estate Const.	245,000	1.6
Real Estate Mortgage	1,550,000	10.1
Other Domestic	1,780,000	11.6
International	5,721,000	37.4
Total	15,300,000	100.0

ANNUAL EARNINGS AND DIVIDENDS PER SHARE

	1993	1992	1991	1990	1989	1988	1987
Earnings Per Share	12.40	8.82	7.75	7.80	d12.10	8.09	0.02
Dividends Per Share	3.12	2.80	2.54	2.33	2.08	1.86	1.66
Dividend Payout %	25.2	31.7	32.8	29.9	...	23.0	N.M.

ANNUAL FINANCIAL DATA

RECORD OF EARNINGS (IN MILLIONS):

	1993	1992	1991	1990	1989	1988	1987
Total Interest Revenue	4,436.0	4,219.0	4,322.0	5,592.0	5,305.0	4,191.0	4,061.0
Total Interest Expense	3,122.0	3,072.0	3,585.0	4,799.0	4,446.0	3,265.0	3,054.0
Net Interest Income	1,314.0	1,147.0	737.0	793.0	859.0	926.0	1,007.0
Prov for Credit Losses	93.0	225.0	238.0	194.0	1,877.0	50.0	862.0
Net Income	ⓘ 1,070.0	761.0	667.0	665.0	d980.0	648.0	1.0
Aver. Shs. Outstg. (000)	82,000	83,000	82,000	81,000	81,000	80,000	73,000

ⓘ Before acctg. change dr$75,000,000.

BALANCE SHEET (IN MILLIONS):

	1993	1992	1991	1990	1989	1988	1987
Cash & Due From Banks	1,750.0	1,384.0	1,747.0	4,149.0	3,331.0	3,618.0	3,737.0
Net Loans	13,876.0	15,698.0	15,241.0	19,305.0	18,421.0	22,801.0	24,886.0
Total Domestic Deposits	10,305.0	10,188.0	9,181.0	13,099.0	13,195.9	13,284.0	11,447.0
Total Foreign Deposits	12,471.0	14,883.0	13,653.0	15,489.0	13,025.0	19,206.0	18,774.0
Long-term Debt	5,597.0	3,992.0	3,081.0	2,650.0	2,435.0	2,450.0	2,571.0
Net Stockholders' Equity	4,534.0	3,809.0	3,412.0	3,024.0	2,386.0	3,499.0	2,889.0
Total Assets	92,082.0	72,448.0	63,959.0	63,596.0	55,658.0	57,942.0	56,521.0
Year End Shs Outstg (000)	81,000	83,000	82,000	81,000	81,000	81,000	77,000

STATISTICAL RECORD:

	1993	1992	1991	1990	1989	1988	1987
Return on Assets %	1.16	1.05	1.04	1.05	...	1.12	...
Return on Equity %	23.60	20.00	19.50	22.00	...	18.50	...
Book Value Per Share	52.89	39.87	35.51	31.16	26.37	43.20	37.52
Average Yield %	4.2	4.7	4.7	6.2	4.5	5.2	4.1
P/E Ratio	6.7-5.3	8.0-5.7	8.9-5.2	6.0-3.7	...	5.1-3.7	N.M
Price Range	83½-65¾	70⅛-50	68-39½	46¾-28½	58¼-34½	41¼-29⅝	55¼-26¼

Statistics are as originally reported.

OFFICERS:
C.S. Sanford, Jr., Chmn. & C.E.O.
G.J. Vojta, Vice-Chmn.
E.B. Shanks, Jr., President
T.T. Yates, Exec. V.P., C.F.O. & Contr.

INCORPORATED: NY, May, 1965

PRINCIPAL OFFICE: 280 Park Avenue, New York, NY 10017

TELEPHONE NUMBER: (212) 250-2500

NO. OF EMPLOYEES: 13,571

ANNUAL MEETING: Third Tues. in April

SHAREHOLDERS: 23,561 (approx.)

INSTITUTIONAL HOLDINGS:
No. of Institutions: 504
Shares Held: 64,050,719

REGISTRAR(S): Bankers Trust Company, New York, NY 10015

TRANSFER AGENT(S): Bankers Trust Company of California, New York, NY 10017

BARD (C.R.), INC.

YIELD 2.3%
P/E RATIO 20.3

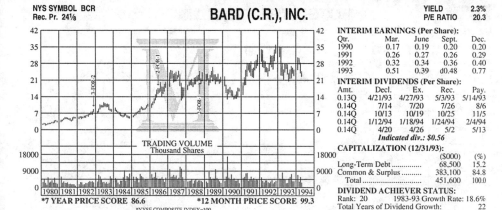

INTERIM EARNINGS (Per Share):

Qtr.	Mar.	June	Sept.	Dec.
1990	0.17	0.19	0.20	0.20
1991	0.26	0.27	0.26	0.29
1992	0.32	0.34	0.36	0.40
1993	0.51	0.39	d0.48	0.77

INTERIM DIVIDENDS (Per Share):

Amt.	Decl.	Ex.	Rec.	Pay.
0.13Q	4/21/93	4/27/93	5/3/93	5/14/93
0.14Q	7/14	7/20	7/26	8/6
0.14Q	10/13	10/19	10/25	11/5
0.14Q	1/12/94	1/18/94	1/24/94	2/4/94
0.14Q	4/20	4/26	5/2	5/13

Indicated div.: $0.56

CAPITALIZATION (12/31/93):

	($000)	(%)
Long-Term Debt	68,500	15.2
Common & Surplus	383,100	84.8
Total	451,600	100.0

TRADING VOLUME
Thousand Shares

*7 YEAR PRICE SCORE 86.6   *12 MONTH PRICE SCORE 99.3
*NYSE COMPOSITE INDEX=100

DIVIDEND ACHIEVER STATUS:
Rank: 20   1983-93 Growth Rate: 18.6%
Total Years of Dividend Growth: 22

RECENT DEVELOPMENTS: For the year ended 12/31/93, net income before an accounting adjustment declined 17.2% to $62.1 million. Sales were down 2% to $970.8 million. The results included a provision equal to cover the proposed $61 million settlement over BCR's involvement in a scandal involving heart surgery equipment. Earnings included a non-recurring gain of $19.4 million, related to the BCR's sale of its entire holding of Ventritex, Inc. common stock, and a charge of $1.8 million, related to plant closings.

PROSPECTS: Operating results will benefit from the recent FDA approval to market the AGIL and SILK balloon angioplasty catheters in the United States. These new catheters should help Bard maintain its 7% share, approximately, in that market. In January, the Defense Logistics Agency announced the exclusion of Bard from receiving any new federal government contracts. However, the Company's existing contracts, less than 2% of total revenues, will run until their expiration date.

BUSINESS

C.R. BARD, INC. is a multinational developer, manufacturer and marketer of health care products. The Company engages in the design, manufacture, packaging, distribution and sale of medical surgical, diagnostic and patient care devices. Bard holds strong positions in cardiovascular, urological, surgical and general health care products. BCR products are marketed worldwide to hospitals, individual health care professionals, extended care facilities, alternate site facilities and the home, employing a combination of direct delivery and medical specialty distributors. Hospitals, physicians and nursing homes purchase approximately 90% of the Company's products.

BUSINESS LINE ANALYSIS

(12/31/93)	Rev(%)	Inc(%)
United States	72.6	60.2
Foreign	27.4	39.8
Total	100.0	100.0

ANNUAL EARNINGS AND DIVIDENDS PER SHARE

	1993	1992	1991	1990	1989	1988	1987
Earnings Per Share	1.19	1.42	1.08	0.76	1.18	1.38	1.07
Dividends Per Share	0.54	0.50	0.46	0.42	0.36	0.28	0.22
Dividend Payout %	45.4	35.2	42.6	55.3	30.5	20.3	10.3

ANNUAL FINANCIAL DATA

RECORD OF EARNINGS (IN THOUSANDS):

	1993	1992	1991	1990	1989	1988	1987
Total Revenues	970,800	990,200	876,000	785,300	777,800	757,500	641,258
Costs and Expenses	806,800	832,200	753,500	691,000	637,900	605,600	511,209
Depreciation & Amort	35,500	35,600	29,500	27,500	24,000	23,500	24,871
Operating Income	128,500	122,400	93,000	66,800	115,900	128,400	105,178
Income Before Taxes	98,900	107,000	76,900	58,500	103,200	123,800	98,962
Income Taxes	36,800	32,000	19,700	18,200	37,800	45,100	36,712
Net Income	①62,100	75,000	57,200	40,300	65,400	78,700	62,250
Aver. Shs. Outstg.	52,197	52,909	53,063	53,266	55,419	57,047	58,156

① Before acctg. change dr$6,100,000.

BALANCE SHEET (IN THOUSANDS):

	1993	1992	1991	1990	1989	1988	1987
Cash and Cash Equivalents	75,000	49,800	33,800	19,900	11,100	24,300	17,058
Accounts Receivable, Net	167,300	178,800	157,200	143,000	131,200	132,900	114,563
Inventories	173,500	181,800	176,600	171,800	155,100	151,000	145,501
Gross Property	260,900	253,000	244,400	230,500	217,700	196,800	179,940
Accumulated Depreciation	92,000	90,200	86,800	83,000	78,100	66,000	56,163
Long-Term Debt	68,500	68,600	68,900	69,800	70,300	41,200	45,211
Net Stockholders' Equity	383,100	392,400	365,700	342,200	333,600	328,600	300,987
Total Assets	798,600	712,500	657,600	612,800	562,600	531,000	487,568
Total Current Assets	421,500	416,900	373,900	341,400	304,800	314,200	289,762
Total Current Liabilities	264,300	215,000	189,900	170,800	123,000	127,700	134,817
Net Working Capital	157,200	201,900	184,000	170,600	181,800	186,500	154,945
Year End Shares Outstg	52,098	52,839	53,019	53,044	54,517	61,362	57,606

STATISTICAL RECORD:

	1993	1992	1991	1990	1989	1988	1987
Operating Profit Margin %	13.2	12.4	10.6	8.5	14.9	17.0	16.4
Book Value Per Share	4.49	5.94	6.90	6.45	6.12	5.36	5.22
Return on Equity %	16.2	19.1	15.6	11.8	19.6	24.0	20.7
Return on Assets %	7.8	10.5	8.7	6.6	11.6	14.8	12.8
Average Yield %	1.9	1.7	2.0	2.4	1.6	1.3	1.2
P/E Ratio	29.6-17.2	25.3-15.8	29.4-13.8	29.6-16.9	22.5-15.9	17.8-12.2	23.5-11.7
Price Range	35¼-20½	35⅞-22½	31¾-14⅞	22½-12⅞	26½-18¾	24⅝-16⅞	25⅛-12½

Statistics are as originally reported.

OFFICERS:
W.H. Longfield, Pres. & C.O.O.
W.C. Bopp, Sr. V.P. & C.F.O.
R.A. Flink, V.P., Gen. Coun. & Sec.
E.L. Parker, Treas.

INCORPORATED: NJ, Feb., 1972

PRINCIPAL OFFICE: 730 Central Ave., Murray Hill, NJ 07974

TELEPHONE NUMBER: (908) 277-8000

NO. OF EMPLOYEES: 8,450 (approx.)

ANNUAL MEETING: In April

SHAREHOLDERS: 8,280 (approx.)

INSTITUTIONAL HOLDINGS:
No. of Institutions: 295
Shares Held: 34,048,183

REGISTRAR(S): First Chicago Trust Co. of New York, New York, NY 10008

TRANSFER AGENT(S): First Chicago Trust Co. of New York, New York, NY 10008

NYS SYMBOL BAX
Rec. Pr. 26

BAXTER INTERNATIONAL INC.

YIELD 3.8%
P/E RATIO ...

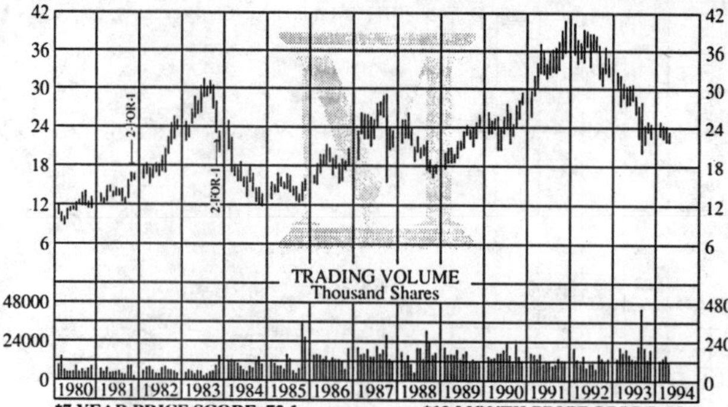
42
36
30
24
18
12
6
2-FOR-1
2-FOR-1
TRADING VOLUME
Thousand Shares
48000
24000
0
1980 1981 1982 1983 1984 1985 1986 1987 1988 1989 1990 1991 1992 1993 1994

***7 YEAR PRICE SCORE 72.1** ***12 MONTH PRICE SCORE 93.1**

*NYSE COMPOSITE INDEX=100

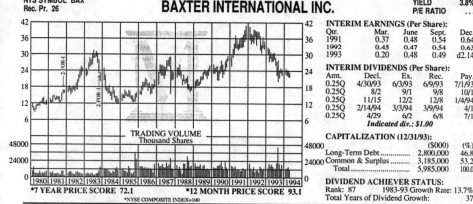

INTERIM EARNINGS (Per Share):

Qtr.	Mar.	June	Sept.	Dec.
1991	0.37	0.48	0.54	0.64
1992	0.45	0.47	0.54	0.63
1993	0.20	0.48	0.49	d2.14

INTERIM DIVIDENDS (Per Share):

Amt.	Decl.	Ex.	Rec.	Pay.
0.25Q	4/30/93	6/3/93	6/9/93	7/1/93
0.25Q	8/2	9/1	9/8	10/1
0.25Q	11/15	12/2	12/8	1/4/94
0.25Q	2/14/94	3/3/94	3/9/94	4/1
0.25Q	4/29	6/2	6/8	7/1

Indicated div.: $1.00

CAPITALIZATION (12/31/93):

	($000)	(%)
Long-Term Debt	2,800,000	46.8
Common & Surplus	3,185,000	53.2
Total	5,985,000	100.0

DIVIDEND ACHIEVER STATUS:
Rank: 87 1983-93 Growth Rate: 13.7%
Total Years of Dividend Growth: 37

RECENT DEVELOPMENTS: For the year ended 12/31/93, net loss before an accounting adjustment amounted to $268 million compared with net income of $561 million a year ago. Sales rose 4.8% to $8.88 billion from $8.47 billion. Earnings included $1.03 billion of pre-tax charges: restructuring charges of $700 million and litigation charges of $330 million. Research and development investment was increased 6% to $337 million.

PROSPECTS: Earnings will be adversely affected by pricing pressure in the health care industry. However, Baxter will continue to invest substantially in research and development in order to bring new products to the market. Earnings should benefit from efforts to streamline sales and distribution operations. The Company received a five-year contract expected to result in purchases of more than $4 billion in Baxter supplies from American Healthcare Systems.

BUSINESS

BAXTER INTERNATIONAL INC. is engaged in the development, distribution, and manufacture of a diversified line of products, systems and services used primarily in the healthcare field. The Medical Specialties segment develops and markets specialized medical products used for cardiac care, dialysis therapy, diagnostic testing, and blood processing. The Medical/Laboratory Products and Distribution segment manufactures and markets products for educational and government laboratories, industrial research and development facilities, and manufacturing facilities. The Company distributes and manufactrues a broad range of products to hospitals, other health care providers and clinical laoratories.

BUSINESS LINE ANALYSIS

(12/31/93)	Rev(%)	Inc($000)
Medical Specialties	36.6	543,000
Medical/laboratory Prods	63.4	(132,000)
Total	100.0	411,000

ANNUAL EARNINGS AND DIVIDENDS PER SHARE

	1993	1992	1991	1990	1989	1988	1987
Earnings Per Share	**d0.97**	**[1] 1.99**	**2.03**	**d0.05**	**1.50**	**1.31**	**[1] 1.10**
Dividends Per Share	**0.965**	**[2] 0.83**	**0.715**	**0.62**	**0.545**	**0.485**	**0.43**
Dividend Payout %	**...**	**41.7**	**35.2**	**...**	**36.3**	**37.0**	**39.1**

[1] Before disc. oper. [2] Bef discont opers

ANNUAL FINANCIAL DATA

	1993	1992	1991	1990	1989	1988	1987
RECORD OF EARNINGS (IN MILLIONS):							
Total Revenues	8,879.0	8,471.0	8,921.0	8,100.0	7,399.0	6,861.0	6,223.0
Costs and Expenses	8,573.0	7,359.0	7,765.0	7,671.0	6,565.0	6,125.0	5,540.0
Depreciation & Amort	494.0	447.0	427.0	383.0	368.0	335.0	314.0
Operating Income	239.0	1,045.0	1,088.0	362.0	766.0	668.0	615.0
Income Bef Income Taxes	d330.0	753.0	805.0	105.0	637.0	518.0	446.0
Income Tax Expense	cr62.0	192.0	214.0	65.0	191.0	130.0	123.0
Net Income	d198.0	[1] 561.0	591.0	40.0	446.0	388.0	331.0
Aver. Shs. Outstg. (000)	277,000	279,000	280,000	253,000	282,000	277,000	238,000
[1] Before disc. op. cr$45,000,000.							
BALANCE SHEET (IN MILLIONS):							
Cash & Equivalents	479.0	32.0	...	...	...	...	...
Receivables, Net	2,017.0	1,799.0	1,939.0	1,743.0	1,743.0	1,437.0	1,279.0
Inventories	1,772.0	1,632.0	1,596.0	1,532.0	1,502.0	1,512.0	1,279.0
Gross Property	4,491.0	4,209.0	3,966.0	3,526.0	3,151.0	2,935.0	2,567.0
Accumulated Depreciation	1,836.0	1,562.0	1,511.0	1,357.0	1,048.0	911.0	791.0
Long-Term Debt	2,800.0	2,433.0	2,249.0	1,729.0	2,052.0	2,246.0	1,641.0
Net Stockholders' Equity	3,185.0	3,795.0	4,373.0	4,092.0	4,246.0	4,041.0	3,713.0
Total Assets	10,545.0	9,155.0	9,340.0	8,517.0	8,503.0	8,550.0	7,638.0
Total Current Assets	4,422.0	3,589.0	4,004.0	3,443.0	3,424.0	3,323.0	2,758.0
Total Current Liabilities	2,933.0	2,368.0	2,357.0	2,324.0	1,859.0	1,886.0	1,877.0
Net Working Capital	1,489.0	1,221.0	1,647.0	1,119.0	1,565.0	1,437.0	881.0
Year End Shs Outstg (000)	277,000	279,000	279,000	279,000	249,000	246,000	240,000
STATISTICAL RECORD:							
Operating Profit Margin %	2.7	12.3	12.2	4.5	10.4	9.7	9.9
Book Value Per Share	2.51	4.68	14.46	13.45	13.52	12.59	11.80
Return on Equity %	...	14.8	13.5	1.0	10.5	9.8	8.7
Return on Assets %	...	6.1	6.3	0.5	5.2	4.5	4.2
Average Yield %	3.7	2.3	2.2	2.5	2.5	2.3	1.9
P/E Ratio	...	20.4-15.3	20.1-12.6	...	17.3-11.7	19.9-12.4	26.6-14.1
Price Range	32¾-20	40½-30½	40⅞-25⅝	29½-20½	25⅞-17½	26⅛-16¼	29¼-15½

Statistics are as originally reported.

OFFICERS:
W.B. Graham, Senior Chmn.
V.R. Loucks, Jr., Chmn. & C.E.O.
R.J. Lambrix, Sr. V.P. & C.F.O.
L.D. Damron, Treasurer

INCORPORATED: DE, Oct., 1931

PRINCIPAL OFFICE: One Baxter Parkway, Deerfield, IL 60015

TELEPHONE NUMBER: (708) 948-2000

FAX: (708) 948-3948

NO. OF EMPLOYEES: 2,651

ANNUAL MEETING: In April

SHAREHOLDERS: 26,593

INSTITUTIONAL HOLDINGS:
No. of Institutions: 654
Shares Held: 179,728,242

REGISTRAR(S): First Chicago Trust Co. of New York, New York, NY 10008

TRANSFER AGENT(S): First Chicago Trust Co. of New York, New York, NY 10008

BB&T FINANCIAL CORP.

YIELD 3.6%
P/E RATIO 9.6

INTERIM EARNINGS (Per Share):

Qtr.	Mar.	June	Sept.	Dec.
1990	0.60	0.62	0.64	0.63
1991	0.64	0.65	0.63	0.65
1992	0.71	0.74	0.72	0.73
1993	0.76	0.77	0.78	0.78

INTERIM DIVIDENDS (Per Share):

Amt.	Decl.	Ex.	Rec.	Pay.
0.25Q	1/26/93	2/23/93	3/1/93	3/15/93
0.25Q	4/28	5/25	6/1	6/15
0.25Q	7/27	8/26	9/1	9/15
0.27Q	10/26	11/24	12/1	12/15
0.27Q	1/25/94	2/23/94	3/1/94	3/15/94

Indicated div.: $1.08

CAPITALIZATION (12/31/93):

	($000)	(%)
Total Deposits	6,995,121	76.4
Total Debt	1,331,061	14.5
Common & Surplus	743,512	8.1
Loan Valuation Reserve	88,235	1.0
Total	9,157,929	100.0

DIVIDEND ACHIEVER STATUS:
Rank: 266   1983-93 Growth Rate: 6.1%
Total Years of Dividend Growth: 17

TRADING VOLUME
Thousand Shares

*7 YEAR PRICE SCORE 116.1   *12 MONTH PRICE SCORE 106.1
*NYSE COMPOSITE INDEX=100

RECENT DEVELOPMENTS: Net income rose 28% to $98.2 million for the year ended 12/31/93. Results were attributed to an increase in interest income, improved credit quality and positive effects resulting from the acquisition of nine thrift institutions during the year. Interest income totaled $559.0 million compared with $543.9 million in 1992 and noninter- est income advanced 25% to $111.7 million. The provision for loan losses was sharply reduced to $17.5 million from $34.0 million. Nonperforming loans were 0.49% of total loans outstanding versus 0.56% last year. During 1993, Company also acquired four insurance agencies with total premium volume of $21.5 million.

BUSINESS

BB&T FINANCIAL CORP., with assets of $9.2 billion, is a bank holding company organized under the laws of the state of North Carolina. The Company has two bank subsidiaries, Branch Banking and Trust Company, Wilson, North Carolina, the oldest and fourth largest bank in North Carolina. Branch Banking and Trust Company of South Carolina, Greenville, South Carolina ranks as one of the ten largest banks in South Carolina. The Company operates 264 offices in 138 Carolina cities. Through its subsidiary banks, BBTF engages in the general banking business of its two-state region serving a wide variety of business and individual customers. BB&T-NC also provides trust, insurance, investment and travel services to customers. BBTF-SC offers trust and investment services.

ANNUAL EARNINGS AND DIVIDENDS PER SHARE

	1993	1992	1991	1990	1989	1988	1987
Earnings Per Share	3.10	2.89	2.57	① 2.49	① 2.49	2.05	1.88
Dividends Per Share	1.02	0.91	0.85	0.81	0.74	0.69	0.65
Dividend Payout %	32.9	31.5	33.1	32.5	32.3	33.7	34.6

① Per primary share

ANNUAL FINANCIAL DATA

RECORD OF EARNINGS (IN MILLIONS):

	1993	1992	1991	1990	1989	1988	1987
Total Interest Income	559.0	493.4	510.2	499.3	459.8	369.5	320.2
Total Interest Expense	230.4	225.1	288.1	307.8	298.7	224.6	178.4
Net Interest Income	328.5	268.4	222.2	191.5	161.1	144.9	141.8
Provision for Loan Losses	17.5	29.0	38.0	19.2	12.2	11.9	13.8
Net Income	98.2	76.1	60.2	53.6	44.2	38.7	33.5
Aver. Shs. Outstg. (000)	31,724	26,313	23,427	21,493	19,337	18,862	18,731

BALANCE SHEET (IN MILLIONS):

	1993	1992	1991	1990	1989	1988	1987
Cash & Due Fr Banks, Nonint-bearing	318.9	280.3	260.7	223.3	362.6	205.2	292.0
Net Loans	6,218.2	4,454.2	4,171.5	3,381.2	3,158.2	2,996.6	2,626.7
Total Domestic Deposits	6,995.1	5,346.3	5,203.5	4,406.4	3,899.4	3,551.8	3,136.4
Long-term Debt	346.7	86.9	86.6	91.8	84.9	85.2	85.4
Net Stockholders' Equity	743.5	560.9	486.5	373.5	311.1	278.0	249.6
Total Assets	9,173.1	6,691.5	6,229.0	5,158.7	4,807.8	4,376.6	3,984.3
Year End Shs Outstg (000)	32,476	26,312	25,348	21,328	19,409	19,213	18,699

STATISTICAL RECORD:

	1993	1992	1991	1990	1989	1988	1987
Return on Assets %	1.07	1.14	0.97	1.04	0.92	0.88	0.84
Return on Equity %	13.20	13.60	12.40	14.40	14.20	13.90	13.40
Book Value Per Share	22.89	21.32	19.19	17.51	16.03	14.47	13.35
Average Yield %	3.1	3.4	4.4	4.7	3.6	...	...
P/E Ratio	11.6-9.4	11.2-7.4	9.4-5.5	8.3-5.6	10.7-7.1	10.0-6.8	11.0-7.4
Price Range	36-29	32⅜-21½	24⅛-14¼	20¾-14	24½-16¼	20½-14	19¾-13¼

Statistics are as originally reported.

LOAN DISTRIBUTION

(12/31/93)	($000)	(%)
Commercial & Industrial	1,007,281	16.0
Real Estate-Construction	423,601	6.7
Real Estate-Mortgage	4,216,650	66.8
Installment & Other	663,278	10.5
Total	6,310,810	100.0

OFFICERS:
J.A. Allison, Chmn. & C.E.O.
H.G. Williamson, Jr., Pres. & C.O.O.
S.E. Reed, Sr. Exec. V.P. & Treas.

PRINCIPAL OFFICE: 223 West Nash Street
Post Office Box 1847, Wilson, NC 27894-1847

TELEPHONE NUMBER: (919) 399-4291
FAX: (919) 399-4871
NO. OF EMPLOYEES: 4,437
ANNUAL MEETING: In April
SHAREHOLDERS: 19,121
INSTITUTIONAL HOLDINGS:
No. of Institutions: 99
Shares Held: 8,403,733

REGISTRAR(S): Branch Banking & Trust Co., Wilson, NC

TRANSFER AGENT(S): Branch Banking & Trust Co., Wilson, NC

BCE INC.

YIELD 7.7%
P/E RATIO N.M

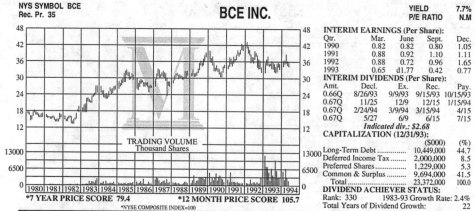

*7 YEAR PRICE SCORE 79.4   *12 MONTH PRICE SCORE 105.7
*NYSE COMPOSITE INDEX=100

TRADING VOLUME
Thousand Shares

INTERIM EARNINGS (Per Share):

Qtr.	Mar.	June	Sept.	Dec.
1990	0.82	0.82	0.80	1.05
1991	0.88	0.92	1.10	1.11
1992	0.88	0.72	0.96	1.65
1993	0.65	d1.77	0.42	0.77

INTERIM DIVIDENDS (Per Share):

Amt.	Decl.	Ex.	Rec.	Pay.
0.66Q	8/26/93	9/9/93	9/15/93	10/15/93
0.67Q	11/25	12/9	12/15	1/15/94
0.67Q	2/24/94	3/9/94	3/15/94	4/15
0.67Q	5/27	6/9	6/15	7/15

Indicated div.: $2.68

CAPITALIZATION (12/31/93):

	($000)	(%)
Long-Term Debt	10,449,000	44.7
Deferred Income Tax	2,000,000	8.5
Preferred Shares	1,229,000	5.3
Common & Surplus	9,694,000	41.5
Total	23,372,000	100.0

DIVIDEND ACHIEVER STATUS:

Rank: 330   1983-93 Growth Rate: 2.4%
Total Years of Dividend Growth: 22

RECENT DEVELOPMENTS: For the year ended 12/31/93, net income from continuing operations was $159.0 million compared with $1.49 billion in 1992. Net income includes an after-tax charge of $624 million related to restructuring at Northern Telecom. Revenues were $19.83 billion, up 1.3%. Bell Canada's performance was negatively affected by intensified competition in the long distance market, weakness in the economy and by higher marketing, sales and depreciation expenses. Comparisons were made with restated prior-year figures, which reflect discontinued operations.

PROSPECTS: BCE will pay $400 million for a 30% interest in Jones Intercable, a U.S. cable operator, and $23 million for interest in two Jones affiliates. BCE will have the option to buy control after eight years. BCE will likely acquire other U.S cable systems. The Company will also focus heavily on telecommunications to improve results. BCE will expand its international business through alliances, joint ventures and investments. BCE and MCI Communications have announced an alliance to develop advanced intelligent network services available in Canada and the United States.

BUSINESS

BCE INC. provides telecommunications services and manufactures and supplies telecommunications equipment. Its Bell Canada subsidiary is Canada's largest supplier of telecommunications services, providing advanced voice, data, and image communications to some seven million customers. BCE owns 52.8% of Northern Telecom Ltd., a leading global supplier of fully digital telecommunications systems; 65.5%, BCE Mobile Communications, a provider of cellular telephone and paging systems. Montreal Trustco Inc., wholly-owned by BCE, markets financial and trust services. BCE owns 70% of Bell-Northern development. Investments are administered by BCE Telecom.

ANNUAL EARNINGS AND DIVIDENDS PER SHARE

	1993	1992	1991	1990	1989	1988	1987
Earnings Per Share	0.21	4.21	4.01	3.50	[1] 3.91	2.96	3.91
Dividends Per Share	2.64	2.60	2.56	2.52	2.48	2.44	2.41
Dividend Payout %	N.M.	61.8	63.8	72.0	63.7	82.4	61.6

[1] Bef. discont. opers.

ANNUAL FINANCIAL DATA

RECORD OF EARNINGS (IN MILLIONS):

	1993	1992	1991	1990	1989	1988	1987
Total Revenues	19,827.0	21,270.0	19,884.0	18,373.0	16,681.0	15,253.0	14,649.0
Depreciation	2,471.0	2,328.0	2,219.0	2,018.0	1,813.0	1,601.0	1,530.0
Operating Profit	1,167.0	39.0	...	...	...	...	...
Total Interest Expense	1,222.0	1,099.0	...	...	...	...	...
Net Income	[1] 159.0	1,390.0	1,329.0	1,147.0	[2] 1,201.0	887.0	1,067.0
Aver. Shs. Outstg. (000)	307,000	307,600	307,649	303,813	297,508	285,427	269,402

[1] Before disc. op. dr$815,000,000.   [2] Before disc. op. dr$440,000,000.

BALANCE SHEET (IN MILLIONS):

	1993	1992	1991	1990	1989	1988	1987
Gross Plant	35,165.0	33,428.0	31,520.0	29,087.0	26,946.0	26,715.0	24,640.0
Accumulated Depreciation	12,857.0	12,044.0	11,469.0	10,513.0	9,655.0	8,763.0	7,768.0
Prop, Plant & Equip, Net	22,308.0	21,384.0	20,051.0	18,574.0	17,291.0	17,952.0	16,872.0
Long-term Debt	10,449.0	8,613.0	7,971.0	7,431.0	7,005.0	7,448.0	7,116.0
Net Stockholders' Equity	10,923.0	12,307.0	11,959.0	11,325.0	10,406.0	9,369.0	9,267.0
Total Assets	36,708.0	48,312.0	45,704.0	41,987.0	39,261.0	28,069.0	26,025.0
Year End Shs Outstg (000)	308,162	305,347	310,292	305,412	302,052	289,546	273,868

STATISTICAL RECORD:

	1993	1992	1991	1990	1989	1988	1987
Book Value Per Share	25.83	28.50	24.11	30.80	29.34	31.97	32.74
Accum. Dep/Gr. Pl %	36.6	36.0	36.4	36.1	35.8	32.8	31.5
Return on Equity %	1.6	12.5	12.4	11.4	12.6	9.5	11.8
Average Yield %	7.5	6.9	6.7	7.2	7.1	8.0	8.5
P/E Ratio	N.M	10.3-7.6	10.6-8.3	11.4-8.6	10.1-7.8	10.6-9.1	8.5-6.0
Price Range	38-32	43¼-32⅛	42⅝-33⅜	40-30¼	39⅜-30½	32⅝-28⅛	33⅜-23½

Statistics are as originally reported.
All figures are in Canadian dollars.

REVENUES

(12/31/93)	($000)	(%)
Canadian Telecom	8,614,000	43.4
Telecom Equipment Manufac	10,550,000	53.2
International Telecom	138,000	0.7
Directories	525,000	2.7
Total	19,827,000	100.0

OFFICERS:
J.R. Cyr, Chmn. of the Board
L.R. Wilson, Pres. & C.E.O.
G.T. McGoey, Exec. V.P. & C.F.O.
INCORPORATED: CN, 1970
PRINCIPAL OFFICE: 2000 McGill College Ave. Suite 2100 Montreal, Quebec H3A 3H7

TELEPHONE NUMBER: (514) 499-7000
FAX: (514) 499-7098
NO. OF EMPLOYEES: 16,864
ANNUAL MEETING: In April
SHAREHOLDERS: 175,619 com.; 455 pfd.
INSTITUTIONAL HOLDINGS:
No. of Institutions: 211
Shares Held: 24,371,471

REGISTRAR(S): The Royal Bank of Scotland, PLC, London, England

TRANSFER AGENT(S): Royal Trust Co., London, England

BECTON, DICKINSON & CO.

YIELD 1.9%
P/E RATIO 13.6

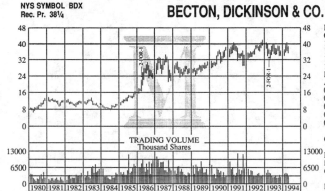

TRADING VOLUME
Thousand Shares

| | 1980 | 1981 | 1982 | 1983 | 1984 | 1985 | 1986 | 1987 | 1988 | 1989 | 1990 | 1991 | 1992 | 1993 | 1994 |

*7 YEAR PRICE SCORE 88.5   *12 MONTH PRICE SCORE 103.9
*NYSE COMPOSITE INDEX=100

INTERIM EARNINGS (Per Share):

Qtr.	Dec.	Mar.	June	Sept.
1990-91	0.38	0.63	0.63	0.80
1991-92	0.28	0.66	0.72	0.93
1992-93	0.33	0.76	0.75	0.98
1993-94	0.33	...	...	...

INTERIM DIVIDENDS (Per Share):

Amt.	Decl.	Ex.	Rec.	Pay.
0.165Q	1/26/93	3/4/93	3/10/93	3/31/93
0.165Q	5/25	6/3	6/9	6/30
0.165Q	7/27	9/2	9/9	9/30
0.165Q	11/23	12/7	12/13	1/3/94
0.185Q	1/25/94	3/4/94	3/10/94	3/31

Indicated div.: $0.74

CAPITALIZATION (9/30/93):

	($000)	(%)
Long-Term Debt	974,635	40.1
Preferred Stock	58,108	2.4
Common & Surplus	1,398,845	57.5
Total	2,431,588	100.0

DIVIDEND ACHIEVER STATUS:
Rank: 201   1983-93 Growth Rate: 8.7%
Total Years of Dividend Growth: 21

RECENT DEVELOPMENTS: For the quarter ended 12/31/93, net income increased 10.1% to $25.7 million compared with $23.3 million, before an accounting adjustment, a year ago. Sales were down slightly to $554.1 million from $560.5 million. The 1992 results were restated. The negative impact of a strong U.S. dollar on foreign currency exchange rates reduced reported revenues by approximately $23 million or 4%, and earnings by about $0.04 per share. Sales of medical supplies and devices fell 1.6% to $296.3 million and diagnostic system sales were down slightly to $257.8 millon.

PROSPECTS: Sales and earnings growth will be driven by volume increases as a changing healthcare market pressures prices. The re-emergence of tuberculosis in the U.S. and other parts of the world is spurring demand for the recently enhanced BACTEC 460 TB system, which offers detection and drug susceptibility testing in less than two weeks, versus the traditional five to seven weeks. The Company's newest generation of cell sorting instrumentation, the FACSORT and the FACS VANTAGE flow cytometers, will also contribute to future revenue growth.

BUSINESS

BECTON, DICKINSON & COMPANY manufactures products for use by health care professionals, medical research institutions, industry and the general public. Products are manufactured at both domestic and foreign locations for sale worldwide. The medical segment includes diabetes care products, intravenous and cardiovascular catheters, operating room supplies, suction products, elastic support products, surgical blades, examination gloves, thermometers and contract packaging services. Products in the diagnostic segment include blood collection products, laboratory ware and suppliers, manual and instrumented microbiology products. In 1993, foreign operations represented 44% of total sales and 32% of operating income.

BUSINESS LINE ANALYSIS

(9/30/93)	Rev(%)	Inc(%)
Medical Supply & Devices	55.1	67.2
Diagnostic Systems	44.9	32.8
Total	100.0	100.0

ANNUAL EARNINGS AND DIVIDENDS PER SHARE

	9/30/93	9/30/92	9/30/91	9/30/90	9/30/89	9/30/88	9/30/87
Earnings Per Share	[1] 2.71	2.58	2.43	2.34	[3] 2.00	[3] 1.85	[4] 1.71
Dividends Per Share	[2] 0.825	0.60	0.58	0.54	0.50	0.43	0.37
Dividend Payout %	30.4	23.3	23.9	23.1	25.0	23.3	21.6

[1] Before acctg. chg.   [2] 2-for-1 stk split,03/01/93   [3] Before disc. oper.   [4] Before extraord. item

ANNUAL FINANCIAL DATA

RECORD OF EARNINGS (IN MILLIONS):

Total Revenues	2,465.4	2,365.3	2,172.2	2,012.7	1,811.5	1,709.4	1,582.0
Costs and Expenses	2,005.2	1,867.1	1,708.5	1,571.5	1,433.7	1,361.1	1,269.9
Depreciation & Amort	189.8	169.6	149.9	135.7	121.9	109.2	92.7
Operating Income	270.4	328.6	313.7	305.5	255.8	239.0	219.3
Income Bef Income Taxes	222.9	269.5	267.3	274.1	227.8	206.3	208.9
Income Tax Provision	10.1	68.7	77.5	91.9	69.8	57.4	67.0
Net Income	[1] 212.8	200.8	189.8	182.3	[2] 158.0	[3] 148.9	[4] 141.8
Aver. Shs. Outstg. (000)	76,930	77,028	77,096	77,320	79,172	80,802	83,096

[1] Before acctg. change dr$141,057,000.   [2] Before disc. op. cr$55,594,000.   [3] Before disc. op. cr$13,087,000.   [4] Before extra. item cr$6,345,000.

BALANCE SHEET (IN MILLIONS):

Cash and Cash Equivalents	64.9	100.5	84.3	72.9	95.1	123.5	189.0
Receivables, Net	557.8	585.1	468.0	422.2	361.0	339.4	295.8
Inventories	445.9	453.4	406.3	397.6	355.2	356.4	305.1
Gross Property	2,363.9	2,294.8	2,097.2	1,924.0	1,655.7	1,434.6	1,185.8
Accumulated Depreciation	960.8	865.3	745.8	647.9	555.1	509.1	430.9
Long-Term Debt	974.6	734.0	739.1	649.3	516.0	500.0	479.6
Net Stockholders' Equity	1,457.0	1,594.9	1,363.8	1,233.6	1,071.5	959.8	861.3
Total Assets	3,087.6	3,177.7	2,780.0	2,593.5	2,270.1	2,067.5	1,891.5
Total Current Assets	1,150.7	1,221.2	1,031.6	961.9	868.6	883.0	842.3
Total Current Liabilities	636.1	713.3	531.3	573.8	567.8	525.8	493.0
Net Working Capital	514.7	507.9	500.3	388.1	300.9	357.2	349.3
Year End Shs Outstg (000)	74,727	75,960	75,482	75,283	76,555	78,886	85,348

STATISTICAL RECORD:

Operating Profit Margin %	11.0	13.9	14.4	15.2	14.1	14.0	13.9
Book Value Per Share	15.83	17.28	15.35	13.61	11.88	10.20	8.23
Return on Equity %	14.6	12.6	13.9	14.8	14.7	15.5	16.5
Return on Assets %	6.9	6.3	6.8	7.0	7.0	7.2	7.5
Average Yield %	...	1.6	1.7	1.6	1.8	1.6	1.3
P/E Ratio	15.0-12.0	16.4-12.5	16.8-11.9	16.4-11.9	15.6-12.1	16.8-12.6	20.2-12.4
Price Range	40¾-32⅝	42⅛-32¼	40¾-29	38⅝-27⅛	31⅛-24¼	31⅛-23¼	34½-21⅛

Statistics are as originally reported.

OFFICERS:
R.V. Gilmartin, Chmn., Pres. & C.E.O.
A.J. Battaglia, Group Pres.
R.A. Reynolds, V.P.-Fin. & Contr.

INCORPORATED: NJ, Nov., 1906

PRINCIPAL OFFICE: One Becton Dr., Franklin Lakes, NJ 07417-1880

TELEPHONE NUMBER: (201) 847-6800
NO. OF EMPLOYEES: 19,000 (approx.)
ANNUAL MEETING: In February
SHAREHOLDERS: 7,413 (approx.)
INSTITUTIONAL HOLDINGS:
No. of Institutions: 362
Shares Held: 29,789,460

REGISTRAR(S): First Chicago Trust Co. of New York, New York, NY 10008

TRANSFER AGENT(S): First Chicago Trust Co. of New York, New York, NY 10008

BEMIS CO., INC.

YIELD 2.3%
P/E RATIO 26.1

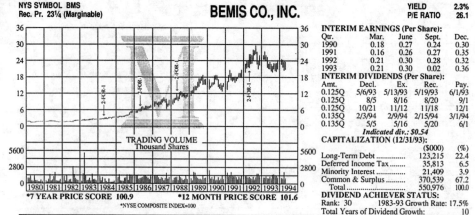

*7 YEAR PRICE SCORE 100.9 *12 MONTH PRICE SCORE 101.6
*NYSE COMPOSITE INDEX=100

TRADING VOLUME
Thousand Shares

INTERIM EARNINGS (Per Share):

Qtr.	Mar.	June	Sept.	Dec.
1990	0.18	0.27	0.24	0.30
1991	0.16	0.26	0.27	0.35
1992	0.21	0.30	0.28	0.32
1993	0.21	0.30	0.02	0.36

INTERIM DIVIDENDS (Per Share):

Amt.	Decl.	Ex.	Rec.	Pay.
0.125Q	5/6/93	5/13/93	5/19/93	6/1/93
0.125Q	8/5	8/16	8/20	9/1
0.125Q	10/21	11/12	11/18	12/1
0.135Q	2/3/94	2/9/94	2/15/94	3/1/94
0.135Q	5/5	5/16	5/20	6/1

Indicated div.: $0.54

CAPITALIZATION (12/31/93):

	($000)	(%)
Long-Term Debt	123,215	22.4
Deferred Income Tax	35,813	6.5
Minority Interest	21,409	3.9
Common & Surplus	370,539	67.2
Total	550,976	100.0

DIVIDEND ACHIEVER STATUS:

Rank: 30   1983-93 Growth Rate: 17.5%
Total Years of Dividend Growth: 10

RECENT DEVELOPMENTS: For the year ended 12/31/93, income before effect of change in accounting principles was $46.1 million compared with $57.3 million in 1992. Revenue advanced 1.9% to $1.20 billion from $1.18 billion in the comparable period last year. The increase in sales was a result of strong operating performances in the coated and laminated film and polyethylene packaging businesses. BMS has announced the completion of the acquisition of Fitchburg Coated Products, a division of Technographics, by its wholly-owned subsidiary, Morgan Adhesives Company.

PROSPECTS: Bemis' performance continues to be adversely affected by poor economic conditions in Europe and a slowly improving U.S. economy. Results in 1994 will be positively affected by a restructuring program which is reducing costs and improving efficiencies. Operating results from recent acquisitions will continue to improve sales levels. The Company has entered into a memorandum of understanding with Hargo Flexible Packaging, under which BMS's wholly owned Curwood, Inc. would acquire the Hargo Health Care business. Terms were not disclosed.

BUSINESS

BEMIS COMPANY, INC. is a major manufacturer of flexible packaging and specialty coated and graphics products. Flexible packaging products include coated and laminated films, polyethylene packaging, packaging machinery, multi-wall paper bags and consumer-size paper packaging, and specialty containers. Specialty coated and graphics products include pressure-sensitive materials, non-woven products and rotogravure cylinders. The primary market for BMS products is the food industry which accounts for about 70% of sales. Other markets include chemicals, agribusiness, pharmaceuticals, printing and graphic arts, and a variety of other industrial end uses.

ANNUAL EARNINGS AND DIVIDENDS PER SHARE

	1993	1992	1991	1990	1989	1988	1987
Earnings Per Share	0.89	①1.11	1.03	0.99	0.90	0.74	0.59
Dividends Per Share	0.50	②0.46	0.42	0.36	0.30	③0.22	0.18
Dividend Payout %	56.2	41.4	40.8	36.4	33.3	29.7	30.5

① Before acctg. chg. ② 2-for-1 stk split, 4/1/92 ③ 100% stk. div., 3/88.

ANNUAL FINANCIAL DATA

RECORD OF EARNINGS (IN MILLIONS):

	1993	1992	1991	1990	1989	1988	1987
Costs and Expenses	1,054.8	1,033.4	999.0	991.2	946.3	951.6	831.6
Depreciation & Amort	47.0	48.3	47.1	42.3	36.8	34.0	30.7
Operating Profit	d1,087.7	d1,065.8	d1,032.8	d1,018.2	d970.9	d973.1	d850.3
Income Bef Income Taxes	74.4	90.3	84.9	81.7	75.9	65.4	54.6
Income Taxes	28.3	33.0	31.9	30.8	28.9	25.8	22.7
Net Income	①46.1	②57.3	53.0	50.9	47.0	39.6	32.0
Aver. Shs. Outstg. (000)	51,767	51,840	51,530	51,402	52,146	53,490	54,414

① Before acctg. change dr$1,746,000. ② Before acctg. change dr$274,000.

BALANCE SHEET (IN MILLIONS):

	1993	1992	1991	1990	1989	1988	1987
Cash and Cash Equivalents	8.9	0.1	1.4	9.2	1.4	1.2	①0.1
Receivables, Net	161.7	166.1	156.8	168.9	151.4	148.3	131.2
Inventories	127.1	128.9	131.3	144.6	113.9	135.8	125.5
Gross Property	676.6	665.9	614.9	597.7	523.8	462.9	418.6
Accumulated Depreciation	261.7	275.2	245.0	227.3	200.2	180.6	159.6
Long-Term Debt	123.2	131.1	128.9	171.1	109.6	119.6	101.7
Net Stockholders' Equity	370.5	361.0	329.2	295.6	266.0	237.4	216.2
Total Assets	789.8	742.7	714.9	756.5	631.6	595.0	545.3
Total Current Assets	337.0	314.6	307.8	344.1	286.4	302.5	275.5
Total Current Liabilities	184.2	160.6	167.1	193.9	171.3	166.3	156.7
Net Working Capital	152.8	154.0	140.6	150.2	115.1	136.3	118.8
Year End Shs Outstg (000)	51,201	51,152	50,986	50,918	50,890	50,098	49,926

① Equal to $77,000.

STATISTICAL RECORD:

	1993	1992	1991	1990	1989	1988	1987
Book Value Per Share	6.75	6.55	5.94	5.26	5.13	4.64	4.23
Return on Equity %	12.4	15.9	16.1	17.2	17.7	16.7	14.8
Return on Assets %	5.8	7.7	7.4	6.7	7.4	6.7	5.9
Average Yield %	2.1	1.9	2.5	2.3	2.0	2.1	2.1
P/E Ratio	30.8-22.3	26.7-17.8	20.1-13.1	18.9-13.0	20.8-12.5	17.2-10.8	17.8-10.8
Price Range	27⅜-19⅞	29⅝-19¾	20¾-13½	18¾-12⅞	18¾-11¼	12¾-8	10½-6⅜

Statistics are as originally reported.

BUSINESS LINE ANALYSIS

(12/31/93)	Rev(%)	Inc(%)
Flexible Packaging		
Prod	75.1	72.2
Special Coat &		
Graph Prod	24.9	27.8
Total	100.0	100.0

OFFICERS:
J.H. Roe, Pres. & C.E.O.
S.W. Johnson, Sr. V.P., Sec. & Gen. Counsel
B.R. Field, III, Sr. V.P., C.F.O. & Treas.
PRINCIPAL OFFICE: 222 S. 9th St., Suite 2300, Minneapolis, MN 55402-4099

TELEPHONE NUMBER: (612) 376-3000
NO. OF EMPLOYEES: 7,565
ANNUAL MEETING: In May
SHAREHOLDERS: 5,649
INSTITUTIONAL HOLDINGS:
No. of Institutions: 143
Shares Held: 10,125,225

REGISTRAR(S):

TRANSFER AGENT(S):

BETZ LABORATORIES INC.

YIELD 3.1%
P/E RATIO 22.2

INTERIM EARNINGS (Per Share):

Qtr.	Mar.	June	Sept.	Dec.
1990	0.50	0.53	0.57	0.52
1991	0.60	0.61	0.65	0.61
1992	0.66	0.67	0.71	0.67
1993	0.62	0.61	0.58	0.24

INTERIM DIVIDENDS (Per Share):

Amt.	Decl.	Ex.	Rec.	Pay.
0.34Q	4/8/93	4/23/93	4/29/93	5/13/93
0.35Q	6/10	7/23	7/29	8/12
0.35Q	8/12	10/22	10/28	11/11
0.35Q	12/9	1/21/94	1/27/94	2/10/94
0.35Q	4/14/94	4/22	4/28	5/12

Indicated div.: $1.40

CAPITALIZATION (12/31/93):

	($000)	(%)
Long-Term Debt	97,500	24.6
Ser A ESOP Conv, 8% Pfd	99,201	25.0
Common & Surplus	200,118	50.4
Total	396,819	100.0

DIVIDEND ACHIEVER STATUS:
Rank: 128   1983-93 Growth Rate: 11.4%
Total Years of Dividend Growth: 28

TRADING VOLUME
Thousand Shares

*7 YEAR PRICE SCORE 92.9   *12 MONTH PRICE SCORE 107.8
*NYSE COMPOSITE INDEX=100

RECENT DEVELOPMENTS: For the year ended 12/31/93, earnings before an accounting change declined 23% to $63.4 million, or $2.05 per share, compared with earnings of $82.0 million in 1992. Sales slipped 3.1% to $684.9 million from $707.0 million last year. For the quarter, net income plunged 61.4% to $7.8 million from $20.1 million a year ago. Sales dropped to $168.4 million compared with $172.6 million for the same quarter last year. Betz Entec, Inc. and Betz Process Chemicals, Inc. posted solid sales gains for the quarter; however, these gains were more than offset by lower sales at Betz PaperChem, Inc. and the Betz Industrial Division. BTL's Canadian subsidiary, Betz Inc., experienced a strong quarter with solid gains in the paper industry in Canada. BTL's Business in Southeast Asia and the Caribbean were up for the quarter as well. Sales in Europe were down approximately 15%, due primarily to currency fluctuations.

BUSINESS

BETZ LABORATORIES INC. produces and sells specialty chemical products for the treatment of water and wastewater and process systems operating in a wide variety of industrial and commercial applications, with particular emphasis on the chemical, petroleum refining, paper and steel industries. Betz also provides technical and laboratory services necessary to utilize Betz products effectively. The Company's products are used chiefly in boilers, water and steam pipes, cooling systems, heat exchangers, air conditioning equipment, water cooled production equipment, pulp and paper mill systems, industrial and municipal intake water and waste effluent, and settling basins and lagoons. The virtue of these products is that they control corrosion, scale formation, foam formation and fouling. Also, the company produces formulated biocides to control the growth of plant and animal life in water used in industrial cooling systems and in water used as a carrier in pulp and paper production, as well as polymers used as retention aids and flocculants in the paper and mining industries and in industrial and municipal water and waste treatment and pollution abatement.

ANNUAL EARNINGS AND DIVIDENDS PER SHARE

	1993	1992	1991	1990	1989	1988	1987
Earnings Per Share	2.05	2.71	2.47	2.12	1.77	1.58	1.30
Dividends Per Share	1.38	1.30	1.16	�böl1.01	0.89	0.80	0.73
Dividend Payout %	67.3	48.0	47.0	47.6	50.3	50.6	56.2

� 100% stk div, 8/9/90

ANNUAL FINANCIAL DATA

RECORD OF EARNINGS (IN THOUSANDS):

Total Revenues	684,872	706,972	665,565	596,805	516,669	447,580	385,868
Costs and Expenses	541,503	536,825	512,701	462,820	403,306	348,631	298,133
Depreciation & Amort	42,083	38,883	33,827	29,869	25,902	22,974	20,122
Operating Earnings	101,286	131,264	119,037	104,116	87,461	75,976	67,614
Earn Bef Income Taxes	104,070	134,171	123,810	107,399	90,920	78,803	70,539
Income Taxes	40,691	52,124	48,286	41,925	35,000	30,418	29,905
Net Income	⏻63,379	82,047	75,524	65,474	55,860	48,385	40,634
Aver. Shs. Outstg.	28,576	28,474	28,547	28,512	30,224	30,747	31,402

⏻ Before acctg. change cr$2,141,000.

BALANCE SHEET (IN THOUSANDS):

Cash & Cash Equivalents	43,921	46,363	59,009	39,781	29,325	8,499	13,207
Receivables, Net	102,882	106,073	93,164	86,191	76,019	67,555	56,611
Inventories	37,346	34,991	35,820	38,442	31,436	34,828	25,197
Gross Property	554,623	509,776	451,694	403,360	344,718	296,599	254,665
Accumulated Depreciation	253,881	221,405	197,064	169,909	143,254	121,629	101,465
Long-Term Debt	97,500	98,000	98,500	99,000	99,500	...	...
Net Stockholders' Equity	299,319	297,689	258,932	220,705	183,454	230,573	205,196
Total Assets	521,129	510,617	475,844	427,356	369,226	318,535	286,901
Total Current Assets	208,635	202,492	200,805	176,374	145,465	120,364	103,202
Total Current Liabilities	92,041	84,137	88,003	77,386	56,793	59,615	56,439
Net Working Capital	116,594	118,355	112,802	98,988	88,672	60,749	46,763
Year End Shs Outstg	28,127	28,520	28,468	28,416	28,428	30,876	30,600

STATISTICAL RECORD:

Operating Profit Margin %	14.8	18.6	17.9	17.4	16.9	17.0	17.5
Book Value Per Share	6.95	6.78	5.41	4.01	2.57	7.12	6.34
Return on Equity %	21.2	27.6	29.2	29.7	30.4	21.0	19.8
Return on Assets %	12.2	16.1	15.9	15.3	15.1	15.2	14.2
Average Yield %	2.7	2.3	2.3	2.8	3.2	3.4	3.1
P/E Ratio	30.7-19.5	24.4-17.8	25.1-15.7	20.4-13.1	17.8-13.4	16.7-13.1	22.4-13.5
Price Range	62⅞-40	66¼-48¼	62-38¾	43¼-27¾	31¼-23⅝	26¼-20⅝	29⅛-17½

Statistics are as originally reported.

OFFICERS:
J.F. McCaughan, Chmn. & C.E.O.
W.R. Cook, Pres. & C.O.O.
R.D. Voncanon, V.P.-Fin. & Treas.
W.C. Brafford, V.P., Sec. & Gen. Coun.

INCORPORATED: PA, Feb., 1957

PRINCIPAL OFFICE: 4636 Somerton Rd.,
Trevose, PA 19053

TELEPHONE NUMBER: (215) 355-3300

FAX: (215) 953-5544

NO. OF EMPLOYEES: 1,266

ANNUAL MEETING: In April

SHAREHOLDERS: 1,710 (approx.)

INSTITUTIONAL HOLDINGS:
No. of Institutions: Not Available
Shares Held: Not Available

REGISTRAR(S): Mellon Bank East,
Pittsburgh, PA 15230

TRANSFER AGENT(S): Mellon Bank East,
Pittsburgh, PA 15230

NYS SYMBOL BKH
Rec. Pr. 20½

BLACK HILLS CORP.

YIELD 6.4%
P/E RATIO 12.3

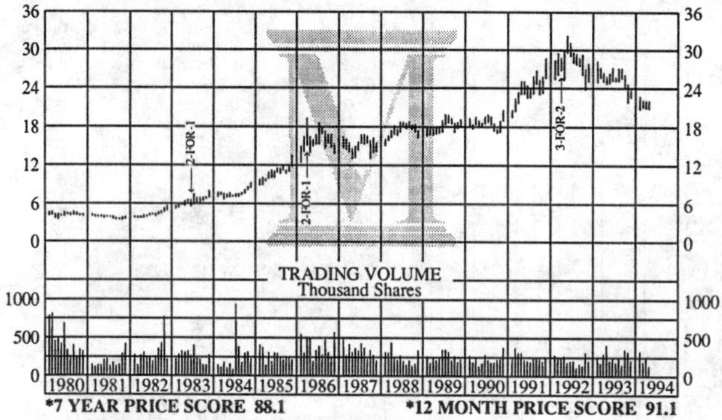

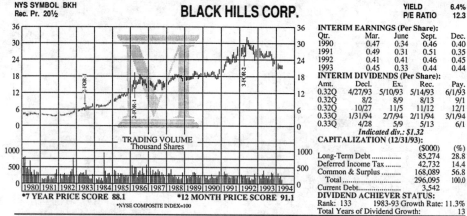

*7 YEAR PRICE SCORE 88.1 *12 MONTH PRICE SCORE 91.1

*NYSE COMPOSITE INDEX=100

INTERIM EARNINGS (Per Share):

Qtr.	Mar.	June	Sept.	Dec.
1990	0.47	0.34	0.46	0.40
1991	0.49	0.31	0.51	0.35
1992	0.41	0.41	0.46	0.45
1993	0.45	0.33	0.44	0.44

INTERIM DIVIDENDS (Per Share):

Amt.	Decl.	Ex.	Rec.	Pay.
0.32Q	4/27/93	5/10/93	5/14/93	6/1/93
0.32Q	8/2	8/9	8/13	9/1
0.32Q	10/27	11/5	11/12	12/1
0.33Q	1/31/94	2/7/94	2/11/94	3/1/94
0.33Q	4/28	5/9	5/13	6/1

Indicated div.: $1.32

CAPITALIZATION (12/31/93):

	($000)	(%)
Long-Term Debt	85,274	28.8
Deferred Income Tax	42,732	14.4
Common & Surplus	168,089	56.8
Total	296,095	100.0
Current Debt	3,542	

DIVIDEND ACHIEVER STATUS:
Rank: 133 1983-93 Growth Rate: 11.3%
Total Years of Dividend Growth: 13

RECENT DEVELOPMENTS: For the year ended 12/31/93, earnings declined to $22.9 million, or $1.66 per share, compared wtih $23.6 million, or $1.73 per share a year ago. Total revenues increased approximately 3% to $139.4 million from $135.3 million last year. The decrease in earnings was due to a decrease in interest income attibutable to lower interest rates and the $1.4 million pre-tax benefit recognized on the PacifiCorp Coal Settlement in the second quarter of 1992. BKH's kilowatthours sales rose 3.5% while coal sales increased 2.3%. Earnings for the fourth quarter were flat: $6.3 million or $0.44 per share versus $6.2 million or $0.45 per share for the same period a year ago. Likewise, revenues for the quarter were $35.8 million compared with $35.3 million for the fourth quarter last year.

BUSINESS

THE BLACK HILLS CORPATION is a diversified company that conducts its electric utility business as Black Hills Power and Light Company and is the owner of Wyodak Resources Development Corporation and Western Production Company. Black Hills Power and Light Company supplies electric service to a 9,300 square-mile area in western South Dakota, northeastern Wyoming, and southeastern Montana. Wyodak Resources Development Corporation is engaged in the mining and sale of coal from its mine located near Gillette, Wyoming. Western Production Company is an oil producing and operating company with interests located in the Rocky Mountain region of Texas.

REVENUES

(12/31/93)	($000)	(%)
Electric	98,155	70.4
Coal Mining	29,822	21.4
Oil & Gas Production	11,396	8.2
Total	139,373	100.0

ANNUAL EARNINGS AND DIVIDENDS PER SHARE

	1993	1992	1991	1990	1989	1988	1987
Earnings Per Share	**1.66**	**1.73**	**1.66**	**1.67**	**[2] 1.60**	**1.53**	**1.45**
Dividends Per Share	**1.28**	**[1] 1.24**	**1.173**	**1.093**	**1.013**	**0.933**	**0.827**
Dividend Payout %	**77.1**	**71.7**	**70.7**	**65.3**	**63.3**	**60.9**	**56.9**

[1] 3-for-2 stk split, 3/3/92 [2] Before disc. oper.

ANNUAL FINANCIAL DATA

RECORD OF EARNINGS (IN THOUSANDS):	1993	1992	1991	1990	1989	1988	1987
Total Operating Revenues	139,373	135,343	133,373	127,498	120,004	283,868	122,398
Deprec, Depl & Amort	16,051	13,860	12,012	9,930	9,484	10,054	10,410
Maintenance	6,869	6,513	6,729	6,088	6,784	7,069	6,047
Total Operating Income	37,786	36,349	35,467	29,474	27,682	26,754	32,707
Interest Expense	8,088	8,587	7,824	4,756	4,267	4,230	3,758
Net Income	22,946	23,638	22,681	22,938	[1] 21,957	[2] 21,166	20,350
Aver. Shs. Outstg.	13,811	13,689	13,675	13,675	13,676	13,665	13,646

[1] Before disc. op. dr$861,000. [2] Before disc. op. cr$1,248,000.

BALANCE SHEET (IN THOUSANDS):	1993	1992	1991	1990	1989	1988	1987
Gross Plant	425,893	391,218	369,303	333,917	310,018	312,987	303,270
Accumulated Depreciation	144,492	132,890	122,574	111,111	101,591	93,245	88,612
Prop, Plant & Equip, Net	281,401	258,328	246,729	222,806	208,427	219,742	214,658
Long-term Debt	85,274	88,816	92,982	78,978	78,939	85,096	78,242
Net Stockholders' Equity	168,089	149,158	141,963	135,329	127,338	120,100	115,051
Total Assets	352,853	330,202	319,895	294,929	272,523	289,992	258,215
Year End Shares Outstg	14,270	13,701	13,675	13,675	13,676	13,650	13,650

STATISTICAL RECORD:	1993	1992	1991	1990	1989	1988	1987
Book Value Per Share	11.78	10.89	10.38	9.90	9.31	8.80	8.09
Op. Inc/Net Pl %	13.4	14.1	14.4	13.2	13.3	12.2	15.2
Dep/Gr. Pl %	3.8	3.5	3.3	3.0	3.1	3.2	3.4
Accum. Dep/Gr. Pl %	33.9	34.0	33.2	33.3	32.8	29.8	29.2
Return on Equity %	13.7	15.8	16.0	16.9	17.2	17.6	17.7
Average Yield %	5.1	4.4	4.9	5.8	5.6	5.5	5.5
P/E Ratio	17.0-13.2	18.6-13.7	17.2-11.7	12.3-10.1	12.4-10.4	12.3-9.8	11.6-9.0
Price Range	28¼-21⅞	32¼-23¾	28⅝-19⅜	20⅝-17	19⅞-16⅝	18⅞-15	16⅞-13

Statistics are as originally reported.

OFFICERS:
D.P. Landguth, Chmn., Pres. & C.E.O.
E.E. Hoyt, Pres. & C.O.O.
D.E. Clement, Sr. V.P.-Fin.
R.R. Basham, Treas. & Sec.

INCORPORATED: SD, Aug., 1941

PRINCIPAL OFFICE: 625 Ninth St., P.O. Box 1400, Rapid City, SD 57709

TELEPHONE NUMBER: (605) 348-1700
FAX: (605) 348-4748
NO. OF EMPLOYEES: 62
ANNUAL MEETING: In May
SHAREHOLDERS: 4,998 common
INSTITUTIONAL HOLDINGS:
No. of Institutions: 83
Shares Held: 3,580,576

REGISTRAR(S): Manufacturers Hanover Trust Co., New York, NY

TRANSFER AGENT(S): Manufacturers Hanover Trust Co., New York, NY

NASDAQ SYMBOL BLOC A
Rec. Pr. 31⅛ (Marginable)

BLOCK DRUG CO., INC.

YIELD 3.3%
P/E RATIO 11.3

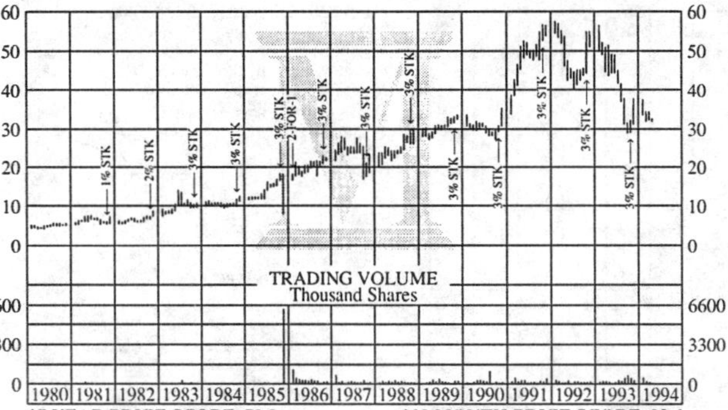

60
50
40
30
20
10
0
1% STK
2% STK
3% STK
3% STK
3% STK
2-FOR-1
3% STK
3% STK
3% STK
3% STK
3% STK
3% STK
3% STK
3% STK
3% STK
TRADING VOLUME
Thousand Shares
6600
3300
0
1980 1981 1982 1983 1984 1985 1986 1987 1988 1989 1990 1991 1992 1993 1994

*7 YEAR PRICE SCORE 79.9 *12 MONTH PRICE SCORE 90.6

*NYSE COMPOSITE INDEX=100

INTERIM EARNINGS (Per Share):

Qtr.	June	Sept.	Dec.	Mar.
1990-91	0.66	0.70	0.70	0.75
1991-92	0.76	0.77	0.73	0.79
1992-93	0.84	0.83	0.79	0.79
1993-94	0.83	0.57	0.56	...

INTERIM DIVIDENDS (Per Share):

Amt.	Decl.	Ex.	Rec.	Pay.
0.25Q	6/8/93	6/15/93	6/21/93	7/1/93
0.25Q	7/27	8/26	9/1	10/1
0.26Q	10/26	11/24	12/1	1/3/94
3%	10/26	11/24	12/1	1/3
0.26Q	1/25/94	2/23/94	3/1/94	4/1

Indicated div.: $1.04

CAPITALIZATION (3/31/93):

	($000)	(%)
Long-Term Debt	19,160	3.7
Deferred Income Tax	8,433	1.7
Common & Surplus	485,298	94.6
Total	512,891	100.0

DIVIDEND ACHIEVER STATUS:
Rank: 174 1983-93 Growth Rate: 10.1%
Total Years of Dividend Growth: 22

RECENT DEVELOPMENTS: For the nine months ended 12/31/93, net sales declined 2.2% to $459.7 million from $470.0 million for the same period in 1992. Net income for the period decreased 20.1% to $37.3 million, or $1.91 per share, compared with $46.7 million, or $2.39 per share, for the same period last year. For the quarter, net sales declined 1.1% to $155.6 million from $157.3 million for the same quarter a year ago. Net income for the quarter was $19.53 million, or $0.56 per share, compared with $19.51 million, or $0.76 per share, for the comparable 1992 quarter. For the quarter ended 9/30/93, net income was $10.8 million, or $0.57 per share, on sales of $153.5 million, compared with net income of $15.8 million, on sales of $159.3 million, for the same period last year.

BUSINESS

BLOCK DRUG CO., INC. develops, manufactures and markets three categories of products: dental products, including consumer oral hygiene amd professional dental products; consumer products, including proprietary over the counter products and household products; and ethical pharmaceuticals. Denture cleansers and adhesives, specialty toothpastes and toothpastes are the key products that comprise the consumer oral hygiene segment. These products include POLIDENT, DENTU-CREME and their line extensions, SUPER POLI-GRIP, WERNET'S AND SUPER WERNET'S, SENSODYNE and PROMISE. Block is a leading manufacturer and marketer of professional dental products for use in chairside patient treatment and dental office infection control. Block's personal care products include: NYTOL Sleep-Aid Tablets, TEGRIN Medicated Shampoos and BC Headache Powder. Household products include 2000 FLUSHES, X-14 brand names. Pharmaceutical products and ethical nonprescription products are manufactured and marketed by Reed & Carnrick. The Division markets products in several medical categories including dermatology, gastroenterology, cardiovascular disease and proctology.

ANNUAL EARNINGS AND DIVIDENDS PER SHARE

	3/31/93	3/31/92	3/31/91	3/31/90	3/31/89	3/31/88	3/31/87
Earnings Per Share	3.25	3.03	2.80	2.41	2.27	1.97	1.70
Dividends Per Share	[1] 0.893	[2] 0.748	[3] 0.636	[4] 0.565	[5] 0.497	[6] 0.45	[7] 0.406
Dividend Payout %	27.5	24.7	22.6	23.6	22.0	22.8	24.0

Note: 3%stk.div.1/3/94. [1] 3% stk div,11/24/92 [2] 3% stk div,11/25/91 [3] 3% stk div, 11/27/90 [4] 3% stk div, 1/2/90 [5] 3% stk div, 1/3/89 [6] 3% stk div, 1/88 [7] 3% stk div, 1/87

ANNUAL FINANCIAL DATA

	3/31/93	3/31/92	3/31/91	3/31/90	3/31/89	3/31/88	3/31/87
RECORD OF EARNINGS (IN THOUSANDS):							
Total Revenues	651,316	585,260	530,854	453,014	424,303	369,102	320,503
Costs and Expenses	561,944	506,252	452,321	388,600	365,757	320,667	278,130
Depreciation & Amort	11,659	10,554	9,471	7,388	5,638	5,157	5,188
Operating Income	77,713	68,454	69,062	57,026	52,908	43,278	37,185
Income Bef Income Taxes	77,713	68,454	69,062	57,026	52,908	43,278	37,185
Total Income Taxes	16,167	11,187	15,852	10,886	9,413	5,330	4,553
Net Income	61,546	57,267	53,210	46,140	43,495	37,948	32,632
Aver. Shs. Outstg.	18,936	18,922	19,035	19,219	19,205	19,214	19,212
BALANCE SHEET (IN THOUSANDS):							
Cash and Cash Equivalents	32,910	30,541	28,793	32,308	32,090	25,146	54,538
Receivables, Net	95,743	87,775	76,735	59,452	54,688	51,120	36,063
Inventories	96,458	89,223	81,214	69,138	68,555	55,135	48,030
Gross Property	259,801	228,007	192,936	152,247	116,354	101,286	85,415
Accumulated Depreciation	70,550	65,567	56,655	46,885	41,888	38,149	31,969
Long-Term Debt	19,160	19,435	19,459	19,660	12,117	17,887	23,872
Net Stockholders' Equity	485,298	446,550	398,736	352,013	311,993	275,979	233,270
Total Assets	726,497	649,608	550,735	460,268	417,748	356,260	317,821
Total Current Assets	254,839	236,173	206,246	179,350	170,447	143,393	150,442
Total Current Liabilities	203,636	166,610	117,626	76,035	81,812	52,475	52,870
Net Working Capital	51,203	69,563	88,620	103,315	88,635	90,918	97,572
Year End Shares Outstg	18,946	18,378	18,896	19,225	19,213	19,198	19,226
STATISTICAL RECORD:							
Operating Profit Margin %	11.9	11.7	13.0	12.6	12.5	11.7	11.6
Book Value Per Share	24.43	23.35	20.18	17.45	15.27	13.59	11.39
Return on Equity %	12.7	12.8	13.3	13.1	13.9	13.8	14.0
Return on Assets %	8.5	8.8	9.7	10.0	10.4	10.7	10.3
Average Yield %	1.8	1.6	2.0	1.8	1.9	2.0	2.0
P/E Ratio	18.2-12.7	19.3-11.5	13.0-10.0	14.5-11.7	13.8-9.2	14.6-8.6	14.0-9.9
Price Range	59¼-41¼	58½-34⅞	36½-27⅞	34¾-28	31⅛-20¾	28⅞-17⅛	23¾-16⅞

Statistics are as originally reported.

OFFICERS:
L. Block, Sr. Chmn.
J.A. Block, Chmn.
T.R. Block, Pres. & Treas.
J.E. Peters, Sr. V.P., Gen. Couns. & Sec.

INCORPORATED: NJ, Mar., 1970

PRINCIPAL OFFICE: 257 Cornelison Ave., Jersey City, NJ 07302-9988

TELEPHONE NUMBER: (201) 434-3000

NO. OF EMPLOYEES: 253

ANNUAL MEETING: In March

SHAREHOLDERS: 181 Cl. A; Cl. B, 5 (approx.)

INSTITUTIONAL HOLDINGS:
No. of Institutions: 66
Shares Held: 5,144,542

REGISTRAR(S):

TRANSFER AGENT(S): American Stock Transfer & Trust Co., 40 Wall Street, New York, NY 10005

NYS SYMBOL HRB
Rec. Pr. 40¾

BLOCK (H & R), INC.

YIELD 2.7%
P/E RATIO 24.1

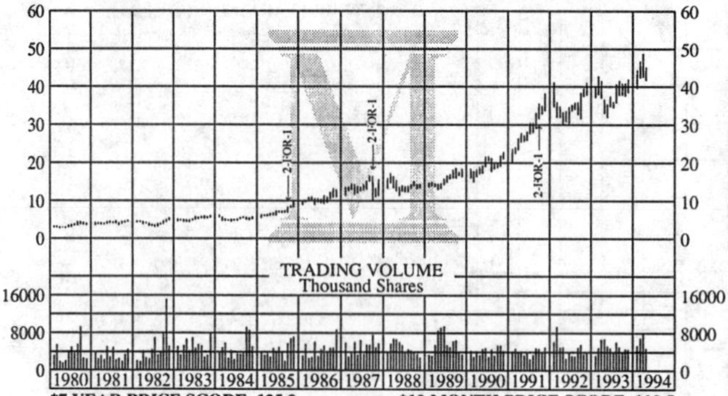

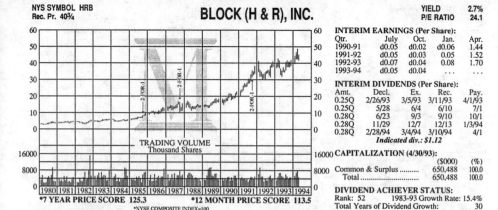

60
50
40
30
20
10
0
2-FOR-1
2-FOR-1
2-FOR-1
TRADING VOLUME
Thousand Shares
16000
8000
0
1980 1981 1982 1983 1984 1985 1986 1987 1988 1989 1990 1991 1992 1993 1994

*7 YEAR PRICE SCORE 125.3 *12 MONTH PRICE SCORE 113.5

*NYSE COMPOSITE INDEX=100

INTERIM EARNINGS (Per Share):

Qtr.	July	Oct.	Jan.	Apr.
1990-91	d0.05	d0.02	d0.06	1.44
1991-92	d0.05	d0.03	0.05	1.52
1992-93	d0.07	d0.04	0.08	1.70
1993-94	d0.05	d0.04	...	...

INTERIM DIVIDENDS (Per Share):

Amt.	Decl.	Ex.	Rec.	Pay.
0.25Q	2/26/93	3/5/93	3/11/93	4/1/93
0.25Q	5/28	6/4	6/10	7/1
0.28Q	6/23	9/3	9/10	10/1
0.28Q	11/29	12/7	12/13	1/3/94
0.28Q	2/28/94	3/4/94	3/10/94	4/1

Indicated div.: $1.12

CAPITALIZATION (4/30/93):

	($000)	(%)
Common & Surplus	650,488	100.0
Total	650,488	100.0

DIVIDEND ACHIEVER STATUS:
Rank: 52 1983-93 Growth Rate: 15.4%
Total Years of Dividend Growth: 30

RECENT DEVELOPMENTS: For the quarter ended 1/31/94, net earnings were $12.6 million, or $0.12 per share, compared with $8.6 million, or $0.08 per share, for the corresponding period last year. Revenues from continuing operations were $6.2 million versus a loss of $2.5 million a year ago. Pretax earnings of CompuServe Incorporated were $29.3 million, up 53.5% from a year earlier. Currently, CompuServe has a total of nearly 1.7 million members worlwide, including more than 100,000 members in Europe. The company is acquiring 60,000 new members per month. H&R Block Tax Services, Inc. incurred a pretax loss of $12.5 million, an increase of 15.3% from the loss of $10.8 million for the same period last year. From 1/1/94 through 3/15/94, worldwide tax services volume increased 1.9% and the number of taxpayers served decreased 0.6% compared with the same period a year ago. The IRS reported that as of 3/18/94 the total number of individual income tax returns filed electronically in 1994 was 11.7 million, an increase of 8.7%.

BUSINESS

H&R BLOCK, INC., is a diversified personal services company providing services in two industry areas. H&R Block Tax Services, Inc., offers tax return preparation and electronic filing services. CompuServe Inc., provides communications and information services to personal computer owners worldwide through CompuServe Information Service. On 1/27/94, HRB completed the sale of its wholly-owned subsidiary, Interim Services Inc., through an initial public offering. On 11/20/93, HRB acquired MECA Software, Inc. for $45.4 million in cash.

BUSINESS LINE ANALYSIS

(4/30/93)	Rev(%)	Inc(%)
Tax Services	48.1	64.7
Computer Services	20.7	25.2
Temporary Help Services	29.5	6.6
Other	1.7	3.5
Total	100.0	100.0

ANNUAL EARNINGS AND DIVIDENDS PER SHARE

	4/30/93	4/30/92	4/30/91	4/30/90	4/30/89	4/30/88	4/30/87
Earnings Per Share	**1.68**	**1.49**	**1.31**	**1.15**	**0.95**	**0.86**	**0.72**
Dividends Per Share	**0.91**	**1 0.805**	**0.675**	**0.55**	**0.46**	**2 0.388**	**0.338**
Dividend Payout %	**54.2**	**54.0**	**33.8**	**47.8**	**48.4**	**45.1**	**47.6**

1 2-for-1 stk split,10/02/91 2 2-for-1 stk split, 10/87

ANNUAL FINANCIAL DATA

	4/30/93	4/30/92	4/30/91	4/30/90	4/30/89	4/30/88	4/30/87
RECORD OF EARNINGS (IN MILLIONS):							
Total Revenues	1,525.3	1,370.7	1,190.8	1,052.7	899.6	794.1	710.4
Costs and Expenses	1,175.4	1,062.2	932.2	822.9	712.1	628.9	561.2
Depreciation & Amort	54.7	44.3	33.0	29.2	25.9	24.9	21.7
Operating Income	295.3	264.3	225.6	200.5	161.6	140.3	127.5
Earn Bef Taxes on Income	295.3	264.3	225.6	200.5	161.6	140.3	127.5
Taxes on Income	114.6	102.0	85.5	77.0	61.4	52.5	54.1
Net Income	180.7	162.3	140.1	123.5	100.2	87.9	73.3
Aver. Shs. Outstg. (000)	107,644	109,154	107,194	107,124	105,726	102,568	102,764
BALANCE SHEET (IN MILLIONS):							
Cash and Cash Equivalents	334.8	274.3	228.2	239.8	252.0	210.9	210.2
Receivables, Net	228.7	271.9	392.4	369.0	315.8	208.4	187.9
Gross Property	320.8	261.0	233.0	210.5	192.4	169.0	147.6
Accumulated Depreciation	172.4	137.5	124.7	113.4	99.5	82.8	68.3
Long-Term Debt	...	...	...	4.9	4.7	4.7	4.8
Net Stockholders' Equity	650.5	613.7	573.6	503.3	445.9	373.7	350.0
Total Assets	1,005.8	962.7	1,035.8	941.5	826.4	676.5	628.7
Total Current Assets	589.9	568.0	648.0	642.2	595.5	440.1	414.1
Total Current Liabilities	329.9	327.8	437.3	411.8	356.7	285.4	260.6
Net Working Capital	260.0	240.2	210.6	230.4	238.8	154.7	153.5
Year End Shs Outstg (000)	106,355	106,598	106,496	105,628	105,011	101,364	102,714
STATISTICAL RECORD:							
Operating Profit Margin %	19.4	19.3	18.9	19.0	18.0	17.7	17.9
Book Value Per Share	4.93	4.61	4.28	3.99	3.56	2.98	2.72
Return on Equity %	27.8	26.4	24.4	24.5	22.5	23.5	21.0
Return on Assets %	18.0	16.9	13.5	13.1	12.1	13.0	11.7
Average Yield %	2.6	2.8	3.6	3.5	3.2	2.9	3.0
P/E Ratio	24.5-17.9	25.7-13.4	17.4-11.5	16.3-11.4	18.2-12.0	19.3-11.6	18.4-12.5
Price Range	41⅛-30⅛	38¼-20	22¾-15	18¾-13⅛	17¼-11⅜	16⅝-10	13¼-9

Statistics are as originally reported.

OFFICERS:
H.W. Bloch, Chmn.
T.M. Bloch, Pres. & C.E.O.
W.P. Anderson, V.P.-Corp. Devel. & C.F.O.
D.W. Ayers, V.P.-Fin. & Treas.

INCORPORATED: MO, 1955

PRINCIPAL OFFICE: 4410 Main Street, Kansas City, MO 64111

TELEPHONE NUMBER: (816) 753-6900

NO. OF EMPLOYEES: 558

ANNUAL MEETING: In September

SHAREHOLDERS: 23,007

INSTITUTIONAL HOLDINGS:
No. of Institutions: 411
Shares Held: 67,743,216

REGISTRAR(S): Boatmen's Trust Co., St.Louis, MO 63101

TRANSFER AGENT(S): Boatmen's Trust Co., St. Louis, MO 63101

NASDAQ SYMBOL BOAT
Rec. Pr. 30 (Marginable)

BOATMEN'S BANCSHARES, INC.

YIELD 4.1%
P/E RATIO 9.8

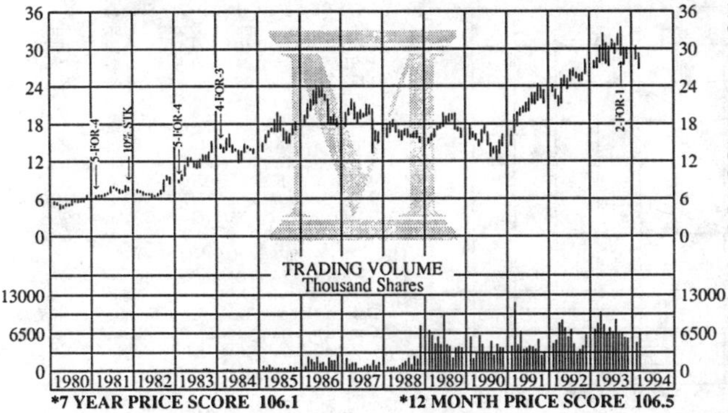

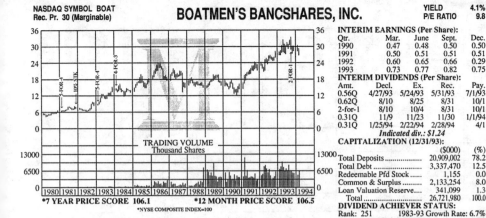

36
30
24
18
12
6
0
5-FOR-4
10% STK
5-FOR-4
4-FOR-3
2-FOR-1
TRADING VOLUME
Thousand Shares
13000
6500
0
1980 1981 1982 1983 1984 1985 1986 1987 1988 1989 1990 1991 1992 1993 1994

***7 YEAR PRICE SCORE 106.1** ***12 MONTH PRICE SCORE 106.5**

*NYSE COMPOSITE INDEX=100

INTERIM EARNINGS (Per Share):

Qtr.	Mar.	June	Sept.	Dec.
1990	0.47	0.48	0.50	0.50
1991	0.50	0.51	0.51	0.51
1992	0.60	0.65	0.66	0.29
1993	0.73	0.77	0.82	0.75

INTERIM DIVIDENDS (Per Share):

Amt.	Decl.	Ex.	Rec.	Pay.
0.56Q	4/27/93	5/24/93	5/31/93	7/1/93
0.62Q	8/10	8/25	8/31	10/1
2-for-1	8/10	10/4	8/31	10/1
0.31Q	11/9	11/23	11/30	1/1/94
0.31Q	1/25/94	2/22/94	2/28/94	4/1

Indicated div.: $1.24

CAPITALIZATION (12/31/93):

	($000)	(%)
Total Deposits	20,909,002	78.2
Total Debt	3,337,470	12.5
Redeemable Pfd Stock	1,155	0.0
Common & Surplus	2,133,254	8.0
Loan Valuation Reserve	341,099	1.3
Total	26,721,980	100.0

DIVIDEND ACHIEVER STATUS:

Rank: 251 1983-93 Growth Rate: 6.7%
Total Years of Dividend Growth: 13

RECENT DEVELOPMENTS: For the year ended 12/31/93, earnings increased 38.8% to a record $317.4 million, or $3.07 per share, from $228.7 million, or $2.29 per share, in 1992. Net interest income rose 11.8% to $981.6 million from $877.7 million last year. Provision for loan losses was reduced by more than half to $60.2 million. For the quarter, earnings more than doubled to $77.1 million, or $0.75 per share, from $32.1 million, or $0.32 per share, for the same period last year. Net interest income rose 8.6% to $248.7 million from $229.1 million in 1992. On 11/30/93, BOAT acquired First Amarillo Bancorporation, Inc., located in Amarillo, Texas with assets of approximately $1.0 billion, in a transaction accounted for as a pooling of interests. During the quarter, BOAT announced plans to acquire Woodland Bancorp, Inc., a retail banking organization in Tulsa, Oklahoma with assets of approximately $65 million.

BUSINESS

BOATMEN'S BANCSHARES, INC. is the largest bank holding company in Missouri. The Corporation's principal office is located in St. Louis, Missouri where its largest subsidiary, The Boatmen's National Bank of St. Louis, is located. The Corporation owns directly substantially all of the capital stock of 51 subsidiary banks, a trust company, a mortgage banking company, a credit life insurance company and an insurance agency. Boatmen's currently operates approximately 400 locations in Arkansas, Illinois, Iowa, Missouri, New Mexico, Oklahoma, Tennessee, and Texas. The business of the Corporation consists primarily of the ownership, supervision and control of its subsidiaries. The Corporation provides its subsidiaries with advice, counsel and specialized services in various fields of financial and banking policy operations. The Corporation also engages in negotiations designed to lead to the acquisition of other banks and closely related businesses.

ANNUAL EARNINGS AND DIVIDENDS PER SHARE

	1993	1992	1991	1990	1989	1988	1987
Earnings Per Share	**3.07**	**2.26**	**2.04**	**1.95**	**1.86**	**1.00**	**2.07**
Dividends Per Share	**[1] 1.15**	**1.09**	**1.07**	**1.06**	**1.015**	**1.00**	**0.92**
Dividend Payout %	**37.5**	**48.3**	**52.6**	**54.4**	**54.6**	**99.5**	**44.4**

[1] 2-for-1 stk split,10/04/93

ANNUAL FINANCIAL DATA

	1993	1992	1991	1990	1989	1988	1987
RECORD OF EARNINGS (IN MILLIONS):							
Total Interest	1,613.6	1,566.1	1,315.8	1,293.9	1,267.1	1,180.0	746.0
Total Interest Expense	632.0	718.7	753.3	808.9	804.8	710.8	437.5
Net Interest Income	981.6	847.5	562.5	485.0	462.3	469.1	308.5
Provision for Loan Losses	60.2	134.6	88.5	69.2	69.4	87.4	41.7
Net Income	317.4	215.5	150.1	135.2	129.2	69.8	81.4
Aver. Shs. Outstg. (000)	104,100	95,530	73,774	69,359	68,360	66,868	38,130
BALANCE SHEET (IN MILLIONS):							
Cash & Due From Banks	1,608.1	1,700.4	1,400.7	1,788.9	1,237.9	1,570.3	969.0
US Government Securities	3,372.9	6,509.1	4,361.3	3,636.9	2,914.8	2,565.2	1,329.1
Obligs Of State & Political Subdiviss	...	...	...	...	...	1,072.8	315.4
Loans, Net	14,484.8	12,340.8	9,520.3	9,032.1	8,811.5	8,757.1	5,289.2
Total Domestic Deposits	20,909.0	18,987.8	13,477.2	13,665.6	10,851.3	11,223.8	7,389.6
Long-term Debt	486.3	380.1	238.1	204.7	214.1	220.5	162.6
Net Stockholders' Equity	2,134.4	1,794.5	1,344.6	1,148.3	1,087.4	1,031.8	670.2
Total Assets	26,654.0	23,386.7	17,634.7	17,468.5	14,542.4	14,675.8	9,884.9
Year End Shs Outstg (000)	104,126	96,556	75,954	69,382	69,315	67,262	38,154
STATISTICAL RECORD:							
Return on Assets %	1.19	0.92	0.85	0.77	0.89	0.48	0.82
Return on Equity %	14.90	12.00	11.20	11.80	11.90	6.80	12.20
Book Value Per Share	20.49	18.57	17.69	16.53	15.67	14.86	16.69
Average Yield %	3.8	4.4	5.5	7.0	5.9	5.9	5.2
P/E Ratio	10.9-8.8	12.5-9.2	11.9-7.1	9.2-6.3	10.6-8.0	18.6-15.0	10.6-6.4
Price Range	33½-26⅞	28¼-20¾	24⅜-14½	17⅞-12¼	19¾-14⅞	18⅝-15	22-13¼

Statistics are as originally reported.

OFFICERS:
A.B. Craig, III, Chmn., Pres. & C.E.O.
S.B. Hayes, III, Vice-Chmn.
J.P. MacCarthy, Vice-Chmn.
J.W. Kienker, Exec. V.P. & C.F.O.

INCORPORATED: MO, Jun., 1946

PRINCIPAL OFFICE: One Boatmen's Plaza
800 Market Street, St. Louis, MO 63101

TELEPHONE NUMBER: (314) 466-6000
FAX: (314) 466-6027
NO. OF EMPLOYEES: 13,025 (approx.)
ANNUAL MEETING: In April
SHAREHOLDERS: 27,968 (approx.)
INSTITUTIONAL HOLDINGS:
No. of Institutions: 286
Shares Held: 50,059,148

REGISTRAR(S):

TRANSFER AGENT(S): Boatmen's Trust Co., St. Louis, MO 63101

BOWL AMERICA INC.

YIELD 3.7%
P/E RATIO 14.8

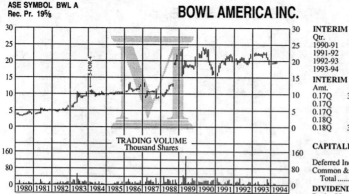

INTERIM EARNINGS (Per Share):

Qtr.	Sept.	Dec.	Mar.	June
1990-91	0.10	0.44	0.63	0.27
1991-92	0.04	0.38	0.63	0.24
1992-93	0.08	0.42	0.63	0.24
1993-94	0.03	0.43	...	...

INTERIM DIVIDENDS (Per Share):

Amt.	Decl.	Ex.	Rec.	Pay.
0.17Q	3/9/93	4/8/93	4/15/93	5/12/93
0.17Q	6/29	7/8	7/14	8/11
0.17Q	9/21	10/7	10/14	11/10
0.18Q	12/7	1/12/94	1/19/94	2/9/94
0.18Q	3/8/94	4/8	4/14	5/11

Indicated div.: $0.72

TRADING VOLUME
Thousand Shares

CAPITALIZATION (6/27/93):

	($000)	(%)
Deferred Income Tax	1,036	3.5
Common & Surplus	28,452	96.5
Total	29,487	100.0

*7 YEAR PRICE SCORE 89.1   *12 MONTH PRICE SCORE 95.1
*NYSE COMPOSITE INDEX=100

DIVIDEND ACHIEVER STATUS:
Rank: 78   1983-93 Growth Rate: 13.9%
Total Years of Dividend Growth: 21

RECENT DEVELOPMENTS: For the thirteen weeks ended 12/26/93, net income increased 2% to $1.2 million. Operating revenues were $7.6 million, up 4.6% from $7.3 million in the same period last year. League linage was up for the period but that increase was more than offset by a decrease in open play linage due to unfavorable bowling weather. Food and beverage sales were flat, while merchandise sales increased partially due to clearance of excess stock at reduced prices. For the twenty-six weeks, net income slipped to $1.3 million, or $0.46 per share, compared with $1.5 million, or $0.50 per share, for the same period a year ago. Operating revenues for the period rose 3.2% to $13.1 million from $12.6 million a year earlier. Operating income decreased to $1.9 million from $2.0 million due to increased operating expenses.

BUSINESS

BOWL AMERICA INC. and its subsidiaries are engaged in the operation of 13 bowling centers in the greater metropolitan area of Washington, D.C., three bowling centers in the greater metropolitan area of Baltimore, Maryland, three bowling centers in the greater metropolitan area of Orlando, Florida, three bowling centers in the greater metropolitan area of Richmond, Virginia, and two bowling centers in the greater metropolitan area of Jacksonville, Florida. These 24 centers contain a total of 896 lanes. The Company's lease of Bowl America Dundalk, a 40-lane bowling center, terminated in the Spring of 1991. Its lease of Bowl America Woodbridge, a 24-lane bowling center, expired in August 1991. The Company has completed construction of a new 40-lane bowling center which replaced Bowl America Woodbridge in August 1991. The Company has received approval of its site plan for an additional 40-lane bowling center in Northern Virginia and will proceed with construction in the near future. On October 31, 1958, the Company acquired entire stock of Shirley Tenpin Bowl, Inc. for 200,000 shares. In July 1970, the Company acquired Lynwood Bowl, located in Woodbridge, Virginia.

ANNUAL EARNINGS AND DIVIDENDS PER SHARE

	6/27/93	6/28/92	6/30/91	7/1/90	7/2/89	7/3/88	6/28/87
Earnings Per Share	1.37	1.29	1.44	1.51	1.42	1.19	0.78
Dividends Per Share	0.68	0.65	0.63	0.59	0.54	0.493	0.28
Dividend Payout %	49.6	50.4	43.8	39.1	38.0	41.5	35.9

ANNUAL FINANCIAL DATA

RECORD OF EARNINGS (IN THOUSANDS):

	6/27/93	6/28/92	6/30/91	7/1/90	7/2/89	7/3/88	6/28/87
Total Revenues	27,300	26,846	27,363	27,339	25,803	23,650	21,336
Costs and Expenses	20,180	19,682	19,632	19,188	18,175	17,168	15,935
Depreciation & Amort	1,416	1,243	1,086	1,126	1,097	1,015	965
Operating Income	5,704	5,920	6,645	7,025	6,532	5,467	4,406
Earn Bef Prov for Inc Taxes	6,324	5,912	6,624	6,987	6,489	5,419	4,346
Income Taxes	2,350	2,195	2,485	2,640	2,421	2,022	2,114
Net Income	3,974	3,717	4,139	4,347	4,068	3,397	2,233
Aver. Shs. Outstg.	2,892	2,892	2,877	2,875	2,871	2,862	2,871

BALANCE SHEET (IN THOUSANDS):

Cash and Cash Equivalents	9,633	9,635	10,586	9,653	9,273	5,935	4,194
Receivables, Net	507	...	...	...	...	79	61
Inventories	635	497	516	549	537	446	439
Gross Property	34,461	32,195	29,723	27,395	24,147	23,551	22,211
Accumulated Depreciation	15,740	14,909	14,626	13,781	12,853	11,866	11,159
Long-Term Debt	...	...	...	132	203	140	175
Obligs Under Cap Lses	...	...	...	...	...	125	156
Net Stockholders' Equity	28,452	26,474	24,482	22,064	19,501	16,820	14,552
Total Assets	31,611	29,471	28,289	25,564	22,879	19,659	17,179
Total Current Assets	11,444	10,665	11,663	10,597	10,184	6,718	4,961
Total Current Liabilities	2,124	2,071	2,911	2,587	2,504	2,045	1,911
Net Working Capital	9,319	8,594	8,752	8,009	7,680	4,673	3,050
Year End Shares Outstg	2,890	2,893	2,874	2,874	2,878	1,910	2,875

STATISTICAL RECORD:

Operating Profit Margin %	20.9	22.1	24.3	25.7	25.3	23.1	20.7
Book Value Per Share	9.84	9.15	8.52	7.68	6.78	8.80	5.05
Return on Equity %	14.0	14.0	16.9	19.7	20.9	20.2	15.3
Return on Assets %	12.6	12.6	14.6	17.0	17.8	17.3	13.0
Average Yield %	3.3	3.2	3.3	3.0	2.8	3.2	2.5
P/E Ratio	16.6-13.9	17.2-14.6	15.4-10.8	16.1-10.4	16.5-10.8	18.4-7.7	17.3-11.1
Price Range	22¾-19	22¼-18⅞	22⅛-15½	24¼-15¾	23½-15⅜	21⅞-9⅛	13½-8⅝

Statistics are as originally reported.

OFFICERS:
L.H. Goldberg, Pres. & Prin. Exec. & Oper. Off.
R. Macklin, Sr. V.P. & Treas.
H. Katzman, Sr. V.P. & Sec.

INCORPORATED: MD, Jul., 1958

PRINCIPAL OFFICE: 6446 Edsall Road, Alexandria, VA 22312

TELEPHONE NUMBER: (703) 941-6300

NO. OF EMPLOYEES: 750 (approx.)

ANNUAL MEETING: In December

SHAREHOLDERS: 647 Cl. A; Cl. B, 42 (approx.)

INSTITUTIONAL HOLDINGS:
No. of Institutions: 20
Shares Held: 495,435

REGISTRAR(S): First American Bank of Washington, Washington, DC 20005

TRANSFER AGENT(S): First American Bank of Washington, Washington, DC 20005

BRISTOL-MYERS SQUIBB CO.

YIELD 5.3%
P/E RATIO 14.5

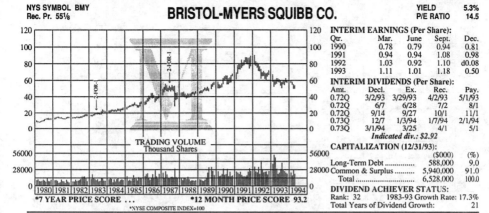

*7 YEAR PRICE SCORE ...   *12 MONTH PRICE SCORE 93.2
*NYSE COMPOSITE INDEX=100

INTERIM EARNINGS (Per Share):

Qtr.	Mar.	June	Sept.	Dec.
1990	0.78	0.79	0.94	0.81
1991	0.94	0.94	1.08	0.98
1992	1.03	0.92	1.10	d0.08
1993	1.11	1.01	1.18	0.50

INTERIM DIVIDENDS (Per Share):

Amt.	Decl.	Ex.	Rec.	Pay.
0.72Q	3/2/93	3/29/93	4/2/93	5/1/93
0.72Q	6/7	6/28	7/2	8/1
0.72Q	9/14	9/27	10/1	11/1
0.73Q	12/7	1/3/94	1/7/94	2/1/94
0.73Q	3/1/94	3/25	4/1	5/1

Indicated div.: $2.92

CAPITALIZATION (12/31/93):

	($000)	(%)
Long-Term Debt	588,000	9.0
Common & Surplus	5,940,000	91.0
Total	6,528,000	100.0

DIVIDEND ACHIEVER STATUS:

Rank: 32   1983-93 Growth Rate: 17.3%
Total Years of Dividend Growth: 21

RECENT DEVELOPMENTS: For the year ended 12/31/93, net income increased 27.4% to $1.96 billion compared with $1.54 billion, from continuing operations, a year ago. Sales were up 2.3% to $11.41 billion from $11.16 billion. Net income includes a special charge of $1.5 billion for potential liabilities and expenses related to breast implant claims, offset by $1 billion of expected insurance proceeds. The decline in sales was largely attributable to the Company's consumer products, which were adversely affected by increased competition in the U.S. analgesics and haircare markets.

PROSPECTS: Price competition and slow revenue growth for Bristol-Myers, and the industry as a whole, will continue to pressure earnings. However, revenues will benefit from the FDA approval for Taxol as a last resort treatment of advanced breast cancer. Pravachol, a cholesterol-lowering drug, will also boost near-term sales. The Company plans to reduce its workforce by 5,000 people, or 10%, by 1996. The restructuring will affect the health-care and consumer businesses, headquarters staff, and the pharmaceutical segment's sales and marketing operations.

BUSINESS

BISTOL-MYERS SQUIBB COM-PANY is involved in health, pharmaceutical and medical related areas. Pharmaceutical Products include prescription medicines, cardiovascular drugs and antibiotics, anti-cancer and central nervous systems drugs, diagnostic agents and other pharmaceutical products. Medical Devices include orthopedic implants, ostomy care and wound management products, surgical instruments and other medical devices. Nonprescription Health Products include infant formulas and other nutritional products, analgesics, vitamins, cough/cold remedies and skin care products. Toiletries and Beauty Aids include hair care preperations, haircoloring, and deodorants.

BUSINESS LINE ANALYSIS

(12/31/93)	Rev(%)	Inc(%)
Pharmaceutical Products................	57.2	78.0
Medical Devices........	14.8	(0.9)
Nonprescrip Health Prods.....................	17.2	16.9
Toiletries & Beauty Aids....................	10.8	6.0
Total	100.0	100.0

ANNUAL EARNINGS AND DIVIDENDS PER SHARE

	1993	1992	1991	1990	1989	1988	1987
Earnings Per Share	3.80 ①	②2.97	3.95	3.33	1.43	2.88	2.47
Dividends Per Share	2.88	2.76	2.40	2.12	2.00	1.68	③1.40
Dividend Payout %	75.8	92.9	60.8	63.7	N.M.	58.3	56.7

① Before disc. oper. ② Before acctg. chg. ③ 2-for-1 stk. split, 6/87.

ANNUAL FINANCIAL DATA

RECORD OF EARNINGS (IN MILLIONS):

	1993	1992	1991	1990	1989	1988	1987
Total Revenues	11,413.0	11,156.0	11,159.0	10,300.0	9,189.0	5,973.0	5,401.0
Costs and Expenses	8,702.0	8,901.0	8,147.0	7,667.0	7,910.0	4,656.0	4,288.0
Depreciation & Amort	308.0	295.0	246.0	244.0	196.0	128.0	116.0
Operating Profit	4,031.0	3,933.0	3,759.0	3,270.0	2,727.0	1,583.0	1,339.0
Earn Bef Income Taxes	2,571.0	1,987.0	2,887.0	2,524.0	1,277.0	1,285.0	1,118.0
Income Taxes	612.0	449.0	831.0	776.0	530.0	456.0	408.0
Net Income	1,959.0	①1,538.0	2,056.0	1,748.0	747.0	829.0	710.0
Aver. Shs. Outstg. (000)	515,000	518,000	521,000	525,000	523,000	288,000	288,000

① Before disc. op. cr$670,000,000; and acctg. chg dr$246,000,000.

BALANCE SHEET (IN MILLIONS):

	1993	1992	1991	1990	1989	1988	1987
Cash and Cash Equivalents	2,729.0	2,385.0	1,583.0	1,958.0	2,282.0	1,710.0	1,578.0
Receivables, Net	1,859.0	1,984.0	1,971.0	1,776.0	1,578.0	946.0	866.0
Inventories	1,322.0	1,490.0	1,451.0	1,366.0	1,139.0	689.0	618.0
Gross Property	5,236.0	5,032.0	4,718.0	4,271.0	3,804.0	2,077.0	1,880.0
Accumulated Depreciation	1,862.0	1,891.0	1,782.0	1,640.0	1,454.0	828.0	738.0
Long-Term Debt	588.0	176.0	135.0	231.0	237.0	215.0	210.0
Net Stockholders' Equity	5,940.0	6,020.0	5,795.0	5,418.0	5,084.0	3,547.0	3,229.0
Total Assets	12,101.0	10,804.0	9,416.0	9,215.0	8,497.0	5,190.0	4,732.0
Total Current Assets	6,570.0	6,621.0	5,567.0	5,670.0	5,552.0	3,566.0	3,264.0
Total Current Liabilities	3,065.0	3,300.0	2,752.0	2,821.0	2,659.0	1,164.0	1,099.0
Net Working Capital	3,505.0	3,321.0	2,815.0	2,849.0	2,893.0	2,402.0	2,165.0
Year End Shs Outstg (000)	512,000	518,000	520,000	524,000	525,000	288,000	288,000

STATISTICAL RECORD:

	1993	1992	1991	1990	1989	1988	1987
Operating Profit Margin %	21.1	17.6	24.8	23.2	11.8	19.9	18.5
Book Value Per Share	11.23	11.33	10.82	9.97	9.26	11.62	10.58
Return on Equity %	33.0	25.5	35.5	32.3	14.7	23.4	22.0
Return on Assets %	16.2	14.2	21.8	19.0	8.8	16.0	15.0
Average Yield %	4.9	3.7	3.2	3.6	3.9	4.0	3.3
P/E Ratio	17.7-13.4	30.3-20.2	22.6-15.5	20.4-15.2	40.6-30.8	16.1-13.2	22.6-11.4
Price Range	67¼-50⅞	90⅛-60	89⅜-61⅛	68-50½		58-44	46½-38⅛	55¾-28¼

Statistics are as originally reported.

OFFICERS:
R.L. Gelb, Chairman
C.A. Heimbold, Pres. & C.E.O.
M.E. Autera, Exec. V.P. & C.F.O.
H.M. Bains, Jr., V.P. & Treas.
INCORPORATED: DE, Aug., 1933
PRINCIPAL OFFICE: 345 Park Ave., New York, NY 10154

TELEPHONE NUMBER: (212) 546-4000
NO. OF EMPLOYEES: 6,732
ANNUAL MEETING: In May
SHAREHOLDERS: 109,185 common
INSTITUTIONAL HOLDINGS:
No. of Institutions: 1,155
Shares Held: 257,830,483

REGISTRAR(S): Manufacturers Hanover Trust Co., New York, NY
Manufacturers Hanover Trust Co. of CA, Los Angeles, CA
TRANSFER AGENT(S): Manufacturers Hanover Trust Co., New York. NY
Manufacturers Hanover Trust Co. of CA, Los Angeles, CA

NYS SYMBOL BU
Rec. Pr. 22¼

BROOKLYN UNION GAS CO.

YIELD 6.1%
P/E RATIO 12.9

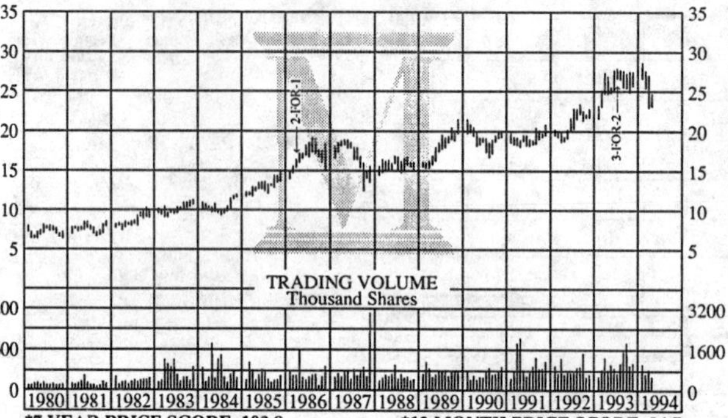

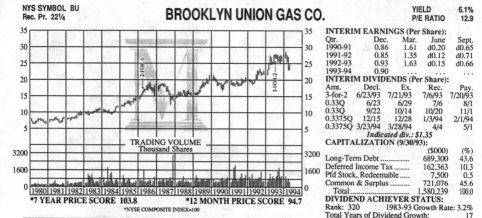

***7 YEAR PRICE SCORE 103.8** ***12 MONTH PRICE SCORE 94.7**

*NYSE COMPOSITE INDEX=100

INTERIM EARNINGS (Per Share):

Qtr.	Dec.	Mar.	June	Sept.
1990-91	0.86	1.61	d0.20	d0.65
1991-92	0.85	1.35	d0.12	d0.71
1992-93	0.93	1.63	d0.15	d0.66
1993-94	0.90	...	...	...

INTERIM DIVIDENDS (Per Share):

Amt.	Decl.	Ex.	Rec.	Pay.
3-for-2	6/23/93	7/21/93	7/6/93	7/20/93
0.33Q	6/23	6/29	7/6	8/1
0.33Q	9/22	10/14	10/20	11/1
0.3375Q	12/15	12/28	1/3/94	2/1/94
0.3375Q	3/23/94	3/28/94	4/4	5/1

Indicated div.: $1.35

CAPITALIZATION (9/30/93):

	($000)	(%)
Long-Term Debt	689,300	43.6
Deferred Income Tax	162,363	10.3
Pfd Stock, Redeemable	7,500	0.5
Common & Surplus	721,076	45.6
Total	1,580,239	100.0

DIVIDEND ACHIEVER STATUS:

Rank: 320 1983-93 Growth Rate: 3.2%

Total Years of Dividend Growth: 17

RECENT DEVELOPMENTS: For the quarter ended 12/31/93, net income advanced 4% to $42.2 million from $40.5 million last year. Revenues were $371.5 million, up 6.6%. Total gas throughput from utility operations was up 6.5% to 48,641 MDTH. For the twelve-month period ended 12/31/93, net income was $78.2 million compared with $63.5 million in the prior year. Revenues were up 10% to $1.23 billion.

PROSPECTS: BU will pursue strategies for growth by marketing technologies for air conditioning, cogeneration, fuel cells, and natural gas powered vehicles. BU subsidiary, Fuel Resources Inc., completed the acquisition of 12 billion cubic feet of proved gas reserves in east Texas. Gas Energy Cogeneration Inc. has interest in a 100-megawatt plant under construction at J.F.K. Airport and a 40-megawatt project planned in Long Island. The Company has essentially completed its exit from the propane business.

BUSINESS

BROOKLYN UNION GAS COMPANY is a natural gas distribution company with diversified businesses in gas exploration and production gas-cogeneration projects. BU distributes natural gas in New York City's boroughs of Brooklyn, Queens and Staten Island with a service area covering 187 square miles and containing 1,117,000 accounts. Gas exploration, production and interstate marketing are conducted through Fuel Resources Inc., a wholly owned subsidiary. This segment, through subsidiaries, owns gas-lease interests in the Gulf of Mexico and has gas properties in West Virginia. The Company is also involved in gas cogeneration projects and equipment sales.

QUARTERLY DATA

(9/30/93)($000)	Rev	Inc
1st Quarter	347,283	40,434
2nd Quarter	489,367	71,737
3rd Quarter	208,531	(6,744)
4th Quarter	160,323	(29,228)

ANNUAL EARNINGS AND DIVIDENDS PER SHARE

	9/30/93	9/30/92	9/30/91	9/30/90	9/30/89	9/30/88	9/30/87
Earnings Per Share	**1.73**	**1.35**	**1.45**	**1.43**	**1.68**	**1.66**	**1.62**
Dividends Per Share	**[1] 1.65**	**1.293**	**1.267**	**1.227**	**1.187**	**1.147**	**1.107**
Dividend Payout %	**95.4**	**96.0**	**87.2**	**86.0**	**70.6**	**69.1**	**68.3**

[1] 3-for-2 stk split,07/21/93

ANNUAL FINANCIAL DATA

	9/30/93	9/30/92	9/30/91	9/30/90	9/30/89	9/30/88	9/30/87
RECORD OF EARNINGS (IN MILLIONS):							
Total Revenues	1,205.5	1,074.9	990.5	993.9	969.2	898.7	924.1
Maintenance	54.7	53.0	51.8	50.4	57.7	56.8	54.0
Prov for Fed Inc Taxes	42.4	30.8	26.7	19.0	26.4	26.4	36.3
Operating Income	123.1	98.4	95.5	93.3	98.0	90.0	88.1
Interest Expense	48.1	42.1	40.5	45.1	41.7	38.4	35.2
Net Income	76.6	59.9	61.8	56.4	64.3	61.7	59.1
Aver. Shs. Outstg. (000)	44,042	42,883	39,894	36,798	35,790	34,687	33,590
BALANCE SHEET (IN MILLIONS):							
Gross Plant	1,729.2	1,614.6	1,504.1	1,381.5	1,282.5	1,211.0	1,088.2
Accumulated Depreciation	423.7	385.9	352.8	318.8	293.1	314.5	285.4
Net Property	1,305.5	1,228.7	1,151.3	1,062.7	989.4	896.5	802.9
Long-term Debt	689.3	682.0	685.4	534.1	553.2	445.0	378.1
Net Stockholders' Equity	728.6	640.1	652.0	555.9	531.1	497.9	467.8
Total Assets	1,897.8	1,748.0	1,717.5	1,460.7	1,445.7	1,257.3	1,129.4
Year End Shs Outstg (000)	46,380	43,452	42,280	37,305	36,290	35,226	34,080
STATISTICAL RECORD:							
Book Value Per Share	15.55	14.55	14.37	13.68	13.36	12.77	12.19
Op. Inc/Net Pl %	9.4	8.0	8.3	8.8	9.9	10.0	11.0
Dep/Gr. Pl %	3.7	4.6	2.8	2.8	2.8	2.7	2.7
Accum. Dep/Gr. Pl %	24.5	23.9	23.5	23.1	22.9	26.0	26.2
Return on Equity %	10.6	9.5	10.2	11.1	13.3	13.7	14.2
Average Yield %	6.7	6.1	6.5	6.4	6.4	7.3	7.1
P/E Ratio	16.1-12.5	17.4-13.8	14.4-12.4	15.0-11.6	12.8-9.2	10.2-8.7	11.7-7.6
Price Range	27⅞-21⅝	23½-18⅝	20⅞-18	21½-16⅝	21½-15⅜	16⅞-14⅜	19-12⅜

Statistics are as originally reported.

OFFICERS:
R.B. Catell, Pres. & C.E.O.
V.D. Enright, Sr. V.P. & C.F.O.
R.R. Wieczorek, V.P. & Treas.

INCORPORATED: NY, Sep., 1895

PRINCIPAL OFFICE: One MetroTech Center, Brooklyn, NY 11201-3850

TELEPHONE NUMBER: (718) 403-2000
FAX: (718) 852-8221
NO. OF EMPLOYEES: 3,711
ANNUAL MEETING: First Thurs. in February
SHAREHOLDERS: 30,925
INSTITUTIONAL HOLDINGS:
No. of Institutions: 149
Shares Held: 11,903,077

REGISTRAR(S): First Chicago Trust Co. of New York, New York, NY 10008

TRANSFER AGENT(S): First Chicago Trust Co. of New York, New York, NY 10008

NASDAQ SYMBOL BRNO
Rec. Pr. $7\frac{5}{8}$ (Marginable)

BRUNO'S, INC.

YIELD 3.1%
P/E RATIO 31.8

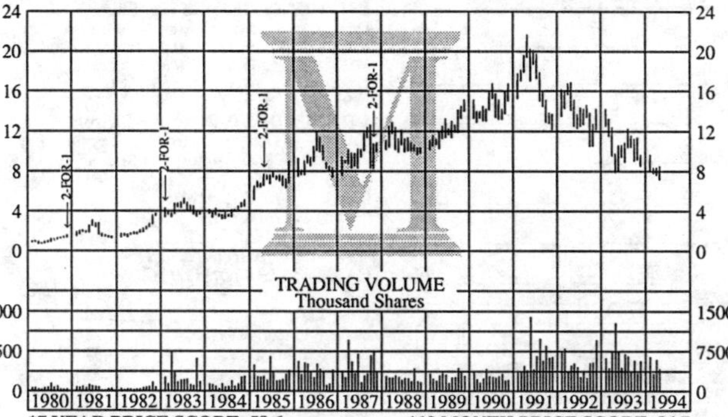

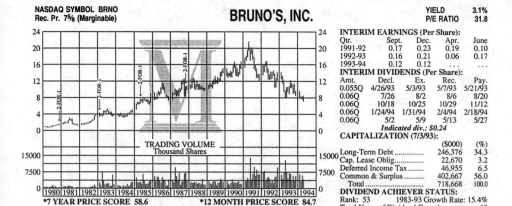

***7 YEAR PRICE SCORE 58.6** ***12 MONTH PRICE SCORE 84.7**
*NYSE COMPOSITE INDEX=100

INTERIM EARNINGS (Per Share):

Qtr.	Sept.	Dec.	Apr.	June
1991-92	0.17	0.23	0.19	0.10
1992-93	0.16	0.21	0.06	0.17
1993-94	0.12	0.12	...	...

INTERIM DIVIDENDS (Per Share):

Amt.	Decl.	Ex.	Rec.	Pay.
0.055Q	4/26/93	5/3/93	5/7/93	5/21/93
0.06Q	7/26	8/2	8/6	8/20
0.06Q	10/18	10/25	10/29	11/12
0.06Q	1/24/94	1/31/94	2/4/94	2/18/94
0.06Q	5/2	5/9	5/13	5/27

Indicated div.: $0.24

CAPITALIZATION (7/3/93):

	($000)	(%)
Long-Term Debt	246,376	34.3
Cap. Lease Oblig.............	22,670	3.2
Deferred Income Tax	46,955	6.5
Common & Surplus	402,667	56.0
Total	718,668	100.0

DIVIDEND ACHIEVER STATUS:
Rank: 53 1983-93 Growth Rate: 15.4%
Total Years of Dividend Growth: 19

RECENT DEVELOPMENTS: For the fourteen weeks ended 1/1/94, net sales increased 2.9% to $768.2 million from $746.9 million for the same period last year. Same store sales declined 0.3% in the quarter, improving from a decline of 2% in the first fiscal quarter. Net income for the quarter was $9.3 million, a 43.7% decrease from $16.6 million for the year-ago quarter. Although sales improved during the quarter, the increase did not offset higher costs associated with BRNO's newer stores, a recent emphasis on customer service, and other promotional expenses. BRNO has reduced its budget for new stores, opting to direct efforts toward remodeling and expanding existing units with the intent of improving overall financial results. During the first six months, BRNO opened five new stores, and the Company plans to open six additional stores by the end of fiscal 1994.

BUSINESS

BRUNO'S INCORPORATED is a leading regional supermarket retailer operating in the southeastern United States. Bruno's operates a total of 257 supermarkets and combination food and drug stores of which 124 are located in Alabama, 91 in Georgia, 17 in Florida, 7 in Mississippi, 9 in Tennessee and 9 in South Carolina. Bruno's attempts to achieve a high sales volume by offering a wide variety of nationally-advertised brands at prices equal to or below those of competing stores. Bruno's also operates seven liquor stores in Florida which are adjacent to supermarkets operated by Bruno's. The Company operates conventional, discount and warehouse supermarkets and combination food and drug stores of various sizes, primarily under five separate store formats. Bruno's 81 Food World supermarkets offer a wide selection of brand-name merchandise in a modern format that includes expanded specialty departments. Bruno's 30 Food Fair supermarkets are designed to operate with a lower overhead and competitive pricing in areas that will not support the volume necessary for a larger supermarket. Bruno's 51 Food Max stores are large "superwarehouse" stores emphasizing an open warehouse appearance with modern decor. Bruno's 14 Bruno's Food and Pharmacy stores are located in markets with suburban shoppers who appreciate "one-stop shopping" and a wide variety of merchandise. Bruno's 57 Piggly Wiggly stores are conventional supermarkets.

ANNUAL EARNINGS AND DIVIDENDS PER SHARE

	7/3/93	6/27/92	6/29/91	6/30/90	7/1/89	7/2/88	6/27/87
Earnings Per Share	**0.60**	**[1] 0.69**	**0.82**	**[2] 0.74**	**[3] 0.59**	**[2] 0.53**	**0.39**
Dividends Per Share	**0.23**	**0.21**	**0.19**	**0.16**	**0.13**	**[4] 0.10**	**0.095**
Dividend Payout %	**38.3**	**30.4**	**23.2**	**21.6**	**22.0**	**18.9**	**24.4**

[1] Before disc. oper. [2] Before extraord. item [3] Before extraord. item & acctg. chg. [4] 2-for-1 stk split, 11/87

ANNUAL FINANCIAL DATA

RECORD OF EARNINGS (IN MILLIONS):							
Total Revenues	2,872.3	2,657.8	2,618.2	2,394.8	2,134.1	1,982.3	1,143.2
Costs and Expenses	2,732.4	2,507.3	2,460.3	2,249.3	2,008.3	1,867.0	1,070.4
Depreciation & Amort	48.7	44.3	41.7	36.4	32.4	29.1	14.0
Operating Income	91.2	106.3	116.2	109.2	93.4	86.1	58.8
Income Bef Income Taxes	73.4	87.1	105.2	95.9	75.2	67.1	57.7
Income Taxes	26.5	30.8	38.5	35.8	27.4	24.4	26.7
Net Income	46.9	[1] 56.4	66.7	[2] 60.1	[3] 47.8	[4] 42.8	31.0
Aver. Shs. Outstg. (000)	78,717	81,874	81,661	81,580	81,529	81,447	78,998

[1] Before disc. op. dr$12,950,000. [2] Before extra. item dr$2,039,000. [3] Before extra. item dr$1,151,000; and acctg. chg cr$3,577,000. [4] Before extra. item dr$2,019,000.

BALANCE SHEET (IN MILLIONS):							
Cash & Cash Equivalents	20.1	19.5	15.7	40.9	23.3	34.9	18.7
Receivables, Net	26.7	39.5	38.4	23.8	23.5	12.1	6.6
Inventories	259.2	236.7	214.8	203.8	182.6	151.4	80.7
Gross Property	738.4	633.2	565.4	487.3	428.6	378.9	232.8
Accumulated Depreciation	194.5	165.4	134.2	109.3	85.7	64.7	50.7
Long-Term Debt	246.4	148.0	150.2	152.7	102.8	124.8	5.3
Capized Lease Obligations	22.7	24.2	25.5	27.4	29.0	30.5	7.2
Net Stockholders' Equity	402.7	422.4	390.2	337.1	290.7	249.7	201.3
Total Assets	916.9	834.7	773.2	728.1	660.7	591.8	300.8
Total Current Assets	313.9	303.2	277.8	276.5	237.3	204.2	111.8
Total Current Liabilities	196.4	192.2	156.2	158.4	187.5	140.0	68.7
Net Working Capital	117.5	111.0	121.5	118.2	49.8	64.1	43.1
Year End Shs Outstg (000)	78,047	81,890	81,768	81,589	81,553	81,491	78,922

STATISTICAL RECORD:							
Operating Profit Margin %	3.2	4.0	4.4	4.6	4.4	4.3	5.1
Book Value Per Share	4.60	4.61	4.19	3.52	2.92	2.39	2.55
Return on Equity %	11.6	13.3	17.1	17.8	16.4	17.1	15.4
Return on Assets %	5.1	6.8	8.6	8.3	7.2	7.2	10.3
Average Yield %	2.1	1.5	1.1	1.1	1.0	0.9	0.9
P/E Ratio	23.8-13.1	24.5-15.2	26.4-14.8	22.6-17.4	25.6-17.2	24.3-18.2	30.8-18.3
Price Range	$14\frac{1}{4}$-$7\frac{7}{8}$	$16\frac{7}{8}$-$10\frac{1}{2}$	$21\frac{5}{8}$-$12\frac{1}{8}$	$16\frac{3}{4}$-$12\frac{7}{8}$	$15\frac{1}{8}$-$10\frac{1}{8}$	$12\frac{7}{8}$-$9\frac{5}{8}$	$12\frac{5}{8}$-$7\frac{1}{2}$

Statistics are as originally reported.

OFFICERS:
R.G. Bruno, Chmn., Pres. & C.E.O.
G.J. Griffin, Exec. V.P. & C.F.O.
R.M. Conley, Sec. & Corp. Couns.

INCORPORATED: AL, Apr., 1959

PRINCIPAL OFFICE: 800 Lakeshore Parkway, Birmingham, AL 35211

TELEPHONE NUMBER: (205) 940-9400

NO. OF EMPLOYEES: 1,441 full-time; 15892 part-time (approx.)

ANNUAL MEETING: In October

SHAREHOLDERS: 5,730 (approx.)

INSTITUTIONAL HOLDINGS:
No. of Institutions: 162
Shares Held: 20,723,724

REGISTRAR(S):

TRANSFER AGENT(S): AmSouth Bank, N.A., Birmingham, AL 35202

CALIFORNIA WATER SERVICE CO.

NYS SYMBOL CWT
Rec. Pr. 35⅝

YIELD 5.6%
P/E RATIO 13.2

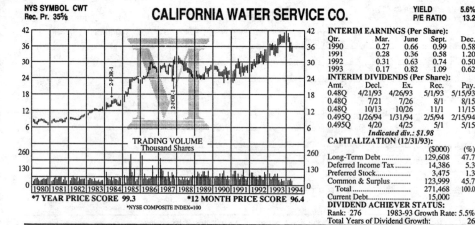

*7 YEAR PRICE SCORE 99.3   *12 MONTH PRICE SCORE 96.4
*NYSE COMPOSITE INDEX=100

INTERIM EARNINGS (Per Share):

Qtr.	Mar.	June	Sept.	Dec.
1990	0.27	0.66	0.99	0.58
1991	0.28	0.36	0.58	1.20
1992	0.31	0.63	0.74	0.50
1993	0.17	0.82	1.09	0.62

INTERIM DIVIDENDS (Per Share):

Amt.	Decl.	Ex.	Rec.	Pay.
0.48Q	4/21/93	4/26/93	5/1/93	5/15/93
0.48Q	7/21	7/26	8/1	8/15
0.48Q	10/13	10/26	11/1	11/15
0.495Q	1/26/94	1/31/94	2/5/94	2/15/94
0.495Q	4/20	4/25	5/1	5/15

Indicated div.: $1.98

CAPITALIZATION (12/31/93):

	($000)	(%)
Long-Term Debt	129,608	47.7
Deferred Income Tax	14,386	5.3
Preferred Stock	3,475	1.3
Common & Surplus	123,999	45.7
Total	271,468	100.0
Current Debt	15,000	

DIVIDEND ACHIEVER STATUS:
Rank: 276   1983-93 Growth Rate: 5.5%
Total Years of Dividend Growth: 26

RECENT DEVELOPMENTS: For the year ended 12/31/93, operating revenue improved 8.5% to $151.7 million from $139.8 million in 1992. Operating income for the year was up 17.2% to $27.9 million from $23.8 million a year ago. Net income rose 23.7% to $15.5 million, or $2.70 per share, from $12.5 million, or $2.18 per share, in 1992. For the quarter, operating revenue increased 8.3% to $35.9 million from $33.2 million for the same period last year. Operating income for the quarter-was up 17.3% to $6.6 million from $5.6 million for the year-ago quarter. Net income rose 25.6% to $3.6 million, or $0.62 per share from $2.9 million, or $0.50 per share, for the same quarter last year. On 1/26/94, CWTR announced that it had applied for listing on the New York Stock Exchange.

BUSINESS

CALIFORNIA WATER SERVICE COMPANY is a public utility water company that owns and operates 21 water systems serving 38 cities and communities and adjacent territories in California with an estimated population of more than 1,400,000. The sole business of the Company consists of the production, purchase, storage, purification, distribution and sale of water for domestic, industrial, public, and irrigation uses, and for fire protection. The Company has 360,700 customers located in Atherton, Bakersfield, Bear Gulch, Broadmoor, Chico, Colma, Commerce, Dixon, East Los Angeles, Hamilton City, Hermosa Beach, King City, Livermore, Los Altos, Marysville, Menlo Park, Oroville, Palos Verdes, Palos Verdes Estates, Portola Valley, Rancho Palos Verdes, Redondo Beach, Rolling Hills Estates, Rolling Hills, Salinas, San Carlos, San Mateo, Selma, South San Francisco, Stockton, Visalia, Westlake, Willows, and Woodside and portions of Cupertino, Los Altos Hills, Montebello, Mountainview, Sunnyvale, Thousand Oaks, and Torrance.

ANNUAL EARNINGS AND DIVIDENDS PER SHARE

	1993	1992	1991	1990	1989	1988	1987
Earnings Per Share	2.70	2.18	2.42	2.50	2.40	2.45	② 2.64
Dividends Per Share	1.92	1.86	1.80	1.74	1.68	1.60	② 1.48
Dividend Payout %	71.1	85.3	74.4	69.6	70.0	65.3	56.1

① Before acctg. chg. ② 2-for-1 stk split, 10/87

ANNUAL FINANCIAL DATA

RECORD OF EARNINGS (IN THOUSANDS):

	1993	1992	1991	1990	1989	1988	1987
Operating Revenue	151,716	139,805	127,176	124,387	117,488	113,755	112,776
Depreciation	10,304	9,412	8,795	8,222	7,841	7,357	6,900
Maintenance	7,250	6,965	7,175	6,998	7,042	6,135	5,688
Net Operating Income	27,855	23,774	24,321	23,370	22,338	22,490	22,990
Total Interest Expense	12,627	11,414	10,777	9,657	9,236	8,634	8,285
Net Income	15,501	12,529	13,928	14,366	13,772	14,074	① 15,001
Aver. Shs. Outstg.	5,689	5,689	5,689	5,689	5,684	5,654	5,551

① Before acctg. change cr$2,196,000.

BALANCE SHEET (IN THOUSANDS):

	1993	1992	1991	1990	1989	1988	1987
Gross Plant	533,213	507,151	474,370	442,017	417,573	393,086	367,412
Accumulated Depreciation	141,510	132,538	124,433	116,608	109,771	103,723	96,404
Net Utility Plant	391,703	374,613	349,937	325,409	307,802	289,363	271,008
First Mortgage Bonds	129,608	122,069	103,505	104,905	86,012	86,959	73,930
Net Stockholders' Equity	127,474	123,049	121,254	117,719	113,404	108,910	104,300
Total Assets	446,619	403,448	393,609	369,055	339,348	313,561	290,963
Year End Shares Outstg	5,689	5,689	5,689	5,689	5,689	5,672	5,566

STATISTICAL RECORD:

	1993	1992	1991	1990	1989	1988	1987
Book Value Per Share	21.80	21.02	20.70	20.08	19.32	18.59	17.70
Op. Inc/Net PI %	7.1	6.3	7.0	7.2	7.3	7.8	8.5
Dep/Gr. Pl %	1.9	1.9	1.9	1.9	1.9	1.9	1.9
Accum. Dep/Gr. Pl %	26.5	26.1	26.2	26.4	26.3	26.4	26.2
Return on Equity %	12.2	10.2	11.5	12.2	12.1	12.9	14.7
Average Yield %	5.2	6.1	6.7	6.9	6.4	5.7	5.4
P/E Ratio	15.3-11.9	16.1-12.0	12.9-9.2	11.4-8.9	12.0-9.8	13.2-9.8	12.1-8.6
Price Range	41¼-32¼	35-26¼	31¼-22¼	28½-22¼	28¾-23½	32¼-24	32-22¾

Statistics are as originally reported.

OFFICERS:

C.H. Stump, Chairman
D.L. Houck, Pres. & C.E.O.
H.C. Ulrich, V.P., C.F.O. & Treas.
H.M. Kasley, Sec. & Legal Counsel

INCORPORATED: CA, Dec., 1926

PRINCIPAL OFFICE: 1720 North First Street, San Jose, CA 95112

TELEPHONE NUMBER: (408) 451-8200
FAX: (408) 437-9185
NO. OF EMPLOYEES: 614
ANNUAL MEETING: In April
SHAREHOLDERS: 4,497 com.; 344 pfd.
INSTITUTIONAL HOLDINGS:
No. of Institutions: 31
Shares Held: 530,424

REGISTRAR(S): First National Bank of Boston, Shareholder Services Division, Boston, MA

TRANSFER AGENT(S): First National Bank of Boston, Shareholder Services Division, Boston, MA

CAMPBELL SOUP CO.

YIELD	2.9%
P/E RATIO	34.5

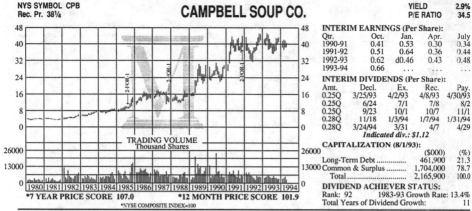

*7 YEAR PRICE SCORE 107.0   *12 MONTH PRICE SCORE 101.9
*NYSE COMPOSITE INDEX=100

TRADING VOLUME Thousand Shares

INTERIM EARNINGS (Per Share):

Qtr.	Oct.	Jan.	Apr.	July
1990-91	0.41	0.53	0.30	0.34
1991-92	0.51	0.64	0.36	0.44
1992-93	0.62	d0.46	0.43	0.48
1993-94	0.66	...	...	...

INTERIM DIVIDENDS (Per Share):

Amt.	Decl.	Ex.	Rec.	Pay.
0.25Q	3/25/93	4/2/93	4/8/93	4/30/93
0.25Q	6/24	7/1	7/8	8/2
0.25Q	9/23	10/1	10/7	11/1
0.28Q	11/18	1/3/94	1/7/94	1/31/94
0.28Q	3/24/94	3/31	4/7	4/29

Indicated div.: $1.12

CAPITALIZATION (8/1/93):

	($000)	(%)
Long-Term Debt	461,900	21.3
Common & Surplus	1,704,000	78.7
Total	2,165,900	100.0

DIVIDEND ACHIEVER STATUS:
Rank: 92   1983-93 Growth Rate: 13.4%
Total Years of Dividend Growth: 11

RECENT DEVELOPMENTS: For the quarter ended 10/31/93, net income was $166 million compared with $152 million last year. Sales increased 4% to $1.76 billion. Prior-year's results were before an accounting change of $249 million. U.S. sales were $1.07 billion, down 3%. Operating earnings were $223 million, down 4%. Biscuit and Bakery posted earnings of $39 million, up 96% from 1992 primarily as a result of the Company's acquiring majority ownership in Amotts in Australia.

PROSPECTS: The Company is launching a series of marketing initiatives, including a new soup advertising campaign, in an effort to increase per-capita consumption. A strategic focus on brand power and cost controls should help profitability. CPB is carefully expanding its private label business in all segments other than soup, cookies, and crackers in order to protect market positions. The International Group should benefit from growing demand in the Pacific Rim.

BUSINESS

CAMPBELL SOUP is a major manufacturer of prepared convenience foods. It is also involved in the fresh foods, refrigerated foods, candy and mail order businesses. Famous brand names include Campbell's, Pepperidge Farm, Swanson, V-8, Franco-American and Mrs. Paul's. Products sold by CPB under these brand names include: canned foods such as ready-to-serve soups, juices, gravies, pasta, meat and vegetables; frozen foods such as dinners, breakfasts and entrees; plus other items including pickles and relishes, various condiments, chocolate, salads and confectionary items. For fiscal year 1993, sales (earnings) were derived: Campbell U.S.A., 69% (98%); Campbell Biscuit and Bakery, 15% (16%); and Campbell International, 16% (d14%).

ANNUAL EARNINGS AND DIVIDENDS PER SHARE

	8/1/93	8/2/92	7/28/91	7/29/90	7/30/89	7/31/88	8/2/87
Earnings Per Share	[1] 1.02	1.95	1.58	0.02	0.05	0.94	0.96
Dividends Per Share	0.72	[2] 0.76	0.71	0.50	0.46	0.42	0.36
Dividend Payout %	70.6	39.0	36.7	N.M.	N.M.	44.9	37.7

[1] Before acctg. chg.   [2] 2-for-1 stk split, 12/24/91

ANNUAL FINANCIAL DATA

RECORD OF EARNINGS (IN MILLIONS):

Total Revenues	6,586.2	6,263.2	6,204.1	6,205.8	5,672.1	4,868.9	4,490.4
Costs and Expenses	5,369.4	5,138.9	5,206.1	5,382.2	4,927.9	4,234.7	3,920.8
Depreciation & Amort	242.2	216.2	208.6	200.9	192.3	170.9	144.6
Operating Income	974.6	908.1	789.4	622.7	551.9	463.3	425.0
Earnings Before Taxes	519.8	799.3	667.4	179.4	106.5	388.6	417.9
Taxes on Earnings	262.6	308.8	265.9	175.0	93.4	147.0	170.6
Net Income	[1] 257.2	490.5	401.5	4.4	13.1	[2] 241.6	247.3
Aver. Shs. Outstg. (000)	251,900	251,700	254,000	259,200	258,600	258,800	259,600

[1] Before acctg. change dr$249,000,000.   [2] Before acctg. change cr$32,500,000.

BALANCE SHEET (IN MILLIONS):

Cash and Cash Equivalents	69.5	117.7	191.7	103.2	147.1	120.8	425.3
Accounts Receivable, Net	646.3	577.1	527.4	624.5	538.0	486.9	338.9
Inventories	804.2	717.9	706.7	819.8	816.0	664.7	623.6
Gross Property	3,584.9	3,209.0	2,921.9	2,734.9	2,543.0	2,539.7	2,355.1
Accumulated Depreciation	1,320.5	1,243.2	1,131.5	1,017.2	1,002.4	1,030.8	1,006.1
Long-Term Debt	461.9	693.3	772.6	805.8	629.2	525.8	380.2
Net Stockholders' Equity	1,704.0	2,027.6	1,793.4	1,691.8	1,778.3	1,895.0	1,736.1
Total Assets	4,897.5	4,353.8	4,149.0	4,115.6	3,932.1	3,609.6	3,090.0
Total Current Assets	1,686.2	1,501.6	1,518.5	1,665.5	1,601.5	1,362.9	1,430.5
Total Current Liabilities	1,850.5	1,299.7	1,278.0	1,298.1	1,232.1	863.3	686.4
Net Working Capital	d164.3	201.9	240.5	367.4	369.4	499.6	744.1
Year End Shs Outstg (000)	251,700	251,168	254,008	258,538	259,158	258,076	260,012

STATISTICAL RECORD:

Operating Profit Margin %	14.8	14.5	12.7	10.0	9.7	9.5	9.5
Book Value Per Share	4.40	6.31	5.35	5.06	5.06	5.42	6.68
Return on Equity %	15.1	24.2	22.4	0.3	0.7	12.7	14.2
Return on Assets %	5.3	11.3	9.7	0.1	0.3	6.7	8.0
Average Yield %	1.8	2.0	2.0	1.9	2.0	2.8	2.5
P/E Ratio	44.5-34.6	23.2-16.2	27.8-17.2	N.M	N.M	19.0-12.9	18.7-12.0
Price Range	45⅜-35¼	45¼-31½	43⅞-27⅛	31-21⅞	30⅜-15¼	17⅝-12	17¾-11⅜

Statistics are as originally reported.

OFFICERS:
D.W. Johnson, Chmn., Pres. & C.E.O.
B. Dorrance, Vice-Chmn.
F.E. Weise, III, Sr. V.P.-Fin. & C.F.O.
B.E. Edgerton, V.P. & Treas.

PRINCIPAL OFFICE: Campbell Place, Camden, NJ 08103-1799

TELEPHONE NUMBER: (609) 342-4800
FAX: (609) 342-3878
NO. OF EMPLOYEES: 6,381
ANNUAL MEETING: In November
SHAREHOLDERS: 29,670 (approx.)
INSTITUTIONAL HOLDINGS:
No. of Institutions: 379
Shares Held: 67,326,896

REGISTRAR(S):

TRANSFER AGENT(S):

CARLISLE COS., INC.

YIELD 2.2%
P/E RATIO 15.4

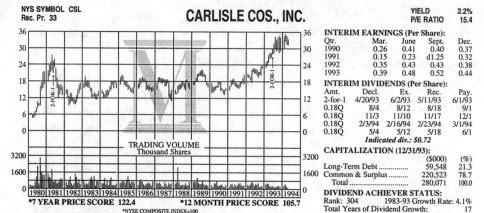

*7 YEAR PRICE SCORE 122.4
*12 MONTH PRICE SCORE 105.7
*NYSE COMPOSITE INDEX=100

INTERIM EARNINGS (Per Share):

Qtr.	Mar.	June	Sept.	Dec.
1990	0.26	0.41	0.40	0.37
1991	0.15	0.23	d1.25	0.32
1992	0.35	0.43	0.43	0.38
1993	0.39	0.48	0.52	0.44

INTERIM DIVIDENDS (Per Share):

Amt.	Decl.	Ex.	Rec.	Pay.
2-for-1	4/20/93	6/2/93	5/11/93	6/1/93
0.18Q	8/4	8/12	8/18	9/1
0.18Q	11/3	11/10	11/17	12/1
0.18Q	2/3/94	2/16/94	2/23/94	3/1/94
0.18Q	5/4	5/12	5/18	6/1

Indicated div.: $0.72

CAPITALIZATION (12/31/93):

	($000)	(%)
Long-Term Debt	59,548	21.3
Common & Surplus	220,523	78.7
Total	280,071	100.0

DIVIDEND ACHIEVER STATUS:
Rank: 304   1983-93 Growth Rate: 4.1%
Total Years of Dividend Growth: 17

RECENT DEVELOPMENTS: For the quarter ended 12/31/93, net income jumped 20% to $6.9 million compared with $5.8 million for the same period in 1992. Sales rose 27% to $151.5 million. Continued improvement in revenues for the Construction Materials segment primarily contributed to higher earnings, as added business from the acquisitions of Versico Inc. and Carlisle Engineered Materials Inc. continued to pay off.

PROSPECTS: Unit sales of custom-molded rubber, plastic products, and heavy-duty brake linings should be boosted by higher production levels in the domestic automotive industry, while growth in the specialty tire division will be driven by increased orders from lawn and tractor markets. Recent acquisitions within the roofing systems business will help to expand its distribution network and its product offerings.

BUSINESS

CARLISLE COMPANY, INC. produces and sells a diverse line of products for industry, primarily of rubber, plastic and metal content. The Construction Materials segment produces elastomeric membranes, adhesives and related products for roofing systems and water barrier applications. Transportation products consist of manufactured rubber and plastic products for the automotive market, brake lining for heavy-duty trucks and off-road vehicles and specialty friction and brakes systems for construction equipment. The General Industry sector produces molded plastic foodservice products and small pneumatic tires.

BUSINESS LINE ANALYSIS

(12/31/93)	Rev(%)	Inc(%)
Construction		
Materials	40.5	45.5
Transportation		
Products	29.0	20.7
General Industry	30.5	33.8
Total	100.0	100.0

ANNUAL EARNINGS AND DIVIDENDS PER SHARE

	1993	1992	1991	1990	1989	1988	1987
Earnings Per Share	1.83	②1.58	②0.43	1.43	1.67	1.08	1.13
Dividends Per Share	①0.68	0.66	0.63	0.61	0.59	0.57	0.56
Dividend Payout %	37.2	41.8	N.M.	42.7	35.3	52.8	49.3

① 2-for-1 stk split, 6/1/93   ② Before disc. oper.

ANNUAL FINANCIAL DATA

RECORD OF EARNINGS (IN THOUSANDS):

	1993	1992	1991	1990	1989	1988	1987
Total Revenues	611,270	528,052	500,771	621,064	553,678	567,386	542,791
Costs and Expenses	541,718	467,985	466,702	560,526	500,907	514,875	483,269
Depreciation & Amort	20,688	18,806	19,427	23,028	21,743	24,392	25,470
Operating Profit	60,029	51,985	43,765	51,204	45,129	51,126	46,938
Earn Bef Income Taxes	46,912	39,720	10,561	36,659	43,538	28,592	31,857
Income Taxes	18,534	15,492	4,007	13,931	16,545	11,208	13,058
Net Income	28,378	②24,228	②6,554	22,728	26,993	17,384	18,799
Aver. Shs. Outstg.	15,478	15,337	15,268	15,906	16,158	16,130	16,710

① Before disc. op. cr$471,000.   ② Before disc. op. dr$14,989,000.

BALANCE SHEET (IN THOUSANDS):

	1993	1992	1991	1990	1989	1988	1987
Cash & Cash Equivalents	51,802	90,605	14,412	17,623	24,081	32,291	...
Receivables, Net	91,158	71,822	75,354	100,095	93,622	...	81,886
Inventories	64,976	49,973	53,380	79,114	67,475	56,495	55,097
Gross Property	318,794	282,996	280,353	296,756	256,108	238,297	248,432
Accumulated Depreciation	176,565	160,945	155,361	173,244	155,255	145,015	144,391
Long-Term Debt	59,548	69,098	48,623	44,501	17,417	21,703	28,111
Net Stockholders' Equity	220,523	204,202	190,088	207,461	208,707	191,031	185,776
Total Assets	420,363	383,528	355,711	373,977	337,855	325,381	308,630
Total Current Assets	236,679	237,226	197,452	212,793	203,019	199,644	164,907
Total Current Liabilities	92,205	75,138	82,134	91,984	86,675	83,427	69,322
Net Working Capital	144,474	162,088	115,318	120,809	116,344	116,217	95,585
Year End Shares Outstg	15,253	15,291	15,254	15,206	16,140	16,106	16,314

STATISTICAL RECORD:

	1993	1992	1991	1990	1989	1988	1987
Operating Profit Margin %	8.0	7.8	2.9	6.0	5.6	5.0	6.3
Book Value Per Share	13.42	12.74	12.34	13.32	12.65	11.62	9.94
Return on Equity %	12.9	11.9	3.4	11.0	12.9	9.1	10.1
Return on Assets %	6.8	6.3	1.8	6.1	8.0	5.3	6.1
Average Yield %	2.4	6.4	7.1	7.7	6.2	7.1	7.3
P/E Ratio	18.9-12.6	15.0-11.2	47.4-34.6	12.7-9.4	13.3-9.6	17.5-12.4	17.3-9.8
Price Range	34½-23⅛	23¾-17⅝	20⅜-14⅞	18⅛-13⅜	22¼-16	18⅞-13⅜	19½-11

Statistics are as originally reported.

OFFICERS:
E.D. Kenna, Chmn.
S.P. Munn, Pres. & C.E.O.
D.J. Hall, Exec. V.P., Treas. & C.F.O.
S.C. Selbach, V.P., Sec. & Gen. Counsel.

INCORPORATED: DE, Sep., 1917; reincorp., DE, May, 1986

PRINCIPAL OFFICE: 101 S. Salina St., Suite 800, Syracuse, NY 13202-1330

TELEPHONE NUMBER: (315) 474-2500
FAX: (315) 474-2008
NO. OF EMPLOYEES: 1,372
ANNUAL MEETING: In April
SHAREHOLDERS: 1,172
INSTITUTIONAL HOLDINGS:
No. of Institutions: 100
Shares Held: 8,412,318

REGISTRAR(S): Harris Trust & Savings Bank, Chicago, IL

TRANSFER AGENT(S): Harris Trust & Savings Bank, Chicago, IL

NASDAQ SYMBOL CCBF
Rec. Pr. 34⅝ (Marginable)

CCB FINANCIAL CORP.

YIELD 3.7%
P/E RATIO 9.9

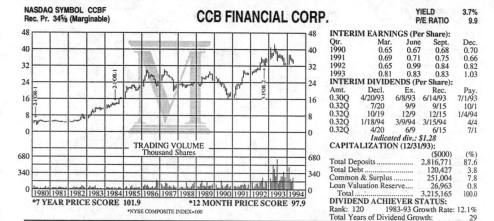

*7 YEAR PRICE SCORE 101.9   *12 MONTH PRICE SCORE 97.9

*NYSE COMPOSITE INDEX=100

INTERIM EARNINGS (Per Share):

Qtr.	Mar.	June	Sept.	Dec.
1990	0.65	0.67	0.68	0.70
1991	0.69	0.71	0.75	0.66
1992	0.65	0.99	0.84	0.82
1993	0.81	0.83	0.83	1.03

INTERIM DIVIDENDS (Per Share):

Amt.	Decl.	Ex.	Rec.	Pay.
0.30Q	4/20/93	6/8/93	6/14/93	7/1/93
0.32Q	7/20	9/9	9/15	10/1
0.32Q	10/19	12/9	12/15	1/4/94
0.32Q	1/18/94	3/9/94	3/15/94	4/4
0.32Q	4/20	6/9	6/15	7/1

Indicated div.: $1.28

CAPITALIZATION (12/31/93):

	($000)	(%)
Total Deposits	2,816,771	87.6
Total Debt	120,427	3.8
Common & Surplus	251,004	7.8
Loan Valuation Reserve	26,963	0.8
Total	3,215,165	100.0

DIVIDEND ACHIEVER STATUS:
Rank: 120   1983-93 Growth Rate: 12.1%
Total Years of Dividend Growth: 29

RECENT DEVELOPMENTS: For the year ended 12/31/93, income, before cumulative effect of changes in accounting principles, was $29.2 million, compared with net income of $25.3 million in 1992, a 15.4% increase. Primary income per share, before cumulative effect of changes in accounting principles, was $3.50, compared with $3.30 in 1992. Total interest income for the year rose 12.3% to $190.7 million from $169.7 million in 1992. For the quarter, net income increased 45.5% to $9.3 million from $6.4 million for the same period last year. Primary income per share was $1.03 per share, compared with $0.82 per share for the year-ago quarter. Total interest income for the quarter was up 29.3% to $54.6 million from $42.3 million for the corresponding 1992 quarter. On 10/15/93, CCBF acquired Citizens Savings, SSB in Lenoir, North Carolina, with total assets at aquisition date of $137 million.

BUSINESS

CCB FINANCIAL CORPORATION is a the bank holding company for Central Carolina Bank and Trust Company, CCB Savings Bank of Lenoir, Inc., SSB, Citizens Savings, SSB and Graham Savings Bank, Inc., SSB. The subsidiary banks conduct a general banking business, offering complete service in the commercial and retail banking, savings and trust fields through 112 offices located primarily in the Piedmont section of North Carolina. The principal activities of the subsidiary banks include the extension of commercial credit and instalment lending, in addition to custodian and safekeeping of securities, safe deposits, night depositories and electronic data processing. CCBF also maintains a complete trust department which provides services including acting as executor and administrator of decedents' estates, trustee of various types of trusts, guardian of estates of minors and incompetents, portfolio managemnt services and investment advice. For corporations, such services include acting as registrar, transfer agent and dividend paying agent for securities, and as trustee for pension and profit-sharing plans. Portfolio management services and investment advice are also available to corporate customers. Non-banking activities engaged through a wholly-owned subsidiary of Republic, Southland Associates Inc., include traditional real estate and insurance sales activities as well as real estate development.

ANNUAL EARNINGS AND DIVIDENDS PER SHARE

	1993	1992	1991	1990	1989	1988	1987
Earnings Per Share	3.50	3.50	2.81	②2.70	②2.78	2.63	③2.27
Dividends Per Share	①1.22	1.515	1.03	0.973	0.92	0.847	0.787
Dividend Payout %	34.9	45.9	36.6	36.0	33.1	32.2	34.7

① 3-for-2 stk split,10/02/92 ② Per primary share ③ Before acctg. chg.

ANNUAL FINANCIAL DATA

RECORD OF EARNINGS (IN MILLIONS):

	1993	1992	1991	1990	1989	1988	1987
Total Interest Income	190.7	169.7	188.2	196.2	188.1	156.8	132.1
Total Interest Expense	73.8	70.6	96.0	110.1	108.6	83.6	64.8
Net Interest Income	116.9	99.1	92.1	86.1	79.5	73.2	67.3
Prov for Loan & Lse Losses	6.5	6.0	7.4	6.3	4.9	3.5	5.1
Net Income	①29.2	25.3	21.5	20.5	21.0	19.7	②17.1
Aver. Shs. Outstg. (000)	8,345	7,664	7,628	7,599	7,559	7,520	7,521

① Before acctg. change dr$1,371,234. ② Before acctg. change cr$1,600,000.

BALANCE SHEET (IN MILLIONS):

Cash & Due From Banks	191.3	129.0	159.6	141.2	140.6	143.0	134.0
US Government Securities	508.8	388.8	297.5	321.7	296.1	238.7	170.0
States & Political Subdiviss	50.3	43.6	55.7	62.8	63.8	59.1	59.4
Net Loans & Lse Financing	2,132.5	1,502.1	1,427.1	1,363.1	1,288.6	1,187.3	1,096.0
Total Domestic Deposits	2,816.8	2,028.5	1,885.6	1,845.1	1,736.3	1,558.5	1,391.0
Long-term Debt	78.7	27.7	25.6	25.7	29.3	30.0	27.0
Net Stockholders' Equity	251.0	189.8	169.8	154.9	141.9	126.8	113.7
Total Assets	3,257.6	2,312.2	2,158.2	2,102.2	1,983.8	1,794.9	1,595.6
Year End Shs Outstg (000)	9,517	7,779	7,640	7,598	7,599	7,523	7,521

STATISTICAL RECORD:

Return on Assets %	0.90	1.10	0.99	0.98	1.06	1.10	1.07
Return on Equity %	11.60	13.30	12.60	13.20	14.80	15.60	15.00
Book Value Per Share	26.37	24.40	22.23	20.38	18.67	16.85	15.12
Average Yield %	3.3	4.7	4.4	4.5	3.6	3.7	3.2
P/E Ratio	12.1-9.3	10.9-8.4	10.6-5.9	10.0-6.0	10.5-8.0	9.1-8.1	13.3-8.6
Price Range	42½-32½	36⅛-27⅞	29⅞-16⅝	26⅞-16⅛	29⅛-22⅛	24-21⅜	30⅛-19⅝

Statistics are as originally reported.

OFFICERS:
W.L. Burns, Jr., Chairman
E.C. Roessler, Pres. & C.E.O.

INCORPORATED: NC, Nov., 1982

PRINCIPAL OFFICE: Central Carolina Bank Building Main and Corcoran Streets P.O. Box 931, Durham, NC 27702

TELEPHONE NUMBER: (919) 683-7777
FAX: (919) 683-7254
NO. OF EMPLOYEES: 1,250
ANNUAL MEETING: In April
SHAREHOLDERS: 4,193
INSTITUTIONAL HOLDINGS:
No. of Institutions: 39
Shares Held: 3,148,024

REGISTRAR(S):

TRANSFER AGENT(S): First Union National Bank of N.C., Charlotte, NC

NASDAQ SYMBOL CFBS
Rec. Pr. 31 (Marginable)

CENTRAL FIDELITY BANKS, INC.

YIELD 3.6%
P/E RATIO 11.7

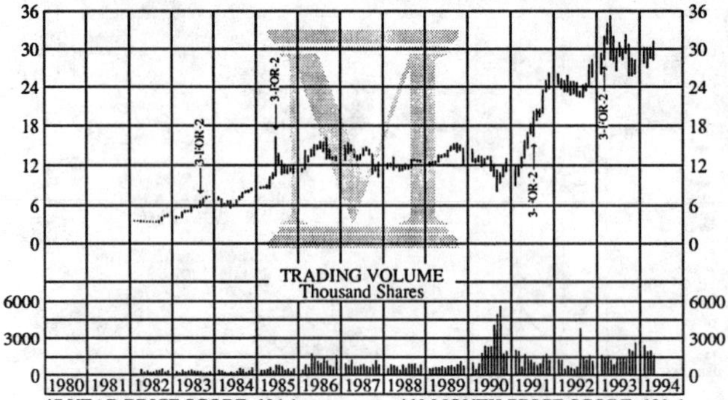

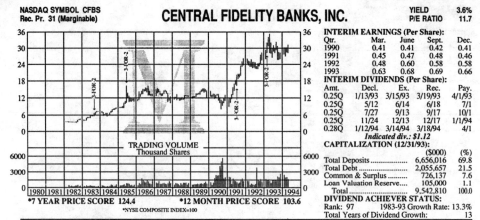

*7 YEAR PRICE SCORE 124.4 *12 MONTH PRICE SCORE 103.6

*NYSE COMPOSITE INDEX=100

INTERIM EARNINGS (Per Share):

Qtr.	Mar.	June	Sept.	Dec.
1990	0.41	0.41	0.42	0.41
1991	0.45	0.47	0.48	0.46
1992	0.48	0.60	0.58	0.58
1993	0.63	0.68	0.69	0.66

INTERIM DIVIDENDS (Per Share):

Amt.	Decl.	Ex.	Rec.	Pay.
0.25Q	1/13/93	3/15/93	3/19/93	4/1/93
0.25Q	5/12	6/14	6/18	7/1
0.25Q	7/27	9/13	9/17	10/1
0.25Q	11/24	12/13	12/17	1/1/94
0.28Q	1/12/94	3/14/94	3/18/94	4/1

Indicated div.: $1.12

CAPITALIZATION (12/31/93):

	($000)	(%)
Total Deposits	6,656,016	69.8
Total Debt	2,055,657	21.5
Common & Surplus	726,137	7.6
Loan Valuation Reserve	105,000	1.1
Total	9,542,810	100.0

DIVIDEND ACHIEVER STATUS:
Rank: 97 1983-93 Growth Rate: 13.3%
Total Years of Dividend Growth: 13

RECENT DEVELOPMENTS: For the year ended 12/31/93, net income increased 31% from $78.5 million for the prior year to $102.9 million. The Company cited steady improvement in the economy and stronger demand for commercial and consumer loans as the primary reasons for results. Interest and fees on loans rose to $359.5 million from $352.0 million in 1992, while income from earning assets increased 6% to $614.0 million. Noninterest income moved up 9% from a year ago to $125.8 million. Credit quality improved as the provision for loan losses was reduced to $79.5 million from $99.8 million. Total loans were up 22% to $4.81 billion with first mortgage real estate, other consumer loans and commercial loans accounting for strong loan volume gains. The net interest margin narrowed to 3.98% from 4.40% in 1992.

BUSINESS

CENTRAL FIDELITY BANKS, INC., with assets of $9.6 billion, is a bank holding company headquartered in Richmond, Virginia. Through its primary subsidiary Central Fidelity Bank and six other bank-related subsidiaries the Company serves only Virginia markets operating 230 branch offices including 29 full-service supermarket locations. CFBS provides a wide variety of financial services including trust and fiduciary services, annuities, private-label mutual funds, insurance and mortgage banking to a broad customer base of individuals, corporations, institutions and governments. Limited international banking services are offered to Virginia-based companies primarily for foreign trade financing.

LOAN DISTRIBUTION

(12/31/93)	($000)	(%)
Commercial & Commercial	1,711,092	35.8
Real Estate Construction	289,199	6.1
Residential Real Estate	1,136,278	23.8
Consumer Second Mortgage	458,294	9.6
Installment	670,487	14.0
Bank Card	509,386	10.7
Total	4,774,736	100.0

ANNUAL EARNINGS AND DIVIDENDS PER SHARE

	1993	1992	1991	1990	1989	1988	1987
Earnings Per Share	**2.66**	**2.25**	**1.87**	**1.65**	**1.57**	**1.42**	**1.34**
Dividends Per Share	**1.06**	**[1] 0.787**	**[2] 0.711**	**0.587**	**0.533**	**0.498**	**0.453**
Dividend Payout %	**39.9**	**35.0**	**38.1**	**35.6**	**34.0**	**35.0**	**33.9**

[1] 3-for-2 stk split,02/23/93 [2] 3-for-2 stk split,07/02/91

ANNUAL FINANCIAL DATA

	1993	1992	1991	1990	1989	1988	1987
RECORD OF EARNINGS (IN MILLIONS):							
Tot Inc Fr Earning Assets	614.0	580.2	560.0	534.3	482.7	400.1	358.3
Total Interest Expense	289.7	285.7	319.4	326.1	286.3	229.9	196.6
Net Interest Income	324.3	294.5	240.6	208.2	196.4	170.2	161.8
Provision for Loan Losses	79.5	99.8	49.8	45.0	17.2	17.1	23.4
Net Income	102.9	78.5	60.4	55.8	54.4	49.5	47.3
Aver. Shs. Outstg. (000)	38,737	34,963	32,396	33,843	34,698	34,844	35,386
BALANCE SHEET (IN MILLIONS):							
Cash & Due From Banks	264.5	280.8	265.7	316.0	244.9	230.7	297.3
US Government Securities	3,193.4	...	...	...	...	...	...
State & Municipal Secur	171.0	...	...	...	...	...	...
Net Loans	4,669.7	3,851.6	3,558.2	3,516.5	3,493.8	3,179.5	2,915.6
Total Domestic Deposits	6,656.0	6,672.5	5,178.0	4,532.8	4,142.3	3,744.5	3,382.4
Long-term Debt	159.9	167.8	22.7	27.0	31.3	36.0	37.7
Net Stockholders' Equity	726.1	603.9	429.4	381.6	378.5	342.9	315.3
Total Assets	9,662.3	8,712.3	6,805.8	6,172.7	5,335.2	4,731.4	4,287.4
Year End Shs Outstg (000)	39,023	38,432	32,716	32,254	34,737	34,711	35,012
STATISTICAL RECORD:							
Return on Assets %	1.07	0.90	0.89	0.90	1.02	1.05	1.10
Return on Equity %	14.20	13.00	14.10	14.60	14.40	14.40	15.00
Book Value Per Share	18.61	15.71	13.13	11.83	10.90	9.88	9.00
Average Yield %	3.5	3.1	4.1	5.2	3.9	4.1	3.6
P/E Ratio	13.3-9.7	12.6-9.9	14.0-4.7	8.8-4.8	9.8-7.6	9.2-7.7	11.5-7.6
Price Range	35¼-25¾	28⅜-22⅜	26⅛-8⅞	14½-8	15⅜-11⅞	13⅛-11	15⅜-10⅛

Statistics are as originally reported.

OFFICERS:
C.L. Saine, Chmn. & Co-C.E.O.
L.N. Miller, Jr., Pres. & Co-C.E.O.
W.F. Shumadine, Jr., President
C.W. Tysinger, Treasurer

INCORPORATED: VA, Dec., 1978

PRINCIPAL OFFICE: 1021 East Cary Street P.O. Box 27602, Richmond, VA 23261

TELEPHONE NUMBER: (804) 782-4000

NO. OF EMPLOYEES: 3,400 (approx.)

ANNUAL MEETING: In May

SHAREHOLDERS: 15,966

INSTITUTIONAL HOLDINGS:
No. of Institutions: 143
Shares Held: 13,252,520

REGISTRAR(S): Central Fidelity Bank, Richmond, VA 23261

TRANSFER AGENT(S): Central Fidelity Bank, Richmond, VA 23261

CENTRAL LOUISIANA ELECTRIC CO., INC.

YIELD 6.1%
P/E RATIO 20.3

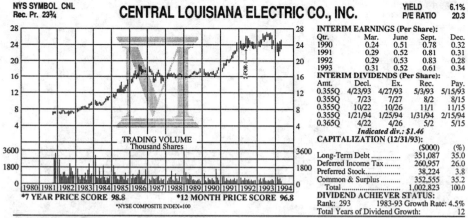

INTERIM EARNINGS (Per Share):

Qtr.	Mar.	June	Sept.	Dec.
1990	0.24	0.51	0.78	0.32
1991	0.29	0.52	0.81	0.31
1992	0.29	0.53	0.83	0.28
1993	0.31	0.52	0.61	0.34

INTERIM DIVIDENDS (Per Share):

Amt.	Decl.	Ex.	Rec.	Pay.
0.355Q	4/23/93	4/27/93	5/3/93	5/15/93
0.355Q	7/23	7/27	8/2	8/15
0.355Q	10/22	10/26	11/1	11/15
0.355Q	1/21/94	1/25/94	1/31/94	2/15/94
0.365Q	4/22	4/26	5/2	5/15

Indicated div.: $1.46

CAPITALIZATION (12/31/93):

	($000)	(%)
Long-Term Debt	351,087	35.0
Deferred Income Tax	260,957	26.0
Preferred Stock	38,224	3.8
Common & Surplus	352,555	35.2
Total	1,002,823	100.0

DIVIDEND ACHIEVER STATUS:
Rank: 293   1983-93 Growth Rate: 4.5%
Total Years of Dividend Growth: 12

RECENT DEVELOPMENTS: For the year ended 12/31/93, net income was $41.8 million compared with $45.2 million last year. Net income includes a net restructuring charge of $6.9 million. The restructuring charge is related to an early retirement and voluntary severance program. Revenues were $382.4 million, up 8.8%. The increase in revenues was primarily due to fuel cost recovery, which has no effect on net income. Favorable weather conditions in 1993 resulted in an 3.5% increase in kilowatthour sales.

PROSPECTS: Results will benefit from lower operating expenses. The Company will eliminate 100 to 150 positions over the next two years, which represents a reduction of about 10% of the workforce. CNL plans to achieve the reduction through attrition, enhanced early retirement and voluntary severance programs that will be offered to eligible employees. CNL is slowing expense growth, reducing capital expenditures and emphasizing business development.

BUSINESS

CENTRAL LOUISIANA ELECTRIC COMPANY renders electric service to approximately 214,000 customers in 62 communities and contiguous rural areas in the State of Louisiana. In November of 1981, CNL was spun off from its holding Company, Celeron. The Company owns or jointly owns four steam electric generating stations, which have an aggregate capacity of 1,686,000 kilowatts. Generating sources are: 54% coal and lignites, 44% natural gas and 2% purchased power.

REVENUES

(12/31/93)	($000)	(%)
Residential	169,876	44.4
Commercial	70,707	18.6
Industrial	84,718	22.2
Other Retail	34,512	9.0
Sales For Resale	4,750	1.2
Transmission	10,877	2.8
Short-Term Sales to other	6,993	1.8
Total	382,433	100.0

ANNUAL EARNINGS AND DIVIDENDS PER SHARE

	1993	1992	1991	1990	1989	1988	1987
Earnings Per Share	1.78	1.93	1.92	1.85	1.78	1.80	1.76
Dividends Per Share	1.41	☐1.37	1.325	1.265	1.205	1.145	1.07
Dividend Payout %	79.2	71.0	69.0	68.4	67.9	63.8	60.8

☐ 2-for-1 stk split, 5/26/92

ANNUAL FINANCIAL DATA

RECORD OF EARNINGS (IN MILLIONS):

	1993	1992	1991	1990	1989	1988	1987
Operating Revenues	382.4	351.6	337.3	334.0	316.5	301.1	304.4
Depreciation	37.3	34.8	34.0	32.9	31.8	30.4	29.8
Maintenance	25.0	26.2	25.8	22.0	21.5	20.0	20.9
Operating Income	64.7	70.4	73.1	73.5	73.6	71.4	72.6
Total Interest Charges	25.8	27.9	30.6	31.7	32.6	30.5	30.7
Net Income	41.8	45.2	44.9	42.5	41.5	43.1	45.0
Aver. Shs. Outstg. (000)	22,350	22,280	22,362	22,494	22,471	22,438	22,378

BALANCE SHEET (IN MILLIONS):

Gross Plant	1,274.8	1,235.6	1,178.3	1,129.3	1,087.8	1,043.7	1,005.5
Accumulated Depreciation	379.8	356.7	327.2	301.0	274.1	246.0	222.6
Total Utility Plant, Net	895.0	879.0	851.0	828.2	813.7	796.7	782.8
Long-term Debt	351.1	310.8	387.4	314.7	255.8	297.6	318.7
Net Stockholders' Equity	390.8	381.5	374.2	337.2	324.3	331.7	322.0
Total Assets	1,161.6	978.2	973.5	921.0	918.6	889.6	860.3
Year End Shs Outstg (000)	22,382	22,306	22,242	22,499	22,482	22,448	22,418

STATISTICAL RECORD:

Book Value Per Share	15.75	15.38	14.84	14.33	13.74	13.12	12.46
Op. Inc/Net Pl %	7.2	8.0	8.6	8.9	9.0	8.9	9.3
Dep/Gr. Pl %	2.9	2.8	2.9	2.9	2.9	2.9	3.0
Accum. Dep/Gr. Pl %	29.8	28.9	27.8	26.7	25.2	23.6	22.1
Return on Equity %	10.9	12.1	12.4	13.2	13.4	13.6	14.7
Average Yield %	5.6	5.6	6.3	7.4	7.2	7.1	6.5
P/E Ratio	15.2-12.9	13.6-11.8	12.8-9.0	9.9-8.5	10.1-8.8	9.4-8.5	10.5-8.1
Price Range	27⅛-23	26¼-22¾	24½-17¼	18¼-15¾	18-15⅝	17-15⅜	18½-14¼

Statistics are as originally reported.

OFFICERS:
G.L. Nesbitt, Pres. & C.E.O.
D.M. Eppler, V.P.-Fin. & Rates & Treas.
V.J. Whittington, Secretary

PRINCIPAL OFFICE: 2030 Donahue Ferry Road, Pineville, LA 71360-5226

TELEPHONE NUMBER: (318) 484-7400
FAX: (318) 484-7465
NO. OF EMPLOYEES: 1,332
ANNUAL MEETING: In April
SHAREHOLDERS: 12,891 (com.)
INSTITUTIONAL HOLDINGS:
No. of Institutions: 119
Shares Held: 8,141,750

REGISTRAR(S):

TRANSFER AGENT(S):

CENTRAL & SOUTH WEST CORP.

YIELD	7.6%
P/E RATIO	13.7

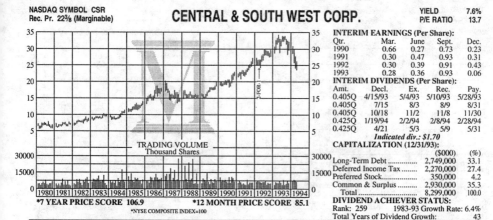

TRADING VOLUME
Thousand Shares

1980|1981|1982|1983|1984|1985|1986|1987|1988|1989|1990|1991|1992|1993|1994

*7 YEAR PRICE SCORE 106.9   ***12 MONTH PRICE SCORE 85.1**

*NYSE COMPOSITE INDEX=100

INTERIM EARNINGS (Per Share):

Qtr.	Mar.	June	Sept.	Dec.
1990	0.66	0.27	0.73	0.23
1991	0.30	0.47	0.93	0.31
1992	0.30	0.39	0.91	0.43
1993	0.28	0.36	0.93	0.06

INTERIM DIVIDENDS (Per Share):

Amt.	Decl.	Ex.	Rec.	Pay.
0.405Q	4/15/93	5/4/93	5/10/93	5/28/93
0.405Q	7/15	8/3	8/9	8/31
0.405Q	10/18	11/2	11/8	11/30
0.425Q	1/19/94	2/2/94	2/8/94	2/28/94
0.425Q	4/21	5/3	5/9	5/31

Indicated div.: $1.70

CAPITALIZATION (12/31/93):

	($000)	(%)
Long-Term Debt	2,749,000	33.1
Deferred Income Tax	2,270,000	27.4
Preferred Stock	350,000	4.2
Common & Surplus	2,930,000	35.3
Total	8,299,000	100.0

DIVIDEND ACHIEVER STATUS:

Rank: 259   1983-93 Growth Rate: 6.4%
Total Years of Dividend Growth: 43

RECENT DEVELOPMENTS: For the year ended 12/31/93, net income fell 19.4% to $308.0 million from $382.0 million last year. Revenues were $3.69 billion, up 12%. The decline in earnings is primarily due to one-time charges associated with organizational restructuring of the Company. Results were also negatively affected by increased operation and maintenance costs primarily associated with the outage at the South Texas Project. This was partially offset by increased kilowatthour sales.

PROSPECTS: The South Texas Project outage continues to negatively impact earnings. The first unit is expected to come back on line in early 1994. The outage has forced CSR to supply customers with electricity from more expensive sources. Central and South West is negotiating to buy El Paso Electric Co., which is currently operating under bankruptcy-court protection. If the buyout is successful, El Paso would be a direct, wholly-owned subsidiary of CSR.

BUSINESS

CENTRAL & SOUTH WEST CORP. is a public utility holding Company with four electric subsidiary companies: Central Power and Light Company, Public Service Company of Oklahoma, Southwestern Electric Power Company and West Texas Utilities Company. These four subsidiaries provide electricity to more than 4 million people in a 152,000 square mile area that encompasses parts of Texas, Oklahoma, Louisiana and Arkansas. CSR also owns five other subsidiaries. Transok, Inc., is an intrastate natural-gas gathering and transmission company. Central and South West Services, Inc., performs financial, engineering and electronic data processing services for the corporation and its subsidiaries. The Company's other three subsidiaries are diversification ventures which include CSW Credit, Inc., Inc., CSW Leasing, Inc. and CSW Energy, Inc.

REVENUES

(12/31/93)	($000)	(%)
Residential	1,160,000	31.5
Commercial	832,000	22.6
Industrial	736,000	19.9
Sales for Resale	179,000	4.9
Other Electric	148,000	4.0
Gas & Other	632,000	17.1
Total	3,687,000	100.0

ANNUAL EARNINGS AND DIVIDENDS PER SHARE

	1993	1992	1991	1990	1989	1988	1987
Earnings Per Share	1.63	2.03	2.00	1.89	1.63	1.72	1.96
Dividends Per Share	1.62	① 1.54	1.46	1.38	1.30	1.22	1.14
Dividend Payout %	99.4	75.9	73.2	72.8	80.0	71.1	58.2

① 2-for-1 stk split, 3/9/92

ANNUAL FINANCIAL DATA

RECORD OF EARNINGS (IN MILLIONS):

Total Revenues	3,687.0	3,289.0	3,047.0	2,744.0	2,549.0	2,512.0	2,436.0
Depreciation & Amort	330.0	308.0	291.0	283.0	277.0	254.0	248.0
Maintenance	197.0	170.0	181.0	164.0	155.0	133.0	124.0
Prov for Fed Inc Taxes	140.0	159.0	182.0	192.0	158.0	122.0	169.0
Operating Income	457.0	591.0	566.0	493.0	492.0	459.0	435.0
Total Interest Charges	269.0	266.0	270.0	322.0	275.0	225.0	181.0
Net Income	① 281.0	404.0	401.0	386.0	337.0	356.0	402.0
Aver. Shs. Outstg. (000)	188,400	188,300	188,300	188,200	188,400	189,200	189,600

① Before acctg. change cr$46,000,000.

BALANCE SHEET (IN MILLIONS):

Gross Plant	11,357.0	11,190.0	10,788.0	10,251.0	9,634.0	9,370.0	8,961.0
Accumulated Depreciation	3,550.0	3,287.0	2,986.0	2,701.0	2,448.0	2,219.0	2,015.0
Utility Plant, Net	7,807.0	7,903.0	7,802.0	7,550.0	7,186.0	7,151.0	6,946.0
Long-term Debt	2,749.0	2,647.0	2,518.0	2,513.0	2,537.0	2,514.0	2,410.0
Net Stockholders' Equity	3,280.0	3,294.0	3,223.0	3,137.0	3,044.0	2,990.0	2,879.0
Total Assets	10,623.0	9,829.0	9,396.0	9,074.0	8,347.0	8,110.0	7,619.0
Year End Shs Outstg (000)	188,405	188,371	188,274	188,204	188,190	188,722	189,624

STATISTICAL RECORD:

Book Value Per Share	15.55	15.54	15.05	14.57	14.07	13.75	13.26
Op. Inc/Net Pl %	5.9	7.5	7.3	6.5	6.8	6.4	6.3
Dep/Gr. Pl %	2.9	2.8	2.7	2.8	2.9	2.7	2.8
Accum. Dep/Gr. Pl %	31.3	29.4	27.7	26.3	25.4	23.7	22.5
Return on Equity %	8.7	12.6	12.8	12.7	11.5	12.3	14.8
Average Yield %	5.2	5.7	6.1	6.7	7.4	7.6	6.8
P/E Ratio	24.6-20.3	14.8-11.9	13.7-10.4	12.2-9.7	12.3-9.1	10.2-8.6	10.3-6.9
Price Range	34¼-28¼	30-24¼	27¼-20⅜	23-18⅜	20⅛-14⅞	17⅜-14¾	20¼-13½

Statistics are as originally reported.

OFFICERS:

E.R. Brooks, Chmn., Pres. & C.E.O.
G.D. Rosilier, Sr. V.P. & C.F.O.
S.J. McDonnell, Treasurer
F.L. Frawley, Corp. Sec. & Sr. Attorney

INCORPORATED: DE, Jul., 1925

PRINCIPAL OFFICE: 1616 Woodall Rodgers Freeway, Dallas, TX 75266-0164

TELEPHONE NUMBER: (214) 777-1000
FAX: (214) 754-1033
NO. OF EMPLOYEES: 8,707
ANNUAL MEETING: Third Thursday in April.
SHAREHOLDERS: 70,000 (approx.)
INSTITUTIONAL HOLDINGS:
No. of Institutions: 473
Shares Held: 86,776,612

REGISTRAR(S): Central & South West Services, Inc., Dallas, TX

TRANSFER AGENT(S): Central & South West Services, Inc., Dallas, TX

CENTURY TELEPHONE ENTERPRISES, INC.

YIELD	1.2%
P/E RATIO	19.5

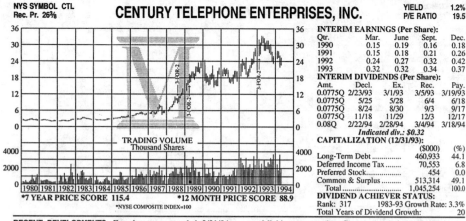

INTERIM EARNINGS (Per Share):

Qtr.	Mar.	June	Sept.	Dec.
1990	0.15	0.19	0.16	0.18
1991	0.15	0.18	0.21	0.26
1992	0.24	0.27	0.32	0.42
1993	0.32	0.32	0.34	0.37

INTERIM DIVIDENDS (Per Share):

Amt.	Decl.	Ex.	Rec.	Pay.
0.0775Q	2/23/93	3/1/93	3/5/93	3/19/93
0.0775Q	5/25	5/28	6/4	6/18
0.0775Q	8/24	8/30	9/3	9/17
0.0775Q	11/18	11/29	12/3	12/17
0.08Q	2/22/94	2/28/94	3/4/94	3/18/94

Indicated div.: $0.32

CAPITALIZATION (12/31/93):

	($000)	(%)
Long-Term Debt	460,933	44.1
Deferred Income Tax	70,553	6.8
Preferred Stock	454	0.0
Common & Surplus	513,314	49.1
Total	1,045,254	100.0

DIVIDEND ACHIEVER STATUS:
Rank: 317   1983-93 Growth Rate: 3.3%
Total Years of Dividend Growth: 20

TRADING VOLUME
Thousand Shares

*7 YEAR PRICE SCORE 115.4   *12 MONTH PRICE SCORE 88.9
*NYSE COMPOSITE INDEX=100

RECENT DEVELOPMENTS: For the quarter ended 3/31/94, consolidated revenues increased 24.9% to $121.0 million. Net income was up 22.0% to $19.2 million from $15.7 million in the first quarter of 1993. During the first quarter, CTL completed the acquisition of Celutel, Inc. Also, CTL completed the acquisition of Kingsley Telephone Co. which serves approximately 2,400 telephone access lines in north-ern Michigan near other Century operations. For the year ended 12/31/93, net income before accounting changes grew 15.1% to $69.0 million from $60.0 million last year. Consolidated revenues increased 20.5% to $433.2 million from $359.6 million in 1992. Telephone revenues increased 17.1% to $348.5 million. Mobile communications revenues jumped 36.4% to $84.7 million.

BUSINESS

CENTURY TELEPHONE ENTERPRISES, INC. is a diversified telecommunications company that provides local telephone, cellular mobile telephone and paging services. Century is one of the twenty largest local exchange telephone companies in the U.S., based on the number of access lines served, and one of the fifteen largest wireline telephone companies operating cellular systems, based on population equivalents. As of 3/31/94, the Company's total number of cellular subscribers in majority owned markets was 160,203.

BUSINESS LINE ANALYSIS

(12/31/93)

	Rev(%)	Inc($000)
Telephone	80.4	114,902
Mobile		
Communications	19.6	9,906
Total	100.0	124,808

ANNUAL EARNINGS AND DIVIDENDS PER SHARE

	1993	1992	1991	1990	1989	1988	1987
Earnings Per Share	1.35	① 1.25	0.80	0.67	0.51	0.58	0.60
Dividends Per Share	0.31	② 0.293	0.287	0.28	③ 0.272	④ 0.264	0.253
Dividend Payout %	23.0	23.4	35.8	41.6	53.7	45.5	42.2

① Before acctg. chg. ② 3-for-2 stk split,01/04/93 ③ 3-for-2 stk split, 3/89 ④ 3-for-2 stock split, 8/88.

ANNUAL FINANCIAL DATA

RECORD OF EARNINGS (IN MILLIONS):

Total Revenues	433.2	356.8	281.0	248.8	213.2	184.0	156.9
Costs and Expenses	231.9	184.2	153.7	140.6	124.9	102.0	77.0
Depreciation & Amort	76.5	62.9	52.2	47.1	41.2	35.6	27.5
Operating Income	124.8	109.6	75.1	61.1	47.2	46.5	52.5
Inc Bef Inc Taxes & Cum Effect Of Acctg Chgs	106.3	92.6	57.5	48.5	32.9	34.4	39.8
Income Taxes	37.3	32.6	20.1	17.4	10.7	11.1	16.5
Net Income	69.0	① 60.0	37.4	31.1	22.2	23.4	23.3
Aver. Shs. Outstg. (000)	51,206	48,500	47,305	46,142	43,451	40,532	39,717

① Before acctg. change dr$15,668,000.

BALANCE SHEET (IN MILLIONS):

Cash and Cash Equivalents	9.8	9.8	11.6	32.6	44.0	16.5	23.7
Receivables, Net	56.2	42.5	44.4	28.0	24.9	18.0	14.6
Inventories	4.4	4.5	3.8	4.0	5.4	5.6	7.1
Gross Property	1,170.4	1,004.4	796.1	734.8	695.8	580.0	528.8
Accumulated Depreciation	342.7	328.5	261.1	243.9	221.7	179.2	148.4
Long-Term Debt	460.9	391.9	254.8	230.7	257.7	180.1	181.6
Net Stockholders' Equity	513.8	385.4	320.0	280.9	256.5	156.1	149.2
Total Assets	1,319.4	1,040.5	764.5	706.4	691.6	497.8	474.8
Total Current Assets	72.5	60.1	61.3	65.9	75.6	40.7	46.0
Total Current Liabilities	179.2	120.7	76.0	83.2	67.9	64.1	56.0
Net Working Capital	d106.7	d60.6	d14.7	d17.3	7.7	d23.5	d10.1
Year End Shs Outstg (000)	51,295	48,897	47,047	46,251	45,782	40,625	39,810

STATISTICAL RECORD:

Book Value Per Share	4.21	3.42	4.36	3.69	3.21	2.96	2.82
Return on Equity %	13.4	15.6	11.7	11.1	8.6	15.3	16.1
Average Yield %	1.1	1.2	1.5	1.4	1.5	2.7	4.0
P/E Ratio	24.7-17.2	23.1-14.7	27.0-19.8	36.4-21.8	47.1-26.2	24.6-10.1	14.0-7.5
Price Range	33⅜-23¼	28⅞-18⅜	21⅝-15⅞	24⅜-14⅝	24-13⅜	14-5¾	8⅛-4⅜

Statistics are as originally reported.

OFFICERS:
C.M. Williams, Chairman
G.F. Post, III, Vice-Chmn., Pres. & C.E.O.
R.S. Ewing, Jr., Sr. V.P. & C.F.O.

INCORPORATED: LA, Apr., 1968

PRINCIPAL OFFICE: 100 Century Park Drive, Monroe, LA 71203

TELEPHONE NUMBER: (318) 388-9500
FAX: (318) 388-9562
NO. OF EMPLOYEES: 2,800 (approx.)
ANNUAL MEETING: In April
SHAREHOLDERS: 5,900 (approx.)
INSTITUTIONAL HOLDINGS:
No. of Institutions: 210
Shares Held: 32,395,775

REGISTRAR(S):

TRANSFER AGENT(S): AmeriTrust Texas, N.A., Dallas, TX 75270

CHEMED CORP.

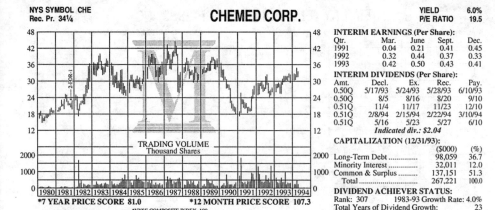

INTERIM EARNINGS (Per Share):

Qtr.	Mar.	June	Sept.	Dec.
1991	0.04	0.21	0.41	0.45
1992	0.32	0.44	0.37	0.33
1993	0.42	0.50	0.43	0.41

INTERIM DIVIDENDS (Per Share):

Amt.	Decl.	Ex.	Rec.	Pay.
0.50Q	5/17/93	5/24/93	5/28/93	6/10/93
0.50Q	8/5	8/16	8/20	9/10
0.51Q	11/4	11/17	11/23	12/10
0.51Q	2/8/94	2/15/94	2/22/94	3/10/94
0.51Q	5/16	5/23	5/27	6/10

Indicated div.: $2.04

CAPITALIZATION (12/31/93):

	($000)	(%)
Long-Term Debt	98,059	36.7
Minority Interest	32,011	12.0
Common & Surplus	137,151	51.3
Total	267,221	100.0

TRADING VOLUME
Thousand Shares

*7 YEAR PRICE SCORE 81.0   ***12 MONTH PRICE SCORE 107.3**
*NYSE COMPOSITE INDEX=100

DIVIDEND ACHIEVER STATUS:
Rank: 307   1983-93 Growth Rate: 4.0%
Total Years of Dividend Growth: 23

RECENT DEVELOPMENTS: For the quarter ended 12/31/93, income from continuing operations totaled $4.0 million, up 27% from the comparable quarter of 1992. Revenues were $137.5 million versus $107.6 million. For the year, income rose 20% to $17.1 million. National Sanitary Supply managed an 8% increase in income to $4.3 million. Roto-Rooter, Inc. reported a 20% increase in income to $8.0 million while Omnicare's income more than doubled to $8.7 million.

PROSPECTS: The acquisition of Patient Care, Inc., a home-healthcare services company, strenghtens CHE's position in a rapidly growing sector of the healthcare business. Omnicare acquired four nursing-home pharmacy operations in 1993; this expansion bodes well for future earnings. The acquisition of The Veratex Group has benefited results and further gains are expected. Roto-Rooter's plumbing and drain-cleaning revenues should move higher.

BUSINESS

CHEMED CORPORATION maintains strategic positions in residential and commercial plumbing and sewer, drain, and pipe-cleaning services; janitorial supply products and services; owned medical and dental supply distribution for the private market; and pharmacy management for the long-term care market. CHE owns 59% of Roto-Rooter Inc., a provider of sewer and drain cleaning and plumbing services; 87% of National Sanitary Supply Co., the largest distributor of sanitary maintenance supplies in the US; 27% of Omnicare, Inc., a long-term pharmacy services affiliate and 100% of The Veratex Group, a medical and dental supply company. The Company acquired Patient Care, Inc., a home-healthcare services provider, in January 1994.

BUSINESS LINE ANALYSIS

(12/31/93)	Rev(%)	Inc(%)
National Sanitary Supply	56.5	31.2
Roto-Rooter	26.0	49.3
Veratex	17.5	19.5
Total	100.0	100.0

ANNUAL EARNINGS AND DIVIDENDS PER SHARE

	1993	1992	1991	1990	1989	1988	1987
Earnings Per Share	1.75	①1.45	①1.10	1.60	2.61	②2.23	2.28
Dividends Per Share	2.10	2.00	1.97	1.96	1.84	1.72	1.60
Dividend Payout %	N.M.	N.M.	N.M.	N.M.	70.5	77.1	70.2

① Before disc. oper. ② Before extraord. item

ANNUAL FINANCIAL DATA

RECORD OF EARNINGS (IN THOUSANDS):

	1993	1992	1991	1990	1989	1988	1987
Total Sales & Service Revs	525,093	400,962	352,282	599,379	591,824	500,647	391,004
Costs and Expenses	493,113	379,434	336,883	555,263	533,888	450,646	341,391
Depreciation & Amort	13,123	9,234	8,101	9,485	8,431	7,048	6,179
Income From Operations	23,163	15,180	9,500	34,631	49,505	42,953	43,434
Income Bef Income Taxes	27,930	22,184	18,022	29,615	43,227	36,406	38,906
Income Taxes	9,278	6,531	5,405	10,361	15,228	13,725	16,705
Equity In Earn Of Affiliate	2,299	1,745	1,179	121	1,116	726	417
Minor Int In Earn Of Subs	3,809	3,147	2,759	2,821	2,933	2,758	2,256
Net Income	①17,142	②14,251	③11,037	16,554	26,182	④20,649	20,362
Aver. Shs. Outstg.	9,778	9,803	10,059	10,371	10,042	9,280	8,939

① Before disc. op. cr$687,000; and acctg. chg cr$1,651,000. ② Before disc. op. cr$1,400,000. ③ Before disc. op. cr$41,930,000. ④ Before disc. op. cr$1,335,000; and extra. item cr$472,000; and acctg. chg cr$1,664,000.

BALANCE SHEET (IN THOUSANDS):

	1993	1992	1991	1990	1989	1988	1987
Cash and Cash Equivalents	15,815	47,704	83,044	1,418	6,545	4,361	4,675
Receivables, Net	63,977	59,576	45,350	81,011	82,696	78,232	64,008
Inventories	54,745	47,581	29,584	55,066	55,216	54,562	37,298
Gross Property	104,710	89,726	67,524	119,573	116,388	105,438	86,721
Accumulated Depreciation	33,952	26,854	23,133	53,577	50,574	44,336	38,176
Long-Term Debt	98,059	103,778	77,928	82,151	85,834	90,405	46,504
Net Stockholders' Equity	137,151	133,511	139,407	112,531	120,774	111,244	113,160
Total Assets	430,253	404,944	364,335	327,545	335,321	322,679	263,765
Total Current Assets	145,214	161,886	163,363	143,852	150,488	143,329	110,388
Total Current Liabilities	127,649	103,957	84,700	94,085	87,980	83,056	68,575
Net Working Capital	17,565	57,929	78,663	49,767	62,508	60,273	41,813
Year End Shares Outstg	9,799	9,759	9,903	10,189	10,262	9,381	8,796

STATISTICAL RECORD:

	1993	1992	1991	1990	1989	1988	1987
Operating Profit Margin %	4.4	3.8	2.7	5.8	8.4	8.6	11.1
Book Value Per Share	2.05	4.46	7.58	5.68	6.30	6.08	7.95
Return on Equity %	12.5	10.7	7.9	14.7	21.7	18.6	18.0
Return on Assets %	4.0	3.5	3.0	5.1	7.8	6.4	7.7
Average Yield %	7.2	7.1	8.7	7.2	5.2	5.1	4.5
P/E Ratio	18.7-14.6	22.3-16.7	25.7-15.7	22.9-11.3	14.8-12.5	17.3-13.2	19.6-11.3
Price Range	32¾-25½	32⅜-24¼	28¼-17¼	36⅝-18	38¾-32½	38½-29½	44⅝-25¾

Statistics are as originally reported.

OFFICERS:
E.L. Hutton, Chmn. & C.E.O.
P.C. Voet, Vice-Chmn. & Exec. V.P.
J.D. Krahulik, Pres. & C.O.O.
INCORPORATED: DE, Apr., 1970
PRINCIPAL OFFICE: 2600 Chemed Center 255 East Fifth Street, Cincinnati, OH 45202-4726

TELEPHONE NUMBER: (513) 762-6900
NO. OF EMPLOYEES: 3,856
ANNUAL MEETING: In May
SHAREHOLDERS: 4,175
INSTITUTIONAL HOLDINGS:
No. of Institutions: 77
Shares Held: 4,513,715

REGISTRAR(S): Mellon Bank, N.A., Pittsburgh, PA

TRANSFER AGENT(S): Mellon Bank, N.A., Pittsburgh, PA

NYS SYMBOL CB
Rec. Pr. 81¾

CHUBB CORP.

YIELD	2.3%
P/E RATIO	20.9

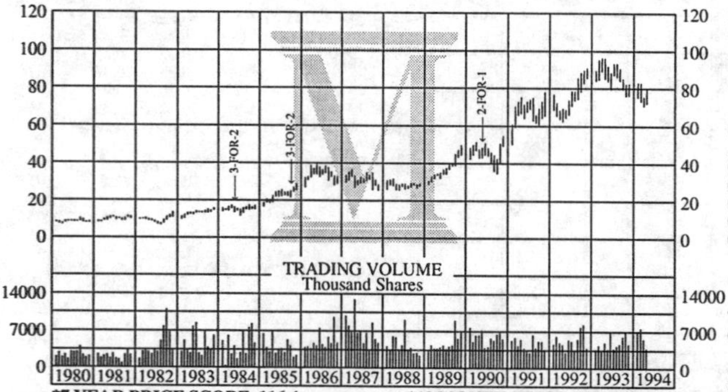

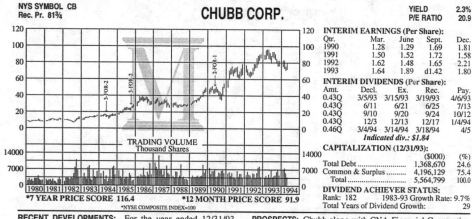

120
100
80
60
40
20
0
3-FOR-2
3-FOR-2
2-FOR-1
TRADING VOLUME
Thousand Shares
14000
7000
0
1980 1981 1982 1983 1984 1985 1986 1987 1988 1989 1990 1991 1992 1993 1994

*7 YEAR PRICE SCORE 116.4 *12 MONTH PRICE SCORE 91.9

*NYSE COMPOSITE INDEX=100

INTERIM EARNINGS (Per Share):

Qtr.	Mar.	June	Sept.	Dec.
1990	1.28	1.29	1.69	1.81
1991	1.50	1.52	1.72	1.58
1992	1.62	1.48	1.65	2.21
1993	1.64	1.89	d1.42	1.80

INTERIM DIVIDENDS (Per Share):

Amt.	Decl.	Ex.	Rec.	Pay.
0.43Q	3/5/93	3/15/93	3/19/93	4/6/93
0.43Q	6/11	6/21	6/25	7/13
0.43Q	9/10	9/20	9/24	10/12
0.43Q	12/3	12/13	12/17	1/4/94
0.46Q	3/4/94	3/14/94	3/18/94	4/5

Indicated div.: $1.84

CAPITALIZATION (12/31/93):

	($000)	(%)
Total Debt	1,368,670	24.6
Common & Surplus	4,196,129	75.4
Total	5,564,799	100.0

DIVIDEND ACHIEVER STATUS:
Rank: 182 1983-93 Growth Rate: 9.7%
Total Years of Dividend Growth: 29

RECENT DEVELOPMENTS: For the year ended 12/31/93, income before extraordinary items and accounting adjustments was $701.1 million, up 13.6% from 1992. Net premiums written were $3.52 billion compared with $3.24 billion a year ago. Property and casualty operations produced underwriting income of $20.0 million. The combined loss and expense ratio was 99.0% as catastrophe losses amounted to $89.0 million down considerably from $175.3 million for the prior year.

PROSPECTS: Chubb along with CNA Financial Corporation and Fireboard Corp., entered into an agreement to pay all future asbestos-related bodily injury claims against Fireboard, a maker of asbestos. An additional $675 million in loss reserves was allocated in third quarter of 1993, bringing total reserves for Fireboard Corporation to $1.25 billion. Underwriting operations are still very sluggish and have not returned to a profitable state. Net premiums written continue to drive earnings.

BUSINESS

THE CHUBB CORPORATION offers commercial and personal property and casualty insurance. It also maintains operations in life and health insurance and real estate development. Chubbs' clients are located in North America, South America, Europe, and the Pacific Rim. The Corporation operates over 100 offices and it ranks in the top 25 among diversified financial service organizations in the United States.

BUSINESS LINE ANALYSIS

(12/31/93)	Rev(%)	Inc(%)
Prop & Casualty	77.6	(1.5)
Life & Health	19.3	99.2
Real Estate	3.1	2.3
Total	100.0	100.0

ANNUAL EARNINGS AND DIVIDENDS PER SHARE

	1993	1992	1991	1990	1989	1988	1987
Earnings Per Share	**3.91**	**6.96**	**6.32**	**6.07**	**4.91**	**4.43**	**4.15**
Dividends Per Share	**1.69**	**1.57**	**1.44**	**[1] 1.28**	**1.14**	**1.045**	**0.87**
Dividend Payout %	**43.2**	**22.6**	**22.8**	**21.1**	**23.2**	**23.6**	**20.9**

[1] 2-for-1 stk split. 5/30/90

ANNUAL FINANCIAL DATA

	1993	1992	1991	1990	1989	1988	1987
RECORD OF EARNINGS (IN MILLIONS):							
Prem Earned & Policy Chrgs	4,306.1	3,852.5	3,671.2	3,398.1	3,190.0	3,299.1	3,162.6
Total Interest Income	1,033.0	938.4	701.0	674.5	611.3	526.2	408.4
Total Revenues	5,499.7	4,940.8	4,513.2	4,247.5	4,022.6	3,980.5	3,714.4
Ins Claims & Policyholders' Bens	3,548.5	2,689.1	2,468.9	2,296.9	2,211.2	2,312.6	2,221.1
Inc Fr Cont Opers Bef Income Taxes	344.5	748.4	683.7	645.7	552.3	457.0	406.0
Fed & Foreign Inc Taxes	0.3	131.3	131.7	123.6	131.5	97.3	75.9
Gain on Sale Of Securities	...	...	65.7	46.3	46.9	d13.0	d14.6
Net Income	[1] 344.2	617.1	552.0	522.1	420.8	359.6	330.1
Aver. Shs. Outstg. (000)	90,549	90,094	88,638	87,364	87,243	84,860	84,860
[1] Before acctg. change dr$20,000,000.							
BALANCE SHEET (IN MILLIONS):							
Cash	4.6	6.7	9.8	11.7	10.3	6.8	6.2
Fixed Maturities	10,186.5	9,737.8	8,392.4	7,220.7	6,845.5	6,119.6	5,196.0
Equity Securities	930.0	738.2	1,143.3	857.7	860.2	664.1	511.7
Policy Loans	179.2	165.3	151.3	133.4	118.2	106.2	102.2
Mortgage Loans	15.1	27.6	35.9	37.1	42.9	47.6	56.2
Total Assets	19,436.9	15,019.2	13,774.7	12,267.7	11,178.6	9,741.2	8,609.4
Benefits and Claims	12,861.9	8,900.8	8,186.8	7,560.6	6,907.6	6,176.0	5,392.2
Net Stockholders' Equity	4,196.1	3,954.4	3,541.6	2,882.6	2,603.7	2,254.8	1,953.4
Year End Shs Outstg (000)	87,709	87,520	86,938	81,912	84,432	81,216	40,608
STATISTICAL RECORD:							
Return on Equity %	8.2	15.6	15.6	18.1	16.2	15.9	16.9
Book Value Per Share	47.84	45.18	40.74	35.19	30.84	27.76	48.10
Average Yield %	2.0	2.0	2.3	2.9	2.9	3.6	2.8
P/E Ratio	24.6-19.4	13.1-9.0	12.3-7.9	9.0-5.7	10.1-5.9	7.4-6.0	9.2-6.4
Price Range	96⅜-76	91-62⅜	78-50	54¾-34⅝	49¾-28⅞	31¾-25⅝	36¾-25½

Statistics are as originally reported.

OFFICERS:
D.R. O'Hare, Chmn. & C.E.O.
P. Chubb, III, Vice-Chmn. & C.F.O.
R.D. Smith, President
P.J. Sempier, V.P. & Treas.

INCORPORATED: NJ, Jun., 1967

PRINCIPAL OFFICE: 15 Mountain View Road P.O. Box 1615, Warren, NJ 07061-1615

TELEPHONE NUMBER: (908) 903-2000

FAX: (908) 903-2003

NO. OF EMPLOYEES: 10,500 (approx.)

ANNUAL MEETING: In April

SHAREHOLDERS: 9,025 (approx.)

INSTITUTIONAL HOLDINGS:
No. of Institutions: 546
Shares Held: 67,857,585

REGISTRAR(S): First Chicago Trust Co. of New York, New York, NY 10008

TRANSFER AGENT(S): First Chicago Trust Co. of New York, New York, NY 10008

NYS SYMBOL CHD
Rec. Pr. 22¼

CHURCH & DWIGHT CO., INC.

YIELD 2.0%
P/E RATIO 15.2

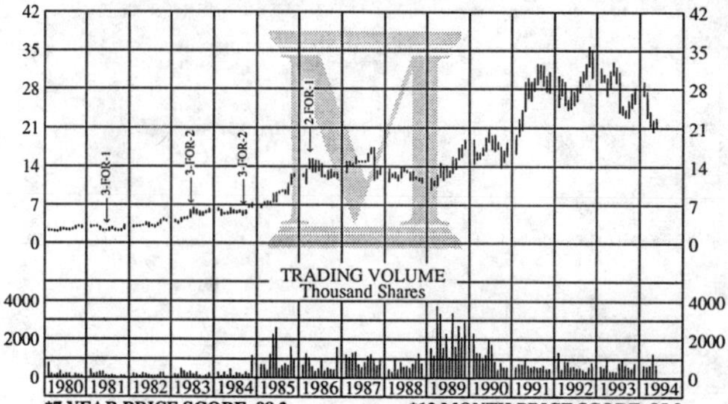

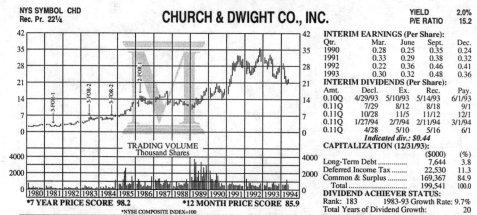

***7 YEAR PRICE SCORE 98.2** ***12 MONTH PRICE SCORE 85.9**

*NYSE COMPOSITE INDEX=100

INTERIM EARNINGS (Per Share):

Qtr.	Mar.	June	Sept.	Dec.
1990	0.28	0.25	0.35	0.24
1991	0.33	0.29	0.38	0.32
1992	0.22	0.36	0.46	0.41
1993	0.30	0.32	0.48	0.36

INTERIM DIVIDENDS (Per Share):

Amt.	Decl.	Ex.	Rec.	Pay.
0.10Q	4/29/93	5/10/93	5/14/93	6/1/93
0.11Q	7/29	8/12	8/18	9/1
0.11Q	10/28	11/5	11/12	12/1
0.11Q	1/27/94	2/7/94	2/11/94	3/1/94
0.11Q	4/28	5/10	5/16	6/1

Indicated div.: $0.44

CAPITALIZATION (12/31/93):

	($000)	(%)
Long-Term Debt	7,644	3.8
Deferred Income Tax	22,530	11.3
Common & Surplus	169,367	84.9
Total	199,541	100.0

DIVIDEND ACHIEVER STATUS:
Rank: 183 1983-93 Growth Rate: 9.7%
Total Years of Dividend Growth: 20

RECENT DEVELOPMENTS: For the year ended 12/31/93, net income was $29.5 million, relatively even with last year's results. Per share earnings increased to $1.46 from $1.45 last year. Results were before an accounting change of $3.2 million. Sales rose 2.1% to $527.5 million. Although sales were depressed by competitive activity in the laundry detergent and dentifrice businesses, profits were maintained through cost controls. For the fourth quarter, income before accounting changes was $7.2 million compared with $8.3 million last year. Sales declined 7.1% to $129.5 million.

PROSPECTS: The Company will continue to face intense competition in the baking soda toothpaste market, as rival toothpaste manufacturers focus on improving their market shares. However, CHD will likely maintain its market share, though higher advertising and promotional costs may reduce margins. New line extensions and the introduction of Armakleen, an aqueous cleaning product for printed circuit boards, could help growth of Specialty Products. In the detergent business, sales growth will likely be marginal as a result of increased price competition.

BUSINESS

CHURCH & DWIGHT COMPANY, INC., is the world's leading producer of sodium bicarbonate, popularly known as baking soda. The Company sells its products, primarily under the Arm & Hammer trademark, to consumers through supermarkets, drug stores and mass merchandisers, and to industrial customers and distributors. CHD operates two business divisions. Consumer Products produces Arm & Hammer products such as baking soda, carpet and room deodorizers, dental care products and laundry products. Specialty Products produces sodium bicarbonate and related products for the food, pharmaceuticals, animal feed and industrial markets.

REVENUES

(12/31/93)	($000)	(%)
Consumer products....	410,400	80.8
Specialty products.....	97,300	19.2
Total	507,700	100.0

ANNUAL EARNINGS AND DIVIDENDS PER SHARE

	1993	1992	1991	1990	1989	1988	1987
Earnings Per Share	**1.46**	**1.45**	**1.34**	**[1] 1.13**	**0.42**	**0.75**	**0.64**
Dividends Per Share	**0.42**	**0.38**	**0.34**	**0.30**	**0.26**	**0.23**	**0.215**
Dividend Payout %	**28.8**	**26.2**	**25.4**	**26.5**	**61.9**	**30.7**	**33.6**

[1] Before extraord. item

ANNUAL FINANCIAL DATA

	1993	1992	1991	1990	1989	1988	1987
RECORD OF EARNINGS (IN THOUSANDS):							
Total Revenues	507,651	516,438	485,487	428,547	387,641	346,779	318,803
Costs and Expenses	461,406	460,117	433,945	384,179	347,353	310,082	286,290
Deprec, Depl & Depreciation	10,622	11,547	11,209	10,525	10,111	9,734	9,271
Income From Operations	35,623	44,774	40,333	33,843	30,176	26,963	23,242
Income Bef Income Taxes	47,796	47,150	42,000	38,973	17,056	24,928	23,345
Income Taxes	18,310	17,647	15,525	15,767	8,408	8,454	9,319
Net Income	[1] 29,486	29,503	26,475	[2] 23,206	8,648	16,474	14,026
Aver. Shs. Outstg.	20,223	20,338	19,831	20,455	20,728	21,985	21,976
[1] Before acctg. change dr$5,647,000. [2] Before extra. item dr$724,000.							
BALANCE SHEET (IN THOUSANDS):							
Cash and Cash Equivalents	9,581	25,596	8,705	45,704	43,321	25,906	45,654
Receivables, Net	56,499	45,597	48,439	42,326	38,348	38,965	31,154
Inventories	52,739	45,603	54,710	40,289	34,864	43,161	33,073
Gross Property	196,443	191,223	178,336	161,557	155,032	159,661	151,459
Accumulated Depreciation	74,248	70,686	64,608	58,502	52,829	48,212	44,032
Long-Term Debt	7,644	7,744	7,811	29,635	52,193	55,586	56,813
Net Stockholders' Equity	169,367	159,051	139,154	118,702	111,555	112,032	116,144
Total Assets	281,741	262,347	244,997	253,479	244,858	243,997	246,161
Total Current Assets	123,453	123,558	116,587	133,318	129,810	112,723	117,598
Total Current Liabilities	68,812	76,581	78,681	84,022	59,841	51,117	46,024
Net Working Capital	54,641	46,977	37,906	49,296	69,969	61,606	71,574
Year End Shares Outstg	20,079	20,335	20,300	20,222	20,712	20,959	22,050
STATISTICAL RECORD:							
Operating Profit Margin %	7.0	8.7	8.3	7.9	7.8	7.8	7.3
Book Value Per Share	8.26	7.62	6.64	5.67	5.18	4.97	4.90
Return on Equity %	17.4	18.5	19.0	19.5	7.8	14.7	12.1
Return on Assets %	10.5	11.2	10.8	9.2	3.5	6.8	5.7
Average Yield %	1.5	1.3	1.4	1.7	1.8	1.8	1.5
P/E Ratio	22.5-15.7	24.7-16.7	24.3-12.1	18.5-12.2	44.9-23.2	18.7-14.7	27.3-18.0
Price Range	32⅞-22⅞	35¾-24¼	32½-16¼	20⅞-13¾	18⅞-9¾	14-11	17½-11½

Statistics are as originally reported.

OFFICERS:
D.C. Minton, Chmn. & C.E.O.
M.A. Bilawsky, V.P., Gen. Couns. & Sec.
A.P. Deasey, V.P.-Fin. & C.F.O.

INCORPORATED: DE, 1925

PRINCIPAL OFFICE: 469 North Harrison St., Princeton, NJ 08543-5297

TELEPHONE NUMBER: (609) 683-5900
FAX: (609) 497-7177
NO. OF EMPLOYEES: 1,096
ANNUAL MEETING: In May
SHAREHOLDERS: 11,600 (approx.)
INSTITUTIONAL HOLDINGS:
No. of Institutions: 99
Shares Held: 10,546,098

REGISTRAR(S): Manufacturers Hanover Trust Co., New York, NY

TRANSFER AGENT(S): Manufacturers Hanover Trust Co., New York, NY

NASDAQ SYMBOL CINF
Rec. Pr. 54¼ (Marginable)

CINCINNATI FINANCIAL CORP.

YIELD 2.4%
P/E RATIO 13.8

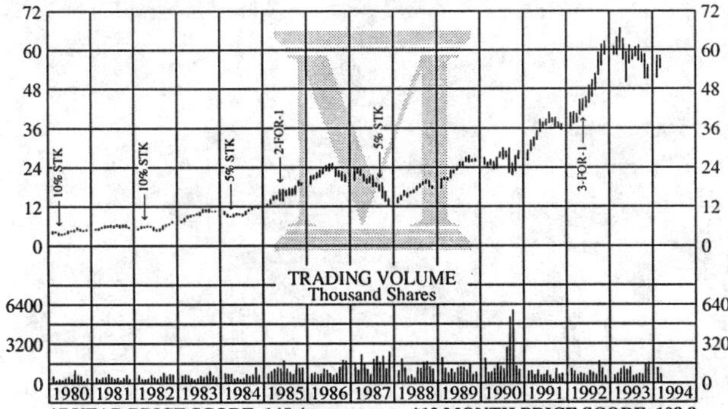

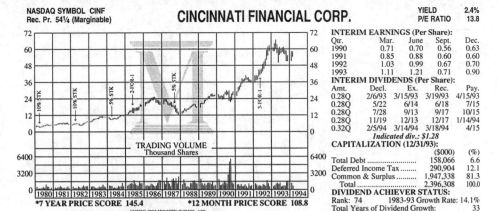

***7 YEAR PRICE SCORE 145.4** ***12 MONTH PRICE SCORE 108.8**

*NYSE COMPOSITE INDEX=100

INTERIM EARNINGS (Per Share):

Qtr.	Mar.	June	Sept.	Dec.
1990	0.71	0.70	0.56	0.63
1991	0.85	0.88	0.60	0.60
1992	1.03	0.99	0.67	0.70
1993	1.11	1.21	0.71	0.90

INTERIM DIVIDENDS (Per Share):

Amt.	Decl.	Ex.	Rec.	Pay.
0.28Q	2/6/93	3/15/93	3/19/93	4/15/93
0.28Q	5/22	6/14	6/18	7/15
0.28Q	7/28	9/13	9/17	10/15
0.28Q	11/19	12/13	12/17	1/14/94
0.32Q	2/5/94	3/14/94	3/18/94	4/15

Indicated div.: $1.28

CAPITALIZATION (12/31/93):

	($000)	(%)
Total Debt	158,066	6.6
Deferred Income Tax	290,904	12.1
Common & Surplus	1,947,338	81.3
Total	2,396,308	100.0

DIVIDEND ACHIEVER STATUS:

Rank: 74 1983-93 Growth Rate: 14.1%

Total Years of Dividend Growth: 33

RECENT DEVELOPMENTS: For the year ended 12/31/93, income, before cumulative effect of an accounting change, was up 18% to $202.2 million, compared with net income of $171.3 million in 1992. Total revenues rose 10.6% to $1.44 billion from $1.30 billion a year ago. Net premiums earned totaled $1.14 billion, a 9.8% increase over $1.04 billion last year. 1993 income included an $11.2 million charge and $2.6 million credit related to the tax effects of the increase in tax rates on unrealized appreciation of investment in equity securities and on accumulated other temporary book-tax differences. Realized gains on investments were $51.5 million, compared with $35.9 million in 1992. For the quarter, net income rose 32.5% to $47.1 million from $35.5 million for the same period last year. Total revenues were up 9.4% to $359.9 million from $329.0 million in 1992.

BUSINESS

CINCINNATI FINANCIAL CORP. has six subsidiary companies, operating principally in the field of insurance. The Cincinnati Insurance Company and the Cincinnati Casualty Company market property and casualty insurance, the Company's main business. Life, health and accident insurance is marketed by the Cincinnati Life Insurance Company. CFC Investment Company supports insurance subsidiaries through leasing, financing and real estate investments.

BUSINESS LINE ANALYSIS

(12/31/93)	Rev(%)	Inc(%)
Property/Casualty	75.7	(1.2)
Life/Health	3.4	0.2
Investment Income	16.6	78.6
Realized Gain on Invest	3.6	18.2
Other	0.8	2.0
Total	100.0	100.0

ANNUAL EARNINGS AND DIVIDENDS PER SHARE

	1993	1992	1991	1990	1989	1988	1987
Earnings Per Share	**3.94**	**3.39**	**2.94**	**2.61**	**2.33**	**2.57**	**1.89**
Dividends Per Share	**1.10**	**[1] 1.00**	**0.883**	**0.79**	**0.687**	**0.567**	**[2] 0.467**
Dividend Payout %	**27.9**	**29.5**	**30.1**	**30.3**	**29.4**	**22.1**	**24.7**

[1] 3-for-1 stk split, 5/18/92 [2] 5% stk div, 10/87

ANNUAL FINANCIAL DATA

	1993	1992	1991	1990	1989	1988	1987
RECORD OF EARNINGS (IN MILLIONS):							
Insurance Premiums	1,140.8	1,038.8	947.6	871.2	813.3	768.4	766.5
Total Interest Income	239.4	218.9	193.2	167.4	149.3	130.9	108.9
Total Revenues	1,442.2	1,304.2	1,161.1	1,048.9	974.4	909.6	883.1
Ins Losses & Policyholder Bens	832.5	766.1	679.9	620.7	577.4	504.9	552.0
Income Bef Income Taxes	267.0	209.2	177.1	149.8	133.2	155.1	103.7
Income Taxes	64.8	37.9	30.9	20.8	18.7	22.2	8.1
Net Realized Gain on Invests	...	...	...	...	...	4.1	2.4
Net Income	[1] 202.2	171.3	146.3	129.0	114.5	128.7	93.2
Aver. Shs. Outstg. (000)	52,066	51,115	49,806	49,425	49,110	48,579	48,306
[1] Before acctg. change cr$13,845,000.							
BALANCE SHEET (IN MILLIONS):							
Cash	48.1	50.0	57.2	39.5	35.1	23.9	26.5
Fixed Matur, At Amortized Cost	1,759.7	1,635.9	1,421.5	1,180.7	1,098.4	1,014.8	871.9
Eq Secur, At Mkt Value	2,318.8	1,972.3	1,604.7	1,049.3	1,100.2	798.8	609.1
Total Assets	4,602.3	4,028.4	3,436.0	2,589.6	2,552.0	2,117.4	1,792.5
Benefits and Claims	2,110.5	1,791.3	1,571.2	1,353.8	1,227.3	1,063.6	962.9
Net Stockholders' Equity	1,947.3	1,713.8	1,441.4	1,006.9	1,020.3	815.6	633.9
Year End Shs Outstg (000)	50,306	49,966	49,584	49,257	48,853	48,639	47,823
STATISTICAL RECORD:							
Book Value Per Share	38.71	34.30	29.07	20.44	20.88	16.77	13.26
Return on Equity %	10.4	10.0	10.1	12.8	11.2	15.8	14.7
Return on Assets %	4.4	4.3	4.3	5.0	4.5	6.1	5.2
Average Yield %	1.9	2.0	2.6	3.1	3.0	3.4	2.6
P/E Ratio	16.9-12.7	18.5-10.5	13.9-8.8	11.4-8.2	11.9-7.6	7.9-5.1	12.7-6.4
Price Range	66¾-50	62¾-35⅝	40⅞-25⅞	29⅞-21½	27⅝-17⅝	20⅜-13⅛	24-12⅛

Statistics are as originally reported.

OFFICERS:
J.J. Schiff, Jr., Chairman
W.H. Zimmer, Vice-Chmn.
R.B. Morgan, Pres. & C.E.O.
R.J. Driehaus, V.P.-Fin. & Treas.
V.H. Beckman, Secretary

INCORPORATED: DE, Sep., 1968

PRINCIPAL OFFICE: P.O. Box 145496, Cincinnati, OH 45250-5496

TELEPHONE NUMBER: (513) 870-2000

FAX: (513) 870-0609

NO. OF EMPLOYEES: 1,976

ANNUAL MEETING: In April

SHAREHOLDERS: 8,850 (approx.)

INSTITUTIONAL HOLDINGS:
No. of Institutions: 138
Shares Held: 16,049,084

REGISTRAR(S):

TRANSFER AGENT(S): At Company's Office

NASDAQ SYMBOL CTAS
Rec. Pr. 30¼ (Marginable)

CINTAS CORP.

YIELD 0.6%
P/E RATIO 29.4

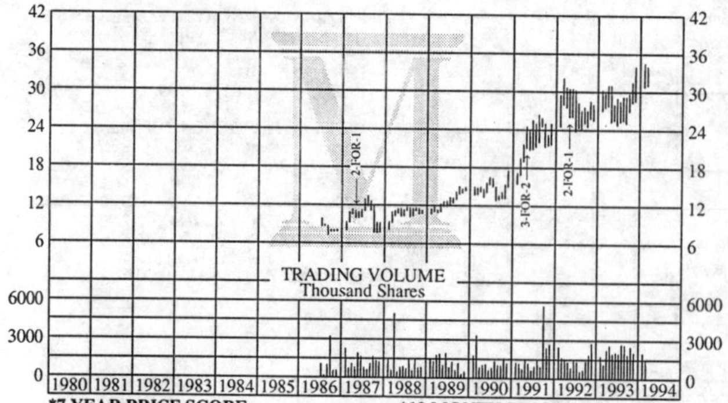

*7 YEAR PRICE SCORE ... *12 MONTH PRICE SCORE 100.5

*NYSE COMPOSITE INDEX=100

INTERIM EARNINGS (Per Share):

Qtr.	Aug.	Nov.	Feb.	May
1990-91	0.17	0.18	0.18	0.22
1991-92	0.14	0.21	0.20	0.24
1992-93	0.21	0.25	0.24	0.27
1993-94	0.23	0.29	...	...

INTERIM DIVIDENDS (Per Share):

Amt.	Decl.	Ex.	Rec.	Pay.
0.14A	2/19/93	3/3/93	3/9/93	4/2/93
0.17A	2/17/94	3/7/94	3/11/94	4/5/94

Indicated div.: $0.17

CAPITALIZATION (5/31/93):

	($000)	(%)
Long-Term Debt	103,611	26.6
Deferred Income Tax	20,464	5.3
Common & Surplus	264,914	68.1
Total	388,989	100.0

DIVIDEND ACHIEVER STATUS:
Rank: 1 1983-93 Growth Rate: 39.5%
Total Years of Dividend Growth: 11

RECENT DEVELOPMENTS: For the quarter ended 11/30/93, revenues were up 17% to $129.8 million from $111.0 million in 1992. Net rental revenue was $114.3 million compared with $97.3 million and net sales were $15.5 million compared with $13.7 million in 1992, increases of 17% and 13% respectively. Growth in the customer base, price increases in established operations and acquisitions accounted for the increase in net rental revenue. Revenues from the sale of uniforms and other direct sale items increased 14% over last year, due to an increase in unit sales. Income from operations, as a percentage of sales, remained at 18% for the quarter. Net income rose 17% to $13.6 million, or $0.29 per share, from $11.6 million, or $0.25 per share a year ago. On 11/1/93, CTAS acquired the Career Apparel Division of Palm Beach Co., Inc., a wholly-owned subsidiary of Plaid Clothing Group. The acquisition did not have a significant impact on sales.

BUSINESS

CINTAS CORPORATION provides a highly specialized service to businesses of all types—from small service companies to major corporations that employ thousands of people. The Company designs, manufactures and implements corporate identity uniform programs throughout the United States. The Company currently occupies 102 facilities located in 95 cities. The corporate offices provide centrally located administrative functions including accounting, finance, marketing and data processing. The Company operates processing plants that house administrative, sales and service personnel and the necessary equipment involved in the cleaning of uniforms and bulk items. Branch operations provide administrative, sales and service functions. The Company operates three distribution facilities and has three manufacturing plants, two producing trous ers and one uniform shirts. The Company owns or leases approximately 2,051 vehicles.

REVENUES

(5/31/93)	($000)	(%)
Net Rentals	404,869	89.4
Net Sales	47,853	10.6
Total	452,722	100.0

ANNUAL EARNINGS AND DIVIDENDS PER SHARE

	5/31/93	5/31/92	5/31/91	5/31/90	5/31/89	5/31/88	5/31/87
Earnings Per Share	0.97	[1] 0.79	0.74	0.63	0.53	0.44	0.36
Dividends Per Share	0.11	[2] 0.095	[3] 0.075	0.055	0.045	0.03	[4] 0.025
Dividend Payout %	11.3	12.0	10.2	8.8	8.6	6.9	7.0

[1] Before acctg. chg. [2] 2-for-1 stk split, 4/2/92 [3] 3-for-2 stk split, 4/2/91 [4] 2-for-1 stk split, 3/16/87.

ANNUAL FINANCIAL DATA

RECORD OF EARNINGS (IN THOUSANDS):							
Total Revenues	452,722	401,563	322,479	284,536	243,619	204,513	163,375
Costs and Expenses	352,648	319,006	255,953	229,251	196,767	166,012	129,765
Depreciation	23,149	19,359	16,402	12,258	10,050	8,246	6,499
Operating Income	76,925	63,198	50,124	43,027	36,802	30,255	27,111
Income Bef Income Taxes	71,303	58,206	48,777	41,626	34,810	27,672	25,087
Income Taxes	26,430	21,716	17,345	15,020	12,752	10,521	11,151
Net Income	44,873	[1] 36,490	31,432	26,606	22,058	17,151	13,936
Aver. Shs. Outstg.	46,411	46,145	42,876	42,476	41,768	39,636	39,126
[1] Before acctg. change cr$2,705,000.							
BALANCE SHEET (IN THOUSANDS):							
Cash and Cash Equivalents	54,969	22,912	18,439	30,374	30,134	18,914	26,914
Accounts Receivable, Net	48,075	40,721	35,261	31,841	27,038	22,154	19,572
Inventories	21,452	25,165	23,209	19,847	17,865	19,866	10,507
Gross Property	263,053	240,462	197,255	144,984	110,849	87,377	69,967
Accumulated Depreciation	82,206	67,507	44,689	33,668	27,920	22,779	17,632
Long-Term Debt	103,611	67,790	58,919	43,568	36,874	48,565	51,149
Net Stockholders' Equity	264,914	225,864	185,632	157,441	133,882	94,382	77,717
Total Assets	454,165	361,261	305,822	254,162	213,640	179,892	161,844
Total Current Assets	187,133	138,729	117,524	115,385	104,708	86,267	77,190
Total Current Liabilities	65,176	51,910	53,368	46,797	37,888	33,101	30,127
Net Working Capital	121,957	86,819	64,156	68,588	66,820	53,166	47,063
Year End Shares Outstg	46,579	46,190	43,421	42,518	42,426	39,825	39,141
STATISTICAL RECORD:							
Operating Profit Margin %	17.0	15.7	15.5	15.1	15.1	14.8	16.6
Book Value Per Share	5.69	4.89	4.28	3.70	3.16	2.37	1.99
Return on Equity %	16.9	16.2	16.9	16.9	16.5	18.2	17.9
Return on Assets %	9.9	10.1	10.3	10.5	10.3	9.5	8.6
Average Yield %	0.4	0.5	0.5	0.4	0.5	0.3	0.3
P/E Ratio	33.1-24.5	33.4-19.5	23.8-17.4	23.8-16.9	22.6-15.6	30.7-17.3	27.4-20.1
Price Range	32⅛-23¾	26⅜-15⅜	17⅝-12⅞	15-10⅝	11¾-8⅛	13½-7⅝	9⅞-7¼

Statistics are as originally reported.

OFFICERS:
R.T. Farmer, Chmn. & C.E.O.
R.J. Kohlhepp, Pres., C.O.O. & Sec.
D.T. Jeanmougin, Sr. V.P.-Fin.
K.L. Carnahan, Treas.

INCORPORATED: OH, 1968; reincorp., WA, Dec., 1986

PRINCIPAL OFFICE: 6800 Cintas Blvd. P.O. Box 625737, Cincinnati, OH 45262-5737

TELEPHONE NUMBER: (513) 459-1200

FAX: (513) 573-4130

NO. OF EMPLOYEES: 7,797

ANNUAL MEETING: In October

SHAREHOLDERS: 1,500 (approx.)

INSTITUTIONAL HOLDINGS:
No. of Institutions: 166
Shares Held: 18,156,899 (adj.)

REGISTRAR(S): Fifth Third Bank, Cincinnati, OH 45263

TRANSFER AGENT(S): Fifth Third Bank, Cincinnati, OH 45263

CIRCUIT CITY STORES, INC.

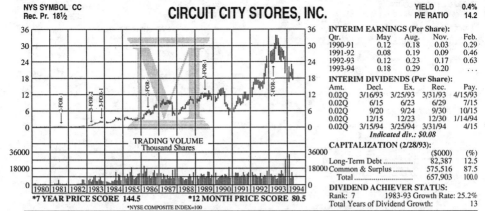

INTERIM EARNINGS (Per Share):

Qtr.	May	Aug.	Nov.	Feb.
1990-91	0.12	0.18	0.03	0.29
1991-92	0.08	0.19	0.09	0.46
1992-93	0.12	0.23	0.17	0.63
1993-94	0.18	0.29	0.20	...

INTERIM DIVIDENDS (Per Share):

Amt.	Decl.	Ex.	Rec.	Pay.
0.02Q	3/16/93	3/25/93	3/31/93	4/15/93
0.02Q	6/15	6/23	6/29	7/15
0.02Q	9/20	9/24	9/30	10/15
0.02Q	12/15	12/23	12/30	1/14/94
0.02Q	3/15/94	3/25/94	3/31/94	4/15

Indicated div.: $0.08

CAPITALIZATION (2/28/93):

	($000)	(%)
Long-Term Debt	82,387	12.5
Common & Surplus	575,516	87.5
Total	657,903	100.0

DIVIDEND ACHIEVER STATUS:
Rank: 7   1983-93 Growth Rate: 25.2%
Total Years of Dividend Growth: 13

TRADING VOLUME
Thousand Shares

*7 YEAR PRICE SCORE 144.5   ***12 MONTH PRICE SCORE 80.5**
*NYSE COMPOSITE INDEX=100

RECENT DEVELOPMENTS: For the quarter ended 11/30/93, net income increased 17% to $19.5 million, or $0.20 per share compared with $16.6 million, or $0.17 a share, in the same period in 1992. Sales rose 26% to $1.02 billion from $805.4 million last year. Comparable store sales increased 5%. Higher sales benefited from contributions of new Superstores and the increase in comparable store sales. As a percentage of sales, gross profit margin decreased to 25.8% from 27.5%, while selling, general and administrative expenses declined to 22.6% from 24.1%.

PROSPECTS: An increasingly competitive retail climate will pressure margins and sales growth. However, increased efficiency in store operating costs and advertising expenditures and contributions from its private label credit card operation will help control expenses. Store expansions should help growth as CC plans to open 180 Superstores and 20 stores for smaller trade areas over a three-year period. The expansion program will place Circuit City in all major metropolitan markets in the U.S., except New York, and will provide an opportunity to increase its overall market share.

BUSINESS

CIRCUIT CITY STORES, INC. (formerly Wards Co., Inc.) is the nation's largest specialty retailer of brand name electronic equipment and consumer appliances including video cassette recorders, cameras, stereo systems, compact disc players, telephones, microwave ovens, washers, dryers, refrigerators, and ranges. It operates 256 Circuit City Superstores, 7 Circuit City stores and 32 Impulse Stores located in California, Nevada, Arizona and Mid-Atlantic and Southern States. The Circuit City Stores offer a full line of merchandise except major appliances. Circuit City Superstores sells a broader selection of the same line of merchandise including major appliances. The Impulse Stores sells smaller electronic products.

ANNUAL EARNINGS AND DIVIDENDS PER SHARE

	2/28/93	2/29/92	2/28/91	2/28/90	2/28/89	2/29/88	2/28/87
Earnings Per Share	1.15	0.83	① 0.61	0.85	0.76	0.56	0.40
Dividends Per Share	0.055	0.05	0.045	② 0.035	0.025	0.018	③ 0.014
Dividend Payout %	4.8	6.1	7.4	4.1	3.3	3.1	3.5

Note: 2-for-1stk.split,3/18/93. ① Before acctg. chg. ② 2-for-1 stk. split, 7/89. ③ 100% stk. div., 5/86.

ANNUAL FINANCIAL DATA

RECORD OF EARNINGS (IN MILLIONS):

	2/28/93	2/29/92	2/28/91	2/28/90	2/28/89	2/29/88	2/28/87
Net Sales & Oper Revs	3,269.8	2,790.2	2,366.9	2,096.6	1,721.5	1,350.4	1,010.7
Costs and Expenses	3,049.0	2,621.4	2,234.6	1,937.8	1,581.6	1,239.2	924.6
Depreciation & Amort	41.7	35.7	29.1	21.9	17.0	13.6	9.4
Operating Income	179.1	133.2	103.2	136.9	122.9	97.6	76.7
Earn Bef Income Taxes	175.3	124.1	91.4	128.1	114.5	89.2	71.5
Provision for Inc Taxes	65.0	45.9	34.8	50.0	45.0	38.8	36.2
Net Income	110.3	78.2	① 56.7	78.1	69.5	50.4	35.3
Aver. Shs. Outstg. (000)	96,140	95,000	93,080	92,136	91,084	89,700	89,000

① Before acctg. change dr$53,500,000.

BALANCE SHEET (IN MILLIONS):

Cash & Cash Equivalents	141.4	71.5	25.2	91.7	46.1	43.9	33.7
Receivables, Net	120.4	93.5	26.6	9.7	11.6	7.1	12.3
Merchandise Inventory	515.8	420.1	389.8	331.2	302.6	208.1	144.4
Gross Property	516.5	437.2	443.9	320.3	255.9	189.4	169.4
Accumulated Depreciation	145.7	117.9	88.4	70.3	49.9	34.2	22.2
Long-Term Debt	82.4	85.4	94.4	93.9	94.7	96.7	101.1
Net Stockholders' Equity	575.5	448.0	366.9	359.3	273.6	201.4	149.3
Total Assets	1,262.9	999.6	874.1	713.7	587.5	433.2	361.6
Total Current Assets	790.9	597.4	450.4	442.2	366.9	265.4	195.5
Total Current Liabilities	373.0	279.0	261.0	222.2	192.2	116.2	98.2
Net Working Capital	417.9	318.4	189.4	220.0	174.7	149.1	97.3
Year End Shs Outstg (000)	95,670	93,866	92,680	91,722	90,468	89,604	88,760

STATISTICAL RECORD:

Operating Profit Margin %	5.5	4.8	4.4	6.5	7.1	7.2	7.6
Book Value Per Share	6.02	4.77	3.96	3.92	3.02	2.25	1.68
Return on Equity %	19.2	17.5	15.4	21.7	25.4	25.0	23.6
Return on Assets %	8.7	7.8	6.5	10.9	11.8	11.6	9.8
Average Yield %	0.3	0.5	0.5	0.3	0.3	0.2	0.2
P/E Ratio	22.7-9.7	15.9-6.9	23.8-7.4	15.9-10.4	15.0-6.1	18.5-7.6	21.6-7.5
Price Range	26⅛-11⅛	13-5⅝	14½-4½	13½-8⅞	11⅜-4⅝	10⅜-4¼	8⅝-3

Statistics are as originally reported.

OFFICERS:
A.L. Wurtzel, Chmn.
R.L. Sharp, Pres. & C.E.O.
M.T. Chalifoux, Sr. V.P. & C.F.O.
P.J. Dunn, Treas.
INCORPORATED: VA, Sep., 1949
PRINCIPAL OFFICE: 9950 Mayland Drive, Richmond, VA 23233-1464

TELEPHONE NUMBER: (804) 527-4000
NO. OF EMPLOYEES: 2,675
ANNUAL MEETING: In June
SHAREHOLDERS: 3,479
INSTITUTIONAL HOLDINGS:
No. of Institutions: 235
Shares Held: 39,369,093

REGISTRAR(S):

TRANSFER AGENT(S):

NASDAQ SYMBOL CBCF
Rec. Pr. 25 (Marginable)

CITIZENS BANKING CORP.

YIELD 3.4%
P/E RATIO 13.2

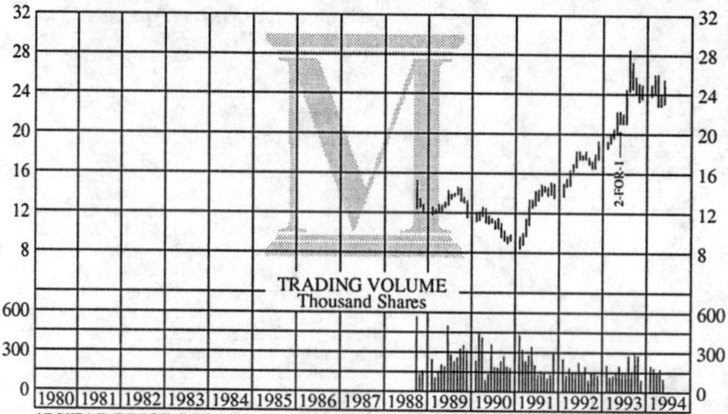

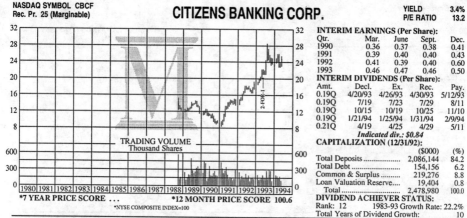

32
28
24
20
16
12
8
2-FOR-1
TRADING VOLUME
Thousand Shares
600
300
0
1980 1981 1982 1983 1984 1985 1986 1987 1988 1989 1990 1991 1992 1993 1994

*7 YEAR PRICE SCORE ... *12 MONTH PRICE SCORE 100.6

*NYSE COMPOSITE INDEX=100

INTERIM EARNINGS (Per Share):

Qtr.	Mar.	June	Sept.	Dec.
1990	0.36	0.37	0.38	0.41
1991	0.39	0.40	0.40	0.43
1992	0.41	0.39	0.40	0.60
1993	0.46	0.47	0.46	0.50

INTERIM DIVIDENDS (Per Share):

Amt.	Decl.	Ex.	Rec.	Pay.
0.19Q	4/20/93	4/26/93	4/30/93	5/12/93
0.19Q	7/19	7/23	7/29	8/11
0.19Q	10/15	10/19	10/25	11/10
0.19Q	1/21/94	1/25/94	1/31/94	2/9/94
0.21Q	4/19	4/25	4/29	5/11

Indicated div.: $0.84

CAPITALIZATION (12/31/92):

	($000)	(%)
Total Deposits	2,086,144	84.2
Total Debt	154,156	6.2
Common & Surplus	219,276	8.8
Loan Valuation Reserve	19,404	0.8
Total	2,478,980	100.0

DIVIDEND ACHIEVER STATUS:
Rank: 12 1983-93 Growth Rate: 22.2%
Total Years of Dividend Growth: 10

RECENT DEVELOPMENTS: For the year ended 12/31/93, net income was $25.8 million, compared with income before cumulative effect of change in accounting principle of $23.5 million last year. Total average earning assets were modestly higher during 1993 compared with 1992 primarily due to the acquisition of National Bank of Royal Oak on 10/1/93. The composition of average earning assets changed as total average loans increased $104.0 million to 70.0% of average earning assets from 67.2% in 1992. This increase was offset in part by a $54.9 million decline in money market investments to 2.9% of average earning assets in 1993 from 5.3% in 1992. Total average interest-bearing liability balances were 0.7% higher in 1993 than in 1992, while average noninterest-bearing deposit balances were 11.3% higher. Average yields on earning assets declined to 7.39% in 1993 from 8.15% in 1992. However, the interest spread on earning assets increased to 4.18% from 4.05% in 1992.

BUSINESS

CITIZENS BANKING CORPORATION is a bank holding company headquartered in Flint, Michigan, and is the parent of Citizens Commercial & Savings Bank, Flint; Second National Bank of Saginaw; Second National Bank of Bay City; National Bank of Royal Oak; State Bank of Standish; Grayling State Bank; Century Life Insurance Company of Michigan, a credit life reinsurance company, and Commercial National Bank, Berwyn, Illinois.

ANNUAL EARNINGS AND DIVIDENDS PER SHARE

	1993	1992	1991	1990	1989	1988	1987
Earnings Per Share	**1.87**	**[1] 1.80**	**1.62**	**1.51**	**1.43**	**1.34**	**1.19**
Dividends Per Share	**0.75**	**[2] 0.69**	**0.645**	**0.60**	**0.555**	**0.495**	**0.48**
Dividend Payout %	**40.1**	**38.4**	**39.9**	**39.7**	**38.8**	**36.9**	**40.3**

Note: 2-for-1stk.split,5/12/93. [1] Before acctg. chg. [2] Bef acctg chge [3] Before extraord. item [4] 50% stk. div., 8/86.

ANNUAL FINANCIAL DATA

	1993	1992	1991	1990	1989	1988	1987
RECORD OF EARNINGS (IN MILLIONS):							
Total Interest Income	166.5	178.8	210.6	221.0	219.1	197.8	177.6
Total Interest Expense	62.1	78.8	111.4	122.9	122.4	107.4	97.9
Net Interest Income	104.3	100.0	99.2	98.1	96.7	90.4	79.7
Provision for Loan Losses	5.6	6.3	6.1	5.6	7.5	5.7	3.8
Net Income	25.8	[1] 23.5	21.1	20.1	19.1	18.0	16.2
Aver. Shs. Outstg. (000)	13,724	13,079	13,061	13,300	13,394	13,440	13,572
[1] Before acctg. change dr$12,905,000. [2] Before extra. item cr$1,960,000.							
BALANCE SHEET (IN MILLIONS):							
Cash & Due From Banks	113.3	121.4	122.9	121.3	132.1	131.4	116.2
Net Loans	1,757.6	1,535.0	1,512.4	1,536.3	1,479.3	1,420.0	1,276.1
Total Domestic Deposits	2,246.8	2,086.1	2,064.0	2,018.3	1,954.8	1,935.5	1,889.9
Long-term Debt	10.9	15.1	20.4	43.3	33.0	19.6	18.1
Net Stockholders' Equity	255.2	219.3	218.2	205.9	196.6	185.1	175.6
Total Assets	2,714.1	2,498.8	2,492.6	2,425.2	2,392.6	2,354.1	2,276.1
Year End Shs Outstg (000)	14,115	13,103	13,079	13,124	13,392	13,406	13,606
STATISTICAL RECORD:							
Return on Assets %	0.95	0.94	0.85	0.83	0.80	0.76	0.71
Return on Equity %	10.10	10.70	9.70	9.80	9.70	9.70	9.20
Book Value Per Share	18.08	16.73	16.68	15.69	14.68	13.80	12.91
Average Yield %	3.2	4.2	5.5	5.6	4.2	3.6	...
P/E Ratio	15.2-9.9	10.7-7.6	9.3-5.2	8.4-5.9	10.2-8.0	11.4-9.0	...
Price Range	28½-18½	19¼-13⅝	15⅛-8⅜	12⅝-8⅞	14⅝-11½	15¼-12⅛	...

Statistics are as originally reported.

OFFICERS:
D.E. Johnson, Jr., Chairman
J.W. Ennest, Vice-Chmn. & C.O.O.
C.R. Weeks, Pres. & C.E.O.
W.G. Schaeffer, Exec. V.P., C.F.O. & Treas.

INCORPORATED: MI, 1982

PRINCIPAL OFFICE: One Citizens Banking Center, Flint, MI 48502

TELEPHONE NUMBER: (810) 766-7500

NO. OF EMPLOYEES: 1,710

ANNUAL MEETING: In April

SHAREHOLDERS: 6,500 (approx.)

INSTITUTIONAL HOLDINGS:
No. of Institutions: 26
Shares Held: 1,385,170

REGISTRAR(S): Mellon Securities Trust Co., Pittsburgh, PA

TRANSFER AGENT(S): Mellon Securities Trust Co., Pittsburgh, PA

NYS SYMBOL CLC
Rec. Pr. 17¾

CLARCOR INC.

YIELD 3.5%
P/E RATIO 15.0

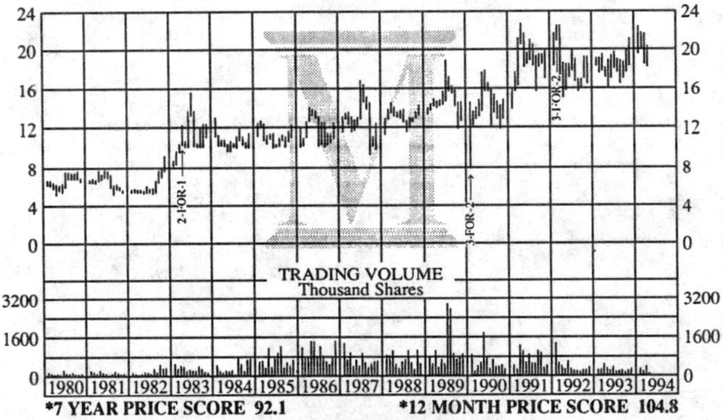

***7 YEAR PRICE SCORE 92.1** ***12 MONTH PRICE SCORE 104.8**

*NYSE COMPOSITE INDEX=100

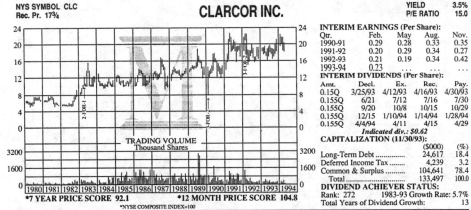

INTERIM EARNINGS (Per Share):

Qtr.	Feb.	May	Aug.	Nov.
1990-91	0.29	0.28	0.33	0.35
1991-92	0.20	0.29	0.34	0.27
1992-93	0.21	0.19	0.34	0.42
1993-94	0.23	...	...	...

INTERIM DIVIDENDS (Per Share):

Amt.	Decl.	Ex.	Rec.	Pay.
0.15Q	3/25/93	4/12/93	4/16/93	4/30/93
0.155Q	6/21	7/12	7/16	7/30
0.155Q	9/20	10/8	10/15	10/29
0.155Q	12/15	1/10/94	1/14/94	1/28/94
0.155Q	4/4/94	4/11	4/15	4/29

Indicated div.: $0.62

CAPITALIZATION (11/30/93):

	($000)	(%)
Long-Term Debt	24,617	18.4
Deferred Income Tax	4,239	3.2
Common & Surplus	104,641	78.4
Total	133,497	100.0

DIVIDEND ACHIEVER STATUS:
Rank: 272 1983-93 Growth Rate: 5.7%
Total Years of Dividend Growth: 13

RECENT DEVELOPMENTS: For the quarter ended 2/26/94, earnings before an accounting change were $3.4 million, or $0.23 per share, compared with earnings of $3.1 million, or $0.21 per share, for the corresponding period last year. Net sales rose 33.3% to $55.9 million, reflecting the contributions from CLC's 1993 acquisitions as well as internal growth in its filtration segment. Operating profit increased 17.1% to $5.9 million. Sales for the consumer products group decreased 12.4%, primarily due to reduced sales volume in metal containers. Including the effect of acquisitions, the filtrations products group sales increased 55%. On 1/31/94, CLC sold the assets and ongoing business of one of its start-up filtration companies, OilpureSystems, to V.S. Company of Kansas City.

BUSINESS

CLARCOR INC. is a manufacturer of filtration products and consumer products. The filtration products group includes five individual companies which provide filtration and purification systems for over-the-road trucking, off-road trucking, off-road construction, farming and mining equipment and railroad industries, food and beverage processing, and general industrial markets. The consumer products group manufactures custom-decorated metal and plastic lithographed containers, composite and paperboard containers, collapsible tubes, promotional products and engineered plastic closures. The precision products group will be divested. During 1993, CLC purchased Airguard Industries, an air filter manufacturer, and Guardian, a specialty air and liquid filter manufacturer, both of which are headquartered in Louisville, Kentucky.

BUSINESS LINE ANALYSIS

(11/30/93)	Rev(%)	Inc(%)
Filtration Products.....	69.3	67.6
Consumer Products ...	30.7	32.4
Total	100.0	100.0

ANNUAL EARNINGS AND DIVIDENDS PER SHARE

	11/30/93	11/30/92	11/30/91	11/30/90	11/30/89	11/30/88	11/30/87
Earnings Per Share	**1.16**	**[1] 1.10**	**[3] 1.24**	**1.37**	**[3] 0.47**	**1.15**	**1.03**
Dividends Per Share	**0.61**	**[2] 0.60**	**[4] 0.55**	**[5] 0.52**	**0.48**	**0.453**	**0.433**
Dividend Payout %	**52.6**	**54.5**	**44.4**	**37.9**	**N.M.**	**39.4**	**41.6**

[1] Before acctg. chg. [2] Bef acctg chge [3] Before disc. oper. [4] 3-for-2 stk split,02/18/92 [5] 3-for-2 stk split, 1/12/90

ANNUAL FINANCIAL DATA

RECORD OF EARNINGS (IN THOUSANDS):							
Total Revenues	225,319	188,625	179,538	214,710	204,112	202,337	180,415
Costs and Expenses	189,957	155,615	143,687	173,122	177,011	164,279	141,238
Depreciation & Amort	6,295	5,380	4,998	7,801	7,117	6,287	6,685
Operating Profit	29,067	27,630	30,853	33,787	19,984	31,771	32,492
Earn Bef Income Taxes	27,078	25,305	28,543	32,556	18,969	33,106	33,849
Income Taxes	9,827	8,796	10,068	12,151	11,028	12,508	15,069
Net Income	17,251	[1] 16,509	[2] 18,475	20,405	[3] 7,941	20,598	18,780
Aver. Shs. Outstg.	14,838	14,973	14,873	...	...	...	...

[1] Before acctg. change dr$2,370,000. [2] Before disc. op. cr$297,000. [3] Before disc. op. dr$824,000.

BALANCE SHEET (IN THOUSANDS):							
Cash and Cash Equivalents	13,838	15,051	9,629	14,810	4,815	20,852	25,427
Receivables, Net	44,152	52,019	35,677	31,951	27,239	27,102	21,959
Inventories	26,996	25,007	28,417	23,855	23,715	20,629	19,945
Gross Property	112,254	95,182	113,923	104,714	102,805	95,701	89,097
Accumulated Depreciation	64,618	59,598	68,211	61,966	58,582	53,638	49,269
Long-Term Debt	24,617	29,325	35,834	35,810	32,634	1,116	1,507
Net Stockholders' Equity	104,641	99,551	95,662	82,689	72,662	125,012	115,015
Total Assets	169,896	161,255	157,999	144,127	131,009	143,842	134,877
Total Current Assets	86,161	93,627	75,207	72,623	58,019	70,028	67,523
Total Current Liabilities	33,288	25,272	20,570	20,758	21,405	14,244	15,899
Net Working Capital	52,873	68,355	54,637	51,865	36,614	55,784	51,624
Year End Shares Outstg	14,819	14,986	14,908	14,846	15,045	17,900	18,099

STATISTICAL RECORD:							
Operating Profit Margin %	12.9	14.6	17.2	15.7	9.8	15.7	18.0
Book Value Per Share	6.00	5.79	5.03	4.13	3.33	5.46	4.92
Return on Equity %	16.5	16.6	19.3	24.7	10.9	16.5	16.3
Return on Assets %	10.2	10.2	11.7	14.2	6.1	14.3	13.9
Average Yield %	3.3	3.2	3.0	4.0	3.1	3.5	3.3
P/E Ratio	18.2-13.8	20.5-13.6	18.2-11.3	13.0-5.7	40.2-25.0	12.6-9.9	16.4-9.0
Price Range	21⅛-16	22½-15	22⅝-14	17⅞-7⅞	18⅞-11¾	14½-11⅜	16⅞-9¼

Statistics are as originally reported.

OFFICERS:
L.E. Gloyd, Chmn., Pres. & C.E.O.
L.P. Harnois, Sr. V.P. & C.F.O.
W.F. Knese, V.P., Treas. & Contr.
M.C. Arne, V.P. & Sec.

INCORPORATED: DE, 1969

PRINCIPAL OFFICE: 2323 Sixth Street P.O. Box 7007, Rockford, IL 61125

TELEPHONE NUMBER: (815) 962-8867

FAX: (815) 962-0417

NO. OF EMPLOYEES: 2,062 (approx.)

ANNUAL MEETING: In March

SHAREHOLDERS: 1,960 (approx.)

INSTITUTIONAL HOLDINGS:
No. of Institutions: 79
Shares Held: 6,901,285

REGISTRAR(S): First Chicago Trust Co. of New York, New York, NY 10008

TRANSFER AGENT(S): First Chicago Trust Co. of New York, New York, NY 10008

CLOROX CO.

YIELD 3.5%
P/E RATIO 16.1

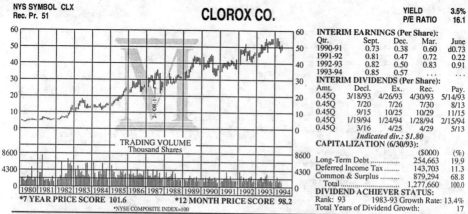

INTERIM EARNINGS (Per Share):

Qtr.	Sept.	Dec.	Mar.	June
1990-91	0.73	0.38	0.60	d0.73
1991-92	0.81	0.47	0.72	0.22
1992-93	0.82	0.50	0.83	0.91
1993-94	0.85	0.57	...	...

INTERIM DIVIDENDS (Per Share):

Amt.	Decl.	Ex.	Rec.	Pay.
0.45Q	3/18/93	4/26/93	4/30/93	5/14/93
0.45Q	7/20	7/26	7/30	8/13
0.45Q	9/15	10/25	10/29	11/15
0.45Q	1/19/94	1/24/94	1/28/94	2/15/94
0.45Q	3/16	4/25	4/29	5/13

Indicated div.: $1.80

CAPITALIZATION (6/30/93):

	($000)	(%)
Long-Term Debt	254,663	19.9
Deferred Income Tax	143,703	11.3
Common & Surplus	879,294	68.8
Total	1,277,660	100.0

DIVIDEND ACHIEVER STATUS:
Rank: 93   1983-93 Growth Rate: 13.4%
Total Years of Dividend Growth: 17

TRADING VOLUME
Thousand Shares

*7 YEAR PRICE SCORE 101.6   *12 MONTH PRICE SCORE 98.2
*NYSE COMPOSITE INDEX=100

RECENT DEVELOPMENTS: For the quarter ended 12/31/93, income from continuing operations rose 13.1% to $30.6 million from $27.0 million a year ago. Sales grew 13.3% to $370.8 million. The increase in sales was a result of a 9% increase in shipments and an increase in CLX's interest in an Argentine business to 90% from 50%. Shipments of household products were up strongly, aided by the introduction of several new products, including Liquid-Plumr build-up remover and Formula 409 glass & surface cleaner.

PROSPECTS: New product introductions and line extensions are expected to remain at a high level and will help fuel future growth. Although these developments will increase investment spending and competition will remain intense, Clorox will continue to focus on cutting $25 million in operating expenses. International shipments, especially to the growing Asia/Pacific and Latin American regions, should continue to increase. For the long term, Clorox will continue its strategic plan of divesting operations that do not fit the Company's product portfolio.

BUSINESS

THE CLOROX COMPANY is a diversified international company whose principal business is to develop, manufacture and market consumer products sold in grocery stores and other retail outlets. In addition, many of these products are included in the line of products sold to food service customers such as schools, hotels and restaurants. Major consumer products inclue: Clorox liquid bleach; Clorox 2 dry bleach; Clorox Pre-Wash and Clorox Detergent. Other name brands are: Formula 409 spray cleaner, Soft Scrub liquid cleanser, Pine-Sol cleaners and Combat insecticides.

QUARTERLY DATA

(6/30/92)($000)	Rev	Inc
1st Quarter	394,657	44,596
2nd Quarter	327,354	27,243
3rd Quarter	435,559	45,420
4th Quarter	476,601	49,792

ANNUAL EARNINGS AND DIVIDENDS PER SHARE

	6/30/93	6/30/92	6/30/91	6/30/90	6/30/89	6/30/88
Earnings Per Share	[1] 3.07	[2] 2.17	0.98	2.80	[3] 2.63	2.46
Dividends Per Share	1.77	1.65	1.53	1.39	1.19	1.00
Dividend Payout %	57.7	76.0	N.M.	49.6	45.2	40.7

[1] Before disc. oper. [2] Before acctg. chg. [3] 2-for-1 stk. split, 6/87.

ANNUAL FINANCIAL DATA

RECORD OF EARNINGS (IN MILLIONS):

Total Revenues	1,634.2	1,717.0	1,646.5	1,484.0	1,356.3	1,259.9
Costs and Expenses	1,254.2	1,371.3	1,446.7	1,217.4	1,104.9	1,015.2
Depreciation & Amort	83.6	89.6	87.0	50.1	44.7	37.5
Operating Profit	296.4	256.1	112.8	216.6	206.7	207.3
Earn Fr Cont Opers Bef Inc Taxes	275.2	210.9	86.2	243.6	229.7	211.8
Provision for Inc Taxes	107.3	93.1	33.4	90.0	84.1	79.2
Net Income	[1] 167.9	[2] 117.8	52.7	153.6	[3] 145.6	132.6
Aver. Shs. Outstg. (000)	54,698	54,366	54,063	54,873	55,333	53,927

[1] Before disc. op. dr$867,000. [2] Before acctg. change dr$19,061,000. [3] Before disc. op. dr$21,416,000.

BALANCE SHEET (IN MILLIONS):

Cash and Cash Equivalents	71.2	69.0	113.9	124.6	233.3	259.3
Receivables, Net	246.0	226.7	219.5	151.5	143.4	139.3
Total Inventories	105.9	110.5	116.3	128.1	110.6	97.4
Gross Property	814.3	865.4	760.6	712.4	572.1	523.2
Accumulated Depreciation	276.2	283.9	238.8	194.9	161.2	147.3
Long-Term Debt	254.7	262.3	406.8	7.5	7.1	29.2
Net Stockholders' Equity	879.3	813.7	784.3	810.5	786.2	712.9
Total Assets	1,649.2	1,614.8	1,602.7	1,137.7	1,213.1	1,156.0
Total Current Assets	531.8	418.3	466.8	418.4	614.8	504.3
Total Current Liabilities	371.6	421.5	348.4	225.6	330.8	314.4
Net Working Capital	160.2	d3.2	118.4	192.8	284.1	189.9
Year End Shs Outstg (000)	54,850	54,545	54,196	54,032	55,398	54,044

STATISTICAL RECORD:

Operating Profit Margin %	18.1	14.9	6.9	14.6	15.2	16.5
Book Value Per Share	7.57	6.13	5.36	13.12	12.39	9.50
Return on Equity %	19.1	14.5	6.7	19.0	18.5	18.6
Return on Assets %	10.2	7.3	3.3	13.5	12.0	11.5
Average Yield %	3.6	3.6	4.0	3.6	3.2	3.3
P/E Ratio	18.0-14.3	24.0-18.2	43.2-35.7	16.2-11.5	16.9-11.5	13.7-10.6
Price Range	55⅜-44	52-39½	42⅜-35	45⅜-32⅛	44½-30⅛	33¾-26⅛

Statistics are as originally reported.

OFFICERS:
G.C. Sullivan, Chmn., Pres. & C.E.O.
E.A. Cutter, Sr. V.P., Gen. Counsel & Sec.
W.F. Ausfahl, Group V.P. & C.F.O.
K.M. Rose, V.P. & Treas.
INCORPORATED: DE, 1986
PRINCIPAL OFFICE: 1221 Broadway, Oakland, CA 94612-1888

TELEPHONE NUMBER: (510) 271-7000
NO. OF EMPLOYEES: 639 (approx.)
ANNUAL MEETING: In November
SHAREHOLDERS: 8,921 (approx.)
INSTITUTIONAL HOLDINGS:
No. of Institutions: 320
Shares Held: 28,032,918

REGISTRAR(S): First Chicago Trust Co. of New York, New York, NY 10008

TRANSFER AGENT(S): First Chicago Trust Co. of New York, New York, NY 10008

NYS SYMBOL KO
Rec. Pr. 40½

COCA-COLA CO.

YIELD 1.9%
P/E RATIO 23.7

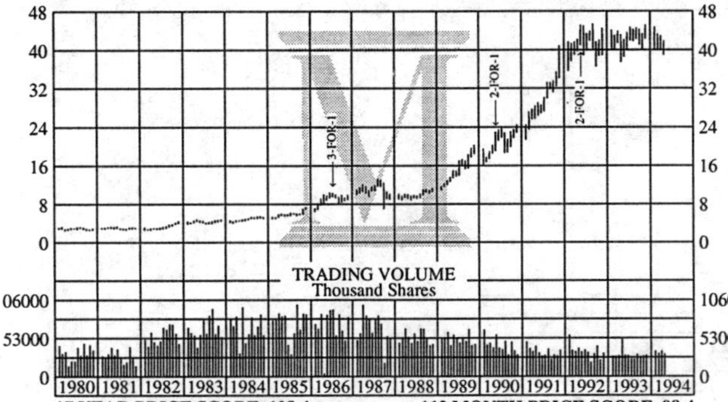

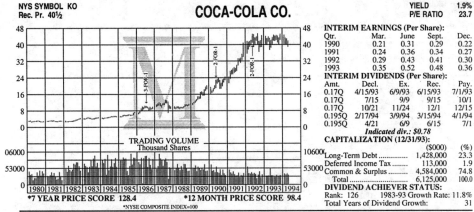

***7 YEAR PRICE SCORE 128.4** ***12 MONTH PRICE SCORE 98.4**

*NYSE COMPOSITE INDEX=100

INTERIM EARNINGS (Per Share):

Qtr.	Mar.	June	Sept.	Dec.
1990	0.21	0.31	0.29	0.22
1991	0.24	0.36	0.34	0.27
1992	0.29	0.43	0.41	0.30
1993	0.35	0.52	0.48	0.36

INTERIM DIVIDENDS (Per Share):

Amt.	Decl.	Ex.	Rec.	Pay.
0.17Q	4/15/93	6/9/93	6/15/93	7/1/93
0.17Q	7/15	9/9	9/15	10/1
0.17Q	10/21	11/24	12/1	12/15
0.195Q	2/17/94	3/9/94	3/15/94	4/1/94
0.195Q	4/21	6/9	6/15	7/1

Indicated div.: $0.78

CAPITALIZATION (12/31/93):

	($000)	(%)
Long-Term Debt	1,428,000	23.3
Deferred Income Tax	113,000	1.9
Common & Surplus	4,584,000	74.8
Total	6,125,000	100.0

DIVIDEND ACHIEVER STATUS:
Rank: 126 1983-93 Growth Rate: 11.8%
Total Years of Dividend Growth: 31

RECENT DEVELOPMENTS: For the year ended 12/31/93, net income was $2.19 billion compared with $1.88 billion in 1992. Increased efficiencies and favorable raw material costs contributed to the gain. Revenues rose 6.8% to $13.96 billion. In Latin America, operating income advanced 16%, led by unit case volume gains in Mexico, Brazil, and Chile. In the Northeast Europe/Middle East group, operating income increased 41%. Coca-Cola Foods posted a 13% in operating income and a 16% increase in unit volume.

PROSPECTS: International sales should increase in the near term due to continued infrastructure investments in the emerging markets of East Central Europe. The foods segment should continue to benefit from higher operating margins, particularly in the juice business. Also, new product introductions such as Nestea and Powerade should continue to help sales and growth potential in North America. For the long term, KO is planning to invest $1 billion a year in markets in China and India.

BUSINESS

THE COCA-COLA BOTTLING COMPANY CONSOLIDATED is the world's largest producer and distributor of soft drinks, soft drink concentrates and syrups. Principal soft drink products are: Coca-Cola, Coca-Cola Classic, Diet Coke, Fanta, Sprite, plus other assorted diet and caffeine-free versions. Coca-Cola Foods markets and processes citrus and other fruit juices and fruit drink products, primarily orange juice. Popular brands include Minute Maid and Hi-C.

BUSINESS LINE ANALYSIS

(12/31/93)	Rev(%)	Inc(%)
Soft Drinks-USA	21.3	17.7
Soft Drinks-International	66.0	78.7
Foods	12.7	3.6
Total	100.0	100.0

ANNUAL EARNINGS AND DIVIDENDS PER SHARE

	1993	1992	1991	1990	1989	1988	1987
Earnings Per Share	**1.68**	**[1] 1.43**	**1.21**	**1.02**	**[4] 0.89**	**0.72**	**0.61**
Dividends Per Share	**0.68**	**[2] 0.56**	**0.48**	**[3] 0.40**	**0.34**	**0.30**	**0.28**
Dividend Payout %	**40.5**	**39.2**	**39.5**	**39.2**	**40.1**	**42.1**	**46.1**

[1] Before acctg. chg. [2] 2-for-1 stk split, 5/12/92 [3] Adj for 2-for-1 stk split, 5/11/90 [4] Before disc. oper.

ANNUAL FINANCIAL DATA

	1993	1992	1991	1990	1989	1988	1987
RECORD OF EARNINGS (IN MILLIONS):							
Net Operating Revenues	13,957.0	13,073.9	11,571.6	10,236.4	8,965.8	8,337.8	7,658.3
Costs and Expenses	10,495.0	9,981.8	8,991.1	8,040.9	7,056.2	6,569.8	6,182.6
Depreciation & Amort	360.0	321.9	261.4	243.9	183.8	169.8	151.9
Operating Income	3,102.0	2,770.1	2,319.0	1,951.6	1,725.8	1,598.3	1,323.8
Income Bef Income Taxes	3,185.0	2,746.1	2,383.3	2,014.4	1,764.3	1,582.1	1,410.2
Income Taxes	997.0	862.3	765.3	632.5	571.5	537.4	494.0
Net Income	2,176.0	1,664.4	1,618.0	1,381.9	[1] 1,192.8	1,044.7	916.1
Aver. Shs. Outstg. (000)	1,302,000	1,316,758	1,332,944	1,337,140	1,383,962	1,458,448	1,509,488
[1] Before disc. op. cr$530,986,000.							
BALANCE SHEET (IN MILLIONS):							
Total Cash & Securities	1,078.0	1,063.0	1,117.2	1,492.1	1,181.7	1,231.2	1,468.3
Receivables, Net	1,243.0	1,085.6	969.6	951.7	820.4	784.0	1,217.0
Inventories	1,049.0	1,018.6	987.8	982.3	789.1	778.8	776.7
Gross Property	5,596.0	5,242.9	4,444.6	3,785.7	3,294.7	2,908.9	2,639.6
Accumulated Depreciation	1,867.0	1,716.6	1,554.8	1,400.2	1,273.5	1,149.8	1,042.0
Long-Term Debt	1,428.0	1,120.1	985.3	535.9	548.7	761.1	803.4
Net Stockholders' Equity	4,584.0	3,888.4	4,425.8	3,849.2	3,485.5	3,345.3	3,223.8
Total Assets	12,021.0	11,051.9	10,222.4	9,278.2	8,282.5	7,450.6	8,355.6
Total Current Assets	4,434.0	4,247.7	4,144.2	4,142.8	3,603.5	3,245.4	4,136.2
Total Current Liabilities	5,171.0	5,303.2	4,117.6	4,296.5	3,657.9	2,868.9	4,118.5
Net Working Capital	d737.0	d1,055.5	26.7	d153.7	d54.4	376.5	17.7
Year End Shs Outstg (000)	1,297,453	1,306,771	1,328,960	1,336,478	1,348,060	1,419,156	1,489,424
STATISTICAL RECORD:							
Operating Profit Margin %	22.2	21.2	20.0	19.1	19.2	19.2	17.3
Book Value Per Share	3.11	2.68	3.10	2.62	2.19	2.11	2.11
Return on Equity %	47.7	48.4	36.6	35.9	34.2	31.2	28.4
Return on Assets %	18.2	17.0	15.8	14.9	14.4	14.0	11.0
Average Yield %	1.6	1.4	1.5	2.0	2.2	3.0	2.8
P/E Ratio	26.9-22.3	31.7-24.9	33.8-17.7	24.0-16.1	23.8-12.8	15.8-12.2	21.7-11.5
Price Range	45⅛-37½	45⅜-35⅝	40⅞-21⅜	24½-16⅜	20¼-10⅞	11⅜-8¾	13¼-7

Statistics are as originally reported.

OFFICERS:
R.C. Goizueta, Chmn. & C.E.O.
J.L. Stahl, Sr.V.P. & C.F.O.
S.E. Shaw, Sec.
L.E. Disley, V.P. & Treas.

INCORPORATED: DE, Sept., 1919

PRINCIPAL OFFICE: One Coca-Cola Plaza, Atlanta, GA 30313

TELEPHONE NUMBER: (404) 676-2121
FAX: (404) 676-5856
NO. OF EMPLOYEES: 34,000
ANNUAL MEETING: In April
SHAREHOLDERS: 163,817
INSTITUTIONAL HOLDINGS:
No. of Institutions: 888
Shares Held: 692,431,011

REGISTRAR(S): First Chicago Trust Company of New York, New York, NY

TRANSFER AGENT(S): First Chicago Trust Company of New York, New York, NY

NYS SYMBOL CL
Rec. Pr. 57⅝

COLGATE-PALMOLIVE CO.

YIELD 2.5%
P/E RATIO 17.0

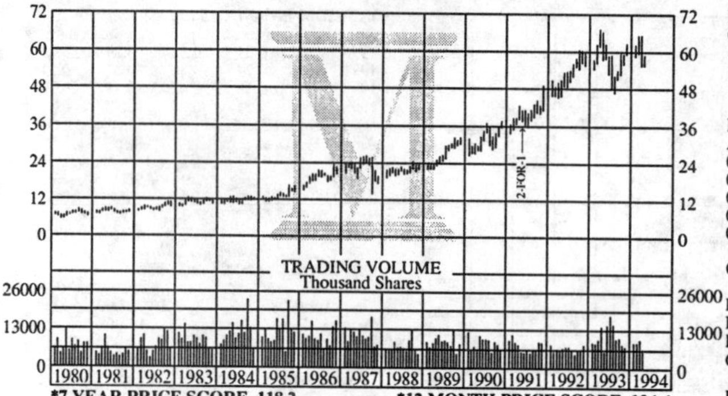

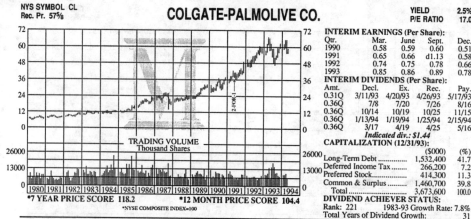

***7 YEAR PRICE SCORE 118.2** ***12 MONTH PRICE SCORE 104.4**

*NYSE COMPOSITE INDEX=100

INTERIM EARNINGS (Per Share):

Qtr.	Mar.	June	Sept.	Dec.
1990	0.58	0.59	0.60	0.51
1991	0.65	0.66	d1.13	0.58
1992	0.74	0.75	0.78	0.66
1993	0.85	0.86	0.89	0.78

INTERIM DIVIDENDS (Per Share):

Amt.	Decl.	Ex.	Rec.	Pay.
0.31Q	3/11/93	4/20/93	4/26/93	5/17/93
0.36Q	7/8	7/20	7/26	8/16
0.36Q	10/14	10/19	10/25	11/15
0.36Q	1/13/94	1/19/94	1/25/94	2/15/94
0.36Q	3/17	4/19	4/25	5/16

Indicated div.: $1.44

CAPITALIZATION (12/31/93):

	($000)	(%)
Long-Term Debt	1,532,400	41.7
Deferred Income Tax	266,200	7.2
Preferred Stock	414,300	11.3
Common & Surplus	1,460,700	39.8
Total	3,673,600	100.0

DIVIDEND ACHIEVER STATUS:
Rank: 221 1983-93 Growth Rate: 7.8%
Total Years of Dividend Growth: 31

RECENT DEVELOPMENTS: For the year ended 12/31/93, net income was $548.1 million compared with $477.0 million last year. Sales rose 2.1% to $7.14 billion, while unit volume increased 5%. Results benefited from a shift in the product mix to higher-margin product categories and an improvement in manufacturing efficiencies. Gross profit margin improved to 47.8% from 47.1% due to product mix changes and capital expenditures directed to savings projects. During the year, capital expenditures increased 14% to $364 million to fund expansion in developing countries and savings projects.

PROSPECTS: CL's presence in both developed and developing markets outside the U.S. will position the Company to take advantage of growth opportunities, especially in the Latin America and Asia/Africa markets. Domestic operations will continue to face intense competition; however, the Company's strategy of shifting the product mix to higher-margin products should enhance profitability. Also, the restructuring of CL's European operations will help increase production efficiency and reduce costs.

BUSINESS

COLGATE-PALMOLIVE COMPANY is a worldwide manufacturer and marketer of consumer products. The Company operates two segments. Oral, Personal and Household Care products consists of toothpastes, toothbrushes, soaps, shampoos, baby products, deodorants, detergents, cleaners, shave products and other similar items. Specialty Marketing consists of pet dietary care products, crystal tableware, and portable fuel for warming food. Principal global trademarks include Colgate, Palmolive, Ajax, Fab, and Science Diet, in addition to various regional tradenames.

BUSINESS LINE ANALYSIS

(12/31/93)	Rev(%)	Inc(%)
Oral, Personal & Househld	87.4	82.3
Specialty Marketing	12.6	17.7
Total	100.0	100.0

ANNUAL EARNINGS AND DIVIDENDS PER SHARE

	1993	1992	1991	1990	1989	1988	1987
Earnings Per Share	**3.38**	**2.92**	**0.77**	**[2] 2.28**	**1.98**	**[3] 1.11**	**0.39**
Dividends Per Share	**1.34**	**1.15**	**[1] 1.02**	**0.90**	**0.78**	**0.79**	**0.695**
Dividend Payout %	**39.7**	**50.2**	**N.M.**	**39.5**	**39.3**	**71.2**	**N.M.**

[1] 2-for-1 stk split,05/16/91 [2] Primary shares [3] Before disc. oper.

ANNUAL FINANCIAL DATA

	1993	1992	1991	1990	1989	1988	1987
RECORD OF EARNINGS (IN MILLIONS):							
Total Revenues	7,141.3	7,007.2	6,060.3	5,691.3	5,038.8	4,734.3	5,647.5
Costs and Expenses	5,977.4	6,016.1	5,632.5	5,010.4	4,506.3	4,347.8	5,373.3
Depreciation & Amort	209.6	192.5	146.2	126.2	97.0	82.0	101.3
Operating Profit	3,411.4	3,298.8	2,764.0	2,570.3	2,195.8	304.5	383.9
Income Bef Income Taxes	836.2	727.9	217.9	511.4	447.0	250.2	122.8
Income Taxes	288.1	250.9	93.0	190.4	166.9	97.6	68.8
Net Income	[1] 548.1	477.0	124.9	321.0	280.0	[2] 152.7	54.0
Aver. Shs. Outstg. (000)	155,900	156,500	135,300	132,200	135,804	136,762	137,154

[1] Before acctg. change dr$358,200,000. [2] Before disc. op. cr$165,134,000.

	1993	1992	1991	1990	1989	1988	1987
BALANCE SHEET (IN MILLIONS):							
Cash & Short-term Invests	...	220.5	245.4	276.4	524.2	365.5	57.1
Receivables, Net	988.3	876.5	744.2	665.7	600.9	589.3	723.3
Inventories	678.0	695.6	675.9	692.4	590.7	629.7	753.4
Gross Property	2,820.2	2,582.4	2,360.6	2,124.3	1,728.7	1,636.3	1,966.3
Accumulated Depreciation	1,053.9	985.6	965.7	761.9	623.2	614.7	764.5
Long-Term Debt	1,532.4	946.5	850.8	1,068.4	1,059.5	674.3	694.1
Net Stockholders' Equity	1,875.0	2,619.8	1,866.3	1,363.6	1,123.2	1,150.6	941.1
Total Assets	5,761.2	5,434.1	4,510.6	4,157.9	3,536.5	3,217.6	3,227.7
Total Current Assets	2,070.4	1,995.1	1,857.7	1,812.7	1,896.9	1,782.8	1,716.5
Total Current Liabilities	1,394.0	1,359.5	1,261.7	1,296.7	989.4	1,071.9	1,277.0
Net Working Capital	676.4	635.6	596.0	516.0	907.5	710.9	439.5
Year End Shs Outstg (000)	149,257	137,268	123,128	95,267	94,509	138,138	107,020
STATISTICAL RECORD:							
Operating Profit Margin %	13.4	11.4	4.6	9.7	8.6	6.4	3.1
Book Value Per Share	...	5.62	5.02	3.99	7.41	8.24	8.68
Return on Equity %	29.2	18.2	6.7	23.5	24.9	13.3	5.7
Return on Assets %	9.5	8.8	2.8	7.7	7.9	4.7	1.7
Average Yield %	2.4	2.2	2.5	2.8	2.9	3.6	3.4
P/E Ratio	19.9-13.8	20.8-15.5	63.8-43.7	16.6-11.6	16.4-11.2	22.3-17.3	67.6-35.9
Price Range	67¼-46¾	60⅝-45⅛	49⅛-33⅝	37¾-26⅜	32½-22⅛	24¾-19¼	26⅜-14

Statistics are as originally reported.

OFFICERS:
R. Mark, Chmn. & C.E.O.
W.S. Shanahan, Pres. & C.O.O.
B.J. Heidtke, V.P. & Corp. Treas.

INCORPORATED: DE, Jul., 1923

PRINCIPAL OFFICE: 300 Park Ave., New York, NY 10022-7499

TELEPHONE NUMBER: (212) 310-2000

NO. OF EMPLOYEES: 28,800 (avg.)

ANNUAL MEETING: In May

SHAREHOLDERS: 36,800 common; 470 pfd.

INSTITUTIONAL HOLDINGS:
No. of Institutions: 602
Shares Held: 83,719,456

REGISTRAR(S): First Chicago Trust Co. of New York, New York, NY 10008

TRANSFER AGENT(S): First Chicago Trust Co. of New York, New York, NY 10008

NASDAQ SYMBOL CGES
Rec. Pr. 20 (Marginable)

COLONIAL GAS CO.

YIELD 6.3%
P/E RATIO 13.2

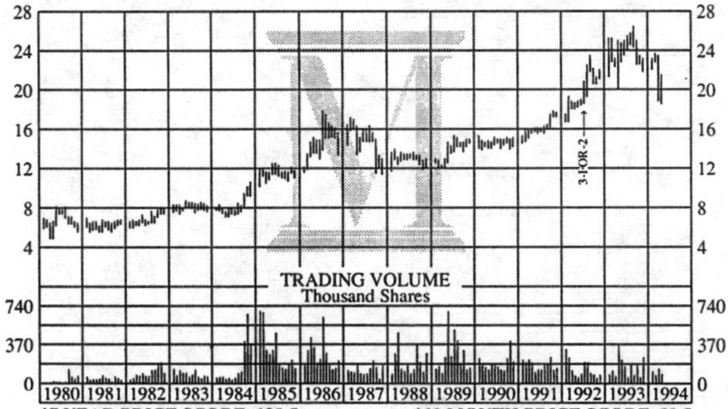

***7 YEAR PRICE SCORE 108.5** ***12 MONTH PRICE SCORE 89.5**

*NYSE COMPOSITE INDEX=100

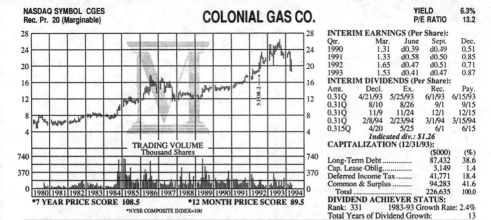

INTERIM EARNINGS (Per Share):

Qtr.	Mar.	June	Sept.	Dec.
1990	1.31	d0.39	d0.49	0.51
1991	1.33	d0.58	d0.50	0.85
1992	1.65	d0.47	d0.51	0.71
1993	1.53	d0.41	d0.47	0.87

INTERIM DIVIDENDS (Per Share):

Amt.	Decl.	Ex.	Rec.	Pay.
0.31Q	4/21/93	5/25/93	6/1/93	6/15/93
0.31Q	8/10	8/26	9/1	9/15
0.31Q	11/9	11/24	12/1	12/15
0.31Q	2/8/94	2/23/94	3/1/94	3/15/94
0.315Q	4/20	5/25	6/1	6/15

Indicated div.: $1.26

CAPITALIZATION (12/31/93):

	($000)	(%)
Long-Term Debt	87,432	38.6
Cap. Lease Oblig.	3,149	1.4
Deferred Income Tax	41,771	18.4
Common & Surplus	94,283	41.6
Total	226,635	100.0

DIVIDEND ACHIEVER STATUS:
Rank: 331 1983-93 Growth Rate: 2.4%
Total Years of Dividend Growth: 13

RECENT DEVELOPMENTS: For the year ended 12/31/93, net income rose 13.0% to $12.0 million, reflecting increased utility operating margin and improved results for the Company's energy trucking subsidiary. The 7.8% improvement in utility operating margin was principally due to three factors: a continued colder than normal weather pattern; a 3.3% increase in firm customers; and 4.9% base rate increase effective 11/1/93. The cooler weather and growing customer base contributed to an increase in firm gas sales of 2.1% or 393,000 Mcf to 18,935,000 Mcf. Weather during 1993 was 2.4% colder than the same period last year and 7.3% colder than normal. For the fourth quarter, net income increased to $6.9 million from $5.6 million a year ago. Utility operating margin rose 10.6% to $25.8 million from $23.3 million for the same period last year.

BUSINESS

COLONIAL GAS COMPANY is primarily a regulated natural gas distribution utility. The Company serves 132,000 utility customers in 24 municipalities located northwest of Boston and on Cape Cod. Through its wholly-owned energy trucking subsidiary, Trangas Inc., the Company also provides over-the-road transportation of liquefied natural gas (LNG), propane and other commodities. The Company's combined natural gas distribution service areas in the Merrimack Valley region northwest of Boston and on Cape Cod cover approximately 622 square miles with a year-round population of approximately 500,000, which increases by approximately 350,000 during the summer tourist season on Cape Cod.

REVENUES

(12/31/93)	($000)	(%)
Residential	106,362	64.0
Commercial & Industrial	53,933	32.4
Interruptible Sales	3,613	2.2
Transportation	816	0.5
Interruptible Transp...	409	0.2
Other	1,128	0.7
Total	166,261	100.0

ANNUAL EARNINGS AND DIVIDENDS PER SHARE

	1993	1992	1991	1990	1989	1988	1987
Earnings Per Share	**1.52**	**1.38**	**1.11**	**0.82**	**1.44**	**1.20**	**1.35**
Dividends Per Share	**1.235**	**[1] 1.213**	**1.193**	**1.167**	**1.14**	**1.113**	**1.087**
Dividend Payout %	**81.3**	**87.9**	**N.M.**	**N.M.**	**79.2**	**92.8**	**80.7**

[1] 3-for-2 stk split, 7/30/92

ANNUAL FINANCIAL DATA

	1993	1992	1991	1990	1989	1988	1987
RECORD OF EARNINGS (IN THOUSANDS):							
Total Revenues	173,819	154,853	137,719	134,298	139,892	124,428	123,805
Depreciation	6,831	5,914	5,488	5,129	4,726	4,388	3,973
Maintenance	5,631	5,477	5,124	5,235	5,335	4,994	4,844
Prov for Fed Inc Taxes	6,111	5,390	3,803	1,651	2,562	3,191	4,444
Interest & Debt Expense	8,141	7,466	8,141	8,445	8,217	7,369	6,740
Net Income	12,022	10,643	8,317	5,695	8,917	9,297	8,004
Aver. Shs. Outstg.	7,931	7,728	7,529	6,963	6,200	6,065	5,948
BALANCE SHEET (IN THOUSANDS):							
Gross Plant	267,719	244,920	220,187	205,341	189,474	177,421	168,004
Accumulated Depreciation	57,857	52,700	48,127	43,823	39,964	36,499	37,240
Prop, Plant & Equip, Net	209,862	192,220	172,060	161,518	149,510	140,922	130,764
Long-term Debt	90,581	94,341	54,248	68,837	74,226	60,559	64,128
Net Stockholders' Equity	94,283	87,771	82,221	80,109	66,568	63,027	58,238
Total Assets	312,118	302,922	264,321	237,836	233,727	212,386	187,897
Year End Shares Outstg	8,030	7,844	7,625	7,449	6,267	6,140	6,036
STATISTICAL RECORD:							
Book Value Per Share	11.39	10.83	10.42	10.38	10.18	9.81	9.18
Dep/Gr. Pl %	2.6	2.4	2.5	2.5	2.5	2.5	2.4
Accum. Dep/Gr. Pl %	21.6	21.5	21.9	21.3	21.1	20.6	22.2
Return on Equity %	12.8	12.1	10.1	7.1	13.4	11.6	13.7
Average Yield %	5.3	6.0	7.4	8.0	8.3	8.7	7.6
P/E Ratio	17.4-13.2	17.0-12.0	16.1-13.1	18.8-16.9	10.7-8.3	11.7-9.7	12.7-8.4
Price Range	26½-20	23½-16⅝	17⅞-14½	15⅝-13⅞	15⅜-12	14-11⅝	17⅛-11⅜

Statistics are as originally reported.

OFFICERS:
F.L. Putnam, Jr., Chmn. & C.E.O.
C.O. Swanson, President
N. Stravropoulos, V.P. & C.F.O.
D.W. Carroll, V.P. & Treas.

INCORPORATED: MA, Jul., 1981

PRINCIPAL OFFICE: 40 Market Street, Lowell, MA 01853

TELEPHONE NUMBER: (508) 458-3171
FAX: (508) 459-2314
NO. OF EMPLOYEES: 83 full-time; 53 part-time
ANNUAL MEETING: In April
SHAREHOLDERS: 3,843
INSTITUTIONAL HOLDINGS:
No. of Institutions: 37
Shares Held: 989,730

REGISTRAR(S):

TRANSFER AGENT(S): First National Bank of Boston, Shareholder Services Division, Boston, MA

NYS SYMBOL CMA
Rec. Pr. 29 1/8

COMERICA, INC.

YIELD 3.8%
P/E RATIO 10.2

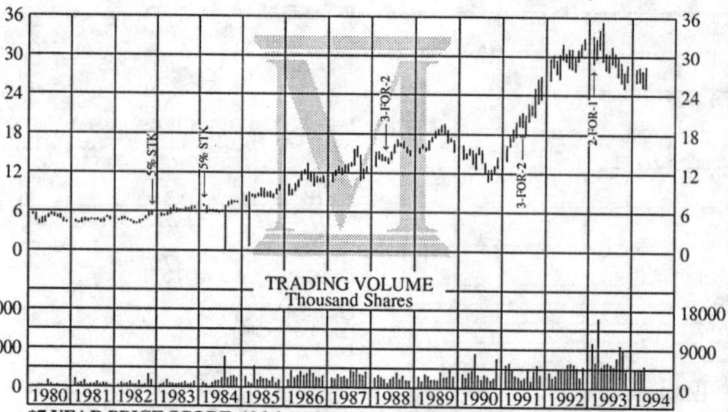

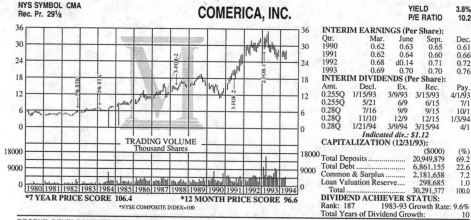

36
30
24
18
12
6
0
5% STK
5% STK
3-FOR-2
3-FOR-2
2-FOR-1
TRADING VOLUME
Thousand Shares
18000
9000
0
1980 1981 1982 1983 1984 1985 1986 1987 1988 1989 1990 1991 1992 1993 1994

***7 YEAR PRICE SCORE 106.4** ***12 MONTH PRICE SCORE 96.6**

*NYSE COMPOSITE INDEX=100

INTERIM EARNINGS (Per Share):

Qtr.	Mar.	June	Sept.	Dec.
1990	0.62	0.63	0.65	0.61
1991	0.62	0.64	0.60	0.66
1992	0.68	d0.14	0.71	0.72
1993	0.69	0.70	0.70	0.76

INTERIM DIVIDENDS (Per Share):

Amt.	Decl.	Ex.	Rec.	Pay.
0.255Q	1/15/93	3/9/93	3/15/93	4/1/93
0.255Q	5/21	6/9	6/15	7/1
0.28Q	7/16	9/9	9/15	10/1
0.28Q	11/10	12/9	12/15	1/3/94
0.28Q	1/21/94	3/9/94	3/15/94	4/1

Indicated div.: $1.12

CAPITALIZATION (12/31/93):

	($000)	(%)
Total Deposits	20,949,879	69.2
Total Debt	6,861,155	22.6
Common & Surplus	2,181,658	7.2
Loan Valuation Reserve	298,685	1.0
Total	30,291,377	100.0

DIVIDEND ACHIEVER STATUS:
Rank: 187 1983-93 Growth Rate: 9.6%
Total Years of Dividend Growth: 10

RECENT DEVELOPMENTS: For 1993, net income totaled $340.6 million, up from $240.4 million for 1992. Results for 1992 included a $128 million pre-tax restructuring charge related to the merger with Manufacturers National. The provision for loan losses was $69.0 million, down considerably from $111.6 million last year. Noninterest income rose 13% to $462.5 million. Nonperforming assets were $209 million or 1.09% of total loans and other real estate compared with $273 million or 1.50% a year ago.

PROSPECTS: Lower credit-related costs have improved earnings. The improvement in credit quality can been seen in the significant reduction of nonperforming loans. The system conversion and technology upgrades related to the merger with Manufacturers National Corp. are near completion. The acquisition of Sugar Creek National (Sugar Land, TX) was completed for $27 million worth of CMA stock. Prospects for the near-term are favorable.

BUSINESS

COMERICA, INC., the 2nd largest bank holding company in Michigan, is the parent of Comerica Bank-Detroit. At 12/31/93 , the Company had assets of approximately $30.3 billion and, in addition to Michigan, operates banks in Illinois, California, Florida and Texas. On June 18, 1992, Comerica merged with Manufacturers National Corp. The banks offer individuals, businesses and governmental agencies a full line of commercial banking services.

LOAN DISTRIBUTION

(12/31/93)	($000)	(%)
Commercial	9,087,000	47.6
International	1,136,000	6.0
Real estate contruction	437,000	2.3
Commercial Mortgage	2,700,000	14.1
Residental Mortgage	1,857,000	9.7
Consumer	3,674,000	19.2
Lease financing	209,000	1.1
Total	19,100,000	100.0

ANNUAL EARNINGS AND DIVIDENDS PER SHARE

	1993	1992	1991	1990	1989	1988	1987
Earnings Per Share	**2.85**	**1.92**	**[2] 2.52**	**[4] 2.52**	**1.55**	**2.26**	**1.38**
Dividends Per Share	**1.045**	**[1] 0.94**	**[3] 0.904**	**0.85**	**0.733**	**0.60**	**[5] 0.50**
Dividend Payout %	**36.7**	**49.0**	**35.9**	**33.8**	**47.3**	**26.5**	**36.3**

[1] 2-for-1 stk split,01/05/93 [2] chg. to reflect 3-for-2- stk split 6/91 [3] 3-for-2 stk split,06/20/91 [4] Per primary share [5] 50% stk. div. 4/88.

ANNUAL FINANCIAL DATA

	1993	1992	1991	1990	1989	1988	1987
RECORD OF EARNINGS (IN MILLIONS):							
Total Interest Income	1,782.9	1,869.7	1,219.0	1,165.8	1,116.5	919.2	822.6
Total Interest Expense	649.3	783.9	624.4	673.6	669.1	523.3	453.7
Net Interest Income	1,133.5	1,085.9	594.7	492.1	447.4	395.9	368.9
Provision for Loan Losses	69.0	113.4	57.9	57.2	103.1	38.7	79.5
Net Income	340.6	226.0	153.4	128.5	77.6	112.0	71.4
Aver. Shs. Outstg. (000)	119,569	113,716	59,484	49,598	47,501	46,862	47,745
BALANCE SHEET (IN MILLIONS):							
Cash & Due From Banks	1,600.7	1,485.5	765.8	627.9	675.1	640.4	553.8
Net Loans	18,801.3	17,509.6	9,090.1	8,178.2	7,704.9	6,790.2	5,852.5
Total Domestic Deposits	19,582.1	19,496.8	11,427.7	10,724.7	9,743.6	9,141.3	8,208.4
Total Foreign Deposits	1,367.8	897.9	13.3	29.8	139.1	108.5	194.3
Long-term Debt	1,460.6	737.0	244.3	263.8	274.3	275.7	193.6
Net Stockholders' Equity	2,181.7	2,029.4	1,052.1	791.2	704.8	668.4	593.0
Total Assets	30,294.9	26,586.8	14,450.8	13,300.4	12,149.5	11,145.5	10,116.0
Year End Shs Outstg (000)	114,871	57,438	62,320	50,006	49,371	47,115	46,572
STATISTICAL RECORD:							
Return on Assets %	1.12	0.85	1.06	0.97	0.64	1.01	0.71
Return on Equity %	15.60	11.10	14.60	16.20	11.00	16.80	12.00
Book Value Per Share	18.99	35.33	16.88	15.82	14.28	14.19	11.25
Average Yield %	3.5	3.2	4.4	6.3	4.2	4.0	3.8
P/E Ratio	12.4-8.8	17.1-13.7	10.7-5.5	6.5-4.3	12.7-9.8	7.6-5.8	11.7-7.6
Price Range	35 1/4-25 1/8	32 3/4-26 1/4	26 7/8-13 7/8	16 3/8-10 3/4	19 5/8-15 1/8	17 1/8-13	16 1/8-10 1/2

Statistics are as originally reported.

OFFICERS:
E.A. Miller, Chmn. & C.E.O.
J.D. Lewis, Vice-Chmn.
M.T. Monahan, President

INCORPORATED: DE, 1973

PRINCIPAL OFFICE: Comerica Tower at Detroit Center, Detroit, MI 48226

TELEPHONE NUMBER: (313) 222-3300
NO. OF EMPLOYEES: 11,424 full-time; 1,763 part-time
ANNUAL MEETING: In April
SHAREHOLDERS: 14,420 (approx.)
INSTITUTIONAL HOLDINGS:
No. of Institutions: 160
Shares Held: 16,258,163

REGISTRAR(S): Norwest Bank Minnesota, N.A., South St. Paul, MN

TRANSFER AGENT(S): Norwest Bank Minnesota, N.A., South St. Paul, MN

COMMERCE BANCSHARES, INC.

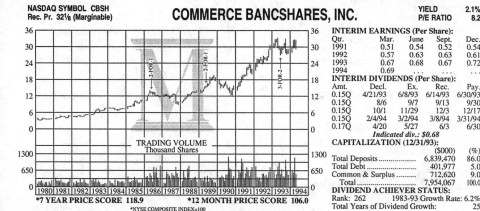

INTERIM EARNINGS (Per Share):

Qtr.	Mar.	June	Sept.	Dec.
1991	0.51	0.54	0.52	0.54
1992	0.57	0.63	0.63	0.61
1993	0.67	0.68	0.67	0.72
1994	0.69	...	...	...

INTERIM DIVIDENDS (Per Share):

Amt.	Decl.	Ex.	Rec.	Pay.
0.15Q	4/21/93	6/8/93	6/14/93	6/30/93
0.15Q	8/6	9/7	9/13	9/30
0.15Q	10/1	11/29	12/3	12/17
0.15Q	2/4/94	3/2/94	3/8/94	3/31/94
0.17Q	4/20	5/27	6/3	6/30

Indicated div.: $0.68

CAPITALIZATION (12/31/93):

	($000)	(%)
Total Deposits	6,839,470	86.0
Total Debt	401,977	5.0
Common & Surplus	712,620	9.0
Total	7,954,067	100.0

DIVIDEND ACHIEVER STATUS:
Rank: 262   1983-93 Growth Rate: 6.2%
Total Years of Dividend Growth: 25

TRADING VOLUME
Thousand Shares

*7 YEAR PRICE SCORE 118.9   ***12 MONTH PRICE SCORE 106.0**

*NYSE COMPOSITE INDEX=100

RECENT DEVELOPMENTS: For the quarter ended 3/31/94, net income was $22.0 million, or $0.69 per share, compared with $21.0 million, or $0.67 per share for the corresponding period a year ago. For the year ended 12/31/93, net income rose 21.3% to $86.9 million, or $2.74 per share, compared with net income of $71.7 million, or $2.44 per share, last year. Net interest income increased to $284.5 million from $247.7 million a year earlier. Non-interest income increased $12.8 million to $121.4 million. Several key products experienced strong growth for the year. Credit card outstandings increased 9.2% to $367.6 million, with a total cardholder base of 400,000 accounts. Sales of mutual funds and annuities exceeded $100 million while investment management, bond and brokerage fees increased 5.7% to $38.4 million. Total assets at year-end were $8.05 billion, up 6.7% from $7.54 billion at year-end 1992.

BUSINESS

COMMERCE BANCSHARES, INC. is a registered bank holding which presently owns or controls all of the outstanding capital stock of 14 banking institutions, all located in Missouri with the exception of Commerce Bank of Omaha N.A., which is located in Nebraska and is limited in its activities to the issuance of credit cards. The company also owns 6 non-banking subsidiaries that are engaged in owning real estate and leasing the same to the Company's banking subsidiaries, underwriting credit life and credit accident and health insurance, selling property and casualty insurance, providing venture capital through a small business investment corporation, mortage banking, and providing discount brokerage services. COMMERCE BANCSHARES now ranks as the third largest multi-bank holding company in the state of Missouri.

LOAN DISTRIBUTION

(12/31/93)	($000)	(%)
Business	1,380,452	34.3
Real Estate-		
Construction	90,102	2.2
Real Estate-Business	533,467	13.3
Real Estate-Personal	734,771	18.3
Consumer	917,683	22.8
Credit card	367,600	9.1
Total	4,024,075	100.0

ANNUAL EARNINGS AND DIVIDENDS PER SHARE

	1993	1992	1991	1990	1989	1988	1987
Earnings Per Share	2.74	①2.44	2.11	②2.01	2.08	1.64	1.30
Dividends Per Share	0.583	0.527	0.50	0.467	③0.42	0.393	0.37
Dividend Payout %	21.3	21.6	23.7	23.2	20.2	24.0	28.5

① 3-for-2 stk split, 4/21/93. ② Before acctg. chg. ③ 2-for-1 stk split, 5/3/89.

ANNUAL FINANCIAL DATA

RECORD OF EARNINGS (IN MILLIONS):

	1993	1992	1991	1990	1989	1988	1987
Total Interest Income	460.4	450.6	508.8	526.9	498.3	414.7	390.7
Total Interest Expense	175.9	202.9	286.2	314.6	291.8	234.1	219.0
Net Interest Income	284.5	247.7	222.7	212.3	206.5	180.6	171.7
Provision for Loan Losses	11.4	19.1	19.0	15.1	15.7	9.2	9.7
Net Income	86.9	71.7	59.8	①57.5	59.0	49.0	40.1
Aver. Shs. Outstg. (000)	31,665	29,396	28,265	28,596	28,361	29,922	30,915

① Before acctg. change cr$2,000,000.

BALANCE SHEET (IN MILLIONS):

	1993	1992	1991	1990	1989	1988	1987
Cash & Due From Banks	534.8	550.7	586.4	756.0	546.5	477.0	564.5
Net Loans & Lse Financing	3,938.2	3,610.3	3,266.5	3,221.1	3,193.3	2,953.7	2,636.5
Total Domestic Deposits	6,839.5	6,458.7	5,850.4	5,764.4	4,987.9	4,683.4	4,469.3
Lg tm Debt & Other Borrow	6.9	7.3	38.1	39.3	10.4	15.5	66.1
Net Stockholders' Equity	712.6	603.7	507.3	457.8	398.0	379.2	359.8
Total Assets	8,047.4	7,541.6	6,765.4	6,709.1	5,829.2	5,444.0	5,269.3
Year End Shs Outstg (000)	31,784	29,719	28,108	27,903	27,254	29,090	30,651

STATISTICAL RECORD:

	1993	1992	1991	1990	1989	1988	1987
Return on Assets %	1.08	0.95	0.88	0.86	1.01	0.90	0.76
Return on Equity %	12.20	11.90	11.80	12.60	14.80	12.90	11.10
Book Value Per Share	22.42	20.31	18.05	16.41	14.60	13.04	11.74
Average Yield %	1.9	3.0	4.0	4.6	3.8	5.0	5.1
P/E Ratio	12.2-9.9	12.6-8.8	11.2-6.7	9.1-6.1	9.4-6.3	8.6-5.8	10.0-6.9
Price Range	33⅜-27	30⅝-21⅜	23⅝-14⅛	18¼-12⅜	19⅝-13⅛	14⅛-9½	12⅞-8⅞

Statistics are as originally reported.

OFFICERS:
D.W. Kemper, Chmn., Pres. & C.E.O.
T.A. Peschka, V.P., Sec. & Gen. Couns.
C.E. Templer, Treas. & Contr.

INCORPORATED: MO, Aug., 1966

PRINCIPAL OFFICE: 1000 Walnut P.O. Box 13686, Kansas City, MO 64199-3686

TELEPHONE NUMBER: (816) 234-2000

NO. OF EMPLOYEES: 4,187 (full-time); 605 (part-time)

ANNUAL MEETING: In April

SHAREHOLDERS: 5,478

INSTITUTIONAL HOLDINGS:
No. of Institutions: 97
Shares Held: 11,512,886

REGISTRAR(S): First Chicago Trust Co. of New York, New York, NY 10008

TRANSFER AGENT(S): First Chicago Trust Co. of New York, New York, NY 10008

COMPASS BANCSHARES INC.

YIELD 3.6%
P/E RATIO 10.9

TRADING VOLUME
Thousand Shares

*7 YEAR PRICE SCORE 125.4   *12 MONTH PRICE SCORE 103.1
*NYSE COMPOSITE INDEX=100

INTERIM EARNINGS (Per Share):

Qtr.	Mar.	June	Sept.	Dec.
1990	0.34	0.41	0.39	0.43
1991	0.41	0.45	0.46	0.48
1992	0.50	0.52	0.52	0.54
1993	0.58	0.60	0.60	...

INTERIM DIVIDENDS (Per Share):

Amt.	Decl.	Ex.	Rec.	Pay.
0.19Q	5/17/93	6/9/93	6/15/93	7/1/93
0.19Q	8/16	9/9	9/15	10/1
0.19Q	11/16	12/9	12/15	1/3/94
0.23Q	2/21/94	3/9/94	3/15/94	4/1
0.23Q	4/18	6/9	6/15	7/1

Indicated div.: $0.92

CAPITALIZATION (12/31/93):

	($000)	(%)
Total Deposits	5,552,826	75.8
Total Debt	1,116,862	15.2
Common & Surplus	545,584	7.5
Loan Valuation Reserve	110,036	1.5
Total	7,325,308	100.0

DIVIDEND ACHIEVER STATUS:
Rank: 79   1983-93 Growth Rate: 13.9%
Total Years of Dividend Growth: 10

RECENT DEVELOPMENTS: For the year ended 12/31/93, net income increased 18% to $89.3 million from $75.4 million in 1992. Pretax income at $137.5 million was up $23.7 million or 21% over 1992; however, income tax expense increased $9.8 million or 26% over last year due to an increase in CBSS's income subject to taxation and an increase in the effective tax rate in 1993 from 34% to 35%. Average earning assets increased 5% over 1992 due to increases in both aver-age loans and trading account securities. Average loans increased 14% in 1993 with much of the increase concentrated in residential mortgage loans, commercial loans and consumer installment loans. Total loans outstanding at year-end increased 11% over last year. The growth in the portfolio resulted from CBSS's ongoing efforts to increase loan originations. Real estate construction loans increased 7% and residential mortgage loans increased 30%.

BUSINESS

COMPASS BANCSHARES INC. is a financial institutions holding company. Compass Bank conducts a general banking and trust business at 89 locations in 48 communities in Alabama. Compass Bank-Houston conducts a general commercial banking business from 13 locations in Houston, Texas and Compass Bank-Dallas conducts a general commercial banking business from 22 banking offices in Dallas and Collin Counties, Texas. River Oaks Trust Company offers a full range of trust services to customers in Texas through its offices in Houston and Dallas. Compass Bank, N.A. conducts a general commercial banking business with five branches in Pensacola and Gulf Breeze, Florida. Compass Bank-Florida conducts business from 16 locations in Jacksonville, Florida and 7 locations in Ft. Walton Beach, Florida. Central Bank of the South primarily provides cash management services to commercial customers of the subsidiary banks.

ANNUAL EARNINGS AND DIVIDENDS PER SHARE

	1993	1992	1991	1990	1989	1988	1987
Earnings Per Share	2.39	2.08	1.80	1.56	1.30	1.27	1.05
Dividends Per Share	0.736	�1 0.646	0.573	0.529	0.502	0.46	0.428
Dividend Payout %	30.8	31.1	31.9	33.9	39.3	36.1	40.9

�1 3-for-2 stk split, 7/6/92

ANNUAL FINANCIAL DATA

RECORD OF EARNINGS (IN MILLIONS):

	1993	1992	1991	1990	1989	1988	1987
Total Interest Income	522.6	516.7	496.5	454.6	423.1	351.2	308.2
Total Interest Expense	197.3	218.0	267.3	282.0	277.8	215.3	180.4
Net Interest Income	325.3	298.7	229.2	172.6	145.4	135.9	127.8
Provision for Loan Losses	36.0	50.0	35.3	20.6	18.4	12.4	12.1
Net Income	89.3	74.4	59.4	48.9	41.9	41.0	33.5
Aver. Shs. Outstg. (000)	36,721	34,790	32,102	31,344	32,288	32,273	31,895

BALANCE SHEET (IN MILLIONS):

Cash & Due From Banks	279.6	321.0	289.1	224.7	248.4	272.5	219.0
Taxable Invest Securities	480.7	893.0	1,691.6	1,079.4	868.0	628.2	555.5
Tax-exempt Invest Secur	109.1	154.6	170.7	184.1	204.9	192.6	333.9
Net Loans	5,038.5	4,361.2	3,548.5	3,068.9	2,804.0	2,557.0	2,251.2
Total Domestic Deposits	5,552.8	5,104.5	4,518.7	3,522.9	3,238.6	2,809.9	2,441.9
Long-term Debt	...	...	7.1	1.9	2.8	3.7	4.6
Net Stockholders' Equity	545.6	488.5	417.1	331.7	307.3	284.2	259.5
Total Assets	7,252.3	6,736.0	6,121.9	4,914.8	4,518.7	4,108.9	3,873.9
Year End Shs Outstg (000)	36,462	34,788	31,647	31,130	31,938	32,174	31,916

STATISTICAL RECORD:

Return on Assets %	1.23	1.10	0.97	0.99	0.93	1.00	0.86
Return on Equity %	16.40	15.20	14.20	14.70	13.60	14.40	12.90
Book Value Per Share	14.96	13.38	12.45	10.66	9.62	8.83	8.13
Average Yield %	3.1	3.1	4.0	5.7	5.2	5.0	3.7
P/E Ratio	11.1-8.7	11.3-8.9	10.8-5.2	6.5-5.4	8.4-6.4	8.2-6.2	14.8-7.1
Price Range	26½-20¾	23½-18½	19⅜-9⅜	10⅛-8½	10⅞-8⅜	10⅜-7⅞	15½-7½

Statistics are as originally reported.

OFFICERS:
D.P. Jones, Jr., Chmn. & C.E.O.
J.W. Powell, Gen. Couns. & Sec.
G.R. Hegel, Chief Fin. Off.

INCORPORATED: AL, 1970

PRINCIPAL OFFICE: 15 South 20th Street, Birmingham, AL 35233

TELEPHONE NUMBER: (205) 933-3000

NO. OF EMPLOYEES: 3,900 (approx.)

ANNUAL MEETING: In May

SHAREHOLDERS: 5,901

INSTITUTIONAL HOLDINGS:
No. of Institutions: 42
Shares Held: 4,814,457

REGISTRAR(S):

TRANSFER AGENT(S): First National Bank of Boston, Shareholder Services Division, Boston, MA

CONAGRA, INC.

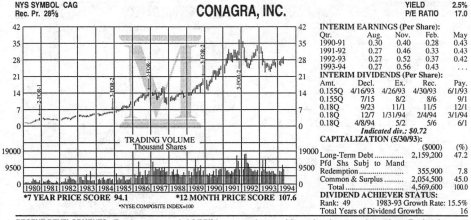

TRADING VOLUME
Thousand Shares

*7 YEAR PRICE SCORE 94.1   *12 MONTH PRICE SCORE 107.6

*NYSE COMPOSITE INDEX=100

INTERIM EARNINGS (Per Share):

Qtr.	Aug.	Nov.	Feb.	May
1990-91	0.30	0.40	0.28	0.43
1991-92	0.27	0.46	0.33	0.43
1992-93	0.27	0.52	0.37	0.42
1993-94	0.27	0.56	0.43	...

INTERIM DIVIDENDS (Per Share):

Amt.	Decl.	Ex.	Rec.	Pay.
0.155Q	4/16/93	4/26/93	4/30/93	6/1/93
0.155Q	7/15	8/2	8/6	9/1
0.18Q	9/23	11/1	11/5	12/1
0.18Q	12/7	1/31/94	2/4/94	3/1/94
0.18Q	4/8/94	5/2	5/6	6/1

Indicated div.: $0.72

CAPITALIZATION (5/30/93):

	($000)	(%)
Long-Term Debt	2,159,200	47.2
Pfd Shs Subj to Mand Redemption	355,900	7.8
Common & Surplus	2,054,500	45.0
Total	4,569,600	100.0

DIVIDEND ACHIEVER STATUS:
Rank: 49   1983-93 Growth Rate: 15.5%
Total Years of Dividend Growth: 16

RECENT DEVELOPMENTS: For the quarter ended 2/27/94, net income was up 14% to $103.7 million, or $0.43 per share, from $91.1 million, or $0.37 per share, for the corresponding period last year. Net sales rose 10% to $5.58 billion from $5.06 billion a year ago. The earnings gain was driven by solid operating profit growth in CAG's prepared food businesses, including its branded grocery products businesses where positive unit volume trends continue. During the quarter, the Company increased its interest in Australia Meat Holdings PTY LTD. (AMH) from 50% to approximately 90%. In March 1994, CAG announced a joint venture with Kellogg USA, Inc., to introduce Health Choice Cereals from Kellogg's. A line of three multi-grain cereals will be in grocery stores across the U.S. in early summer.

BUSINESS

CONAGRA, INC. is an international food concern with two main divisions: Basic Food Companies and Finance Companies. Basic Food Companies operates in three industry segments: Agri-Products include crop protection chemicals, fertilizers, and health care products for livestock. Trading and Processing consists of commodities, food ingredients, processed products and serving domestic and international food industry customers. Prepared Foods comprise branded self-stable & frozen foods, poultry & meats, seafood and pet & home sewing accessories. Finance Companies provide specialized, self-financed financial services to the food industry.

BUSINESS LINE ANALYSIS

(5/31/93)	Rev(%)	Inc(%)
Agri-Products	12.4	9.6
Trading & Processing	10.9	11.7
Prepared Foods	76.7	78.7
Total	100.0	100.0

ANNUAL EARNINGS AND DIVIDENDS PER SHARE

	5/30/93	5/31/92	5/26/91	5/28/90	5/28/89	5/29/88	5/31/87
Earnings Per Share	[1] 1.58	1.50	1.42	1.25	1.09	0.86	0.82
Dividends Per Share	0.56	0.48	0.415	[2] 0.357	0.309	0.268	[3] 0.231
Dividend Payout %	35.4	32.0	...	28.6	28.4	31.1	28.1

[1] Before acctg. chg. [2] 3-for-2 stock split paid 12/1/89 [3] 2-for-1 stk. split, 12/86.

ANNUAL FINANCIAL DATA

RECORD OF EARNINGS (IN MILLIONS):

Total Revenues	21,519.1	21,219.0	19,504.7	15,501.2	11,340.4	9,475.0	9,001.6
Costs and Expenses	20,377.7	20,012.0	18,464.3	14,862.1	10,794.3	9,088.4	8,598.4
Depreciation & Amort	277.0	319.3	250.8	129.7	101.7	89.5	81.6
Operating Income	864.4	887.7	789.6	509.4	444.5	297.0	321.5
Income Bef Income Taxes	631.4	587.7	515.2	356.9	312.2	240.1	271.5
Income Taxes	239.9	215.3	204.0	125.2	114.3	85.4	122.8
Net Income	[1] 391.5	372.4	311.2	231.7	197.9	154.7	148.7
Aver. Shs. Outstg. (000)	233,000	231,900	205,350	184,785	180,831	178,173	178,992

[1] Before acctg. change dr$121,200,000.

BALANCE SHEET (IN MILLIONS):

Cash and Cash Equivalents	447.0	535.9	966.5	333.5	607.0	167.8	194.9
Receivables, Net	1,421.4	1,290.4	1,228.9	1,305.8	1,099.9	755.9	604.3
Inventories	2,439.2	2,373.9	2,019.8	1,648.8	1,383.1	1,096.1	864.0
Gross Property	3,719.0	3,364.3	2,740.1	1,703.5	1,397.1	1,166.6	1,002.1
Accumulated Depreciation	1,330.8	1,087.5	798.6	668.9	572.2	470.5	400.2
Long-Term Debt	2,159.2	2,124.4	2,093.0	635.4	560.1	489.9	428.7
Net Stockholders' Equity	2,410.4	2,588.3	2,173.5	1,098.0	958.2	824.0	735.8
Total Assets	9,988.7	9,758.7	9,420.3	4,804.2	4,278.2	3,042.9	2,482.5
Total Current Assets	4,486.7	4,371.2	4,342.9	3,347.8	3,160.4	2,076.2	1,707.1
Total Current Liabilities	4,272.6	4,081.3	4,087.4	2,967.5	2,651.5	1,636.1	1,236.6
Net Working Capital	214.1	289.9	255.5	380.3	508.9	440.1	470.5
Year End Shs Outstg (000)	251,710	231,963	209,511	184,094	180,917	175,545	175,545

STATISTICAL RECORD:

Operating Profit Margin %	4.0	4.2	4.0	3.3	3.9	3.1	3.6
Book Value Per Share	...	...	...	4.59	4.61	4.22	3.71
Return on Equity %	19.1	16.7	17.1	21.1	20.8	19.0	20.6
Return on Assets %	3.9	3.8	3.3	4.8	4.6	5.1	6.0
Average Yield %	1.9	1.6	2.0	2.2	2.4	2.1	2.0
P/E Ratio	22.6-15.5	24.3-14.9	18.0-10.7	16.1-10.3	13.9-9.6	19.6-10.8	17.4-10.5
Price Range	35¾-24½	36½-22⅜	25½-15⅛	20⅛-12⅞	15⅛-10½	16⅞-9¼	14¼-8⅝

Statistics are as originally reported.

OFFICERS:
P.B. Fletcher, Chmn. & C.E.O.
P.B. Fletcher, Sr. V.P.-Human Res.
S.L. Key, Exec. V.P. & C.F.O.

INCORPORATED: DE, Jan., 1976

PRINCIPAL OFFICE: One ConAgra Dr., Omaha, NE 68102-5001

TELEPHONE NUMBER: (402) 595-4000

NO. OF EMPLOYEES: 11,288 (approx.)

ANNUAL MEETING: In September

SHAREHOLDERS: 19,813 (approx.)

INSTITUTIONAL HOLDINGS:
No. of Institutions: 357
Shares Held: 85,136,668

REGISTRAR(S): Manufacturers Hanover Trust Co., New York, NY

TRANSFER AGENT(S): Manufacturers Hanover Trust Co., New York, NY

CONNECTICUT WATER SERVICE, INC.

YIELD 6.5%
P/E RATIO 12.6

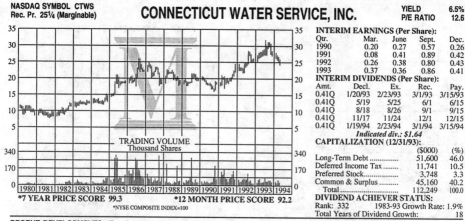

TRADING VOLUME
Thousand Shares

| | 1980 | 1981 | 1982 | 1983 | 1984 | 1985 | 1986 | 1987 | 1988 | 1989 | 1990 | 1991 | 1992 | 1993 | 1994 |

*7 YEAR PRICE SCORE 99.3   *12 MONTH PRICE SCORE 92.2
*NYSE COMPOSITE INDEX=100

INTERIM EARNINGS (Per Share):

Qtr.	Mar.	June	Sept.	Dec.
1990	0.20	0.27	0.57	0.26
1991	0.08	0.41	0.89	0.42
1992	0.26	0.38	0.80	0.43
1993	0.37	0.36	0.86	0.41

INTERIM DIVIDENDS (Per Share):

Amt.	Decl.	Ex.	Rec.	Pay.
0.41Q	1/20/93	2/23/93	3/1/93	3/15/93
0.41Q	5/19	5/25	6/1	6/15
0.41Q	8/18	8/26	9/1	9/15
0.41Q	11/17	11/24	12/1	12/15
0.41Q	1/19/94	2/23/94	3/1/94	3/15/94

Indicated div.: $1.64

CAPITALIZATION (12/31/93):

	($000)	(%)
Long-Term Debt	51,600	46.0
Deferred Income Tax	11,741	10.5
Preferred Stock	3,748	3.3
Common & Surplus	45,160	40.2
Total	112,249	100.0

DIVIDEND ACHIEVER STATUS:
Rank: 332   1983-93 Growth Rate: 1.9%
Total Years of Dividend Growth: 18

RECENT DEVELOPMENTS: For the year ended 12/31/93, net income applicable to common stockholders was up 8.2% to $5.5 million compared with $5.1 million a year ago. Revenues rose 2.5% to $38.1 million from $37.2 million. Operating results benefited from the hot, dry summer, which increased water consumption by 2.2%. Other major factors were the refinancing of more than $24 million of long-term debt at more favorable interest rates; financing of capital improvements solely through internally generated funds and continuation of stringent cost-reduction programs throughout the Company. The improved results are particularly noteworthy when taking into consideration that CTWS did not seek or receive a rate increase. The Company plans to seek out opportunities in acquiring or managing viable water utilities. A growing number of small water utilities are considering contract operations or outright ownership by large water utilities due to regulatory conditions and financial problems.

BUSINESS

CONNECTICUT WATER SERVICE, INC. is the parent company of The Connecticut Water Company which supplies water to approximately 60,000 customers for residential, commercial, industrial and municipal purposes throughout 31 towns in the State of Connecticut. The Connecticut Water Company operates through three, non-contiguous operating regions. The Company represents the second largest investor-owned water system in the State of Connecticut in terms of operating revenues and utility plant investment. The area served has an estimated population of 209,000. The Connecticut Water Company's water system consists of some 950 miles of water main with reservoir storage capacity of approximately 6.8 billion gallons. The safe dependable yield from the Connecticut Water Company's 78 active wells and 20 reservoirs is approximately 39 million gallons per-day. Water supply sources vary among the regions, but from the systems as a whole, about 55% of the total dependable yield comes from reservoirs and 45% from wells.

ANNUAL EARNINGS AND DIVIDENDS PER SHARE

	1993	1992	1991	1990	1989	1988	1987
Earnings Per Share	2.00	1.87	1.80	1.30	1.71	1.86	⫞ 1.80
Dividends Per Share	1.64	1.61	1.60	1.57	1.56	1.53	1.52
Dividend Payout %	82.0	86.1	88.9	N.M.	91.2	82.3	84.4

⫞ Before acctg. chg.

ANNUAL FINANCIAL DATA

RECORD OF EARNINGS (IN THOUSANDS):

	1993	1992	1991	1990	1989	1988	1987
Operating Revenues	38,131	37,190	37,372	32,301	29,804	28,378	26,273
Depreciation	3,037	2,912	2,877	2,748	2,491	2,201	2,041
Maintenance	1,793	1,474	1,834	1,578	1,261	1,211	1,008
Income Taxes	3,710	3,163	2,834	1,851	1,693	2,272	2,855
Operating Income	9,983	10,033	10,402	8,712	8,773	8,086	7,192
Total Interest & Debt Exp	4,338	4,872	5,321	5,650	5,206	4,401	3,368
Net Income	5,567	5,149	4,877	2,983	3,721	3,966	⫞ 3,761
Aver. Shs. Outstg.	2,769	2,729	2,686	2,272	2,148	2,117	2,085

⫞ Before acctg. change cr$1,004,000.

BALANCE SHEET (IN THOUSANDS):

Gross Plant	177,698	172,241	168,451	163,567	155,294	143,113	127,293
Accumulated Depreciation	40,130	36,544	33,319	30,464	27,854	25,484	23,320
Net Utility Plant	137,568	135,697	135,132	133,103	127,440	117,629	103,973
Long-term Debt	51,600	51,600	52,412	52,953	54,067	49,243	41,338
Net Stockholders' Equity	48,908	46,910	45,359	44,894	38,075	34,371	33,434
Total Assets	163,080	149,696	148,625	145,379	140,555	129,790	115,335
Year End Shares Outstg	2,790	2,751	2,711	2,668	2,168	2,132	2,106

STATISTICAL RECORD:

Book Value Per Share	16.19	15.68	15.30	15.05	15.27	15.05	14.69
Op. Inc/Net Pl %	7.3	7.4	7.7	6.5	6.9	6.9	6.9
Dep/Gr. Pl %	1.7	1.7	1.7	1.7	1.6	1.5	1.6
Accum. Dep/Gr. Pl %	22.6	21.2	19.8	18.6	17.9	17.8	18.3
Return on Equity %	12.1	11.7	11.5	7.3	11.0	12.1	11.9
Average Yield %	5.7	6.4	7.7	8.5	7.9	7.6	7.1
P/E Ratio	15.9-12.6	15.2-11.6	13.6-9.4	16.0-12.3	12.6-10.4	12.2-9.5	13.9-9.9
Price Range	31⅞-25¼	28½-21¾	24½-17	20¾-16	21½-17¾	22¾-17¾	25-17¾

Statistics are as originally reported.

OFFICERS:
W.C. Stewart, Chairman
M.T. Chiaraluce, Pres. & C.E.O.
B.L. Lenz, Sr. V.P.-Fin. & Acctg. & Treas.
V.F. Susco, Jr., V.P.-Admin. & Sec.

INCORPORATED: CT, Feb., 1956

PRINCIPAL OFFICE: 93 West Main Street, Clinton, CT 06413

TELEPHONE NUMBER: (203) 669-8636

NO. OF EMPLOYEES: 23

ANNUAL MEETING: In April

SHAREHOLDERS: 3,209

INSTITUTIONAL HOLDINGS:
No. of Institutions: 20
Shares Held: 409,471

REGISTRAR(S):

TRANSFER AGENT(S): State Street Bank & Trust Co., Boston, MA 02266

CONSOLIDATED EDISON CO. OF NEW YORK, INC.

YIELD 7.1%
P/E RATIO 10.5

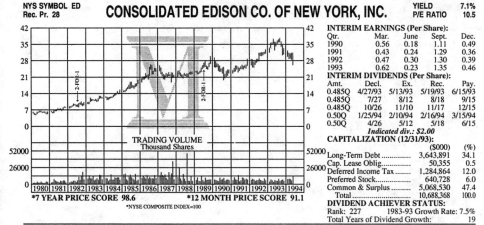

TRADING VOLUME
Thousand Shares

*7 YEAR PRICE SCORE 98.6   *12 MONTH PRICE SCORE 91.1

*NYSE COMPOSITE INDEX=100

INTERIM EARNINGS (Per Share):

Qtr.	Mar.	June	Sept.	Dec.
1990	0.56	0.18	1.11	0.49
1991	0.43	0.24	1.29	0.36
1992	0.47	0.30	1.30	0.39
1993	0.62	0.23	1.35	0.46

INTERIM DIVIDENDS (Per Share):

Amt.	Decl.	Ex.	Rec.	Pay.
0.485Q	4/27/93	5/13/93	5/19/93	6/15/93
0.485Q	7/27	8/12	8/18	9/15
0.485Q	10/26	11/10	11/17	12/15
0.50Q	1/25/94	2/10/94	2/16/94	3/15/94
0.50Q	4/26	5/12	5/18	6/15

Indicated div.: $2.00

CAPITALIZATION (12/31/93):

	($000)	(%)
Long-Term Debt	3,643,891	34.1
Cap. Lease Oblig.	50,355	0.5
Deferred Income Tax	1,284,864	12.0
Preferred Stock	640,728	6.0
Common & Surplus	5,068,530	47.4
Total	10,688,368	100.0

DIVIDEND ACHIEVER STATUS:
Rank: 227   1983-93 Growth Rate: 7.5%
Total Years of Dividend Growth: 19

RECENT DEVELOPMENTS: For the year ended 12/31/93, net income was $659.5 million compared with $604.1 million last year. Revenues were $6.27 billion, up 5.6%. Electric sales volume in the Company's service territory, excluding sales to other utilities, increased 3.3% from 1992. Firm gas sales volume increased 0.6% and steam sales were unchanged. The increase in electric sales was primarily due to increased air-conditioning usage.

PROSPECTS: The Company's reliance on power purchases to supply new capacity will limit cash flow and earnings growth. However, Con Ed has taken steps to reduce its obligations to non-utility generators. Management has terminated five contracts with non-utility generators by making payments of $122 million. The Public Service Commission has authorized full recovery of the payments. ED's construction expenditure plans are $4 billion over the next 5 years.

BUSINESS

CONSOLIDATED EDISON CO. supplies electric service in all of New York City (except part of Queens) and most of Westchester County, a service area with a population of more than 8 million. It also supplies gas in Manhattan, The Bronx and parts of Queens and Westchester, and steam in part of Manhattan. Most governmental customers within the Company's service territory receive electric service from the New York Power Authority through the Company's facilities.

BUSINESS LINE ANALYSIS

(12/31/93)	Rev(%)	Inc(%)
Electric	81.9	85.8
Gas	12.9	11.2
Steam	5.2	3.0
Total	100.0	100.0

ANNUAL EARNINGS AND DIVIDENDS PER SHARE

	1993	1992	1991	1990	1989	1988	1987
Earnings Per Share	2.66	2.46	2.32	2.34	2.49	2.47	2.21
Dividends Per Share	1.94	1.90	1.86	1.82	① 1.72	1.60	1.48
Dividend Payout %	72.9	77.2	80.2	77.8	69.1	64.9	67.0

① 2-for-1 stk split, 06/30/89

ANNUAL FINANCIAL DATA

RECORD OF EARNINGS (IN MILLIONS):

	1993	1992	1991	1990	1989	1988	1987
Total Revenues	6,265.4	5,932.9	5,873.1	5,738.9	5,550.6	5,108.8	5,094.4
Depreciation & Amort.	403.7	380.9	359.8	342.8	324.9	308.1	292.3
Maintenance	570.8	529.0	520.9	509.5	483.1	447.2	447.1
Income Taxes	366.0	318.3	282.3	289.2	296.2	291.4	356.4
Operating Income	951.1	880.4	813.1	800.8	783.7	773.2	724.0
Net Interest Charges	298.1	291.6	289.7	255.3	235.6	212.5	207.4
Net Income	658.5	604.1	566.9	571.5	606.1	599.3	550.1
Aver. Shs. Outstg. (000)	233,981	231,129	228,283	228,189	228,065	227,937	232,031

BALANCE SHEET (IN MILLIONS):

	1993	1992	1991	1990	1989	1988	1987
Gross Plant	13,750.9	13,190.6	12,520.7	11,922.0	11,365.7	10,867.7	10,407.6
Accumulated Depreciation	3,594.8	3,461.0	3,257.7	3,106.8	2,954.4	2,797.0	2,664.6
Net Utility Plant	10,156.2	9,729.7	9,263.0	8,815.2	8,411.2	8,070.7	7,743.0
Long-term Debt	3,694.2	3,546.5	3,420.2	3,370.8	3,150.0	2,889.4	2,907.3
Net Stockholders' Equity	5,709.3	5,528.1	5,241.2	5,138.0	5,021.1	4,847.4	4,652.6
Total Assets	13,483.5	11,596.1	11,107.9	10,685.6	10,349.5	9,551.7	9,384.0
Year End Shs Outstg (000)	234,373	233,932	228,326	228,232	228,151	227,993	227,876

STATISTICAL RECORD:

	1993	1992	1991	1990	1989	1988	1987
Book Value Per Share	21.63	20.89	20.18	19.73	19.21	18.44	17.58
Op. Inc/Net Pl %	9.4	9.0	8.8	9.1	9.3	9.6	9.4
Dep/Gr. Pl %	2.9	2.9	2.9	2.9	2.9	2.8	2.8
Accum. Dep/Gr. Pl %	26.1	26.2	26.0	26.1	26.0	25.7	25.6
Return on Equity %	11.7	11.1	10.9	11.2	12.2	12.5	12.0
Average Yield %	5.7	6.6	7.3	7.4	6.6	7.3	6.6
P/E Ratio	14.2-11.4	13.4-10.2	12.4-9.7	12.5-8.4	12.0-8.9	9.7-8.3	11.8-8.5
Price Range	37¾-30¼	32⅞-25	28¾-22½	29¼-19¾	29⅞-22¼	23¾-20⅜	26-18¾

Statistics are as originally reported.

OFFICERS:
E.R. McGrath, Chmn., Pres. & C.E.O.
R.J. McCann, Exec. V.P. & C.F.O.
J.F. Cioffi, Treasurer

INCORPORATED: NY, Nov., 1884

PRINCIPAL OFFICE: Four Irving Place, New York, NY 10003

TELEPHONE NUMBER: (212) 460-4600
NO. OF EMPLOYEES: 18,718
ANNUAL MEETING: In May
SHAREHOLDERS: 171,321 (common); preferred, 15,870
INSTITUTIONAL HOLDINGS:
No. of Institutions: 412
Shares Held: 67,912,394

REGISTRAR(S): Chemical Bank, New York, NY

TRANSFER AGENT(S): At Company's Office

CONSOLIDATED NATURAL GAS CO.

YIELD 5.1%
P/E RATIO 17.5

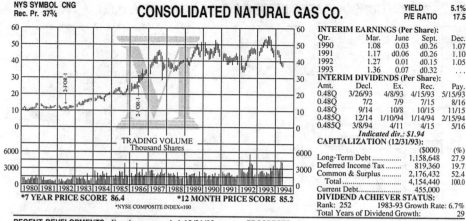

INTERIM EARNINGS (Per Share):

Qtr.	Mar.	June	Sept.	Dec.
1990	1.08	0.03	d0.26	1.07
1991	1.17	d0.06	d0.26	1.10
1992	1.27	0.01	d0.15	1.05
1993	1.36	0.07	d0.32	...

INTERIM DIVIDENDS (Per Share):

Amt.	Decl.	Ex.	Rec.	Pay.
0.48Q	3/26/93	4/8/93	4/15/93	5/15/93
0.48Q	7/2	7/9	7/15	8/16
0.48Q	9/14	10/8	10/15	11/15
0.485Q	12/14	1/10/94	1/14/94	2/15/94
0.485Q	3/8/94	4/11	4/15	5/16

Indicated div.: $1.94

CAPITALIZATION (12/31/93):

	($000)	(%)
Long-Term Debt	1,158,648	27.9
Deferred Income Tax	819,360	19.7
Common & Surplus	2,176,432	52.4
Total	4,154,440	100.0
Current Debt	455,000	

DIVIDEND ACHIEVER STATUS:
Rank: 252   1983-93 Growth Rate: 6.7%
Total Years of Dividend Growth: 29

TRADING VOLUME
Thousand Shares

| 1980 | 1981 | 1982 | 1983 | 1984 | 1985 | 1986 | 1987 | 1988 | 1989 | 1990 | 1991 | 1992 | 1993 | 1994 |

*7 YEAR PRICE SCORE 86.4   *12 MONTH PRICE SCORE 85.2

*NYSE COMPOSITE INDEX=100

RECENT DEVELOPMENTS: For the year ended 12/31/93, net income excluding the cumulative effects of an accounting change was $188.5 million compared with $195.0 million last year. Revenues were $3.18 billion, up 26%. Results in 1992 benefited from certain deferred tax benefits under the previous accounting standard. Operating income from CNG's gas distribution utilities was down 3.5% to $125.5 million. Operating income from interstate gas transmission operations was $98 million, up 16.7%.

PROSPECTS: Prospects are encouraging. Wellhead prices for natural gas are on the rise in what appears to be a turnaround in market fundamentals. The exploration and production results should improve due to the recent firming of natural gas prices. Through the completion of the 135-mile natural gas pipeline in Virginia, CNG is accommodating fast-growing residential markets. Eventually, the pipeline will serve eight Virginia counties where natural gas service is not yet available.

BUSINESS

CONSOLIDATED NATURAL GAS operates a pipeline subsidiary and operates distribution subsidiaries serving Ohio, Pennsylvania, Virginia, West Virginia, New York and the northeast U.S. Exploration and production operations are conducted through CNG Producing Co., in the Gulf of Mexico and southern and western U.S., and Canada and CNG Development Co., in the Appalachian area.

REVENUES

(12/31/93)	($000)	(%)
Gas Sales-Resid & Comml	1,595,142	50.1
Gas Sales-Industrial	55,347	1.7
Gas Sales-Wholesale	422,698	13.3
Nonregulated Gas Sales	541,849	17.0
Other	569,049	17.9
Total	3,184,085	100.0

ANNUAL EARNINGS AND DIVIDENDS PER SHARE

	1993	1992	1991	1990	1989	1988	1987
Earnings Per Share	2.22	2.19	1.94	1.91	2.20	2.34	2.24
Dividends Per Share	1.92	1.90	1.88	1.84	1.76	1.64	1.50
Dividend Payout %	86.5	86.8	96.9	96.3	80.0	70.1	67.0

ANNUAL FINANCIAL DATA

RECORD OF EARNINGS (IN MILLIONS):

	1993	1992	1991	1990	1989	1988	1987
Total Operating Revenues	3,184.1	2,520.9	2,607.0	2,714.9	2,801.9	2,467.8	2,321.6
Depreciation & Amort	294.6	287.8	284.7	281.8	275.2	242.6	209.5
Maintenance	87.2	79.1	72.9	62.8	60.8	57.5	53.1
Operating Income	257.4	273.6	230.1	248.3	253.8	221.9	229.2
Total Interest Charges	79.5	83.4	87.8	92.9	77.9	62.8	56.5
Net Income	① 188.5	195.0	168.6	163.8	181.8	192.9	186.0
Aver. Shs. Outstg. (000)	92,808	89,128	86,837	85,683	82,492	82,498	83,214

① Before acctg. change cr$17,422,000.

BALANCE SHEET (IN MILLIONS):

	1993	1992	1991	1990	1989	1988	1987
Gross Plant	3,916.3	3,874.9	3,738.4	3,612.8	5,559.4	5,080.9	4,807.4
Accumulated Depreciation	...	3,212.2	3,010.8	2,820.8	2,205.9	2,067.5	1,947.4
Net Prop, Plant & Equip	3,916.3	3,874.9	3,738.4	3,612.8	3,353.4	3,013.4	2,860.0
Long-term Debt	1,158.6	1,112.0	1,159.1	1,128.5	890.6	661.6	631.0
Net Stockholders' Equity	2,176.4	2,132.8	1,889.8	1,844.6	1,671.9	1,634.8	1,598.2
Total Assets	5,409.6	5,241.8	5,011.1	5,006.0	4,601.2	4,109.4	3,946.9
Year End Shs Outstg (000)	92,934	92,557	87,322	86,327	82,526	82,421	82,948

STATISTICAL RECORD:

	1993	1992	1991	1990	1989	1988	1987
Book Value Per Share	23.42	23.04	21.64	21.37	20.26	19.83	19.27
Op. Inc/Net Pl %	6.6	7.1	6.2	6.9	7.6	7.4	8.0
Dep/Gr. Pl %	9.9	9.8	9.8	9.7	4.9	4.8	4.4
Accum. Dep/Gr. Pl %	...	45.3	44.6	43.8	39.7	40.7	40.5
Return on Equity %	8.7	9.1	8.9	8.9	10.9	11.8	11.6
Average Yield %	3.9	4.6	4.5	3.9	4.0	4.3	4.0
P/E Ratio	27.3-21.0	22.2-15.3	23.2-19.5	27.7-21.5	23.4-16.9	17.8-14.4	20.8-12.7
Price Range	55⅜-42⅝	48⅝-33½	45-37⅞	52⅞-41	51½-37⅛	41¾-33¾	46⅝-28½

Statistics are as originally reported.

OFFICERS:
G.A. Davidson, Jr., Chmn. & C.E.O.
L.D. Johnson, Exec. V.P. & C.F.O.
J.V. Whitacre, Treasurer

INCORPORATED: DE, Jul., 1942

PRINCIPAL OFFICE: CNG Tower, 625 Liberty Ave., Pittsburgh, PA 15222-3199

TELEPHONE NUMBER: (412) 227-1000
FAX: (412) 227-1306
NO. OF EMPLOYEES: 7,615
ANNUAL MEETING: In May
SHAREHOLDERS: 42,859
INSTITUTIONAL HOLDINGS:
No. of Institutions: 441
Shares Held: 41,760,472

REGISTRAR(S): Society National Bank, Cleveland, OH

TRANSFER AGENT(S): Society National Bank, Cleveland, OH

CONSUMERS WATER CO.

YIELD 6.9%
P/E RATIO 10.8

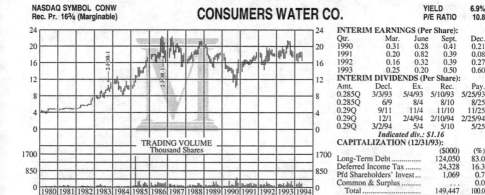

*7 YEAR PRICE SCORE 84.0   *12 MONTH PRICE SCORE 97.9

*NYSE COMPOSITE INDEX=100

INTERIM EARNINGS (Per Share):

Qtr.	Mar.	June	Sept.	Dec.
1990	0.31	0.28	0.41	0.21
1991	0.20	0.82	0.39	0.08
1992	0.16	0.32	0.39	0.27
1993	0.25	0.20	0.50	0.60

INTERIM DIVIDENDS (Per Share):

Amt.	Decl.	Ex.	Rec.	Pay.
0.285Q	3/3/93	5/4/93	5/10/93	5/25/93
0.285Q	6/9	8/4	8/10	8/25
0.29Q	9/11	11/4	11/10	11/25
0.29Q	12/1	2/4/94	2/10/94	2/25/94
0.29Q	3/2/94	5/4	5/10	5/25

Indicated div.: $1.16

CAPITALIZATION (12/31/93):

	($000)	(%)
Long-Term Debt	124,050	83.0
Deferred Income Tax	24,328	16.3
Pfd Shareholders' Invest	1,069	0.7
Common & Surplus	...	0.0
Total	149,447	100.0

DIVIDEND ACHIEVER STATUS:
Rank: 247   1983-93 Growth Rate: 6.9%
Total Years of Dividend Growth: 36

RECENT DEVELOPMENTS: For the year ended 12/31/93, net income from continuing operations before the sales of properties declined 4.6% to $8.1 million compared with $8.5 million the previous year. Revenues were up 5.7% to $89.1 million from $84.2 million. Results include an additional reserve of $1.1 million to reflect the cost of winding up the affairs of Consumers' subsidiary, Burlington Homes of New England, Inc. The Company announced its intention to sell Burlington and had taken a charge of $4.2 million in the third quarter to provide for losses expected in connection with the sale. Consumers' Ohio subsidiary closed the sale of its Washington Court House Division on 12/16/93, for a gain of $3 million, or $0.41 per share. Revenues at C/P Utility Services Company, Inc. rose 11% to almost $11 million, primarily attributable to low margin water-meter installation work. Activity in higher margin technical and engineering areas decreased.

BUSINESS

CONSUMERS WATER CO. is a holding company that owns and operates water utilities, a manufactured housing business and a utility services company. Consumers currently owns eleven utilities in six states that serve the water and wastewater needs of over 226,000 customers. CONW's manufactured housing business builds mobile and modular homes for sale to developers and dealers. Consumers' utility services company provides operational and technical services primarily to water utilities and industrial clients. In Illinois, the Consumers Illinois Water Company operates six divisions serving 61,141 customers; in Ohio, The Ohio Water Service Company with seven divisions serves 76,649 customers; in Pennsylvania, three different water companies serve 36,968 customers; in New Jersey, The Garden State Water Company with three divisions and the Califon Water Company serve 28,415 customers; in Maine, The Maine Water Company with four divisions and the Camden and Rockland Water Company serve 9,780 customers. The Company also has locations in Connecticut, Florida and New Hampshire.

ANNUAL EARNINGS AND DIVIDENDS PER SHARE

	1993	1992	1991	1990	1989	1988	1987
Earnings Per Share	1.63	1.14	⒈1.46	⒈1.21	1.15	1.59	1.51
Dividends Per Share	1.145	1.125	1.105	1.085	1.05	0.98	0.90
Dividend Payout %	70.2	98.7	75.7	89.7	91.3	61.6	59.6

⒈ Before disc. oper.

ANNUAL FINANCIAL DATA

RECORD OF EARNINGS (IN THOUSANDS):

Operating Revenue	89,084	89,615	85,205	81,589	87,098	87,891	80,467
Depreciation & Amort	7,994	7,694	6,358	5,994	6,017	5,763	4,883
Prov for Fed Inc Taxes	4,128	4,182	3,091	3,204	3,018	3,528	5,050
Operating Income	22,845	23,146	20,569	20,389	20,922	20,631	21,014
Interest Expense	11,127	11,128	11,307	12,182	12,058	9,633	8,361
Net Income	⒈12,003	8,022	⒉9,418	⒊7,346	6,883	9,421	8,870
Aver. Shs. Outstg.	7,320	7,007	6,429	6,025	5,959	5,898	5,838

⒈ Before disc. op. dr$6,084,000.   ⒉ Before disc. op. cr$1,800,000.   ⒊ Before disc. op. dr$9,292,000.

BALANCE SHEET (IN THOUSANDS):

Gross Plant	382,005	362,667	336,885	315,750	312,657	288,448	264,175
Accumulated Depreciation	64,460	61,354	56,631	53,598	55,420	50,969	47,204
Net Prop, Plant & Equip	317,545	301,313	280,254	262,152	257,237	237,479	216,971
Long-term Debt	124,050	119,832	101,410	105,420	99,958	89,146	83,163
Net Stockholders' Equity	96,938	85,321	81,173	65,099	72,588	70,967	66,351
Total Assets	371,657	343,569	315,154	302,550	302,045	282,561	257,195
Year End Shares Outstg	8,041	7,130	6,892	6,060	5,982	5,914	5,843

STATISTICAL RECORD:

Op. Inc/Net Pl %	7.2	7.7	7.3	7.8	8.1	8.7	9.7
Accum. Dep/Gr. Pl %	16.9	16.9	16.8	17.0	17.7	17.7	17.9
Return on Equity %	12.4	9.4	11.6	11.3	9.5	13.3	13.4
Average Yield %	5.9	6.6	6.9	7.7	6.0	5.3	4.8
P/E Ratio	13.2-10.4	17.3-12.5	12.7-9.4	15.1-8.3	17.8-12.8	13.4-9.9	14.9-9.9
Price Range	21½-17	19¾-14¼	18½-13¾	18¼-10	20½-14¾	21¼-15¾	22½-15

Statistics are as originally reported.

OFFICERS:
P.L. Haynes, Pres. & C.E.O.
J.F. Isacke, Sr. V.P. & C.F.O.
B.R. Mullany, V.P. & Sec.

INCORPORATED: ME, Feb., 1926

PRINCIPAL OFFICE: Three Canal Plaza,
Portland, ME 04101

TELEPHONE NUMBER: (207) 773-6438

NO. OF EMPLOYEES: 743

ANNUAL MEETING: In May

SHAREHOLDERS: 5,500 (approx.)

INSTITUTIONAL HOLDINGS:
No. of Institutions: 37
Shares Held: 1,054,579

REGISTRAR(S):

TRANSFER AGENT(S): At Company's Office

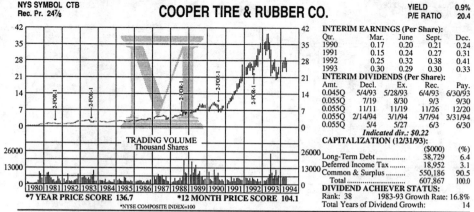

NYS SYMBOL CTB
Rec. Pr. 24⅞

COOPER TIRE & RUBBER CO.

YIELD 0.9%
P/E RATIO 20.4

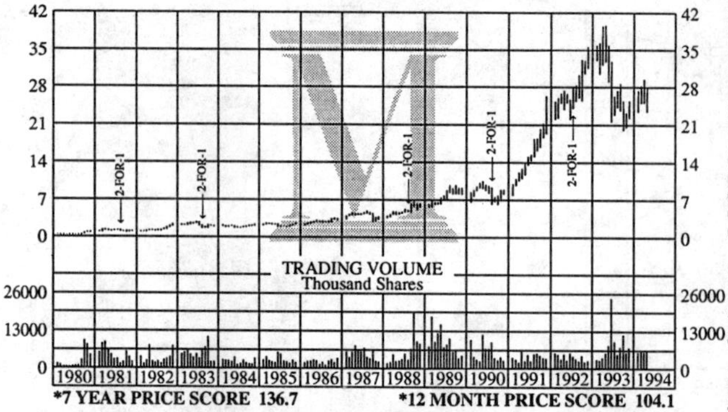

***7 YEAR PRICE SCORE 136.7** ***12 MONTH PRICE SCORE 104.1**

*NYSE COMPOSITE INDEX=100

INTERIM EARNINGS (Per Share):

Qtr.	Mar.	June	Sept.	Dec.
1990	0.17	0.20	0.21	0.24
1991	0.15	0.24	0.27	0.31
1992	0.25	0.32	0.38	0.41
1993	0.30	0.29	0.30	0.33

INTERIM DIVIDENDS (Per Share):

Amt.	Decl.	Ex.	Rec.	Pay.
0.045Q	5/4/93	5/28/93	6/4/93	6/30/93
0.055Q	7/19	8/30	9/3	9/30
0.055Q	11/11	11/19	11/26	12/20
0.055Q	2/14/94	3/1/94	3/7/94	3/31/94
0.055Q	5/4	5/27	6/3	6/30

Indicated div.: $0.22

CAPITALIZATION (12/31/93):

	($000)	(%)
Long-Term Debt	38,729	6.4
Deferred Income Tax	18,952	3.1
Common & Surplus	550,186	90.5
Total	607,867	100.0

DIVIDEND ACHIEVER STATUS:

Rank: 38 1983-93 Growth Rate: 16.8%

Total Years of Dividend Growth: 14

RECENT DEVELOPMENTS: For the quarter ended 12/31/93, net income dropped 18% to $27.8 million compared with $33.8 million for the comparable period in 1992. Revenues rose slightly to $295.0 million. For the year ended 12/31/93, net income slid 6% to $102.2 million compared with $108.2 million last year, while sales rose 2% to $1.19 billion. During the fiscal year, the market for replacement tires remained depressed compared with a year ago, although industry-wide pricing pressures also narrowed operating margins. Sales volume strengthened for engineered products.

PROSPECTS: Although the market for replacement tires seems to be in the early stages of recovery, the industry is currently characterized by intense pricing competition, which may stall earnings growth. Profits are expected to remain near levels of a year ago. Still, the Company has positioned itself well for longer-term growth, evidenced in the agreement to produce a new private brand tire which will be shipped in early 1994. Meanwhile, demand for engineered rubber products continues to be strong.

BUSINESS

COOPER TIRE & RUBBER COMPANY specializes in the manufacturing and marketing of rubber products for consumers and industrial users. Products include automobile and truck tires, inner tubes, vibration control products, hose and tubing, automotive body sealing products and specialty seating components. CTB markets its products nationally and internationally through well-established channels of distribution. Represented among its customers are automobile manufacturing companies, independent distributors and dealers, oil companies, large retail chains and industrial manufacturers.

QUARTERLY DATA

(12/31/93)($000)	Rev	Inc
1st Quarter	280,100	25,196
2nd Quarter	292,566	24,024
3rd Quarter	326,107	25,155
4th Quarter	294,875	27,835

ANNUAL EARNINGS AND DIVIDENDS PER SHARE

	1993	1992	1991	1990	1989	1988	1987
Earnings Per Share	**1.22**	**[1] 1.30**	**0.96**	**0.81**	**0.71**	**0.50**	**0.38**
Dividends Per Share	**0.20**	**[2] 0.17**	**0.13**	**[3] 0.105**	**0.086**	**0.07**	**0.058**
Dividend Payout %	**16.4**	**13.1**	**13.5**	**13.0**	**12.1**	**14.0**	**15.3**

[1] Before acctg. chg. [2] 2-for-1 stk split, 7/1/92 [3] 2-for-1 stk split, 8/20/90

ANNUAL FINANCIAL DATA

	1993	1992	1991	1990	1989	1988	1987
RECORD OF EARNINGS (IN MILLIONS):							
Total Revenues	1,194.2	1,176.0	1,001.6	896.8	869.6	750.9	669.3
Costs and Expenses	981.3	966.0	840.6	759.6	749.2	661.6	591.3
Depreciation & Amort	46.4	38.1	32.0	27.6	23.4	19.9	18.4
Operating Profit	228.9	230.6	180.9	156.8	142.3	109.3	97.4
Income Bef Income Taxes	164.3	169.8	124.5	104.9	92.6	64.9	53.1
Provision for Inc Taxes	62.0	61.7	45.0	38.4	34.4	23.9	22.4
Net Income	102.2	[1] 108.2	79.4	66.5	58.2	41.1	30.7
Aver. Shs. Outstg. (000)	83,350	83,357	82,738	82,391	82,077	81,583	81,258
[1] Before acctg. change dr$64,960,000.							
BALANCE SHEET (IN MILLIONS):							
Cash	25.8	55.1	24.4	10.1	49.6	38.7	72.6
Accounts Receivable, Net	182.2	181.2	152.7	127.0	126.4	120.4	115.5
Total Inventories	111.1	75.0	78.0	121.4	70.7	67.9	61.0
Gross Property	807.2	700.6	596.5	520.9	426.3	356.4	289.4
Accumulated Depreciation	279.3	240.2	207.9	186.1	163.8	143.4	127.0
Long-Term Debt	38.7	48.1	47.5	85.3	59.0	60.2	61.3
Capized Lease Obligations	...	...	6.0	5.8	6.7	7.6	8.7
Net Stockholders' Equity	550.2	471.5	439.6	369.0	310.1	257.8	221.6
Total Assets	889.6	796.9	670.6	616.5	519.9	442.6	413.3
Total Current Assets	332.0	314.7	261.7	267.8	249.2	229.2	250.5
Total Current Liabilities	127.2	139.6	117.4	100.5	98.9	86.1	96.2
Net Working Capital	204.9	175.2	144.3	167.3	150.3	143.1	154.3
Year End Shs Outstg (000)	83,582	83,511	82,962	82,519	82,259	81,821	81,383
STATISTICAL RECORD:							
Operating Profit Margin %	14.0	14.6	12.9	12.2	11.2	9.2	8.9
Book Value Per Share	6.58	5.65	5.30	4.47	3.77	3.15	2.72
Return on Equity %	18.6	22.9	18.1	18.0	18.8	15.9	13.8
Return on Assets %	11.5	13.6	11.8	10.8	11.2	9.3	7.4
Average Yield %	0.7	0.6	0.8	1.3	1.1	1.3	1.5
P/E Ratio	32.5-16.4	27.4-17.0	27.5-8.2	13.0-7.7	13.7-7.9	13.8-7.0	13.2-7.2
Price Range	39⅝-20	35⅝-22⅛	26⅜-7⅞	10½-6¼	9¾-5⅝	6⅞-3½	5-2¾

Statistics are as originally reported.

OFFICERS:
I.W. Gorr, Chmn. & C.E.O.
P.W. Rooney, Pres. & C.O.O.
J.A. Reinhardt, Exec. V.P. & C.F.O.
W.C. Hattendorf, Treas.

INCORPORATED: DE, Mar., 1930

PRINCIPAL OFFICE: 701 Lima Avenue, Findlay, OH 45840

TELEPHONE NUMBER: (419) 423-1321

FAX: (419) 424-4108

NO. OF EMPLOYEES: 7,607

ANNUAL MEETING: In May

SHAREHOLDERS: 8,096

INSTITUTIONAL HOLDINGS:
No. of Institutions: 196
Shares Held: 29,306,681

REGISTRAR(S): Society National Bank, Cleveland, OH

TRANSFER AGENT(S): Society National Bank, Cleveland, OH

CRAWFORD & CO.

YIELD	3.3%
P/E RATIO	14.3

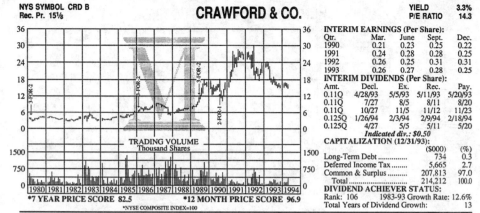

TRADING VOLUME
Thousand Shares

*7 YEAR PRICE SCORE 82.5   *12 MONTH PRICE SCORE 96.9
*NYSE COMPOSITE INDEX=100

INTERIM EARNINGS (Per Share):

Qtr.	Mar.	June	Sept.	Dec.
1990	0.21	0.23	0.25	0.22
1991	0.24	0.28	0.28	0.25
1992	0.26	0.25	0.31	0.31
1993	0.26	0.27	0.28	0.25

INTERIM DIVIDENDS (Per Share):

Amt.	Decl.	Ex.	Rec.	Pay.
0.11Q	4/28/93	5/5/93	5/11/93	5/20/93
0.11Q	7/27	8/5	8/11	8/20
0.11Q	10/27	11/5	11/12	11/23
0.125Q	1/26/94	2/3/94	2/9/94	2/18/94
0.125Q	4/27	5/5	5/11	5/20

Indicated div.: $0.50

CAPITALIZATION (12/31/93):

	($000)	(%)
Long-Term Debt	734	0.3
Deferred Income Tax	5,665	2.7
Common & Surplus	207,813	97.0
Total	214,212	100.0

DIVIDEND ACHIEVER STATUS:
Rank: 106   1983-93 Growth Rate: 12.6%
Total Years of Dividend Growth: 13

RECENT DEVELOPMENTS: For the year ended 12/31/93, revenues totaled $576.3 million, a 3.6% decrease from record revenues of $597.7 million in 1992. Net income before accounting changes totaled $38.1 million compared with $40.4 million for 1992. The revenue decline was a result of fewer weather-related property assignments during 1993 compared with 1992, when the Company generated $19.0 million in hurricane revenues. Also, lower claims frequency and competitive pricing pressures in the self-insured market segment inhibited growth in 1993. HealthCare Management Services experienced only modest revenue growth, reflecting clients' caution over the direction of the government's health plan.

BUSINESS

CRAWFORD & CO. is a diversified services firm which provides claims services, risk management services, healthcare management and risk control services to insurance companies, corporations and self-insured entities. The Company is not owned by or affiliated with any insurance company. Claims Services (including risk management services) provides claims administration services to insurance companies and self-insured clients. Health Care Management services include vocational services and medical care management services.

REVENUES

(12/31/93)	($000)	(%)
U.S. Operations	533,582	92.6
Foreign Operations....	42,716	7.4
Total	576,298	100.0

ANNUAL EARNINGS AND DIVIDENDS PER SHARE

	1993	1992	1991	1990	1989	1988	1987
Earnings Per Share	1.06	1.13	1.05	0.91	0.79	0.54	0.47
Dividends Per Share	0.52	0.40	0.35	① 0.32	② 0.26	0.214	0.194
Dividend Payout %	49.1	35.4	33.3	35.2	32.9	39.6	41.3

① 2-for-1 stk split, 07/90   ② 3-for-2 stk split, 6/89

ANNUAL FINANCIAL DATA

RECORD OF EARNINGS (IN THOUSANDS):

	1993	1992	1991	1990	1989	1988	1987
Total Revenues	576,298	597,745	538,027	449,225	374,029	294,349	265,093
Costs and Expenses	495,669	514,113	460,728	388,188	320,770	253,263	224,601
Depreciation & Amort	15,779	16,715	15,607	10,461	9,306	10,646	11,990
Operating Income	64,850	66,917	61,692	50,576	43,953	30,440	28,502
Income Bef Income Taxes	64,850	66,917	61,692	50,576	43,953	30,440	28,502
Income Taxes	26,800	26,500	24,250	18,450	16,250	11,600	12,100
Net Income	38,050	40,417	37,442	32,126	27,703	18,840	16,402
Aver. Shs. Outstg.	35,984	35,835	35,656	35,395	35,218	35,092	35,014

BALANCE SHEET (IN THOUSANDS):

	1993	1992	1991	1990	1989	1988	1987
Cash and Cash Equivalents	69,291	57,065	53,509	34,061	59,142	45,909	35,123
Receivables, Net	142,614	155,420	143,297	136,065	100,354	80,707	79,208
Gross Property	99,415	98,560	100,659	86,198	68,179	65,780	68,723
Accumulated Depreciation	62,979	56,925	52,512	41,014	37,822	36,000	33,960
Long-Term Debt	734	1,806	2,489	9,280	1,241	1,474	3,972
Net Stockholders' Equity	207,813	191,069	165,543	140,791	119,378	99,789	87,721
Total Assets	316,759	304,045	292,512	271,128	200,883	165,335	156,761
Total Current Assets	248,739	228,705	210,509	186,300	163,198	128,891	116,253
Total Current Liabilities	95,552	108,564	120,160	117,502	77,637	55,912	52,968
Net Working Capital	153,187	120,141	90,349	68,798	85,561	72,979	63,285
Year End Shares Outstg	36,030	35,904	35,720	35,543	35,304	35,134	35,044

STATISTICAL RECORD:

	1993	1992	1991	1990	1989	1988	1987
Book Value Per Share	5.77	5.32	4.63	3.96	3.38	2.84	2.50
Return on Equity %	18.3	21.2	22.6	22.8	23.2	18.9	18.7
Return on Assets %	12.0	13.3	12.8	11.9	13.8	11.4	10.5
Average Yield %	2.6	1.7	1.6	2.3	2.0	3.2	2.7
P/E Ratio	22.9-14.2	26.5-15.6	27.1-14.4	20.1-11.1	22.9-9.3	14.4-10.4	20.2-10.4
Price Range	24¼-15	30-17⅝	28½-15⅛	18¼-10⅛	18⅛-7⅜	7¾-5⅝	9½-4⅞

Statistics are as originally reported.

OFFICERS:
F.L. Minix, Chmn., Pres. & C.E.O.
D.R. Chapman, Exec. V.P.-Fin. & C.F.O.
J.F. Osten, V.P., Gen. Counsel & Sec.

INCORPORATED: GA, 1943

PRINCIPAL OFFICE: 5620 Glenridge Drive.
N.E., Atlanta, GA 30342

TELEPHONE NUMBER: (404) 256-0830

NO. OF EMPLOYEES: 7,390

ANNUAL MEETING: In April

SHAREHOLDERS: 1,481 (cl. A); 1,287 (cl. B)

INSTITUTIONAL HOLDINGS:
No. of Institutions: 57
Shares Held: 13,813,437

REGISTRAR(S): Trust Company Bank, Atlanta, GA

TRANSFER AGENT(S): Trust Company Bank, Atlanta, GA

CROMPTON & KNOWLES CORP.

YIELD 2.6%
P/E RATIO 18.4

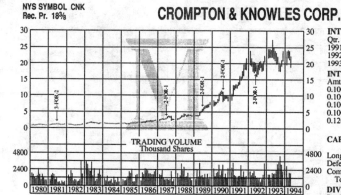

TRADING VOLUME
Thousand Shares

| | 1980 | 1981 | 1982 | 1983 | 1984 | 1985 | 1986 | 1987 | 1988 | 1989 | 1990 | 1991 | 1992 | 1993 | 1994 |

*7 YEAR PRICE SCORE 139.8   *12 MONTH PRICE SCORE 102.3
*NYSE COMPOSITE INDEX=100

INTERIM EARNINGS (Per Share):

Qtr.	Mar.	June	Sept.	Dec.
1991	0.17	0.22	0.17	0.18
1992	0.20	0.26	0.20	0.21
1993	0.24	0.30	0.22	0.24

INTERIM DIVIDENDS (Per Share):

Amt.	Decl.	Ex.	Rec.	Pay.
0.10Q	4/13/93	5/3/93	5/7/93	5/28/93
0.10Q	7/21	8/2	8/6	8/27
0.10Q	10/20	11/1	11/5	11/26
0.10Q	1/25/94	2/7/94	2/11/94	2/25/94
0.12Q	4/11	5/2	5/6	5/27

Indicated div.: $0.48

CAPITALIZATION (12/25/93):

	($000)	(%)
Long-Term Debt	14,000	5.4
Deferred Income Tax	4,727	1.8
Common & Surplus	239,996	92.8
Total	258,723	100.0

DIVIDEND ACHIEVER STATUS:
Rank: 24   1983-93 Growth Rate: 18.4%
Total Years of Dividend Growth: 17

RECENT DEVELOPMENTS: For the three months ended 12/31/93, net income was $12.5 million compared with $7.4 million in the similar period of 1992. Sales rose to $142.9 million from $137.6 million. Net income was $52.0 million, up 52% from the prior year. Sales totaled $558.3 million versus $517.7 million for 1992. Results from the specialty process equipment and controls business more than offset the slow sales growth in the dye businesses. The equipment backlog amounted to $38 million, 12% above the 1992 level.

PROSPECTS: The weak demand from the European market is adversely affecting sales and hindering the strong growth that the Company is anticipating. The strength of the domestic carpet industry along with increased demand for paper dyes and specialty ingredients continues to combat the current softness of the apparel dye market. The specialty process equipment and controls business continues to deliver solid performances. Domestic shipments have increased and reflect positively on results.

BUSINESS

CROMPTON & KNOWLES CORP. produces and markets specialty chemicals and equipment which it markets in North America, Europe, Latin America and Asia. Specialty chemicals is one of America's largest dye producers and a major participant in the specialty food and pharmaceutical ingredients business. Through this segment the Company also produces organic intermediates, flavors and food colors. CNK's other core business, specialty process equipment and controls, manufactures extrusion systems and related electronic controls for industries such as plastics and packaging.

BUSINESS LINE ANALYSIS

(12/26/93)	Rev(%)	Inc(%)
Specialty Chemicals..	72.9	72.4
Specialty Process.......		
Equipment &		
Controls.................	27.1	27.6
Total	100.0	100.0

ANNUAL EARNINGS AND DIVIDENDS PER SHARE

	12/25/93	12/26/92	12/28/91	12/29/90	12/30/89	12/31/88	12/26/87
Earnings Per Share	1.00	① 0.87	0.73	0.61	0.50	② 0.36	0.25
Dividends Per Share	0.38	0.305	0.248	0.197	0.145	0.108	③ 0.085
Dividend Payout %	38.0	35.1	33.9	32.2	29.0	30.2	34.4

① Before acctg. chg. & extraord. loss ② Before disc. oper. ③ 2-for-1 stk. split, 5/87.

ANNUAL FINANCIAL DATA

RECORD OF EARNINGS (IN THOUSANDS):

Total Revenues	558,348	517,718	450,228	390,032	355,817	289,787	237,469
Costs and Expenses	463,911	433,285	378,478	330,643	306,902	254,611	212,606
Depreciation & Amort.	12,076	11,635	10,028	7,984	6,474	5,280	4,121
Operating Profit	82,361	72,743	61,722	51,405	42,441	29,896	20,742
Earn Bef Income Taxes	82,473	68,337	56,600	47,260	38,588	26,943	20,076
Income Taxes	30,515	25,072	20,659	17,250	14,087	10,098	8,326
Net Income	51,958	①43,265	35,941	30,010	24,501	②16,845	11,750
Aver. Shs. Outstg.	52,176	49,967	49,317	49,270	49,064	47,239	48,168

① Before extra. item dr$3,000,000. ② Before disc. op. dr$1,517,000.

BALANCE SHEET (IN THOUSANDS):

Cash & Cash Equivalents	9,284	2,441	8,483	11,320	4,863	7,677	3,250
Inventories	113,932	115,688	111,108	95,111	69,583	63,082	48,703
Gross Property	173,312	163,114	134,823	123,481	90,677	78,798	62,244
Accumulated Depreciation	73,387	64,287	54,669	46,772	39,830	35,113	33,159
Long-Term Debt	14,000	24,000	76,118	70,330	41,213	44,594	12,927
Net Stockholders' Equity	239,996	211,452	140,763	117,565	98,901	81,921	75,805
Total Assets	363,246	360,715	308,562	282,644	217,850	205,642	135,229
Total Current Assets	220,396	207,383	185,235	164,442	127,216	120,584	94,069
Total Current Liabilities	95,439	102,593	85,712	88,340	71,068	72,352	40,922
Net Working Capital	124,957	104,790	99,523	76,102	56,148	48,232	53,147
Year End Shares Outstg	51,292	51,082	47,908	47,554	49,064	46,860	47,608

STATISTICAL RECORD:

Operating Profit Margin %	14.8	14.1	13.7	13.2	11.9	10.3	8.7
Book Value Per Share	4.68	4.14	2.94	2.47	2.02	1.14	1.43
Return on Equity %	21.6	20.5	25.5	25.5	24.8	20.6	15.5
Return on Assets %	14.3	12.3	11.6	10.6	11.2	8.2	8.7
Average Yield %	1.7	1.5	1.6	2.1	2.5	3.1	2.8
P/E Ratio	27.3-17.6	27.4-18.4	29.6-11.6	29.6-11.6	19.1-11.1	15.8-7.5	12.5-6.9	15.0-9.0
Price Range	27¼-17⅝	23⅞-16	21⅝-8½	11¾-6¾	7⅞-3¾	4½-2½	3¾-2¼

Statistics are as originally reported.

OFFICERS:
V.A. Calarco, Chmn., Pres. & C.E.O.
C.J. Marsden, V.P.-Fin. & C.F.O.

INCORPORATED: MA, Feb., 1900

PRINCIPAL OFFICE: One Station Place
Metro Center, Stamford, CT 06902

TELEPHONE NUMBER: (203) 353-5400
FAX: (203) 353-5424
NO. OF EMPLOYEES: 2,352
ANNUAL MEETING: In April
SHAREHOLDERS: 3,973
INSTITUTIONAL HOLDINGS:
No. of Institutions: 142
Shares Held: 24,084,494

REGISTRAR(S): Chase Manhattan Bank,
N.A., New York, NY 10031

TRANSFER AGENT(S): Chase Manhattan
Bank, N.A., New York, NY 10031

NYS SYMBOL CSX
Rec. Pr. 73⅛

CSX CORP.

YIELD 2.4%
P/E RATIO 21.1

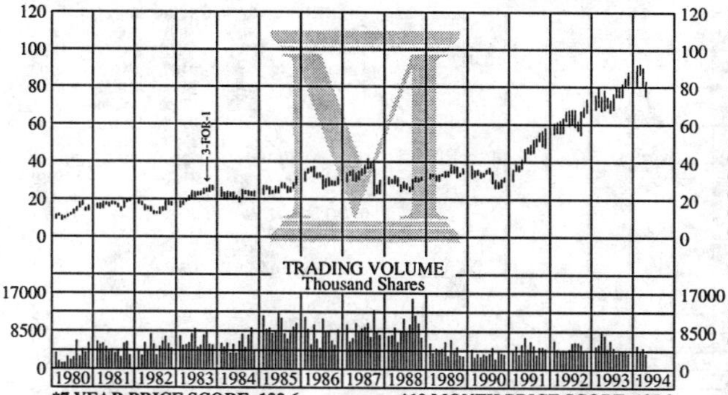

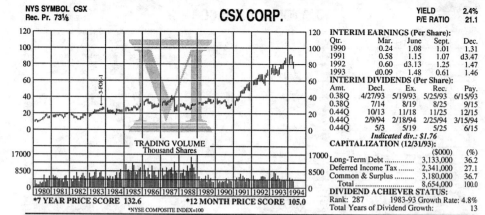

***7 YEAR PRICE SCORE 132.6** ***12 MONTH PRICE SCORE 105.0**

*NYSE COMPOSITE INDEX=100

INTERIM EARNINGS (Per Share):

Qtr.	Mar.	June	Sept.	Dec.
1990	0.24	1.08	1.01	1.31
1991	0.58	1.15	1.07	d3.47
1992	0.60	d3.13	1.25	1.47
1993	d0.09	1.48	0.61	1.46

INTERIM DIVIDENDS (Per Share):

Amt.	Decl.	Ex.	Rec.	Pay.
0.38Q	4/27/93	5/19/93	5/25/93	6/15/93
0.38Q	7/14	8/19	8/25	9/15
0.44Q	10/13	11/18	11/25	12/15
0.44Q	2/9/94	2/18/94	2/25/94	3/15/94
0.44Q	5/3	5/19	5/25	6/15

Indicated div.: $1.76

CAPITALIZATION (12/31/93):

	($000)	(%)
Long-Term Debt	3,133,000	36.2
Deferred Income Tax	2,341,000	27.1
Common & Surplus	3,180,000	36.7
Total	8,654,000	100.0

DIVIDEND ACHIEVER STATUS:
Rank: 287 1983-93 Growth Rate: 4.8%
Total Years of Dividend Growth: 13

RECENT DEVELOPMENTS: For the quarter ended 12/31/93, net income was $151 million compared with $152 million last year. Results were aided by strong performances at each CSX unit, offsetting the impact of depressed export coal demand. Revenues rose 3.1% to $2.32 billion. Rail income improved 5% to $219.0 million. Container shipping income surged 40% to $63 million with strong results from the Asia/Middle East/Europe routes.

PROSPECTS: Earnings should improve as CSX improves its operating efficiency, although barge and rail results will be adversely affected by a continued weak export coal market. CSX Transportation Inc. will benefit from increased automotive and metal shipments, as well as from ongoing productivity improvements. The Intermodal unit should increase its market share with new business, as transcontinental traffic volume continues to grow.

BUSINESS

CSX CORPORATION is an international, multimodal transportation company with interests in rail freight, ocean container shipping, intermodal carriage, barging, trucking, warehousing and distribution. The rail system, CSX Transportation Inc., operates in 20 states, the District of Columbia and Ontario, Canada. Service is provided over 18,905 route-miles using a fleet of 2,965 locomotives. Sea-Land Services Inc., the ocean-container shipping unit, has a fleet of 88 vessels and serves 100 ports in 70 countries and territories. American Commercial Lines Inc. provides inland marine operations through its barging unit, American Commercial Barge Line Company (ACBL). Non-transportation interests include CSX Real Property Inc. and two resort properties.

REVENUES

(12/31/93)	($000)	(%)
Transportation	8,767	98.1
Non-transportation	173	1.9
Total	8,940	100.0

ANNUAL EARNINGS AND DIVIDENDS PER SHARE

	1993	1992	1991	1990	1989	1988	1987
Earnings Per Share	3.46	0.19	[1] d0.75	[2] 3.63	[2] 4.09	d0.33	2.78
Dividends Per Share	1.58	1.52	1.43	1.40	1.28	1.29	1.18
Dividend Payout %	45.7	N.M.	...	38.6	31.3	...	42.4

[1] Before acctg. chg. [2] Before disc. oper.

ANNUAL FINANCIAL DATA

	1993	1992	1991	1990	1989	1988	1987
RECORD OF EARNINGS (IN MILLIONS):							
Total Operating Revenue	8,940.0	8,734.0	8,636.0	8,205.0	7,745.0	7,592.0	8,043.0
Operating Expenses	7,455.0	7,941.0	8,036.0	6,917.0	6,429.0	6,954.0	6,604.0
Depreciation	572.0	527.0	501.0	473.0	447.0	467.0	544.0
Operating Income	913.0	266.0	99.0	815.0	869.0	171.0	895.0
Earn Bef Income Taxes	633.0	d7.0	d113.0	537.0	692.0	d60.0	682.0
Income Tax Exp (benefit)	274.0	cr27.0	cr37.0	172.0	265.0	cr22.0	250.0
Net Income	359.0	20.0	[1] d76.0	[2] 365.0	[3] 427.0	[4] d38.0	[5] 432.0
Aver. Shs. Outstg. (000)	103,915	102,907	100,489	98,252	101,230	146,451	154,814

[1] Before acctg. change dr$196,000,000. [2] Before disc. op. cr$51,000,000. [3] Before disc. op. cr$25,000,000. [4] Before disc. op. cr$185,000,000. [5] Before acctg. change dr$294,000,000.

	1993	1992	1991	1990	1989	1988	1987
BALANCE SHEET (IN MILLIONS):							
Cash and Cash Equivalents	499.0	530.0	465.0	609.0	591.0	625.0	921.0
Receivables, Net	776.0	605.0	728.0	728.0	645.0	896.0	876.0
Gross Property	15,853.0	15,702.0	15,176.0	14,927.0	14,262.0	14,048.0	14,843.0
Accumulated Depreciation	5,065.0	5,066.0	4,999.0	4,936.0	4,610.0	4,417.0	4,681.0
Long-Term Debt	3,133.0	3,245.0	2,804.0	3,025.0	2,727.0	3,032.0	3,162.0
Net Properties	10,788.0	10,636.0	10,177.0	9,991.0	9,652.0	9,631.0	10,162.0
Net Stockholders' Equity	3,180.0	2,975.0	3,182.0	3,541.0	3,397.0	3,392.0	5,008.0
Total Assets	13,420.0	13,049.0	12,798.0	12,804.0	12,298.0	13,026.0	13,231.0
Total Current Assets	1,571.0	1,421.0	1,535.0	1,725.0	1,711.0	2,435.0	2,390.0
Total Current Liabilities	2,275.0	2,280.0	2,477.0	2,303.0	2,331.0	3,061.0	1,898.0
Net Working Capital	d704.0	d859.0	d942.0	d578.0	d620.0	d626.0	492.0
Year End Shs Outstg (000)	104,143	103,476	102,378	98,540	97,696	106,683	155,446
STATISTICAL RECORD:							
Operating Profit Margin %	10.2	3.0	1.1	9.9	11.2	2.3	11.1
Book Value Per Share	30.53	28.75	31.08	35.93	33.24	30.39	31.25
Return on Equity %	11.3	0.7	...	10.3	12.6	...	8.6
Return on Assets %	2.7	0.2	...	2.9	3.5	...	3.3
Average Yield %	2.0	2.4	3.3	4.4	3.7	4.5	3.7
P/E Ratio	25.5-19.2	N.M	...	10.5-7.2	9.4-7.3	...	17.4-9.2
Price Range	88⅛-66⅜	73⅝-54½	58-29¾	38⅛-26	38⅝-29¾	32½-24⅜	41¾-22⅛

Statistics are as originally reported.

OFFICERS:
J.W. Snow, Chmn., Pres. & C.E.O.
J. Ermer, Sr. V.P.-Fin.
A.A. Rudnick, V.P., Sec. & Gen. Coun.
W.H. Sparrow, V.P. & Treas.

PRINCIPAL OFFICE: One James Center 901 East Cary Street, Richmond, VA 23219

TELEPHONE NUMBER: (804) 782-1400
FAX: (804) 782-1409
NO. OF EMPLOYEES: 47,063
ANNUAL MEETING: In May
SHAREHOLDERS: 59,714 Common.
INSTITUTIONAL HOLDINGS:
No. of Institutions: 581
Shares Held: 64,285,681

REGISTRAR(S):

TRANSFER AGENT(S):

DAYTON-HUDSON CORP.

YIELD 2.1%
P/E RATIO 16.2

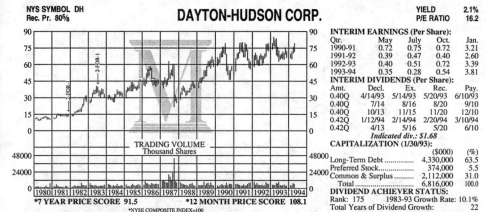

TRADING VOLUME
Thousand Shares

| | 1980 | 1981 | 1982 | 1983 | 1984 | 1985 | 1986 | 1987 | 1988 | 1989 | 1990 | 1991 | 1992 | 1993 | 1994 |

*7 YEAR PRICE SCORE 91.5   *12 MONTH PRICE SCORE 108.1
*NYSE COMPOSITE INDEX=100

INTERIM EARNINGS (Per Share):

Qtr.	May	July	Oct.	Jan.
1990-91	0.72	0.75	0.72	3.21
1991-92	0.39	0.47	0.40	2.60
1992-93	0.40	0.51	0.72	3.39
1993-94	0.35	0.28	0.54	3.81

INTERIM DIVIDENDS (Per Share):

Amt.	Decl.	Ex.	Rec.	Pay.
0.40Q	4/14/93	5/14/93	5/20/93	6/10/93
0.40Q	7/14	8/16	8/20	9/10
0.40Q	10/13	11/15	11/20	12/10
0.42Q	1/12/94	2/14/94	2/20/94	3/10/94
0.42Q	4/13	5/16	5/20	6/10

Indicated div.: $1.68

CAPITALIZATION (1/30/93):

	($000)	(%)
Long-Term Debt	4,330,000	63.5
Preferred Stock	374,000	5.5
Common & Surplus	2,112,000	31.0
Total	6,816,000	100.0

DIVIDEND ACHIEVER STATUS:
Rank: 175   1983-93 Growth Rate: 10.1%
Total Years of Dividend Growth: 22

RECENT DEVELOPMENTS: For the quarter ended 10/30/93, net income was $43 million compared with $57 million in 1992. Revenues grew 7% to $4.63 billion. Same-store revenues increased 1% from a year ago. Target recorded an increase in operating income on a 6% increase in same-store revenues. Mervyn's operating profit decreased significantly on a 7% decrease in same-store revenues. Gross margins fell due to reductions in everyday pricing. The department store division's profit was flat as higher markups on certain merchandise buys were offset by heavier promotional selling.

PROSPECTS: In response to disappointing results at Mervyn's, DH has focused on improving inventory management; however, a more aggressive pricing strategy and weak same-store sales will continue to hamper earnings. DH will continue to monitor costs by reducing advertising expenses and improving distribution efficiency and productivity. Target's expansion into the Chicago market should improve results. For the long term, DH plans to invest $1.3 billion in new stores, remodels and other capital support, including the upgrading of distribution and operational systems.

BUSINESS

DAYTON HUDSON CORPORATION is a diversified general merchandise retailer. Target is a national discount store chain offering low prices with stores selling hardlines and fashion softgoods; Mervyn's is a moderate-priced department store chain specializing in trend-right active and casual apparel and home softlines. The Department Store Division, operates three groups of full-service, full-line department stores under the names of Dayton's stores, Hudson's stores and Marshall Field Stores, offering moderate to better merchandise.

BUSINESS LINE ANALYSIS

(1/3/93)	Rev(%)	Inc(%)
Target	57.9	52.8
Mervyn's	25.2	26.2
Department Store		
Division	16.8	21.0
Total	100.0	100.0

ANNUAL EARNINGS AND DIVIDENDS PER SHARE

	1/30/93	2/1/92	2/2/91	2/3/90	1/28/89	1/30/88	1/31/87
Earnings Per Share	5.02	3.86	①5.41	5.37	3.45	2.41	②2.62
Dividends Per Share	1.52	1.44	1.32	1.12	1.02	0.92	0.84
Dividend Payout %	30.3	37.3	24.4	20.9	29.6	38.2	32.1

① Before acctg. chg.   ② Before disc. oper. & extraord. item

ANNUAL FINANCIAL DATA

RECORD OF EARNINGS (IN MILLIONS):

Revenues	17,927.0	16,115.0	14,739.0	13,644.0	12,204.0	10,677.3	9,259.1
Costs and Expenses	16,420.0	14,835.0	13,386.0	12,384.0	11,224.0	9,894.8	①8,464.7
Depreciation	459.0	410.0	369.0	315.0	290.0	231.0	...
Operating Income	1,048.0	870.0	984.0	945.0	690.0	551.6	611.7
Earn Bef Income Taxes	611.0	472.0	659.0	678.0	472.0	399.8	494.2
Income Taxes	228.0	171.0	249.0	268.0	185.0	171.4	239.2
Net Income	383.0	301.0	412.0	410.0	287.0	228.4	②255.0
Aver. Shs. Outstg. (000)	71,600	71,500	71,300	76,300	83,300	94,800	97,300

① Incl. Dep.   ② Before disc. op. cr$87,300,000; and extra. item dr$32,300,000.

BALANCE SHEET (IN MILLIONS):

Cash and Cash Equivalents	117.0	96.0	92.0	103.0	53.0	175.1	223.8
Accounts Receivable, Net	1,514.0	1,430.0	1,407.0	1,138.0	1,223.0	1,073.5	1,052.5
Inventories	2,618.0	2,381.0	2,016.0	1,827.0	1,669.0	1,623.3	1,312.5
Gross Property	7,760.0	6,961.0	6,133.0	4,873.0	4,706.0	4,091.2	3,324.7
Accumulated Depreciation	2,197.0	1,859.0	1,608.0	1,350.0	1,220.0	985.4	807.5
Long-Term Debt	4,330.0	4,227.0	3,682.0	2,510.0	2,383.0	1,683.4	1,244.9
Capital Lease Obligations	...	...	...	...	...	135.3	131.6
Net Stockholders' Equity	2,486.0	2,231.0	2,427.0	2,132.0	1,861.0	1,986.0	2,179.5
Total Assets	10,337.0	9,485.0	8,524.0	6,684.0	6,523.0	6,075.5	5,282.0
Total Current Assets	4,414.0	4,032.0	3,658.0	3,107.0	2,981.0	2,908.3	2,617.4
Total Current Liabilities	2,964.0	2,580.0	2,422.0	2,195.0	2,003.0	1,985.8	1,424.6
Net Working Capital	1,450.0	1,452.0	1,236.0	912.0	978.0	922.5	1,192.8
Year End Shs Outstg (000)	71,384	71,235	71,062	70,874	70,874	85,775	97,369

STATISTICAL RECORD:

Operating Profit Margin %	5.8	5.4	6.7	6.9	5.7	5.2	6.6
Book Value Per Share	29.59	26.03	28.82	24.73	23.97	23.15	22.38
Return on Equity %	15.4	13.5	20.0	23.4	15.4	11.5	11.7
Return on Assets %	3.7	3.2	4.8	6.1	4.4	3.8	4.8
Average Yield %	2.2	2.1	2.1	2.1	2.8	2.2	1.7
P/E Ratio	16.4-12.0	20.8-13.9	14.7-8.5	12.5-7.2	13.2-8.2	26.1-8.9	22.3-15.3
Price Range	79¼-58	80¼-53¾	79½-46¼	67-38¾	45½-28¼	63-21½	58½-40

Statistics are as originally reported.

OFFICERS:
K.A. Macke, Chmn. & C.E.O.
H.T. DeNero, Vice-Chmn.
S.E. Watson, Pres.

INCORPORATED: MN, 1902

PRINCIPAL OFFICE: 777 Nicollet Mall,
Minneapolis, MN 55402

TELEPHONE NUMBER: (612) 370-6948
FAX: (612) 370-5502
NO. OF EMPLOYEES: 170,000
ANNUAL MEETING: In May
SHAREHOLDERS: 12,196
INSTITUTIONAL HOLDINGS:
No. of Institutions: 437
Shares Held: 58,126,626

REGISTRAR(S): First Chicago Trust Co. of
New York, New York, NY 10008

TRANSFER AGENT(S): First Chicago Trust
Co. of New York, New York, NY 10008

NYS SYMBOL DF
Rec. Pr. 28⅞

DEAN FOODS CO.

YIELD 2.2%
P/E RATIO 17.8

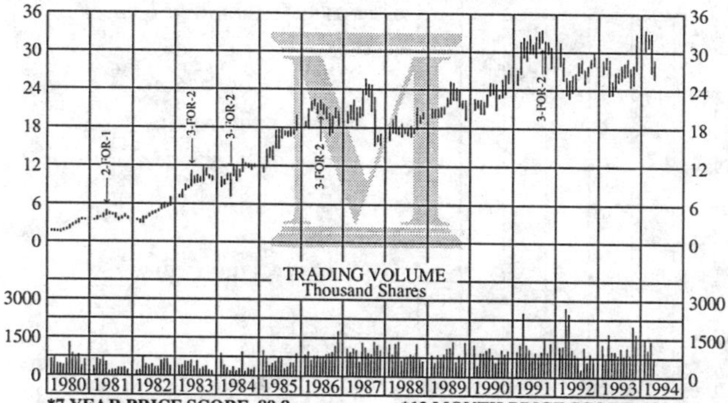

*7 YEAR PRICE SCORE 89.8 *12 MONTH PRICE SCORE 103.4

*NYSE COMPOSITE INDEX=100

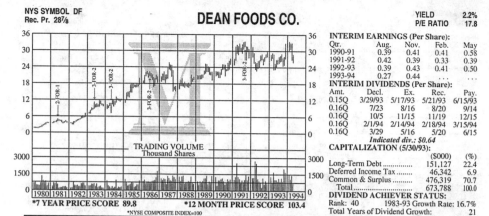

INTERIM EARNINGS (Per Share):

Qtr.	Aug.	Nov.	Feb.	May
1990-91	0.39	0.41	0.41	0.58
1991-92	0.42	0.39	0.33	0.39
1992-93	0.39	0.43	0.41	0.50
1993-94	0.27	0.44	...	...

INTERIM DIVIDENDS (Per Share):

Amt.	Decl.	Ex.	Rec.	Pay.
0.15Q	3/29/93	5/17/93	5/21/93	6/15/93
0.16Q	7/23	8/16	8/20	9/14
0.16Q	10/5	11/15	11/19	12/15
0.16Q	2/1/94	2/14/94	2/18/94	3/15/94
0.16Q	3/29	5/16	5/20	6/15

Indicated div.: $0.64

CAPITALIZATION (5/30/93):

	($000)	(%)
Long-Term Debt	151,127	22.4
Deferred Income Tax	46,342	6.9
Common & Surplus	476,319	70.7
Total	673,788	100.0

DIVIDEND ACHIEVER STATUS:
Rank: 40 1983-93 Growth Rate: 16.7%
Total Years of Dividend Growth: 21

RECENT DEVELOPMENTS: For the quarter ended 11/28/93, net income increased to $17.5 million from $17.2 million. Sales rose 0.8% to $577.1 million. Although processing costs associated with the intake of the year's vegetable crop rose, vegetable operations experienced improved margins as reduced inventories resulted in lower promotional activity and higher price levels. Pickle operations experienced higher volumes but lower margins, as weather related crop problems resulted in higher raw product and plant costs. In the dairy segment, income and revenues were flat.

PROSPECTS: Although pressures on vegetable pricing and margins are still evident, inventory levels have become more balanced which should improve long-term results. Also, the pickle business should continue its recovery from weather related crop shortages in the Midwest, as improved pricing levels support margin growth. Meanwhile, the dairy markets will likely remain steady in the near term. The Company terminated negotiations to acquire the dairy operations of Flav-O-Rich.

BUSINESS

DEAN FOODS COMPANY is a food processor and distributor engaged primarily in two business segments: Dairy Products and Specialty Food Products. The dairy products segment includes: fluid milk and related dairy products; ice cream and natural cheeses such as aged cheddar. The specialty food products segment includes: canned and frozen vegetables; pickles; relishes and salad dressings; non-dairy creamers; sauces; puddings; dips and salads. DF also operates a transportation business which concentrates on refrigerated and frozen cartage.

BUSINESS LINE ANALYSIS

(5/30/93)	Rev(%)	Inc(%)
Dairy Products	64.1	59.1
Specialty Food Products	35.9	40.9
Total	100.0	100.0

ANNUAL EARNINGS AND DIVIDENDS PER SHARE

	5/30/93	5/31/92	5/26/91	5/27/90	5/28/89	5/29/88	5/31/87
Earnings Per Share	1.73	1.53	1.79	1.53	1.52	1.07	1.03
Dividends Per Share	0.57	0.506	0.453	0.41	0.37	0.333	[1] 0.279
Dividend Payout %	32.9	33.1	25.3	26.9	24.3	31.3	27.1

[1] 3-for-2 stk split, 6/86

ANNUAL FINANCIAL DATA

	5/30/93	5/31/92	5/26/91	5/27/90	5/28/89	5/29/88	5/31/87
RECORD OF EARNINGS (IN MILLIONS):							
Total Revenues	2,274.3	2,289.4	2,158.0	1,987.5	1,683.6	1,551.8	1,434.6
Costs and Expenses	2,144.7	2,112.5	1,975.1	1,837.6	1,555.2	1,424.4	1,321.8
Depreciation & Amort	3.7	50.3	47.0	38.6	32.0	35.7	27.0
Operating Income	126.0	126.6	135.9	111.3	96.4	91.7	85.8
Income Before Taxes	114.8	105.5	124.3	102.1	101.8	76.5	82.8
Provision for Inc Taxes	46.4	43.5	51.8	40.8	41.4	33.8	41.7
Net Income	68.4	62.0	72.5	61.2	60.4	42.8	41.1
BALANCE SHEET (IN MILLIONS):							
Cash & Temp Cash Invests	41.6	34.0	44.1	43.5	70.0	53.8	51.1
Accts & Notes Receiv, Net	146.5	152.5	151.6	140.6	121.4	111.2	100.0
Inventories	179.0	168.0	174.5	164.9	112.0	91.8	79.4
Gross Property	770.9	694.2	624.5	561.7	452.0	392.8	354.1
Accumulated Depreciation	327.1	278.4	248.6	224.6	198.0	181.1	159.2
Long-Term Debt	151.1	155.5	150.0	146.6	84.2	48.9	47.0
Net Stockholders' Equity	476.3	430.4	416.6	362.8	293.2	265.7	236.4
Total Assets	892.8	857.2	817.0	744.8	586.7	499.2	450.1
Total Current Assets	406.1	397.0	399.5	372.4	320.2	270.3	239.1
Total Current Liabilities	207.7	213.4	201.0	189.6	163.7	139.9	124.2
Net Working Capital	198.4	183.6	198.4	182.9	156.5	130.4	114.8
Year End Shs Outstg (000)	39,689	39,604	40,709	40,623	39,458	40,269	40,154
STATISTICAL RECORD:							
Operating Profit Margin %	5.5	5.5	6.3	5.6	5.7	5.9	6.0
Book Value Per Share	11.11	10.00	9.36	8.16	7.26	6.42	5.60
Return on Equity %	14.4	14.4	17.4	16.9	20.6	16.1	17.4
Return on Assets %	7.7	7.2	8.9	8.2	10.3	8.6	9.1
Average Yield %	2.1	1.7	1.9	1.8	2.0	1.6	1.4
P/E Ratio	18.2-13.2	21.9-16.3	15.2-11.2	16.5-12.6	14.0-10.5	23.9-14.1	21.8-16.3
Price Range	31½-22¾	33½-24⅞	27¼-20⅛	25¼-19¼	21¼-16	25⅝-15⅛	22½-16¾

Statistics are as originally reported.

OFFICERS:
H.M. Dean, Chmn. & C.E.O.
T.L. Rose, Pres. & C.O.O.
D.I. Hecox, Treasurer

INCORPORATED: DE, May, 1968

PRINCIPAL OFFICE: 3600 North River Road, Franklin Park, IL 60131

TELEPHONE NUMBER: (312) 625-6200
FAX: (708) 671-8741
NO. OF EMPLOYEES: 5,565 (approx.)
ANNUAL MEETING: In September
SHAREHOLDERS: 4,067 (approx.)
INSTITUTIONAL HOLDINGS:
No. of Institutions: 158
Shares Held: 14,383,490

REGISTRAR(S): Harris Trust & Savings Bank, Chicago, IL

TRANSFER AGENT(S): Harris Trust & Savings Bank, Chicago, IL

DELUXE CORP.

YIELD 5.3%
P/E RATIO 15.9

TRADING VOLUME
Thousand Shares

*7 YEAR PRICE SCORE 82.3   *12 MONTH PRICE SCORE 85.3

*NYSE COMPOSITE INDEX=100

INTERIM EARNINGS (Per Share):

Qtr.	Mar.	June	Sept.	Dec.
1990	0.42	0.45	0.53	0.63
1991	0.49	0.52	0.54	0.63
1992	0.58	0.57	0.60	0.67
1993	0.62	0.03	0.45	0.61

INTERIM DIVIDENDS (Per Share):

Amt.	Decl.	Ex.	Rec.	Pay.
0.35Q	5/12/93	5/18/93	5/24/93	6/7/93
0.36Q	8/13	8/17	8/23	9/7
0.36Q	11/12	11/16	11/22	12/6
0.36Q	2/10/94	2/15/94	2/22/94	3/7/94
0.36Q	5/9	5/17	5/23	6/6

Indicated div.: $1.44

CAPITALIZATION (12/31/93):

	($000)	(%)
Long-Term Debt	110,755	11.6
Deferred Income Tax	42,119	4.4
Common & Surplus	801,249	84.0
Total	954,123	100.0

DIVIDEND ACHIEVER STATUS:
Rank: 43   1983-93 Growth Rate: 16.4%
Total Years of Dividend Growth: 33

RECENT DEVELOPMENTS: For the year ended 12/31/93, net income fell 30% to $141.9 million. Sales increased 3.1% to $1.58 billion from $1.53 billion. The 1993 results included a $60 million pretax restructuring charge taken in the second quarter to close 16 check printing facilities. However, only 14 of the facilities were closed and at a cost less than previously estimated. Thus, DLX reduced the total restructuring charge to $49 million and recorded a credit of $11 million in the fourth quarter.

PROSPECTS: The check-printing industry is expected to decline as people are increasingly paying their bills electronically. DLX has responded by restructuring the check printing division and reducing costs. Also, DLX has entered the electronic business forms and payment systems industries. Consolidation of financial institutions is also pressuring margins as banks demand lower prices. Operations are expanding internationally with a manufacturing facility in the U.K. and plans to open a printing facility in Canada early in 1994.

BUSINESS

DELUXE CORPORATION specializes in the production and sale of checks, deposit tickets, and related forms for use by banks and their depositors. The Company has three business segments: Payment Systems, 71% of sales, provides check printing, electronic funds transfer, ATM card services, new account verification services, and credit reporting services; Business Systems, 13%, manufactures and supplies computer and business forms, record keeping systems, and related office products; and Consumer Specialty Products, 16%, manufactures and distributes greeting cards, gift wrap, stationery, and other products for household use. The Company has more than 85 printing plants located throughout the country to provide service to customers in all 50 states.

BUSINESS LINE ANALYSIS

(12/31/93)	Rev(%)	Inc(%)
Payment Systems	67.6	78.4
Business Systems	15.0	10.9
Consumer Specialty Prods	17.4	10.7
Total	100.0	100.0

ANNUAL EARNINGS AND DIVIDENDS PER SHARE

	1993	1992	1991	1990	1989	1988	1987
Earnings Per Share	1.71	2.42	2.18	2.03	1.79	1.68	1.74
Dividends Per Share	1.42	1.34	1.22	1.10	0.98	0.86	0.76
Dividend Payout %	83.0	55.4	56.0	54.2	54.7	51.2	43.7

ANNUAL FINANCIAL DATA

RECORD OF EARNINGS (IN MILLIONS):

	1993	1992	1991	1990	1989	1988	1987
Total Revenues	1,581.8	1,534.4	1,474.5	1,413.6	1,315.8	1,196.0	948.0
Costs and Expenses	1,277.6	1,145.5	1,110.5	1,088.0	1,027.1	931.1	707.6
Depreciation & Amort	72.3	66.6	76.0	51.0	44.9	38.1	30.4
Income From Operations	231.8	322.2	288.0	274.6	243.8	226.8	209.9
Income Bef Income Taxes	235.9	324.8	295.5	282.5	246.3	226.6	236.6
Provision for Inc Taxes	94.1	122.0	112.6	110.3	93.7	83.3	88.1
Net Income	141.9	202.8	182.9	172.2	152.6	143.4	148.5
Aver. Shs. Outstg. (000)	82,936	83,861	84,005	84,638	85,346	85,255	85,242

BALANCE SHEET (IN MILLIONS):

Cash and Cash Equivalents	221.8	380.9	317.3	114.5	45.0	22.0	158.8
Receivables, Net	178.1	141.3	111.7	125.1	126.8	110.2	101.1
Inventories	85.3	65.1	68.0	71.9	62.9	62.5	54.1
Gross Property	779.9	729.9	687.4	640.0	600.5	527.5	468.3
Accumulated Depreciation	378.3	340.8	314.2	283.9	254.6	225.5	200.5
Long-Term Debt	110.8	115.5	110.6	11.9	10.2	10.9	12.9
Net Stockholders' Equity	801.2	829.8	748.0	675.8	630.6	567.7	490.8
Total Assets	1,252.0	1,199.6	1,099.1	923.9	847.0	786.1	866.3
Total Current Assets	522.4	611.2	539.0	344.3	262.7	219.9	337.3
Total Current Liabilities	297.9	224.4	208.0	199.3	167.8	167.1	315.1
Net Working Capital	224.5	386.9	330.9	145.0	94.8	52.8	22.2
Year End Shs Outstg (000)	82,549	83,797	83,938	84,075	85,212	85,365	85,050

STATISTICAL RECORD:

Operating Profit Margin %	14.7	21.0	19.5	19.4	18.5	19.0	22.1
Book Value Per Share	6.15	7.77	6.93	5.88	5.23	4.29	3.35
Return on Equity %	17.7	24.4	24.5	25.5	24.2	25.3	30.3
Return on Assets %	11.3	16.9	16.6	18.6	18.0	18.2	17.1
Average Yield %	3.6	3.1	3.0	3.5	3.3	3.5	2.4
P/E Ratio	28.0-18.6	20.2-15.8	22.2-15.0	17.7-13.1	20.0-13.4	16.9-12.5	24.3-11.5
Price Range	47⅞-31¾	49-38⅛	48½-32⅝	35⅞-26⅝	35¾-24	28⅜-21	42¼-20

Statistics are as originally reported.

OFFICERS:
H.V. Haverty, Chmn., Pres. & C.E.O.
C.M. Osborne, Sr. V.P. & C.F.O.
D.G. Stephens, V.P. & Treas.

INCORPORATED: MN, Mar., 1920

PRINCIPAL OFFICE: 1080 West County Road F, Saint Paul, MN 55126-8201

TELEPHONE NUMBER: (612) 483-7111
FAX: (612) 481-4163
NO. OF EMPLOYEES: 9,222
ANNUAL MEETING: In May
SHAREHOLDERS: 11,256
INSTITUTIONAL HOLDINGS:
No. of Institutions: 387
Shares Held: 48,751,686

REGISTRAR(S): The Bank of New York, New York, NY

TRANSFER AGENT(S): The Bank of New York, New York, NY

DIBRELL BROTHERS, INC.

YIELD 4.4%
P/E RATIO 8.1

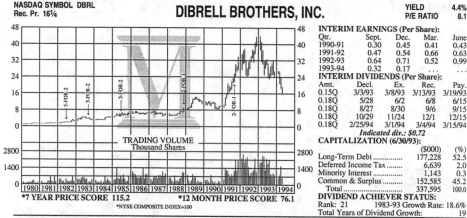

*7 YEAR PRICE SCORE 115.2   *12 MONTH PRICE SCORE 76.1
*NYSE COMPOSITE INDEX=100

INTERIM EARNINGS (Per Share):

Qtr.	Sept.	Dec.	Mar.	June
1990-91	0.30	0.45	0.41	0.43
1991-92	0.47	0.54	0.66	0.63
1992-93	0.64	0.71	0.52	0.99
1993-94	0.32	0.17	...	...

INTERIM DIVIDENDS (Per Share):

Amt.	Decl.	Ex.	Rec.	Pay.
0.15Q	3/3/93	3/8/93	3/13/93	3/19/93
0.18Q	5/28	6/2	6/8	6/15
0.18Q	8/27	8/30	9/6	9/15
0.18Q	10/29	11/24	12/1	12/15
0.18Q	2/25/94	3/1/94	3/4/94	3/15/94

Indicated div.: $0.72

CAPITALIZATION (6/30/93):

	($000)	(%)
Long-Term Debt	177,228	52.5
Deferred Income Tax	6,639	2.0
Minority Interest	1,143	0.3
Common & Surplus	152,585	45.2
Total	337,595	100.0

DIVIDEND ACHIEVER STATUS:
Rank: 21   1983-93 Growth Rate: 18.6%
Total Years of Dividend Growth: 19

RECENT DEVELOPMENTS: For the six months ended 12/31/93, net income before the cumulative effect of accounting changes was $6.5 million, or $0.49 per share, compared with $18.0 million, or $1.35 per share, last year. Net sales decreased 19.4% to $439.9 million compared with $545.9 million last year. Net sales for tobacco operations decreased 26.6% to $270.6 million and the volume of tobacco sold decreased 12.4%. For the quarter, net income

was $2.2 million, or $0.17 per share, compared with $9.5 million, or $0.71 per share, the year before. Net sales decreased 8.1% to $266.2 million compared with $289.6 million last year. Net sales for tobacco operations decreased 11.2% to $168.3 million. The decreases in tobacco sales, primarily in Brazil, Malawi and China, as well as delayed sales in the U.S., are attributed to a surplus of tobacco in the world market.

BUSINESS

DIBRELL BROTHERS, INC. is involved in two international businesses: the purchasing, processing and selling of leaf tobacco and the purchasing and selling of cut flowers. The Company's principal business is buying and processing leaf tobacco in the United States and foreign countries for sale to manufacturers of cigarettes and other tobacco products. The Company, through Florimex Verwaltungsgesellschaft mbH, a subsidiary headquartered in Nurnberg, Germany, is in the business of buying and selling cut flowers around the world. Baardse B.V., a subsidiary of the Company, is a flower exporter located in Holland.

ANNUAL EARNINGS AND DIVIDENDS PER SHARE

	6/30/93	6/30/92	6/30/91	6/30/90	6/30/89	6/30/88	6/30/87
Earnings Per Share	① 2.87	② 2.31	1.60	④ 1.10	1.11	0.95	d0.08
Dividends Per Share	0.69	③ 0.57	0.46	0.39	⑤ 0.33	0.31	0.24
Dividend Payout %	24.0	24.7	28.8	35.3	29.9	32.8	...

① Before acctg. chg. ② Before extraord. item ③ 2-for-1 stk split, 9/16/91 ④ Before disc. oper. ⑤ 2-for-1 stk split, 12/15/88

ANNUAL FINANCIAL DATA

RECORD OF EARNINGS (IN MILLIONS):

Total Revenues	1,065.4	1,081.1	1,003.0	765.4	685.3	555.0	308.1
Costs and Expenses	977.6	994.0	942.0	730.0	648.7	521.6	300.8
Depreciation & Amort	19.7	20.0	11.4	10.3	9.0	6.8	3.7
Operating Income	68.1	67.1	49.6	25.1	27.6	26.6	3.6
Income Bef Income Taxes	58.3	43.2	31.3	18.9	19.5	16.3	d2.2
Income Taxes	20.1	16.6	12.4	6.3	6.6	5.4	cr0.6
Inc Applic to Minority Int	0.5	0.2	0.5	0.6	0.3	0.7	⑧ cr0.1
Net Income	39.3	① 30.6	21.2	② 14.6	14.6	12.7	d1.1
Aver. Shs. Outstg. (000)	...	...	13,225	13,225	13,225	13,448	13,942

① Before extra. item dr$327,000. ② Before disc. op. dr$2,573,000. ⑧ Equal to cr$93,000.

BALANCE SHEET (IN MILLIONS):

Cash and Cash Equivalents	12.3	15.2	29.2	24.6	7.2	19.2	10.0
Receivables, Net	209.9	233.7	180.8	162.5	93.3	71.3	43.8
Inventories	174.6	152.5	107.8	80.5	83.2	86.2	55.9
Gross Property	181.1	166.9	146.2	104.3	100.5	83.3	48.5
Accumulated Depreciation	45.7	36.4	39.6	34.6	29.9	22.9	21.2
Long-Term Debt	177.2	202.0	202.8	90.9	85.2	84.4	...
Net Stockholders' Equity	152.6	120.4	97.3	81.3	75.1	63.8	57.7
Total Assets	639.8	630.5	539.3	431.4	302.9	290.1	159.7
Total Current Assets	405.1	414.2	322.0	271.5	187.3	179.5	111.6
Total Current Liabilities	279.5	292.4	221.8	245.1	129.8	129.8	94.6
Net Working Capital	125.6	121.8	100.1	26.4	57.5	49.6	17.0
Year End Shs Outstg (000)	13,302	13,255	13,225	13,225	13,225	13,225	13,785

STATISTICAL RECORD:

Operating Profit Margin %	6.4	6.2	4.9	3.3	4.0	4.8	1.2
Book Value Per Share	6.74	4.29	5.37	5.17	4.61	3.97	4.18
Return on Equity %	25.1	25.4	21.8	18.0	19.4	19.9	...
Return on Assets %	6.0	4.9	3.9	3.4	4.8	4.4	...
Average Yield %	2.1	1.7	2.1	3.8	2.9	4.3	3.8
P/E Ratio	15.3-8.0	18.9-10.5	21.1-5.8	11.0-7.5	12.6-7.3	9.7-5.4	...
Price Range	44-23	43¾-24¼	33¾-9¼	12⅛-8¼	14¼-8¼	9¼-5⅛	7½-5

Statistics are as originally reported.

OFFICERS:
C.B. Owen, Jr., Chmn., C.E.O. & Pres.
T.H. Faucett, Sr. V.P. & C.F.O.
J.O. Hunnicutt, III, V.P. & Sec.
J.M. Dail, V.P. & Treas.

INCORPORATED: VA, Aug., 1904

PRINCIPAL OFFICE: 512 Bridge St., Danville, VA 24543-0681

TELEPHONE NUMBER: (804) 792-0180
FAX: (804) 791-0377
NO. OF EMPLOYEES: 707 (approx.)
ANNUAL MEETING: In October
SHAREHOLDERS: 3,249
INSTITUTIONAL HOLDINGS:
No. of Institutions: 64
Shares Held: 5,282,016

REGISTRAR(S): First Union National Bank of N.C., Charlotte, NC

TRANSFER AGENT(S): First Union National Bank of N.C., Charlotte, NC

DIEBOLD, INC.

YIELD 2.1%
P/E RATIO 17.7

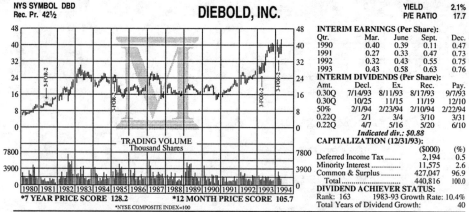

INTERIM EARNINGS (Per Share):

Qtr.	Mar.	June	Sept.	Dec.
1990	0.40	0.39	0.11	0.47
1991	0.27	0.33	0.47	0.73
1992	0.32	0.43	0.55	0.75
1993	0.43	0.58	0.63	0.76

INTERIM DIVIDENDS (Per Share):

Amt.	Decl.	Ex.	Rec.	Pay.
0.30Q	7/14/93	8/11/93	8/17/93	9/7/93
0.30Q	10/25	11/15	11/19	12/10
50%	2/1/94	2/23/94	2/10/94	2/22/94
0.22Q	2/1	3/4	3/10	3/31
0.22Q	4/7	5/16	5/20	6/10

Indicated div.: $0.88

CAPITALIZATION (12/31/93):

	($000)	(%)
Deferred Income Tax	2,194	0.5
Minority Interest	11,575	2.6
Common & Surplus	427,047	96.9
Total	440,816	100.0

DIVIDEND ACHIEVER STATUS:
Rank: 163   1983-93 Growth Rate: 10.4%
Total Years of Dividend Growth: 40

RECENT DEVELOPMENTS: For the year ended 12/31/93, net income increased 17.6% to $48.4 million from $41.1 million the previous year. Sales were up 14.4% to $623.3 million from $543.9 million. Net income was affected by the combination of a higher tax rate in 1993 as well as an unusually low tax rate in 1992 due to the settlement of a tax case. Results benefited from a strong backlog of orders at the beginning of the period. DBD experienced significant growth in orders outside the United States, which is consistent with the Company's strategy to penetrate foreign markets.

PROSPECTS: DBD will benefit from an agreement for the purchase of 50% of OLTP ATM Systems in Caracas, Venezuela. OLTP ATM distributes, installs, and services Diebold Automated Teller Machines (ATMs), and physical and electronic security products in Venezuela. Upon completion of the purchase, the acquired company will be renamed Diebold OLTP Systems. Expansion into China, Mexico, and Venezuela, as well as the point of sale market and healthcare industry, should help DBD achieve steady long-term growth.

BUSINESS

DIEBOLD, INC. is engaged in the automation of self-service transactions, security products, and customer service. Electronic and retail products dispense currency and documents of value, transfer funds, validate checks, authorize credit and perform other point-of-sale functions. Products are used in financial service applications in financial, retail, transportation, government, petroleum, and other industry groups. The Company manufactures electronic and physical security systems. The financial group has traditionally consisted of banks, savings and loan associations and credit unions.

REVENUES

(12/31/93)	($000)	(%)
Products....................	367,385	58.9
Services	255,892	41.1
Total	623,277	100.0

ANNUAL EARNINGS AND DIVIDENDS PER SHARE

	1993	1992	1991	1990	1989	1988	1987
Earnings Per Share	2.40	2.05	1.80	1.37	1.83	②1.59	1.81
Dividends Per Share	1.20	①1.12	1.067	1.00	0.933	0.867	0.80
Dividend Payout %	5.0	54.5	59.3	73.2	50.9	54.6	44.1

Note: 50%stk.div.2/22/94. ① Bef acctg chge ② Before acctg. chg.

ANNUAL FINANCIAL DATA

RECORD OF EARNINGS (IN THOUSANDS):

	1993	1992	1991	1990	1989	1988	1987
Total Revenues	623,277	543,852	506,217	476,054	468,883	450,571	439,063
Costs and Expenses	540,581	477,549	449,109	431,303	411,369	403,658	383,841
Depreciation & Amort	13,606	12,502	12,808	12,564	11,892	10,334	8,735
Operating Income	69,090	53,801	44,300	32,187	45,622	36,579	46,487
Income Bef Income Taxes	70,515	54,836	49,166	37,478	53,863	43,870	55,143
Taxes on Income	22,141	13,699	13,421	10,367	17,633	12,530	19,375
Net Income	48,374	①41,137	35,745	27,111	36,230	②31,340	35,768
Aver. Shs. Outstg.	30,231	20,050	19,893	19,838	19,790	19,764	19,743

① Before acctg. change dr$17,932,000. ② Before acctg. change cr$4,484,000.

BALANCE SHEET (IN THOUSANDS):

	1993	1992	1991	1990	1989	1988	1987
Cash and Cash Equivalents	71,913	55,970	68,303	85,452	80,440	91,632	84,226
Receivables, Net	129,256	120,691	118,849	106,727	117,280	109,041	105,316
Inventories	74,983	80,750	106,147	96,000	76,757	85,423	93,058
Gross Property	146,400	141,491	133,972	135,336	120,826	117,708	101,151
Accumulated Depreciation	85,740	80,890	75,523	70,723	64,896	58,156	49,184
Long-Term Debt	...	...	2,000	3,250	4,500	5,000	6,000
Net Stockholders' Equity	427,047	399,674	396,908	378,128	379,532	360,791	341,125
Total Assets	609,019	558,914	535,593	519,932	489,649	454,737	441,638
Total Current Assets	313,326	292,387	321,368	313,314	289,338	298,563	298,528
Total Current Liabilities	138,571	117,612	115,779	116,022	89,991	74,806	88,853
Net Working Capital	174,755	174,775	205,589	197,292	199,347	223,757	209,675
Year End Shares Outstg	30,260	20,081	19,963	19,848	19,805	19,751	19,740

STATISTICAL RECORD:

	1993	1992	1991	1990	1989	1988	1987
Operating Profit Margin %	11.1	9.9	8.8	6.8	9.7	8.1	10.6
Book Value Per Share	14.11	19.90	19.88	19.05	19.16	18.27	17.28
Return on Equity %	11.3	10.3	9.0	7.2	9.5	8.7	10.5
Return on Assets %	7.9	7.4	6.7	5.2	7.4	6.9	8.1
Average Yield %	3.6	4.6	5.6	5.8	5.0	4.8	3.9
P/E Ratio	25.7-16.3	13.4-10.1	13.1-8.2	15.2-9.8	11.6-8.8	13.4-9.5	14.9-7.7
Price Range	41⅛-26	27½-20¾	23½-14¾	20⅞-13⅜	21¼-16⅛	21⅜-15⅛	27-13⅞

Statistics are as originally reported.

OFFICERS:
R.W. Mahoney, Chmn., Pres. & C.E.O.
R.P. Barone, Vice-Chmn.
G.F. Morris, Exec. V.P. & C.F.O.
R.J. Warren, V.P. & Treas.
INCORPORATED: OH, 1876
PRINCIPAL OFFICE: P.O. Box 8230, Canton, OH 44711-8230

TELEPHONE NUMBER: (216) 489-4000
NO. OF EMPLOYEES: 571
ANNUAL MEETING: In April
SHAREHOLDERS: 1,932 (approx.)
INSTITUTIONAL HOLDINGS:
No. of Institutions: 167
Shares Held: 16,315,144

REGISTRAR(S): Society National Bank, Cleveland, OH

TRANSFER AGENT(S): Society National Bank, Cleveland, OH

NYS SYMBOL D
Rec. Pr. 40

DOMINION RESOURCES, INC.

YIELD 6.4%
P/E RATIO 12.8

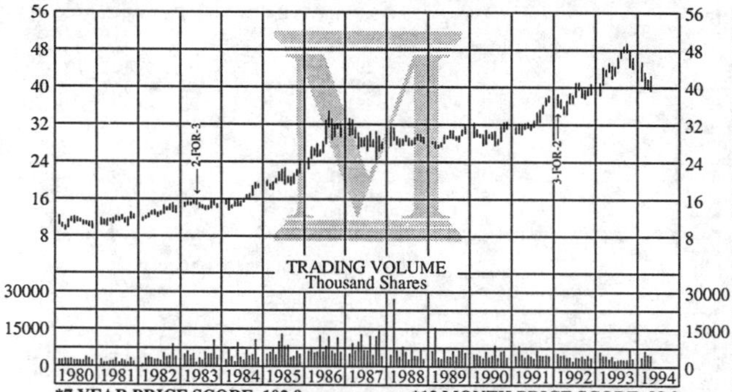

*7 YEAR PRICE SCORE 102.9 *12 MONTH PRICE SCORE 93.0

*NYSE COMPOSITE INDEX=100

INTERIM EARNINGS (Per Share):

Qtr.	Mar.	June	Sept.	Dec.
1991	0.67	0.57	1.15	0.54
1992	0.59	0.38	0.92	0.77
1993	0.75	0.63	1.20	0.55

INTERIM DIVIDENDS (Per Share):

Amt.	Decl.	Ex.	Rec.	Pay.
0.615Q	4/16/93	5/24/93	5/28/93	6/20/93
0.615Q	7/16	8/24	8/30	9/20
0.635Q	10/18	11/24	12/1	12/20
0.635Q	2/18/94	2/24/94	3/2/94	3/20/94
0.635Q	4/15	5/24	5/31	6/20

Indicated div.: $2.54

CAPITALIZATION (12/31/93):

	($000)	(%)
Long-Term Debt	4,750,500	42.0
Deferred Income Tax	1,893,000	16.8
Preferred Stock	818,000	7.2
Common & Surplus	3,841,900	34.0
Total	11,303,400	100.0

DIVIDEND ACHIEVER STATUS:
Rank: 297 1983-93 Growth Rate: 4.3%
Total Years of Dividend Growth: 18

RECENT DEVELOPMENTS: For the year ended 12/31/93, net income was $516.6 million compared with $428.9 million last year. Revenues were $4.43 billion, up 17%. Virginia Power's results were positively affected by hotter weather in 1993. Retail kilowatthour sales were up 6.4%. Non-utility earnings benefited from Dominion Energy's increased investments in natural gas production, which increased from 9.2 billion cubic feet (Bcf) in 1992 to 33 Bcf in 1993.

PROSPECTS: Dominion Resources' 1993 performance will be difficult to match in 1994. Utility and non-utilitiy operations benefitted from favorable weather conditions in 1993. Virginia Power faces potential competition for industrial, commercial and some government customers from cogeneration units that might directly serve those customers. Dominion's non-utility businesses will likely continue to be important contributors to earnings. Dominion Energy has doubled its natural gas reserves to more than 225 billion cubic feet.

BUSINESS

DOMINION RESOURCES, INC. is a holding company for Virginia Electric & Power Co., which provides electric services for more than 1.8 million customers in Virginia and Northeastern North Carolina. Dominion Capital, a subsidiary, provides investment management services to the holding company and other nonutility subsidiaries. Dominion Lands, Inc. is involved in joint venture real estate development. Dominion Energy has investment or ownership interest in non-utility electric power generation products and is also involved in joint ventures for natural gas and oil exploration.

REVENUES

(12/31/93)	($000)	(%)
Electric utility	4,187,300	94.4
Nonutility	246,600	5.6
Total	4,433,900	100.0

ANNUAL EARNINGS AND DIVIDENDS PER SHARE

	1993	1992	1991	1990	1989	1988	1987
Earnings Per Share	**3.12**	**[1] 2.66**	**2.94**	**2.92**	**2.76**	**3.01**	**3.03**
Dividends Per Share	**2.48**	**2.40**	**[2] 2.313**	**2.233**	**2.153**	**2.073**	**1.993**
Dividend Payout %	**79.5**	**90.2**	**78.7**	**76.5**	**78.0**	**68.8**	**65.9**

[1] Before acctg. chg. [2] 3-for-2 stk split,01/24/92

ANNUAL FINANCIAL DATA

	1993	1992	1991	1990	1989	1988	1987
RECORD OF EARNINGS (IN MILLIONS):							
Total Oper Revenues & Inc	4,433.9	3,791.1	3,785.7	3,532.5	3,699.9	3,344.1	3,251.2
Depreciation & Amort	593.9	560.0	553.2	423.4	468.2	497.7	405.6
Maintenance	279.5	280.6	304.6	281.2	299.3	275.0	278.5
Prov for Fed Inc Taxes	210.2	203.6	210.7	196.1	165.8	124.3	250.9
Operating Income	1,127.3	1,029.2	1,095.0	1,050.1	1,039.7	972.2	1,047.0
Net Income	516.6	[1] 428.9	459.9	445.7	410.7	438.4	430.5
Aver. Shs. Outstg. (000)	165,700	161,100	156,500	152,550	148,800	145,500	142,350
[1] Before acctg. change cr$15,600,000.							
BALANCE SHEET (IN MILLIONS):							
Gross Plant	15,009.0	14,416.8	13,580.1	12,845.4	12,282.5	11,441.8	10,664.3
Accumulated Depreciation	4,802.1	4,724.9	4,302.4	3,886.5	3,549.5	3,223.9	2,847.9
Prop, Plant & Equip, Net	10,206.9	9,691.9	9,277.7	8,958.9	8,733.0	8,217.9	7,816.4
Long-term Debt	4,750.5	4,404.1	4,393.3	4,395.6	4,540.6	4,176.6	3,800.3
Net Stockholders' Equity	4,659.9	4,391.5	4,147.9	3,920.6	3,739.4	3,573.9	3,389.0
Total Assets	13,349.5	12,615.1	11,201.4	10,990.9	11,033.5	10,282.3	9,656.5
Year End Shs Outstg (000)	168,123	163,843	158,851	154,789	150,900	147,150	143,993
STATISTICAL RECORD:							
Book Value Per Share	22.85	21.74	21.48	20.43	19.60	19.29	18.79
Op. Inc/Net Pl %	11.0	10.6	11.8	11.7	11.9	11.8	13.4
Dep/Gr. Pl %	3.4	3.1	3.3	3.3	3.8	4.3	3.8
Accum. Dep/Gr. Pl %	32.0	32.8	31.7	30.3	28.9	28.2	26.7
Return on Equity %	11.6	10.4	11.9	12.3	12.0	13.6	14.3
Average Yield %	5.7	6.4	6.8	7.4	7.3	7.1	6.9
P/E Ratio	15.9-12.3	15.4-12.8	13.0-10.2	11.2-9.5	11.5-9.7	10.5-9.1	11.0-8.0
Price Range	49½-38¼	41-34⅛	38⅛-29⅞	32⅝-27⅝	31⅞-26⅞	31½-27¼	33¼-24⅜

Statistics are as originally reported.

OFFICERS:
T.E. Capps, Chmn., Pres. & C.E.O.
J.F. Betts, Vice-Chmn.
O.J. Peterson, III, Sr. V.P. & C.F.O.
L.R. Robertson, V.P. & Treas.

INCORPORATED: VA, Feb., 1983

PRINCIPAL OFFICE: Riverfront Plaza-West Tower 901 East Byrd St., Richmond, VA 23219-6532

TELEPHONE NUMBER: (804) 775-5700
FAX: (804) 775-5819
NO. OF EMPLOYEES: 1,640
ANNUAL MEETING: In April
SHAREHOLDERS: 154,331
INSTITUTIONAL HOLDINGS:
No. of Institutions: 390
Shares Held: 64,357,373

REGISTRAR(S): Mellon Financial Securities, New York, NY

TRANSFER AGENT(S): Mellon Financial Securities, New York, NY

DONNELLEY (R. R.) & SONS CO.

YIELD 2.0%
P/E RATIO 24.0

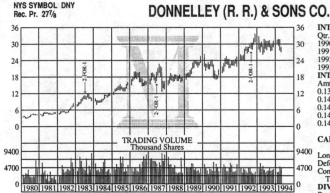

INTERIM EARNINGS (Per Share):

Qtr.	Mar.	June	Sept.	Dec.
1990	0.28	0.33	0.41	0.44
1991	0.19	0.28	0.41	0.44
1992	0.23	0.34	0.47	0.47
1993	d0.14	0.34	0.45	0.51

INTERIM DIVIDENDS (Per Share):

Amt.	Decl.	Ex.	Rec.	Pay.
0.13Q	4/22/93	5/6/93	5/12/93	6/2/93
0.14Q	7/22	8/5	8/11	9/1
0.14Q	10/28	11/4	11/11	12/1
0.14Q	1/27/94	2/1/94	2/7/94	3/1/94
0.14Q	4/28	5/5	5/11	6/1

Indicated div.: $0.56

CAPITALIZATION (12/31/93):

	($000)	(%)
Long-Term Debt	673,422	24.1
Deferred Income Tax	272,959	9.8
Common & Surplus	1,843,991	66.1
Total	2,790,372	100.0

DIVIDEND ACHIEVER STATUS:
Rank: 172   1983-93 Growth Rate: 10.2%
Total Years of Dividend Growth: 24

TRADING VOLUME
Thousand Shares

*7 YEAR PRICE SCORE 99.8   *12 MONTH PRICE SCORE 98.8
*NYSE COMPOSITE INDEX=100

RECENT DEVELOPMENTS: For the year ended 12/31/93, net income before an accounting adjustment declined 23.8% to $178.9 million compared with $234.7 million a year ago. Sales rose 4.6% to $4.39 billion from $4.19 billion. Earnings included a net gain from restructuring of $60.8 million, primarily related to the closing of a Chicago manufacturing facility. Capital investment totaled $484 million, including $178 million for acquisitions and joint venture investments. The Company's investments were also directed toward expanding and upgrading current operations.

PROSPECTS: Donnelley will proceed with efforts to improve operating efficiencies and lower costs. Future operations and expansion will be funded by a strong cash flow and growth in credit facilities. Sales will be aided by global expansion into new markets. Strong demand for financial printing, global software services, and services for book publishers should continue in the near term. However, catalog volume will be adversely affected by the elimination of the Sears catalog. The Company anticipates capital investment of $375 million in 1994.

BUSINESS

R.R. DONNELLEY & SONS COMPANY provides printing and related services to publishers of magazines and books, as well as merchandisers, the telephone industry, financial institutions and other firms requiring substantial amounts of printing. The Company is the largest supplier of commercial printing services in the U.S. and produces catalogs and tabloids, magazines, books, directories and financial printing. Services provided to customers are presswork and binding, along with all pre-press operations necessary to create a printing image, and planning for truck, rail and air distribution of the printed product.

QUARTERLY DATA

(12/31/93)	Rev	Inc
1st Quarter	960,341	(22,108)
2nd Quarter	993,964	52,771
3rd Quarter	1,123,848	69,451
4th Quarter	1,309,608	78,806

ANNUAL EARNINGS AND DIVIDENDS PER SHARE

	1993	1992	1991	1990	1989	1988	1987
Earnings Per Share	1.16	1.51	1.32	1.45	1.42	1.32	1.40
Dividends Per Share	0.54	①0.51	0.50	0.48	0.44	0.39	②0.35
Dividend Payout %	46.6	33.8	37.9	33.0	30.9	29.5	25.0

① 2-for-1 stk split,09/01/92 ② 2-for-1 stk. split, 5/87.

ANNUAL FINANCIAL DATA

RECORD OF EARNINGS (IN MILLIONS):

Total Revenues	4,387.8	4,193.1	3,914.8	3,497.9	3,122.3	2,878.4	2,482.9
Costs and Expenses	3,787.4	3,529.4	3,310.5	2,941.9	2,622.5	2,403.5	2,063.5
Depreciation & Amort	274.8	258.2	241.2	194.3	167.1	161.8	140.3
Operating Income	325.6	405.5	363.1	361.8	332.7	313.1	279.0
Inc Fr Cont Opers Bef Income Taxes	276.6	361.0	320.2	360.2	352.2	317.1	356.5
Income Taxes	97.6	126.4	115.3	134.4	130.3	111.8	138.3
Net Income	109.4	234.7	204.9	225.8	221.9	205.3	218.2
Aver. Shs. Outstg. (000)	154,600	155,400	155,340	155,456	155,674	155,422	155,744

BALANCE SHEET (IN MILLIONS):

Cash & Equivalents	10.7	12.3	24.1	59.9	27.7	31.8	38.6
Receivables, Net	825.2	791.9	689.4	685.9	526.1	517.4	462.6
Invent. Principally At LIFO Cost	243.7	198.0	160.4	159.2	159.4	157.8	172.8
Gross Property	3,361.3	3,022.9	2,854.1	2,643.1	2,233.6	2,028.5	1,868.5
Accumulated Depreciation	1,686.8	1,490.7	1,307.4	1,158.8	1,023.5	902.7	777.7
Long-Term Debt	673.4	522.6	527.5	647.1	62.6	121.0	193.8
Net Stockholders' Equity	1,844.0	1,849.0	1,730.4	1,595.6	1,445.8	1,296.4	1,155.1
Total Assets	3,654.0	3,410.2	3,403.8	3,343.1	2,507.3	2,346.3	2,086.4
Total Current Assets	1,109.9	1,021.6	972.9	991.6	726.4	686.5	650.6
Total Current Liabilities	685.4	611.7	726.5	676.8	602.1	546.4	383.7
Net Working Capital	424.5	409.9	246.4	314.8	124.3	140.1	266.9
Year End Shs Outstg (000)	154,158	155,029	155,350	154,930	155,806	155,370	158,608

STATISTICAL RECORD:

Operating Profit Margin %	7.4	9.7	9.3	10.3	10.7	10.9	11.2
Book Value Per Share	8.76	9.03	8.24	7.31	7.72	6.81	5.76
Return on Equity %	9.7	12.7	11.8	14.2	15.3	15.8	18.9
Return on Assets %	4.9	6.9	6.0	6.8	8.8	8.8	10.5
Average Yield %	1.8	1.8	2.2	2.2	2.1	2.3	2.0
P/E Ratio	28.2-22.5	22.4-15.7	19.4-14.8	18.2-11.8	18.0-12.1	14.7-11.4	16.3-9.1
Price Range	32¾-26⅛	33¾-23¾	25⅝-19½	26⅜-17⅛	25⅝-17⅛	19⅜-15	22¾-12¾

Statistics are as originally reported.

OFFICERS:
J.R. Walter, Chmn. & C.E.O.
J.R. Donnelley, Vice-Chmn.
F.R. Jarc, Exec. V.P. & C.F.O.
R.G. Eidell, Sr. V.P. & Treas.
INCORPORATED: DE, May, 1956
PRINCIPAL OFFICE: 77 West Wacker Drive, Chicago, IL 60601-1696

TELEPHONE NUMBER: (312) 326-8000
FAX: (312) 326-8557
NO. OF EMPLOYEES: 34,000 (approx.)
ANNUAL MEETING: In March
SHAREHOLDERS: 10,400 (approx.)
INSTITUTIONAL HOLDINGS:
No. of Institutions: 436
Shares Held: 113,121,831

REGISTRAR(S): First Chicago Trust Co. of New York, New York, NY 10008

TRANSFER AGENT(S): First Chicago Trust Co. of New York, New York, NY 10008

DOVER CORP.

YIELD 1.8%
P/E RATIO 25.7

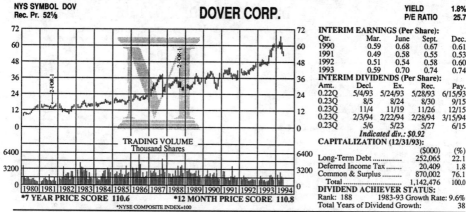

TRADING VOLUME
Thousand Shares

| | 1980 | 1981 | 1982 | 1983 | 1984 | 1985 | 1986 | 1987 | 1988 | 1989 | 1990 | 1991 | 1992 | 1993 | 1994 |

*7 YEAR PRICE SCORE 110.6   *12 MONTH PRICE SCORE 110.8
*NYSE COMPOSITE INDEX=100

INTERIM EARNINGS (Per Share):

Qtr.	Mar.	June	Sept.	Dec.
1990	0.59	0.68	0.67	0.61
1991	0.49	0.58	0.55	0.53
1992	0.51	0.54	0.58	0.60
1993	0.59	0.70	0.74	0.74

INTERIM DIVIDENDS (Per Share):

Amt.	Decl.	Ex.	Rec.	Pay.
0.22Q	5/4/93	5/24/93	5/28/93	6/15/93
0.23Q	8/5	8/24	8/30	9/15
0.23Q	11/4	11/19	11/26	12/15
0.23Q	2/3/94	2/22/94	2/28/94	3/15/94
0.23Q	5/6	5/23	5/27	6/15

Indicated div.: $0.92

CAPITALIZATION (12/31/93):

	($000)	(%)
Long-Term Debt	252,065	22.1
Deferred Income Tax	20,409	1.8
Common & Surplus	870,002	76.1
Total	1,142,476	100.0

DIVIDEND ACHIEVER STATUS:
Rank: 188   1983-93 Growth Rate: 9.6%
Total Years of Dividend Growth: 38

RECENT DEVELOPMENTS: For the year ended 12/31/93, net income increased 22.5% to $158.3 million compared with $129.1 million, before an accounting adjustment, a year ago. Sales rose 9.3% to $2.48 billion from $2.27 billion. Earnings growth was primarily attributable to Dover Resources, Dover Industries, and Dover Technologies International. Operating earnings at Dover Resources increased 20% to $70.3 million. The Company completed 13 separate acquisitions for a total cost of approximately $321 million.

PROSPECTS: Earnings will continue to benefit from strong internal growth at Dover Resources. However, growth in 1994 is not expected to match that of 1993. Operating results will benefit from the Dover Diversified subsidiary's acquisition of Thermal Equipment Company of California and Phoenix Refrigeration of Georgia. Dynapert, which makes through-hole assembly equipment, will be merged into the Universal Instruments Company operations of Dover Technologies.

BUSINESS

DOVER CORPORATION groups its products and services into the following five segments: Dover Resources Inc., includes oilfield operations, domestic oil and gas drilling, Logic Controls, compressor valves for air conditioners and refrigerators. Dover Elevators International involves the manufacture, sale, installation, and servicing of elevators. Dover Technologies include automatic electronic circuitry assembly equipment, component insertion machines, microwave, and R.F. filters. Dover Industries encompasses rotary lifts, food services, and engineered machinery. Dover Diversified includes heat exchangers, bearings, pressure vessels, metals and fabrics, and marine products.

BUSINESS LINE ANALYSIS

(12/31/93)	Rev(%)	Inc(%)
Dover Elevator Intl....	31.3	21.1
Dover Resources.......	19.0	26.2
Dover Diversified......	9.8	14.7
Dover Industries........	20.2	22.4
Dover Technologies ..	19.7	15.6
Total	100.0	100.0

ANNUAL EARNINGS AND DIVIDENDS PER SHARE

	1993	1992	1991	1990	1989	1988	1987
Earnings Per Share	2.77	2.23	2.15	2.55	2.28	2.22	1.66
Dividends Per Share	0.90	① 0.86	0.82	0.76	0.70	② 0.62	0.51
Dividend Payout %	32.5	38.6	38.1	29.8	30.7	27.9	30.8

① Bef acctg chge ② 2-for-1 stk split, 9/88

ANNUAL FINANCIAL DATA

RECORD OF EARNINGS (IN MILLIONS):

Total Revenues	2,483.9	2,271.6	2,195.8	2,210.3	2,120.4	1,953.8	1,585.5
Costs and Expenses	2,153.1	1,990.9	1,947.1	1,879.5	1,806.1	1,650.2	1,339.6
Depreciation & Amort	77.0	77.5	85.4	77.5	78.8	73.8	61.9
Operating Profit	253.9	203.2	163.3	253.3	235.5	229.8	184.0
Earn Bef Taxes on Income	245.5	200.3	204.1	244.1	227.0	224.8	180.9
Fed & Other Taxes on Inc	87.3	71.2	75.9	88.4	83.0	79.0	69.2
Net Income	158.3	① 129.1	128.2	155.7	144.0	145.8	111.7
Aver. Shs. Outstg. (000)	57,110	57,988	59,750	61,169	63,250	65,726	67,552

① Before acctg. change cr$564,000.

BALANCE SHEET (IN MILLIONS):

Cash and Cash Equivalents	96.3	101.2	127.4	152.4	175.8	84.5	191.2
Receivables, Net	475.2	389.3	368.0	389.3	389.2	363.8	283.9
Inventories	294.3	250.2	227.3	246.3	236.5	272.4	232.9
Gross Property	714.6	678.1	649.1	636.0	598.5	553.7	444.0
Accumulated Depreciation	431.3	426.9	397.9	367.6	326.4	285.6	231.1
Long-Term Debt	252.1	1.2	6.3	21.0	26.7	27.8	26.6
Net Stockholders' Equity	870.0	804.9	828.4	787.7	746.8	741.1	672.0
Total Assets	1,773.7	1,426.1	1,356.6	1,468.4	1,406.4	1,365.6	1,150.2
Total Current Assets	903.6	774.0	756.4	814.7	823.1	738.8	721.7
Total Current Liabilities	595.8	572.4	475.5	608.0	577.3	540.8	412.6
Net Working Capital	307.8	201.6	280.9	206.7	245.8	198.0	309.1
Year End Shs Outstg (000)	57,163	57,085	58,958	59,971	62,243	65,208	66,254

STATISTICAL RECORD:

Operating Profit Margin %	10.2	8.9	7.4	11.5	11.1	11.8	11.6
Book Value Per Share	5.68	7.81	8.96	7.37	7.51	6.69	7.06
Return on Equity %	18.2	16.0	15.5	19.8	19.3	19.7	16.6
Return on Assets %	8.9	9.1	9.5	10.6	10.2	10.7	9.7
Average Yield %	1.7	2.0	2.1	2.2	2.1	2.0	1.7
P/E Ratio	22.3-16.2	21.4-17.2	20.3-16.0	16.2-10.8	17.3-12.0	16.5-12.0	23.6-13.3
Price Range	61⅞-45	47⅝-38¼	43¾-34½	41¼-27½	39½-27¼	36⅜-26⅝	38⅞-21⅞

Statistics are as originally reported.

OFFICERS:
G.L. Roubos, Chmn.
T.L. Reece, Pres. & C.E.O.
J.F. McNiff, V.P.-Fin.

INCORPORATED: DE, 1947

PRINCIPAL OFFICE: 280 Park Avenue, New York, NY 10017-1292

TELEPHONE NUMBER: (212) 922-1640
FAX: (212) 922-1656
NO. OF EMPLOYEES: 20,445
ANNUAL MEETING: In April
SHAREHOLDERS: 10,000 (approx.)
INSTITUTIONAL HOLDINGS:
No. of Institutions: 284
Shares Held: 35,829,714

REGISTRAR(S): Harris Trust Co. of N.Y., New York, NY 10005

TRANSFER AGENT(S): Harris Trust Co. of N.Y., New York, NY 10005

NYS SYMBOL DUK
Rec. Pr. 35½

DUKE POWER CO.

YIELD 5.3%
P/E RATIO 12.7

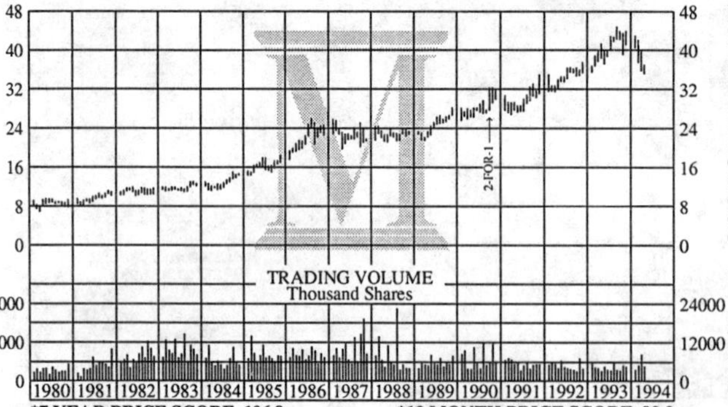

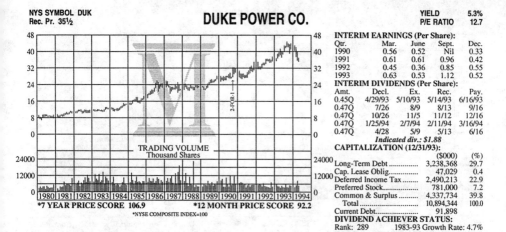

48
40
32
24
16
8
0
2-FOR-1
TRADING VOLUME
Thousand Shares
24000
12000
0
1980 1981 1982 1983 1984 1985 1986 1987 1988 1989 1990 1991 1992 1993 1994

*7 YEAR PRICE SCORE 106.9 *12 MONTH PRICE SCORE 92.2

*NYSE COMPOSITE INDEX=100

INTERIM EARNINGS (Per Share):

Qtr.	Mar.	June	Sept.	Dec.
1990	0.56	0.52	Nil	0.33
1991	0.61	0.61	0.96	0.42
1992	0.45	0.36	0.85	0.55
1993	0.63	0.53	1.12	0.52

INTERIM DIVIDENDS (Per Share):

Amt.	Decl.	Ex.	Rec.	Pay.
0.45Q	4/29/93	5/10/93	5/14/93	6/16/93
0.47Q	7/26	8/9	8/13	9/16
0.47Q	10/26	11/5	11/12	12/16
0.47Q	1/25/94	2/7/94	2/11/94	3/16/94
0.47Q	4/28	5/9	5/13	6/16

Indicated div.: $1.88

CAPITALIZATION (12/31/93):

	($000)	(%)
Long-Term Debt	3,238,368	29.7
Cap. Lease Oblig.	47,029	0.4
Deferred Income Tax	2,490,213	22.9
Preferred Stock	781,000	7.2
Common & Surplus	4,337,734	39.8
Total	10,894,344	100.0
Current Debt	91,898	

DIVIDEND ACHIEVER STATUS:
Rank: 289 1983-93 Growth Rate: 4.7%
Total Years of Dividend Growth: 18

RECENT DEVELOPMENTS: For the year ended 12/31/93, net income was $626.4 million, up 23.3% from $508.1 million last year. Revenues were $4.28 billion, up 8.1%. Total electric sales were up 7.1%. Residential sales were up 9.4% and general service sales were up 6.9%. The increased sales were the result of a colder winter and a hotter summer. Reflecting an improving economy, total industrial sales were up 4.3%.

PROSPECTS: Capital expenditures will increase substantially. Engineers have discovered microscopic cracking in steam generators at three nuclear stations. New generators will be needed for the plants to continue operating safely and reliably. A unit is scheduled for replacement each year, beginning in 1995. Also, the Company is planning for a plant-modernization program and construction of 16 combustion turbines beginning in 1995.

BUSINESS

DUKE POWER COMPANY provides electricity to 1.7 million people in a 20,000 square-mile service area in the central portion of North Carolina and western portion of South Carolina. DUK's three nuclear generating stations, eight coal-fired stations and 27 hydroelectric stations produced 84 billion kilowatt-hours of electricity in 1993. Duke Power also owns Nantahala Power and Light Co. which serves more than 50,000 customers in a five county area in western North Carolina. Total electric revenues reached $4.3 billion, with approximately 70% of sales in North Carolina and 30% in South Carolina.

QUARTERLY DATA

(12/31/93)	Rev	Inc
1st Quarter	1,007,783	188,522
2nd Quarter	987,218	169,111
3rd Quarter	1,289,994	283,411
4th Quarter	996,881	173,021

ANNUAL EARNINGS AND DIVIDENDS PER SHARE

	1993	1992	1991	1990	1989	1988	1987
Earnings Per Share	2.80	2.21	2.60	2.40	2.57	[2] 1.95	2.20
Dividends Per Share	1.84	1.76	1.68	[1] 1.60	1.52	1.44	1.37
Dividend Payout %	65.7	79.6	64.6	66.7	59.3	73.8	62.3

[1] 2-for-1 stk split, 9/28/90. [2] Before acctg. chg.

ANNUAL FINANCIAL DATA

	1993	1992	1991	1990	1989	1988	1987
RECORD OF EARNINGS (IN MILLIONS):							
Total Revenues	4,281.9	3,961.5	3,817.0	3,681.5	3,639.3	3,627.0	3,705.8
Depreciation & Amort	657.1	660.9	619.8	405.8	410.9	417.5	411.2
Maintenance Of Plant Facil	375.5	403.2	354.7	403.8	348.9	383.3	375.1
Income Taxes	410.7	303.3	296.1	252.4	296.0	248.5	378.3
Electric Operating Income	814.1	724.7	706.8	642.8	704.6	629.6	658.0
Total Interest Deductions	258.9	301.6	274.1	251.3	234.8	227.6	230.7
Net Income	626.4	508.1	583.6	538.2	571.6	[1] 448.1	500.2
Aver. Shs. Outstg. (000)	204,859	204,819	203,431	202,570	202,554	202,533	202,500
[1] Before acctg. change cr$102,255,000.							
BALANCE SHEET (IN MILLIONS):							
Gross Plant	14,072.7	15,192.8	14,524.4	13,806.9	12,833.7	11,804.5	10,813.2
Accumulated Depreciation	4,837.4	6,071.3	5,638.0	5,167.1	4,771.9	4,323.9	3,859.9
Prop, Plant & Equip, Net	9,235.4	9,121.5	8,886.4	8,639.8	8,061.8	7,480.5	6,953.3
Total Long-term Debt	3,285.4	3,202.4	3,159.6	3,102.7	2,822.4	2,728.8	2,723.4
Net Stockholders' Equity	5,118.7	4,930.1	4,796.9	4,558.8	4,331.8	4,127.9	3,928.1
Total Assets	12,193.1	10,801.8	10,470.6	10,083.5	9,542.4	8,890.6	8,511.8
Year End Shs Outstg (000)	300,000	204,859	204,700	202,584	202,563	202,544	202,518
STATISTICAL RECORD:							
Book Value Per Share	14.46	20.26	19.86	18.84	18.05	17.01	15.98
Op. Inc/Net Pl %	0.1	0.1	0.1	0.1	0.1	0.1	0.1
Accum. Dep/Gr. Pl %	0.3	0.3	0.4	0.4	0.4	0.4	0.4
Return on Equity %	12.2	10.9	12.8	12.5	14.0	11.6	13.7
Average Yield %	4.6	5.1	5.4	5.5	6.1	6.3	6.0
P/E Ratio	16.0-12.6	17.0-14.2	13.5-10.3	13.5-10.6	11.0-8.3	12.6-10.8	11.8-9.0
Price Range	44⅞-35⅝	37½-31⅜	35-26¾	32⅜-25½	28¼-21⅜	24½-21⅛	25⅞-19¾

Statistics are as originally reported.

OFFICERS:
W.H. Grigg, Chmn., Pres. & C.E.O.
W.L. Foust, Pres.-Duke Merchandising
R.J. Osborne, V.P. & C.F.O.

INCORPORATED: NC, Jun., 1964

PRINCIPAL OFFICE: 422 South Church St., Charlotte, NC 28242-0001

TELEPHONE NUMBER: (704) 594-0887
FAX: (704) 373-8038
NO. OF EMPLOYEES: 18,274
ANNUAL MEETING: In April
SHAREHOLDERS: 125,881 (common)
INSTITUTIONAL HOLDINGS:
No. of Institutions: 431
Shares Held: 102,540,475

REGISTRAR(S): First Union National Bank of N.C., Charlotte, NC

TRANSFER AGENT(S): At Company's Office

DUN & BRADSTREET CORP.

YIELD 4.6%
P/E RATIO 23.4

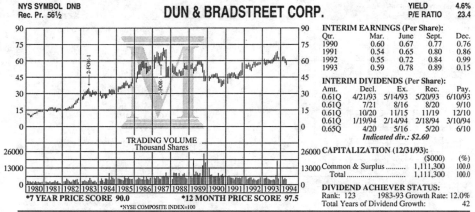

TRADING VOLUME
Thousand Shares

| 1980|1981|1982|1983|1984|1985|1986|1987|1988|1989|1990|1991|1992|1993|1994 |

7 YEAR PRICE SCORE 90.0 *NYSE COMPOSITE INDEX=100 **12 MONTH PRICE SCORE 97.5**

INTERIM EARNINGS (Per Share):

Qtr.	Mar.	June	Sept.	Dec.
1990	0.60	0.67	0.77	0.76
1991	0.54	0.65	0.80	0.86
1992	0.55	0.72	0.84	0.99
1993	0.59	0.78	0.89	0.15

INTERIM DIVIDENDS (Per Share):

Amt.	Decl.	Ex.	Rec.	Pay.
0.61Q	4/21/93	5/14/93	5/20/93	6/10/93
0.61Q	7/21	8/16	8/20	9/10
0.61Q	10/20	11/15	11/19	12/10
0.61Q	1/19/94	2/14/94	2/18/94	3/10/94
0.65Q	4/20	5/16	5/20	6/10
		Indicated div.: $2.60		

CAPITALIZATION (12/31/93):

	($000)	(%)
Common & Surplus	1,111,300	100.0
Total	1,111,300	100.0

DIVIDEND ACHIEVER STATUS:
Rank: 123   1983-93 Growth Rate: 12.0%
Total Years of Dividend Growth: 42

RECENT DEVELOPMENTS: For the quarter ended 12/31/93 net income totaled $192.9 million, a 9.3% gain from the similar quarter of 1992. Results excluded $166.7 million in restructuring charges. A significant amount of the charges were for the consolidation of data centers and back-office accounting functions and reducing worldwide real estate costs.

PROSPECTS: Note: Moody's Investors Service is a wholly-owned subsidiary of The Dun & Bradstreet Corporation. Consequently, no evaluations or projections are made.

BUSINESS

THE DUN & BRADSTREET CORPORATION serves its customers through five business segments: Marketing Information Services, with 1993 revenue (operating income) contribution of 40% (31%), served by IMS International, Nielsen Marketing Research, and Nielsen Media Research. Risk Management and Business Marketing Information Services, 33% (42%), served by D&B Information Services, Moody's Investors Service, and Interactive Data. Software Services, 10% (5%), served by D&B Software, Sales Technologies, and Erisco. Directory Information Services, 10% (19%), served by Reuben H. Donnelley. Other Business Services, 7% (3%), served by D&B Plan Services, NCH Promotional Services, Dataquest and Gartner Group.

BUSINESS LINE ANALYSIS

(12/31/93)	Rev(%)	Inc(%)
Marketing Info Services	39.6	33.8
Risk Mgmt & Bus Mktg Info..............	33.2	42.6
Software Services......	10.1	(3.4)
Directory Info Services	9.6	23.6
Other Business Services	7.5	3.4
Total	100.0	100.0

ANNUAL EARNINGS AND DIVIDENDS PER SHARE

	1993	1992	1991	1990	1989	1988	1987
Earnings Per Share	2.42	3.10	2.85	2.80	3.14	2.67	2.58
Dividends Per Share	2.40	2.25	2.15	2.09	1.935	1.68	① 1.445
Dividend Payout %	99.2	72.6	75.4	74.6	61.6	62.9	56.0

① 2-for-1 stk. split, 6/87.

ANNUAL FINANCIAL DATA

RECORD OF EARNINGS (IN MILLIONS):

	1993	1992	1991	1990	1989	1988	1987
Operating Revenue	4,710.4	4,750.7	4,642.8	4,817.7	4,321.8	4,267.4	3,359.2
Costs and Expenses	3,784.2	3,585.9	3,554.3	3,697.8	3,174.1	3,244.6	① 2,564.3
Depreciation & Amort	373.7	378.9	350.9	349.0	249.9	219.2	...
Operating Income	552.5	785.9	737.6	770.9	897.8	803.5	637.7
Inc Bef Prov for Income Taxes	588.0	795.2	730.6	751.8	914.7	790.7	660.5
Provision for Inc Taxes	159.3	241.7	222.1	243.6	328.4	291.7	267.5
Net Income	38.1	553.5	508.5	508.2	586.4	499.0	393.0
Aver. Shs. Outstg. (000)	177,181	178,346	178,556	181,566	186,884	187,093	152,051
① Incl. Dep.							

BALANCE SHEET (IN MILLIONS):

	1993	1992	1991	1990	1989	1988	1987
Cash and Cash Equivalents	668.6	539.5	310.5	337.7	759.7	1,069.5	313.4
Receivables, Net	1,275.3	1,164.2	1,228.7	1,209.3	1,007.9	1,278.7	892.9
Inventories	18.9	18.8	18.7	36.9	56.2	56.6	56.1
Gross Property	1,885.8	1,837.7	1,855.6	1,863.2	1,743.6	1,542.3	1,201.7
Accumulated Depreciation	1,024.7	972.9	901.9	828.2	762.8	683.6	518.4
Net Stockholders' Equity	1,111.3	2,156.0	2,161.1	2,080.1	2,184.7	2,093.2	1,663.8
Total Assets	5,170.4	4,914.9	4,777.4	4,754.4	5,184.2	5,023.8	3,316.8
Total Current Assets	2,122.4	1,930.4	1,767.4	1,785.5	2,012.6	2,716.7	1,517.6
Total Current Liabilities	2,044.1	1,644.6	1,527.1	1,676.1	1,720.5	1,919.4	835.7
Net Working Capital	78.3	285.8	240.3	109.4	292.0	797.3	681.9
Year End Shs Outstg (000)	170,282	178,235	178,450	178,622	185,164	187,188	152,007

STATISTICAL RECORD:

	1993	1992	1991	1990	1989	1988	1987
Operating Profit Margin %	11.7	16.5	15.9	16.0	20.8	18.8	19.0
Book Value Per Share	...	4.76	4.32	3.77	4.32	5.78	6.69
Return on Equity %	38.6	25.7	23.5	24.4	26.8	23.8	23.6
Return on Assets %	8.3	11.3	10.6	10.7	11.3	9.9	11.8
Average Yield %	3.9	4.1	4.4	4.9	3.8	3.3	2.5
P/E Ratio	28.3-23.0	19.1-16.3	20.4-13.7	17.4-12.9	19.2-13.1	21.5-17.2	27.8-17.2
Price Range	68½-55¾	59⅛-50⅝	58-39⅛	48⅝-36⅛	60¼-41¼	57½-45⅞	71¾-44½

Statistics are as originally reported.

OFFICERS:
C.W. Moritz, Chairman
R.E. Weissman, Pres. & C.E.O.
E.A. Bescherer, Jr., Exec. V.P.-Fin. & C.F.O.

INCORPORATED: DE, Feb., 1973

PRINCIPAL OFFICE: 200 Nyala Farms, Westport, CT 06880

TELEPHONE NUMBER: (203) 222-4200

NO. OF EMPLOYEES: 50,400 (approx.)

ANNUAL MEETING: In April

SHAREHOLDERS: 15,512

INSTITUTIONAL HOLDINGS:
No. of Institutions: 703
Shares Held: 135,081,674

REGISTRAR(S): First Chicago Trust Co. of New York, New York, NY 10008

TRANSFER AGENT(S): First Chicago Trust Co. of New York, New York, NY 10008

EATON VANCE CORP.

YIELD 2.2%
P/E RATIO 8.7

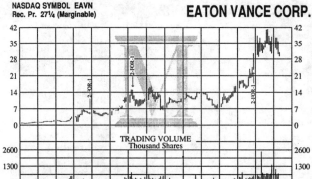

*7 YEAR PRICE SCORE 161.2   *12 MONTH PRICE SCORE 92.7

*NYSE COMPOSITE INDEX=100

TRADING VOLUME
Thousand Shares

INTERIM EARNINGS (Per Share):

Qtr.	Jan.	Apr.	July	Oct.
1990-91	0.31	0.44	0.53	0.47
1991-92	0.64	0.52	0.78	0.59
1992-93	0.62	0.86	1.19	0.41
1993-94	0.67	...	...	...

INTERIM DIVIDENDS (Per Share):

Amt.	Decl.	Ex.	Rec.	Pay.
0.12Q	4/15/93	4/26/93	4/30/93	5/10/93
0.12Q	7/16	7/26	7/30	8/9
0.14Q	10/15	10/25	10/29	11/8
0.14Q	1/7/94	1/25/94	1/31/94	2/14/94
0.15Q	4/15	4/25	4/29	5/9

Indicated div.: $0.60

CAPITALIZATION (10/31/93):

	($000)	(%)
Long-Term Debt	73,228	24.6
Deferred Income Tax	77,128	25.9
Minority Interest	2,340	0.8
Common & Surplus	145,300	48.7
Total	297,996	100.0

DIVIDEND ACHIEVER STATUS:
Rank: 23   1983-93 Growth Rate: 18.5%
Total Years of Dividend Growth: 12

RECENT DEVELOPMENTS: For the three months ended 1/31/94, income before accounting change was $6.4 million, or $0.67 per share, compared with $4.9 million, or $0.62 per share, last year. Assets under management on 1/31/94 totaled $16.3 billion, up 37% from a year ago. Investment management sales of $1.4 billion exceeded sales of $800 million for the same period a year ago by 68%. Fund shareholders redeemed $454 million, 34% more than the $338 million redeemed the year before. As a result of the increased assets under management, investment management revenues rose to $42 million, 29% higher than the comparable year-ago quarter, including an increase in distribution income to $20.9 million from $15.9 million. The Company's gold mining activities posted a loss of $0.04 per share as a result of reductions in the market values of the securities held in two partnerships.

BUSINESS

EATON VANCE CORP. has five main lines of business: (1) management of investment companies, distribution of investment company shares, and investment counseling for individuals and institutions; (2) custodial, trust and banking services, and mutual fund custody, accounting and pricing services through a 77.3% interest in Investors Bank & Trust Company, a state-chartered and FDIC insured bank; (3) real estate investment and consulting through a wholly-owned subsidiary, Northeast Properties, Inc.; (4) the development of precious metal properties through wholly-owned Fulcrum Management, Inc. and MinVen, Inc., and (5) oil and gas activities through wholly-owned Energex Corporation and Marblehead Energy Corporation.

BUSINESS LINE ANALYSIS

(10/31/93)	Rev(%)	Inc(%)
Investment		
Management	76.2	91.5
Banking	19.6	7.5
Real Estate	2.7	2.3
Mining, Oil & Gas	1.5	(1.3)
Total	100.0	100.0

ANNUAL EARNINGS AND DIVIDENDS PER SHARE

	10/31/93	10/31/92	10/31/91	10/31/90	10/31/89	10/31/88	10/31/87
Earnings Per Share	3.09	2.49	1.75	1.03	0.99	1.37	1.35
Dividends Per Share	0.49	☐ 0.36	0.29	0.235	0.205	0.185	0.15
Dividend Payout %	15.9	14.5	16.6	22.9	20.8	13.5	11.1

☐ 2-for-1 stk split,12/8/92

ANNUAL FINANCIAL DATA

RECORD OF EARNINGS (IN THOUSANDS):

	10/31/93	10/31/92	10/31/91	10/31/90	10/31/89	10/31/88	10/31/87
Total Income	189,145	152,979	119,564	94,126	64,395	46,104	50,559
Costs and Expenses	☐ 100,813	89,196	☐ 74,327	☐ 52,568	☐ 38,217	☐ 21,562	☐ 22,712
Depreciation & Amort	...	3,804	...	...	...	...	...
Operating Income	47,440	35,818	22,721	23,143	16,595	17,641	20,359
Income Bef Income Taxes	47,011	33,133	21,079	16,380	13,531	17,037	20,279
Income Taxes	19,670	13,826	8,361	8,706	6,207	6,633	9,582
Eq In Inc Of Unconsol Sub	...	...	...	...	...	337	853
Net Income	27,341	19,307	12,718	7,674	7,324	10,741	11,550
Aver. Shs. Outstg	8,848	7,752	7,290	7,500	7,440	7,831	8,552

☐ Incl. Dep.

BALANCE SHEET (IN THOUSANDS):

	10/31/93	10/31/92	10/31/91	10/31/90	10/31/89	10/31/88	10/31/87
Cash and Cash Equivalents	108,861	99,933	99,957	82,056	90,769	10,890	6,109
Receivables, Net	5,930	10,523	6,790	4,094	16,512	1,917	3,857
Gross Property	6,339	5,007	3,821	3,366	4,392	3,025	2,731
Long-Term Debt	73,228	78,358	63,961	50,633	62,907	14,169	7,500
Net Stockholders' Equity	145,300	77,479	59,604	47,932	43,884	37,356	41,804
Total Assets	425,547	330,293	277,795	223,987	241,773	77,395	80,903
Total Current Assets	116,181	111,800	108,030	86,977	107,855	13,222	10,443
Total Current Liabilities	123,927	108,609	104,785	85,500	100,225	7,443	10,249
Net Working Capital	d7,746	3,191	3,245	1,477	7,630	5,779	194
Year End Shares Outstg	9,134	7,495	7,389	7,291	7,499	7,380	8,440

STATISTICAL RECORD:

	10/31/93	10/31/92	10/31/91	10/31/90	10/31/89	10/31/88	10/31/87
Return on Equity %	18.8	24.9	21.3	16.0	16.7	28.8	27.6
Return on Assets %	6.4	5.9	4.6	3.4	3.0	13.9	14.3
Average Yield %	1.4	1.6	2.4	2.2	1.6	1.9	1.3
P/E Ratio	13.3-9.4	12.2-6.2	9.5-4.5	13.7-7.2	14.3-11.1	8.6-5.5	12.1-4.8
Price Range	41¼-29	30½-15½	16½-7¾	14-7⅜	14⅛-11	11¾-7½	16⅜-6½

Statistics are as originally reported.

OFFICERS:
L.T. Clay, Chairman
H.D. Brigham, Jr., V.P. & Chmn.
M.D. Gardner, President
C.H. Jones, V.P. & Treas.

INCORPORATED: MD, May, 1959

PRINCIPAL OFFICE: 24 Federal Street, Boston, MA 02110

TELEPHONE NUMBER: (617) 482-8260

NO. OF EMPLOYEES: 356

ANNUAL MEETING: In January

SHAREHOLDERS: 1,116 (approx.)

INSTITUTIONAL HOLDINGS:
No. of Institutions: 69
Shares Held: 3,257,572

REGISTRAR(S): Bank of Boston, Boston, MA 02102

TRANSFER AGENT(S): Bank of Boston, Boston, MA 02102

EG&G, INC.

YIELD 3.9%
P/E RATIO 10.3

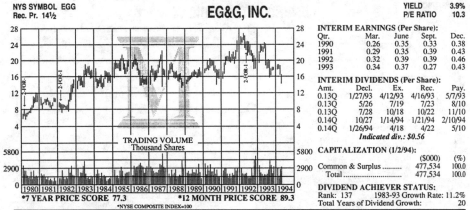

TRADING VOLUME
Thousand Shares

| 1980|1981|1982|1983|1984|1985|1986|1987|1988|1989|1990|1991|1992|1993|1994 |

*7 YEAR PRICE SCORE 77.3   *12 MONTH PRICE SCORE 89.3

*NYSE COMPOSITE INDEX=100

INTERIM EARNINGS (Per Share):

Qtr.	Mar.	June	Sept.	Dec.
1990	0.26	0.35	0.33	0.38
1991	0.29	0.35	0.39	0.43
1992	0.32	0.39	0.39	0.46
1993	0.34	0.37	0.27	0.43

INTERIM DIVIDENDS (Per Share):

Amt.	Decl.	Ex.	Rec.	Pay.
0.13Q	1/27/93	4/12/93	4/16/93	5/7/93
0.13Q	5/26	7/19	7/23	8/10
0.13Q	7/28	10/18	10/22	11/10
0.14Q	10/27	1/14/94	1/21/94	2/10/94
0.14Q	1/26/94	4/18	4/22	5/10

Indicated div.: $0.56

CAPITALIZATION (1/2/94):

	($000)	(%)
Common & Surplus	477,534	100.0
Total	477,534	100.0

DIVIDEND ACHIEVER STATUS:

Rank: 137   1983-93 Growth Rate: 11.2%
Total Years of Dividend Growth: 20

RECENT DEVELOPMENTS: For the quarter ended 1/2/94, net income before accounting changes dropped 6% to $24.2 million compared with $25.9 million for the same period a year ago. Revenues slid 7% to $640.7 million. The decrease in earnings was primarily attributed to depressed results for the Department of Energy Support segment, while shrinking revenues for the Aerospace segment continued to hamper profits. However, income rose for the Components, Defense, and Technical services segments.

PROSPECTS: Lower demand for defense-related products and services by the Department of Energy are negating positive revenue and earnings growth for the other units, and the unrecoverability of these earnings due to government budget cuts will continue to constrain results. In addition, weak economic conditions in Europe are stifling the otherwise strong performances of the Instruments and Components businesses. Any chance for a near-term earnings recovery is slim.

BUSINESS

EG&G INCORPORATED provides advanced scientific and technical products and services worldwide. The Instruments segment develops equipment for airport and industrial security and scientific instruments. The Components segment provides mechnical, optical, and electronic devices. Technical services provide vehicle and lubricant testing and support services. Components and subsystems are produced for aviation and aerospace industries. The Defense segment supports the national defense with technical products and with research, management, and field services. The Department of Energy Support segment provides site management, engineering services, precision instrument and components production.

BUSINESS LINE ANALYSIS

(01/02/94)	Rev(%)	Inc(%)
Technical Services.....	23.6	44.1
DOE Support	51.1	25.9
Instruments................	8.8	6.8
Mechanical		
Components...........	9.0	15.9
Optoelectronics..........	7.5	7.3
Total	100.0	100.0

ANNUAL EARNINGS AND DIVIDENDS PER SHARE

	1/2/94	1/3/93	12/29/91	12/31/90	12/31/89	12/31/88	12/31/87
Earnings Per Share	1.41	1.56	1.45	1.30	1.20	1.15	1.00
Dividends Per Share	0.52	0.48	0.42	0.38	0.34	0.30	0.28
Dividend Payout %	36.9	...	28.9	29.2	28.3	26.1	28.0

ANNUAL FINANCIAL DATA

RECORD OF EARNINGS (IN MILLIONS):

Total Sales	2,697.9	2,788.8	2,688.5	2,474.3	1,650.2	1,406.3	1,247.5
Costs and Expenses	2,539.3	2,629.4	2,529.6	2,336.6	1,526.2	1,283.6	1,154.0
Depreciation & Amort	37.8	36.3	33.7	30.0	25.5	24.6	21.2
Income From Operations	120.8	123.2	125.2	107.7	98.4	98.0	81.0
Income Bef Income Taxes	121.9	121.1	120.4	107.2	99.8	97.4	81.0
Prov for Fed & Non-U.S. Inc Taxes	42.3	33.3	39.1	33.2	29.9	28.7	25.5
Net Income	59.1	87.8	81.2	74.0	69.9	68.7	55.5
Aver. Shs. Outstg. (000)	56,504	56,385	55,901	56,989	58,262	59,778	55,516

BALANCE SHEET (IN MILLIONS):

Cash and Cash Equivalents	72.2	69.8	63.0	34.2	28.6	41.9	32.0
Accounts Receivable	237.6	261.9	249.7	235.2	237.5	201.8	169.6
Inventories	121.6	114.2	115.7	113.9	117.0	100.9	84.1
Gross Property	327.4	301.9	267.5	230.3	208.5	186.4	148.9
Accumulated Depreciation	221.3	205.8	181.6	159.8	135.4	118.0	96.5
Long-Term Debt	...	...	...	...	8.9	14.8	21.4
Net Stockholders' Equity	477.5	473.6	420.7	369.6	349.0	332.3	271.4
Total Assets	768.8	749.7	697.9	675.2	643.4	539.3	515.5
Total Current Assets	465.0	482.8	455.9	407.6	407.3	364.4	307.8
Total Current Liabilities	237.1	235.3	241.4	257.9	256.2	173.2	198.0
Net Working Capital	227.9	247.5	214.5	149.7	151.2	191.2	109.8
Year End Shs Outstg (000)	56,132	56,813	56,496	56,176	57,994	60,022	55,576

STATISTICAL RECORD:

Operating Profit Margin %	4.5	4.4	4.7	4.4	6.0	7.0	6.5
Book Value Per Share	5.45	5.80	5.21	3.80	3.88	4.81	4.20
Return on Equity %	16.7	18.5	19.3	20.0	20.0	20.7	20.4
Return on Assets %	10.3	11.7	11.6	11.0	10.9	12.7	10.8
Average Yield %	2.6	2.2	2.1	2.2	2.1	1.8	1.6
P/E Ratio	17.4-11.2	17.1-11.5	17.7-11.0	15.8-10.8	15.2-11.7	17.0-11.6	22.6-13.5
Price Range	24½-15¾	26¾-17⅞	25-15½	20½-14	18¼-14¼	19½-13⅜	22⅝-13½

Statistics are as originally reported.

OFFICERS:

J.M. Kucharski, Chmn., Pres. & C.E.O.
M. Gross, V.P., General Counsel & Clerk
P.A. Broadbent, Treasurer

INCORPORATED: MA, Nov., 1947

PRINCIPAL OFFICE: 45 William Street,
Wellesley, MA 02181

TELEPHONE NUMBER: (617) 237-5100
FAX: (617) 431-4255
NO. OF EMPLOYEES: 34,000 (approx.)
ANNUAL MEETING: In April
SHAREHOLDERS: 15,396
INSTITUTIONAL HOLDINGS:
No. of Institutions: 237
Shares Held: 38,976,772 (adj.)

REGISTRAR(S):

TRANSFER AGENT(S): First National Bank
of Boston, Shareholder Services Division,
Boston, MA

EMERSON ELECTRIC CO.

YIELD	2.6%
P/E RATIO	15.9

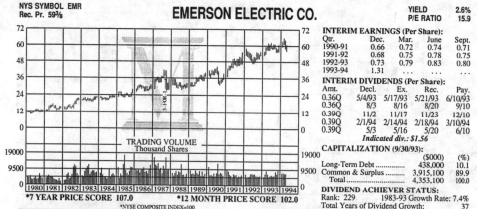

7 YEAR PRICE SCORE 107.0
12 MONTH PRICE SCORE 102.0
*NYSE COMPOSITE INDEX=100

INTERIM EARNINGS (Per Share):

Qtr.	Dec.	Mar.	June	Sept.
1990-91	0.66	0.72	0.74	0.71
1991-92	0.68	0.75	0.78	0.75
1992-93	0.73	0.79	0.83	0.80
1993-94	1.31	...	...	...

INTERIM DIVIDENDS (Per Share):

Amt.	Decl.	Ex.	Rec.	Pay.
0.36Q	5/4/93	5/17/93	5/21/93	6/10/93
0.36Q	8/3	8/16	8/20	9/10
0.39Q	11/2	11/17	11/23	12/10
0.39Q	2/1/94	2/14/94	2/18/94	3/10/94
0.39Q	5/3	5/16	5/20	6/10

Indicated div.: $1.56

CAPITALIZATION (9/30/93):

	($000)	(%)
Long-Term Debt	438,000	10.1
Common & Surplus	3,915,100	89.9
Total	4,353,100	100.0

DIVIDEND ACHIEVER STATUS:
Rank: 229   1983-93 Growth Rate: 7.4%
Total Years of Dividend Growth: 37

RECENT DEVELOPMENTS: For the quarter ended 12/31/93, net income rose 9% to $178.0 million compared with $163.2 million for the same period in 1992. Net sales climbed 1% to $2.01 billion. Gains were led by double-digit sales increases for the appliance components and fractional motor businesses, driven by strong end-market demand. In addition, the professional tools business reported slight gains while the consumer tool joint ventures experienced healthy sales growth.

PROSPECTS: EMR's profitability has benefited greatly from its focus on improving operating margins, and is now concentrating on the expansion of its worldwide sales base through heavy investment in new products. Revenue growth should also benefit from EMR's aggressive expansion through acquisition as well as from its willingness to form joint ventures.

BUSINESS

EMERSON ELECTRIC COMPANY is a global manufacturer of a broad range of electrical-electronic products and systems that are sold through independent distributors and to OEM's. EMR produces instruments related to control systems and processing measurements for continuous processing industry. Commercial and industrial components and systems products include various motor driven systems such as solid, air and gas control devices. Consumer products offer a variety of tools and accessories primarily for the residential markets, including console humidifiers, electric waste disposers, hot water dispensers, automatic dishwashers and ventilating equipment.

BUSINESS LINE ANALYSIS

(09/30/93)	Rev(%)	Inc(%)
Commercial & Industrial	59.8	53.3
Appliance & Const-Related	40.2	45.3
Corporate & Other Items		1.4
Total	100.0	100.0

ANNUAL EARNINGS AND DIVIDENDS PER SHARE

	9/30/93	9/30/92	9/30/91	9/30/90	9/30/89	9/30/88	9/30/87
Earnings Per Share	3.15	2.96	2.83	2.75	2.63	2.31	2.00
Dividends Per Share	1.47	1.395	1.335	1.275	1.155	1.03	①0.98
Dividend Payout %	47.7	47.1	47.2	46.4	43.9	44.6	49.0

① 3-for-1 stk. split, 9/87.

ANNUAL FINANCIAL DATA

RECORD OF EARNINGS (IN MILLIONS):

	9/30/93	9/30/92	9/30/91	9/30/90	9/30/89	9/30/88	9/30/87
Total Revenues	8,173.8	7,706.0	7,427.0	7,573.4	7,071.3	6,651.5	6,170.3
Costs and Expenses	6,555.7	6,219.5	5,981.2	6,160.9	5,767.5	5,427.7	5,033.1
Depreciation & Amort	340.7	295.2	294.4	269.3	230.8	228.3	214.3
Operating Income	1,277.4	1,191.3	1,151.4	1,143.2	1,073.0	995.5	922.9
Earnings Bef Income Tax	1,112.0	1,043.9	1,003.1	989.0	954.0	859.8	810.6
Income Tax	403.9	381.0	371.2	375.8	366.0	331.0	343.4
Net Income	708.1	662.9	631.9	613.2	588.0	528.8	467.2
Aver. Shs. Outstg. (000)	225,083	224,252	223,589	223,150	223,760	229,246	233,860

BALANCE SHEET (IN MILLIONS):

	9/30/93	9/30/92	9/30/91	9/30/90	9/30/89	9/30/88	9/30/87
Cash and Cash Equivalents	101.9	80.2	102.4	98.3	112.7	108.0	130.3
Receivables, Net	1,392.1	1,364.8	1,316.5	1,410.0	1,240.4	1,162.0	1,091.9
Total Inventories	1,298.3	1,278.2	1,348.6	1,391.6	1,286.0	1,334.6	1,257.8
Gross Property	3,586.6	3,252.2	2,993.8	2,793.5	2,335.3	2,168.2	2,081.8
Accumulated Depreciation	1,706.5	1,557.7	1,410.4	1,257.7	1,137.6	1,046.7	955.5
Long-Term Debt	438.0	448.0	450.2	496.2	418.9	481.4	553.0
Net Stockholders' Equity	3,915.1	3,729.8	3,256.9	2,989.9	3,073.4	2,820.1	2,702.5
Total Assets	7,814.5	6,627.0	6,364.4	6,376.4	5,408.0	5,027.0	4,867.8
Total Current Assets	3,074.3	2,977.0	2,988.6	3,138.7	2,850.5	2,763.5	2,655.4
Total Current Liabilities	2,692.6	1,811.9	2,093.8	2,335.9	1,533.2	1,438.0	1,324.8
Net Working Capital	381.7	1,165.1	894.8	802.8	1,317.3	1,325.5	1,330.6
Year End Shs Outstg (000)	224,763	224,308	224,069	223,328	222,842	225,378	231,310

STATISTICAL RECORD:

	9/30/93	9/30/92	9/30/91	9/30/90	9/30/89	9/30/88	9/30/87
Operating Profit Margin %	15.6	15.5	15.5	15.1	15.2	15.0	15.0
Book Value Per Share	9.26	11.68	9.83	8.74	10.24	8.80	8.08
Return on Equity %	18.1	17.8	19.4	20.5	19.1	18.8	17.3
Return on Assets %	9.1	10.0	9.9	9.6	10.9	10.5	9.6
Average Yield %	2.6	2.7	2.9	3.4	3.3	3.3	2.9
P/E Ratio	19.8-16.7	19.6-15.8	19.4-13.0	16.1-11.2	15.2-11.2	15.6-11.8	20.9-13.4
Price Range	62⅜-52¾	58-46¾	55-36⅞	44⅜-30¾	39⅞-29½	36-27¼	41⅞-26¾

Statistics are as originally reported.

OFFICERS:
C.F. Knight, Chmn. & C.E.O.
A.E. Suter, Senior Vice-Chmn. & C.O.O.
J.J. Adorjan, President

INCORPORATED: MO, Sep., 1890

PRINCIPAL OFFICE: 8000 West Florissant Ave. P.O. Box 4100, Saint Louis, MO 63136

TELEPHONE NUMBER: (314) 553-2000
FAX: (314) 553-3527
NO. OF EMPLOYEES: 71,600 (avg.)
ANNUAL MEETING: In February
SHAREHOLDERS: 32,700 (approx.)
INSTITUTIONAL HOLDINGS:
No. of Institutions: 743
Shares Held: 150,276,142

REGISTRAR(S): Boatmen's Trust Co., St.Louis, MO 63101

TRANSFER AGENT(S): Boatmen's Trust Co., St. Louis, MO 63101

EMPIRE DISTRICT ELECTRIC COMPANY

YIELD 7.4%
P/E RATIO 15.0

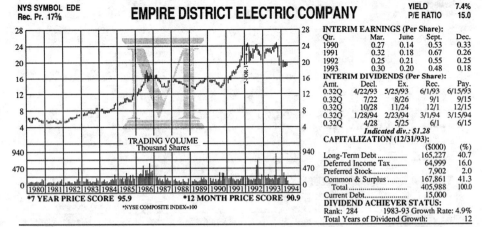

*7 YEAR PRICE SCORE 95.9   *12 MONTH PRICE SCORE 90.9

*NYSE COMPOSITE INDEX=100

INTERIM EARNINGS (Per Share):

Qtr.	Mar.	June	Sept.	Dec.
1990	0.27	0.14	0.53	0.33
1991	0.32	0.18	0.67	0.26
1992	0.25	0.21	0.55	0.25
1993	0.30	0.20	0.48	0.18

INTERIM DIVIDENDS (Per Share):

Amt.	Decl.	Ex.	Rec.	Pay.
0.32Q	4/22/93	5/25/93	6/1/93	6/15/93
0.32Q	7/22	8/26	9/1	9/15
0.32Q	10/28	11/24	12/1	12/15
0.32Q	1/28/94	2/23/94	3/1/94	3/15/94
0.32Q	4/28	5/25	6/1	6/15

Indicated div.: $1.28

CAPITALIZATION (12/31/93):

	($000)	(%)
Long-Term Debt	165,227	40.7
Deferred Income Tax	64,999	16.0
Preferred Stock	7,902	2.0
Common & Surplus	167,861	41.3
Total	405,988	100.0

Current Debt....................... 15,000

DIVIDEND ACHIEVER STATUS:

Rank: 284   1983-93 Growth Rate: 4.9%
Total Years of Dividend Growth: 12

RECENT DEVELOPMENTS: For the year ended 12/31/93, operating revenues increased 12.6% to $168.4 million from $150.3 million in 1992. Net income slipped 5.8% to $15.9 million from $16.9 million in 1992. Earnings per share were $1.16 for 1993 compared with $1.26 for 1992. The earnings for the year were negatively affected by additional purchased power costs associated with previously reported outages of some of the Company's generating stations. The Company continues to expense rather than defer these additional purchased power costs. Earnings for the fourth quarter of 1993 were $0.18 per share on revenues of $40.4 million and net income of $2.6 million. Earnings for the same period in 1992 were $0.25 per share on revenues of $37.8 million and net income of $3.4 million.

BUSINESS

EMPIRE DISTRICT ELECTRIC COMPANY provides electric service to a 10,000 square-mile area in southwest Missouri, southeast Kansas, northeast Oklahoma and northwest Arkansas. The Company also provides water service in three incorporated communities in Missouri.

ELECTRIC REVENUES

(12/31/93)	($000)	(%)
Residential	68,477	40.9
Commercial	50,264	30.0
Industrial	28,880	17.2
Public Authorities	3,419	2.0
Wholesale On-		
System	8,038	4.8
Miscellaneous	2,302	1.4
Wholesale Off-		
System	6,244	3.7
Total	167,624	100.0

ANNUAL EARNINGS AND DIVIDENDS PER SHARE

	1993	1992	1991	1990	1989	1988	1987
Earnings Per Share	1.16	1.26	1.43	1.28	1.47	1.53	1.48
Dividends Per Share	1.28	① 1.257	1.22	② 1.172	1.122	1.072	1.015
Dividend Payout %	N.M.	99.8	85.3	92.0	76.4	70.2	68.8

① 2-for-1 stk split, 1/30/92 ② Bef acctg chge

ANNUAL FINANCIAL DATA

RECORD OF EARNINGS (IN THOUSANDS):

Total Operating Revenues	168,439	150,302	150,442	141,612	133,361	153,805	150,148
Depreciation	18,248	17,346	16,495	14,224	13,097	12,474	11,672
Maintenance & Repairs	10,632	10,301	9,378	9,347	8,914	9,583	10,329
Prov for Fed Inc Taxes	7,666	8,380	9,278	7,436	7,360	8,670	10,647
Operating Income	29,291	30,090	31,761	27,071	26,678	25,553	23,487
Total Interest Charges	13,189	12,961	12,789	11,335	10,048	8,425	7,433
Net Income	15,936	16,905	18,768	① 15,473	17,347	17,656	16,835
Aver. Shs. Outstg.	13,416	13,120	12,812	11,740	11,420	11,155	10,918

① Before acctg. change cr$3,335,000.

BALANCE SHEET (IN THOUSANDS):

Gross Plant	587,079	546,713	519,282	499,835	458,290	421,029	390,818
Accumulated Depreciation	193,522	179,268	165,894	153,237	143,508	133,162	124,956
Total Prop, Plant & Equip	393,557	367,445	353,388	346,598	314,782	287,867	265,862
Long-term Debt	165,227	143,619	142,214	142,310	127,483	113,481	88,479
Net Stockholders' Equity	175,763	171,195	165,012	157,949	138,942	131,956	124,507
Total Assets	463,617	406,731	387,363	378,562	345,047	319,831	290,112
Year End Shares Outstg	13,571	13,285	12,986	12,668	11,577	11,290	11,048

STATISTICAL RECORD:

Book Value Per Share	12.37	12.29	12.08	11.75	11.17	10.75	10.22
Op. Inc/Net Pl %	7.4	8.2	9.0	7.8	8.5	8.9	8.8
Dep/Gr. Pl %	3.0	3.0	3.0	2.8	2.9	2.8	2.8
Accum. Dep/Gr. Pl %	33.0	32.8	31.9	30.7	31.3	31.6	32.0
Return on Equity %	9.1	9.9	11.4	9.9	12.6	13.7	13.9
Average Yield %	5.8	5.6	6.3	8.0	7.6	7.2	6.6
P/E Ratio	21.4-16.5	19.6-16.0	16.9-10.3	12.3-10.6	11.0-9.0	10.5-9.0	11.6-9.4
Price Range	24⅞-19⅛	24¾-20⅛	24⅛-14¾	15¾-13⅝	16⅛-13¼	16-13¾	17-13¾

Statistics are as originally reported.

OFFICERS:
R.L. Lamb, President
V.E. Brill, V.P.-Fin.
G.C. Hunter, Treas. & Sec.

PRINCIPAL OFFICE: 602 Joplin Street,
Joplin, MO 64802

TELEPHONE NUMBER: (417) 623-4700
FAX: (417) 625-5155
NO. OF EMPLOYEES: 639
ANNUAL MEETING: 4th Thursday in April
SHAREHOLDERS: 9,700 com.; 1,474 pfd.
INSTITUTIONAL HOLDINGS:
No. of Institutions: 54
Shares Held: 1,776,057

REGISTRAR(S):

TRANSFER AGENT(S):

ENGELHARD CORP.

YIELD 1.7%
P/E RATIO N.M

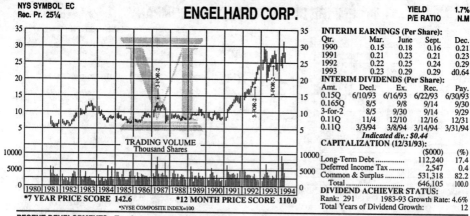

*7 YEAR PRICE SCORE 142.6   *12 MONTH PRICE SCORE 110.0
*NYSE COMPOSITE INDEX=100

INTERIM EARNINGS (Per Share):

Qtr.	Mar.	June	Sept.	Dec.
1990	0.15	0.18	0.16	0.21
1991	0.21	0.23	0.21	0.23
1992	0.22	0.25	0.24	0.29
1993	0.23	0.29	0.29	d0.64

INTERIM DIVIDENDS (Per Share):

Amt.	Decl.	Ex.	Rec.	Pay.
0.15Q	6/10/93	6/16/93	6/22/93	6/30/93
0.165Q	8/5	9/8	9/14	9/30
3-for-2	8/5	9/30	9/14	9/29
0.11Q	11/4	12/10	12/16	12/31
0.11Q	3/3/94	3/8/94	3/14/94	3/31/94

Indicated div.: $0.44

CAPITALIZATION (12/31/93):

	($000)	(%)
Long-Term Debt	112,240	17.4
Deferred Income Tax	2,547	0.4
Common & Surplus	531,318	82.2
Total	646,105	100.0

DIVIDEND ACHIEVER STATUS:
Rank: 291   1983-93 Growth Rate: 4.6%
Total Years of Dividend Growth: 12

RECENT DEVELOPMENTS: For the quarter ended 12/31/93, a net loss of $61.6 million was posted compared with net income of $28.1 million in the comparable period of 1992. Results included a nonrecurring charge of $91.8 million. Sales declined to $539.4 million from $546.1 million. For the year ended 12/31/93, income before accounting adjustments totaled $16.7 million versus $100.1 million for 1992. Sales were $2.15 billion, down from $2.40 billion for the prior year. Results included nonrecurring charges of $85.5 million.

PROSPECTS: Emerging markets in Eastern and Western Europe, Pacific Rim and Asia will present opportunities for EC. Global concern for the environment will strengthen the Environmental Catalyst business. In order to capitalize on the opportunities in the industry the Company will have to focus efforts on the development of new technology. The Pigment and Additives business is expected to improve pricing. As the economy returns to full strength excess capacity in the paper, paint, and plastics industry should be reduced.

BUSINESS

ENGELHARD CORPORATION is a provider of specialty chemical products, engineered materials and precious metals management services. The catalysts and chemicals segment manufactures catalysts, chemical products and process technologies for the petroleum refining, chemical, pharmaceutical, and automotive industries. The pigments and additives segment manufactures coatings and extender pigments for the paper industry and pigments and additives for the paint, coatings, and plastics industries. The engineered materials and precious metals management segment manufactures fabricated metallurgical products and engineered materials and is engaged in precious metals refining, dealing, and management.

ANNUAL EARNINGS AND DIVIDENDS PER SHARE

	1993	1992	1991	1990	1989	1988	1987
Earnings Per Share	0.17	☒1.00	0.87	0.70	d0.77	0.63	0.71
Dividends Per Share	☒0.42	0.251	0.329	0.302	0.249	0.24	0.231
Dividend Payout %	N.M.	37.7	37.8	43.3	...	38.0	32.5

☒ 3-for-2 stk split,09/30/92   ☒ Before acctg. chg.

ANNUAL FINANCIAL DATA

RECORD OF EARNINGS (IN MILLIONS):

	1993	1992	1991	1990	1989	1988	1987
Total Revenues	2,150.9	2,399.7	2,436.4	2,942.2	2,403.0	2,350.7	2,479.2
Costs and Expenses	2,087.3	2,183.3	2,224.3	2,749.9	2,474.0	2,196.9	2,348.5
Deprec, Depl & Amort	68.2	73.8	77.8	74.4	68.8	56.7	44.4
Earnings From Operations	d4.6	142.6	134.2	117.8	d139.9	97.1	86.4
Earn Bef Income Taxes	d4.7	133.9	117.6	93.7	d126.5	87.2	99.7
Income Tax Exp (benefit)	cr21.4	33.7	29.6	23.4	cr49.0	23.4	29.9
Net Income	☒16.7	☒100.1	87.9	70.3	d77.5	63.7	69.8
Aver. Shs. Outstg. (000)	96,792	100,287	101,129	100,580	101,100	100,905	98,098

☒ Before acctg. change dr$16,000,000.   ☒ Before acctg. change dr$89,509,000.

BALANCE SHEET (IN MILLIONS):

	1993	1992	1991	1990	1989	1988	1987
Cash and Cash Equivalents	25.6	31.3	36.2	46.9	41.0	49.1	120.6
Receivables	230.6	257.3	302.5	315.9	327.1	325.4	368.4
Inventories	216.3	241.4	230.2	249.8	278.7	275.7	205.1
Gross Property	1,171.0	1,115.6	1,079.8	1,068.2	1,020.5	1,012.5	799.2
Accumulated Depreciation	676.6	624.5	569.8	528.1	468.8	405.5	367.0
Long-Term Debt	112.2	113.9	114.5	119.4	220.1	221.3	119.2
Net Stockholders' Equity	531.3	647.2	756.6	709.8	636.9	760.4	730.1
Total Assets	1,279.1	1,279.5	1,256.1	1,320.0	1,339.6	1,413.2	1,216.3
Total Current Assets	516.6	568.7	575.6	618.1	653.0	657.0	700.1
Total Current Liabilities	462.7	366.2	378.2	482.3	475.0	354.6	297.5
Net Working Capital	53.8	202.5	197.5	135.8	178.0	302.4	402.6
Year End Shs Outstg (000)	95,946	98,528	100,879	100,221	100,308	100,616	101,700

STATISTICAL RECORD:

	1993	1992	1991	1990	1989	1988	1987
Operating Profit Margin %	...	5.9	5.5	4.0	...	4.1	3.5
Book Value Per Share	5.54	6.57	7.50	7.08	6.35	7.56	7.18
Return on Equity %	3.1	15.5	11.6	9.9	...	8.4	9.6
Return on Assets %	1.3	7.8	7.0	5.3	...	4.5	5.7
Average Yield %	1.7	1.3	2.9	3.4	2.6	2.8	2.4
P/E Ratio	N.M	24.4-13.9	17.5-8.6	15.0-10.7	...	15.3-11.5	18.3-9.2
Price Range	29⅞-19⅜	24⅜-13⅞	15¼-7½	10½-7½	11½-7⅝	9⅝-7¼	13-6½

Statistics are as originally reported.

OFFICERS:
O.R. Smith, Pres. & C.E.O.
R.L. Guyett, Sr. V.P. & C.F.O.
A.A. Dornbusch, II, V.P. & Gen. Counsel
M.A. Sperduto, Treas.

PRINCIPAL OFFICE: 101 Wood Ave., Iselin, NJ 08830

TELEPHONE NUMBER: (908) 205-5000

NO. OF EMPLOYEES: 6,030

ANNUAL MEETING: In May

SHAREHOLDERS: 9,280

INSTITUTIONAL HOLDINGS:
No. of Institutions: 172
Shares Held: 22,984,665

REGISTRAR(S):

TRANSFER AGENT(S):

ENNIS BUSINESS FORMS, INC.

YIELD 4.1%
P/E RATIO 11.8

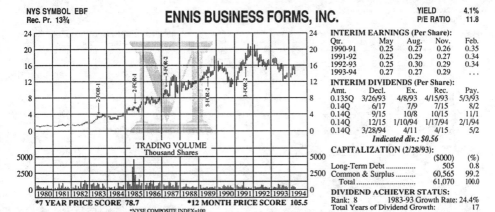

INTERIM EARNINGS (Per Share):

Qtr.	May	Aug.	Nov.	Feb.
1990-91	0.25	0.27	0.26	0.35
1991-92	0.25	0.29	0.27	0.34
1992-93	0.25	0.30	0.29	0.34
1993-94	0.27	0.27	0.29	...

INTERIM DIVIDENDS (Per Share):

Amt.	Decl.	Ex.	Rec.	Pay.
0.135Q	3/26/93	4/8/93	4/15/93	5/3/93
0.14Q	6/17	7/9	7/15	8/2
0.14Q	9/15	10/8	10/15	11/1
0.14Q	12/15	1/10/94	1/17/94	2/1/94
0.14Q	3/28/94	4/11	4/15	5/2

Indicated div.: $0.56

CAPITALIZATION (2/28/93):

	($000)	(%)
Long-Term Debt	505	0.8
Common & Surplus	60,565	99.2
Total	61,070	100.0

DIVIDEND ACHIEVER STATUS:
Rank: 8   1983-93 Growth Rate: 24.4%
Total Years of Dividend Growth: 17

*7 YEAR PRICE SCORE 78.7   *12 MONTH PRICE SCORE 105.5
*NYSE COMPOSITE INDEX=100

RECENT DEVELOPMENTS: For the quarter ended 11/30/93, net income was essentially flat at $4.9 million. Sales were up 2.4% to $34.6 million compared with $33.8 million a year ago. The increase in sales was attributable to the acquisition of Weaver Badge and Novelties, an award ribbon company in June of 1993. Earnings were pressured by smaller profit margins in the award ribbon business and increased raw material and labor costs in the forms business.

PROSPECTS: The office supply industry is consolidating as larger companies are actively pursuing the acquisition of smaller companies. Admore, Inc. should post strong earnings; however, sales probably will not be sufficient to offset declining business form sales. EBF's cash flow from operations continues to be adequate to sustain operations, meet debt repayment requirements and fund capital additions.

BUSINESS

ENNIS BUSINESS FORMS prints and constructs a broad line of business forms for national distribution. About 85% of the business forms manufactured are custom and semi-custom, constructed a variety of sizes, colors, number of parts and quantities on an individual job basis depending upon the customers' specifications. Connolly Tool & Machine Co., a subsidiary, designs and manufacturers tools, dies and special machinery for customers located primarily in the Southwestern part of the U.S. Ennis also offers presentation folders manufactured by its Admore, Inc. subsidiary. The Company operates thirteen manufacturing locations in twelve states.

QUARTERLY DATA

(2/28/93)($000)	Rev	Inc
1st Quarter	31,233	4,572
2st Quarter	33,180	5,313
3nd Quarter	33,782	4,938
4rd Quarter	31,084	5,869

ANNUAL EARNINGS AND DIVIDENDS PER SHARE

	2/28/93	2/29/92	2/28/91	2/28/90	2/28/89	2/29/88	2/28/87
Earnings Per Share	1.21	① 1.14	1.12	1.05	0.92	0.74	0.55
Dividends Per Share	0.53	0.51	0.47	② 0.41	0.32	③ 0.22	0.127
Dividend Payout %	43.8	43.9	40.5	37.1	31.7	29.2	22.4

① Before disc. oper. & acctg. chg. ② 3-for-2 stk split, 7/03/89 ③ 3-for-2 stk split, 3/87

ANNUAL FINANCIAL DATA

RECORD OF EARNINGS (IN THOUSANDS):

Total Revenues	129,279	131,810	126,164	129,606	128,170	117,511	111,878
Costs and Expenses	92,847	95,696	91,124	94,992	96,339	88,537	87,517
Depreciation & Amort	4,392	4,368	3,694	3,486	3,372	3,249	3,097
Income From Operations	31,789	31,402	30,926	30,588	27,856	25,099	20,570
Earns Fr Cont Opers Bef Inc Taxes	32,276	32,303	32,776	32,669	29,287	25,857	23,085
Income Taxes	11,584	11,536	11,676	11,642	10,448	10,106	10,523
Net Income	① 20,692	② 20,767	21,100	21,027	18,839	15,751	12,562
Aver. Shs. Outstg.	17,558	18,244	18,858	19,910	20,411	21,270	22,562

① Before disc. op. cr$560,000. ② Before disc. op. dr$1,051,000.

BALANCE SHEET (IN THOUSANDS):

Cash and Cash Equivalents	22,597	25,077	25,513	26,389	16,018	19,544	25,347
Receivables, Net	15,653	16,106	15,496	16,688	16,880	15,413	15,087
Invent, At Lower Of Cost Or Mkt	7,901	7,216	8,081	9,810	11,420	12,378	11,981
Gross Property	64,258	65,482	57,624	54,463	52,092	51,831	50,075
Accumulated Depreciation	43,735	41,811	37,379	34,024	31,586	29,735	27,061
Long-Term Debt	505	2,396	3,163	4,172	5,843	6,865	7,876
Net Stockholders' Equity	60,565	66,485	55,830	60,737	52,954	49,586	53,950
Total Assets	75,923	81,244	73,208	79,192	73,826	74,241	79,374
Total Current Assets	48,928	51,035	50,927	55,527	46,797	48,725	53,390
Total Current Liabilities	12,087	9,631	10,203	10,074	10,080	12,619	12,642
Net Working Capital	36,841	41,404	40,724	45,453	36,717	36,106	40,748
Year End Shares Outstg	17,199	18,235	18,300	19,591	19,877	20,591	22,224

STATISTICAL RECORD:

Operating Profit Margin %	24.6	23.8	24.5	23.6	21.7	21.4	18.4
Book Value Per Share	3.28	3.41	3.05	3.10	2.66	2.37	2.38
Return on Equity %	34.2	31.2	37.8	34.6	35.6	31.8	23.3
Return on Assets %	27.3	25.6	28.8	26.6	25.5	21.2	15.8
Average Yield %	2.9	3.2	3.4	2.7	2.9	2.0	1.8
P/E Ratio	17.9-12.6	18.8-9.5	15.3-9.5	17.5-11.3	13.5-10.3	18.6-10.6	15.0-11.4
Price Range	21⅛-14⅞	21⅜-10⅞	17⅛-10⅝	18⅜-11⅞	12⅜-9½	13¾-7⅞	8¼-6¼

Statistics are as originally reported.

OFFICERS:
K.A. McCrady, Chmn. & C.E.O.
C.F. Ray, Pres. & C.O.O.
V. DiTommaso, Treas.

INCORPORATED: TX, Dec., 1909

PRINCIPAL OFFICE: 107 North Sherman Street, Ennis, TX 75119

TELEPHONE NUMBER: (214) 875-6581

FAX: (214) 875-4915

NO. OF EMPLOYEES: 1,290

ANNUAL MEETING: In June

SHAREHOLDERS: 2,336

INSTITUTIONAL HOLDINGS:
No. of Institutions: 99
Shares Held: 9,090,695

REGISTRAR(S): Society National Bank, Cleveland, OH

TRANSFER AGENT(S): Society National Bank, Cleveland, OH

EXXON CORP.

YIELD 4.7%
P/E RATIO 14.6

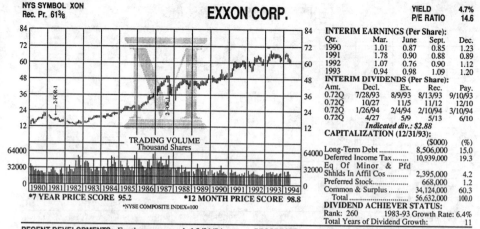

*7 YEAR PRICE SCORE 95.2   *12 MONTH PRICE SCORE 98.8

TRADING VOLUME
Thousand Shares

*NYSE COMPOSITE INDEX=100

INTERIM EARNINGS (Per Share):

Qtr.	Mar.	June	Sept.	Dec.
1990	1.01	0.87	0.85	1.23
1991	1.78	0.90	0.88	0.89
1992	1.07	0.76	0.90	1.12
1993	0.94	0.98	1.09	1.20

INTERIM DIVIDENDS (Per Share):

Amt.	Decl.	Ex.	Rec.	Pay.
0.72Q	7/28/93	8/9/93	8/13/93	9/10/93
0.72Q	10/27	11/5	11/12	12/10
0.72Q	1/26/94	2/4/94	2/10/94	3/10/94
0.72Q	4/27	5/9	5/13	6/10

Indicated div.: $2.88

CAPITALIZATION (12/31/93):

	($000)	(%)
Long-Term Debt	8,506,000	15.0
Deferred Income Tax	10,939,000	19.3
Eq Of Minor & Pfd Shhlds In Affil Cos	2,395,000	4.2
Preferred Stock	668,000	1.2
Common & Surplus	34,124,000	60.3
Total	56,632,000	100.0

DIVIDEND ACHIEVER STATUS:

Rank: 260   1983-93 Growth Rate: 6.4%
Total Years of Dividend Growth: 11

RECENT DEVELOPMENTS: For the quarter ended 3/31/94, net income fell 2% to $1.16 billion compared with $1.19 billion for the comparable period in 1993. Meanwhile, revenues dropped 5% to $27.84 billion. Income from exploration and production activities suffered under low crude oil prices, but was stabilized by higher sales of natural gas. The decrease in earnings was buffered by significant improvements for refining and marketing operations as a result of favorable petroleum product margins and lower operating expenses.

PROSPECTS: Despite plummeting oil prices, upstream operations will remain healthy as a result of increasing operating efficiencies, higher natural gas prices, and a number of new projects. Opportunities for growth are being taken advantage of with major projects being undertaken in Australia and the U.K. In addition, major expansion efforts are being initiated in the Asia-Pacific region. Worldwide efforts to reorganize operations will continue to improve margins as underperforming units are divested.

BUSINESS

EXXON CORPORATION's principal business is energy, involving exploration for and production of crude oil and natural gas, manufacturing of petroleum products, transportation and sale of crude oil, natural gas and petroleum products, and exploration for and mining and sale of coal. Exxon Chemical is a major manufacturer and marketer of petrochemicals. Exxon is also engaged in exploration for and mining of minerals in addition to coal. Exxon conducts extensive research programs in support of these businesses. Exxon owns 70% of Imperial Oil.

BUSINESS LINE ANALYSIS

(12/31/93)	Rev(%)	Inc(%)
United States	20.8	29.1
Other Western Hemisphere	15.8	5.5
Eastern Hemisphere	63.4	65.4
Total	100.0	100.0

ANNUAL EARNINGS AND DIVIDENDS PER SHARE

	1993	1992	1991	1990	1989	1988	1987
Earnings Per Share	4.21	① 3.82	4.45	3.96	② 2.32	3.95	3.43
Dividends Per Share	2.88	② 2.83	2.68	2.47	2.30	2.15	③ 1.90
Dividend Payout %	68.4	74.1	60.2	62.4	99.1	54.4	55.4

① Before acctg. chg. ② Bef acctg chge ③ 2-for-1 stk. split, 9/87.

ANNUAL FINANCIAL DATA

RECORD OF EARNINGS (IN MILLIONS):

	1993	1992	1991	1990	1989	1988	1987
Total Revenue	111,211.0	117,106.0	116,492.0	116,940.0	96,285.0	88,563.0	83,335.0
Costs and Expenses	97,344.0	103,744.0	102,173.0	101,643.0	82,207.0	74,175.0	70,836.0
Depreciation & Depletion	4,884.0	5,044.0	4,824.0	5,545.0	5,002.0	4,790.0	4,239.0
Operating Profit	9,631.0	9,126.0	10,409.0	10,709.0	9,948.0	10,577.0	9,078.0
Income Bef Income Taxes	8,052.0	7,287.0	8,518.0	...	...	...	...
Net Income	5,280.0	①4,810.0	5,600.0	5,010.0	②2,975.0	5,260.0	4,840.0
Aver. Shs. Outstg. (000)	1,242,000	1,242,000	1,244,000	1,248,000	1,412,000	1,333,000	1,412,000

① Before acctg. change dr$40,000,000. ② Before acctg. change cr$535,000,000.

BALANCE SHEET (IN MILLIONS):

	1993	1992	1991	1990	1989	1988	1987
Cash and Cash Equivalents	1,652.0	1,515.0	1,587.0	1,379.0	2,016.0	2,409.0	2,531.0
Notes & Accts Receiv, Net	6,860.0	8,079.0	8,540.0	9,574.0	7,787.0	6,094.0	6,278.0
Inventories	5,472.0	5,807.0	6,081.0	6,386.0	5,622.0	5,151.0	...
Gross Property	111,135.0	110,738.0	112,440.0	107,599.0	99,556.0	89,723.0	86,219.0
Accumulated Depreciation	49,173.0	48,939.0	48,576.0	44,911.0	39,131.0	35,664.0	32,785.0
Long-Term Debt	8,506.0	8,637.0	8,582.0	7,687.0	9,275.0	4,689.0	5,021.0
Net Stockholders' Equity	34,792.0	33,776.0	34,927.0	33,055.0	30,244.0	31,767.0	33,626.0
Total Assets	84,145.0	85,030.0	87,560.0	87,707.0	83,219.0	74,293.0	74,042.0
Total Current Assets	14,859.0	16,424.0	17,012.0	18,336.0	16,576.0	14,846.0	15,391.0
Total Current Liabilities	18,590.0	19,663.0	20,854.0	24,025.0	21,984.0	17,479.0	15,296.0
Net Working Capital	d3,731.0	d3,239.0	d3,842.0	d5,689.0	d5,408.0	d2,633.0	95.0
Year End Shs Outstg (000)	1,242,000	1,242,000	1,242,000	1,245,000	1,250,000	1,289,000	1,379,000

STATISTICAL RECORD:

	1993	1992	1991	1990	1989	1988	1987
Operating Profit Margin %	8.1	7.1	8.2	8.3	9.4	10.8	9.9
Book Value Per Share	27.48	26.57	27.42	25.78	23.39	24.64	24.38
Return on Equity %	15.2	14.2	16.0	15.2	9.8	16.6	14.4
Return on Assets %	6.3	5.7	6.4	5.7	3.6	7.1	6.5
Average Yield %	4.5	4.7	4.8	4.9	5.0	5.4	4.7
P/E Ratio	16.4-13.7	17.1-14.1	13.9-11.2	13.9-11.3	22.3-17.5	12.1-8.1	14.7-9.0
Price Range	69-57¾	65½-53¾	61⅞-49⅝	55⅛-44⅞	51⅝-40½	47¾-32	50⅜-30⅞

Statistics are as originally reported.

OFFICERS:
L.R. Raymond, Chmn. & C.E.O.
C.R. Sitter, Pres.
E.A. Robinson, V.P. & Treas.

INCORPORATED: NJ, Aug., 1882

PRINCIPAL OFFICE: 225 E. John W. Carpenter Freeway, Irving, TX 75062-2298

TELEPHONE NUMBER: (214) 444-1000
NO. OF EMPLOYEES: 91,000
ANNUAL MEETING: In April
SHAREHOLDERS: 620,467
INSTITUTIONAL HOLDINGS:
No. of Institutions: 927
Shares Held: 475,150,613

REGISTRAR(S):

TRANSFER AGENT(S):

NYS SYMBOL FDO
Rec. Pr. 14¾

FAMILY DOLLAR STORES, INC.

YIELD 2.3%
P/E RATIO 12.6

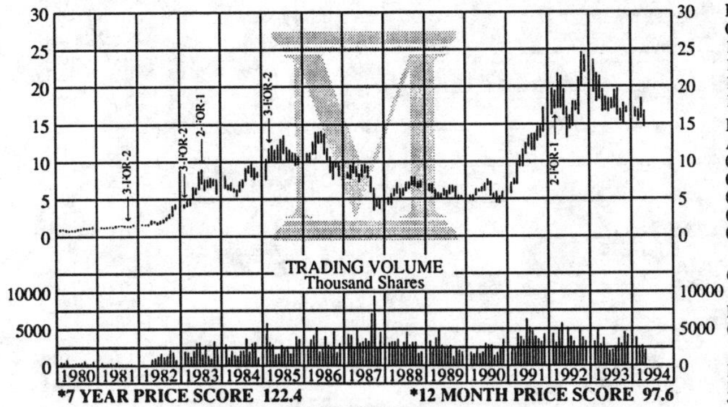

3-FOR-2
3-FOR-2
2-FOR-1
3-FOR-2
2-FOR-1
TRADING VOLUME
Thousand Shares
1980 1981 1982 1983 1984 1985 1986 1987 1988 1989 1990 1991 1992 1993 1994

***7 YEAR PRICE SCORE 122.4** ***12 MONTH PRICE SCORE 97.6**

*NYSE COMPOSITE INDEX=100

INTERIM EARNINGS (Per Share):

Qtr.	Nov.	Feb.	May	Aug.
1990-91	0.14	0.22	0.22	0.15
1991-92	0.21	0.32	0.27	0.20
1992-93	0.25	0.37	0.31	0.22
1993-94	0.27	...	...	...

INTERIM DIVIDENDS (Per Share):

Amt.	Decl.	Ex.	Rec.	Pay.
0.075Q	5/14/93	6/9/93	6/15/93	7/15/93
0.075Q	8/16	9/9	9/15	10/15
0.075Q	11/15	12/9	12/15	1/14/94
0.085Q	1/20/94	3/9/94	3/15/94	4/15
0.085Q	5/13	6/9	6/15	7/15

Indicated div.: $0.34

CAPITALIZATION (8/31/93):

	($000)	(%)
Deferred Income Tax	16,195	4.8
Common & Surplus	323,282	95.2
Total	339,477	100.0

DIVIDEND ACHIEVER STATUS:
Rank: 16 1983-93 Growth Rate: 20.0%
Total Years of Dividend Growth: 17

RECENT DEVELOPMENTS: For the quarter ended 11/30/93, net income was $14.9 million compared with $13.8 million last year. Sales totaled $335.1 million, up 10.0% from last year. Results were before an accounting change of $1.1 million. Results benefited from growth in existing stores and in new stores opened in the Company's store expansion program. Sales in existing stores increased 0.7%. During the quarter, the Company opened 46 new stores and closed five stores.

PROSPECTS: A new price reduction program and increased sales in existing and new stores should boost earnings potential. Profit margins should increase as a result of continued emphasis on increasing sales in higher margin departments and reducing sales in lower margin departments, as well as from a stronger Family Dollar brand label merchandise program.

BUSINESS

FAMILY DOLLAR STORES, INC. operated 2,062 discount stores as of 11/31/93. The stores are located in a contiguous 33 state area ranging as far northwest as Wisconsin, northeast to Massachusetts, southeast to Florida and southwest to Texas. The stores' relatively small size, generally 6,000 to 8,000 square feet, gives FDO flexibility to open them in various markets from small rural towns to large urban centers. The stores are located in strip shopping centers or as freestanding buildings convenient to FDO's low and middle income customer base. The merchandise is sold in a no-frills, low overhead, self-service environment on a cash and carry basis. Most merchandise is priced at $17.99 or less.

QUARTERLY DATA

(08/31/93)	Rev	Inc
1st Quarter	304,608	13,787
2nd Quarter	356,461	20,789
3rd Quarter	310,081	17,455
4th Quarter	326,281	12,398

ANNUAL EARNINGS AND DIVIDENDS PER SHARE

	8/31/93	8/31/92	8/31/91	8/31/90	8/31/89	8/31/88	8/31/87
Earnings Per Share	**1.15**	**1.00**	**0.73**	**0.52**	**0.39**	**0.49**	**0.43**
Dividends Per Share	**0.29**	**[1] 0.25**	**0.215**	**0.195**	**0.175**	**0.155**	**0.135**
Dividend Payout %	**25.2**	**25.0**	**29.7**	**37.5**	**44.9**	**31.6**	**31.4**

[1] 2-for-1 stk split, 2/27/92

ANNUAL FINANCIAL DATA

	8/31/93	8/31/92	8/31/91	8/31/90	8/31/89	8/31/88	8/31/87
RECORD OF EARNINGS (IN MILLIONS):							
Total Revenues	1,297.4	1,158.7	989.3	874.4	756.9	669.5	560.3
Costs and Expenses	1,177.3	1,055.0	912.5	814.1	709.8	620.4	510.2
Depreciation & Amort	17.2	14.7	13.1	12.7	12.0	10.1	8.5
Operating Profit	d819.8	d733.8	d636.1	d570.6	d498.0	237.2	212.6
Income Bef Income Taxes	102.9	88.9	63.7	47.6	35.1	44.2	46.8
Income Taxes	38.5	33.3	23.5	18.9	13.6	16.8	22.0
Net Income	64.4	55.7	40.2	28.7	21.5	27.3	24.8
Aver. Shs. Outstg. (000)	56,250	55,911	55,585	55,482	55,480	56,055	58,004
BALANCE SHEET (IN MILLIONS):							
Cash and Cash Equivalents	5.7	1.7	25.0	4.6	0.7	7.0	13.3
Receivables, Net	12.4	12.8	7.1	4.9	2.5	...	...
Inventories	379.4	339.0	258.9	239.5	212.4	178.9	142.4
Gross Property	226.0	199.2	173.1	161.1	151.4	134.4	111.1
Accumulated Depreciation	95.9	82.4	69.9	59.0	47.7	36.6	28.6
Net Stockholders' Equity	323.3	271.8	227.3	197.1	179.1	167.3	159.6
Total Assets	537.4	478.0	399.3	355.1	324.0	290.7	242.0
Total Current Assets	402.5	358.7	293.7	251.7	219.0	191.6	158.6
Total Current Liabilities	196.6	188.5	157.5	143.8	131.7	112.7	74.7
Net Working Capital	205.9	170.3	136.2	107.9	87.2	78.9	83.9
Year End Shs Outstg (000)	56,352	56,038	55,760	55,486	55,481	55,478	58,121
STATISTICAL RECORD:							
Operating Profit Margin %	...	...	...	...	...	6.5	8.3
Book Value Per Share	5.74	4.85	4.08	3.55	3.23	3.02	2.75
Return on Equity %	19.9	20.5	17.7	14.6	12.0	16.3	15.5
Return on Assets %	12.0	11.6	10.1	8.1	6.6	9.4	10.2
Average Yield %	1.5	1.3	1.9	3.2	2.9	2.5	2.0
P/E Ratio	20.5-13.2	24.6-13.1	24.0-8.0	14.7-8.7	18.3-12.5	16.3-8.7	23.0-8.1
Price Range	23⅝-15⅛	24⅝-13⅛	17¼-5¾	7⅝-4½	7⅛-4⅞	8-4¼	9⅞-3½

Statistics are as originally reported.

OFFICERS:
L. Levine, Chmn., C.E.O., Pres. & C.O.O.
G.R. Mahoney, Jr., V.P. & Gen. Couns.
C.M. Sowers, Sr. V.P.-Fin.

INCORPORATED: DE, Nov., 1969

PRINCIPAL OFFICE: 10401 Old Monroe Road, Matthews, NC 28105

TELEPHONE NUMBER: (704) 847-6961

NO. OF EMPLOYEES: 1,224 full time; 6,900 part-time

ANNUAL MEETING: In January

SHAREHOLDERS: 2,208 (approx.)

INSTITUTIONAL HOLDINGS:
No. of Institutions: 173
Shares Held: 31,643,678

REGISTRAR(S): Chemical Bank, New York, NY

TRANSFER AGENT(S): Chemcial Bank, New York, NY

NYS SYMBOL FRT
Rec. Pr. 24¾

FEDERAL REALTY INVESTMENT TRUST

YIELD 6.3%
P/E RATIO 51.6

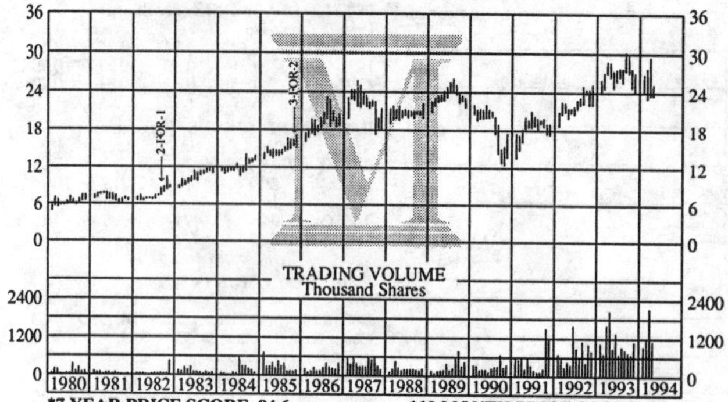

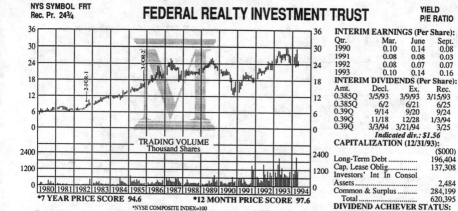

*7 YEAR PRICE SCORE 94.6   *12 MONTH PRICE SCORE 97.6

*NYSE COMPOSITE INDEX=100

INTERIM EARNINGS (Per Share):

Qtr.	Mar.	June	Sept.	Dec.
1990	0.10	0.14	0.08	0.03
1991	0.08	0.08	0.03	0.06
1992	0.08	0.07	0.07	0.08
1993	0.10	0.14	0.16	0.19

INTERIM DIVIDENDS (Per Share):

Amt.	Decl.	Ex.	Rec.	Pay.
0.385Q	3/5/93	3/9/93	3/15/93	4/15/93
0.385Q	6/2	6/21	6/25	7/15
0.39Q	9/14	9/20	9/24	10/15
0.39Q	11/18	12/28	1/3/94	1/14/94
0.39Q	3/3/94	3/21/94	3/25	4/15

Indicated div.: $1.56

CAPITALIZATION (12/31/93):

	($000)	(%)
Long-Term Debt	196,404	31.7
Cap. Lease Oblig.	137,308	22.1
Investors' Int In Consol Assets	2,484	0.4
Common & Surplus	284,199	45.8
Total	620,395	100.0

DIVIDEND ACHIEVER STATUS:
Rank: 228   1983-93 Growth Rate: 7.5%
Total Years of Dividend Growth: 26

RECENT DEVELOPMENTS: For the year ended 12/31/93, funds from operations increased 38% to $41.5 million from $30.0 million in 1992, reflecting the combination of contributions from FRT's new acquisitions, improved results from the base portfolio, and decreased interest expense. Rental income increased 18% to $105.9 millionin 1993 from $90.0 million in 1992. If adjusted for properties sold and acquired during 1993 and 1992, rental income increased $7.8 million or 8.8% to $96.3 million from $88.5 million in 1992. During the year, The Trust leased 880,000 square feet at an average rent of $13.51 per square foot compared to the previous average rent per square foot for the same spaces of $11.35, a 19% increase. At 12/31/93, FRT's overall portfolio was 95% leased compared to 96% leased a year ago. Shopping centers operated in both periods were 96% leased at year-end versus 97% leased a year ago.

BUSINESS

FEDERAL REALTY INVESTMENT TRUST is an equity real estate investment trust specializing in the ownership, management and redevelopment of prime community and neighborhood shopping centers. The Trust's portfolio currently contains 48 shopping centers containing 10.5 million square feet located principally along the east coast region between the New York metropolitan area and Richmond, Virginia.

REVENUES

(12/31/93)	($000)	(%)
Rental	105,948	91.8
Interest	3,894	3.4
Other Property	5,495	4.8
Total	115,337	100.0

ANNUAL EARNINGS AND DIVIDENDS PER SHARE

	1993	1992	1991	1990	1989	1988	1987
Earnings Per Share	0.60	[1] 0.30	[2] 0.25	0.35	0.82	0.68	0.47
Dividends Per Share	1.56	1.525	1.49	1.42	1.36	1.23	1.11
Dividend Payout %	N.M.	N.M.	N.M.	N.M.	N.M.	N.M.	N.M.

[1] Before realized gain [2] Before extraord. item

ANNUAL FINANCIAL DATA

	1993	1992	1991	1990	1989	1988	1987
RECORD OF EARNINGS (IN THOUSANDS):							
Total Revenue	115,337	100,197	97,652	90,949	82,852	68,108	60,419
Costs and Expenses	[1] 41,518	33,857	32,618	30,308	28,386	22,918	20,470
Depreciation & Amort	...	23,033	21,922	19,091	16,174	12,121	9,529
Operating Income	48,444	43,307	43,112	41,550	38,292	33,069	30,420
Inc Fr Cont Opers Bef Income Taxes	16,894	9,925	5,026	6,340	12,378	9,820	6,338
Investors' Share Of Opers	780	437	641	499	381	546	293
Net Income	[2] 16,114	[3] 9,488	[4] 4,385	5,841	11,997	9,274	6,045
Aver. Shs. Outstg.	27,009	22,767	17,304	16,695	14,672	13,684	12,979

[1] Incl. Dep. [2] Before extra. item cr$2,016,000. [3] Before extra. item dr$58,000. [4] Before extra. item cr$415,000.

	1993	1992	1991	1990	1989	1988	1987
BALANCE SHEET (IN THOUSANDS):							
Cash and Cash Equivalents	9,635	36,316	43,387	25,064	50,118	15,431	67,951
Receivables, Net	31,442	28,256	24,442	24,919	30,941	27,168	16,787
Long-Term Debt	196,404	216,293	241,469	229,847	231,711	247,460	250,996
Obligs Under Cap Lses	137,308	125,619	126,393	128,016	128,535	108,870	30,423
Net Stockholders' Equity	284,199	222,878	151,480	129,346	146,114	95,668	100,292
Total Assets	690,943	603,811	563,091	551,319	564,441	475,689	402,315
Total Current Assets	60,576	80,840	82,271	63,216	93,478	51,460	91,620
Total Current Liabilities	70,548	36,396	43,879	63,390	56,281	21,158	18,028
Net Working Capital	d9,972	44,444	38,392	d174	37,197	30,302	73,592
Year End Shares Outstg	28,018	24,718	19,687	16,716	16,642	13,529	13,529
STATISTICAL RECORD:							
Book Value Per Share	10.14	9.02	7.69	7.74	8.78	7.07	7.41
Return on Equity %	5.7	4.3	2.9	4.5	8.2	9.7	6.0
Return on Assets %	2.3	1.6	0.8	1.1	2.1	2.0	1.5
Average Yield %	5.8	6.9	8.6	8.2	5.8	6.0	5.2
P/E Ratio	50.4-39.8	84.2-62.5	84.0-54.5	75.9-43.1	78.8-62.9	57.1-48.7	54.8-36.7
Price Range	30¼-23⅞	25¼-18¾	21-13⅝	22-12½	26-20¾	22¼-19	25¾-17¼

Statistics are as originally reported.

OFFICERS:
S.J. Guttman, Pres. & C.E.O.
C.R. Mack, V.P., Sec., Sec. & Gen. Counsel
M.J. Morrow, V.P.-Fin. & Treas.

INCORPORATED: MD, 1962

PRINCIPAL OFFICE: 4800 Hampden Lane, Suite 500, Bethesda, MD 20814

TELEPHONE NUMBER: (301) 652-3360
FAX: (301) 961-9328
NO. OF EMPLOYEES: 143
ANNUAL MEETING: In May
SHAREHOLDERS: 4,136
INSTITUTIONAL HOLDINGS:
No. of Institutions: 124
Shares Held: 13,323,205

REGISTRAR(S):

TRANSFER AGENT(S): American Stock Transfer Co., 40 Wall St., 46th Floor, New York, NY 10005

FIFTH THIRD BANCORP

YIELD	2.1%
P/E RATIO	16.0

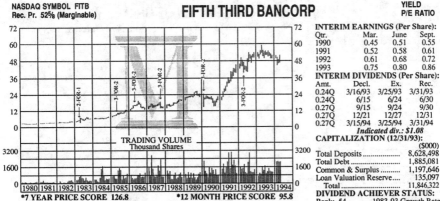

*7 YEAR PRICE SCORE 126.8   *12 MONTH PRICE SCORE 95.8

*NYSE COMPOSITE INDEX=100

INTERIM EARNINGS (Per Share):

Qtr.	Mar.	June	Sept.	Dec.
1990	0.45	0.51	0.55	0.54
1991	0.52	0.58	0.61	0.62
1992	0.61	0.68	0.72	0.74
1993	0.75	0.80	0.86	0.87

INTERIM DIVIDENDS (Per Share):

Amt.	Decl.	Ex.	Rec.	Pay.
0.24Q	3/16/93	3/25/93	3/31/93	4/15/93
0.24Q	6/15	6/24	6/30	7/15
0.27Q	9/15	9/24	9/30	10/15
0.27Q	12/21	12/27	12/31	1/15/94
0.27Q	3/15/94	3/25/94	3/31/94	4/15

Indicated div.: $1.08

CAPITALIZATION (12/31/93):

	($000)	(%)
Total Deposits	8,628,498	72.8
Total Debt	1,885,081	15.9
Common & Surplus	1,197,646	10.1
Loan Valuation Reserve	135,097	1.2
Total	11,846,322	100.0

DIVIDEND ACHIEVER STATUS:
Rank: 54   1983-93 Growth Rate: 15.4%
Total Years of Dividend Growth: 21

RECENT DEVELOPMENTS: For the year ended 12/31/93, net income was $196.4 million compared to $164.1 million in 1992. Total assets were $11.97 billion versus $10.21 billion in 1992. For the quarter, net income was $52.3 million compared to $44.3 million a year ago. Return on average equity for the year was 18.2% and return on average assets was 1.80%. Consumer loans and leases were up 34% and residen-

tial mortgage loans rose 12% over 1992. Commercial loans and leases increased 12% over last year. Nonperforming assets were .27 percent of total loans, leases, and other real estate owned. New merchant processing customers such as The Kroger Company and the addition of over 40 new financial institutions to FITB's Jeanie® automated teller network increased data processing income by 17% over 1992.

BUSINESS

FIFTH THIRD BANCORP is a bank holding company with its primary subsidiary, the Fifth Third Bank, headquartered in Cincinnati, Ohio. The Bank provides full service banking to individuals as well as to industry and governmental subdivisions. Fifth Third currently has 290 Banking Centers, including 63 seven-day a week locations. It has made a strong impact on the Cincinnati retail banking market through a great variety of services, including the Jeanie electronic funds transfer system which consists of automated teller machines and telephone banking and features a bill payment service. The service is used by banks and savings and loans in three states. The Bank also provides fiduciary services through its Trust Division. The banking services provided to industry and government include demand and time deposit accounts, certificates of deposit, and all types of loans. The Bank further serves the requirements of Cincinnati commercial enterprises by offering financial counseling, freight payment, automated payroll programs, cash management, cashiering, and other computer based services.

ANNUAL EARNINGS AND DIVIDENDS PER SHARE

	1993	1992	1991	1990	1989	1988	1987
Earnings Per Share	3.28	2.75	2.33	2.05	1.86	1.75	③ 1.35
Dividends Per Share	0.99	① 0.86	0.76	② 0.727	0.60	0.52	④ 0.453
Dividend Payout %	30.2	31.3	32.6	35.5	32.3	29.8	33.5

① 3-for-2 stk split, 4/16/92 ② 50% stk div, 1/13/90 ③ Before acctg. chg. ④ 50% stk. div. 4/86 & 10/87.

ANNUAL FINANCIAL DATA

RECORD OF EARNINGS (IN MILLIONS):

Total Interest Income	727.3	694.5	713.5	696.6	649.8	415.6	308.9
Total Interest Expense	291.0	300.3	381.3	402.9	374.7	226.8	166.3
Net Interest Income	436.4	394.2	332.2	293.6	275.1	188.8	142.6
Provision for Credit Losses	44.5	65.3	55.7	39.9	36.5	26.1	18.9
Net Income	196.4	164.1	138.2	120.4	108.3	84.2	① 60.1
Aver. Shs. Outstg. (000)	59,952	59,632	59,632	59,201	58,847	58,263	48,222	44,310

① Before acctg. change cr$7,455,000.

BALANCE SHEET (IN MILLIONS):

Cash & Due From Banks	580.9	565.9	501.2	564.2	453.4	361.2	315.9
Total Loans & Leases	8,675.9	7,360.1	5,716.3	5,412.0	5,083.9	3,695.4	2,715.3
Total Domestic Deposits	8,458.9	7,461.2	6,672.1	6,383.0	5,780.8	4,090.2	3,182.6
Foreign Office	169.6	70.7	15.1	2.2	2.8	3.5	1.0
Long-term Debt	282.9	254.1	12.8	13.5	12.6	12.2	12.8
Net Stockholders' Equity	1,197.6	1,005.2	879.5	782.7	699.3	508.6	402.0
Total Assets	11,966.0	10,213.3	8,826.1	7,955.8	7,143.0	5,245.8	4,051.5
Year End Shs Outstg (000)	61,402	59,832	59,375	59,081	58,713	49,089	44,409

STATISTICAL RECORD:

Return on Assets %	1.64	1.61	1.57	1.51	1.52	1.60	1.48
Return on Equity %	16.40	16.30	15.70	15.40	15.50	16.50	14.90
Book Value Per Share	19.50	16.80	14.81	13.25	11.91	10.36	9.05
Average Yield %	1.8	1.8	2.3	3.7	2.6	3.0	2.8
P/E Ratio	18.0-15.1	19.6-14.5	19.5-8.4	12.0-7.3	14.2-10.6	11.6-8.1	13.8-10.0
Price Range	59-49½	54-39¾	45½-19⅝	24⅝-15	26½-19¾	20¼-14⅛	18⅝-13½

Statistics are as originally reported.

OFFICERS:
G.A. Schaefer, Jr., Pres. & C.E.O.
P.M. Brumm, Sr. V.P. & C.F.O.
M.K. Keating, Sr. V.P., Couns. & Sec.
N.E. Arnold, Treasurer

INCORPORATED: OH, 1974

PRINCIPAL OFFICE: 38 Fountain Square Plaza, Cincinnati, OH 45263

TELEPHONE NUMBER: (513) 579-5300

NO. OF EMPLOYEES: 4,938

ANNUAL MEETING: In March

SHAREHOLDERS: 11,302

INSTITUTIONAL HOLDINGS:
No. of Institutions: 166
Shares Held: 26,680,441

REGISTRAR(S): Fifth Third Bank, Cincinnati, OH 45263

TRANSFER AGENT(S): Fifth Third Bank, Cincinnati, OH 45263

NASDAQ SYMBOL FBOH
Rec. Pr. 25 (Marginable)

FIRST BANCORPORATION OF OHIO

YIELD 3.8%
P/E RATIO 11.5

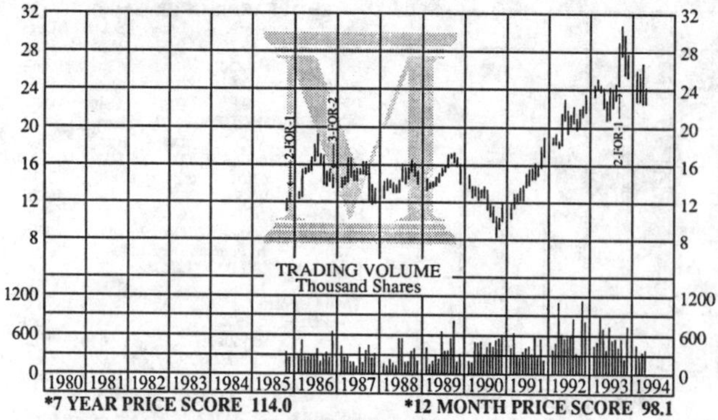

32
28
24
20
16
12
8
2-FOR-1
3-FOR-2
2-FOR-1
TRADING VOLUME
Thousand Shares
1200
600
0
1980 1981 1982 1983 1984 1985 1986 1987 1988 1989 1990 1991 1992 1993 1994

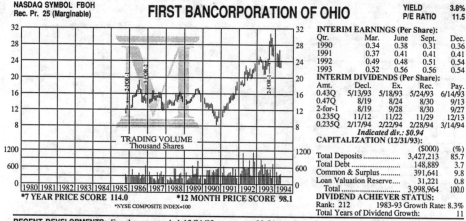

*7 YEAR PRICE SCORE 114.0 *12 MONTH PRICE SCORE 98.1

*NYSE COMPOSITE INDEX=100

INTERIM EARNINGS (Per Share):

Qtr.	Mar.	June	Sept.	Dec.
1990	0.34	0.38	0.31	0.36
1991	0.37	0.41	0.41	0.41
1992	0.49	0.48	0.51	0.54
1993	0.52	0.56	0.56	0.54

INTERIM DIVIDENDS (Per Share):

Amt.	Decl.	Ex.	Rec.	Pay.
0.43Q	5/13/93	5/18/93	5/24/93	6/14/93
0.47Q	8/19	8/24	8/30	9/13
2-for-1	8/19	9/28	8/30	9/27
0.235Q	11/12	11/22	11/29	12/13
0.235Q	2/17/94	2/22/94	2/28/94	3/14/94

Indicated div.: $0.94

CAPITALIZATION (12/31/93):

	($000)	(%)
Total Deposits	3,427,213	85.7
Total Debt	148,889	3.7
Common & Surplus	391,641	9.8
Loan Valuation Reserve	31,221	0.8
Total	3,998,964	100.0

DIVIDEND ACHIEVER STATUS:
Rank: 212 1983-93 Growth Rate: 8.3%
Total Years of Dividend Growth: 11

RECENT DEVELOPMENTS: For the year ended 12/31/93, net income was a record $55.2 million, or $2.19 per share, compared with $50.7 million, or $2.02 per share, in 1992. Total interest income slipped to $277.7 million from $294.9 million last year. Net interest income was $184.5 million, up from $180.0 million a year ealier. For the quarter, net income was $13.6 million, or $0.54 per share, versus $13.7 million, or $0.54 per share, for the corresponding period last year. Net interest income was $46.2 million, down from $46.5 million a year ago. Both total interest income and interest expense declined an equal amount. Net interest income after provisions was $45.0 million, up from $40.8 million for the same period last year. At 12/31/93, total assets amounted to $4.00 billion compared with $3.92 billion at the end of 1992.

BUSINESS

FIRST BANCORP OF OHIO is a bank holding company that provides, through its subsidiaries, a wide range of banking, fiduciary, financial and investment services to corporate, institutional and individual customers throughout Northern Ohio and Southern Florida. FBOH directs the overall policies and financial resources of the subsidiaries, but the day-to-day affairs, including lending practices, services, and interest rates, are managed by their own officers and directors.

LOAN DISTRIBUTION

(12/31/93)	($000)	(%)
Comml, Financial & Agri	430,118	18.0
Loans to Individuals	597,875	24.9
Real Estate	1,311,788	54.7
Lease Financing	56,682	2.4
Total	2,396,463	100.0

ANNUAL EARNINGS AND DIVIDENDS PER SHARE

	1993	1992	1991	1990	1989	1988	1987
Earnings Per Share	2.19	2.02	1.58	[2] 1.39	1.60	1.56	1.56
Dividends Per Share	[1] 0.90	0.825	0.803	0.763	0.731	0.688	0.619
Dividend Payout %	41.1	40.8	51.0	54.9	45.9	44.1	39.7

[1] 2-for-1 stk split,09/28/93 [2] Before acctg. chg.

ANNUAL FINANCIAL DATA

	1993	1992	1991	1990	1989	1988	1987
RECORD OF EARNINGS (IN MILLIONS):							
Total Interest Income	277.7	294.9	315.6	326.5	293.6	224.1	204.3
Total Interest Expense	93.2	114.9	163.7	185.9	165.1	116.3	100.9
Net Interest Income	184.5	180.0	151.9	140.5	128.5	107.8	103.4
Prov for Possible Loan Losses	6.6	17.4	11.4	11.7	7.1	5.0	6.0
Net Income	55.2	50.7	39.6	34.9	38.6	[1] 33.9	33.9
Aver. Shs. Outstg. (000)	25,219	25,158	25,110	25,108	24,176	21,742	21,726
[1] Before acctg. change cr$1,282,000.							
BALANCE SHEET (IN MILLIONS):							
Cash & Due From Banks	222.3	210.9	190.7	215.2	198.4	197.3	154.0
Net Loans	2,365.2	2,292.6	2,223.5	2,130.9	1,925.1	1,715.3	1,367.1
Total Domestic Deposits	3,427.2	3,384.1	3,267.8	3,229.2	2,843.8	2,648.2	2,264.0
Net Stockholders' Equity	391.6	358.3	327.4	307.9	296.5	258.5	238.0
Total Assets	3,996.7	3,916.2	3,765.7	3,722.1	3,334.2	3,048.9	2,638.4
Year End Shs Outstg (000)	25,249	25,196	25,117	25,108	24,178	21,764	21,732
STATISTICAL RECORD:							
Return on Assets %	1.38	1.29	1.05	0.94	1.16	1.11	1.28
Return on Equity %	14.10	14.20	12.10	11.30	13.00	13.10	14.20
Book Value Per Share	15.51	14.22	13.04	12.26	12.26	11.88	10.95
Average Yield %	3.5	4.0	5.5	6.6	4.8	4.7	4.3
P/E Ratio	14.0-9.5	11.6-8.8	12.0-6.5	10.8-5.9	10.9-8.3	10.7-7.9	10.7-7.5
Price Range	30¾-20¾	23½-17⅞	19-10¼	15-8¼	17⅜-13¼	16⅝-12⅜	16¾-11¾

Statistics are as originally reported.

OFFICERS:
H.L. Flood, Pres. & C.E.O.
T.E. Patton, Sr. V.P. & Sec.
G.J. Elek, Sr. V.P. & Treas.

PRINCIPAL OFFICE: 106 South Main Street, Akron, OH 44308

TELEPHONE NUMBER: (216) 384-8000

FAX: (216) 253-1849

NO. OF EMPLOYEES: 2,747

ANNUAL MEETING: In April

SHAREHOLDERS: 6,673

INSTITUTIONAL HOLDINGS:
No. of Institutions: 70
Shares Held: 2,982,032

REGISTRAR(S): First National Bank of Ohio, Akron Ohio 44308

TRANSFER AGENT(S):

FIRST EMPIRE STATE CORP.

YIELD 1.4%
P/E RATIO 10.0

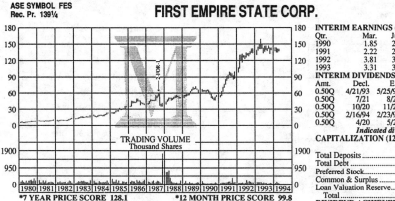

INTERIM EARNINGS (Per Share):

Qtr.	Mar.	June	Sept.	Dec.
1990	1.85	2.02	2.12	1.92
1991	2.22	2.24	2.37	2.49
1992	3.81	3.82	2.85	2.93
1993	3.31	3.42	3.52	3.62

INTERIM DIVIDENDS (Per Share):

Amt.	Decl.	Ex.	Rec.	Pay.
0.50Q	4/21/93	5/25/93	6/1/93	6/29/93
0.50Q	7/21	8/26	9/1	9/28
0.50Q	10/20	11/24	12/1	12/28
0.50Q	2/16/94	2/23/94	3/1/94	3/30/94
0.50Q	4/20	5/25	6/1	6/29

Indicated div.: $2.00

CAPITALIZATION (12/31/93):

	($000)	(%)
Total Deposits	7,353,261	70.4
Total Debt	2,177,257	20.8
Preferred Stock	40,000	0.4
Common & Surplus	683,994	6.5
Loan Valuation Reserve	195,878	1.9
Total	10,450,390	100.0

DIVIDEND ACHIEVER STATUS:
Rank: 70   1983-93 Growth Rate: 14.3%
Total Years of Dividend Growth: 13

TRADING VOLUME
Thousand Shares

1980|1981|1982|1983|1984|1985|1986|1987|1988|1989|1990|1991|1992|1993|1994

*7 YEAR PRICE SCORE 128.1   *12 MONTH PRICE SCORE 99.8
*NYSE COMPOSITE INDEX=100

RECENT DEVELOPMENTS: For the year ended 12/31/93, net income was $102.0 million, or $13.87 per share, compared with $97.9 million, or $13.41 per share, in 1992. Average earning assets were $10.0 billion in 1993, up 9% from last year. The taxable-equivalent net interest income was $474.8 million, up 8% from last year's $438.6 million. Net interest income, expressed as an annualized percentage of average earnings, was 4.76% compared with 4.79% in 1992. The spread between the yield on earning assets and the rate paid on interest-bearing liabilities widened slightly to 4.33% in 1993 from 4.29% in 1992. Non-interest income, excluding securities gains, rose 12% to $109.7 million (includes a full year's income from acquisitions made in 1992).

BUSINESS

FIRST EMPIRE STATE CORPORATION is a regional bank holding company. Its banking subsidiaries are Manufacturers and Traders Trust Company and The East New York Savings Bank both of which are wholly owned. M&T Bank is a New York-chartered commercial bank with 106 offices throughout Western New York State and New York's Southern Tier, 13 offices in the Hudson Valley of New York State plus offices in New York City, Albany, Syracuse, and Nassau, The Bahamas. East New York, is a New York-chartered savings bank with 19 offices in metropolitan New York City. M&T Bank's subsidiaries include M&T Capital Corporation, a venture capital company, M&T Financial Corporation, an equipment leasing company, M&T Mortgage Corporation, a mortgage banking company, and M&T Discount Brokerage Services, Inc., a discount securities broker.

LOAN DISTRIBUTION

(12/31/93)	($000)	(%)
Commercial, Financial &	1,419,039	19.3
Agricultural		
Real Estate-Construction	51,384	0.7
Real estate-Mortgage	4,540,177	61.8
Consumer	1,337,293	18.2
Total	7,347,893	100.0

ANNUAL EARNINGS AND DIVIDENDS PER SHARE

	1993	1992	1991	1990	1989	1988	1987
Earnings Per Share	13.87	13.41	9.32	7.91	①7.04	6.02	4.78
Dividends Per Share	1.90	1.60	1.40	1.25	1.10	0.95	②0.80
Dividend Payout %	13.7	11.9	15.0	15.8	15.6	15.8	16.7

① Before acctg. chg. ② 100% stk. div. 9/87.

ANNUAL FINANCIAL DATA

RECORD OF EARNINGS (IN MILLIONS):

	1993	1992	1991	1990	1989	1988	1987
Total Interest Income	740.6	756.5	769.0	657.4	576.6	492.5	423.3
Total Interest Expense	269.9	323.6	440.2	426.9	384.4	306.8	245.0
Net Interest Income	470.8	432.9	328.8	230.4	192.2	185.8	178.3
Prov for Possible Cr Losses	80.0	85.0	63.4	27.4	15.3	13.9	9.8
Net Income	102.0	97.9	67.2	53.9	①50.7	44.5	40.3
Aver. Shs. Outstg. (000)	7,097	7,033	6,905	6,818	7,199	7,385	5,547

① Before acctg. change dr$9,455,000.

BALANCE SHEET (IN MILLIONS):

	1993	1992	1991	1990	1989	1988	1987
Cash & Due From Banks	195.8	264.5	269.2	235.8	271.8	253.9	202.1
U S Treasury & Fed Agcy	...	...	15.6	60.8	937.4	846.2	633.3
Obligs Of State & Political Subdiviss	...	...	128.4	164.1	100.8	113.8	119.9
Loans & Leases, Net	7,065.2	6,832.1	5,946.3	5,297.9	4,315.6	3,915.2	3,420.9
Total Domestic Deposits	7,164.2	7,959.3	7,248.1	6,029.4	4,672.2	4,702.7	4,095.5
Deposits At Foreign Office	189.1	117.8	226.2	171.6	198.4	354.7	281.9
Long-term Debt	75.6	75.7	9.5	3.2	13.1	13.5	23.3
Net Stockholders' Equity	724.0	626.8	535.8	437.2	406.3	388.1	382.1
Total Assets	10,365.0	9,587.9	9,171.1	7,715.4	6,233.8	5,908.1	5,176.9
Year End Shs Outstg (000)	8,097	6,840	6,708	6,630	6,836	7,021	7,631

STATISTICAL RECORD:

	1993	1992	1991	1990	1989	1988	1987
Return on Assets %	0.98	1.02	0.73	0.70	0.81	0.75	0.78
Return on Equity %	14.10	15.60	12.50	12.30	12.50	11.50	10.50
Book Value Per Share	84.47	85.79	73.91	65.94	59.44	55.28	50.07
Average Yield %	1.3	1.3	1.8	2.2	1.8	2.0	1.7
P/E Ratio	11.5-9.4	10.6-7.4	10.7-5.6	8.5-5.9	10.3-7.3	9.3-6.5	12.3-7.3
Price Range	159-130¼	142-99	99¾-52½	67½-47	72½-51⅜	56¼-39	59-35

Statistics are as originally reported.

OFFICERS:
P.B. Murray, Chairman
R.G. Wilmers, Pres. & C.E.O.
J.L. Vardon, Exec. V.P. & C.F.O.
W.C. Rappolt, Exec. V.P. & Treas.

INCORPORATED: NY, Nov., 1969

PRINCIPAL OFFICE: One M&T Plaza P.O. Box 223, Buffalo, NY 14240-0223

TELEPHONE NUMBER: (716) 842-5138

NO. OF EMPLOYEES: 4,400

ANNUAL MEETING: In April

SHAREHOLDERS: 3,985

INSTITUTIONAL HOLDINGS:
No. of Institutions: 104
Shares Held: 3,198,154

REGISTRAR(S): First National Bank of Boston, Shareholder Services Division, Boston, MA

TRANSFER AGENT(S): First National Bank of Boston, Shareholder Services Division, Boston, MA

NASDAQ SYMBOL FHWN
Rec. Pr. 27¼ (Marginable)

FIRST HAWAIIAN INC.

YIELD 4.3%
P/E RATIO 11.3

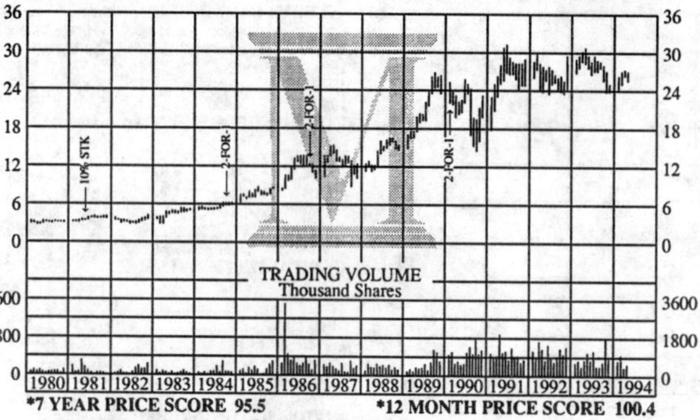

36
30
24
18
12
6
0
10% STK
2-FOR-1
2-FOR-1
2-FOR-1
TRADING VOLUME
Thousand Shares
3600
1800
0
1980 1981 1982 1983 1984 1985 1986 1987 1988 1989 1990 1991 1992 1993 1994

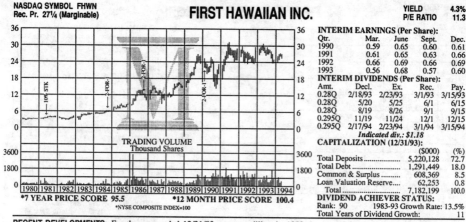

***7 YEAR PRICE SCORE 95.5** ***12 MONTH PRICE SCORE 100.4**

*NYSE COMPOSITE INDEX=100

INTERIM EARNINGS (Per Share):

Qtr.	Mar.	June	Sept.	Dec.
1990	0.59	0.65	0.60	0.61
1991	0.61	0.65	0.63	0.66
1992	0.66	0.69	0.66	0.69
1993	0.56	0.68	0.57	0.60

INTERIM DIVIDENDS (Per Share):

Amt.	Decl.	Ex.	Rec.	Pay.
0.28Q	2/18/93	2/23/93	3/1/93	3/15/93
0.28Q	5/20	5/25	6/1	6/15
0.28Q	8/19	8/26	9/1	9/15
0.295Q	11/19	11/24	12/1	12/15
0.295Q	2/17/94	2/23/94	3/1/94	3/15/94

Indicated div.: $1.18

CAPITALIZATION (12/31/93):

	($000)	(%)
Total Deposits	5,220,128	72.7
Total Debt	1,291,449	18.0
Common & Surplus	608,369	8.5
Loan Valuation Reserve	62,253	0.8
Total	7,182,199	100.0

DIVIDEND ACHIEVER STATUS:
Rank: 90 1983-93 Growth Rate: 13.5%
Total Years of Dividend Growth: 11

RECENT DEVELOPMENTS: For the year ended 12/31/93, net income was $78.2 million compared with $86.9 million in the comparable period of 1992. The decrease in earnings resulted primarily from a slowdown in earnings growth caused by the economic recession in Hawaii. Results were before an accounting credit of $3.7 million. Total interest income was $441.6 million, down 9.2% from $486.3 million. Net interest income increased to $278.1 million from $268.6 million in 1992 due to a 2.3% increase in average earning assets and a 7 basis point increase in net interest margin. At 12/31/93, total deposits were $5.22 billion, up 2.6% from 1992. This increase was primarily attributable to the acquisition of Pioneer Federal Savings Bank. Total loans and leases increased 15.3% to $5.07 billion, representing 69.7% of total assets.

BUSINESS

FIRST HAWAIIAN INC. is a bank holding company. Its principal subsidiary, First Hawaiian Bank, was founded in 1858 and is the oldest financial institution on the islands. The bank presently has 59 branches throughout Hawaii, two in Guam, an offshore branch in Grand Cayman, British West Indies and a representative office in Tokyo, Japan. Other major subsidiaries include Pioneer Federal Savings Bank with 19 branches statewide; First Hawaiian Creditcorp, Inc., the state's third largest financial services loan company with 10 branches statewide and a branch in Guam; and First Hawaiian Leasing, Inc., which is primarily engaged in commercial equipment and vehicle leasing.

LOAN DISTRIBUTION

(12/31/93)	($000)	(%)
Commercial, Fincl & Agric	1,208,912	23.9
Real Est-Construction	317,036	6.3
Real Est-Comml & Resident	2,668,589	52.6
Consumer	459,910	9.1
Lease Financing	201,449	4.0
Foreign	210,913	4.2
Total	4,396,018	100.0

ANNUAL EARNINGS AND DIVIDENDS PER SHARE

	1993	1992	1991	1990	1989	1988	1987
Earnings Per Share	**2.41**	**2.70**	**2.55**	**2.45**	**2.14**	**1.62**	**1.32**
Dividends Per Share	**1.35**	**1.06**	**0.95**	**[1] 0.83**	**0.70**	**0.575**	**0.475**
Dividend Payout %	**56.2**	**39.3**	**37.3**	**33.9**	**32.7**	**35.5**	**36.0**

[1] 2-for-1 stk split, 1/26/90

ANNUAL FINANCIAL DATA

	1993	1992	1991	1990	1989	1988	1987
RECORD OF EARNINGS (IN MILLIONS):							
Total Interest Income	441.6	486.3	523.6	498.9	431.1	347.7	295.2
Total Interest Expense	163.5	217.7	270.9	283.7	249.7	196.1	171.6
Net Interest Income	278.1	268.6	252.7	215.2	181.5	151.6	123.6
Prov for Loan & Lse Losses	13.3	12.8	10.3	9.1	9.0	5.8	6.2
Net Income	[1] 78.2	86.9	81.7	71.5	57.4	43.3	35.5
Aver. Shs. Outstg. (000)	32,505	32,225	32,079	29,175	26,909	26,859	26,831
[1] Before acctg. change cr$3,650,000.							
BALANCE SHEET (IN MILLIONS):							
Cash & Due From Banks	436.1	325.7	354.0	324.2	276.8	270.1	172.7
Net Loans & Leases	5,004.6	4,339.6	4,274.2	3,221.9	2,772.6	2,356.1	1,900.6
Total Domestic Deposits	4,968.6	4,901.7	5,146.8	4,487.1	4,174.5	3,587.0	3,284.7
Foreign	251.6	186.5	189.9	290.4	337.8	186.6	115.4
Long-term Debt	221.8	71.1	61.6	49.9	60.5	60.9	62.9
Net Stockholders' Equity	608.4	562.2	498.3	446.8	281.1	242.1	210.8
Total Assets	7,269.1	6,553.4	6,510.6	5,509.4	5,080.1	4,238.6	3,942.7
Year End Shs Outstg (000)	32,543	32,502	32,079	32,079	26,909	26,909	26,830
STATISTICAL RECORD:							
Return on Assets %	1.08	1.33	1.26	1.30	1.13	1.02	0.90
Return on Equity %	12.90	15.50	16.40	16.00	20.40	17.90	16.80
Book Value Per Share	18.69	17.30	15.53	13.93	10.45	9.00	7.86
Average Yield %	5.0	4.0	3.9	4.1	3.4	4.1	3.9
P/E Ratio	12.8-9.9	11.0-8.7	12.3-7.0	10.5-5.9	12.5-7.0	10.2-6.9	11.6-6.7
Price Range	30¾-23¾	29¾-23½	31¼-17¾	25¾-14½	26¾-14⅞	16½-11¼	15⅜-8⅞

Statistics are as originally reported.

OFFICERS:
W.A. Dods, Jr., Chmn. & C.E.O.
J.A. Hoag, President
H.H. Karr, Exec. V.P. & Treas.
H.E. Wolff, Sr. V.P. & Sec.

INCORPORATED: DE, Jul., 1974

PRINCIPAL OFFICE: P.O. Box 3200, Honolulu, HI 96847

TELEPHONE NUMBER: (808) 525-7000

NO. OF EMPLOYEES: 2,695

ANNUAL MEETING: In April

SHAREHOLDERS: 5,151

INSTITUTIONAL HOLDINGS:
No. of Institutions: 85
Shares Held: 9,257,883

REGISTRAR(S): First Hawaiian Bank, Honolulu, HI

TRANSFER AGENT(S): First Hawaiian Bank, Honolulu, HI

FIRST OF AMERICA BANK CORP.

YIELD 4.2%
P/E RATIO 9.0

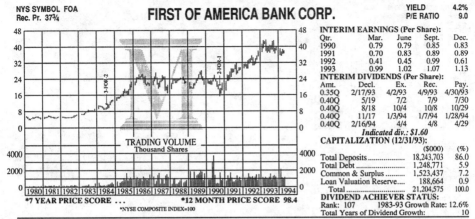

INTERIM EARNINGS (Per Share):

Qtr.	Mar.	June	Sept.	Dec.
1990	0.79	0.79	0.85	0.83
1991	0.70	0.83	0.89	0.89
1992	0.41	0.45	0.99	0.61
1993	0.99	1.02	1.07	1.13

INTERIM DIVIDENDS (Per Share):

Amt.	Decl.	Ex.	Rec.	Pay.
0.35Q	2/17/93	4/2/93	4/9/93	4/30/93
0.40Q	5/19	7/2	7/9	7/30
0.40Q	8/18	10/4	10/8	10/29
0.40Q	11/17	1/3/94	1/7/94	1/28/94
0.40Q	2/16/94	4/4	4/8	4/29

Indicated div.: $1.60

CAPITALIZATION (12/31/93):

	($000)	(%)
Total Deposits	18,243,703	86.0
Total Debt	1,248,771	5.9
Common & Surplus	1,523,437	7.2
Loan Valuation Reserve	188,664	0.9
Total	21,204,575	100.0

DIVIDEND ACHIEVER STATUS:
Rank: 107   1983-93 Growth Rate: 12.6%
Total Years of Dividend Growth: 10

RECENT DEVELOPMENTS: For the three months ended 12/31/93, net income rose 6% from the prior-year period to $65.8 million. Net income for the twelve months ended 12/31/93 was $247.4 million compared with $219.3 million for 1992. Results benefited from higher fee income and growth in credit card loans. Credit card loans increased 18% and consumer installment loans moved up 19%. The Company originated over $3.0 billion in residential mortgages as the mortgage servicing portfolio totaled $6.3 billion.

PROSPECTS: The combination of income produced from trust services, mortgage banking operations and credit card fees is providing a boost to the bottom line. Cost-control methods have been effective and contributed positively to results. The core community banking business has become more efficient and consequently allowed for the expansion of mortgage banking, financial services and credit card business lines. Earning assets have grown as a result.

BUSINESS

FIRST OF AMERICA CORPORATION is a bank holding company serving rural, urban and metropolitan areas in Michigan, Indiana and Illinois through 572 offices. The Company's primary lines of business are retail consumer banking, retail commercial banking, trust and investment services, and correspondent banking. Non-banking subsidiaries provide mortgage, trust, data processing, discount brokerage, revolving credit and investment advisory services.

LOAN DISTRIBUTION

(12/31/93)	($000)	(%)
Consumer	5,062,173	35.2
Commercial, Fin. & Agric.	2,148,663	14.9
Commercial Real Estate	2,902,549	20.1
Residential Real Estate	3,914,914	27.2
Loans held for sale	365,856	2.6
Total	14,394,155	100.0

ANNUAL EARNINGS AND DIVIDENDS PER SHARE

	1993	1992	1991	1990	1989	1988	1987
Earnings Per Share	4.20	①2.86	3.32	3.26	③2.94	3.08	2.97
Dividends Per Share	1.50	1.31	1.22	②1.125	1.05	0.925	0.825
Dividend Payout %	35.7	45.8	36.7	34.5	35.7	30.0	27.8

① Before acctg. chg. ② 2-for-1 stk split, 10/19/90 ③ Per primary share

ANNUAL FINANCIAL DATA

RECORD OF EARNINGS (IN MILLIONS):

	1993	1992	1991	1990	1989	1988	1987
Total Interest Income	1,511.0	1,596.1	1,259.9	1,235.6	1,171.8	793.2	685.4
Total Interest Expense	608.9	721.3	654.2	687.5	651.2	422.2	363.0
Net Interest Income	902.0	874.8	605.7	548.1	520.6	371.0	322.4
Provision for Loan Losses	84.7	78.8	45.6	29.4	30.5	21.6	16.6
Net Income	247.4	①169.5	134.9	131.6	122.9	88.8	78.3
Aver. Shs. Outstg. (000)	57,417	54,842	36,030	35,245	35,470	45,264	20,090

① Before acctg. change dr$21,956,000.

BALANCE SHEET (IN MILLIONS):

	1993	1992	1991	1990	1989	1988	1987
Cash & Due From Banks	903.5	919.0	884.7	909.9	859.0	639.1	521.5
Net Loans	14,205.5	13,579.2	11,325.7	9,386.6	8,241.0	6,151.3	5,344.2
Total Domestic Deposits	18,243.7	18,035.6	15,020.8	12,541.2	11,366.4	8,675.4	7,554.5
Long-term Debt	254.2	254.1	220.7	137.0	124.7	107.8	119.0
Net Stockholders' Equity	1,523.4	1,335.5	1,073.6	994.2	947.9	722.8	631.7
Total Assets	21,230.5	20,146.8	16,755.0	14,038.6	12,792.7	9,769.4	8,679.9
Year End Shs Outstg (000)	59,521	57,014	36,022	35,844	35,516	49,672	22,022

STATISTICAL RECORD:

	1993	1992	1991	1990	1989	1988	1987
Return on Assets %	1.17	0.84	0.81	0.94	0.96	0.91	0.90
Return on Equity %	16.20	12.70	12.60	13.20	13.00	12.30	12.40
Book Value Per Share	25.59	22.12	25.21	23.11	21.25	10.58	19.68
Average Yield %	3.8	3.9	4.9	5.5	4.5	4.2	3.8
P/E Ratio	10.3-8.7	13.2-10.1	9.6-5.5	7.9-4.7	9.5-6.5	16.3-12.3	9.1-5.7
Price Range	43¼-36½	37⅞-29	31¾-18¼	25⅞-15⅜	28-19⅛	25⅛-19	27-16⅞

Statistics are as originally reported.

OFFICERS:
D.R. Smith, Chmn. & C.E.O.
R.D. Klein, Vice-Chmn.-Corp. Development
R.F. Chormann, Pres. & C.O.O.

PRINCIPAL OFFICE: 211 South Rose Street, Kalamazoo, MI 49007

TELEPHONE NUMBER: (616) 376-9000
FAX: (616) 376-7079
NO. OF EMPLOYEES: 13,330
ANNUAL MEETING: In April
SHAREHOLDERS: 28,400
INSTITUTIONAL HOLDINGS:
No. of Institutions: 122
Shares Held: 13,570,212

REGISTRAR(S):

TRANSFER AGENT(S):

NASDAQ SYMBOL FTEN
Rec. Pr. 41½ (Marginable)

FIRST TENNESSEE NATIONAL CORP.

YIELD 4.0%
P/E RATIO 9.7

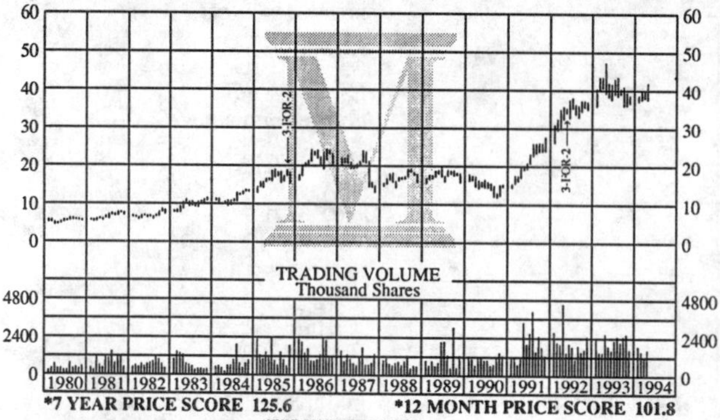

***7 YEAR PRICE SCORE 125.6** ***12 MONTH PRICE SCORE 101.8**

*NYSE COMPOSITE INDEX=100

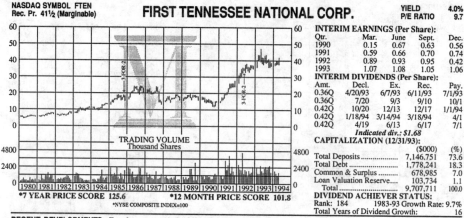

INTERIM EARNINGS (Per Share):

Qtr.	Mar.	June	Sept.	Dec.
1990	0.15	0.67	0.63	0.56
1991	0.59	0.66	0.70	0.74
1992	0.89	0.93	0.95	0.42
1993	1.07	1.08	1.05	1.06

INTERIM DIVIDENDS (Per Share):

Amt.	Decl.	Ex.	Rec.	Pay.
0.36Q	4/20/93	6/7/93	6/11/93	7/1/93
0.36Q	7/20	9/3	9/10	10/1
0.42Q	10/20	12/13	12/17	1/1/94
0.42Q	1/18/94	3/14/94	3/18/94	4/1
0.42Q	4/19	6/13	6/17	7/1

Indicated div.: $1.68

CAPITALIZATION (12/31/93):

	($000)	(%)
Total Deposits	7,146,751	73.6
Total Debt	1,778,241	18.3
Common & Surplus	678,985	7.0
Loan Valuation Reserve	103,734	1.1
Total	9,707,711	100.0

DIVIDEND ACHIEVER STATUS:
Rank: 184 1983-93 Growth Rate: 9.7%
Total Years of Dividend Growth: 16

RECENT DEVELOPMENTS: For the year ended 12/31/93 net income totaled $120.7 million compared with $89.2 million for 1992. Net interest income was $346.6 million versus $322.9 million in the prior year. Noninterest income rose 20% to $270.5 million as mortgage banking income soared to $28.2 million from $10.5 million. Mortgage banking income benefited from the acquisition of Maryland National Mortgage Corp. Income from trust service operations increased to $22.3 million from $20.1 million while both bank card income and deposit services income rose 9% to $26.4 million and $56.2 million respectively. The provision for loan losses was reduced 25% from last year to $34.5 million. Nonperforming loans were also reduced to $25.4 million from $30.0 million a year earlier. The loan portfolio increased 17% to $5.16 billion. Consumer loan growth was up 37% for the year while commercial loans were 15% higher.

BUSINESS

FIRST TENNESSEE NATIONAL CORPORATION is a $9.6 billion bank holding company and ranks among the 65 largest bank holding companies in the nation. With principal offices in Memphis, Tennessee, the Company operates 214 banking locations in twenty Tennessee counties and 4 locations in Mississippi. Through its principal subsidiary, First Tennessee National Association and other banking and bank-related subsidiaries, FTEN provides a broad range of financial services including: general banking for consumers and small businesses, corporations, and financial institutions, mortgage banking services; trust, fiduciary and agency services; check clearing; discount brokerage; venture capital; equipment financing and credit life insurance services; investment and financial advisory services; mutual fund sales and check processing software and systems. It is the largest Tennessee-headquartered bank holding company in terms of assets.

ANNUAL EARNINGS AND DIVIDENDS PER SHARE

	1993	1992	1991	1990	1989	1988	1987
Earnings Per Share	**4.26**	**3.19**	**2.69**	**2.01**	**1.21**	**2.23**	**1.46**
Dividends Per Share	**1.44**	**[1] 1.20**	**1.12**	**1.067**	**0.933**	**0.827**	**0.773**
Dividend Payout %	**33.8**	**37.6**	**41.6**	**53.2**	**76.9**	**37.1**	**53.0**

[1] 3-for-2 stk split, 5/26/92

ANNUAL FINANCIAL DATA

	1993	1992	1991	1990	1989	1988	1987
RECORD OF EARNINGS (IN MILLIONS):							
Total Interest Income	586.5	599.2	579.7	600.2	582.5	500.5	444.1
Total Interest Expense	239.9	276.3	314.8	357.6	357.3	286.2	252.6
Net Interest Income	346.6	322.9	264.8	242.6	225.2	214.3	191.5
Provision for Loan Losses	34.5	43.2	53.6	63.6	63.9	25.4	52.3
Net Income	120.7	89.2	63.8	47.9	28.8	52.3	32.9
Aver. Shs. Outstg. (000)	28,325	27,972	23,669	23,865	23,780	23,516	22,466
BALANCE SHEET (IN MILLIONS):							
Cash & Due From Banks	602.4	496.5	542.8	509.0	558.2	637.1	626.3
US Treas & Other US Govt Agencies	338.4	341.8	1,697.7	1,041.3	980.0	725.2	638.5
State & Municipalities	56.4	88.3	115.4	150.8	197.0	254.3	282.4
Total Net Loans	5,164.3	4,425.6	3,848.5	3,747.9	3,599.8	3,531.8	3,530.3
Total Domestic Deposits	7,146.8	6,916.8	6,040.5	5,343.2	4,949.4	4,656.8	4,477.3
Long-term Debt	448.2	396.8	676.1	327.9	332.9	295.4	317.0
Net Stockholders' Equity	679.0	597.5	437.6	397.8	380.7	372.5	327.1
Total Assets	9,608.8	8,925.8	7,903.7	6,707.7	6,397.5	5,972.0	5,761.8
Year End Shs Outstg (000)	28,326	28,123	23,750	23,565	23,907	23,721	22,592
STATISTICAL RECORD:							
Return on Assets %	1.26	1.00	0.81	0.71	0.45	0.88	0.57
Return on Equity %	17.80	14.90	14.60	12.00	7.60	14.00	10.00
Book Value Per Share	23.97	21.25	18.42	16.88	15.93	15.71	14.48
Average Yield %	3.5	3.7	5.3	7.1	5.3	4.9	4.2
P/E Ratio	11.1-8.4	11.9-8.2	10.3-5.3	9.0-5.9	16.4-12.9	8.7-6.4	16.5-9.0
Price Range	47¼-35¾	38-26¼	27⅝-14⅜	18-11⅞	19⅞-15⅝	19⅜-14⅜	24⅛-13⅛

Statistics are as originally reported.

OFFICERS:
R. Terry, Chmn. & C.E.O.
R. Horn, Pres. & C.O.O.
S.S. Bies, Exec. V.P. & C.F.O.
T.A. Fehrman, V.P. & Treas.

INCORPORATED: TN, 1968

PRINCIPAL OFFICE: 165 Madison Avenue, Memphis, TN 38103

TELEPHONE NUMBER: (901) 523-4444
FAX: (901) 523-4336
NO. OF EMPLOYEES: 5,653 (approx.)
ANNUAL MEETING: In April
SHAREHOLDERS: 7,893
INSTITUTIONAL HOLDINGS:
No. of Institutions: 152
Shares Held: 13,115,697

REGISTRAR(S):

TRANSFER AGENT(S): Bank of Boston, Boston, MA 02102

FIRST UNION CORP.

YIELD 3.6%
P/E RATIO 9.5

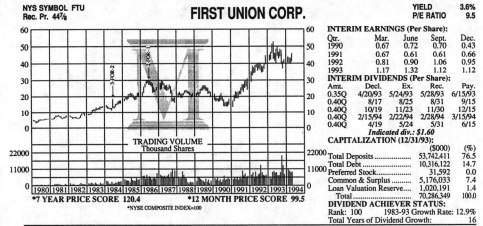

*7 YEAR PRICE SCORE 120.4   *12 MONTH PRICE SCORE 99.5
*NYSE COMPOSITE INDEX=100

TRADING VOLUME
Thousand Shares

INTERIM EARNINGS (Per Share):

Qtr.	Mar.	June	Sept.	Dec.
1990	0.67	0.72	0.70	0.43
1991	0.67	0.61	0.61	0.66
1992	0.81	0.90	1.06	0.95
1993	1.17	1.32	1.12	1.12

INTERIM DIVIDENDS (Per Share):

Amt.	Decl.	Ex.	Rec.	Pay.
0.35Q	4/20/93	5/24/93	5/28/93	6/15/93
0.40Q	8/17	8/25	8/31	9/15
0.40Q	10/19	11/23	11/30	12/15
0.40Q	2/15/94	2/22/94	2/28/94	3/15/94
0.40Q	4/19	5/24	5/31	6/15

Indicated div.: $1.60

CAPITALIZATION (12/31/93):

	($000)	(%)
Total Deposits	53,742,411	76.5
Total Debt	10,316,122	14.7
Preferred Stock	31,592	0.0
Common & Surplus	5,176,033	7.4
Loan Valuation Reserve	1,020,191	1.4
Total	70,286,349	100.0

DIVIDEND ACHIEVER STATUS:
Rank: 100   1983-93 Growth Rate: 12.9%
Total Years of Dividend Growth: 16

RECENT DEVELOPMENTS: FTU announced plans to acquire BancFlorida Financial Corp. in a stock swap worth $168 million. BancFlorida, headquartered in Naples, FL, has 37 offices and $1.5 billion in assets. For the quarter ended 12/31/93, net income totaled $195.3 million. Results benefited from lower credit costs, increased noninterest income and improved credit quality.

PROSPECTS: In an effort to retain depositors seeking higher yields, FTU acquired Lieber and Co., the manager of the $3.3 billion Evergreen mutual fund family. First Union has already begun training its branch bankers to sell mutual funds; the addition of Lieber will bring the total number of funds offered to 28. The proposed acquisition of BancFlorida will establish Company presence in Southwest Florida.

BUSINESS

FIRST UNION COPORATION, one of the nation's largest bank holding companies, provides a wide range of commercial and retail banking and trust services through the third largest branch banking network in the nation. As of 12/31/93, FTU had assets of $70.8 billion and operated 1302 banking offices in seven states and the District of Columbia as well as 222 non-banking offices nationwide. FTU also provides mortgage banking, home equity lending, consumer lending, asset-based financing, insurance, export trading and brokerage services.

LOAN DISTRIBUTION

(12/31/93)	($000)	(%)
Commercial, Finl & Agric	13,233,725	28.0
Real Est-Construc & Other	1,664,694	3.5
Real Estate-Mortgage	5,834,894	12.4
Lease Financing	962,599	2.0
Foreign	304,267	0.7
Retail	25,210,057	53.4
Total	47,210,236	100.0

ANNUAL EARNINGS AND DIVIDENDS PER SHARE

	1993	1992	1991	1990	1989	1988	1987
Earnings Per Share	4.73	3.72	2.55	2.52	2.40	2.76	2.55
Dividends Per Share	1.50	1.28	1.12	1.08	1.00	0.86	0.77
Dividend Payout %	31.7	34.4	43.9	42.9	41.7	31.2	30.2

ANNUAL FINANCIAL DATA

RECORD OF EARNINGS (IN MILLIONS):

	1993	1992	1991	1990	1989	1988	1987
Total Interest Income	4,556.3	3,509.3	4,647.4	3,518.1	2,903.4	2,453.8	2,179.1
Total Interest Expense	1,790.4	1,501.2	2,743.0	2,239.9	1,873.3	1,415.5	1,190.1
Net Interest Income	2,765.9	2,008.2	1,904.4	1,278.2	1,030.0	1,038.3	989.0
Provision for Loan Losses	221.8	249.7	648.3	177.7	80.6	61.1	82.3
Net Income	817.5	515.2	318.7	304.3	256.2	296.9	283.1
Aver. Shs. Outstg. (000)	167,692	130,344	112,114	108,046	106,925	107,748	111,183

BALANCE SHEET (IN MILLIONS):

	1993	1992	1991	1990	1989	1988	1987
Cash & Due From Banks	3,352.0	2,624.5	2,559.1	2,241.4	2,002.9	2,358.8	1,834.1
Loans, Net	45,856.0	32,675.5	31,446.5	25,787.0	21,578.6	18,673.2	15,125.1
Total Domestic Deposits	53,742.4	39,389.5	36,597.7	27,680.1	21,498.3	20,033.3	17,425.3
Long-term Debt	3,061.9	2,521.8	2,063.7	1,190.9	871.5	634.1	654.3
Net Stockholders' Equity	5,207.6	3,831.7	3,112.5	2,565.6	2,076.1	1,923.5	1,794.4
Total Assets	70,787.0	51,332.4	45,972.1	40,771.9	32,115.0	28,942.2	27,629.5
Year End Shs Outstg (000)	170,338	136,052	121,065	109,173	107,164	106,966	110,403

STATISTICAL RECORD:

	1993	1992	1991	1990	1989	1988	1987
Return on Assets %	1.15	1.00	0.69	0.75	0.80	1.03	1.02
Return on Equity %	15.70	13.40	10.20	11.90	12.30	15.40	15.80
Book Value Per Share	30.39	27.93	24.62	23.19	19.37	17.98	16.25
Average Yield %	3.3	3.5	5.0	6.0	4.3	4.0	3.4
P/E Ratio	11.2-7.9	12.1-7.8	12.2-5.3	8.7-5.5	11.3-8.2	8.7-7.0	11.6-6.4
Price Range	53⅛-37¼	44⅞-29⅛	31-13½	22-13¾	27-19⅝	23⅞-19¼	29½-16¼

Statistics are as originally reported.

OFFICERS:
E.E. Crutchfield, Jr., Chmn. & C.E.O.
B.J. Walker, Vice-Chmn.
J.R. Georgius, President

INCORPORATED: NC, Dec., 1967

PRINCIPAL OFFICE: Two First Union Center, Charlotte, NC 28288-0570

TELEPHONE NUMBER: (704) 374-6787
NO. OF EMPLOYEES: 32,861
ANNUAL MEETING: In April
SHAREHOLDERS: 3,117 pfd.; 37,955 com.
INSTITUTIONAL HOLDINGS:
No. of Institutions: 520
Shares Held: 97,316,762

REGISTRAR(S): First Union National Bank of N.C., Charlotte, NC

TRANSFER AGENT(S): First Union National Bank of N.C., Charlotte, NC

NYS SYMBOL FVB
Rec. Pr. 37¼

FIRST VIRGINIA BANKS, INC.

YIELD 3.3%
P/E RATIO 10.4

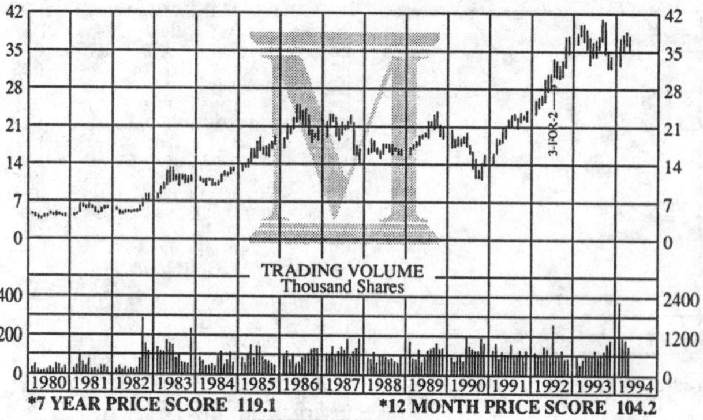

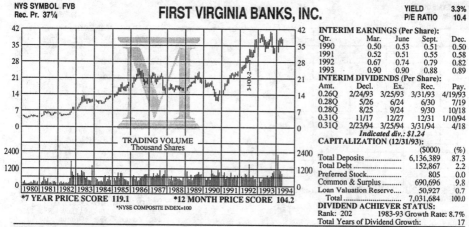

*7 YEAR PRICE SCORE 119.1 *12 MONTH PRICE SCORE 104.2
*NYSE COMPOSITE INDEX=100

INTERIM EARNINGS (Per Share):

Qtr.	Mar.	June	Sept.	Dec.
1990	0.50	0.53	0.51	0.50
1991	0.52	0.51	0.55	0.58
1992	0.67	0.74	0.79	0.82
1993	0.90	0.90	0.88	0.89

INTERIM DIVIDENDS (Per Share):

Amt.	Decl.	Ex.	Rec.	Pay.
0.26Q	2/24/93	3/25/93	3/31/93	4/19/93
0.28Q	5/26	6/24	6/30	7/19
0.28Q	8/25	9/24	9/30	10/18
0.31Q	11/17	12/27	12/31	1/10/94
0.31Q	2/23/94	3/25/94	3/31/94	4/18

Indicated div.: $1.24

CAPITALIZATION (12/31/93):

	($000)	(%)
Total Deposits	6,136,389	87.3
Total Debt	152,867	2.2
Preferred Stock	805	0.0
Common & Surplus	690,696	9.8
Loan Valuation Reserve	50,927	0.7
Total	7,031,684	100.0

DIVIDEND ACHIEVER STATUS:
Rank: 202 1983-93 Growth Rate: 8.7%
Total Years of Dividend Growth: 17

RECENT DEVELOPMENTS: For the quarter ended 12/31/93, net income increased 9% from the corresponding 1992 period to $29.0 million. The provision for loan losses was sharply reduced to $1.4 million from $4.2 million. For the year ended 12/31/93, net income was $116.0 million compared with $97.5 million for 1992. FVB cited the rise in consumer automobile lending (up over 25%) as one of the principal reasons for the record results. Total loans rose 6%.

PROSPECTS: FVB's efforts to increase indirect automobile financing revenue are paying off as automobile lending is up. Results are also benefiting from the refinancing activity in the real estate market. In response to customer demand for non-traditional, higher-yield products, the Company's offerings of annuities, brokerage services, mutual fund packages along with trust services have given a substantial boost to revenue.

BUSINESS

FIRST VIRGINIA BANKS, INC., with assets of $7.0 billion, provides mortgage banking, consumer finance, insurance, and lease financing services through its subsidiaries. In addition to 268 banking offices located in Virginia, FVB has 37 offices in Maryland located in Baltimore and around Washington, D.C., and 20 offices serving eastern Tennessee. The Company also operates a variety of other financial businesses, including: mortgage servicing; underwriting credit life and disability insurance; an insurance agency; and second mortgage loans.

LOAN DISTRIBUTION

(12/31/93)	($000)	(%)
Consumer	3,144,337	71.2
Real Estate	949,188	21.5
Comm'l, Fin & Agric	321,428	7.3
Total	4,414,953	100.0

ANNUAL EARNINGS AND DIVIDENDS PER SHARE

	1993	1992	1991	1990	1989	1988	1987
Earnings Per Share	**3.57**	**3.02**	**2.17**	**2.03**	**2.13**	**1.93**	**1.83**
Dividends Per Share	**1.08**	**[1] 0.963**	**0.893**	**0.84**	**0.787**	**0.733**	**0.68**
Dividend Payout %	**30.3**	**31.9**	**41.2**	**41.3**	**36.9**	**37.9**	**37.1**

[1] 3-for-2 stk split, 7/28/92

ANNUAL FINANCIAL DATA

	1993	1992	1991	1990	1989	1988	1987
RECORD OF EARNINGS (IN MILLIONS):							
Total Interest Income	504.8	525.3	515.8	501.4	471.6	420.4	390.7
Total Interest Expense	165.0	204.8	260.3	264.9	243.1	211.1	188.3
Net Interest Income	339.8	320.4	255.6	236.6	228.5	209.2	202.4
Provision for Loan Losses	6.5	17.4	14.0	13.4	11.0	11.4	11.7
Net Income	116.0	97.5	69.6	65.1	67.4	60.9	56.3
Aver. Shs. Outstg. (000)	32,512	32,252	32,093	32,027	31,583	31,523	30,702
BALANCE SHEET (IN MILLIONS):							
Cash & Nonint-bearing Deps In Banks	326.1	381.4	361.0	291.3	314.1	287.9	264.6
US Govt & Agencies Secur	1,904.7	1,871.3	1,507.1	949.8	762.6	811.1	817.9
State & Municipal Obligs	235.4	253.9	257.9	271.1	238.6	224.1	233.4
Net Loans	4,036.4	3,793.0	3,470.6	3,390.5	3,294.8	3,150.8	2,791.6
Total Domestic Deposits	6,136.4	6,013.7	5,350.0	4,715.9	4,426.7	4,223.1	3,913.8
Long-term Debt	1.0	5.2	11.5	11.8	37.5	38.1	43.7
Net Stockholders' Equity	691.5	607.4	540.1	497.7	454.6	412.2	368.1
Total Assets	7,036.9	6,840.5	6,119.3	5,384.1	5,124.0	4,795.8	4,432.8
Year-end Shs Outstg (000)	32,444	32,185	32,093	32,009	31,563	31,533	30,744
STATISTICAL RECORD:							
Return on Assets %	1.65	1.42	1.14	1.21	1.31	1.27	1.27
Return on Equity %	16.80	16.00	12.90	13.10	14.80	14.80	15.30
Book Value Per Share	21.29	18.85	16.80	15.51	14.37	13.03	11.93
Average Yield %	3.0	3.1	4.7	5.3	4.0	4.3	3.6
P/E Ratio	11.5-8.9	12.5-7.7	11.1-6.5	10.0-5.5	11.2-7.5	9.7-7.8	12.8-7.7
Price Range	41-31¾	37⅞-23⅜	24-14⅛	20⅜-11¼	23¾-15⅞	18⅝-15⅛	23⅜-14⅛

Statistics are as originally reported.

OFFICERS:
R.H. Zalokar, Chmn. & C.E.O.
P.H. Geithner, Jr., Pres. & Chief Admin. Off
R.F. Bowman, V.P., Treas. & C.F.O.
T.P. Jennings, V.P. & Gen. Couns.
INCORPORATED: VA, Oct., 1949
PRINCIPAL OFFICE: One First Virginia Plaza 6400 Arlington Boulevard, Falls Church, VA 22042-2336

TELEPHONE NUMBER: (703) 241-4000
FAX: (703) 241-3090
NO. OF EMPLOYEES: 4,651 (full-time equivalent)
ANNUAL MEETING: In April
SHAREHOLDERS: 18,878
INSTITUTIONAL HOLDINGS:
No. of Institutions: 158
Shares Held: 10,954,153

REGISTRAR(S): Security Trust Company, N.A., Baltimore, MD

TRANSFER AGENT(S): Security Trust Company, N.A., Baltimore, MD

FIRSTAR CORP.

YIELD 3.6%
P/E RATIO 10.9

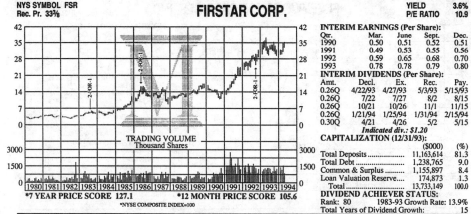

*7 YEAR PRICE SCORE 127.1   *12 MONTH PRICE SCORE 105.6
*NYSE COMPOSITE INDEX=100

INTERIM EARNINGS (Per Share):

Qtr.	Mar.	June	Sept.	Dec.
1990	0.50	0.51	0.52	0.51
1991	0.49	0.53	0.55	0.56
1992	0.59	0.65	0.68	0.70
1993	0.78	0.78	0.79	0.80

INTERIM DIVIDENDS (Per Share):

Amt.	Decl.	Ex.	Rec.	Pay.
0.26Q	4/22/93	4/27/93	5/3/93	5/15/93
0.26Q	7/22	7/27	8/2	8/15
0.26Q	10/21	10/26	11/1	11/15
0.26Q	1/21/94	1/25/94	1/31/94	2/15/94
0.30Q	4/21	4/26	5/2	5/15

Indicated div.: $1.20

CAPITALIZATION (12/31/93):

	($000)	(%)
Total Deposits	11,163,614	81.3
Total Debt	1,238,765	9.0
Common & Surplus	1,155,897	8.4
Loan Valuation Reserve	174,873	1.3
Total	13,733,149	100.0

DIVIDEND ACHIEVER STATUS:
Rank: 80   1983-93 Growth Rate: 13.9%
Total Years of Dividend Growth: 15

RECENT DEVELOPMENTS: For the year ended 12/31/93, net income rose 23% to $204.3 million from $166.0 million for 1992. Results benefited from an 11.2% increase in consumer loans and a 13.5% jump in commercial loans. Non-interest income improved as a result of higher demand for fee-based products, specifically trust and investment management products, which posted a 13.8% gain. The return on average assets improved to 1.59% from 1.36% in the prior year.

PROSPECTS: The emphasis on credit quality standards and the diversification of risks are reflected in the continued improvement of FSR's asset quality. Non-performing assets continue their downward trend. The Company's growth strategy includes acquiring a network of community-based banks in the Upper Midwest. The acquisitions of banks in Wisconsin, Iowa and Illinois netted assets of $655 million and there are other acquisitions pending.

BUSINESS

FIRSTAR CORPORATION, with $13.8 billion in assets, is the largest bank holding company headquartered in Wisconsin. It has 37 banks with 200 offices in Wisconsin, Iowa, Minnesota, Illinois, Florida and Arizona. Bank subsidiaries provide financial services including issuing and servicing credit cards, engaging in correspondent banking and providing trust and investment services. Nonbank subsidiaries provide retail brokerage services, trust and investment services, title insurance, business insurance, and consumer and credit insurance.

LOAN DISTRIBUTION

(12/31/93)	($000)	(%)
Commercial & Industrial	2,470,454	27.5
Real Estate-Construction	209,181	2.3
Real Estate-Mortgage	1,739,608	19.4
Foreign	31,269	0.3
Other Commercial	855,249	9.5
Consumer	3,678,057	41.0
Total	8,983,818	100.0

ANNUAL EARNINGS AND DIVIDENDS PER SHARE

	1993	1992	1991	1990	1989	1988	1987
Earnings Per Share	3.15	2.62	2.13	2.05	1.87	2.44	d1.38
Dividends Per Share	1.00	① 0.80	0.705	0.635	0.545	0.49	0.45
Dividend Payout %	31.8	30.5	33.0	31.0	29.2	20.1	...

① 2-for-1 stk split, 10/1/92

ANNUAL FINANCIAL DATA

RECORD OF EARNINGS (IN MILLIONS):

	1993	1992	1991	1990	1989	1988	1987
Total Interest Revenue	867.0	898.5	981.7	763.1	727.8	619.8	545.8
Total Interest Expense	298.9	359.4	501.1	427.9	406.4	325.9	301.1
Net Interest Income	568.1	539.2	480.6	335.1	321.4	293.9	244.7
Credit Loss Provision	24.6	44.8	50.3	37.2	43.6	33.6	166.9
Net Income	204.3	166.0	134.3	97.6	87.2	① 109.9	d49.1
Aver. Shs. Outstg. (000)	63,747	61,879	60,998	45,578	44,582	42,832	40,824

① Before extra. item cr$22,422,000.

BALANCE SHEET (IN MILLIONS):

	1993	1992	1991	1990	1989	1988	1987
Cash & Due From Banks	1,229.0	1,290.0	1,070.5	966.8	863.6	828.0	781.3
Loans-net	8,808.9	7,943.0	7,394.0	5,681.1	5,253.7	4,903.3	4,519.7
Total Domestic Deposits	11,163.6	10,884.1	10,063.4	7,494.3	6,810.4	6,220.6	5,789.9
Foreign Offices	...	...	...	28.6	24.9	72.9	161.7
Long-term Debt	126.3	157.9	143.8	161.3	165.8	167.4	66.8
Net Stockholders' Equity	1,155.9	1,048.4	916.3	659.5	580.1	506.7	412.5
Total Assets	13,794.0	13,168.9	12,309.5	9,382.9	8,607.9	7,841.9	7,256.7
Year End Shs Outstg (000)	64,919	62,640	61,132	46,472	44,634	42,964	40,902

STATISTICAL RECORD:

	1993	1992	1991	1990	1989	1988	1987
Return on Assets %	1.48	1.26	1.09	1.04	1.01	1.40	...
Return on Equity %	17.70	15.80	14.70	14.80	15.00	21.70	...
Book Value Per Share	17.81	16.73	14.98	14.18	12.98	11.78	10.06
Average Yield %	3.0	2.9	3.8	4.5	3.6	4.1	3.6
P/E Ratio	11.8-9.3	12.2-8.8	11.4-6.0	8.3-5.4	9.4-6.9	5.6-4.3	...
Price Range	37¼-29⅜	31⅞-23⅛	24½-12¾	17-11	17½-12⅞	13½-10⅜	16-8⅞

Statistics are as originally reported.

OFFICERS:
R.L. Fitzsimonds, Chmn. & C.E.O.
J.A. Becker, Pres. & C.O.O.
W.H. Risch, Sr. V.P.-Fin. & Treas.

INCORPORATED: WI, 1929

PRINCIPAL OFFICE: 777 East Wisconsin Ave., Milwaukee, WI 53202

TELEPHONE NUMBER: (414) 765-4321
FAX: (414) 765-4349
NO. OF EMPLOYEES: 6,929 (full-time); part-time, 2,251.
ANNUAL MEETING: In April
SHAREHOLDERS: 9,717
INSTITUTIONAL HOLDINGS:
No. of Institutions: 52
Shares Held: 6,882,588

REGISTRAR(S): First Wisconsin Trust Co., Milwaukee, WI

TRANSFER AGENT(S): First Wisconsin Trust Co., Milwaukee, WI

NYS SYMBOL FLE
Rec. Pr. 20⅜

FLEETWOOD ENTERPRISES, INC.

YIELD 2.5%
P/E RATIO 16.0

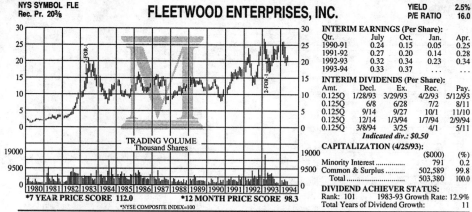

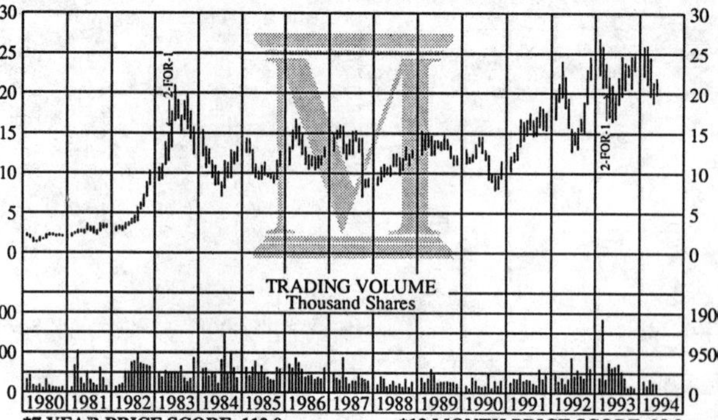
30
25
20
15
10
5
0
2-FOR-1
2-FOR-1
TRADING VOLUME
Thousand Shares
19000
9500
0
1980 1981 1982 1983 1984 1985 1986 1987 1988 1989 1990 1991 1992 1993 1994

*7 YEAR PRICE SCORE 112.0 *12 MONTH PRICE SCORE 98.3

*NYSE COMPOSITE INDEX=100

INTERIM EARNINGS (Per Share):

Qtr.	July	Oct.	Jan.	Apr.
1990-91	0.24	0.15	0.05	0.25
1991-92	0.27	0.20	0.14	0.28
1992-93	0.32	0.34	0.23	0.34
1993-94	0.33	0.37	...	...

INTERIM DIVIDENDS (Per Share):

Amt.	Decl.	Ex.	Rec.	Pay.
0.125Q	1/28/93	3/29/93	4/2/93	5/12/93
0.125Q	6/8	6/28	7/2	8/11
0.125Q	9/14	9/27	10/1	11/10
0.125Q	12/14	1/3/94	1/7/94	2/9/94
0.125Q	3/8/94	3/25	4/1	5/11

Indicated div.: $0.50

CAPITALIZATION (4/25/93):

	($000)	(%)
Minority Interest	791	0.2
Common & Surplus	502,589	99.8
Total	503,380	100.0

DIVIDEND ACHIEVER STATUS:
Rank: 101 1983-93 Growth Rate: 12.9%
Total Years of Dividend Growth: 11

RECENT DEVELOPMENTS: For the quarter ended 1/23/94, net income was $12.1 million versus $10.8 million in the same period last year. Revenues were $548.6 million, up 23.3% from $445.0 in 1993. Improved results were led by a sales increase for the housing group of 32% to $251.7 million. Unit volume grew 23% to 13,475 homes. Recreational vehicle revenues reached a record third-quarter high, up to $278.3 million. Domestic motor home sales rose 24% to $164 million on a 21% increase in unit volume to 3,266 units.

PROSPECTS: FLE will continue to see growth in revenues and earnings driven primarily by a resurgence in demand for manufactured housing. However, the strong profits in the housing group are being dampened by lower profits from the recreational vehicle group which is experiencing margin pressure. An improving economy and a pick-up in consumer confidence should help turn this situation around. Future results will benefit from new product introductions although price competition is expected to be tough.

BUSINESS

FLEETWOOD ENTERPRISES, INC. is a major producer of recreational vehicles and manufactured homes. FLE's motor homes, travel trailers and folding trailers are used for leisure-time activities, including vacation, sightseeing and fishing trips. FLE offers financing to its Recreational Vehicle (RV) dealers and customers through Fleetwood Credit Corp., while a supply group produces components for both Fleetwood and other companies. FLE operates 17 RV and 27 housing factories in 17 states and Canada. Products are marketed through 3,500 independent dealer locations.

BUSINESS LINE ANALYSIS

(4/25/93)	Rev(%)	Inc(%)
Recreational Vehicles	57.2	47.3
Manufactured Housing	39.8	39.9
Supply Operations.....	1.0	2.4
Finance Operations....	2.0	10.4
Total	100.0	100.0

ANNUAL EARNINGS AND DIVIDENDS PER SHARE

	4/25/93	4/26/92	4/28/91	4/29/90	4/30/89	4/24/88	4/30/87
Earnings Per Share	**1.23**	**0.88**	**0.69**	**1.21**	**1.53**	**1.04**	**0.85**
Dividends Per Share	**0.45**	**0.43**	**0.40**	**0.35**	**0.31**	**0.28**	**0.24**
Dividend Payout %	**36.6**	**48.9**	**58.4**	**28.9**	**20.3**	**26.9**	**28.2**

ANNUAL FINANCIAL DATA

	4/25/93	4/26/92	4/28/91	4/29/90	4/30/89	4/24/88	4/30/87
RECORD OF EARNINGS (IN MILLIONS):							
Total Operating Revenues	1,941.9	1,589.3	1,400.9	1,549.4	1,618.5	1,406.0	1,259.3
Costs and Expenses	1,842.8	1,519.6	1,351.5	1,459.5	1,504.4	1,331.0	1,184.8
Depreciation Expense	15.6	15.1	15.1	13.9	12.0	10.3	9.7
Operating Income	83.5	54.7	34.3	76.0	102.1	64.7	64.8
Inc Bef Prov for Income Taxes	91.3	64.1	46.6	86.7	113.7	73.4	73.0
Income Taxes	34.8	23.9	16.2	31.6	43.3	28.1	34.3
Eq In Net Inc Of Unconsol Subs	...	...	...	...	...	2.9	1.0
Minor Int In Net Inc Subs	[1] cr0.1	...	...	...	...	...	...
Net Income	56.6	40.2	30.4	55.0	70.5	48.2	39.7
Aver. Shs. Outstg. (000)	45,961	45,648	44,584	45,510	46,106	46,364	46,730
[1] Equal to cr$65,000.							
BALANCE SHEET (IN MILLIONS):							
Cash and Cash Equivalents	158.5	197.1	170.3	155.4	180.5	136.0	144.5
Receivables, Net	525.7	418.4	317.5	370.3	285.2	113.0	110.5
Inventories	154.7	112.3	94.1	106.3	118.2	96.5	86.9
Gross Property	282.9	247.0	230.6	219.9	190.0	160.5	141.1
Accumulated Depreciation	110.5	96.6	86.9	76.5	67.3	57.5	51.2
Net Stockholders' Equity	502.6	468.0	428.1	424.3	400.6	343.9	316.5
Total Assets	1,061.9	915.0	764.6	817.5	717.9	514.0	482.2
Total Current Assets	838.9	727.8	581.9	632.0	583.9	360.1	353.9
Total Current Liabilities	438.7	345.3	255.3	315.7	252.3	160.4	155.1
Net Working Capital	400.2	382.5	326.7	316.2	331.5	199.7	198.9
Year End Shs Outstg (000)	45,667	45,606	43,786	44,616	45,816	45,804	46,660
STATISTICAL RECORD:							
Operating Profit Margin %	4.3	3.4	2.4	4.9	6.3	4.6	5.1
Book Value Per Share	11.01	10.26	9.78	9.51	8.74	7.51	6.78
Return on Equity %	11.3	8.6	7.1	13.0	17.6	14.0	12.6
Return on Assets %	5.3	4.4	4.0	6.7	9.8	9.4	8.2
Average Yield %	2.4	3.0	3.6	2.7	2.8	2.4	...
P/E Ratio	20.0-10.4	20.9-11.6	21.5-11.6	12.7-9.1	8.7-5.6	15.4-6.7	19.7-12.2
Price Range	24⅝-12¾	18⅜-10¼	14⅝-7⅞	15⅜-11	13⅜-8½	16-7	16¾-10⅜

Statistics are as originally reported.

OFFICERS:
J.C. Crean, Chmn. & C.E.O.
G.F. Kummer, Pres. & C.O.O.
P.M. Bingham, Fin. V.P. & C.F.O.

INCORPORATED: DE, Sep., 1977; reincorp., CA, 1957

PRINCIPAL OFFICE: 3125 Myers Street, Riverside, CA 92503-5527

TELEPHONE NUMBER: (714) 351-3500

NO. OF EMPLOYEES: 4,452 (approx.)

ANNUAL MEETING: In September

SHAREHOLDERS: 940 (approx.)

INSTITUTIONAL HOLDINGS:
No. of Institutions: 163
Shares Held: 14,934,680

REGISTRAR(S):

TRANSFER AGENT(S):

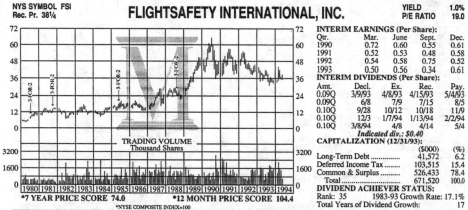

NYS SYMBOL FSI
Rec. Pr. 38¼

FLIGHTSAFETY INTERNATIONAL, INC.

YIELD 1.0%
P/E RATIO 19.0

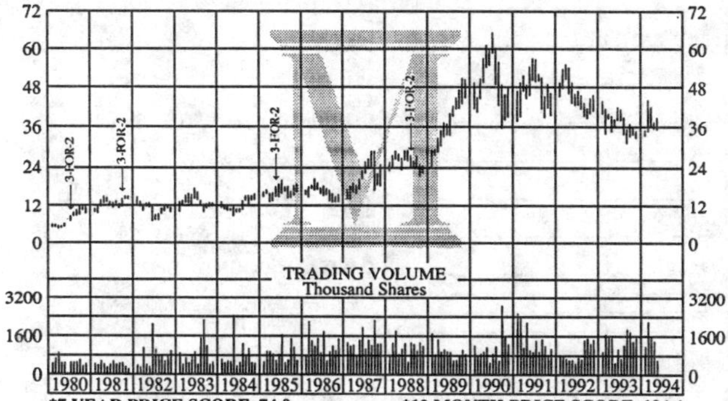

*7 YEAR PRICE SCORE 74.0 *12 MONTH PRICE SCORE 104.4

*NYSE COMPOSITE INDEX=100

INTERIM EARNINGS (Per Share):

Qtr.	Mar.	June	Sept.	Dec.
1990	0.72	0.60	0.55	0.61
1991	0.52	0.53	0.48	0.58
1992	0.54	0.58	0.75	0.52
1993	0.50	0.56	0.34	0.61

INTERIM DIVIDENDS (Per Share):

Amt.	Decl.	Ex.	Rec.	Pay.
0.09Q	3/9/93	4/8/93	4/15/93	5/4/93
0.09Q	6/8	7/9	7/15	8/5
0.10Q	9/28	10/12	10/18	11/9
0.10Q	12/3	1/7/94	1/13/94	2/2/94
0.10Q	3/8/94	4/8	4/14	5/4

Indicated div.: $0.40

CAPITALIZATION (12/31/93):

	($000)	(%)
Long-Term Debt	41,572	6.2
Deferred Income Tax	103,515	15.4
Common & Surplus	526,433	78.4
Total	671,520	100.0

DIVIDEND ACHIEVER STATUS:
Rank: 35 1983-93 Growth Rate: 17.1%
Total Years of Dividend Growth: 17

RECENT DEVELOPMENTS: For the three months ended 12/31/93, net income totaled $19.6 million, a gain of 9.4% from the similar period of 1992. Revenues climbed to $76.8 million from $68.5 million, paced by a 13% hike in training revenues. Net income for 1993 was $66.4 million versus $82.3 million for 1992. Higher depreciation costs and narrower profit margins on government contracts and product sales were responsible for lower results. Total revenue grew 6.7% to $297.1 million because of increased demand for business aviation and airline training.

PROSPECTS: Training revenue is benefiting from strong demand from business aviation and major airline companies. Sales of visual systems is also boosting training revenue. The Company's Flight Academy in Vero Beach, Florida is turning in results below satisfactory levels. Capabilities are being upgraded with the addition of new higher technology simulators but sales of simulators to third parties are down. The Company's government contract services subsidiary is struggling with lower revenues and narrowing operating margins.

BUSINESS

FLIGHTSAFETY INTERNATIONAL, INC., offers high technology training to operators of aircraft, ships, electrical utilities, steam generating and processing plants. Simulators are used that enable trainees to practice and perfect normal and emergency procedures under controlled conditions. FSI's clients include: corporations, commercial airlines, ship operators, military and other government agencies, including 20 aircraft manufacturers. The Company operates 38 learning centers with more than 160 flight simulators in the U.S., Montreal and Toronto, Canada and two locations in France.

BUSINESS LINE ANALYSIS

(12/31/93)	Rev(%)	Inc(%)
Training Revenue......	82.4	85.6
Sales of Manufact Prods......................	17.6	14.4
Total	100.0	100.0

ANNUAL EARNINGS AND DIVIDENDS PER SHARE

	1993	1992	1991	1990	1989	1988	1987
Earnings Per Share	**2.01**	**2.39**	**2.11**	**[1] 2.48**	**1.93**	**1.48**	**1.25**
Dividends Per Share	**0.37**	**0.30**	**0.25**	**0.21**	**0.17**	**[2] 0.147**	**0.133**
Dividend Payout %	**18.4**	**12.6**	**11.8**	**8.5**	**8.8**	**9.9**	**10.7**

[1] Before acctg. chg. [2] 50% stk. div., 8/88.

ANNUAL FINANCIAL DATA

RECORD OF EARNINGS (IN THOUSANDS):							
Total Revenues	297,096	278,435	267,641	283,392	231,297	182,732	135,934
Costs and Expenses	151,575	132,362	131,101	125,409	100,268	79,041	52,572
Depreciation & Amort	44,337	39,951	36,337	30,937	26,548	23,099	14,979
Operating Profit	101,184	106,122	100,203	127,046	104,481	80,592	68,383
Income Bef Income Taxes	109,549	128,015	110,594	119,785	103,691	78,353	67,987
Income Taxes	43,135	45,706	38,152	44,064	38,084	28,339	26,174
Net Income	66,414	82,309	72,442	[1] 75,721	65,607	50,014	41,813
Aver. Shs. Outstg.	33,089	34,410	34,307	34,171	33,991	33,790	33,609
[1] Before acctg. change cr$9,011,000.							
BALANCE SHEET (IN THOUSANDS):							
Cash and Cash Equivalents	181,049	278,676	204,803	158,782	107,601	72,281	78,572
Accounts Receivable, Net	48,963	41,358	46,029	37,994	31,624	31,901	17,450
Inventories	14,605	9,858	...	...	...	...	...
Gross Property	744,408	680,903	614,099	570,051	493,624	427,703	390,834
Accumulated Depreciation	291,030	247,219	209,527	179,795	152,931	132,765	112,140
Long-Term Debt	41,572	44,630	29,653	35,086	33,760	38,778	39,894
Net Stockholders' Equity	526,433	564,409	490,433	423,234	336,560	273,917	228,037
Total Assets	753,934	814,486	690,594	620,998	524,584	451,397	390,989
Total Current Assets	253,203	338,349	259,825	204,327	145,931	123,170	98,127
Total Current Liabilities	75,078	106,846	75,367	77,590	60,287	49,822	41,937
Net Working Capital	178,125	231,503	184,458	126,737	85,644	73,348	56,190
Year End Shares Outstg	32,008	34,457	34,371	34,245	34,078	33,876	33,683
STATISTICAL RECORD:							
Operating Profit Margin %	34.1	38.1	37.4	44.8	45.2	44.1	50.3
Book Value Per Share	16.45	16.38	14.27	12.36	9.88	8.09	6.77
Return on Equity %	12.6	14.6	14.8	17.9	19.5	18.3	18.3
Return on Assets %	8.8	10.1	10.5	12.2	12.5	11.1	10.7
Average Yield %	1.0	0.6	0.5	0.4	0.5	0.6	0.6
P/E Ratio	21.9-15.7	23.1-16.3	27.0-17.9	26.3-14.3	26.4-12.5	19.8-14.2	23.3-11.4
Price Range	44-31⅝	55¼-39	57-37¾	65¼-35½	51-24⅛	29¼-21	28⅞-14⅛

Statistics are as originally reported.

OFFICERS:
A.L. Ueltschi, Chmn. & Pres.
K.W. Motschwiller, V.P. & Treas.
P.P. Mullen, Secretary

INCORPORATED: NY, Mar., 1951

PRINCIPAL OFFICE: Marine Air Terminal/La Guardia Airport, Flushing, NY 11371-1061

TELEPHONE NUMBER: (718) 565-4100
FAX: (718) 565-4134
NO. OF EMPLOYEES: 292
ANNUAL MEETING: In April
SHAREHOLDERS: 8,625 (approx.)
INSTITUTIONAL HOLDINGS:
No. of Institutions: 168
Shares Held: 15,457,470

REGISTRAR(S): Chase Manhattan Bank, N.A., New York, NY 10031

TRANSFER AGENT(S): Chase Manhattan Bank, N.A., New York, NY 10031

NYS SYMBOL FPC
Rec. Pr. 26⅞

FLORIDA PROGRESS CORP.

YIELD 7.4%
P/E RATIO 12.1

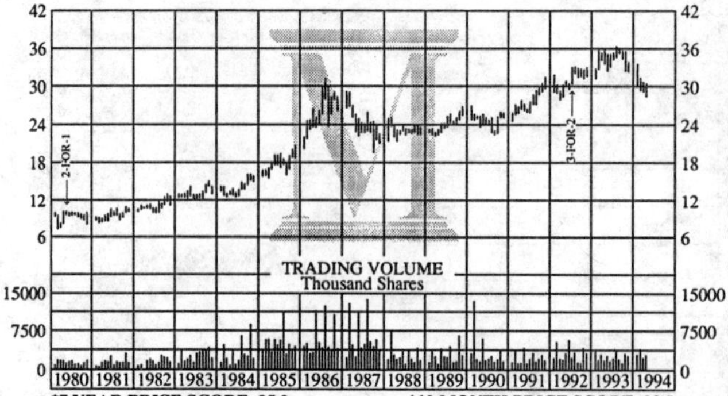

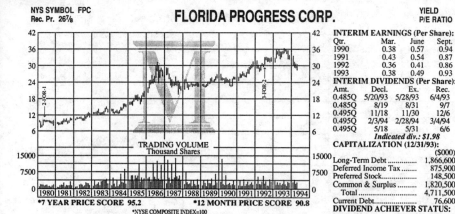

*7 YEAR PRICE SCORE 95.2 *12 MONTH PRICE SCORE 90.8

*NYSE COMPOSITE INDEX=100

INTERIM EARNINGS (Per Share):

Qtr.	Mar.	June	Sept.	Dec.
1990	0.38	0.57	0.94	0.44
1991	0.43	0.54	0.87	0.33
1992	0.36	0.41	0.86	0.41
1993	0.38	0.49	0.93	0.42

INTERIM DIVIDENDS (Per Share):

Amt.	Decl.	Ex.	Rec.	Pay.
0.485Q	5/20/93	5/28/93	6/4/93	6/20/93
0.485Q	8/19	8/31	9/7	9/20
0.495Q	11/18	11/30	12/6	12/20
0.495Q	2/3/94	2/28/94	3/4/94	3/20/94
0.495Q	5/18	5/31	6/6	6/20

Indicated div.: $1.98

CAPITALIZATION (12/31/93):

	($000)	(%)
Long-Term Debt	1,866,600	39.6
Deferred Income Tax	875,900	18.6
Preferred Stock	148,500	3.2
Common & Surplus	1,820,500	38.6
Total	4,711,500	100.0
Current Debt	76,600	

DIVIDEND ACHIEVER STATUS:
Rank: 305 1983-93 Growth Rate: 4.1%
Total Years of Dividend Growth: 41

RECENT DEVELOPMENTS: For the year ended 12/31/93, net income before accounting changes was $195.8 million compared with $175.7 million last year. Revenues were $2.45 billion, up 16.9%. Improved operating results at Florida Power was the primary reason for FPC's improved results. Retail kilowatt-hour sales rose 5.3% due to customer growth and higher customer usage. A voluntary, early retirement program offered to more than 200 employees resulted in a negative earnings impact of $3.4 million.

PROSPECTS: Earnings in 1994 will be negatively affected by approximately $8 million due to a early retirement program announced in December of 1993. Conditions remain depressed in Florida's real estate market. These factors continue to hurt FPC's ability to market and sell its real estate properties. This will adversely affect diversified operations results. However, higher earnings at Electric Fuels Corp., and Mid-Continent Life Insurance Co., should help mitigate lower results from real estate operations.

BUSINESS

FLORIDA PROGRESS CORPORATION is a diversifed utility holding company whose principal subsidiary is Florida Power Corp. and whose diversified operations include coal mining, real estate, and financial services. Florida Power services over 1.2 million customers in 32 counties along the Gulf Coast through the central ridge sector of Florida. The territory comprises about 20,000 square miles with a population of more than 4.4 million.

BUSINESS LINE ANALYSIS

(12/31/93)	Rev(%)	Inc(%)
Utility	79.9	88.5
Diversified	20.1	11.5
Total	100.0	100.0

ANNUAL EARNINGS AND DIVIDENDS PER SHARE

	1993	1992	1991	1990	1989	1988	1987
Earnings Per Share	**2.22**	**2.06**	**[2] 2.16**	**[2] 2.33**	**2.45**	**2.35**	**2.49**
Dividends Per Share	**1.95**	**[1] 1.904**	**1.843**	**1.777**	**1.72**	**1.667**	**1.613**
Dividend Payout %	**87.8**	**92.4**	**85.3**	**76.1**	**70.3**	**70.1**	**64.7**

[1] 3-for-2 stk split,07/30/92 [2] Before disc. oper.

ANNUAL FINANCIAL DATA

	1993	1992	1991	1990	1989	1988	1987
RECORD OF EARNINGS (IN MILLIONS):							
Total Revenues	2,449.0	2,095.3	2,074.7	2,010.8	2,129.4	2,002.0	1,957.6
Depreciation	299.9	268.7	266.3	161.1	195.7	190.4	143.4
Maintenance	136.8	139.7	134.8	126.2	137.6	117.8	112.7
Prov for Fed Inc Taxes	110.4	88.5	91.9	102.4	88.8	63.6	122.2
Income From Operations	442.6	404.8	415.4	434.1	410.2	365.7	443.6
Interest Expense	141.1	134.2	146.1	144.4	131.2	117.3	120.1
Net Income	196.6	175.7	[1] 174.5	[2] 179.8	187.1	179.8	187.8
Aver. Shs. Outstg. (000)	88,300	85,400	80,850	76,950	76,650	76,650	75,450

[1] Before disc. op. dr$2,400,000. [2] Before disc. op. dr$15,000,000.

	1993	1992	1991	1990	1989	1988	1987
BALANCE SHEET (IN MILLIONS):							
Gross Plant	6,066.0	5,645.5	5,199.3	4,924.3	4,690.4	4,452.5	4,311.7
Accumulated Depreciation	2,033.0	1,809.9	1,657.7	1,503.9	1,383.4	1,252.4	1,142.1
Prop, Plant & Equip, Net	4,033.0	3,835.6	3,541.6	3,420.4	3,307.0	3,200.1	3,169.6
Long-term Debt	1,866.6	1,656.4	1,581.1	1,326.2	1,126.7	1,050.0	1,117.1
Net Stockholders' Equity	1,969.0	1,953.6	1,818.7	1,657.8	1,605.8	1,550.4	1,498.2
Total Assets	5,638.8	5,333.0	5,024.9	5,045.9	4,634.0	4,303.5	4,131.9
Year End Shs Outstg (000)	89,260	87,530	82,933	77,551	76,577	76,577	76,577
STATISTICAL RECORD:							
Book Value Per Share	20.40	19.85	19.14	18.37	17.92	17.20	16.52
Op. Inc/Net Pl %	11.0	10.6	11.7	12.7	12.4	11.4	14.0
Dep/Gr. Pl %	4.2	4.0	4.3	3.5	3.9	3.6	3.5
Accum. Dep/Gr. Pl %	35.8	34.5	34.2	32.8	31.6	29.9	28.2
Return on Equity %	10.1	9.4	10.1	11.5	12.4	12.4	13.4
Average Yield %	5.8	6.2	6.6	7.2	7.0	7.2	6.6
P/E Ratio	16.4-14.1	16.1-13.5	14.6-11.3	11.6-9.6	11.0-9.0	10.7-9.1	11.7-7.9
Price Range	36⅜-31¼	33¼-27⅞	31½-24⅜	27-22⅜	26⅞-22⅛	25⅛-21⅜	29¼-19⅝

Statistics are as originally reported.

OFFICERS:
Dr. J.B. Critchfield, Chmn. & C.E.O.
R. Korpan, Pres. & C.O.O.
J.K. Heinicka, Sr. V.P. & C.F.O.

INCORPORATED: FL, Jan., 1982

PRINCIPAL OFFICE: Barnett Tower One Progress Plaza, Saint Petersburg, FL 33701

TELEPHONE NUMBER: (813) 824-6400

NO. OF EMPLOYEES: 7,301

ANNUAL MEETING: In April

SHAREHOLDERS: 44,870

INSTITUTIONAL HOLDINGS:
No. of Institutions: 249
Shares Held: 29,161,777

REGISTRAR(S): Chemical Bank, New York, NY

TRANSFER AGENT(S): Chemical Bank, New York, NY

FLOWERS INDUSTRIES, INC.

YIELD 4.5%
P/E RATIO 50.7

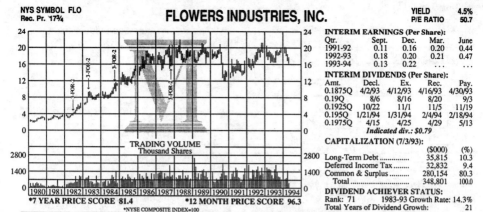

INTERIM EARNINGS (Per Share):

Qtr.	Sept.	Dec.	Mar.	June
1991-92	0.11	0.16	0.20	0.44
1992-93	0.18	0.20	0.21	0.47
1993-94	0.13	0.22	...	...

INTERIM DIVIDENDS (Per Share):

Amt.	Decl.	Ex.	Rec.	Pay.
0.1875Q	4/2/93	4/12/93	4/16/93	4/30/93
0.19Q	8/6	8/16	8/20	9/3
0.1925Q	10/22	11/1	11/5	11/19
0.195Q	1/21/94	1/31/94	2/4/94	2/18/94
0.1975Q	4/15	4/25	4/29	5/13

Indicated div.: $0.79

CAPITALIZATION (7/3/93):

	($000)	(%)
Long-Term Debt	35,815	10.3
Deferred Income Tax	32,832	9.4
Common & Surplus	280,154	80.3
Total	348,801	100.0

TRADING VOLUME
Thousand Shares

*7 YEAR PRICE SCORE 81.4   *12 MONTH PRICE SCORE 96.3
*NYSE COMPOSITE INDEX=100

DIVIDEND ACHIEVER STATUS:
Rank: 71   1983-93 Growth Rate: 14.3%
Total Years of Dividend Growth: 21

RECENT DEVELOPMENTS: For the 12 weeks ended 12/18/93, net income was $8.2 million compared with $7.5 million last year. Sales advanced 6.5% to $234.2 million. Manufacturing costs increased due to increases in the cost of raw materials, wages, and fringe benefits. Volume grew both in units and in poundage; however, difficult pricing and higher ingredient costs constrained profit margins.

PROSPECTS: The Company is nearing the end of a two-year capital expenditure program to improve automation and add capacity to the frozen food business. Therefore, the Company's near-term focus will be on improving margins, which have been constrained recently by higher costs and difficult pricing. Bakery products will continue to face competition from private-label brands at grocery stores.

BUSINESS

FLOWERS INDUSTRIES, INC. operates in the packaged foods industry, serving primarily the grocery, food service, restaurant and fast-food markets. The Company produces a variety of branded food products, including: fresh and frozen breads, buns, specialty rolls, cakes and snacks, frozen specialty vegetables, batter-dipped and breaded vegetables, and fruits and desserts. Products are distributed primarily in the Southeast, Central and Western United States, and are sold chiefly to restaurants, fast-food chains, wholesalers, institutions, supermarkets and vending companies. Major brands include Beebo, Nature's Own, Stilwell, Cobblestone Mill, Blue Bird, and Sunbeam.

QUARTERLY DATA

(07/03/93)($000)	Rev	Inc
1st Quarter	210,684	6,444
2nd Quarter	219,950	7,461
3rd Quarter	211,339	7,692
4th Quarter	320,159	17,564

ANNUAL EARNINGS AND DIVIDENDS PER SHARE

	7/3/93	6/27/92	6/29/91	6/30/90	7/1/89	7/2/88	6/27/87
Earnings Per Share	1.07	0.92	0.71	① 0.98	0.85	① 1.18	0.79
Dividends Per Share	0.755	0.715	0.674	0.627	0.55	② 0.47	0.395
Dividend Payout %	70.6	77.7	94.9	64.0	64.7	39.8	50.0

① Before extraord. item   ② 3-for-2 stk split, 11/87

ANNUAL FINANCIAL DATA

RECORD OF EARNINGS (IN THOUSANDS):

Total Revenues	972,142	888,722	831,199	843,477	789,291	749,871	803,047
Costs and Expenses	874,972	797,856	750,340	749,960	706,750	654,869	721,364
Depreciation & Amort	33,137	33,438	31,639	29,125	25,727	23,393	23,003
Operating Income	64,033	57,428	49,220	64,392	56,814	71,609	58,680
Income Bef Income Taxes	60,032	49,236	39,799	55,939	47,497	62,036	48,213
Fed & State Income Taxes	20,871	17,571	15,754	21,686	17,945	20,560	20,568
Net Income	39,161	31,665	24,045	① 34,253	29,552	② 41,476	27,645
Aver. Shs. Outstg.	36,520	34,350	34,040	34,777	34,848	35,197	35,196

① Before extra. item dr$4,955,000.   ② Before acctg. change cr$1,757,000.

BALANCE SHEET (IN THOUSANDS):

Cash and Cash Equivalents	17,162	14,262	11,042	17,424	25,958	23,643	21,463
Receivables, Net	82,267	75,789	68,961	66,786	70,246	68,079	55,158
Total Inventories	48,856	49,481	41,726	38,112	36,873	36,387	34,130
Gross Property	516,384	482,916	452,405	424,313	413,554	332,238	332,238
Accumulated Depreciation	225,266	205,284	179,344	153,516	146,502	111,722	116,560
Long-Term Debt	35,815	95,397	92,240	91,563	101,825	102,997	107,554
Net Stockholders' Equity	280,154	218,266	206,310	215,766	208,477	198,217	177,747
Total Assets	490,948	462,113	434,905	439,207	448,037	433,575	399,401
Total Current Assets	151,127	142,995	124,421	125,231	136,527	131,241	114,671
Total Current Liabilities	119,604	98,966	86,680	76,970	88,103	79,292	76,886
Net Working Capital	31,523	44,029	37,741	48,261	48,424	51,949	37,785
Year End Shares Outstg	37,699	34,335	33,602	34,425	34,458	34,529	34,895

STATISTICAL RECORD:

Operating Profit Margin %	6.6	6.5	5.9	7.6	7.2	9.5	7.3
Book Value Per Share	7.23	6.20	6.09	6.22	5.82	5.60	4.95
Return on Equity %	14.0	14.5	11.7	15.9	14.2	20.9	15.6
Return on Assets %	8.0	6.9	5.5	7.8	6.6	9.6	6.9
Average Yield %	4.1	4.0	4.5	3.8	2.9	2.4	2.2
P/E Ratio	19.2-15.3	23.1-16.0	24.3-18.0	21.3-12.1	24.9-19.1	18.6-13.9	26.1-18.5
Price Range	20½-16⅜	21¼-14¾	17¼-12¾	20⅞-11⅞	21⅛-16¼	22-16⅜	20⅝-14⅝

Statistics are as originally reported.

OFFICERS:
A.R. McMullian, Chmn. & C.E.O.
R.P. Crozer, Vice-Chmn.
H. Varnedoe, III, Pres. & C.O.O.
C.M. Wood, III, Sr. V.P. & C.F.O.

INCORPORATED: DE, May, 1968; reincorp., GA, Dec., 1987

PRINCIPAL OFFICE: U.S. Highway 19 P.O. Box 1338, Thomasville, GA 31792

TELEPHONE NUMBER: (912) 226-9110

NO. OF EMPLOYEES: 1,142 (approx.)

ANNUAL MEETING: In October

SHAREHOLDERS: 3,320

INSTITUTIONAL HOLDINGS:
No. of Institutions: 114
Shares Held: 13,895,021

REGISTRAR(S):

TRANSFER AGENT(S): Citizens & Southern Trust Co. N.A., Atlanta, GA 30302

FPL GROUP, INC.

YIELD 9.0%
P/E RATIO 12.0

*NYSE COMPOSITE INDEX=100

*7 YEAR PRICE SCORE 89.0   *12 MONTH PRICE SCORE 92.2

INTERIM EARNINGS (Per Share):

Qtr.	Mar.	June	Sept.	Dec.
1991	0.44	0.46	1.15	0.25
1992	0.43	0.60	1.05	0.56
1993	0.50	0.60	0.75	0.45

INTERIM DIVIDENDS (Per Share):

Amt.	Decl.	Ex.	Rec.	Pay.
0.62Q	5/10/93	5/24/93	5/28/93	6/15/93
0.62Q	8/16	8/23	8/27	9/15
0.62Q	11/15	11/19	11/26	12/15
0.62Q	2/14/94	2/18/94	2/25/94	3/15/94
0.42Q	5/9	5/23	5/27	6/15

Indicated div.: $2.48

CAPITALIZATION (12/31/93):

	($000)	(%)
Long-Term Debt	3,748,983	35.7
Cap. Lease Oblig.	271,498	2.6
Deferred Income Tax	1,835,858	17.5
Preferred Stock	548,250	5.2
Common & Surplus	4,100,607	39.0
Total	10,505,196	100.0

DIVIDEND ACHIEVER STATUS:
Rank: 313   1983-93 Growth Rate: 3.5%
Total Years of Dividend Growth: 47

RECENT DEVELOPMENTS: For the year ended 12/31/93, net income was $428.7 million compared with $466.9 million in 1992. Revenues were $5.35 billion, up 3%. Net income includes a non-recurring net charge of $84.8 million related to a major cost reduction program at Florida Power & Light Co. Florida Power & Light Co.'s net income contribution excluding the charge was $510 million, up 8.3%. FPL's results benefited from a 4.6% increase in electric energy sales reflecting the addition of 77,000 new customers and higher usage per customer.

PROSPECTS: The Company has announced that as many as 1,700 positions will be eliminated as part of a cost-reduction program. The cost-reduction program should enable the Company to keep rates stable for customers and remain competitive in the utility industry. FPL will continue to divest selected non-utility businesses. Nonutility operations are beginning to have an impact on FPL's consolidated results. Subsidiary, ESI Energy will likely benefit from stricter pollution requirements.

BUSINESS

FPL GROUP is a holding Company whose principal operating subsidiary is Florida Power & Light Company, which is engaged in the generation, transmission, distribution and sale of electric energy. FPL supplies service throughout most of the east and lower west coasts of Florida. The service territory contains 27,650 square miles with a population of about 6.2 million. FPL represents nearly 98% of FPL Group's revenues. During 1991, the insurance operations of Colonial Penn, previously the largest non-utility operations, were sold.

ANNUAL EARNINGS AND DIVIDENDS PER SHARE

	1993	1992	1991	1990	1989	1988	1987
Earnings Per Share	2.30	2.65	☐2.31	d2.86	3.12	3.42	3.10
Dividends Per Share	2.47	2.43	2.39	2.34	2.26	2.18	2.10
Dividend Payout %	N.M.	91.7	N.M.	...	72.4	63.7	67.7

☐ Before disc. oper.

ANNUAL FINANCIAL DATA

RECORD OF EARNINGS (IN MILLIONS):

	1993	1992	1991	1990	1989	1988	1987
Total Operating Revenues	5,316.3	5,193.3	5,249.4	6,289.0	6,179.8	5,853.5	...
Depreciation & Amort	598.4	554.2	518.1	617.0	758.3	615.9	446.8
Maint Of Utility Plant	...	...	...	408.1	385.5	372.8	...
Income Taxes	250.5	261.4	171.3	53.7	172.6	202.0	242.7
Operating Income	974.0	1,033.8	877.0	6.0	913.9	921.9	681.2
Interest Expense	409.8	410.2	411.1	352.2	341.4	331.3	306.4
Net Income	428.7	466.9	240.6	d391.0	410.4	447.8	402.9
Aver. Shs. Outstg. (000)	186,777	176,458	163,101	136,732	131,639	131,106	130,031

BALANCE SHEET (IN MILLIONS):

	1993	1992	1991	1990	1989	1988	1987
Gross Plant	15,880.7	14,972.4	13,771.3	12,962.4	12,166.5	11,533.7	10,485.1
Accumulated Depreciation	5,591.3	5,106.1	4,690.4	4,506.6	4,087.8	3,593.4	2,912.0
Tot Prop, Plt & Equip, Net	10,289.5	9,866.3	9,080.9	8,455.9	8,078.7	7,940.2	7,573.1
Long-term Debt	4,020.5	4,280.5	3,947.8	3,863.4	3,465.4	3,411.9	3,325.1
Net Stockholders' Equity	4,648.9	4,387.4	3,850.2	3,682.4	3,971.5	3,800.6	3,638.6
Total Assets	13,078.0	12,306.3	11,281.8	12,953.6	12,325.3	11,793.3	9,986.5
Year End Shs Outstg (000)	190,066	182,788	170,756	161,065	133,342	131,122	130,031

STATISTICAL RECORD:

	1993	1992	1991	1990	1989	1988	1987
Book Value Per Share	21.57	20.99	19.64	19.63	24.65	23.61	23.82
Op. Inc/Net Pl %	9.5	10.5	9.7	0.1	11.3	11.6	9.0
Dep/Gr. Pl %	3.8	3.8	3.8	4.9	6.4	5.5	4.3
Accum. Dep/Gr. Pl %	35.8	34.8	34.7	35.6	34.7	32.1	27.8
Return on Equity %	9.4	11.0	6.5	...	10.8	12.4	11.7
Average Yield %	6.5	6.9	7.3	7.5	6.9	7.2	7.1
P/E Ratio	17.8-15.4	14.5-12.1	16.1-12.2	...	11.8-9.3	9.5-8.1	11.3-7.9
Price Range	41-35½	38⅜-32	37¼-28⅛	36½-26⅛	36¾-29	32½-27¾	34⅞-24⅜

Statistics are as originally reported.

OFFICERS:
J.L. Broadhead, Chmn. & C.E.O.
P.J. Evanson, V.P. & C.F.O.
D.L. Samil, Treasurer

INCORPORATED: FL, Sep., 1984
PRINCIPAL OFFICE: 700 Universe Blvd., Juno Beach, FL 33408

TELEPHONE NUMBER: (407) 694-4000
NO. OF EMPLOYEES: 1,976
ANNUAL MEETING: In May
SHAREHOLDERS: 57,345
INSTITUTIONAL HOLDINGS:
No. of Institutions: 451
Shares Held: 71,397,446

REGISTRAR(S): Bank of Boston, Boston, MA 02102

TRANSFER AGENT(S): Bank of Boston, Boston, MA 02102

ASE SYMBOL FRS
Rec. Pr. 14⅝

FRISCH'S RESTAURANTS, INC.

YIELD 1.6%
P/E RATIO 18.5

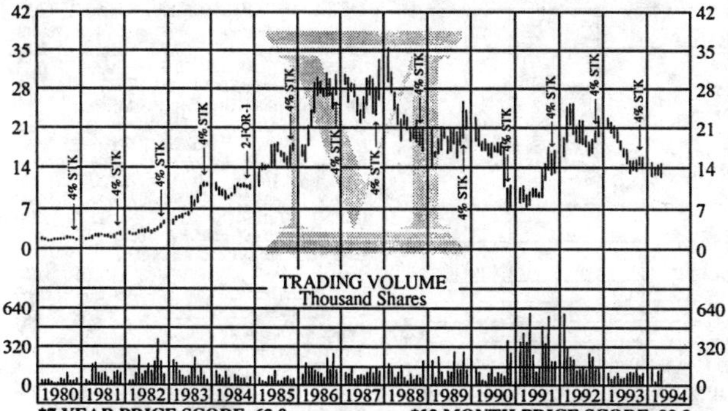

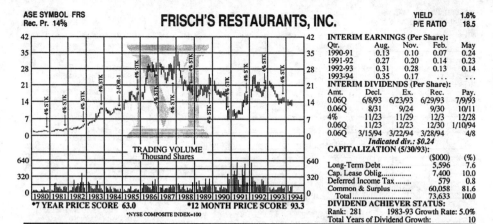

42
35
28
21
14
7
0
4% STK
2-FOR-1
TRADING VOLUME
Thousand Shares
640
320
1980 1981 1982 1983 1984 1985 1986 1987 1988 1989 1990 1991 1992 1993 1994

*7 YEAR PRICE SCORE 63.0 *12 MONTH PRICE SCORE 93.3

*NYSE COMPOSITE INDEX=100

INTERIM EARNINGS (Per Share):

Qtr.	Aug.	Nov.	Feb.	May
1990-91	0.13	0.10	0.07	0.24
1991-92	0.27	0.20	0.14	0.23
1992-93	0.31	0.28	0.13	0.14
1993-94	0.35	0.17	...	...

INTERIM DIVIDENDS (Per Share):

Amt.	Decl.	Ex.	Rec.	Pay.
0.06Q	6/8/93	6/23/93	6/29/93	7/9/93
0.06Q	8/31	9/24	9/30	10/11
4%	11/23	11/29	12/3	12/28
0.06Q	11/23	12/23	12/30	1/10/94
0.06Q	3/15/94	3/22/94	3/28/94	4/8

Indicated div.: $0.24

CAPITALIZATION (5/30/93):

	($000)	(%)
Long-Term Debt	5,596	7.6
Cap. Lease Oblig.	7,400	10.0
Deferred Income Tax	579	0.8
Common & Surplus	60,058	81.6
Total	73,633	100.0

DIVIDEND ACHIEVER STATUS:
Rank: 281 1983-93 Growth Rate: 5.0%
Total Years of Dividend Growth: 10

RECENT DEVELOPMENTS: For the twenty-eight weeks ended 12/12/93, net earnings decreased 11% to $3.3 million compared with $3.7 million last year. Total revenue rose 11% to $88.7 million from $80.0 million a year ago. FRS continued to modernize its existing restaurants, remodeling 23 Big Boys and five other properties, which contributed to lower earnings because much of the asset base replaced had not been fully depreciated. For the twelve weeks, revenue rose 9% to a record $38.3 million, from $35.0 million in 1992. Net earnings decreased 39% to $1.1 million from $1.8 million last year. Higher revenue came from sales of new Big Boy restaurants and from increases in same store sales. New restaurants, which contributed significantly to revenue increases, had a minor impact on earnings due to higher opening expenses. One new Big Boy restaurant was opened.

BUSINESS

FRISCH'S RESTAURANTS, INC. operates and licenses family restaurants with drive-through service under the names Frisch's Big Boy and Kip's Big Boy and operates restaurants under the name Hardee's. These restaurants are located in Ohio, Indiana, Kentucky, Florida, Oklahoma and Texas. Additionally, the Company operates two hotels with restaurants and two specialty restaurants in metropolitan Cincinnati, where it is headquartered. Trademarks which the Company has the right to use include "Frisch's," "Big Boy," "Kip's," "Hardee's," "Quality Hotel," and "Prime'n Wine."

QUARTERLY DATA

(5/30/93)($000)	Rev	Inc
1st Quarter	45,037	1,917
2nd Quarter	35,003	1,789
3rd Quarter	33,219	781
4th Quarter	35,728	905

ANNUAL EARNINGS AND DIVIDENDS PER SHARE

	5/30/93	5/31/92	6/2/91	6/3/90	5/28/89	5/29/88	5/31/87
Earnings Per Share	**0.85**	**0.84**	**0.52**	**0.49**	**0.33**	**0.54**	**0.43**
Dividends Per Share	**0.221**	**[1] 0.213**	**0.205**	**0.197**	**0.189**	**0.167**	**0.161**
Dividend Payout %	**26.1**	**25.4**	**39.7**	**39.6**	**59.2**	**31.5**	**36.9**

Note: 4%stk.div.12/28/93. [1] 4% stk div, 11/22/91

ANNUAL FINANCIAL DATA

	5/30/93	5/31/92	6/2/91	6/3/90	5/28/89	5/29/88	5/31/87
RECORD OF EARNINGS (IN THOUSANDS):							
Total Revenue	148,987	138,330	144,501	146,842	147,117	143,739	139,823
Costs and Expenses	130,844	120,621	130,064	132,189	134,121	129,203	125,863
Depreciation & Amort	8,362	8,176	8,004	7,766	7,625	7,542	7,014
Operating Income	9,781	9,533	6,433	6,887	5,370	6,994	6,946
Earn Bef Income Taxes	8,440	8,143	4,677	5,006	3,319	5,356	5,246
Total Income Taxes	3,048	2,847	1,430	1,909	1,304	1,949	2,422
Net Income	5,392	5,296	3,247	3,097	[1] 2,015	3,407	2,824
Aver. Shs. Outstg.	6,123	6,069	6,041	6,041	6,041	6,203	6,204
[1] Before acctg. change cr$951,064.							
BALANCE SHEET (IN THOUSANDS):							
Cash	547	2,953	1,680	2,611	2,925	8,075	4,781
Receivables, Net	1,512	1,803	1,986	1,660	1,313	1,254	1,278
Total Inventories	3,223	3,186	3,238	3,442	3,069	3,296	2,647
Gross Property	142,100	127,540	127,084	121,068	120,057	113,943	104,356
Accumulated Depreciation	63,588	61,396	57,911	54,161	52,905	50,982	46,475
Long-Term Debt	5,596	1,454	6,094	5,382	4,467	6,293	8,296
Obligs Under Capized Lses	7,400	7,952	8,561	9,165	10,623	10,345	6,513
Net Stockholders' Equity	60,058	56,140	52,038	50,119	48,314	46,490	43,703
Total Assets	97,730	86,625	87,199	84,737	83,591	84,941	79,455
Total Current Assets	7,858	10,306	8,288	9,015	8,631	16,467	14,260
Total Current Liabilities	19,094	16,026	15,555	15,145	14,598	15,093	14,642
Net Working Capital	d11,236	d5,720	d7,266	d6,130	d5,967	1,374	d382
Yr End Com & Com Equiv Shs Outstg	6,123	6,125	5,809	5,587	5,588	6,035	5,985
STATISTICAL RECORD:							
Operating Profit Margin %	6.6	6.9	4.5	4.7	3.6	4.9	5.0
Book Value Per Share	9.53	8.88	8.65	8.64	8.30	7.39	6.98
Return on Equity %	9.0	9.4	6.2	6.2	4.2	7.3	6.5
Return on Assets %	5.5	6.1	3.7	3.7	2.4	4.0	3.6
Average Yield %	1.1	1.7	1.4	1.0	0.7	0.6	0.7
P/E Ratio	30.1-18.9	20.7-8.8	44.0-13.2	52.5-28.4	N.M	62.1-40.6	71.4-34.4
Price Range	26½-16⅝	18¼-7¾	23¾-7⅛	26¾-14½	37-17½	34¾-22¾	32⅛-15½

Statistics are as originally reported.

OFFICERS:
J.C. Maier, Chmn.
C.F. Maier, Pres. & C.E.O.
L.J. Ullman, Sr. V.P. & C.F.O.
D.H. Walker, Treas.

INCORPORATED: OH, Oct., 1947

PRINCIPAL OFFICE: 2800 Gilbert Avenue, Cincinnati, OH 45206

TELEPHONE NUMBER: (513) 961-2660

FAX: (513) 559-5160

NO. OF EMPLOYEES: 447 (approx.)

ANNUAL MEETING: In October

SHAREHOLDERS: 2,208 (approx.)

INSTITUTIONAL HOLDINGS:
No. of Institutions: 26
Shares Held: 2,371,345

REGISTRAR(S):

TRANSFER AGENT(S): Mellon Bank, N.A., Pittsburgh, PA

NASDAQ SYMBOL FULL
Rec. Pr. 34¾ (Marginable)

FULLER (H.B.) CO.

YIELD 1.7%
P/E RATIO 20.9

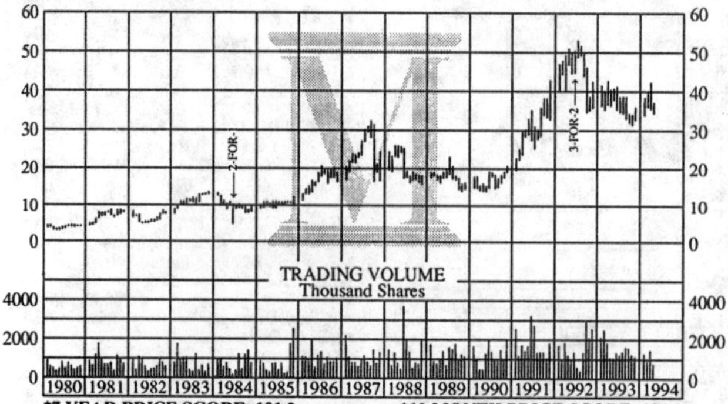

***7 YEAR PRICE SCORE 101.2** ***12 MONTH PRICE SCORE 104.3**

*NYSE COMPOSITE INDEX=100

INTERIM EARNINGS (Per Share):

Qtr.	Feb.	May	Aug.	Nov.
1991-92	0.43	0.73	0.73	0.66
1992-93	0.21	0.63	0.63	0.11
1993-94	0.29	...	...	...

INTERIM DIVIDENDS (Per Share):

Amt.	Decl.	Ex.	Rec.	Pay.
0.14Q	4/15/93	4/20/93	4/26/93	5/10/93
0.14Q	7/15	7/21	7/27	8/10
0.14Q	10/16	10/21	10/27	11/10
0.14Q	12/2	1/20/94	1/26/94	2/10/94
0.145Q	4/21/94	4/26	5/2	5/12

Indicated div.: $0.58

CAPITALIZATION (11/30/93):

	($000)	(%)
Long-Term Debt	60,261	19.0
Deferred Income Tax	2,073	0.7
Minor Int In Consol Sub	5,183	1.6
Series A Preferred Stock	306	0.1
Common & Surplus	249,090	78.6
Total	316,913	100.0

DIVIDEND ACHIEVER STATUS:
Rank: 129 1983-93 Growth Rate: 11.4%
Total Years of Dividend Growth: 26

RECENT DEVELOPMENTS: For the quarter ended 2/28/94, earnings increased to $4.0 million compared with earnings (before accounting changes) of $2.7 million in the same period last year. Net sales rose 6% to $242.5 million from $228.1 million a year ago. Sales by the North American operations were up 15% compared with the same period in 1993. The Adhesives, Sealants and Coatings Division produced a sales increase of 14% over first quarter 1993, primarily due to strong sales by the Structural group. The Specialty Group produced a sales increase of 17% with substantial growth in Industrial Coatings Division sales and significant growth in the sales of Linear Products Division and TEC Incorporated. Sales by the European operations were down 10% while Latin American sales were up 2% compared with the first quarter of 1993. Asia/Pacific sales were up 12% from the same period last year.

BUSINESS

H.B. FULLER COMPANY and its subsidiaries are principally engaged in the manufacture and distribution of industrial adhesives, coatings, sealants, caulks, putties, glazing tapes, mastics and related products in the United States and Canada. The Company also manufactures and distributes cleaners, sanitizers and pesticides for dairy, food and beverage industry through its Monarch Chemicals Division. The Company's subsidiary, Kativo Chemical Industries, S.A. and its subsidiaries manufacture and distribute paints, adhesives, plastics, printing inks and related chemical products in Central America, Panama, Mexico and South America. LW-Fuller GmbH, the Company's subsidiary in West Germany, is a manufacturer of specialty waxes and hot melt compounds for packaging, rubber and electro-technical industries as well as other industrial markets. The Company has 53 plants and technical service centers in 30 U.S. metropolitan areas, and manufacturing and sales operations in 32 countries worldwide.

ANNUAL EARNINGS AND DIVIDENDS PER SHARE

	11/30/93	11/30/92	11/30/91	11/30/90	11/30/89	11/30/88	11/30/87
Earnings Per Share	**1.55**	**2.55**	**2.00**	**1.53**	**1.09**	**1.47**	**1.79**
Dividends Per Share	**0.54**	**[1] 0.464**	**0.41**	**0.397**	**0.383**	**0.35**	**0.27**
Dividend Payout %	**34.8**	**18.2**	**20.5**	**25.9**	**35.1**	**23.9**	**15.1**

[1] 3-for-2 stk split, 6/2/92

ANNUAL FINANCIAL DATA

RECORD OF EARNINGS (IN THOUSANDS):

Total Revenues	975,287	933,720	852,930	792,230	753,374	685,034	597,061
Costs and Expenses	[1] 921,817	830.748	764,362	712,715	683,420	619.782	533.638
Depreciation & Amort	...	31,566	28,722	27,604	23,945	18,822	15,675
Operating Income	53,470	71,406	59,846	51,911	46,009	46,430	47,748
Earn Bef Income Taxes	40,853	60,947	47,428	37,075	30,309	36,047	42,912
Income Taxes	19,191	24,716	19,173	15,234	13,936	14,361	16,320
Net Earns Of Subs Applic to Minor Int	cr39	609	568	696	702	605	780
Net Income	[2] 21,701	35,622	27,687	21,145	15,671	21,081	25,812
Aver. Shs. Outstg.	14,018	13,989	13,854	13,799	14,358	14.387	14,379

[1] Incl. Dep. [2] Before acctg. change dr$11,717,000.

BALANCE SHEET (IN THOUSANDS):

Cash & Cash Equivalents	17,377	29,070	15,197	13,994	10,404	17,953	19,949
Receivables, Net	139,326	133,876	122,860	110,695	103,033	102,898	83,077
Inventories	123.794	116,200	106,901	106,629	93,522	89,522	72,424
Gross Property	419,612	394,821	351,496	330,181	293,902	255,021	205,432
Accumulated Depreciation	187,065	171,668	144,118	127,840	107,271	93,416	78,527
Long-Term Debt	60,261	53,457	71,814	88,240	100,974	98,473	33,015
Net Stockholders' Equity	249,396	255,040	219,050	197,191	186,515	178,871	161,355
Total Assets	564,521	561,204	508,911	489,634	455,172	434,293	329,636
Total Current Assets	295,854	299,234	259,567	242,293	215,770	217,990	181,732
Total Current Liabilities	175,949	168,417	150,788	146,196	120,125	113,919	95,134
Net Working Capital	119,905	130,817	108,779	96,097	95,645	104,071	86,598
Year End Shares Outstg	13,898	13,825	13,707	13,521	14,033	14,214	14,190

STATISTICAL RECORD:

Operating Profit Margin %	5.5	7.6	7.0	6.6	6.1	6.8	8.0
Book Value Per Share	16.44	17.08	14.15	12.35	10.71	9.71	11.18
Return on Equity %	8.7	14.0	12.6	10.7	8.4	11.8	16.0
Return on Assets %	3.8	6.3	5.4	4.3	3.4	4.9	7.8
Average Yield %	1.5	1.1	1.3	2.3	2.1	1.7	1.1
P/E Ratio	27.6-20.2	20.9-13.5	21.4-9.8	13.6-9.0	21.0-12.7	17.6-10.6	18.1-9.1
Price Range	42¾-31¼	53¼-34½	42⅞-19½	20⅞-13¾	22⅞-13⅞	25⅞-15⅝	32⅜-16⅜

Statistics are as originally reported.

OFFICERS:
A.L. Andersen, Chmn. & C.E.O.
W. Kissling, Pres. & C.O.O.
J.W. Bolanos, V.P., C.F.O. & Treas.

INCORPORATED: MN, Dec., 1915

PRINCIPAL OFFICE: 2400 Energy Park Dr., Saint Paul, MN 55108-1591

TELEPHONE NUMBER: (612) 645-3401

FAX: (612) 645-6936

NO. OF EMPLOYEES: 816 (approx.)

ANNUAL MEETING: In April

SHAREHOLDERS: 3,210

INSTITUTIONAL HOLDINGS:
No. of Institutions: 98
Shares Held: 5,282,421

REGISTRAR(S): Norwest Bank Minnesota, N.A., St. Paul, MN

TRANSFER AGENT(S): Norwest Bank Minnesota, N.A., St. Paul, MN

GANNETT CO., INC.

YIELD 2.6%
P/E RATIO 18.9

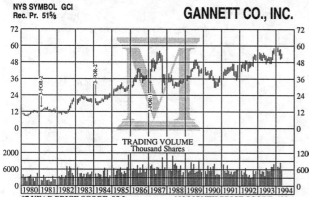

INTERIM EARNINGS (Per Share):

Qtr.	Mar.	June	Sept.	Dec.
1991	0.32	0.61	0.42	0.68
1992	0.39	0.69	0.56	0.79
1993	0.46	0.78	0.61	0.88

INTERIM DIVIDENDS (Per Share):

Amt.	Decl.	Ex.	Rec.	Pay.
0.32Q	2/23/93	3/8/93	3/12/93	4/1/93
0.32Q	5/4	6/7	6/11	7/1
0.33Q	8/24	9/13	9/17	10/1
0.33Q	10/26	12/6	12/10	1/3/94
0.33Q	2/22/94	3/7/94	3/11/94	4/1

Indicated div.: $1.32

CAPITALIZATION (12/26/93):

	($000)	(%)
Long-Term Debt	850,686	28.7
Deferred Income Tax	205,314	6.9
Common & Surplus	1,907,920	64.4
Total	2,963,920	100.0

DIVIDEND ACHIEVER STATUS:
Rank: 219   1983-93 Growth Rate: 8.0%
Total Years of Dividend Growth: 22

TRADING VOLUME
Thousand Shares

*7 YEAR PRICE SCORE 95.2   ***12 MONTH PRICE SCORE 103.1**
*NYSE COMPOSITE INDEX=100

RECENT DEVELOPMENTS: For the year ended 12/26/93, net income increased 15.1% to $397.8 million compared with $345.7 million, before an accounting adjustment, the previous year. Revenues were up 3.3% to $3.64 billion from $3.47 billion. Results included a profit contribution from USA Today and a significant earnings recovery in the broadcast operations. Broadcast revenues increased 7.2% to $397.2 million. Newspaper revenues advanced 5.7% to $2.84 billion.

PROSPECTS: The Company will enhance earnings by increasing efficiency and controlling costs. The advertising business will be challenged by tentative consumer confidence and cautious spending due to higher tax liabilities and downsizing in corporate America. The Honolulu Advertiser will continue to make a significant contribution to advertising revenues. USA Today, the nations largest newspaper, should continue to post growth in profits.

BUSINESS

GANNET COOMPANY, INC. is a diversified news and information company that publishes newspapers, operates broadcasting stations and outdoor advertising businesses, and is engaged in research, marketing, commercial printing, a newswire data services and news programming. The Company has facilities in 41 states, the District of Columbia, Canada, Guam, the U.S., Virgin Islands, London, Paris, Switzerland, Hong Kong and Singapore. Gannett's is the largest U.S. newspaper group, with 82 daily newspapers, including USA Today, 50 non-daily publications and USA Weekend, a weekly newspaper magazine. The Company owns and operates 10 television stations. Gannett Outdoor is the largest outdoor advertising group in North America, with operations in 11 states and Canada.

BUSINESS LINE ANALYSIS

(12/26/93)	Rev(%)	Inc(%)
Newspaper		
Publishing..............	82.8	87.0
Broadcasting.............	10.9	11.1
Outdoor Advert	6.3	1.9
Total	100.0	100.0

ANNUAL EARNINGS AND DIVIDENDS PER SHARE

	12/26/93	12/27/92	12/29/91	12/30/90	12/31/89	12/25/88	12/27/87
Earnings Per Share	2.72	2.40	2.00	2.36	2.47	2.26	1.98
Dividends Per Share	1.29	1.25	1.24	1.20	1.08	1.00	① 0.92
Dividend Payout %	47.4	52.1	62.0	50.8	43.7	44.2	46.5

① 2-for-1 stk split, 1/87

ANNUAL FINANCIAL DATA

RECORD OF EARNINGS (IN MILLIONS):

	12/26/93	12/27/92	12/29/91	12/30/90	12/31/89	12/25/88	12/27/87
Total Operating Revenues	3,641.6	3,469.0	3,382.0	3,441.6	3,518.2	3,314.5	3,079.4
Costs and Expenses	2,717.6	2,653.8	2,623.3	2,568.7	2,571.6	2,449.6	2,257.3
Depreciation & Amort	209.6	197.9	199.8	194.0	190.1	177.2	161.1
Operating Income	714.4	617.3	558.9	678.8	756.5	687.7	661.1
Income Bef Income Taxes	668.5	574.3	502.7	618.0	647.5	607.5	590.4
Income Taxes	270.7	228.6	201.1	241.0	250.0	243.0	271.0
Net Income	397.8	① 345.7	301.6	377.0	397.5	364.5	319.4
Aver. Shs. Outstg. (000)	146,474	144,148	150,783	160,047	161,253	161,622	161,704

① Before acctg. change dr$146,000,000.

BALANCE SHEET (IN MILLIONS):

Cash and Cash Equivalents	75.5	73.3	70.7	56.2	55.6	48.7	26.9
Receivables, Net	584.1	454.3	444.6	469.1	485.9	458.8	439.8
Inventories	53.1	48.1	51.4	66.5	61.1	84.2	64.7
Gross Property	2,794.6	2,693.3	2,593.5	2,473.0	2,344.3	2,178.4	1,993.7
Accumulated Depreciation	1,316.3	1,218.1	1,108.6	1,000.8	916.9	800.9	682.1
Long-Term Debt	850.7	1,080.8	1,335.4	848.6	922.5	1,134.7	1,094.3
Net Stockholders' Equity	1,907.9	1,580.1	1,539.5	2,063.1	1,995.8	1,786.4	1,609.4
Total Assets	3,823.8	3,609.0	3,684.1	3,826.1	3,782.8	3,792.8	3,510.3
Total Current Assets	758.0	631.4	636.1	668.7	671.0	665.0	601.2
Total Current Liabilities	455.1	431.6	443.8	500.2	477.8	500.8	474.8
Net Working Capital	302.8	199.9	192.3	168.5	193.2	164.2	126.4
Year End Shs Outstg (000)	146,967	144,402	143,753	158,991	160,971	161,057	161,967

STATISTICAL RECORD:

Operating Profit Margin %	19.6	17.8	16.5	19.7	21.5	20.7	21.5
Book Value Per Share	2.77	1.49	0.91	3.80	3.23	1.61	1.32
Return on Equity %	20.8	21.9	19.6	18.3	19.9	20.4	19.8
Return on Assets %	10.4	9.6	8.2	9.9	10.5	9.6	9.1
Average Yield %	2.5	2.6	3.0	3.2	2.6	2.9	2.2
P/E Ratio	21.4-17.2	22.5-17.2	23.5-17.6	18.9-12.5	20.2-14.0	17.6-12.9	28.4-13.1
Price Range	58¼-46¾	54-41¼	47-35⅛	44½-29½	49⅞-34½	39⅞-29¼	56¼-26

Statistics are as originally reported.

OFFICERS:
J.J. Curley, Chmn., Pres. & C.E.O.
D.H. McCorkindale, Vice Chmn. & C.F.O.
J.L. Thomas, Sr. V.P. & Treas.
T.L. Chapple, Sec. & Gen. Counsel

INCORPORATED: NY, Dec., 1923; reincorp., DE, May, 1972

PRINCIPAL OFFICE: 1100 Wilson Boulevard, Arlington, VA 22234

TELEPHONE NUMBER: (703) 284-6000

NO. OF EMPLOYEES: 36,500

ANNUAL MEETING: In May

SHAREHOLDERS: 14,000 approx.

INSTITUTIONAL HOLDINGS:
No. of Institutions: 562
Shares Held: 113,580,631

REGISTRAR(S): Norwest Bank Minnesota, N.A., St. Paul, MN

TRANSFER AGENT(S): Norwest Bank Minnesota, N.A., St. Paul, MN

NYS SYMBOL GEC
Rec. Pr. 55½

GEICO CORP.

YIELD 1.8%
P/E RATIO 15.3

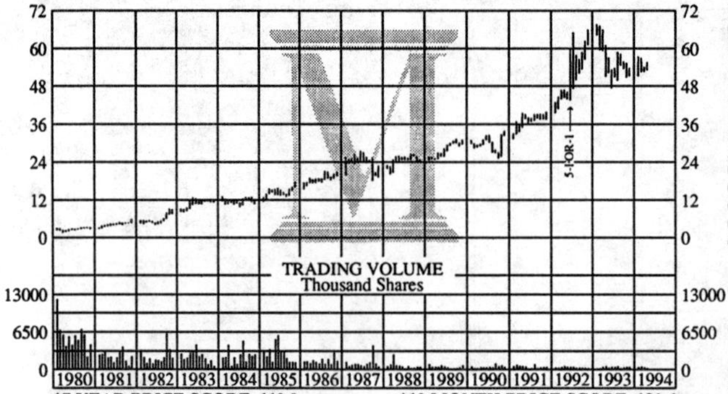

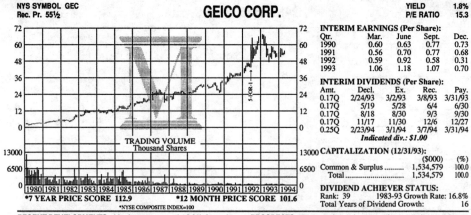

72
60
48
36
24
12
0
5-FOR-1
TRADING VOLUME
Thousand Shares
13000
6500
0
1980 1981 1982 1983 1984 1985 1986 1987 1988 1989 1990 1991 1992 1993 1994

*7 YEAR PRICE SCORE 112.9 *12 MONTH PRICE SCORE 101.6

*NYSE COMPOSITE INDEX=100

INTERIM EARNINGS (Per Share):

Qtr.	Mar.	June	Sept.	Dec.
1990	0.60	0.63	0.77	0.73
1991	0.56	0.70	0.77	0.68
1992	0.59	0.92	0.58	0.31
1993	1.06	1.18	1.07	0.70

INTERIM DIVIDENDS (Per Share):

Amt.	Decl.	Ex.	Rec.	Pay.
0.17Q	2/24/93	3/2/93	3/8/93	3/31/93
0.17Q	5/19	5/28	6/4	6/30
0.17Q	8/18	8/30	9/3	9/30
0.17Q	11/17	11/30	12/6	12/27
0.25Q	2/23/94	3/1/94	3/7/94	3/31/94

Indicated div.: $1.00

CAPITALIZATION (12/31/93):

	($000)	(%)
Common & Surplus	1,534,579	100.0
Total	1,534,579	100.0

DIVIDEND ACHIEVER STATUS:
Rank: 39 1983-93 Growth Rate: 16.8%
Total Years of Dividend Growth: 16

RECENT DEVELOPMENTS: Net income surged 126% from the corresponding 1992 period to $50.2 million for the three months ended 12/31/93. Revenue advanced 11% to $610.6 million. For the year ended 12/31/93, net income before accounting adjustments was $286.4 million versus $172.8 million in 1992. Results were attributed to improved underwriting results. Revenue was $2.64 billion, up from $2.42 billion last year. Property/casualty premiums earned were 10% above the prior year.

PROSPECTS: Property/casualty operations continue to benefit from premium growth and recent but modest rate increases. Growth is expected to continue in polices and premiums. Underwriting results are benefiting from fewer weather-related charges. GEC maintains very tight control over costs and underwriting standards. The acceleration of bodily injury claims frequency appears to be moving at a slower pace. The severity of claims is increasing at a Company predicted level.

BUSINESS

GEICO CORPORATION is primarily an insurance organization whose principal subsidiary, Government Employees Insurance Co., is a property and casualty insurer engaged in writing preferred-risk private passenger automobile insurance and homeowners' insurance. Criterion Life Insurance Company writes structured settlement annuities for its property/casualty affiliates. GEICO Indemnity Co., writes standard-risk private passenger automobile and motorcycle insurance with emphasis on marketing to military personnel. Southern Heritage Insurance Co., writes preferred-risk auto and other personal lines through independent agents.

BUSINESS LINE ANALYSIS

(12/31/93)	Rev(%)	Inc(%)
Property & Casualty..	98.3	97.5
Reinsurance	0.1	1.2
Life & Health	0.5	(0.4)
Finance	0.5	1.3
Other.........................	0.6	0.4
Total	100.0	100.0

ANNUAL EARNINGS AND DIVIDENDS PER SHARE

	1993	1992	1991	1990	1989	1988	1987
Earnings Per Share	4.01	2.39	2.70	2.73	2.75	2.38	1.80
Dividends Per Share	0.68	① 0.60	0.456	0.40	0.36	0.328	0.272
Dividend Payout %	17.0	25.1	16.9	14.7	13.1	13.8	15.1

① 5-for-1 stk split, 6/4/92

ANNUAL FINANCIAL DATA

	1993	1992	1991	1990	1989	1988	1987
RECORD OF EARNINGS (IN MILLIONS):							
Premiums	2,283.5	2,084.5	1,888.4	1,692.5	1,621.4	1,556.9	1,435.5
Total Interest Income	11.5	16.5	20.0	23.6	29.2	31.2	...
Total Revenues	2,638.3	2,420.0	2,147.0	1,934.9	1,939.4	1,756.9	1,580.2
Losses & Loss Adjust Exps	1,821.8	1,725.0	1,450.1	1,328.5	1,265.2	1,260.7	1,132.0
Income Bef Income Taxes	378.6	218.0	241.0	222.8	255.4	145.6	164.5
Income Taxes	92.2	45.2	44.6	14.4	42.4	11.2	14.3
Realized Gains on Invests, Net	...	...	...	...	...	54.6	27.7
Net Income	① 286.4	172.8	196.4	208.4	213.1	189.0	177.9
Aver. Shs. Outstg. (000)	71,417	72,387	72,855	76,397	77,522	79,303	83,365
① Before acctg. change dr$8,814,000.							
BALANCE SHEET (IN MILLIONS):							
Cash	18.4	16.1	24.7	35.7	22.7	20.3	17.4
U.S. Treas Secs & Govt Corps & Agencies	1,014.2	...	...	...	...	...	...
Common Stocks	687.1	724.1	750.4	603.2	691.8	...	...
Total Assets	4,831.4	4,377.6	4,085.8	3,575.9	3,434.4	3,060.6	2,845.8
Benefits and Claims	2,630.8	2,535.4	2,283.1	2,032.6	1,893.1	1,754.6	1,832.3
Net Stockholders' Equity	1,534.6	1,292.5	1,184.3	970.0	898.1	707.4	634.7
Year End Shs Outstg (000)	708,345	71,184	71,047	74,253	75,882	77,200	80,995
STATISTICAL RECORD:							
Return on Equity %	18.7	13.4	16.6	21.5	23.7	26.7	28.0
Book Value Per Share	2.17	18.16	16.67	13.06	11.84	9.16	7.84
Average Yield %	1.2	1.1	1.3	1.4	1.3	1.4	1.2
P/E Ratio	16.9-11.8	27.6-16.6	14.8-11.6	12.4-9.2	11.4-8.9	15.5-11.9	15.2-10.0
Price Range	67⅝-47⅜	66-39⅝	39⅞-31¼	33⅞-25⅛	31¼-24½	26⅜-20¼	27⅜-18

Statistics are as originally reported.

OFFICERS:
E.H. Utley, Vice-Chmn.
W.A. Sparks, Jr., Exec. V.P. & C.F.O.
C.G. Schara, Treasurer

INCORPORATED: DE, Nov., 1978

PRINCIPAL OFFICE: One GEICO Plaza, Washington, DC 20076-0001

TELEPHONE NUMBER: (301) 986-3000

NO. OF EMPLOYEES:

ANNUAL MEETING: In May

SHAREHOLDERS: 3,203

INSTITUTIONAL HOLDINGS:
No. of Institutions: 141
Shares Held: 60,032,180

REGISTRAR(S): Riggs National Bank of Washington, D.C., 808 17th Street, N.W., Suite 240, Washington, DC 20006-3950
Chemical Bank, New York, NY

TRANSFER AGENT(S): Riggs National Bank of Washington, D.C., 808 17th Street, N.W., Suite 240, Washington, DC 20006-3950
Chemical Bank, New York, NY

GENERAL BINDING CORP.

YIELD 2.5%
P/E RATIO 16.6

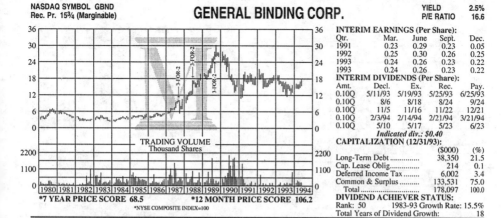

TRADING VOLUME
Thousand Shares

*7 YEAR PRICE SCORE 68.5   *12 MONTH PRICE SCORE 106.2

*NYSE COMPOSITE INDEX=100

INTERIM EARNINGS (Per Share):

Qtr.	Mar.	June	Sept.	Dec.
1991	0.23	0.29	0.23	0.05
1992	0.25	0.30	0.26	0.25
1993	0.24	0.26	0.23	0.22
1993	0.24	0.26	0.23	0.22

INTERIM DIVIDENDS (Per Share):

Amt.	Decl.	Ex.	Rec.	Pay.
0.10Q	5/11/93	5/19/93	5/25/93	6/25/93
0.10Q	8/6	8/18	8/24	9/24
0.10Q	11/5	11/16	11/22	12/21
0.10Q	2/3/94	2/14/94	2/21/94	3/21/94
0.10Q	5/10	5/17	5/23	6/23

Indicated div.: $0.40

CAPITALIZATION (12/31/93):

	($000)	(%)
Long-Term Debt	38,350	21.5
Cap. Lease Oblig.	214	0.1
Deferred Income Tax	6,002	3.4
Common & Surplus	133,531	75.0
Total	178,097	100.0

DIVIDEND ACHIEVER STATUS:
Rank: 50   1983-93 Growth Rate: 15.5%
Total Years of Dividend Growth: 18

RECENT DEVELOPMENTS: For the year ended 12/31/93, net income decreased 8% to $15.0 million, or $0.95 per share, compared with $16.4 million, or $1.04 per share, last year. Sales advanced 2% to $376.1 million from $368.6 million in 1992. For the quarter, earnings decreased 9% to $3.5 million, or $0.22 per share, compared with $3.9 million, or $0.25 per share in the 1992 fourth quarter. Sales increased 8% to $96.8 million versus $89.2 million in the corresponding period last

year. The earnings shortfall in 1993 was primarily due to the economy in GBND's overseas markets. The company adopted SFAS No. 109 on 1/31/93 and thus restated prior periods. The effect of the restatement upon the fourth quarter and full year ended 12/31/92 was an increase in income tax expense of $81,000 and $324,000, respectively, which resulted in a decrease in earnings per share of $0.02 for the year-to-date period.

BUSINESS

GENERAL BINDING CORP. is engaged primarily in the design, manufacture and distribution in the U.S. and abroad binding and laminating systems, paper shredders and other presentation products including machines and related supplies. The Company's product are marketed under the GBC, Velobind, Shredmaster and U.S. RingBinder names. Therm A-Bind Systems binds loose pages, by thermal-activated adhesives, into soft and hard cover books. Plastic Binding punches and binds various printed material into booklets. In addition it markets a variety of customized metal looseleaf binders, indexes, folders and other items. Laminating Systems seals pages between layers of clear plastic film. Sizes up to thirty-six inches wide and one inch thick can be handled. Photo ID Systems laminates identification cards and coded signature cards into ID cards, and badges. Plastic pouches used are manufactured by the Company. U.S. Ring Binder Corp., a domestic subsidiary of GBC, is a manufacturer of metal loose leaf elements for loose leaf binder manufacturers throughout North America. Standard three ring metals are primarily produced at U.S. Ring's plant in Singapore.

ANNUAL EARNINGS AND DIVIDENDS PER SHARE

	1993	1992	1991	1990	1989	1988	1987
Earnings Per Share	0.95	1.06	0.80	0.86	1.26	0.93	③0.59
Dividends Per Share	0.40	0.37	0.33	0.29	①0.273	②0.187	④0.13
Dividend Payout %	42.1	34.9	41.3	33.7	21.7	20.1	22.0

① 50% stk div, 8/31/89   ② 3-for-2 stk split, 6/6/88   ③ Inc before disc. oper.   ④ 50% stk div, 9/24/87

ANNUAL FINANCIAL DATA

RECORD OF EARNINGS (IN THOUSANDS):

	1993	1992	1991	1990	1989	1988	1987
Total Revenues	376,138	368,643	311,199	303,670	283,691	250,626	212,005
Costs and Expenses	336,267	325,893	280,275	272,292	248,436	220,920	187,274
Depreciation & Amort	10,747	10,775	8,239	7,439	6,131	5,878	5,480
Operating Profit	29,124	31,975	24,220	27,535	29,324	24,918	19,251
Income Bef Income Taxes	24,305	27,348	20,255	21,378	28,763	24,457	16,721
Income Taxes	9,311	10,644	7,656	7,723	8,658	9,601	7,122
Net Income	14,994	16,704	12,599	13,655	20,105	14,856	①9,599
Aver. Shs. Outstg.	15,777	15,797	15,819	15,889	15,962	16,077	16,115

① Before disc. op. cr$1,274,000.

BALANCE SHEET (IN THOUSANDS):

	1993	1992	1991	1990	1989	1988	1987
Cash and Cash Equivalents	4,462	10,769	14,466	22,442	6,151	15,921	19,052
Receivables, Net	63,701	57,262	54,980	48,149	51,046	46,530	39,404
Invent, At Lower Of FIFO Cost/mkt	65,636	62,095	58,069	52,940	52,974	45,398	35,902
Gross Property	124,599	114,435	108,894	93,402	84,613	75,057	70,628
Accumulated Depreciation	62,504	56,525	51,563	47,104	40,631	36,811	33,687
Long-Term Debt	38,350	32,530	35,530	2,530	4,667	4,558	5,127
Capital Leases	214	306	44	264	475	624	. . .
Net Stockholders' Equity	133,531	127,588	119,047	113,620	104,534	92,163	83,613
Total Assets	251,109	239,966	237,773	191,728	173,437	161,227	144,369
Total Current Assets	145,351	141,189	138,871	135,412	120,366	117,980	102,769
Total Current Liabilities	64,760	67,148	71,552	63,641	54,021	56,474	49,330
Net Working Capital	80,591	74,041	67,319	71,771	66,345	61,506	53,439
Year End Shares Outstg	15,761	15,782	15,814	15,982	15,927	15,968	16,124

STATISTICAL RECORD:

	1993	1992	1991	1990	1989	1988	1987
Operating Profit Margin %	7.7	8.7	7.3	7.9	10.3	9.5	9.1
Book Value Per Share	6.57	6.16	5.59	7.08	6.47	5.67	5.08
Return on Equity %	11.2	13.1	10.6	12.0	19.2	16.1	11.5
Return on Assets %	6.0	7.0	5.3	7.1	11.6	9.2	6.6
Average Yield %	2.6	2.1	2.1	1.4	1.1	1.3	1.7
P/E Ratio	20.3-12.1	20.3-13.7	25.6-13.4	32.3-15.1	24.0-14.0	21.3-9.9	17.5-8.8
Price Range	19¼-11½	21½-14½	20½-10¾	27¾-13	30¼-17⅝	19⅝-9⅛	10½-5¼

Statistics are as originally reported.

OFFICERS:
W.N. Lane, III, Chmn.
R. Grua, Pres. & C.E.O.
S. Rubin, V.P., Sec. & Gen. Coun.
E.J. McNulty, V.P. & C.F.O.

INCORPORATED: DE, 1947

PRINCIPAL OFFICE: One GBC Plaza, Northbrook, IL 60062-4195

TELEPHONE NUMBER: (708) 272-3700

FAX: (708) 272-1389

NO. OF EMPLOYEES: 1,782

ANNUAL MEETING: In May

SHAREHOLDERS: 411 com.; 1 Cl. B.

INSTITUTIONAL HOLDINGS:
No. of Institutions: 30
Shares Held: 4,108,338

REGISTRAR(S): Harris Trust & Savings Bank, Chicago, IL

TRANSFER AGENT(S): Harris Trust & Savings Bank, Chicago, IL

NYS SYMBOL GE
Rec. Pr. 94⅞

GENERAL ELECTRIC CO.

YIELD 2.7%
P/E RATIO 19.5

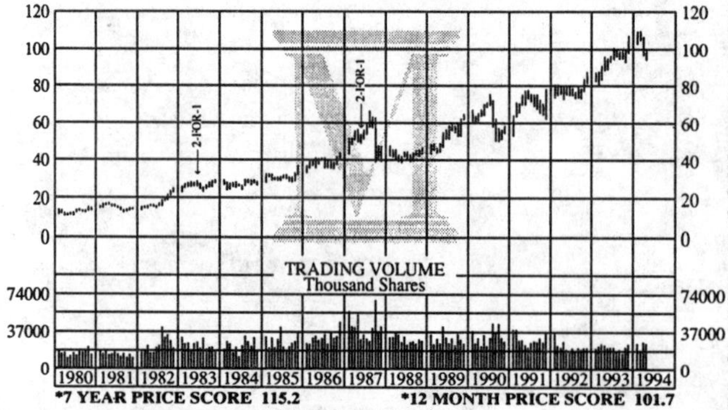

120
100
80
60
40
20
0
2-FOR-1
2-FOR-1
TRADING VOLUME
Thousand Shares
74000
37000
0
1980 1981 1982 1983 1984 1985 1986 1987 1988 1989 1990 1991 1992 1993 1994

*7 YEAR PRICE SCORE 115.2 *12 MONTH PRICE SCORE 101.7

*NYSE COMPOSITE INDEX=100

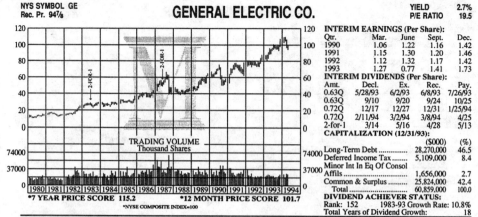

INTERIM EARNINGS (Per Share):

Qtr.	Mar.	June	Sept.	Dec.
1990	1.06	1.22	1.16	1.42
1991	1.15	1.30	1.20	1.46
1992	1.12	1.32	1.17	1.42
1993	1.27	0.77	1.41	1.73

INTERIM DIVIDENDS (Per Share):

Amt.	Decl.	Ex.	Rec.	Pay.
0.63Q	5/28/93	6/2/93	6/8/93	7/26/93
0.63Q	9/10	9/20	9/24	10/25
0.72Q	12/17	12/27	12/31	1/25/94
0.72Q	2/11/94	3/2/94	3/8/94	4/25
2-for-1	3/14	5/16	4/28	5/13

CAPITALIZATION (12/31/93):

	($000)	(%)
Long-Term Debt	28,270,000	46.5
Deferred Income Tax	5,109,000	8.4
Minor Int In Eq Of Consol Affils	1,656,000	2.7
Common & Surplus	25,824,000	42.4
Total	60,859,000	100.0

DIVIDEND ACHIEVER STATUS:
Rank: 152 1983-93 Growth Rate: 10.8%
Total Years of Dividend Growth: 18

RECENT DEVELOPMENTS: For the quarter ended 12/31/93, net income rose 10% to $1.48 billion compared with $1.34 billion for the same period in 1992 in spite of the absence of income from the divested Aerospace unit. Revenues rose 12% to $18.09 billion. Eleven of twelve business units reported improved operating profits for the year while ten led by Plastics, GE Capital Services, NBC and Power Systems achieved double-digit increases. Also, all businesses except for Aircraft Engines improved their operating margins.

PROSPECTS: GE is benefiting in all areas from management's attempts to restructure and streamline the entire organization. Healthy profit growth for the Industrial and Power Systems segments should continue to benefit from productivity improvements as well as from increasing demand for electrical distribution and control products. GE Capital Services will be aided by shrinking overhead costs, while profits from the Broadcasting segment will strengthen alongside higher advertising revenues.

BUSINESS

GENERAL ELECTRIC COMPANY is engaged in the development, manufacture, and marketing of a wide variety of products for the generatíon, transmission, distribution, control and utilization of electricity. The Company's products include lamps; major appliances for the home; industrial automation products and components; motors; electrical distribution and control equipment; locomotives; power generation and delivery products; nuclear reactors, nuclear power support services and fuel assemblies; commerical and military aircraft jet engines; materials, including engineered plastics, sillicones, and cutting materials; and a wide variety of high technology products, including products used in defense and medical diagnostic applications.

BUSINESS LINE ANALYSIS

(12/31/93)	Rev(%)	Inc(%)
Aircraft Engines	10.5	8.3
Appliances	8.9	3.9
Broadcasting	4.9	2.8
Industrial	11.8	8.2
Materials & Power System	18.7	20.6
Tech Products & Services	6.7	7.4
GECS & All Other	38.5	48.8
Total	100.0	100.0

ANNUAL EARNINGS AND DIVIDENDS PER SHARE

	1993	1992	1991	1990	1989	1988	1987
Earnings Per Share	**5.18**	**[1] 5.02**	**[2] 5.10**	**4.85**	**4.36**	**3.75**	**[3] 2.33**
Dividends Per Share	**2.52**	**2.24**	**2.04**	**1.88**	**1.64**	**1.40**	**[4] 1.29**
Dividend Payout %	**48.7**	**44.6**	**40.0**	**38.8**	**37.6**	**37.3**	**55.4**

Note: 2-for-1stk.split,5/13/94. [1] Before disc. oper. [2] Before acctg. chg. [3] Before extraord. item [4] 2-for-1 stk. split, 5/87.

ANNUAL FINANCIAL DATA

RECORD OF EARNINGS (IN MILLIONS):

Total Revenues	60,562.0	57,073.0	60,236.0	58,414.0	54,574.0	50,089.0	40,515.0
Costs and Expenses	28,825.0	27,519.0	31,363.0	31,421.0	29,731.0	28,066.0	34,092.0
Deprec, Depl & Amort	3,261.0	2,818.0	2,832.0	2,508.0	2,256.0	2,266.0	1,544.0
Operating Profit	28,476.0	26,736.0	26,041.0	24,485.0	22,587.0	19,757.0	4,879.0
Earn Bef Income Taxes	6,575.0	6,273.0	6,436.0	6,147.0	5,703.0	4,721.0	3,207.0
Provision for Inc Taxes	2,151.0	1,968.0	2,001.0	1,844.0	1,764.0	1,335.0	1,088.0
Net Income	[1] 4,424.0	[2] 4,305.0	[3] 4,435.0	4,303.0	3,939.0	3,386.0	[4] 2,119.0
Aver. Shs. Outstg. (000)	1,708,000	1,714,000	1,738,000	1,776,000	1,808,000	1,804,000	1,824,000

[1] Before disc. op. cr$753,000,000; and acctg. chg dr$862,000,000. [2] Before disc. op. cr$420,000,000. [3] Before acctg. change dr$1,799,000,000. [4] Before extra. item dr$62,000,000.

BALANCE SHEET (IN MILLIONS):

Cash and Cash Equivalents	3,657.0	65,327.0	47,194.0	44,725.0	33,565.0	26,866.0	2,692.0
Current Receivables	8,195.0	7,150.0	7,324.0	7,806.0	6,976.0	6,780.0	6,782.0
Inventories	3,824.0	4,574.0	6,398.0	6,707.0	6,655.0	6,486.0	6,265.0
Gross Property	38,179.0	35,655.0	34,004.0	30,572.0	[1] 15,646.0	[1] 13,611.0	18,572.0
Accumulated Depreciation	16,951.0	15,268.0	15,028.0	13,941.0	...	...	9,317.0
Long-Term Debt	28,270.0	25,376.0	22,682.0	21,043.0	16,110.0	15,082.0	4,491.0
Net Stockholders' Equity	25,824.0	23,459.0	21,683.0	21,680.0	20,890.0	18,466.0	16,480.0
Total Assets	251,506.0	192,876.0	168,259.0	153,884.0	128,344.0	110,865.0	98,920.0
Total Current Assets	95,240.0	44,464.0	24,720.0	59,238.0	47,196.0	40,132.0	15,739.0
Total Current Liabilities	55,729.0	20,475.0	2,611.0	93,022.0	73,902.0	61,800.0	12,671.0
Net Working Capital	39,511.0	23,989.0	22,109.0	d33,784.0	d26,706.0	d21,668.0	3,068.0
Year End Shs Outstg (000)	1,708,000	1,710,000	1,728,000	1,746,000	1,810,000	1,804,000	1,806,000

[1] Net

STATISTICAL RECORD:

Operating Profit Margin %	47.0	46.8	43.2	41.9	41.4	39.4	12.0
Book Value Per Share	9.05	8.16	6.87	7.07	6.67	5.50	6.67
Return on Equity %	17.1	18.4	20.5	19.8	18.9	18.3	12.9
Return on Assets %	1.8	2.2	2.6	2.8	3.1	3.1	2.1
Average Yield %	2.7	2.8	3.1	3.0	3.0	3.2	2.5
P/E Ratio	41.3-31.2	34.9-29.0	30.6-20.8	31.1-20.6	29.7-20.0	25.5-20.5	57.0-33.3
Price Range	107-80⅞	87½-72¾	78⅛-53	75½-50	64¾-43½	47⅞-38⅜	66⅜-38¾

Statistics are as originally reported.

OFFICERS:
J.F. Welch, Jr., Chmn. & C.E.O.
P. Fresco, Vice-Chmn.
D.D. Dammerman, Sr. V.P.-Fin.

INCORPORATED: NY, Apr., 1892

PRINCIPAL OFFICE: 3135 Easton Turnpike, Fairfield, CT 06431-0001

TELEPHONE NUMBER: (203) 373-2211

NO. OF EMPLOYEES: 222,000 (approx.)

ANNUAL MEETING: In April

SHAREHOLDERS: 457,000 (approx.)

INSTITUTIONAL HOLDINGS:
No. of Institutions: 1,309
Shares Held: 449,398,464

REGISTRAR(S): The Bank of New York, New York, NY

TRANSFER AGENT(S): The Bank of New York, New York, NY

GENERAL HOST CORP.

YIELD 6.8%
P/E RATIO ...

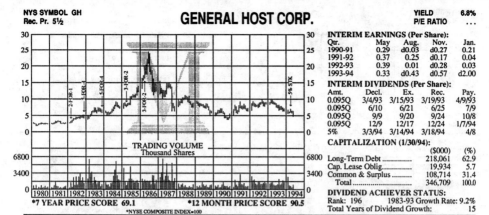

*7 YEAR PRICE SCORE 69.1   *12 MONTH PRICE SCORE 90.5
*NYSE COMPOSITE INDEX=100

INTERIM EARNINGS (Per Share):

Qtr.	May	Aug.	Nov.	Jan.
1990-91	0.29	d0.03	d0.27	0.21
1991-92	0.37	0.25	d0.17	0.04
1992-93	0.39	0.01	d0.28	0.03
1993-94	0.33	d0.43	d0.57	d2.00

INTERIM DIVIDENDS (Per Share):

Amt.	Decl.	Ex.	Rec.	Pay.
0.095Q	3/4/93	3/15/93	3/19/93	4/9/93
0.095Q	6/10	6/21	6/25	7/9
0.095Q	9/9	9/20	9/24	10/8
0.095Q	12/9	12/17	12/24	1/7/94
5%	3/3/94	3/14/94	3/18/94	4/8

CAPITALIZATION (1/30/94):

	($000)	(%)
Long-Term Debt	218,061	62.9
Cap. Lease Oblig.	19,934	5.7
Common & Surplus	108,714	31.4
Total	346,709	100.0

DIVIDEND ACHIEVER STATUS:
Rank: 196   1983-93 Growth Rate: 9.2%
Total Years of Dividend Growth: 15

RECENT DEVELOPMENTS: For the year year ended 1/30/94, GH incurred a loss of $56.1 million, or $2.67 per share, compared with net income of $5.3 million, or $0.15 per share, last year. Results include a reserve of $22.9 million for the closing of 26 unprofitable stores in the South Florida, Orlando, and Nashville markets. Also included is a loss of $17.7 million from the net equity loss and write-down of the Company's investment in Sunbelt Nursery Group, Inc. Sales for the year increased to $568.6 million from $557.8 million for the prior year. The addition of seven new stores in 1993 and the sales from the temporary Christmas boutiques of $11.2 million contributed to the sales increase. Also, the Company implemented an inventory reduction program in January 1994 to dispose of outdated and excess inventory.

BUSINESS

GENERAL HOST CORPORATION operates the nation's largest chain of specialty retail stores devoted to the sale of lawn and garden products, crafts and Christmas merchandise. Frank's Nursery & Crafts stores carry garden products and craft merchandise. As of 1/30/94, GH operated 265 stores in 16 states. Generally located on three-acre sites, new stores built over the past several years are prototyped models containing 20,000 square feet with easily accessible extension of the indoor selling space. The yard features a rotating selection of live goods including annuals, perennials, trees and shrubs. GH also owns a 49.5% interest in Sunbelt Nursery Group, Inc.

REVENUES

(1/30/94)($000)	($000)	(%)
Lawn & Garden	147,837	26.0
Live Nursery	136,464	24.0
Crafts	181,953	32.0
Christmas	90,976	16.0
Pet	11,372	2.0
Total	568,602	100.0

ANNUAL EARNINGS AND DIVIDENDS PER SHARE

	1/30/94	1/31/93	1/26/92	1/27/91	1/28/90	1/29/89	1/31/88
Earnings Per Share	d2.67	0.16	③ d0.48	0.21	④ ⑤ d0.23	⑥ d0.31	
Dividends Per Share	0.375	0.355	0.335	0.315	0.295	0.28	0.24
Dividend Payout %	...	N.M.	69.8	N.M.	N.M.	...	...

Note: 5%stk.div.4/8/94. ① Bef. disc. oper. ② Bef. extraord. loss ③ Bef. extraord. item

ANNUAL FINANCIAL DATA

RECORD OF EARNINGS (IN THOUSANDS):

Total Revenues	569,940	564,788	539,320	519,573	508,946	478,470	402,262
Costs and Expenses	575,985	519,372	486,331	481,013	471,009	447,601	380,812
Depreciation & Amort	24,610	21,179	20,325	19,572	19,011	17,580	14,549
Operating Profit	d7,779	24,237	32,664	18,988	18,926	13,289	6,901
Income Bef Income Taxes	d53,906	1,005	14,601	d2,764	d7,887	d7,724	d14,790
Prov (ben) for Inc Taxes	cr16,389	cr1,848	5,460	cr6,609	cr8,768	cr3,140	cr7,451
Net Eq Loss & Write-down Of Invests	dr17,703	...	...	...	...	...	...
Minority Interest	...	...	438	...	...	...	...
Net Income	① d55,220	② 2,853	③ 8,703	3,845	④ 881	⑤ d4,584	⑥ d7,339
Aver. Shs. Outstg.	20,697	18,989	18,921	19,402	20,330	20,917	24,809

① Before disc. op. dr$840,000. ② Before disc. op. dr$381,000. ③ Before disc. op. cr$5,940,000; and extra. item dr$860,000. ④ Before disc. op. dr$3,424,000. ⑤ Before disc. op. dr$12,200,000; and extra. item dr$4,500,000. ⑥ Before disc. op. cr$64,127,000.

BALANCE SHEET (IN THOUSANDS):

Cash and Cash Equivalents	62,975	77,993	61,691	65,590	110,438	117,605	94,762
Receivables, Net	7,109	9,611	3,734	8,712	16,092	12,037	29,766
Total Inventories	87,807	121,161	83,978	...	...	...	77,007
Gross Property	413,966	386,843	337,904	323,031	307,682	312,155	280,901
Accumulated Depreciation	133,756	113,255	94,748	77,819	61,366	58,183	42,776
Long-Term Debt	218,061	256,327	160,362	167,923	196,436	216,335	146,653
Capital Lease Obligations	19,934	...	...	...	...	...	...
Net Stockholders' Equity	108,714	154,358	155,389	148,632	153,678	171,621	199,015
Total Assets	478,205	531,019	435,304	445,735	505,893	532,656	489,807
Total Current Assets	167,896	222,421	158,522	159,635	217,450	228,290	206,423
Total Current Liabilities	117,371	91,879	96,244	99,395	126,969	117,114	107,967
Net Working Capital	50,525	130,542	62,278	60,240	90,481	111,179	98,456
Year End Shares Outstg	21,017	18,980	18,874	18,780	19,950	20,855	20,935

STATISTICAL RECORD:

Operating Profit Margin %	...	4.3	6.1	3.7	3.7	2.8	1.7
Book Value Per Share	4.31	7.13	7.18	6.69	6.50	7.23	8.59
Return on Equity %	...	1.8	5.6	2.6	0.6	...	...
Return on Assets %	...	0.5	2.0	0.9	0.2	...	...
Average Yield %	4.6	4.3	4.7	5.8	4.0	3.0	2.2
P/E Ratio	...	66.7-43.3	20.1-10.9	35.6-18.8	N.M	...	...
Price Range	10⅛-6¼	10-6½	9¼-5	7⅛-3¾	9½-5¼	11¼-7½	15½-6¼

Statistics are as originally reported.

OFFICERS:
H.J. Ashton, Chmn., Pres. & C.E.O.
J.C. Ficarro, V.P., General Coun. & Sec.
R.M. Lovejoy, V.P. & Treas.
INCORPORATED: NY, Jun., 1911
PRINCIPAL OFFICE: 1 Station Place, Stamford, CT 06902

TELEPHONE NUMBER: (203) 357-9900
NO. OF EMPLOYEES: 7,216
ANNUAL MEETING: In May
SHAREHOLDERS: 3,701 (approx.)
INSTITUTIONAL HOLDINGS:
No. of Institutions: 64
Shares Held: 7,213,971

REGISTRAR(S): Chemical Bank, New York, NY

TRANSFER AGENT(S): Chemical Bank, New York, NY

NYS SYMBOL GIS
Rec. Pr. 50¾

GENERAL MILLS, INC.

YIELD 3.7%
P/E RATIO 15.6

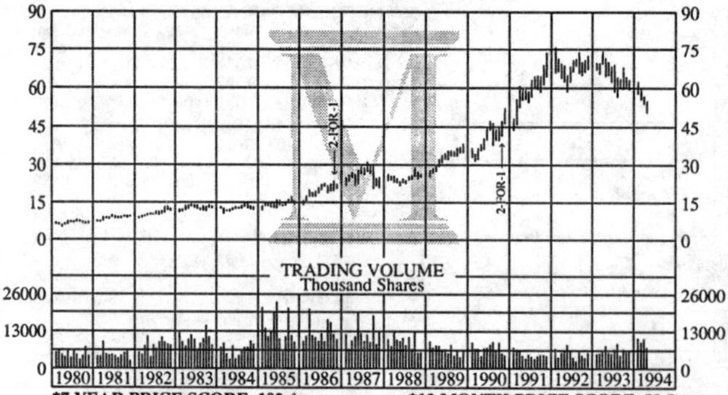

*7 YEAR PRICE SCORE 102.4 *12 MONTH PRICE SCORE 89.8

*NYSE COMPOSITE INDEX=100

INTERIM EARNINGS (Per Share):

Qtr.	Aug.	Nov.	Feb.	May
1991-92	0.86	0.77	0.80	0.62
1992-93	0.97	0.85	0.86	0.42
1993-94	1.04	0.88	0.91	...

INTERIM DIVIDENDS (Per Share):

Amt.	Decl.	Ex.	Rec.	Pay.
0.47Q	6/29/93	7/2/93	7/9/93	8/2/93
0.47Q	9/20	10/4	10/8	11/1
0.47Q	12/13	1/4/94	1/10/94	2/1/94
0.47Q	2/14/94	4/4	4/8	5/2

Indicated div.: $1.88

CAPITALIZATION (5/30/93):

	($000)	(%)
Long-Term Debt	1,268,300	43.1
Deferred Income Tax	457,600	15.5
Common & Surplus	1,218,500	41.4
Total	2,944,400	100.0

DIVIDEND ACHIEVER STATUS:
Rank: 81 1983-93 Growth Rate: 13.9%
Total Years of Dividend Growth: 29

RECENT DEVELOPMENTS: For the quarter ended 11/28/93, net income was $140.7 million compared with $138.1 million last year. Sales advanced 4.1% to $2.18 billion. Consumer Foods sales increased 2% to $1.51 billion. Yoplait and Betty Crocker products reported strong profit growth. Big G cereal unit volume decreased 5% due to competitive promotional efforts. North American sales grew 4% at Red Lobster. The Olive Garden's North American operations posted a 14% gain in sales.

PROSPECTS: In the near term, the rate of sales and earnings growth will likely slow; however, the Company should experience significant contributions from Big G Cereals as a result of competitive promotions and new product introductions. Encouraging results from the Company's China Coast units have prompted the Company to open an additional 16 stores in the Midwest, Southwest, and Southeast.

BUSINESS

GENERAL MILLS, INC., is a leading producer of packaged consumer foods and one of North America's largest operators of full-service restaurants. Consumer Foods include Big G cereals, snack products, dessert mixes, side dishes, flour, baking mix, yogurt and frozen seafoods. Brand names include Cheerios, Wheaties and Total cereals; plus Betty Crocker, Bisquick, Yoplait and Gorton's. International Food operations include General Mills Canada Inc. Restaurant operations consist of Red Lobster seafood restaurants and The Olive Garden Italian restaurants.

ANNUAL EARNINGS AND DIVIDENDS PER SHARE

	5/30/93	5/31/92	5/26/91	5/27/90	5/28/89	5/29/88	5/31/87
Earnings Per Share	**3.10**	**[1] 3.05**	**[1] 2.82**	**[1] 2.28**	**[1] [3] 1.93**	**[1] 1.53**	**1.25**
Dividends Per Share	**1.58**	**1.38**	**[2] 1.19**	**1.02**	**0.87**	**0.72**	**[4] 0.59**
Dividend Payout %	**51.0**	**45.2**	**42.2**	**44.8**	**45.2**	**47.2**	**47.2**

[1] Bef. disc. oper. [2] 2-for-1 stk split, 11/90 [3] Bef. acctg. chg. [4] 2-for-1 stk split, 11/86

ANNUAL FINANCIAL DATA

RECORD OF EARNINGS (IN MILLIONS):							
Total Revenues	8,134.6	7,777.8	7,153.2	6,448.3	5,620.6	5,178.8	5,189.3
Costs and Expenses	6,942.8	6,627.7	6,108.1	5,623.1	4,923.3	4,558.3	[1] 4,590.4
Depreciation & Amort	274.2	247.4	218.4	180.1	152.3	140.0	...
Operating Income	917.6	902.7	826.7	645.1	545.0	480.5	467.2
Earn Bef Income Taxes	844.0	844.5	765.6	612.7	517.5	442.8	433.2
Income Taxes	337.9	338.9	301.4	239.0	202.2	177.4	211.2
Net Income	506.1	[2] 505.6	[3] 464.2	[4] 373.7	[5] 315.3	[6] 265.4	222.0
Aver. Shs. Outstg. (000)	163,100	165,700	164,500	164,400	163,900	174,000	177,400

[1] Incl. Dep. [2] Before disc. op. dr$10,000,000. [3] Before disc. op. cr$8,500,000. [4] Before disc. op. cr$7,700,000. [5] Before disc. op. cr$169,000,000; and acctg. chg dr$70,000,000. [6] Before disc. op. cr$17,700,000.

BALANCE SHEET (IN MILLIONS):							
Cash and Cash Equivalents	100.0	0.5	39.8	70.8	10.6	14.6	179.7
Receivables, Net	429.7	440.6	450.4	370.0	356.1	310.6	236.7
Inventories	439.0	487.2	493.6	394.4	370.1	423.5	388.6
Gross Property	4,239.5	3,909.3	3,337.1	2,883.2	2,404.0	2,139.0	1,939.1
Accumulated Depreciation	1,379.9	1,260.7	1,095.8	948.7	815.9	762.6	689.6
Long-Term Debt	1,268.3	920.5	879.0	688.5	536.3	361.5	285.5
Net Stockholders' Equity	1,218.5	1,370.9	1,113.5	809.7	731.9	648.5	730.4
Total Assets	4,650.8	4,305.0	3,901.8	3,289.5	2,888.1	2,671.9	2,280.4
Total Current Assets	1,076.9	1,034.6	1,082.3	910.1	841.3	985.9	865.9
Total Current Liabilities	1,558.8	1,371.7	1,272.4	1,173.2	1,038.4	1,191.4	923.0
Net Working Capital	d481.9	d337.1	d190.1	d263.1	d197.1	d205.5	d57.1
Year End Shs Outstg (000)	160,500	165,500	165,100	163,200	161,200	167,310	176,464

STATISTICAL RECORD:							
Operating Profit Margin %	11.3	11.6	11.6	10.0	9.7	9.3	9.0
Book Value Per Share	7.59	7.79	6.26	4.57	4.19	3.44	3.82
Return on Equity %	41.5	36.9	41.7	46.2	43.1	40.9	30.4
Return on Assets %	10.9	11.7	11.9	11.4	10.9	9.9	9.7
Average Yield %	2.3	2.4	2.9	3.2	3.4	2.8	3.1
P/E Ratio	24.5-19.0	24.1-14.3	18.4-11.1	17.0-11.1	15.1-11.3	20.3-13.3	19.5-11.6
Price Range	75⅞-58¾	73⅝-43½	52-31⅜	38½-25¼	29-21⅝	31⅛-20⅜	23¾-14⅛

Statistics are as originally reported.

OFFICERS:
H.B. Atwater, Jr., Chmn. & C.E.O.
M.H. Willes, Vice-Chmn.
J.R. Lee, Vice-Chmn.
S.W. Sanger, President

INCORPORATED: DE, Jun., 1928

PRINCIPAL OFFICE: One General Mills Blvd., Minneapolis, MN 55426

TELEPHONE NUMBER: (612) 540-2311

NO. OF EMPLOYEES: 8,743 (approx.)

ANNUAL MEETING: In September

SHAREHOLDERS: 13,892

INSTITUTIONAL HOLDINGS:
No. of Institutions: 663
Shares Held: 107,951,619

REGISTRAR(S): Harris Trust & Savings Bank, Chicago, IL

TRANSFER AGENT(S): Harris Trust & Savings Bank, Chicago, IL

NYS SYMBOL GRN
Rec. Pr. 122¼

GENERAL RE CORP.

YIELD 1.6%
P/E RATIO 15.2

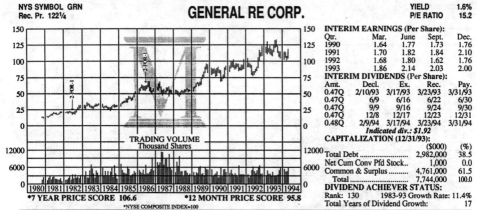

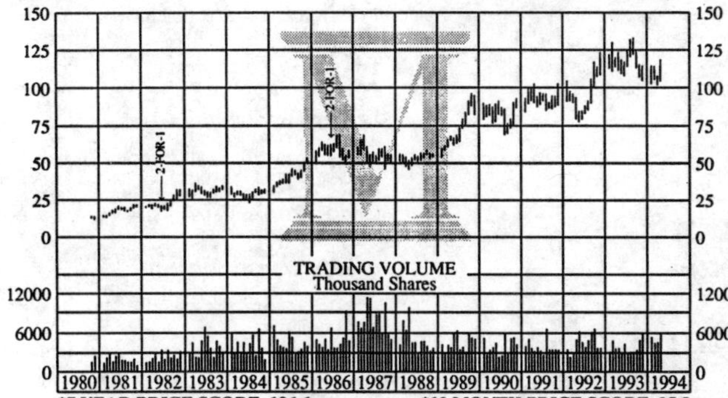
150
125
100
75
50
25
0
2-FOR-1
2-FOR-1
TRADING VOLUME
Thousand Shares
12000
6000
0
1980 1981 1982 1983 1984 1985 1986 1987 1988 1989 1990 1991 1992 1993 1994

*7 YEAR PRICE SCORE 106.6 *12 MONTH PRICE SCORE 95.8

*NYSE COMPOSITE INDEX=100

INTERIM EARNINGS (Per Share):

Qtr.	Mar.	June	Sept.	Dec.
1990	1.64	1.77	1.73	1.76
1991	1.70	1.82	1.84	2.10
1992	1.68	1.80	1.62	1.76
1993	1.86	2.14	2.03	2.00

INTERIM DIVIDENDS (Per Share):

Amt.	Decl.	Ex.	Rec.	Pay.
0.47Q	2/10/93	3/17/93	3/23/93	3/31/93
0.47Q	6/9	6/16	6/22	6/30
0.47Q	9/9	9/16	9/24	9/30
0.47Q	12/8	12/17	12/23	12/31
0.48Q	2/9/94	3/17/94	3/23/94	3/31/94

Indicated div.: $1.92

CAPITALIZATION (12/31/93):

	($000)	(%)
Total Debt	2,982,000	38.5
Net Cum Conv Pfd Stock..	1,000	0.0
Common & Surplus	4,761,000	61.5
Total	7,744,000	100.0

DIVIDEND ACHIEVER STATUS:
Rank: 130 1983-93 Growth Rate: 11.4%
Total Years of Dividend Growth: 17

RECENT DEVELOPMENTS: For the three months ended 12/31/93, net income was $171.1 million, up 13% from the comparable period of 1992. Premiums written advanced to $625.1 million from $582.7 million. Income before accounting adjustments, for the twelve months ended 12/31/93, was $696.8 million versus $596.4 million for 1992. Underwriting operations posted a loss of $36.5 million, much narrower than the $207.4 million loss recorded a year ago. The international reinsurance business benefited from stronger demand and better pricing.

PROSPECTS: General Re Asset Management, providing investment services to reinsurance clients, is now operational and has acquired accounts. General Re Financial Products continues to experience solid growth and more profits are expected. The Company will gradually expand into Southeast Asia and Latin America and offices in France and Madrid will be opened sometime this year. Premium growth is exceeding expectations and trends in Europe are well above anticipated levels but underwriting results for international operations are not meeting expected levels.

BUSINESS

THE GENERAL RE CORPORATION is a holding company. Through its insurance subsidiaries, the Company provides reinsurance insurance and related services throughout the United States and in more than 30 countries. The principal subsidiary is General Reinsurance Corp., which is the largest professional property/casualty reinsurer domiciled in the United States.

REVENUES

(12/31/93)	($000)	(%)
Premiums Earned	2,446,000	68.7
Net Investment Income	755,000	21.2
Other Income	200,000	5.6
Realized Gains on Invests	159,000	4.5
Total	3,560,000	100.0

ANNUAL EARNINGS AND DIVIDENDS PER SHARE

	1993	1992	1991	1990	1989	1988	1987
Earnings Per Share	**8.11**	**[1] 6.84**	**7.46**	**6.89**	**6.52**	**5.44**	**4.79**
Dividends Per Share	**1.88**	**1.80**	**1.68**	**1.52**	**1.36**	**1.20**	**1.00**
Dividend Payout %	**23.2**	**26.3**	**22.5**	**22.1**	**20.9**	**22.1**	**20.9**

[1] Before acctg. chg.

ANNUAL FINANCIAL DATA

RECORD OF EARNINGS (IN MILLIONS):

	1993	1992	1991	1990	1989	1988	1987
Premiums Earned	2,446.0	2,319.0	2,241.0	2,102.0	1,908.0	2,044.0	2,774.0
Net Investment Income	755.0	755.0	752.0	706.0	673.0	570.0	563.0
Total Revenues	3,560.0	3,387.0	3,207.0	2,993.0	2,774.0	...	...
Claims & Claim Expenses	1,723.0	1,829.0	1,618.0	1,446.0	1,326.0	1,444.0	2,042.0
Income Bef Income Taxes	885.0	721.0	793.0	738.0	736.0	...	...
Income Tax Expense	188.0	125.0	136.0	124.0	138.0	63.0	74.0
Net Income	[1] 697.0	[2] 596.0	657.0	614.0	599.0	[3] 513.0	511.0
Aver. Shs. Outstg. (000)	85,000	86,000	87,000	88,000	91,000	95,000	101,000

[1] Before acctg. change cr$14,000,000. [2] Before acctg. change cr$61,000,000. [3] Before disc. op. dr$33,000,000.

BALANCE SHEET (IN MILLIONS):

	1993	1992	1991	1990	1989	1988	1987
Cash	615.0	157.0	84.0	59.0	27.0	22.0	34.0
Fixed Maturs-amortized Cost	1,925.0	2,322.0	8,078.0	7,644.0	6,888.0	6,185.0	6,297.0
Equity Securities, At Mkt	2,726.0	2,157.0	1,827.0	1,286.0	1,342.0	1,037.0	943.0
Accrued Invest Income	240.0	204.0	210.0	200.0	193.0	162.0	163.0
Benefits and Claims	9,292.0	7,619.0	7,149.0	6,720.0	6,354.0	6,033.0	6,121.0
Net Stockholders' Equity	4,762.0	4,228.0	3,912.0	3,270.0	3,084.0	2,695.0	2,563.0
Year End Shs Outstg (000)	84,000	85,000	87,000	87,000	90,000	93,000	98,000

STATISTICAL RECORD:

	1993	1992	1991	1990	1989	1988	1987
Return on Equity %	14.6	14.1	16.8	18.8	19.4	19.0	19.9
Book Value Per Share	56.68	49.73	44.95	37.59	34.27	28.98	26.15
Average Yield %	1.6	1.8	1.8	1.9	1.8	2.3	1.7
P/E Ratio	16.4-12.9	18.1-11.3	13.8-11.2	13.5-10.0	14.8-8.3	10.9-8.4	14.4-9.6
Price Range	133⅜-104	123½-77	102¾-83	93¼-69	96¼-54⅜	59⅜-45½	68⅞-46

Statistics are as originally reported.

OFFICERS:
R.E. Ferguson, Chmn., Pres. & C.E.O.
J.C. Etling, Vice-Chmn.
J.P. Brandon, V.P. & C.F.O.
E.F. Rondepierre, V.P. & Gen. Couns.

PRINCIPAL OFFICE: Financial Centre 695 East Main St. P.O. Box 10351, Stamford, CT 06904-2351

TELEPHONE NUMBER: (203) 328-5000

NO. OF EMPLOYEES:

ANNUAL MEETING: In May

SHAREHOLDERS: 4,213

INSTITUTIONAL HOLDINGS:
No. of Institutions: 616
Shares Held: 72,479,670

REGISTRAR(S): American Stock Transfer & Trust Co., 40 Wall Street, New York, NY 10005

TRANSFER AGENT(S): American Stock Transfer & Trust Co., 40 Wall Street, New York, NY 10005

ASE SYMBOL GFS A
Rec. Pr. 21

GIANT FOOD INC.

YIELD 3.4%
P/E RATIO 13.7

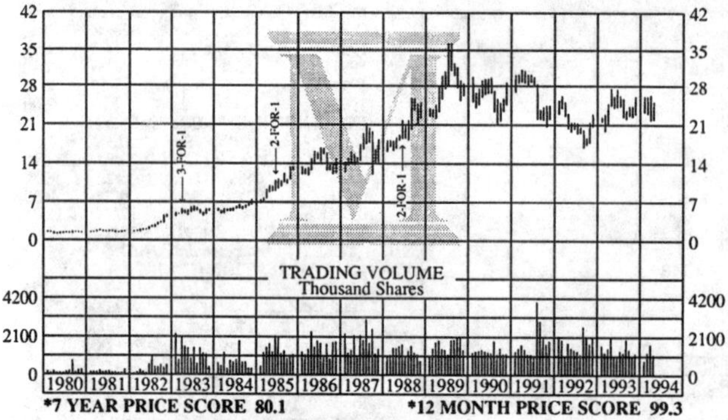

***7 YEAR PRICE SCORE 80.1** ***12 MONTH PRICE SCORE 99.3**

*NYSE COMPOSITE INDEX=100

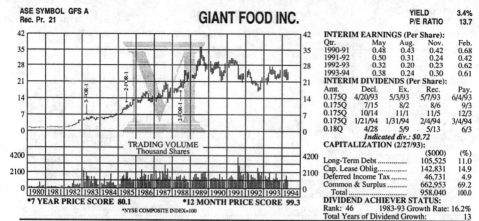

INTERIM EARNINGS (Per Share):

Qtr.	May	Aug.	Nov.	Feb.
1990-91	0.48	0.43	0.42	0.68
1991-92	0.50	0.31	0.24	0.42
1992-93	0.32	0.20	0.23	0.62
1993-94	0.38	0.24	0.30	0.61

INTERIM DIVIDENDS (Per Share):

Amt.	Decl.	Ex.	Rec.	Pay.
0.175Q	4/20/93	5/3/93	5/7/93	6/4/93
0.175Q	7/15	8/2	8/6	9/3
0.175Q	10/14	11/1	11/5	12/3
0.175Q	1/21/94	1/31/94	2/4/94	3/4/94
0.18Q	4/28	5/9	5/13	6/3

Indicated div.: $0.72

CAPITALIZATION (2/27/93):

	($000)	(%)
Long-Term Debt	105,525	11.0
Cap. Lease Oblig.	142,831	14.9
Deferred Income Tax	46,731	4.9
Common & Surplus	662,953	69.2
Total	958,040	100.0

DIVIDEND ACHIEVER STATUS:
Rank: 46 1983-93 Growth Rate: 16.2%
Total Years of Dividend Growth: 13

RECENT DEVELOPMENTS: For the year ended 2/26/94, earnings before an accounting change increased to $91.3 million, or $1.53 per share, compared with earnings of $81.5 million, or $1.37 per share, for the previous year. Sales rose 2.7% to $3.57 billion from $3.47 billion last year. For the quarter, the series of winter storms that hit GFS's region helped contribute to a sales increase of 4.2%. For stores in operation both years, the increase was 2.1%. Earnings for the quarter amounted to $36.3 million, or $0.61 per share, compared with $36.7 million, or $0.62 per share, a year ago. The Company opened four food-drug stores during fiscal 1994 and closed two smaller stores, resulting in a net increase of store space of 209,000 square feet. On 4/20/94, GFS opened its first Delaware store. The Company plans to open four food-drug stores during the 1995 fiscal year.

BUSINESS

GIANT FOOD INC. operates a chain of 157 supermarkets selling retail, food and general merchandise in the Delaware, Washington, Maryland and Virginia vicinities. Giant supermarkets are all self-service and offer a full line of nationally advertised groceries, meat, produce, dairy products, seafood, tobacco, flowers and household items. The Company also sells groceries, frozen foods, bakery products and dairy products under its own private label. Unbranded items such as meat and produce are marketed in the Company's supermarkets. Giant operates three freestanding drug stores.

QUARTERLY DATA

(2/27/93)($000)	Rev	Inc
1st Quarter	803,020	19,102
2nd Quarter	778,586	11,959
3rd Quarter	778,547	13,758
4th Quarter	1,112,428	36,687

ANNUAL EARNINGS AND DIVIDENDS PER SHARE

	2/27/93	2/29/92	2/23/91	2/24/90	2/25/89	2/27/88	2/28/87
Earnings Per Share	**1.37**	**1.47**	**2.01**	**1.80**	**1.63**	**1.26**	**0.78**
Dividends Per Share	**0.675**	**0.645**	**0.575**	**0.50**	**0.40**	**[1] 0.323**	**0.288**
Dividend Payout %	**49.3**	**43.9**	**28.6**	**27.8**	**24.5**	**26.2**	**37.1**

[1] 3-for-1 stk. split, 3/83 & 2-for-1 stk. split, 6/88 & 6/85.

ANNUAL FINANCIAL DATA

RECORD OF EARNINGS (IN MILLIONS):							
Total Revenues	3,472.6	3,489.8	3,349.5	3,248.9	2,987.2	2,721.3	2,528.5
Costs and Expenses	3,224.9	3,238.4	3,063.8	2,991.0	2,759.8	2,528.9	[1] 2,426.0
Depreciation & Amort	94.9	92.0	82.4	71.1	57.0	49.7	...
Operating Income	152.8	159.4	203.4	186.8	170.3	142.7	102.5
Income Bef Income Taxes	132.3	142.1	192.1	179.2	159.1	131.7	93.3
Provision for Inc Taxes	50.8	54.9	73.2	70.8	61.1	56.2	46.8
Net Income	81.5	87.2	118.9	108.4	98.0	75.6	46.5
Aver. Shs. Outstg. (000)	59,648	59,447	59,257	60,095	60,166	60,126	60,026
[1] Incl. Dep.							
BALANCE SHEET (IN MILLIONS):							
Cash and Cash Equivalents	185.2	151.4	168.3	181.9	178.7	147.6	105.6
Receivables	32.7	28.1	26.7	26.1	28.0	26.0	22.1
Total Inventories	223.9	207.3	211.4	206.6	191.0	183.3	156.7
Gross Property	1,329.9	1,281.4	1,126.2	982.7	856.3	763.8	670.3
Accumulated Depreciation	531.2	462.4	395.5	343.0	298.1	261.9	225.0
Long-Term Debt	105.5	113.4	98.4	100.4	101.7	108.0	81.6
Obligs Under Cap Lses	142.8	142.9	147.0	141.2	131.7	126.8	118.8
Net Stockholders' Equity	663.0	621.0	555.7	493.1	427.7	355.6	299.9
Total Assets	1,296.6	1,251.3	1,175.0	1,080.8	982.5	885.0	759.4
Total Current Assets	461.6	404.6	421.7	421.8	404.5	364.8	291.1
Total Current Liabilities	307.1	296.2	296.0	275.4	258.1	239.6	212.6
Net Working Capital	154.5	108.4	125.7	146.4	146.4	125.2	78.5
Year End Shs Outstg (000)	59,690	59,620	58,979	59,757	60,163	60,152	60,090
STATISTICAL RECORD:							
Operating Profit Margin %	4.4	4.6	6.1	5.7	5.7	5.2	4.1
Book Value Per Share	11.11	10.42	9.42	8.25	7.11	5.91	4.99
Return on Equity %	12.3	14.0	21.4	22.0	22.9	21.3	15.5
Return on Assets %	6.3	7.0	10.1	10.0	10.0	8.5	6.1
Average Yield %	3.1	2.5	2.3	1.7	1.9	2.0	2.0
P/E Ratio	19.2-12.3	21.3-14.0	14.9-10.5	20.1-12.3	15.9-9.8	16.8-9.5	21.5-15.2
Price Range	26¼-16⅞	31¼-20⅝	29⅞-21⅛	36¼-22⅛	25⅞-16	21⅛-12	16¾-11⅞

Statistics are as originally reported.

OFFICERS:
I. Cohen, Chmn. & C.E.O.
P.L. Manos, Pres.
D.B. Sykes, Sr. V.P.-Fin., Sec. & Treas.

INCORPORATED: DE, 1935

PRINCIPAL OFFICE: 6300 Sheriff Road, Landover, MD 20785

TELEPHONE NUMBER: (301) 341-4100

NO. OF EMPLOYEES: 3,223

ANNUAL MEETING: In September

SHAREHOLDERS: 26,220 cl. A non-voting com; 1, cl. AC com.; 1, Cl. AL com.

INSTITUTIONAL HOLDINGS:
No. of Institutions: 201
Shares Held: 19,817,207

REGISTRAR(S): American Stock Transfer Co., 40 Wall St., 46th Floor, New York, NY 10005

TRANSFER AGENT(S): American Stock Transfer Co., 40 Wall St., 46th Floor, New York, NY 10005

GILLETTE CO., (THE)

YIELD	1.6%
P/E RATIO	33.6

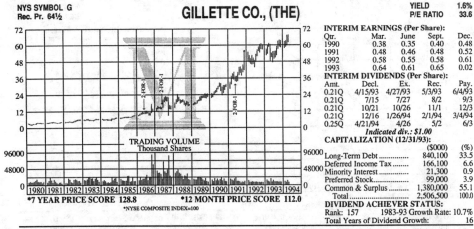

INTERIM EARNINGS (Per Share):

Qtr.	Mar.	June	Sept.	Dec.
1990	0.38	0.35	0.40	0.48
1991	0.48	0.46	0.48	0.52
1992	0.58	0.55	0.58	0.61
1993	0.64	0.61	0.65	0.02

INTERIM DIVIDENDS (Per Share):

Amt.	Decl.	Ex.	Rec.	Pay.
0.21Q	4/15/93	4/27/93	5/3/93	6/4/93
0.21Q	7/15	7/27	8/2	9/3
0.21Q	10/21	10/26	11/1	12/3
0.21Q	12/16	1/26/94	2/1/94	3/4/94
0.25Q	4/21/94	4/26	5/2	6/3

Indicated div.: $1.00

CAPITALIZATION (12/31/93):

	($000)	(%)
Long-Term Debt	840,100	33.5
Deferred Income Tax	166,100	6.6
Minority Interest	21,300	0.9
Preferred Stock	99,000	3.9
Common & Surplus	1,380,000	55.1
Total	2,506,500	100.0

TRADING VOLUME
Thousand Shares

*7 YEAR PRICE SCORE 128.8   *12 MONTH PRICE SCORE 112.0
*NYSE COMPOSITE INDEX=100

DIVIDEND ACHIEVER STATUS:

Rank: 157	1983-93 Growth Rate: 10.7%
Total Years of Dividend Growth:	16

RECENT DEVELOPMENTS: For the year ended 12/31/93, net income before an accounting adjustment fell 16.8% to $426.9 million compared with $513.4 million the previous year. Sales were up 4.8% to $5.41 billion. Earnings include a non-recurring fourth quarter charge of $164.1 million related to a realignment program. Toiletries and cosmetic sales improved but operating profits were down sharply reflecting heavy costs associated with the launch of the Gillette Series line of toiletries.

PROSPECTS: Sales and earnings growth will be driven by blades and razor products. The Gillette Series will contribute to improved profits in the toiletries and cosmetics product lines. The Company will reduce costs in its personal-care business by eliminating 2,000 positions overseas, closing facilities, and converting multi-product manufacturing plants into single-product facilities which are more efficient. Gillette will also add about 2,000 jobs in other areas to offset the eliminations. Cost savings are not anticipated until 1995.

BUSINESS

THE GILLETTE COMPANY is a consumer products firm engaged in the development, manufacture and sale of a wide range of products for personal care. Major lines include blades and razors, toiletries and cosmetics, stationery products, Braun electric shavers and small appliances and Oral-B oral care products. Gillette is the market leader of blades and razors in North America and most other areas of the world. The Company holds a major position in North America in sales of toiletries and writing instruments. Braun markets electric shavers in Germany, Europe, North America and Japan.

ANNUAL EARNINGS AND DIVIDENDS PER SHARE

	1993	1992	1991	1990	1989	1988	1987
Earnings Per Share	1.92	2.32	1.94	1.60	1.35	1.22	1.00
Dividends Per Share	0.81	0.695	⬜ 0.62	0.54	0.48	0.43	⬜ 0.37
Dividend Payout %	42.2	30.0	30.9	32.8	34.6	35.1	37.0

⬜ 2-for-1 stk split,05/23/91 ⬜ 2-for-1 stk. split, 5/87.

ANNUAL FINANCIAL DATA

RECORD OF EARNINGS (IN MILLIONS):

Total Revenues	5,410.8	5,162.8	4,683.9	4,344.6	3,818.5	3,581.2	3,166.8
Costs and Expenses	4,367.6	3,984.8	3,629.6	3,394.9	3,005.3	2,826.0	2,526.4
Depreciation & Amort	218.5	210.9	192.7	177.0	149.1	141.2	125.1
Profit From Operations	824.7	967.1	861.6	772.7	664.1	614.0	515.3
Income Bef Income Taxes	682.7	829.7	694.1	593.2	473.6	448.6	383.6
Income Taxes	255.8	316.3	266.7	225.3	188.9	180.1	153.7
Net Income	⬜ 426.9	513.4	427.4	367.9	284.7	268.5	229.9
Aver. Shs. Outstg. (000)	220,400	219,500	211,300	194,114	193,444	219,118	230,144

⬜ Before acctg. change dr$138,600,000.

BALANCE SHEET (IN MILLIONS):

Receivables, Net	1,226.9	1,186.1	1,083.9	1,015.7	828.5	729.1	680.1
Inventories	874.6	852.4	785.2	758.4	688.2	653.4	594.5
Gross Property	2,575.9	2,413.6	2,125.0	1,986.1	1,680.5	1,550.6	1,437.8
Accumulated Depreciation	1,361.4	1,338.2	1,193.6	1,124.5	935.7	867.5	773.4
Long-Term Debt	840.1	554.2	742.2	1,045.7	1,041.0	1,675.2	839.6
Net Stockholders' Equity	1,479.0	1,496.4	1,157.1	865.4	670.0	d84.6	599.4
Total Assets	5,102.3	4,189.9	3,886.7	3,671.3	3,114.0	2,867.9	2,731.2
Total Current Assets	2,528.0	2,336.2	2,177.8	2,093.5	1,854.5	1,739.7	1,578.2
Total Current Liabilities	1,760.3	1,560.8	1,484.6	1,307.9	1,061.3	965.4	960.5
Net Working Capital	767.7	775.4	693.2	785.6	793.2	774.3	617.7
Year End Shs Outstg (000)	220,890	220,169	219,179	194,436	193,700	193,234	230,700

STATISTICAL RECORD:

Operating Profit Margin %	15.2	18.7	18.4	17.8	17.4	17.1	16.3
Book Value Per Share	2.10	4.38	3.00	...	...	...	1.48
Return on Equity %	28.9	34.3	36.9	N.M.	N.M.	...	38.4
Return on Assets %	8.4	12.3	11.0	10.0	9.1	9.4	8.4
Average Yield %	1.5	1.3	1.5	2.0	2.3	2.2	2.3
P/E Ratio	33.2-24.7	26.4-18.9	28.9-14.6	20.4-13.6	18.4-12.2	20.1-12.0	23.0-8.9
Price Range	63¾-47⅜	61¼-43⅞	56⅛-28¼	32⅝-21¾	24⅞-16½	24½-14⅝	23-8⅞

Statistics are as originally reported.

OFFICERS:
A.M. Zeien, Chmn. & C.E.O.
J.E. Mullaney, Vice-Chmn.-Legal & Sec.
T.F. Skelly, Sr. V.P.-Fin.

INCORPORATED: DE, Sep., 1917

PRINCIPAL OFFICE: Prudential Tower Bldg., Boston, MA 02199

TELEPHONE NUMBER: (617) 421-7000
NO. OF EMPLOYEES: 4,542
ANNUAL MEETING: In April
SHAREHOLDERS: 20,056
INSTITUTIONAL HOLDINGS:
No. of Institutions: 714
Shares Held: 156,828,983

REGISTRAR(S): First National Bank of Boston, Shareholder Services Division, Boston, MA

TRANSFER AGENT(S): First National Bank of Boston, Shareholder Services Division, Boston, MA

GLATFELTER (P.H.) CO.

YIELD 4.4%
P/E RATIO 33.8

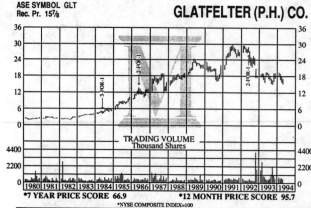

INTERIM EARNINGS (Per Share):

Qtr.	Mar.	June	Sept.	Dec.
1991	0.45	0.39	0.38	0.46
1992	0.33	0.35	0.27	0.32
1993	Nil	0.21	0.07	0.19

INTERIM DIVIDENDS (Per Share):

Amt.	Decl.	Ex.	Rec.	Pay.
0.175Q	6/23/93	7/2/93	7/9/93	8/1/93
0.175Q	9/22	10/4	10/8	11/1
0.175Q	12/22	1/10/94	1/14/94	2/1/94
0.175Q	3/16/94	4/6	4/12	5/1

Indicated div.: $0.70

CAPITALIZATION (12/31/93):

	($000)	(%)
Long-Term Debt	150,000	20.8
Deferred Income Tax	130,509	18.1
Common & Surplus	441,400	61.1
Total	721,909	100.0

TRADING VOLUME
Thousand Shares

DIVIDEND ACHIEVER STATUS:
Rank: 27   1983-93 Growth Rate: 18.0%
Total Years of Dividend Growth: 10

*7 YEAR PRICE SCORE 66.9   *12 MONTH PRICE SCORE 95.7
*NYSE COMPOSITE INDEX=100

RECENT DEVELOPMENTS: Net income for the year ended 12/31/93, before accounting changes and unusual charges, decreased to $20.4 million from $56.5 million in 1992. Revenues slid 12.3% to $473.5 million from $540.1 million the previous year. Restructuring costs of $16.4 million related to the elimination of 180 jobs were partially offset by a gain of $1.5 million on the sale of Ecusta's airplane and a credit of $1.5 million due to updated estimates of post-retirement benefits.

PROSPECTS: With the gradual recovery of the U.S. economy, Glatfelter may begin to see some improvement in its markets. The Company's printing papers business remains depressed because of overcapacity in the industry. It is expected that the supply/demand imbalance will shift towards GLT's favor later in the year, leading the way to price relief and improved results. The Company plans to eliminate 100 more jobs at its Pisgah Forest, N.C., plant, part of the Ecusta division, by mid-1994.

BUSINESS

P.H. GLATFELTER CO. makes printing papers and tobacco and other specialty papers. Its Spring Grove facility is an integrated paper manufacturing plant, producing a substantial part of its fiber requirements from wood. The Pisgah Forest mill produces flax fiber pulp used to manufacture tobacco products and utilizes purchased virgin wood pulp to manufacture nearly all of Ecusta's printing and other specialty papers. The Neenah mill recycles a wide range of wastepapers to provide its principal fiber raw material. The Glatfelter Pulp Wood Co. is responsible for woodlands management. Ecusta Fibres Ltd., a wholly-owned Canadian subsidiary, buys and processes flax straw. The Glatfelter family holds 38.3% of common and Ruane, Cunniff & Co. controls 10.8%.

REVENUES

(12/31/93)	($000)	(%)
Printing Papers	341,528	72.1
Tobacco & other	131,981	27.9
Total	473,509	100.0

ANNUAL EARNINGS AND DIVIDENDS PER SHARE

	1993	1992	1991	1990	1989	1988	1987
Earnings Per Share	0.46	1.27	1.67	1.88	1.92	1.70	1.13
Dividends Per Share	0.70	② 0.675	0.60	0.55	0.50	0.35	0.273
Dividend Payout %	N.M.	53.1	35.9	29.3	26.0	20.6	24.2

② 2-for-1 stk split,05/14/92

ANNUAL FINANCIAL DATA

RECORD OF EARNINGS (IN THOUSANDS):

	1993	1992	1991	1990	1989	1988	1987
Total	482,005	547,839	577,000	633,373	622,726	589,310	442,114
Costs and Expenses	392,437	425,185	423,121	458,649	440,206	420,001	318,681
Depreciation & Depletion	38,132	31,893	30,694	30,023	27,231	23,200	19,011
Operating Profit	82,753	125,806	165,229	189,071	196,977	185,835	134,088
Income Bef Income Taxes	35,383	90,761	123,185	144,534	149,769	135,910	96,214
Tot Fed & State Inc Taxes	14,974	34,217	47,136	56,202	56,905	53,678	41,187
Net Income	① 20,409	56,544	76,049	88,332	92,864	82,232	55,027
Aver. Shs. Outstg.	44,315	44,674	45,600	47,004	48,296	48,416	48,980

① Before acctg. change dr$4,193,000.

BALANCE SHEET (IN THOUSANDS):

	1993	1992	1991	1990	1989	1988	1987
Cash and Cash Equivalents	46,366	3,093	44,760	28,549	2,765	4,686	3,361
Receivables, Net	34,340	38,540	42,777	49,815	43,872	185,489	39,691
Inventories	98,930	88,423	89,192	86,016	77,854	78,832	77,338
Gross Property	918,038	752,034	675,770	632,666	601,753	551,027	509,264
Accumulated Depreciation	296,925	265,264	245,948	217,994	191,103	168,450	149,021
Long-Term Debt	150,000	...	...	...	...	52,700	179,200
Net Stockholders' Equity	441,400	457,940	447,331	412,867	382,069	335,752	279,269
Total Assets	842,087	648,464	630,115	598,842	550,015	663,048	616,415
Total Current Assets	180,941	130,527	176,962	164,686	124,587	269,334	120,561
Total Current Liabilities	81,477	97,136	97,251	103,658	98,314	220,827	85,153
Net Working Capital	99,464	33,391	79,711	61,028	26,273	48,507	35,408
Year End Shares Outstg	43,987	44,057	44,629	45,175	46,976	48,022	48,472

STATISTICAL RECORD:

	1993	1992	1991	1990	1989	1988	1987
Operating Profit Margin %	10.7	16.6	21.3	22.8	24.9	24.8	23.6
Book Value Per Share	10.03	10.37	10.02	9.13	8.12	6.98	5.75
Return on Equity %	4.6	12.4	17.0	21.4	24.3	24.5	19.7
Return on Assets %	2.4	8.7	12.1	14.8	16.9	12.4	8.9
Average Yield %	4.0	2.9	2.4	2.8	2.3	2.1	1.8
P/E Ratio	42.4-32.9	23.2-13.7	17.9-12.2	12.3-8.6	12.8-9.6	11.3-8.5	16.7-10.4
Price Range	19½-15⅛	29½-17⅜	29⅞-20⅜	23⅛-16⅛	24½-18½	19⅛-14½	18⅞-11¾

Statistics are as originally reported.

OFFICERS:
T.C. Norris, Chmn., Pres. & C.E.O.
R.W. Wand, V.P. & Treas.
R.S. Wood, Sec. & Asst. Treas.

INCORPORATED: PA, Dec., 1905

PRINCIPAL OFFICE: 228 S. Main Street, Spring Grove, PA 17362

TELEPHONE NUMBER: (717) 225-4711
FAX: (717) 225-6834
NO. OF EMPLOYEES: 1,079
ANNUAL MEETING: In April
SHAREHOLDERS: 5,030
INSTITUTIONAL HOLDINGS:
No. of Institutions: 107
Shares Held: 15,790,908

REGISTRAR(S): Wachovia Bank & Trust Co., N.A., Winston-Salem, NC 27102

TRANSFER AGENT(S): Wachovia Bank & Trust Co., N.A., Winston-Salem, NC 27102

NASDAQ SYMBOL GLDC
Rec. Pr. 8⅛ (Marginable)

GOLDEN ENTERPRISES, INC.

YIELD	5.5%
P/E RATIO	35.3

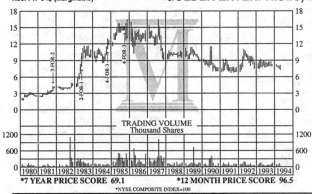

TRADING VOLUME
Thousand Shares

*7 YEAR PRICE SCORE 69.1   *12 MONTH PRICE SCORE 96.5
*NYSE COMPOSITE INDEX=100

INTERIM EARNINGS (Per Share):

Qtr.	Aug.	Nov.	Feb.	May
1990-91	0.15	0.08	0.03	0.09
1991-92	0.11	0.10	0.10	0.07
1992-93	0.14	0.09	0.08	0.09
1993-94	0.09	0.04	0.01	...

INTERIM DIVIDENDS (Per Share):

Amt.	Decl.	Ex.	Rec.	Pay.
0.11Q	4/7/93	4/13/93	4/19/93	4/28/93
0.11Q	7/7	7/13	7/19	7/28
0.1125Q	9/27	10/4	10/8	10/27
0.1125Q	1/5/94	1/10/94	1/17/94	1/26/94
0.1125Q	3/28	4/5	4/11	4/27
		Indicated div.: $0.45		

CAPITALIZATION (5/31/93):

	($000)	(%)
Deferred Income Tax	2,531	4.9
Common & Surplus	49,084	95.1
Total	51,615	100.0

DIVIDEND ACHIEVER STATUS:
Rank: 91   1983-93 Growth Rate: 13.5%
Total Years of Dividend Growth: 16

RECENT DEVELOPMENTS: For the nine months ended 2/28/94, total revenues were $96.4 million, compared with $101.0 million for the same period last year. Net income was $1.7 million, compared with $3.9 million for the year-ago period. For the quarter, total revenues were $33.0 million, compared with $36.2 million for the same quarter last year. Net income was $116,609, compared with $975,830 for the corresponding 1993 quarter. The decline in net income is attributed to poor quality in potatoes that were available during the quarter, higher costs of other raw materials, the cost of complying with new nutritional labelling requirements on snack food packages, and the continuation of high advertising expenses associated with market specific campaigns to improve customer awareness of GLDC's brands.

BUSINESS

GOLDEN ENTERPRISES, INC. is a holding concern which owns all of the stock of three subsidiaries: Golden Flake Snack Foods, Inc., a wholly owned subsidiary, manufactures and distributes a variety of food products, such as potato chips, tortilla chips, fried pork skins, cheese curls, corn chips, peanut butter, cheese filled sandwiches, onion rings and popcorn. The Company sells its products through its own sales organization to commercial establishments which sell food products in Alabama, and in parts of Tennessee, Kentucky, Georgia, Florida, Mississippi, Arkansas, Louisiana, North Carolina, South Carolina, and Missouri. Steel City Bolt & Screw, Inc., a wholly owned subsidiary, manufactures and distributes special bolts and other fasteners and sells all types of headed and threaded products manufactured by others. All of the manufacturing is done at its principal place of business in Birmingham, Alabama. Nall & Associates, Inc., a wholly owned subsidiary, is principally engaged in the business of representing numerous manufactures of nuts, bolts, and other fasteners and in selling their products. Nall & Associates operates throughout the southeast and southwest.

ANNUAL EARNINGS AND DIVIDENDS PER SHARE

	5/31/93	5/31/92	5/31/91	5/31/90	5/31/89	5/31/88	5/31/87
Earnings Per Share	0.40	0.38	0.35	0.35	0.42	①0.52	0.61
Dividends Per Share	0.425	0.405	0.37	0.83	0.29	0.25	0.218
Dividend Payout %	N.M.	N.M.	N.M.	N.M.	69.0	48.1	35.7
① Before acctg. chg.							

ANNUAL FINANCIAL DATA

RECORD OF EARNINGS (IN THOUSANDS):

Total Revenues	134,893	132,561	130,424	134,872	127,511	130,086	123,341
Costs and Expenses	122,957	120,693	118,307	122,439	112,778	111,967	101,306
Depreciation & Amort	3,993	4,330	5,069	5,667	6,467	7,397	7,586
Operating Income	7,943	7,538	7,048	6,766	8,266	10,723	14,448
Income Bef Income Taxes	7,940	7,531	7,034	6,743	8,231	10,665	14,359
Total Prov for Inc Taxes	2,959	2,756	2,633	2,304	2,840	3,927	6,406
Net Income	4,981	4,775	4,401	4,439	5,391	①6,738	7,953
Aver. Shs. Outstg.	12,596	12,637	12,707	12,781	12,815	12,992	13,066
① Before acctg. change cr$1,025,000.							

BALANCE SHEET (IN THOUSANDS):

Cash and Cash Equivalents	16,444	15,882	15,312	11,625	19,198	17,053	13,500
Receivables, Net	9,622	9,274	9,272	9,588	9,879	9,465	8,792
Inventories	5,326	5,246	6,172	5,969	5,908	5,493	5,211
Gross Property	72,771	72,824	71,553	70,880	66,806	66,182	62,777
Accumulated Depreciation	49,884	47,808	44,646	40,070	35,405	32,245	27,478
Net Stockholders' Equity	49,084	50,103	50,614	51,813	58,483	58,010	55,646
Total Assets	58,097	58,902	60,251	61,011	68,528	68,358	65,451
Total Current Assets	33,597	32,641	32,487	29,466	36,696	33,711	28,816
Total Current Liabilities	6,195	5,911	6,923	6,027	6,279	6,819	5,321
Net Working Capital	27,402	26,730	25,564	23,438	30,417	26,892	23,495
Year End Shares Outstg	12,600	12,639	12,668	12,755	12,802	12,895	13,071

STATISTICAL RECORD:

Operating Profit Margin %	5.9	5.7	5.4	5.0	6.5	8.2	11.7
Book Value Per Share	3.90	3.96	4.00	4.06	4.57	4.50	4.26
Return on Equity %	10.1	9.5	8.7	8.6	9.2	11.6	14.3
Return on Assets %	8.6	8.1	7.3	7.3	7.9	9.9	12.2
Average Yield %	4.8	5.1	4.0	8.2	2.9	2.0	1.7
P/E Ratio	27.5-17.2	24.3-17.8	32.9-20.0	32.5-25.0	25.6-22.0	31.7-17.3	26.2-16.8
Price Range	11-6⅞	9¼-6¾	11½-7	11⅜-8¾	10¾-9¼	16½-9	16-10¼
Statistics are as originally reported.							

OFFICERS:
S.Y. Bashinsky, Sr., Chairman
J.S. Stein, Pres. & C.E.O.
J.H. Shannon, V.P. & Sec.

INCORPORATED: DE, Dec., 1967

PRINCIPAL OFFICE: 2101 Magnolia Ave. South Suite 212, Birmingham, AL 35205

TELEPHONE NUMBER: (205) 326-6101

FAX: (205) 326-6148

NO. OF EMPLOYEES: 61 (approx.)

ANNUAL MEETING: In September

SHAREHOLDERS: 649 (approx.)

INSTITUTIONAL HOLDINGS:
No. of Institutions: 23
Shares Held: 1,371,753

REGISTRAR(S): AmSouth Bank, N.A., Birmingham, AL 35202

TRANSFER AGENT(S): AmSouth Bank, N.A., Birmingham, AL 35202

NYS SYMBOL GDW
Rec. Pr. 39⅝

GOLDEN WEST FINANCIAL CORP.

YIELD	0.8%
P/E RATIO	9.3

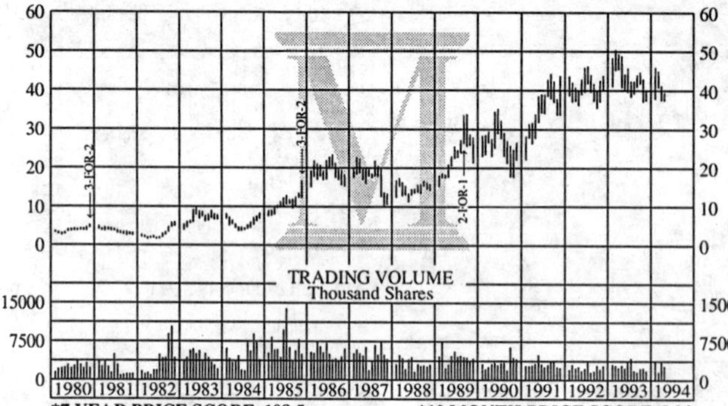

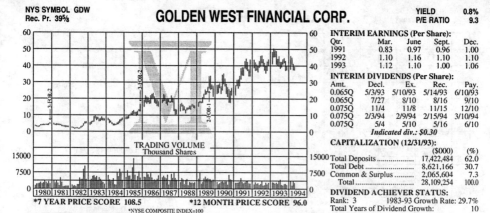

***7 YEAR PRICE SCORE 108.5** ***12 MONTH PRICE SCORE 96.0**

*NYSE COMPOSITE INDEX=100

INTERIM EARNINGS (Per Share):

Qtr.	Mar.	June	Sept.	Dec.
1991	0.83	0.97	0.96	1.00
1992	1.10	1.16	1.10	1.10
1993	1.12	1.10	1.00	1.06

INTERIM DIVIDENDS (Per Share):

Amt.	Decl.	Ex.	Rec.	Pay.
0.065Q	5/3/93	5/10/93	5/14/93	6/10/93
0.065Q	7/27	8/10	8/16	9/10
0.075Q	11/4	11/8	11/15	12/10
0.075Q	2/3/94	2/9/94	2/15/94	3/10/94
0.075Q	5/4	5/10	5/16	6/10

Indicated div.: $0.30

CAPITALIZATION (12/31/93):

	($000)	(%)
Total Deposits	17,422,484	62.0
Total Debt	8,621,166	30.7
Common & Surplus	2,065,604	7.3
Total	28,109,254	100.0

DIVIDEND ACHIEVER STATUS:

Rank: 3 1983-93 Growth Rate: 29.7%

Total Years of Dividend Growth: 10

RECENT DEVELOPMENTS: For the quarter ended 12/31/93, net income declined 3% from the corresponding 1992 quarter to $67.9 million. Results benefited from an extraordinary gain of $17 million. The provision for loan losses increased to $25.0 million from $11.5 million a year ago. For 1993, net income was $273.9 million compared with $283.5 million for 1992. Results were adversely affected by the California real estate recession. The provision for possible loan losses totaled $65.8 million, up 52% from the prior-year.

PROSPECTS: GDW has proposed a takeover bid for California Federal Bank. The acquisition of California Federal would mark the Company's entry into Nevada and Georgia markets. The Company acquired PriMerit Bank's Arizona deposits and sold $133 million of savings in two Ohio branches. GDW continues to contend with the real estate recession in its home state despite the brisk mortgage business. GDW's strong balance sheet has provided some protection.

BUSINESS

GOLDEN WEST FINANCIAL is a savings and loan holding company which has as its principal asset World Savings & Loan Association. World Savings is a federally-chartered savings and loan association with operations in California and 7 other states. It operates as a financial intermediary attracting deposits (primarily in the form of savings accounts) and investing funds in loans and securities backed by residential real estate. With a total of 227 branches, World Savings has one of the largest branch networks in the U.S.

LOAN DISTRIBUTION

(12/31/93)	($000)	(%)
1-to-4 Family Dwelling	20,197,613	83.6
Over 4-Family Dwelling	3,785,673	15.7
Commercial Property	153,396	0.6
Construction & Land.	2,987	0.1
Savings Accounts	32,012	0.1
Total	24,171,681	100.0

ANNUAL EARNINGS AND DIVIDENDS PER SHARE

	1993	1992	1991	1990	1989	1988	1987
Earnings Per Share	**4.28**	**4.46**	**3.76**	**2.87**	**2.51**	**[2] 2.21**	**2.42**
Dividends Per Share	**0.27**	**0.23**	**0.19**	**0.165**	**[1] 0.15**	**0.125**	**0.105**
Dividend Payout %	**6.3**	**5.2**	**5.1**	**5.7**	**6.0**	**5.7**	**4.3**

[1] 2-for-1 stk split, 9/8/89 [2] 2-for1 stock split, payable 09/08/89

ANNUAL FINANCIAL DATA

	1993	1992	1991	1990	1989	1988	1987
RECORD OF EARNINGS (IN MILLIONS):							
Total Interest Income	1,870.2	1,984.5	2,214.6	2,098.3	1,906.3	1,383.0	1,205.7
Total Interest Expense	1,137.4	1,267.2	1,582.8	1,601.5	1,485.3	1,006.3	832.0
Net Interest Income	732.8	717.3	631.8	496.8	421.0	376.7	373.7
Prov for Possible Loan Losses	65.8	43.2	30.2	13.6	6.7	1.9	6.0
Earn Bef Taxes on Income	457.4	463.7	386.7	282.7	246.2	215.1	249.0
Taxes on Income	183.5	180.2	148.1	101.2	88.3	76.8	97.4
Net Income	273.9	283.5	238.6	181.5	157.9	138.3	[1] 151.6
Aver. Shs. Outstg. (000)	63,978	63,578	63,442	63,137	62,906	62,781	62,610
[1] Before extra. item dr$4,759,000.							
BALANCE SHEET (IN MILLIONS):							
Cash & Sec. Etc.	2,417.9	1,179.9	1,289.3	1,343.5	1,562.0	1,548.6	896.0
Investments and Advances	1,915.4	2,149.1	2,336.6	2,775.8	2,240.9	2,333.2	2,505.2
Loans Receivable, Net	23,912.6	21,968.7	20,087.4	17,730.4	15,011.0	12,121.0	8,811.5
Savings Accounts	...	...	...	...	...	...	8,427.4
Long-term Debt	1,220.1	921.7	625.1	426.2	113.7	113.5	...
Net Stockholders' Equity	2,065.6	1,727.4	1,449.1	1,220.4	1,046.3	896.4	792.1
Total Assets	28,829.3	25,890.9	24,297.8	22,562.1	19,520.6	16,721.0	12,835.5
Year End Shs Outstg (000)	63,929	63,925	63,499	63,330	63,002	62,821	62,658
STATISTICAL RECORD:							
Return on Equity %	13.3	16.4	16.5	14.9	15.1	15.4	19.1
Return on Assets %	1.0	1.1	1.0	0.8	0.8	0.8	1.2
Book Value Per Share	32.31	27.02	22.82	19.27	16.61	14.27	12.64
Average Yield %	0.6	0.6	0.6	0.6	0.6	0.9	0.6
P/E Ratio	11.8-8.7	10.4-8.0	11.8-5.9	12.3-6.1	13.4-6.1	7.9-5.1	9.3-4.2
Price Range	50⅜-37⅛	46¼-35½	44¼-22¼	35¼-17⅝	33¾-15⅜	17⅜-11¼	22⅝-10¼

Statistics are as originally reported.

OFFICERS:
H.M. Sandler, Chmn. & C.E.O.
M.O. Sandler, Chmn. & C.E.O.
R.W. Kettell, President

PRINCIPAL OFFICE: 1901 Harrison Street, Oakland, CA 94612

TELEPHONE NUMBER: (510) 446-3420
FAX: (510) 446-4259
NO. OF EMPLOYEES: 4,019
ANNUAL MEETING: In April
SHAREHOLDERS: 1,925
INSTITUTIONAL HOLDINGS:
No. of Institutions: 232
Shares Held: 39,256,786

REGISTRAR(S):

TRANSFER AGENT(S):

ASE SYMBOL GRC
Rec. Pr. 25½

GORMAN-RUPP CO.

YIELD 2.8%
P/E RATIO 16.6

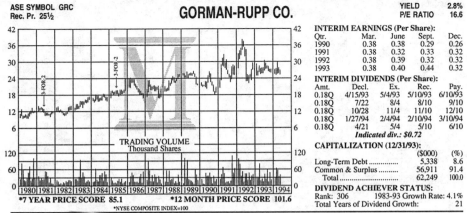

7 YEAR PRICE SCORE 85.1 **12 MONTH PRICE SCORE 101.6**
*NYSE COMPOSITE INDEX=100

INTERIM EARNINGS (Per Share):

Qtr.	Mar.	June	Sept.	Dec.
1990	0.38	0.38	0.29	0.26
1991	0.38	0.32	0.33	0.32
1992	0.38	0.39	0.32	0.32
1993	0.38	0.40	0.44	0.32

INTERIM DIVIDENDS (Per Share):

Amt.	Decl.	Ex.	Rec.	Pay.
0.18Q	4/15/93	5/4/93	5/10/93	6/10/93
0.18Q	7/22	8/4	8/10	9/10
0.18Q	10/28	11/4	11/10	12/10
0.18Q	1/27/94	2/4/94	2/10/94	3/10/94
0.18Q	4/21	5/4	5/10	6/10

Indicated div.: $0.72

CAPITALIZATION (12/31/93):

	($000)	(%)
Long-Term Debt	5,338	8.6
Common & Surplus	56,911	91.4
Total	62,249	100.0

DIVIDEND ACHIEVER STATUS:
Rank: 306   1983-93 Growth Rate: 4.1%
Total Years of Dividend Growth: 21

RECENT DEVELOPMENTS: For the year ended 12/31/93, net sales amounted to $131.5 million, up 4.4% from net sales of $126.0 million in 1992. Net income was $8.8 million, or $1.54 per share, compared with income of $8.0 million, or $1.39 per share, before the effect of accounting changes, in 1992. The cumulative effect of a change in accounting prin- ciples in 1992 reduced income from operations by $11.9 million, or $2.07 per share, which resulted in a net loss of $3.9 million, or $0.68 per share. For the fourth quarter ended 12/31/93, net sales totaled $31.3 million, up from $27.5 million a year ago. Net income was flat at $1.8 million or $0.32 per share.

BUSINESS

GORMAN-RUPP CO. designs, manufactures and sells pumps and related equipment for use in construction, industrial, petroleum, agricultural, water and wastewater, original equipment, fire, military and other liquid-handling applications. Its product line is composed of pump models ranging in rated capacity from less than one gallon per minute up to 200,000 gallons per minute. The types of pumps the Company produces include self-priming centrifugal, standard centrifugal, magnetic drive centrifugal, rotary gear, diaphragm, bellows and oscillating. The pumps have drives that range from 1/35 horsepower electric motors up to much larger electric motors or internal combustion engines. The Company's larger pumps are sold principally for use in the construction, industrial, sewage and waste handling fields; for pumping refined petroleum products, including the ground refueling of aircraft; for agricultural applications; and for fire fighting. Many of the Company's smallest pumps are sold to customers for incorporation into such products as X-ray processing equipment, gas air-conditioning equipment, office copy machines, chemical feeding, instrumentation and ice cube making machinery; photographic processing and soft drink dispensing equipment; laser cooling applications; graphic arts equipment; and floor cleaning equipment.

ANNUAL EARNINGS AND DIVIDENDS PER SHARE

	1993	1992	1991	1990	1989	1988	1987
Earnings Per Share	1.54	① 1.39	1.34	1.28	1.19	1.14	1.02
Dividends Per Share	0.72	② 0.683	0.671	0.65	0.641	0.59	0.56
Dividend Payout %	46.8	49.2	49.8	51.0	54.2	51.5	54.9

① Before acctg. chg. ② 3-for-2 stk split, 7/13/92

ANNUAL FINANCIAL DATA

RECORD OF EARNINGS (IN THOUSANDS):

	1993	1992	1991	1990	1989	1988	1987
Total Income	132,124	126,540	124,100	120,422	114,965	84,386	75,863
Costs and Expenses	113,992	109,856	107,873	104,483	99,833	70,943	62,839
Depreciation & Amort	4,274	4,025	3,874	3,709	3,723	2,604	2,254
Operating Profit	33,288	31,496	30,530	29,309	28,375	23,944	21,888
Income Bef Income Taxes	13,858	12,659	12,353	12,230	11,409	10,839	10,770
Income Taxes	5,063	4,693	4,664	4,888	4,638	4,221	4,851
Net Income	8,795	① 7,966	7,689	7,342	6,771	6,618	5,919
Aver. Shs. Outstg.	5,726	5,730	5,730	5,730	5,730	5,790	5,819

① Before acctg. change dr$11,886,000.

BALANCE SHEET (IN THOUSANDS):

Cash & Cash Equivalents	2,782	3,402	3,043	3,643	3,002	3,575	14,977
Receivables, Net	26,628	21,895	21,886	20,348	18,704	17,303	11,340
Inventories	25,614	23,991	27,893	25,647	26,070	22,062	12,435
Gross Property	70,726	62,670	60,672	54,723	50,097	45,612	37,675
Accumulated Depreciation	33,891	31,863	29,834	28,589	25,618	22,817	20,785
Long-Term Debt	5,338	668	6,238	2,437	2,187	1,151	. . .
Net Stockholders' Equity	56,911	52,759	61,256	57,310	53,711	50,476	48,248
Total Assets	98,706	86,434	85,131	77,643	74,560	68,695	57,119
Total Current Assets	55,746	50,152	53,642	50,531	48,793	44,118	39,663
Total Current Liabilities	14,382	12,380	14,471	14,805	15,871	14,789	6,588
Net Working Capital	41,364	37,772	39,171	35,726	32,922	29,329	33,075
Year End Shares Outstg	5,720	5,730	5,730	5,730	5,730	5,730	5,819

STATISTICAL RECORD:

Operating Profit Margin %	10.5	10.0	10.0	10.2	9.9	12.8	14.2
Book Value Per Share	9.95	9.21	10.69	10.00	9.37	8.81	8.29
Return on Equity %	15.5	15.1	12.6	12.8	12.6	13.1	12.3
Return on Assets %	8.9	9.2	9.0	9.5	9.1	9.6	10.4
Average Yield %	2.6	2.3	2.5	2.9	2.7	2.6	2.8
P/E Ratio	19.8-16.2	27.4-16.0	24.3-15.3	20.7-14.1	22.4-18.1	22.4-16.9	22.9-16.4
Price Range	30½-24⅞	38⅛-22¼	32⅝-20½	26½-18	26⅝-21½	25½-19¼	23⅜-16¾

Statistics are as originally reported.

OFFICERS:
J.C. Gorman, Chmn. & C.E.O.
J.A. Walter, Pres.
K.E. Dudley, Treas.

INCORPORATED: OH, Apr., 1934

PRINCIPAL OFFICE: 305 Bowman Street,
Mansfield, OH 44903

TELEPHONE NUMBER: (419) 755-1011

FAX: (419) 755-1233

NO. OF EMPLOYEES: 306 approx.

ANNUAL MEETING: In April

SHAREHOLDERS: 748

INSTITUTIONAL HOLDINGS:
No. of Institutions: 47
Shares Held: 3,029,825

REGISTRAR(S): National City Bank,
Cleveland. OH 44114

TRANSFER AGENT(S): National City Bank,
Cleveland. OH 44114

NYS SYMBOL GWW
Rec. Pr. 65

GRAINGER (W.W.), INC.

YIELD 1.2%
P/E RATIO 22.6

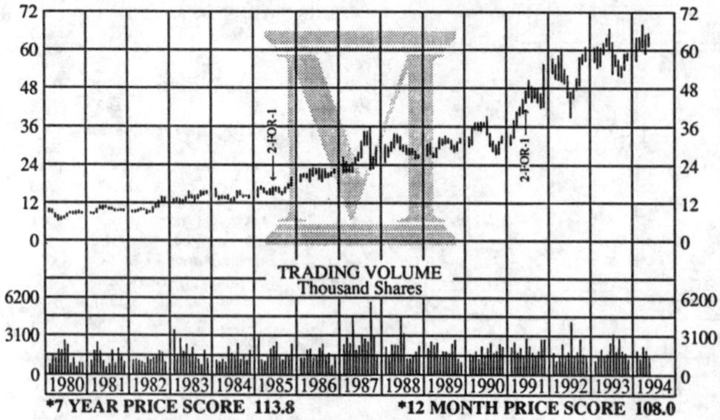

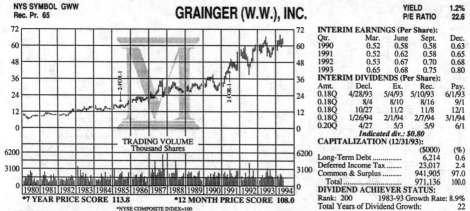

*7 YEAR PRICE SCORE 113.8 *12 MONTH PRICE SCORE 108.0

*NYSE COMPOSITE INDEX=100

INTERIM EARNINGS (Per Share):

Qtr.	Mar.	June	Sept.	Dec.
1990	0.52	0.58	0.58	0.63
1991	0.52	0.62	0.58	0.65
1992	0.53	0.67	0.70	0.68
1993	0.65	0.68	0.75	0.80

INTERIM DIVIDENDS (Per Share):

Amt.	Decl.	Ex.	Rec.	Pay.
0.18Q	4/28/93	5/4/93	5/10/93	6/1/93
0.18Q	8/4	8/10	8/16	9/1
0.18Q	10/27	11/2	11/8	12/1
0.18Q	1/26/94	2/1/94	2/7/94	3/1/94
0.20Q	4/27	5/3	5/9	6/1

Indicated div.: $0.80

CAPITALIZATION (12/31/93):

	($000)	(%)
Long-Term Debt	6,214	0.6
Deferred Income Tax	23,017	2.4
Common & Surplus	941,905	97.0
Total	971,136	100.0

DIVIDEND ACHIEVER STATUS:
Rank: 200 1983-93 Growth Rate: 8.9%
Total Years of Dividend Growth: 22

RECENT DEVELOPMENTS: For the year ended 12/31/93, net income before an accounting adjustment increased 8.8% to $149.3 million compared with $137.2 million a year ago. Sales rose 11.2% to $2.63 billion from $2.36 billion. The Company recently opened two zone distribution centers, each approximating 200,000 square feet in size: Ontario, California, 11/93; and Atlanta, 1/94. The Ontario location supports twenty-three branches in the Los Angeles area and the Atlanta location supports nineteen branches in the Southeast.

PROSPECTS: The Company will accelerate efforts to expand sales and establish a national distribution system for sanitary supplies and equipment with the recent formation of Grainger Sanitary Supplies and Equipment. This action combined the Company's Jani-Serv and Ball Industries sanitary supply distribution businesses with the Grainger Division's lines of sanitary supply products. Ball Industries will continue as the Company's cleaning chemical mixing operation. Operations will be enhanced by the recently opened distribution centers.

BUSINESS

W.W. GRAINGER, INC., is a nationwide distributor of equipment, components, and supplies to the commercial, industrial, contractor and institutional markets. Products include motors, fans, blowers, pumps, compressors, air and power tools, heating and air conditioning equipments, as well as other items offered in its Wholesale Net Price Catalog which features over 42,400 products. Grainger serves its over one million customers from regional distribution facilities in Chicago, IL, Kansas City, MO, Los Angeles, CA, and Greenville County, SC through a nationwide network of 334 branches in 50 states. Other Business Units includes Allied Safety Inc., Ball Industries, Bossert Industrial Supply, Inc., Grainger Sanitary Supplies and Equipment, Lab Saftey Supply, and Parts Co. of America.

QUARTERLY DATA

(12/31/93)($000)	Rev	Inc
1st Quarter	606,183	33,365
2nd Quarter	660,407	35,445
3rd Quarter	698,835	38,714
4th Quarter	662,973	40,923

ANNUAL EARNINGS AND DIVIDENDS PER SHARE

	1993	1992	1991	1990	1989	1988	1987
Earnings Per Share	**2.88**	**2.58**	**2.37**	**2.31**	**2.20**	**1.96**	**1.57**
Dividends Per Share	**0.705**	**0.65**	**[1] 0.61**	**0.565**	**0.50**	**0.43**	**0.39**
Dividend Payout %	**24.5**	**25.2**	**25.7**	**24.4**	**22.8**	**21.9**	**24.8**

[1] 2-for-1 stk split,06/10/91

ANNUAL FINANCIAL DATA

	1993	1992	1991	1990	1989	1988	1987
RECORD OF EARNINGS (IN MILLIONS):							
Total Revenues	2,628.4	2,364.4	2,077.2	1,935.2	1,727.5	1,535.5	1,320.8
Costs and Expenses	2,317.1	2,086.9	1,837.4	1,689.6	1,502.8	1,329.1	1,140.8
Depreciation & Amort	59.2	49.1	35.6	41.9	33.6	28.5	22.7
Operating Earnings	252.2	228.4	204.2	203.7	191.1	177.8	157.4
Earn Bef Income Taxes	250.0	227.2	209.4	208.5	196.5	179.7	162.5
Income Taxes	100.8	90.0	81.7	81.7	76.9	70.9	72.0
Net Income	[1] 149.3	137.2	127.7	126.8	119.6	108.8	90.5
Aver. Shs. Outstg. (000)	51,911	53,257	54,001	54,905	54,520	55,574	57,688
[1] Before acctg. change dr$820,000.							
BALANCE SHEET (IN MILLIONS):							
Cash and Cash Equivalents	2.6	44.8	141.0	147.5	81.4	79.2	58.4
Receivables, Net	344.3	305.4	262.7	257.3	255.4	206.5	169.6
Inventories	466.2	432.2	443.3	416.7	412.4	329.9	342.2
Gross Property	716.8	626.7	553.0	520.8	481.5	465.4	379.7
Accumulated Depreciation	307.4	274.0	241.4	209.2	179.2	156.8	129.2
Long-Term Debt	6.2	6.9	11.3	14.5	2.8	16.5	7.0
Net Stockholders' Equity	941.9	931.2	860.4	815.4	731.7	635.5	581.2
Total Assets	1,376.7	1,310.5	1,216.6	1,162.4	1,065.2	936.2	832.1
Total Current Assets	823.9	794.3	854.3	828.6	755.2	619.6	574.2
Total Current Liabilities	381.4	315.5	280.2	268.5	261.6	236.9	200.9
Net Working Capital	442.5	478.8	574.0	560.0	493.6	382.7	373.3
Year End Shs Outstg (000)	50,685	52,376	52,913	54,108	54,498	42,344	55,424
STATISTICAL RECORD:							
Operating Profit Margin %	9.6	9.7	9.8	10.5	11.1	11.6	11.9
Book Value Per Share	18.58	17.78	16.26	15.07	13.43	15.01	10.49
Return on Equity %	15.8	14.7	14.8	15.5	16.3	17.1	15.6
Return on Assets %	10.8	10.5	10.5	10.9	11.2	11.6	10.9
Average Yield %	1.2	1.3	1.4	1.7	1.7	1.5	1.4
P/E Ratio	23.2-17.9	23.6-15.1	23.4-12.8	17.0-11.8	15.1-12.0	17.2-12.6	22.9-13.8
Price Range	66¾-51⅝	61-39	55½-30¼	39¼-27¼	33⅛-26¼	33¾-24⅝	35⅞-21⅝

Statistics are as originally reported.

OFFICERS:
D.W. Grainger, Chmn. & Pres.
J.D. Fluno, Vice-Chmn.

INCORPORATED: IL, 1928

PRINCIPAL OFFICE: 5500 W. Howard St., Skokie, IL 60077-2699

TELEPHONE NUMBER: (708) 982-9000
FAX: (708) 982-3489
NO. OF EMPLOYEES: 10,219
ANNUAL MEETING: In April
SHAREHOLDERS: 2,100
INSTITUTIONAL HOLDINGS:
No. of Institutions: 349
Shares Held: 32,338,204

REGISTRAR(S): First National Bank of Boston, Shareholder Services Division, Boston, MA

TRANSFER AGENT(S): First National Bank of Boston, Shareholder Services Division, Boston, MA

GREAT LAKES CHEMICAL CORP.

YIELD 0.7%
P/E RATIO 14.3

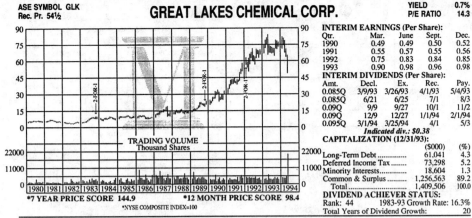

7 YEAR PRICE SCORE 144.9   **12 MONTH PRICE SCORE 98.4**
*NYSE COMPOSITE INDEX=100

TRADING VOLUME
Thousand Shares

INTERIM EARNINGS (Per Share):

Qtr.	Mar.	June	Sept.	Dec.
1990	0.49	0.49	0.50	0.52
1991	0.55	0.57	0.55	0.56
1992	0.75	0.83	0.84	0.85
1993	0.90	0.98	0.96	0.98

INTERIM DIVIDENDS (Per Share):

Amt.	Decl.	Ex.	Rec.	Pay.
0.085Q	3/9/93	3/26/93	4/1/93	5/4/93
0.085Q	6/21	6/25	7/1	8/3
0.09Q	9/9	9/27	10/1	11/2
0.09Q	12/9	12/27	1/1/94	2/1/94
0.095Q	3/1/94	3/25/94	4/1	5/3

Indicated div.: $0.38

CAPITALIZATION (12/31/93):

	($000)	(%)
Long-Term Debt	61,041	4.3
Deferred Income Tax	73,298	5.2
Minority Interests	18,604	1.3
Common & Surplus	1,256,563	89.2
Total	1,409,506	100.0

DIVIDEND ACHIEVER STATUS:
Rank: 44   1983-93 Growth Rate: 16.3%
Total Years of Dividend Growth: 20

RECENT DEVELOPMENTS: For the quarter ended 12/31/93, net income rose 14.8% from the comparable quarter of 1992 to $69.9 million. Sales increased 6.4% to $430.4 million. For the year ended 12/31/93, net income totaled $272.8 million compared with $232.7 million for 1992. Sales were $1.79 billion, up 19.8% from the prior year. Results were limited by the soft European economy, weak demand for furfural derivative products and the strength of the dollar against weak foreign currencies.

PROSPECTS: Strong demand for derivative products has facilities operating at unprecedented levels. In order to meet demand, GLK has increased derivative production and raised bromine capacity levels. Octel Associates, as part of its extended agreement with DuPont, is supplying additional quantities of antiknock compound to Mexico. Octel also completed the initiative to make the Company less susceptible to currency fluctuations.

BUSINESS

GREAT LAKES CHEMICAL CORPORATION is the world's leading producer of bromine, brominated specialty chemicals, and furfural derivatives. The Company has more than 50 sales, production, and distribution facilities in the U.S., Europe, and Japan. Through subsidiaries and affiliates, GLK is a leader in global specialty chemical markets. The Company has an 87.8% interest in Octel Associates.

BUSINESS LINE ANALYSIS

(12/31/93)	Rev(%)	Inc(%)
United States	47.3	34.9
Foreign	52.7	65.1
Total	100.0	100.0

ANNUAL EARNINGS AND DIVIDENDS PER SHARE

	1993	1992	1991	1990	1989	1988	1987
Earnings Per Share	3.82	3.27	2.23	2.01	1.76	1.49	0.84
Dividends Per Share	0.34	① 0.30	0.26	0.22	② 0.19	0.175	0.15
Dividend Payout %	8.9	9.2	11.7	11.0	10.8	11.5	18.0

① 2-for-1 stk split, 1/31/92   ② 2-for-1 stk split, 10/31/89

ANNUAL FINANCIAL DATA

RECORD OF EARNINGS (IN MILLIONS):

	1993	1992	1991	1990	1989	1988	1987
Total Revenues	1,827.8	1,538.2	1,347.9	1,113.5	847.7	616.0	501.0
Costs and Expenses	1,304.8	1,075.0	948.0	752.6	591.5	436.6	376.3
Depreciation & Depletion	62.5	58.4	49.8	43.3	36.9	28.6	25.9
Operating Profit	460.5	404.7	350.1	317.7	219.3	150.9	98.7
Income Before Taxes	383.4	332.7	225.5	209.4	167.9	143.5	85.0
Income Taxes	110.6	100.0	68.0	68.6	45.0	40.2	29.5
Net Income	272.8	232.7	157.5	140.8	122.9	103.3	55.5
Aver. Shs. Outstg. (000)	71,329	71,164	70,700	70,287	69,885	69,659	66,468

BALANCE SHEET (IN MILLIONS):

	1993	1992	1991	1990	1989	1988	1987
Cash & Cash Equivalents	179.7	140.8	81.0	60.6	30.4	12.2	5.6
Receivables, Net	383.1	340.9	294.6	301.5	229.6	102.3	93.7
Total Inventories	275.1	258.0	240.3	223.5	165.8	90.1	92.3
Gross Property	830.8	738.1	693.4	611.8	487.0	409.1	367.0
Accumulated Depreciation	362.8	308.2	287.8	248.1	211.1	174.7	148.6
Long-Term Debt	61.0	45.6	139.8	75.7	113.7	19.3	42.1
Net Stockholders' Equity	1,256.6	1,052.9	900.3	744.2	590.9	482.2	392.6
Total Assets	1,900.9	1,732.0	1,649.1	1,406.3	1,097.4	663.8	577.1
Total Current Assets	856.9	773.2	640.9	608.2	447.1	222.9	209.7
Total Current Liabilities	367.7	431.1	302.9	307.1	210.4	122.6	108.7
Net Working Capital	489.2	342.2	338.0	301.1	236.6	100.2	101.1
Year End Shs Outstg (000)	71,275	71,410	70,924	70,443	70,099	69,654	69,580

STATISTICAL RECORD:

	1993	1992	1991	1990	1989	1988	1987
Book Value Per Share	12.84	10.55	9.47	7.64	6.11	6.18	4.87
Return on Equity %	0.2	0.2	0.2	0.2	0.2	0.2	0.1
Return on Assets %	0.1	0.1	0.1	0.1	0.1	0.2	0.1
Average Yield%	0.5	0.5	0.6	0.8	1.0	1.2	1.1
P/E Ratio	22.0-16.9	21.8-15.4	26.0-13.6	17.0-10.2	13.6-8.0	11.1-8.2	22.9-10.7
Price Range	84-64½	71⅜-50¼	58-30⅜	34-20⅜	24-14⅛	16½-12⅛	19¼-9

Statistics are as originally reported.

OFFICERS:
E. Kampen, Chmn., Pres. & C.E.O.
R.T. Jeffares, V.P.-Fin. & C.F.O.
R.R. Ferguson, Treas. & Sec.

INCORPORATED: MI, 1933; reincorp., DE, Sep., 1970

PRINCIPAL OFFICE: One Great Lakes Boulevard, West Lafayette, IN 47906-0200

TELEPHONE NUMBER: (317) 497-6100

NO. OF EMPLOYEES: 7,000 (approx.)

ANNUAL MEETING: In May

SHAREHOLDERS: 4,850

INSTITUTIONAL HOLDINGS:
No. of Institutions: 396
Shares Held: 57,320,135

REGISTRAR(S): Harris Trust Co. of N.Y., New York, NY 10005

TRANSFER AGENT(S): Harris Trust Co. of N.Y., New York, NY 10005

GREAT WESTERN FINANCIAL CORP.

YIELD 5.4%
P/E RATIO 61.2

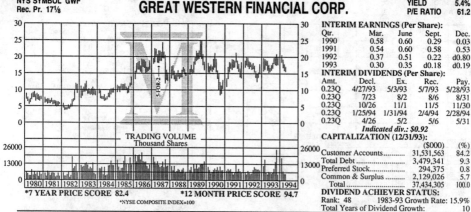

INTERIM EARNINGS (Per Share):

Qtr.	Mar.	June	Sept.	Dec.
1990	0.58	0.60	0.29	0.03
1991	0.54	0.60	0.58	0.53
1992	0.37	0.51	0.22	d0.80
1993	0.30	0.35	d0.18	d0.19

INTERIM DIVIDENDS (Per Share):

Amt.	Decl.	Ex.	Rec.	Pay.
0.23Q	4/27/93	5/3/93	5/7/93	5/28/93
0.23Q	7/23	8/2	8/6	8/31
0.23Q	10/26	11/1	11/5	11/30
0.23Q	1/25/94	1/31/94	2/4/94	2/28/94
0.23Q	4/26	5/2	5/6	5/31

Indicated div.: $0.92

CAPITALIZATION (12/31/93):

	($000)	(%)
Customer Accounts	31,531,563	84.2
Total Debt	3,479,341	9.3
Preferred Stock	294,375	0.8
Common & Surplus	2,129,026	5.7
Total	37,434,305	100.0

DIVIDEND ACHIEVER STATUS:
Rank: 48   1983-93 Growth Rate: 15.9%
Total Years of Dividend Growth: 10

TRADING VOLUME
Thousand Shares

*7 YEAR PRICE SCORE 82.4   *12 MONTH PRICE SCORE 94.7
*NYSE COMPOSITE INDEX=100

RECENT DEVELOPMENTS: A net loss of $18.2 million was posted for the three months ended 12/31/93. The Company attributed the loss to a high level of provisions for loan and real estate losses and restructuring charges of $30 million. For 1993, net income was $62.4 million compared with $53.9 million for 1992. Nonperforming assets fell to $1.13 billion or 2.90% of total assets. The acquisition of HomeFed Bank of San Diego enchanced the retail banking network by 119 branches and $4.1 billion in deposits.

PROSPECTS: Great Western's primary focus is the reduction of nonperforming assets. The completion of four bulk sales during 1993 reduced nonperforming assets to less than 3% of total assets. New real-estate loan volumes are down because of the weak California economy. The consumer finance division continues to contribute excellent results. GWF was successful in its bid to acquire the deposits and branch banking network of the HomeFed Bank of San Diego. The assets were acquired through a sealed-bid process with Resolution Trust Corp.

BUSINESS

GREAT WESTERN FINANCIAL CORPORATION is a multi-regional financial services company. Its operations are concentrated in three areas: retail banking, real estate services and consumer finance. The primary emphasis is on real estate lending as the company operates 187 offices in 20 states. The retail banking division has 400 branch offices in California and Florida and consumer finance maintains 508 offices spread across 23 states.

LOAN DISTRIBUTION

(12/31/93)	($000)	(%)
Real Estate	29,112,599	93.0
Consumer	2,207,897	7.0
Total	31,320,496	100.0

ANNUAL EARNINGS AND DIVIDENDS PER SHARE

	1993	1992	1991	1990	1989	1988	1987
Earnings Per Share	0.28	[1] 0.30	2.25	1.50	0.78	1.95	1.67
Dividends Per Share	0.92	[2] 0.91	0.87	0.83	0.79	0.75	[3] 0.66
Dividend Payout %	N.M.	N.M.	38.7	55.3	N.M.	38.5	39.5

[1] Before acctg. chg.   [2] Bef acctg chge   [3] 150% stk. div. 5/87.

ANNUAL FINANCIAL DATA

RECORD OF EARNINGS (IN MILLIONS):

	1993	1992	1991	1990	1989	1988	1987
Total Interest Income	2,680.8	3,091.1	3,718.8	4,073.1	3,667.5	2,901.1	2,450.2
Total Interest Expense	1,297.9	1,668.7	2,453.5	2,905.1	2,711.7	2,056.5	1,723.2
Net Interest Income	1,382.9	1,422.4	1,265.3	1,168.0	955.8	844.6	727.0
Provision for Loan Losses	463.0	420.0	149.9	285.0	232.0	84.8	84.0
Earnings Before Taxes	92.0	95.5	505.4	275.7	214.4	407.3	423.8
Taxes on Income	30.0	41.6	207.3	82.6	114.3	158.9	213.7
Net Income	62.0	[1] 53.9	298.1	193.1	100.1	248.4	210.1
Aver. Shs. Outstg. (000)	132,008	130,736	129,132	128,501	128,939	127,505	123,193

[1] Before acctg. change cr$31,094,000.

BALANCE SHEET (IN MILLIONS):

	1993	1992	1991	1990	1989	1988	1987
Cash & Sec. Etc.	1,846.8	1,660.5	1,397.5	1,819.8	1,889.8	1,675.3	1,803.6
Investments and Advances	4,429.8	5,035.1	5,296.6	5,488.1	778.0	653.7	503.3
Loans Receivable, Net	30,162.4	30,185.4	31,261.0	30,548.5	33,187.0	29,143.6	25,158.0
Net Stockholders' Equity	2,423.4	2,449.7	2,321.1	2,075.8	1,988.3	1,983.2	1,851.9
Total Assets	38,348.4	38,439.2	39,599.6	39,405.8	37,176.4	32,815.2	28,631.4
Year End Shs Outstg (000)	132,616	130,814	128,876	128,537	128,437	128,224	124,563

STATISTICAL RECORD:

	1993	1992	1991	1990	1989	1988	1987
Return on Equity %	2.6	2.2	12.8	9.3	5.0	12.5	11.3
Return on Assets %	0.2	0.1	0.8	0.5	0.3	0.8	0.7
Book Value Per Share	16.05	16.48	17.01	16.15	15.48	15.47	14.87
Average Yield %	5.1	5.6	5.4	5.6	4.0	5.0	3.6
P/E Ratio	74.6-54.5	66.7-41.7	9.4-4.9	14.1-5.7	32.2-18.8	8.9-6.5	14.6-7.2
Price Range	20⅞-15¼	20-12½	21¼-11	21⅛-8½	25⅛-14⅝	17⅜-12⅝	24⅜-12

Statistics are as originally reported.

OFFICERS:
J.F. Montgomery, Chmn. & C.E.O.
J.F. Maher, Pres. & C.O.O.
C.F. Geuther, Exec. V.P. & C.F.O.

PRINCIPAL OFFICE: 9200 Oakdale Avenue, Chatsworth, CA 91311-6519

TELEPHONE NUMBER: (818) 775-3411
NO. OF EMPLOYEES: 16,016
ANNUAL MEETING: In April
SHAREHOLDERS: 14,330 (approx.)
INSTITUTIONAL HOLDINGS:
No. of Institutions: 281
Shares Held: 106,073,646

REGISTRAR(S):

TRANSFER AGENT(S):

NYS SYMBOL GMP
Rec. Pr. 25⅛

GREEN MOUNTAIN POWER CORP.

YIELD 8.4%
P/E RATIO 11.4

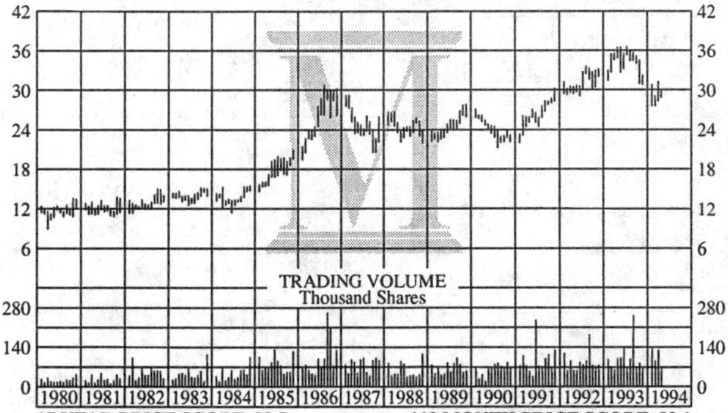

42
36
30
24
18
12
6
TRADING VOLUME
Thousand Shares
280
140
0
1980 1981 1982 1983 1984 1985 1986 1987 1988 1989 1990 1991 1992 1993 1994

***7 YEAR PRICE SCORE 93.5** ***12 MONTH PRICE SCORE 92.1**

*NYSE COMPOSITE INDEX=100

INTERIM EARNINGS (Per Share):

Qtr.	Mar.	June	Sept.	Dec.
1990	0.88	0.31	0.47	0.63
1991	0.79	0.48	0.53	0.65
1992	0.89	0.32	0.59	0.74
1993	0.93	0.17	0.41	0.69

INTERIM DIVIDENDS (Per Share):

Amt.	Decl.	Ex.	Rec.	Pay.
0.525Q	5/20/93	6/11/93	6/17/93	6/30/93
0.53Q	8/31	9/10	9/16	9/30
0.53Q	12/8	12/14	12/20	12/30
0.53Q	3/8/94	3/14/94	3/18/94	3/31/94
0.53Q	5/19	6/10	6/16	6/30

Indicated div.: $2.12

CAPITALIZATION (12/31/93):

	($000)	(%)
Long-Term Debt	79,800	35.7
Cap. Lease Oblig.	11,029	4.9
Deferred Income Tax	26,355	11.8
Redeemable Cum Pfd Stk.	9,385	4.2
Common & Surplus	97,149	43.4
Total	223,718	100.0

DIVIDEND ACHIEVER STATUS:

Rank: 326 1983-93 Growth Rate: 2.8%
Total Years of Dividend Growth: 19

RECENT DEVELOPMENTS: For the year ended 12/31/93 net income fell 10.3% to $10.6 million from $11.9 million last year. Revenues were $147.3 million, up 1.4%. GMP's earnings were negatively affected by unfavorable results reported by the Green Mountain Propane Gas subsidiary and restructuring charges. Results were also negatively affected by an increase in power supply expenses.

PROSPECTS: The Company accepted a rate agreement that will, if approved by the Vermont Public Service Board, generate nearly $4 million in additional annual revenue. The settlement also provides for full recovery of $4.3 million in costs incurred by GMP relating to the Pine Street Barge Canal Superfund proceedings. The increase is needed to offset the increased cost of purchased electricity.

BUSINESS

GREEN MOUNTAIN POWER CORPORATION is an electric utility serving 79,100 retail customers in Vermont. GMP also sells electricity at wholesale to other utilities, three of which receive almost all of their power requirements from the Company. GMP's service territory cuts across central Vermont in a 25-mile wide strip from Lake Champlain to the Connecticut River, and also includes three non-contiguous population centers in southern Vermont. GMP has a whole or partial ownership interest in generational facilities that supply 40% of its total capacity of 417 megawatts. The balance of the generating capacity and 60% of the energy GMP distributes is purchased from other utilities. GMP holds a 30% interest in Vermont Electric Power, which owns nearly all of the transmission network that services Vermont.

REVENUES

(12/31/93)	($000)	(%)
Retail	130,061	88.3
Sales for Resales	14,441	9.8
Other	2,751	1.9
Total	147,253	100.0

ANNUAL EARNINGS AND DIVIDENDS PER SHARE

	1993	1992	1991	1990	1989	1988	1987
Earnings Per Share	**2.20**	**2.54**	**2.45**	**2.29**	**2.36**	**2.41**	**2.63**
Dividends Per Share	**2.11**	**2.08**	**2.04**	**2.00**	**1.95**	**1.89**	**1.83**
Dividend Payout %	**95.9**	**81.9**	**83.3**	**87.3**	**82.6**	**78.4**	**69.6**

ANNUAL FINANCIAL DATA

	1993	1992	1991	1990	1989	1988	1987
RECORD OF EARNINGS (IN THOUSANDS):							
Operating Revenues	147,253	145,240	143,555	147,633	144,028	128,613	129,811
Depreciation & Amort	8,572	8,065	7,046	6,754	5,907	5,440	5,338
Maintenance	4,352	4,692	4,340	4,377	4,822	5,514	4,155
Prov for Fed Inc Taxes	6,249	6,915	6,022	4,970	5,048	4,357	6,721
Operating Income	14,826	16,412	14,514	13,708	12,175	11,101	12,448
Total Interest Charges	6,828	6,819	6,972	6,865	5,479	4,579	4,453
Net Income	10,631	11,852	10,456	8,966	9,028	9,246	10,331
Aver. Shs. Outstg.	4,457	4,345	3,919	3,729	3,697	3,688	3,672
BALANCE SHEET (IN THOUSANDS):							
Gross Plant	246,968	233,828	219,880	208,220	183,479	164,155	151,934
Accumulated Depreciation	64,226	58,516	58,970	54,486	50,152	44,932	40,463
Prop, Plant & Equip, Net	182,742	175,312	160,910	153,734	133,327	119,223	111,471
Long-term Debt	90,829	79,594	68,897	73,423	56,992	41,558	42,624
Net Stockholders' Equity	106,534	102,220	97,280	82,029	72,833	71,592	71,167
Total Assets	291,854	257,218	229,216	214,940	189,072	170,157	159,998
Year End Shares Outstg	4,520	4,414	4,292	3,768	3,697	3,694	3,681
STATISTICAL RECORD:							
Book Value Per Share	20.72	20.08	20.38	19.09	18.79	18.39	18.12
Op. Inc/Net Pl %	8.1	9.4	9.0	8.9	9.1	9.3	11.2
Dep/Gr. Pl %	3.5	3.4	3.2	3.2	3.2	3.3	3.5
Accum. Dep/Gr. Pl %	26.0	25.0	26.8	26.2	27.3	27.4	26.6
Return on Equity %	10.9	12.8	12.0	12.5	13.0	13.6	15.5
Average Yield %	6.3	6.6	7.8	8.3	7.8	7.8	7.4
P/E Ratio	16.6-14.0	13.2-11.4	12.3-9.0	11.8-9.3	11.8-9.4	11.1-9.1	11.1-7.8
Price Range	36⅝-30¾	33⅝-29	30¼-22	27⅛-21¼	27⅞-22⅛	26¾-22	29¼-20½

Statistics are as originally reported.

OFFICERS:
D.G. Hyde, Pres. & C.E.O.
C.L. Dutton, V.P. & General Counsel
E.M. Norse, V.P., C.F.O. & Treas.

INCORPORATED: VT, Apr., 1893

PRINCIPAL OFFICE: 25 Green Mountain Drive, South Burlington, VT 05403

TELEPHONE NUMBER: (802) 864-5731
FAX: (802) 865-9129
NO. OF EMPLOYEES: 388
ANNUAL MEETING: In May
SHAREHOLDERS: 6,852 Com.; 6 Pfd.
INSTITUTIONAL HOLDINGS:
No. of Institutions: 39
Shares Held: 808,518

REGISTRAR(S): Manufacturers Hanover Trust Co., New York, NY

TRANSFER AGENT(S): Manufacturers Hanover Trust Co., New York, NY

NYS SYMBOL GTE
Rec. Pr. 32⅝

GTE CORP.

YIELD 5.8%
P/E RATIO 31.7

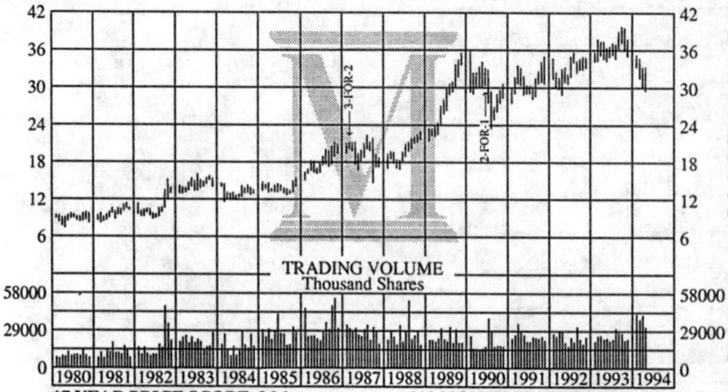

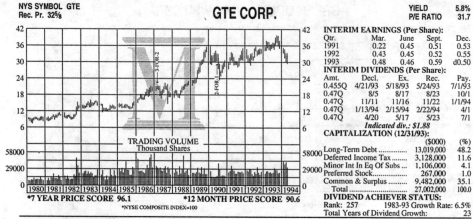

***7 YEAR PRICE SCORE 96.1** ***12 MONTH PRICE SCORE 90.6**

*NYSE COMPOSITE INDEX=100

INTERIM EARNINGS (Per Share):

Qtr.	Mar.	June	Sept.	Dec.
1991	0.22	0.45	0.51	0.53
1992	0.43	0.45	0.52	0.55
1993	0.48	0.46	0.59	d0.50

INTERIM DIVIDENDS (Per Share):

Amt.	Decl.	Ex.	Rec.	Pay.
0.455Q	4/21/93	5/18/93	5/24/93	7/1/93
0.47Q	8/5	8/17	8/23	10/1
0.47Q	11/11	11/16	11/22	1/1/94
0.47Q	1/13/94	2/15/94	2/22/94	4/1
0.47Q	4/20	5/17	5/23	7/1

Indicated div.: $1.88

CAPITALIZATION (12/31/93):

	($000)	(%)
Long-Term Debt	13,019,000	48.2
Deferred Income Tax	3,128,000	11.6
Minor Int In Eq Of Subs	1,106,000	4.1
Preferred Stock	267,000	1.0
Common & Surplus	9,482,000	35.1
Total	27,002,000	100.0

DIVIDEND ACHIEVER STATUS:
Rank: 257 1983-93 Growth Rate: 6.5%
Total Years of Dividend Growth: 23

RECENT DEVELOPMENTS: For the year ended 12/31/93, income from continuing operations was $990.0 million compared with $1.79 billion last year. Income includes a net non-recurring charge of $1.84 billion related to restructuring. Revenues were $19.75 billion, down 1.2%. The number of cellular customers increased 45% in 1993. Total cellular subscribers are approaching 1.6 million.

PROSPECTS: In 1/94, GTE announced plans to restructure and cut 17,000 jobs, or 13% of its work force. GTE's management believes the action is necessary to compete effectively in the multimedia age. The streamlining will include about 12,500 hourly workers and 4,500 salaried employees. As part of the plan, GTE will combine its Spacenet satellite communications operations with its Government Systems unit.

BUSINESS

GTE CORPORATION has three major business segments: telephone operations, telecommunications products and services, and electrical products. GTE has other subsidiaries engaged in financing, insurance, leasing and other activities offering financial and related services primarily to GTE operating companies. In March, 1991, GTE and Contel Corporation merged operations. With the merger, GTE is now the largest U.S. based local exchange telephone company and the second-largest cellular-telephone operator in the United States. The Company's telephone operating subsidiaries in the U.S. served approximately 21.4 million access lines in 40 states as of 12/31/92 and provided many types of communications services from homes and offices to industry and national defense.

REVENUES

(12/31/93)	($000)	(%)
Telephone Opers	15,829,000	80.2
Telecomm Products & Svces	3,919,000	19.8
Total	19,748,000	100.0

ANNUAL EARNINGS AND DIVIDENDS PER SHARE

	1993	1992	1991	1990	1989	1988	1987
Earnings Per Share	1.03	[1] [2] 1.95	[1] 1.69	2.26	2.08	1.79	1.65
Dividends Per Share	1.835	1.73	1.61	[3] 1.49	1.37	1.28	[4] 1.23
Dividend Payout %	N.M.	88.7	95.3	65.9	65.9	71.5	74.8

[1] Before disc. oper. [2] Before extraord. item [3] 2-for-1 stk split, 6/22/90 [4] 3-for-2 stk split, 2/87

ANNUAL FINANCIAL DATA

	1993	1992	1991	1990	1989	1988	1987
RECORD OF EARNINGS (IN MILLIONS):							
Total Revenues and Sales	19,748.0	19,984.0	19,621.0	18,374.0	17,424.4	16,459.9	15,421.0
Costs and Expenses	13,764.0	12,479.0	12,625.0	12,169.0	11,613.8	10,849.2	9,794.7
Depreciation & Amort	3,419.0	3,289.0	3,254.0	2,753.0	2,621.3	2,559.1	2,473.7
Operating Income	2,565.0	4,216.0	3,742.0	3,452.0	3,189.2	3,051.6	3,152.7
Income Bef Income Taxes	1,558.0	2,754.0	2,191.0	2,230.0	2,064.1	1,841.0	1,752.0
Income Tax Provision	568.0	967.0	662.0	689.0	646.8	616.3	633.1
Net Income	[1] 990.0	[2] 1,787.0	[3] 1,529.0	1,541.0	1,417.3	1,224.7	1,118.8
Aver. Shs. Outstg. (000)	945,000	905,000	882,000	664,000	659,298	657,178	658,342

[1] Before extra. item dr$90,000,000. [2] Before disc. op. dr$48,000,000; and extra. item dr$52,000,000; and acctg. chg dr$2,441,000,000. [3] Before disc. op. cr$51,000,000.

	1993	1992	1991	1990	1989	1988	1987
BALANCE SHEET (IN MILLIONS):							
Cash & Temp Cash Invests	322.0	354.0	517.0	431.0	395.8	307.0	170.8
Receivables, Net	4,164.0	3,676.0	3,869.0	3,652.0	3,499.0	3,159.9	2,665.7
Inventories	659.0	814.0	910.0	1,376.0	1,416.1	1,263.9	1,283.8
Gross Property	47,259.0	47,429.0	45,612.0	38,796.0	36,661.7	34,681.6	32,251.4
Accumulated Depreciation	18,539.0	17,609.0	16,289.0	14,264.0	12,961.4	11,694.8	10,249.4
Long-Term Debt	13,019.0	14,182.0	16,049.0	11,974.0	10,909.4	9,704.7	9,587.3
Net Stockholders' Equity	9,749.0	10,250.0	11,516.0	9,313.0	8,678.6	8,933.3	8,617.2
Total Assets	41,575.0	42,144.0	42,437.0	33,769.0	31,986.5	31,103.9	28,745.2
Total Current Assets	5,948.0	6,296.0	7,566.0	5,874.0	5,597.3	5,611.9	4,335.1
Total Current Liabilities	7,933.0	7,511.0	7,226.0	5,711.0	5,703.2	5,870.1	4,611.0
Net Working Capital	d1,985.0	d1,215.0	340.0	163.0	d105.9	d258.2	d275.9
Year End Shs Outstg (000)	951,762	939,530	888,900	669,392	660,602	652,578	651,100
STATISTICAL RECORD:							
Book Value Per Share	7.75	8.30	9.76	11.52	11.75	12.01	10.57
Return on Equity %	10.3	17.7	13.5	16.9	16.9	14.2	13.5
Average Yield %	5.0	5.4	5.2	5.0	4.8	6.4	6.6
P/E Ratio	38.7-33.1	18.3-14.8	20.7-16.3	15.9-10.4	17.1-10.3	12.8-9.4	13.6-8.9
Price Range	39⅞-34⅛	35¾-28⅞	35-27½	36-23½	35⅝-21½	23-16⅞	22⅜-14¾

Statistics are as originally reported.

OFFICERS:
K.B. Foster, Vice-Chmn.
M.T. Masin, Vice-Chmn.
C.R. Lee, Pres. & C.E.O.

INCORPORATED: NY, Feb., 1935

PRINCIPAL OFFICE: One Stamford Forum, Stamford, CT 06904

TELEPHONE NUMBER: (203) 965-2000
FAX: (203) 965-2520
NO. OF EMPLOYEES: 117,000 (approx.)
ANNUAL MEETING: In April
SHAREHOLDERS: 567,000
INSTITUTIONAL HOLDINGS:
No. of Institutions: 993
Shares Held: 412,870,375

REGISTRAR(S): GTE Shareholder Services Inc.(T/A), North Quincy, MA 02171
State Street Bank & Trust Co., Boston, MA 02266

TRANSFER AGENT(S): GTE Shareholder Services Inc.(T/A), North Quincy, MA 02171
State Street Bank & Trust Co., Boston, MA 02266

NYS SYMBOL HRD
Rec. Pr. 21¼

HANNAFORD BROS. CO.

YIELD 1.8%
P/E RATIO 16.0

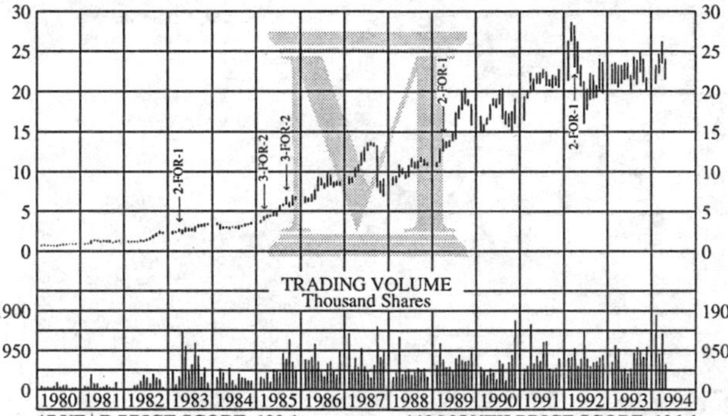

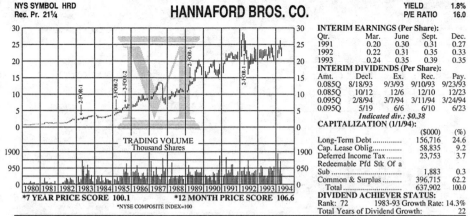

***7 YEAR PRICE SCORE 100.1** ***12 MONTH PRICE SCORE 106.6**

*NYSE COMPOSITE INDEX=100

INTERIM EARNINGS (Per Share):

Qtr.	Mar.	June	Sept.	Dec.
1991	0.20	0.30	0.31	0.27
1992	0.22	0.31	0.35	0.33
1993	0.24	0.35	0.39	0.35

INTERIM DIVIDENDS (Per Share):

Amt.	Decl.	Ex.	Rec.	Pay.
0.085Q	8/18/93	9/3/93	9/10/93	9/23/93
0.085Q	10/12	12/6	12/10	12/23
0.095Q	2/8/94	3/7/94	3/11/94	3/24/94
0.095Q	5/19	6/6	6/10	6/23

Indicated div.: $0.38

CAPITALIZATION (1/1/94):

	($000)	(%)
Long-Term Debt	156,716	24.6
Cap. Lease Oblig.	58,835	9.2
Deferred Income Tax	23,753	3.7
Redeemable Pfd Stk Of a Sub	1,883	0.3
Common & Surplus	396,715	62.2
Total	637,902	100.0

DIVIDEND ACHIEVER STATUS:
Rank: 72 1983-93 Growth Rate: 14.3%
Total Years of Dividend Growth: 22

RECENT DEVELOPMENTS: For the year ended 1/2/94, net income was $54.6 million compared with $49.2 million last year. Results were before an accounting credit of $2.1 million. Sales declined 0.5% to $2.05 billion. Same store sales declined 2.0%. Gross margin decreased 0.6% to $511.0 million and operating profit increased 8.9% to $111.5 million.

PROSPECTS: In response to increased competition among wholesale clubs and lower sales along the Canadian border, the Company has adopted a strong competitive pricing and merchandising platform. In the meantime, an ongoing restructuring program coupled with expense control measures should contribute to earnings growth.

BUSINESS

HANNAFORD BROTHERS COMPANY is involved in the retail food and drug business through supermarkets, drug stores and supermarket/drug combination stores. It operates 93 supermarkets throughout Maine and in parts of New York, New Hampshire, Massachusetts and Vermont under the names Shop 'n Save, Alexander's, Martin's and Sun Foods. In addition, the Company operates 38 separate pharmacies within its supermarkets or combination stores. In May 1992, HRD sold 34 of its 41 retail drug stores to Rite Aid Corporation. Wholesale sales are made to 20 independent customers in which Hannaford has no ownership interest. The Sobey Family of Nova Scotia owns 25.6% of HRD.

ANNUAL EARNINGS AND DIVIDENDS PER SHARE

	1/1/94	1/2/93	12/28/91	12/29/90	12/31/89	12/31/88	1/2/88
Earnings Per Share	**1.33**	**1.21**	**1.08**	**1.06**	**[2] 0.95**	**0.77**	**0.65**
Dividends Per Share	**0.34**	**0.30**	**[1] 0.26**	**0.22**	**[3] 0.18**	**0.16**	**0.14**
Dividend Payout %	**25.6**	**24.8**	**24.1**	**20.7**	**18.8**	**20.8**	**21.5**

[1] 2-for-1 stk split,03/11/92 [2] Before acctg. chg. [3] 2-for-1 stk split, 2/89

ANNUAL FINANCIAL DATA

	1/1/94	1/2/93	12/28/91	12/29/90	12/31/89	12/31/88	1/2/88
RECORD OF EARNINGS (IN MILLIONS):							
Sales & Other Revenues	2,054.9	2,066.0	2,008.0	1,687.6	1,520.6	1,261.7	1,033.4
Costs and Expenses	1,887.0	1,908.7	1,863.9	1,569.4	1,420.0	1,181.5	964.8
Depreciation & Amort	56.4	54.9	50.7	35.5	28.1	23.8	18.2
Operating Profit	111.5	102.4	93.4	82.7	358.0	337.9	271.8
Earn Bef Income Taxes	92.2	81.7	72.6	69.7	62.4	48.7	45.1
Income Taxes	37.6	32.5	29.3	27.5	25.0	18.8	20.3
Minority Interest	...	...	...	...	...	0.9	0.7
Net Income	[1] 54.6	49.2	43.4	42.2	[2] 37.4	28.9	24.1
Aver. Shs. Outstg. (000)	41,049	40,520	39,939	39,435	38,869	37,512	37,036
[1] Before acctg. change cr$2,100,000. [2] Before acctg. change cr$1,874,000.							
BALANCE SHEET (IN MILLIONS):							
Cash and Cash Equivalents	97.4	99.8	33.2	[1] 0.0	6.7	3.7	6.3
Receivables, Net	23.7	21.4	18.3	16.4	11.6	11.8	8.2
Inventories	129.9	124.9	150.0	148.9	112.2	92.6	74.7
Gross Property	711.6	656.3	600.9	524.9	408.2	330.5	269.8
Accumulated Depreciation	223.9	190.6	158.2	116.9	94.6	78.7	77.2
Long-Term Debt	156.7	171.6	165.3	159.5	94.3	77.0	52.4
Obligs Under Cap Lses	58.8	54.9	49.3	49.0	29.8	23.2	19.0
Net Stockholders' Equity	398.6	348.6	300.6	258.8	216.8	169.9	140.1
Total Assets	795.4	768.6	705.5	629.2	470.2	387.2	304.4
Total Current Assets	255.7	250.1	205.6	169.7	133.1	110.4	91.0
Total Current Liabilities	136.8	144.9	137.5	115.3	95.6	83.4	64.9
Net Working Capital	118.8	105.2	68.1	54.5	37.5	27.0	26.2
Year End Shs Outstg (000)	41,211	40,776	40,148	39,629	39,063	37,740	37,172
[1] Equal to $49,000.							
STATISTICAL RECORD:							
Operating Profit Margin %	5.4	5.0	4.7	4.9	4.8	4.5	4.9
Book Value Per Share	8.48	7.31	6.08	5.23	4.96	4.10	3.50
Return on Equity %	13.8	14.2	14.6	16.5	17.5	17.3	17.2
Return on Assets %	6.9	6.4	6.1	6.7	8.0	7.5	7.9
Average Yield %	1.5	1.3	1.3	1.2	1.2	1.6	1.4
P/E Ratio	18.8-15.0	23.7-13.2	21.1-15.2	19.2-14.0	21.4-11.2	15.4-10.9	21.0-10.6
Price Range	25-20	28⅝-16	22¾-16⅜	20⅜-14⅞	20⅜-10⅝	11⅞-8⅜	13⅝-6⅞

Statistics are as originally reported.

OFFICERS:
J.L. Moody, Jr., Chmn.
H.G. Farrington, Pres. & C.E.O.
N.E. Brackett, Sr. V.P. & C.F.O.

INCORPORATED: ME, Dec., 1902

PRINCIPAL OFFICE: 145 Pleasant Hill Rd., Scarborough, ME 04074

TELEPHONE NUMBER: (207) 883-2911
FAX: (207) 885-3165
NO. OF EMPLOYEES: 1,972
ANNUAL MEETING: In May
SHAREHOLDERS: 5,934
INSTITUTIONAL HOLDINGS:
No. of Institutions: 95
Shares Held: 14,529,628

REGISTRAR(S): Continental Stock Transfer & Trust Co., New York, NY

TRANSFER AGENT(S): Continental Stock Transfer & Trust Co., New York, NY

NYS SYMBOL H
Rec. Pr. 34¾

HARCOURT GENERAL, INC.

YIELD 1.7%
P/E RATIO 17.0

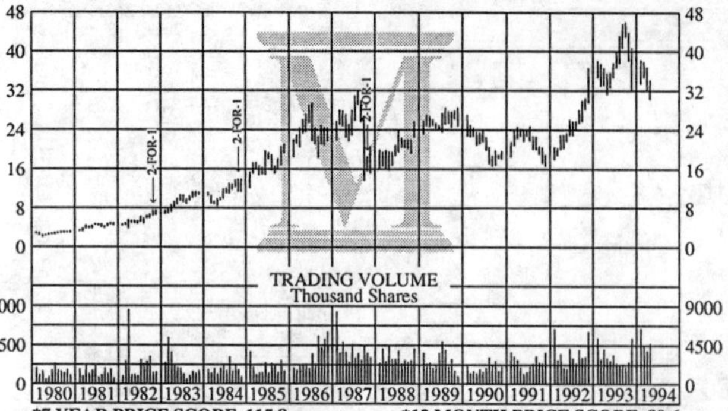

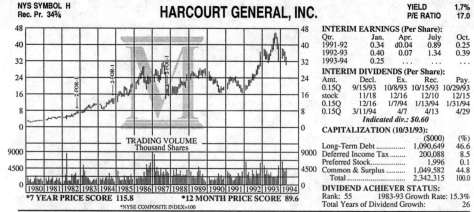

*7 YEAR PRICE SCORE 115.8 *12 MONTH PRICE SCORE 89.6

*NYSE COMPOSITE INDEX=100

INTERIM EARNINGS (Per Share):

Qtr.	Jan.	Apr.	July	Oct.
1991-92	0.34	d0.04	0.89	0.25
1992-93	0.40	0.07	1.34	0.39
1993-94	0.25	...	...	...

INTERIM DIVIDENDS (Per Share):

Amt.	Decl.	Ex.	Rec.	Pay.
0.15Q	9/15/93	10/8/93	10/15/93	10/29/93
stock	11/18	12/16	12/10	12/15
0.15Q	12/16	1/7/94	1/13/94	1/31/94
0.15Q	3/11/94	4/7	4/13	4/29

Indicated div.: $0.60

CAPITALIZATION (10/31/93):

	($000)	(%)
Long-Term Debt	1,090,649	46.6
Deferred Income Tax	200,088	8.5
Preferred Stock	1,996	0.1
Common & Surplus	1,049,582	44.8
Total	2,342,315	100.0

DIVIDEND ACHIEVER STATUS:
Rank: 55 1983-93 Growth Rate: 15.3%
Total Years of Dividend Growth: 26

RECENT DEVELOPMENTS: For the quarter ended 1/31/94, net income decreased 25.6% to $20.0 million compared with $26.8 million, from continuing operations, a year ago. However, 1/31/93 earnings included a non-recurring gain of $12.2 million. Revenues were up 3.1% to $832.2 million. Operating earnings from the specialty retailing segment increased 5.4% to $37.0 million. Comparisons were made with restated results. The Company spun off its theater operations to shareholders on 12/15/93.

PROSPECTS: The specialty retailing operations will be enhanced by improved levels of consumer confidence. However, restructuring and downsizing in corporate America should contribute to fluctuations in consumer confidence. The school textbook adoption schedule will result in increased demand over the next several years. Harcourt is preparing for 1995 by committing approximately $100 million to educational publishing product development in the current year.

BUSINESS

HARCOURT GENERAL, INC. engages primarily in publishing and specialty retailing. Harcourt also maintains leadership positions in insurance. Speciality retailing includes Neiman Marcus (65%-owned), which manages Neiman Marcus, Bergdorf Goodman, Contempo Casuals and NM Direct mail order businesses. The Harcourt Brace subsidiary is a leading domestic and international publisher in the educational, scientific, technical, medical, legal and trade fields. Insurance primarily consists of the underwriting of individual accident, health, life and credit insurance policies. Professional services provides human resources consulting services to large and small corporations worldwide.

BUSINESS LINE ANALYSIS

(10/31/93)	Rev(%)	Inc(%)
Publishing	25.8	39.3
Specialty Retail	55.2	33.2
Insurance	15.0	19.6
Professional Services.	4.0	7.9
Total	100.0	100.0

ANNUAL EARNINGS AND DIVIDENDS PER SHARE

	10/31/93	10/31/92	10/31/91	10/31/90	10/31/89	10/31/88	10/31/87
Earnings Per Share	**2.08**	**[1] 1.44**	**d3.88**	**1.51**	**[2] 1.43**	**[2] 1.12**	**[2] 1.18**
Dividends Per Share	**0.57**	**0.53**	**0.49**	**0.45**	**0.41**	**0.37**	**[3] 0.345**
Dividend Payout %	**27.4**	**36.8**	**...**	**29.8**	**28.7**	**33.0**	**29.2**

[1] Before extraord. item & acctg. chg. [2] Before disc. oper. [3] 2-for-1 stk. split, 10/87.

ANNUAL FINANCIAL DATA

RECORD OF EARNINGS (IN MILLIONS):							
Revenues	3,655.7	3,716.9	3,587.8	2,149.5	1,913.8	2,323.8	1,039.7
Costs and Expenses	3,172.2	3,302.2	3,412.4	2,033.2	1,762.8	2,064.9	885.4
Depreciation & Amort	169.3	173.6	315.2	62.5	58.6	85.4	44.6
Operating Earnings	314.3	241.1	d139.8	53.7	92.4	173.6	109.7
Earn Bef Income Taxes	262.1	187.0	d359.7	175.9	180.1	132.9	120.8
Income Tax Exp (benefit)	96.6	72.9	cr69.9	61.4	71.0	46.7	34.3
Minority Interest	...	...	3.3	3.3	3.3	3.3	...
Net Income	[1] 165.5	[2] 114.1	d293.1	111.3	[3] 105.9	[4] 82.9	[5] 86.5
Aver. Shs. Outstg. (000)	79,600	79,139	78,876	73,823	73,842	73,557	73,579

[1] Before disc. op. cr$5,843,000. [2] Before extra. item cr$419,557,000; and acctg. chg dr$39,196,000. [3] Before disc. op. cr$865,935,000. [4] Before disc. op. cr$4,855,000. [5] Before disc. op. dr$17,100,000.

BALANCE SHEET (IN MILLIONS):							
Cash and Cash Equivalents	466.9	430.7	1,619.0	1,634.4	1,687.8	22.9	91.6
Receivables, Net	493.4	399.3	318.2	199.5	190.7	207.3	208.5
Inventories	470.5	411.1	417.6	276.9	251.2	258.6	246.1
Gross Property	796.4	1,507.4	1,413.1	794.2	697.1	956.6	851.7
Accumulated Depreciation	279.8	655.9	584.3	218.5	168.3	332.9	276.3
Long-Term Debt	1,090.6	1,086.1	980.2	803.1	737.9	868.9	686.7
Net Stockholders' Equity	1,051.6	924.4	472.8	1,629.0	1,548.9	605.0	542.3
Total Assets	5,976.8	5,287.1	6,208.3	3,068.4	3,403.6	1,897.5	1,647.4
Total Current Assets	1,503.9	1,294.0	2,553.2	2,196.9	2,208.1	570.9	615.3
Total Current Liabilities	791.9	745.6	2,554.1	580.6	1,081.7	344.4	339.3
Net Working Capital	712.1	548.3	d0.8	1,616.2	1,126.5	226.5	276.0
Year End Shs Outstg (000)	77,307	76,292	75,160	69,589	69,325	68,626	68,270

STATISTICAL RECORD:							
Operating Profit Margin %	8.6	6.5	...	2.5	4.8	7.5	10.6
Book Value Per Share	8.40	6.64	0.54	20.71	19.76	6.93	6.13
Return on Equity %	15.7	12.3	...	6.8	6.8	13.7	16.0
Return on Assets %	2.8	2.2	...	3.6	3.1	4.4	5.3
Average Yield %	1.5	1.9	2.4	2.1	1.6	1.8	1.5
P/E Ratio	22.2-15.0	25.4-12.5	...	17.9-10.9	19.9-16.2	23.0-14.1	26.9-11.7
Price Range	46⅛-31¼	36⅝-18	24¾-16½	27-16½	28½-23⅛	25¾-15¾	31¾-13¾

Statistics are as originally reported.

OFFICERS:
R.A. Smith, Chairman
R.J. Tarr, Jr., Pres. & C.E.O.
J.R. Cook, Sr. V.P. & C.F.O.

INCORPORATED: DE, 1950

PRINCIPAL OFFICE: 27 Boylston St., Chestnut Hill, MA 02167

TELEPHONE NUMBER: (617) 232-8200
NO. OF EMPLOYEES: 3,223
ANNUAL MEETING: In March
SHAREHOLDERS: 9,245 com.; 847 ser. A pfd
INSTITUTIONAL HOLDINGS:
No. of Institutions: 251
Shares Held: 41,249,742

REGISTRAR(S):

TRANSFER AGENT(S):

NYS SYMBOL JH
Rec. Pr. 22¼

HARLAND (JOHN H.) CO.

YIELD 4.4%
P/E RATIO 13.7

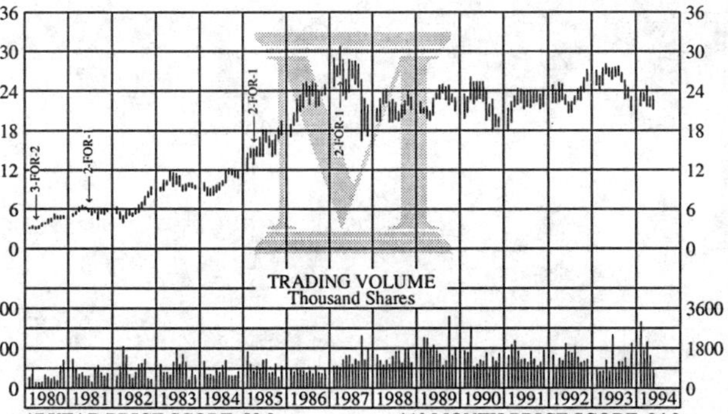

***7 YEAR PRICE SCORE 83.3** ***12 MONTH PRICE SCORE 94.0**

*NYSE COMPOSITE INDEX=100

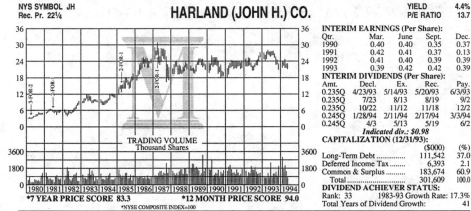

INTERIM EARNINGS (Per Share):

Qtr.	Mar.	June	Sept.	Dec.
1990	0.40	0.40	0.35	0.37
1991	0.42	0.41	0.37	0.13
1992	0.41	0.40	0.39	0.39
1993	0.39	0.42	0.42	0.39

INTERIM DIVIDENDS (Per Share):

Amt.	Decl.	Ex.	Rec.	Pay.
0.235Q	4/23/93	5/14/93	5/20/93	6/3/93
0.235Q	7/23	8/13	8/19	9/2
0.235Q	10/22	11/12	11/18	12/2
0.245Q	1/28/94	2/11/94	2/17/94	3/3/94
0.245Q	4/3	5/13	5/19	6/2

Indicated div.: $0.98

CAPITALIZATION (12/31/93):

	($000)	(%)
Long-Term Debt	111,542	37.0
Deferred Income Tax	6,393	2.1
Common & Surplus	183,674	60.9
Total	301,609	100.0

DIVIDEND ACHIEVER STATUS:
Rank: 33 1983-93 Growth Rate: 17.3%
Total Years of Dividend Growth: 41

RECENT DEVELOPMENTS: For the year ended 12/31/93, net income declined 7.3% to $52.5 million compared with $56.6 million the previous year. Sales increased 16.7% to $519.5 million from $445.0 million. The acquisition of Rocky Mountain Bank Note, the nation's fourth largest check printer, provided greater market penetration, boosting revenues and check units. Harland completed two common stock repurchase programs totaling 3.8 million shares.

PROSPECTS: The Company will make efforts to reduce costs and generate growth in a changing check printing environment. The changing market is attributable to the emergence of alternative distribution channels and consolidating financial institutions, which are intensifying price competition. Harland should realize further efficiency gains as a result of the continued intergration of Rocky Mountain Bank Note and Interchecks. Future results will benefit from the recent acquisition of Marketing Profiles, Inc.

BUSINESS

JOHN H. HARLAND COMPANY is a financial stationer primarily involved in the printing of checks and related items. Principal products consist of MICR encoded checks, deposit tickets and related forms for financial institutions and their customers. Financial institutions include commercial banks, savings & loan associations, brokerage firms and insurance companies. The Company offers a number of different styles of pocket checks, including checks incorporating multi-colored background scenes, three-to-the-page personal checks, three-to-the-page business checks, voucher checks, window checks and carbonized payroll checks. JH operates 50 printing plants nationwide and in Puerto Rico.

QUARTERLY DATA

(12/31/93)($000)	Rev	Inc
1st Quarter	133,504	13,119
2nd Quarter	129,979	14,127
3rd Quarter	129,922	13,318
4th Quarter	126,081	11,958

ANNUAL EARNINGS AND DIVIDENDS PER SHARE

	1993	1992	1991	1990	1989	1988	1987
Earnings Per Share	**1.62**	**1.59**	**[1] 1.33**	**1.52**	**1.54**	**1.41**	**1.26**
Dividends Per Share	**0.94**	**0.90**	**0.86**	**0.78**	**0.68**	**0.58**	**[2] 0.42**
Dividend Payout %	**58.0**	**56.6**	**64.2**	**51.3**	**44.2**	**41.1**	**33.3**

[1] Before acctg. chg. [2] 2-for-1 stk split, 3/87

ANNUAL FINANCIAL DATA

	1993	1992	1991	1990	1989	1988	1987
RECORD OF EARNINGS (IN THOUSANDS):							
Total Revenues	519,486	444,980	378,659	371,346	344,734	333,315	287,732
Costs and Expenses	423,477	356,777	281,507	265,321	240,432	239,881	207,810
Depreciation & Amort	35,102	29,662	22,684	20,871	18,042	16,380	11,733
Income From Operations	87,307	83,530	74,468	85,154	86,260	77,054	68,190
Income Bef Income Taxes	85,674	88,267	79,702	90,577	91,778	81,260	73,326
Income Taxes	33,152	31,629	29,882	33,410	33,727	27,936	29,773
Net Income	52,522	56,638	[1] 49,820	57,167	58,052	53,323	43,553
Aver. Shs. Outstg.	32,460	35,689	37,469	37,604	37,797	37,934	34,529
[1] Before acctg. change dr$2,385,000.							
BALANCE SHEET (IN THOUSANDS):							
Cash and Cash Equivalents	28,124	19,283	71,423	44,584	78,856	57,776	51,384
Receivables, Net	70,354	56,700	47,956	59,326	53,816	52,472	38,775
Inventories	26,000	27,121	24,234	23,877	21,809	19,536	13,065
Gross Property	305,042	278,283	251,693	264,653	234,163	211,150	156,946
Accumulated Depreciation	152,656	130,554	111,566	109,940	90,721	77,716	56,514
Long-Term Debt	111,542	12,622	11,661	12,649	11,276	11,232	...
Net Stockholders' Equity	183,674	256,222	292,263	295,686	272,596	244,367	189,309
Total Assets	356,451	339,880	351,554	356,638	321,081	295,364	224,855
Total Current Assets	134,895	110,659	150,389	138,009	162,777	137,770	111,812
Total Current Liabilities	43,979	59,466	35,053	28,401	24,016	29,665	35,546
Net Working Capital	90,916	51,193	115,336	109,608	138,761	108,105	76,266
Year End Shares Outstg	30,486	34,049	36,570	37,355	37,572	37,682	34,472
STATISTICAL RECORD:							
Operating Profit Margin %	16.8	18.8	19.7	22.9	25.0	23.1	23.7
Book Value Per Share	4.25	6.42	7.99	7.92	7.26	6.48	5.49
Return on Equity %	28.6	22.1	17.0	19.3	21.3	21.8	23.0
Return on Assets %	14.7	16.7	14.2	16.0	18.1	18.1	19.4
Average Yield %	3.8	3.8	4.1	3.5	3.1	2.7	1.8
P/E Ratio	17.4-12.9	17.1-12.9	18.3-13.4	17.2-11.8	16.2-12.7	17.2-13.7	24.4-13.0
Price Range	28⅛-20⅞	27¼-20½	24⅜-17⅞	26⅛-17⅞	25-19½	24¼-19¼	30¾-16⅜

Statistics are as originally reported.

OFFICERS:
R.R. Woodson, Chmn., Pres. & C.E.O.
I.W. Lang, Sr. V.P. & Sec.
W.M. Dollar, V.P., Treas. & C.F.O.

INCORPORATED: GA, Jun., 1923

PRINCIPAL OFFICE: 2939 Miller Road, Decatur, GA 30035

TELEPHONE NUMBER: (404) 981-9460
FAX: (404) 593-5619
NO. OF EMPLOYEES: 911
ANNUAL MEETING: In April
SHAREHOLDERS: 5,705
INSTITUTIONAL HOLDINGS:
No. of Institutions: 225
Shares Held: 21,189,679

REGISTRAR(S): Trust Company Bank, Atlanta, GA

TRANSFER AGENT(S): Trust Company Bank, Atlanta, GA

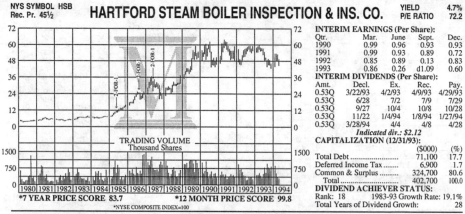

NYS SYMBOL HSB
Rec. Pr. 45½

HARTFORD STEAM BOILER INSPECTION & INS. CO.

YIELD 4.7%
P/E RATIO 72.2

*7 YEAR PRICE SCORE 83.7   *12 MONTH PRICE SCORE 99.8

*NYSE COMPOSITE INDEX=100

INTERIM EARNINGS (Per Share):

Qtr.	Mar.	June	Sept.	Dec.
1990	0.99	0.96	0.93	0.93
1991	0.99	0.93	0.89	0.72
1992	0.85	0.89	0.13	0.83
1993	0.86	0.26	d1.09	0.60

INTERIM DIVIDENDS (Per Share):

Amt.	Decl.	Ex.	Rec.	Pay.
0.53Q	3/22/93	4/2/93	4/9/93	4/29/93
0.53Q	6/28	7/2	7/9	7/29
0.53Q	9/27	10/4	10/8	10/28
0.53Q	11/22	1/4/94	1/8/94	1/27/94
0.53Q	3/28/94	4/4	4/8	4/28

Indicated div.: $2.12

CAPITALIZATION (12/31/93):

	($000)	(%)
Total Debt	71,100	17.7
Deferred Income Tax	6,900	1.7
Common & Surplus	324,700	80.6
Total	402,700	100.0

DIVIDEND ACHIEVER STATUS:
Rank: 18   1983-93 Growth Rate: 19.1%
Total Years of Dividend Growth: 28

RECENT DEVELOPMENTS: For the three months ended 12/31/93, net income was $12.4 million, down 28% from the comparable period of 1992. Insurance premiums were $87.2 million, a very modest decline from $87.8 million a year ago. The focus on risk selection, price increases and coverage adjustments were the reasons for the flat results. For the twelve months ended 12/31/93, income including $20 million in restructuring charges was $13.1 million compared with $56.3 million for 1992. Engineering services recorded flat revenues due to delays in the authorization of projects.

PROSPECTS: The restructuring of operations and a sharper focus on engineering services should improve the earnings picture. The reduction of the workforce should also offer benefits in the future. Insurance operations have been hit with intense price competition and a high number of weather-related catastrophes. Correcting prior under-pricing and re-underwriting major accounts is underway and has been successful so far. This process entails non-renewal of poor risks, price increases and changes in the conditions of coverage.

BUSINESS

HARTFORD STEAM BOILER INSPECTION & INSURANCE COMPANY offers engineering services and property insurance that help protect people, property and the environment. The core business is boiler and machinery and all risk property insurance for commercial and industrial facilities. Other areas include environmental services, property insurance and products and services for the international market. Subsidiaries include The Boiler Inspection and Insurance Co. of Canada, Radian Corp., and Engineering Insurance Group.

REVENUES

(12/31/93)	($000)	(%)
Insurance Premiums..	349,200	54.9
Engineering Services.	231,500	36.4
Investment Income	29,300	4.6
Realized Invest Gains	26,100	4.1
Total	636,100	100.0

ANNUAL EARNINGS AND DIVIDENDS PER SHARE

	1993	1992	1991	1990	1989	1988	1987
Earnings Per Share	0.63	①2.71	3.53	3.80	3.78	3.46	2.61
Dividends Per Share	2.12	②2.03	1.85	1.70	1.50	1.15	③0.95
Dividend Payout %	N.M.	74.9	52.4	44.7	39.7	33.2	36.4

① Before acctg. chg.   ② Bef acctg chge   ③ 2-for-1 stk. split, 4/87.

ANNUAL FINANCIAL DATA

RECORD OF EARNINGS (IN THOUSANDS):

	1993	1992	1991	1990	1989	1988	1987
Insurance Premiums	349,200	350,100	323,303	298,600	286,792	291,794	283,490
Net Investment Income	29,300	36,500	41,449	42,403	41,679	35,773	35,497
Total Revenues	636,100	682,100	630,433	562,373	500,977	458,742	421,663
Claims & Adjustment	199,100	177,700	141,510	111,206	95,606	102,263	101,092
Income Before Taxes	16,900	73,400	101,036	110,489	109,645	96,001	82,048
Income Taxes	3,800	17,100	27,168	31,741	32,074	25,342	21,404
Gain on Sale Of Securities	...	...	...	...	...	...	7,259
Net Income	①13,100	②56,300	73,868	78,748	77,571	70,659	60,644
Aver. Shs. Outstg.	20,700	20,800	20,950	20,741	20,520	20,409	20,476

① Before acctg. change dr$3,600,000.   ② Before acctg. change dr$15,100,000.

BALANCE SHEET (IN THOUSANDS):

	1993	1992	1991	1990	1989	1988	1987
Cash	7,300	8,700	5,985	11,644	5,572	5,183	17,243
Fixed Maturities	154,900	151,600	154,613	194,172	190,261	231,248	205,660
Equity Securities, At Mkt	290,000	309,900	332,769	251,499	302,163	224,904	210,410
Total Assets	877,900	888,000	888,542	827,317	794,510	730,143	701,674
Benefits and Claims	383,700	305,200	272,118	268,793	283,689	301,421	292,301
Net Stockholders' Equity	324,700	374,300	409,321	355,251	335,472	266,476	216,745
Year End Shares Outstg	20,500	20,700	21,018	20,833	20,599	20,442	20,348

STATISTICAL RECORD:

	1993	1992	1991	1990	1989	1988	1987
Return on Equity %	4.0	15.0	18.0	22.2	23.1	26.5	28.0
Book Value Per Share	15.84	18.08	19.47	17.05	16.29	13.04	10.65
Average Yield %	4.1	3.9	3.4	3.2	3.2	3.8	3.3
P/E Ratio	95.0-67.7	21.9-16.7	18.1-13.1	16.3-11.4	15.7-9.2	10.8-6.5	14.0-7.8
Price Range	59⅞-42⅝	59¼-45⅛	63¾-46⅛	62⅛-43½	59¼-34¾	37¼-22½	36⅝-20¼

Statistics are as originally reported.

OFFICERS:
W. Wilde, Chmn. & C.E.O.
G.W. Kreh, President
R.W. Trainer, Sr. V.P., Treas. & C.F.O.
R.K. Price, Sr. V.P. & Corp. Sec.
INCORPORATED: CT, 1866
PRINCIPAL OFFICE: One State Street, Hartford, CT 06102

TELEPHONE NUMBER: (203) 722-1866
FAX: (203) 722-5107
NO. OF EMPLOYEES: 4,000 (approx.)
ANNUAL MEETING: In April
SHAREHOLDERS: 5,764
INSTITUTIONAL HOLDINGS:
No. of Institutions: 177
Shares Held: 10,418,735

REGISTRAR(S): First National Bank of Boston, Shareholder Services Division, Boston, MA

TRANSFER AGENT(S): First National Bank of Boston, Shareholder Services Division, Boston, MA

HASBRO, INC.

YIELD 0.8%
P/E RATIO 15.1

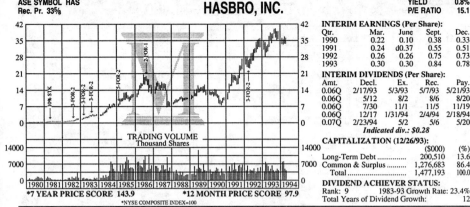

*7 YEAR PRICE SCORE 143.9   *12 MONTH PRICE SCORE 97.9

*NYSE COMPOSITE INDEX=100

INTERIM EARNINGS (Per Share):

Qtr.	Mar.	June	Sept.	Dec.
1990	0.22	0.10	0.38	0.33
1991	0.24	d0.37	0.55	0.51
1992	0.26	0.26	0.75	0.73
1993	0.30	0.30	0.84	0.78

INTERIM DIVIDENDS (Per Share):

Amt.	Decl.	Ex.	Rec.	Pay.
0.06Q	2/17/93	5/3/93	5/7/93	5/21/93
0.06Q	5/12	8/2	8/6	8/20
0.06Q	7/30	11/1	11/5	11/19
0.06Q	12/17	1/31/94	2/4/94	2/18/94
0.07Q	2/23/94	5/2	5/6	5/20

Indicated div.: $0.28

CAPITALIZATION (12/26/93):

	($000)	(%)
Long-Term Debt	200,510	13.6
Common & Surplus	1,276,683	86.4
Total	1,477,193	100.0

DIVIDEND ACHIEVER STATUS:
Rank: 9   1983-93 Growth Rate: 23.4%
Total Years of Dividend Growth: 12

RECENT DEVELOPMENTS: For the year ended 12/26/93, net income increased 11.6% to $200.0 million compared with $179.2 million in 1992. Revenues were up 8.1% to $2.75 billion. Earnings included a pre-tax restructuring charge of $15.5 million. The promoted brands group was led by Kenner due in part to the continued enthusiasm for Littlest Pet Shop and Jurassic Park items. Hasbro Toy began to benefit from an up-turn in several of its products.

PROSPECTS: Operating results will be fueled by a mix of new and existing products. The Company will make its initial foray into the juvenile products market with the 1-2-3 High Chair, which is scheduled for release in the spring. In April, Hasbro agreed to acquire Western Publishing Group Inc.'s puzzles and games for $105 million. Included in the transaction are two popular games for adults, Pictionary and Balderdash, and the largest line of puzzles in the nation. Western Publishing has annual sales of approximately $130 million.

BUSINESS

HASBRO INCORPORATED is the world's largest toy manufacturer, offering a diverse line of toys, board and card games, dolls, preschool toys, boys' and girls' action toys as well as infant care products. In 1984, HAS acquired Milton Bradley Co. Hasbro's extensive portfolio was further strengthened and expanded with the 1991 acquisition of Tonka Corp., which in addition to the well-known Tonka products also included Parker Bros. and Kenner. The Company's products now include Milton Bradley games and puzzles, Parker Bros. games, G.I. Joe, Fashion Plates, Fantastic Flowers, Playskool, Tonka trucks and the Kenner products including Easy Bake Oven and Play-Doh.

BUSINESS LINE ANALYSIS

(12/26/93)	Rev(%)	Inc(%)
United States	60.8	68.9
Foreign	39.2	31.1
Total	100.0	100.0

ANNUAL EARNINGS AND DIVIDENDS PER SHARE

	12/26/93	12/27/92	12/29/91	12/30/90	12/31/89	12/25/88	12/27/87
Earnings Per Share	2.22	2.01	0.94	1.03	1.04	0.83	0.55
Dividends Per Share	0.23	0.19	0.153	0.127	0.10	0.075	0.06
Dividend Payout %	10.4	9.5	16.3	12.3	9.6	9.1	11.0

ANNUAL FINANCIAL DATA

RECORD OF EARNINGS (IN MILLIONS):

Net Revenues	2,747.2	2,541.1	2,141.1	1,520.0	1,409.7	1,357.9	1,345.1
Costs and Expenses	2,360.6	2,183.0	1,874.4	1,339.2	1,196.7	1,152.9	1,160.5
Depreciation & Amort	100.6	62.1	81.9	39.7	42.9	51.0	52.1
Operating Profit	351.2	324.5	237.4	160.3	170.1	154.1	132.5
Earn Bef Income Taxes	325.2	292.2	145.6	152.4	156.8	131.4	99.6
Income Taxes	125.2	113.2	63.9	63.3	64.6	59.0	51.4
Net Income	200.0	① 179.0	81.7	89.2	92.2	72.4	48.2
Aver. Shs. Outstg. (000)	90,031	89,086	86,983	87,119	88,779	79,548	83,345
① Before acctg. change cr$214,000.							

BALANCE SHEET (IN MILLIONS):

Cash and Cash Equivalents	186.3	126.0	120.6	289.3	278.2	231.8	161.8
Receivables, Net	...	...	...	...	...	...	352.8
Inventories	250.1	217.9	208.4	137.4	142.7	116.3	133.6
Gross Property	413.0	363.1	325.0	252.8	236.8	226.2	228.3
Accumulated Depreciation	133.2	111.8	99.9	83.6	67.0	61.2	52.1
Long-Term Debt	200.5	206.2	380.3	56.9	57.6	126.6	127.1
Net Stockholders' Equity	1,276.7	1,105.6	955.3	867.8	802.3	703.2	641.5
Total Assets	2,293.0	2,082.8	1,950.1	1,284.8	1,246.5	1,111.9	1,076.0
Total Current Assets	1,301.1	1,116.9	1,025.2	861.6	806.9	736.0	692.6
Total Current Liabilities	748.3	701.3	593.8	357.6	384.1	272.5	303.9
Net Working Capital	552.8	415.6	431.4	504.0	422.8	463.5	388.7
Year End Shs Outstg (000)	87,795	87,176	86,184	84,744	88,067	79,280	79,280

STATISTICAL RECORD:

Operating Profit Margin %	12.8	12.8	11.1	10.5	12.1	11.3	9.8
Book Value Per Share	7.01	4.76	3.52	7.46	6.21	6.30	5.51
Return on Equity %	15.7	16.2	8.5	10.3	11.5	10.3	7.5
Return on Assets %	8.7	8.6	4.2	6.9	7.4	6.5	4.5
Average Yield %	0.7	0.6	0.8	1.2	0.8	0.8	0.5
P/E Ratio	18.1-12.7	17.8-11.5	29.0-10.8	14.1-7.4	15.6-9.7	13.7-9.6	32.0-12.0
Price Range	40⅛-28⅛	35⅞-23⅛	27¼-10⅛	14⅜-7½	16¼-10⅛	11⅜-8	17⅝-6⅝

Statistics are as originally reported.

OFFICERS:
A.G. Hassenfeld, Chmn., Pres. & C.E.O.
B.J. Alperin, Vice-Chmn.
J.T. O'Neill, Exec. V.P. & & C.F.O.
D.M. Robbins, Sr. V.P., Couns. & Sec.

INCORPORATED: RI, Jan., 1926

PRINCIPAL OFFICE: 1027 Newport Ave., Pawtucket, RI 02862-1059

TELEPHONE NUMBER: (401) 431-8697
FAX: (401) 431-8400
NO. OF EMPLOYEES: 3,498
ANNUAL MEETING: In May
SHAREHOLDERS: 2,350 (approx.)
INSTITUTIONAL HOLDINGS:
No. of Institutions: 335
Shares Held: 63,314,507

REGISTRAR(S): First National Bank of Boston, Shareholder Services Division, Boston, MA

TRANSFER AGENT(S): First National Bank of Boston, Shareholder Services Division, Boston, MA

HAVERTY FURNITURE COS., INC.

YIELD 1.7%
P/E RATIO 18.5

7 YEAR PRICE SCORE 140.3 **12 MONTH PRICE SCORE 95.3**
*NYSE COMPOSITE INDEX=100

TRADING VOLUME
Thousand Shares

INTERIM EARNINGS (Per Share):				
Qtr.	Mar.	June	Sept.	Dec.
1990	0.18	0.10	0.17	0.31
1991	0.07	0.03	0.05	0.11
1992	0.09	0.01	0.13	0.29
1993	0.21	0.14	0.21	0.34

INTERIM DIVIDENDS (Per Share):				
Amt.	Decl.	Ex.	Rec.	Pay.
50%	5/7/93	7/1/93	6/15/93	6/30/93
0.0675Q	8/6	8/10	8/16	8/25
0.0675Q	11/5	11/8	11/15	11/24
0.0675Q	2/8/94	2/14/94	2/18/94	2/28/94
0.0675Q	5/6	5/10	5/16	5/25

Indicated div.: $0.27

CAPITALIZATION (12/31/93):

	($000)	(%)
Long-Term Debt	94,197	43.9
Common & Surplus	120,418	56.1
Total	214,615	100.0

DIVIDEND ACHIEVER STATUS:
Rank: 214   1983-93 Growth Rate: 8.2%
Total Years of Dividend Growth: 19

RECENT DEVELOPMENTS: For the year ended 12/31/93, net income more than doubled to $9.7 million compared with $4.5 million in 1992. Net sales amounted to $322.9 million, up 14.5% from $282.0 million in 1992. Earnings per share were $0.91 versus $0.53 last year. For the quarter, net income was $3.9 million, up 52% from $2.6 million a year ago. Earnings per share were $0.34 versus $0.29 in the fourth quarter last year. Net sales were up 12.3% to $92.1 million

from $82.0 million in the same period last year. Comparable-store sales were up 12.0% in the fourth quarter, resulting in a 13.1% gain for 1993 as a whole. HAVT's performance benefited from the general resurgence in consumer purchases of home furnishings. The company is concentrating on upgrading its merchandise line as well as remodeling and expanding its showrooms.

BUSINESS

HAVERTY FURNITURE COMPANIES, INC. currently operates 89 retail furnishings stores in eleven states throughout the Southeast and Southwest, including four stores dedicated to the Thomasville line and 23 stores which feature Thomasville galley displays. Haverty maintains and warehouses inventory for prompt delivery of merchandise sold. Customers may purchase on credit terms. Haverty carries its own customer accounts receivable. The Company provides attractive and conveniently located stores, professional employees and full service, including financing of customer accounts on the basis of satisfactory terms. To accomplish this, the Company has maintained a continual program of store relocation, modernization of older units, and upgrading of its merchandising. The relocation program, principally a shift to suburban areas, has been completed. To complement these retail units and provide prompt delivery of merchandise to customers, the Company operates a warehouse in each city in which it is located.

QUARTERLY DATA

(12/31/93)($000)	Rev	Inc
1st Quarter	77,734	1,902
2nd Quarter	71,876	1,534
3rd Quarter	81,179	2,396
4th Quarter	92,070	3,884

ANNUAL EARNINGS AND DIVIDENDS PER SHARE

	1993	1992	1991	1990	1989	1988	1987
Earnings Per Share	0.91	0.53	0.27	0.75	0.90	0.88	0.98
Dividends Per Share	[1] 0.33	0.257	0.253	0.247	0.24	0.235	0.23
Dividend Payout %	36.3	48.7	95.0	32.7	26.7	26.7	23.5

[1] 3-for-2 stk split,07/01/93

ANNUAL FINANCIAL DATA

RECORD OF EARNINGS (IN THOUSANDS):

	1993	1992	1991	1990	1989	1988	1987
Total Revenues	333,359	292,511	257,956	260,799	242,974	239,968	229,289
Costs and Expenses	300,024	268,882	238,741	235,472	219,270	217,080	204,661
Depreciation & Amort	6,875	6,069	5,479	5,232	4,934	4,590	3,948
Operating Income	26,460	17,560	13,736	20,095	18,770	18,298	20,680
Income Bef Income Taxes	15,650	7,188	3,555	8,795	10,903	10,905	14,631
Total Income Taxes	5,934	2,656	1,315	2,364	3,110	3,251	5,929
Net Income	9,716	4,532	2,240	6,431	7,793	7,654	8,702
Aver. Shs. Outstg.	10,733	8,571	8,492	8,552	8,670	8,726	8,885

BALANCE SHEET (IN THOUSANDS):

Cash & Cash Equivalents	614	1,189	1,741	1,481	2,938	4,069	2,120
Receivables, Net	138,823	112,502	92,931	97,682	78,748	78,280	74,077
Inventories, At LIFO	54,739	50,573	49,483	50,443	44,616	40,159	39,677
Gross Property	112,374	102,320	95,567	88,715	90,943	85,930	80,898
Accumulated Depreciation	44,935	41,024	37,668	33,234	29,861	25,660	22,074
Long-Term Debt	94,197	79,630	74,406	80,149	77,229	74,505	63,111
Capital Lease Obligations	...	...	...	...	6,163	6,573	7,497
Net Stockholders' Equity	120,418	83,567	80,804	80,969	76,960	72,469	66,877
Total Assets	264,353	229,184	208,653	208,862	191,097	186,882	178,194
Total Current Assets	195,174	165,637	148,345	150,905	127,440	123,484	117,008
Total Current Liabilities	47,441	62,170	49,155	43,264	26,077	28,779	36,901
Net Working Capital	147,733	103,467	99,190	107,641	101,363	94,705	80,107
Year End Shares Outstg	8,190	5,084	8,467	8,515	8,576	8,720	8,721

STATISTICAL RECORD:

Operating Profit Margin %	7.9	6.0	5.3	7.7	7.7	7.6	9.0
Book Value Per Share	14.70	16.44	9.54	9.51	8.97	8.31	7.67
Return on Equity %	8.1	5.4	2.8	7.9	10.1	10.6	13.0
Return on Assets %	3.7	2.0	1.1	3.1	4.1	4.1	4.9
Average Yield %	2.2	3.0	4.1	4.0	3.1	3.1	2.6
P/E Ratio	21.6-12.0	21.7-10.4	27.8-18.1	10.7-6.0	10.0-7.2	10.2-7.2	12.2-6.1
Price Range	19⅝-10⅞	11½-5½	7½-4⅞	8-4½	9-6½	9-6⅜	12-6

Statistics are as originally reported.

OFFICERS:
R. Haverty, Chmn.
F.S. McGaughey, Jr., Pres. & C.E.O.
D.L. Fink, Sr. V.P.-Fin. & C.F.O.
H.G. Wells, Jr., V.P. & Treas.

INCORPORATED: MD, Sep., 1929

PRINCIPAL OFFICE: 866 W. Peachtree St., N.W., Atlanta, GA 30308-1123

TELEPHONE NUMBER: (404) 881-1911

NO. OF EMPLOYEES: 332

ANNUAL MEETING: In April

SHAREHOLDERS: 1,863 com.; 500, cl. A com. (approx.)

INSTITUTIONAL HOLDINGS:
No. of Institutions: 34
Shares Held: 1,490,508

REGISTRAR(S): Wachovia Bank of North Carolina, N.A., P.O. Box 3001, Winston-Salem, NC 27102

TRANSFER AGENT(S): Wachovia Bank of North Carolina, N.A., P.O. Box 3001, Winston-Salem, NC 27102

NYS SYMBOL HE
Rec. Pr. 31¾

HAWAIIAN ELECTRIC INDUSTRIES, INC.

YIELD 7.3%
P/E RATIO 13.4

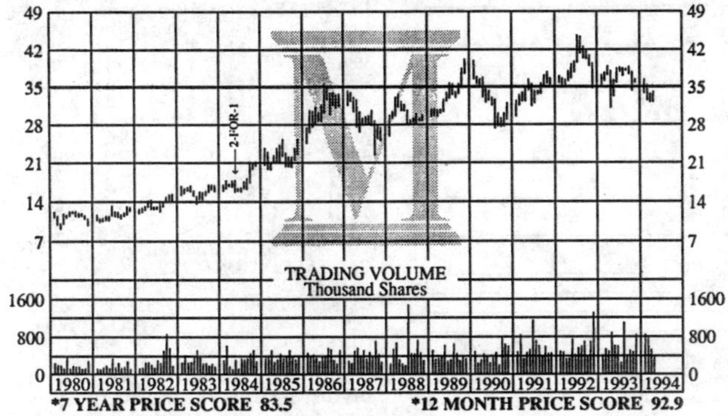

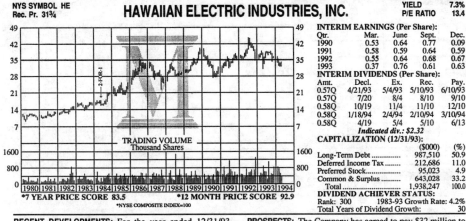

*7 YEAR PRICE SCORE 83.5 *12 MONTH PRICE SCORE 92.9

*NYSE COMPOSITE INDEX=100

INTERIM EARNINGS (Per Share):

Qtr.	Mar.	June	Sept.	Dec.
1990	0.53	0.64	0.77	0.09
1991	0.58	0.59	0.64	0.59
1992	0.55	0.64	0.68	0.67
1993	0.37	0.76	0.61	0.63

INTERIM DIVIDENDS (Per Share):

Amt.	Decl.	Ex.	Rec.	Pay.
0.57Q	4/21/93	5/4/93	5/10/93	6/10/93
0.57Q	7/20	8/4	8/10	9/10
0.58Q	10/19	11/4	11/10	12/10
0.58Q	1/18/94	2/4/94	2/10/94	3/10/94
0.58Q	4/19	5/4	5/10	6/13

Indicated div.: $2.32

CAPITALIZATION (12/31/93):

	($000)	(%)
Long-Term Debt	987,510	50.9
Deferred Income Tax	212,686	11.0
Preferred Stock	95,023	4.9
Common & Surplus	643,028	33.2
Total	1,938,247	100.0

DIVIDEND ACHIEVER STATUS:
Rank: 300 1983-93 Growth Rate: 4.2%
Total Years of Dividend Growth: 30

RECENT DEVELOPMENTS: For the year ended 12/31/93, income from continuing operations edged downward to $61.7 million. Revenues were $1.14 billion, up 10.7%. Results for 1993 include a charge of $15 million to establish an additional reserve to cover the settlement of a lawsuit filed by the Hawaii Insurance Commissioner and Hawaii Insurance Guaranty Association against HE. Operating income at Hawaiian Electric Co. and its subsidiaries was up 15% due primarily to rate increases.

PROSPECTS: The Company has agreed to pay $32 million to the Insurance Commissioner in return for a dismissal of the lawsuit and a release of claims against HE. The lawsuit relates to HE's former insurance subsidiary, Hawaiian Insurance Group (HIG). HE discontinued HIG in 1992 due to soaring insurance claims from Hurricane Iniki. The state insurance commissioner alleged that HIG was mismanaged as a part of HE. The settlement is subject to court approval.

BUSINESS

HAWAIIAN ELECTRIC INDUSTRIES, INC. is a Hawaii-based electric utility holding company with subsidiaries in energy, banking, maritime freight transportation and real estate development. The three utilities supply electricity to about 95% of Hawaii's population. Diversified manufacturing and a large tourist business are the major factors in the local economy. Non-utility companies include: American Savings Bank, HEI Investment Corporation, Hawaiian Tug and Barge Corporation, Malama Pacific Corporation and Hawaiian Electric Renewable Systems, Inc.

BUSINESS LINE ANALYSIS

(12/31/93)	Rev(%)	Inc(%)
Electric Utility	77.0	75.8
Savings Bank	17.5	28.0
Other	5.5	-3.8
Total	100.0	100.0

ANNUAL EARNINGS AND DIVIDENDS PER SHARE

	1993	1992	1991	1990	1989	1988	1987
Earnings Per Share	**2.38**	**[1] 2.54**	**2.40**	**2.02**	**3.06**	**2.90**	**2.20**
Dividends Per Share	**2.29**	**2.25**	**2.21**	**2.17**	**2.07**	**1.95**	**1.83**
Dividend Payout %	**96.2**	**88.6**	**92.1**	**N.M.**	**67.6**	**67.2**	**83.2**

[1] Before disc. oper.

ANNUAL FINANCIAL DATA

	1993	1992	1991	1990	1989	1988	1987
RECORD OF EARNINGS (IN MILLIONS):							
Total Revenues	1,142.2	1,031.4	1,083.8	1,010.8	884.1	732.7	635.1
Depreciation & Amort	64.3	61.9	61.9	54.7	48.5	39.5	38.7
Operating Income	157.6	136.2	131.2	116.3	131.9	117.1	112.3
Interest Expense	46.2	40.4	43.6	41.2	38.1	34.3	37.0
Net Income	[1] 61.7	[2] 61.7	54.8	43.6	64.1	55.0	37.8
Aver. Shs. Outstg. (000)	25,938	24,275	22,882	21,559	20,960	18,984	17,208
[1] Before disc. op. dr$13,025,000. [2] Before disc. op. dr$73,297,000.							
BALANCE SHEET (IN MILLIONS):							
Gross Plant	2,221.2	2,002.9	1,857.7	1,707.2	1,574.1	1,425.1	1,281.4
Accumulated Depreciation	678.2	615.1	572.9	517.6	467.5	422.5	385.7
Prop, Plant & Equip, Net	1,543.0	1,387.8	1,284.8	1,189.7	1,106.6	1,002.6	895.7
Long-term Debt	987.5	776.6	798.6	683.5	698.3	643.8	359.5
Net Stockholders' Equity	738.1	633.0	668.4	599.0	583.0	514.3	403.6
Total Assets	4,521.6	4,142.8	3,904.5	3,673.9	3,130.3	2,683.2	1,279.2
Year End Shs Outstg (000)	27,675	24,762	23,867	21,918	21,266	20,681	17,504
STATISTICAL RECORD:							
Book Value Per Share	21.44	20.06	21.89	20.33	19.93	18.23	19.59
Op. Inc/Net Pl %	10.2	9.8	10.2	9.8	11.9	11.7	12.5
Dep/Gr. Pl %	...	...	...	...	...	...	3.1
Accum. Dep/Gr. Pl %	30.5	30.7	30.8	30.3	29.7	29.6	30.1
Return on Equity %	8.9	10.6	8.9	8.0	12.1	11.2	10.0
Average Yield %	6.6	5.7	6.6	6.5	5.9	6.6	6.5
P/E Ratio	16.3-13.0	17.6-13.7	15.8-12.2	19.8-13.5	13.2-9.6	11.6-8.9	15.6-10.1
Price Range	38⅞-31	44⅝-34¾	37⅞-29⅜	40-27¼	40¼-29⅜	33⅝-25⅞	34¼-22¼

Statistics are as originally reported.

OFFICERS:
R.F. Clarke, Pres. & C.E.O.
R.F. Mougeot, Financial V.P. & C.F.O.
C.H. Lau, Treasurer

INCORPORATED: HI, Jul., 1981

PRINCIPAL OFFICE: 900 Richards Street, Honolulu, HI 96813

TELEPHONE NUMBER: (808) 543-5662
FAX: (808) 543-7966
NO. OF EMPLOYEES: 3,399
ANNUAL MEETING: In April
SHAREHOLDERS: 40,466
INSTITUTIONAL HOLDINGS:
No. of Institutions: 120
Shares Held: 7,487,115

REGISTRAR(S):

TRANSFER AGENT(S): First Chicago Trust Co. of New York, New York, NY 10008

NYS SYMBOL HNZ
Rec. Pr. 33½

HEINZ (H.J.) CO.

YIELD 3.9%
P/E RATIO 24.6

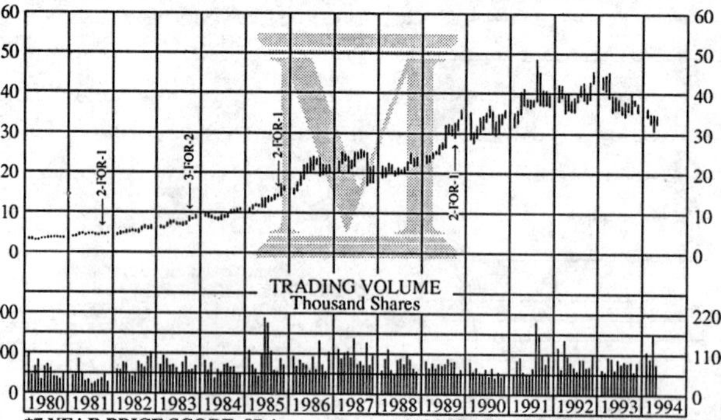

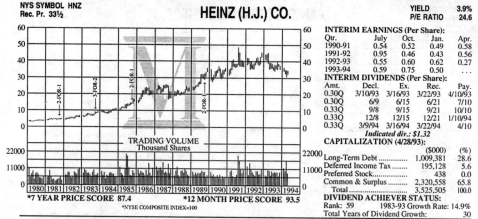

*7 YEAR PRICE SCORE 87.4 *12 MONTH PRICE SCORE 93.5

*NYSE COMPOSITE INDEX=100

INTERIM EARNINGS (Per Share):

Qtr.	July	Oct.	Jan.	Apr.
1990-91	0.54	0.52	0.49	0.58
1991-92	0.95	0.46	0.43	0.56
1992-93	0.55	0.60	0.62	0.27
1993-94	0.59	0.75	0.50	...

INTERIM DIVIDENDS (Per Share):

Amt.	Decl.	Ex.	Rec.	Pay.
0.30Q	3/10/93	3/16/93	3/22/93	4/10/93
0.30Q	6/9	6/15	6/21	7/10
0.33Q	9/8	9/15	9/21	10/10
0.33Q	12/8	12/15	12/21	1/10/94
0.33Q	3/9/94	3/16/94	3/22/94	4/10

Indicated div.: $1.32

CAPITALIZATION (4/28/93):

	($000)	(%)
Long-Term Debt	1,009,381	28.6
Deferred Income Tax	195,128	5.6
Preferred Stock	438	0.0
Common & Surplus	2,320,558	65.8
Total	3,525,505	100.0

DIVIDEND ACHIEVER STATUS:
Rank: 59 1983-93 Growth Rate: 14.9%
Total Years of Dividend Growth: 30

RECENT DEVELOPMENTS: For the quarter ended 2/27/94, net income was $128.6 million, or $0.50 per share, compared with $162.3 million, or $0.62 per share, for the corresponding period a year earlier. Sales totaled $1.71 billion, down 3.2% from $1.77 billion a year ago. Volume gains occurred in Heinz grocery ketchup, various Heinz Pet Products brands, foodservice products and Heinz beans. These gains were partially offset by volume declines in Weight Watchers businesses (both meetings and foods) and StarKist tuna. Price increases occurred in many of the company's core products both domestically and overseas. Gross profit decreased 4.3% to $671.1 million. The ratio of gross profit to sales fell to 39.2% from 39.7% for the same period last year. Operating income was $247.3 million, down $38.1 million or 13.3% from $285.4 million a year ago.

BUSINESS

H.J. HEINZ COMPANY packs and sells canned foods, including: ketchup, soups, baby and junior foods, beans, canned prepared meals, pickles, vinegar, and other specialties, under the Heinz label and trademark '57 Varieties.' Under the StarKist label it produces tuna products; cat food under the 9-Lives label; and frozen potato and onion products under Ore-Ida. Weight Watchers prepares diet foods and operates weight control meetings. Overseas, Heinz has factories in England, Holland, Belgium, Italy, Australia, Venezuela, Ireland, Denmark, Portugal, Korea and Japan.

BUSINESS LINE ANALYSIS

(4/28/93)	Rev(%)	Inc(%)
Domestic	57.0	48.0
United Kingdom	12.0	12.5
Continental Europe	15.5	22.4
Canada	5.3	7.5
Asia/Pacific	8.0	6.8
Other	2.2	2.8
Total	100.0	100.0

ANNUAL EARNINGS AND DIVIDENDS PER SHARE

	4/28/93	4/29/92	5/1/91	5/2/90	5/3/89	4/27/88	4/29/87
Earnings Per Share	[1] 2.04	2.40	2.13	1.90	1.67	1.46	1.24
Dividends Per Share	1.11	0.99	0.87	0.75	0.645	0.56	0.463
Dividend Payout %	54.4	41.3	41.0	39.5	38.6	38.5	37.4

[1] Before acctg. chg.

ANNUAL FINANCIAL DATA

RECORD OF EARNINGS (IN MILLIONS):							
Total Revenues	7,103.4	6,581.9	6,647.1	6,085.7	5,800.9	5,244.2	4,639.5
Costs and Expenses	6,007.6	5,485.0	5,413.9	4,995.2	4,849.3	4,422.9	3,936.6
Depreciation & Amort	234.9	211.8	196.1	168.5	148.1	133.3	109.9
Operating Income	860.9	1,106.5	1,037.1	921.9	803.5	688.0	593.0
Income Bef Income Taxes	715.8	984.3	903.0	811.4	724.9	622.6	564.6
Income Taxes	185.8	346.1	335.0	307.0	284.7	236.6	226.1
Net Income	[1] 529.9	638.3	568.0	504.5	440.2	386.0	338.5
Aver. Shs. Outstg. (000)	259,789	266,339	266,629	266,078	263,568	265,412	273,670
[1] Before acctg. change dr$133,630,000.							
BALANCE SHEET (IN MILLIONS):							
Cash and Cash Equivalents	224.3	273.1	314.0	241.1	237.7	252.8	564.7
Receivables, Net	978.9	830.8	678.1	640.8	507.5	491.9	446.3
Inventories	1,185.4	1,034.9	967.9	993.6	902.7	797.1	746.9
Gross Property	3,328.4	2,979.8	2,764.5	2,495.5	2,184.1	2,025.7	1,725.0
Accumulated Depreciation	1,166.1	1,067.7	1,041.7	927.8	818.1	771.8	688.3
Long-Term Debt	1,009.4	178.4	716.9	875.2	693.5	524.4	585.6
Net Stockholders' Equity	2,321.0	2,367.4	2,274.9	1,886.9	1,777.2	1,593.9	1,392.9
Total Assets	6,821.3	5,931.9	4,935.4	4,487.5	4,001.8	3,605.1	3,364.2
Total Current Assets	2,623.4	2,280.3	2,119.8	2,013.7	1,775.2	1,664.4	1,856.8
Total Current Liabilities	2,866.3	2,844.0	1,429.7	1,280.0	1,115.9	1,074.7	1,034.8
Net Working Capital	d242.9	d563.7	690.1	733.7	659.3	589.7	822.1
Year End Shs Outstg (000)	254,365	254,057	259,435	253,518	256,962	255,236	257,278
STATISTICAL RECORD:							
Operating Profit Margin %	12.1	16.8	15.6	15.1	13.9	13.1	12.8
Book Value Per Share	3.73	4.67	5.88	4.89	4.56	4.35	4.61
Return on Equity %	22.8	27.0	25.0	26.7	24.8	24.2	24.3
Return on Assets %	7.8	10.8	11.5	11.2	11.0	10.7	10.1
Average Yield %	2.8	2.5	2.7	2.6	2.9	2.6	2.4
P/E Ratio	22.3-17.2	20.3-13.1	17.4-12.9	18.9-11.8	15.0-11.2	17.7-11.5	19.5-11.8
Price Range	45½-35⅛	48⅝-31½	37-27½	35⅞-22½	25-18¾	25⅞-16¾	24⅛-14⅝

Statistics are as originally reported.

OFFICERS:
A.F. O'Reilly, Chmn., Pres. & C.E.O.
J.J. Bogdanovich, Vice-Chmn.
D.R. Williams, Sr. V.P. & C.F.O.
P.F. Renne, V.P. & Treas.

INCORPORATED: PA, Jul., 1900

PRINCIPAL OFFICE: 600 Grant St., Pittsburgh, PA 15219

TELEPHONE NUMBER: (412) 456-5700

NO. OF EMPLOYEES: 2,717 (approx.)

ANNUAL MEETING: In September

SHAREHOLDERS: 18,128 (approx.)

INSTITUTIONAL HOLDINGS:
No. of Institutions: 535
Shares Held: 140,200,015

REGISTRAR(S): Mellon Bank, N.A., Pittsburgh, PA

TRANSFER AGENT(S): Mellon Bank, N.A., Pittsburgh, PA

NYS SYMBOL HP
Rec. Pr. 26¼

HELMERICH & PAYNE, INC.

YIELD 1.8%
P/E RATIO 26.0

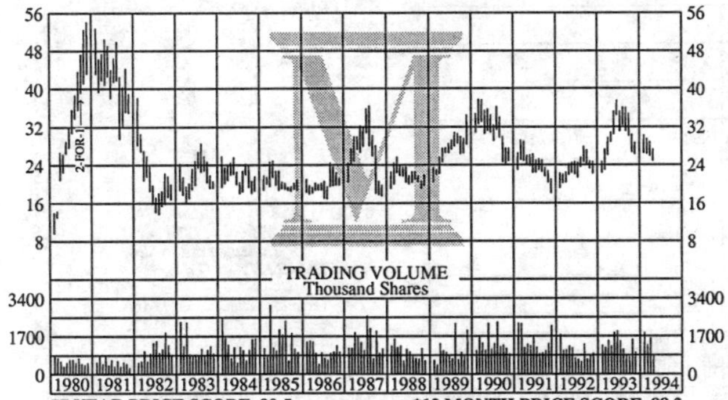

***7 YEAR PRICE SCORE 90.5** ***12 MONTH PRICE SCORE 88.3**

*NYSE COMPOSITE INDEX=100

INTERIM EARNINGS (Per Share):

Qtr.	Dec.	Mar.	June	Sept.
1990-91	0.57	0.12	0.11	0.08
1991-92	0.21	0.09	0.12	0.03
1992-93	0.30	0.30	0.20	0.21
1993-94	0.30	...	...	...

INTERIM DIVIDENDS (Per Share):

Amt.	Decl.	Ex.	Rec.	Pay.
0.12Q	3/3/93	5/10/93	5/14/93	6/1/93
0.12Q	6/2	8/10	8/16	9/1
0.12Q	9/1	11/8	11/15	12/1
0.12Q	12/1	2/9/94	2/15/94	3/1/94
0.12Q	3/3/94	5/10	5/16	6/1

Indicated div.: $0.48

CAPITALIZATION (9/30/93):

	($000)	(%)
Long-Term Debt	3,600	0.7
Deferred Income Tax	44,723	8.0
Common & Surplus	508,927	91.3
Total	557,250	100.0

DIVIDEND ACHIEVER STATUS:

Rank: 308 1983-93 Growth Rate: 4.0%
Total Years of Dividend Growth: 17

RECENT DEVELOPMENTS: For the quarter ended 12/31/93, net income increased slightly to $7.3 million compared with $7.2 million for the comparable period in 1992. Revenues slipped 1% to $82.2 million. The Contract Drilling Division reported a 37% increase in pre-tax earnings as a result of increased domestic offshore drilling activity and increasing profitability in certain foreign markets. Lower prices and production volumes for both natural gas and oil resulted in lower operating earnings for the Company's Oil and Gas division.

PROSPECTS: Increased domestic offshore drilling activity reflecting increasing worldwide demand for energy along with the favorable rate of growth for operations in Venezuela and Colombia should directly contribute to earnings for the contract drilling group. However, the oil and gas group will most likely post flat earnings in the near term due to lower product prices and production. Low interest rates and favorable market conditions will spur growth in the real-estate segment while improved margins and volumes should benefit the chemicals unit.

BUSINESS

HELMERICH & PAYNE, INC. is a diversified, energy-oriented company engaged primarily in exploration for and production of crude oil and natural gas and in contract drilling of oil and gas wells for the petroleum industry. The Company also manufactures and distributes odorants for use in the gas transmission and distribution industry and engages as well in the ownership, development, and operation of commercial real estate.

BUSINESS LINE ANALYSIS

(9/30/93) ($000)	Rev	Inc
1st Quarter	82,998	7,219
2nd Quarter	83,351	7,268
3rd Quarter	73,607	4,931
4th Quarter	75,141	5,132

ANNUAL EARNINGS AND DIVIDENDS PER SHARE

	9/30/93	9/30/92	9/30/91	9/30/90	9/30/89	9/30/88	9/30/87
Earnings Per Share	**1.01**	**0.45**	**0.88**	**1.97**	**0.94**	**0.83**	**0.91**
Dividends Per Share	**0.48**	**0.47**	**0.46**	**0.445**	**0.425**	**0.405**	**0.39**
Dividend Payout %	**47.5**	**N.M.**	**52.3**	**22.6**	**45.2**	**48.8**	**42.9**

ANNUAL FINANCIAL DATA

	9/30/93	9/30/92	9/30/91	9/30/90	9/30/89	9/30/88	9/30/87
RECORD OF EARNINGS (IN THOUSANDS):							
Total Revenues	315,097	239,700	213,946	238,544	171,169	160,565	158,879
Costs and Expenses	223,243	167,255	138,160	129,273	91,234	85,521	80,901
Deprec, Depl & Amort	48,609	47,738	40,345	41,550	41,651	37,642	34,212
Operating Income	43,245	24,707	35,441	67,721	38,284	37,402	43,766
Inc Bef Fed Income Taxes	42,320	24,075	35,061	70,381	32,400	31,119	37,081
Income Taxes	17,368	8,641	12,280	22,194	9,812	6,286	10,101
Net Income	24,550	10,849	21,241	47,562	22,700	20,150	22,016
Aver. Shs. Outstg.	24,307	24,210	24,182	24,178	24,167	24,167	24,187
BALANCE SHEET (IN THOUSANDS):							
Cash and Cash Equivalents	70,765	50,714	70,054	134,481	121,067	116,916	118,026
Accounts Receivable, Net	56,305	42,819	37,532	37,755	31,323	29,485	28,951
Inventories	17,646	17,611	16,697	10,059	8,786	7,748	8,639
Gross Property	873,322	848,793	783,416	703,381	694,410	650,372	621,222
Accumulated Depreciation	514,524	484,197	446,894	420,689	401,932	369,424	349,250
Long-Term Debt	3,600	8,339	5,693	5,648	49,087	70,715	74,732
Net Stockholders' Equity	508,927	493,286	491,133	479,485	443,396	430,804	420,833
Total Assets	610,935	585,504	575,168	582,927	591,229	576,473	571,348
Total Current Assets	150,499	133,128	142,175	200,661	168,308	161,799	158,945
Total Current Liabilities	46,414	35,881	33,963	53,920	53,949	26,524	23,806
Net Working Capital	104,085	97,247	108,212	146,741	114,359	135,275	135,139
Year End Shares Outstg	24,637	24,577	24,487	24,485	24,173	24,166	24,187
STATISTICAL RECORD:							
Operating Profit Margin %	13.7	10.3	16.6	28.4	22.4	23.3	27.5
Book Value Per Share	20.66	20.07	20.06	19.58	18.34	17.83	17.40
Return on Equity %	4.8	2.2	4.3	9.9	5.1	4.7	5.2
Return on Assets %	4.0	1.9	3.7	8.2	3.8	3.5	3.9
Average Yield %	1.6	2.0	1.9	1.4	1.5	1.8	1.4
P/E Ratio	37.1-22.0	61.9-42.5	33.2-20.5	19.2-12.2	36.7-21.7	31.0-22.9	40.0-19.2
Price Range	37½-22¼	27⅞-19⅛	29¼-18	37¾-24	34½-20⅜	25¾-19	36⅜-17½

Statistics are as originally reported.

OFFICERS:
W.H. Helmerich, III, Chmn.
H. Helmerich, Pres. & C.E.O.
S.R. Mackey, V.P., Gen. Counsel & Sec.
D.E. Fears, V.P.-Fin.

INCORPORATED: DE, Feb., 1940

PRINCIPAL OFFICE: Utica at 21st St., Tulsa, OK 74114

TELEPHONE NUMBER: (918) 742-5531

NO. OF EMPLOYEES: 325

ANNUAL MEETING: In March

SHAREHOLDERS: 1,273

INSTITUTIONAL HOLDINGS:
No. of Institutions: 181
Shares Held: 14,602,222

REGISTRAR(S): Liberty National Bank & Trust Co., Oklahoma City, OK 73125

TRANSFER AGENT(S): Liberty National Bank & Trust Co., Oklahoma City, OK 73125

NYS SYMBOL HSY
Rec. Pr. 42½

HERSHEY FOODS CORP.

YIELD 2.8%
P/E RATIO 12.8

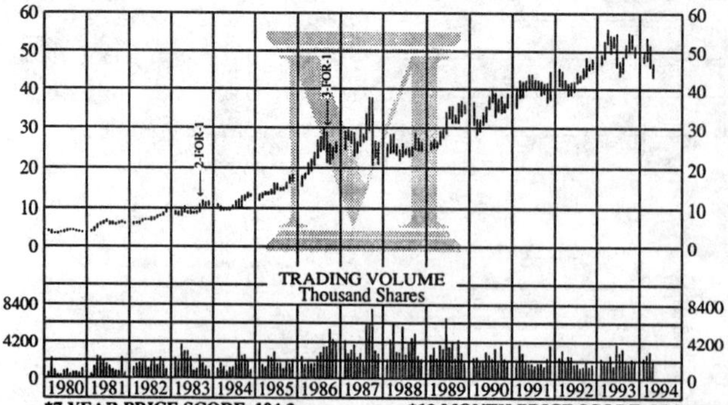

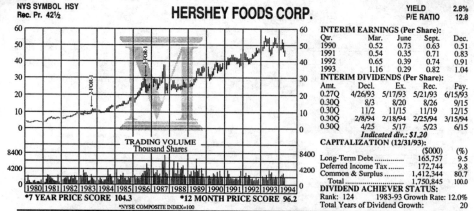

*7 YEAR PRICE SCORE 104.3 *12 MONTH PRICE SCORE 96.2

*NYSE COMPOSITE INDEX=100

INTERIM EARNINGS (Per Share):

Qtr.	Mar.	June	Sept.	Dec.
1990	0.52	0.73	0.63	0.51
1991	0.54	0.35	0.71	0.83
1992	0.65	0.39	0.74	0.91
1993	1.16	0.29	0.82	1.04

INTERIM DIVIDENDS (Per Share):

Amt.	Decl.	Ex.	Rec.	Pay.
0.27Q	4/26/93	5/17/93	5/21/93	6/15/93
0.30Q	8/3	8/20	8/26	9/15
0.30Q	11/2	11/15	11/19	12/15
0.30Q	2/8/94	2/18/94	2/25/94	3/15/94
0.30Q	4/25	5/17	5/23	6/15

Indicated div.: $1.20

CAPITALIZATION (12/31/93):

	($000)	(%)
Long-Term Debt	165,757	9.5
Deferred Income Tax	172,744	9.8
Common & Surplus	1,412,344	80.7
Total	1,750,845	100.0

DIVIDEND ACHIEVER STATUS:

Rank: 124 1983-93 Growth Rate: 12.0%

Total Years of Dividend Growth: 20

RECENT DEVELOPMENTS: For the year ended 12/31/93, net income was $297.2 million compared with $242.6 million last year. Results were before an accounting change of $103.9 million. Sales increased 8.3% to $3.49 million as a result of significant contributions from Hershey's Hugs, Hershey's Cookies 'n' Mint chocolate bar, and Amazin' Fruit gummy bears. Hershey Chocolate U.S.A. and Hershey Pasta Group posted strong sales and market share gains.

PROSPECTS: Several overseas acquisitions should continue to contribute to sales growth at Hershey International. HSY's ongoing program to modernize and expand production capacity will help reduce production costs and improve margins, while line extensions and new product introductions should boost future earnings growth. The 1993 introductions of Hugs and the Cookies 'n' Mint chocolate bar have already produced favorable results.

BUSINESS

HERSHEY FOODS COPORATION produces a broad line of chocolate, confectionery and pasta products, including chocolate bars, breakfast cocoa, baking and chocolate syrup. Principal U.S. brands include Hershey's, Reese's, Peter Paul and Ludens. Canadian operations include these brands plus Oh Henry, Life Savers and Planters. Hershey Pasta Group produces eight regional brands led by San Giorgio, Ronzoni and American Beauty. Hershey International Manufactures and exports chocolate and confectionery products. In August 1988, HSY acquired Cadbury Schweppes' U.S. confectionary business, Peter Paul/Cadbury. In February 1990, HSY acquired Ronzoni Foods Corp.

BUSINESS LINE ANALYSIS

(12/31/93)	Rev(%)	Inc(%)
Domestic	88.3	97.7
International	11.7	2.3
Total	100.0	100.0

ANNUAL EARNINGS AND DIVIDENDS PER SHARE

	1993	1992	1991	1990	1989	1988	1987
Earnings Per Share	**3.31**	**2.69**	**2.43**	**2.39**	**1.90**	**[1] 1.60**	**1.64**
Dividends Per Share	**1.14**	**1.03**	**0.94**	**0.99**	**0.74**	**0.66**	**0.58**
Dividend Payout %	**34.4**	**38.3**	**38.7**	**41.4**	**38.9**	**39.8**	**35.4**

[1] Before disc. oper.

ANNUAL FINANCIAL DATA

RECORD OF EARNINGS (IN MILLIONS):	1993	1992	1991	1990	1989	1988	1987
Total Revenues	3,488.2	3,219.8	2,899.2	2,715.6	2,421.0	2,168.0	2,433.8
Costs and Expenses	2,837.3	2,694.5	2,423.5	2,255.6	2,044.9	1,850.1	2,069.1
Depreciation & Amort	113.1	97.1	85.4	73.9	65.7	51.9	70.6
Operating Income	537.9	428.2	390.3	386.1	310.3	266.1	294.1
Income Bef Income Taxes	510.9	401.0	363.5	361.5	289.9	236.1	269.4
Income Taxes	213.6	158.4	143.9	145.6	118.9	91.6	121.2
Net Income	[1] 297.2	242.6	219.5	215.9	171.1	[2] 144.5	148.2
Aver. Shs. Outstg. (000)	89,757	90,186	90,186	90,186	90,186	90,186	90,186

[1] Before acctg. change dr$103,908,000. [2] Before disc. op. cr$69,443,000.

BALANCE SHEET (IN MILLIONS):	1993	1992	1991	1990	1989	1988	1987
Cash and Cash Equivalents	16.0	203.2	71.1	26.6	52.5	70.1	15.0
Receivables, Net	380.5	220.1	159.8	143.0	121.9	166.8	121.5
Inventories	453.4	457.2	436.9	379.1	309.8	308.8	285.4
Gross Property	2,041.8	1,797.4	1,581.3	1,323.6	1,150.3	1,018.9	1,260.3
Accumulated Depreciation	580.9	501.4	435.6	371.5	320.4	282.9	397.3
Long-Term Debt	165.8	174.3	282.9	273.4	216.1	233.0	306.1
Net Stockholders' Equity	1,412.3	1,465.3	1,335.3	1,243.5	1,117.1	1,005.9	832.4
Total Assets	2,855.1	2,672.9	2,341.8	2,078.8	1,814.1	1,764.7	1,645.2
Total Current Assets	889.0	940.0	744.5	661.8	567.6	619.1	484.9
Total Current Liabilities	813.8	736.9	470.7	341.2	285.7	345.4	299.8
Net Working Capital	75.2	203.0	273.7	320.6	281.8	273.7	185.1
Year End Shs Outstg (000)	87,613	90,186	90,186	90,186	90,186	90,186	90,186
STATISTICAL RECORD:							
Operating Profit Margin %	15.4	13.3	13.5	14.2	12.8	12.3	12.1
Book Value Per Share	10.72	11.81	10.13	9.16	8.25	7.04	6.33
Return on Equity %	21.0	16.6	16.4	17.4	15.3	14.4	17.8
Return on Assets %	10.4	9.1	9.4	10.4	9.4	8.2	9.0
Average Yield %	2.3	2.4	2.4	2.9	2.4	2.6	2.0
P/E Ratio	16.9-13.1	18.0-14.2	18.3-14.5	16.6-11.8	19.4-13.0	17.9-13.7	27.4-15.0
Price Range	55⅞-43½	48⅜-38¼	44½-35⅛	39⅝-28¼	36⅞-24¾	28⅝-21⅞	37¾-20¾

Statistics are as originally reported.

OFFICERS:
K.L. Wolfe, Chmn. & C.E.O.
J.P. Viviano, Pres. & C.O.O.
W.F. Christ, Sr. V.P. & C.F.O.
W. Lehr, Jr., V.P. & Sec.
T.C. Fitzgerald, V.P. & Treas.

INCORPORATED: DE, Oct., 1927

PRINCIPAL OFFICE: 100 Crystal A Drive, Hershey, PA 17033

TELEPHONE NUMBER: (717) 534-6799

FAX: (717) 534-6724

NO. OF EMPLOYEES: 1,945 full-time; 1,600 part-time

ANNUAL MEETING: Last Monday in April

SHAREHOLDERS: 22,673

INSTITUTIONAL HOLDINGS:
No. of Institutions: 384
Shares Held: 28,052,908

REGISTRAR(S):

TRANSFER AGENT(S):

NYS SYMBOL HB
Rec. Pr. 36⅜

HILLENBRAND INDUSTRIES, INC.

YIELD 1.6%
P/E RATIO 18.8

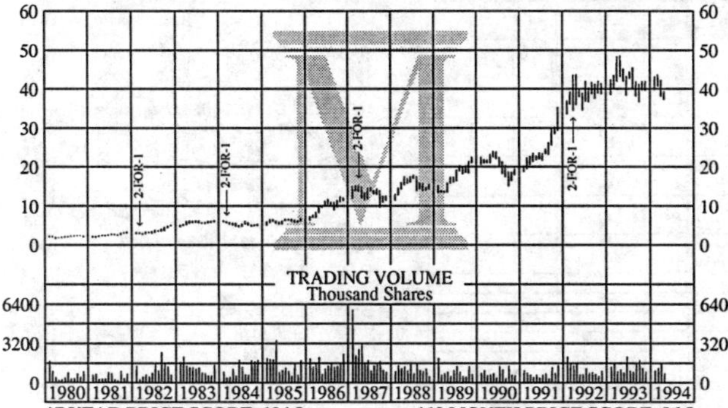

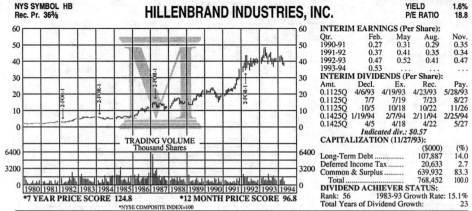

*7 YEAR PRICE SCORE 124.8 *12 MONTH PRICE SCORE 96.8

*NYSE COMPOSITE INDEX=100

INTERIM EARNINGS (Per Share):

Qtr.	Feb.	May	Aug.	Nov.
1990-91	0.27	0.31	0.29	0.35
1991-92	0.37	0.41	0.35	0.34
1992-93	0.47	0.52	0.41	0.47
1993-94	0.53	...	...	...

INTERIM DIVIDENDS (Per Share):

Amt.	Decl.	Ex.	Rec.	Pay.
0.1125Q	4/6/93	4/19/93	4/23/93	5/28/93
0.1125Q	7/7	7/19	7/23	8/27
0.1125Q	10/5	10/18	10/22	11/26
0.1425Q	1/19/94	2/7/94	2/11/94	2/25/94
0.1425Q	4/5	4/18	4/22	5/27

Indicated div.: $0.57

CAPITALIZATION (11/27/93):

	($000)	(%)
Long-Term Debt	107,887	14.0
Deferred Income Tax	20,633	2.7
Common & Surplus	639,932	83.3
Total	768,452	100.0

DIVIDEND ACHIEVER STATUS:
Rank: 56 1983-93 Growth Rate: 15.1%
Total Years of Dividend Growth: 23

RECENT DEVELOPMENTS: For the three months ended 11/27/93, income from continuing operations was $33.3 million, up 13% from the comparable period of 1992. For the fiscal year ended 11/27/93, income from continuing operations totaled $132.5 million compared with $111.2 million for the 1992 fiscal year. The funeral services segment reported a 17% jump in operating profit. Increased insurance in force and stronger demand for new casket models was cited.

PROSPECTS: The introduction of new products from Medeco Security Locks, Inc., and new casket models from Batesville in addition to cost control measures and realized efficiences have provided a boost to results. Hill-Rom continues to benefit from strong demand for the new bed lines, Advance 2000 and Affinity. The introduction of new products by SSI in addition to growth in care services will continue.

BUSINESS

HILLENBRAND INDUSTRIES, INC., is the parent company of six wholly owned and separately managed operating companies. The companies are organized into Industrial and Insurance groups and serve four diversified market segments. The Industrial Group consists of: Hill-Rom Co., Inc., the leading producer of electric hospital beds, patient room furniture and handling equipment. SSI Medical Services Inc., provides rental therapy units. BLOCK Medical Inc., is a provider of home infusion therapy products. Medeco Security Locks, Inc., is a producer of high-security mechanical locks and Batesville Casket Co., is the leading producer of burial caskets. Forecorp, Inc., the insurance company, provides pre-need funeral planning services.

QUARTERLY DATA

(11/27/93) ($000)	Rev	Inc
1st Quarter	348,432	33,559
2nd Quarter	365,398	37,387
3rd Quarter	340,599	29,975
4th Quarter	393,484	44,897

ANNUAL EARNINGS AND DIVIDENDS PER SHARE

	11/27/93	11/30/92	11/30/91	12/1/90	12/2/89	12/3/88	11/28/87
Earnings Per Share	**1.86**	**1.47**	**1.22**	**1.03**	**1.01**	**0.93**	**0.75**
Dividends Per Share	**0.45**	**0.35**	**0.29**	**0.275**	**0.25**	**0.20**	**1 0.175**
Dividend Payout %	**24.2**	**23.8**	**23.7**	**10.7**	**24.8**	**21.5**	**23.2**

1 2-for-1 stk split, 2/87

ANNUAL FINANCIAL DATA

	11/27/93	11/30/92	11/30/91	12/1/90	12/2/89	12/3/88	11/28/87
RECORD OF EARNINGS (IN MILLIONS):							
Net Revenues	1,447.9	1,429.8	1,198.9	1,106.6	1,138.3	884.3	724.6
Costs and Expenses	1,100.9	1,125.1	946.1	875.1	916.9	680.0	544.4
Depreciation & Amort	112.7	115.3	95.0	94.0	81.0	68.8	54.4
Operating Income	234.3	189.4	157.8	137.4	140.5	135.4	125.8
Inc Fr Cont Opers Bef Income Taxes	221.5	171.3	145.7	126.3	127.3	120.4	110.4
Income Taxes	89.1	65.8	56.5	50.7	52.3	50.7	53.0
Net Income	1 132.5	2 105.5	89.2	75.7	75.0	69.7	57.4
Aver. Shs. Outstg. (000)	71,407	71,915	72,885	73,971	74,376	75,116	76,244

1 Before disc. op. cr$13,332,000. 2 Before acctg. change cr$10,747,000.

	11/27/93	11/30/92	11/30/91	12/1/90	12/2/89	12/3/88	11/28/87
BALANCE SHEET (IN MILLIONS):							
Cash & Cash Equivalents	210.2	150.0	54.9	86.8	49.0	28.2	50.6
Receivables, Net	253.8	248.9	198.0	185.8	181.8	185.1	146.2
Inventories	90.9	111.6	111.1	109.6	103.6	84.8	72.8
Gross Property	787.2	784.1	703.4	660.3	612.4	525.1	135.5
Accumulated Depreciation	460.4	477.0	406.0	346.8	274.1	213.9	170.7
Long-Term Debt	107.9	185.1	103.6	108.1	113.4	117.9	123.7
Net Stockholders' Equity	639.9	547.7	490.8	436.5	405.1	353.3	312.4
Total Assets	2,270.7	1,935.2	1,532.2	1,267.7	1,009.8	734.7	660.5
Total Current Assets	574.0	533.4	383.5	400.1	342.3	306.0	284.0
Total Current Liabilities	290.0	254.4	226.8	183.9	150.2	154.1	138.7
Net Working Capital	284.0	279.0	156.6	216.2	192.1	151.9	145.2
Year End Shs Outstg (000)	71,263	71,580	72,659	73,221	74,226	74,592	75,538
STATISTICAL RECORD:							
Operating Profit Margin %	16.2	13.2	13.2	12.4	12.3	15.3	17.4
Book Value Per Share	7.04	5.37	4.26	4.59	4.14	3.58	3.12
Return on Equity %	20.7	19.3	18.2	17.3	18.5	19.7	18.4
Return on Assets %	5.8	5.5	5.8	6.0	7.4	9.5	8.7
Average Yield %	1.1	0.9	1.1	1.4	1.4	1.4	1.4
P/E Ratio	26.1-19.6	29.7-22.8	28.9-15.4	23.5-14.8	22.4-13.1	19.2-12.2	20.5-12.8
Price Range	48⅝-36½	43⅝-33½	35¼-18¾	24-15⅛	22⅝-13¼	17⅞-11⅜	15⅜-9⅝

Statistics are as originally reported.

OFFICERS:
D.A. Hillenbrand, Chmn.
W. Hillenbrand, Pres. & C.E.O.
T.E. Brewer, Sr. V.P., C.F.O. & Treas.
M.R. Lindenmeyer, V.P. & Gen. Couns.

INCORPORATED: IN, Aug., 1969

PRINCIPAL OFFICE: 700 State Route 46 East, Batesville, IN 47006-9166

TELEPHONE NUMBER: (812) 934-7000

NO. OF EMPLOYEES: 1,333 (approx.)

ANNUAL MEETING: In April

SHAREHOLDERS: 18,630 (approx.)

INSTITUTIONAL HOLDINGS:
No. of Institutions: 185
Shares Held: 24,576,959

REGISTRAR(S): Harris Trust & Savings Bank, Chicago, IL

TRANSFER AGENT(S): Harris Trust & Savings Bank, Chicago, IL

HOME BENEFICIAL CORP.

YIELD 3.7%
P/E RATIO 38.4

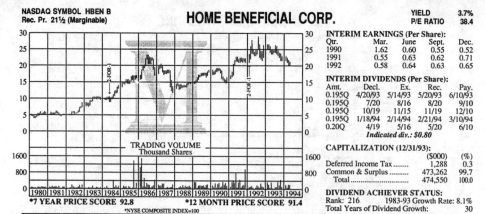

*7 YEAR PRICE SCORE 92.8   *12 MONTH PRICE SCORE 91.4
*NYSE COMPOSITE INDEX=100

INTERIM EARNINGS (Per Share):

Qtr.	Mar.	June	Sept.	Dec.
1990	1.62	0.60	0.55	0.52
1991	0.55	0.63	0.62	0.71
1992	0.58	0.64	0.63	0.65

INTERIM DIVIDENDS (Per Share):

Amt.	Decl.	Ex.	Rec.	Pay.
0.195Q	4/20/93	5/14/93	5/20/93	6/10/93
0.195Q	7/20	8/16	8/20	9/10
0.195Q	10/19	11/15	11/19	12/10
0.195Q	1/18/94	2/14/94	2/21/94	3/10/94
0.20Q	4/19	5/16	5/20	6/10

Indicated div.: $0.80

CAPITALIZATION (12/31/93):

	($000)	(%)
Deferred Income Tax	1,288	0.3
Common & Surplus	473,262	99.7
Total	474,550	100.0

DIVIDEND ACHIEVER STATUS:

Rank: 216   1983-93 Growth Rate: 8.1%
Total Years of Dividend Growth: 30

RECENT DEVELOPMENTS: For the year ended 12/31/93, net income was $42.6 million, or $2.35 per share, compared with net income of $46.5 million, or $2.50 per share, before an accounting change in 1992. Revenues for 1993 totaled $213.2 million, up from $211.5 million last year. Premium income of $116.4 million was down 1.3% from the $117.9 million for 1992 due primarily to reduced sales this year. Investment income, net of expenses, increased to $96.9 million with $10.8 million being attributed to realized investment gains versus $93.6 million of which $2.9 million were realized gains during 1992. At year-end 1993, total life insurance in force increased to $9.9 billion. For the quarter, net income fell to $10.0 million, or $0.56 per share, versus $12.0 million, or $0.65 per share, for the same period in 1992.

BUSINESS

HOME BENEFICIAL CORPORATION is a holding company located in the state of Virginia with one principal operating subsidiary, Home Beneficial Life Insurance Company (the Life Company), which is engaged in the life and accident and health insurance business. The Life Company sells group life insurance and substantially all the forms of ordinary insurance, including universal life, whole life, term and annuities, together with accidental death and disability riders. In addition, the Life Company participates in several group life insurance programs as a reinsurer and also assumes reinsurance on a faculative (individual risk) basis from two other life insurance companies. The Life Company's business is concentrated in six Mid-Atlantic states and the District of Columbia and its policies are marketed through its own sales force of approximately 1,275 full time personnel.

REVENUES

(12/31/93)	($000)	(%)
Premiums	116,369	54.6
Net Investment	96,874	45.4
Total	213,243	100.0

ANNUAL EARNINGS AND DIVIDENDS PER SHARE

	1993	1992	1991	1990	1989	1988	1987
Earnings Per Share	2.35	[1]2.50	2.51	[3]3.29	2.13	1.98	1.71
Dividends Per Share	0.775	[2]0.76	0.69	0.645	0.59	0.555	0.52
Dividend Payout %	33.0	30.4	27.5	19.6	27.8	28.1	30.4

[1] Before acctg. chg.   [2] 2-for-1 stk split, 1/3/92

ANNUAL FINANCIAL DATA

RECORD OF EARNINGS (IN MILLIONS):

	1993	1992	1991	1990	1989	1988	1987
Premiums	116.4	117.9	103.5	102.2	99.6	103.9	103.4
Net Investment Income	96.9	93.6	93.9	136.8	87.9	83.9	81.1
Total Revenues	213.2	211.5	197.4	239.1	187.4	187.8	184.5
Benefits & Claims	94.6	88.4	76.1	77.7	75.4	78.7	80.3
Inc Fr Cont Opers Bef Income Taxes	63.9	68.7	70.9	...	66.2	62.0	...
Total Income Taxes	21.3	22.3	23.5	45.6	21.9	19.5	21.0
Realized Invest Losses	...	...	...	...	...	[2]d0.0	[3]d0.0
Net Income	42.6	[1]46.5	47.4	66.6	44.3	42.5	38.0
Aver. Shs. Outstg. (000)	18,126	18,600	18,869	20,274	20,838	21,520	22,276

[1] Before acctg. change dr$29,444,884.   [2] Equal to d$29,000.   [3] Equal to d$26,000.

BALANCE SHEET (IN MILLIONS):

	1993	1992	1991	1990	1989	1988	1987
Cash	6.0	3.3	2.6	1.3	2.3	1.7	1.8
Fixed Matur, At Amortized Cost	705.7	561.7	459.9	428.5	420.4	414.7	415.5
Equity Securities, At Mkt	27.3	28.6	28.4	23.3	25.9	23.3	22.4
Policy Loans	52.7	52.1	50.8	48.1	46.5	45.5	44.8
Mtge Loans on Real Estate	316.4	382.5	489.3	518.4	494.9	423.5	418.2
Total Assets	1,280.2	1,248.4	1,205.3	1,159.8	1,110.8	1,069.4	1,020.1
Benefits and Claims	747.3	727.2	712.9	696.7	679.3	641.5	624.9
Net Stockholders' Equity	473.3	460.4	456.9	430.1	403.4	396.8	366.0
Year End Shs Outstg (000)	17,939	18,527	18,716	19,103	20,693	21,486	21,532

STATISTICAL RECORD:

	1993	1992	1991	1990	1989	1988	1987
Book Value Per Share	26.38	24.85	24.41	22.52	19.50	18.47	17.00
Return on Equity %	9.0	10.1	10.4	15.5	11.0	10.7	10.4
Return on Assets %	3.3	3.7	3.9	5.7	4.0	4.0	3.7
Average Yield %	3.2	3.0	3.6	3.8	3.5	4.0	3.2
P/E Ratio	11.3-9.1	11.6-8.4	9.1-6.4	5.9-4.5	8.8-6.8	7.6-6.5	12.0-6.9
Price Range	26½-21½	29-21	22¾-16	19¼-14¾	18¾-14½	15-12¾	20½-11¾

Statistics are as originally reported.

OFFICERS:
R.W. Wiltshire, Sr., Chairman
R.W. Wiltshire, Jr., Pres. & C.E.O.
J.M. Wiltshire, Jr., V.P., Sec. & Couns.
W.V. Collins, V.P. & Sec.
D.M. Westerhouse, Jr., Treasurer

INCORPORATED: VA, Mar., 1970

PRINCIPAL OFFICE: 3901 West Broad Street
P.O. Box 27572, Richmond, VA 23261

TELEPHONE NUMBER: (804) 358-8431

NO. OF EMPLOYEES: 1,275

ANNUAL MEETING: In April

SHAREHOLDERS: 1,800

INSTITUTIONAL HOLDINGS:
No. of Institutions: 39
Shares Held: 5,904,272 (adj.)

REGISTRAR(S): Jefferson National Bank,
Charlottesville, VA 23241

TRANSFER AGENT(S):

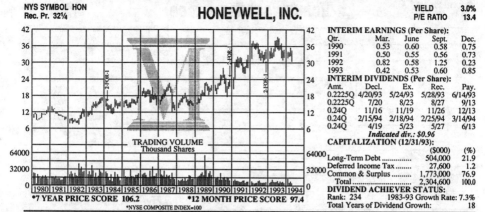

NYS SYMBOL HON
Rec. Pr. 32¼

HONEYWELL, INC.

YIELD 3.0%
P/E RATIO 13.4

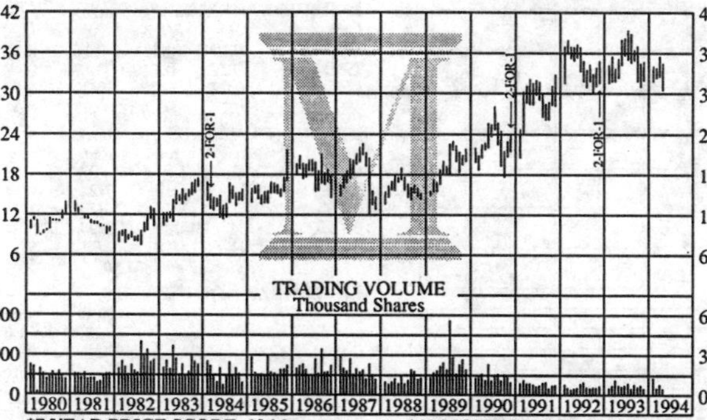

42
36
30
24
18
12
6
2-FOR-1
2-FOR-1
2-FOR-1
TRADING VOLUME
Thousand Shares
64000
32000
0
1980 1981 1982 1983 1984 1985 1986 1987 1988 1989 1990 1991 1992 1993 1994

*7 YEAR PRICE SCORE 106.2 *12 MONTH PRICE SCORE 97.4
*NYSE COMPOSITE INDEX=100

INTERIM EARNINGS (Per Share):

Qtr.	Mar.	June	Sept.	Dec.
1990	0.53	0.60	0.58	0.75
1991	0.50	0.55	0.56	0.73
1992	0.82	0.58	1.25	0.23
1993	0.42	0.53	0.60	0.85

INTERIM DIVIDENDS (Per Share):

Amt.	Decl.	Ex.	Rec.	Pay.
0.2225Q	4/20/93	5/24/93	5/28/93	6/14/93
0.2225Q	7/20	8/23	8/27	9/13
0.24Q	11/16	11/19	11/26	12/13
0.24Q	2/15/94	2/18/94	2/25/94	3/14/94
0.24Q	4/19	5/23	5/27	6/13

Indicated div.: $0.96

CAPITALIZATION (12/31/93):

	($000)	(%)
Long-Term Debt	504,000	21.9
Deferred Income Tax	27,600	1.2
Common & Surplus	1,773,000	76.9
Total	2,304,600	100.0

DIVIDEND ACHIEVER STATUS:
Rank: 234 1983-93 Growth Rate: 7.3%
Total Years of Dividend Growth: 18

RECENT DEVELOPMENTS: For the quarter ended 12/31/93, net income more than tripled to $112.6 million compared with $32.1 million for the same period in 1992. However, figures for the previous year include special charges of $113.9 million. Sales slipped 5% to $1.62 billion. Home and Building Control continued to contribute to earnings through a 22% increase in operating profit as a result of improved market share. Meanwhile, Industrial Control reported disappointing earnings due to higher R&D expenses.

PROSPECTS: Due to the fact that current levels of business activity for Space and Aviation show no signs of recovery, near-term profits are expected to remain somewhat erratic. In addition, the effects of adverse currency translations will hamper future earnings for the otherwise healthy Home and Building Control unit. Meanwhile, HON is aggressively expanding its research and development spending, especially related to the Industrial Control and Space/Aviation Control units.

BUSINESS

HONEYWELL INCORPORATED operations are engaged in the design, development, manufacture, marketing and service of systems and products in three industry segments. Home and Buildings include automation, energy management, environmental controls and fire and security systems for commercial and residential systems. Industrial provides customers with products and digital systems for industrial process and manufacturing automation. Space and Aviation provides controls and guidance systems for commercial and military aircraft, space and satellite applications.

BUSINESS LINE ANALYSIS

(12/31/93)	Rev(%)	Inc(%)
United States	65.8	67.5
Europe	23.5	24.7
Other areas	10.7	7.8
Total	100.0	100.0

ANNUAL EARNINGS AND DIVIDENDS PER SHARE

	1993	1992	1991	1990	1989	1988	1987
Earnings Per Share	2.40	1 2 2.88	2.35	4 2.45	4 3.23	d5.11	1.44
Dividends Per Share	0.907	3 0.841	0.769	5 0.703	0.566	0.525	0.506
Dividend Payout %	37.9	29.2	32.7	28.7	17.5	...	35.2

1 Before extraord. item & acctg. chg. 2 Before acctg. chg. 3 2-for-1 stk split,12/21/92 4 Before disc. oper. 5 2-for-1 stk split,12/26/90

ANNUAL FINANCIAL DATA

	1993	1992	1991	1990	1989	1988	1987
RECORD OF EARNINGS (IN MILLIONS):							
Total Revenues	5,963.0	6,222.6	6,192.9	6,309.1	6,058.6	7,148.3	6,679.3
Costs and Expenses	5,147.8	5,412.0	5,350.7	5,475.3	5,417.7	6,741.9	5,899.6
Depreciation & Amort	284.9	292.7	286.0	283.0	247.8	283.1	262.1
Operating Income	530.3	517.9	556.2	550.8	393.1	123.3	517.6
Income Bef Income Taxes	478.5	634.7	509.4	516.4	675.9	d200.9	411.9
Income Taxes	156.3	234.8	178.3	144.6	125.6	234.0	158.2
Net Income	322.2	1 399.9	331.1	2 371.8	3 550.3	d434.9	253.7
Aver. Shs. Outstg. (000)	134,200	138,500	140,900	151,800	170,400	170,400	176,400

1 Before extra. item dr$8,600,000. 2 Before disc. op. cr$10,100,000. 3 Before disc. op. cr$53,800,000.

	1993	1992	1991	1990	1989	1988	1987
BALANCE SHEET (IN MILLIONS):							
Cash and Cash Equivalents	256.1	346.2	508.2	367.9	254.1	180.4	404.7
Receivables, Net	1,534.0	1,534.0	1,286.4	1,242.0	1,475.0	1,448.7	1,102.6
Inventories	760.1	827.6	904.3	972.3	1,071.6	1,134.5	1,099.2
Gross Property	2,549.4	2,497.9	2,446.6	2,315.8	2,280.9	2,540.4	2,431.6
Accumulated Depreciation	1,487.4	1,384.4	1,300.4	1,165.5	1,092.0	1,181.7	1,054.8
Long-Term Debt	504.0	512.1	639.8	616.3	692.5	800.7	677.9
Net Stockholders' Equity	1,773.0	1,790.4	1,850.8	1,696.9	1,918.2	1,731.3	2,245.3
Total Assets	4,598.1	4,870.1	4,806.7	4,746.2	5,258.2	5,089.1	5,285.2
Total Current Assets	2,550.2	2,707.8	2,698.9	2,582.2	2,800.7	2,763.6	2,606.5
Total Current Liabilities	1,856.1	1,969.2	2,095.0	2,175.1	2,415.8	2,394.0	2,096.1
Net Working Capital	694.1	738.6	603.9	407.1	384.9	369.6	510.4
Year End Shs Outstg (000)	131,560	136,680	139,656	141,562	159,996	172,512	170,112
STATISTICAL RECORD:							
Operating Profit Margin %	8.9	8.3	9.0	8.7	6.5	1.7	7.7
Book Value Per Share	9.76	9.04	9.44	7.90	8.23	6.58	9.62
Return on Equity %	18.2	22.3	17.9	21.9	28.7	...	11.3
Return on Assets %	7.0	8.2	6.9	7.8	10.5	...	4.8
Average Yield %	2.6	2.5	2.9	3.1	3.0	3.2	2.9
P/E Ratio	16.4-12.9	13.2-10.5	13.9-8.7	11.5-7.2	7.1-4.6	...	15.7-8.5
Price Range	39⅜-31	38-30¼	32¾-20½	28⅛-17⅝	23-14⅞	19⅛-13⅝	22⅝-12¼

Statistics are as originally reported.

OFFICERS:
M.R. Bonsignore, Chmn. & C.E.O.
D.L. Moore, Pres. & C.O.O.
W.L. Trubeck, Sr. V.P. & C.F.O.

INCORPORATED: DE, Oct., 1927

PRINCIPAL OFFICE: Honeywell Plaza, Minneapolis, MN 55408-1792

TELEPHONE NUMBER: (612) 951-1000
FAX: (612) 870-3875
NO. OF EMPLOYEES: 7,113 (approx.)
ANNUAL MEETING: In April
SHAREHOLDERS: 22,880
INSTITUTIONAL HOLDINGS:
No. of Institutions: 460
Shares Held: 52,211,716

REGISTRAR(S): Chemical Bank, New York, NY

TRANSFER AGENT(S): Chemical Bank, New York, NY

HORMEL (GEORGE A.) & CO.

YIELD 2.5%
P/E RATIO 14.5

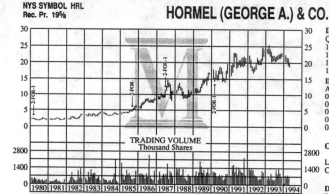

TRADING VOLUME
Thousand Shares

| 1980 | 1981 | 1982 | 1983 | 1984 | 1985 | 1986 | 1987 | 1988 | 1989 | 1990 | 1991 | 1992 | 1993 | 1994 |

*7 YEAR PRICE SCORE 99.8   *12 MONTH PRICE SCORE 94.6
*NYSE COMPOSITE INDEX=100

INTERIM EARNINGS (Per Share):

Qtr.	Jan.	Apr.	July	Oct.
1989-90	0.19	0.18	0.16	0.48
1990-91	0.27	0.21	0.17	0.48
1991-92	0.22	0.26	0.21	0.55
1992-93	0.25	0.28	0.25	0.57

INTERIM DIVIDENDS (Per Share):

Amt.	Decl.	Ex.	Rec.	Pay.
0.11Q	3/22/93	4/12/93	4/17/93	5/15/93
0.11Q	5/24	7/19	7/24	8/15
0.11Q	9/27	10/18	10/23	11/15
0.125Q	11/24	1/14/94	1/22/94	2/15/94
0.125Q	3/28/94	4/18	4/23	5/15

Indicated div.: $0.50

CAPITALIZATION (10/30/93):

	($000)	(%)
Long-Term Debt	5,700	1.0
Common & Surplus	570,888	99.0
Total	576,588	100.0

DIVIDEND ACHIEVER STATUS:

Rank: 94   1983-93 Growth Rate: 13.4%
Total Years of Dividend Growth: 26

RECENT DEVELOPMENTS: For the 13 weeks ended 1/29/94, net income was $20.6 million compared with $18.3 million last year. Sales increased 5.0% to $716.2 million, aided by increased tonnage volume of core brands and newly introduced meat and food products. Prior-year's results were before an accounting change of $127.5 million. The Grocery Products Division posted strong results with the help of solid volume increases from Spam luncheon meat, Dinty Moore stew, and Mary Kitchen hash.

PROSPECTS: Hormel continues to invest in new equipment to improve productivity and efficiency in an effort to support steady demand for its extensive lines of branded, value-added products. HRL will continue to introduce new products and further extend current lines, as private label businesses increase competition. An agreement with Zwanenberg de Mexico to sell HRL's branded, processed meat products in Mexico will provide HRL with a strong presence in this growing market.

BUSINESS

GEORGE A. HORMEL & COMPANY and its subsidiaries produce and market thousands of processed, packaged food products. The principal products of the Company are meat and meat products, hams, sausages, wieners, sliced bacon, luncheon meats, stews, chilies, hash and meat spreads. The products are sold fresh, frozen, cured, smoked, cooked or canned. The majority of products are sold under the Hormel name. Other tradenames include Spam, Wranglers, Light & Lean, Frank'N Stuff, Farm Fresh, Dinty Moore, Black Label, Top Shelf and Mary Kitchen, By George, Kids Kitchen and Old Smokehouse. Through two wholly-owned subsidiaries, the Company is a producer and marketer of whole and processed turkey products and grain-fed, farm-raised catfish.

QUARTERLY DATA

(10/30/93)($000)

	Rev	Inc
1st Quarter	682,102	19,254
2nd Quarter	676,686	21,636
3rd Quarter	677,835	19,143
4th Quarter	817,374	44,637

ANNUAL EARNINGS AND DIVIDENDS PER SHARE

	10/30/93	10/31/92	10/26/91	10/28/90	10/28/89	10/29/88	10/31/87
Earnings Per Share	1.31	1.24	1.13	1.01	0.91	0.79	0.60
Dividends Per Share	0.44	0.36	0.30	0.26	0.22	0.18	① 0.15
Dividend Payout %	33.6	29.0	26.5	25.7	24.2	22.9	25.0

① 2-for-1 stk split, 6/87

ANNUAL FINANCIAL DATA

RECORD OF EARNINGS (IN MILLIONS):

Total Revenues	2,854.0	2,813.7	2,836.2	2,681.2	2,340.5	2,292.8	2,314.1
Costs and Expenses	2,666.5	2,628.2	2,666.2	2,525.6	2,193.8	2,158.5	2,192.7
Depreciation & Amort	32.2	39.0	36.3	35.6	36.9	35.5	33.5
Operating Income	155.3	146.5	133.7	120.0	109.8	98.8	87.9
Earn Bef Income Taxes	161.1	151.1	137.9	121.4	110.8	95.4	79.9
Income Taxes	60.4	55.9	51.5	44.2	40.7	35.2	33.9
Net Income	① 100.8	95.2	86.4	77.1	70.1	60.2	45.9

① Before acctg. change dr$127,529,000.

BALANCE SHEET (IN MILLIONS):

Cash and Cash Equivalents	172.4	225.5	172.1	102.4	78.3	68.9	64.3
Receivables, Net	230.9	189.8	192.5	194.4	169.5	158.6	151.8
Inventories	208.1	185.9	176.4	184.3	165.0	143.0	136.4
Gross Property	585.3	543.9	533.8	514.0	511.9	512.9	497.6
Accumulated Depreciation	340.3	327.5	302.0	278.9	267.5	249.9	233.7
Long-Term Debt	5.7	7.6	22.8	24.5	19.2	20.4	48.8
Net Stockholders' Equity	570.9	644.3	583.4	513.8	470.9	418.7	373.1
Total Assets	1,093.6	913.0	856.8	799.4	727.4	706.5	698.0
Total Current Assets	619.9	609.1	546.4	486.9	417.0	376.0	366.0
Total Current Liabilities	227.1	207.9	200.3	193.1	188.0	219.5	218.0
Net Working Capital	392.8	401.2	346.2	293.8	229.0	156.5	148.0
Year End Shs Outstg (000)	76,672	76,627	76,641	76,664	76,652	76,652	76,736

STATISTICAL RECORD:

Operating Profit Margin %	5.4	5.2	4.7	4.5	4.7	4.3	3.8
Book Value Per Share	6.50	7.88	7.02	6.08	5.57	4.87	4.25
Return on Equity %	17.7	14.8	14.8	15.0	14.9	14.4	12.3
Return on Assets %	9.2	10.4	10.1	9.6	9.6	8.5	6.6
Average Yield %	1.9	1.7	1.5	…	1.6	1.6	1.3
P/E Ratio	19.5-15.5	20.0-13.5	20.5-14.2	19.6-13.9	18.7-11.1	17.6-11.2	24.6-13.5
Price Range	25½-20¼	24¾-16¼	23⅛-16	19¾-14	17-10⅛	13¾-8¾	14¾-8⅛

Statistics are as originally reported.

OFFICERS:
R.L. Knowlton, Chmn. & C.E.O.
J.W. Johnson, Pres. & C.E.O.
D.J. Hodapp, Exec. V.P. & C.F.O.

INCORPORATED: DE, Sep., 1928

PRINCIPAL OFFICE: 1 Hormel Place, Austin, MN 55912-3680

TELEPHONE NUMBER: (507) 437-5611

NO. OF EMPLOYEES: 1,469 (approx.)

ANNUAL MEETING: Last Tuesday in January

SHAREHOLDERS: 7,186 (approx.)

INSTITUTIONAL HOLDINGS:
No. of Institutions: 105
Shares Held: 20,183,606

REGISTRAR(S): Norwest Bank Minnesota, N.A., St. Paul, MN

TRANSFER AGENT(S): Norwest Bank Minnesota, N.A., St. Paul, MN

HOUGHTON MIFFLIN CO.

YIELD 1.8%
P/E RATIO 20.6

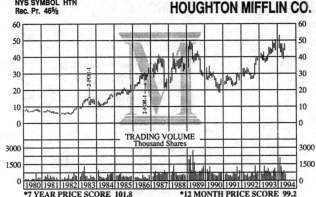

7 YEAR PRICE SCORE 101.8 **12 MONTH PRICE SCORE 99.2**
*NYSE COMPOSITE INDEX=100

TRADING VOLUME
Thousand Shares

INTERIM EARNINGS (Per Share):

Qtr.	Mar.	June	Sept.	Dec.
1990	d0.85	0.81	1.88	d0.58
1991	d1.09	0.87	2.36	d0.39
1992	d0.98	0.82	2.46	d0.92
1993	d1.08	0.32	3.00	0.02

INTERIM DIVIDENDS (Per Share):

Amt.	Decl.	Ex.	Rec.	Pay.
0.205Q	4/28/93	5/6/93	5/12/93	5/26/93
0.205Q	8/2	8/5	8/11	8/25
0.215Q	10/27	11/4	11/10	11/24
0.215Q	1/26/94	2/3/94	2/9/94	2/23/94
0.215Q	4/27	5/5	5/11	5/25

Indicated div.: $0.86

CAPITALIZATION (12/31/93):

	($000)	(%)
Long-Term Debt	26,438	10.6
Common & Surplus	224,082	89.4
Total	250,520	100.0

DIVIDEND ACHIEVER STATUS:
Rank: 235 1983-93 Growth Rate: 7.3%
Total Years of Dividend Growth: 11

RECENT DEVELOPMENTS: For the year ended 12/31/93, net income before an extraordinary charge increased 64.5% to $31.4 million compared with $19.1 million a year ago. Sales were up 1.8% to $463.0 million from $454.7 million. The earnings included $10.6 million in non-recurring charges: workforce restructuring costs of $7.5 million, $2.2 million in costs related to relocation of the Company's headquarters, and $900,00 charge associated with the warehouse closing in Newark, California. The after-tax cost was $6.6 million.

PROSPECTS: Results will be adversely affected by reduced state text-book adoption opportunities in Houghton's most profitable business, school publishing. However, state adoptions in California, the largest of the 22 states that purchase text-books in bulk, and Florida are expected in 1995. Completion of the McDougal, Littell acquisition should significantly expand HTN's secondary school business. The Company agreed to acquire McDougal Littell in a transaction valued at $138 million.

BUSINESS

HOUGHTON MIFFLIN COMPANY has four principal subsidiaries: The Riverside Publishing Co., a publisher of educational materials; Houghton Mifflin Canada Limited, a purveyor of educational materials; Ticknor & Fields, Inc., a trade book imprint, and HMR, Inc., which manages the Company's investment in real estate, marketable securities, and other short-term cash equivalent investments. HTN's principal business is publishing and its operations are classified into two industry segments: textbooks and other educational materials and services for the school and college markets; and general publishing, including fiction, nonfiction, children's books, dictionary and reference materials.

BUSINESS LINE ANALYSIS

(12/31/93)	Rev(%)	Inc(%)
Textbooks & Other....	77.2	84.4
General Publishing....	22.8	15.6
Total	100.0	100.0

ANNUAL EARNINGS AND DIVIDENDS PER SHARE

	1993	1992	1991	1990	1989	1988	1987
Earnings Per Share	2.27	①1.35	1.75	1.27	1.62	1.70	1.66
Dividends Per Share	0.83	②0.79	0.75	0.71	0.67	0.63	0.59
Dividend Payout %	36.6	58.5	42.9	55.9	41.4	37.1	35.5

① Before acctg. chg. ② Bef acctg chge

ANNUAL FINANCIAL DATA

RECORD OF EARNINGS (IN THOUSANDS):

	1993	1992	1991	1990	1989	1988	1987
Total Revenues	462,969	454,706	466,801	421,600	404,359	368,289	343,416
Costs and Expenses	372,238	368,116	383,230	353,125	331,810	295,479	272,101
Depreciation & Amort	39,361	42,280	39,419	34,227	32,546	32,163	32,415
Operating Income	51,370	44,310	44,152	34,248	40,003	40,647	38,900
Inc Bef Taxes on Income	49,023	28,444	40,446	31,257	37,007	38,872	41,798
Taxes on Inc Bef Acctg Chgs	17,650	9,373	15,369	13,222	13,997	14,771	18,182
Net Income	①31,373	②19,071	25,077	18,035	23,010	24,101	23,616
Aver. Shs. Outstg.	13,823	14,029	14,314	14,255	14,214	14,160	14,193

① Before acctg. change dr$1,002,000. ② Before acctg. change dr$14,657,000.

BALANCE SHEET (IN THOUSANDS):

	1993	1992	1991	1990	1989	1988	1987
Total	85,349	68,635	92,804	77,434	37,335	22,622	35,148
Receivables, Net	104,489	86,867	90,972	83,633	87,247	75,277	65,125
Inventories	64,000	61,547	67,781	74,234	70,682	65,565	60,086
Gross Property	103,161	114,663	113,637	150,985	143,497	91,271	129,591
Accumulated Depreciation	36,991	40,619	36,451	74,005	70,298	25,959	69,607
Long-Term Debt	26,438	52,608	52,975	52,985	28,973	2,262	1,980
Net Stockholders' Equity	224,082	199,839	223,181	209,504	199,850	185,233	169,479
Total Assets	398,221	371,421	381,780	366,496	321,176	261,967	247,595
Total Current Assets	267,849	233,771	268,362	250,903	210,316	175,600	163,273
Total Current Liabilities	111,270	83,934	92,083	92,617	81,880	66,681	68,343
Net Working Capital	156,579	149,837	176,279	158,286	128,436	108,919	94,930
Year End Shares Outstg	14,526	14,411	14,281	14,259	14,235	14,177	14,121

STATISTICAL RECORD:

	1993	1992	1991	1990	1989	1988	1987
Operating Profit Margin %	11.1	9.7	9.5	8.1	9.9	11.0	11.3
Book Value Per Share	14.07	12.34	14.91	13.90	12.82	12.65	11.60
Return on Equity %	14.0	9.5	11.2	8.6	11.5	13.0	13.9
Return on Assets %	7.9	5.1	6.6	4.9	7.2	9.2	9.5
Average Yield %	1.9	2.4	2.9	2.7	1.7	1.9	1.9
P/E Ratio	22.2-16.0	29.5-19.7	17.4-12.7	27.1-14.5	31.0-17.4	25.0-14.3	24.9-12.5
Price Range	50⅜-36⅜	39⅞-26⅝	30⅜-22¼	34⅜-18⅜	50¼-28⅛	42½-24⅜	41⅜-20¾

Statistics are as originally reported.

OFFICERS:
N.F. Darehshori, Chmn., Pres. & C.E.O.
S.O. Jaeger, Exec. V.P., C.F.O. & Treas.
P.D. Weaver, Sr. V.P. & Gen. Counsel

INCORPORATED: MA, 1908

PRINCIPAL OFFICE: One Beacon Street, Boston, MA 02108

TELEPHONE NUMBER: (617) 351-5000
FAX: (617) 573-4914
NO. OF EMPLOYEES: 285
ANNUAL MEETING: In April
SHAREHOLDERS: 1,420
INSTITUTIONAL HOLDINGS:
No. of Institutions: 109
Shares Held: 8,301,020

REGISTRAR(S):

TRANSFER AGENT(S):

HOUSEHOLD INTERNATIONAL, INC.

YIELD	3.7%
P/E RATIO	11.3

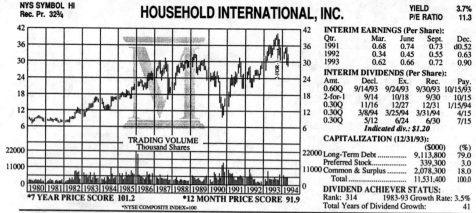

7 YEAR PRICE SCORE 101.2   **12 MONTH PRICE SCORE 91.9**

*NYSE COMPOSITE INDEX=100

INTERIM EARNINGS (Per Share):

Qtr.	Mar.	June	Sept.	Dec.
1991	0.68	0.74	0.73	d0.52
1992	0.34	0.45	0.55	0.63
1993	0.62	0.66	0.72	0.90

INTERIM DIVIDENDS (Per Share):

Amt.	Decl.	Ex.	Rec.	Pay.
0.60Q	9/14/93	9/24/93	9/30/93	10/15/93
2-for-1	9/14	10/18	9/30	10/15
0.30Q	11/16	12/27	12/31	1/15/94
0.30Q	3/8/94	3/25/94	3/31/94	4/15
0.30Q	5/12	6/24	6/30	7/15

Indicated div.: $1.20

CAPITALIZATION (12/31/93):

	($000)	(%)
Long-Term Debt	9,113,800	79.0
Preferred Stock	339,300	3.0
Common & Surplus	2,078,300	18.0
Total	11,531,400	100.0

DIVIDEND ACHIEVER STATUS:

Rank: 314   1983-93 Growth Rate: 3.5%
Total Years of Dividend Growth: 41

RECENT DEVELOPMENTS: For the quarter ended 12/31/93, net income rose 55.5% from the corresponding 1992 period to $93.0 million. Results were attributed to solid growth in the credit card business, as domestic managed receivables increased 5%. Operations in the United Kingdom turned in income of $6.5 million versus a loss of $8 million a year ago. For 1993, net income was $298.7 million or 56.5% above the prior year. Results were aided by a 51% jump in the finance and banking unit's income to $303.2 million.

PROSPECTS: The consumer lending environment is favorable as managed receivables are on the rise. Reduced credit losses and lower nonaccruing loans should continue to translate into earnings growth in the future. Most of the Company's foreign operations are showing improved results, particularly in the United Kingdom. The GM credit card portfolio is making strong contibutions and the delinquency percentage is acceptable.

BUSINESS

HOUSEHOLD INTERNATIONAL, INC., with over 85% of its receivables in the U.S., is a major provider of consumer finance, banking services, consumer life insurance and investment products. Its subsidiaries include: Household Finance Corp., the nation's oldest and largest consumer finance company; Household Credit Services, the 7th-largest issuer of VISA and MasterCards; Household Retail Services, the second largest private label credit card issuer; Household Bank, f.s.b., the 12th-largest thrift and the 4th-largest mortgage servicer in the country; and Alexander Hamilton Life Insurance Co., which ranks in the top 3% of North American life insurance companies in terms of assets.

BUSINESS LINE ANALYSIS

(12/31/93)	Inc($000)	Rev(%)
Finance & Banking	24,362.5	73.9
Individual Life Insur.	6,959.0	21.1
Corporate	84.3	0.3
Liquidating Comm.		
Lines	1,555.7	4.7
Total	32,961.5	100.0

ANNUAL EARNINGS AND DIVIDENDS PER SHARE

	1993	1992	1991	1990	1989	1988	1987
Earnings Per Share	2.91	1.97	1.58	② 3.03	② 2.94	② 2.49	2.79
Dividends Per Share	① 1.17	1.138	1.108	1.08	1.07	1.017	0.947
Dividend Payout %	40.2	57.9	70.3	35.7	36.5	40.9	34.0

① 2-for-1 stk split,10/18/93 ② Before disc. oper. ③ Primary shares

ANNUAL FINANCIAL DATA

RECORD OF EARNINGS (IN MILLIONS)

	1993	1992	1991	1990	1989	1988	1987
Total Revenues	4,454.5	4,180.6	4,593.9	4,319.7	3,490.1	2,637.4	3,440.5
Costs and Expenses	4,003.8	3,902.6	4,394.1	3,971.0	3,157.1	2,345.1	3,099.2
Operating Income	450.7	278.0	199.8	348.7	333.0	292.3	341.3
Income Bef Income Taxes	450.7	278.0	199.8	348.7	333.0	292.3	341.3
Income Taxes	152.0	87.1	50.0	113.4	114.6	108.6	119.8
Net Income	298.7	190.9	149.8	235.3	① 218.4	② 183.7	221.5
Aver. Shs. Outstg. (000)	94,800	86,000	83,000	71,000	70,800	69,400	75,600

① Before disc. op. cr$21,100,000. ② Before disc. op. cr$63,000,000.

BALANCE SHEET (IN MILLIONS)

	1993	1992	1991	1990	1989	1988	1987
Cash and Cash Equivalents	9,112.5	7,645.6	6,710.2	5,723.3	4,366.9	3,358.7	2,243.1
Receivables, Net	19,563.0	18,960.6	18,987.1	21,802.6	20,016.7	16,123.2	13,260.1
Gross Property	434.3	397.4	423.8	347.9	319.8	212.7	371.9
Long-Term Debt	9,113.8	9,014.4	9,594.5	9,561.3	7,915.9	6,565.9	6,265.3
Net Stockholders' Equity	2,417.6	1,881.6	1,829.3	1,612.9	1,343.7	1,251.0	1,009.7
Total Assets	32,961.5	31,128.4	29,982.3	29,454.7	26,162.7	21,032.4	16,985.8
Total Current Assets	28,675.5	26,606.2	25,697.3	27,525.9	24,383.6	19,481.9	15,690.4
Total Current Liabilities	13,158.2	13,283.6	12,110.0	12,618.8	11,926.6	9,592.7	7,769.7
Net Working Capital	15,517.3	13,322.6	13,585.3	14,907.1	12,457.0	9,889.2	7,920.7
Year End Shs Outstg (000)	94,448	82,876	79,553	71,596	70,614	69,887	69,590

STATISTICAL RECORD:

	1993	1992	1991	1990	1989	1988	1987
Book Value Per Share	22.00	18.65	19.17	18.77	16.91	16.79	13.32
Return on Equity %	12.4	10.1	8.2	14.6	16.3	14.7	21.9
Return on Assets %	0.9	0.6	0.5	0.8	0.8	0.9	1.3
Average Yield %	4.5	4.5	4.9	5.9	3.8	4.0	4.0
P/E Ratio	13.9-9.3	15.4-10.5	19.9-8.7	8.8-3.2	11.2-7.9	12.2-7.9	11.2-5.8
Price Range	40½-27	30¼-20¾	31½-13¾	26⅝-9¾	32¾-23¼	30½-19¾	31¼-16¼

Statistics are as originally reported.

OFFICERS:
D.C. Clark, Chmn. & C.E.O.

INCORPORATED: DE, Feb., 1981

PRINCIPAL OFFICE: 2700 Sanders Road, Prospect Heights, IL 60070-2799

TELEPHONE NUMBER: (708) 564-5000
NO. OF EMPLOYEES: 14,108
ANNUAL MEETING: In May
SHAREHOLDERS: 14,632 (common); pfd., 2,988
INSTITUTIONAL HOLDINGS:
No. of Institutions: 318
Shares Held: 33,542,838

REGISTRAR(S):

TRANSFER AGENT(S): Harris Trust & Savings Bank, Chicago, IL

NYS SYMBOL HUB B
Rec. Pr. 57⅝

HUBBELL INC.

YIELD 2.8%
P/E RATIO 27.4

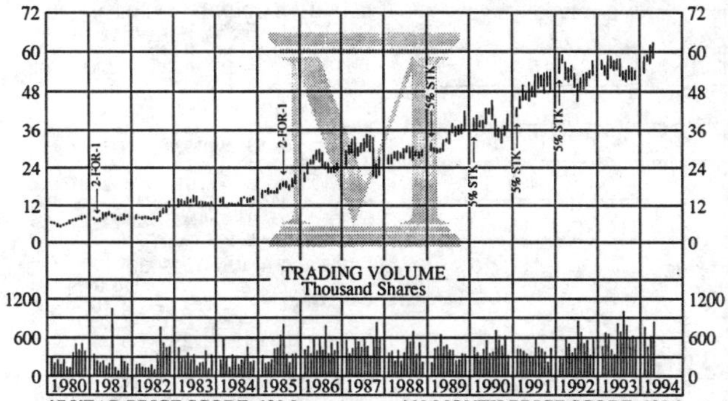

***7 YEAR PRICE SCORE 103.2** ***12 MONTH PRICE SCORE 109.3**

*NYSE COMPOSITE INDEX=100

INTERIM EARNINGS (Per Share):

Qtr.	Mar.	June	Sept.	Dec.
1990	0.68	0.71	0.66	0.70
1991	0.71	0.75	0.69	0.72
1992	0.74	0.77	0.72	0.74
1993	0.76	0.79	0.74	d0.19

INTERIM DIVIDENDS (Per Share):

Amt.	Decl.	Ex.	Rec.	Pay.
0.40Q	3/9/93	3/16/93	3/22/93	4/12/93
0.41Q	6/16	6/22	6/28	7/12
0.41Q	9/9	9/14	9/20	10/11
0.41Q	12/15	12/20	12/27	1/11/94
0.41Q	3/14/94	3/22/94	3/28/94	4/11

Indicated div.: $1.64

CAPITALIZATION (12/31/93):

	($000)	(%)
Long-Term Debt	2,700	0.5
Deferred Income Tax	4,572	0.8
Common & Surplus	557,660	98.7
Total	564,932	100.0

DIVIDEND ACHIEVER STATUS:
Rank: 108 1983-93 Growth Rate: 12.6%
Total Years of Dividend Growth: 33

RECENT DEVELOPMENTS: For the year ended 12/31/93, net income was $66.3 million, or $2.10 per share, versus income of $94.1 million, or $2.97 per share, before an accounting change in 1992. Included in the results for 1993 was a $50.0 million fourth quarter pretax charge for the estimated costs of a restructuring program. Net sales increased 5.9% to $832.4 million from $786.1 million last year. The sales improvement was due to continued growth at the Ohio Brass subsidiary, inclusion of Hipotronics Inc.(acquired in November 1992) and the E.M. Wiegmann & Co., Inc. (acquired in March 1993), as well as improved sales through distributors and home centers. At 12/31/93, the backlog of orders was approximately $60.4 million, up from the $54.7 million reported at the end of 1992. On 3/16/94, HUB announced that it had entered into an agreement to purchase A.B. Chance Industries, Inc.

BUSINESS

HUBBELL INCORPORATED is an international manufacturer of electrical and electronic products serving a broad range of industrial, commerical, telecommunications, and utility markets. Operations are reported in three segments. Low Voltage products are in the range of less than 600 volts and are sold principally to distributors and represent stock items. This segment consists of standard and special application wiring device products, lighting fixtures, low voltage industrial controls and remanufactured refrigeration compressors. High Voltage products are in the more than 600 volt range and are generally sold directly to the user and represent products made to customer's order. This segment comprises wire and cable, insulators and surge arresters. The Other segment consists of products not classified on a voltage basis. This segment includes standard and special application enclosures, fittings, switch and outlet boxes, wire management components and systems, and data transmission and telecommunications equipment. The Company operates facilities in the United States, Canada, Puerto Rico, Mexico, Singapore and the United Kingdom.

ANNUAL EARNINGS AND DIVIDENDS PER SHARE

	1993	1992	1991	1990	1989	1988	1987
Earnings Per Share	**2.10**	**[1] 2.97**	**2.87**	**2.74**	**2.52**	**2.25**	**1.97**
Dividends Per Share	**1.62**	**[2] 1.561**	**[3] 1.43**	**1.352**	**[4] 1.06**	**0.872**	**0.76**
Dividend Payout %	**77.1**	**52.6**	**49.8**	**49.3**	**42.1**	**38.7**	**38.5**

[1] Before acctg. chg. [2] 5% stk div, 1/6/92 [3] 5% stk div, 1/7/91 [4] 5% stk div, 2/89

ANNUAL FINANCIAL DATA

	1993	1992	1991	1990	1989	1988	1987
RECORD OF EARNINGS (IN THOUSANDS):							
Total Revenues	832,423	786,078	756,126	719,509	668,765	614,237	581,087
Costs and Expenses	732,084	641,339	615,403	590,645	547,222	501,869	477,251
Depreciation & Amort	30,098	26,813	22,222	17,728	16,570	14,950	14,101
Operating Income	70,241	117,926	118,501	111,136	104,973	97,418	89,735
Income Bef Income Taxes	81,494	130,678	129,418	124,655	116,714	106,402	99,253
Income Taxes	15,188	36,588	38,821	38,633	37,350	35,114	36,724
Net Income	66,306	[1] 94,090	90,597	86,022	79,364	71,288	62,529
Aver. Shs. Outstg.	31,620	31,643	31,570	31,414	31,478	31,735	31,612
[1] Before acctg. change dr$16,506,000.							
BALANCE SHEET (IN THOUSANDS):							
Cash & Temp Cash Invests	44,231	28,255	91,614	103,269	101,144	66,871	61,416
Accounts Receivable, Net	109,987	115,639	93,666	91,869	83,838	71,118	67,268
Inventories	181,699	177,910	140,760	141,293	127,966	124,355	106,470
Gross Property	336,667	315,564	292,253	264,297	227,210	209,006	194,376
Accumulated Depreciation	182,046	162,225	144,638	132,498	119,248	106,563	94,167
Long-Term Debt	2,700	2,700	8,100	8,100	8,100	8,100	8,270
Net Stockholders' Equity	557,660	541,327	518,906	468,733	427,818	392,530	357,236
Total Assets	874,298	806,688	685,341	624,706	576,286	523,462	468,891
Total Current Assets	362,081	329,867	343,715	354,156	341,038	278,774	261,086
Total Current Liabilities	230,206	200,466	110,776	105,107	101,478	88,337	80,786
Net Working Capital	131,875	129,401	232,939	249,049	239,560	190,437	180,300
Year End Shares Outstg	31,259	31,185	31,153	29,531	29,526	31,247	31,163
STATISTICAL RECORD:							
Operating Profit Margin %	8.4	15.0	15.7	15.4	15.7	15.9	15.4
Book Value Per Share	15.71	15.44	15.55	15.39	14.17	12.24	11.04
Return on Equity %	11.9	17.4	17.5	18.4	18.6	18.2	17.5
Return on Assets %	7.6	11.7	13.2	13.8	13.8	13.6	13.3
Average Yield %	3.0	3.0	3.0	3.5	3.0	3.1	2.7
P/E Ratio	28.0-24.2	20.2-15.1	18.8-14.0	16.5-11.6	16.6-11.4	13.8-11.2	17.5-10.7
Price Range	58⅞-50¾	60-44⅞	53⅞-40⅛	45⅛-31⅞	41¾-28¾	31-25⅛	34½-21

Statistics are as originally reported.

OFFICERS:
G.J. Ratcliffe, Chmn., Pres. & C.E.O.
J.H. Biggart, Jr., Treas.
J.K. Braun, Asst. Treas.
R.W. Davies, Gen. Couns. & Sec.

INCORPORATED: CT, May, 1905

PRINCIPAL OFFICE: 584 Derby Milford Rd. P.O. Box 549, Orange, CT 06477-4024

TELEPHONE NUMBER: (203) 799-4100

FAX: (203) 799-4333

NO. OF EMPLOYEES: 5,885

ANNUAL MEETING: In May

SHAREHOLDERS: 1,405 Cl. A com.; 5,628 Cl. B.

INSTITUTIONAL HOLDINGS:
No. of Institutions: 226
Shares Held: 15,550,544 Cl. B

REGISTRAR(S): Manufacturers Hanover Trust Co., New York, NY

TRANSFER AGENT(S): Manufacturers Hanover Trust Co., New York, NY

HUNT MANUFACTURING CO.

YIELD 2.3%
P/E RATIO 24.4

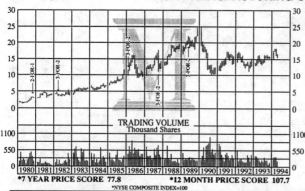

TRADING VOLUME
Thousand Shares

1980 1981 1982 1983 1984 1985 1986 1987 1988 1989 1990 1991 1992 1993 1994

*7 YEAR PRICE SCORE 77.8   *12 MONTH PRICE SCORE 107.7

*NYSE COMPOSITE INDEX=100

INTERIM EARNINGS (Per Share):

Qtr.	Feb.	May	Aug.	Nov.
1991-92	0.14	0.20	0.24	0.25
1992-93	0.16	0.22	0.24	Nil
1993-94	0.19	…	…	…

INTERIM DIVIDENDS (Per Share):

Amt.	Decl.	Ex.	Rec.	Pay.
0.0875Q	4/16/93	4/20/93	4/26/93	5/4/93
0.0875Q	6/25	6/29	7/6	7/14
0.0875Q	10/28	11/2	11/8	11/16
0.09Q	12/16	12/22	12/29	1/6/94
0.09Q	4/14/94	4/19/94	4/25/94	5/3

Indicated div.: $0.36

CAPITALIZATION (11/28/93):

	($000)	(%)
Long-Term Debt	3,003	2.5
Deferred Income Tax	1,230	1.0
Common & Surplus	116,267	96.5
Total	120,500	100.0

DIVIDEND ACHIEVER STATUS:

Rank: 125   1983-93 Growth Rate: 12.0%
Total Years of Dividend Growth: 26

RECENT DEVELOPMENTS: For the year ended 11/28/93, net income increased 12.2% to $14.9 million. Sales were up 9% to $256.2 million. Both of the Company's business segments posted higher sales. The office products sales growth was led by an increase in sales of office furniture products, while mechanical and electromechanical office products contributed to a lesser extent. The art/craft products sales growth was largely attributable to higher sales of mounting and laminating products.

PROSPECTS: Despite distribution consolidation, lower prices, and troubled European economies, the Company should continue to report revenue and earnings growth. However, these pressures will further necessitate efforts to control costs. Strong cash flows being generated by operating activities will be used to fund continuing debt reduction activities. New products and business efforts in office and data products, foam board, crafts, and laminating are likely to have considerable impact on results in 1994.

BUSINESS

HUNT MANUFACTURING CO. is a producer and distributor of office and art/craft products. The Company manufactures more than 10,000 items and distributes them to more than 60 countries. These include office products such as pencil sharpeners, paper punches, paper shredders, paper trimmers, letter openers, air cleaners, and staplers; metal office files, racks, desk organizers, machine stands, fax and printer cabinets, and cash boxes; furniture for computers and the home/office; acoustical covers for printers; budget office furniture, and data product accessories. Art/craft products include Speedball dip pens, paints, inks, calligraphy kits, and screen and block printing products.

REVENUES

(11/28/93)	($000)	(%)
Mechanical & Electromech	70,047	27.3
Office Furniture	44,233	17.3
Desktop Accessories	28,182	11.0
Mounting & Laminating	68,734	26.8
Art Supplies	27,569	10.8
Hobby/Craft	17,385	6.8
Total	256,150	100.0

ANNUAL EARNINGS AND DIVIDENDS PER SHARE

	11/28/93	11/29/92	12/1/91	12/2/90	12/3/89	11/27/88	11/29/87
Earnings Per Share	0.93	0.83	0.60	0.75	1.17	1.01	0.77
Dividends Per Share	0.35	0.34	0.32	0.31	①0.267	0.227	②0.193
Dividend Payout %	37.6	41.0	53.3	41.3	22.8	22.5	25.3

① 3-for-2 stk split, 5/89   ② 3-for-2 stk split, 10/87

ANNUAL FINANCIAL DATA

RECORD OF EARNINGS (IN THOUSANDS):

Total Revenues	256,150	234,929	228,622	220,099	203,444	178,755	150,291
Costs and Expenses	223,925	204,477	202,090	192,909	169,077	146,706	123,202
Depreciation & Amort	7,664	7,558	7,467	6,866	5,560	5,769	4,319
Operating Income	24,561	22,894	19,065	20,324	28,807	26,280	22,770
Income Bef Income Taxes	24,038	21,609	17,118	18,737	29,430	25,939	21,623
Income Taxes	9,110	8,307	7,532	6,726	10,626	9,772	9,245
Net Income	14,928	13,302	9,586	12,011	18,804	16,167	12,378
Aver. Shs. Outstg.	16,107	16,104	16,080	16,083	16,080	16,059	16,032

BALANCE SHEET (IN THOUSANDS):

Cash & Cash Equivalents	10,778	6,013	8,738	7,532	15,839	17,424	9,335
Accounts Receivable, Net	39,472	39,565	39,278	36,485	34,176	30,302	26,107
Total Inventories	27,960	25,007	28,250	30,233	26,406	17,573	17,441
Gross Property	88,950	81,840	78,756	76,926	60,356	53,334	46,709
Accumulated Depreciation	42,333	39,185	35,074	30,788	26,764	22,718	19,527
Long-Term Debt	3,003	6,160	17,271	26,498	9,674	10,790	12,364
Net Stockholders' Equity	116,267	107,456	102,384	99,539	90,029	75,660	63,060
Total Assets	156,317	144,170	151,824	154,361	127,947	112,970	96,777
Total Current Assets	80,842	72,302	77,181	74,880	76,839	65,557	53,114
Total Current Liabilities	33,714	26,850	29,531	24,391	23,741	22,366	17,881
Net Working Capital	47,128	45,452	47,650	50,489	53,098	43,191	35,233
Year End Shares Outstg	16,107	16,082	16,095	16,054	16,106	16,077	16,023

STATISTICAL RECORD:

Operating Profit Margin %	9.6	9.7	8.3	9.2	14.2	14.7	15.2
Book Value Per Share	5.54	4.95	4.50	4.19	4.57	3.73	3.03
Return on Equity %	12.8	12.4	9.4	12.1	20.9	21.4	19.6
Return on Assets %	9.5	9.2	6.3	7.8	14.7	14.3	12.8
Average Yield %	2.4	2.4	2.2	1.8	1.3	1.4	1.4
P/E Ratio	17.6-14.0	20.8-13.6	28.8-19.0	33.2-13.7	21.2-14.1	19.4-12.9	23.1-12.7
Price Range	16⅜-13	17¼-11¼	17¼-11⅜	24⅞-10¼	24¾-16½	19⅝-13	17¾-9¾

Statistics are as originally reported.

OFFICERS:
R.J. Naples, Chmn. & C.E.O.
R.B. Fritsch, Pres. & C.O.O.
W.E. Chandler, Sr. V.P.-C.F.O. & Sec.

INCORPORATED: PA, Nov., 1962

PRINCIPAL OFFICE: 230 South Broad St., Philadelphia, PA 19102-4167

TELEPHONE NUMBER: (215) 732-7700
FAX: (215) 875-5331
NO. OF EMPLOYEES: 2,200 (approx.)
ANNUAL MEETING: In April
SHAREHOLDERS: 1,200 (approx.)
INSTITUTIONAL HOLDINGS:
No. of Institutions: 50
Shares Held: 5,699,150

REGISTRAR(S): Mellon Bank (East) N.A., Philadelphia, PA

TRANSFER AGENT(S): Mellon Bank (East), N.A., Philadelphia, PA

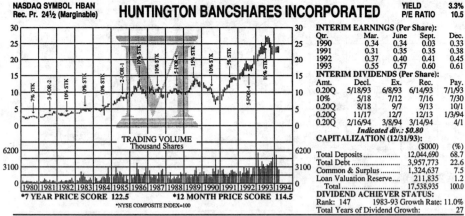

NASDAQ SYMBOL HBAN
Rec. Pr. 24½ (Marginable)

HUNTINGTON BANCSHARES INCORPORATED

YIELD 3.3%
P/E RATIO 10.5

INTERIM EARNINGS (Per Share):

Qtr.	Mar.	June	Sept.	Dec.
1990	0.34	0.34	0.03	0.33
1991	0.31	0.35	0.35	0.38
1992	0.37	0.40	0.41	0.45
1993	0.55	0.57	0.60	0.61

INTERIM DIVIDENDS (Per Share):

Amt.	Decl.	Ex.	Rec.	Pay.
0.20Q	5/18/93	6/8/93	6/14/93	7/1/93
10%	5/18	7/12	7/16	7/30
0.20Q	8/18	9/7	9/13	10/1
0.20Q	11/17	12/7	12/13	1/3/94
0.20Q	2/16/94	3/8/94	3/14/94	4/1

Indicated div.: $0.80

CAPITALIZATION (12/31/93):

	($000)	(%)
Total Deposits	12,044,690	68.7
Total Debt	3,957,773	22.6
Common & Surplus	1,324,637	7.5
Loan Valuation Reserve	211,835	1.2
Total	17,538,935	100.0

DIVIDEND ACHIEVER STATUS:
Rank: 147   1983-93 Growth Rate: 11.0%
Total Years of Dividend Growth: 27

TRADING VOLUME
Thousand Shares

*7 YEAR PRICE SCORE 122.5   *12 MONTH PRICE SCORE 114.5

*NYSE COMPOSITE INDEX=100

RECENT DEVELOPMENTS: For the year ended 12/31/93, net income was $236.9 million, up 47.1% from $161.0 million earned in 1992. Return on average assets was 1.41%, up from 1.06% a year ago. Return on average equity was 19.48% versus 14.99% last year. For the quarter, net income increased 44.5% to $63.4 million from $43.8 million in 1992, and return on average assets was 1.44% versus 1.09% one year ago. Return on average equity was 19.6% compared with 15.59% last year. For the full year, net interest margin was 5.20%, up from 5.12% last year. Non-performing assets declined to $139.6 million, or 1.27% of total loans and other real estate, at year-end 1993 from $163.2 million, or 1.70% of total loans and other real estate one year ago. At 12/31/93, HBAN's allowance for loan losses totaled $211.8 million, or 1.93% of total loans, up from $153.7 million, or 1.61% of total loans at the end of 1992. The allowance for loan losses currently represents 274.4% of non-performing loans.

BUSINESS

HUNTINGTON BANCSHARES INCORPORATED is a regional bank holding company headquartered in Columbus, Ohio. The Company's banking subsidiaries operate 352 offices in Ohio, Florida, Illinois, Indiana, Kentucky, Michigan, Pennsylvania, and West Virginia. In addition, the Company's mortgage, trust, investment banking and automobile finance subsidiaries manage 89 offices in the eight states mentioned as well as Connecticut, Delaware, Maryland, Massachusetts, New Jersey, North Carolina, Rhode Island, and Virginia. International banking services are maintained through the headquarters office in Columbus and an additional branch located in the Cayman Islands.

LOAN DISTRIBUTION

(12/31/93)	($000)	(%)
Commercial	3,434,738	31.4
Tax-free	71,525	0.7
Real Estate-Construction	337,585	3.1
Real Estate-Commercial	1,214,575	11.1
Real Estate-Residential	1,470,242	13.4
Consumer	3,943,666	36.0
Direct Lease Financing	481,597	4.5
Total	10,953,928	100.0

ANNUAL EARNINGS AND DIVIDENDS PER SHARE

	1993	1992	1991	1990	1989	1988	1987
Earnings Per Share	2.31	1.64	1.38	1.00	1.33	1.22	0.69
Dividends Per Share	① 0.709	② 0.60	③ 0.561	④ 0.523	⑤ 0.42	0.435	⑥ 0.343
Dividend Payout %	30.7	36.7	40.6	52.1	31.7	35.8	49.5

① 10% stk div,07/12/93 ② 5-for-4 stk split, 8/03/92 ③ 5% stk div, 7/9/91 ④ 10% stk div, 7/31/90 ⑤ 15% stk div, 7/31/89 ⑥ 10% stk div, 7/87

ANNUAL FINANCIAL DATA

RECORD OF EARNINGS (IN MILLIONS):

	1993	1992	1991	1990	1989	1988	1987
Total Interest Income	1,236.3	1,022.8	1,035.7	1,102.3	1,020.1	774.4	682.5
Total Interest Expense	440.1	412.6	558.1	678.4	631.2	446.9	374.9
Net Interest Income	796.2	610.2	477.5	423.9	389.0	327.6	307.5
Provision for Loan Losses	79.3	75.7	56.7	71.0	39.9	26.3	76.0
Net Income	236.9	139.0	117.0	85.2	108.0	87.6	47.8
Aver. Shs. Outstg. (000)	102,651	84,799	84,655	93,188	89,276	75,574	68,653

BALANCE SHEET (IN MILLIONS):

	1993	1992	1991	1990	1989	1988	1987
Cash & Due From Banks	704.0	599.9	634.7	718.7	866.4	829.4	791.9
US Treas & Fed Agencies	3,785.7	2,825.0	2,174.9	2,024.8	2,344.0	1,076.2	1,104.0
States & Political Subdiviss	232.7	222.7	293.6	340.1	406.5	356.6	394.1
Net Loans	10,742.1	8,043.8	7,558.6	7,552.2	7,032.0	5,815.3	5,206.7
Total Domestic Deposits	11,681.1	9,668.6	9,435.3	9,087.8	8,570.3	7,035.5	6,371.9
Total Foreign Deposits	363.6	284.1	75.4	27.1	19.3	71.1	229.9
Long-term Debt	762.3	269.6	136.7	141.4	152.6	152.6	154.2
Net Stockholders' Equity	1,324.6	941.4	853.0	785.5	720.7	570.4	511.7
Total Assets	17,618.7	13,894.9	12,332.6	11,808.8	11,679.8	9,506.0	8,835.9
Year End Shs Outstg (000)	103,809	84,899	84,533	93,002	81,341	76,111	68,600

STATISTICAL RECORD:

	1993	1992	1991	1990	1989	1988	1987
Return on Assets %	1.34	1.00	0.95	0.72	0.92	0.92	0.54
Return on Equity %	17.90	14.80	13.70	10.80	15.00	15.40	9.30
Book Value Per Share	12.76	11.09	10.09	8.45	8.86	7.49	7.46
Average Yield %	3.0	3.4	5.0	5.4	3.6	4.5	3.4
P/E Ratio	11.9-8.4	12.9-8.5	10.5-5.6	14.0-6.9	11.7-7.7	9.6-7.2	17.0-12.0
Price Range	27½-19½	21⅛-13⅞	14½-7¾	12⅞-6⅜	14⅛-9¼	11⅛-8⅜	11¾-8¼

OFFICERS:
F. Wobst, Chmn. & C.E.O.
W.L. Hoskins, Vice-Chmn.
Z. Sofia, Pres., C.O.O. & Treas.

INCORPORATED: MD, Apr., 1966

PRINCIPAL OFFICE: Huntington Center, 41 South High Street, Columbus, OH 43287

TELEPHONE NUMBER: (614) 480-8300
NO. OF EMPLOYEES: 8,395
ANNUAL MEETING: In April
SHAREHOLDERS: 27,531
INSTITUTIONAL HOLDINGS:
No. of Institutions: 165
Shares Held: 19,674,258

REGISTRAR(S):

TRANSFER AGENT(S): Huntington National Bank, Stock Transfer Department, Columbus, OH 43287

NYS SYMBOL ITW
Rec. Pr. 40⅛

ILLINOIS TOOL WORKS, INC.

YIELD 1.3%
P/E RATIO 21.8

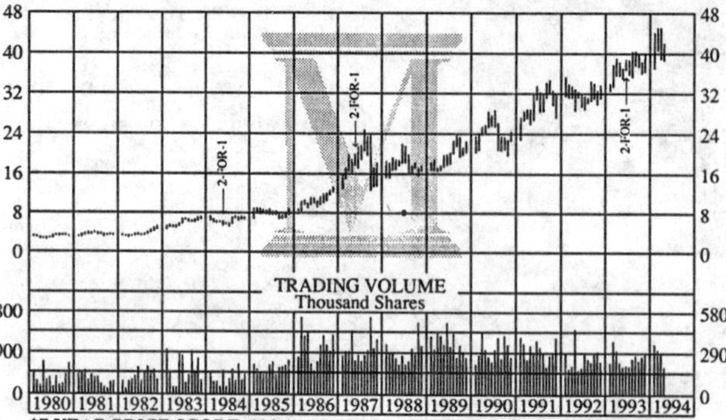

*7 YEAR PRICE SCORE 114.4 *12 MONTH PRICE SCORE 107.2
*NYSE COMPOSITE INDEX=100

INTERIM EARNINGS (Per Share):

Qtr.	Mar.	June	Sept.	Dec.
1990	0.38	0.46	0.42	0.42
1991	0.38	0.43	0.41	0.42
1992	0.36	0.46	0.44	0.46
1993	0.38	0.49	0.45	0.52

INTERIM DIVIDENDS (Per Share):

Amt.	Decl.	Ex.	Rec.	Pay.
0.13Q	10/15/93	11/2/93	11/8/93	12/1/93
0.13Q	12/10	1/31/94	2/4/94	3/1/94
0.13Q	2/18/94	5/2	5/6	6/1
0.13Q	5/6	8/1	8/5	9/1

Indicated div.: $0.52

CAPITALIZATION (12/31/93):

	($000)	(%)
Long-Term Debt	375,641	21.7
Deferred Income Tax	92,470	5.4
Common & Surplus	1,258,669	72.9
Total	1,726,780	100.0

DIVIDEND ACHIEVER STATUS:
Rank: 102 1983-93 Growth Rate: 12.9%
Total Years of Dividend Growth: 31

RECENT DEVELOPMENTS: Net income increased 7.5% to $206.6 million from $192.1 million for the year ended 12/31/93. Revenues for the year were $3.16 billion, up 12.4% from $2.81 billion in 1992. The Engineered Components segment posted significant increases in revenue and operating income as a result of the Miller acquisition and increased sales volume in U.S. automotive and construction markets. Revenues were flat for the Industrial Systems and Consumables segments due to a decrease in international revenues.

PROSPECTS: ITW will continue to benefit from a U.S. economy that is strengthening, especially in the automotive, construction and general industrial markets. Ongoing cost reduction programs in its European businesses will help ITW offset weak conditions there. Foreign currency translation will continue to adversely affect earnings. Revenues and earnings will continue to be enhanced by the operations of fully integrated Miller Group. ITW will see improvement in operating income as a result of continued company-wide cost- control efforts.

BUSINESS

ILLINOIS TOOL WORKS, INC. manufactures engineered components, industrial systems and consumables, and specialty mechanical and chemical products. Engineered Components produces short lead-time plastic and metal components and small assemblies, metal fasteners and adhesives. Industrial Systems and Consumables manufactures systems and related consumables for packaging, quality assurance, tooling and specialty applications. The Company serves the appliance, automotive and truck, electronics, agricultural and telecommunications markets with 250 operations in 33 countries.

QUARTERLY DATA

(12/31/93) ($000)	Rev	Inc
1st Quarter	750,022	42,027
2nd Quarter	829,318	54,799
3rd Quarter	779,536	50,946
4th Quarter	800,305	58,798

ANNUAL EARNINGS AND DIVIDENDS PER SHARE

	1993	1992	1991	1990	1989	1988	1987
Earnings Per Share	**1.83**	**1.72**	**1.63**	**1.67**	**1.53**	**1.33**	**1.03**
Dividends Per Share	**1 0.49**	**0.45**	**0.40**	**0.33**	**0.27**	**0.22**	**2 0.195**
Dividend Payout %	**26.8**	**26.2**	**24.6**	**19.7**	**17.6**	**16.5**	**18.9**

1 2-for-1 stk split,06/21/93 2 2-for-1 stk split, 5/87

ANNUAL FINANCIAL DATA

	1993	1992	1991	1990	1989	1988	1987
RECORD OF EARNINGS (IN MILLIONS):							
Operating Revenues	3,159.2	2,811.6	2,639.7	2,544.2	2,172.7	1,929.8	1,698.4
Costs and Expenses	2,641.9	2,323.9	2,201.4	2,097.3	1,784.9	1,582.1	1,400.9
Depreciation & Amort	131.7	125.3	115.4	102.1	84.7	75.1	57.8
Operating Income	385.6	362.4	322.9	344.7	303.2	272.7	239.6
Income Bef Income Taxes	335.9	309.8	287.8	299.9	269.0	232.8	199.8
Income Taxes	129.3	117.7	107.2	117.5	105.2	92.8	93.6
Net Income	206.6	192.1	180.6	182.4	163.8	140.0	106.2
Aver. Shs. Outstg. (000)	112,979	111,746	111,178	108,872	107,028	105,350	103,272
BALANCE SHEET (IN MILLIONS):							
Cash & Equivalents	35.4	31.2	93.1	46.8	30.9	26.7	32.1
Trade Receivables	544.2	492.2	483.0	474.1	380.2	316.5	287.3
Inventories	403.9	400.6	427.2	468.0	365.2	315.6	291.3
Gross Property	1,205.9	1,073.3	1,014.6	916.9	768.2	661.3	599.2
Accumulated Depreciation	622.1	549.2	488.9	433.3	354.7	318.5	280.5
Long-Term Debt	375.6	252.0	307.1	430.6	334.4	225.9	309.5
Net Stockholders' Equity	1,258.7	1,339.7	1,212.1	1,091.8	871.1	744.7	608.5
Total Assets	2,336.9	2,204.2	2,257.1	2,150.3	1,688.0	1,380.2	1,284.9
Total Current Assets	1,093.6	1,004.8	1,088.0	1,143.5	824.2	713.6	674.2
Total Current Liabilities	546.1	512.7	646.0	528.4	383.8	321.4	341.8
Net Working Capital	547.5	492.1	442.0	615.1	440.4	392.3	332.4
Year End Shs Outstg (000)	113,150	112,013	111,436	109,609	107,332	105,588	103,560
STATISTICAL RECORD:							
Operating Profit Margin %	12.2	12.9	12.2	13.5	14.0	14.1	14.1
Book Value Per Share	7.91	8.78	7.73	7.27	5.42	5.31	4.05
Return on Equity %	16.4	14.3	14.9	16.7	18.8	18.8	17.4
Return on Assets %	8.8	8.7	8.0	8.5	9.7	10.1	8.3
Average Yield %	1.3	1.4	1.4	1.4	1.3	1.2	1.0
P/E Ratio	22.1-17.8	20.6-16.6	21.3-14.0	17.2-11.8	15.5-10.8	16.4-11.4	24.0-12.3
Price Range	40½-32½	35⅜-28½	34¾-22⅞	28¾-19⅝	23¾-16½	21⅞-15⅛	24¾-12⅝

Statistics are as originally reported.

OFFICERS:
J.D. Nichols, Chmn. & C.E.O.
H.R. Crowther, Vice-Chmn.
S.S. Hudnut, Sr. V.P. & Gen. Counsel
M.J. Robinson, V.P. & Treas.

INCORPORATED: DE, Jun., 1961

PRINCIPAL OFFICE: 3600 West Lake Ave., Glenview, IL 60025-5811

TELEPHONE NUMBER: (708) 724-7500
FAX: (708) 657-4261
NO. OF EMPLOYEES: 19,000
ANNUAL MEETING: In May
SHAREHOLDERS: 3,600 approx.
INSTITUTIONAL HOLDINGS:
No. of Institutions: 357
Shares Held: 80,855,893

REGISTRAR(S): Continental Bank, N.A., Chicago, IL 60697

TRANSFER AGENT(S): Continental Bank, N.A., Chicago, IL 60697

INDIANA ENERGY, INC.

YIELD 5.1%
P/E RATIO 11.9

TRADING VOLUME
Thousand Shares

*7 YEAR PRICE SCORE 111.1   *12 MONTH PRICE SCORE 93.7

*NYSE COMPOSITE INDEX=100

INTERIM EARNINGS (Per Share):

Qtr.	Dec.	Mar.	June	Sept.
1989-90	1.00	1.26	0.02	d0.27
1990-91	0.66	1.31	d0.20	d0.09
1991-92	0.80	1.10	d0.08	d0.09
1992-93	1.49	1.28	0.05	d0.29

INTERIM DIVIDENDS (Per Share):

Amt.	Decl.	Ex.	Rec.	Pay.
0.3825Q	7/30/93	8/12/93	8/18/93	9/1/93
3-for-2	7/30	10/4	9/17	10/1
0.255Q	10/29	11/10/94	11/17	12/1
0.255Q	1/10/94	2/9	2/15/94	3/1/94
0.255Q	4/29	5/9	5/13	6/1

Indicated div.: $1.02

CAPITALIZATION (9/30/93):

	($000)	(%)
Long-Term Debt	164,901	33.4
Deferred Income Tax	70,874	14.3
Common & Surplus	258,647	52.3
Total	494,422	100.0

DIVIDEND ACHIEVER STATUS:
Rank: 254   1983-93 Growth Rate: 6.6%
Total Years of Dividend Growth: 18

RECENT DEVELOPMENTS: For the quarter ended 12/31/93, net income was $15.2 million compared with $20.7 million last year. Revenues were $151.9 million, down 2.3%. Net income in the comparable period of 1992 includes a gain of $7.1 million related to the sale of a subsidiary. Results for 1993 benefited from weather that was 10% colder than 1992. Net income for the twelve month period ended 12/31/93 was $29.1 million versus $33.6 million in 1992.

PROSPECTS: Indiana Gas is requesting a $10 to $12 million rate increase to recover cost associated with cleanup efforts to comply with current environmental standards and increased costs for post-retirement benefits under FAS 106. The Company serves a growing territory with a good combination of commercial and residential customers. IEI will continue its efforts in acquiring additional natural gas distributors throughout the state of Indiana.

BUSINESS

INDIANA ENERGY, INC., is a gas distribution and related-services holding company. IEI's principal subsidiary, Indiana Gas Company, provides gas utility service to more than 421,000 customers in north central, central, and southern portions of Indiana. Terre Haute Gas Corp. and Richmond Gas Corp. were acquired in July 1990. Both companies are public utilities providing local distribution of natural gas in the state of Indiana. While the Companies technically still exist as separate corporate entities, their business operations were merged with Indiana Gas' in 1991. IEI Investments is a wholly-owned subsidiary formed to group the operations and financing of non-regulated businesses. IEI has two wholly-owned subsidiaries, IGC Energy and EnTrade Corp.

ANNUAL EARNINGS AND DIVIDENDS PER SHARE

	9/30/93	9/30/92	9/30/91	9/30/90	9/30/89	9/30/88	9/30/87
Earnings Per Share	2.43	1.74	1.67	1.91	1.92	1.83	③ 1.29
Dividends Per Share	① 1.3775	1.45	1.39	1.32	② 1.24	1.130	1.070
Dividend Payout %	56.7	83.3	83.2	69.5	64.6	61.7	82.9

① 3-for-2 stk split,10/04/93 ② 2-for-1 stock split, 2/2/89 ③ Before acctg. chg.

ANNUAL FINANCIAL DATA

RECORD OF EARNINGS (IN THOUSANDS):

Total Revenues	713,049	805,357	672,502	572,491	344,676	322,890	303,364
Depreciation & Amort	26,806	25,136	23,568	22,243	20,682	19,177	17,318
Prov for Fed Inc Taxes	16,823	14,821	12,672	12,357	12,785	11,489	11,123
Operating Income	58,266	50,367	52,264	46,960	44,271	42,775	35,316
Interest Expense	16,820	14,624	15,041	12,539	11,663	10,940	10,968
Net Income	34,578	23,969	23,051	21,749	21,157	20,091	① 14,147
Aver. Shs. Outstg.	14,250	13,804	13,778	11,469	11,010	10,992	10,952

① Before acctg. change cr$2,479,000.

BALANCE SHEET (IN THOUSANDS):

Gross Plant	773,174	725,312	667,252	597,850	517,687	485,445	449,391
Accumulated Depreciation	267,629	248,677	226,082	206,537	180,973	165,801	145,855
Net Utility Plant	505,545	476,635	441,170	391,313	336,714	319,644	303,536
Long-term Debt	164,901	150,311	161,135	102,946	121,330	114,642	96,655
Net Stockholders' Equity	258,647	232,310	226,026	221,261	159,919	152,029	124,045
Total Assets	631,280	627,719	556,008	544,238	398,872	388,061	356,951
Year End Shares Outstg	14,973	13,846	13,781	13,723	11,010	11,009	10,966

STATISTICAL RECORD:

Book Value Per Share	17.28	15.33	14.96	12.99	12.71	11.99	11.31
Op. Inc/Net Pl %	11.5	10.6	11.8	12.0	13.1	13.4	11.6
Dep/Gr. Pl %	3.5	3.5	3.5	3.7	4.0	4.0	3.9
Accum. Dep/Gr. Pl %	34.6	34.3	33.9	34.5	35.0	34.2	32.5
Return on Equity %	13.4	10.3	10.2	9.8	13.2	13.2	11.4
Average Yield %	6.3	7.8	8.1	9.2	9.9	12.0	11.0
P/E Ratio	15.4-11.7	11.5-10.1	12.3-8.4	8.7-6.5	7.6-5.5	5.9-4.5	9.1-6.1
Price Range	24⅞-18⅞	20-17½	20½-14	16½-12½	14⅝-10½	10¾-8⅛	11¾-7⅞

Statistics are as originally reported.

OFFICERS:
D.M. Amundson, Chairman
L.A. Ferger, Pres. & C.E.O.
N.C. Ellerbrook, V.P., Treas. & C.F.O.

INCORPORATED: IN, Oct., 1985

PRINCIPAL OFFICE: 1630 North Meridian Street, Indianapolis, IN 46202-1496

TELEPHONE NUMBER: (317) 926-3351

NO. OF EMPLOYEES: 1,135 full-time (Indiana Gas)

ANNUAL MEETING: In January

SHAREHOLDERS: 11,144

INSTITUTIONAL HOLDINGS:
No. of Institutions: 85
Shares Held: 3,040,364

REGISTRAR(S): Continental Bank, N.A., Chicago, IL 60697

TRANSFER AGENT(S): Continental Bank, N.A., Chicago, IL 60697

NYS SYMBOL IFF
Rec. Pr. 36¼

INTERNATIONAL FLAVORS & FRAGRANCES

YIELD 3.0%
P/E RATIO 22.1

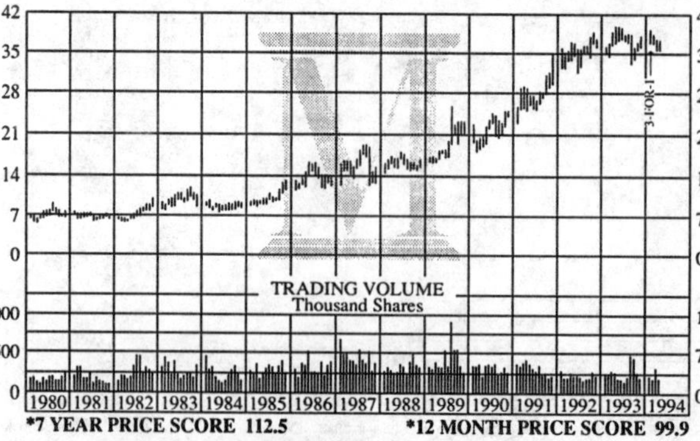

***7 YEAR PRICE SCORE 112.5** ***12 MONTH PRICE SCORE 99.9**

*NYSE COMPOSITE INDEX=100

INTERIM EARNINGS (Per Share):

Qtr.	Mar.	June	Sept.	Dec.
1990	0.36	0.40	0.35	0.25
1991	0.41	0.43	0.37	0.26
1992	0.44	0.48	0.43	0.19
1993	0.49	0.53	0.43	0.33

INTERIM DIVIDENDS (Per Share):

Amt.	Decl.	Ex.	Rec.	Pay.
0.75Q	9/14/93	9/22/93	9/28/93	10/12/93
0.81Q	12/14	12/21	12/28	1/11/94
3-for-1	12/14	1/20/94	12/28	1/19
0.27Q	2/8/94	3/16	3/22/94	4/8
0.27Q	5/12	6/16	6/22	7/8

Indicated div.: $1.08

CAPITALIZATION (12/31/93):

	($000)	(%)
Deferred Income Tax........	11,099	1.2
Common & Surplus..........	891,869	98.8
Total............................	902,968	100.0

DIVIDEND ACHIEVER STATUS:
Rank: 138 1983-93 Growth Rate: 11.2%
Total Years of Dividend Growth: 32

RECENT DEVELOPMENTS: For the year ended 12/31/93, net income increased 14.6% to $202.5 million compared with $176.7 million, before an accounting adjustment, a year ago. Sales were up 5.5% to $1.19 billion from $1.13 billion. The improved operating results were attained despite the adverse effects of a strong U.S. dollar on foreign currency exchange rates and a soft global economy. For the quarter ended 12/31/93, net income rose 61% to $35.7 million compared with $22.0 million a year ago. However, prior year results included a one-time charge of $13 million.

PROSPECTS: Efforts to expand existing facilities and the Company's penetration into new markets will boost future revenues. In addition, the balance sheet is free of long-term debt and the Company expects to finance capital expenditure programs and share repurchase programs through internally generated funds. Sales in Western Europe should continue to grow, despite a soft economy, and International Flavors & Fragrances will proceed with plans to enhance its market share in the developing economies of Eastern Europe.

BUSINESS

INTERNATIONAL FLAVORS & FRAGRANCES, INC. supplies compounds that enhance the aroma or taste of other manufacturers' products. It is one of the largest companies in its field producing and marketing on an international basis. Fragrance products are sold to makers of perfumes and cosmetics, hair and other personal care products, soaps and detergents, household and other cleaning products and area fresheners. Approximately 60% of total sales come from fragrances and aroma chemicals. The remainder came from the sale of flavors, principally to the food and beverage industries for use in such consumer products as soft drinks, snacks, dairy, meat and other processed foods, pharmaceuticals, and animal foods.

ANNUAL EARNINGS AND DIVIDENDS PER SHARE

	1993	1992	1991	1990	1989	1988	1987
Earnings Per Share	**1.78**	**[2] 1.53**	**1.47**	**1.37**	**1.22**	**1.13**	**0.94**
Dividends Per Share	**[1] 1.00**	**0.907**	**0.80**	**0.72**	**0.64**	**0.533**	**0.413**
Dividend Payout %	**56.2**	**59.3**	**54.4**	**52.6**	**52.6**	**47.1**	**43.8**

Note: 3-for-1stk.split,1/19/94. [1] Adj for 3-for-1 stk split, 01/20/94 [2] Before acctg. chg.

ANNUAL FINANCIAL DATA

	1993	1992	1991	1990	1989	1988	1987
RECORD OF EARNINGS (IN MILLIONS):							
Total Revenues	1,188.6	1,126.4	1,017.0	962.8	869.5	839.5	745.9
Costs and Expenses	847.6	828.8	733.4	695.3	631.1	605.8	546.3
Depreciation	35.1	34.0	29.4	28.2	24.3	22.7	20.7
Operating Profit	381.3	354.8	316.4	296.7	266.3	260.7	223.5
Inc Bef Taxes on Income	323.8	281.5	269.5	252.1	223.1	209.3	175.4
Taxes on Income	121.3	104.8	100.8	95.4	84.5	80.6	68.4
Net Income	202.5	[1] 176.7	168.7	156.7	138.6	128.7	107.0
Aver. Shs. Outstg. (000)	113,925	115,454	114,642	38,122	37,993	37,881	37,750
[1] Before acctg. change dr$6,089,000.							
BALANCE SHEET (IN MILLIONS):							
Cash & Mktable Securities	187.2	210.8	134.0	128.5	289.0	235.6	252.5
Receivables, Net	234.3	208.9	187.2	178.3	166.7	...	...
Inventories	302.9	297.7	290.3	278.5	254.1	241.6	223.4
Gross Property	610.6	553.8	563.1	516.6	445.1	414.3	393.6
Accumulated Depreciation	287.2	267.5	273.5	249.8	208.6	186.1	174.3
Net Stockholders' Equity	891.9	977.1	960.1	898.2	764.9	695.4	659.9
Total Assets	1,225.3	1,267.6	1,217.4	1,129.4	969.6	882.3	874.6
Total Current Assets	879.0	965.1	917.7	852.9	723.9	646.1	646.0
Total Current Liabilities	226.6	194.7	180.8	157.9	140.2	126.5	151.5
Net Working Capital	652.4	770.4	736.9	695.0	583.7	519.6	494.5
Year End Shs Outstg (000)	112,060	38,421	38,166	38,168	38,068	37,918	37,824
STATISTICAL RECORD:							
Operating Profit Margin %	25.7	23.4	25.0	24.9	24.6	25.1	24.0
Book Value Per Share	7.96	25.43	25.15	23.53	20.09	18.34	17.45
Return on Equity %	22.7	18.1	17.6	17.4	18.1	18.5	16.2
Return on Assets %	16.5	13.9	13.9	13.9	14.3	14.6	12.2
Average Yield %	2.7	2.6	2.8	3.3	3.0	3.3	2.6
P/E Ratio	22.4-18.5	25.3-20.6	23.8-15.6	6.1-4.4	7.1-4.4	5.3-4.2	6.8-4.4
Price Range	39⅞-33	38¾-31½	35-22⅞	25-18¼	25⅞-16⅛	18⅛-14⅜	19⅜-12⅜

Statistics are as originally reported.

OFFICERS:
E.P. Grisanti, Chmn. & Pres.
T.H. Hoppel, V.P., Fin. & Treas.
S.A. Block, V.P.-Law & Sec.

INCORPORATED: NY, Dec., 1909

PRINCIPAL OFFICE: 521 West 57th Street, New York, NY 10019-2960

TELEPHONE NUMBER: (212) 765-5500

NO. OF EMPLOYEES: 4,371

ANNUAL MEETING: In May

SHAREHOLDERS: 4,588

INSTITUTIONAL HOLDINGS:
No. of Institutions: 425
Shares Held: 21,964,359

REGISTRAR(S): The Bank of New York, New York, NY

TRANSFER AGENT(S): The Bank of New York, New York, NY

NYS SYMBOL IPG
Rec. Pr. 32

INTERPUBLIC GROUP OF COMPANIES, INC.

YIELD 1.8%
P/E RATIO 19.8

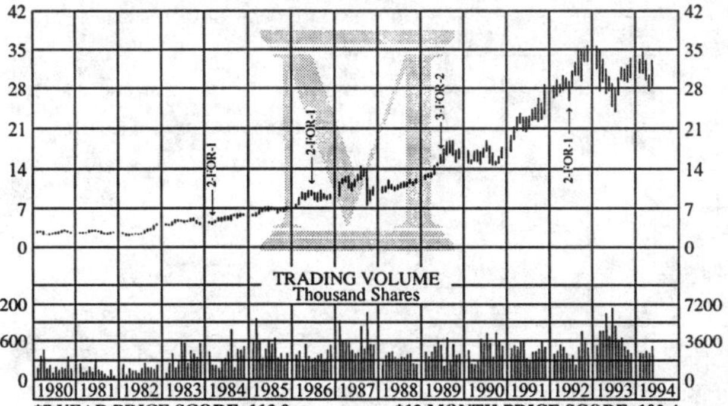

42
35
28
21
14
7
0
2-FOR-1
2-FOR-1
3-FOR-2
2-FOR-1
TRADING VOLUME
Thousand Shares
7200
3600
0
1980 1981 1982 1983 1984 1985 1986 1987 1988 1989 1990 1991 1992 1993 1994

***7 YEAR PRICE SCORE 113.9** ***12 MONTH PRICE SCORE 102.4**

*NYSE COMPOSITE INDEX=100

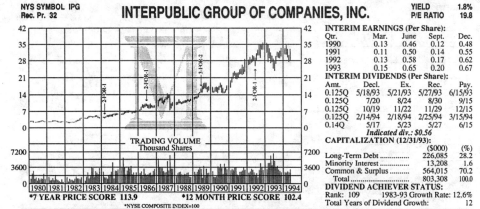

INTERIM EARNINGS (Per Share):

Qtr.	Mar.	June	Sept.	Dec.
1990	0.13	0.46	0.12	0.48
1991	0.11	0.50	0.14	0.55
1992	0.13	0.58	0.17	0.62
1993	0.15	0.65	0.20	0.67

INTERIM DIVIDENDS (Per Share):

Amt.	Decl.	Ex.	Rec.	Pay.
0.125Q	5/18/93	5/21/93	5/27/93	6/15/93
0.125Q	7/20	8/24	8/30	9/15
0.125Q	10/19	11/22	11/29	12/15
0.125Q	2/14/94	2/18/94	2/25/94	3/15/94
0.14Q	5/17	5/23	5/27	6/15

Indicated div.: $0.56

CAPITALIZATION (12/31/93):

	($000)	(%)
Long-Term Debt	226,085	28.2
Minority Interest	13,208	1.6
Common & Surplus	564,015	70.2
Total	803,308	100.0

DIVIDEND ACHIEVER STATUS:

Rank: 109 1983-93 Growth Rate: 12.6%
Total Years of Dividend Growth: 12

RECENT DEVELOPMENTS: For the year ended 12/31/93, net income before an accounting adjustment increased 11.9% to $125.3 million compared with $111.9 million the previous year. Revenues were down 3.3% to $1.79 billion from $1.86 billion. Revenues from U.S. operations were up 3.8% to $585.2 million from $563.7 million. International revenues declined 6.5% to $1.21 billion from $1.29 billion.

PROSPECTS: The Company will continue to benefit from a strong cash position which has helped reduce interest expense. Interpublic executed a purchase agreement with WPP Group Ltd. to acquire Scali, McCabe, Sloves, Inc. The acquisition does not include Fallon, McElligott, Inc., Morton Goldberg Associates or Scali's operations in Brazil, the Netherlands, or Germany. At the closing, $32.9 million will be paid to WPP. Scali will become part of the Lowe Group, one of the IPG's advertising networks.

BUSINESS

INTERPUBLIC GROUP OF COMPANIES, INC. is a large organization of advertising agencies. The agencies owned include: McCann-Erickson Worldwide, Lintas: Worldwide, Dailey & Associates and The Lowe Group. The Company also offers advertising agency services through association arrangements with local agencies in various parts of the world. Other activities conducted by IPG within the area of marketing communications include market research, sales promotion, product development, direct marketing, telemarketing, and other related services.

BUSINESS LINE ANALYSIS

(12/31/93)	Rev(%)	Inc(%)
United States	33.8	36.6
Europe	39.5	31.0
Far East	15.9	17.1
Latin America	6.0	13.2
Other International	4.8	2.1
Total	100.0	100.0

ANNUAL EARNINGS AND DIVIDENDS PER SHARE

	1993	1992	1991	1990	1989	1988	1987
Earnings Per Share	**[1] 1.67**	**[1] 1.50**	**1.30**	**1.19**	**1.05**	**0.90**	**0.75**
Dividends Per Share	**0.49**	**[2] 0.45**	**0.41**	**0.37**	**[3] 0.322**	**0.257**	**0.22**
Dividend Payout %	**29.3**	**30.0**	**31.5**	**31.1**	**30.6**	**28.3**	**29.3**

[1] Before acctg. chg. [2] 2-for-1 stk split, 6/16/92 [3] 3-for-2 stk split, 6/89

ANNUAL FINANCIAL DATA

	1993	1992	1991	1990	1989	1988	1987
RECORD OF EARNINGS (IN MILLIONS):							
Total Income	1,793.9	1,856.0	1,677.5	1,368.2	1,256.9	1,191.9	970.7
Costs and Expenses	1,493.1	1,576.0	1,421.8	1,172.1	1,081.9	1,034.3	845.2
Depreciation & Amort	42.5	39.6	36.9	27.6	22.3	19.1	15.9
Operating Profit	258.2	240.4	218.8	168.4	152.6	138.5	109.7
Inc Bef Prov for Income Taxes	231.8	207.2	185.3	149.5	137.6	128.3	101.0
Total Prov for Inc Taxes	99.8	91.3	87.7	72.5	68.1	67.8	51.4
Eq In Net Earn Of Unconsol Affil	0.9	2.8	2.2	6.1	6.0	4.3	3.0
Inc Applic to Minor Ints	7.6	6.7	5.2	3.1	4.9	4.7	3.2
Net Income	124.8	[1] 111.9	94.6	80.1	70.6	60.1	49.3
Aver. Shs. Outstg. (000)	75,216	74,975	72,860	67,349	67,334	66,214	65,796
[1] Before acctg. change dr$24,640,000.							
BALANCE SHEET (IN MILLIONS):							
Cash and Cash Equivalents	322.4	290.7	276.4	216.4	123.0	180.0	180.8
Receivables, Net	1,525.7	1,460.2	1,705.6	1,656.0	1,225.3	1,092.9	...
Gross Property	387.7	342.2	333.1	305.5	225.8	195.3	152.2
Accumulated Depreciation	171.0	161.7	146.3	126.7	93.8	83.2	68.8
Long-Term Debt	226.1	200.2	170.5	144.5	36.5	42.6	21.3
Net Stockholders' Equity	564.0	511.2	586.8	509.7	367.6	332.9	280.0
Total Assets	2,869.8	2,623.3	2,784.3	2,584.1	1,740.7	1,600.0	1,346.9
Total Current Assets	2,003.2	1,914.8	2,031.6	1,914.8	1,372.8	1,296.8	1,129.9
Total Current Liabilities	1,836.0	1,690.2	1,853.6	1,769.3	1,210.5	1,116.8	946.5
Net Working Capital	167.2	224.5	178.0	145.5	162.4	180.1	183.4
Year End Shs Outstg (000)	74,801	75,063	75,427	73,477	69,138	69,892	66,298
STATISTICAL RECORD:							
Operating Profit Margin %	14.4	13.0	13.0	12.3	12.1	11.6	11.3
Book Value Per Share	0.97	1.50	1.80	1.77	3.54	3.30	3.29
Return on Equity %	22.2	21.9	16.1	15.7	19.2	18.1	17.6
Return on Assets %	4.4	4.3	3.4	3.1	4.1	3.8	3.7
Average Yield %	1.6	1.5	1.8	2.2	2.1	2.3	2.0
P/E Ratio	21.3-14.3	23.8-17.2	22.0-13.0	16.0-12.3	18.1-11.5	13.6-10.6	19.3-10.2
Price Range	35⅝-23⅞	35¾-25¾	28⅝-16⅞	19-14⅝	19-12⅛	12⅜-9⅝	14½-7⅝

Statistics are as originally reported.

OFFICERS:
P.H. Geier, Jr., Chmn., Pres. & C.E.O.
E.P. Beard, Exec. V.P. & C.F.O.
C. Rudge, Sr. V.P., Gen. Couns. & Sec.

INCORPORATED: DE, Sep., 1930

PRINCIPAL OFFICE: 1271 Ave. of the Americas, New York, NY 10020

TELEPHONE NUMBER: (212) 399-8000
FAX: (212) 399-8130
NO. OF EMPLOYEES: 8,904
ANNUAL MEETING: In May
SHAREHOLDERS: 2,516
INSTITUTIONAL HOLDINGS:
No. of Institutions: 208
Shares Held: 27,671,442

REGISTRAR(S):

TRANSFER AGENT(S):

NYS SYMBOL JP
Rec. Pr. 48½

JEFFERSON-PILOT CORP.

YIELD 3.5%
P/E RATIO 11.1

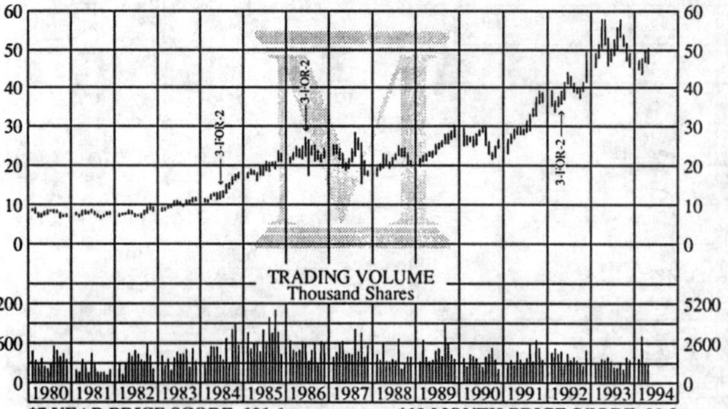

*7 YEAR PRICE SCORE 121.6 *12 MONTH PRICE SCORE 99.0

*NYSE COMPOSITE INDEX=100

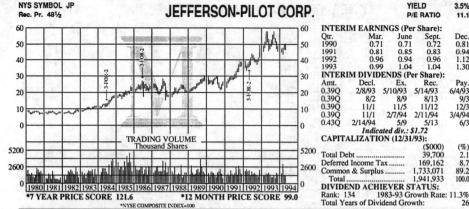

INTERIM EARNINGS (Per Share):

Qtr.	Mar.	June	Sept.	Dec.
1990	0.71	0.71	0.72	0.81
1991	0.81	0.85	0.83	0.94
1992	0.96	0.94	0.96	1.12
1993	0.99	1.04	1.04	1.30

INTERIM DIVIDENDS (Per Share):

Amt.	Decl.	Ex.	Rec.	Pay.
0.39Q	2/8/93	5/10/93	5/14/93	6/4/93
0.39Q	8/2	8/9	8/13	9/3
0.39Q	11/1	11/5	11/12	12/3
0.39Q	11/1	2/7/94	2/11/94	3/4/94
0.43Q	2/14/94	5/9	5/13	6/3

Indicated div.: $1.72

CAPITALIZATION (12/31/93):

	($000)	(%)
Total Debt	39,700	2.1
Deferred Income Tax	169,162	8.7
Common & Surplus	1,733,071	89.2
Total	1,941,933	100.0

DIVIDEND ACHIEVER STATUS:
Rank: 134 1983-93 Growth Rate: 11.3%
Total Years of Dividend Growth: 26

RECENT DEVELOPMENTS: For the year ended 12/31/93, income before accounting adjustments was $219.3 million compared with $203.2 million for 1992. Revenues moved up to $1.25 billion from $1.20 billion. The improved results reflect increased sales of new life insurance products. New life insurance written totaled $7.11 billion compared with $5.01 billion in 1992. Revenues from the communications business improved 12% to $145.0 million as life and annuity revenue increased 3% to 170.4 million. Accident and health revenues were flat.

PROSPECTS: Life insurance operations continue to drive earnings and the trend is likely to continue. Annuity sales to individuals are encouraging and should get better as new marketing efforts are realized. The new Independent Marketing Organization distribution system is in its early stages of operation but the Company anticipates benefits in the form of increased revenue. Stricter underwriting standards are one of the steps being taken to improve profitability in the accident and health segment.

BUSINESS

JEFFERSON PILOT CORPORATION is the parent of Jefferson-Pilot Life Insurance Company, which offers both group and individual life insurance, health insurance, annuity and pension products. Other subsidiaries provide fire and casualty insurance, title insurance and mutual fund sales and management services. Jefferson-Pilot Communications Co. provides information and entertainment services through three network television and thirteen radio stations.

BUSINESS LINE ANALYSIS

(12/31/93)	Rev(%)	Inc(%)
Life Insurance	79.2	81.1
Other Insurance	4.1	4.1
Communications	11.6	8.9
Other	5.1	6.0
Total	100.0	100.0

ANNUAL EARNINGS AND DIVIDENDS PER SHARE

	1993	1992	1991	1990	1989	1988	1987
Earnings Per Share	4.36	3.99	3.43	2.94	2.43	1.72	2.47
Dividends Per Share	1.51	1.30	[1] 1.093	0.987	0.893	0.84	0.787
Dividend Payout %	34.6	32.6	31.9	33.6	36.7	48.8	31.8

[1] 3-for-2 stk split,04/15/92

ANNUAL FINANCIAL DATA

	1993	1992	1991	1990	1989	1988	1987
RECORD OF EARNINGS (IN MILLIONS):							
Tot Prem & Other Considerations	669.8	658.4	658.3	661.3	659.2	781.1	698.4
Net Investment Income	369.6	360.9	352.8	342.1	333.5	313.8	298.0
Total Revenues	1,246.6	1,202.3	1,173.5	1,162.6	1,140.2	1,223.5	1,052.3
Death Benefits	...	105.0	104.1	111.4	100.3	112.9	115.3
Inc Bef Income Taxes & Acctg Chang	322.0	285.6	244.8	221.6	197.9	138.8	129.9
Income Taxes	102.8	82.4	69.1	64.0	60.2	42.5	68.4
Gain Fr Sales Of Invests, Net	...	...	...	...	...	5.0	56.5
Net Income	[1] 219.3	203.2	175.7	157.6	137.7	101.2	147.7
Aver. Shs. Outstg. (000)	50,252	50,952	51,319	53,636	56,589	58,602	59,588
[1] Before acctg. change dr$24,109,000.							
BALANCE SHEET (IN MILLIONS):							
Cash	34.6	197.9	165.1	128.7	176.3	214.0	17.5
Debt Secur, At Amortized Cost	3,221.9	2,773.8	2,571.7	2,327.4	2,229.7	...	...
Eq Secur, Principally At Mkt	833.4	837.9	784.0	610.0	780.0	...	...
Policy Loans	214.6	220.7	227.9	231.8	236.7	247.9	262.3
Mtge Loans on Real Estate	583.6	561.0	541.2	535.7	506.1	498.8	511.8
Total Assets	5,640.6	5,235.8	4,925.2	4,454.9	4,529.6	4,174.1	3,889.8
Benefits and Claims	3,196.5	2,949.9	2,786.8	2,610.3	2,475.7	2,308.5	2,182.9
Net Stockholders' Equity	1,733.1	1,686.8	1,563.0	1,353.0	1,474.7	1,336.0	1,243.2
Year End Shs Outstg (000)	49,464	50,439	51,292	51,785	56,054	57,822	59,019
STATISTICAL RECORD:							
Book Value Per Share	35.04	33.44	30.47	26.13	26.31	23.11	21.06
Return on Equity %	12.7	12.0	11.2	11.7	9.3	7.6	11.9
Return on Assets %	3.9	3.9	3.6	3.5	3.0	2.4	3.8
Average Yield %	2.9	3.1	3.5	3.8	3.6	4.0	3.6
P/E Ratio	13.3-10.4	12.4-8.4	11.4-6.7	10.2-7.4	12.5-8.2	15.0-10.3	18.5-10.0
Price Range	57⅞-45½	49½-33⅜	39⅛-22⅞	29⅞-21⅝	30⅜-19⅞	25-17⅛	28⅜-15⅜

Statistics are as originally reported.

OFFICERS:
R.H. Spilman, Chairman
D.A. Stonecipher, Pres. & C.E.O.
D.R. Glass, Sr. V.P. & C.F.O.

INCORPORATED: NC, Jan., 1968

PRINCIPAL OFFICE: 100 North Greene Street P.O. Box 21008, Greensboro, NC 27420

TELEPHONE NUMBER: (919) 691-3000

NO. OF EMPLOYEES: 3,900 (approx.)

ANNUAL MEETING: In May

SHAREHOLDERS: 9,881

INSTITUTIONAL HOLDINGS:
No. of Institutions: 279
Shares Held: 22,072,867

REGISTRAR(S): First Union National Bank of N.C., Charlotte, NC

TRANSFER AGENT(S): First Union National Bank of N.C., Charlotte, NC

NYS SYMBOL JCI
Rec. Pr. 47⅞

JOHNSON CONTROLS, INC.

YIELD 3.0%
P/E RATIO 14.1

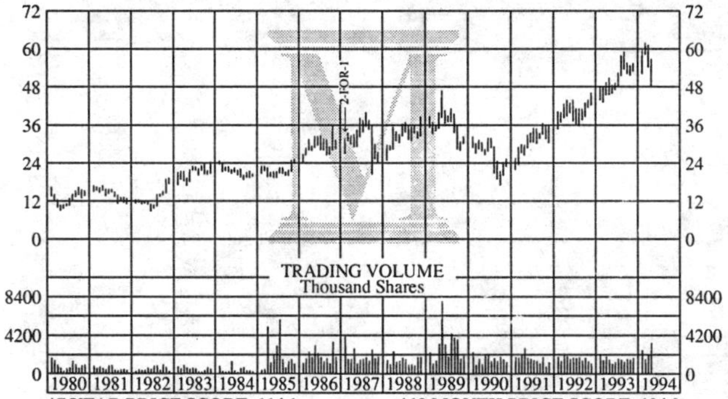

***7 YEAR PRICE SCORE 114.1** ***12 MONTH PRICE SCORE 104.0**

*NYSE COMPOSITE INDEX=100

INTERIM EARNINGS (Per Share):

Qtr.	Dec.	Mar.	June	Sept.
1990-91	0.57	0.20	0.69	0.73
1991-92	0.66	0.36	0.86	0.98
1992-93	0.80	0.48	0.98	1.06
1993-94	0.87	...	...	...

INTERIM DIVIDENDS (Per Share):

Amt.	Decl.	Ex.	Rec.	Pay.
0.34Q	1/27/93	3/1/93	3/5/93	3/31/93
0.34Q	5/26	5/28	6/4	6/30
0.34Q	7/28	8/30	9/3	9/30
0.36Q	11/17	11/29	12/3	1/3/94
0.36Q	1/26/94	2/28/94	3/4/94	3/31

Indicated div.: $1.44

CAPITALIZATION (9/30/93):

	($000)	(%)
Long-Term Debt	500,400	31.4
Deferred Income Tax	11,100	0.7
Preferred Stock	168,100	10.6
Common & Surplus	910,900	57.3
Total	1,590,500	100.0

DIVIDEND ACHIEVER STATUS:
Rank: 269 1983-93 Growth Rate: 5.9%
Total Years of Dividend Growth: 18

RECENT DEVELOPMENTS: For the quarter ended 12/31/93, net income increased 17% to $38.1 million compared with $32.7 million for the same period in 1992. Sales also rose 5% to $1.59 billion. Profit gains were driven by a substantial increase in sales of automotive seating, reflecting a higher level of activity in the North American market as well as participation in several successful new domestic vehicle programs, offset by lower earnings for European automotive sales.

PROSPECTS: Johnson Controls should post higher earnings in fiscal 1994. The strong levels of production scheduled by automakers for 1994 should translate into higher orders for the Company's automobile seats. Earnings will also benefit from JCI's large market share for automobile seating. Meanwhile, higher orders for control systems for both new and existing buildings will aid profits of the control systems business. Stable demand for plastic bottles alongside increased revenues for European operations should bolster earnings for the plastics unit.

BUSINESS

JOHNSON CONTROLS, INC. is a market leader in facility services and control systems, automotive seating systems, plastic packaging and automotive batteries. The Controls segment installs and services control systems for temperature and lighting control and services mechanical equipment. The Automotive division offers complete seating systems and components. Plastics produces containers for household use as well as injection molding tools and plastic components for the auto industry. The Battery segment supplies automotive and specialty batteries.

BUSINESS LINE ANALYSIS

(09/30/93)	Rev(%)	Inc(%)
Automotive	41.4	37.9
Controls	33.0	28.2
Plastics	14.6	20.9
Battery	11.0	13.0
Total	100.0	100.0

ANNUAL EARNINGS AND DIVIDENDS PER SHARE

	9/30/93	9/30/92	9/30/91	9/30/90	9/30/89	9/30/88	9/30/87
Earnings Per Share	**1 3.16**	**2.86**	**2.19**	**2.13**	**2.55**	**2.83**	**2.20**
Dividends Per Share	**1.36**	**1.28**	**1.24**	**1.20**	**1.16**	**1.10**	**2 1.06**
Dividend Payout %	**43.0**	**44.8**	**56.6**	**56.3**	**45.5**	**38.9**	**48.2**

1 Before acctg. chg. 2 100% stk div, 12/86

ANNUAL FINANCIAL DATA

	9/30/93	9/30/92	9/30/91	9/30/90	9/30/89	9/30/88	9/30/87
RECORD OF EARNINGS (IN MILLIONS):							
Total Revenues	6,181.7	5,156.5	4,559.0	4,504.0	3,683.6	3,099.6	2,676.8
Costs and Expenses	5,645.1	4,659.9	4,133.3	4,094.6	3,334.9	2,773.7	2,400.9
Depreciation & Amort	238.3	231.1	196.9	181.4	143.7	115.6	97.9
Operating Income	298.3	265.5	228.8	228.0	205.0	210.3	178.0
Income Bef Income Taxes	250.7	227.7	176.0	172.8	178.9	186.5	171.0
Income Taxes	112.8	104.7	80.9	80.4	81.4	83.0	81.4
Net Income	1 137.9	123.0	95.1	92.4	97.5	103.5	89.6
Aver. Shs. Outstg. (000)	40,800	40,100	39,600	39,400	37,100	36,600	37,817
1 Before acctg. change dr$122,000,000.							
BALANCE SHEET (IN MILLIONS):							
Cash & Cash Equivalents	87.7	96.2	91.7	54.3	27.0	20.0	20.3
Receivables, Net	912.1	899.4	780.9	765.6	667.8	592.9	463.2
Inventories	281.3	316.0	287.4	319.0	270.4	256.8	211.1
Gross Property	2,367.0	2,125.9	1,791.7	1,654.1	1,375.3	1,194.3	1,003.9
Accumulated Depreciation	1,153.4	968.6	805.9	675.3	537.1	434.3	355.6
Long-Term Debt	500.4	503.3	490.6	483.0	445.1	342.1	198.2
Net Stockholders' Equity	1,079.0	1,194.2	1,064.0	1,035.5	977.9	852.5	770.4
Total Assets	3,230.8	3,179.5	2,841.0	2,798.8	2,415.0	2,013.3	1,739.1
Total Current Assets	1,532.0	1,524.3	1,376.1	1,290.6	1,100.8	958.5	790.1
Total Current Liabilities	1,284.9	1,245.2	1,105.3	1,099.4	837.9	695.7	651.1
Net Working Capital	247.1	279.1	270.8	191.2	262.9	262.8	139.0
Year End Shs Outstg (000)	38,800	40,100	39,600	39,400	39,400	36,400	36,903
STATISTICAL RECORD:							
Operating Profit Margin %	4.8	5.1	5.0	5.1	5.6	6.8	6.7
Book Value Per Share	15.19	17.44	16.33	15.37	14.91	18.25	15.60
Return on Equity %	12.8	10.3	8.9	8.9	10.0	12.1	11.6
Return on Assets %	4.3	3.9	3.3	3.3	4.0	5.1	5.2
Average Yield %	...	3.2	4.2	4.9	3.1	3.5	3.5
P/E Ratio	N.M	16.1-12.1	16.7-10.0	15.1-8.0	18.3-10.9	13.6-8.7	18.2-9.3
Price Range	59⅛-43	46⅛-34⅝	36⅝-21⅞	32¼-17⅛	46¾-27⅞	38½-24¾	40-20½

Statistics are as originally reported.

OFFICERS:
J.H. Keyes, Chmn. & C.E.O.
S.A. Roell, V.P. & C.F.O.
J.P. Kennedy, V.P., Sec. & General Counsel

INCORPORATED: WI, Jul., 1900

PRINCIPAL OFFICE: 5757 N. Green Bay Ave. P.O. Box 591, Milwaukee, WI 53201

TELEPHONE NUMBER: (414) 228-1200
NO. OF EMPLOYEES: 6,814
ANNUAL MEETING: In January
SHAREHOLDERS: 21,033
INSTITUTIONAL HOLDINGS:
No. of Institutions: 262
Shares Held: 24,121,077

REGISTRAR(S): First Wisconsin Trust Co., Milwaukee, WI

TRANSFER AGENT(S): First Wisconsin Trust Co., Milwaukee, WI

NYS SYMBOL JNJ
Rec. Pr. 44

JOHNSON & JOHNSON

YIELD 2.6%
P/E RATIO 16.1

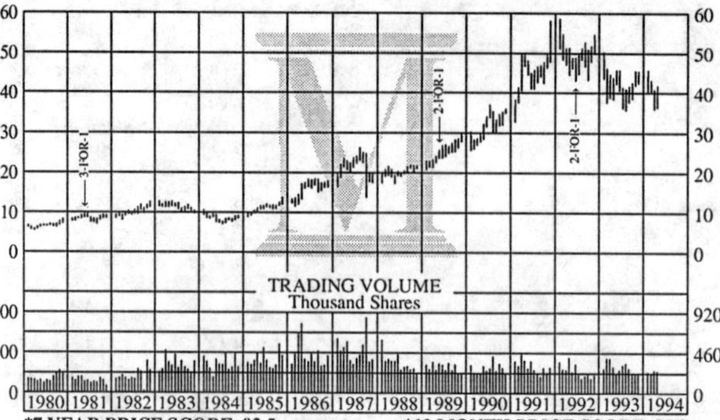

*7 YEAR PRICE SCORE 93.5 *12 MONTH PRICE SCORE 95.3

*NYSE COMPOSITE INDEX=100

INTERIM EARNINGS (Per Share):

Qtr.	Mar.	June	Sept.	Dec.
1991	0.63	0.61	0.54	0.42
1992	0.68	0.68	0.63	0.47
1993	0.77	0.75	0.70	0.52

INTERIM DIVIDENDS (Per Share):

Amt.	Decl.	Ex.	Rec.	Pay.
0.26Q	7/26/93	8/11/93	8/17/93	9/7/93
0.26Q	10/25	11/9	11/16	12/7
0.26Q	1/4/94	2/9/94	2/15/94	3/8/94
0.29Q	4/28	5/11	5/17	6/7

Indicated div.: $1.16

CAPITALIZATION (1/2/94):

	($000)	(%)
Long-Term Debt	1,493,000	21.1
Common & Surplus	5,568,000	78.9
Total	7,061,000	100.0

DIVIDEND ACHIEVER STATUS:
Rank: 73 1983-93 Growth Rate: 14.2%
Total Years of Dividend Growth: 31

RECENT DEVELOPMENTS: For the year ended 1/2/94, net income increased 10% to $1.79 billion compared with $1.63 billion a year ago. Sales were up 2.8% to $14.14 billion from $13.75 billion. Professional sales rose 4.1% to $4.82 billion led by Lifescan blood glucose monitoring products, and Protectiv catheter safety system products. Pharmaceutical sales grew 3.5% to $4.49 billion led by domestic operations. International revenues felt the impact of pricing pressures in Germany and Italy.

PROSPECTS: Sales growth will be pressured by cost containment measures in Europe, Germany and Italy in particular, and by the progressive shift towards managed health care in the United States. Earnings will benefit from a streamlined workforce which was reduced by 3,300 to 81,600 employees, despite the addition of 900 employees from the recent acquisition of RoC S.A., a consumer skin care products company based in France.

BUSINESS

JOHNSON & JOHNSON is engaged in the manufacture and sale of a broad range of products in the health care and other fields. The Consumer segment consists of toiletries and hygienic products. The Professional segment includes ligatures and sutures, mechanical wound closure products, diagnostic products, dental products, medical equipment and devices, surgical dressings, surgical apparel and accessories, surgical instruments and related items. The Pharmaceutical segment consists of prescription drugs including contraceptives and therapeutics, antifungal, and dermatological products.

BUSINESS LINE ANALYSIS

(1/2/94) ($000)	Rev(%)	Inc(%)
United States	50.9	46.8
Europe	28.5	40.1
West Hemisphere exc U.S.	9.4	6.1
Africa, Asia & Pacific	11.2	7.0
Total	100.0	100.0

ANNUAL EARNINGS AND DIVIDENDS PER SHARE

	1/2/94	1/3/93	12/29/91	12/30/90	12/31/89	1/1/89	1/3/88
Earnings Per Share	2.74	[1] 2.46	2.20	1.72	1.63	1.43	1.21
Dividends Per Share	1.01	0.89	0.77	0.655	0.56	0.48	0.405
Dividend Payout %	36.9	36.2	35.1	38.2	34.5	33.6	33.3

[1] Before acctg. chg.

ANNUAL FINANCIAL DATA

RECORD OF EARNINGS (IN MILLIONS):							
Costs and Expenses	11,127.0	10,916.0	9,790.0	8,870.0	7,682.0	7,205.0	6,447.0
Depreciation & Amort	617.0	560.0	493.0	474.0	414.0	391.0	356.0
Operating Profit	d10,562.0	d10,349.0	d9,303.0	d8,406.0	d7,377.0	d6,922.0	d6,186.0
Earn Bef Prov for Taxes on Inc	2,332.0	2,207.0	2,038.0	1,623.0	1,514.0	1,396.0	1,193.0
Provision for Taxes on Inc	545.0	582.0	577.0	480.0	432.0	422.0	360.0
Net Income	1,787.0	[1] 1,625.0	1,461.0	1,143.0	1,082.0	974.0	833.0
Aver. Shs. Outstg. (000)	652,000	660,000	662,000	666,000	666,000	681,000	690,000

[1] Before acctg. change dr$595,000,000.

BALANCE SHEET (IN MILLIONS):							
Cash and Cash Equivalents	476.0	878.0	792.0	931.0	583.0	660.0	741.0
Receivables, Net	2,506.0	2,182.0	2,001.0	1,751.0	1,516.0	1,318.0	1,120.0
Inventories	1,717.0	1,742.0	1,702.0	1,543.0	1,353.0	1,273.0	1,165.0
Gross Property	[1] 4,406.0	[1] 4,115.0	[1] 3,667.0	[1] 3,247.0	[1] 2,846.0	[1] 2,493.0	3,642.0
Accumulated Depreciation	...	...	...	...	...	...	1,392.0
Long-Term Debt	1,493.0	1,365.0	1,301.0	1,316.0	1,170.0	1,166.0	733.0
Net Stockholders' Equity	5,568.0	5,171.0	5,626.0	4,900.0	4,148.0	3,503.0	3,485.0
Total Assets	12,242.0	11,884.0	10,513.0	9,506.0	7,919.0	7,119.0	6,546.0
Total Current Assets	5,217.0	5,423.0	4,933.0	4,664.0	3,776.0	3,503.0	3,272.0
Total Current Liabilities	3,212.0	3,427.0	2,689.0	2,623.0	1,927.0	1,868.0	1,763.0
Net Working Capital	2,005.0	1,996.0	2,244.0	2,041.0	1,849.0	1,635.0	1,509.0
Year End Shs Outstg (000)	643,000	655,000	666,000	666,000	666,000	666,000	688,000

[1] Net

STATISTICAL RECORD:							
Book Value Per Share	7.22	6.80	7.34	6.30	5.17	4.35	4.16
Return on Equity %	32.1	31.4	26.0	23.3	26.1	27.8	23.9
Return on Assets %	14.6	13.7	13.9	12.0	13.7	13.7	12.7
Average Yield %	2.3	1.7	1.7	2.1	2.2	2.4	2.0
P/E Ratio	18.4-13.0	23.9-17.5	26.5-15.0	21.6-14.9	18.3-12.7	15.4-12.2	22.0-11.5
Price Range	50⅜-35⅝	58¾-43	58⅛-32¾	37⅛-25⅝	29¾-20¾	22-17⅜	26⅜-13¾

Statistics are as originally reported.

OFFICERS:
R.S. Larsen, Chmn. & C.E.O.
R.E. Campbell, Vice-Chmn.
R.N. Wilson, Vice-Chmn.
J.H. Heisen, Treasurer

INCORPORATED: NJ, Nov., 1887

PRINCIPAL OFFICE: One Johnson & Johnson Plaza, New Brunswick, NJ 08933

TELEPHONE NUMBER: (908) 524-0400
FAX: (908) 214-0332
NO. OF EMPLOYEES: 81,600
ANNUAL MEETING: In April
SHAREHOLDERS: 96,100
INSTITUTIONAL HOLDINGS:
No. of Institutions: 1,089
Shares Held: 377,615,120

REGISTRAR(S): First Chicago Trust Co. of New York, New York, NY 10008

TRANSFER AGENT(S): First Chicago Trust Co. of New York, New York, NY 10008

NYS SYMBOL JOS		
Rec. Pr. 17⅜		

JOSTENS, INC.

YIELD 5.1%
P/E RATIO ...

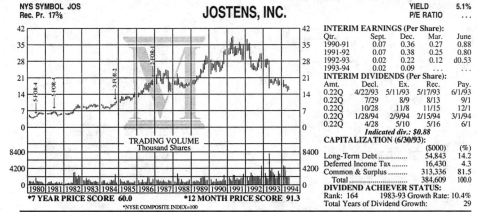

TRADING VOLUME
Thousand Shares

1980 1981 1982 1983 1984 1985 1986 1987 1988 1989 1990 1991 1992 1993 1994

*7 YEAR PRICE SCORE 60.0 ***12 MONTH PRICE SCORE 91.3**

*NYSE COMPOSITE INDEX=100

INTERIM EARNINGS (Per Share):

Qtr.	Sept.	Dec.	Mar.	June
1990-91	0.07	0.36	0.27	0.88
1991-92	0.07	0.38	0.25	0.80
1992-93	0.02	0.22	0.12	d0.53
1993-94	0.02	0.09	...	...

INTERIM DIVIDENDS (Per Share):

Amt.	Decl.	Ex.	Rec.	Pay.
0.22Q	4/22/93	5/11/93	5/17/93	6/1/93
0.22Q	7/29	8/9	8/13	9/1
0.22Q	10/28	11/8	11/15	12/1
0.22Q	1/28/94	2/9/94	2/15/94	3/1/94
0.22Q	4/28	5/10	5/16	6/1

Indicated div.: $0.88

CAPITALIZATION (6/30/93):

	($000)	(%)
Long-Term Debt	54,843	14.2
Deferred Income Tax	16,430	4.3
Common & Surplus	313,336	81.5
Total	384,609	100.0

DIVIDEND ACHIEVER STATUS:
Rank: 164   1983-93 Growth Rate: 10.4%
Total Years of Dividend Growth: 29

RECENT DEVELOPMENTS: For the quarter ended 12/31/93, net income declined 60.5% to $3.9 million compared with $9.9 million a year ago. Sales were up slightly to $223.4 million from $222.2 million. Earnings were adversely affected by a weak performance in the Jostens Learning segment. The Company's School products and Recognition businesses reported sales and earnings increases. Jostens entered into a letter of intent to sell its Sportswear business.

PROSPECTS: Jostens is currently proceeding with reengineering efforts across its product lines. Earnings will be pressured by weak results from Jostens Learning, while the rest of the business divisions are expected to post improved results. The School Product and the Recognition businesses should continue to report growth in operating results. The Company is in the midst of a consulting study undertaking a comprehensive review of Jostens Learning Corp.'s marketplace, product line and business strategies.

BUSINESS

JOSTENS, INC., is a leading provider of products and services for the youth, education, sports award and recognition markets. Primary products include yearbooks, class rings, graduation products, student photography packages, technology-based educational products and services, customized sales and service awards, sports awards, customized-imprinted sportswear and customized products for university alumni. The Company has three operating groups with 43 plant and office facilities in the United States and Canada. Customers are served by more than 9,000 employees and 1,300 independent sales representatives.

QUARTERLY DATA

(6/30/93)($000)	Rev	Inc
1st Quarter	153,943	-3,300
2nd Quarter	222,188	9,881
3rd Quarter	184,964	5,458
4th Quarter	353,753	24,136

ANNUAL EARNINGS AND DIVIDENDS PER SHARE

	6/30/93	6/30/92	6/30/91	6/30/90	6/30/89	6/30/88	6/30/87
Earnings Per Share	① d0.18	1.50	1.58	1.51	1.39	② 0.99	② 1.05
Dividends Per Share	0.88	0.85	0.81	0.74	0.66	0.58	③ 0.50
Dividend Payout %	...	56.7	51.3	49.0	47.5	58.6	47.6

① Before acctg. chg. ② Before disc. oper. ③ 2-for-1 stk. split, 11/86.

ANNUAL FINANCIAL DATA

RECORD OF EARNINGS (IN THOUSANDS):

Total Revenues	914,848	876,395	859,878	787,503	696,352	560,022	587,256
Costs and Expenses	③913,937	748,747	725,049	665,612	582,874	471,009	491,958
Depreciation & Amort	...	21,307	22,957	18,868	19,620	12,624	12,159
Operating Income	911	106,341	111,872	103,023	93,858	76,389	83,139
Income Bef Income Taxes	...	97,636	101,623	93,815	86,881	71,535	74,356
Income Taxes	3,206	36,223	37,459	33,605	32,516	27,185	35,765
Net Income	②d7,947	61,413	64,164	60,210	54,365	④44,350	⑤38,591

① Incl. Dep. ② Before acctg. change dr$4,150,000. ③ Before disc. op. ④ Before disc. op. cr$42,183,000. ⑤ Before disc. op. cr$6,121,000.

BALANCE SHEET (IN THOUSANDS):

Cash & Short-term Invests	13,564	45,345	15,522	26,916	67,969	140,556	79,225
Receivables, Net	217,850	196,743	193,535	149,842	117,843	80,959	90,307
Inventories	131,186	114,847	115,327	109,743	98,045	83,832	82,717
Gross Property	218,891	195,694	180,651	160,548	141,323	110,638	129,191
Accumulated Depreciation	130,003	108,571	94,461	79,351	67,011	57,080	60,680
Long-Term Debt	54,843	55,335	31,633	53,247	75,091	92,243	11,816
Net Stockholders' Equity	313,336	326,893	296,232	257,337	222,250	175,703	112,892
Total Assets	583,341	565,357	530,183	473,435	452,787	407,215	360,717
Total Current Assets	379,265	369,918	335,974	295,659	290,268	310,800	255,224
Total Current Liabilities	198,732	164,122	190,649	157,783	153,534	139,269	129,306
Net Working Capital	180,533	205,796	145,325	137,876	136,734	171,531	125,918
Year End Shares Outstg	45,425	41,145	40,875	40,066	39,441	38,725	35,828

STATISTICAL RECORD:

Operating Profit Margin %	0.1	12.1	13.0	13.1	13.5	13.6	14.2
Book Value Per Share	5.97	6.60	5.85	4.94	4.29	3.91	2.63
Return on Equity %	...	18.8	21.7	23.4	24.5	25.2	34.2
Return on Assets %	...	10.9	12.1	12.7	12.0	10.9	10.7
Average Yield %	3.9	2.8	2.4	2.7	2.7	3.0	2.5
P/E Ratio	...	24.9-15.8	24.4-18.0	21.9-14.9	21.9-13.0	18.3-13.3	23.8-14.4
Price Range	29-16½	37⅜-23¾	38⅝-28½	33-22½	30⅜-18⅛	22¾-16½	25-15⅛

Statistics are as originally reported.

OFFICERS:
R.P. Jensen, Chmn.
J.W. Stodder, Vice-Chmn.
R.C. Buhrmaster, Pres. & C.E.O.

INCORPORATED: MN, Jul., 1906

PRINCIPAL OFFICE: 5501 Norman Ctr. Drive, Minneapolis, MN 55437-1088

TELEPHONE NUMBER: (612) 830-3300

NO. OF EMPLOYEES: 9,000

ANNUAL MEETING: In October

SHAREHOLDERS: 9,400 (approx.)

INSTITUTIONAL HOLDINGS:
No. of Institutions: 221
Shares Held: 23,152,149

REGISTRAR(S): Norwest Bank Minnesota, N.A., St. Paul, MN

TRANSFER AGENT(S): Norwest Bank of St. Paul, St. Paul, MN

NYS SYMBOL KM
Rec. Pr. 15¼

K MART CORP.

YIELD 6.3%
P/E RATIO 9.1

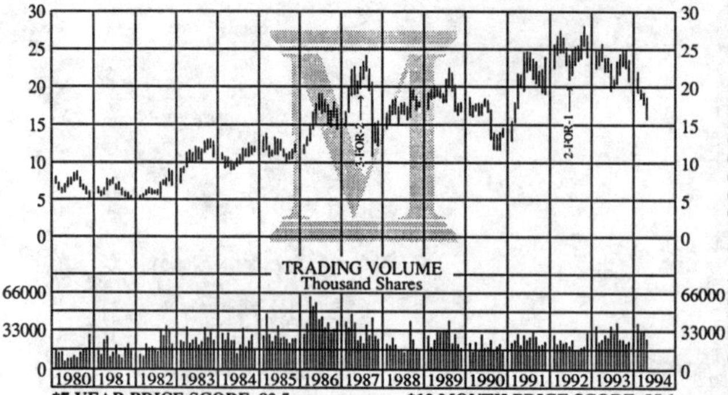

30
25
20
15
10
5
0
3-FOR-2
2-FOR-1
TRADING VOLUME
Thousand Shares
66000
33000
0
1980
1981
1982
1983
1984
1985
1986
1987
1988
1989
1990
1991
1992
1993
1994

*7 YEAR PRICE SCORE 83.5 *12 MONTH PRICE SCORE 85.1

*NYSE COMPOSITE INDEX=100

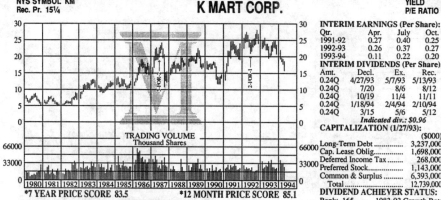

INTERIM EARNINGS (Per Share):

Qtr.	Apr.	July	Oct.	Jan.
1991-92	0.27	0.40	0.25	1.06
1992-93	0.26	0.37	0.27	1.15
1993-94	0.11	0.22	0.20	d1.35

INTERIM DIVIDENDS (Per Share):

Amt.	Decl.	Ex.	Rec.	Pay.
0.24Q	4/27/93	5/7/93	5/13/93	6/14/93
0.24Q	7/20	8/6	8/12	9/13
0.24Q	10/19	11/4	11/11	12/13
0.24Q	1/18/94	2/4/94	2/10/94	3/14/94
0.24Q	3/15	5/6	5/12	6/13

Indicated div.: $0.96

CAPITALIZATION (1/27/93):

	($000)	(%)
Long-Term Debt	3,237,000	25.4
Cap. Lease Oblig.	1,698,000	13.3
Deferred Income Tax	268,000	2.1
Preferred Stock	1,143,000	9.0
Common & Surplus	6,393,000	50.2
Total	12,739,000	100.0

DIVIDEND ACHIEVER STATUS:

Rank: 165 1983-93 Growth Rate: 10.4%

Total Years of Dividend Growth: 29

RECENT DEVELOPMENTS: For the year ended 1/26/94, the Company reported a loss from continuing operations of $328.0 million compared with income of $882.0 million last year. Sales advanced 10.1% to $34.16 billion. Gross margin decreased to 24.9% from 26.5% of sales due to a reduction and changing mix of merchandise purchases. Kmart announced plans to replace 500 discount stores with larger ones, which resulted in a $1.35 billion pretax charge to year-end earnings.

PROSPECTS: Kmart is seeking shareholder approval to sell 20% to 30% stakes in each of its Builders Square, Sports Authority, Office Max, and Borders units to the public. Meanwhile, the discontinuation of PACE Membership Warehouse and sale of PayLess Drug Stores will allow KM to focus more on improving its core retailing business. The focus will be on improving the Company's cost structure primarily through an inventory reduction program.

BUSINESS

K MART CORP. is one of the world's largest mass merchandise retailers. The Company operates 2,435 general merchandise and 2,537 specialty retail stores in the United States, the Czech Republic, Slovakia, Canada and Puerto Rico. General merchandise includes 2,422 Kmart discount stores and four Super Kmart Centers, which feature grocery items in addition to general merchandise. Specialty retailing includes Waldenbooks, the nation's largest bookstore chain, operating 1,260 stores; Builders Square, which manages 165 do-it-yourself home improvement retail stores; 179 OfficeMax stores; 31 Borders book superstores; and 56 Sports Authority stores.

BUSINESS LINE ANALYSIS

(1/27/93)	Rev(%)	Inc(%)
General Merchandise.	70.2	86.0
Specialty Retail	29.8	14.0
Total	100.0	100.0

ANNUAL EARNINGS AND DIVIDENDS PER SHARE

	1/27/93	1/29/92	1/30/91	1/31/90	1/25/89	1/27/88	1/28/87
Earnings Per Share	2.06	2.02	1.89	0.81	2.00	1.70	1.42
Dividends Per Share	0.91	0.875	0.85	0.78	0.64	[1] 0.56	0.487
Dividend Payout %	44.2	43.4	45.0	96.9	32.0	32.9	34.3

[1] 3-for-2 stk split, 6/87

ANNUAL FINANCIAL DATA

	1/27/93	1/29/92	1/30/91	1/31/90	1/25/89	1/27/88	1/28/87
RECORD OF EARNINGS (IN MILLIONS):							
Gross Operating Revenues	38,124.0	34,969.0	32,452.0	29,898.0	27,688.0	25,978.0	24,152.0
Costs and Expenses	35,581.0	32,678.0	30,376.0	28,566.0	25,661.0	24,076.0	[1] 22,775.0
Depreciation & Amort	685.0	589.0	531.0	461.0	437.0	401.0	...
Operating Income	1,858.0	1,702.0	1,545.0	871.0	1,590.0	1,501.0	1,377.0
Income Bef Income Taxes	1,426.0	1,301.0	1,146.0	515.0	1,244.0	1,171.0	1,028.0
Income Taxes	485.0	442.0	390.0	192.0	441.0	479.0	458.0
Net Income	941.0	859.0	756.0	323.0	803.0	692.0	582.0
Aver. Shs. Outstg. (000)	458,000	426,000	400,000	401,000	401,000	407,000	403,000
[1] Incl. Dep.							
BALANCE SHEET (IN MILLIONS):							
Cash	611.0	565.0	278.0	353.0	948.0	449.0	521.0
Inventories	8,752.0	7,546.0	6,891.0	6,933.0	5,671.0	5,571.0	5,153.0
Gross Property	11,029.0	9,559.0	8,339.0	7,507.0	7,034.0	6,537.0	6,076.0
Accumulated Depreciation	4,624.0	4,294.0	3,978.0	3,657.0	3,138.0	2,793.0	2,482.0
Long-Term Debt	3,237.0	2,287.0	1,701.0	1,480.0	1,358.0	1,191.0	1,011.0
Capital Lease Obligations	1,698.0	1,638.0	1,598.0	1,549.0	1,588.0	1,557.0	1,600.0
Net Stockholders' Equity	7,536.0	6,891.0	5,384.0	4,972.0	5,009.0	4,409.0	3,939.0
Total Assets	18,931.0	15,999.0	13,899.0	13,145.0	12,126.0	11,106.0	10,578.0
Total Current Assets	10,509.0	8,990.0	7,896.0	7,984.0	7,146.0	6,373.0	6,064.0
Total Current Liabilities	5,495.0	4,308.0	4,377.0	4,299.0	3,492.0	3,370.0	3,531.0
Net Working Capital	5,014.0	4,682.0	3,519.0	3,685.0	3,654.0	3,003.0	2,533.0
Year End Shs Outstg (000)	407,000	404,000	400,000	399,000	399,000	399,000	404,000
STATISTICAL RECORD:							
Operating Profit Margin %	4.9	4.9	4.8	2.9	5.7	5.8	5.7
Book Value Per Share	13.15	12.63	13.46	12.46	12.55	11.05	9.75
Return on Equity %	12.5	12.5	14.0	6.5	16.0	15.7	14.8
Return on Assets %	5.0	5.4	5.4	2.5	6.6	6.2	5.5
Average Yield %	3.7	4.7	5.6	4.0	3.7	3.2	3.2
P/E Ratio	13.7-10.1	12.3-6.3	9.9-6.2	28.0-20.3	9.9-7.3	14.2-6.3	13.5-7.9
Price Range	28⅛-20⅞	24¾-12¾	18⅝-11⅝	22⅜-16¼	19⅞-14½	24⅛-10¾	19⅛-11¼

Statistics are as originally reported.

OFFICERS:
J.E. Antonini, Chmn., Pres. & C.E.O.
T.F. Murasky, Exec. V.P. & C.F.O.
J.P. Churilla, V.P. & Treas.
N.W. LaDuke, V.P. & Sec.

INCORPORATED: MI, Mar., 1916

PRINCIPAL OFFICE: 3100 West Big Beaver Rd., Troy, MI 48084

TELEPHONE NUMBER: (313) 643-1000

NO. OF EMPLOYEES: 48,688 (approx.)

ANNUAL MEETING: In May

SHAREHOLDERS: 46,321

INSTITUTIONAL HOLDINGS:
No. of Institutions: 668
Shares Held: 150,609,772

REGISTRAR(S): NBD Bank, N.A., Securities Transfer Services, Detroit, MI 02266

TRANSFER AGENT(S): NBD Bank, N.A., Securities Transfer Services, Detroit, MI 02266

NYS SYMBOL K
Rec. Pr. 52 1/4

KELLOGG CO.

YIELD 2.6%
P/E RATIO 17.8

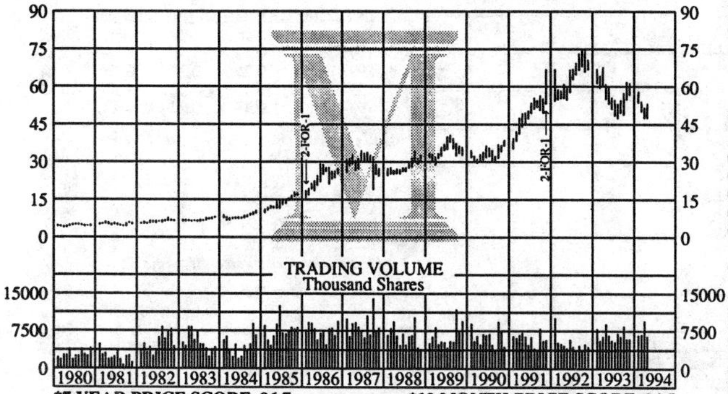

*7 YEAR PRICE SCORE 96.7 *12 MONTH PRICE SCORE 94.5

*NYSE COMPOSITE INDEX=100

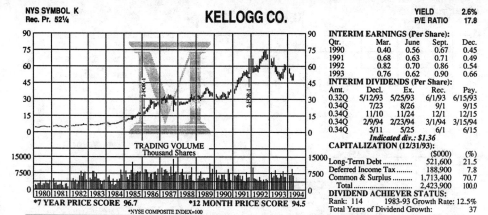

INTERIM EARNINGS (Per Share):

Qtr.	Mar.	June	Sept.	Dec.
1990	0.40	0.56	0.67	0.45
1991	0.68	0.63	0.71	0.49
1992	0.82	0.70	0.86	0.54
1993	0.76	0.62	0.90	0.66

INTERIM DIVIDENDS (Per Share):

Amt.	Decl.	Ex.	Rec.	Pay.
0.32Q	5/12/93	5/25/93	6/1/93	6/15/93
0.34Q	7/23	8/26	9/1	9/15
0.34Q	11/10	11/24	12/1	12/15
0.34Q	2/9/94	2/23/94	3/1/94	3/15/94
0.34Q	5/11	5/25	6/1	6/15

Indicated div.: $1.36

CAPITALIZATION (12/31/93):

	($000)	(%)
Long-Term Debt	521,600	21.5
Deferred Income Tax	188,900	7.8
Common & Surplus	1,713,400	70.7
Total	2,423,900	100.0

DIVIDEND ACHIEVER STATUS:
Rank: 114 1983-93 Growth Rate: 12.5%
Total Years of Dividend Growth: 37

RECENT DEVELOPMENTS: For the year ended 12/31/93, net income was $680.7 million compared with $682.8 million in 1992. Sales decreased 1.7% to $6.30 billion. Selling and administrative expenses increased to 35.5% of sales from 34.6% in 1992. Global ready-to-eat cereal volume grew significantly during the year. For the quarter ended 12/31/93, net income was $149.5 million compared with $127.9 million last year. Sales increased 10.2% to $1.57 billion.

PROSPECTS: An increase in domestic prices and productivity improvements should help results; however, K will continue to face intense competition from private-label brands. As a result of increased competition, K will continue aggressive advertising and promotional campaigns for established brands such as Corn Flakes, Raisin Bran and Frosted Flakes. Difficult recessionary conditions in several major markets will continue to affect international results.

BUSINESS

KELLOGG CO. is the world's leading producer of ready-to-eat-cereal products. It also manufactures a wide variety of food products in the United States and abroad, including frozen pies, toaster pastries, frozen waffles, cereal bars, snack items and other convenience foods. Brand names include: Kellogg's, Mrs. Smith's, and Eggo. Products are manufactured in 17 countries and distributed in 150 countries, including Asia, Australia, Europe, Africa and Latin America.

QUARTERLY DATA

(12/31/93) ($000)	Rev	Inc
1st Quarter	1,518,400	179,200
2nd Quarter	1,541,600	142,700
3rd Quarter	1,669,200	209,300
4th Quarter	1,566,200	149,500

ANNUAL EARNINGS AND DIVIDENDS PER SHARE

	1993	1992	1991	1990	1989	1988	1987
Earnings Per Share	2.94	2.86	2.51	2.08	[3] 1.73	1.95	1.60
Dividends Per Share	1.32	[1] 1.20	[2] 1.075	0.96	0.86	0.76	0.645
Dividend Payout %	44.9	42.0	42.8	46.2	49.7	39.0	40.3

[1] Bef acctg chge [2] 2-for-1 stk split,12/17/91 [3] Before acctg. chg.

ANNUAL FINANCIAL DATA

	1993	1992	1991	1990	1989	1988	1987
RECORD OF EARNINGS (IN MILLIONS):							
Gross Operating Revenues	6,293.9	6,227.4	5,801.2	5,176.3	4,634.5	4,368.2	3,798.7
Costs and Expenses	4,961.3	4,896.3	4,535.9	4,095.2	3,751.6	3,415.0	2,988.7
Depreciation	265.2	231.5	222.8	200.2	167.6	139.7	113.1
Operating Income	1,067.4	1,099.6	1,042.5	880.9	715.3	813.5	696.9
Earn Bef Income Taxes	1,034.1	1,070.4	984.2	814.7	667.0	774.7	665.7
Income Taxes	353.4	387.6	378.2	311.9	244.9	294.3	269.8
Net Income	680.7	[1] 682.8	606.0	502.8	[2] 422.1	480.4	395.9
Aver. Shs. Outstg. (000)	231,500	238,900	241,200	241,600	244,200	246,376	247,336
[1] Before acctg. change dr$251,600,000. [2] Before acctg. change cr$48,100,000.							
BALANCE SHEET (IN MILLIONS):							
Cash & Temporary Invests	98.1	126.3	178.0	100.5	80.3	185.0	126.2
Receivables, Net	622.3	585.3	483.5	500.6	355.2	404.6	275.1
Inventories	403.1	416.4	401.1	359.7	394.0	362.2	310.9
Gross Property	4,272.5	3,993.7	3,889.7	3,672.0	3,302.4	2,916.4	2,418.0
Accumulated Depreciation	1,504.1	1,331.0	1,243.2	1,076.6	896.1	784.5	679.2
Long-Term Debt	521.6	314.9	15.2	295.6	371.4	272.1	290.4
Net Stockholders' Equity	1,713.4	1,945.2	2,159.8	1,901.8	1,634.4	1,483.2	1,211.4
Total Assets	4,237.1	4,015.0	3,925.8	3,749.4	3,390.4	3,297.9	2,680.9
Total Current Assets	1,245.1	1,236.6	1,173.0	1,041.4	906.1	1,063.2	801.9
Total Current Liabilities	1,214.6	1,071.0	1,324.4	1,109.6	1,037.2	1,183.5	853.4
Net Working Capital	30.5	165.6	d151.4	d68.2	d131.1	d120.3	d51.5
Year End Shs Outstg (000)	227,920	237,319	240,463	241,317	243,752	245,856	246,816
STATISTICAL RECORD:							
Operating Profit Margin %	17.0	17.7	18.0	17.0	15.4	18.6	18.3
Book Value Per Share	7.26	7.97	8.77	7.62	6.56	5.82	4.59
Return on Equity %	39.7	35.1	28.1	26.4	25.8	32.4	32.7
Return on Assets %	16.1	17.0	15.4	13.4	12.4	14.6	14.8
Average Yield %	2.3	1.8	2.1	2.8	2.5	2.6	2.4
P/E Ratio	23.1-16.1	26.4-19.0	26.7-13.9	18.6-14.1	23.6-16.7	17.6-12.6	21.5-11.9
Price Range	67 7/8-47 1/4	75 3/8-54 3/8	67-35	38 3/4-29 3/8	40 7/8-28 7/8	34 1/4-24 1/2	34 3/8-19

Statistics are as originally reported.

OFFICERS:
A.G. Langbo, Chmn. & C.E.O.
C.W. Elliott, Exec. V..-Admin. & C.F.O.
R.M. Clark, Sr. V.P., Couns. & Sec.
C.E. French, V.P.-Fin. & Treas.

INCORPORATED: DE, Dec., 1922

PRINCIPAL OFFICE: One Kellogg Square, Battle Creek, MI 49016-3599

TELEPHONE NUMBER: (616) 961-2000

NO. OF EMPLOYEES: 2,197

ANNUAL MEETING: In April

SHAREHOLDERS: 20,273 (approx.)

INSTITUTIONAL HOLDINGS:
No. of Institutions: 499
Shares Held: 166,652,206

REGISTRAR(S): Harris Trust & Savings Bank, Chicago, IL

TRANSFER AGENT(S): Harris Trust & Savings Bank, Chicago, IL

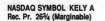

KELLY SERVICES, INC.

NASDAQ SYMBOL KELY A
Rec. Pr. 26¾ (Marginable)

YIELD 2.7%
P/E RATIO 22.7

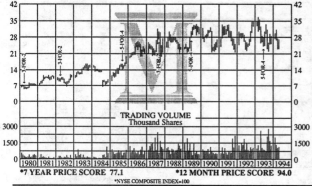

TRADING VOLUME
Thousand Shares

*7 YEAR PRICE SCORE 77.1   *12 MONTH PRICE SCORE 94.0
*NYSE COMPOSITE INDEX=100

INTERIM EARNINGS (Per Share):

Qtr.	Mar.	June	Sept.	Dec.
1990	0.42	0.48	0.56	0.43
1991	0.22	0.26	0.30	0.24
1992	0.17	0.22	0.30	0.34
1993	0.18	0.27	0.37	0.36

INTERIM DIVIDENDS (Per Share):

Amt.	Decl.	Ex.	Rec.	Pay.
0.16Q	5/18/93	5/24/93	5/28/93	6/11/93
0.16Q	8/17	8/23	8/27	9/10
0.16Q	11/16	11/19	11/26	12/10
0.16Q	2/16/94	2/22/94	2/28/94	3/14/94
0.18Q	5/18	5/24	5/31	6/14
			Indicated div.: $0.72	

CAPITALIZATION (1/2/94):

	($000)	(%)
Common & Surplus	386,219	100.0
Total	386,219	100.0

DIVIDEND ACHIEVER STATUS:
Rank: 64   1983-93 Growth Rate: 14.6%
Total Years of Dividend Growth: 22

RECENT DEVELOPMENTS: For the year ended 1/2/94, sales reached $1.95 billion, a 14% increase over the 1992 sales level of $1.71 billion. Net earnings rose 13.6% to $44.6 million from $39.2 million last year. Earnings per share in 1993 were $1.18 versus $1.04 per share in 1992 after adjusting for the 5-for-4 stock split of 5/93. For the quarter, sales were $504.3 million, a 6.2% increase over the $474.9 million reported in 1992. Net earnings rose 4.1% to $13.6 million from $13.1 million last year. Earnings per share for the quarter amounted to $0.36 per share versus 1992 earnings of $0.35 per share, as adjusted for the 1993 stock split. For the quarter ended 10/3/93, sales were $519.1 million, a 14.7% increase over 1992 sales of $452.4 million. Net earnings of $14.0 million rose 22.9% over 1992 net earnings of $11.4 million. Record sales were reported in all major service lines in the United States.

BUSINESS

KELLY SERVICES, INC. is a service organization that provides temporary help in the areas of office clerical, marketing, technical, industrial, nursing and home health care and other business services to a diversified group of customers. KELLY OFFICE SERVICES: provides guaranteed temporary office help to accomodate customers' needs caused by absences due to vacations and illness, for planned programs and for unexpected or short-term work volume increases. KELLY MARKETING: offers coordinated marketing support services for everything from market surveys to direct selling. KELLY LIGHT INDUSTRIAL: supplies semi-skilled light industrial services for a variety of needs. KELLY TECHNICAL: puts a wide range of technical and scientific assistance at the disposal of business when and where it is needed. KELLY ASSISTED LIVING: provides a wide range of paraprofessional nursing services for in-the-home care.

QUARTERLY DATA

(01/02/94)($000)	Rev	Inc
1st Quarter................	450,654	6,879
2nd Quarter...............	482,034	10,009
3rd Quarter................	517,585	14,028
4th Quarter................	504,261	13,643

ANNUAL EARNINGS AND DIVIDENDS PER SHARE

	1/2/94	1/3/93	12/29/91	12/31/90	12/31/89	1/1/89	1/3/88
Earnings Per Share	1.18	1.04	1.02	1.90	1.89	1.60	1.34
Dividends Per Share	0.632	0.584	0.576	0.528	①0.462	0.384	②0.329
Dividend Payout %	53.6	56.2	56.3	27.8	24.4	23.9	24.5
① 5-for-4 stk split, 6/89 ② 3-for-2 stk. split, 9/87.							

ANNUAL FINANCIAL DATA

RECORD OF EARNINGS (IN MILLIONS):

Total Revenues	1,954.5	1,722.5	1,437.9	1,470.5	1,377.5	1,269.4	1,161.4
Costs and Expenses	1,874.0	1,647.5	1,367.8	1,348.7	1,256.6	1,162.7	1,063.1
Depreciation	16.6	14.0	9.8	8.8	7.9	7.4	6.4
Operating Profit	63.9	350.1	322.2	372.0	360.2	325.1	299.5
Earn Bef Income Taxes	70.9	61.0	60.2	113.0	112.9	99.4	91.9
Total Income Taxes	26.3	21.8	21.6	41.8	42.1	39.0	41.5
Net Income	44.6	39.2	38.6	71.2	70.8	60.3	50.5
Aver. Shs. Outstg. (000)	37,728	37,668	37,616	37,586	37,548	37,510	37,514

BALANCE SHEET (IN MILLIONS):

Cash and Cash Equivalents	181.0	184.3	227.5	217.4	189.3	147.2	101.3
Accounts Receivable, Net	248.2	209.0	170.8	163.5	154.4	135.5	123.1
Gross Property	112.1	107.3	80.7	62.6	58.0	55.3	47.7
Accumulated Depreciation	43.8	37.9	29.2	24.8	24.0	24.5	20.2
Net Stockholders' Equity	386.2	367.3	355.0	337.8	283.7	229.9	184.2
Total Assets	542.1	496.1	479.4	443.8	394.3	326.4	261.8
Total Current Assets	447.1	408.6	411.5	393.2	353.9	292.2	232.1
Total Current Liabilities	155.9	128.8	124.4	106.0	110.6	96.5	77.6
Net Working Capital	291.2	279.8	287.0	287.2	243.4	195.7	154.5
Year End Shs Outstg (000)	37,755	37,706	37,624	37,603	37,570	37,520	37,501

STATISTICAL RECORD:

Operating Profit Margin %	3.3	3.5	4.2	7.7	8.2	7.8	7.9
Book Value Per Share	10.23	9.74	9.43	8.98	7.55	6.13	4.91
Return on Equity %	11.5	10.7	10.9	21.1	25.0	26.2	27.4
Return on Assets %	8.2	7.9	8.1	16.0	18.0	18.5	19.3
Average Yield %	2.2	2.0	2.1	2.0	1.7	1.5	1.3
P/E Ratio	31.0-18.6	33.7-21.4	32.7-21.2	17.0-11.4	17.8-11.4	18.9-12.9	23.6-13.1
Price Range	36⅜-22	35-22¼	33⅜-21⅝	32¼-21⅝	33⅜-21½	30⅜-20¾	31⅝-17½
Statistics are as originally reported.							

OFFICERS:
W.R. Kelly, Chairman
T.E. Adderley, Pres. & C.E.O.
R.F. Stoner, Sr. V.P., C.F.O., Treas. & Contr.

INCORPORATED: DE, Aug., 1952

PRINCIPAL OFFICE: 999 W. Big Beaver Rd., Troy, MI 48084

TELEPHONE NUMBER: (810) 362-4444

NO. OF EMPLOYEES: 4,300 Perm.; 630,000 Temp.

ANNUAL MEETING: In May

SHAREHOLDERS: 1,323 Cl. A.; 320 Cl. B.

INSTITUTIONAL HOLDINGS:
No. of Institutions: 111
Shares Held: 14,645,670

REGISTRAR(S): NBD Bank, N.A., Securities Transfer Services, Detroit, MI 02266

TRANSFER AGENT(S): NBD Bank, N.A., Securities Transfer Services, Detroit, MI 02266

KENAN TRANSPORT CO.

YIELD 1.3%
P/E RATIO 12.6

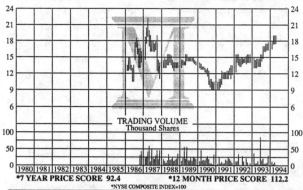

TRADING VOLUME
Thousand Shares

*7 YEAR PRICE SCORE 92.4   ***12 MONTH PRICE SCORE 112.2**
*NYSE COMPOSITE INDEX=100

INTERIM EARNINGS (Per Share):

Qtr.	Mar.	June	Sept.	Dec.
1990	0.25	0.09	0.18	0.12
1991	0.27	0.20	0.26	0.36
1992	0.35	0.27	0.28	0.39
1993	0.39	0.31	0.32	0.43

INTERIM DIVIDENDS (Per Share):

Amt.	Decl.	Ex.	Rec.	Pay.
0.0575Q	3/15/93	3/25/93	3/31/93	4/15/93
0.06Q	6/15	6/24	6/30	7/15
0.06Q	9/15	9/24	9/30	10/15
0.06Q	12/15	12/27	12/31	1/15/94
0.06Q	3/15/94	3/25/94	3/31/94	4/15

Indicated div.: $0.24

CAPITALIZATION (12/31/93):

	($000)	(%)
Deferred Income Tax	7,299	16.3
Common & Surplus	37,363	83.7
Total	44,662	100.0

DIVIDEND ACHIEVER STATUS:
Rank: 230   1983-93 Growth Rate: 7.4%
Total Years of Dividend Growth: 10

RECENT DEVELOPMENTS: For the year ended 12/31/93, revenue increased 6% to $57.1 million from $53.8 million last year. Net income increased 12% to $3.4 million from $3.1 million in 1992. Earnings per share were $1.45 compared with $1.29 last year. For the fourth quarter, revenue increased 4% to $15.0 million from $14.4 million in the same period last year. Net income was $1.0 million, an increase of $111,000 and 12%. Earnings per share were $0.43 compared with $0.39 in 1992. Growth in revenue for the quarter was a result of increased demand for transportation of petroleum products, propane gas and contract chemicals. The revenue growth combined with effective control over operating expenses produced record earnings. For the year, KTCO's operating ratio was 88.9%. The operating ratio for the year was 90.5%.

BUSINESS

KENAN TRANSPORT COMPANY is a tank truck carrier serving the petroleum, propane gas and chemical industries in the southeastern United States. KTCO conducts bulk trucking operations intrastate in Virginia, North Carolina, South Carolina, Georgia, and Florida and interstate between these five states and points throughout the United States. It is ranked among the fifteen largest tank truck carriers in the country. KTCO transports a wide variety of products including gasoline to service stations; petroleum products to wholesalers and industrial plants; propane gas to agricultural, rural and industrial consumers and liquid and dry bulk chemicals to manufacturers. Each of the products transported requires specialized trailers and experienced personnel with special skills necessary for safe and efficient handling of these varied bulk materials.

QUARTERLY DATA

(12/31/93)($000)	Rev	Inc
1st Quarter	14,120	910
2nd Quarter	13,770	745
3rd Quarter	14,157	755
4th Quarter	15,016	1,025

ANNUAL EARNINGS AND DIVIDENDS PER SHARE

	1993	1992	1991	1990	1989	1988	1987
Earnings Per Share	1.45	1.29	1.08	0.64	1.07	① 1.24	1.27
Dividends Per Share	0.235	0.225	0.215	0.205	0.19	0.175	0.165
Dividend Payout %	16.6	17.4	19.9	32.0	17.8	14.1	13.0

① Before acctg. chg.

ANNUAL FINANCIAL DATA

RECORD OF EARNINGS (IN THOUSANDS):

	1993	1992	1991	1990	1989	1988	1987
Operating Revenue	57,063	53,750	49,175	48,392	46,271	47,585	50,011
Operating Expenses	46,710	44,307	40,659	41,762	37,894	38,599	40,071
Depreciation	4,932	4,741	4,722	4,469	4,377	4,197	4,286
Operating Income	5,421	4,702	3,794	2,161	4,000	4,789	5,654
Inc Bef Prov for Income Taxes	5,778	5,086	4,296	2,527	4,178	4,859	5,505
Provision for Inc Taxes	2,343	2,032	1,743	1,021	1,668	1,937	2,529
Net Income	3,435	3,054	2,553	1,506	2,510	① 2,922	2,976
Aver. Shs. Outstg.	2,368	2,359	2,355	2,355	2,355	2,351	2,344

① Before acctg. change cr$1,500,000.

BALANCE SHEET (IN THOUSANDS):

	1993	1992	1991	1990	1989	1988	1987
Cash and Cash Equivalents	11,996	10,816	9,147	7,499	4,436	3,099	4,095
Receivables, Net	5,856	4,157	3,622	3,524	3,520	3,781	3,701
Gross Property	55,661	52,330	49,381	46,763	45,676	44,673	42,476
Accumulated Depreciation	22,914	22,753	21,481	19,699	17,384	17,517	16,584
Long-Term Debt	...	...	...	...	...	...	2,979
Net Operating Property	32,747	29,577	27,900	27,064	28,292	27,156	25,892
Net Stockholders' Equity	37,363	34,348	31,767	29,727	28,710	26,614	22,512
Total Assets	54,727	48,568	44,640	42,215	40,182	38,042	37,605
Total Current Assets	20,831	17,884	15,711	14,145	10,866	9,850	10,663
Total Current Liabilities	10,065	8,840	7,333	6,765	5,134	5,621	4,247
Net Working Capital	10,766	9,044	8,378	7,380	5,732	4,229	6,416
Year End Shares Outstg	2,370	2,360	2,355	2,355	2,355	2,352	2,345

STATISTICAL RECORD:

	1993	1992	1991	1990	1989	1988	1987
Operating Profit Margin %	9.5	8.7	7.7	4.5	8.6	10.1	11.3
Book Value Per Share	15.76	14.55	13.49	12.62	12.19	10.92	9.20
Return on Equity %	9.2	8.9	8.0	5.1	8.7	11.0	13.2
Return on Assets %	6.3	6.3	5.7	3.6	6.2	7.7	7.9
Average Yield %	1.5	1.6	1.9	1.8	1.3	1.3	1.0
P/E Ratio	12.2-9.0	12.0-9.5	12.5-8.3	21.9-14.1	14.5-12.1	12.5-10.1	17.5-8.7
Price Range	17¾-13	15½-12¼	13½-9		14-9	15½-13	15½-12½	22¼-11

Statistics are as originally reported.

OFFICERS:
F.H. Kenan, Chmn. & C.E.O.
L.P. Shaffer, Pres. & C.O.O.
W.L. Boone, V.P.-Fin., C.F.O. & Sec.

INCORPORATED: NC, 1949

PRINCIPAL OFFICE: University Square-West, 143 W. Franklin St., P.O. Box 2729, Chapel Hill, NC 27515-2729

TELEPHONE NUMBER: (919) 967-8221

FAX: (919) 967-1546

NO. OF EMPLOYEES: 95

ANNUAL MEETING: In May

SHAREHOLDERS: 538 common

INSTITUTIONAL HOLDINGS:
No. of Institutions: 18
Shares Held: 684,239

REGISTRAR(S):

TRANSFER AGENT(S): First Union National Bank of N.C., Charlotte, NC

KEYCORP

	YIELD	3.9%
	P/E RATIO	10.4

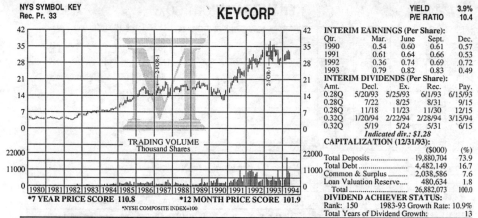

*7 YEAR PRICE SCORE 110.8   *12 MONTH PRICE SCORE 101.9
*NYSE COMPOSITE INDEX=100

INTERIM EARNINGS (Per Share):

Qtr.	Mar.	June	Sept.	Dec.
1990	0.54	0.60	0.61	0.57
1991	0.61	0.64	0.66	0.53
1992	0.36	0.74	0.69	.72
1993	0.79	0.82	0.83	0.49

INTERIM DIVIDENDS (Per Share):

Amt.	Decl.	Ex.	Rec.	Pay.
0.28Q	5/20/93	5/25/93	6/1/93	6/15/93
0.28Q	7/22	8/25	8/31	9/15
0.28Q	11/18	11/23	11/30	12/15
0.32Q	1/20/94	2/22/94	2/28/94	3/15/94
0.32Q	5/19	5/24	5/31	6/15

Indicated div.: $1.28

CAPITALIZATION (12/31/93):

	($000)	(%)
Total Deposits	19,880,704	73.9
Total Debt	4,482,149	16.7
Common & Surplus	2,038,586	7.6
Loan Valuation Reserve	480,634	1.8
Total	26,882,073	100.0

DIVIDEND ACHIEVER STATUS:
Rank: 150   1983-93 Growth Rate: 10.9%
Total Years of Dividend Growth: 13

RECENT DEVELOPMENTS: On 3/1/94, the merger between Key Corp. and Society Corporation was completed. For the year ended 12/31/93, net income before restructuring charges was $403.9 million, up from $316.7 million in 1992. Restructuring charges of $64.8 million were related to the Society Corp. merger. The level of nonperforming assets and charge-offs continued their declining trend to 1.24% and 0.55% of total loans respectively. Comparisons were made with restated 1992 figures.

PROSPECTS: The merger with Society Corporation yields a $60 billion bank holding company with 1300 offices in 18 states. Upon completion of the transaction, the company will be called KeyCorp and headquartered in Ohio. Society Corp., a $26 billion bank holding company, maintains one of the largest investment management businesses in the nation and also provides specialty finance and large corporate banking services. These services are expected to complement KEY's strengths.

BUSINESS

KEYCORP is a multi-regional bank. Banking offices serve individual consumers, small-to-medium sized businesses, and municipalities in eight states: Alaska, Maine, Oregon, Washington State, New York (upstate New York and Long Island, exclusive of New York City), Wyoming, Idaho, and Utah. Non-bank services include trust, leasing, discount brokerage, finance, investment management, credit life reinsurance, mortgage banking, and data processing.

LOAN DISTRIBUTION

(12/31/93)	($000)	(%)
Commercial, Fin. & Agri.	4,388,185	24.5
Real Estate-Const.	623,245	3.5
Real Estate-Resident Mtge	4,574,503	25.6
Real Estate-Comm Mtge	2,119,857	11.8
Consumer	3,266,772	18.3
Loans Held For Sale	1,648,611	9.2
Lease Finance & Foreign	1,276,474	7.1
Total	17,897,647	100.0

ANNUAL EARNINGS AND DIVIDENDS PER SHARE

	1993	1992	1991	1990	1989	1988	1987
Earnings Per Share	2.93	2.51	2.45	[2] 2.32	0.05	2.10	1.88
Dividends Per Share	1.19	[1] 0.98	0.92	0.88	0.80	0.68	[3] 0.60
Dividend Payout %	40.6	39.0	37.6	38.0	N.M.	32.5	32.0

[1] 2-for-1 stk split,03/23/93 [2] Before acctg. chg. [3] 2-for-1 stk. split, 2/87.

ANNUAL FINANCIAL DATA

RECORD OF EARNINGS (IN MILLIONS):

	1993	1992	1991	1990	1989	1988	1987
Total Interest Income	1,871.3	1,903.4	1,384.1	1,486.9	987.1	825.4	741.0
Total Interest Expense	672.3	773.0	697.3	862.6	561.3	465.5	411.9
Net Interest Income	1,199.0	1,130.4	686.8	624.3	425.8	359.8	329.1
Provision for Loan Losses	72.2	147.4	79.8	94.7	51.6	24.9	18.1
Net Income	347.2	301.2	163.0	[1] 155.2	110.0	100.1	90.9
Aver. Shs. Outstg. (000)	118,323	117,349	66,569	66,893	46,672	46,814	47,516

[1] Before acctg. change cr$2,714,000.

BALANCE SHEET (IN MILLIONS):

	1993	1992	1991	1990	1989	1988	1987
Cash & Due From Banks	1,375.6	1,345.1	850.3	999.5	783.2	745.7	624.0
Net Loans	17,417.0	15,699.0	9,417.4	9,895.1	6,719.9	6,175.4	5,641.2
Total Domestic Deposits	17,866.2	17,542.8	11,377.8	11,933.2	7,741.1	7,415.2	7,041.6
Total Foreign Deposits	2,014.5	1,115.2	157.3	184.9	683.4	260.5	238.7
Long-term Debt	952.7	886.1	177.1	183.2	122.2	182.5	186.0
Net Stockholders' Equity	2,038.6	1,868.1	1,116.7	1,005.2	746.2	689.5	618.8
Total Assets	27,007.3	24,978.3	15,404.5	15,110.2	10,903.3	10,009.6	9,077.3
Year End Sh Outstg (000)	117,377	116,726	66,057	65,537	43,496	44,356	44,090

STATISTICAL RECORD:

	1993	1992	1991	1990	1989	1988	1987
Return on Assets %	1.29	1.21	1.06	1.03	1.01	1.00	1.00
Return on Equity %	17.00	16.10	14.60	15.40	14.70	14.50	14.70
Book Value Per Share	17.37	15.49	16.90	15.34	16.58	14.98	13.47
Average Yield %	3.7	3.4	4.4	5.9	4.4	4.0	3.6
P/E Ratio	12.7-9.3	13.3-9.7	10.7-6.2	7.6-5.2	8.7-7.1	9.0-7.4	10.6-7.0
Price Range	37¼-27¼	33½-24¼	26¼-15¼	17⅝-12	20¼-16½	18⅞-15½	20-13¼

Statistics are as originally reported.

OFFICERS:
V.J. Riley, Jr., Chmn. & C.E.O.
R.W. Gillespie, Pres. & C.O.O.
C.B. Chase, Exec. V.P. & Gen. Couns.
L. Irving, Exec. V.P. & Treas.
INCORPORATED: OH, 1958
PRINCIPAL OFFICE: 127 Public Square, Cleveland, OH 44114-1306

TELEPHONE NUMBER: (216) 689-3000
NO. OF EMPLOYEES: 30,000
ANNUAL MEETING: In May
SHAREHOLDERS: 46,777
INSTITUTIONAL HOLDINGS:
No. of Institutions: 317
Shares Held: 55,633,658

REGISTRAR(S):

TRANSFER AGENT(S):

KEYSTONE INTERNATIONAL, INC.

YIELD 3.3%
P/E RATIO 81.9

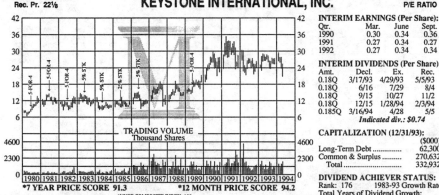

INTERIM EARNINGS (Per Share):

Qtr.	Mar.	June	Sept.	Dec.
1990	0.30	0.34	0.36	0.31
1991	0.27	0.34	0.27	d0.22
1992	0.27	0.34	0.34	0.27

INTERIM DIVIDENDS (Per Share):

Amt.	Decl.	Ex.	Rec.	Pay.
0.18Q	3/17/93	4/29/93	5/5/93	5/19/93
0.18Q	6/16	7/29	8/4	8/18
0.18Q	9/15	10/27	11/2	11/17
0.18Q	12/15	1/28/94	2/3/94	2/23/94
0.185Q	3/16/94	4/28	5/5	5/18

Indicated div.: $0.74

CAPITALIZATION (12/31/93):

	($000)	(%)
Long-Term Debt	62,300	18.7
Common & Surplus	270,632	81.3
Total	332,932	100.0

TRADING VOLUME
Thousand Shares

*7 YEAR PRICE SCORE 91.3   *12 MONTH PRICE SCORE 94.2
*NYSE COMPOSITE INDEX=100

DIVIDEND ACHIEVER STATUS:
Rank: 176   1983-93 Growth Rate: 10.1%
Total Years of Dividend Growth: 22

RECENT DEVELOPMENTS: For the quarter ended 12/31/93, net income remained flat at $9.5 million, while net sales rose 1% to $131.0 million from $129.9 million. Earnings were negatively impacted by unfavorable translation effects resulting from the stronger dollar. Meanwhile, order rate for the quarter dropped by 8% from last year's levels due to significantly lower orders in December. However, January 1994 orders were up by 23% over last year's totals.

PROSPECTS: Restructuring efforts scheduled to be completed in 1994 should cut operating costs through relocations of several plants to Mexico. Stringent environmental standards to ensure safety measures when handling highly volatile products will boost earnings in the safety and environment segment. Also, new product offerings, including bellows seal valves, steam conditioning valves and metal-sealed valves, will lift sales.

BUSINESS

KEYSTONE INTERNATIONAL, INC. primarily designs, manufactures and markets on a worldwide basis valves and other specialized industrial products that control the flow of liquids, gas and solid materials, including food and beverage, water and sewage, petroleum production and refining, natural gas, chemical, pulp and paper and power. Keystone is one of the leading manufacturers of specialty valves in the world.

BUSINESS LINE ANALYSIS

(12/31/93)	Rev(%)	Rev(%)
United States	44.9	37.2
Europe, Mid East & Africa	30.0	35.2
Asia-Pacific	19.0	23.3
N. & S. Amer., except U.S	6.1	4.3
Total	100.0	100.0

ANNUAL EARNINGS AND DIVIDENDS PER SHARE

	1993	1992	1991	1990	1989	1988	1987
Earnings Per Share	1.12	1.22	[1] 0.66	1.31	[2] 1.10	0.96	0.68
Dividends Per Share	0.71	0.67	0.56	0.59	[3] 0.532	0.44	0.41
Dividend Payout %	63.4	54.9	84.8	45.0	48.4	45.8	60.0

[1] Before acctg. chg. [2] Before disc. oper. [3] 5-for-4 stk split, 5/25/89

ANNUAL FINANCIAL DATA

RECORD OF EARNINGS (IN THOUSANDS):

	1993	1992	1991	1990	1989	1988	1987
Total Revenues	516,140	528,372	520,496	446,232	375,709	346,010	292,224
Costs and Expenses	420,940	425,292	443,740	343,696	287,676	270,952	227,985
Depreciation & Amort	24,537	22,749	22,492	18,965	16,930	12,796	12,621
Operating Income	70,663	80,331	54,264	83,571	71,103	62,262	51,618
Inc Bef Income Taxes & Acctg Chg	62,121	69,854	43,107	72,089	59,713	51,080	38,239
Income Taxes	22,985	27,313	20,273	28,064	22,953	19,206	15,915
Net Income	[1] 39,136	42,541	[2] 22,834	44,025	[3] 36,760	31,874	22,324
Aver. Shs. Outstg.	35,085	34,902	34,676	33,654	33,515	33,301	33,270

[1] Before acctg. change cr$1,879,000. [2] Before acctg. change dr$4,928,000. [3] Before disc. op. dr$558,000.

BALANCE SHEET (IN THOUSANDS):

	1993	1992	1991	1990	1989	1988	1987
Cash and Cash Equivalents	19,873	29,390	12,467	32,335	29,695	30,699	22,914
Receivs (princpally Trade), Net	119,750	105,304	117,056	101,883	85,053	73,202	68,660
Inventories	134,608	138,034	156,027	130,621	116,225	113,325	100,458
Gross Property	274,890	257,009	255,032	204,630	169,407	155,823	156,360
Accumulated Depreciation	140,037	133,035	123,411	95,896	80,261	72,263	64,517
Long-Term Debt	62,300	14,312	58,365	48,221	51,465	69,762	82,496
Net Stockholders' Equity	270,632	252,609	239,373	231,312	198,831	180,537	163,452
Total Assets	456,500	438,099	458,752	417,441	365,856	339,697	330,256
Total Current Assets	279,744	277,533	290,217	269,849	234,092	220,546	195,445
Total Current Liabilities	107,917	156,931	147,049	120,452	103,277	79,100	68,892
Net Working Capital	171,827	120,602	143,168	149,397	130,815	141,446	126,553
Year End Shares Outstg	35,142	34,927	34,658	33,586	33,500	33,313	33,195

STATISTICAL RECORD:

	1993	1992	1991	1990	1989	1988	1987
Operating Profit Margin %	13.7	15.2	10.4	18.7	18.9	18.0	17.7
Book Value Per Share	7.70	7.23	6.91	6.89	5.94	5.42	4.92
Return on Equity %	14.5	16.8	9.5	19.0	18.5	17.7	13.7
Return on Assets %	8.6	9.7	5.0	10.5	10.0	9.4	6.8
Average Yield %	2.7	2.6	1.9	2.4	3.0	2.9	2.8
P/E Ratio	26.0-20.5	24.9-17.5	53.6-35.6	22.7-14.4	19.3-13.2	20.1-12.1	27.9-14.7
Price Range	29⅛-23	30⅜-21⅜	35⅜-23½	29¾-18⅞	21¼-14½	19¼-11⅝	19-10

Statistics are as originally reported.

OFFICERS:
R.A. LeBlanc, Chmn. & C.E.O.
M.D. Clark, Pres. & C.O.O.
M.E. Baldwin, V.P. & C.F.O.

INCORPORATED: TX, 1947

PRINCIPAL OFFICE: 9600 West Gulf Bank Drive, Houston, TX 77040

TELEPHONE NUMBER: (713) 466-1176

FAX: (713) 466-6328

NO. OF EMPLOYEES: 571 (approx.)

ANNUAL MEETING: In May

SHAREHOLDERS: 2,126 (approx.)

INSTITUTIONAL HOLDINGS:
No. of Institutions: 174
Shares Held: 19,625,283

REGISTRAR(S):

TRANSFER AGENT(S): Continental Stock Transfer & Trust Co., New York, NY

NYS SYMBOL KMB
Rec. Pr. 56 3/8

KIMBERLY-CLARK CORP.

YIELD 3.1%
P/E RATIO 17.7

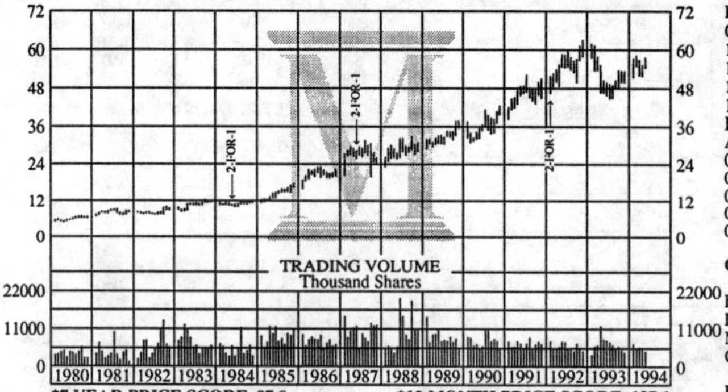

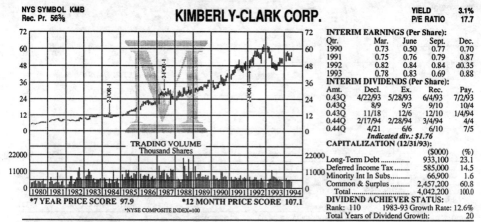

*7 YEAR PRICE SCORE 97.9 *12 MONTH PRICE SCORE 107.1
*NYSE COMPOSITE INDEX=100

INTERIM EARNINGS (Per Share):

Qtr.	Mar.	June	Sept.	Dec.
1990	0.73	0.50	0.77	0.70
1991	0.75	0.76	0.79	0.87
1992	0.82	0.84	0.84	d0.35
1993	0.78	0.83	0.69	0.88

INTERIM DIVIDENDS (Per Share):

Amt.	Decl.	Ex.	Rec.	Pay.
0.43Q	4/22/93	5/28/93	6/4/93	7/2/93
0.43Q	8/9	9/3	9/10	10/4
0.43Q	11/18	12/6	12/10	1/4/94
0.44Q	2/17/94	2/28/94	3/4/94	4/4
0.44Q	4/21	6/6	6/10	7/5

Indicated div.: $1.76

CAPITALIZATION (12/31/93):

	($000)	(%)
Long-Term Debt	933,100	23.1
Deferred Income Tax	585,000	14.5
Minority Int In Subs	66,900	1.6
Common & Surplus	2,457,200	60.8
Total	4,042,200	100.0

DIVIDEND ACHIEVER STATUS:
Rank: 110 1983-93 Growth Rate: 12.6%
Total Years of Dividend Growth: 20

RECENT DEVELOPMENTS: For the year ended 12/31/93, net income increased 48.1% to $510.9 million compared with $345.0 million in 1992. Revenues for the year fell slightly to $6.97 billion from $7.09 billion. Sales were negatively affected by lower selling prices for disposable diapers, feminine care products and facial tissue in the U.S. and changing currency exchange rates for Canada and Europe. Improved earnings were a result, in part, of higher sales volumes for Huggies Pull-Ups training pants and baby wipes.

PROSPECTS: Prospects look good for Kimberly-Clark as sales volumes are increasing in many of its businesses. However, foreign currency translation will continue to have adverse affects on the Company's earnings. Profitability will be maintained by keeping costs down and expanding products into different markets. Results for KMB's consumer and industrial bathroom tissue businesses are suffering due to overcapacity and weak prices.

BUSINESS

KIMBERLY-CLARK CORP. manufactures household, personal care and health care products, as well as newsprint and premium business, correspondence and specialty papers. The Class I segment includes tissue products; infant, child, feminine and incontinence care products; industrial and commercial wipers; health care products; and related products. Class II includes newsprint, printing papers, premium papers, premium business and correspondence papers, tobacco industry papers and products, technical papers, and related products. Class III includes airline services, commercial air transportation and other products and services.

BUSINESS LINE ANALYSIS

(12/31/93)	Rev(%)	Inc($000)
United States	72.6	94.9
Canada	7.8	(3.5)
Europe	12.6	0.1
Asia & Latin America	7.0	8.5
Total	100.0	100.0

ANNUAL EARNINGS AND DIVIDENDS PER SHARE

	1993	1992	1991	1990	1989	1988	1987
Earnings Per Share	**3.18**	[1] **2.15**	**3.18**	**2.70**	**2.63**	**2.36**	**1.87**
Dividends Per Share	**1.70**	[2] **1.64**	**1.45**	**1.345**	**1.175**	**0.78**	[3] **0.695**
Dividend Payout %	**53.5**	**76.3**	**45.6**	**49.8**	**44.7**	**33.1**	**37.3**

[1] Before acctg. chges [2] 2-for-1 stk split, 1/3/92 [3] 2-for-1 stk. split, 5/87.

ANNUAL FINANCIAL DATA

	1993	1992	1991	1990	1989	1988	1987
RECORD OF EARNINGS (IN MILLIONS):							
Total Revenues	6,972.9	7,091.1	6,776.9	6,407.3	5,733.6	5,393.5	4,884.7
Costs and Expenses	5,883.5	6,259.0	5,769.6	5,413.4	4,849.3	4,565.3	4,112.6
Depreciation	295.9	289.0	265.5	240.3	210.9	187.6	186.0
Operating Profit	793.5	543.1	741.8	753.6	673.4	640.6	586.1
Income Bef Income Taxes	713.0	461.9	684.3	660.8	630.8	583.9	534.1
Provision for Inc Taxes	284.4	186.3	236.1	277.2	242.4	229.8	230.5
Sh Of Net Inc Of Eq Cos	98.0	82.9	72.8	58.2	49.3	46.0	35.3
Minor Owners' Shs Of Subs' Net Inc	15.7	13.5	12.7	9.7	13.9	21.5	13.7
Net Income	510.9	[1] 345.0	508.3	432.1	423.8	378.6	325.2
Aver. Shs. Outstg. (000)	160,900	160,400	160,000	160,000	161,200	160,800	174,400
[1] Before acctg. change dr$210,000,000.							
BALANCE SHEET (IN MILLIONS):							
Cash & Cash Equivalents	34.8	41.1	42.8	60.2	164.3	84.1	89.7
Receivables, Net	832.4	856.9	691.1	623.1	624.8	584.9	519.9
Inventories	775.9	719.7	686.0	668.0	615.5	566.5	525.4
Gross Property	6,372.8	5,974.1	5,591.8	5,188.0	4,753.6	4,154.3	3,768.0
Accumulated Depreciation	2,330.0	2,199.3	1,981.6	1,801.7	1,712.7	1,579.0	1,431.2
Long-Term Debt	933.1	994.6	874.7	728.5	745.1	743.3	686.9
Net Stockholders' Equity	2,457.2	2,191.1	2,519.7	2,259.7	2,085.8	1,865.6	1,571.9
Total Assets	6,380.7	6,029.1	5,650.4	5,283.9	4,923.0	4,267.6	3,885.7
Total Current Assets	1,675.2	1,682.6	1,474.8	1,397.1	1,443.2	1,235.5	1,135.0
Total Current Liabilities	1,908.5	1,822.8	1,433.3	1,466.2	1,263.2	979.4	996.1
Net Working Capital	d233.3	d140.2	41.5	d69.1	180.0	256.1	138.9
Year End Shs Outstg (000)	160,900	160,759	160,077	159,834	161,400	161,200	160,348
STATISTICAL RECORD:							
Operating Profit Margin %	11.4	7.7	10.9	11.8	11.7	11.9	12.0
Book Value Per Share	15.27	13.63	15.74	14.14	12.92	11.57	9.80
Return on Equity %	20.8	15.7	20.2	19.1	20.3	20.3	20.7
Return on Assets %	8.0	5.7	9.0	8.2	8.6	8.9	8.4
Average Yield %	3.2	3.0	3.2	3.7	3.5	2.8	2.7
P/E Ratio	19.5-14.0	29.4-21.5	16.4-11.9	15.9-11.4	14.4-10.9	13.9-9.8	16.9-10.6
Price Range	62-44 5/8	63 1/4-46 1/4	52 1/4-38	42 7/8-30 3/4	37 3/4-28 3/4	32 7/8-23 1/8	31 5/8-19 3/4

Statistics are as originally reported.

OFFICERS:
W.R. Sanders, Chmn. & C.E.O.
J.W. Donehower, Sr. V.P. & C.F.O.
D.M. Crook, V.P. & Sec.
W.A. Gamron, V.P. & Treas.

INCORPORATED: DE, Jun., 1928

PRINCIPAL OFFICE: P.O. Box 619100 DFW Airport Station, Dallas, TX 75261-9100

TELEPHONE NUMBER: (214) 830-1200
FAX: (214) 830-1490
NO. OF EMPLOYEES: 42,131
ANNUAL MEETING: In April
SHAREHOLDERS: 25,121
INSTITUTIONAL HOLDINGS:
No. of Institutions: 606
Shares Held: 107,742,934

REGISTRAR(S): First National Bank of Boston, Shareholder Services Division, Boston, MA

TRANSFER AGENT(S): First National Bank of Boston, Shareholder Services Division, Boston, MA

NYS SYMBOL KU
Rec. Pr. 25

KU ENERGY CORP.

YIELD 6.6%
P/E RATIO 11.8

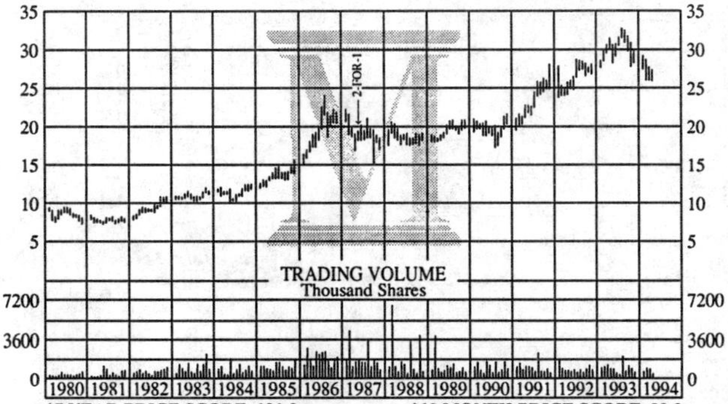

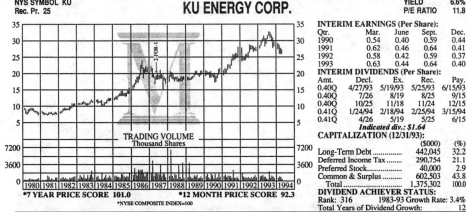

***7 YEAR PRICE SCORE 101.0** ***12 MONTH PRICE SCORE 92.3**

*NYSE COMPOSITE INDEX=100

INTERIM EARNINGS (Per Share):

Qtr.	Mar.	June	Sept.	Dec.
1990	0.54	0.40	0.59	0.44
1991	0.62	0.46	0.64	0.41
1992	0.58	0.42	0.59	0.37
1993	0.63	0.44	0.64	0.40

INTERIM DIVIDENDS (Per Share):

Amt.	Decl.	Ex.	Rec.	Pay.
0.40Q	4/27/93	5/19/93	5/25/93	6/15/93
0.40Q	7/26	8/19	8/25	9/15
0.40Q	10/25	11/18	11/24	12/15
0.41Q	1/24/94	2/18/94	2/25/94	3/15/94
0.41Q	4/26	5/19	5/25	6/15

Indicated div.: $1.64

CAPITALIZATION (12/31/93):

	($000)	(%)
Long-Term Debt	442,045	32.2
Deferred Income Tax	290,754	21.1
Preferred Stock	40,000	2.9
Common & Surplus	602,503	43.8
Total	1,375,302	100.0

DIVIDEND ACHIEVER STATUS:
Rank: 316 1983-93 Growth Rate: 3.4%
Total Years of Dividend Growth: 12

RECENT DEVELOPMENTS: For the quarter ended 3/31/94, net income was $25.0 million, up 4.9% from $23.8 million in 1993. Revenues were $166.5 million, up 7.9%. First quarter income reflects a one-time recovery of about $3.2 million resulting from the resolution of a coal contract dispute. KU's sales of electricity were 11% above the same period of 1993. The improved results for the quarter were primarily due to weather related growth in sales and lower interest charges.

PROSPECTS: In January 1994, KU filed an application with the Kentucky Public Service Commission to implement an environmental surcharge as a means to recover the costs of complying with Federal Clean Air Legislation. In response to a changing marketplace, KU will pursue nonregulated opportunities. KU's nonregulated investment strategy will focus on independent power projects and equipment leases to other utilities.

BUSINESS

KU ENERGY CORP. is a holding company for Kentucky Utilities, which furnishes electricity to about 437,000 customers, 77 Kentucky counties and in five counties in southwestern Virginia. Among the principal industries in the territory served are coal mining, automotive and related industries, agriculture, primary metals processing, crude oil production, pipeline transportation, and the manufacture of electrical and other machinery and of paper and paper products. Virtually all of KU's electric generation is coal-fired.

REVENUES

(12/31/93)	($000)	(%)
Residential	210,759	34.7
Commercial	138,271	22.8
Industrial	111,857	18.4
Mine Power	34,977	5.8
Public Authorities	48,142	7.9
Other Electric Utilities	62,463	10.3
Miscellaneous & Other	139	0.1
Total	606,608	100.0

ANNUAL EARNINGS AND DIVIDENDS PER SHARE

	1993	1992	1991	1990	1989	1988	1987
Earnings Per Share	**2.11**	**1.96**	**2.13**	**[1] 1.97**	**[1] 2.02**	**1.94**	**1.72**
Dividends Per Share	**1.60**	**1.56**	**1.50**	**1.46**	**1.40**	**1.34**	**[2] 1.29**
Dividend Payout %	**75.8**	**79.6**	**70.4**	**74.1**	**69.3**	**69.1**	**75.0**

[1] Before acctg. chg. [2] 2-for-1 stk. split, 5/87.

ANNUAL FINANCIAL DATA

	1993	1992	1991	1990	1989	1988	1987
RECORD OF EARNINGS (IN MILLIONS):							
Operating Revenues	606.6	576.3	587.7	553.8	531.9	559.8	553.2
Depreciation	60.8	58.9	58.3	56.2	54.8	51.7	49.9
Maintenance	59.5	61.3	58.6	52.6	48.1	47.8	37.2
Prov for Fed Inc Taxes	47.8	41.0	45.8	42.3	45.1	48.4	60.7
Operating Income	104.5	105.3	109.5	102.2	107.1	106.5	110.6
Interest Expense	32.7	40.9	38.1	37.3	36.6	36.6	36.8
Net Income	80.0	74.2	80.6	80.1	[1] 82.3	79.3	73.7
Aver. Shs. Outstg. (000)	37,818	37,818	37,818	37,818	37,818	37,818	37,818
[1] Before acctg. change cr$11,470,000.							
BALANCE SHEET (IN MILLIONS):							
Gross Plant	2,163.5	1,992.6	1,917.1	1,595.3	1,557.2	1,525.6	1,507.6
Accumulated Depreciation	880.0	823.5	771.0	718.7	670.7	620.1	571.8
Prop, Plant & Equip, Net	1,283.6	1,169.1	1,146.0	876.6	886.5	905.5	935.8
Long-term Debt	442.0	444.0	408.2	409.0	396.9	397.4	397.5
Net Stockholders' Equity	642.5	623.3	608.2	586.5	598.1	565.8	546.8
Total Assets	1,609.6	1,473.7	1,425.7	1,162.1	1,133.4	1,108.0	1,082.0
Year End Shs Outstg (000)	37,818	37,818	37,818	37,818	37,818	37,818	37,818
STATISTICAL RECORD:							
Book Value Per Share	15.93	15.42	15.02	14.45	13.94	13.01	12.42
Op. Inc/Net Pl %	8.1	9.0	9.6	11.7	12.1	11.8	11.8
Accum. Dep/Gr. Pl %	40.7	41.3	40.2	45.1	43.1	40.6	37.9
Return on Equity %	12.4	11.9	13.3	13.7	14.5	14.9	14.5
Average Yield %	5.3	5.9	6.3	7.5	7.2	7.0	6.9
P/E Ratio	15.5-13.1	14.7-12.1	13.2-9.2	11.0-8.8	10.3-8.8	10.6-9.0	12.9-8.7
Price Range	32¾-27⅝	28¾-23¾	28⅛-19½	21⅝-17¼	20⅞-17⅞	20⅝-17½	22¼-15

Statistics are as originally reported.

OFFICERS:
J.T. Newton, Chmn. & Pres.
W.N. English, Treasurer
G.S. Brooks, II, Corp. Sec. & Gen. Coun.

PRINCIPAL OFFICE: One Quality Street, Lexington, KY 40507

TELEPHONE NUMBER: (606) 288-1155
FAX: (606) 288-1125
NO. OF EMPLOYEES: 307
ANNUAL MEETING: In April
SHAREHOLDERS: 23,798 common; 1,872 preferred
INSTITUTIONAL HOLDINGS:
No. of Institutions: 130
Shares Held: 8,320,120

REGISTRAR(S): Harris Trust & Savings Bank, Chicago, IL

TRANSFER AGENT(S): Illinois Stock Transfer Co., Chicago, IL 60606
Harris Trust & Savings Bank, Chicago, IL

LA-Z-BOY CHAIR CO.

YIELD 2.1%
P/E RATIO 17.1

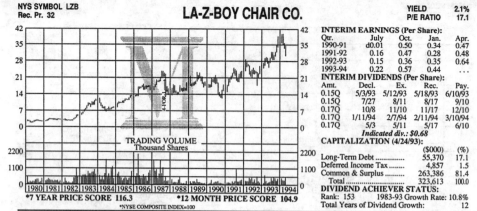

*7 YEAR PRICE SCORE 116.3   *12 MONTH PRICE SCORE 104.9
*NYSE COMPOSITE INDEX=100

TRADING VOLUME
Thousand Shares

INTERIM EARNINGS (Per Share):

Qtr.	July	Oct.	Jan.	Apr.
1990-91	d0.01	0.50	0.34	0.47
1991-92	0.16	0.47	0.28	0.48
1992-93	0.15	0.36	0.35	0.64
1993-94	0.22	0.57	0.44	...

INTERIM DIVIDENDS (Per Share):

Amt.	Decl.	Ex.	Rec.	Pay.
0.15Q	5/3/93	5/12/93	5/18/93	6/10/93
0.15Q	7/27	8/11	8/17	9/10
0.17Q	10/8	11/10	11/17	12/10
0.17Q	1/11/94	2/7/94	2/11/94	3/10/94
0.17Q	5/3	5/11	5/17	6/10

Indicated div.: $0.68

CAPITALIZATION (4/24/93):

	($000)	(%)
Long-Term Debt	55,370	17.1
Deferred Income Tax	4,857	1.5
Common & Surplus	263,386	81.4
Total	323,613	100.0

DIVIDEND ACHIEVER STATUS:
Rank: 153   1983-93 Growth Rate: 10.8%
Total Years of Dividend Growth: 12

RECENT DEVELOPMENTS: For the quarter ended 1/22/94, net income was up 25% to $8.0 million compared with $6.4 million a year ago. Sales totaled $192.6 million, up 13.4% from $169.8 million in the same period last year. La-Z-Boy experienced strong sales volumes in each of its five operating units, especially at Hammary, which primarily produces occasional tables. Other products showing improved sales included modulars, sofas, sleepers and reclining sofas.

PROSPECTS: The outlook for the near term is positive with sales and profits being traditionally strong around the end of a fiscal year. La-Z-Boy has announced that construction will soon begin on a new upholstery factory in Arkansas. Cost of the facility is estimated at $7 million. Increased capacity will result as the existing older 200,000 square foot plant is replaced by a plant with over 350,000 square feet.

BUSINESS

LA-Z-BOY CHAIR COMPANY is the largest manufacturer of reclining chairs in the United States and one of the largest in the world. The Company operates through six separate divisions. The La-Z-Boy recliner is the most well-known product and has expanded in other lines of furniture. La-Z-Boy sleep sofas, swivel rockers, modular seating units, and stationary sofas and loveseats are some of the Company's popular products. LZB operates 24 manufacturing plants in the U.S. and Canada. The Company is also a volume supplier of seating and quality wood furniture to the contract market which includes offices, hotels, hospitals, and clinics.

QUARTERLY DATA

(4/24/93)($000)	Rev	Inc
1st Quarter	140,003	2,783
2nd Quarter	175,877	6,507
3rd Quarter	169,810	6,391
4th Quarter	198,432	11,603

ANNUAL EARNINGS AND DIVIDENDS PER SHARE

	4/24/93	4/25/92	4/27/91	4/28/90	4/29/89	4/30/88	4/25/87
Earnings Per Share	1.50	1.39	1.30	1.58	1.54	①1.45	1.34
Dividends Per Share	0.60	0.57	0.56	0.52	0.44	0.40	②0.375
Dividend Payout %	40.0	41.0	43.1	32.9	29.0	27.6	28.0

① Before extraord. item ② 4-for-1 stk. split, 9/87.

ANNUAL FINANCIAL DATA

RECORD OF EARNINGS (IN THOUSANDS):

Total Revenues	684,122	619,471	608,032	592,273	553,187	486,793	419,991
Costs and Expenses	623,229	561,103	550,702	528,261	491,106	429,220	366,215
Depreciation & Amort	14,061	14,840	14,039	13,735	13,607	14,203	9,033
Operating Income	46,832	43,528	43,291	50,277	48,474	43,370	44,743
Income Bef Income Taxes	45,299	39,905	38,370	45,535	43,974	42,024	44,947
Total Tax Expense	18,015	14,805	15,009	17,282	16,508	15,543	20,283
Net Income	27,284	25,100	23,361	28,253	27,466	26,481	24,664
Aver. Shs. Outstg.	18,172	18,064	17,941	17,868	17,886	18,285	18,400

BALANCE SHEET (IN THOUSANDS):

Cash & Cash Equivalents	28,808	21,737	12,960	6,720	18,159	13,207	22,565
Receivables, Net	184,258	168,264	156,953	155,955	143,141	130,584	113,834
Inventories	60,487	57,808	60,407	69,568	65,641	66,822	45,475
Gross Property	191,169	185,789	173,888	158,683	146,409	139,340	123,189
Accumulated Depreciation	100,762	92,349	78,380	69,542	66,564	55,180	49,701
Long-Term Debt	55,370	55,912	62,187	69,066	70,641	76,215	23,270
Net Stockholders' Equity	263,386	246,359	229,217	214,585	194,293	178,765	165,344
Total Assets	401,064	376,722	363,085	361,856	349,007	336,592	269,887
Total Current Assets	278,976	253,579	238,222	240,411	235,822	219,438	186,911
Total Current Liabilities	77,451	69,148	65,233	70,119	76,875	72,374	71,576
Net Working Capital	201,525	184,431	172,989	170,292	158,947	147,064	115,335
Year End Shares Outstg	18,195	18,135	17,979	17,905	17,078	18,024	18,424

STATISTICAL RECORD:

Operating Profit Margin %	6.8	7.0	7.1	8.5	8.8	8.9	10.7
Book Value Per Share	13.29	12.32	11.43	10.61	9.88	8.46	8.97
Return on Equity %	10.4	10.2	10.2	13.2	14.1	14.8	14.9
Return on Assets %	6.8	6.7	6.4	7.8	7.9	7.9	9.1
Average Yield %	2.6	2.8	3.3	2.6	2.7	2.2	2.4
P/E Ratio	19.2-11.8	18.1-10.9	16.9-9.5	14.7-10.7	12.3-8.8	16.3-9.0	13.5-9.7
Price Range	28¾-17¾	25⅛-15⅛	22-12⅜	23¼-16⅞	19-13½	23⅝-13	18⅛-13

Statistics are as originally reported.

OFFICERS:
C.T. Knabusch, Chmn. & Pres.
E.J. Shoemaker, Vice-Chmn. & Exec. V.P.- Engineering
G.M. Hardy, Sec. & Treas.

INCORPORATED: MI, May, 1941

PRINCIPAL OFFICE: 1284 N. Telegraph Rd., Monroe, MI 48161-3390

TELEPHONE NUMBER: (313) 242-1444

NO. OF EMPLOYEES: 377

ANNUAL MEETING: In July

SHAREHOLDERS: 2,929

INSTITUTIONAL HOLDINGS:
No. of Institutions: 72
Shares Held: 3,834,093

REGISTRAR(S):

TRANSFER AGENT(S):

LABATT (JOHN) LTD.

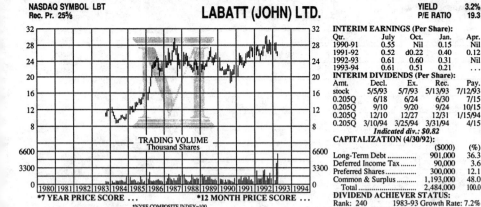

TRADING VOLUME
Thousand Shares

*7 YEAR PRICE SCORE ...   *12 MONTH PRICE SCORE ...
*NYSE COMPOSITE INDEX=100

INTERIM EARNINGS (Per Share):

Qtr.	July	Oct.	Jan.	Apr.
1990-91	0.55	Nil	0.15	Nil
1991-92	0.52	d0.22	0.40	0.12
1992-93	0.61	0.60	0.31	Nil
1993-94	0.61	0.51	0.21	...

INTERIM DIVIDENDS (Per Share):

Amt.	Decl.	Ex.	Rec.	Pay.
stock	5/5/93	5/7/93	5/13/93	7/12/93
0.205Q	6/18	6/24	6/30	7/15
0.205Q	9/10	9/20	9/24	10/15
0.205Q	12/10	12/27	12/31	1/15/94
0.205Q	3/10/94	3/25/94	3/31/94	4/15

Indicated div.: $0.82

CAPITALIZATION (4/30/92):

	($000)	(%)
Long-Term Debt	901,000	36.3
Deferred Income Tax	90,000	3.6
Preferred Shares	300,000	12.1
Common & Surplus	1,193,000	48.0
Total	2,484,000	100.0

DIVIDEND ACHIEVER STATUS:
Rank: 240   1983-93 Growth Rate: 7.2%
Total Years of Dividend Growth: 21

RECENT DEVELOPMENTS: For the quarter ended 10/31/93, earnings from continuing operations slid to $47.0 million from $51.0 million for the corresponding period last year. The positive impact of improved brewing segment earnings was more than offset by a decline in entertainment segment earnings, as well as by higher interest expense. In addition, segment earnings last year were favorably affected by the inclusion of certain items of sundry income. Gross sales totaled $805.0 million, down from $824.0 million a year ago. The brewing segment's net sales increased by 7% over last year to $470.0 million. Net sales for the entertainment segment were down 10% from last year, totaling $189.0 million. The company's share of the Canadian market was boosted to a record 44% in 1993, primarily due to the success of Labatt Genuine Draft and Labatt Ice Beer.

BUSINESS

JOHN LABATT LIMITED's two primary businesses are beverage (brewing) and broadcasting. The brewing segment is comprised of three divisions: Labatt Breweries of Canada, Labatt's USA and Labatt Breweries of Europe. The entertainment segment has three divisions: the JLL Broadcast Group, the Toronto Blue Jays Baseball Club and the John Labatt Entertainment Group. The company operates principally in Canada, the United States and Europe--specifically the United Kingdom and Italy. At the end of 1992, Labatt completed the disposition of its food-related businesses. On 6/4/93, the Company completed the distribution of the Canadian dairy operations directly to the common shareholders.

ANNUAL EARNINGS AND DIVIDENDS PER SHARE

	4/30/93	4/30/92	4/30/91	4/30/90	4/30/89	4/30/88	4/30/87
Earnings Per Share	③1.32	①0.83	1.10	②2.00	1.80	1.92	1.73
Dividends Per Share	0.815	0.785	0.75	0.71	0.655	0.58	0.522
Dividend Payout %	61.7	94.6	68.2	35.5	36.4	30.2	30.2

① Before disc. oper. ② Amounts in Canadian dollars ③ 2-for-1 stk. split, 7/86 & 9/83.

ANNUAL FINANCIAL DATA

RECORD OF EARNINGS (IN MILLIONS):

	4/30/93	4/30/92	4/30/91	4/30/90	4/30/89	4/30/88	4/30/87
Total Revenue	2,135.0	3,837.0	4,760.0	4,681.0	4,856.8	4,611.0	3,782.2
Costs and Expenses	1,807.0	3,415.0	4,350.0	4,283.0	4,466.5	4,209.0	3,423.1
Depreciation & Amort	89.0	125.0	150.0	134.0	127.0	114.3	90.3
Operating Income	239.0	297.0	260.0	264.0	193.9	220.8	209.0
Earn Bef Income Taxes	194.0	130.0	158.0	231.0	184.9	227.8	221.8
Total Income Taxes	64.0	37.0	50.0	72.0	56.6	85.9	95.4
Net Income	133.0	①85.0	109.0	169.0	135.1	140.6	125.2
Aver. Shs. Outstg. (000)	80,000	77,560	76,180	75,090	73,990	73,363	72,391

① Before disc. oper.

BALANCE SHEET (IN MILLIONS):

Cash and Cash Equivalents	276.0	766.0	300.0	300.0	515.2	200.0	200.0
Accounts Receivable	286.0	406.0	409.0	418.0	307.3	301.5	373.9
Total Inventories	192.0	359.0	444.0	397.0	344.7	407.9	355.0
Gross Property	1,320.0	1,715.0	2,032.0	1,843.0	1,554.5	1,523.1	1,291.1
Accumulated Depreciation	784.0	688.0	775.0	662.0	552.7	531.0	453.7
Long-Term Debt	932.0	901.0	688.0	821.0	821.7	772.3	673.7
Net Stockholders' Equity	1,206.0	1,493.0	1,404.0	1,367.0	1,108.8	867.7	770.9
Total Assets	3,020.0	3,320.0	3,138.0	2,946.0	2,756.5	2,538.0	2,355.0
Total Current Assets	1,187.0	1,634.0	1,234.0	1,184.0	1,226.9	964.1	985.4
Total Current Liabilities	1,703.0	836.0	913.0	628.0	683.0	736.0	780.7
Net Working Capital	255.0	798.0	321.0	556.0	543.9	228.1	204.7
Year End Shs Outstg (000)	85,000	78,350	76,560	75,790	74,630	73,792	72,730

STATISTICAL RECORD:

Operating Profit Margin %	11.2	7.7	5.5	5.6	4.0	4.8	5.5
Book Value Per Share	14.19	15.23	14.42	14.08	12.85	11.76	10.60
Return on Equity %	11.0	5.7	7.8	12.4	12.2	16.2	16.2
Return on Assets %	4.4	2.6	3.5	5.7	4.9	5.5	5.3
Average Yield %	3.3	3.3	2.9	2.8	2.3	2.7	
P/E Ratio		33.4-24.2	22.6-16.7	13.8-10.6	14.6-11.4	15.5-10.5	14.5-8.2
Price Range	30⅜-18⅜	27¾-20⅛	24⅞-18⅜	27½-21⅛	26¼-20½	29¾-20⅛	25-14¼

Statistics are as originally reported. Figures are in Canadian dollars.
Figures for 1993 reflect the disposition of the Food and Dairy segments.

OFFICERS:
S. Pollock, Chmn.
S.M. Oland, Vice-Chmn. & Group Chmn.
G.S. Taylor, Pres. & C.E.O.
G.S. Branget, Treas.

PRINCIPAL OFFICE: Labatt House, BCE Place 181 Bay Street, Suite 200, P.O Toronto, Ontario, Canada M5J 2T3

TELEPHONE NUMBER: (416) 865-6000
FAX: (416) 865-6074
NO. OF EMPLOYEES: 5,700
ANNUAL MEETING: In September
SHAREHOLDERS: 12,500
INSTITUTIONAL HOLDINGS:
No. of Institutions: 62
Shares Held: 8,449,012

REGISTRAR(S): The R-M Trust Company, Toronto, Ontario, Canada M5C 2W9

TRANSFER AGENT(S): The R-M Trust Company, Toronto, Ontario, Canada M5C 2W9

LANCE, INC.

YIELD 5.3%
P/E RATIO 18.0

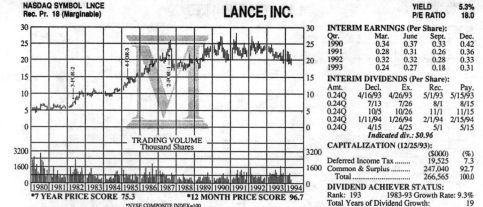

*7 YEAR PRICE SCORE 75.3   ***12 MONTH PRICE SCORE 96.7**
*NYSE COMPOSITE INDEX=100

INTERIM EARNINGS (Per Share):

Qtr.	Mar.	June	Sept.	Dec.
1990	0.34	0.37	0.33	0.42
1991	0.28	0.31	0.26	0.36
1992	0.32	0.32	0.28	0.33
1993	0.24	0.27	0.18	0.31

INTERIM DIVIDENDS (Per Share):

Amt.	Decl.	Ex.	Rec.	Pay.
0.24Q	4/16/93	4/26/93	5/1/93	5/15/93
0.24Q	7/13	7/26	8/1	8/15
0.24Q	10/5	10/26	11/1	11/15
0.24Q	1/11/94	1/26/94	2/1/94	2/15/94
0.24Q	4/15	4/25	5/1	5/15

Indicated div.: $0.96

CAPITALIZATION (12/25/93):

	($000)	(%)
Deferred Income Tax	19,525	7.3
Common & Surplus	247,040	92.7
Total	266,565	100.0

DIVIDEND ACHIEVER STATUS:
Rank: 193   1983-93 Growth Rate: 9.3%
Total Years of Dividend Growth: 19

RECENT DEVELOPMENTS: For the year ended 12/25/93, net income decreased to $30.8 million, or $0.99 per share, compared with $39.1 million, or $1.25 per share, last year. Net sales and other operating revenue were up 2.5% to $472.8 million compared with $461.4 million last year. For the quarter, net income decreased to $9.7 million, or $0.31 per share, compared with $10.4 million, or $0.33 per share, last year. Net sales and other operating revenue were up 4.6% to $147 million compared with $140.6 million last year. The decrease in net income is attributed primarily to higher production costs at LNCE's Vista Bakery plant, lower sales of higher margin products, an increase in selling expenses and the impact of the enactment of the new federal tax act which increased the corporate tax rate to 35%. The increase in net sales and other operating revenue is attributed primarily to increased unit volume.

BUSINESS

LANCE, INC. manufactures snack foods and bakery products that are sold and distributed through the Company's own sales organization to service stations, drug stores, restaurants, supermarkets, and similar establishments. Through its subsidiary, Midwest Biscuit Co., Lance manufactures cookies and crackers, which are sold to wholesale grocers, supermarket chains and distributors. Through its Nutrition-Pak subsidiary, the Company manufactures nutritional food products on a contractual basis. In addition, the Company's Tri Plas, Inc. subsidiary, manufactures injection molded plastic containers which are sold through its own sales organization principally to food processing and retail fast food industries.

QUARTERLY DATA

(12/25/93)($000)	Rev	Inc
1st Quarter	106,423	7,058
2nd Quarter	113,184	8,442
3rd Quarter	106,140	5,638
4th Quarter	147,039	9,660

ANNUAL EARNINGS AND DIVIDENDS PER SHARE

	12/25/93	12/26/92	12/28/91	12/29/90	12/30/89	12/31/88	12/26/87
Earnings Per Share	0.99	1.25	1.21	1.46	1.42	1.23	1.17
Dividends Per Share	0.96	0.92	0.88	0.82	0.72	0.66	① 0.585
Dividend Payout %	97.0	73.6	72.0	56.2	50.7	53.7	50.0

① 2-for-1 stk. split, 8/87.

ANNUAL FINANCIAL DATA

RECORD OF EARNINGS (IN THOUSANDS):

Net Sales & Other Oper Revs	472,786	461,449	449,861	445,962	432,140	407,683	380,020
Costs and Expenses	402,847	383,856	377,048	363,552	350,257	331,205	305,055
Depreciation	24,747	23,227	21,823	20,184	18,607	17,197	16,011
Profit From Operations	45,192	54,366	50,990	62,226	63,276	59,281	58,954
Income Bef Income Taxes	50,707	60,162	58,673	70,463	69,864	60,381	64,588
Total Income Taxes	19,531	21,018	20,961	24,736	25,001	21,238	26,609
Net Income	① 31,176	39,144	37,712	45,727	44,863	39,143	37,979
Aver. Shs. Outstg.	31,236	31,299	31,268	31,377	31,622	31,745	32,447

① Before acctg. change dr$378,000.

BALANCE SHEET (IN THOUSANDS):

Cash and Cash Equivalents	39,556	58,973	75,902	60,692	64,373	53,219	69,010
Receivables, Net	36,713	36,551	35,651	32,627	32,423	30,315	27,948
Inventories	33,673	32,131	27,728	32,981	33,251	33,171	20,255
Gross Property	356,058	345,310	319,558	301,641	270,959	251,230	225,683
Accumulated Depreciation	182,419	166,799	165,802	146,899	130,620	115,620	105,888
Net Stockholders' Equity	247,040	252,126	242,344	231,882	220,219	199,087	187,808
Total Assets	308,474	313,446	300,290	288,621	276,331	255,620	241,843
Total Current Assets	109,942	127,655	139,281	126,300	130,047	116,705	117,213
Total Current Liabilities	31,490	32,232	29,466	28,614	28,742	31,956	30,739
Net Working Capital	78,452	95,423	109,815	97,686	101,305	84,749	86,474
Year End Shares Outstg	31,001	31,279	31,283	31,252	31,592	31,610	31,965

STATISTICAL RECORD:

Operating Profit Margin %	9.6	11.8	11.3	14.0	14.6	14.5	15.5
Book Value Per Share	7.97	8.06	7.75	7.42	6.97	6.30	5.88
Return on Equity %	12.6	15.5	15.6	19.7	20.4	19.7	20.2
Return on Assets %	10.1	12.5	12.6	15.8	16.2	15.3	15.7
Average Yield %	4.4	3.8	3.6	3.5	3.4	3.4	2.7
P/E Ratio	24.8-19.0	21.8-17.0	23.3-16.5	18.7-13.2	17.6-12.1	17.7-13.6	22.2-14.3
Price Range	24¾-19	27¼-21¼	28¼-20	27¼-19¼	25-17¼	21¾-16¾	26-16¾

Statistics are as originally reported.

OFFICERS:
J.W. Disher, Chmn., Pres. & C.E.O.
E.D. Leake, Treas. & Asst. Sec.
J.W. Helms, Jr., Sec. & Asst. Treas.

INCORPORATED: NC, Dec., 1926

PRINCIPAL OFFICE: 8600 South Blvd.,
Charlotte, NC 28232

TELEPHONE NUMBER: (704) 554-1421

FAX: (704) 554-5562

NO. OF EMPLOYEES: 5,838

ANNUAL MEETING: In April

SHAREHOLDERS: 5,835

INSTITUTIONAL HOLDINGS:
No. of Institutions: 78
Shares Held: 11,489,960

REGISTRAR(S):

TRANSFER AGENT(S): Wachovia Bank & Trust Co., N.A., Winston-Salem, NC 27102

LEE ENTERPRISES, INC.

	YIELD	2.5%
	P/E RATIO	18.5

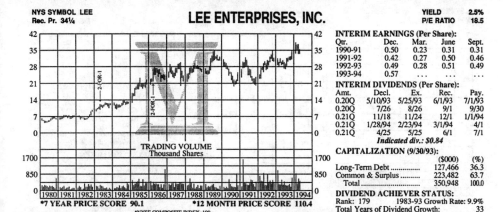

*NYSE COMPOSITE INDEX=100

*7 YEAR PRICE SCORE 90.1   *12 MONTH PRICE SCORE 110.4

TRADING VOLUME
Thousand Shares

INTERIM EARNINGS (Per Share):

Qtr.	Dec.	Mar.	June	Sept.
1990-91	0.50	0.23	0.31	0.31
1991-92	0.42	0.27	0.50	0.46
1992-93	0.49	0.28	0.51	0.49
1993-94	0.57	...	...	...

INTERIM DIVIDENDS (Per Share):

Amt.	Decl.	Ex.	Rec.	Pay.
0.20Q	5/10/93	5/25/93	6/1/93	7/1/93
0.20Q	7/26	8/26	9/1	9/30
0.21Q	11/18	11/24	12/1	1/1/94
0.21Q	1/28/94	2/23/94	3/1/94	4/1
0.21Q	4/25	5/25	6/1	7/1

Indicated div.: $0.84

CAPITALIZATION (9/30/93):

	($000)	(%)
Long-Term Debt	127,466	36.3
Common & Surplus	223,482	63.7
Total	350,948	100.0

DIVIDEND ACHIEVER STATUS:
Rank: 179   1983-93 Growth Rate: 9.9%
Total Years of Dividend Growth: 33

RECENT DEVELOPMENTS: For the quarter ended 12/31/93, net income increased 15.8% to $13.3 million compared with $11.5 million a year ago. Revenues rose 6% to $102.1 million from $96.3 million. The improved results reflected strong advertising revenues due primarily to greater classified advertising. The growth in classified advertising was attributable to strengthened automotive and real estate segments and higher levels of advertising by individual customers.

PROSPECTS: Increased taxes and interest rates may adversely affect consumer spending, and subsequently advertising, in the near term. The NAPP subsidiary will benefit from the exit of a major European producer of newspaper letterpress printing plates. Upon this exit, NAPP and BASF entered into a distribution agreement for the European market. The agreement provides for payment in U.S. dollars which substantially reduces NAPP's exposure to foreign currency exchange rates.

BUSINESS

LEE ENTERPRISES, INC. is a diversified media company in the business information and entertainment industry. It publishes daily newspapers in Illinois, Iowa, Minnesota, Montana, Nebraska, North and South Dakota, Oregon, and Wisconsin; operates television stations in Hawaii, Arizona, Nebraska, Oregon and West Virginia; participates in cable television services in Iowa and Wisconsin; and serves the graphic arts industry through NAPP Systems Inc., the world's leading producer of photosensitive polymer printing plates for newspapers. Lee and its subsidiaries purchase newprint, from its core raw material, from U.S. and Canadian producers. The Company owns and operates 8 television stations, and publishes 19 daily newspapers and 34 weekly publications.

REVENUES

(9/30/93)	($000)	(%)
Newspapers	223,423	61.3
Broadcasting.............	81,284	22.5
Media Products & Services	58,651	16.2
Total	363,358	100.0

ANNUAL EARNINGS AND DIVIDENDS PER SHARE

	9/30/93	9/30/92	9/30/91	9/30/90	9/30/89	9/30/88	9/30/87
Earnings Per Share	1.76	1.65	1.35	1.82	1.74	1.63	1.74
Dividends Per Share	0.80	0.77	0.76	0.72	0.68	0.64	0.60
Dividend Payout %	45.5	46.7	56.3	39.6	39.1	39.3	34.5

ANNUAL FINANCIAL DATA

RECORD OF EARNINGS (IN THOUSANDS):

Total Operating Revenue	372,907	363,918	346,260	287,477	269,463	252,537	237,555
Costs and Expenses	266,992	258,889	251,933	200,574	187,256	171,017	161,664
Depreciation & Amort	24,776	23,726	23,868	17,336	13,981	12,641	11,625
Operating Income	81,139	81,303	70,459	69,567	68,226	68,879	64,266
Inc Bef Taxes on Income	67,930	66,006	53,244	60,631	62,833	61,536	75,816
Income Taxes	26,694	27,514	21,743	17,137	19,786	20,615	31,243
Net Income	41,236	38,492	31,501	43,494	43,047	40,921	44,573
Aver. Shs. Outstg.	23,460	23,341	23,292	23,928	24,794	25,082	25,624

BALANCE SHEET (IN THOUSANDS):

Cash and Cash Equivalents	62,572	48,071	18,324	16,105	20,506	29,689	25,158
Receivables, Net	45,421	45,638	41,835	50,824	34,195	30,728	36,341
Inventories	11,177	12,489	13,934	11,955	3,552	2,934	2,294
Gross Property	204,413	197,652	196,369	188,365	140,796	119,105	106,070
Accumulated Depreciation	129,057	120,854	112,189	101,255	78,765	72,462	64,676
Long-Term Debt	127,466	153,174	166,074	177,743	76,327	73,840	75,553
Net Stockholders' Equity	223,482	203,812	183,035	173,343	176,382	167,196	152,009
Total Assets	482,317	474,830	459,269	465,777	328,800	307,837	295,589
Total Current Assets	135,122	125,925	94,457	91,057	69,652	74,035	71,861
Total Current Liabilities	91,708	85,991	76,925	85,280	50,774	41,811	44,526
Net Working Capital	43,414	39,934	17,532	5,777	18,878	32,224	27,335
Year End Shares Outstg	23,100	23,128	23,070	23,247	24,198	24,717	24,846

STATISTICAL RECORD:

Operating Profit Margin %	21.8	22.3	20.3	24.2	25.3	27.3	27.1
Return on Equity %	18.5	18.9	17.2	25.1	24.4	24.5	29.3
Return on Assets %	8.5	8.1	6.9	9.3	13.1	13.3	15.1
Average Yield %	2.6	2.7	2.9	2.8	2.3	2.5	2.4
P/E Ratio	19.9-15.3	21.1-13.9	23.6-14.9	17.1-10.9	20.0-14.2	18.0-13.3	17.2-11.5
Price Range	35-27	34⁷⁄₈-23	31⁷⁄₈-20⅛	31⅛-19¾	34¼-24¾	29⅜-21¾	29⁷⁄₈-20

Statistics are as originally reported.

OFFICERS:
L.G. Schermer, Chmn.
R.D. Gottlieb, Pres. & C.E.O.
L.L. Bloom, V.P.-Fin., C.F.O. & Treas.

INCORPORATED: DE, Sep., 1950

PRINCIPAL OFFICE: 400 Putnam Building
215 N. Main St., Davenport, IA 52801-1924

TELEPHONE NUMBER: (319) 383-2100

NO. OF EMPLOYEES: 639 (approx.)

ANNUAL MEETING: In January

SHAREHOLDERS: 3,381 com.; 3,191 class B.

INSTITUTIONAL HOLDINGS:
No. of Institutions: 100
Shares Held: 8,668,720

REGISTRAR(S): First Chicago Trust Co. of New York, New York, NY 10008

TRANSFER AGENT(S): First Chicago Trust Co. of New York, New York, NY 10008

LEGG MASON, INC.

YIELD	2.1%
P/E RATIO	6.3

TRADING VOLUME
Thousand Shares

1980	1981	1982	1983	1984	1985	1986	1987	1988	1989	1990	1991	1992	1993	1994

*7 YEAR PRICE SCORE 120.7   ***12 MONTH PRICE SCORE 95.6**
*NYSE COMPOSITE INDEX=100

INTERIM EARNINGS (Per Share):

Qtr.	June	Sept.	Dec.	Mar.
1990-91	0.30	0.33	0.24	0.35
1991-92	0.37	0.41	0.50	0.58
1992-93	0.74	0.61	0.59	0.66
1993-94	0.68	0.94	0.81	...

INTERIM DIVIDENDS (Per Share):

Amt.	Decl.	Ex.	Rec.	Pay.
5-for-4	7/27/93	9/27/93	9/8/93	9/24/93
0.10Q	7/27	10/4	10/8	10/25
0.10Q	10/18	12/10	12/16	1/10/94
0.10Q	1/21/94	3/11/94	3/17/94	4/11
0.10Q	4/15	6/10	6/16	7/11

Indicated div.: $0.40

CAPITALIZATION (3/31/93):

	($000)	(%)
Common & Surplus	176,928	100.0
Total	176,928	100.0

DIVIDEND ACHIEVER STATUS:

Rank: 6	1983-93 Growth Rate: 26.7%
Total Years of Dividend Growth:	10

RECENT DEVELOPMENTS: Net income for the three months ended 12/31/93 was $9.9 million compared with $7.0 million in the comparable quarter of 1992. Revenues totaled $103.1 million, up 21% from the prior-year period. Investment advisory and related fee revenues jumped 30% from last year to $16.8 million as investment banking revenues increased 25% to $23.3 million. Commission revenues were $35.4 million, up 19%. For the first nine months, net income was $21.5 million while revenues were $301.2 million.

PROSPECTS: LM has established Legg Mason Trust Co. to provide clients with personal and employee benefit plan trust services. The robust activity of the market continues to provide the record earnings, particularly for the investment advisory business. In order to maintain a satisfactory level of growth once the activity cools off, LM is developing new products and services, implementing measures to increase productivity and paying attention to expense control.

BUSINESS

LEGG MASON, INC. is a holding company which provides securities brokerage, investment advisory, corporate and public finance, and mortgage banking services to individuals, institutions, corporations and municipalities. The Company serves brokerage clients through 83 offices. As investment advisors, the Company manages $15 billion in assets for private accounts and mutual funds. Its mortgage banking subsidiaries have direct and master servicing responsibility for $16 billion of commercial mortgages.

REVENUES

(3/31/93)	($000)	(%)
Commissions	117,305	34.9
Principal		
Transactions	55,000	16.4
Invest Advis & Rltd		
Fees	50,915	15.1
	66	
Invest banking	575	19.8
Interest	23,973	7.1
Other	22,579	6.7
Total	336,347	100.0

ANNUAL EARNINGS AND DIVIDENDS PER SHARE

	3/31/93	3/31/92	3/31/91	3/31/90	3/31/89	3/31/88	3/31/87
Earnings Per Share	2.61	1.86	1.22	① 1.10	0.56	0.70	1.17
Dividends Per Share	0.296	0.264	0.232	0.20	0.18	0.164	② 0.136
Dividend Payout %	11.3	14.2	19.1	18.1	32.1	23.3	11.6

Note: 5-for-4stk.split,9/24/93. ① Per primary share ② 5-for-4 stk. split, 9/86.

ANNUAL FINANCIAL DATA

RECORD OF EARNINGS (IN THOUSANDS):

Principal Transactions	55,000	53,191	61,808	56,527	50,249	46,432	28,317
Commissions	117,305	112,556	91,233	99,954	79,841	92,008	75,724
Total Revenues	336,347	292,356	242,723	243,676	213,447	215,571	148,651
Compensation & Benefits	193,857	164,595	132,277	132,639	114,512	122,506	82,793
Interest Expense	11,629	13,433	14,198	17,095	18,521	11,454	7,764
Sell, Gen. & Admin. Exp.	243,055	212,171	178,901	179,654	160,759	163,680	107,519
Earn Bef Income Taxes	48,983	35,015	21,222	19,532	9,633	12,728	19,812
Income Taxes	18,780	13,898	8,309	7,687	3,628	5,152	9,517
Net Income	30,203	21,117	12,913	11,845	6,005	7,576	10,295
Aver. Shs. Outstg. (000)	11,574	11,386	10,626	10,719	10,685	10,765	8,823

BALANCE SHEET (IN THOUSANDS):

Cash & Marketable Secs.	204,864	221,837	161,605	33,740	74,513	108,221	94,173
Customer Receivables	208,273	164,960	176,350	269,800	210,322	186,749	186,945
Rec Fr Brokers & Dealers	8,296	5,533	3,949	10,078	13,104	16,160	12,360
Securities Inventory	112,082	94,648	64,562	53,316	42,415	64,053	68,943
Total Assets	640,454	579,883	496,266	432,556	419,202	444,097	430,188
Payable to Customers	267,316	236,979	241,383	201,919	188,497	180,830	182,195
Long-Term Debt	34,597	35,020	35,120	35,120	35,120	35,545	36,369	36,419
Net Stockholders' Equity	176,928	147,957	126,363	116,080	107,794	104,057	98,399
Year End Shares Outstg	11,248	11,062	10,379	10,310	10,424	10,461	10,469

STATISTICAL RECORD:

Return on Assets %	4.7	3.6	2.6	2.7	1.4	1.7	2.4
Return on Equity %	17.1	14.3	10.2	10.2	5.6	7.3	10.5
Book Value Per Share	15.73	13.38	12.18	11.26	10.34	9.95	9.40
Average Yield %	1.6	1.8	2.1	1.9	2.0	1.2	0.8
P/E Ratio	8.3-5.8	10.5-5.4	11.0-6.9	11.8-7.5	18.3-13.6	28.0-10.9	17.4-10.9
Price Range	21⅝-15¼	19½-10⅛	13⅜-8⅜	13-8¼	10¼-7⅝	19⅝-7⅝	20⅜-12¾

Statistics are as originally reported.

OFFICERS:
R.A. Mason, Chmn. & C.E.O.
C.A. Bacigalupo, Sr. V.P. & Sec.
T.C. Scheve, Treasurer

PRINCIPAL OFFICE: 111 South Calvert Street, P.O. Box 1476, Baltimore, MD 21203-1476

TELEPHONE NUMBER: (410) 539-0000

NO. OF EMPLOYEES: 2,436

ANNUAL MEETING: In July

SHAREHOLDERS: 1,857

INSTITUTIONAL HOLDINGS:
No. of Institutions: Not Available
Shares Held: Not Available

REGISTRAR(S):

TRANSFER AGENT(S):

LEGGETT & PLATT, INC.

	YIELD	1.6%
	P/E RATIO	17.5

TRADING VOLUME
Thousand Shares

*7 YEAR PRICE SCORE 157.6   *12 MONTH PRICE SCORE 103.3
*NYSE COMPOSITE INDEX=100

INTERIM EARNINGS (Per Share):

Qtr.	Mar.	June	Sept.	Dec.
1990	0.36	0.37	0.30	d0.18
1991	0.22	0.28	0.34	0.28
1992	0.38	0.39	0.46	0.41
1993	0.48	0.51	0.54	0.56

INTERIM DIVIDENDS (Per Share):

Amt.	Decl.	Ex.	Rec.	Pay.
0.13Q	5/12/93	5/24/93	5/28/93	6/15/93
0.14Q	8/11	8/23	8/27	9/15
0.14Q	11/10	11/19	11/26	12/15
0.15Q	2/9/94	2/18/94	2/25/94	3/15/94
0.15Q	5/12	5/23	5/27	6/15

Indicated div.: $0.60

CAPITALIZATION (12/31/93):

	($000)	(%)
Long-Term Debt	165,800	22.9
Deferred Income Tax	43,200	6.0
Common & Surplus	515,600	71.1
Total	724,600	100.0

DIVIDEND ACHIEVER STATUS:
Rank: 139   1983-93 Growth Rate: 11.2%
Total Years of Dividend Growth: 24

RECENT DEVELOPMENTS: For the year ended 12/31/93, net income increased 31.5% to $85.9 million from $65.4 million in 1992. Sales were up 16.1% to $1.53 billion compared with $1.32 billion the previous year. The 1992 figures were restated to reflect pooling of interests in the 1993 acquisition of Hanes Holding Co. Profit margins remained favorable due to recent acquisitions performing in line with expectations. As a result, growth in operating profits exceeded growth in sales.

PROSPECTS: Recent acquisitions including Hanes Holding Company, VWR Textiles and Supplies and several wire mill operations will continue to enhance results for LEG. These acquisitions are expected to increase 1994 sales by $250 million and improve earnings by $0.15 to $0.20 per share. Operating efficiencies will result from higher production volume and tighter control over expenses. Future performance will benefit from efforts to better utilize human and capital resources.

BUSINESS

LEGGETT & PLATT, INC. specializes in manufacturing and marketing components and other related products for the home furnishings industry and diversified markets. Principle products for the home furnishings industry include a broad line of components used by companies that make furniture and bedding for homes, offices and institutions. Select lines of sleep-related finished furniture and carpet cushioning materials are also produced and sold in these markets. The Company's diversified products have manufacturing technologies and processes similar to those used in making its home furnishings products. However, the diversified products are sold in many different markets, unrelated to the home furnishings industry.

BUSINESS LINE ANALYSIS

(12/31/93)	Rev(%)	Inc(%)
Furnishings Products	75.2	77.8
Diversified	24.8	22.2
Total	100.0	100.0

ANNUAL EARNINGS AND DIVIDENDS PER SHARE

	1993	1992	1991	1990	1989	1988	1987
Earnings Per Share	2.09	1.64	1.11	0.84	1.33	1.11	1.14
Dividends Per Share	0.54	☐ 0.57	0.425	0.41	0.355	0.31	0.21
Dividend Payout %	25.8	34.8	38.3	49.1	26.8	28.1	18.4

☐ 2-for-1 stk split, 6/16/92

ANNUAL FINANCIAL DATA

RECORD OF EARNINGS (IN MILLIONS):

	1993	1992	1991	1990	1989	1988	1987
Total Revenues	1,526.7	1,170.5	1,081.8	1,088.6	991.6	809.9	649.2
Costs and Expenses	1,324.8	1,023.5	967.3	986.9	874.7	719.0	565.1
Depreciation & Amort	45.3	38.2	36.4	34.4	28.4	23.9	17.6
Operating Profit	156.6	108.8	78.1	87.7	88.5	67.0	66.5
Earn Bef Income Taxes	141.0	99.8	63.9	50.6	75.7	60.0	64.0
Income Taxes	55.1	37.3	24.5	21.2	29.8	22.3	26.6
Net Income	85.9	62.5	39.4	29.4	45.9	37.7	37.5
Aver. Shs. Outstg. (000)	41,100	38,052	35,450	35,218	34,698	34,172	32,936

BALANCE SHEET (IN MILLIONS):

	1993	1992	1991	1990	1989	1988	1987
Cash and Cash Equivalents	0.4	4.0	5.3	3.3	2.9	7.0	29.6
Total Receivables	...	156.8	140.8	...	...	...	...
Total Inventories	209.1	161.1	157.3	172.0	144.2	122.4	92.8
Gross Property	571.2	438.5	418.1	380.0	350.1	295.5	223.4
Accumulated Depreciation	258.1	207.8	184.0	155.2	140.9	119.3	95.5
Long-Term Debt	165.8	101.5	179.4	212.8	147.5	106.8	83.6
Net Stockholders' Equity	515.6	425.2	332.6	302.6	281.6	245.4	209.5
Total Assets	901.9	678.0	656.1	676.1	568.3	477.6	384.3
Total Current Assets	435.6	340.2	321.7	342.4	292.8	250.5	208.2
Total Current Liabilities	166.2	118.6	110.6	128.0	112.7	103.1	78.0
Net Working Capital	269.4	221.6	211.1	214.5	180.1	147.3	130.2
Year End Shs Outstg (000)	40,318	38,165	35,299	34,921	34,472	34,046	32,210

STATISTICAL RECORD:

	1993	1992	1991	1990	1989	1988	1987
Operating Profit Margin %	10.3	9.3	7.2	6.2	8.9	8.3	10.3
Book Value Per Share	9.84	9.59	7.75	7.13	7.41	6.60	6.15
Return on Equity %	16.7	14.7	11.8	9.7	16.3	15.4	17.9
Return on Assets %	9.5	9.2	6.0	4.4	8.1	7.9	9.8
Average Yield %	1.3	2.1	2.6	2.8	2.4	2.4	1.5
P/E Ratio	24.0-15.7	21.5-11.4	17.2-11.7	22.6-11.9	13.2-8.9	14.0-9.7	16.5-8.9
Price Range	50⅛-32¾	35¼-18¾	19⅛-13	19-10	17½-11⅞	15½-10¾	18½-10

Statistics are as originally reported.

OFFICERS:
H.M. Cornell, Jr., Chmn. & C.E.O.
F.E. Wright, Pres. & C.O.O.
T.D. Sherman, V.P., Gen. Couns. & Sec.

INCORPORATED: MO, 1901

PRINCIPAL OFFICE: No. 1—Leggett Rd., Carthage, MO 64836

TELEPHONE NUMBER: (417) 358-8131
FAX: (417) 358-6045
NO. OF EMPLOYEES: 13,000 (approx.)
ANNUAL MEETING: In May
SHAREHOLDERS: 6,969 (approx.)
INSTITUTIONAL HOLDINGS:
No. of Institutions: 143
Shares Held: 10,751,487

REGISTRAR(S): Mellon Securities Trust Co., New York, NY

TRANSFER AGENT(S): Mellon Securities Trust Company, New York, NY

LG&E ENERGY CORP.

YIELD 5.9%
P/E RATIO 21.3

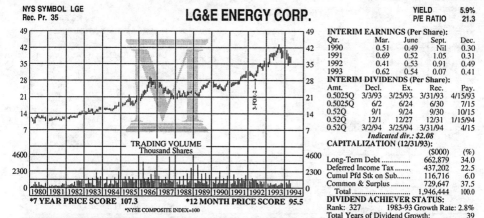

INTERIM EARNINGS (Per Share):

Qtr.	Mar.	June	Sept.	Dec.
1990	0.51	0.49	Nil	0.30
1991	0.69	0.52	1.05	0.31
1992	0.41	0.53	0.91	0.49
1993	0.62	0.54	0.07	0.41

INTERIM DIVIDENDS (Per Share):

Amt.	Decl.	Ex.	Rec.	Pay.
0.5025Q	3/3/93	3/25/93	3/31/93	4/15/93
0.5025Q	6/2	6/24	6/30	7/15
0.52Q	9/1	9/24	9/30	10/15
0.52Q	12/1	12/27	12/31	1/15/94
0.52Q	3/2/94	3/25/94	3/31/94	4/15

Indicated div.: $2.08

CAPITALIZATION (12/31/93):

	($000)	(%)
Long-Term Debt	662,879	34.0
Deferred Income Tax	437,202	22.5
Cumul Pfd Stk on Sub	116,716	6.0
Common & Surplus	729,647	37.5
Total	1,946,444	100.0

DIVIDEND ACHIEVER STATUS:
Rank: 327   1983-93 Growth Rate: 2.8%
Total Years of Dividend Growth: 39

TRADING VOLUME
Thousand Shares

| 1980 | 1981 | 1982 | 1983 | 1984 | 1985 | 1986 | 1987 | 1988 | 1989 | 1990 | 1991 | 1992 | 1993 | 1994 |

*7 YEAR PRICE SCORE 107.3   ***12 MONTH PRICE SCORE 95.5**

*NYSE COMPOSITE INDEX=100

RECENT DEVELOPMENTS: For the year ended 12/31/93, income from continuing operations was $86.8 million compared with $78.6 million last year. Revenues were $900.0 million, up 7.8%. The improved results reflect a return to more normal weather patterns in the Company's service area in Kentucky. Non-utility earnings benefitted from strong construction profits by LG&E Power. Income from continuing operations for the quarter ended 12/31/93 was $15.0 million compared with $16.0 million in the prior year.

PROSPECTS: The Company has agreed to sell its partnership interest in Natural Gas Clearinghouse to NOVA of Alberta. NGE expects to post a pre-tax gain of $87 million from the sale. LGE has a competitive rate structure, low-risk service territory, and clean coal-fired generating capacity. It is not expected that LGE will need additional plant generating capacity until the end of the decade. Consequently, LGE will have limited capital spending requirements.

BUSINESS

LG&E ENERGY CORP. is a diversified energy-services holding company which supplies electricity and natural gas to an estimated 577,000 people in Louisville and surrounding territory in Kentucky. Natural gas is purchased from Texas Gas Transmission Corp. and on the spot-market when possible. Ohio Valley Transmission Corp., a wholly-owned subsidiary, owns and operates Indiana properties. Electric and gas revenues were derived: residential, 33.2% (53.9%); commercial and industrial, 47.1% (35.3%); public authorities, 9.4% (7.8%); and miscellaneous, 10.2 (3.1%). In 1992, revenues were derived from electric, 74.7% and gas, 25.3%.

BUSINESS LINE ANALYSIS

(12/31/93)	Rev(%)	Inc(%)
Electric	63.5	84.8
Gas	22.8	8.6
Non-Utility	13.7	6.6
Total	100.0	100.0

ANNUAL EARNINGS AND DIVIDENDS PER SHARE

	1993	1992	1991	1990	1989	1988	1987
Earnings Per Share	2.47	2.34	2.57	[2] 2.30	2.13	2.47	2.23
Dividends Per Share	2.027	[1] 1.965	1.907	1.863	1.823	1.783	1.743
Dividend Payout %	82.2	84.0	74.1	81.0	85.5	72.3	78.3

[1] 3-for-2 stk split, 5/18/92   [2] Before extraord. item

ANNUAL FINANCIAL DATA

RECORD OF EARNINGS (IN MILLIONS):

	1993	1992	1991	1990	1989	1988	1987
Total Revenues	900.0	834.7	715.0	699.0	676.9	659.7	631.2
Depreciation & Amort	79.9	79.7	76.7	55.6	55.3	50.7	48.1
Maintenance	...	...	49.6	48.5	52.0	52.5	53.5
Net Operating Income	193.0	182.1	137.4	137.0	127.6	129.8	119.4
Interest Charges	48.2	51.2	52.7	53.7	51.1	...	45.6
Net Income	[1] 80.8	75.6	83.0	91.4	66.6	75.6	76.2
Aver. Shs. Outstg. (000)	32,689	32,307	32,256	31,857	31,271	30,615	29,945

[1] Before disc. op. cr$7,435,000.

BALANCE SHEET (IN MILLIONS):

Gross Plant	2,464.1	2,373.5	2,285.5	2,215.2	2,277.4	2,109.6	1,941.1
Accumulated Depreciation	823.1	754.4	693.2	631.4	582.8	507.7	464.2
Utility Plant, Net	1,641.0	1,619.1	1,592.2	1,583.7	1,694.6	1,602.0	1,476.9
Long-term Debt	662.9	686.1	686.5	687.4	613.3	560.1	...
Net Stockholders' Equity	846.4	802.0	791.5	766.0	719.9	696.0	660.7
Total Assets	2,284.8	2,160.6	2,054.2	2,001.4	1,905.3	1,763.1	1,664.5
Year End Shs Outstg (000)	32,956	32,328	32,284	32,106	31,532	30,908	30,224

STATISTICAL RECORD:

Book Value Per Share	22.14	21.20	20.89	20.22	19.12	18.70	17.96
Op. Inc/Net Pl %	11.8	11.2	8.6	8.7	7.5	8.1	8.1
Dep/Gr. Pl %	3.2	3.4	3.4	2.5	2.4	2.4	2.5
Accum. Dep/Gr. Pl %	33.4	31.8	30.3	28.5	25.6	24.1	23.9
Return on Equity %	9.5	9.4	10.5	9.6	9.3	10.9	11.5
Average Yield %	5.3	6.0	6.6	7.2	7.4	8.1	7.4
P/E Ratio	17.6-13.7	15.5-12.4	12.5-9.9	12.2-10.2	13.1-10.0	9.6-8.1	12.2-9.0
Price Range	43⅜-33¾	36⅜-29⅛	32-25⅜	28-23½	27⅞-21⅜	23¾-20⅛	27⅛-20⅛

Statistics are as originally reported.

OFFICERS:
R.W. Hale, Chmn., Pres. & C.E.O.
E.J. Casey, Jr., Exec. V.P. & C.F.O.
C.A. Markel, III, Corp. V.P.-Fin. & Treas.

INCORPORATED: KY, Nov., 1989

PRINCIPAL OFFICE: 220 West Main St. P.O. Box 32030, Louisville, KY 40232-2030

TELEPHONE NUMBER: (502) 627-2000
NO. OF EMPLOYEES: 3,767
ANNUAL MEETING: In May
SHAREHOLDERS: 32,575
INSTITUTIONAL HOLDINGS:
No. of Institutions: 155
Shares Held: 8,704,915

REGISTRAR(S):

TRANSFER AGENT(S): At Company's Office Continental Stock Transfer & Trust Co., New York, NY

LILLY (ELI) & CO.

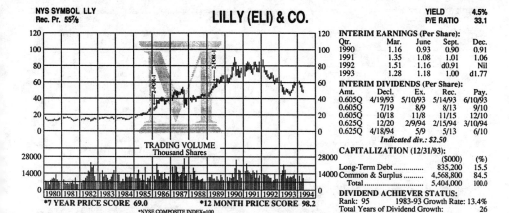

INTERIM EARNINGS (Per Share):

Qtr.	Mar.	June	Sept.	Dec.
1990	1.16	0.93	0.90	0.91
1991	1.35	1.08	1.01	1.06
1992	1.51	1.16	d0.91	Nil
1993	1.28	1.18	1.00	d1.77

INTERIM DIVIDENDS (Per Share):

Amt.	Decl.	Ex.	Rec.	Pay.
0.605Q	4/19/93	5/10/93	5/14/93	6/10/93
0.605Q	7/19	8/9	8/13	9/10
0.605Q	10/18	11/8	11/15	12/10
0.625Q	12/20	2/9/94	2/15/94	3/10/94
0.625Q	4/18/94	5/9	5/13	6/10

Indicated div.: $2.50

CAPITALIZATION (12/31/93):

	($000)	(%)
Long-Term Debt	835,200	15.5
Common & Surplus	4,568,800	84.5
Total	5,404,000	100.0

DIVIDEND ACHIEVER STATUS:
Rank: 95   1983-93 Growth Rate: 13.4%
Total Years of Dividend Growth: 26

TRADING VOLUME
Thousand Shares

*7 YEAR PRICE SCORE 69.0   ***12 MONTH PRICE SCORE 98.2**
*NYSE COMPOSITE INDEX=100

RECENT DEVELOPMENTS: For the year ended 12/31/93, net income before an accounting adjustment declined 40.7% to $491.1 million compared with $827.6 million a year ago. Sales were up 4.6% to $6.45 billion from $6.17 billion. The earnings include a restructuring charge of $856 million for the voluntary early-retirement program, consolidation and rationalization of certain operations, streamlining, and impaired manufacturing assets and write-offs.Pharmaceutical sales rose 7% to $4.75 billion.

PROSPECTS: Margins will be pressured by competitive pricing conditions due to the negotiating power of large customers. Lilly is restructuring operations to reduce costs and improve efficiencies in the changing healthcare industry. Sales will be led by Axid, Humatrope, Humulin, Prozac, and Vancocin HCI. LLY plans to build a new five-story $150 million multipurpose bulk pharmaceutical manufacturing facility to be located at the Company's existing Tippecanoe Laboratories complex in Indiana.

BUSINESS

ELI LILLY & CO. is a global research-based corporation that develops, manufactures, and markets pharmaceuticals, including Ceclor, Keflex®, Kefzol®, lorabid, Nebcin®, Tazidime®, and Vancocin HCI. Medical devices and diagnostics include intravenous fluid-delivery and control systems, implantable cardiac pacemakers and defibrillators, external cardiac defibrillators and monitors, coronary angioplasty catheter systems, peripheral and coronary atherectomy catheter systems, patient vital-signs measurement and monitoring systems, and diagnostic products that include tests incorporating monclonal antibodies. Central-nervous-system agents include Prozac and Darvon®. Other major groups are diabetic-care products which include Humulin and Iletin® and animal health products, that includes Rumensin®, Micotil, Tylan and Coban.

REVENUES

(12/31/93)	($000)	(%)
Anti-Infectives	1,731,400	26.8
Central Nervous System	1,393,600	21.6
Med Devices & Diagnostics	1,254,000	19.4
Diabetic Care	687,400	10.7
Animal Health	439,100	6.8
All Other	946,900	14.7
Total	6,452,400	100.0

ANNUAL EARNINGS AND DIVIDENDS PER SHARE

	1993	1992	1991	1990	1989	1988	1987
Earnings Per Share	1.67	① 2.81	4.50	3.90	3.20	2.67	③ 1.42
Dividends Per Share	2.42	2.20	2.00	1.64	② 1.35	1.15	1.00
Dividend Payout %	N.M.	78.3	44.4	42.1	42.2	43.2	70.7

① Before acctg. chg. ② 2-for-1 stk split, 4/28/89 ③ Before disc. oper.

ANNUAL FINANCIAL DATA

RECORD OF EARNINGS (IN MILLIONS):

	1993	1992	1991	1990	1989	1988	1987
Total Revenues	6,452.4	6,167.3	5,725.7	5,191.6	4,175.6	4,069.7	3,643.8
Costs and Expenses	5,401.5	4,643.7	3,657.9	3,404.7	2,781.5	2,818.9	2,875.8
Depreciation & Amort	398.3	368.1	299.5	247.5	229.3	204.0	184.3
Operating Income	652.6	1,155.5	1,768.3	1,539.4	1,164.8	1,046.8	583.7
Inc Bef Income Taxes & Acctg Chges	701.9	1,182.3	1,879.2	1,599.0	1,329.9	1,115.8	595.0
Income Taxes	210.8	354.7	564.5	471.7	390.4	354.8	184.5
Net Income	① 491.1	② 827.6	1,314.7	1,127.3	939.5	761.0	③ 410.5
Aver. Shs. Outstg. (000)	294,289	294,478	294,224	289,993	294,507	287,374	294,014

① Before acctg. change dr$10,900,000. ② Before acctg. change dr$118,900,000. ③ Before disc. op. cr$233,200,000.

BALANCE SHEET (IN MILLIONS):

	1993	1992	1991	1990	1989	1988	1987
Cash and Cash Equivalents	987.1	728.3	782.4	750.8	652.0	761.5	1,030.9
Receivables, Net	1,284.1	1,051.1	1,126.0	878.7	845.8	761.7	931.5
Inventories	1,103.0	938.4	796.9	673.0	599.5	674.3	615.5
Gross Property	6,566.5	6,148.1	5,568.6	4,515.8	3,478.4	3,047.2	2,757.9
Accumulated Depreciation	2,366.3	2,076.0	1,786.1	1,579.1	1,363.8	1,240.6	1,115.4
Long-Term Debt	835.2	582.3	395.5	277.0	269.5	387.7	365.7
Net Stockholders' Equity	4,568.8	4,892.1	4,966.1	3,467.5	3,757.1	3,225.3	3,042.6
Total Assets	9,623.6	8,672.8	8,298.6	7,142.8	5,848.0	5,262.7	5,254.9
Total Current Assets	3,697.1	3,006.0	2,939.3	2,501.3	2,274.4	2,414.7	2,724.1
Total Current Liabilities	2,928.0	2,398.6	2,272.0	2,817.6	1,328.8	1,288.8	1,448.2
Net Working Capital	769.1	607.4	667.3	d316.3	945.6	1,125.9	1,275.9
Year End Shs Outstg (000)	292,748	292,686	292,623	267,138	278,816	274,242	278,737

STATISTICAL RECORD:

	1993	1992	1991	1990	1989	1988	1987
Operating Profit Margin %	10.1	18.7	30.9	29.7	27.9	25.7	16.0
Book Value Per Share	14.22	15.14	15.52	11.22	11.85	10.27	9.50
Return on Equity %	10.7	16.9	26.5	32.5	25.0	23.6	13.5
Return on Assets %	5.1	9.5	15.8	15.8	16.1	14.5	7.8
Average Yield %	4.6	3.0	2.6	2.2	2.4	2.8	2.4
P/E Ratio	37.1-26.1	31.2-20.6	18.9-15.0	23.2-15.1	21.4-13.2	17.2-13.2	37.9-20.3
Price Range	62-43⅝	87¾-57¾	85⅛-67½	90⅜-58¾	68½-42⅜	45⅞-35⅜	53⅞-28⅞

Statistics are as originally reported.

OFFICERS:
R.L. Tobias, Chmn. & C.E.O.
J.M. Cornelius, V.P.-Fin. & C.F.O.

INCORPORATED: IN, Jan., 1901

PRINCIPAL OFFICE: Lilly Corporate Center, Indianapolis, IN 46285

TELEPHONE NUMBER: (317) 276-2000
FAX: (317) 276-3492
NO. OF EMPLOYEES: 4,447
ANNUAL MEETING: Third Monday in April
SHAREHOLDERS: 40,917
INSTITUTIONAL HOLDINGS:
No. of Institutions: 681
Shares Held: 177,956,581

REGISTRAR(S): At Company's Office

TRANSFER AGENT(S): At Company's Office

NASDAQ SYMBOL LICI A
Rec. Pr. 24¼ (Marginable)

LILLY INDUSTRIES, INC.

YIELD	1.2%
P/E RATIO	31.5

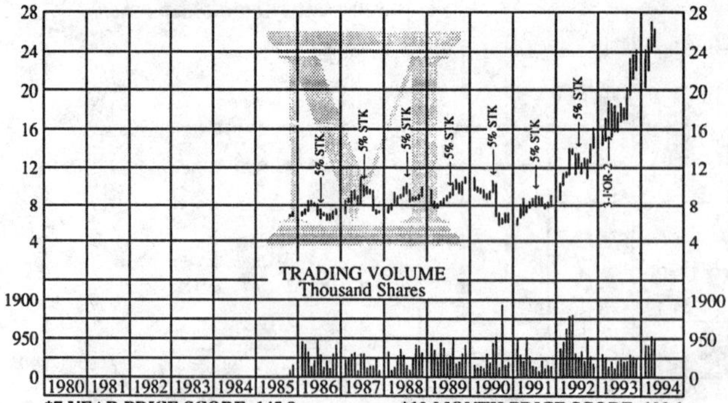

5% STK
5% STK
5% STK
5% STK
5% STK
5% STK
5% STK
3-FOR-2
TRADING VOLUME
Thousand Shares
1980 1981 1982 1983 1984 1985 1986 1987 1988 1989 1990 1991 1992 1993 1994

*7 YEAR PRICE SCORE 145.8 *12 MONTH PRICE SCORE 123.1
*NYSE COMPOSITE INDEX=100

INTERIM EARNINGS (Per Share):

Qtr.	Feb.	May	Aug.	Nov.
1990-91	0.01	0.12	0.15	0.13
1991-92	0.11	0.21	0.25	0.26
1992-93	0.15	0.27	0.30	0.33
1993-94	0.20	...	...	...

INTERIM DIVIDENDS (Per Share):

Amt.	Decl.	Ex.	Rec.	Pay.
0.09Q	6/25/93	9/3/93	9/10/93	10/1/93
0.09Q	10/4	12/7	12/13	1/3/94
0.10Q	1/28/94	3/7/94	3/11/94	4/1
3-for-2	4/21	6/2	5/12	6/1
0.07Q	4/21	6/6	6/10	7/1

Indicated div.: $0.28

CAPITALIZATION (11/30/93):

	($000)	(%)
Long-Term Debt	40,621	33.4
Common & Surplus	81,128	66.6
Total	121,749	100.0

DIVIDEND ACHIEVER STATUS:
Rank: 111 1983-93 Growth Rate: 12.6%
Total Years of Dividend Growth: 10

RECENT DEVELOPMENTS: For the year ended 11/30/93, net income was $16.2 million compared with $12.7 million last year. Net sales increased 20% to $284.3 million from $236.5 million a year ago. For the quarter, net income increased 29.1% to a record $5.2 million from $4.0 million last year. Net sales were a record $81.2 million compared to $60.5 million in 1992, an increase of 34%. Approximately 80% of the sales growth was attributable to the North American liquid industrial coatings business acquired from ICI Paints on 5/7/93. Costs and expenses increased to $71.7 million compared to $53.6 million last year. Increases in operating expenses and interest expense were also primarily associated with the acquired business. Improved earnings were the result of increased sales and operational efficiencies.

BUSINESS

LILLY INDUSTRIES, INC. designs, manufactures and sells coatings and other specialities that add high value or enhance customers' or potential customers' products. The Company is one of the ten largest North American manufacturers of industrial paints and coatings. Lilly supplies customers world wide from twenty-three plants; nineteen in the United States, two in Canada, one in Taiwan and one in West Germany. Lilly and its subsidiaries formulate, manufacture and sell industrial coatings that are applied to wood, plastic and metal surfaces by a variety of manufactures. London Laboratories formulates and sells silver and copper plating chemicals for non-conductive surfaces that results in mirrors, thermos bottles, Christmas tree ornaments and other products. American Finishes, Inc., in addition to industrial coating, sells automotive finishes primarily for the automotive after market. Lilly-Ram Industries produces gelcoats and related items for the marine, transportation, cultured marble and tub and shower markets. Perfection Paint produces trade sales coatings for the homeowner and contractor plus other specialty coatings.

ANNUAL EARNINGS AND DIVIDENDS PER SHARE

	11/30/93	11/30/92	11/30/91	11/30/90	11/30/89	11/30/88	11/30/87
Earnings Per Share	**1.05**	**0.82**	**0.41**	**0.61**	**0.75**	**0.68**	**0.60**
Dividends Per Share	**0.357**	[1] **0.334**	[2] **0.318**	[3] **0.298**	[4] **0.26**	[5] **0.231**	[6] **0.211**
Dividend Payout %	**34.0**	**40.7**	**78.3**	**48.7**	**34.3**	**33.9**	**35.0**

Note: 3-for-2stk.split,6/1/94. [1] 5% stk div, 7/20/92 [2] 5% stk div, 7/19/91 [3] 5% stk div, 8/15/90 [4] 5% stk div, 8/15/89 [5] 5% stk div, 8/88 [6] 5% stk div, 8/87

ANNUAL FINANCIAL DATA

RECORD OF EARNINGS (IN THOUSANDS):							
Total Revenues	284,325	236,476	213,282	231,615	212,230	196,764	183,596
Costs and Expenses	251,009	209,673	194,004	207,641	187,344	175,742	162,384
Depreciation & Amort	3,746	3,965	6,966	6,672	4,586	3,133	2,785
Operating Income	29,570	22,838	12,312	17,302	20,300	17,889	18,427
Income Bef Income Taxes	27,939	21,907	10,774	16,872	20,687	18,478	18,777
Income Taxes	11,784	9,201	4,417	6,850	8,399	7,550	8,599
Minority Shareholders' Int	...	...	...	...	cr286	cr356	cr94
Net Income	16,155	12,706	6,357	10,022	12,574	11,284	10,272
Aver. Shs. Outstg.	15,415	15,459	15,667	16,438	16,576	16,616	17,008
BALANCE SHEET (IN THOUSANDS):							
Cash and Cash Equivalents	7,459	10,826	14,088	5,031	10,636	11,911	8,627
Accounts Receivable, Net	39,936	29,601	28,698	30,912	32,460	25,962	25,111
Total Inventory	22,727	14,653	17,318	19,796	22,843	17,214	16,428
Gross Property	69,805	63,510	64,387	62,989	59,503	50,925	47,794
Accumulated Depreciation	36,029	32,939	30,870	27,381	23,743	20,946	17,915
Long-Term Debt	40,621	10,361	16,638	23,016	21,105	5,829	3,137
Net Stockholders' Equity	81,128	70,125	74,187	73,185	74,482	65,987	58,755
Total Assets	167,044	117,049	127,342	125,371	129,025	101,357	96,814
Total Current Assets	70,221	55,300	60,706	56,471	67,187	56,368	51,555
Total Current Liabilities	36,951	28,169	30,301	21,958	26,798	20,000	25,549
Net Working Capital	33,270	27,131	30,405	34,513	40,389	36,368	26,006
Year End Shares Outstg	15,011	14,817	15,652	15,755	16,574	17,993	16,736
STATISTICAL RECORD:							
Operating Profit Margin %	10.4	9.7	5.8	7.5	9.6	9.1	10.0
Book Value Per Share	1.71	2.97	2.89	2.73	3.10	3.07	2.83
Return on Equity %	19.9	18.1	8.6	13.7	16.9	17.1	17.5
Return on Assets %	9.7	10.9	5.0	8.0	9.7	11.1	10.6
Average Yield %	1.8	2.7	4.3	3.6	2.8	2.7	2.4
P/E Ratio	23.1-13.7	19.7-10.5	22.0-14.0	18.0-9.4	14.7-10.2	15.3-10.3	18.3-11.5
Price Range	24¼-14⅜	16⅛-8⅝	9-5¾	11-5¾	11-7⅝	10⅜-7	11-6⅞

Statistics are as originally reported.

OFFICERS:
D.W. Huemme, Chmn., Pres. & C.E.O.
R.J. Klusas, V.P., C.F.O. & Sec.

INCORPORATED: IN, Nov., 1988

PRINCIPAL OFFICE: 733 South West Street, Indianapolis, IN 46225

TELEPHONE NUMBER: (317) 687-6700

NO. OF EMPLOYEES: 1,175 (approx.)

ANNUAL MEETING: In April

SHAREHOLDERS: 1,815 Cl. A. 76 Cl. B.

INSTITUTIONAL HOLDINGS:
No. of Institutions: 40
Shares Held: 4,219,798

REGISTRAR(S): Bank One, Indianapolis, N.A., Bank One Center/ Tower, Indianapolis, IN 46204

TRANSFER AGENT(S): Bank One, Indianapolis, N.A., Bank One Center/Tower, Indianapolis, IN 46204

NYS SYMBOL LNC
Rec. Pr. 40½

LINCOLN NATIONAL CORP.

YIELD 4.0%
P/E RATIO 10.0

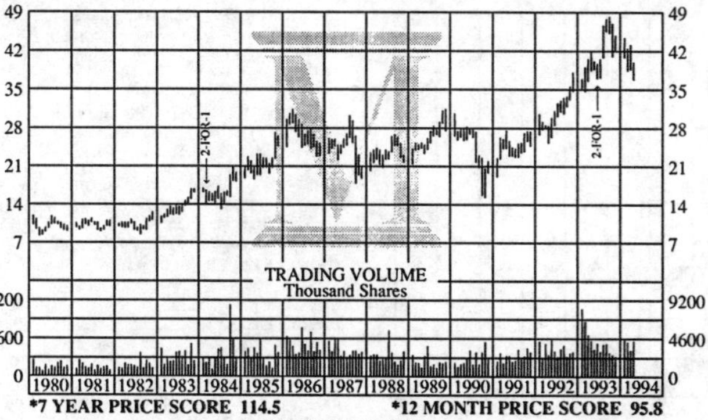

49
42
35
28
21
14
7
2-FOR-1
2-FOR-1
TRADING VOLUME
Thousand Shares
9200
4600
0
1980 1981 1982 1983 1984 1985 1986 1987 1988 1989 1990 1991 1992 1993 1994

***7 YEAR PRICE SCORE 114.5** ***12 MONTH PRICE SCORE 95.8**

*NYSE COMPOSITE INDEX=100

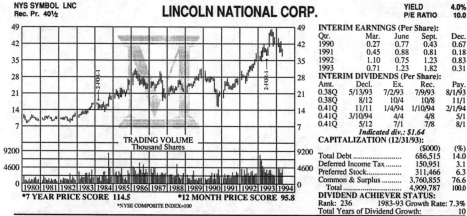

INTERIM EARNINGS (Per Share):

Qtr.	Mar.	June	Sept.	Dec.
1990	0.27	0.77	0.43	0.67
1991	0.45	0.88	0.81	0.18
1992	1.10	0.75	1.23	0.83
1993	0.71	1.23	1.82	0.31

INTERIM DIVIDENDS (Per Share):

Amt.	Decl.	Ex.	Rec.	Pay.
0.38Q	5/13/93	7/2/93	7/9/93	8/1/93
0.38Q	8/12	10/4	10/8	11/1
0.41Q	11/11	1/4/94	1/10/94	2/1/94
0.41Q	3/10/94	4/4	4/8	5/1
0.41Q	5/12	7/1	7/8	8/1

Indicated div.: $1.64

CAPITALIZATION (12/31/93):

	($000)	(%)
Total Debt	686,515	14.0
Deferred Income Tax	150,951	3.1
Preferred Stock	311,466	6.3
Common & Surplus	3,760,855	76.6
Total	4,909,787	100.0

DIVIDEND ACHIEVER STATUS:
Rank: 236 1983-93 Growth Rate: 7.3%
Total Years of Dividend Growth: 10

RECENT DEVELOPMENTS: Net income for the quarter ended 12/31/93 declined sharply to $31.5 million from $76.3 million in the corresponding 1992 period. Results included a $98.5 million charge for the loss on the sale of an asset. However, the property/casualty business contributed $45.6 million in income reflecting the benefits of underwriting controls. Life insurance and annuities segment had income of $65.7 million while the life-health reinsurance business reported a loss of $21.6 million.

PROSPECTS: Results from the property and casualty business are benefiting from tight underwriting controls. First Penn-Pacific Life Insurance Co. is performing well and the annuities and pensions segment continues to record increases in the number of assets under management. LNC agreed to sell most of its managed health care operations. Claims from California's January earthquake are expected to amount to $15 million as claims from the winter storms in the Eastern and Midwestern US will amount to $18 million.

BUSINESS

LINCOLN NATIONAL CORPORATION, a multi-line holding company, is one of the nation's largest diversified financial services companies. Subsidiaries provide, on a national basis, individual life insurance, employee benefits and property-casualty insurance. Through its subsidiaries, Lincoln National writes more individual life insurance than any other publicly-held group.

BUSINESS LINE ANALYSIS

(12/31/93)	Rev(%)	Inc(%)
Property-Casualty	27.0	43.8
Life Insur & Annuities	34.5	58.6
Life-Health Reinsurance	23.3	4.7
Employee Life-Health Ben	15.6	14.6
Other Operations	-0.4	-21.7
Total	100.0	100.0

ANNUAL EARNINGS AND DIVIDENDS PER SHARE

	1993	1992	1991	1990	1989	1988	1987
Earnings Per Share	**4.06**	**3.91**	**2.30**	**2.14**	**[2] 3.03**	**2.06**	**2.59**
Dividends Per Share	**[1] 1.52**	**1.46**	**1.36**	**1.30**	**1.24**	**1.18**	**1.08**
Dividend Payout %	**37.4**	**37.4**	**59.1**	**60.6**	**40.9**	**57.3**	**41.8**

[1] 2-for-1 stk split,06/28/93 [2] Per primary share

ANNUAL FINANCIAL DATA

	1993	1992	1991	1990	1989	1988	1987
RECORD OF EARNINGS (IN MILLIONS):							
Insurance Premiums	5,356.8	5,298.9	6,730.2	6,328.6	5,961.2	5,714.7	5,481.3
Net Investment Income	2,146.5	1,987.3	1,799.3	1,653.4	1,580.2	1,439.5	1,337.3
Total Revenue	8,289.8	8,034.1	9,169.0	8,489.6	8,081.1	7,312.3	6,960.1
Bens & Settlement Exps	5,628.3	5,700.4	6,886.8	6,358.1	5,939.8	5,370.4	5,192.0
Inc Bef Fed Income Taxes	587.8	424.7	198.8	200.1	330.3	180.1	275.0
Income Taxes	172.5	61.8	cr9.6	8.7	61.5	cr5.3	39.0
Gain on Sale Of Securities	...	...	...	...	...	d38.6	0.8
Net Income	[1] 415.3	362.9	208.4	191.5	268.9	146.7	236.9
Aver. Shs. Outstg. (000)	102,307	92,977	90,659	86,086	83,900	84,000	87,470
[1] Before acctg. change dr$96,431,000.							
BALANCE SHEET (IN MILLIONS):							
Fixed Matur, At Amortized Costs	...	18,352.3	16,037.3	14,211.3	13,076.7	10,462.9	9,144.5
Eq Secur, At Mkt Value	1,080.3	923.4	1,025.5	833.7	868.3	570.4	447.2
Policy Loans	595.1	563.5	530.3	485.4	456.8	480.3	471.5
Mtge Loans on Real Estate	3,301.0	3,135.1	3,144.6	3,230.1	3,053.8	2,845.1	2,531.7
Total Assets	48,380.4	39,671.7	34,094.8	27,597.3	25,070.1	20,964.3	18,003.9
Benefits and Claims	28,383.0	24,954.3	22,122.4	18,989.4	17,071.9	14,680.7	12,607.1
Net Stockholders' Equity	4,072.3	2,951.2	2,776.5	2,393.7	2,391.8	2,244.3	2,197.1
Year End Shs Outstg (000)	94,183	84,142	92,548	88,001	84,076	83,112	84,966
STATISTICAL RECORD:							
Book Value Per Share	39.93	31.37	26.63	25.45	26.08	24.60	23.51
Return on Equity %	10.2	12.3	7.5	8.0	11.2	6.5	10.8
Return on Assets %	0.9	0.9	0.6	0.7	1.1	0.7	1.3
Average Yield %	3.7	4.6	5.8	5.7	4.7	5.0	4.5
P/E Ratio	11.9-8.6	9.8-6.5	12.0-8.3	14.3-7.2	10.4-7.1	13.0-9.8	11.7-6.9
Price Range	48¼-34¾	38⅛-25¼	27⅝-19	30⅝-15⅜	31½-21⅜	26¾-20⅛	30¼-17⅞

Statistics are as originally reported.

OFFICERS:
I.M. Rolland, Chmn. & C.E.O.
R.A. Anker, Pres. & C.O.O.
R.C. Vaughan, Sr. V.P. & C.F.O.
C.S. Womack, Secretary

PRINCIPAL OFFICE: 1300 S. Clinton St. P.O. Box 1110. Fort Wayne, IN 46802

TELEPHONE NUMBER: (219) 455-2000

NO. OF EMPLOYEES: 11,980

ANNUAL MEETING: In May

SHAREHOLDERS: 14,260

INSTITUTIONAL HOLDINGS:
No. of Institutions: 230
Shares Held: 27,881,800

REGISTRAR(S):

TRANSFER AGENT(S):

LIQUI-BOX CORP.

YIELD 1.1%
P/E RATIO 22.3

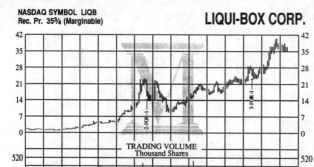

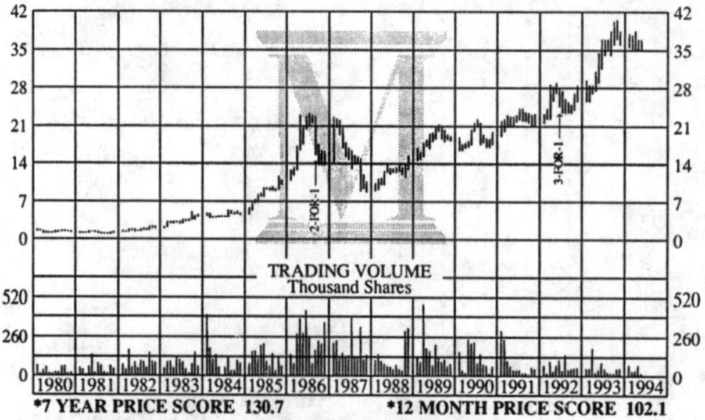

7 YEAR PRICE SCORE 130.7　　**12 MONTH PRICE SCORE 102.1**
*NYSE COMPOSITE INDEX=100

TRADING VOLUME
Thousand Shares

INTERIM EARNINGS (Per Share):				
Qtr.	Mar.	June	Sept.	Dec.
1991	0.32	0.48	0.47	0.21
1992	0.33	0.52	0.54	0.35
1993	0.40	0.62	0.58	0.40

INTERIM DIVIDENDS (Per Share):				
Amt.	Decl.	Ex.	Rec.	Pay.
0.09Q	3/15/93	3/26/93	4/1/93	4/15/93
0.10Q	6/15	6/25	7/1	7/15
0.10Q	9/15	9/27	10/1	10/15
0.10Q	12/15	12/27	1/1/94	1/15/94
0.10Q	3/15/94	3/25/94	4/1	4/15

Indicated div.: $0.40

CAPITALIZATION (1/1/94):

	($000)	(%)
Cap. Lease Oblig.	55	0.1
Deferred Income Tax	1,355	2.0
Common & Surplus	65,210	97.9
Total	66,620	100.0

DIVIDEND ACHIEVER STATUS:
Rank: 37　　1983-93 Growth Rate: 16.9%
Total Years of Dividend Growth: 15

RECENT DEVELOPMENTS: For the year ended 1/1/94, earnings increased 15% to $12.9 million from $11.3 million in 1992. Earnings per share were $2.00 in 1993, up from $1.73 in 1992. Sales were $130.1 million in 1993, up 12% from $116.1 million last year. For the quarter ended 1/1/94, net income rose 14% to $2.6 million compared with $2.3 million in the corresponding period a year ago. Earnings per share rose to $0.40 versus $0.35 last year. Sales were $28.4 million, up 16% from $24.5 million in fourth quarter 1992. Revenues were up across all lines of business. Strong gains were achieved in domestic operations. In addition, European gains were achieved by the acquisition of the liquid Packaging Divisions of Sonoco Products Co.

BUSINESS

LIQUI-BOX CORPORATION designs and manufactures environmentally friendly bag-in-box packaging, blow molded containers and bulk liquid dispensing systems for the beverage, wine, dairy, processed foods, specialty chemicals and bottled water industries. The Company markets its products in more than 45 countries. The Company operates 12 plants in the United States and one in Europe.

QUARTERLY DATA

(01/01/94) ($000)	Rev	Inc
1st Quarter	28,080	2,583
2nd Quarter	35,072	3,995
3rd Quarter	38,540	3,776
4th Quarter	28,389	2,583

ANNUAL EARNINGS AND DIVIDENDS PER SHARE

	1/1/94	1/2/93	1/4/92	12/29/90	12/30/89	12/31/88	1/2/88
Earnings Per Share	2.00	1.73	1.48	1.46	1.23	1.18	0.81
Dividends Per Share	0.38	0.346	0.333	0.317	0.267	0.22	0.20
Dividend Payout %	19.0	20.0	22.5	21.7	21.7	19.0	24.6

ANNUAL FINANCIAL DATA

RECORD OF EARNINGS (IN THOUSANDS)							
Total Revenues	130,081	116,117	107,790	113,130	102,760	90,365	72,001
Costs and Expenses	102,066	89,661	83,468	88,480	83,071	73,239	58,936
Depreciation & Amort	6,067	6,983	7,087	7,005	5,244	4,253	3,790
Operating Income	21,948	19,473	17,235	17,645	14,445	12,873	9,275
Income Bef Income Taxes	21,594	18,848	16,421	16,386	14,111	13,078	9,554
Taxes on Income	8,657	7,598	6,790	6,510	5,460	4,909	3,871
Net Income	12,937	11,250	9,631	9,876	8,651	8,169	5,683
Aver. Shs. Outstg.	6,484	6,495	6,512	6,769	7,025	6,927	6,978
BALANCE SHEET (IN THOUSANDS)							
Cash and Cash Equivalents	6,376	9,710	4,171	5,208	2,298	2,784	2,190
Accounts Receivable, Net	14,224	10,672	9,617	9,349	9,285	8,060	6,076
Inventories	19,805	14,121	12,005	9,740	8,975	9,053	8,541
Gross Property	75,648	67,334	68,655	65,081	61,750	50,151	44,046
Accumulated Depreciation	48,138	43,518	40,868	34,991	29,227	25,000	21,266
Long-Term Debt	...	...	511	10,068	3,421	1,781	2,130
Capital Lease Obligations	55	105	155	336	463	650	845
Net Stockholders' Equity	65,210	55,972	47,740	42,130	42,305	33,204	27,607
Total Assets	86,072	68,974	63,512	64,223	64,161	46,511	41,487
Total Current Assets	44,341	37,088	27,189	25,283	21,538	20,454	18,031
Total Current Liabilities	19,452	10,384	12,104	7,568	14,318	6,938	7,059
Net Working Capital	24,889	26,704	15,085	17,715	7,220	13,516	10,972
Year End Shares Outstg	6,360	6,383	6,407	6,509	6,987	6,771	6,834
STATISTICAL RECORD:							
Operating Profit Margin %	16.9	16.8	16.0	15.6	14.1	14.2	12.9
Book Value Per Share	8.54	7.56	6.21	5.19	4.74	4.90	4.04
Return on Equity %	19.8	20.1	20.2	23.4	20.4	24.6	20.6
Return on Assets %	15.0	16.3	15.2	15.4	13.5	17.6	13.7
Average Yield %	1.2	1.4	1.5	1.6	1.5	1.8	1.3
P/E Ratio	20.3-12.8	16.8-12.5	16.5-12.9	15.3-11.3	17.4-11.8	13.1-7.5	27.9-10.6
Price Range	40½-25½	29-21⅝	24⅜-19⅛	22⅜-16½	21⅜-14½	15½-8⅞	22⅝-8⅝

Statistics are as originally reported.

OFFICERS:
S.B. Davis, Chmn., Pres., C.E.O. & Treas.
R.S. Hamilton, Vice-Chmn.
P.J. Linn, Exec. V.P. & Sec.

INCORPORATED: OH, 1961

PRINCIPAL OFFICE: 6950 Worthington-Galena Road, Worthington, OH 43085

TELEPHONE NUMBER: (614) 888-9280

FAX: (614) 888-0982

NO. OF EMPLOYEES: 720 (approx.)

ANNUAL MEETING: In April

SHAREHOLDERS: 865

INSTITUTIONAL HOLDINGS:
No. of Institutions: 39
Shares Held: 461,191

REGISTRAR(S):

TRANSFER AGENT(S): Huntington National Bank, Stock Transfer Department, Columbus, OH 43287

NYS SYMBOL LDG
Rec. Pr. 34⅛

LONGS DRUG STORES CORP.

YIELD 3.3%
P/E RATIO 14.3

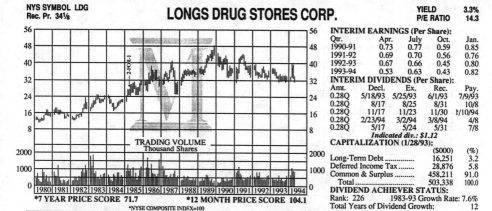

*7 YEAR PRICE SCORE 71.7   *12 MONTH PRICE SCORE 104.1
*NYSE COMPOSITE INDEX=100

TRADING VOLUME
Thousand Shares

INTERIM EARNINGS (Per Share):

Qtr.	Apr.	July	Oct.	Jan.
1990-91	0.73	0.77	0.59	0.85
1991-92	0.69	0.70	0.56	0.76
1992-93	0.67	0.66	0.45	0.80
1993-94	0.53	0.63	0.43	0.82

INTERIM DIVIDENDS (Per Share):

Amt.	Decl.	Ex.	Rec.	Pay.
0.28Q	5/18/93	5/25/93	6/1/93	7/9/93
0.28Q	8/17	8/25	8/31	10/8
0.28Q	11/17	11/23	11/30	1/10/94
0.28Q	2/23/94	3/2/94	3/8/94	4/8
0.28Q	5/17	5/24	5/31	7/8

Indicated div.: $1.12

CAPITALIZATION (1/28/93):

	($000)	(%)
Long-Term Debt	16,251	3.2
Deferred Income Tax	28,876	5.8
Common & Surplus	458,211	91.0
Total	503,338	100.0

DIVIDEND ACHIEVER STATUS:
Rank: 226   1983-93 Growth Rate: 7.6%
Total Years of Dividend Growth: 12

RECENT DEVELOPMENTS: For the year ended 1/27/94, net income was $49.8 million compared with $53.0 million last year. Results were before an accounting credit of $3.0 million. Sales increased 1.0% to $2.50 billion. Sales in LDG's primary market remained soft due to difficult economic conditions in California and Hawaii. Gross margin increased to 25.4% from 24.7% of sales. During the year, the Company opened 12 new stores and added 20 stores through the acquisition of Bill's Drug Stores.

PROSPECTS: Near-term earnings will continue to be affected by difficult economic conditions in California and Hawaii. A conversion program to scanning systems will favor earnings growth in the longer term. The POS system will improve inventory control, increase productivity and lower merchandising costs, resulting in improved gross margins. LDG plans to build four new small-format pharmacies in order to take advantage of profitable markets that it otherwise would not have entered.

BUSINESS

LONGS DRUG STORES CORP. operates a chain of 307 super drug stores located in California, Hawaii, Nevada, Alaska, and Colorado. These stores primarily sell nationally advertised brand-name merchandise in four core segments: Pharmacy, Photo, Cosmetics and Greeting Cards. Certain liquors, drugs and other items are sold under private label to reduce selling prices. LDG stores range in size from about 15,000 to 25,000 sq. ft. except for three older, smaller stores. The stores are operated on a self-service basis except for the prescription drug, photo and some liquor departments. Operations are decentralized. Each store manager is responsible for purchasing and pricing.

QUARTERLY DATA

(1/28/93)($000)	Rev	Inc
1st Quarter	601,695	13,693
2nd Quarter	613,395	13,529
3rd Quarter	593,669	9,275
4th Quarter	666,716	16,496

ANNUAL EARNINGS AND DIVIDENDS PER SHARE

	1/28/93	1/30/92	1/31/91	1/25/90	1/26/89	1/28/88	1/29/87
Earnings Per Share	2.58	2.71	2.94	3.01	2.75	2.33	1.78
Dividends Per Share	1.10	1.06	1.00	0.92	0.84	0.78	0.74
Dividend Payout %	42.6	39.1	34.0	30.6	31.0	33.5	41.6

ANNUAL FINANCIAL DATA

RECORD OF EARNINGS (IN MILLIONS):

Total Revenues	2,475.5	2,365.9	2,333.8	2,110.6	1,925.5	1,772.5	1,635.4
Costs and Expenses	2,359.6	2,251.4	2,214.2	1,991.4	1,816.6	1,669.9	⬚1,560.5
Depreciation & Amort	28.4	23.3	21.3	18.2	16.2	14.3	...
Operating Income	87.5	91.3	98.2	101.0	92.7	88.3	74.9
Inc Bef Taxes on Income	87.5	91.3	98.2	101.0	92.7	88.3	74.9
Taxes on Income	34.5	35.9	38.6	39.7	36.8	39.1	36.3
Net Income	53.0	55.4	59.6	61.3	55.9	49.2	38.6
Aver. Shs. Outstg. (000)	20,538	20,417	20,291	20,378	20,277	...	...
⬚ Incl. Dep.							

BALANCE SHEET (IN MILLIONS):

Cash & Equivalents	16.1	12.0	9.7	24.6	21.8	20.3	13.0
Pharmacy & Other Receivs	40.5	36.8	40.2	27.3	23.0	15.7	13.3
Inventories	273.9	268.3	251.2	224.8	196.7	192.3	181.0
Gross Property	538.0	495.3	440.1	391.5	352.6	321.3	301.2
Accumulated Depreciation	171.4	148.3	129.6	110.7	94.8	81.9	71.5
Long-Term Debt	16.3	18.5	20.5	22.4	...	...	...
Net Stockholders' Equity	458.2	423.2	379.3	335.8	309.1	299.8	290.4
Total Assets	709.2	672.8	623.1	566.7	507.6	474.0	442.4
Total Current Assets	342.6	325.8	312.7	285.9	249.8	234.5	212.7
Total Current Liabilities	205.9	204.7	197.6	185.4	179.6	155.8	136.5
Net Working Capital	136.7	121.0	115.1	100.5	70.2	78.7	76.2
Year End Shs Outstg (000)	20,413	20,441	20,170	20,132	19,993	20,545	21,142

STATISTICAL RECORD:

Operating Profit Margin %	3.5	3.9	4.2	4.8	4.8	5.0	4.6
Book Value Per Share	22.45	20.70	18.80	16.68	15.46	14.59	13.74
Return on Equity %	11.6	13.1	15.7	18.3	18.1	16.4	13.3
Return on Assets %	7.5	8.2	9.6	10.8	11.0	10.4	8.7
Average Yield %	3.0	2.8	2.6	2.6	2.2	2.5	2.3
P/E Ratio	15.5-12.6	16.4-11.4	15.3-11.3	16.1-11.5	13.6-10.7	17.6-10.8	21.8-15.0
Price Range	40-32½	44⅜-30⅞	44⅞-33¼	48½-34½	37⅜-29⅜	41-25⅛	38¾-26⅝

Statistics are as originally reported.

OFFICERS:
R.M. Long, Chmn. & C.E.O.
S.D. Roath, Pres.
O.D. Jones, Sr. V.P.-Prop. & Sec.
W.G. Combs, V.P.-Admin. & Treas.
INCORPORATED: CA, Oct., 1946; reincorp., MD, May, 1985
PRINCIPAL OFFICE: 141 North Civic Dr., Walnut Creek, CA 94596

TELEPHONE NUMBER: (510) 210-6726
FAX: (510) 210-6886
NO. OF EMPLOYEES: 1,096 approx.
ANNUAL MEETING: In January
SHAREHOLDERS: 4,994 approx.
INSTITUTIONAL HOLDINGS:
No. of Institutions: 166
Shares Held: 8,437,934

REGISTRAR(S):

TRANSFER AGENT(S):

LORAL CORP.

YIELD 1.6%
P/E RATIO 14.9

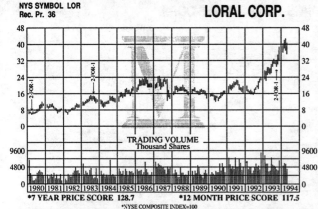

*7 YEAR PRICE SCORE 128.7   *12 MONTH PRICE SCORE 117.5

*NYSE COMPOSITE INDEX=100

TRADING VOLUME
Thousand Shares

INTERIM EARNINGS (Per Share):

Qtr.	June	Sept.	Dec.	Mar.
1990-91	0.36	0.42	0.41	0.60
1991-92	0.42	0.47	0.48	0.64
1992-93	0.36	0.47	0.53	0.69
1993-94	0.49	0.56	0.68	...

INTERIM DIVIDENDS (Per Share):

Amt.	Decl.	Ex.	Rec.	Pay.
0.28Q	7/27/93	8/23/93	8/27/93	9/15/93
100%	9/3	10/8	9/28	10/7
0.14Q	10/26	11/23	11/30	12/15
0.14Q	1/25/94	2/18/94	2/25/94	3/15/94
0.14Q	3/9	5/23	5/27	6/15

Indicated div.: $0.56

CAPITALIZATION (3/31/93):

	($000)	(%)
Long-Term Debt	490,806	29.2
Common & Surplus	1,187,853	70.8
Total	1,678,659	100.0

DIVIDEND ACHIEVER STATUS:
Rank: 185   1983-93 Growth Rate: 9.7%
Total Years of Dividend Growth: 17

RECENT DEVELOPMENTS: For the three months ended 12/31/93, net income was $56.9 million compared with $41.4 million last year. Sales declined 4.3% to $902.0 million. Bookings totaled $875 million compared with $1.30 billion last year, while backlog was $3.44 billion compared with $4.07 billion. Space Systems/Loral reported sales of $164.6 million, booking of $42.8 million, and backlog of $866.2 million. Additionally, Loral agreed to buy IBM Federal Systems Company for approximately $1.50 billion.

PROSPECTS: In the near term, earnings and bookings should increase moderately, as LOR should benefit from increasing margins and continuing operating improvements. A diverse program base will reduce LOR's dependence on any one program and allow LOR to concentrate on its core business segments. New contracts should help business at the CI segment. Meanwhile, the Company will focus on reducing debt and improving liquidity.

BUSINESS

LORAL CORP. primarily designs and manufactures defense electronics. The Company's principal business areas are: electronic combat (self-protection); command, control, communications and intelligence; training and simulation; tactical weapons systems and guidance; reconnaissance and surveillance; and space systems. U.S. Government agencies accounted for 63% of sales, and foreign governments accounted for 14%. In October 1990, Loral acquired Ford Aerospace Corporation, a leading defense electronics and space systems company for approximately $150 million. In August 1992, Loral acquired Loral Vought Systems from LTV Corp. for $261.3 million.

QUARTERLY DATA

(3/31/93)($000)	Rev	Inc
1st Quarter	681,300	51,449
2nd Quarter	738,902	64,860
3rd Quarter	941,141	76,367
4th Quarter	974,060	103,578

ANNUAL EARNINGS AND DIVIDENDS PER SHARE

	3/31/93	3/31/92	3/31/91	3/31/90	3/31/89	3/31/88	3/31/87
Earnings Per Share	①②2.07	2.00	1.78	③1.54	③1.21	1.51	1.18
Dividends Per Share	0.49	0.46	0.52	0.30	0.33	0.23	0.28
Dividend Payout %	10.6	11.5	14.7	9.8	13.7	7.7	11.9

Note: 100%stk.div.10/7/93. ① Before extraord. item ② Before acctg. chg. ③ Before disc. oper.

ANNUAL FINANCIAL DATA

RECORD OF EARNINGS (IN MILLIONS):

Total Revenues	3,335.4	2,881.8	2,126.8	1,274.3	1,187.0	1,440.8	690.0
Costs and Expenses	2,885.1	2,461.0	1,811.2	1,046.9	988.0	1,186.9	554.4
Depreciation & Amort	154.0	128.6	100.1	78.7	66.2	73.1	30.6
Operating Income	296.3	292.2	215.5	148.7	132.8	180.7	105.1
Inc Fr Contin Oper Bef Income Taxes	255.5	241.0	165.8	123.1	94.9	121.9	98.7
Income Taxes	94.6	89.2	61.3	45.5	34.6	47.5	41.3
Minority Interest	2.6	28.7	11.7	...	...	...	...
Net Income	①159.1	121.8	90.4	②77.5	③60.3	④74.3	57.5

① Before extra. item dr$17,776,000; and acctg. chg dr$233,377,000. ② Before disc. op. cr$707,000. ③ Before disc. oper. cr$27,326,000. ④ Before disc. op. cr$24,956,000.

BALANCE SHEET (IN MILLIONS):

Cash and Cash Equivalents	116.9	191.1	75.1	105.0	87.5	27.4	43.1
Receivables, Net	883.5	673.6	715.6	359.7	246.6	293.5	283.0
Inventories	324.7	320.8	365.1	270.0	226.7	297.8	271.7
Gross Property	1,271.5	1,098.3	980.8	714.2	524.9	581.5	586.6
Accumulated Depreciation	489.8	408.5	321.5	256.3	199.5	159.2	112.3
Long-Term Debt	490.8	561.7	783.7	419.1	423.2	583.6	667.2
Net Stockholders' Equity	1,187.9	997.3	672.0	584.5	517.9	438.3	362.9
Total Assets	3,228.1	2,658.6	2,532.2	1,535.2	1,461.5	1,414.8	1,466.9
Total Current Assets	1,365.2	1,204.4	1,177.5	748.8	898.2	631.3	605.6
Total Current Liabilities	754.7	608.2	719.8	436.2	435.4	326.0	359.9
Net Working Capital	610.5	596.1	457.7	312.6	462.8	305.4	245.6
Year End Shs Outstg (000)	82,532	63,778	51,882	51,208	51,030	50,640	48,030

STATISTICAL RECORD:

Operating Profit Margin %	8.9	10.1	10.1	11.7	11.2	12.5	15.2
Book Value Per Share	7.88	11.16	7.25	6.10	6.09	2.26	0.23
Return on Equity %	13.4	12.2	13.4	13.3	11.6	17.0	15.8
Return on Assets %	4.9	4.6	3.6	5.1	4.1	5.3	3.9
Average Yield %	2.5	2.4	3.5	1.8	1.9	1.2	1.4
P/E Ratio	11.5-7.4	11.4-8.1	9.9-6.8	12.3-8.9	16.8-12.7	24.6-12.5	21.3-14.8
Price Range	23¾-15⅜	22¾-16⅛	17½-12⅛	19-13¾	20¼-15¼	24⅝-12½	24⅜-17

Statistics are as originally reported.

OFFICERS:
B.L. Schwartz, Chmn. & C.E.O.
F.C. Lanza, Pres. & C.O.O.
M.P. DeBlasio, Sr. V.P.-Fin.
M.B. Targoff, Sr. V.P. & Sec.

INCORPORATED: NY, Feb., 1948

PRINCIPAL OFFICE: 600 Third Avenue, New York, NY 10016

TELEPHONE NUMBER: (212) 697-1105

FAX: (212) 661-8988

NO. OF EMPLOYEES: 3,332 (approx.)

ANNUAL MEETING: In July

SHAREHOLDERS: 2,967 (approx.)

INSTITUTIONAL HOLDINGS:
No. of Institutions: 219
Shares Held: 20,779,499

REGISTRAR(S):

TRANSFER AGENT(S):

LOUISIANA-PACIFIC CORP.

YIELD 1.4%
P/E RATIO 15.1

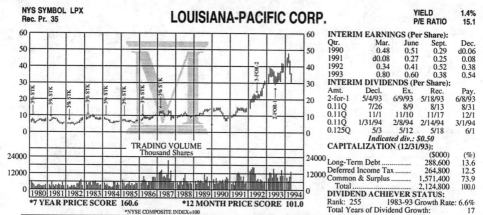

INTERIM EARNINGS (Per Share):

Qtr.	Mar.	June	Sept.	Dec.
1990	0.48	0.51	0.29	d0.06
1991	d0.08	0.27	0.25	0.08
1992	0.34	0.41	0.52	0.38
1993	0.80	0.60	0.38	0.54

INTERIM DIVIDENDS (Per Share):

Amt.	Decl.	Ex.	Rec.	Pay.
2-for-1	5/4/93	6/9/93	5/18/93	6/8/93
0.11Q	7/26	8/9	8/13	8/31
0.11Q	11/1	11/10	11/17	12/1
0.11Q	1/31/94	2/8/94	2/14/94	3/1/94
0.125Q	5/3	5/12	5/18	6/1

Indicated div.: $0.50

CAPITALIZATION (12/31/93):

	($000)	(%)
Long-Term Debt	288,600	13.6
Deferred Income Tax	264,800	12.5
Common & Surplus	1,571,400	73.9
Total	2,124,800	100.0

DIVIDEND ACHIEVER STATUS:
Rank: 255   1983-93 Growth Rate: 6.6%
Total Years of Dividend Growth: 17

TRADING VOLUME Thousand Shares

*7 YEAR PRICE SCORE 160.6   *12 MONTH PRICE SCORE 101.0
*NYSE COMPOSITE INDEX=100

RECENT DEVELOPMENTS: For the year ended 12/31/93, net income increased 43.8% to $254.4 million from $176.9 million in 1992. Revenue for the year advanced 14.9% to $2.51 billion from $2.18 billion. Record results were achieved despite a loss of $59 million in the pulp segment. Louisiana-Pacific experienced sales growth in lumber and structured panel products. Export sales were down 25.6% to $252.3 million from $339.2 million. Total operating profit rose 46.4% to $503.4 million.

PROSPECTS: Louisiana-Pacific is positioned well with its staff and operations to take advantage of the improving building products market. Favorable selling prices and increasing demand, coupled with an economy in the early stages of recovery, indicate promise for future earnings growth. LPX has adopted a new technology with known environmental advantages. Its Red Bluff, Ca. plant is one of two in the country to introduce a formaldehyde-emission-free gluing process.

BUSINESS

LOUISIANA-PACIFIC CORP., spun-off from Georgia-Pacific in 1973, is the leading redwood manufacturer and one of the largest producers of lumber in the world. The Company also manufactures pulp, hardboard, Inner-Seal OSB, plywood, medium density fiberboard, particleboard and windows and doors. Sales are derived: redwood lumber, 3%; other lumber, 27%; structural panels, 41%, other panels, 7%; other building products, 14%; and pulp, 8%. LPX owns or has long term rights on more than 2.0 million acres of timberlands and operates 125 facilities in 26 states and two provinces in Canada and Mexico. In June 1988, LPX completed the spin-off of Fibreboard Corp.

BUSINESS LINE ANALYSIS

(12/31/93)	Rev(%)	Inc($000)
Building Products	96.6	562
Pulp	3.4	(59)
Total	100.0	503

ANNUAL EARNINGS AND DIVIDENDS PER SHARE

	1993	1992	1991	1990	1989	1988	1987
Earnings Per Share	2.32	1.63	0.51	1.23	2.52	③1.77	1.63
Dividends Per Share	①0.43	②0.39	0.36	0.518	0.488	0.445	0.40
Dividend Payout %	18.5	23.9	69.7	42.3	19.4	25.0	24.3

① 2-for-1 stk split,06/09/93 ② 3-for-2 stock split, 6/8/92 ③ Before disc. oper. & extraord. item

ANNUAL FINANCIAL DATA

RECORD OF EARNINGS (IN MILLIONS):

	1993	1992	1991	1990	1989	1988	1987
Total Revenues	2,511.3	2,184.7	1,702.1	1,793.3	2,009.5	1,799.4	1,921.6
Costs and Expenses	1,945.7	1,765.8	1,481.2	1,535.5	1,595.4	1,471.1	1,562.0
Depreciation & Amort	133.0	121.4	114.6	152.3	141.8	145.1	114.1
Operating Profit	482.8	339.1	141.5	183.7	335.9	258.6	278.9
Income Before Taxes	427.6	283.1	87.4	137.0	291.9	214.1	208.3
Income Taxes	173.2	106.2	31.5	45.9	99.3	78.9	83.3
Net Income	①254.4	176.9	55.9	91.1	192.6	299.6	125.0
Aver. Shs. Outstg. (000)	109,670	108,500	107,980	111,060	114,600	114,630	114,750

① Before acctg. change dr$10,400,000.

BALANCE SHEET (IN MILLIONS):

	1993	1992	1991	1990	1989	1988	1987
Cash & Cash Equivalents	261.6	228.1	190.8	209.1	352.8	256.4	3.8
Receivables, Net	110.9	113.0	79.7	71.2	94.1	86.6	108.2
Inventories	234.7	192.3	184.3	220.8	203.3	189.1	216.0
Gross Property	2,112.8	1,944.7	1,868.9	1,773.7	1,511.0	1,337.1	1,466.0
Accumulated Depreciation	966.9	874.4	802.8	736.9	684.0	619.3	627.6
Long-Term Debt	288.6	386.3	492.7	588.7	529.5	369.6	524.7
Net Stockholders' Equity	1,571.4	1,361.0	1,203.6	1,166.7	1,176.5	1,137.1	1,044.2
Total Assets	2,466.3	2,206.0	2,107.1	2,104.1	2,031.7	1,796.4	1,971.0
Total Current Assets	614.1	539.1	461.4	509.1	653.6	536.3	345.0
Total Current Liabilities	317.2	295.5	259.5	195.5	180.0	162.8	225.5
Net Working Capital	296.9	243.6	201.9	313.6	473.6	373.5	119.5
Year End Shs Outstg (000)	110,181	109,218	107,734	107,610	114,034	111,826	115,002

STATISTICAL RECORD:

	1993	1992	1991	1990	1989	1988	1987
Operating Profit Margin %	17.2	13.6	6.2	8.1	15.1	12.3	12.8
Book Value Per Share	14.26	12.46	11.17	10.84	10.32	10.17	9.08
Return on Equity %	16.2	13.0	4.6	7.8	16.4	26.3	12.0
Return on Assets %	10.3	8.0	2.7	4.3	9.5	16.7	6.3
Average Yield %	1.2	1.7	3.0	4.7	4.1	4.2	3.9
P/E Ratio	18.2-12.4	19.3-9.0	29.6-17.1	18.4-8.2	8.6-5.6	10.6-7.2	12.9-6.9
Price Range	42⅛-28¾	31½-14⅝	15⅜-8⅞	15⅛-6¾	14½-9⅜	12½-8½	13¼-7⅛

Statistics are as originally reported.

OFFICERS:
H.A. Merlo, Chmn. & Pres.
W.L. Hebert, Treas. & C.F.O.
A.C. Kirchhof, Jr., Gen. Couns. & Sec.

INCORPORATED: DE, Jul., 1972

PRINCIPAL OFFICE: 111 S.W. 5th Avenue, Portland, OR 97204

TELEPHONE NUMBER: (503) 221-0800
FAX: (503) 796-0204
NO. OF EMPLOYEES: 1,768
ANNUAL MEETING: In May
SHAREHOLDERS: 16,974
INSTITUTIONAL HOLDINGS:
No. of Institutions: 364
Shares Held: 61,665,664

REGISTRAR(S): First Chicago Trust Co. of New York, New York, NY 10008

TRANSFER AGENT(S): First Chicago Trust Co. of New York, New York, NY 10008

LOWE'S COS., INC.

YIELD 0.5%
P/E RATIO 20.8

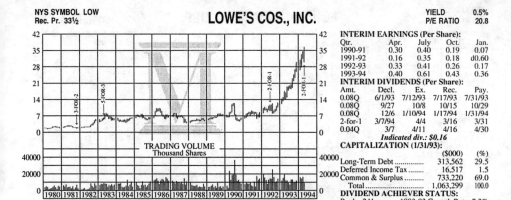

*7 YEAR PRICE SCORE 192.5 *12 MONTH PRICE SCORE 135.3
*NYSE COMPOSITE INDEX=100

TRADING VOLUME
Thousand Shares

INTERIM EARNINGS (Per Share):

Qtr.	Apr.	July	Oct.	Jan.
1990-91	0.30	0.40	0.19	0.07
1991-92	0.16	0.35	0.18	d0.60
1992-93	0.33	0.41	0.26	0.17
1993-94	0.40	0.61	0.43	0.36

INTERIM DIVIDENDS (Per Share):

Amt.	Decl.	Ex.	Rec.	Pay.
0.08Q	6/1/93	7/12/93	7/17/93	7/31/93
0.08Q	9/27	10/8	10/15	10/29
0.08Q	12/6	1/10/94	1/17/94	1/31/94
2-for-1	3/7/94	4/4	3/16	3/31
0.04Q	3/7	4/11	4/16	4/30

Indicated div.: $0.16

CAPITALIZATION (1/31/93):

	($000)	(%)
Long-Term Debt	313,562	29.5
Deferred Income Tax	16,517	1.5
Common & Surplus	733,220	69.0
Total	1,063,299	100.0

DIVIDEND ACHIEVER STATUS:

Rank: 241   1983-93 Growth Rate: 7.2%
Total Years of Dividend Growth: 16

RECENT DEVELOPMENTS: For the year ended 1/31/94, net income was $131.8 million compared with $84.7 million in 1993. Sales increased 18.0% to $4.54 billion, while comparable store sales increased 10%. Results were aided by increased sales and higher margins. As a percentage of sales, gross margin increased to 23.8% from 23.4%, while SG&A expenses declined to 16.7% from 17.3%. The improvement in margins was aided by a higher proportion of retail sales and by a favorable product mix.

PROSPECTS: Lowe's is experiencing significant sales and earnings gains as a result of its conversion into a large store format. Lowe's will continue to emphasize its Everyday Competitive Pricing program and a wider product selection, while relying less on promotional advertising. The program should also continue to help increase sales volumes and margin dollars, while reducing expenses as a percentage of sales. For 1994, expansion plans call for the opening of 50 to 55 superstores.

BUSINESS

LOWE'S COMPANIES, INC. is a specialty retailer that combines the merchandise, sales and service of a home improvement center, a building materials supplier and a consumer-durables retailer to serve the do-it-yourself home improvement and construction markets. As of 1/31/94, 311 retail stores were in operation in 20 states, located principally in the South Atlantic and South Central regions of the U.S. Contributions to sales were: 16%, Structural Lumber; 24%, Building Commodities & Millwork; 17%, Home Decorating; 10%, Kitchen, Bathroom & Laundry; 6%, Heating Cooling & Water System; 5%, Home Entertainment; 11%, Yard, Patio & Garden; 5%, Tools; and 6%, Special Order.

QUARTERLY DATA

(1/31/93)($000)	Rev	Inc
1st Quarter	883,283	23,779
2nd Quarter	1,061,645	29,718
3rd Quarter	991,192	18,900
4th Quarter	910,298	12,323

ANNUAL EARNINGS AND DIVIDENDS PER SHARE

	1/31/93	1/31/92	1/31/91	1/31/90	1/31/89	1/31/88	1/31/87
Earnings Per Share	1.16	0.09	0.96	1.00	0.92	② 0.71	③ 0.71
Dividends Per Share	① 0.28	0.27	0.26	0.24	0.225	0.21	0.195
Dividend Payout %	24.1	N.M.	27.2	23.9	24.6	29.8	27.7

Note: 2-for-1stk.split,3/31/94. ① 2-for-1 stk split, 6/29/92 ② Before acctg. chg. ③ Before extraord. item

ANNUAL FINANCIAL DATA

RECORD OF EARNINGS (IN MILLIONS):

Total Revenues	3,846.4	3,056.2	2,833.1	2,650.5	2,516.9	2,442.2	2,283.5
Costs and Expenses	3,635.1	2,976.1	2,664.0	2,476.4	2,349.1	2,283.6	2,131.1
Depreciation	69.8	58.3	51.4	46.1	41.2	38.5	30.5
Operating Income	141.5	21.9	117.7	128.0	126.6	120.0	121.9
Pre-tax Earnings	125.9	5.0	100.3	108.8	105.6	90.8	108.1
Income Taxes	41.2	cr1.5	29.2	33.9	36.4	34.8	53.0
Net Income	84.7	6.5	71.1	74.9	69.2	① 56.0	② 55.1
Aver. Shs. Outstg. (000)	73,076	73,026	74,428	74,556	75,496	79,438	78,058

① Before acctg. change cr$5,226,000. ② Before extra. item dr$2,885,000.

BALANCE SHEET (IN MILLIONS):

Cash and Cash Equivalents	54.8	30.8	50.1	55.6	60.3	43.9	50.0
Receivables, Net	61.8	122.2	96.4	123.1	128.4	127.4	118.7
Inventories	594.2	602.8	460.8	407.7	379.4	373.8	368.1
Gross Property	1,067.9	869.8	776.5	706.2	641.6	587.5	530.1
Accumulated Depreciation	280.7	256.8	235.1	198.4	161.7	134.5	116.9
Long-Term Debt	313.6	113.7	159.2	167.9	190.1	186.2	153.0
Net Stockholders' Equity	733.2	668.6	682.7	645.6	586.9	582.4	540.5
Total Assets	1,608.9	1,441.2	1,203.1	1,147.4	1,085.8	1,027.3	969.2
Total Current Assets	745.6	770.1	616.5	595.9	577.6	552.5	546.9
Total Current Liabilities	499.6	589.0	337.7	307.9	285.7	231.9	257.3
Net Working Capital	245.9	181.1	278.8	288.1	291.8	320.6	289.6
Year End Shs Outstg (000)	72,973	72,880	72,920	74,510	74,278	78,996	79,248

STATISTICAL RECORD:

Operating Profit Margin %	3.7	0.7	4.2	4.8	5.0	4.9	5.3
Book Value Per Share	10.05	9.17	9.36	8.66	7.90	7.37	6.82
Return on Equity %	11.6	1.0	10.4	11.6	11.8	9.6	10.2
Return on Assets %	5.3	0.5	5.9	6.5	6.4	5.4	5.7
Average Yield %	1.4	1.8	1.5	1.8	2.2	1.8	1.2
P/E Ratio	21.9-13.8	N.M	25.9-9.6	16.1-10.4	13.5-8.9	23.1-10.7	29.2-15.8
Price Range	25⅜-16	18⅝-11½	24⅞-9¼	16⅛-10⅜	12¼-8⅛	16⅜-7⅝	20¾-11¼

Statistics are as originally reported.

OFFICERS:

R.L. Strickland, Chmn.
L.G. Herring, Pres. & C.E.O.
H.B. Underwood, II, Sr. V.P., C.F.O. & Treas.

INCORPORATED: NC, Aug., 1952

PRINCIPAL OFFICE: P.O. Box 1111, North Wilkesboro, NC 28656

TELEPHONE NUMBER: (910) 651-4766
FAX: (910) 651-4766
NO. OF EMPLOYEES: 2,893
ANNUAL MEETING: In May
SHAREHOLDERS: 5,007
INSTITUTIONAL HOLDINGS:
No. of Institutions: 201
Shares Held: 19,537,149

REGISTRAR(S): Wachovia Bank & Trust Co., N.A., Winston-Salem, NC 27102

TRANSFER AGENT(S): Wachovia Bank & Trust Co., N.A., Winston-Salem, NC 27102

LUBY'S CAFETERIAS, INC.

YIELD 2.5%
P/E RATIO 17.5

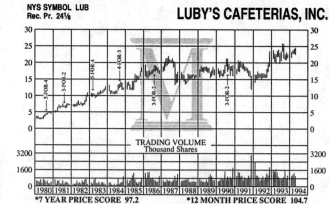

INTERIM EARNINGS (Per Share):

Qtr.	Nov.	Feb.	May	Aug.
1990-91	0.28	0.26	0.33	0.31
1991-92	0.24	0.26	0.33	0.31
1992-93	0.29	0.29	0.36	0.37
1993-94	0.32	0.33	...	...

INTERIM DIVIDENDS (Per Share):

Amt.	Decl.	Ex.	Rec.	Pay.
0.135Q	4/14/93	6/7/93	6/11/93	6/28/93
0.15Q	7/12	9/3	9/10	9/27
0.15Q	10/14	12/13	12/17	1/3/94
0.15Q	1/13/94	3/7/94	3/11/94	3/28
0.15Q	4/12	6/6	6/10	6/27

Indicated div.: $0.60

TRADING VOLUME
Thousand Shares

1980|1981|1982|1983|1984|1985|1986|1987|1988|1989|1990|1991|1992|1993|1994

*7 YEAR PRICE SCORE 97.2   *12 MONTH PRICE SCORE 104.7
*NYSE COMPOSITE INDEX=100

CAPITALIZATION (8/31/93):

	($000)	(%)
Common & Surplus	238,948	100.0
Total	238,948	100.0

DIVIDEND ACHIEVER STATUS:
Rank: 112   1983-93 Growth Rate: 12.6%
Total Years of Dividend Growth: 20

RECENT DEVELOPMENTS: For the quarter ended 11/30/93, net income before accounting changes rose 10% to $8.6 million compared with $7.9 million for the comparable period in 1992. Sales rose 6% to $94.2 million compared with $88.6 million for the same period last year. The implementation of a new marketing program contributed to sales growth. One new cafeteria was opened in Leavenworth, Kansas, while another opened in Grapevine, Texas.

PROSPECTS: A new marketing campaign which includes new menu entrees and a redesigned restaurant layout should boost revenues. Presently, increasing competition from other restaurant franchises is slightly hampering revenues, although new restaurants are contributing to sales growth. LUB has initiated credit card service in all its cafeterias and is conducting consumer research to more effectively respond to the prevailing market conditions.

BUSINESS

LUBY'S CAFETERIAS, INC. owns and operates one of the nation's largest cafeteria chains in the Southwest and Florida. As of 8/31/93, Luby's operated 169 cafeterias in ten states comprised of four in New Mexico, eleven in Arizona, three in Arkansas, five in Florida, two in Kansas, one in Louisiana, two in Missouri, nine in Oklahoma, six in Tennessee and 126 in Texas. The cafeterias are typically located convenient to shopping and business developments, as well as to residential areas. They cater primarily to shoppers, store and office personnel at lunch and to families at dinner. Generally from 10,000 to 11,000 square feet in area, a cafeteria can typically accommodate 300 customers.

ANNUAL EARNINGS AND DIVIDENDS PER SHARE

	8/31/93	8/31/92	8/31/91	8/31/90	8/31/89	8/31/88	8/31/87
Earnings Per Share	1.31	1.19	1.18	1.17	1.08	1.01	0.87
Dividends Per Share	0.555	0.51	0.47	① 0.435	0.387	0.343	0.303
Dividend Payout %	42.4	42.9	39.8	37.2	35.8	34.1	35.0

① 3-for-2 stk split, 8/3/90

ANNUAL FINANCIAL DATA

RECORD OF EARNINGS (IN THOUSANDS):

Total Revenues	367,757	346,359	328,236	311,325	283,252	254,301	232,858
Costs and Expenses	297,700	282,708	267,985	253,000	230,937	206,548	186,960
Depreciation & Amort	15,415	14,453	12,994	11,385	9,921	8,636	7,381
Income From Operations	54,642	49,198	47,257	46,940	42,394	39,117	38,517
Income Bef Income Taxes	56,216	50,517	48,848	48,512	44,377	41,247	41,750
Income Taxes	20,687	17,924	16,502	16,412	14,895	13,738	18,085
Net Income	35,529	32,593	32,346	32,100	29,482	27,509	23,665
Aver. Shs. Outstg.	27,195	27,344	27,392	27,365	27,352	27,350	27,344
BALANCE SHEET (IN THOUSANDS):							
Cash and Cash Equivalents	34,305	12,294	14,200	12,327	15,266	20,177	20,448
Trade Account & Other Receivs	602	241	190	157	251	468	400
Food & Supply Inventories	3,426	3,642	4,267	3,732	4,574	3,427	2,378
Gross Property	348,187	330,250	304,373	269,240	231,209	196,265	165,775
Accumulated Depreciation	103,401	89,705	77,565	65,288	55,720	46,895	39,216
Long-Term Debt	...	1,384	1,851	2,328	2,832	3,515	3,931
Net Stockholders' Equity	238,948	217,251	202,782	182,968	162,635	143,697	125,578
Total Assets	302,099	273,852	260,704	235,344	210,102	184,534	162,205
Total Current Assets	43,818	18,430	21,225	18,447	21,949	25,928	24,892
Total Current Liabilities	43,324	38,865	40,400	32,546	28,562	23,022	20,361
Net Working Capital	494	d20,435	d19,175	d14,099	d6,613	2,906	4,531
Year End Shares Outstg	27,227	27,134	27,398	27,374	27,359	27,350	27,350
STATISTICAL RECORD:							
Operating Profit Margin %	14.9	14.2	14.4	15.1	15.0	15.4	16.5
Book Value Per Share	8.78	8.01	7.40	6.68	5.94	5.25	4.59
Return on Equity %	14.9	15.0	16.0	17.5	18.1	19.1	18.8
Return on Assets %	11.8	11.9	12.4	13.6	14.0	14.9	14.6
Average Yield %	2.4	2.4	2.9	2.4	2.3	2.2	1.7
P/E Ratio	19.8-15.1	19.7-11.8	17.6-10.2	18.2-13.4	17.5-14.2	17.0-13.4	25.1-15.4
Price Range	25⅞-19¾	23½-14	20¾-12	21¼-15⅝	18⅞-15⅜	17⅛-13½	21⅞-13⅜

Statistics are as originally reported.

OFFICERS:
J.B. Lahourcade, Chmn.
R. Erben, Pres. & C.E.O.
J.E. Curtis, Jr., Sr. V.P., C.F.O. & Treas.

INCORPORATED: TX, 1959; reincorp., DE, Dec., 1991

PRINCIPAL OFFICE: 2211 Northeast Loop 410 P.O. Box 33069, San Antonio, TX 78265-3069

TELEPHONE NUMBER: (210) 654-9000

NO. OF EMPLOYEES: 1,306 (approx.)

ANNUAL MEETING: In January

SHAREHOLDERS: 2,877 (approx.)

INSTITUTIONAL HOLDINGS:
No. of Institutions: 142
Shares Held: 10,780,993

REGISTRAR(S): AmeriTrust Texas, N.A., Dallas, TX 75270

TRANSFER AGENT(S): AmeriTrust Texas, N.A., Dallas, TX 75270

MACNEAL-SCHWENDLER CORP.

YIELD 4.9%
P/E RATIO 13.7

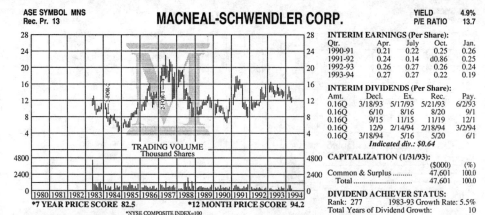

*7 YEAR PRICE SCORE 82.5   *12 MONTH PRICE SCORE 94.2
*NYSE COMPOSITE INDEX=100

INTERIM EARNINGS (Per Share):

Qtr.	Apr.	July	Oct.	Jan.
1990-91	0.21	0.22	0.25	0.26
1991-92	0.24	0.14	d0.86	0.25
1992-93	0.26	0.27	0.26	0.24
1993-94	0.27	0.27	0.22	0.19

INTERIM DIVIDENDS (Per Share):

Amt.	Decl.	Ex.	Rec.	Pay.
0.16Q	3/18/93	5/17/93	5/21/93	6/2/93
0.16Q	6/10	8/16	8/20	9/1
0.16Q	9/15	11/15	11/19	12/1
0.16Q	12/9	2/14/94	2/18/94	3/2/94
0.16Q	3/18/94	5/16	5/20	6/1

Indicated div.: $0.64

CAPITALIZATION (1/31/93):

	($000)	(%)
Common & Surplus	47,601	100.0
Total	47,601	100.0

DIVIDEND ACHIEVER STATUS:
Rank: 277   1983-93 Growth Rate: 5.5%
Total Years of Dividend Growth: 10

RECENT DEVELOPMENTS: For the year ended 1/31/94, revenues increased 3% to $79.6 million from $77.2 million a year ago. A total of 77% of revenue was derived from MSC/NASTRAN, the Company's principal computer-aided engineering analysis software product, and 13% of revenue was derived from MSC/ARIES, the Company's geometric modeling and automatic meshing software. The increase in total revenue primarily results from increased paid-up license sales of MSC/NASTRAN throughout the world. Net income for the year increased 14.5% to $11.4 million from $10.0 million in the prior year. Operating results for the year were unfavorably affected by $1.5 million due to exchange rate variances principally related to the functional currency of the Company's European and Far East subsidiaries.

BUSINESS

MACNEAL SCHWENDLER CORP. is a provider of finite element modeling and analysis products to the computer-aided engineering (CAE) market. The Company also is a leading provider of other products for the CAE market, including pre- and post-processing geometric modeling products. The Company''s four major product lines are MSC/NASTRAN, MSC/ARIES, MSC/EMAS and MSC/DYTRAN. These products are used by engineers and designers to model structures and assemblies and then analyze prior to manufacture their strength, dynamic response and heat transfer characteristics as well as electromagnetic reactions. The Company's products are marketed worldwide through offices in the United States, Europe and the Far East.

ANNUAL EARNINGS AND DIVIDENDS PER SHARE

	1/31/93	1/31/92	1/31/91	1/31/90	1/31/89	1/31/88	1/31/87
Earnings Per Share	1.03	d0.12	0.94	0.82	0.73	0.74	0.58
Dividends Per Share	0.48	0.46	0.38	0.31	0.26	[1]0.175	0.095
Dividend Payout %	46.6	...	40.4	37.8	36.0	23.6	16.4

[1] 2-for-1 stk. split, 3/87.

ANNUAL FINANCIAL DATA

RECORD OF EARNINGS (IN THOUSANDS):

Revenues	65,474	55,826	56,611	45,016	39,873	34,530	27,078
Costs and Expenses	42,686	49,047	33,866	28,702	24,646	19,011	[1]15,386
Depreciation & Amort	4,758	7,491	6,154	3,277	2,254	1,405	...
Operating Income	18,030	d712	16,591	13,037	12,973	14,114	11,692
Income Bef Income Taxes	18,708	d699	16,984	14,897	13,576	15,115	12,692
Provision for Inc Taxes	6,548	761	5,775	5,065	4,722	6,046	5,687
Net Income	12,160	d1,460	11,209	9,832	8,854	9,069	7,005
Aver. Shs. Outstg.	11,843	11,852	11,926	12,019	12,186	12,206	12,181

[1] Incl. Dep.

BALANCE SHEET (IN THOUSANDS):

Cash and Cash Equivalents	19,873	12,833	10,300	11,376	18,394	18,836	15,937
Receivables, Net	13,999	12,647	17,865	13,482	10,129	8,565	6,894
Gross Property	21,488	24,015	21,586	17,031	12,869	9,239	6,617
Accumulated Depreciation	10,233	10,860	9,630	6,712	4,558	3,271	2,300
Net Stockholders' Equity	47,601	40,268	48,377	43,221	38,161	34,448	27,217
Total Assets	68,860	58,689	68,421	59,627	50,455	42,925	32,327
Total Current Assets	39,135	27,997	31,075	27,826	30,174	28,697	23,776
Total Current Liabilities	21,259	12,761	13,035	10,682	8,837	6,540	4,002
Net Working Capital	17,876	15,236	18,040	17,144	21,337	22,157	19,774
Year End Shares Outstg	11,858	11,774	11,846	11,993	12,024	12,222	12,181

STATISTICAL RECORD:

Operating Profit Margin %	27.5	...	29.3	29.0	32.5	40.9	43.2
Book Value Per Share	2.57	2.01	2.06	1.93	2.25	2.18	1.92
Return on Equity %	25.5	...	23.2	22.7	23.2	26.3	25.7
Return on Assets %	17.7	...	16.4	16.5	17.5	21.1	21.7
Average Yield %	3.8	3.6	4.0	2.9	1.9	1.0	0.7
P/E Ratio	15.4-9.3	...	13.3-6.9	16.3-10.2	26.7-10.8	31.1-15.9	28.0-16.2
Price Range	15⅞-9⅝	18-7¾	12½-6½	13⅜-8⅜	19½-7⅞	23-11¾	16¼-9⅜

Statistics are as originally reported.

OFFICERS:
R.H. MacNeal, Chmn. & C.E.O.
L. McArthur, Pres. & C.O.O.
L.A. Greco, C.F.O. & Sec.

INCORPORATED: CA, 1963

PRINCIPAL OFFICE: 815 Colorado Blvd., Los Angeles, CA 90041

TELEPHONE NUMBER: (213) 258-9111

FAX: (213) 259-3838

NO. OF EMPLOYEES: 300

ANNUAL MEETING: In June

SHAREHOLDERS: 389

INSTITUTIONAL HOLDINGS:
No. of Institutions: 71
Shares Held: 8,251,056

REGISTRAR(S): Chemical Trust Company of California, Los Angeles, CA

TRANSFER AGENT(S): Chemical Trust Company of California, Los Angeles, CA

MADISON GAS & ELECTRIC CO.

YIELD 5.7%
P/E RATIO 14.4

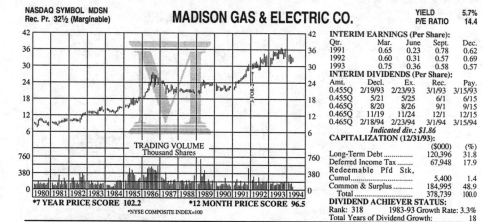

*7 YEAR PRICE SCORE 102.2   *12 MONTH PRICE SCORE 96.5

*NYSE COMPOSITE INDEX=100

INTERIM EARNINGS (Per Share):

Qtr.	Mar.	June	Sept.	Dec.
1991	0.65	0.23	0.78	0.62
1992	0.60	0.31	0.57	0.69
1993	0.75	0.36	0.58	0.57

INTERIM DIVIDENDS (Per Share):

Amt.	Decl.	Ex.	Rec.	Pay.
0.455Q	2/19/93	2/23/93	3/1/93	3/15/93
0.455Q	5/21	5/25	6/1	6/15
0.465Q	8/20	8/26	9/1	9/15
0.465Q	11/19	11/24	12/1	12/15
0.465Q	2/18/94	2/23/94	3/1/94	3/15/94

Indicated div.: $1.86

CAPITALIZATION (12/31/93):

	($000)	(%)
Long-Term Debt	120,396	31.8
Deferred Income Tax	67,948	17.9
Redeemable Pfd Stk,		
Cumul.	5,400	1.4
Common & Surplus	184,995	48.9
Total	378,739	100.0

DIVIDEND ACHIEVER STATUS:
Rank: 318   1983-93 Growth Rate: 3.3%
Total Years of Dividend Growth: 18

RECENT DEVELOPMENTS: For the year ended 12/31/93, MDSN reported net income of $24.7 million, up 3.6% from $23.8 million the previous year. Revenues were up 7.1% to $244.1 million compared with $228.0 million in 1992. The Company realized higher sales as a result of continued economic growth in its service operations. Expansion of business and ongoing cost containment programs also helped MDSN achieve improved results. While operating income dropped 2.4% to $34.2 million from $35.1 million, operating income as a percentage of sales moved downward to 14% from 16.4%. For the quarter ended 12/31/93, net income was down 17.5% to $6.2 million from $7.5 million last year. Revenues for the quarter edged up 1.1% to $67.4 million from $66.6 million. Operating profit as a percentage of sales fell to 12.7% from 15.4% due to a decrease of 17.3% in income from operations to $8.5 million.

BUSINESS

MADISON GAS & ELECTRIC COMPANY is a public utility engaged in the generation and transmission of electric energy and its distribution in Madison and its environs, (250 sq. miles) and in the purchase, transportation, and distribution of natural gas in Madison and its immediate surrounding territory (962 sq. miles). MDSN supplies electric service to 115,262 customers, of whom 103,010 were located in the cities of Fitchburg, Madison, Middleton, and Monona, and 12,252 in adjacent areas. MDSN supplies gas service to 92,372 customers in the cities of Madison, Middleton, Monona, Fitchburg, Lodi, and Verona; 13 villages; and all or parts of 29 townships.

BUSINESS LINE ANALYSIS

(12/31/93)	Rev(%)	Inc(%)
Electric	60.3	77.2
Gas	39.7	22.8
Total	100.0	100.0

ANNUAL EARNINGS AND DIVIDENDS PER SHARE

	1993	1992	1991	1990	1989	1988	1987
Earnings Per Share	2.26	2.18	2.28	2.04	1.95	1.99	1.93
Dividends Per Share	1.84	① 1.79	1.747	1.72	1.68	1.633	1.593
Dividend Payout %	81.4	82.1	76.6	84.3	86.3	82.2	82.4

① 3-for-2 stk split, 1/22/92

ANNUAL FINANCIAL DATA

RECORD OF EARNINGS (IN THOUSANDS):

	1993	1992	1991	1990	1989	1988	1987
Total Oper Revenues	244,133	228,002	232,200	220,568	217,588	214,323	202,133
Depreciation & Amort	21,791	21,427	21,025	22,098	19,878	18,231	21,007
Maintenance	13,029	12,544	13,170	11,538	12,588	10,954	9,943
Prov for Fed Inc Taxes	12,389	11,253	13,010	10,972	7,718	9,053	7,159
Net Oper Income	34,230	35,062	36,374	34,798	33,606	31,331	30,257
Net Interest Expense	11,624	13,436	12,684	14,198	14,553	12,457	11,749
Net Income	24,675	23,807	24,880	22,029	20,596	20,538	19,627
Aver. Shs. Outstg.	10,704	10,697	10,696	10,530	10,290	10,032	9,839

BALANCE SHEET (IN THOUSANDS):

Gross Plant	671,497	651,397	638,456	623,160	604,943	578,336	545,260
Accumulated Depreciation	302,904	284,248	265,278	245,427	279,515	261,315	244,818
Total Utility Plant	368,593	367,149	373,178	377,733	325,428	317,021	300,442
Long-term Debt	120,396	122,363	124,859	135,813	140,842	141,806	132,738
Net Stockholders' Equity	190,395	185,967	182,013	176,168	167,153	159,362	150,853
Total Assets	465,364	460,046	455,065	450,334	407,325	388,449	364,715
Year End Shares Outstg	10,720	10,697	10,697	10,680	10,415	10,188	9,943

STATISTICAL RECORD:

Book Value Per Share	17.26	16.86	16.47	15.93	15.45	15.01	14.51
Op. Inc/Net Pl %	9.3	9.5	9.7	9.2	10.3	9.9	10.1
Dep/Gr. Pl %	3.2	3.3	3.3	3.5	3.3	3.2	3.9
Accum. Dep/Gr. Pl %	45.1	43.6	41.5	39.4	46.2	45.2	44.9
Return on Equity %	13.3	13.2	14.1	12.9	12.8	13.4	13.6
Average Yield %	5.5	5.7	6.7	7.7	7.5	7.8	7.2
P/E Ratio	16.3-13.4	15.8-13.1	13.4-9.4	11.6-10.2	12.8-10.2	11.0-10.1	12.8-10.3
Price Range	36¾-30¼	34½-28½	30⅝-21½	23⅝-20⅞	25-19⅞	21⅞-20	24⅝-19⅞

Statistics are as originally reported.

OFFICERS:
F.C. Vondrasek, Chairman
D.C. Mebane, Pres., C.O.O., & C.E.O.
J.T. Krzos, V.P.-Fin.
G.J. Wolter, V.P.-Admin. & Sec.
T.A. Hanson, Treasurer
INCORPORATED: WI, Apr., 1896
PRINCIPAL OFFICE: 133 S. Blair Street P.O. Box 1231, Madison, WI 53701-1231

TELEPHONE NUMBER: (608) 252-7923
NO. OF EMPLOYEES: 723
ANNUAL MEETING: In May
SHAREHOLDERS: 16,152
INSTITUTIONAL HOLDINGS:
No. of Institutions: 54
Shares Held: 1,203,653

REGISTRAR(S): Harris Trust & Savings Bank, Chicago, IL

TRANSFER AGENT(S): Harris Trust & Savings Bank, Chicago, IL

MARK TWAIN BANCSHARES, INC.

YIELD 3.3%
P/E RATIO 12.9

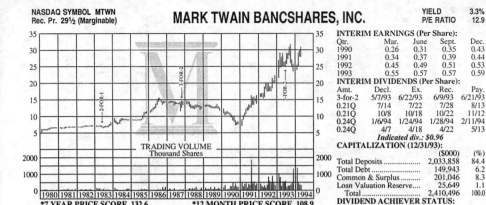

INTERIM EARNINGS (Per Share):

Qtr.	Mar.	June	Sept.	Dec.
1990	0.26	0.31	0.35	0.43
1991	0.34	0.37	0.39	0.44
1992	0.45	0.49	0.51	0.53
1993	0.55	0.57	0.57	0.59

INTERIM DIVIDENDS (Per Share):

Amt.	Decl.	Ex.	Rec.	Pay.
3-for-2	5/7/93	6/22/93	6/9/93	6/21/93
0.21Q	7/14	7/22	7/28	8/13
0.21Q	10/8	10/18	10/22	11/12
0.24Q	1/6/94	1/24/94	1/28/94	2/11/94
0.24Q	4/7	4/18	4/22	5/13

Indicated div.: $0.96

CAPITALIZATION (12/31/93):

	($000)	(%)
Total Deposits	2,033,858	84.4
Total Debt	149,943	6.2
Common & Surplus	201,046	8.3
Loan Valuation Reserve	25,649	1.1
Total	2,410,496	100.0

DIVIDEND ACHIEVER STATUS:
Rank: 190   1983-93 Growth Rate: 9.5%
Total Years of Dividend Growth: 23

TRADING VOLUME
Thousand Shares

*7 YEAR PRICE SCORE 132.6   ***12 MONTH PRICE SCORE 108.9**
*NYSE COMPOSITE INDEX=100

RECENT DEVELOPMENTS:

For the year ended 12/31/93, net income increased 22.4% to $33.1 million from $27.0 million in 1992. Total interest income was down a slight 1% to $164.2 million compared with $165.9 million the previous year. MTWN's solid financial performance resulted from the Company's continued strong net interest margin, increasing revenues from the fee groups, continuing low loan losses, improved efficiency levels due to only small increases in overhead expenses and steady loan growth. Banking opera-

tions benefited from strong net interest margins during the year, finishing up at 4.98% compared with 4.62%. The provision for loan losses in 1993 was $5.9 million compared with $8.2 million in 1992. Record levels of profitability were achieved in the Company's brokerage, bond and trust divisions. The mortgage division, although adversely affected by $2.9 million in write-downs in the value of MTWN's servicing portfolio, was profitable for the year and is expected to do better in 1994.

BUSINESS

MARK TWAIN BANCSHARES, INC. owns or controls substantially all of the capital stock of three banks: Mark Twain Bank, which operates eighteen separate locations in the metropolitan St. Louis area, Mark Twain Kansas City Bank, which operates five separate locations in the metropolitan Kansas City area, and Mark Twain Illinois Bank, which operates four locations on the Illinois side of the St. Louis metropolitan area. On 2/10/93, MTWN acquired First National Bank of Shawnee, Kansas, which operates three locations on the Kansas side of the Kansas City metropolitan area. Mark Twain Properties, Inc. owns, holds under lease or manages property by present banking centers. Mark Twain Community Development Corp. provides services and housing opportunities for low-and moderate-income persons. Tarquad Corp. acts as a trustee of deeds of trust for MTWN's subsidiaries. Mark Twain Asset Recovery, Inc. purchases certain assets acquired by subsidiary banks in collection of loans.

ANNUAL EARNINGS AND DIVIDENDS PER SHARE

	1993	1992	1991	1990	1989	1988	1987
Earnings Per Share	2.28	1.98	1.55	1.35	1.37	1.27	② 1.07
Dividends Per Share	① 0.807	0.68	0.613	0.587	0.52	0.453	③ 0.40
Dividend Payout %	35.4	34.3	39.5	43.6	37.9	35.6	37.3

① Adj for 3-for-2 stk split, 6/22/93 ② Before extraord. item ③ 3-for-2 stk. split, 11/87.

ANNUAL FINANCIAL DATA

RECORD OF EARNINGS (IN MILLIONS):

	1993	1992	1991	1990	1989	1988	1987
Total Interest Income	164.2	165.9	189.2	192.7	184.9	165.5	129.9
Total Interest Expense	59.3	73.7	106.0	116.9	112.3	95.6	74.0
Net Interest Income	105.0	92.1	83.2	75.7	72.5	69.9	55.9
Provision for Loan Losses	5.9	8.2	14.1	7.4	4.5	4.1	3.2
Net Income	33.1	27.0	19.6	16.1	16.2	14.3	① 11.2
Aver. Shs. Outstg. (000)	14,494	13,653	12,649	12,047	11,683	11,236	10,289

① Before extra. item dr$773,000.

BALANCE SHEET (IN MILLIONS):

	1993	1992	1991	1990	1989	1988	1987
Cash & Due From Banks	100.8	105.5	102.4	101.2	113.5	116.7	97.0
Loans, Net	1,580.1	1,417.0	1,451.3	1,484.2	1,363.7	1,293.2	1,133.5
Total Domestic Deposits	2,033.9	1,891.4	1,844.4	1,857.3	1,668.8	1,636.2	1,425.4
Long-term Debt	22.4	26.3	27.4	32.2	33.1	34.0	37.3
Net Stockholders' Equity	201.0	167.4	148.8	116.6	109.5	99.4	79.1
Total Assets	2,408.0	2,213.1	2,170.4	2,127.7	1,949.2	1,834.7	1,602.6
Year End Shs Outstg (000)	14,594	13,496	13,434	11,688	11,424	11,385	9,968

STATISTICAL RECORD:

	1993	1992	1991	1990	1989	1988	1987
Return on Assets %	1.37	1.22	0.90	0.76	0.83	0.78	0.70
Return on Equity %	16.40	16.10	13.20	13.80	14.80	14.40	14.10
Book Value Per Share	13.78	12.40	11.08	9.98	9.34	8.48	7.65
Average Yield %	3.0	3.6	5.2	6.0	4.1	3.4	3.1
P/E Ratio	13.9-9.4	11.3-7.8	10.5-4.5	9.2-5.4	9.9-8.5	11.5-9.4	13.6-10.7
Price Range	31¾-21½	22⅜-15⅜	16⅜-7	12⅜-7¼	13⅝-11⅝	14⅝-12	14⅝-11½

Statistics are as originally reported.

OFFICERS:
A.J. Siteman, Chairman
J.P. Dubinsky, Pres. & C.E.O.
K. Miller, Sr. V.P.-Fin. & C.F.O.
C.A. Wattenberg, Jr., Sr. V.P. & Sec.

INCORPORATED: MO, Apr., 1967

PRINCIPAL OFFICE: 8820 Ladue Road, St. Louis, MO 63124

TELEPHONE NUMBER: (314) 727-1000
FAX: (314) 889-0784
NO. OF EMPLOYEES: 1,000 (approx.)
ANNUAL MEETING: In May
SHAREHOLDERS: 2,135 (approx.)
INSTITUTIONAL HOLDINGS:
No. of Institutions: 50
Shares Held: 3,281,429

REGISTRAR(S): Society National Bank, Cleveland, OH

TRANSFER AGENT(S): Society National Bank, Cleveland, OH

MARSH & McLENNAN COMPANIES, INC.

YIELD 3.3%
P/E RATIO 19.3

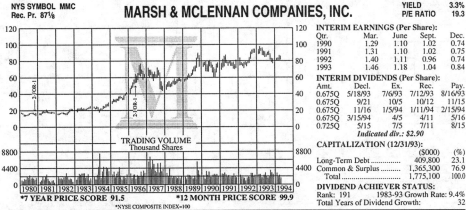

INTERIM EARNINGS (Per Share):

Qtr.	Mar.	June	Sept.	Dec.
1990	1.29	1.10	1.02	0.74
1991	1.31	1.10	1.02	0.75
1992	1.40	1.11	0.96	0.74
1993	1.46	1.18	1.04	0.84

INTERIM DIVIDENDS (Per Share):

Amt.	Decl.	Ex.	Rec.	Pay.
0.675Q	5/18/93	7/6/93	7/12/93	8/16/93
0.675Q	9/21	10/5	10/12	11/15
0.675Q	11/16	1/5/94	1/11/94	2/15/94
0.675Q	3/15/94	4/5	4/11	5/16
0.725Q	5/15	7/5	7/11	8/15

Indicated div.: $2.90

CAPITALIZATION (12/31/93):

	($000)	(%)
Long-Term Debt	409,800	23.1
Common & Surplus	1,365,300	76.9
Total	1,775,100	100.0

DIVIDEND ACHIEVER STATUS:
Rank: 191   1983-93 Growth Rate: 9.4%
Total Years of Dividend Growth: 32

TRADING VOLUME
Thousand Shares

*7 YEAR PRICE SCORE 91.5   *12 MONTH PRICE SCORE 99.9

*NYSE COMPOSITE INDEX=100

RECENT DEVELOPMENTS: Net income advanced 15% to $62.6 million for the three months ended 12/31/93. Revenue increased to $779.8 million from $705.2 million in the similar period of 1992, paced by a 40% gain in investment management revenues. Insurance services revenues were up 11% to $422.5 million. For 1993, income was $332.4 million versus $303.8 million in 1992. Revenues were up to $3.16 billion from last year's $2.94 billion.

PROSPECTS: Insurance services revenue is a driving force behind earnings. The investment management business continues to make positive contributions with increased revenue and a growth in asset levels due primarily to improved institutional and mutual fund sales through its subsidiary, Putnam Investments. Pricing problems still persist in the property casualty markets and the wait for stable pricing will probably continue into the near term.

BUSINESS

MARSH & McLENNAN COMPANIES, INC. is engaged in the worldwide business of providing retail and wholesale insurance services, principally as a broker or consultant for insurers, insurance underwriters and other brokers. Marsh & McLennan Inc., the major subsidiary, is the largest insurance broker in the world. Other subsidiaries render advisory services in the area of employee benefits and compensation consulting, management consulting, economic consulting, environmental consulting and investment management services.

REVENUES

(12/31/93)	($000)	(%)
Insurance Services	1,790,500	56.6
Consulting	854,800	27.0
Investment Mgt	518,100	16.4
Total	3,163,400	100.0

ANNUAL EARNINGS AND DIVIDENDS PER SHARE

	1993	1992	1991	1990	1989	1988	1987
Earnings Per Share	4.52	4.21	4.18	4.15	4.10	4.09	4.06
Dividends Per Share	2.70	① 2.65	2.60	2.55	2.50	2.425	2.15
Dividend Payout %	59.7	62.9	62.2	61.4	61.0	59.3	53.0

① Bef acctg chge

ANNUAL FINANCIAL DATA

RECORD OF EARNINGS (IN MILLIONS):

	1993	1992	1991	1990	1989	1988	1987
Revenue	3,163.4	2,937.0	2,779.2	2,723.0	2,427.7	2,272.4	2,147.1
Costs and Expenses	2,570.6	2,396.0	2,281.1	2,195.7	1,918.2	1,757.0	1,596.9
Operating Income	592.8	541.0	498.1	527.3	509.5	515.4	550.2
Income Bef Income Taxes	558.6	519.3	526.8	528.8	517.3	516.4	567.3
Income Taxes	226.2	215.5	221.3	224.7	222.4	220.1	265.2
Net Income	332.4	① 303.8	305.5	304.1	294.9	296.3	302.1
Aver. Shs. Outstg. (000)	73,500	72,200	73,100	73,300	71,900	72,400	74,400

① Before acctg. change dr$40,100,000.

BALANCE SHEET (IN MILLIONS):

Cash and Cash Equivalents	332.0	371.1	349.0	304.6	293.0	252.2	344.1
Net Receivables	853.0	827.0	690.0	748.2	618.1	535.6	502.5
Gross Property	1,226.9	1,196.7	1,177.4	1,139.2	1,018.5	912.4	581.6
Accumulated Depreciation	538.8	488.9	443.4	379.8	337.1	292.9	228.3
Long-Term Debt	409.8	411.2	318.0	319.9	319.4	266.2	16.4
Net Stockholders' Equity	1,365.3	1,102.9	1,035.0	1,085.3	873.0	755.1	791.7
Total Assets	3,546.6	3,088.4	2,382.2	2,411.2	2,035.2	1,830.0	1,634.4
Total Current Assets	1,312.4	1,260.4	1,039.0	1,052.8	911.1	787.8	846.6
Total Current Liabilities	1,109.9	1,016.5	736.0	732.6	624.9	626.4	638.3
Net Working Capital	202.5	243.9	303.0	320.2	286.2	161.4	208.3
Year End Shs Outstg (000)	73,932	73,275	71,841	73,521	72,426	71,515	73,856

STATISTICAL RECORD:

Book Value Per Share	18.47	15.05	14.41	14.76	12.05	10.56	10.72
Return on Equity %	24.3	27.5	29.5	28.0	33.8	39.2	38.2
Return on Assets %	9.4	9.8	12.8	12.6	14.5	16.2	18.5
Average Yield %	3.1	3.2	3.3	3.6	3.5	4.6	3.7
P/E Ratio	21.6-17.0	22.4-16.9	20.9-16.5	19.5-14.4	21.9-13.4	14.6-11.1	17.7-10.8
Price Range	97⅝-77	94½-71¼	87¼-69⅛	81-59¾	89¾-55⅛	59¾-45¼	72-43¾

Statistics are as originally reported.

OFFICERS:
A.C. Smith, Chairman
R. Clements, President
F.J. Borelli, Sr. V.P. & C.F.O.
G.F. Van Gundy, Sec. & Gen. Couns.

INCORPORATED: DE, Mar., 1969

PRINCIPAL OFFICE: 1166 Avenue of the Americas, New York, NY 10036

TELEPHONE NUMBER: (212) 345-5000

FAX: (212) 345-5669

NO. OF EMPLOYEES: 25,800

ANNUAL MEETING: In May

SHAREHOLDERS: 11,313

INSTITUTIONAL HOLDINGS:
No. of Institutions: 451
Shares Held: 47,791,200

REGISTRAR(S): Harris Trust Co. of N.Y., New York, NY 10005

TRANSFER AGENT(S): Harris Trust Co. of N.Y., New York, NY 10005

NASDAQ SYMBOL MRIS
Rec. Pr. 22¼ (Marginable)

MARSHALL & ILSLEY CORP.

YIELD 2.7%
P/E RATIO 11.8

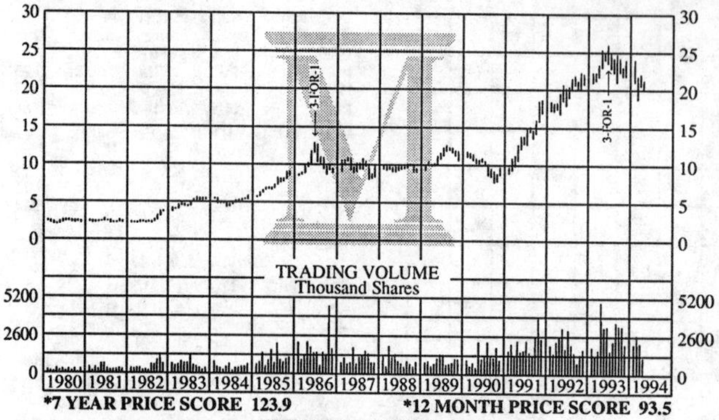

30
25
20
15
10
5
0
3-FOR-1
3-FOR-1
TRADING VOLUME
Thousand Shares
5200
2600
0
1980
1981
1982
1983
1984
1985
1986
1987
1988
1989
1990
1991
1992
1993
1994

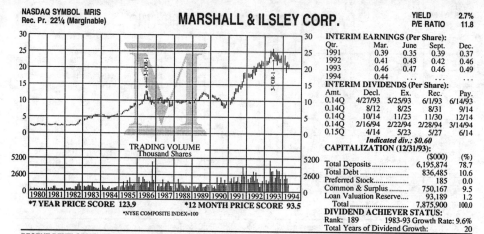

*7 YEAR PRICE SCORE 123.9 *12 MONTH PRICE SCORE 93.5

*NYSE COMPOSITE INDEX=100

INTERIM EARNINGS (Per Share):

Qtr.	Mar.	June	Sept.	Dec.
1991	0.39	0.35	0.39	0.37
1992	0.41	0.43	0.42	0.46
1993	0.46	0.47	0.46	0.49
1994	0.44	...	...	...

INTERIM DIVIDENDS (Per Share):

Amt.	Decl.	Ex.	Rec.	Pay.
0.14Q	4/27/93	5/25/93	6/1/93	6/14/93
0.14Q	8/12	8/25	8/31	9/14
0.14Q	10/14	11/23	11/30	12/14
0.14Q	2/16/94	2/22/94	2/28/94	3/14/94
0.15Q	4/14	5/23	5/27	6/14

Indicated div.: $0.60

CAPITALIZATION (12/31/93):

	($000)	(%)
Total Deposits	6,195,874	78.7
Total Debt	836,485	10.6
Preferred Stock	185	0.0
Common & Surplus	750,167	9.5
Loan Valuation Reserve	93,189	1.2
Total	7,875,900	100.0

DIVIDEND ACHIEVER STATUS:
Rank: 189 1983-93 Growth Rate: 9.6%
Total Years of Dividend Growth: 20

RECENT DEVELOPMENTS: For the quarter ended 3/31/94, net income decreased 9% to $28.2 million, or $0.44 per share, from $31.0 million, or $0.46 per share, for the same quarter last year. The reduction in net income is attributed primarily to a narrowing of the margin between the yields on loans and investments and the cost of deposits. This reduction was partially offset by an increase in loan growth. On 5/31/94, MRIS completed the acquisition of Valley Bancorporation, a $4.6 billion bank holding company headquartered in Appleton, Wisconsin, for stock valued at more than $760 million. Valley, which has 160 banking offices, provides a complete range of banking services, including insurance, trust services, securities, credit card servicing and bank support services.

BUSINESS

MARSHALL & ILSLEY CORP. is a multibank holding company headquartered in Milwaukee, Wisconsin. M&I Marshall and Ilsley Bank is the Corporation's lead bank. The Corporation has 35 affiliated banks serving the state from 129 banking offices and one bank in Phoenix, Arizona with 12 offices. In addition, the holding company has a leasing company with fourteen offices, an investment management company, two mortgage banking companies, an insurance subsidiary, a venture capital company, a data services company with six offices, and trust companies in Wisconsin, Arizona, and Florida.

LOAN DISTRIBUTION

(12/31/93)	($000)	(%)
Commercial, Financial & Agricultural	1,861,757	34.7
Industrial Development Revenue Bonds	27,821	0.5
Real Estate	2,530,752	47.1
Personal	711,194	13.2
Lease Financing	239,561	4.5
Total	5,371,085	100.0

ANNUAL EARNINGS AND DIVIDENDS PER SHARE

	1993	1992	1991	1990	1989	1988	1987
Earnings Per Share	1.87	[2] 1.73	1.50	1.08	1.28	1.16	1.05
Dividends Per Share	[1] 0.543	[3] 0.48	0.43	0.39	0.35	0.31	0.277
Dividend Payout %	29.0	27.8	28.7	36.0	27.3	26.7	26.3

[1] 3-for-1 stk split,06/01/93 [2] Before acctg. chg. [3] Bef acctg chge

ANNUAL FINANCIAL DATA

	1993	1992	1991	1990	1989	1988	1987
RECORD OF EARNINGS (IN MILLIONS):							
Total Interest Income	487.5	532.1	607.9	641.8	612.0	525.0	431.8
Total Interest Expense	178.4	224.3	318.9	366.4	358.4	294.6	241.5
Net Interest Income	309.2	307.8	289.0	275.4	253.5	230.4	190.3
Provision for Loan Losses	9.1	15.2	20.6	39.8	12.3	8.3	8.7
Net Income	125.5	[1] 116.6	99.3	71.3	85.4	76.2	57.9
Aver. Shs. Outstg. (000)	67,047	67,523	66,162	65,943	66,797	66,170	55,023
[1] Before acctg. change dr$7,387,000.							
BALANCE SHEET (IN MILLIONS):							
Cash & Due From Banks	479.5	491.8	551.9	614.5	516.5	515.6	436.6
U.S. Treasury Securities	...	...	...	...	...	...	32.6
Net Loans	5,277.9	4,792.8	4,699.6	4,699.1	4,567.7	4,021.7	3,039.5
Total Domestic Deposits	6,195.9	6,212.1	6,133.1	5,979.6	5,585.3	5,211.1	4,318.8
Long-term Borrowings	202.8	130.2	182.3	178.4	148.9	177.0	143.1
Net Stockholders' Equity	750.4	760.6	675.0	599.2	564.2	497.7	389.4
Total Assets	7,970.2	7,850.3	7,627.8	7,460.1	7,150.8	6,774.9	5,555.8
Year End Shs Outstg (000)	66,425	64,356	63,491	62,610	63,744	63,219	51,888
STATISTICAL RECORD:							
Return on Assets %	1.57	1.49	1.30	0.96	1.19	1.12	1.04
Return on Equity %	16.70	15.30	14.70	11.90	15.10	15.30	14.90
Book Value Per Share	11.29	11.82	10.63	9.57	8.85	7.87	7.50
Average Yield %	2.3	2.5	3.1	4.0	3.2	3.2	2.9
P/E Ratio	13.9-11.2	12.9-9.8	12.4-5.9	11.0-7.2	9.9-7.3	8.7-7.9	10.5-7.7
Price Range	26-20⅞	22¼-16⅞	18⅝-8⅞	11⅞-7¾	12⅝-9⅜	10⅛-9⅛	11-8⅛

Statistics are as originally reported.

OFFICERS:
J.B. Wigdale, Chmn. & C.E.O.
E.I. Van Housen, Vice-Chmn.
D.J. Kuester, President
M.A. Hatfield, Sr. V.P., Sec. & Treas.

INCORPORATED: WI, Feb., 1959

PRINCIPAL OFFICE: 770 North Water Street, Milwaukee, WI 53202

TELEPHONE NUMBER: (414) 765-7801

NO. OF EMPLOYEES: 7,000

ANNUAL MEETING: In April

SHAREHOLDERS: 10,400

INSTITUTIONAL HOLDINGS:
No. of Institutions: 128
Shares Held: 24,378,616

REGISTRAR(S): The Bank of New York, New York, NY

TRANSFER AGENT(S): The Bank of New York, New York, NY

MARTIN MARIETTA CORP.

YIELD 2.1%
P/E RATIO 10.0

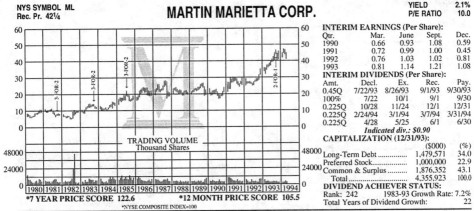

TRADING VOLUME
Thousand Shares

*7 YEAR PRICE SCORE 122.6   *12 MONTH PRICE SCORE 105.5
*NYSE COMPOSITE INDEX=100

INTERIM EARNINGS (Per Share):

Qtr.	Mar.	June	Sept.	Dec.
1990	0.66	0.93	1.08	0.59
1991	0.72	0.99	1.00	0.45
1992	0.76	1.03	1.02	0.81
1993	0.81	1.14	1.21	1.08

INTERIM DIVIDENDS (Per Share):

Amt.	Decl.	Ex.	Rec.	Pay.
0.45Q	7/22/93	8/26/93	9/1/93	9/30/93
100%	7/22	10/1	9/1	9/30
0.225Q	10/28	11/24	12/1	12/31
0.225Q	2/24/94	3/1/94	3/7/94	3/31/94
0.225Q	4/28	5/25	6/1	6/30

Indicated div.: $0.90

CAPITALIZATION (12/31/93):

	($000)	(%)
Long-Term Debt	1,479,571	34.0
Preferred Stock	1,000,000	22.9
Common & Surplus	1,876,352	43.1
Total	4,355,923	100.0

DIVIDEND ACHIEVER STATUS:
Rank: 242   1983-93 Growth Rate: 7.2%
Total Years of Dividend Growth: 22

RECENT DEVELOPMENTS: In April, the Company lost its bidding war with Northrop to acquire Grumman Corporation. For the quarter ended 12/31/93, net income increased 30.4% to $450.3 million. Sales rose 58.5% to $9.44 billion. Results were aided by the acquisition of GE Aerospace. Electronics posted operating margins of 9.3% on sales of $3.90 billion. The Space Group reported sales of $3.40 billion, up 13%. The Materials Group recorded an 11% increase in sales to $450 million.

PROSPECTS: Although the acquisition of GE Aerospace has increased debt levels, it will fuel sales and earnings growth and position the Company to capitalize on market synergies among its commercial, civil government and international lines of businesses. Additionally, the acquisition of General Dynamics' Space Systems Division will complement the Company's established position in the large payload market. Despite ML's unsuccessful bid to acquire Grumman Corp., the Company will continue to seek growth opportunities.

BUSINESS

MARTIN MARIETTA CORP. engages in the design, manufacture and integration of systems and products in the fields of space, defense, electronics, information managment, energy and materials. Astronautics (accounting for 35% of 1993 sales) consists of space launch vehicles, spacecraft, space and ground-based strategic systems and the Space Shuttle external tank. Electronics, Information and Missiles (54%) consists of missiles, electronic systems for precision guidance and air defense programs, electro-optical target acquisition and navigation systems and information management and engineering systems. Materials (5%) consists of aggregates operations and magnesia specialties. Other operations (6%) include research for the Department of Energy and real estate activities.

BUSINESS LINE ANALYSIS

(12/31/93)	Rev(%)	Inc(%)
Electronics	40.1	38.9
Space	35.2	29.0
Information	14.2	14.8
Services	4.7	3.3
Materials	4.6	9.0
Energy & Other	1.2	5.0
Total	100.0	100.0

ANNUAL EARNINGS AND DIVIDENDS PER SHARE

	1993	1992	1991	1990	1989	1988	1987
Earnings Per Share	4.25	②3.61	3.15	3.26	2.91	③3.01	2.13
Dividends Per Share	①0.87	0.76	0.75	0.693	0.612	0.55	0.53
Dividend Payout %	23.5	11.0	11.9	10.7	10.5	9.0	12.4

① 2-for-1 stk split, 10/1/93 ② 2-for-1 stock split,10/01/93 ③ Before extraord. item

ANNUAL FINANCIAL DATA

RECORD OF EARNINGS (IN MILLIONS):

	1993	1992	1991	1990	1989	1988	1987
Total Revenues	9,435.7	5,954.3	6,075.4	6,125.9	5,796.2	5,727.5	5,165.1
Costs and Expenses	8,297.2	5,179.0	5,312.9	5,467.6	5,124.5	5,132.2	4,585.0
Deprec, Depl & Amort	350.0	226.1	225.1	215.8	207.0	198.6	173.3
Earnings From Operations	788.5	549.2	537.5	442.5	464.6	396.7	406.8
Earn Bef Taxes on Inc & Acctg Chge	725.3	512.4	420.8	435.2	429.3	475.2	380.0
Taxes on Income	275.0	167.0	107.7	107.6	122.4	155.4	149.4
Net Income	①450.3	345.4	313.1	327.6	306.9	②319.8	230.7
Aver. Shs. Outstg. (000)	95,347	95,869	99,341	100,530	105,542	106,304	108,636

① Before acctg. change dr$429,432,000. ② Before extra. item cr$39,100,000.

BALANCE SHEET (IN MILLIONS):

	1993	1992	1991	1990	1989	1988	1987
Cash & Cash Equivalents	373.1	239.6	170.6	87.5	67.6	76.6	153.5
Receivables, Net	1,674.2	851.5	860.9	807.5	779.7	735.7	555.1
Inventories	358.7	300.9	538.9	458.3	539.7	443.3	369.4
Gross Property	3,804.3	3,144.2	3,049.3	2,843.1	2,626.0	2,501.7	2,202.5
Accumulated Depreciation	2,111.6	1,887.1	1,733.8	1,502.4	1,325.0	1,204.2	1,066.8
Long-Term Debt	1,479.6	474.7	595.9	463.3	477.5	483.8	281.9
Net Stockholders' Equity	2,876.4	1,945.2	1,803.9	1,541.0	1,355.0	1,200.6	907.7
Total Assets	7,744.9	3,599.6	3,896.9	3,610.5	3,505.4	3,319.0	2,794.1
Total Current Assets	2,448.2	1,434.3	1,616.5	1,400.6	1,440.6	1,291.3	1,130.2
Total Current Liabilities	1,810.1	586.2	948.0	993.6	926.3	908.6	813.5
Net Working Capital	638.1	848.1	668.5	407.0	514.3	382.7	316.6
Year End Shs Outstg (000)	95,697	94,458	99,060	97,732	101,628	105,638	105,810

STATISTICAL RECORD:

	1993	1992	1991	1990	1989	1988	1987
Operating Profit Margin %	8.4	9.2	8.8	7.2	8.0	6.9	7.9
Book Value Per Share	30.06	20.59	18.21	15.77	13.33	11.37	8.58
Return on Equity %	15.7	17.8	17.4	21.3	22.7	26.6	25.4
Return on Assets %	5.8	9.6	8.0	9.1	8.8	9.6	8.3
Average Yield %	2.2	2.5	2.9	3.4	2.7	2.5	2.3
P/E Ratio	5.8-4.0	4.9-3.5	4.8-3.4	7.4-5.3	9.2-6.5	8.0-6.4	13.3-8.2
Price Range	46⅝-32	35¼-25	30¼-21¼	24⅛-17⅛	26¾-18⅞	24⅛-19⅛	28¼-17½

Statistics are as originally reported.

OFFICERS:
N.R. Augustine, Chmn. & C.E.O.
A.T. Young, Pres. & C.O.O.
M.C. Bennett, Sr. V.P. & C.F.O.
J.L. McGregor, Treasurer
K.T. Sheehan, Secretary
INCORPORATED: MD, Oct., 1961
PRINCIPAL OFFICE: 6801 Rockledge Drive, Bethesda, MD 20817

TELEPHONE NUMBER: (301) 897-6000
FAX: (301) 897-6083
NO. OF EMPLOYEES: 2,409
ANNUAL MEETING: In April
SHAREHOLDERS: 10,952
INSTITUTIONAL HOLDINGS:
No. of Institutions: 366
Shares Held: 33,171,676

REGISTRAR(S): First Chicago Trust Co. of New York, New York, NY 10008
Maryland National Bank, Baltimore, MD 21201

TRANSFER AGENT(S): First Chicago Trust Co. of New York, New York, NY 10008
Maryland National Bank, Baltimore, MD 21201

NYS SYMBOL MAS
Rec. Pr. 28⅜

MASCO CORP.

YIELD 2.4%
P/E RATIO 26.0

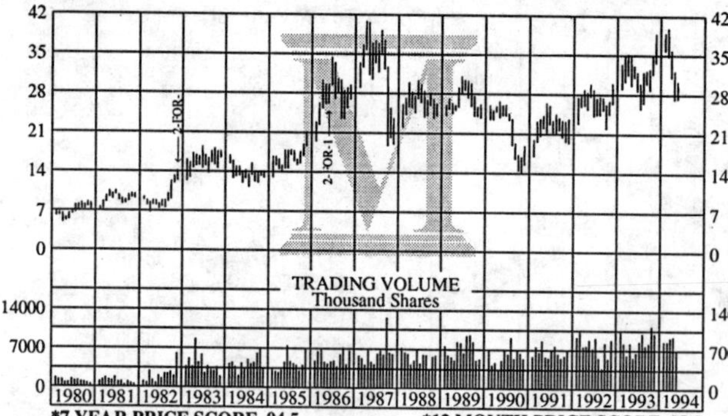

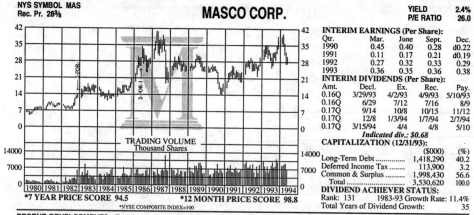

*7 YEAR PRICE SCORE 94.5 *12 MONTH PRICE SCORE 98.8

*NYSE COMPOSITE INDEX=100

INTERIM EARNINGS (Per Share):

Qtr.	Mar.	June	Sept.	Dec.
1990	0.45	0.40	0.28	d0.22
1991	0.11	0.17	0.21	d0.19
1992	0.27	0.32	0.33	0.29
1993	0.36	0.35	0.36	0.38

INTERIM DIVIDENDS (Per Share):

Amt.	Decl.	Ex.	Rec.	Pay.
0.16Q	3/29/93	4/2/93	4/9/93	5/10/93
0.16Q	6/29	7/12	7/16	8/9
0.17Q	9/14	10/8	10/15	11/12
0.17Q	12/8	1/3/94	1/7/94	2/7/94
0.17Q	3/15/94	4/4	4/8	5/10

Indicated div.: $0.68

CAPITALIZATION (12/31/93):

	($000)	(%)
Long-Term Debt	1,418,290	40.2
Deferred Income Tax	113,900	3.2
Common & Surplus	1,998,430	56.6
Total	3,530,620	100.0

DIVIDEND ACHIEVER STATUS:
Rank: 131 1983-93 Growth Rate: 11.4%
Total Years of Dividend Growth: 35

RECENT DEVELOPMENTS: For the year ended 12/31/93, net income increased 20.8% to $221.1 million compared with $183.1 million in 1992. Sales rose 10.2% to $3.89 billion from $3.53 billion. Building and home improvement products achieved all-time record sales and earnings. Home furnishings products posted a 15% increase in operating profit to $69 million.

PROSPECTS: Supported by economic recovery, sales and earnings will increase as the Company continues to experience market share growth. Strength in the housing market and improved consumer confidence should benefit the home improvement and home furnishings segments while the home furnishings group will continue to benefit from recent acquisitions, capital expenditures and cost reduction programs.

BUSINESS

MASCO CORP. manufactures building, home improvement and home furnishings products. Masco's building and home improvement segment includes faucets, plumbing fittings, kitchen and bathroom cabinets, bathtubs and whirlpools, builders' hardware, venting and ventilating equipment, insulation products and water pumps. Home furnishings and other specialty products include high-quality furniture and other home furnishings products, giftware, and recreational accessories. Brand-names include Delta, Delex, Peerless, Artistic and Epic faucets; Merillat kitchen and bathroom cabinets; Weiser and Baldwin locks, Brass-Craft and Plumb Shop plumbing fittings; Thermador and Waste King appliances.

BUSINESS LINE ANALYSIS

(12/31/93)	Rev(%)	Inc(%)
Building & Home Improvement	56.3	85.7
Home Furnishings Products	43.7	14.3
Total	100.0	100.0

ANNUAL EARNINGS AND DIVIDENDS PER SHARE

	1993	1992	1991	1990	1989	1988	1987
Earnings Per Share	**1.45**	**1.21**	**0.30**	**0.91**	**1.42**	**2.10**	**1.65**
Dividends Per Share	**0.65**	**0.61**	**0.57**	**0.54**	**0.50**	**0.44**	**0.38**
Dividend Payout %	**44.8**	**50.4**	**N.M.**	**59.3**	**35.2**	**21.0**	**23.0**

ANNUAL FINANCIAL DATA

	1993	1992	1991	1990	1989	1988	1987
RECORD OF EARNINGS (IN MILLIONS):							
Total Revenues	3,886.0	3,525.0	3,141.0	3,209.0	3,150.5	2,438.6	2,023.3
Costs and Expenses	3,366.2	3,052.0	2,790.0	2,752.7	2,656.5	1,967.8	1,603.8
Depreciation & Amort	116.0	114.5	102.7	93.5	89.1	74.6	63.3
Operating Profit	403.8	358.5	248.3	362.8	405.0	396.2	356.2
Income Bef Income Taxes	362.6	304.8	97.6	235.9	327.1	421.4	334.5
Income Taxes	141.5	121.7	52.7	97.1	106.2	133.1	115.7
Net Income	221.1	183.1	44.9	138.8	220.9	288.3	218.8
Aver. Shs. Outstg. (000)	152,700	151,700	149,900	152,600	155,600	137,500	132,500
BALANCE SHEET (IN MILLIONS):							
Cash and Cash Equivalents	124.9	54.3	70.3	68.9	113.1	143.1	304.5
Receivables	610.1	547.8	497.0	480.5	512.9	372.0	330.8
Inventories	824.1	781.7	738.9	753.4	712.3	550.9	446.7
Gross Property	1,683.4	1,554.0	1,460.2	1,375.0	1,252.6	920.8	830.3
Accumulated Depreciation	588.2	523.5	460.1	404.9	372.0	268.7	215.0
Long-Term Debt	1,418.3	1,487.1	1,369.3	1,334.3	1,153.2	999.2	938.0
Net Stockholders' Equity	1,998.4	1,886.9	1,798.9	1,774.0	1,858.4	1,546.1	1,370.9
Total Assets	4,021.1	3,986.6	3,785.8	3,760.7	3,640.8	2,999.2	2,850.1
Total Current Assets	1,643.8	1,465.5	1,375.9	1,365.2	1,393.3	1,137.9	1,100.3
Total Current Liabilities	490.4	491.5	513.8	551.8	539.5	377.7	481.1
Net Working Capital	1,153.4	974.0	862.1	813.3	853.7	760.2	619.3
Year End Shs Outstg (000)	152,850	152,470	151,010	147,760	155,620	136,810	132,590
STATISTICAL RECORD:							
Operating Profit Margin %	10.4	10.2	7.9	11.3	12.9	16.2	17.6
Book Value Per Share	9.12	8.26	7.73	7.67	7.91	7.11	5.96
Return on Equity %	11.1	9.7	2.5	7.8	11.9	18.6	16.0
Return on Assets %	5.5	4.6	1.2	3.7	6.1	9.6	7.7
Average Yield %	2.0	2.3	2.6	2.6	1.8	1.7	1.3
P/E Ratio	26.8-17.6	24.8-18.2	88.3-56.7	29.4-15.7	21.9-16.7	14.5-10.5	24.8-11.4
Price Range	38⅞-25½	30-22	26½-17	26¾-14¼	31⅛-23¾	30⅜-22	40⅞-18¾

Statistics are as originally reported.

OFFICERS:
R.A. Manoogian, Chmn. & C.E.O.
W.B. Lyon, Pres. & C.O.O.
R.G. Mosteller, Sr. V.P.-Fin.
G. Bright, V.P. & Sec.

INCORPORATED: MI, Dec., 1929; reincorp., DE, 1968

PRINCIPAL OFFICE: 21001 Van Born Rd., Taylor, MI 48180

TELEPHONE NUMBER: (313) 274-7400

FAX: (313) 563-5975

NO. OF EMPLOYEES: 3,107 (approx.)

ANNUAL MEETING: In May

SHAREHOLDERS: 2,659

INSTITUTIONAL HOLDINGS:
No. of Institutions: 389
Shares Held: 100,346,917

REGISTRAR(S): NBD Bank, N.A., Securities Transfer Services, Detroit, MI 02266

TRANSFER AGENT(S): NBD Bank, N.A., Securities Transfer Services, Detroit, MI 02266

NYS SYMBOL MA
Rec. Pr. 38⅞

MAY DEPARTMENT STORES CO. (THE)

YIELD 2.7%
P/E RATIO 15.0

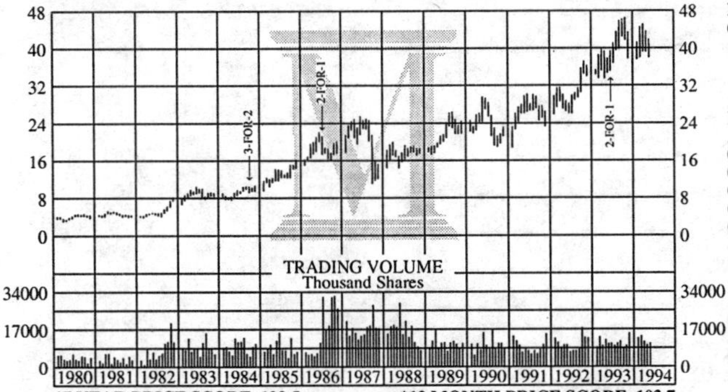

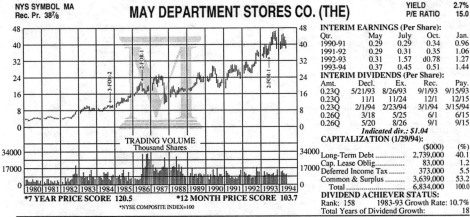

***7 YEAR PRICE SCORE 120.5** ***12 MONTH PRICE SCORE 103.7**

*NYSE COMPOSITE INDEX=100

INTERIM EARNINGS (Per Share):

Qtr.	May	July	Oct.	Jan.
1990-91	0.29	0.29	0.34	0.96
1991-92	0.29	0.31	0.35	1.06
1992-93	0.31	1.57	d0.78	1.27
1993-94	0.37	0.45	0.51	1.44

INTERIM DIVIDENDS (Per Share):

Amt.	Decl.	Ex.	Rec.	Pay.
0.23Q	5/21/93	8/26/93	9/1/93	9/15/93
0.23Q	11/1	11/24	12/1	12/15
0.23Q	2/1/94	2/23/94	3/1/94	3/15/94
0.26Q	3/18	5/25	6/1	6/15
0.26Q	5/20	8/26	9/1	9/15

Indicated div.: $1.04

CAPITALIZATION (1/29/94):

	($000)	(%)
Long-Term Debt	2,739,000	40.1
Cap. Lease Oblig.	83,000	1.2
Deferred Income Tax	373,000	5.5
Common & Surplus	3,639,000	53.2
Total	6,834,000	100.0

DIVIDEND ACHIEVER STATUS:
Rank: 158 1983-93 Growth Rate: 10.7%
Total Years of Dividend Growth: 18

RECENT DEVELOPMENTS: For the year ended 1/29/94, net income was $711 million compared with $603 million in 1992. Revenues increased 3.4% to $11.53 billion, while net retail sales increased 7.6% to $11.02 billion. Comparable store sales increased 4.6%. As a percentage of sales, selling, general and administrative expenses fell to 19.9% from 21.5%. Results benefited from lower expenses, the closings of unprofitable stores, and the consolidation of four of the Company's department store divisions.

PROSPECTS: The consolidation of four of the Company's department stores fits in with the Company's strategy to strengthen operations by lowering expenses and increasing efficiencies. Also, the move of May Merchandising Company to St. Louis from New York will enable the Company to respond faster to emerging trends and offer a greater merchandising mix. A five-year, $4.6 billion capital spending plan will boost the department store division to more than 400 stores and the Payless division to nearly 4,800 stores.

BUSINESS

MAY DEPARTMENT STORES COMPANY owns 4,080 stores, consisting of 301 department stores and 3,779 Payless ShoeSource stores. The Department store segment operates 8 chains including: Lord & Taylor, Foley's, Hecht's, Robinsons-May, Famous-Barr, Kaufmann's, Filene's and Meier & Frank. Payless ShoeSource, the nation's largest chain of self-service family shoe stores, operates in 49 states, Puerto Rico and the District of Columbia. Thalhimers was acquired for $317 million in 1990, and was consolidated with Hecht's division in January 1992.

BUSINESS LINE ANALYSIS

(1/29/94)	Rev(%)	Inc(%)
Department Stores	82.2	85.0
Payless ShoeSource	17.8	15.0
Total	100.0	100.0

ANNUAL EARNINGS AND DIVIDENDS PER SHARE

	1/29/94	1/30/93	2/1/92	2/2/91	2/3/90	1/28/89	1/30/88
Earnings Per Share	2.77	2.36	2.01	1.94	[2] 1.82	[3] 1.71	[2] 1.45
Dividends Per Share	1.335	[1] 0.825	0.805	0.77	0.692	0.622	0.558
Dividend Payout %	48.2	35.0	40.0	39.7	38.0	36.4	38.4

[1] 2-for-1 stk split,06/15/93 [2] Before disc. oper. [3] Earnings before discontin oper.

ANNUAL FINANCIAL DATA

RECORD OF EARNINGS (IN MILLIONS):							
Revenues	11,529.0	11,150.0	10,615.0	10,066.0	9,602.0	11,742.0	10,581.0
Costs and Expenses	9,758.0	9,552.0	9,184.0	8,730.0	8,301.0	10,402.0	9,455.0
Depreciation & Amort	348.0	341.0	319.0	294.0	269.0	330.0	270.0
Operating Profit	3,619.0	3,459.0	3,276.0	3,088.0	3,021.0	3,289.0	2,875.0
Earn Bef Income Taxes	1,178.0	791.0	796.0	762.0	799.0	781.0	743.0
Provision for Inc Taxes	467.0	188.0	281.0	262.0	284.0	278.0	299.0
Net Income	711.0	603.0	515.0	500.0	[1] 515.0	[2] 503.0	444.0
Aver. Shs. Outstg. (000)	250,000	249,000	248,000	249,000	267,000	294,000	304,000

[1] Before disc. op. dr$17,000,000. [2] Before disc. op. cr$31,000,000.

BALANCE SHEET (IN MILLIONS):							
Cash and Cash Equivalents	46.0	172.0	207.0	80.0	92.0	124.0	172.0
Accounts Receivable, Net	2,394.0	2,367.0	2,404.0	2,494.0	2,274.0	2,160.0	1,670.0
Merchandise Inventories	2,020.0	1,791.0	1,741.0	1,628.0	1,491.0	1,788.0	1,481.0
Gross Property	5,047.0	4,731.0	4,540.0	4,180.0	3,736.0	4,421.0	3,870.0
Accumulated Depreciation	1,636.0	1,573.0	1,389.0	1,195.0	1,070.0	1,315.0	1,238.0
Long-Term Debt	2,739.0	2,782.0	3,918.0	3,565.0	3,003.0	2,483.0	...
Capital Lease Obligations	83.0	97.0	...	...	...	...	...
Net Stockholders' Equity	3,639.0	3,181.0	2,781.0	2,467.0	2,319.0	3,050.0	2,726.0
Total Assets	8,800.0	8,545.0	8,728.0	8,295.0	7,802.0	8,144.0	6,181.0
Total Current Assets	4,679.0	4,654.0	4,574.0	4,377.0	4,053.0	4,168.0	3,381.0
Total Current Liabilities	1,771.0	1,975.0	1,522.0	1,742.0	1,994.0	2,074.0	1,560.0
Net Working Capital	2,908.0	2,679.0	3,052.0	2,635.0	2,059.0	2,094.0	1,821.0
Year End Shs Outstg (000)	248,000	248,000	247,000	246,000	249,000	298,000	298,000

STATISTICAL RECORD:							
Operating Profit Margin %	12.3	11.3	10.5	10.4	10.7	8.6	8.1
Book Value Per Share	12.18	10.26	8.63	7.44	7.04	8.13	9.14
Return on Equity %	19.5	19.0	18.5	20.3	22.2	16.5	16.3
Return on Assets %	8.1	7.1	5.9	6.0	6.6	6.2	7.2
Average Yield %	3.3	2.6	3.3	3.2	3.2	3.6	3.0
P/E Ratio	16.8-12.1	15.9-11.0	15.0-9.3	15.3-9.7	14.0-9.2	11.7-8.4	17.7-7.7
Price Range	46½-33½	37¼-25⅞	30¼-18¾	29⅝-18⅞	26⅜-17⅜	20-14⅜	25½-11⅛

Statistics are as originally reported.

OFFICERS:
D.C. Farrell, Chmn. & C.E.O.
J.T. Loeb, President
J.R. Kniffen, Sr. V.P. & Treas.
R.A. Brickson, V.P., Sec. & Sr. Couns.

INCORPORATED: NY, Jun., 1910

PRINCIPAL OFFICE: 611 Olive St., Saint Louis, MO 63101-1799

TELEPHONE NUMBER: (314) 342-6300

NO. OF EMPLOYEES: 35,298 (approx)

ANNUAL MEETING: In May

SHAREHOLDERS: 23,030 (approx.)

INSTITUTIONAL HOLDINGS:
No. of Institutions: 616
Shares Held: 177,932,351

REGISTRAR(S): Boatmen's Trust Co., St.Louis, MO 63101

TRANSFER AGENT(S): Boatmen's Trust Co., St. Louis, MO 63101

NYS SYMBOL MCD
Rec. Pr. 57⅞

MCDONALD'S CORP.

YIELD 0.7%
P/E RATIO 19.8

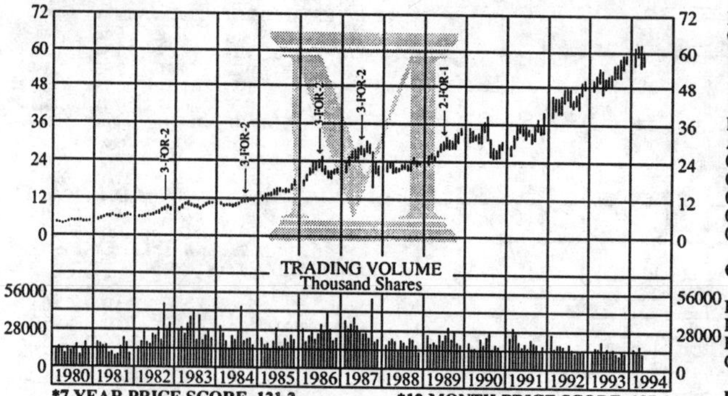

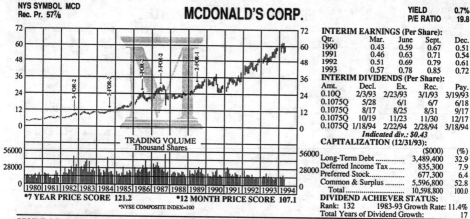

*7 YEAR PRICE SCORE 121.2 *12 MONTH PRICE SCORE 107.1

*NYSE COMPOSITE INDEX=100

INTERIM EARNINGS (Per Share):

Qtr.	Mar.	June	Sept.	Dec.
1990	0.43	0.59	0.67	0.51
1991	0.46	0.63	0.71	0.54
1992	0.51	0.69	0.79	0.61
1993	0.57	0.78	0.85	0.72

INTERIM DIVIDENDS (Per Share):

Amt.	Decl.	Ex.	Rec.	Pay.
0.10Q	2/3/93	2/23/93	3/1/93	3/19/93
0.1075Q	5/28	6/1	6/7	6/18
0.1075Q	8/17	8/25	8/31	9/17
0.1075Q	10/19	11/23	11/30	12/17
0.1075Q	1/18/94	2/22/94	2/28/94	3/18/94

Indicated div.: $0.43

CAPITALIZATION (12/31/93):

	($000)	(%)
Long-Term Debt	3,489,400	32.9
Deferred Income Tax	835,300	7.9
Preferred Stock	677,300	6.4
Common & Surplus	5,596,800	52.8
Total	10,598,800	100.0

DIVIDEND ACHIEVER STATUS:
Rank: 132 1983-93 Growth Rate: 11.4%
Total Years of Dividend Growth: 17

RECENT DEVELOPMENTS: For the quarter ended 12/31/93, net income increased 16% to $264.5 million compared with $227.9 million for the same period in 1992. Total revenues rose 6% to $1.93 billion. Meanwhile, systemwide sales grew 8% to $6.15 billion. The steady growth in sales was attributed to the addition of 900 restaurants in 1993 as well as to increased sales volume at existing stores. Earnings were boosted by improvements in margins for franchised restaurants.

PROSPECTS: Revenues should continue to benefit from McDonald's value program which permits MCD to introduce several new menu strategies including Extra-Value Meals, Happy Meals and other special offerings. Meanwhile, cost reduction strategies will continue to improve margins. International business remains a key contributor to growth due to expansion. MCD plans to accelerate new restaurant openings over the next several years, ranging from 700-900 units yearly.

BUSINESS

MCDONALD'S CORP. develops, licenses, leases and services a worldwide system of restaurants. Units serve a standardized menu of moderately priced food consisting of hamburgers, cheeseburgers, chicken sandwiches, salads, desserts and beverages. There are 9,001 units operated by franchisees, 2,510 units operated by the Company, and 1,209 units operated by affiliates. There are 12,752 MCD restaurants in 59 countries. Revenues were derived from: Company owned units sales, 44%; and franchised restaurants, 56%. Independent operators normally lease on a 20-year basis with rental derived as a percentage of sales, with a minimum fixed rent.

BUSINESS LINE ANALYSIS

(12/31/93)	Rev(%)	Inc(%)
U.S.	53.1	54.8
Europe/Africa/Middle East	30.2	27.5
Canada	7.5	5.6
Asia/Pacific	6.7	9.6
Latin America	2.5	2.5
Total	100.0	100.0

ANNUAL EARNINGS AND DIVIDENDS PER SHARE

	1993	1992	1991	1990	1989	1988	1987
Earnings Per Share	**2.91**	**2.60**	**2.35**	**2.20**	**1.95**	**1.72**	**[2] 1.45**
Dividends Per Share	**0.422**	**0.393**	**0.363**	**0.333**	**[1] 0.314**	**0.273**	**[3] 0.243**
Dividend Payout %	**14.4**	**15.1**	**15.4**	**15.1**	**16.1**	**16.0**	**16.8**

[1] 2-for-1 stk split, 6/89 [2] Before acctg. chg. [3] 3-for-2 stk split, 6/87

ANNUAL FINANCIAL DATA

	1993	1992	1991	1990	1989	1988	1987
RECORD OF EARNINGS (IN MILLIONS):							
Total Revenues	7,408.1	7,133.3	6,695.0	6,639.6	6,142.0	5,566.3	4,893.5
Costs and Expenses	4,917.7	4,780.8	4,616.1	4,645.7	4,319.0	3,958.5	3,452.8
Depreciation & Amort	568.4	554.9	514.2	493.3	364.0	324.0	279.0
Operating Profit	1,984.0	1,861.6	1,678.5	1,595.9	2,350.0	2,099.2	1,858.9
Inc Bef Prov for Income Taxes	1,675.7	1,448.1	1,299.4	1,246.3	1,157.0	1,046.5	958.8
Provision for Inc Taxes	593.2	489.5	439.8	444.0	430.0	400.6	409.7
Net Income	1,082.5	958.6	859.6	802.3	727.0	645.9	[1] 549.1
Aver. Shs. Outstg. (000)	355,900	363,200	358,100	359,000	371,000	376,918	379,476
[1] Before acctg. change cr$47,400,000.							
BALANCE SHEET (IN MILLIONS):							
Cash & Equivalents	185.8	436.5	220.2	142.8	137.0	184.4	183.2
Receivables, Net	314.6	279.6	274.4	255.0	234.0	204.0	...
Invent, At Cost, Not In Excess Of Mkt	43.5	43.5	42.6	42.9	46.0	48.5	48.5
Gross Property	13,459.0	12,658.0	12,368.0	11,535.5	9,874.0	8,647.8	7,393.0
Accumulated Depreciation	3,377.6	3,060.6	2,809.5	2,488.4	2,116.0	1,847.5	1,573.4
Long-Term Debt	3,489.4	3,176.4	4,267.4	4,428.7	3,901.0	3,111.1	2,685.1
Net Stockholders' Equity	6,274.1	5,892.4	4,835.1	4,182.3	3,550.0	3,412.8	2,916.7
Total Assets	12,035.2	11,681.2	11,349.1	10,667.5	9,175.0	8,158.7	6,981.6
Total Current Assets	662.8	864.7	646.0	549.0	495.0	516.4	483.6
Total Current Liabilities	1,102.0	1,544.6	1,287.9	1,198.7	1,017.0	1,003.6	856.2
Net Working Capital	d439.2	d679.9	d641.9	d649.7	d522.0	d487.2	d372.6
Year End Shs Outstg (000)	353,700	363,600	358,700	359,100	362,000	375,476	377,712
STATISTICAL RECORD:							
Operating Profit Margin %	26.8	26.1	25.1	24.0	23.8	23.1	23.7
Book Value Per Share	14.65	13.26	11.62	10.02	8.35	8.25	7.03
Return on Equity %	17.3	16.3	17.8	19.2	20.5	18.9	18.8
Return on Assets %	9.0	8.2	7.6	7.5	7.9	7.9	7.9
Average Yield %	0.8	0.9	1.1	1.0	1.1	1.2	1.1
P/E Ratio	20.3-15.6	19.4-14.7	17.0-11.1	17.5-11.4	17.9-11.8	14.9-11.9	21.0-10.8
Price Range	59⅛-45½	50⅜-38¼	39⅞-26⅛	38½-25	34⅞-23	25½-20⅜	30½-15⅝

Statistics are as originally reported.

OFFICERS:
F.L. Turner, Senior Chmn.
M.R. Quinlan, Chmn. & C.E.O.
J.M. Greenberg, Vice-Chmn. & C.F.O.
E.H. Rensi, Pres. & C.O.O.

INCORPORATED: DE, Mar., 1965

PRINCIPAL OFFICE: Kroc Drive, Oak Brook, IL 60521

TELEPHONE NUMBER: (708) 575-3000
FAX: (708) 575-5004
NO. OF EMPLOYEES: 167,000 (approx.)
ANNUAL MEETING: In May
SHAREHOLDERS: 458,400 com.
INSTITUTIONAL HOLDINGS:
No. of Institutions: 795
Shares Held: 228,370,557

REGISTRAR(S): First Chicago Trust Co. of New York, New York, NY 10008

TRANSFER AGENT(S): First Chicago Trust Co. of New York, New York, NY 10008

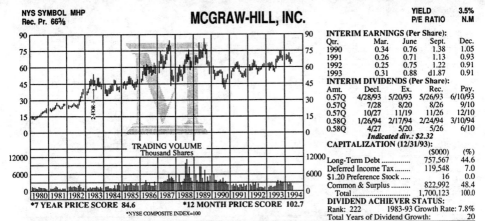

MCGRAW-HILL, INC.

YIELD 3.5%
P/E RATIO N.M

INTERIM EARNINGS (Per Share):

Qtr.	Mar.	June	Sept.	Dec.
1990	0.34	0.76	1.38	1.05
1991	0.26	0.71	1.13	0.93
1992	0.25	0.75	1.22	0.91
1993	0.31	0.88	d1.87	0.91

INTERIM DIVIDENDS (Per Share):

Amt.	Decl.	Ex.	Rec.	Pay.
0.57Q	4/28/93	5/20/93	5/26/93	6/10/93
0.57Q	7/28	8/20	8/26	9/10
0.57Q	10/27	11/19	11/26	12/10
0.58Q	1/26/94	2/17/94	2/24/94	3/10/94
0.58Q	4/27	5/20	5/26	6/10

Indicated div.: $2.32

CAPITALIZATION (12/31/93):

	($000)	(%)
Long-Term Debt	757,567	44.6
Deferred Income Tax	119,548	7.0
$1.20 Preference Stock	16	0.0
Common & Surplus	822,992	48.4
Total	1,700,123	100.0

DIVIDEND ACHIEVER STATUS:
Rank: 222   1983-93 Growth Rate: 7.8%
Total Years of Dividend Growth: 20

TRADING VOLUME
Thousand Shares

*7 YEAR PRICE SCORE 84.6   ***12 MONTH PRICE SCORE 102.7**

*NYSE COMPOSITE INDEX=100

RECENT DEVELOPMENTS: For the year ended 12/31/93, net income amounted to $11.4 million compared with $153.2 million, before an accounting adjustment, a year ago. Revenues were up 7.1% to $2.20 billion. The earnings included $229.8 million ($160.8 million after taxes) of non-recurring charges related to the acquisition of its partner's 50% interest in Macmillan/McGraw-Hill School Publishing Company. Results reflect MHP's 50% interest in Macmillan/McGraw-Hill through 9/30/93 and 100% for the balance of the year.

PROSPECTS: Financial Services will continue to benefit from a strong new issue market, the introduction of new products, and expansion of international operations. Information and Publication Services earnings should improve as a result of cost-containment efforts and a better advertising climate. However, publishing revenues will be adversely affected by a soft college publishing market and weak economic conditions in Europe and Canada.

BUSINESS

MCGRAW-HILL, INC., a multimedia publishing and information services company, serves worldwide markets in education, business, industry, professions and government. As a multimedia company, McGraw-Hill provides information in print through books, magazines and newsletters; online over electronic networks; over the air by television, satellite and FM sideband; and on software, videotape, facsimile and compact disks. McGraw-Hill produces information in many frequencies-instantly, daily, weekly, monthly, annually-to meet growing and changing customer requirements in a global marketplace.

BUSINESS LINE ANALYSIS

(12/31/93)	Rev(%)	Inc(%)
Info & Media		
Services	37.9	29.0
Educat & Pro		
Publishing..............	30.4	14.0
Financial Services	31.7	57.0
Total	100.0	100.0

ANNUAL EARNINGS AND DIVIDENDS PER SHARE

	1993	1992	1991	1990	1989	1988	1987
Earnings Per Share	0.23	☐ 3.13	3.03	3.53	☐ 0.82	3.83	3.27
Dividends Per Share	2.28	2.24	2.20	2.16	2.05	1.84	1.68
Dividend Payout %	N.M.	71.6	72.6	61.2	N.M.	48.0	51.4

☐ Before acctg. chg.

ANNUAL FINANCIAL DATA

RECORD OF EARNINGS (IN MILLIONS):

Operating Revenue	2,195.5	2,050.5	1,943.0	1,938.6	1,789.0	1,818.0	1,751.2
Costs and Expenses	1,992.9	1,692.1	1,601.3	1,546.7	1,689.8	1,627.0	1,417.5
Depreciation & Amort	139.6	74.3	72.1	66.8	45.9	66.2	65.6
Operating Profit	292.7	284.1	269.6	325.2	273.3	274.3	268.2
Inc Bef Taxes on Income	66.3	267.3	258.3	302.6	86.6	379.6	299.1
Provision for Taxes on Inc	54.8	114.1	110.3	130.1	46.8	194.1	134.3
Net Income	11.4	☐ 153.2	148.0	172.5	☐ 39.8	185.5	164.8
Aver. Shs. Outstg. (000)	49,189	48,889	48,821	48,819	48,725	48,475	50,410

☐ Before acctg. change dr$124,587,000.   ☐ Before acctg. change cr$8,000,000.

BALANCE SHEET (IN MILLIONS):

Cash and Cash Equivalents	48.0	13.2	16.6	20.6	34.6	24.5	49.7
Receivables, Net	731.1	617.6	624.2	655.3	...	...	...
Total Inventories	215.2	188.5	192.1	188.0	166.5	309.8	239.6
Gross Property	753.5	669.6	646.1	620.5	533.2	518.0	481.7
Accumulated Depreciation	408.1	384.9	357.5	328.9	299.7	274.4	235.2
Long-Term Debt	757.6	358.7	437.3	507.6	377.6	1.9	3.9
Net Stockholders' Equity	823.0	908.8	999.0	954.3	880.2	922.8	825.3
Total Assets	3,084.2	2,508.1	2,525.2	2,533.6	2,208.2	1,758.4	1,637.6
Total Current Assets	1,131.8	911.0	942.3	961.1	839.7	883.7	792.8
Total Current Liabilities	1,068.9	840.7	818.7	844.7	792.5	726.3	676.0
Net Working Capital	62.9	70.3	123.6	116.4	47.2	157.5	116.8
Year End Shs Outstg (000)	49,414	49,134	49,049	48,932	44,014	48,531	48,221

STATISTICAL RECORD:

Operating Profit Margin %	2.9	13.9	13.9	16.8	3.0	6.9	15.3
Book Value Per Share	7.19	7.23	8.60	7.48	10.61	8.56	8.53
Return on Equity %	1.4	16.9	14.8	18.1	4.5	20.1	20.0
Return on Assets %	0.4	6.1	5.9	6.8	1.8	10.5	10.1
Average Yield %	3.5	3.7	3.8	4.3	2.9	3.0	2.6
P/E Ratio	N.M	21.2-16.9	21.4-16.4	17.3-11.3	N.M	19.8-12.2	25.8-13.1
Price Range	75¼-55¼	66½-53	64¾-49¾	61⅛-39⅞	86⅛-53½	76-46¾	84½-43

Statistics are as originally reported.

OFFICERS:
J.L. Dionne, Chmn. & C.E.O.
H. McGraw, III, Pres. & C.O.O.
R.J. Bahash, Exec. V.P. & C.F.O.
R.N. Landes, Exec. V.P., Sec. & Couns.
INCORPORATED: NY, Dec., 1925
PRINCIPAL OFFICE: 1221 Avenue of the Americas, New York, NY 10020

TELEPHONE NUMBER: (212) 512-2000
FAX: (212) 512-3514
NO. OF EMPLOYEES: 1,821
ANNUAL MEETING: In April
SHAREHOLDERS: 4,042 com.; 40 pfd.
INSTITUTIONAL HOLDINGS:
No. of Institutions: 372
Shares Held: 31,767,072

REGISTRAR(S): Manufacturers Hanover Trust Co., New York, NY
Manufacturers Hanover Trust Co. of CA, Los Angeles, CA

TRANSFER AGENT(S): Manufacturers Hanover Trust Co., New York, NY
Manufacturers Hanover Trust Co. of CA, Los Angeles, CA

MEDTRONIC, INC.

YIELD 0.9%
P/E RATIO 18.8

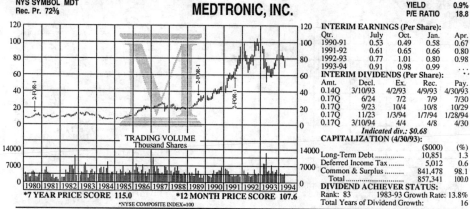

INTERIM EARNINGS (Per Share):

Qtr.	July	Oct.	Jan.	Apr.
1990-91	0.53	0.49	0.58	0.67
1991-92	0.61	0.65	0.66	0.80
1992-93	0.77	1.01	0.80	0.98
1993-94	0.91	0.98	0.99	...

INTERIM DIVIDENDS (Per Share):

Amt.	Decl.	Ex.	Rec.	Pay.
0.14Q	3/10/93	4/2/93	4/9/93	4/30/93
0.17Q	6/24	7/2	7/9	7/30
0.17Q	9/23	10/4	10/8	10/29
0.17Q	11/23	1/3/94	1/7/94	1/28/94
0.17Q	3/10/94	4/4	4/8	4/30

Indicated div.: $0.68

CAPITALIZATION (4/30/93):

	($000)	(%)
Long-Term Debt	10,851	1.3
Deferred Income Tax	5,012	0.6
Common & Surplus	841,478	98.1
Total	857,341	100.0

DIVIDEND ACHIEVER STATUS:
Rank: 83   1983-93 Growth Rate: 13.8%
Total Years of Dividend Growth: 16

TRADING VOLUME
Thousand Shares

*7 YEAR PRICE SCORE 115.0   ***12 MONTH PRICE SCORE 107.6**
*NYSE COMPOSITE INDEX=100

RECENT DEVELOPMENTS: For the quarter ended 1/28/94, net income increased 19% to $56.9 million compared with $47.8 million a year ago. Sales were up 8.6% to $334.6 million from $308.2 million. The improved earnings were primarily attributable to solid sales gains, strong margins and cost containment efforts. Results also benefitted from strong sales of the Medtronic Elite II dual chamber rate responsive pacemaker which, along with Medtronic CapSure pacing leads, fueled revenue growth for the Bradycardia Pacing business.

PROSPECTS: Earnings will be enhanced by strong sales in the Pacing business and ongoing efforts to control costs. Revenues should improve as a result of the Food and Drug Administration's clearance for commercial sale of Transvene leads. Operations will benefit from the acquisition of Electromedics, Inc. The agreement provides that Electromedics shareholders will receive $8.875 in Medtronic stock tax-free or $6.875 cash for each share of Electromedics stock. The merger is subject to shareholder and regulatory approval.

BUSINESS

MEDTRONIC, INC. is a medical technology company serving the worldwide marketplace with technically sophisticated products and services designed to improve cardiovascular and neurological health. The Company is a major provider of prosthetic heart valves, membrane oxygenators, therapeutic catheters, vascular graphs, nerve and muscle stimulation devices, drug delivery systems and other innovative, high quality products. The Company's activities are grouped in five medical categories: bradycardia pacing, tachyarrhythmia management, cardiovascular surgery, vascular therapy and neurological stimulation. Most of its products are physcian prescribed therapeutic devices.

BUSINESS LINE ANALYSIS

(4/30/93)	Rev(%)	Inc(%)
United States	58.0	70.3
Europe	29.6	17.0
Other International	12.4	12.7
Total	100.0	100.0

ANNUAL EARNINGS AND DIVIDENDS PER SHARE

	4/30/93	4/30/92	4/30/91	4/30/90	4/30/89	4/30/88	4/30/87
Earnings Per Share	[1] 3.56	2.71	2.25	2.02	1.83	1.58	1.32
Dividends Per Share	0.52	[2] 0.458	0.38	[3] 0.325	0.28	0.24	0.21
Dividend Payout %	14.6	16.9	16.9	16.1	15.3	15.2	16.0

[1] Before acctg. chg. [2] 2-for-1 stk split,08/30/91 [3] 2-for-1 stock split, 8/89

ANNUAL FINANCIAL DATA

RECORD OF EARNINGS (IN MILLIONS):

Total Revenues	1,328.2	1,176.9	1,021.4	836.6	741.7	653.3	502.0
Costs and Expenses	1,033.1	871.5	768.5	632.2	567.4	494.2	369.9
Depreciation & Amort	69.6	59.4	46.5	39.4	44.6	29.0	26.4
Operating Income	277.1	246.0	206.4	165.0	129.7	130.1	105.8
Earn Bef Income Taxes	313.5	242.9	196.2	159.9	150.4	131.1	108.7
Income Taxes	101.9	81.4	62.9	51.2	52.9	44.6	34.9
Net Income	197.2	161.5	133.4	108.7	97.4	86.5	73.8
Aver. Shs. Outstg. (000)	59,416	59,606	59,290	54,014	53,374	54,758	56,288

BALANCE SHEET (IN MILLIONS):

Cash and Cash Equivalents	156.0	110.4	113.0	51.6	51.3	78.5	113.7
Accounts Receivable, Net	350.0	332.9	300.0	253.1	211.1	202.6	146.7
Total Inventories	189.1	173.2	139.4	128.0	119.6	107.3	84.1
Gross Property	550.5	497.6	426.0	360.4	307.2	264.3	240.1
Accumulated Depreciation	267.7	240.8	208.8	182.3	155.9	136.0	125.0
Long-Term Debt	10.9	8.6	7.9	8.0	7.8	9.1	5.5
Net Stockholders' Equity	841.5	796.5	683.2	541.0	473.6	395.9	387.0
Total Assets	1,286.5	1,163.5	1,024.1	856.5	759.6	640.8	559.7
Total Current Assets	774.7	695.9	612.1	478.8	421.2	420.8	365.9
Total Current Liabilities	348.1	308.6	292.0	260.4	231.6	188.8	125.6
Net Working Capital	426.6	387.3	320.1	218.3	189.6	232.1	240.2
Year End Shs Outstg (000)	57,820	59,431	59,532	54,220	53,560	53,280	56,244

STATISTICAL RECORD:

Operating Profit Margin %	20.9	20.9	20.2	19.7	17.5	19.9	21.1
Book Value Per Share	12.14	11.13	9.11	7.34	6.06	6.39	6.07
Return on Equity %	25.1	20.3	19.5	20.1	20.6	21.9	19.1
Return on Assets %	16.4	13.9	13.0	12.7	12.8	13.5	13.2
Average Yield %	0.6	0.7	1.0	1.2	1.3	1.1	1.2
P/E Ratio	29.4-17.8	34.8-14.3	20.4-13.1	17.6-9.5	13.7-9.4	17.2-10.1	17.5-8.1
Price Range	104½-63	94¼-38⅝	46-29½	35½-19¼	25-17⅛	27⅛-16	23⅛-10¾

Statistics are as originally reported.

OFFICERS:
W.R. Wallin, Chmn.
W.W. George, Pres. & C.E.O.
R.E. Lund, Sr. V.P., Gen. Counsel & Sec.
R.L. Ryan, Sr. V.P. & C.F.O.

INCORPORATED: MN, 1957

PRINCIPAL OFFICE: 7000 Central Avenue N.E., Minneapolis, MN 55432-3576

TELEPHONE NUMBER: (612) 574-4000
FAX: (612) 574-4879
NO. OF EMPLOYEES: 9,247
ANNUAL MEETING: In August
SHAREHOLDERS: 12,276
INSTITUTIONAL HOLDINGS:
No. of Institutions: 449
Shares Held: 40,014,705

REGISTRAR(S): Norwest Trust Company, New York, NY
Chase Manhattan Bank, N.A., New York, NY 10031

TRANSFER AGENT(S): Norwest Trust Company, New York, NY
Chase Manhattan Bank, N.A., New York, NY 10031

NYS SYMBOL MES
Rec. Pr. 39½

MELVILLE CORP.

YIELD 3.8%
P/E RATIO 13.2

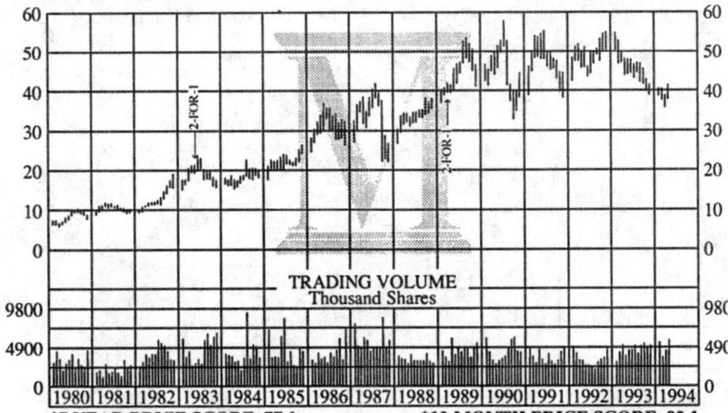

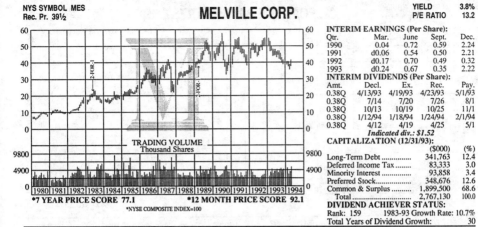

60
50
40
30
20
10
0
2-FOR-1
2-FOR-1
TRADING VOLUME
Thousand Shares
9800
4900
0
1980 1981 1982 1983 1984 1985 1986 1987 1988 1989 1990 1991 1992 1993 1994

*7 YEAR PRICE SCORE 77.1 *12 MONTH PRICE SCORE 92.1

*NYSE COMPOSITE INDEX=100

INTERIM EARNINGS (Per Share):

Qtr.	Mar.	June	Sept.	Dec.
1990	0.04	0.72	0.59	2.24
1991	d0.06	0.54	0.50	2.21
1992	d0.17	0.70	0.49	0.32
1993	d0.24	0.67	0.35	2.22

INTERIM DIVIDENDS (Per Share):

Amt.	Decl.	Ex.	Rec.	Pay.
0.38Q	4/13/93	4/19/93	4/23/93	5/1/93
0.38Q	7/14	7/20	7/26	8/1
0.38Q	10/13	10/19	10/25	11/1
0.38Q	1/12/94	1/18/94	1/24/94	2/1/94
0.38Q	4/12	4/19	4/25	5/1

Indicated div.: $1.52

CAPITALIZATION (12/31/93):

	($000)	(%)
Long-Term Debt	341,763	12.4
Deferred Income Tax	83,333	3.0
Minority Interest	93,858	3.4
Preferred Stock	348,676	12.6
Common & Surplus	1,899,500	68.6
Total	2,767,130	100.0

DIVIDEND ACHIEVER STATUS:
Rank: 159 1983-93 Growth Rate: 10.7%
Total Years of Dividend Growth: 30

RECENT DEVELOPMENTS: For the year ended 12/31/93, net income was $331.8 million compared with $156.0 million last year. Prior-year's results were before an accounting change of $22.6 million. Sales increased slightly to $10.44 billion. Same store sales increased 0.1%. CVS, This End Up, and Linens 'n Things recorded strong results. However, the apparel segment, primarily Marshalls and Wilsons, was affected by a shift in consumer spending to more durable and home related goods.

PROSPECTS: The Company has focused on improving its core and growth businesses through a strategic realignment program. Although the Company is experiencing soft economic conditions in several markets, new stores and remodelings and improved information systems should enhance the Company's competitive position. In the long term, MES should benefit from the prescription drug segment, reflecting more favorable demographic changes such as an aging population.

BUSINESS

MELVILLE CORP. operates 7,246 specialty retail stores. The apparel segment includes: Marshalls, discount apparel; Wilsons, leather apparel; and Bob's, Casual Clothing. The footwear segment consists of: Meldisco, leased footwear departments in Kmart Stores; Thom McAn, footwear for men, women and children; and FootAction, athletic footwear. Drug, health and beauty aids are sold through CVS and Freddy's. The toys and household furnishings sector includes: Kay-Bee toy stores; Linens 'n Things, brand name linens; and This End Up, furniture. Circus World and Peoples Drug Stores were acquired in 1990.

BUSINESS LINE ANALYSIS

(12/31/93)	Rev(%)	Inc(%)
Drugs, Health & Beauty	37.8	30.8
Apparel	32.6	28.6
Footwear	16.4	26.6
Toys & Household Furnishings	13.2	14.0
Total	100.0	100.0

ANNUAL EARNINGS AND DIVIDENDS PER SHARE

	1993	1992	1991	1990	1989	1988	1987
Earnings Per Share	**3.00**	**[1] 1.34**	**3.20**	**3.59**	**3.56**	**3.26**	**2.63**
Dividends Per Share	**1.52**	**1.48**	**1.44**	**1.42**	**[2] 1.30**	**1.05**	**0.88**
Dividend Payout %	**50.7**	**N.M.**	**45.0**	**39.6**	**36.5**	**64.4**	**33.5**

[1] Before acctg. chg. [2] 2-for-1 stk split, 3/89.

ANNUAL FINANCIAL DATA

	1993	1992	1991	1990	1989	1988	1987
RECORD OF EARNINGS (IN MILLIONS):							
Total Revenues	10,435.4	10,432.8	9,886.2	8,686.8	7,554.0	6,780.4	5,930.3
Costs and Expenses	9,620.5	9,870.9	9,039.5	7,908.1	6,795.3	6,108.7	5,334.7
Depreciation & Amort	191.6	201.0	177.1	114.4	97.8	82.2	72.0
Operating Profit	623.3	360.9	669.6	664.2	660.9	589.5	523.6
Earn Bef Income Taxes	599.5	335.5	640.1	633.3	648.7	585.6	518.6
Income Taxes	220.4	125.7	242.9	202.0	208.0	188.0	190.7
Minority Int In Net Earn	47.3	53.8	50.5	46.0	42.6	43.1	42.5
Net Income	331.8	[1] 156.0	346.7	385.3	398.1	354.5	285.4
Aver. Shs. Outstg. (000)	105,069	104,418	103,376	102,841	107,640	108,877	108,650
[1] Before acctg. change dr$22,551,000.							
BALANCE SHEET (IN MILLIONS):							
Cash & Cash Equivalents	81.0	145.1	78.7	111.1	368.8	298.4	341.8
Accounts Receivable, Net	244.0	245.2	213.5	148.8	126.4	111.1	82.9
Inventories	1,858.8	1,806.6	1,875.2	1,656.2	1,288.4	1,200.9	1,006.2
Gross Property	1,900.8	1,831.5	1,800.9	1,578.7	1,302.1	1,151.3	964.8
Accumulated Depreciation	584.0	606.5	687.6	588.6	507.3	458.4	398.8
Long-Term Debt	341.8	349.0	418.3	428.0	389.8	5.2	12.4
Obligs Under Cap Lses	...	...	...	...	...	43.3	45.9
Net Stockholders' Equity	2,248.2	2,077.9	2,091.6	1,853.6	1,620.0	1,708.0	1,460.6
Total Assets	4,272.4	4,214.1	4,085.2	3,662.2	3,031.8	2,736.2	2,231.1
Total Current Assets	2,398.4	2,441.7	2,370.0	2,113.2	1,874.5	1,693.6	1,488.6
Total Current Liabilities	1,328.1	1,380.9	1,330.2	1,202.3	855.3	823.6	568.7
Net Working Capital	1,070.3	1,060.8	1,039.8	911.0	1,019.2	870.0	919.9
Year End Shs Outstg (000)	105,346	104,733	104,212	102,936	102,679	109,011	108,734
STATISTICAL RECORD:							
Operating Profit Margin %	6.0	3.5	6.8	7.6	8.7	8.7	8.8
Book Value Per Share	13.82	12.36	12.22	10.46	9.36	12.84	12.08
Return on Equity %	14.8	7.5	16.6	20.8	24.6	20.8	19.6
Return on Assets %	7.8	3.7	8.5	10.5	13.1	13.0	12.8
Average Yield %	3.2	3.0	3.1	3.1	2.9	3.2	2.7
P/E Ratio	18.3-13.0	41.0-31.7	17.3-12.0	16.1-9.1	15.1-10.4	11.8-8.2	16.0-8.4
Price Range	54¾-38⅞	55-42½	55¼-38¼	57¾-32¾	53⅝-36⅞	38⅜-26⅝	42-22⅛

Statistics are as originally reported.

OFFICERS:
S.P. Goldstein, Chmn. & C.E.O.
H. Rosenthal, Pres. & C.O.O.
R.D. Huth, Exec. V.P. & C.F.O.

INCORPORATED: NY, May, 1914

PRINCIPAL OFFICE: One Theall Rd., Rye, NY 10580

TELEPHONE NUMBER: (914) 925-4000
NO. OF EMPLOYEES: 15,728
ANNUAL MEETING: In April
SHAREHOLDERS: 5,520
INSTITUTIONAL HOLDINGS:
No. of Institutions: 474
Shares Held: 81,082,213

REGISTRAR(S): Chemical Bank, New York, NY

TRANSFER AGENT(S): Chemical Bank, New York, NY

NASDAQ SYMBOL MRBK
Rec. Pr. 18¾ (Marginable)

MERCANTILE BANKSHARES CORP.

YIELD 3.6%
P/E RATIO 10.4

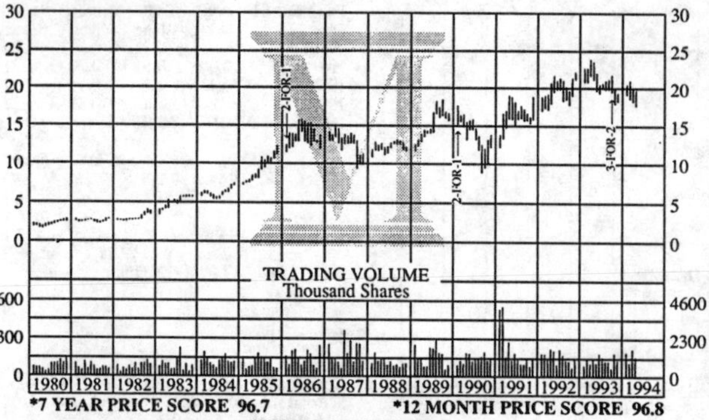

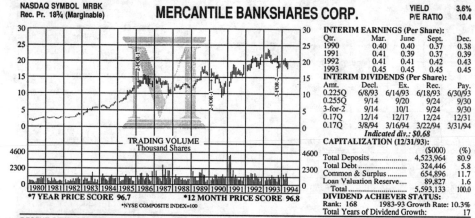

*7 YEAR PRICE SCORE 96.7 *12 MONTH PRICE SCORE 96.8

*NYSE COMPOSITE INDEX=100

INTERIM EARNINGS (Per Share):

Qtr.	Mar.	June	Sept.	Dec.
1990	0.40	0.40	0.37	0.38
1991	0.41	0.39	0.37	0.39
1992	0.41	0.41	0.42	0.43
1993	0.45	0.45	0.45	0.45

INTERIM DIVIDENDS (Per Share):

Amt.	Decl.	Ex.	Rec.	Pay.
0.225Q	6/8/93	6/14/93	6/18/93	6/30/93
0.255Q	9/14	9/20	9/24	9/30
3-for-2	9/14	10/1	9/24	9/30
0.17Q	12/14	12/17	12/24	12/31
0.17Q	3/8/94	3/16/94	3/22/94	3/31/94

Indicated div.: $0.68

CAPITALIZATION (12/31/93):

	($000)	(%)
Total Deposits	4,523,964	80.9
Total Debt	324,446	5.8
Common & Surplus	654,896	11.7
Loan Valuation Reserve	89,827	1.6
Total	5,593,133	100.0

DIVIDEND ACHIEVER STATUS:
Rank: 168 1983-93 Growth Rate: 10.3%
Total Years of Dividend Growth: 17

RECENT DEVELOPMENTS: For the year ended 12/31/93, net income rose 8% to $82.4 million from $76.3 million in 1992. on a per share basis, 1993 earnings were $1.80 compared with $1.67 in the previous year. Deposits at year-end remained flat at $4.52 billion. The provision for loan losses for 1993 decreased to $12.6 million compared with $45.3 million in 1992. During 1993, investment securities, federal funds sold and securities purchased under agreements to resell increased only modestly to 30% of year-end total assets. Total assets at year-end were $5.55 billion. For the quarter ended 12/31/93, net income rose 7% to $20.9 million from $19.6 million for the same period last year. On a per share basis, earnings were $0.46 per share compared with $0.42 per share for the year-ago quarter.

BUSINESS

MERCANTILE BANKSHARES CORPORATION is a multibank holding company. Its principal affiliates are 17 banks and a mortgage banking company. The affiliated banks are engaged in a general personal and corporate banking business. The Corporation's largest bank, Mercantile-Safe Deposit and Trust Company, also provides a full range of trust services. PERSONAL BANKING Services, operated through 128 retail banking offices, include deposit vehicles such as checking accounts, NOW accounts, Money Market Deposit Accounts, CDs, and IRAs. CORPORATE BANKING: Each affiliate pursues a commercial banking program serving local businesses. The primary corporate banking effort for medium and large companies is centered at Mercantile-Safe Deposit. Corporate banking services include the making of various types of commercial and real estate loans, accepting deposits, cash management and short-term money market investing. The TRUST Department provides fiduciary services to individuals, corporations and charitable institutions. Trust services for individuals include estate planning, investment management and custodial services. Employee benefit plans, master and directed trustee and corporate financial services are provided to businesses; endowment trust to nonprofit institutions. MORTGAGE BANKING: Through offices in Maryland and Delaware, Mercantile Mortgage Corp. generates and services real estate mortgage loans and construction loans, as principal and as agent.

ANNUAL EARNINGS AND DIVIDENDS PER SHARE

	1993	1992	1991	1990	1989	1988	1987
Earnings Per Share	**1.80**	**[1] 1.67**	**1.56**	**1.55**	**1.60**	**1.39**	**1.20**
Dividends Per Share	**0.64**	**0.58**	**0.57**	**0.543**	**[2] 0.483**	**0.416**	**0.37**
Dividend Payout %	**35.6**	**23.1**	**24.5**	**23.4**	**20.1**	**20.1**	**20.5**

[1] 3-for-2 stock split,10/01/93 [2] 2-for-1 stock split, 12/31/89.

ANNUAL FINANCIAL DATA

	1993	1992	1991	1990	1989	1988	1987
RECORD OF EARNINGS (IN MILLIONS):							
Total Interest Income	370.8	394.6	436.2	431.0	374.4	308.3	263.9
Total Interest Expense	133.2	166.1	227.6	230.9	194.1	154.9	129.7
Net Interest Income	237.6	228.5	208.6	200.1	180.3	153.4	134.1
Provision for Loan Losses	12.6	45.3	20.9	15.0	9.2	8.7	5.1
Net Income	82.4	76.3	70.6	68.9	62.0	53.4	46.1
Aver. Shs. Outstg. (000)	45,901	45,777	45,182	44,470	38,770	38,505	38,340
BALANCE SHEET (IN MILLIONS):							
Cash & Due From Banks	161.5	212.9	201.0	237.6	217.7	211.8	234.5
Loans, Net	3,487.6	3,401.2	3,309.0	3,258.3	2,851.1	2,582.2	2,309.2
Total Domestic Deposits	4,524.0	4,517.2	4,273.9	3,988.1	3,367.4	3,011.1	2,709.7
Long-term Debt	32.4	15.1	16.6	17.3	23.1	28.9	33.9
Net Stockholders' Equity	654.9	598.1	542.1	486.6	402.3	353.3	314.7
Total Assets	5,554.0	5,459.6	5,182.9	4,885.6	4,018.0	3,642.5	3,328.7
Year End Shs Outstg (000)	45,997	45,777	45,374	44,572	39,027	38,568	38,463
STATISTICAL RECORD:							
Return on Assets %	1.48	1.40	1.36	1.41	1.54	1.47	1.38
Return on Equity %	12.60	12.80	13.00	14.20	15.40	15.10	14.60
Book Value Per Share	14.24	13.07	11.95	10.92	10.31	9.16	8.18
Average Yield %	3.1	3.0	3.7	4.1	3.2	3.5	3.0
P/E Ratio	13.3-10.0	13.2-10.2	12.2-7.8	11.4-5.7	11.5-7.3	9.4-7.8	12.6-7.8
Price Range	23⅞-18	22⅛-17	19-12⅛	17⅝-8⅞	18⅜-11⅝	13⅛-10⅞	15⅛-9⅜

Statistics are as originally reported.

OFFICERS:
H.F. Baldwin, Chmn. & C.E.O.
D.W. Dodge, Vice-Chmn.
E.K. Dunn, Jr., President
C.C. McGuire, Jr., Sr. V.P. & Treas.
J.A. O'Connor, Jr., Sr. V.P. & Sec.

INCORPORATED: MD, May, 1969

PRINCIPAL OFFICE: Two Hopkins Plaza P.O. Box 1477, Baltimore, MD 21203

TELEPHONE NUMBER: (410) 237-5900

NO. OF EMPLOYEES: 2,724

ANNUAL MEETING: In April

SHAREHOLDERS: 7,617

INSTITUTIONAL HOLDINGS:
No. of Institutions: 117
Shares Held: 12,972,248

REGISTRAR(S):

TRANSFER AGENT(S): Mercantile Safe & Deposit Trust Co., Baltimore, MD 21203

NYS SYMBOL MRK
Rec. Pr. 30¼

MERCK & CO., INC.

YIELD 3.7%
P/E RATIO 16.2

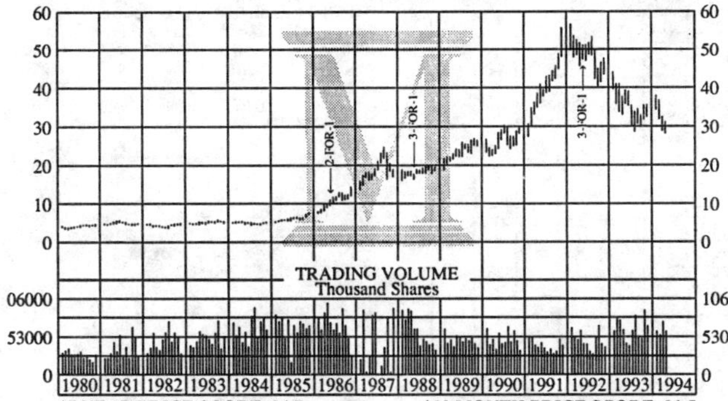

*7 YEAR PRICE SCORE 84.7 *12 MONTH PRICE SCORE 91.5

*NYSE COMPOSITE INDEX=100

INTERIM EARNINGS (Per Share):

Qtr.	Mar.	June	Sept.	Dec.
1990	0.34	0.40	0.40	0.38
1991	0.42	0.48	0.48	0.46
1992	0.48	0.56	0.55	0.53
1993	0.54	0.15	0.62	0.56

INTERIM DIVIDENDS (Per Share):

Amt.	Decl.	Ex.	Rec.	Pay.
0.25Q	2/23/93	3/2/93	3/8/93	4/1/93
0.25Q	5/25	6/2	6/8	7/1
0.28Q	7/27	9/2	9/9	10/1
0.28Q	11/23	12/2	12/8	1/3/94
0.28Q	2/22/94	3/2/94	3/8/94	4/1

Indicated div.: $1.12

CAPITALIZATION (12/31/93):

	($000)	(%)
Long-Term Debt	1,120,800	9.1
Minority Interests..............	1,144,400	9.3
Common & Surplus	10,021,700	81.6
Total	12,286,900	100.0

DIVIDEND ACHIEVER STATUS:
Rank: 14 1983-93 Growth Rate: 20.8%
Total Years of Dividend Growth: 10

RECENT DEVELOPMENTS: For the year ended 12/31/93, net income declined 11.5% to $2.17 billion compared with $2.45 billion, before an accounting adjustment, a year ago. Sales rose 8.6% to $10.50 billion from $9.66 billion. The earnings included $775 million of pre-tax charges related to restructuring. Income was adversely affected by the acquisition of Medco Containment Services, the divestiture of Calgon Water Management, and the negative impact of a strong U.S. dollar on foreign currency exchange rates.

PROSPECTS: Merck is combining its managed-care operations with the recently acquired Medco, a leader in information-based prescription drug management, to form a new business unit called the Merck-Medco U.S. Managed Care Division. The new division will be involved in the rapidly expanding managed healthcare segment of the U.S. prescription drug market. Vasotec will benefit from the Food and Drug Administration's clearance for new and expanded use.

BUSINESS

MERCK & CO. is engaged in the business of discovering, developing, producing, and marketing products and services for the maintenance or restoration of health. MRK's business is divided into two industry segments: Human and Animal Health Products and Specialty Chemical Products. Human and animal health products include therapeutic and preventive agents for the treatment of human disorders. Human and animal health products also include poultry breeding stock, agricultural chemicals, antihypertensive and cardiovascular products. Animal health/agricultural products include anthelmintics and antiparasitics for the control of parasites.

BUSINESS LINE ANALYSIS

(12/31/93)	Rev(%)	Inc(%)
Human/Animal Health	95.1	94.0
Specialty Chemical....	4.9	6.0
Total	100.0	100.0

ANNUAL EARNINGS AND DIVIDENDS PER SHARE

	1993	1992	1991	1990	1989	1988	1987
Earnings Per Share	**1.87**	**[1] 2.12**	**1.83**	**1.52**	**1.26**	**1.02**	**0.74**
Dividends Per Share	**1.03**	**[2] 0.92**	**0.77**	**0.637**	**0.547**	**[3] 0.426**	**0.272**
Dividend Payout %	**55.1**	**43.4**	**42.1**	**41.9**	**43.4**	**41.9**	**36.7**

[1] Before acctg. chg. [2] 3-for-1 stk split, 5/26/92 [3] 3-for-1 stk. split, 5/88.

ANNUAL FINANCIAL DATA

RECORD OF EARNINGS (IN MILLIONS):							
Total Revenues	10,498.2	9,662.5	8,602.7	7,671.5	6,550.5	5,939.5	5,061.3
Costs and Expenses	6,972.8	5,867.4	5,239.0	4,766.1	4,092.5	3,867.8	3,482.1
Depreciation & Amort	386.5	303.6	254.0	254.0	221.7	204.9	210.0
Operating Profit	5,086.7	4,603.1	4,097.5	3,505.4	2,986.8	2,535.6	1,934.9
Income Before Taxes	3,102.7	3,563.6	3,166.7	2,698.8	2,283.0	1,871.0	1,405.2
Taxes on Income	936.5	1,117.0	1,045.0	917.6	787.6	664.2	498.8
Net Income	2,166.2	[1] 2,446.6	2,121.7	1,781.2	1,495.4	1,206.8	906.4
Aver. Shs. Outstg. (000)	1,156,500	1,153,500	1,159,900	1,172,100	1,188,300	1,186,800	1,221,300
[1] Before acctg. change dr$462,400,000.							
BALANCE SHEET (IN MILLIONS):							
Cash & Short-term Invests	1,542.3	1,093.5	1,411.8	1,197.3	1,143.5	1,550.0	1,148.2
Accounts Receivable	2,094.3	1,736.9	1,545.5	1,345.8	1,265.6	1,022.8	1,076.5
Inventories	1,641.7	1,182.6	991.3	892.6	779.7	657.7	659.6
Gross Property	7,172.8	6,530.9	5,606.8	4,630.5	3,993.9	3,590.5	3,337.3
Accumulated Depreciation	2,278.2	2,259.8	2,102.3	1,908.8	1,701.4	1,519.8	1,389.3
Long-Term Debt	1,120.8	495.7	493.7	124.1	117.8	142.8	167.4
Net Stockholders' Equity	10,021.7	5,002.9	4,916.2	3,834.4	3,520.6	2,855.8	2,116.7
Total Assets	19,927.5	11,086.0	9,498.5	8,029.8	6,756.7	6,127.5	5,680.0
Total Current Assets	5,734.6	4,399.7	4,310.8	3,766.3	3,409.8	3,389.3	3,006.9
Total Current Liabilities	5,895.7	3,617.3	2,814.3	2,827.1	1,907.3	1,909.0	2,208.6
Net Working Capital	d161.1	782.4	1,496.5	939.2	1,502.5	1,480.3	798.3
Year End Shs Outstg (000)	1,253,935	1,144,698	1,159,529	1,160,974	1,186,224	1,190,220	1,181,988
STATISTICAL RECORD:							
Operating Profit Margin %	29.9	36.1	36.1	34.6	34.1	31.4	27.1
Book Value Per Share	2.69	4.24	4.24	3.30	2.97	2.40	1.79
Return on Equity %	21.6	48.9	43.2	46.5	42.5	42.3	42.8
Return on Assets %	10.9	22.1	22.3	22.2	22.1	19.7	16.0
Average Yield %	2.8	1.9	1.9	2.4	2.4	2.4	1.4
P/E Ratio	23.6-15.3	26.7-19.1	30.4-15.0	20.0-14.7	21.3-14.9	19.5-15.7	33.4-18.2
Price Range	44⅛-28⅝	56⅝-40½	55⅝-27⅜	30⅜-22⅜	26⅞-18¾	19⅞-16	24¾-13½

Statistics are as originally reported.

OFFICERS:
P.R. Vagelos, Chmn. & C.E.O.
J.C. Lewent, Sr. V.P.-Fin. & C.F.O.
C.A. Abramson, V.P. & Sec.
C. Dorsa, Treas.

INCORPORATED: NJ, Jun., 1927

PRINCIPAL OFFICE: P.O. Box 100 One Merck Drive, Whitehouse Station, NJ 08889-0100

TELEPHONE NUMBER: (908) 594-4000

NO. OF EMPLOYEES: 5,222

ANNUAL MEETING: In April

SHAREHOLDERS: 111,228

INSTITUTIONAL HOLDINGS:
No. of Institutions: 1,003
Shares Held: 216,134,848

REGISTRAR(S):

TRANSFER AGENT(S):

NASDAQ SYMBOL MSEX
Rec. Pr. 17 (Marginable)

MIDDLESEX WATER CO.

YIELD 6.2%
P/E RATIO 12.8

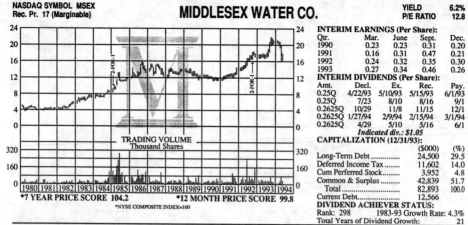

7 YEAR PRICE SCORE 104.2 · **12 MONTH PRICE SCORE 99.8**
*NYSE COMPOSITE INDEX=100

INTERIM EARNINGS (Per Share):

Qtr.	Mar.	June	Sept.	Dec.
1990	0.23	0.23	0.31	0.20
1991	0.16	0.31	0.47	0.21
1992	0.24	0.32	0.35	0.30
1993	0.27	0.34	0.46	0.26

INTERIM DIVIDENDS (Per Share):

Amt.	Decl.	Ex.	Rec.	Pay.
0.25Q	4/22/93	5/10/93	5/15/93	6/1/93
0.25Q	7/23	8/10	8/16	9/1
0.2625Q	10/29	11/8	11/15	12/1
0.2625Q	1/27/94	2/9/94	2/15/94	3/1/94
0.2625Q	4/29	5/10	5/16	6/1

Indicated div.: $1.05

CAPITALIZATION (12/31/93):

	($000)	(%)
Long-Term Debt	24,500	29.5
Deferred Income Tax	11,602	14.0
Cum Perferred Stock	3,952	4.8
Common & Surplus	42,839	51.7
Total	82,893	100.0

Current Debt.................. 12,566

DIVIDEND ACHIEVER STATUS:

Rank: 298   1983-93 Growth Rate: 4.3%
Total Years of Dividend Growth: 21

RECENT DEVELOPMENTS: For the year ended 12/31/93, MSEX reported a 22.8% increase in net income to $5.5 million from $4.5 million in 1992. Revenues were up 11.4% to $34.1 million compared with $30.6 million the previous year. The increase in earnings was attributed to higher sales due to a rate increase granted in April 1993 and increased sales during the summer months. Also having a positive effect on results were reduced interest charges and the continued control of expenses. Both MSEX and its wholly-owned subsidiary, Tidewater Utilities, remain subject to the regulations of various Federal and State agencies concerning water quality standards. For the three months ended 12/31/93, net income slid 6.3% to $1.1 million from $1.2 million despite a revenue increase of 12.9% to $8.4 million.

BUSINESS

MIDDLESEX WATER COMPANY is engaged in the business of supplying water for domestic, commercial, industrial, and fire protection purposes. Located approximately 30 miles southwest of New York City, the Company supplies water on a retail basis to a population of 209,000 in South Plainfield, Metuchen, Carteret, Woodbridge, Edison, portions of Clark and, on a wholesale basis, to the Township of Edison and the Borough of Highland Park, Old Bridge Municipal Utilites Authority Borough of Sayreville and, under special contract, to East Brunswick.

REVENUES

(12/31/93)	($000)	(%)
Residential	14,042	39.6
Commercial	4,170	11.8
Industrial	6,481	18.3
Fire Protection	4,312	12.2
Contract Sales & Other	6,474	18.2
Total	35,479	100.0

ANNUAL EARNINGS AND DIVIDENDS PER SHARE

	1993	1992	1991	1990	1989	1988	1987
Earnings Per Share	1.33	1.20	1.14	0.96	0.91	1.14	1.00
Dividends Per Share	1.012	⒈0.97	0.945	0.925	0.898	0.868	0.837
Dividend Payout %	76.1	80.8	82.9	96.4	98.6	76.0	83.3

⒈ 2-for-1 stk split, 10/2/92

ANNUAL FINANCIAL DATA

RECORD OF EARNINGS (IN THOUSANDS):

	1993	1992	1991	1990	1989	1988	1987
Operating Revenues	35,479	30,861	29,853	26,417	23,499	24,034	22,370
Depreciation	2,376	1,961	1,834	1,592	1,398	1,317	1,251
Maintenance	1,460	1,389	1,295	1,380	1,501	1,418	1,468
Prov for Fed Inc Taxes	3,072	2,351	2,377	1,426	1,415	1,781	1,974
Operating Income	8,225	7,248	7,056	6,013	5,315	5,820	5,169
Total Interest Charges	3,014	3,267	3,156	2,828	2,998	2,509	2,127
Net Income	5,480	4,462	4,105	3,467	2,987	3,626	3,199
Aver. Shs. Outstg.	3,924	3,568	3,477	3,439	3,090	3,031	3,003

BALANCE SHEET (IN THOUSANDS):

	1993	1992	1991	1990	1989	1988	1987
Gross Plant	125,223	118,525	101,697	99,214	93,218	84,034	79,993
Accumulated Depreciation	19,677	17,796	16,075	14,804	13,675	12,777	12,035
Prop, Plant & Equip, Net	105,547	100,729	85,621	84,411	79,543	71,257	67,958
Long-term Debt	24,500	38,800	45,350	39,350	39,350	39,350	29,350
Net Stockholders' Equity	46,790	44,057	35,608	34,580	34,197	30,078	28,941
Total Assets	125,676	113,843	100,014	93,093	92,058	88,827	76,142
Year End Shares Outstg	3,979	3,891	3,503	3,456	3,423	3,046	3,017

STATISTICAL RECORD:

	1993	1992	1991	1990	1989	1988	1987
Book Value Per Share	10.77	10.29	9.80	9.61	9.58	9.39	9.08
Op. Inc/Net Pl %	7.8	7.2	8.2	7.1	6.7	8.2	7.6
Dep/Gr. Pl %	1.9	1.7	1.8	1.6	1.5	1.6	1.6
Accum. Dep/Gr. Pl %	15.7	15.0	15.8	14.9	14.7	15.2	15.0
Return on Equity %	11.7	10.1	12.0	10.4	9.1	12.7	11.7
Average Yield %	5.2	6.0	7.3	7.7	7.0	6.6	6.1
P/E Ratio	16.5-12.6	15.4-11.5	12.8-9.9	13.4-11.7	15.7-12.5	12.6-10.5	15.4-12.3
Price Range	22-16¾	18½-13¾	14½-11¼	12⅞-11¼	14¼-11⅜	14⅜-12	15⅜-12¼

Statistics are as originally reported.

OFFICERS:
J.R. Tompkins, Chmn., Pres. & C.E.O.
E.C. Gere, Sr. V.P. & C.F.O.
M.F. Reynolds, Sec. & Treas.

INCORPORATED: NJ, 1897

PRINCIPAL OFFICE: 1500 Ronson Road,
P.O.Box 1500, Iselin, NJ 08830-0452

TELEPHONE NUMBER: (908) 634-1500
FAX: (908) 750-5981
NO. OF EMPLOYEES: 133
ANNUAL MEETING: In May
SHAREHOLDERS: 2,007
INSTITUTIONAL HOLDINGS:
No. of Institutions: 22
Shares Held: 727,414

REGISTRAR(S):

TRANSFER AGENT(S): Registrar & Transfer
Co., Cranford, NJ 07016

NYS SYMBOL MIL
Rec. Pr. 52

MILLIPORE CORP.

YIELD 1.1%
P/E RATIO 38.0

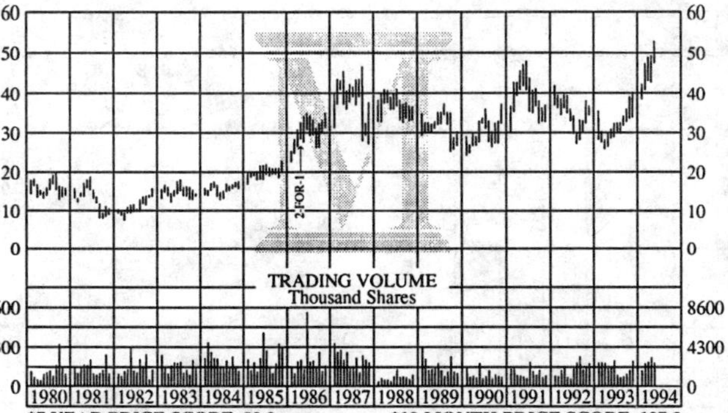

***7 YEAR PRICE SCORE 82.2** ***12 MONTH PRICE SCORE 127.3**

*NYSE COMPOSITE INDEX=100

INTERIM EARNINGS (Per Share):

Qtr.	Mar.	June	Sept.	Dec.
1990	0.47	0.50	0.37	d0.34
1991	0.55	0.56	0.40	0.66
1992	0.30	0.17	0.46	0.24
1993	0.03	0.46	0.38	0.50

INTERIM DIVIDENDS (Per Share):

Amt.	Decl.	Ex.	Rec.	Pay.
0.13Q	2/11/93	3/22/93	3/26/93	4/23/93
0.14Q	6/10	6/21	6/25	7/23
0.14Q	9/9	9/20	9/24	10/22
0.14Q	12/9	12/27	12/31	1/28/94
0.14Q	2/10/94	3/21/94	3/25/94	4/22

Indicated div.: $0.56

CAPITALIZATION (12/31/93):

	($000)	(%)
Long-Term Debt	102,047	18.1
Common & Surplus	461,154	81.9
Total	563,201	100.0

DIVIDEND ACHIEVER STATUS:
Rank: 148 1983-93 Growth Rate: 11.0%
Total Years of Dividend Growth: 23

RECENT DEVELOPMENTS: MIL has decided to divest its Waters Chromatography business unit and to explore options to leave its non-membrane business in order to shift operating emphasis to its membrane business unit. Therefore, quarterly results reflect only the performance of the membrane business unit. For the quarter ended 12/31/93, net income from continuing operations nearly doubled to $14.0 million compared with restated earnings of $7.3 million for the same period a year ago. Revenues rose 9% to $113.7 million.

PROSPECTS: MIL's decision to leave the chromatography and non-membrane businesses bodes well for earnings growth as demand heats up for membrane products utilized in the research, environmental, pharmaceutical and biotechnology markets. New product offerings which include sample handling devices, gas purification products, filter cartridges, DNA sequencing kits and a family of information management systems will benefit sales.

BUSINESS

MILLIPORE CORP. manufactures and sells products which are used for the analysis and purification of fluids as well as the analysis, synthesis and sequencing of nucleic acids and peptides. The principal separation and synthesis technologies utilized by the Company are based on membrane filter products. These technologies and products are used in a wide range of industries including the pharmaceutical, biotechnology, microelectronics, environmental, chemical and food and beverage industries.

BUSINESS LINE ANALYSIS

(12/31/93)	Rev(%)	Inc(%)
Americas	38.1	26.4
Europe	32.8	42.0
Pacific	29.1	31.6
Total	100.0	100.0

ANNUAL EARNINGS AND DIVIDENDS PER SHARE

	1993	1992	1991	1990	1989	1988	1987
Earnings Per Share	**1.75**	**[1] 1.17**	**2.17**	**1.00**	**1.90**	**1.96**	**1.70**
Dividends Per Share	**0.54**	**[2] 0.50**	**0.46**	**0.42**	**0.38**	**0.34**	**0.30**
Dividend Payout %	**30.9**	**42.7**	**21.2**	**42.0**	**20.0**	**17.4**	**17.6**

[1] Before acctg. chg. [2] Bef discont opers

ANNUAL FINANCIAL DATA

	1993	1992	1991	1990	1989	1988	1987
RECORD OF EARNINGS (IN THOUSANDS):							
Total Revenues	445,366	777,001	747,979	703,162	657,515	621,893	528,743
Costs and Expenses	350,399	681,304	633,657	635,821	564,232	522,568	441,005
Depreciation & Amort	23,775	33,993	29,181	28,741	24,757	23,504	23,036
Operating Income	71,192	61,704	85,141	38,600	68,526	75,821	64,702
Income Bef Income Taxes	63,223	51,485	77,915	35,416	67,363	72,728	63,617
Income Taxes	14,225	11,584	17,531	7,615	14,483	18,180	15,904
Net Income	[1] 48,998	[2] 39,901	60,384	27,801	52,880	54,548	47,713
Aver. Shs. Outstg.	27,951	28,242	27,857	27,870	27,886	27,892	28,119

[1] Before disc. op. dr$10,851,000; and extra. item dr$3,544,000. [2] Before acctg. change dr$6,718,000.

	1993	1992	1991	1990	1989	1988	1987
BALANCE SHEET (IN THOUSANDS):							
Cash and Cash Equivalents	40,642	70,451	76,261	55,239	57,447	36,211	28,359
Accounts Receivable, Net	99,655	182,370	199,782	191,763	168,172	166,717	151,089
Inventories	65,187	161,794	149,205	150,023	137,068	136,019	114,531
Gross Property	357,966	471,441	443,967	404,078	333,361	298,614	259,247
Accumulated Depreciation	163,071	210,377	188,499	168,416	144,120	136,026	116,767
Long-Term Debt	102,047	103,240	102,452	103,347	104,048	104,978	5,497
Net Stockholders' Equity	461,154	452,835	478,160	434,853	406,948	365,547	330,918
Total Assets	702,604	786,957	783,706	734,339	650,621	576,149	479,757
Total Current Assets	356,961	429,965	441,728	411,823	376,469	346,853	301,178
Total Current Liabilities	120,287	206,512	191,017	187,132	130,362	97,576	135,183
Net Working Capital	236,674	223,453	250,711	224,691	246,107	249,277	165,995
Year End Shares Outstg	28,003	27,974	27,956	27,849	27,860	27,919	27,909
STATISTICAL RECORD:							
Operating Profit Margin %	16.0	7.9	11.4	5.5	10.4	12.2	12.2
Book Value Per Share	16.37	15.22	16.28	14.72	13.44	12.03	11.86
Return on Equity %	10.6	8.8	12.6	6.4	13.0	14.9	14.4
Return on Assets %	7.0	5.1	7.7	3.8	8.1	9.5	9.9
Average Yield %	1.6	1.4	1.2	1.4	1.2	0.9	0.8
P/E Ratio	23.0-14.8	35.9-23.2	22.1-13.7	37.3-24.3	19.7-13.3	21.0-16.6	27.4-16.0
Price Range	40¼-25⅞	42-27⅛	47⅞-29¾	37¼-24¼	37⅜-25¼	41⅛-32⅝	46½-27⅛

Statistics are as originally reported.

OFFICERS:
J.H. Gilmartin, Chmn., Pres. & C.E.O.

INCORPORATED: MA, May, 1954

PRINCIPAL OFFICE: 80 Ashby Rd., Bedford, MA 01730-2271

TELEPHONE NUMBER: (617) 275-9200

FAX: (617) 275-5550

NO. OF EMPLOYEES: 5,772

ANNUAL MEETING: In April

SHAREHOLDERS: 4,173

INSTITUTIONAL HOLDINGS:
No. of Institutions: 246
Shares Held: 21,623,422

REGISTRAR(S): First National Bank of Boston, Shareholder Services Division, Boston, MA

TRANSFER AGENT(S): First National Bank of Boston, Shareholder Services Division, Boston, MA

MINE SAFETY APPLIANCES CO.

YIELD 2.3%
P/E RATIO 22.9

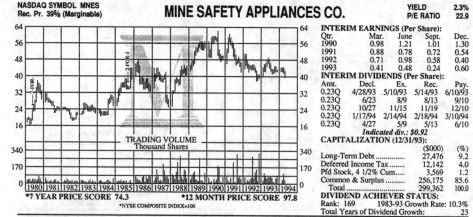

*7 YEAR PRICE SCORE 74.3   *12 MONTH PRICE SCORE 97.8

*NYSE COMPOSITE INDEX=100

INTERIM EARNINGS (Per Share):

Qtr.	Mar.	June	Sept.	Dec.
1990	0.98	1.21	1.01	1.30
1991	0.88	0.78	0.72	0.54
1992	0.71	0.98	0.58	0.40
1993	0.41	0.48	0.24	0.60

INTERIM DIVIDENDS (Per Share):

Amt.	Decl.	Ex.	Rec.	Pay.
0.23Q	4/28/93	5/10/93	5/14/93	6/10/93
0.23Q	6/23	8/9	8/13	9/10
0.23Q	10/27	11/15	11/19	12/10
0.23Q	1/17/94	2/14/94	2/18/94	3/10/94
0.23Q	4/27	5/9	5/13	6/10

Indicated div.: $0.92

CAPITALIZATION (12/31/93):

	($000)	(%)
Long-Term Debt	27,476	9.2
Deferred Income Tax	12,142	4.0
Pfd Stock, 4 1/2% Cum.	3,569	1.2
Common & Surplus	256,175	85.6
Total	299,362	100.0

DIVIDEND ACHIEVER STATUS:
Rank: 169   1983-93 Growth Rate: 10.3%
Total Years of Dividend Growth: 23

RECENT DEVELOPMENTS: For the year ended 12/31/93, net income from continuing operations was $10.6 million or $1.73 per share compared with $16.7 million or $2.27 in the same period of 1992. Sales were down 14.6% to $429.2 million from $502.4 million. The most significant factor affecting sales was decreased shipments of gas masks to the U.S. military which peaked in 1992 due to the Middle East conflict. Also, delays in production on one large contract, caused by a technical difficulty on a subcontractor-provided component, has negatively affected military sales. Higher margins on current contracts, due to improved cost performance, are providing a partial offset to the decline in sales. As stagnant conditions continued in the industrial economy, overall sales to U.S. commercial markets remained essentially flat. Sales of portable instruments continued to grow while sales of breathing apparatus were reduced. Sales in Europe remained depressed and currency exchange rates have been unfavorable.

BUSINESS

MINE SAFETY APPLIANCES CO.'s primary business is the manufacture and sale of products designed to safeguard the safety and health of workers throughout the world. Principal products include respiratory protective equipment that is air-purifying, air-supplied and self-contained in design. MSA also produces instruments that monitor and analyze workplace environments and control industrial processes. Personal protective products include head, eye and face, body and hearing protectors. For the mining industry, MSA provides mine lighting, rockdusting equipment, firefighting foam and foam application equipment. MSA health-related products include emergency care items, hospital filters and instruments and heart pacemaker power cells. MSA also manufactures specialized high-efficiency space filters with applications ranging from safeguarding clean rooms to the protection of sophisticated electronic equipment. Many of these products have wide application for workers in industries that include manufacturing, public utilities, chemicals, petroleum, construction, transportation, municipal fire departments, the military and hazardous materials clean-up.

ANNUAL EARNINGS AND DIVIDENDS PER SHARE

	1993	1992	1991	1990	1989	1988	1987
Earnings Per Share	1.73	① 2.67	2.92	4.50	4.19	3.67	2.11
Dividends Per Share	0.92	0.89	0.88	0.82	0.73	0.60	0.56
Dividend Payout %	53.2	33.3	30.1	18.2	17.4	16.4	26.5

① Before acctg. chg. ② Before disc. oper.

ANNUAL FINANCIAL DATA

RECORD OF EARNINGS (IN THOUSANDS):

Gross Operating Revenues	435,105	512,121	510,347	482,918	427,044	406,264	387,425
Costs and Expenses	394,656	460,437	452,905	410,232	360,700	343,109	341,867
Depreciation	17,294	16,831	17,927	14,991	13,758	15,255	15,793
Operating Income	23,155	34,853	39,515	57,695	52,586	47,900	29,765
Income Bef Income Taxes	18,241	27,810	34,956	51,115	45,147	40,997	22,960
Income Taxes	7,686	11,107	16,305	21,911	17,640	16,766	8,918
Net Income	10,555	② 16,703	18,651	29,204	27,507	24,231	14,042
Aver. Shs. Outstg.	6,069	6,225	6,353	6,471	6,545	6,592	6,628

② Before disc. op. dr$5,067,000; and acctg. chg dr$8,964,000.

BALANCE SHEET (IN THOUSANDS):

Cash and Cash Equivalents	46,434	55,409	54,636	68,575	44,507	40,187	29,728
Receivables, Net	81,897	75,779	83,962	86,315	77,397	76,872	70,987
Total Inventories	81,454	87,784	100,452	88,933	87,830	77,242	68,909
Gross Property	306,691	305,908	314,221	307,583	270,263	261,571	251,823
Accumulated Depreciation	153,162	149,763	141,673	130,142	111,535	108,387	96,762
Long-Term Debt	27,476	28,868	23,009	24,606	22,544	19,040	18,224
Net Stockholders' Equity	259,744	263,194	279,176	279,511	249,269	234,729	215,329
Total Assets	407,884	407,772	436,350	443,151	387,106	360,914	337,022
Total Current Assets	224,609	232,412	254,225	258,225	221,270	204,245	177,117
Total Current Liabilities	60,410	55,125	68,770	70,525	57,633	54,093	53,361
Net Working Capital	164,199	177,287	185,455	187,700	163,637	150,152	123,756
Year End Shares Outstg	6,012	6,079	6,276	6,397	6,507	6,588	6,601

STATISTICAL RECORD:

Operating Profit Margin %	5.3	6.8	7.7	11.9	12.3	11.8	7.7
Book Value Per Share	42.61	42.71	43.91	43.14	37.76	35.09	32.08
Return on Equity %	4.1	6.3	6.7	10.4	11.0	10.3	6.5
Return on Assets %	2.6	4.1	4.3	6.6	7.1	6.7	4.2
Average Yield %	2.1	2.0	1.7	1.5	1.5	1.7	1.6
P/E Ratio	28.3-23.0	19.1-14.1	20.7-14.4	13.8-10.4	13.6-10.1	12.4-6.9	20.9-11.8
Price Range	49-39¾	51-37¾	60½-42	62-47	57-42½	45½-25½	44-25

Statistics are as originally reported.

OFFICERS:
J.T. Ryan, III, Chmn., Pres. & C.E.O.
J.E. Herald, V.P.-Fin. & C.F.O.
D.H. Cuozzo, Sec.

INCORPORATED: PA, Jan., 1917

PRINCIPAL OFFICE: 121 Gamma Dr., RIDC Industrial Park O'Hara Township, Pittsburgh, PA 15238

TELEPHONE NUMBER: (412) 967-3000
FAX: (412) 967-3452
NO. OF EMPLOYEES: 626 (approx.)
ANNUAL MEETING: In April
SHAREHOLDERS: 331 (approx.); 100 pfd.
INSTITUTIONAL HOLDINGS:
No. of Institutions: 49
Shares Held: 3,094,312

REGISTRAR(S):

TRANSFER AGENT(S): Mellon Bank, N.A., Pittsburgh, PA

NYS SYMBOL MMM
Rec. Pr. 49⅜

MINNESOTA MINING & MANUFACTURING CO.

YIELD 3.6%
P/E RATIO 8.5

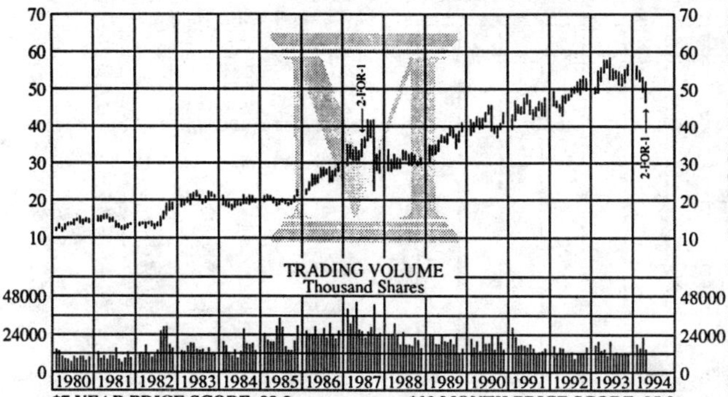
70
60
50
40
30
20
10
2-FOR-1
2-FOR-1
TRADING VOLUME
Thousand Shares
48000
24000
0
1980
1981
1982
1983
1984
1985
1986
1987
1988
1989
1990
1991
1992
1993
1994

***7 YEAR PRICE SCORE 99.3** ***12 MONTH PRICE SCORE 95.0**

*NYSE COMPOSITE INDEX=100

INTERIM EARNINGS (Per Share):

Qtr.	Mar.	June	Sept.	Dec.
1990	1.51	1.54	1.52	1.34
1991	1.37	1.36	1.35	1.18
1992	1.40	1.45	1.48	1.32
1993	1.51	1.51	1.47	1.33

INTERIM DIVIDENDS (Per Share):

Amt.	Decl.	Ex.	Rec.	Pay.
0.83Q	8/9/93	8/16/93	8/20/93	9/12/93
0.83Q	11/8	11/15	11/19	12/12
0.88Q	2/14/94	2/18/94	2/25/94	3/12/94
2-for-1	2/14	4/11	3/15	4/8
0.44Q	5/10	5/16	5/20	6/12

Indicated div.: $1.76

CAPITALIZATION (12/31/93):

	($000)	(%)
Long-Term Debt	796,000	10.4
Minority Interest	376,000	4.9
Common & Surplus	6,512,000	84.7
Total	7,684,000	100.0

DIVIDEND ACHIEVER STATUS:
Rank: 243 1983-93 Growth Rate: 7.2%
Total Years of Dividend Growth: 35

RECENT DEVELOPMENTS: For the year ended 12/31/93, net income increased 2.2% to $1.26 billion compared with $1.24 billion in 1992. Sales increased slightly to $14.02 billion from $13.88 billion the previous year. Earnings were up despite a small decrease in operating earnings. Negative currency translation led to significant reductions in both operating income and net income. Operating margins improved in the U.S. as a result of strong cost control efforts. Sales volume outside the U.S. increased by 7%.

PROSPECTS: The Company will experience a volume increase in the U.S. as a result of an improving economy. While European and Japanese markets are still showing signs of weakness, markets in Latin America and Asia outside of Japan are showing solid economic growth. Innovative products will continue to provide revenue growth for the Company. MMM will soon market a steel wool-type pad that doesn't scratch non-stick cookware.

BUSINESS

MINNESOTA MINING & MANUFACTURING CO. (3M) is a worldwide producer of a diverse variety of industrial and consumer products. The Company operates three business sectors. Industrial and Consumer produces adhesive tapes, abrasives, specialty chemicals, roofing granules, decorative products and products for the aerospace, automotive and industrial markets. Products also include Scotch tape and Post-It notes. Information, Imaging and Electronic products include films, videocassettes, computer disks, laser imagers and fiber optics. Life Sciences, provides products and services for health and safety.

BUSINESS LINE ANALYSIS

(12/31/93)	Rev(%)	Inc(%)
Industrial & Consumer	38.2	43.2
Inform, Imaging & Electr	32.3	13.8
Life Sciences	29.5	43.0
Total	100.0	100.0

ANNUAL EARNINGS AND DIVIDENDS PER SHARE

	1993	1992	1991	1990	1989	1988	1987
Earnings Per Share	**5.82**	**[1] 5.65**	**5.26**	**5.91**	**5.60**	**5.09**	**4.02**
Dividends Per Share	**3.32**	**3.20**	**3.12**	**2.92**	**2.60**	**2.12**	**[2] 1.86**
Dividend Payout %	**57.1**	**56.6**	**59.3**	**49.4**	**46.4**	**42.0**	**46.3**

Note: 2-for-1stk.split,4/8/94. [1] Before acctg. chg. [2] 2-for-1 stk. split, 6/87.

ANNUAL FINANCIAL DATA

RECORD OF EARNINGS (IN MILLIONS):							
Total Revenues	14,020.0	13,883.0	13,340.0	13,021.0	11,990.0	10,581.0	9,429.0
Costs and Expenses	10,988.0	10,802.0	10,412.0	9,981.0	9,079.0	8,697.0	7,287.0
Depreciation & Amort	1,076.0	1,087.0	969.0	849.0	761.0	1.0	564.0
Operating Income	1,956.0	1,994.0	1,959.0	2,191.0	2,150.0	1,883.0	1,578.0
Income Bef Income Taxes	2,002.0	1,947.0	1,877.0	2,135.0	2,099.0	1,882.0	1,565.0
Income Taxes	707.0	687.0	691.0	798.0	825.0	728.0	647.0
Minority Interest	32.0	24.0	32.0	29.0	30.0	...	...
Net Income	1,263.0	[1] 1,236.0	1,154.0	1,308.0	1,244.0	1,154.0	918.0
Aver. Shs. Outstg. (000)	217,000	219,000	220,000	221,000	222,000	227,000	229,000

[1] Before acctg. change dr$3,000,000.

BALANCE SHEET (IN MILLIONS):							
Cash and Cash Equivalents	656.0	722.0	502.0	591.0	887.0	897.0	594.0
Account Receivable-net	2,610.0	2,394.0	2,362.0	2,367.0	2,075.0	1,727.0	1,615.0
Inventories	2,401.0	2,315.0	2,292.0	2,355.0	2,120.0	1,831.0	1,770.0
Gross Property	11,488.0	10,828.0	10,080.0	9,383.0	7,938.0	6,665.0	6,119.0
Accumulated Depreciation	6,658.0	6,036.0	5,414.0	4,994.0	4,231.0	3,592.0	3,188.0
Long-Term Debt	796.0	687.0	764.0	760.0	885.0	406.0	435.0
Net Stockholders' Equity	6,512.0	6,599.0	6,293.0	6,110.0	5,378.0	5,514.0	5,060.0
Total Assets	12,197.0	11,955.0	11,083.0	11,079.0	9,776.0	8,922.0	8,031.0
Total Current Assets	6,363.0	6,209.0	5,585.0	5,729.0	5,382.0	4,741.0	4,229.0
Total Current Liabilities	3,282.0	3,241.0	3,236.0	3,339.0	2,721.0	2,371.0	1,931.0
Net Working Capital	3,081.0	2,968.0	2,349.0	2,390.0	2,661.0	2,370.0	2,298.0
Year End Shs Outstg (000)	215,000	219,000	219,000	220,000	223,000	224,000	227,000

STATISTICAL RECORD:							
Operating Profit Margin %	14.0	14.4	14.7	16.8	17.9	17.8	16.7
Book Value Per Share	30.29	30.13	28.74	27.77	24.12	24.62	22.29
Return on Equity %	19.4	18.7	18.3	21.4	23.1	20.9	18.1
Return on Assets %	10.4	10.3	10.4	11.8	12.7	12.9	11.4
Average Yield %	6.2	6.6	7.1	7.1	7.3	6.9	5.8
P/E Ratio	10.1-8.4	9.5-7.6	9.3-7.4	7.7-6.2	7.3-5.4	6.6-5.4	10.4-5.6
Price Range	58½-48⅝	53½-42¾	48¾-39⅛	45¾-36⅞	41-30⅛	33¾-27⅝	41¾-22½

Statistics are as originally reported.

OFFICERS:
L.D. DeSimone, Chmn. & C.E.O.
G. Agostini, Sr. V.P.-Fin.
A.D. Levi, V.P. & Sec.

INCORPORATED: MN, Jul., 1902; reincorp., DE, Jun., 1929

PRINCIPAL OFFICE: 3M Center, St. Paul, MN 55144-1000

TELEPHONE NUMBER: (612) 733-1110

NO. OF EMPLOYEES: 11,719

ANNUAL MEETING: In May

SHAREHOLDERS: 80,967

INSTITUTIONAL HOLDINGS:
No. of Institutions: 896
Shares Held: 143,773,247

REGISTRAR(S): Norwest Bank Minnesota, N.A., St. Paul, MN

TRANSFER AGENT(S): Norwest Bank Minnesota, N.A., St. Paul, MN

MINNESOTA POWER & LIGHT CO.

YIELD 7.6%
P/E RATIO 12.3

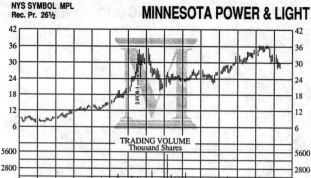

TRADING VOLUME
Thousand Shares

*7 YEAR PRICE SCORE 91.8   *12 MONTH PRICE SCORE 90.0
*NYSE COMPOSITE INDEX=100

INTERIM EARNINGS (Per Share):

Qtr.	Mar.	June	Sept.	Dec.
1990	0.64	0.56	0.74	0.43
1991	0.54	0.42	0.80	0.70
1992	0.54	0.65	0.46	0.66
1993	0.62	0.45	0.59	0.49

INTERIM DIVIDENDS (Per Share):

Amt.	Decl.	Ex.	Rec.	Pay.
0.495Q	4/21/93	5/10/93	5/14/93	6/1/93
0.495Q	7/21	8/10	8/16	9/1
0.495Q	10/27	11/8	11/15	12/1
0.505Q	1/26/94	2/9/94	2/15/94	3/1/94
0.505Q	4/27	5/10	5/16	6/1

Indicated div.: $2.02

CAPITALIZATION (12/31/93):

	($000)	(%)
Long-Term Debt	596,144	42.8
Deferred Income Tax	187,436	13.4
Preferred Stock	48,547	3.5
Common & Surplus	562,625	40.3
Total	1,394,752	100.0

DIVIDEND ACHIEVER STATUS:
Rank: 280   1983-93 Growth Rate: 5.1%
Total Years of Dividend Growth: 23

RECENT DEVELOPMENTS: For the year ended 12/31/93, net income was $62.6 million compared with $68.5 million last year. Revenues were $505.5 million, up 3.3%. The decline in earnings reflect increased property taxes and other costs in its electric utility operations and lower earnings from its investment portfolio and utility-related businesses. Revenues from MPL's water utilities were up 29% to $62.1 million. For the quarter ended 12/31/93, net income was $14.4 million, down 26%.

PROSPECTS: In January 1994, MPL filed for a retail electric rate increase which, if approved by the Minnesota Public Utilities Commission, would add $34 million to annual revenues by 1995. The Company's water utility subsidiaries have been granted more than $13 million in rate relief. Revenues will be negatively impacted as a result of the August 1 shutdown of National Steel Pellet Company's taconite production facility at Keewatin, Minnesota, a large electric customer.

BUSINESS

MINNESOTA POWER & LIGHT CO. is primarily engaged in the generation, purchase, transmission, distribution and sale of electric energy within a service area of 26,000 square miles located in 16 counties in central and northeastern Minnesota. Electric service in northern Wisconsin is provided by its by subsidiary, Superior Water, Light & Power Co., which also sells water and natural gas. Non-electric businesses include BNI Coal, Ltd., which mines and sells lignite coal. Lake Superior Paper Industries, a joint venture mill that makes supercalendered paper; water and wastewater treatment utilities in Florida and the Carolinas.

BUSINESS LINE ANALYSIS

(12/31/93)	Rev(%)	Inc(%)
Electric	81.0	81.2
Water	12.3	14.4
Coal	4.7	4.2
Gas	2.0	0.2
Total	100.0	100.0

ANNUAL EARNINGS AND DIVIDENDS PER SHARE

	1993	1992	1991	1990	1989	1988	1987
Earnings Per Share	2.20	① 2.31	2.46	2.37	2.90	2.35	2.34
Dividends Per Share	1.98	② 1.94	1.90	1.86	1.78	1.72	1.66
Dividend Payout %	90.0	84.0	77.2	78.5	61.4	73.0	70.9

① Before extraord. item ② Bef extraord item

ANNUAL FINANCIAL DATA

RECORD OF EARNINGS (IN MILLIONS):

Operating Revenues	505.5	489.4	484.1	477.5	463.9	460.5	426.1
Depreciation	43.5	39.1	37.2	35.7	36.6	40.2	38.7
Maintenance	26.7	24.8	26.1	26.8	29.0	26.1	25.7
Income Taxes	20.8	19.5	12.2	16.3	14.1	19.6	26.1
Operating Income	77.5	76.9	69.3	72.6	72.2	73.3	66.5
Total Interest Charges	43.5	47.5	50.2	46.6	44.9	42.1	39.4
Net Income	62.6	① 68.5	75.5	74.6	88.9	72.9	70.0
Aver. Shs. Outstg. (000)	26,987	29,442	30,362	29,600	29,044	28,915	27,550

① Before extra. item cr$4,831,000.

BALANCE SHEET (IN MILLIONS):

Gross Plant	1,601.7	1,553.4	1,489.3	1,414.5	1,424.3	1,350.3	1,262.6
Accumulated Depreciation	535.9	505.1	473.4	437.3	425.2	406.4	360.3
Net Plant	1,065.9	1,048.2	1,015.9	977.2	999.2	943.9	902.3
Long-term Debt	596.1	542.0	534.0	520.3	517.1	509.0	489.0
Net Stockholders' Equity	611.2	538.0	524.7	578.9	566.6	548.6	522.4
Total Assets	1,760.5	1,679.1	1,642.1	1,619.5	1,553.7	1,483.8	1,411.8
Year End Shs Outstg (000)	31,207	29,453	29,475	31,932	29,105	28,946	27,629

STATISTICAL RECORD:

Book Value Per Share	18.03	16.58	16.02	16.36	17.46	16.86	16.50
Op. Inc/Net Pl %	7.3	7.3	6.8	7.4	7.2	7.8	7.4
Dep/Gr. Pl %	2.7	2.5	2.5	2.5	2.6	3.0	3.1
Accum. Dep/Gr. Pl %	33.5	32.5	31.8	30.9	29.8	30.1	28.5
Return on Equity %	10.6	13.2	15.1	13.5	16.6	14.1	14.5
Average Yield %	6.0	6.0	6.5	7.5	7.0	7.2	6.1
P/E Ratio	16.6-13.6	14.2-12.0	13.2-10.6	13.2-10.6	9.5-7.9	11.3-8.9	15.1-8.3
Price Range	36½-30	35-29⅝	32½-26	27⅜-22¼	27⅜-22⅜	26½-21	35¼-19½

Statistics are as originally reported.

OFFICERS:
A.J. Sandbulte, Chmn., Pres. & C.E.O.
J.R. McDonald, Exec. V.P.-Fin. & Dev.
D.G. Gartzke, V.P.-Fin. & C.F.O.
P.R. Halverson, Gen. Couns. & Corp. Sec.
INCORPORATED: MN, 1906
PRINCIPAL OFFICE: 30 West Superior Street, Duluth, MN 55802-2093

TELEPHONE NUMBER: (218) 722-2641
FAX: (218) 723-3996
NO. OF EMPLOYEES: 2,587
ANNUAL MEETING: In May
SHAREHOLDERS: 27,000 (common)
INSTITUTIONAL HOLDINGS:
No. of Institutions: 127
Shares Held: 4,561,397

REGISTRAR(S): First Bank - Duluth, Duluth, MN

TRANSFER AGENT(S): At Company's Office

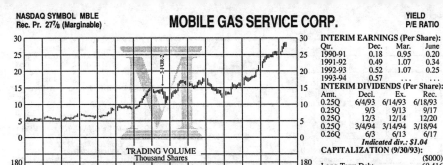

NASDAQ SYMBOL MBLE
Rec. Pr. 27⅞ (Marginable)

MOBILE GAS SERVICE CORP.

YIELD 3.7%
P/E RATIO 14.7

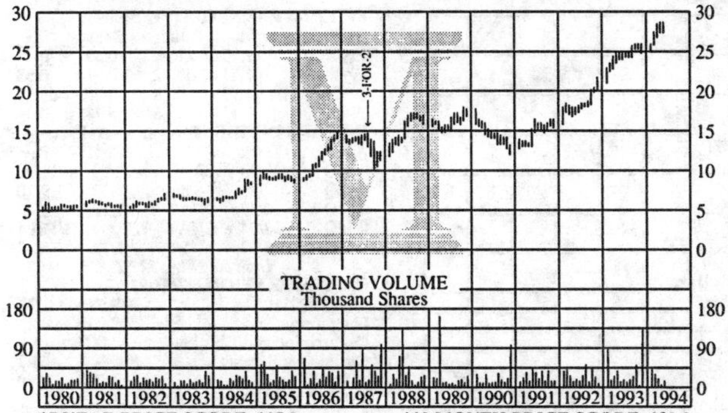

INTERIM EARNINGS (Per Share):

Qtr.	Dec.	Mar.	June	Sept.
1990-91	0.18	0.95	0.20	0.15
1991-92	0.49	1.07	0.34	0.06
1992-93	0.52	1.07	0.25	d0.05
1993-94	0.57	...	...	...

INTERIM DIVIDENDS (Per Share):

Amt.	Decl.	Ex.	Rec.	Pay.
0.25Q	6/4/93	6/14/93	6/18/93	7/1/93
0.25Q	9/3	9/13	9/17	10/1
0.25Q	12/3	12/14	12/20	1/1/94
0.25Q	3/4/94	3/14/94	3/18/94	4/1
0.26Q	6/3	6/13	6/17	7/1

Indicated div.: $1.04

CAPITALIZATION (9/30/93):

	($000)	(%)
Long-Term Debt	60,416	61.2
Deferred Income Tax	4,872	4.9
4.90% Cum Pfd Stock	600	0.6
Common & Surplus	32,831	33.3
Total	98,719	100.0
Current Debt	1,548	

DIVIDEND ACHIEVER STATUS:
Rank: 278   1983-93 Growth Rate: 5.4%
Total Years of Dividend Growth: 16

TRADING VOLUME
Thousand Shares

*7 YEAR PRICE SCORE 115.9   *12 MONTH PRICE SCORE 109.9
*NYSE COMPOSITE INDEX=100

RECENT DEVELOPMENTS: For the quarter ended 12/31/93, net income was $1.6 million, or $0.57 per share, compared with $1.4 million, or $0.52 per share, for the same period last year. Operating revenues for the year rose 17.4% to $17.2 million from $14.7 million for the year-ago quarter. Gas revenues increased 18.4% to $16.4 million from $13.9 million for the same quarter last year. The increases in revenues were primarily due to a rise in natural gas prices and increased volumes of gas delivered. Volumes of gas sold to temperature sensitive customers (residential and small commercial) increased 13% for the quarter. Merchandise sales and jobbing revenues remained flat at $813,000.

BUSINESS

MOBILE GAS SERVICE CORP. is a natural gas utility is engaged principally in the distribution of natural gas to customers in southwest Alabama. The Company serves nearly 100,000 residential, commercial and industrial customers. Gas sales to these customers are categorized as utility operations which are regulated by the Alabama Public Service Commission. Nonutility operations include the delivery of of gas for industrial customers, appliance sales activities, and contract and consulting work for utilities and industrial customers.

REVENUES

(9/30/93)	($000)	(%)
Residential Sales	35,204	64.8
Commercial Sales	7,723	14.2
Industrial-Firm	727	1.3
Industrial-Interruptible	4,123	7.6
Transportation	5,927	10.9
Other	588	1.1
Total	54,292	100.0

ANNUAL EARNINGS AND DIVIDENDS PER SHARE

	9/30/93	9/30/92	9/30/91	9/30/90	9/30/89	9/30/88	9/30/87
Earnings Per Share	1.79	1.96	1.48	1.01	1.22	1.42	1.13
Dividends Per Share	0.96	0.90	0.86	0.82	0.78	0.74	① 0.706
Dividend Payout %	53.6	45.9	58.1	81.2	63.9	52.1	62.5

① 3-for-2 stk. split, 7/87.

ANNUAL FINANCIAL DATA

RECORD OF EARNINGS (IN THOUSANDS):

Total Revenues	56,817	53,622	50,742	49,050	46,094	58,119	62,226
Depreciation	3,468	3,029	2,862	2,643	2,377	2,218	2,133
Maintenance	1,249	1,664	1,127	1,077	965	1,075	902
Prov for Fed Inc Taxes	2,752	2,074	1,375	953	991	1,618	2,039
Operating Income	9,928	9,404	7,576	5,900	5,754	6,616	6,597
Interest Expense	2,909	2,008	2,116	2,123	1,987	1,081	1,456
Net Income	4,920	5,368	4,052	2,765	3,316	3,866	3,070
Aver. Shs. Outstg.	2,733	2,726	2,718	2,709	2,702	2,694	2,685

BALANCE SHEET (IN THOUSANDS):

Gross Plant	110,345	86,414	75,733	72,094	65,172	58,100	53,816
Accumulated Depreciation	26,532	24,233	22,194	20,087	17,979	16,692	15,299
Prop, Plant & Equip, Net	83,813	62,181	53,539	52,007	47,193	41,408	38,517
Net Stockholders' Equity	33,431	31,021	28,004	26,197	25,561	24,263	22,300
Lg tm Debt (less Curr Matur)	60,416	26,833	14,765	16,205	17,145	9,485	10,837
Total Assets	116,839	80,531	67,281	62,871	58,748	51,211	49,568
Year End Shares Outstg	2,736	2,729	2,721	2,712	2,705	2,697	2,688

STATISTICAL RECORD:

Book Value Per Share	12.00	11.15	10.07	9.44	9.23	8.77	8.07
Op. Inc/Net Pl %	11.8	15.1	14.2	11.3	12.2	16.0	17.1
Dep/Gr. Pl %	3.1	3.5	3.8	3.7	3.6	3.8	4.0
Accum. Dep/Gr. Pl %	24.0	28.0	29.3	27.9	27.6	28.7	28.4
Return on Equity %	14.7	17.3	14.5	10.6	13.0	15.9	13.8
Average Yield %	4.1	4.8	5.9	5.5	4.8	5.1	5.6
P/E Ratio	14.5-11.7	11.1-8.0	11.1-8.6	17.6-11.9	14.8-12.1	12.1-8.3	13.1-9.1
Price Range	26-21	21¾-15¾	16½-12¾	17¾-12	18-14¾	17¼-11¾	14¾-10¼

Statistics are as originally reported.

OFFICERS:
W.J. Hearin, Chairman
W.L. Hovell, Pres. & C.E.O.
C.P. Huffman, C.F.O., Treas. & Asst. Sec.
G.E. Downing, Jr., Sec. & Gen. Couns.
INCORPORATED: AL, May, 1933
PRINCIPAL OFFICE: 2828 Dauphin Street, Mobile, AL 36606

TELEPHONE NUMBER: (205) 476-2720
FAX: (205) 478-5817
NO. OF EMPLOYEES: 33
ANNUAL MEETING: in Jan.
SHAREHOLDERS: 1,085 com.
INSTITUTIONAL HOLDINGS:
No. of Institutions: 18
Shares Held: 315,997

REGISTRAR(S): AmSouth Bank, N.A., Birmingham, AL 35202

TRANSFER AGENT(S): AmSouth Bank, N.A., Birmingham, AL 35202

MONSANTO CO.

YIELD 3.1%
P/E RATIO 19.6

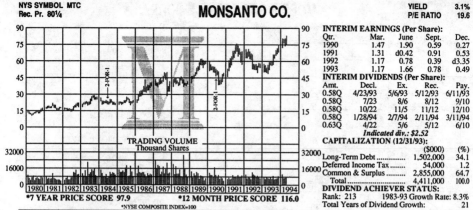

INTERIM EARNINGS (Per Share):

Qtr.	Mar.	June	Sept.	Dec.
1990	1.47	1.90	0.59	0.27
1991	1.31	d0.42	0.91	0.53
1992	1.17	0.78	0.39	d3.35
1993	1.17	1.66	0.78	0.49

INTERIM DIVIDENDS (Per Share):

Amt.	Decl.	Ex.	Rec.	Pay.
0.58Q	4/23/93	5/6/93	5/12/93	6/11/93
0.58Q	7/23	8/6	8/12	9/10
0.58Q	10/22	11/5	11/12	12/10
0.58Q	1/28/94	2/7/94	2/11/94	3/11/94
0.63Q	4/22	5/6	5/12	6/10

Indicated div.: $2.52

CAPITALIZATION (12/31/93):

	($000)	(%)
Long-Term Debt	1,502,000	34.1
Deferred Income Tax	54,000	1.2
Common & Surplus	2,855,000	64.7
Total	4,411,000	100.0

TRADING VOLUME
Thousand Shares

DIVIDEND ACHIEVER STATUS:
Rank: 213   1983-93 Growth Rate: 8.3%
Total Years of Dividend Growth: 21

*7 YEAR PRICE SCORE 97.9   *12 MONTH PRICE SCORE 116.0
*NYSE COMPOSITE INDEX=100

RECENT DEVELOPMENTS: Income from continuing operations was $58 million for the three months ended 12/31/93, reversing a $413 million loss in the comparable period of 1992. Sales rose slightly to $1.88 billion from $1.87 billion. The chemical group reported increased demand from US and Latin American markets. Searle, the pharmaceutical division, cited the introduction of new products as the primary reason for improved results. For 1993, income from continuing operations was $494 million.

PROSPECTS: MTC acquired Ortho Consumer Products Division from Chevron Corp., for $400 million. Ortho is the second leading producer of lawn and garden related products; Monsanto is the leader. Plans to restructure selected research investments, consolidate and close facilities, write down assets and sell non-strategic businesses have improved results and better focused operations. Roundup herbicides continue to reach record volumes worldwide.

BUSINESS

MONSANTO CO. is one of the largest chemical companies in the US. Products include herbicides, detergents, phosphates, fibers, plastics, resins, rubber, specialty chemicals, control valves, pharmaceuticals, and aspartame. Some of the Company's trade names include Lasso and Roundup, herbicides; Saflex, a plastic interlayer; Cytotec, an ulcer preventive drug, Calan, a calcium channel blocker and Equal, Nutrasweet, Simplesse, and Simple Pleasures.

QUARTERLY DATA

(12/31/93)($000)	Rev	Inc
1st Quarter	1,941,000	141,000
2nd Quarter	2,230,000	200,000
3rd Quarter	1,849,000	95,000
4th Quarter	1,882,000	58,000

ANNUAL EARNINGS AND DIVIDENDS PER SHARE

	1993	1992	1991	1990	1989	1988	1987
Earnings Per Share	4.10	① d1.01	2.33	③ 4.23	5.02	4.14	2.82
Dividends Per Share %	2.30	② 2.20	2.045	④ 1.91	1.65	1.48	1.38
Dividend Payout %	56.1	...	87.8	45.2	32.9	36.0	48.8

① Before disc. oper. & acctg. chg. ② Bef discont opers ③ Before extraord. item ④ 2-for-1 stk split, 6/90

ANNUAL FINANCIAL DATA

RECORD OF EARNINGS (IN MILLIONS):

	1993	1992	1991	1990	1989	1988	1987
Total Revenues	7,902.0	7,763.0	8,864.0	8,995.0	8,681.0	8,293.0	7,639.0
Costs and Expenses	7,011.0	7,468.0	8,055.0	7,851.0	7,377.0	7,107.0	6,680.0
Depreciation & Amort	572.0	765.0	751.0	739.0	690.0	703.0	679.0
Operating Income	810.0	58.0	570.0	909.0	1,078.0	955.0	734.0
Income Bef Income Taxes	729.0	d174.0	442.0	809.0	1,015.0	893.0	673.0
Income Taxes	235.0	cr48.0	146.0	263.0	336.0	302.0	237.0
Net Income	494.0	① d126.0	296.0	546.0	679.0	591.0	436.0
Aver. Shs. Outstg. (000)	120,000	123,000	127,000	127,000	129,000	135,000	143,000	155,000

① Before disc. op. cr$578,000,000.

BALANCE SHEET (IN MILLIONS):

	1993	1992	1991	1990	1989	1988	1987
Cash and Cash Equivalents	273.0	729.0	189.0	204.0	253.0	221.0	223.0
Receivables, Net	1,787.0	1,800.0	1,843.0	1,669.0	1,503.0	1,422.0	1,374.0
Inventories	1,224.0	1,156.0	1,349.0	1,270.0	1,197.0	1,170.0	1,081.0
Gross Property	7,382.0	7,602.0	7,902.0	7,620.0	6,937.0	6,926.0	6,730.0
Accumulated Depreciation	4,580.0	4,597.0	4,540.0	4,128.0	3,764.0	3,780.0	3,654.0
Long-Term Debt	1,502.0	1,423.0	1,877.0	1,652.0	1,471.0	1,408.0	1,564.0
Net Stockholders' Equity	2,855.0	3,005.0	3,654.0	4,089.0	3,941.0	3,800.0	3,901.0
Total Assets	8,640.0	9,085.0	9,227.0	9,236.0	8,604.0	8,461.0	8,455.0
Total Current Assets	3,672.0	4,060.0	3,711.0	3,513.0	3,248.0	3,097.0	3,003.0
Total Current Liabilities	2,295.0	2,548.0	2,175.0	2,190.0	1,922.0	1,980.0	1,8(0).0
Net Working Capital	1,377.0	1,512.0	1,536.0	1,323.0	1,326.0	1,117.0	1,203.0
Year End Shs Outstg (000)	116,000	120,000	123,000	126,000	132,000	138,000	148,000

STATISTICAL RECORD:

	1993	1992	1991	1990	1989	1988	1987
Operating Profit Margin %	10.3	0.7	6.4	10.1	12.4	11.5	9.6
Book Value Per Share	14.36	16.16	19.22	21.14	17.11	14.57	13.16
Return on Equity %	17.3	...	8.1	13.4	17.2	15.6	11.2
Return on Assets %	5.7	...	3.2	5.9	7.9	7.0	5.2
Average Yield %	3.7	3.6	3.4	3.9	3.2	3.6	3.5
P/E Ratio	18.3-11.9	...	32.6-19.7	14.2-9.2	12.4-8.0	11.2-8.9	17.8-10.1
Price Range	75-48⅞	71¼-49¾	76-46	60⅛-38¾	62⅛-40¼	46¼-36¾	50⅛-28½

Statistics are as originally reported.

OFFICERS:
R.J. Mahoney, Chmn. & C.E.O.
R.B. Shapiro, Pres. & C.O.O.
F.A. Stroble, Sr. V.P. & C.F.O.
R.W. Duesenberg, Sr. V.P., Sec. & Couns.

INCORPORATED: DE, Apr., 1933

PRINCIPAL OFFICE: 800 N. Lindbergh
Blvd., Saint Louis, MO 63167

TELEPHONE NUMBER: (314) 694-1000

FAX: (314) 694-8421

NO. OF EMPLOYEES: 1,462

ANNUAL MEETING: Fourth Friday in April

SHAREHOLDERS: 19,482

INSTITUTIONAL HOLDINGS:
No. of Institutions: 625
Shares Held: 86,833,782

REGISTRAR(S): First National Bank of
Boston, Shareholder Services Division,
Boston, MA

TRANSFER AGENT(S): First National Bank
of Boston. Shareholder Services Division,
Boston, MA

NYS SYMBOL JPM
Rec. Pr. 65

MORGAN (J. P.) & CO. INC.

YIELD 4.2%
P/E RATIO 7.6

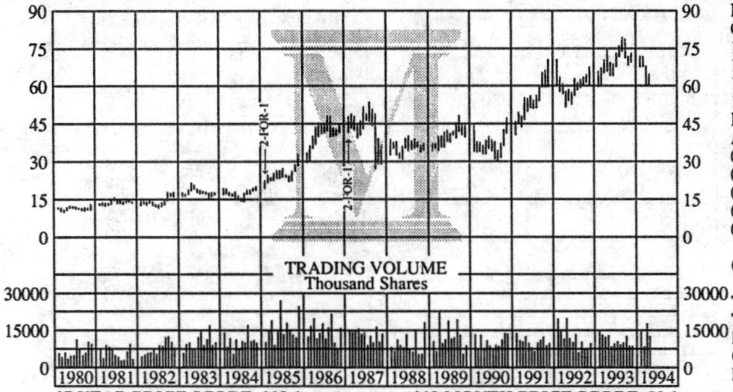

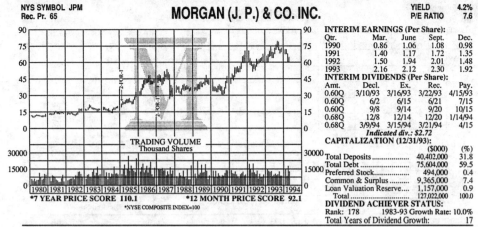

*7 YEAR PRICE SCORE 110.1 *12 MONTH PRICE SCORE 92.1

*NYSE COMPOSITE INDEX=100

INTERIM EARNINGS (Per Share):

Qtr.	Mar.	June	Sept.	Dec.
1990	0.86	1.06	1.08	0.98
1991	1.40	1.17	1.72	1.35
1992	1.50	1.94	2.01	1.48
1993	2.16	2.12	2.30	1.92

INTERIM DIVIDENDS (Per Share):

Amt.	Decl.	Ex.	Rec.	Pay.
0.60Q	3/10/93	3/16/93	3/22/93	4/15/93
0.60Q	6/2	6/15	6/21	7/15
0.60Q	9/8	9/14	9/20	10/15
0.68Q	12/8	12/14	12/20	1/14/94
0.68Q	3/9/94	3/15/94	3/21/94	4/15

Indicated div.: $2.72

CAPITALIZATION (12/31/93):

	($000)	(%)
Total Deposits	40,402,000	31.8
Total Debt	75,604,000	59.5
Preferred Stock	494,000	0.4
Common & Surplus	9,365,000	7.4
Loan Valuation Reserve	1,157,000	0.9
Total	127,022,000	100.0

DIVIDEND ACHIEVER STATUS:
Rank: 178 1983-93 Growth Rate: 10.0%
Total Years of Dividend Growth: 17

RECENT DEVELOPMENTS: For the three months ended 12/31/93, net income rose 77% from the prior-year period to $392 million. Results benefited from a 19% increase in net interest revenue and a 69% jump in noninterest revenue, paced by a $406 million gain in trading revenue. For 1993, income before accounting adjustments was $1.72 billion, up 53% from 1992. Comparisons were made with restated 1992 results. Increased demand for risk management and emerging market products and services aided results.

PROSPECTS: For JPM, strong earnings delivered an impressive 22% return on equity. Fee income is a driving force behind the increased results. Trading revenue is well-balanced across Company products and geographic locations. Trading revenue is particularly strong in Europe and in emerging markets. It is benefiting from the decline of European interest rates. The increase in assets under management is boosting investment management fee income. Loan demand is soft but prospects for the long-term are favorable.

BUSINESS

J.P. MORGAN & CO., INC. is a global financial firm providing a wide range of financial services to corporations, governments, financial institutions, institutional investors, financially sophisticated individuals, private firms, and nonprofit organizations. Activities include providing corporate finance advice and executing financing transactions; underwriting, trading, and investing in securities, providing trust, agency, and operational services; and serving as an investment advisor and manager. The Company's principal subsidiary is Morgan Guaranty Trust Company of New York.

LOAN DISTRIBUTION

(12/31/93)	($000)	(%)
Commercial & Industrial	11,316,000	46.4
Financial Institution	7,180,000	29.4
Collateral by Real Estate	724,000	3.0
Foreign Governments	1,149,000	4.7
Other	4,011,000	16.5
Total	24,380,000	100.0

ANNUAL EARNINGS AND DIVIDENDS PER SHARE

	1993	1992	1991	1990	1989	1988	1987
Earnings Per Share	**8.48**	**6.92**	**[1] 5.63**	**[2] 3.99**	**d7.04**	**5.38**	**0.39**
Dividends Per Share	**2.40**	**2.18**	**1.98**	**1.82**	**1.66**	**1.50**	**[3] 1.36**
Dividend Payout %	**28.3**	**38.5**	**35.2**	**45.6**	**...**	**27.9**	**N.M.**

[1] Before extraord. item [2] Before acctg. chg. [3] 100% stk div, 1/87

ANNUAL FINANCIAL DATA

	1993	1992	1991	1990	1989	1988	1987
RECORD OF EARNINGS (IN MILLIONS):							
Total Interest Revenue	7,442.0	7,281.0	7,786.0	8,430.0	8,657.0	6,282.0	5,487.0
Total Interest Expense	5,670.0	5,573.0	6,302.0	7,272.0	7,513.0	4,512.0	3,891.0
Net Interest Income	1,772.0	1,708.0	1,484.0	1,158.0	1,144.0	1,770.0	1,596.0
Provision for Credit Losses	...	55.0	40.0	50.0	2,045.0	200.0	960.0
Net Income	1,586.0	1,382.0	[1] 1,114.0	[2] 775.0	d1,275.0	1,002.0	83.0

[1] Before extra. item cr$32,000,000. [2] Before acctg. change cr$230,000,000.

	1993	1992	1991	1990	1989	1988	1987
BALANCE SHEET (IN MILLIONS):							
Cash and Due From Banks	1,008.0	1,149.0	1,555.0	2,200.0	1,951.0	2,561.0	2,622.0
Net Loans	23,223.0	25,180.0	26,378.0	25,712.0	26,030.0	26,842.0	28,923.0
Total Domestic Deposits	7,082.0	5,804.0	6,756.0	9,111.0	8,827.0	12,622.0	13,965.0
Total Foreign Deposits	33,320.0	26,715.0	30,220.0	28,446.0	30,331.0	29,847.0	30,022.0
Long-term Debt	5,276.0	5,443.0	5,395.0	4,723.0	4,690.0	4,052.0	2,754.0
Net Stockholders' Equity	9,859.0	7,066.0	6,068.0	5,189.0	4,495.0	5,778.0	5,036.0
Total Assets	133,888.0	102,941.0	103,468.0	93,103.0	88,964.0	83,923.0	75,414.0
Year End Shs Outstg (000)	193,000	192,000	190,000	186,000	184,000	181,000	182,000
STATISTICAL RECORD:							
Return on Assets %	1.29	1.34	1.08	0.83	...	1.19	0.11
Return on Equity %	17.50	19.60	18.40	14.90	...	17.30	1.60
Book Value Per Share	48.52	34.23	29.34	25.24	21.74	30.57	26.30
Average Yield %	3.5	3.6	3.6	4.7	4.0	4.2	3.4
P/E Ratio	9.4-7.0	10.2-7.4	12.5-7.2	11.8-7.4	...	7.5-5.7	N.M
Price Range	79⅜-59⅜	70½-51½	70½-40½	47¼-29⅝	48⅛-34	40¼-30¾	53⅝-27

Statistics are as originally reported.

OFFICERS:
D. Weatherstone, Chairman
D.A. Warner, III, President
B.S. Stokes, Secretary

INCORPORATED: DE, Dec., 1968

PRINCIPAL OFFICE: 60 Wall Street, New York, NY 10260-0060

TELEPHONE NUMBER: (212) 483-2323

NO. OF EMPLOYEES: 14,368

ANNUAL MEETING: In May

SHAREHOLDERS: 28,061

INSTITUTIONAL HOLDINGS:
No. of Institutions: 825
Shares Held: 125,975,190

REGISTRAR(S): First Chicago Trust Co. of New York, New York, NY 10008

TRANSFER AGENT(S): First Chicago Trust Co. of New York, New York, NY 10008

MYERS INDUSTRIES INC.

YIELD 0.9%
P/E RATIO 15.3

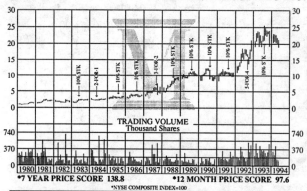

7 YEAR PRICE SCORE 138.8   **12 MONTH PRICE SCORE 97.6**

*NYSE COMPOSITE INDEX=100

TRADING VOLUME
Thousand Shares

INTERIM EARNINGS (Per Share):

Qtr.	Mar.	June	Sept.	Dec.
1990	0.18	0.28	0.22	0.30
1991	0.16	0.28	0.20	0.30
1992	0.23	0.35	0.24	0.36
1993	0.29	0.38	0.26	0.38

INTERIM DIVIDENDS (Per Share):

Amt.	Decl.	Ex.	Rec.	Pay.
10%	7/27/93	8/9/93	8/13/93	8/31/93
0.045Q	7/27	9/3	9/10	10/1
0.045Q	10/27	12/6	12/10	1/3/94
0.045Q	1/18/94	3/7/94	3/11/94	4/1
0.045Q	4/28	6/6	6/10	7/1

Indicated div.: $0.18

CAPITALIZATION (12/31/93):

	($000)	(%)
Long-Term Debt	10,655	8.3
Deferred Income Tax	2,064	1.6
Common & Surplus	115,287	90.1
Total	128,006	100.0

DIVIDEND ACHIEVER STATUS:

Rank: 170   1983-93 Growth Rate: 10.3%
Total Years of Dividend Growth: 17

RECENT DEVELOPMENTS:

For the year ended 12/31/93, net income increased 17% to $15.4 million from $13.1 million a year ago. Net sales for the year were up 7% to a record $245.1 million from $229.3 million in 1992. Each of the Company's business segments increased in unit volume for the year. A 7% increase in the Distribution segment's sales was the result of expanded market coverage, new product introductions and the acquisition of a distributor. Sales in the Manufacturing segment increased 7% due primarily to sustained demand for existing consumer and industrial product lines and concentrated sales and marketing efforts. For the quarter, net income rose 13% to $4.6 million from $4.1 million for the same period last year. Net sales for the quarter increased 4% to $66.0 million from $63.6 million for the year-ago quarter.

BUSINESS

MYERS INDUSTRIES, INC. is a diversified manufacturer of reusable plastic storage systems and other polymer and metal products for domestic and international markets, and a specialized nationwide distributor of tools, equipment and supplies for the tire servicing and transportation industries. The Company's manufacturing plants are located in Ohio, Kentucky, North Carolina and Missouri. The Company has 42 aftermarket distribution centers in the United States.

QUARTERLY DATA

(12/31/93)($000)	Rev	Inc
1st Quarter	54,407	3,269
2nd Quarter	63,559	4,376
3rd Quarter	61,186	3,134
4th Quarter	65,984	4,616

ANNUAL EARNINGS AND DIVIDENDS PER SHARE

	1993	1992	1991	1990	1989	1988	1987
Earnings Per Share	1.31	1.17	0.95	0.97	0.87	0.74	0.47
Dividends Per Share	0.18	① 0.15	② 0.135	③ 0.123	④ 0.112	③ 0.102	⑤ 0.095
Dividend Payout %	13.7	12.9	14.2	12.7	12.8	13.9	19.9

Note: 10% stk div 8/31/93 ① 5-for-4 stk split, 9/1/92 ② 10% stk div, 8/12/91 ③ 10% stk split, 8/31/90 ④ 10% stk div, 9/01/89 ⑤ 3-for-2 stk split, 9/87

ANNUAL FINANCIAL DATA

RECORD OF EARNINGS (IN THOUSANDS):

	1993	1992	1991	1990	1989	1988	1987
Total Revenues	245,136	229,255	195,581	202,104	194,772	183,811	131,710
Costs and Expenses	211,519	200,154	170,322	175,933	169,832	161,752	117,086
Depreciation	7,077	5,922	5,677	5,399	5,031	4,569	3,289
Operating Income	26,540	23,179	19,583	20,772	19,909	17,489	11,336
Income Bef Income Taxes	25,449	21,837	17,844	17,992	16,216	13,865	9,576
Income Taxes	10,054	8,727	7,308	7,234	6,595	5,797	4,358
Net Income	15,395	13,110	10,536	10,758	9,621	8,068	5,218
Aver. Shs. Outstg.	11,778	11,250	11,090	11,057	11,022	10,984	10,909

BALANCE SHEET (IN THOUSANDS):

	1993	1992	1991	1990	1989	1988	1987
Cash & Temp Cash Invests	1,662	3,416	3,156	2,515	2,472	1,633	1,804
Receivables, Net	40,405	38,310	30,605	30,702	30,084	29,127	24,877
Inventories	34,942	30,877	25,132	27,778	26,000	25,239	23,725
Gross Property	105,308	91,976	76,378	70,296	61,046	55,410	47,632
Accumulated Depreciation	47,613	41,313	37,041	31,597	27,033	22,651	17,677
Long-Term Debt	10,655	24,917	14,560	25,362	29,834	38,433	35,502
Net Stockholders' Equity	115,287	83,883	72,454	63,194	53,293	44,767	38,003
Total Assets	152,386	142,081	113,030	116,373	111,104	109,669	103,402
Total Current Assets	78,922	74,893	60,723	63,311	61,479	58,853	52,171
Total Current Liabilities	24,381	31,686	25,346	26,346	26,398	24,796	28,326
Net Working Capital	54,541	43,207	35,377	36,965	35,082	34,057	23,845
Year End Shares Outstg	12,223	11,275	11,101	11,069	11,042	10,996	10,915

STATISTICAL RECORD:

	1993	1992	1991	1990	1989	1988	1987
Operating Profit Margin %	10.8	10.1	10.0	10.3	10.2	9.5	8.6
Book Value Per Share	8.36	6.23	5.56	4.66	3.69	2.79	2.08
Return on Equity %	13.4	15.6	14.5	17.0	18.1	18.0	13.7
Return on Assets %	10.1	9.2	9.3	9.2	8.7	7.4	5.0
Average Yield %	0.8	0.9	1.3	1.2	1.1	1.5	1.7
P/E Ratio	19.1-14.6	18.1-9.6	12.8-8.8	12.8-8.6	13.2-10.5	12.7-6.3	15.9-7.3
Price Range	25-19⅛	21-11⅛	12⅛-8⅜	12⅜-8⅜	11½-9⅛	9⅜-4⅝	7⅝-3½

Statistics are as originally reported.

OFFICERS:
S.E. Myers, Pres. & C.E.O.
M.I. Wiskind, Sr. V.P. & Sec.
G.J. Stodnick, V.P.-Fin. & C.F.O.

INCORPORATED: OH, Jan., 1955

PRINCIPAL OFFICE: 1293 South Main St., Akron, OH 44301

TELEPHONE NUMBER: (216) 253-5592

FAX: (216) 253-6568

NO. OF EMPLOYEES: 1,600

ANNUAL MEETING: In April

SHAREHOLDERS: 1,530 (approx.)

INSTITUTIONAL HOLDINGS:
No. of Institutions: 43
Shares Held: 2,867,520

REGISTRAR(S): First Chicago Trust Company of New York, New York, NY 10005

TRANSFER AGENT(S): First Chicago Trust Company of New York, New York, NY 10005

NACCO INDUSTRIES INC.

YIELD 1.3%
P/E RATIO 40.7

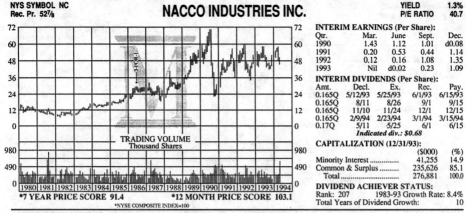

INTERIM EARNINGS (Per Share):

Qtr.	Mar.	June	Sept.	Dec.
1990	1.43	1.12	1.01	d0.08
1991	0.20	0.53	0.44	1.14
1992	0.12	0.16	1.08	1.35
1993	Nil	d0.02	0.23	1.09

INTERIM DIVIDENDS (Per Share):

Amt.	Decl.	Ex.	Rec.	Pay.
0.165Q	5/12/93	5/25/93	6/1/93	6/15/93
0.165Q	8/11	8/26	9/1	9/15
0.165Q	11/10	11/24	12/1	12/15
0.165Q	2/9/94	2/23/94	3/1/94	3/15/94
0.17Q	5/11	5/25	6/1	6/15

Indicated div.: $0.68

CAPITALIZATION (12/31/93):

	($000)	(%)
Minority Interest	41,255	14.9
Common & Surplus	235,626	85.1
Total	276,881	100.0

DIVIDEND ACHIEVER STATUS:
Rank: 207   1983-93 Growth Rate: 8.4%
Total Years of Dividend Growth: 10

TRADING VOLUME
Thousand Shares

*7 YEAR PRICE SCORE 91.4   *12 MONTH PRICE SCORE 103.1
*NYSE COMPOSITE INDEX=100

RECENT DEVELOPMENTS: For the year ended 12/31/93, net income was $11.6 million compared with $22.9 million last year. Results for 1993 include an extraordinary charge of $3.3 million resulting from the costs associated with the retirement of debt. Revenues were $1.55 billion, up 4.4%. NACCO Materials Handling Group reported a net loss of $5.1 million compared with net income of $1.3 million last year. North American Coal Corp. reported net income of $16 million, down 18%. Hamilton Beach/Proctor Silex had net income of $2.0 million compared with $4.5 million in 1992.

PROSPECTS: Market acceptance for new Hyster and Yale products has been strong. However, Hyster and Yale's results continue to be negatively affected by weak market conditions in Europe and Japan. Also, startup costs for new facilties and new products have been hampering profit margins. NC is integrating Hyster and Yale manufacturing operations to strengthen its long-term cost effectiveness. Programs have also been put into place that further strengthen Hyster and Yale dealer networks.

BUSINESS

NACCO INDUSTRIES, INC. is a holding company with four operating subsidaries: NACCO Materials Handling Group, The North American Coal Corp., Hamilton Beach/Proctor-Silex, Inc., and the Kitchen Collection, Inc. NACCO Materials Handling Group is a world leader in the design and manufacture of forklift trucks, marketed under the Hyster and Yale brand names. North American Coal mines and markets lignite coal primarily, as fuel for power generation by electric utilities. Hamilton Beach/Proctor-Silex is a leading manufactuer of small electric appliances. The Kitchen Collection is a national specialty retailer of kitchenware and small electric appliances.

BUSINESS LINE ANALYSIS

(12/31/93)	Rev(%)	Inc(%)
NAACO Materials Handling	58.4	39.1
Hamilton Beach/Proctor-Si ...	22.9	11.6
North American Coal	14.9	43.6
Kitchen Collection	3.5	4.7
Bellaire	0.3	1.0
Total	100.0	100.0

ANNUAL EARNINGS AND DIVIDENDS PER SHARE

	1993	1992	1991	1990	1989	1988	1987
Earnings Per Share	1.30	①2.71	2.31	3.49	6.08	5.08	3.75
Dividends Per Share	0.655	0.635	0.615	0.595	0.575	0.55	0.515
Dividend Payout %	50.4	23.4	26.6	17.0	18.9	21.7	27.5

① Before extraord. item

ANNUAL FINANCIAL DATA

RECORD OF EARNINGS (IN MILLIONS):

	1993	1992	1991	1990	1989	1988	1987
Total Revenues	1,549.4	1,481.5	1,369.2	1,385.0	1,187.6	616.5	494.5
Costs and Expenses	1,377.9	1,295.3	1,189.9	1,193.3	992.7	523.7	388.1
Deprec, Depl & Amort	78.1	67.9	66.5	64.3	52.3	32.2	32.1
Operating Profit	93.4	118.3	112.7	127.4	142.6	60.6	74.3
Income Bef Income Taxes	24.7	43.5	30.0	50.0	92.3	60.3	47.9
Provision for Inc Taxes	13.5	19.4	9.5	19.1	38.3	15.3	13.5
Minority Interest	cr0.4	...	...	...	...	...	0.4
Net Income	①11.6	②24.1	20.5	30.9	53.9	45.0	34.0
Aver. Shs. Outstg. (000)	8,938	8,891	8,878	8,877	8,874	8,850	9,047

① Before extra. item dr$3,292,000.   ② Before extra. item dr$110,000,000.

BALANCE SHEET (IN MILLIONS):

	1993	1992	1991	1990	1989	1988	1987
Cash & Cash Equivalents	29.1	33.8	52.3	100.8	172.0	95.0	146.2
Receivables, Net	200.1	181.2	201.0	215.5	180.0	94.8	74.1
Inventories	238.2	235.5	225.1	259.1	252.6	118.4	72.9
Gross Property	782.2	745.1	674.8	627.1	549.0	433.8	437.7
Accumulated Depreciation	286.0	248.0	211.5	170.8	131.9	121.2	132.8
Long-Term Debt	...	...	...	...	596.6	54.7	198.7
Capized Lease Obligations	...	...	...	...	126.4	133.6	144.4
Net Stockholders' Equity	235.6	239.6	350.3	352.9	300.8	246.0	205.5
Total Assets	1,642.5	1,664.3	1,608.5	1,722.0	1,680.2	837.0	702.6
Total Current Assets	504.8	495.9	531.6	657.6	701.7	357.3	293.2
Total Current Liabilities	397.5	330.6	373.7	408.5	462.4	226.7	83.7
Net Working Capital	107.3	165.3	157.9	249.1	239.2	130.6	209.5
Year End Shs Outstg (000)	8,036	8,935	8,882	8,878	8,876	8,870	8,829

STATISTICAL RECORD:

	1993	1992	1991	1990	1989	1988	1987
Operating Profit Margin %	6.0	8.0	8.2	9.2	12.0	9.8	15.0
Book Value Per Share	...	...	...	...	...	20.36	23.27
Return on Equity %	4.9	10.1	5.9	8.8	17.9	18.3	16.5
Return on Assets %	0.7	1.4	1.3	1.8	3.2	5.4	4.8
Average Yield %	1.3	1.3	1.4	1.3	1.3	1.8	2.0
P/E Ratio	44.8-32.3	22.1-12.6	24.6-12.6	20.2-6.3	9.2-5.1	8.0-4.2	8.6-5.0
Price Range	58¼-42	60-34¼	56⅞-29	70½-22	56-31¼	40¾-21¼	32¼-18¾

Statistics are as originally reported.

OFFICERS:
W. Smith, Chmn.
A.M. Rankin, Jr., Pres. & C.E.O.
F.B. O'Brien, Sr. V.P. & C.F.O.
C.A. Bittenbender, V.P., Couns. & Sec.
INCORPORATED: DE
PRINCIPAL OFFICE: 5875 Landerbrook Drive, Mayfield Heights, OH 44124-4017

TELEPHONE NUMBER: (216) 449-9600
NO. OF EMPLOYEES: 10,879
ANNUAL MEETING: In May
SHAREHOLDERS: 900 Cl. A com.; 700 Cl. B
INSTITUTIONAL HOLDINGS:
No. of Institutions: 99
Shares Held: 5,037,554

REGISTRAR(S): Society National Bank, Cleveland, OH

TRANSFER AGENT(S): Society National Bank, Cleveland, OH

NASH-FINCH CO.

YIELD 4.4%
P/E RATIO 11.3

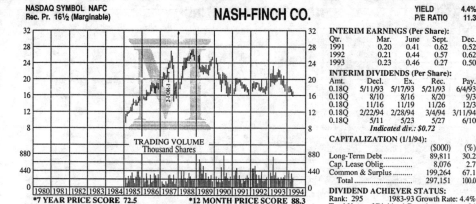

*7 YEAR PRICE SCORE 72.5 *12 MONTH PRICE SCORE 88.3
*NYSE COMPOSITE INDEX=100

INTERIM EARNINGS (Per Share):

Qtr.	Mar.	June	Sept.	Dec.
1991	0.20	0.41	0.62	0.52
1992	0.21	0.44	0.57	0.62
1993	0.23	0.46	0.27	0.50

INTERIM DIVIDENDS (Per Share):

Amt.	Decl.	Ex.	Rec.	Pay.
0.18Q	5/11/93	5/17/93	5/21/93	6/4/93
0.18Q	8/10	8/16	8/20	9/3
0.18Q	11/16	11/19	11/26	12/3
0.18Q	2/22/94	2/28/94	3/4/94	3/11/94
0.18Q	5/11	5/23	5/27	6/10

Indicated div.: $0.72

CAPITALIZATION (1/1/94):

	($000)	(%)
Long-Term Debt	89,811	30.2
Cap. Lease Oblig.	8,076	2.7
Common & Surplus	199,264	67.1
Total	297,151	100.0

DIVIDEND ACHIEVER STATUS:
Rank: 295   1983-93 Growth Rate: 4.4%
Total Years of Dividend Growth: 24

RECENT DEVELOPMENTS: For the year ended 1/1/94, net earnings were down 20.9% to $15.9 million compared with $20.1 million in 1992. Total revenues increased 8.3% to $2.72 billion from $2.52 billion the previous year. Record sales were achieved primarily due to the contributions from the Baltimore-based military wholesale division acquired at the end of 1992 and the 16-store Easter group acquired in mid-year. The decline in earnings was due to non-recurring charges associated with a debt-workout acquisition of 23

stores in North Carolina, certain bad debts and other contingencies and the higher federal tax rate. Work has begun on a new supermarket in Spearfish, South Dakota, which involves the conversion of an existing building to a 33,500-square-foot Family Thrift Center. The store is scheduled to open in the second quarter of 1994. NAFC also began construction on a 30,000-square-foot addition to what is currently its largest Econofoods superwarehouse store.

BUSINESS

NASH-FINCH COMPANY is one of the largest food wholesalers in the country, supplying products to approximately 700 affiliated and independent supermarkets and some 5,000 other independent retailers and military bases in 29 states. The Company also owns and operates approximately 90 supermarkets, warehouse stores and mass merchandise stores in 13 states and produce marketing subsidiaries in California.

ANNUAL EARNINGS AND DIVIDENDS PER SHARE

	1/1/94	1/2/93	12/28/91	12/29/90	12/30/89	12/31/88	1/2/88
Earnings Per Share	1.46	1.85	1.75	1.64	1.21	1.67	1.75
Dividends Per Share	0.72	0.70	0.70	0.69	0.67	0.65	⑪0.57
Dividend Payout %	49.3	37.8	40.0	42.1	55.4	38.9	32.6

⑪ 100% stk. div., 6/87.

ANNUAL FINANCIAL DATA

RECORD OF EARNINGS (IN MILLIONS):

Total Revenues	2,723.5	2,515.4	2,343.3	2,374.9	2,223.8	2,097.8	1,943.3
Costs and Expenses	2,657.6	2,446.5	2,277.4	2,311.7	2,171.2	2,037.7	1,881.2
Depreciation & Amort	29.1	27.0	26.1	25.6	23.2	20.2	18.4
Operating Profit	36.8	41.9	39.8	37.6	29.4	40.0	43.7
Earn Bef Income Taxes	26.7	32.6	30.8	29.0	21.2	29.0	32.9
Income Taxes	10.8	12.5	11.7	11.1	8.0	10.9	14.4
Net Income	15.9	20.1	19.1	17.8	13.2	18.2	18.5
Aver. Shs. Outstg. (000)	10,872	10,872	10,871	10,870	10,868	10,881	10,576

BALANCE SHEET (IN MILLIONS):

Cash and Cash Equivalents	0.9	0.8	0.6	0.6	12.8	0.7	0.5
Accts & Notes Receiv, Net	96.0	97.3	67.2	55.3	48.9	58.3	52.3
Inventories	186.6	205.0	167.1	172.8	145.1	155.6	151.5
Gross Property	382.6	359.6	323.1	294.8	260.9	244.9	213.3
Accumulated Depreciation	196.4	184.3	159.3	138.7	117.2	102.1	98.3
Long-Term Debt	89.8	92.1	80.4	71.8	75.0	63.0	61.8
Capized Lease Obligations	8.1	2.0	2.1	2.5	2.9	3.2	5.2
Net Stockholders' Equity	199.3	191.2	178.8	167.4	157.0	151.0	140.9
Total Assets	521.7	513.6	429.6	416.2	380.8	388.3	352.2
Total Current Assets	294.9	309.8	239.9	234.1	212.3	220.0	209.3
Total Current Liabilities	215.0	213.7	155.0	158.0	128.2	153.1	127.6
Net Working Capital	79.9	96.1	84.9	76.1	84.1	66.9	81.7
Year End Shs Outstg (000)	10,873	10,872	10,871	10,871	10,869	10,865	11,224

STATISTICAL RECORD:

Operating Profit Margin %	1.4	1.7	1.7	1.6	1.3	1.9	2.3
Book Value Per Share	17.45	17.59	16.45	15.40	14.45	13.90	12.55
Return on Equity %	8.0	10.5	10.7	10.7	8.4	12.0	13.1
Return on Assets %	3.0	3.9	4.4	4.3	3.5	4.7	5.3
Average Yield %	3.6	3.9	3.8	3.4	2.9	2.9	2.7
P/E Ratio	15.9-11.6	10.7-8.8	11.6-9.2	15.4-9.6	21.5-17.4	16.5-10.5	15.4-8.3
Price Range	23¼-17	19⅞-16¼	20¼-16⅛	25¼-15¾		26-21 27½-17½	27-14½

Statistics are as originally reported.

OFFICERS:
H.B. Finch, Jr., Chmn. & C.E.O.
A.N. Flaten, Jr., Pres. & C.O.O.
R.F. Nash, V.P. & Treas.
N.R. Soland, V.P., Sec. & Couns.

INCORPORATED: DE, 1921

PRINCIPAL OFFICE: 7600 France Avenue
South P.O. Box 355, Minneapolis, MN
55440-0355

TELEPHONE NUMBER: (612) 832-0534

NO. OF EMPLOYEES: 6,000 full-time; 5,900 part-time

ANNUAL MEETING: In May

SHAREHOLDERS: 2,074

INSTITUTIONAL HOLDINGS:
No. of Institutions: 51
Shares Held: 3,578,825

REGISTRAR(S): Norwest Bank Minnesota,
N.A., St. Paul, MN

TRANSFER AGENT(S): Norwest Bank
Minnesota, N.A., St. Paul, MN

NYS SYMBOL NFG
Rec. Pr. 29¾

NATIONAL FUEL GAS COMPANY

YIELD 5.2%
P/E RATIO 15.3

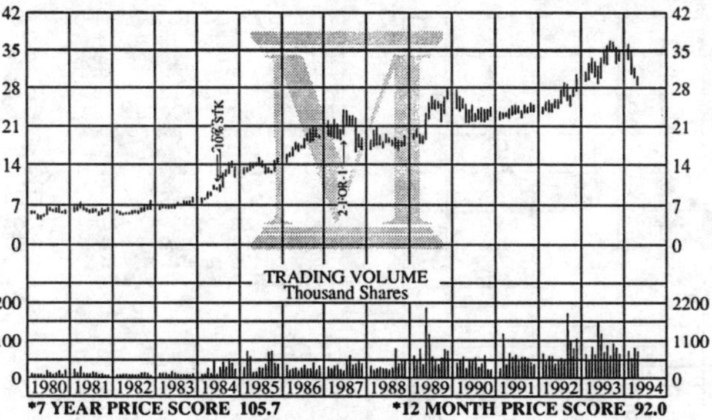

42
35
28
21
14
7
0
10% STK
2-FOR-1
TRADING VOLUME
Thousand Shares
2200
1100
0
1980 1981 1982 1983 1984 1985 1986 1987 1988 1989 1990 1991 1992 1993 1994

*7 YEAR PRICE SCORE 105.7 *12 MONTH PRICE SCORE 92.0

*NYSE COMPOSITE INDEX=100

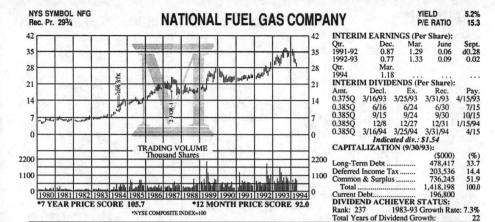

INTERIM EARNINGS (Per Share):

Qtr.	Dec.	Mar.	June	Sept.
1991-92	0.87	1.29	0.06	d0.28
1992-93	0.77	1.33	0.09	0.02
Qtr.		Mar.		
1994	1.18	...	...	...

INTERIM DIVIDENDS (Per Share):

Amt.	Decl.	Ex.	Rec.	Pay.
0.375Q	3/16/93	3/25/93	3/31/93	4/15/93
0.385Q	6/16	6/24	6/30	7/15
0.385Q	9/15	9/24	9/30	10/15
0.385Q	12/8	12/27	12/31	1/15/94
0.385Q	3/16/94	3/25/94	3/31/94	4/15

Indicated div.: $1.54

CAPITALIZATION (9/30/93):

	($000)	(%)
Long-Term Debt	478,417	33.7
Deferred Income Tax	203,536	14.4
Common & Surplus	736,245	51.9
Total	1,418,198	100.0
Current Debt	196,800	

DIVIDEND ACHIEVER STATUS:
Rank: 237 1983-93 Growth Rate: 7.3%
Total Years of Dividend Growth: 22

RECENT DEVELOPMENTS: For the quarter ended 12/31/93, income before an accounting adjustment was $27.8 million compared with net income of $25.9 million last year. Revenues were $1.04 billion, up 10%. Earnings reported by the Pipeline and Storage segment were up 20% primarily because of the approval of a favorable rate settlement and the receipt of a refund of prior cost. Utility Operation's earnings declined 5.5% due to the timing of gas cost adjustments.

PROSPECTS: FERC Order 636 should benefit the pipeline and storage operations by stabilizing earnings and cash flow. Future exploration and production earnings will benefit from increased production. Disappointing rate decisions in the New York and Pennsylvania jurisdictions have authorized NFG lower-than-industry returns on equity. However, the lower return in New York is partially offset by the stable nature of the Company's earnings in that jurisdiction, mainly due to a weather-normalization clause.

BUSINESS

NATIONAL FUEL GAS COMPANY is the public utility holding company of National Fuel Gas Supply, National Fuel Gas Distribution Corp., Seneca Resources, Penn-York Energy Corp., Empire Exploration, Inc., Utility Constructors, Inc. and National Fuel Resources Inc. These operations are involved in all phases of the natural gas marketing, industry: exploration, production, purchasing, gathering, transmission, storage, sale at wholesale, and distribution, together with by-product operations. Seneca Resources Corp. also markets timber and coal. Other subsidiaries included Highland Land & Minerals Inc., a sawmill operation, Data-Track, Inc., a collection service and Enerop Corporation.

QUARTERLY DATA

(9/30/93)	Rev($)	Inc($)
First Qtr	294,220	38,542
Second Qtr	391,790	57,195
Third Qtr	185,525	14,993
Fourth Qtr	148,847	11,643

ANNUAL EARNINGS AND DIVIDENDS PER SHARE

	9/30/93	9/30/92	9/30/91	9/30/90	9/30/89	9/30/88	9/30/87
Earnings Per Share	**2.16**	**1.94**	**1.63**	**1.83**	**1.93**	**1.65**	**[1] 1.49**
Dividends Per Share	**1.52**	**1.48**	**1.44**	**1.38**	**1.30**	**1.23**	**[2] 1.17**
Dividend Payout %	**70.4**	**76.3**	**88.3**	**75.4**	**67.4**	**74.5**	**78.5**

[1] Before extraord. item [2] 2-for-1 stk. split, 6/87.

ANNUAL FINANCIAL DATA

RECORD OF EARNINGS (IN MILLIONS):							
Operating Revenues	1,020.4	919.8	865.1	892.0	855.8	768.9	737.2
Maintenance	24.3	22.4	20.5	18.7	20.1	21.1	21.4
Prov for Fed Inc Taxes	41.0	35.2	23.3	27.5	25.8	18.7	24.8
Operating Income	122.3	113.6	98.4	102.3	98.0	79.1	69.4
Total Interest Charges	51.9	59.0	61.3	57.8	51.6	41.3	39.4
Net Income	75.2	60.3	49.0	52.0	52.4	42.6	[1] 35.9
Aver. Shs. Outstg. (000)	34,939	31,153	29,996	28,404	27,191	25,885	24,134
[1] Before extra. item cr$6,570,000.							
BALANCE SHEET (IN MILLIONS):							
Gross Plant	2,039.4	1,918.4	1,772.5	1,625.3	1,472.6	1,353.2	1,238.3
Accumulated Depreciation	561.4	502.0	458.8	418.9	385.1	350.7	319.0
Prop, Plant & Equip, Net	1,478.0	1,416.4	1,313.8	1,206.4	1,087.5	1,002.4	919.3
Long-term Debt	478.4	479.5	442.1	397.4	383.9	297.2	266.3
Net Stockholders' Equity	736.2	632.3	542.1	484.0	464.2	406.1	393.5
Total Assets	1,801.5	1,760.8	1,560.8	1,436.7	1,311.6	1,176.9	1,119.4
Year End Shs Outstg (000)	36,661	33,856	30,927	28,532	28,245	25,936	25,864
STATISTICAL RECORD:							
Book Value Per Share	20.08	18.68	17.53	16.96	16.44	15.66	15.21
Op. Inc/Net Pl %	8.3	8.0	7.5	8.5	9.0	7.9	7.6
Dep/Gr. Pl %	3.4	2.9	2.9	2.7	3.0	3.2	2.9
Accum. Dep/Gr. Pl %	27.5	26.2	25.9	25.8	26.2	25.9	25.8
Return on Equity %	10.2	9.5	9.0	10.7	11.3	10.5	9.1
Average Yield %	4.6	5.5	6.1	5.6	5.7	6.6	5.8
P/E Ratio	17.2-13.4	15.7-12.0	15.5-13.6	15.1-11.8	14.4-9.3	12.6-10.0	16.1-10.9
Price Range	36⅞-28¾	30½-23¼	25¼-22⅛	27⅝-21⅝	27⅞-17⅞	20¾-16½	24-16¼

Statistics are as originally reported.

OFFICERS:
B.J. Kennedy, Chmn., Pres. & C.E.O.
J.P. Pawlowski, Treasurer
R.M. DiValerio, Secretary

INCORPORATED: NJ, Dec., 1902

PRINCIPAL OFFICE: 30 Rockefeller Plaza, New York, NY 10112

TELEPHONE NUMBER: (212) 541-7533
FAX: (212) 541-7841
NO. OF EMPLOYEES: 3,329
ANNUAL MEETING: In February
SHAREHOLDERS: 22,893
INSTITUTIONAL HOLDINGS:
No. of Institutions: 153
Shares Held: 11,132,670

REGISTRAR(S): Manufacturers Hanover Trust Co., New York, NY

TRANSFER AGENT(S): Manufacturers Hanover Trust Co., New York, NY

NASDAQ SYMBOL NPBC
Rec. Pr. 39½ (Marginable)

NATIONAL PENN BANCSHARES, INC.

YIELD 1.9%
P/E RATIO 19.8

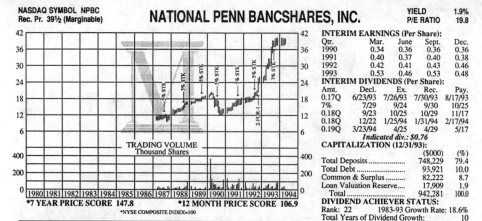

7 YEAR PRICE SCORE 147.8
12 MONTH PRICE SCORE 106.9
*NYSE COMPOSITE INDEX=100

TRADING VOLUME
Thousand Shares

INTERIM EARNINGS (Per Share):

Qtr.	Mar.	June	Sept.	Dec.
1990	0.34	0.36	0.36	0.36
1991	0.40	0.37	0.40	0.38
1992	0.42	0.41	0.43	0.46
1993	0.53	0.46	0.53	0.48

INTERIM DIVIDENDS (Per Share):

Amt.	Decl.	Ex.	Rec.	Pay.
0.17Q	6/23/93	7/26/93	7/30/93	8/17/93
7%	7/29	9/24	9/30	10/25
0.18Q	9/23	10/25	10/29	11/17
0.18Q	12/22	1/25/94	1/31/94	2/17/94
0.19Q	3/23/94	4/25	4/29	5/17

Indicated div.: $0.76

CAPITALIZATION (12/31/93):

	($000)	(%)
Total Deposits	748,229	79.4
Total Debt	93,921	10.0
Common & Surplus	82,222	8.7
Loan Valuation Reserve	17,909	1.9
Total	942,281	100.0

DIVIDEND ACHIEVER STATUS:
Rank: 22   1983-93 Growth Rate: 18.6%
Total Years of Dividend Growth: 10

RECENT DEVELOPMENTS: For the year ended 12/31/93, total profits rose 17.6% to $13.3 million. Assets increased to $934 million, up 20.3% from $776 million in 1992. Of the $158 million increase, $73 million is attributable to the acquisition of Chestnut Hill National bank on 12/1/93, $25 million to the purchase of two First Lehigh Bank branches, and $60 million from internal growth. Aggregate loan outstandings increased 21.7% to $720 million compared with $592 million in 1992.

While Chestnut Hill National Bank added $46 million and the First Lehigh Bank branch purchases added $15 million, NPBC's internal growth was responsible for $67 million of the increased loans. This growth has occured throughout all of NPBC's major lending areas, particularly residential mortgages, home equity loans, construction and investment property lending, and to a lesser extent, commercial loans.

BUSINESS

NATIONAL PENN BANCSHARES, INC. is a bank holding company. Through its banking subsidiary, National Penn Bank, National Penn operates 30 offices in Berks, Bucks, Chester, Lehigh, Montgomery and Philadelphia counties. In addition, National Penn has two wholly-owned non-bank subsidiaries engaged in activities related to the business of banking.

LOAN DISTRIBUTION

(12/31/93)	($000)	(%)
Commerical & Industrial	68,599	9.3
Loans Purch & Carry Secur	1,008	0.1
Loans to Financial Instit	2,063	0.3
Real Estate	643,105	87.2
Individual	22,979	3.1
Lease Finance Receivables	27	0.0
Total	737,781	100.0

ANNUAL EARNINGS AND DIVIDENDS PER SHARE

	1993	1992	1991	1990	1989	1988	1987
Earnings Per Share	1.96	1.69	1.52	1.41	1.30	1.21	1.05
Dividends Per Share	① 0.68	② 0.559	③ 0.507	④ 0.463	⑤ 0.413	⑥ 0.359	⑦ 0.289
Dividend Payout %	34.7	33.0	33.2	32.6	31.6	29.6	27.7

① 7% stk div,09/24/93 ② 5% stk div,08/25/92 ③ 5% stk div,09/30/91 ④ 5% stk div, 10/16/90 ⑤ 5% stock dividend, 10/16/89. ⑥ 5% stk. div., 10/88 ⑦ 5% stk. div. 10/87.

ANNUAL FINANCIAL DATA

RECORD OF EARNINGS (IN THOUSANDS):

	1993	1992	1991	1990	1989	1988	1987
Total Interest Income	71,272	69,073	71,709	61,353	57,824	46,249	40,203
Total Interest Expense	23,839	26,699	36,387	32,912	31,710	23,346	19,988
Net Interest Income	47,433	42,374	35,322	28,441	26,114	22,903	20,215
Prov for Loan & Lse Losses	5,145	6,225	4,817	1,845	1,300	1,825	2,465
Net Income	⑧ 12,808	11,313	10,100	9,305	8,605	⑨ 7,867	6,700
Aver. Shs. Outstg.	6,783	6,697	6,623	6,601	6,589	6,535	6,123

⑧ Before acctg. change cr$500,000. ⑨ Before acctg. change dr$215,000.

BALANCE SHEET (IN THOUSANDS):

	1993	1992	1991	1990	1989	1988	1987
Cash & Due From Banks	23,310	17,193	24,324	23,440	20,842	19,606	13,569
Loans & Leases-net	719,856	591,513	520,300	505,950	390,282	328,681	279,390
Total Domestic Deposits	748,229	631,186	616,617	600,359	482,331	411,304	374,369
Long-term Debt	51,089	41,110	25,079	6,700	3,000	3,000	3,000
Net Stockholders' Equity	82,222	70,700	61,609	54,618	48,558	42,023	35,309
Total Assets	933,736	775,888	739,512	726,531	572,740	493,855	427,405
Year End Shares Outstg	6,855	6,731	6,622	6,613	6,295	5,959	5,606

STATISTICAL RECORD:

	1993	1992	1991	1990	1989	1988	1987
Return on Assets %	1.37	1.46	1.37	1.28	1.50	1.59	1.57
Return on Equity %	15.60	16.00	16.40	17.00	17.00	18.70	19.00
Book Value Per Share	11.99	10.50	9.30	8.26	7.71	7.05	6.30
Average Yield %	2.1	2.6	3.2	2.8	2.4	2.5	2.6
P/E Ratio	21.4-12.7	15.5-9.8	12.3-8.4	14.7-8.5	14.7-12.3	14.1-10.2	11.9-9.0
Price Range	40¼-23⅞	26⅛-16½	18½-12¾	20⅝-11⅞	19⅛-16	16⅞-12¼	12½-9½

Statistics are as originally reported.

OFFICERS:
L.T. Jilk, Jr., Chm.
W.R. Weidner, Pres. & C.E.O.
W.H. Sayre, E.V.P.
G.L. Rhoads, Treasurer
S.L. Spayd, Secretary

INCORPORATED: PA, Jan., 1982

PRINCIPAL OFFICE: P.O. Box 547,
Boyertown, PA 19512-0547

TELEPHONE NUMBER: (610) 369-6128
FAX: (610) 369-6349
NO. OF EMPLOYEES: 509 (full & part-time)
ANNUAL MEETING: In April
SHAREHOLDERS: 2,710
INSTITUTIONAL HOLDINGS:
No. of Institutions: 7
Shares Held: 61,047

REGISTRAR(S):

TRANSFER AGENT(S):

NYS SYMBOL NSI
Rec. Pr. 25½

NATIONAL SERVICE INDUSTRIES, INC.

YIELD 4.2%
P/E RATIO 16.3

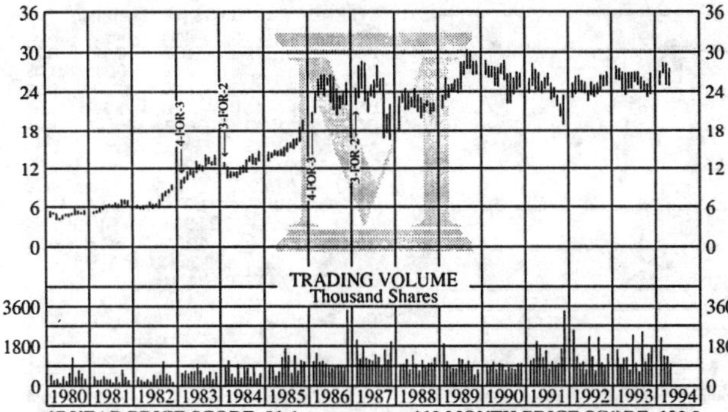

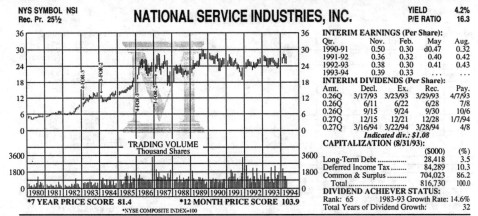

*7 YEAR PRICE SCORE 81.4 *12 MONTH PRICE SCORE 103.9

*NYSE COMPOSITE INDEX=100

INTERIM EARNINGS (Per Share):

Qtr.	Nov.	Feb.	May	Aug.
1990-91	0.50	0.30	d0.47	0.32
1991-92	0.36	0.32	0.40	0.42
1992-93	0.38	0.30	0.41	0.43
1993-94	0.39	0.33	...	...

INTERIM DIVIDENDS (Per Share):

Amt.	Decl.	Ex.	Rec.	Pay.
0.26Q	3/17/93	3/23/93	3/29/93	4/7/93
0.26Q	6/11	6/22	6/28	7/8
0.26Q	9/15	9/24	9/30	10/6
0.27Q	12/15	12/21	12/28	1/7/94
0.27Q	3/16/94	3/22/94	3/28/94	4/8

Indicated div.: $1.08

CAPITALIZATION (8/31/93):

	($000)	(%)
Long-Term Debt	28,418	3.5
Deferred Income Tax	84,289	10.3
Common & Surplus	704,023	86.2
Total	816,730	100.0

DIVIDEND ACHIEVER STATUS:
Rank: 65 1983-93 Growth Rate: 14.6%
Total Years of Dividend Growth: 32

RECENT DEVELOPMENTS: For the three months ended 11/30/93, net income rose slightly to $19.2 million from $18.6 million in the similar period of 1992. Sales advanced 6% to $459.9 million, the modest increase was due to weak chemical sales in Europe and Canada and flat results from the textile division. The lighting equipment segment posted an 11.7% increase in sales to $182.1 million.

PROSPECTS: Despite soft market demand, the lighting equipment division continues to increase sales and plans to further increase market share are being formulated. The chemicals unit is suffering from weak European markets. Canadian markets are performing below Company expectations while domestic markets are turning in satisfactory results. Textile rentals have benefited from acquisitions.

BUSINESS

NATIONAL SERVICE INDUSTRIES, INC. is a diversified manufacturing and service company with operations in six separate divisions. The lighting equipment division manufactures a wide variety of lighting equipment for commercial, industrial, institutional, and residential use. The textile rental division rents textile items to restaurants and lodging, hospitals, clinics, nursing homes and industrial. The chemical division manufactures a broad line of specialty chemicals for industrial and commercial maintenance, sanitation and housekeeping. Other divisions include, Marketing Services, Envelope, and Insulation Services.

BUSINESS LINE ANALYSIS

(08/31/93)	Rev(%)	Inc(%)
Lighting Equipment	38.4	29.4
Textile Rental	30.3	37.4
Chemical	17.6	25.4
Other	13.7	7.8
Total	100.0	100.0

ANNUAL EARNINGS AND DIVIDENDS PER SHARE

	8/31/93	8/31/92	8/31/91	8/31/90	8/31/89	8/31/88	8/31/87
Earnings Per Share	1.52	1.50	0.65	2.02	1.92	1.75	1.54
Dividends Per Share	1.04	1.00	0.96	0.92	0.84	0.76	[1] 0.64
Dividend Payout %	68.4	66.7	N.M.	45.5	43.8	43.4	41.6

[1] 3-for-2 stk split, 1/27/87

ANNUAL FINANCIAL DATA

	8/31/93	8/31/92	8/31/91	8/31/90	8/31/89	8/31/88	8/31/87
RECORD OF EARNINGS (IN MILLIONS):							
Total Revenues	1,804.8	1,633.8	1,601.7	1,647.8	1,539.5	1,414.2	1,326.9
Costs and Expenses	1,608.7	1,455.9	1,501.9	1,448.8	1,359.7	1,252.1	1,173.0
Depreciation & Amort	62.1	53.8	50.2	42.8	36.3	31.0	27.3
Operating Income	134.0	124.1	49.6	156.2	143.6	131.0	126.5
Inc Bef Prov for Income Taxes	119.5	116.9	48.6	155.7	148.0	133.2	132.4
Provision for Inc Taxes	44.4	42.8	16.4	56.0	53.3	47.1	56.7
Net Income	75.1	74.1	32.2	99.7	94.7	86.1	75.7
Aver. Shs. Outstg. (000)	49,556	49,539	49,540	49,389	49,255	49,258	49,278
BALANCE SHEET (IN MILLIONS):							
Cash and Cash Equivalents	20.6	109.6	87.6	125.2	129.0	134.0	122.9
Receivables, Net	250.0	204.0	199.0	202.2	193.7	181.9	171.4
Inventories	171.5	151.7	165.0	178.1	173.5	163.8	152.0
Gross Property	724.0	679.5	649.3	581.0	510.2	451.2	398.8
Accumulated Depreciation	358.9	339.2	307.0	280.1	249.4	222.8	196.2
Long-Term Debt	28.4	28.4	31.4	27.5	20.8	21.4	21.5
Net Stockholders' Equity	704.0	683.0	660.6	675.4	612.7	558.2	508.2
Total Assets	1,087.5	1,042.4	1,012.0	962.1	887.8	825.3	760.3
Total Current Assets	556.9	567.5	549.3	576.5	570.1	552.4	519.4
Total Current Liabilities	243.7	209.8	197.7	142.4	133.6	126.0	114.6
Net Working Capital	313.2	357.8	351.6	434.1	436.5	426.4	404.9
Year End Shs Outstg (000)	49,561	49,538	49,602	...	49,255	49,255	49,278
STATISTICAL RECORD:							
Operating Profit Margin %	7.4	7.6	3.1	9.5	9.3	9.3	9.5
Book Value Per Share	11.63	12.06	11.65	...	11.87	10.99	10.12
Return on Equity %	10.7	10.9	4.9	14.8	15.5	15.4	14.9
Return on Assets %	6.9	7.1	3.2	10.4	10.7	10.4	10.0
Average Yield %	4.1	4.0	4.1	3.6	3.2	3.6	2.8
P/E Ratio	18.3-15.2	18.0-15.0	43.5-29.2	14.2-11.0	15.8-11.1	14.0-10.4	18.6-10.7
Price Range	27⅞-23⅛	27-22½	28¼-19	28¾-22⅛	30⅜-21⅜	24½-18¼	28⅝-16½

Statistics are as originally reported.

OFFICERS:
E. Zaban, Chmn.
D.R. Riddle, Pres. & C.E.O.
J.R. Hipps, Sr. V.P.-Fin.
K.W. Murphy, Sec. & Asst. Couns.

INCORPORATED: DE, Aug., 1928

PRINCIPAL OFFICE: 1420 Peachtree St. N.E., Atlanta, GA 30309-3002

TELEPHONE NUMBER: (404) 853-1000

FAX: (404) 883-1015

NO. OF EMPLOYEES: 22,200 (approx.)

ANNUAL MEETING: In January

SHAREHOLDERS: 7,262

INSTITUTIONAL HOLDINGS:
No. of Institutions: 205
Shares Held: 28,258,088

REGISTRAR(S): Wachovia Bank & Trust Co., N.A., Winston-Salem, NC 27102

TRANSFER AGENT(S): Wachovia Bank & Trust Co., N.A., Winston-Salem, NC 27102

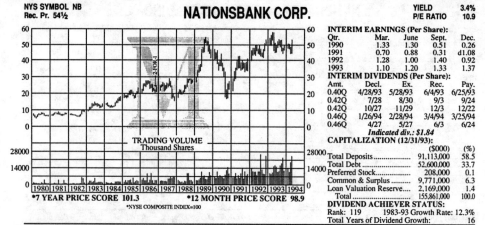

NYS SYMBOL NB
Rec. Pr. 54½

NATIONSBANK CORP.

YIELD 3.4%
P/E RATIO 10.9

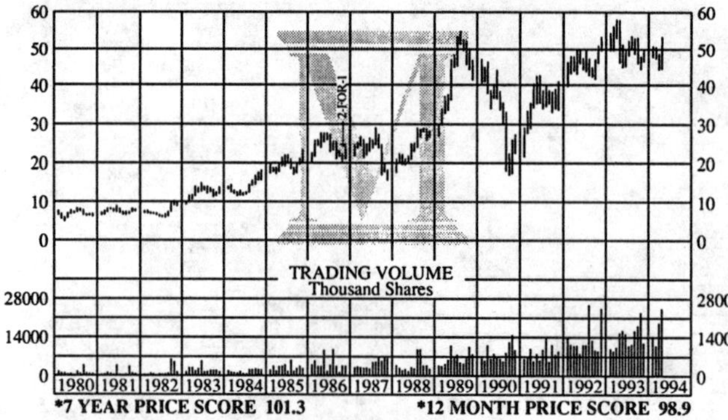

***7 YEAR PRICE SCORE 101.3** ***12 MONTH PRICE SCORE 98.9**

*NYSE COMPOSITE INDEX=100

INTERIM EARNINGS (Per Share):

Qtr.	Mar.	June	Sept.	Dec.
1990	1.33	1.30	0.51	0.26
1991	0.70	0.88	0.31	d1.08
1992	1.28	1.00	1.40	0.92
1993	1.10	1.20	1.33	1.37

INTERIM DIVIDENDS (Per Share):

Amt.	Decl.	Ex.	Rec.	Pay.
0.40Q	4/28/93	5/28/93	6/4/93	6/25/93
0.42Q	7/28	8/30	9/3	9/24
0.42Q	10/27	11/29	12/3	12/22
0.46Q	1/26/94	2/28/94	3/4/94	3/25/94
0.46Q	4/27	5/27	6/3	6/24

Indicated div.: $1.84

CAPITALIZATION (12/31/93):

	($000)	(%)
Total Deposits	91,113,000	58.5
Total Debt	52,600,000	33.7
Preferred Stock	208,000	0.1
Common & Surplus	9,771,000	6.3
Loan Valuation Reserve	2,169,000	1.4
Total	155,861,000	100.0

DIVIDEND ACHIEVER STATUS:
Rank: 119 1983-93 Growth Rate: 12.3%
Total Years of Dividend Growth: 16

RECENT DEVELOPMENTS: For the three months ended 12/31/93, net income rose 59% from the corresponding 1992 period to $373 million. Results benefited from a 33% reduction in credit loss provisions to $100 million and a 33% increase in noninterest income to $615 million. For 1993, income before accounting method adjustments was $1.30 billion compared with $1.15 billion for 1993. The Company cited improved credit quality and internal loan growth of 10% as the principal reasons for stronger results.

PROSPECTS: During 1993, the Company acquired MNC Financial Inc., Chrysler First, Chicago Research and Trading Group and US WEST Financial Services Inc. These strategic acquisitions are consistent with NB's objective of expanding nonbank services, diversification of earnings and becoming more competitive with nonbank institutions. Efforts to further strenghten credit quality have been successful as nonperforming assets and net charge-offs maintain a downward trend.

BUSINESS

NATIONSBANK CORP. (formerly NCNB Corp.) is the nation's third largest banking company with total assets of $158 billion and 1,930 banking centers in nine states and the District of Columbia. It was created by the December 31, 1991 combination of NCNB Corp. and C&S/Sovran Corp. The Company provides diversified financial services, including general, international and merchant banking, consumer and commercial finance, leasing, factoring, and trust services.

LOAN DISTRIBUTION

(12/31/93)	($000)	(%)
Commercial	52,442,000	57.9
Residential Mortgage	12,801,000	14.1
Home Equity	2,565,000	2.8
Bank Card	3,728,000	4.1
Other Consumer	17,063,000	18.9
Foreign	978,000	1.1
Factored Accts Receivable	1,001,000	1.1
Total	90,578,000	100.0

ANNUAL EARNINGS AND DIVIDENDS PER SHARE

	1993	1992	1991	1990	1989	1988	1987
Earnings Per Share	**5.00**	**4.60**	**0.76**	**3.40**	**4.62**	**2.90**	**2.03**
Dividends Per Share	**1.64**	**1.51**	**1.48**	**1.42**	**1.10**	**0.94**	**0.86**
Dividend Payout %	**32.8**	**32.8**	**N.M.**	**41.8**	**23.8**	**32.4**	**42.4**

ANNUAL FINANCIAL DATA

	1993	1992	1991	1990	1989	1988	1987
RECORD OF EARNINGS (IN MILLIONS):							
Tot Inc Fr Earning Assets	8,207.0	7,780.0	9,398.0	5,727.0	5,292.0	2,464.0	2,129.0
Total Interest Expense	3,570.0	3,682.0	5,599.0	3,911.0	3,589.0	1,567.0	1,307.0
Net Interest Income	4,637.0	4,098.0	3,799.0	1,816.0	1,703.0	897.0	822.0
Provision for Credit Losses	430.0	715.0	1,582.0	505.0	239.0	122.0	195.0
Net Income	[1] 1,301.0	1,145.0	202.0	366.0	447.0	252.0	167.0
Aver. Shs. Outstg. (000)	258,000	244,000	226,000	102,000	92,000	85,000	82,000
[1] Before acctg. change cr$200,000,000.							
BALANCE SHEET (IN MILLIONS):							
Cash and Due From Banks	...	...	...	...	...	...	1,812.0
Net Loans and Leases	89,838.0	71,260.0	67,503.0	36,436.0	33,944.0	18,677.0	16,830.0
Total Domestic Deposits	87,079.0	80,690.0	86,715.0	48,496.0	46,427.0	19,814.0	18,245.0
Total Foreign Deposits	4,034.0	2,037.0	1,360.0	1,726.0	2,149.0	857.0	1,305.0
Long-term Debt	8,352.0	3,066.0	2,876.0	1,697.0	1,465.0	493.0	497.0
Net Stockholders' Equity	9,979.0	7,814.0	6,518.0	3,208.0	2,962.0	1,942.0	1,510.0
Total Assets	157,686.0	118,059.0	110,319.0	65,285.0	66,191.0	29,848.0	28,915.0
Year End Shs Outstg (000)	271,000	253,000	231,000	103,000	101,000	86,000	85,000
STATISTICAL RECORD:							
Return on Assets %	0.83	0.97	0.18	0.56	0.68	0.84	0.58
Return on Equity %	13.00	14.70	3.10	11.40	15.10	13.00	11.10
Book Value Per Share	36.06	30.42	26.60	28.72	26.85	22.52	17.76
Average Yield %	3.2	3.2	4.6	4.4	2.7	4.0	3.9
P/E Ratio	11.6-8.9	11.6-8.6	56.3-28.3	13.9-5.0	11.9-5.8	10.0-6.0	14.3-7.6
Price Range	58-44½	53⅜-39⅝	42¾-21½	47¼-16⅞	55-27	29⅛-17½	29⅛-15½

Statistics are as originally reported.

OFFICERS:
H.L. McColl, Jr., Chmn. & C.E.O.
J.H. Hance, Vice-Chmn. & C.F.O.
K.D. Lewis, President

INCORPORATED: NC, Jul., 1968

PRINCIPAL OFFICE: NationsBank Corporate Center, Charlotte, NC 28255

TELEPHONE NUMBER: (704) 386-5000
NO. OF EMPLOYEES: 57,463
ANNUAL MEETING: In April
SHAREHOLDERS: 108,435
INSTITUTIONAL HOLDINGS:
No. of Institutions: 643
Shares Held: 149,763,972

REGISTRAR(S):

TRANSFER AGENT(S): Chemical Bank, New York, NY

NYS SYMBOL NBD
Rec. Pr. 29¼

NBD BANCORP, INC.

YIELD 4.1%
P/E RATIO 9.8

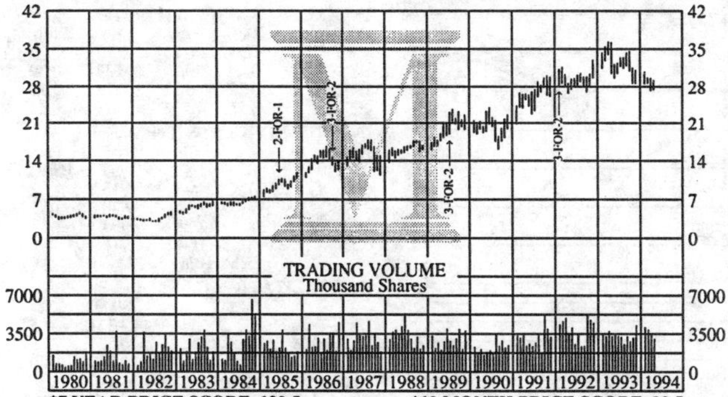

***7 YEAR PRICE SCORE 102.5** ***12 MONTH PRICE SCORE 93.5**

*NYSE COMPOSITE INDEX=100

INTERIM EARNINGS (Per Share):

Qtr.	Mar.	June	Sept.	Dec.
1990	0.61	0.61	0.64	0.64
1991	0.59	0.63	0.61	0.66
1992	0.62	0.56	0.23	0.70
1993	0.71	0.76	0.77	0.74

INTERIM DIVIDENDS (Per Share):

Amt.	Decl.	Ex.	Rec.	Pay.
0.27Q	3/15/93	4/13/93	4/19/93	5/10/93
0.27Q	6/21	7/14	7/20	8/10
0.27Q	9/20	10/14	10/20	11/10
0.27Q	12/20	1/13/94	1/20/94	2/10/94
0.30Q	3/21/94	4/13	4/19	5/10

Indicated div.: $1.20

CAPITALIZATION (12/31/93):

	($000)	(%)
Total Deposits	29,821,107	74.0
Total Debt	6,789,786	16.9
Common & Surplus	3,248,599	8.1
Loan Valuation Reserve	423,030	1.0
Total	40,282,522	100.0

DIVIDEND ACHIEVER STATUS:
Rank: 103 1983-93 Growth Rate: 12.9%
Total Years of Dividend Growth: 27

RECENT DEVELOPMENTS: For the quarter ended 12/31/93, net income rose to $119.0 million from $111.8 million in the comparable quarter of 1992. The provision for loan losses was $19.8 million, a sharp reduction from $57.2 million a year earlier. For the twelve months ended 12/31/93, income before accounting method changes was $481.8 million versus $338.0 million for 1992. The provision for loan losses declined 48% to $119.7 million.

PROSPECTS: Credit quality is steadily improving as nonperforming assets have been reduced considerably. A wider net interest margin is benefiting interest income and results from noninterest operations are boosting income. The acquisition of INB Financial Corp., a $6.2 billion Indianapolis bank, will make NBD the largest bank-holding company in Michigan and Indiana based on total assets.

BUSINESS

NBD BANCORP, INC. is a regional bank holding company with assets of $40.8 billion. It operates banks in Michigan, Illinois, Indiana, Ohio and Florida markets and bank-related subsidiaries engaged in commercial finance, mortgage banking, insurance, trust services, leasing, consumer credit processing and securities trading. Its principal subsidiary, NBD Bank, N.A., is the 16th largest bank in the country. NBD Bancorp offers a broad array of financial services to corporate, retail and trust customers across the country and around the world.

LOAN DISTRIBUTION

(12/31/93)	($000)	(%)
Commercial	13,794,714	54.0
Real Estate-Construction	789,248	3.1
Real Estate-Mortgage	2,560,539	10.0
Consumer	6,758,171	26.5
Lease Financing	284,805	1.1
Foreign	1,107,413	4.3
Mortgages Held For Sale	255,902	1.0
Total	25,550,792	100.0

ANNUAL EARNINGS AND DIVIDENDS PER SHARE

	1993	1992	1991	1990	1989	1988	1987
Earnings Per Share	**2.98**	**①2.11**	**2.49**	**2.50**	**2.39**	**2.14**	**1.54**
Dividends Per Share	**1.08**	**②1.02**	**0.933**	**0.893**	**③0.751**	**0.605**	**0.533**
Dividend Payout %	**36.2**	**48.3**	**37.5**	**35.7**	**31.4**	**28.3**	**34.6**

① Before acctg. chg. ② 3-for-2 stk split, 1/7/92 ③ 3-for-2 stk. split, 6/89

ANNUAL FINANCIAL DATA

	1993	1992	1991	1990	1989	1988	1987
RECORD OF EARNINGS (IN MILLIONS):							
Total Interest Income	2,622.8	2,843.8	2,386.9	2,408.4	2,281.9	1,935.3	1,720.7
Total Interest Expense	1,064.7	1,334.0	1,378.9	1,516.6	1,447.2	1,178.1	1,038.3
Net Interest Income	1,558.1	1,509.8	1,008.0	891.8	834.7	757.1	682.4
Prov for Possible Cr Losses	119.7	228.5	95.8	65.8	55.1	46.0	115.1
Net Income	①481.8	②338.0	293.0	274.8	258.8	227.2	162.2
Aver. Shs. Outstg. (000)	161,253	160,716	117,598	109,892	108,178	105,984	104,331
① Before acctg. change cr$3,950,000. ② Before acctg. change dr$37,885,000.							
BALANCE SHEET (IN MILLIONS):							
Cash & Due From Banks	2,405.7	2,549.3	1,507.3	1,417.1	1,668.8	1,913.4	1,936.6
Loans & Leases, Net	25,127.8	24,725.9	17,457.4	16,061.2	15,117.2	14,444.6	12,989.9
Total Domestic Deposits	27,755.1	29,187.6	20,624.3	19,851.8	18,362.4	17,932.5	16,671.1
Foreign Office Deposits	2,066.0	1,813.1	1,568.4	1,394.2	1,443.7	1,562.3	1,494.9
Long-term Debt	1,434.9	975.4	450.0	222.6	265.0	390.5	447.9
Net Stockholders' Equity	3,248.6	2,940.9	2,089.5	1,860.3	1,673.8	1,503.5	1,350.8
Total Assets	40,775.9	40,937.2	29,513.5	26,746.6	25,771.3	24,176.2	23,353.6
Year End Shs Outstg (000)	160,715	160,386	115,917	109,425	107,948	106,968	106,442
STATISTICAL RECORD:							
Return on Assets %	1.18	0.83	0.99	1.03	1.00	0.94	0.69
Return on Equity %	14.80	11.50	14.00	14.80	15.50	15.10	12.00
Book Value Per Share	20.21	18.34	18.03	17.00	15.51	14.06	12.58
Average Yield %	3.3	3.4	3.7	4.5	3.8	3.9	3.6
P/E Ratio	12.2-9.6	15.7-12.7	12.1-8.3	9.6-6.5	9.9-6.7	8.3-6.4	11.6-7.5
Price Range	36⅜-28⅝	33⅛-26¾	30⅛-20¾	23⅞-16⅛	23⅝-16⅛	17¾-13⅝	17⅞-11½

Statistics are as originally reported.

OFFICERS:
V.G. Istock, Chmn. & C.E.O.
T.H. Jeffs, II, Pres. & C.O.O.
L. Betanzos, Exec. V.P., Treas. & C.F.O.
D.T. Lis, Sr. V.P. & Sec.

INCORPORATED: DE, Jul., 1972

PRINCIPAL OFFICE: 611 Woodward Ave., Detroit, MI 48226

TELEPHONE NUMBER: (313) 225-1000

NO. OF EMPLOYEES: 18,543 (full-time equivalent)

ANNUAL MEETING: In May

SHAREHOLDERS: 26,100

INSTITUTIONAL HOLDINGS:
No. of Institutions: 347
Shares Held: 71,939,912 (adj.)

REGISTRAR(S): NBD Bank, N.A., Securities Transfer Services, Detroit, MI 02266

TRANSFER AGENT(S): NBD Bank, N.A., Securities Transfer Services, Detroit, MI 02266

NYS SYMBOL NPR
Rec. Pr. 22⅛

NEW PLAN REALTY TRUST

YIELD 6.0%
P/E RATIO 23.0

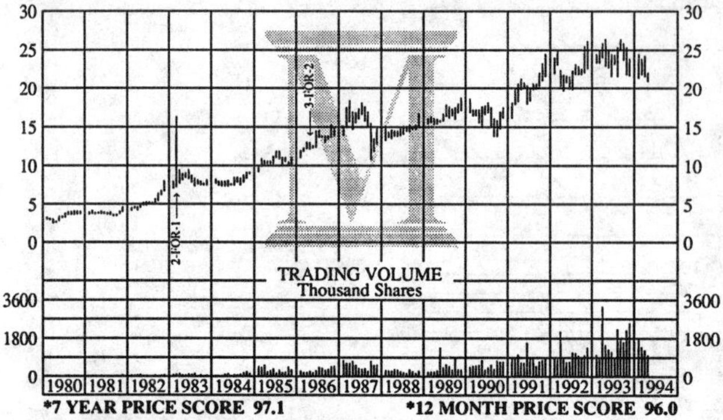

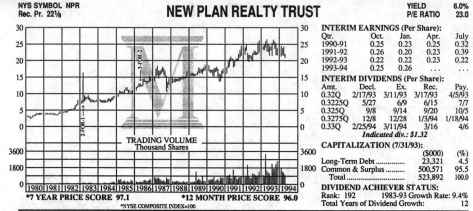

30
25
20
15
10
5
0
3-FOR-2
2-FOR-1
TRADING VOLUME
Thousand Shares
3600
1800
0
1980 1981 1982 1983 1984 1985 1986 1987 1988 1989 1990 1991 1992 1993 1994

***7 YEAR PRICE SCORE 97.1** ***12 MONTH PRICE SCORE 96.0**

*NYSE COMPOSITE INDEX=100

INTERIM EARNINGS (Per Share):

Qtr.	Oct.	Jan.	Apr.	July
1990-91	0.25	0.23	0.25	0.32
1991-92	0.26	0.20	0.23	0.39
1992-93	0.22	0.22	0.23	0.22
1993-94	0.25	0.26	...	...

INTERIM DIVIDENDS (Per Share):

Amt.	Decl.	Ex.	Rec.	Pay.
0.32Q	2/17/93	3/11/93	3/17/93	4/5/93
0.3225Q	5/27	6/9	6/15	7/7
0.325Q	9/8	9/14	9/20	10/5
0.3275Q	12/8	12/28	1/3/94	1/18/94
0.33Q	2/25/94	3/11/94	3/16	4/6

Indicated div.: $1.32

CAPITALIZATION (7/31/93):

	($000)	(%)
Long-Term Debt	23,321	4.5
Common & Surplus	500,571	95.5
Total	523,892	100.0

DIVIDEND ACHIEVER STATUS:
Rank: 192 1983-93 Growth Rate: 9.4%
Total Years of Dividend Growth: 12

RECENT DEVELOPMENTS: For the six months ended 1/31/94, revenues rose 28% to a record $46.8 million from $36.5 million for the same period last year. Net income for the period increased 19% to a record $25.0 million, or $0.51 per share, from $21.1 million, or $0.44 per share, for the year-ago period. Funds from operations rose 21% to $29.2 million, compared with $24.3 million for the same period last year. The Trust's operating gains reflect rising occupancy levels at its properties and the investment of nearly $400 million in real estate over the last 30 months, including the purchase of 39 shopping centers, factory outlet centers and garden apartment properties. Since fiscal year-end, 12 properties have been acquired. As of 2/16/94, the Trust had 110 properties in 18 states.

BUSINESS

NEW PLAN REALTY TRUST is the nation's largest real estate investment trust. The trust owns 110 properties in 18 states, including traditional shopping centers, factory outlet centers, garden apartment properties and other real estate. The trust has been publicly-owned since 1962 and has been a real estate investment trust since 1972.

REVENUES

(7/31/93)	($000)	(%)
Rental Inc & Rel Rev	65,308	85.6
Int & Div Inc	11,001	14.4
Total	76,309	100.0

ANNUAL EARNINGS AND DIVIDENDS PER SHARE

	7/31/93	7/31/92	7/31/91	7/31/90	7/31/89	7/31/88	7/31/87
Earnings Per Share	**0.89**	**1.08**	**1.05**	**1.01**	**0.95**	**0.88**	**0.80**
Dividends Per Share	**1.285**	**1.23**	**1.15**	**1.07**	**0.99**	**0.91**	**0.83**
Dividend Payout %	**N.M.**	**N.M.**	**N.M.**	**N.M.**	**N.M.**	**N.M.**	**N.M.**

ANNUAL FINANCIAL DATA

	7/31/93	7/31/92	7/31/91	7/31/90	7/31/89	7/31/88	7/31/87
RECORD OF EARNINGS (IN THOUSANDS):							
Gross Operating Revenues	76,309	64,692	57,383	54,123	43,541	37,320	35,859
Costs and Expenses	23,826	17,690	15,944	16,691	13,357	11,764	12,255
Operating Income	44,909	41,951	37,234	33,870	27,019	22,988	21,199
Inc Fr Cont Opers Bef Income Taxes	43,229	49,446	39,878	35,047	27,111	23,450	17,966
Net Income	43,229	49,446	39,878	35,047	27,111	23,450	17,966
Aver. Shs. Outstg.	48,838	45,971	38,138	34,844	28,620	26,734	22,585
BALANCE SHEET (IN THOUSANDS):							
Cash and Cash Equivalents	150,301	219,322	281,863	141,495	170,844	90,016	92,135
Receivables, Net	29,955	38,565	24,450	18,295	11,890	5,803	17,453
Gross Property	...	...	...	...	...	...	274
Accumulated Depreciation	...	...	...	...	...	...	97
Long-Term Debt	23,321	17,494	18,643	22,713	22,746	22,523	26,714
Net Stockholders' Equity	500,571	506,339	437,206	279,490	274,199	161,866	159,368
Total Assets	534,248	530,827	461,913	307,678	301,282	187,320	189,280
Total Current Assets	181,720	258,909	307,120	160,723	183,300	96,589	110,592
Total Current Liabilities	1,548	1,442	1,274	1,305	1,248	1,120	3,198
Net Working Capital	180,173	257,467	305,846	159,418	182,051	95,468	107,394
Year End Shares Outstg	48,957	48,385	44,491	35,151	34,713	26,847	26,643
STATISTICAL RECORD:							
Return on Equity %	8.6	9.8	9.1	12.5	9.9	14.5	11.3
Return on Assets %	8.1	9.3	8.6	11.4	9.0	12.5	9.5
Book Value Per Share	10.22	10.46	9.83	7.95	7.90	6.03	5.98
Average Yield %	5.4	5.4	5.7	6.6	5.8	6.1	5.7
P/E Ratio	29.6-24.2	24.2-18.2	23.3-15.4	18.4-13.6	19.7-16.1	19.0-15.1	23.0-13.4
Price Range	26⅜-21½	26⅛-19⅝	24½-16⅛	18⅝-13¾	18¾-15¼	16¾-13¼	18⅜-10¾

Statistics are as originally reported.

OFFICERS:
W. Newman, Chmn. & C.E.O.
A. Laubich, Pres. & C.O.O.
W. Kirshenbaum, V.P. & Treas.
S.F. Siegel, Sec. & Gen. Couns.

PRINCIPAL OFFICE: 1120 Avenue Of The Americas, New York, NY 10036

TELEPHONE NUMBER: (212) 869-3000

NO. OF EMPLOYEES: 198

ANNUAL MEETING:

SHAREHOLDERS: 10,600

INSTITUTIONAL HOLDINGS:
No. of Institutions: 119
Shares Held: 8,037,643

REGISTRAR(S): The First National Bank of Boston, Boston, MA 02102

TRANSFER AGENT(S): The First National Bank of Boston, Boston MA 02102

NORDSON CORP.

YIELD	0.9%
P/E RATIO	29.2

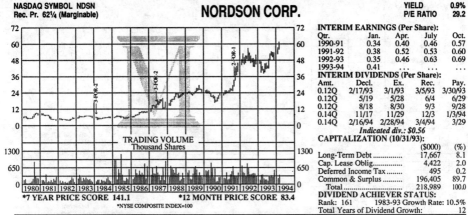

INTERIM EARNINGS (Per Share):

Qtr.	Jan.	Apr.	July	Oct.
1990-91	0.34	0.40	0.46	0.57
1991-92	0.38	0.52	0.53	0.60
1992-93	0.35	0.46	0.63	0.69
1993-94	0.41	...	...	...

INTERIM DIVIDENDS (Per Share):

Amt.	Decl.	Ex.	Rec.	Pay.
0.12Q	2/17/93	3/1/93	3/5/93	3/30/93
0.12Q	5/19	5/28	6/4	6/29
0.12Q	8/18	8/30	9/3	9/28
0.14Q	11/17	11/29	12/3	1/3/94
0.14Q	2/16/94	2/28/94	3/4/94	3/29

Indicated div.: $0.56

CAPITALIZATION (10/31/93):

	($000)	(%)
Long-Term Debt	17,667	8.1
Cap. Lease Oblig.	4,422	2.0
Deferred Income Tax	495	0.2
Common & Surplus	196,405	89.7
Total	218,989	100.0

DIVIDEND ACHIEVER STATUS:
Rank: 161   1983-93 Growth Rate: 10.5%
Total Years of Dividend Growth: 12

TRADING VOLUME
Thousand Shares

*7 YEAR PRICE SCORE 141.1   *12 MONTH PRICE SCORE 83.4
*NYSE COMPOSITE INDEX=100

RECENT DEVELOPMENTS: For the quarter ended 1/30/94, net sales increased 4% to $104.7 million compared with $100.3 million last year. Income increased to $7.8 million, or $0.41 per share, compared with income before a $4.8 million charge for an accounting change of $6.7 million, or $0.35 per share last year. Sales volume increased in all of NDSN's geographic areas, with strong gains across Latin America and the Pacific Rim. NDSN also realized solid sales growth in North America, and experienced accelerated activity in key industries in Japan, Europe and several western regions, including Sweden and the United Kingdom. Approximately 60% of NDSN's sales come from abroad. Increased earnings results were also attributed to product sales mix, improvements in manufacturing efficiency and reduced debt levels.

BUSINESS

NORDSON CORPORATION develops, manufactures and markets worldwide industrial application equipment, along with the software and application technologies that enhance its use. Company customers produce consumer and industrial products by processes in which use of adhesives, sealants, coatings, and other challenging technology-oriented materials are important. In the packaging and product assembly business, Nordson designs, engineers and manufactures equipment to melt, pump, transfer and apply a variety of adhesives, sealants, caulking and other materials. These compounds are used in the manufacture and sealing of packages, and in numerous industrial production and processing application. In the powder and liquid finishing businesses, Nordson designs, engineers and manufactures coating equipment ranging from relatively simple manual systems to sophisticated, programmable, automatic systems. These specialized systems are designed to solve coating problems and help keep Nordson's customers productive and profitable.

ANNUAL EARNINGS AND DIVIDENDS PER SHARE

	10/31/93	11/1/92	11/3/91	10/28/90	10/29/89	10/30/88	11/1/87
Earnings Per Share	2.13	2.03	1.77	1.52	1.76	1.55	1.17
Dividends Per Share	0.48	0.44	① 0.40	0.36	0.32	0.28	② 0.24
Dividend Payout %	22.5	21.7	22.6	23.7	18.2	18.1	20.5

① Adj for 2-for-1 stk split, 9/25/91 ② 3-for-2 stk. split, 4/87.

ANNUAL FINANCIAL DATA

RECORD OF EARNINGS (IN THOUSANDS):

Total Revenues	461,557	425,618	387,962	344,904	282,098	245,028	205,175
Costs and Expenses	377,076	341,645	314,952	282,027	220,877	188,935	159,862
Depreciation & Amort	17,107	16,679	14,747	13,076	8,427	6,875	5,848
Operating Profit	67,374	67,294	58,263	49,801	52,794	49,218	39,465
Income Bef Income Taxes	62,248	60,767	51,960	44,802	51,787	48,559	39,737
Income Taxes	21,473	21,230	18,173	15,456	17,600	16,976	15,030
Net Income	① 40,775	39,537	33,787	29,346	34,187	31,583	24,707
Aver. Shs. Outstg.	19,184	19,471	19,093	19,266	19,386	20,340	21,040

① Before acctg. change dr$4,784,000.

BALANCE SHEET (IN THOUSANDS):

Cash and Cash Equivalents	23,363	13,009	10,481	8,837	5,753	16,065	42,095
Receivables, Net	129,103	127,308	102,801	95,019	79,092	60,194	52,530
Inventories	84,661	87,674	78,471	68,027	68,662	41,794	28,772
Gross Property	146,939	139,102	124,881	118,042	100,001	66,875	57,428
Accumulated Depreciation	68,250	61,730	50,441	43,353	35,783	26,741	22,357
Long-Term Debt	17,667	22,075	22,172	22,261	17,742	11,019	11,031
Obligs Under Cap Lses	4,422	4,748	3,359	3,240	2,396	2,230	1,777
Net Stockholders' Equity	196,405	177,720	152,714	130,374	106,918	89,109	101,205
Total Assets	357,970	346,297	296,930	269,523	235,551	162,912	164,212
Total Current Assets	241,672	231,836	193,915	173,924	156,168	119,837	126,377
Total Current Liabilities	116,281	126,698	106,911	107,831	102,334	55,797	45,849
Net Working Capital	125,391	105,138	87,004	66,093	53,834	64,040	80,528
Year End Shares Outstg	18,726	18,752	18,754	18,794	18,810	19,176	20,688

STATISTICAL RECORD:

Operating Profit Margin %	14.6	15.8	15.0	14.4	18.7	20.1	19.2
Book Value Per Share	9.03	7.79	6.87	5.99	4.98	4.56	4.81
Return on Equity %	20.8	22.2	22.1	22.5	32.0	35.4	24.4
Return on Assets %	11.4	11.4	11.4	10.9	14.5	19.4	15.0
Average Yield %	1.0	0.9	1.2	1.7	1.2	1.4	1.6
P/E Ratio	25.7-18.0	28.1-21.2	26.0-12.5	17.3-11.1	16.7-12.4	15.5-9.3	16.9-8.4
Price Range	54¾-38¼	57-43	46-22⅛	26¼-16⅞	29½-22	24⅛-14½	20-9⅞

Statistics are as originally reported.

OFFICERS:
E.T. Nord, Chmn.
W.P. Madar, Pres. & C.E.O.
E.P. Campbell, Exec.V.P. & C.O.O.
N.D. Pellecchia, V.P.-Fin. & Treas.
W.D. Ginn, Sec.

INCORPORATED: OH, 1954

PRINCIPAL OFFICE: 28601 Clemens Road, Westlake, OH 44145

TELEPHONE NUMBER: (216) 892-1580

FAX: (216) 892-9507

NO. OF EMPLOYEES: 3,151

ANNUAL MEETING: In March

SHAREHOLDERS: 2,845

INSTITUTIONAL HOLDINGS:
No. of Institutions: 95
Shares Held: 4,487,143

REGISTRAR(S): Society National Bank, Cleveland, OH

TRANSFER AGENT(S): Society National Bank, Cleveland, OH

NASDAQ SYMBOL NOBE
Rec. Pr. 41¼ (Marginable)

NORDSTROM, INC.

YIELD 0.8%
P/E RATIO 26.1

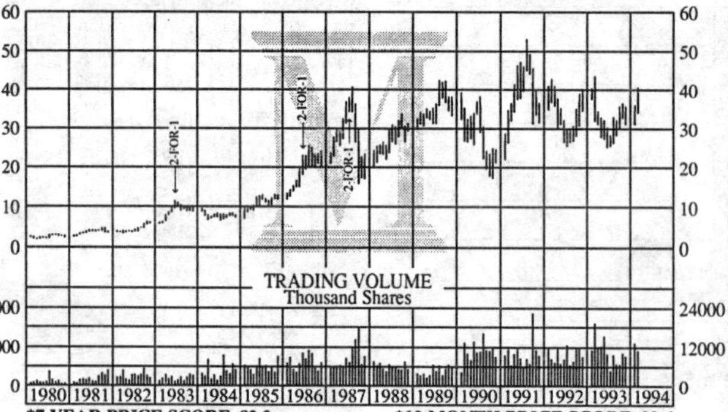

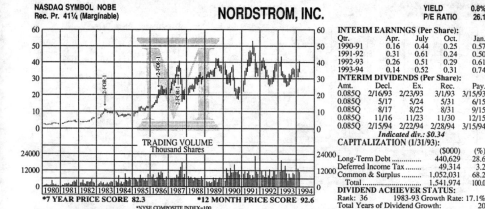

*7 YEAR PRICE SCORE 82.3 *12 MONTH PRICE SCORE 92.6
*NYSE COMPOSITE INDEX=100

INTERIM EARNINGS (Per Share):

Qtr.	Apr.	July	Oct.	Jan.
1990-91	0.16	0.44	0.25	0.57
1991-92	0.31	0.61	0.24	0.50
1992-93	0.26	0.51	0.29	0.61
1993-94	0.14	0.52	0.31	0.74

INTERIM DIVIDENDS (Per Share):

Amt.	Decl.	Ex.	Rec.	Pay.
0.085Q	2/16/93	2/23/93	3/1/93	3/15/93
0.085Q	5/17	5/24	5/31	6/15
0.085Q	8/17	8/25	8/31	9/15
0.085Q	11/16	11/23	11/30	12/15
0.085Q	2/15/94	2/22/94	2/28/94	3/15/94

Indicated div.: $0.34

CAPITALIZATION (1/31/93):

	($000)	(%)
Long-Term Debt	440,629	28.6
Deferred Income Tax	49,314	3.2
Common & Surplus	1,052,031	68.2
Total	1,541,974	100.0

DIVIDEND ACHIEVER STATUS:
Rank: 36 1983-93 Growth Rate: 17.1%
Total Years of Dividend Growth: 20

RECENT DEVELOPMENTS: For the year ended 1/31/94, net earnings increased 2.8% to $140.4 million, or $1.71 per share, from $136.6 million, or $1.67 per share, last year. Sales increased 4.9% to $3.59 billion from $3.42 billion last year. For the quarter ended 1/31/94, net earnings increased 22.1% to $61.0 million, or $0.74 per share, from $50.0 million, or $0.61 per share, last year. Sales increased 3.6% to $1.11 billion from $1.07 billion last year, primarily due to a continuing improvement in sales trends and reduced markdowns on merchandise inventories. Net earnings were reduced by $3.0 million after income taxes for expenses and property losses resulting from the earthquake in Southern California. For the quarter, net earnings increased 8.7% to $25.5 million on sales of $769.4 million, from $23.3 million on sales of $737.3 million last year.

BUSINESS

NORDSTROM, INC. operates 52 large specialty stores in Washington, Oregon, California, Utah, Alaska, Virginia, New Jersey, Illinois, Maryland and Minnesota, selling a wide selection of apparel, shoes and accessories for women, men and children. The Company also operates sixteen clearance stores under the name "Nordstrom Rack" which serve as outlets for clearance merchandise from the Company's large specialty stores. The Racks also purchase merchandise directly from manufacturers. The Racks are located in Washington, Oregon, California, Utah, Virginia and Maryland. The Company also operates four smaller specialty stores under the name "Place Two" in Washington, one clearance store in Arizona under the name "Last Chance" and leased shoe departments in 11 department stores in Hawaii.

QUARTERLY DATA

(1/31/93)($000)	Rev	Inc
1st Quarter	663,809	41,357
2nd Quarter	951,616	80,469
3rd Quarter	737,301	31,330
4th Quarter	1,069,253	64,059

ANNUAL EARNINGS AND DIVIDENDS PER SHARE

	1/31/93	1/31/92	1/31/91	1/31/90	1/31/89	1/31/88	1/31/87
Earnings Per Share	**1.67**	**1.66**	**1.42**	**1.41**	**1.51**	**1.13**	**0.91**
Dividends Per Share	**0.32**	**0.31**	**0.30**	**0.28**	**0.22**	**[1] 0.18**	**[2] 0.13**
Dividend Payout %	**19.2**	**18.7**	**21.1**	**19.9**	**14.6**	**15.9**	**14.3**

[1] 2-for-1 stk split, 6/87 [2] 2-for-1 stk split, 6/86

ANNUAL FINANCIAL DATA

	1/31/93	1/31/92	1/31/91	1/31/90	1/31/89	1/31/88	1/31/87
RECORD OF EARNINGS (IN MILLIONS):							
Total Revenues	3,422.0	3,179.8	2,893.9	2,671.1	2,327.9	1,920.2	1,629.9
Costs and Expenses	3,138.4	2,904.9	2,662.4	2,427.7	2,086.2	1,728.1	1,457.5
Depreciation & Amort	102.8	96.0	85.6	70.9	60.6	50.1	46.7
Operating Income	180.8	178.9	145.9	172.6	181.1	142.0	125.7
Earnings Bef Income Tax	222.1	217.2	178.3	179.4	198.4	162.7	140.2
Income Taxes	85.5	81.4	62.5	64.5	75.1	70.0	67.3
Net Income	136.6	135.8	115.8	114.9	123.3	92.7	72.9
Aver. Shs. Outstg. (000)	81,893	81,780	81,675	81,528	...	81,759	81,612
BALANCE SHEET (IN MILLIONS):							
Cash and Cash Equivalents	29.1	14.7	24.7	33.1	16.1	4.9	18.4
Accounts Receivable, Net	603.2	608.2	575.5	536.3	481.6	404.6	118.9
Merchandise Inventories	536.7	506.6	448.3	420.0	403.8	312.7	257.3
Gross Property	1,385.1	1,327.2	1,184.9	994.3	837.6	696.1	578.5
Accumulated Depreciation	560.9	470.8	378.7	302.4	243.6	193.4	154.3
Long-Term Debt	440.6	502.2	457.7	418.5	346.5	215.3	116.2
Obligs Under Capized Lses	...	...	21.0	22.1	23.0	24.0	24.8
Net Stockholders' Equity	1,052.0	939.2	826.4	733.3	639.9	533.2	451.2
Total Assets	2,053.2	2,041.9	1,902.6	1,707.4	1,511.7	1,234.3	892.0
Total Current Assets	1,219.8	1,177.6	1,090.4	1,011.1	914.9	730.2	401.7
Total Current Liabilities	511.2	553.9	551.8	489.9	448.2	394.7	270.5
Net Working Capital	708.6	623.7	538.5	521.3	466.8	335.5	131.2
Year End Shs Outstg (000)	81,975	81,844	81,738	81,585	81,465	81,371	80,982
STATISTICAL RECORD:							
Operating Profit Margin %	5.3	5.6	5.0	6.5	7.8	7.4	7.7
Book Value Per Share	12.83	11.48	10.11	8.99	7.86	6.55	5.57
Return on Equity %	13.0	14.5	14.0	15.7	19.3	17.4	16.2
Return on Assets %	6.7	6.7	6.1	6.7	8.2	7.5	8.2
Average Yield %	0.9	0.8	1.1	0.8	0.8	0.6	0.7
P/E Ratio	25.6-15.3	31.9-13.3	27.6-12.1	30.1-21.1	22.5-13.1	36.1-13.9	28.2-13.0
Price Range	42¾-25½	53-22	39¼-17¼	42½-29¾	34-19¾	40¾-15¾	25⅝-11⅞

Statistics are as originally reported.

OFFICERS:
B.A. Nordstrom, Co-Chmn.
J.N. Nordstrom, Co-Chmn.
J.F. Nordstrom, Co.-Chmn.
J.A. McMillan, Co-Chmn.
R.A. Johnson, Co-Pres.
D.J. Hume, Co-Pres.
INCORPORATED: WA, 1946
PRINCIPAL OFFICE: 1501 Fifth Avenue, Seattle, WA 98101-1603

TELEPHONE NUMBER: (206) 628-2111
FAX: (206) 628-1707
NO. OF EMPLOYEES: 10,494 (approx.)
ANNUAL MEETING: In May
SHAREHOLDERS: 36,190 (approx.)
INSTITUTIONAL HOLDINGS:
No. of Institutions: 252
Shares Held: 34,674,387

REGISTRAR(S): First Interstate Bank of California, Los Angeles, CA

TRANSFER AGENT(S): First Interstate Bank of California, Los Angeles, CA

NORTH CAROLINA NATURAL GAS CORP.

YIELD 4.7%
P/E RATIO 13.3

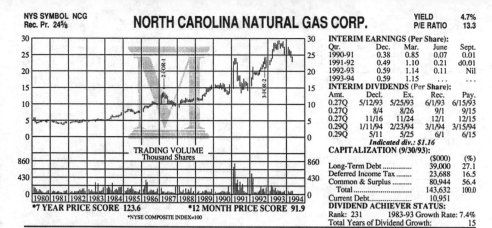

7 YEAR PRICE SCORE 123.6   **12 MONTH PRICE SCORE 91.9**
*NYSE COMPOSITE INDEX=100

INTERIM EARNINGS (Per Share):

Qtr.	Dec.	Mar.	June	Sept.
1990-91	0.38	0.85	0.07	0.01
1991-92	0.49	1.10	0.21	d0.01
1992-93	0.59	1.14	0.11	Nil
1993-94	0.59	1.15	...	...

INTERIM DIVIDENDS (Per Share):

Amt.	Decl.	Ex.	Rec.	Pay.
0.27Q	5/12/93	5/25/93	6/1/93	6/15/93
0.27Q	8/4	8/26	9/1	9/15
0.27Q	11/16	11/24	12/1	12/15
0.29Q	1/11/94	2/23/94	3/1/94	3/15/94
0.29Q	5/11	5/25	6/1	6/15

Indicated div.: $1.16

CAPITALIZATION (9/30/93):

	($000)	(%)
Long-Term Debt	39,000	27.1
Deferred Income Tax	23,688	16.5
Common & Surplus	80,944	56.4
Total	143,632	100.0
Current Debt	10,951	

DIVIDEND ACHIEVER STATUS:

Rank: 231   1983-93 Growth Rate: 7.4%
Total Years of Dividend Growth: 15

RECENT DEVELOPMENTS: For the quarter ended 12/31/93, net income increased 15.4% to $3.7 million, or 0.59 per share, from $3.2 million, or $0.59 per share, for the same period last year. This increase was due primarily to an increase in the natural gas throughput volume, a more favorable sales mix and lower interest rates on short-term bank loans. Operating revenues for the quarter declined 18.1% to $42.1 million from $51.4 million for the corresponding 1992 quarter. The decline in operating revenues was offset by a decline in the cost of gas to $26.9 million, compared with $37.2 million for the year-ago quarter. As a result, gross margin increased 6.5% to $15.1 million from $14.2 million for the same quarter last year.

BUSINESS

NORTH CAROLINA NATURAL GAS CORP. is engaged in the transmission and distribution of natural gas through approximately 980 miles of transmission pipeline and approximately 2,448 miles of distribution mains. Natural gas is sold under regulated rates to approximately 127,000 residential, commercial, industrial and municipal customers in 63 cities and towns and four municipal gas distribution systems in eastern and southcentral North Carolina. The Company purchases and transports natural gas under long-term contracts with Transcontinental Gas Pipe Line Corporation, Columbia Gas Transmission Corporation and several major oil and gas producers. A small volume of gas is purchased from NCNG Exploration Corporation, a subsidiary of the Company. The Company also serves propane gas to approximately 8,000 customers and sells gas appliances and home insulation services to gas customers and new home builders.

QUARTERLY DATA

(9/30/93)($000)	Rev	Inc
1st Quarter	51,396	4,093
2nd Quarter	53,916	7,391
3rd Quarter	38,638	1,852
4th Quarter	29,195	1,756

ANNUAL EARNINGS AND DIVIDENDS PER SHARE

	9/30/93	9/30/92	9/30/91	9/30/90	9/30/89	9/30/88	9/30/87
Earnings Per Share	1.84	1.79	1.31	1.40	1.53	1.35	1.17
Dividends Per Share	1.08	[1]1.00	0.933	0.893	0.80	0.733	[2]0.667
Dividend Payout %	58.7	55.9	71.4	63.8	52.4	54.2	57.1

[1] 3-for-2 stk split, 11/2/92 [2] 2-for-1 stk. split, 3/87.

ANNUAL FINANCIAL DATA

RECORD OF EARNINGS (IN THOUSANDS):

Operating Revenues	173,145	150,510	126,601	128,539	143,186	136,216	136,096
Depreciation	6,891	6,125	5,360	4,853	4,578	4,291	4,004
Maintenance	2,873	3,184	2,915	2,131	2,036	1,878	1,922
Prov for Fed Inc Taxes	4,942	3,990	3,274	2,557	3,819	3,430	4,139
Operating Income	15,092	14,231	10,951	10,343	11,309	10,307	9,398
Total Utility Int Charges	4,424	5,011	5,227	4,716	4,261	3,965	4,187
Net Income	10,977	9,697	7,014	7,441	8,058	7,085	6,081
Aver. Shs. Outstg.	5,981	5,414	5,362	5,311	5,279	5,247	5,220

BALANCE SHEET (IN THOUSANDS):

Gross Plant	224,946	210,761	187,879	167,361	152,143	140,719	132,853
Accumulated Depreciation	72,403	66,348	60,673	55,717	51,383	47,161	43,232
Gas Utility Plant, Net	152,543	144,412	127,205	111,644	100,760	93,559	89,621
Long-term Debt	39,000	45,088	23,452	27,741	30,030	32,319	34,608
Net Stockholders' Equity	80,944	57,413	51,967	49,106	45,696	41,407	37,762
Total Assets	194,178	186,550	151,714	138,472	123,356	115,564	111,301
Year End Shares Outstg	6,301	5,448	5,388	5,337	5,296	5,265	5,234

STATISTICAL RECORD:

Book Value Per Share	12.85	10.54	9.65	9.20	8.63	7.86	7.22
Op. Inc/Net Pl %	9.9	9.9	8.6	9.3	11.2	11.0	10.5
Dep/Gr. Pl %	3.1	2.9	2.9	2.9	3.0	3.0	3.0
Accum. Dep/Gr. Pl %	32.2	31.5	32.3	33.3	33.8	33.5	32.5
Return on Equity %	13.6	16.9	13.5	15.2	17.6	17.1	16.1
Average Yield %	4.2	5.0	5.0	6.1	5.9	7.0	5.8
P/E Ratio	16.0-11.9	13.6-8.7	18.3-10.2	11.7-9.2	10.4-7.3	8.8-6.7	11.6-8.0
Price Range	29⅜-21⅞	24⅜-15½	24-13⅜	16⅜-12⅞	15⅞-11⅛	11⅞-9	13⅝-9⅜

Statistics are as originally reported.

OFFICERS:
C.B. Wells, Pres. & C.E.O.
G.A. Teele, Sr. V.P. & C.F.O.
C.C. Dew, V.P. & Treas.
D.W. McCoy, Sec.

INCORPORATED: DE, Oct., 1955

PRINCIPAL OFFICE: 150 Rowan Street
P.O.Box 909, Fayetteville, NC 28302

TELEPHONE NUMBER: (910) 483-0315
FAX: (910) 483-0336
NO. OF EMPLOYEES: 517
ANNUAL MEETING: In January
SHAREHOLDERS: 5,381 (approx.)
INSTITUTIONAL HOLDINGS:
No. of Institutions: 40
Shares Held: 721,095

REGISTRAR(S):

TRANSFER AGENT(S): Wachovia Bank of North Carolina, N.A., P.O. Box 3001, Winston-Salem, NC 27102

NYS SYMBOL NSP
Rec. Pr. 40¾

NORTHERN STATES POWER CO.

YIELD 6.3%
P/E RATIO 14.1

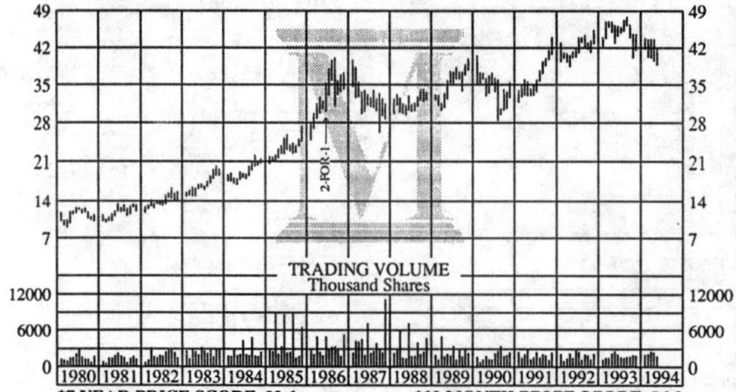

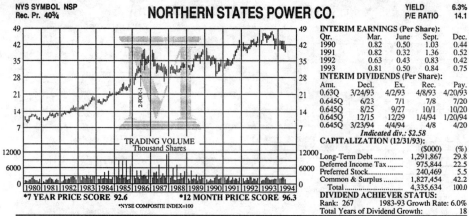

*7 YEAR PRICE SCORE 92.6 *12 MONTH PRICE SCORE 96.3

*NYSE COMPOSITE INDEX=100

INTERIM EARNINGS (Per Share):

Qtr.	Mar.	June	Sept.	Dec.
1990	0.82	0.50	1.03	0.44
1991	0.82	0.32	1.36	0.52
1992	0.63	0.43	0.83	0.42
1993	0.81	0.50	0.84	0.75

INTERIM DIVIDENDS (Per Share):

Amt.	Decl.	Ex.	Rec.	Pay.
0.63Q	3/24/93	4/2/93	4/8/93	4/20/93
0.645Q	6/23	7/1	7/8	7/20
0.645Q	8/25	9/27	10/1	10/20
0.645Q	12/15	12/29	1/4/94	1/20/94
0.645Q	3/23/94	4/4/94	4/8	4/20

Indicated div.: $2.58

CAPITALIZATION (12/31/93):

	($000)	(%)
Long-Term Debt	1,291,867	29.8
Deferred Income Tax	975,844	22.5
Preferred Stock	240,469	5.5
Common & Surplus	1,827,454	42.2
Total	4,335,634	100.0

DIVIDEND ACHIEVER STATUS:
Rank: 267 1983-93 Growth Rate: 6.0%
Total Years of Dividend Growth: 18

RECENT DEVELOPMENTS: For the year ended 12/31/93, net income was $211.7 million compared with income of $160.9 million in 1992. Revenues were $2.40 billion, up 11.3%. Contributing to the improved results were higher rates, more favorable weather in 1993 and improved profitability from non-regulated operations. Partially offsetting these increases were higher costs for purchased power and other operating expenses.

PROSPECTS: The Company has a healthy and diverse service territory, well-managed nuclear units, and limited Clean Air Act exposure. However, NSP's increasing reliance on purchased power, in addition to a sizable capital expenditure program, will require continued constructive regulatory treatment to support earnings growth. NSP could invest up to $360 million in its non-regulated subsidiary, NRG Group, Inc. over the next five years, which would increase its risk profile.

BUSINESS

NORTHERN STATES POWER COMPANY, an operating holding company, provides electric energy to customers in parts of Minnesota, Wisconsin, North and South Dakota, and Michigan's Upper Peninsula. NSP generates, transmits and distributes electric power to 1.3 million customers and distributes gas to more than 380,000 people in its 49,000 square mile service area. The Company also supplies telephone service in the Minot, North Dakota area.

REVENUES

(12/31/93)	($000)	(%)
Electric	1,974,916	82.2
Gas	429,076	17.8
Total	2,403,992	100.0

ANNUAL EARNINGS AND DIVIDENDS PER SHARE

	1993	1992	1991	1990	1989	1988	1987
Earnings Per Share	**3.02**	**[1] 2.31**	**[3] 3.02**	**[3] 2.79**	**3.24**	**3.11**	**3.01**
Dividends Per Share	**2.55**	**[2] 2.47**	**2.37**	**2.27**	**2.17**	**2.07**	**1.96**
Dividend Payout %	**84.4**	**N.M.**	**78.5**	**81.4**	**67.0**	**66.6**	**65.1**

[1] Before acctg. chg. [2] Bef acctg chge [3] Before disc. oper.

ANNUAL FINANCIAL DATA

RECORD OF EARNINGS (IN MILLIONS):							
Total Revenues	2,404.0	2,159.5	2,201.2	2,064.5	1,989.7	2,006.5	1,770.3
Depreciation & Amort	264.5	242.9	215.6	215.6	209.9	208.6	170.5
Maintenance	161.4	180.6	182.5	172.0	151.1	172.3	153.6
Prov for Fed Inc Taxes	128.3	90.7	117.3	114.4	108.5	117.1	119.5
Operating Income	303.9	256.0	305.5	288.8	306.7	303.2	264.6
Total Interest Charges	108.1	103.7	106.1	108.6	106.0	102.7	95.6
Net Income	211.7	206.4	[1] 207.0	[2] 193.0	222.0	214.8	204.9
Aver. Shs. Outstg. (000)	65,211	62,641	62,566	62,541	62,541	62,541	62,541

[1] Before disc. op. cr$17,035,000. [2] Before disc. op. cr$2,516,000.

BALANCE SHEET (IN MILLIONS):							
Gross Plant	7,775.9	7,349.5	6,979.0	6,703.0	6,475.7	6,210.5	5,969.7
Accumulated Depreciation	3,561.8	3,223.8	2,982.0	2,748.5	2,579.5	2,351.7	2,107.2
Net Utility Plant	4,214.1	4,125.7	3,997.0	3,954.6	3,896.2	3,858.8	3,862.5
Long-term Debt	1,291.9	1,299.9	1,233.9	1,239.5	1,262.7	1,275.7	1,248.5
Net Stockholders' Equity	2,067.9	1,897.6	1,877.3	1,827.6	1,786.5	1,777.3	1,669.1
Total Assets	5,587.7	4,977.7	4,750.9	4,762.3	4,592.8	4,495.5	4,401.2
Year End Shs Outstg (000)	66,880	62,598	62,541	62,541	62,541	62,541	62,541
STATISTICAL RECORD:							
Book Value Per Share	26.28	25.91	25.21	24.43	23.77	22.82	21.89
Op. Inc/Net Pl %	7.2	6.2	7.6	7.3	7.9	7.9	6.9
Dep/Gr. Pl %	3.4	3.2	3.3	3.2	3.2	3.4	2.9
Accum. Dep/Gr. Pl %	45.8	43.9	42.7	41.0	39.8	37.9	35.3
Return on Equity %	10.2	8.5	11.0	10.6	12.4	12.1	12.3
Average Yield %	5.8	5.9	6.3	6.6	6.2	6.5	5.9
P/E Ratio	15.9-13.3	19.6-16.7	14.6-10.5	14.5-10.2	12.3-9.3	11.0-9.4	13.2-8.7
Price Range	47⅞-40⅛	45⅝-38½	44-31¾	40½-28⅜	40-30¼	34¼-29¼	39¾-26¼

Statistics are as originally reported.

OFFICERS:
J.J. Howard, Chmn. & C.E.O.
E. Theisen, Pres. & C.O.O.
H.M. Winston, V.P., Sec. & Fin. Couns.
E.J. McIntyre, V.P. & C.F.O.

INCORPORATED: MN, Jun., 1909

PRINCIPAL OFFICE: 414 Nicollet Mall, Minneapolis, MN 55401

TELEPHONE NUMBER: (612) 330-5500

NO. OF EMPLOYEES: 8,231

ANNUAL MEETING: In April

SHAREHOLDERS: 72,525

INSTITUTIONAL HOLDINGS:
No. of Institutions: 281
Shares Held: 18,367,414

REGISTRAR(S): Norwest Bank Minneasota, N.A., Minneapolis, MN

TRANSFER AGENT(S): At Company's Office

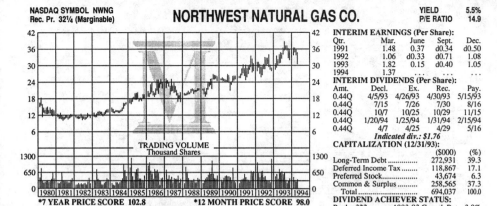

NASDAQ SYMBOL NWNG
Rec. Pr. 32¼ (Marginable)

NORTHWEST NATURAL GAS CO.

YIELD 5.5%
P/E RATIO 14.9

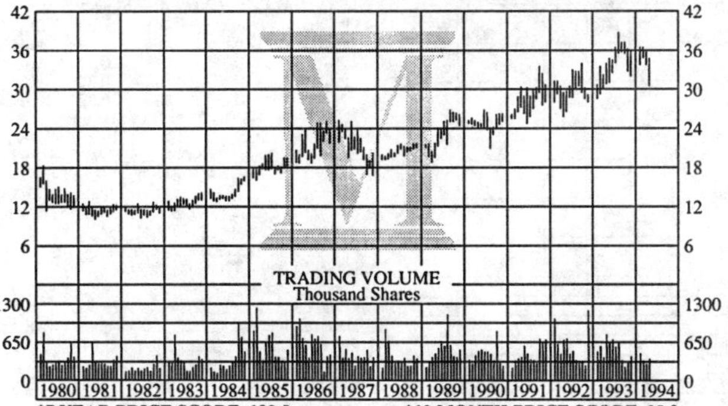

42
36
30
24
18
12
6
TRADING VOLUME
Thousand Shares
1300
650
0
1980 1981 1982 1983 1984 1985 1986 1987 1988 1989 1990 1991 1992 1993 1994

***7 YEAR PRICE SCORE 102.8** ***12 MONTH PRICE SCORE 98.0**

*NYSE COMPOSITE INDEX=100

INTERIM EARNINGS (Per Share):

Qtr.	Mar.	June	Sept.	Dec.
1991	1.48	0.37	d0.34	d0.50
1992	1.06	d0.33	d0.71	1.08
1993	1.82	0.15	d0.40	1.05
1994	1.37	...	...	...

INTERIM DIVIDENDS (Per Share):

Amt.	Decl.	Ex.	Rec.	Pay.
0.44Q	4/5/93	4/26/93	4/30/93	5/15/93
0.44Q	7/15	7/26	7/30	8/16
0.44Q	10/7	10/25	10/29	11/15
0.44Q	1/20/94	1/25/94	1/31/94	2/15/94
0.44Q	4/7	4/25	4/29	5/16

Indicated div.: $1.76

CAPITALIZATION (12/31/93):

	($000)	(%)
Long-Term Debt	272,931	39.3
Deferred Income Tax	118,867	17.1
Preferred Stock	43,674	6.3
Common & Surplus	258,565	37.3
Total	694,037	100.0

DIVIDEND ACHIEVER STATUS:

Rank: 323 1983-93 Growth Rate: 3.0%

Total Years of Dividend Growth: 18

RECENT DEVELOPMENTS: For the year ended 12/31/93, net income was $37.6 million compared with $15.8 million in 1992. Revenues for the year advanced 31% to $358.7 million from $274.4 million last year. Earnings per share were $2.61 versus $1.11 last year. Gas utility operations benefited from weather that was 3% colder than average and 22% colder than 1992, which was the warmest year in 97 years in the Company's service territory. Gas sales and transportation to residential, commercial, and industrial firm customers were 581 million therms in 1993, up from 474 million therms last year. Deliveries to the industrial interruptible market at 463 million therms were down from 591 million therms last year. The Company had 372,427 customers at year-end 1993. For the quarter ended 12/31/93, net income was $14.7 million versus $13.7 million in the comparable period last year. Revenues for the period were $120.8 million, up 24%.

BUSINESS

NORTHWEST NATURAL GAS CO. is principally engaged in the distribution of natural gas to customers in western Oregon and southwestern Washington, including the Portland metropolitan area. NWNG has four subsidiaries: Oregon Natural Gas Development Corporation, NNG Financial Corporation, NNG Energy Systems Inc. and Pacific Square Corporation. Oregon Natural is engaged in natural gas exploration, development and production, and, through Westar Marketing Company, a partnership between Oregon Natural and a subsidiary of Questar Pipeline Corporation, in the purchase, marketing and arranging for transportation of natural gas in Oregon and other western states. Energy Systems, through its wholly-owned subsidiary, Agrico Cogeneration Corporation, owns a 25 megawatt cogeneration plant near Fresno, California. The Financial Corp. holds financial investments as a limited partner in four solar electric generating systems, four windmill projects and a hydroelectric project, all located in California, and in a low-income housing project in Portland. Pacific Square is engaged in real estate management, principally in connection with two office buildings in Portland and other Company-owned properties adjacent to those buildings.

ANNUAL EARNINGS AND DIVIDENDS PER SHARE

	1993	1992	1991	1990	1989	1988	1987
Earnings Per Share	**2.61**	**1.11**	**1.01**	**2.43**	**2.37**	**2.00**	**[1] 1.80**
Dividends Per Share	**1.75**	**1.72**	**1.69**	**1.65**	**1.61**	**1.57**	**1.56**
Dividend Payout %	**67.0**	**N.M.**	**N.M.**	**67.9**	**67.9**	**78.5**	**86.7**

[1] Before acctg. chg.

ANNUAL FINANCIAL DATA

	1993	1992	1991	1990	1989	1988	1987
RECORD OF EARNINGS (IN THOUSANDS):							
Total Operating Revenues	358,717	274,366	295,938	296,281	260,924	277,564	308,917
Deprec, Depl & Amort	39,683	33,035	33,623	27,967	...	...	...
Prov for Fed Inc Taxes	...	...	...	...	15,769	13,004	14,784
Income From Operations	83,917	49,726	41,883	68,225	45,991	39,893	38,710
Total Int Charges - Net	25,107	26,733	26,591	24,333	18,770	16,350	18,297
Net Income	37,647	15,775	14,377	30,724	28,420	23,720	[1] 20,521
Aver. Shs. Outstg.	13,074	11,909	11,698	11,522	10,799	10,553	10,329
[1] Before acctg. change cr$4,195,000.							
BALANCE SHEET (IN THOUSANDS):							
Gross Plant	840,030	779,274	722,069	668,664	623,114	567,489	504,407
Accumulated Depreciation	255,282	233,385	207,165	183,404	163,678	147,923	132,149
Utility Plant - Net	584,748	545,889	514,904	485,260	459,436	419,566	372,258
Long-term Debt	272,931	253,766	252,995	215,230	220,503	182,290	162,019
Net Stockholders' Equity	302,239	296,522	247,297	251,573	240,283	215,691	194,324
Total Assets	849,036	731,834	731,494	687,835	611,386	542,130	495,521
Year End Shares Outstg	13,177	12,973	11,785	11,604	11,430	10,641	10,460
STATISTICAL RECORD:							
Book Value Per Share	19.62	18.62	18.35	18.91	18.06	16.88	16.38
Op. Inc/Net Pl %	14.4	9.1	8.1	14.1	10.0	9.5	10.4
Dep/Gr. Pl %	4.7	4.2	4.7	4.2	3.7	4.1	3.7
Accum. Dep/Gr. Pl %	30.4	29.9	28.7	27.4	26.3	26.1	26.2
Return on Equity %	13.2	5.9	6.6	13.9	13.6	13.0	11.8
Average Yield %	5.2	5.8	5.8	6.9	7.1	7.7	7.4
P/E Ratio	14.8-10.9	30.6-23.2	33.2-24.5	11.1-8.6	11.3-7.9	10.9-9.6	14.0-9.3
Price Range	38¾-28½	34-25¾	33½-24¾	26⅞-20⅞	26⅞-18¾	21¾-19⅛	25¼-16¾

Statistics are as originally reported.

OFFICERS:
R.L. Ridgley, Pres. & C.E.O.
B.R. DeBolt, Sr. V.P.-Fin. & C.F.O.
D.J. Wilson, Treas. & Contr.
C.J. Rue, Sec. & Asst. Treas.

INCORPORATED: OR, Jan., 1910

PRINCIPAL OFFICE: 220 N.W. Second Ave., Portland, OR 97209

TELEPHONE NUMBER: (503) 226-4211

NO. OF EMPLOYEES: 1,328

ANNUAL MEETING: In May

SHAREHOLDERS: 13,717 com.; 149 conv. pref.

INSTITUTIONAL HOLDINGS:
No. of Institutions: 99
Shares Held: 3,718,206

REGISTRAR(S): United States National Bank of Oregon, Portland, OR 97204

TRANSFER AGENT(S): At Company's Office

NORTHWESTERN PUBLIC SERVICE CO.

YIELD 6.1%
P/E RATIO 13.9

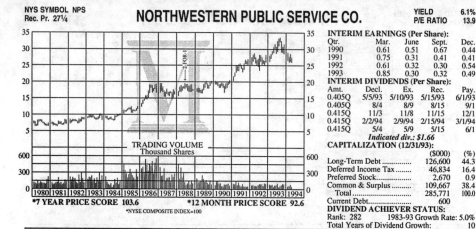

*7 YEAR PRICE SCORE 103.6   ***12 MONTH PRICE SCORE 92.6**
*NYSE COMPOSITE INDEX=100

TRADING VOLUME
Thousand Shares

INTERIM EARNINGS (Per Share):

Qtr.	Mar.	June	Sept.	Dec.
1990	0.61	0.51	0.67	0.44
1991	0.75	0.31	0.41	0.41
1992	0.61	0.32	0.30	0.54
1993	0.85	0.30	0.32	0.49

INTERIM DIVIDENDS (Per Share):

Amt.	Decl.	Ex.	Rec.	Pay.
0.405Q	5/5/93	5/10/93	5/15/93	6/1/93
0.405Q	8/4	8/9	8/15	9/1
0.415Q	11/3	11/8	11/15	12/1
0.415Q	2/2/94	2/9/94	2/15/94	3/1/94
0.415Q	5/4	5/9	5/15	6/1

Indicated div.: $1.66

CAPITALIZATION (12/31/93):

	($000)	(%)
Long-Term Debt	126,600	44.3
Deferred Income Tax	46,834	16.4
Preferred Stock	2,670	0.9
Common & Surplus	109,667	38.4
Total	285,771	100.0
Current Debt	600	

DIVIDEND ACHIEVER STATUS:
Rank: 282   1983-93 Growth Rate: 5.0%
Total Years of Dividend Growth: 10

RECENT DEVELOPMENTS: For the year ended 12/31/93, net income increased 10.7% to $15.2 million, on total revenues of $153.3 million, up 28.6% from 1992. Electric operating revenues increased 6.8% to $70.1 million from $65.6 million in 1992. Retail electric kwh sales increased 7.9% to 964,477,000 kwh from 894,077 kwh last year, while sales to wholesale customers, representing primarily kwh sales to other utilities in the power pool, increased 19.6% to 191,170,000 kwh from 159,785,000 kwh in 1992. More favorable weather patterns in 1993 resulted in increases in electric fuel-related costs and gas sold. Natural gas operating revenue increased 24.5% to $65.0 million from $52.2 million last year. Colder weather patterns during the 1993 heating season resulted in a 20.1% increase in gas sales to 15,511,000 mcf from 12,910,000 mcf in 1992.

BUSINESS

NORTHWESTERN PUBLIC SERVICE COMPANY is an electric and gas utility engaged in generating, transmitting, distributing and selling electric energy in eastern South Dakota, where it furnishes electric service to 54,288 customers in more than 100 communities and adjacent rural areas. The Company also purchases, distributes, sells, and transports natural gas to 73,228 customers in four communities in Nebraska and 53 communities in eastern South Dakota.

BUSINESS LINE ANALYSIS

(12/31/93)	Rev(%)	Inc(%)
Electric	45.7	83.7
Gas	42.5	12.2
Other	11.8	4.1
Total	100.0	100.0

ANNUAL EARNINGS AND DIVIDENDS PER SHARE

	1993	1992	1991	1990	1989	1988	1987
Earnings Per Share	1.96	1.77	1.88	2.23	2.04	1.72	1.67
Dividends Per Share	1.63	1.59	1.535	1.475	1.415	①1.351	1.25
Dividend Payout %	83.2	89.8	81.6	66.1	69.4	78.6	75.1

① 2-for-1 stock split, 6/88.

ANNUAL FINANCIAL DATA

RECORD OF EARNINGS (IN THOUSANDS):

	1993	1992	1991	1990	1989	1988	1987
Total Revenues	153,257	119,197	122,900	114,150	115,961	115,518	108,067
Depreciation	11,559	11,062	10,506	10,986	9,979	9,742	9,491
Maintenance	6,368	5,889	5,836	5,217	5,540	5,486	4,863
Operating Income	20,306	19,574	20,575	19,755	19,198	19,823	18,448
Interest Expense, Net	8,945	8,105	7,244	6,804	6,886	6,981	7,459
Net Income	15,190	13,721	14,815	17,506	16,123	13,876	13,659
Aver. Shs. Outstg.	7,677	7,677	7,677	7,677	7,677	7,677	7,677

BALANCE SHEET (IN THOUSANDS):

Gross Plant	369,105	351,818	335,105	316,081	303,238	293,620	286,420
Accumulated Depreciation	130,610	122,085	113,205	107,117	99,186	92,076	85,461
Total Utility Plant, Net	238,495	229,733	221,900	208,964	204,052	201,544	200,959
Long-term Debt	126,600	106,422	92,003	78,236	79,469	80,702	81,935
Net Stockholders' Equity	112,337	109,781	111,369	108,903	103,301	98,719	97,074
Total Assets	343,574	313,452	297,761	283,073	272,260	264,810	263,681
Year End Shares Outstg	7,677	7,677	7,677	7,677	7,677	7,677	7,677

STATISTICAL RECORD:

Book Value Per Share	14.29	13.95	13.78	13.43	12.68	12.05	11.68
Op. Inc/Net Pl %	8.5	8.5	9.4	9.5	9.4	9.8	9.2
Dep/Gr. Pl %	3.1	3.1	3.1	3.2	3.3	3.3	3.3
Accum. Dep/Gr. Pl %	35.4	34.7	33.8	33.9	32.7	31.4	29.8
Return on Equity %	13.5	12.5	13.7	16.6	16.1	14.6	14.8
Average Yield %	5.5	6.1	6.5	7.9	7.7	7.7	7.3
P/E Ratio	17.1-13.4	16.2-13.3	14.3-10.8	9.2-7.5	9.9-8.1	11.3-9.1	11.7-8.8
Price Range	33½-26¼	28¾-23½	26⅞-20¼	20½-16¾	20¼-16½	19½-15⅝	19½-14⅝

Statistics are as originally reported.

OFFICERS:
R.A. Wilkens, Chairman
M.D. Lewis, Pres. & C.E.O.
A.D. Dietrich, V.P.-Legal & Corp. Sec.
R.R. Hylland, V.P.-Fin. & Corp. Devel.

INCORPORATED: DE, Nov., 1923

PRINCIPAL OFFICE: 33 Third St. SE P.O. Box 1318, Huron, SD 57350-1318

TELEPHONE NUMBER: (605) 352-8411

NO. OF EMPLOYEES: 473

ANNUAL MEETING: In May

SHAREHOLDERS: 8,231

INSTITUTIONAL HOLDINGS:
No. of Institutions: 29
Shares Held: 1,232,939

REGISTRAR(S): Norwest Bank Minnesota, N.A., South St. Paul, MN

TRANSFER AGENT(S): Norwest Bank Minnesota, N.A., South St. Paul, MN

NUCOR CORP.

YIELD 0.3%
P/E RATIO 47.3

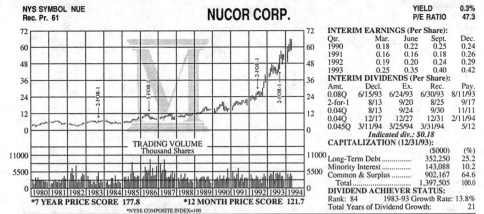

*7 YEAR PRICE SCORE 177.8 *12 MONTH PRICE SCORE 121.7
*NYSE COMPOSITE INDEX=100

TRADING VOLUME
Thousand Shares

INTERIM EARNINGS (Per Share):

Qtr.	Mar.	June	Sept.	Dec.
1990	0.18	0.22	0.25	0.24
1991	0.16	0.16	0.18	0.26
1992	0.19	0.20	0.24	0.29
1993	0.25	0.35	0.40	0.42

INTERIM DIVIDENDS (Per Share):

Amt.	Decl.	Ex.	Rec.	Pay.
0.08Q	6/15/93	6/24/93	6/30/93	8/11/93
2-for-1	8/13	9/20	8/25	9/17
0.04Q	8/13	9/24	9/30	11/11
0.04Q	12/17	12/27	12/31	2/11/94
0.045Q	3/11/94	3/25/94	3/31/94	5/12

Indicated div.: $0.18

CAPITALIZATION (12/31/93):

	($000)	(%)
Long-Term Debt	352,250	25.2
Minority Interest	143,088	10.2
Common & Surplus	902,167	64.6
Total	1,397,505	100.0

DIVIDEND ACHIEVER STATUS:
Rank: 84   1983-93 Growth Rate: 13.8%
Total Years of Dividend Growth: 21

RECENT DEVELOPMENTS: For the year ended 12/31/93, net income rose 27.3% to $123.5 million from 79.2 million in 1992. Sales increased 39.2% to $2.25 billion from $1.62 billion in the prior year. Steel joist production increased slightly to 417,000 tons. Improved operating results were helped by an increase in steel production of 32.9% to 5.7 million tons. Revenues were enhanced due to a 41.1% increase, to 4.9 million tons, in steel sales to outside customers.

PROSPECTS: The outlook for earnings growth is positive as economic conditions continue to improve. However, Nucor will have to fight hard to remain the industry leader as a wave of new low-cost, high-quality steel producers enter the market. This could cause problems for Nucor in the form of intense price competition and scrap metal shortages. Expansion of two sheet steel mills to be completed by mid-1994 will increase the Company's capacity by more than 70%.

BUSINESS

NUCOR CORP. is engaged in the manufacture of steel and steel products. The Nucor Steel Division produces merchant bar and structural steel products, and is a major supplier of steel angles. The Vulcraft Division is the nation's largest producer of steel joists and joist girders for building construction. Approximately 80% of steel production is sold to outside customers, with the balance being used internally by several other divisions.

QUARTERLY DATA

(12/31/93)($000)	Rev	Inc
1st Quarter	489,779	21,745
2nd Quarter	564,933	30,417
3rd Quarter	587,281	34,807
4th Quarter	611,746	36,540

ANNUAL EARNINGS AND DIVIDENDS PER SHARE

	1993	1992	1991	1990	1989	1988	1987
Earnings Per Share	1.42	0.92	0.75	0.88	0.68	③0.84	0.60
Dividends Per Share	0.27	①0.138	②0.127	0.118	0.108	0.097	0.088
Dividend Payout %	19.0	15.0	17.0	13.4	15.9	7.6	14.6

① 2-for-1 stk split,09/20/93 ② 2-for-1 stk split, 6/22/92 ③ Before disc. oper.

ANNUAL FINANCIAL DATA

RECORD OF EARNINGS (IN MILLIONS):

	1993	1992	1991	1990	1989	1988	1987
Total Revenues	2,253.7	1,619.2	1,465.5	1,481.6	1,269.0	1,061.4	851.0
Costs and Expenses	1,931.2	1,396.4	1,276.2	1,278.6	1,095.7	895.0	727.0
Depreciation	122.3	97.8	93.6	85.0	76.6	56.3	41.8
Operating Profit	287.9	201.9	162.7	188.5	163.8	172.2	137.7
Earn Bef Fed Inc Taxes	187.1	117.3	95.8	111.2	85.6	107.6	83.2
Income Taxes	63.6	38.1	31.1	36.2	27.8	36.7	32.7
Net Income	123.5	79.2	64.7	75.1	57.8	109.4	50.5
Aver. Shs. Outstg. (000)	86,909	86,584	86,240	85,764	85,372	84,896	84,616

BALANCE SHEET (IN MILLIONS):

	1993	1992	1991	1990	1989	1988	1987
Cash & Short-term Invests	27.3	25.5	38.3	51.6	32.6	26.4	...
Accounts Receivable	202.2	132.1	109.5	126.7	107.0	97.4	80.1
Inventories	215.0	206.4	186.1	136.6	139.5	123.2	73.3
Gross Property	1,821.0	1,574.1	1,261.5	1,086.4	1,048.0	942.3	618.5
Accumulated Depreciation	460.0	448.3	414.2	363.1	294.2	240.4	199.2
Long-Term Debt	352.3	246.8	72.8	28.8	156.0	113.2	35.5
Net Stockholders' Equity	902.2	784.2	711.6	652.8	584.4	532.3	428.0
Total Assets	1,829.3	1,490.4	1,181.6	1,038.4	1,033.8	949.7	654.1
Total Current Assets	468.2	364.6	334.3	315.1	280.0	247.8	234.7
Total Current Liabilities	350.5	272.0	229.2	225.6	193.6	216.1	147.5
Net Working Capital	117.7	92.6	105.1	89.5	86.5	31.7	87.2
Year End Shs Outstg (000)	87,073	86,737	86,418	85,951	85,600	85,152	84,784

STATISTICAL RECORD:

	1993	1992	1991	1990	1989	1988	1987
Operating Profit Margin %	8.9	7.7	6.5	8.0	7.6	10.4	9.7
Book Value Per Share	10.36	9.04	8.23	7.59	6.83	6.25	5.05
Return on Equity %	13.7	10.1	9.1	11.5	9.9	20.6	11.8
Return on Assets %	6.8	5.3	5.5	7.2	5.6	11.5	7.7
Average Yield %	0.6	0.5	0.7	0.7	0.8	0.9	0.9
P/E Ratio	40.3-26.8	43.5-22.8	29.8-19.0	23.3-13.8	24.8-16.5	14.6-10.9	20.6-12.3
Price Range	57¼-38	40-21	22⅜-14¼	20½-12⅛	16⅞-11¼	12¼-9⅛	12⅜-7⅜

Statistics are as originally reported.

OFFICERS:
F.K. Iverson, Chmn. & C.E.O.
J.D. Correnti, Pres. & C.O.O.
S. Siegel, Vice-Chmn., C.F.O., Treas. & Sec.

INCORPORATED: DE, Mar., 1958

PRINCIPAL OFFICE: 2100 Rexford Rd.., Charlotte, NC 28211

TELEPHONE NUMBER: (704) 366-7000
FAX: (704) 362-4208
NO. OF EMPLOYEES: 1,844
ANNUAL MEETING: In May
SHAREHOLDERS: 13,630
INSTITUTIONAL HOLDINGS:
No. of Institutions: 351
Shares Held: 30,513,672

REGISTRAR(S):

TRANSFER AGENT(S): First Union National Bank of N.C., Charlotte, NC

NWNL COS., INC.

YIELD 2.6%
P/E RATIO 12.0

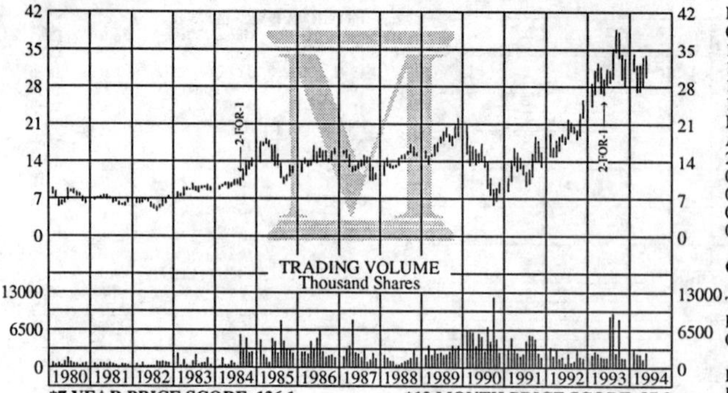

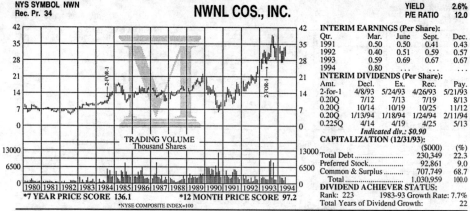

***7 YEAR PRICE SCORE 136.1** ***12 MONTH PRICE SCORE 97.2**

*NYSE COMPOSITE INDEX=100

INTERIM EARNINGS (Per Share):

Qtr.	Mar.	June	Sept.	Dec.
1991	0.50	0.50	0.41	0.43
1992	0.40	0.51	0.59	0.57
1993	0.59	0.69	0.67	0.67
1994	0.80	...	...	...

INTERIM DIVIDENDS (Per Share):

Amt.	Decl.	Ex.	Rec.	Pay.
2-for-1	4/8/93	5/24/93	4/26/93	5/21/93
0.20Q	7/12	7/13	7/19	8/13
0.20Q	10/14	10/19	10/25	11/12
0.20Q	1/13/94	1/18/94	1/24/94	2/11/94
0.225Q	4/14	4/19	4/25	5/13

Indicated div.: $0.90

CAPITALIZATION (12/31/93):

	($000)	(%)
Total Debt	230,349	22.3
Preferred Stock	92,861	9.0
Common & Surplus	707,749	68.7
Total	1,030,959	100.0

DIVIDEND ACHIEVER STATUS:

Rank: 223 1983-93 Growth Rate: 7.7%

Total Years of Dividend Growth: 22

RECENT DEVELOPMENTS: For the year ended 12/31/93, income, before extraordinary charges and cumulative effect of accounting changes, was $82.5 million, compared with income, before cumulative effect of accounting changes, of $60.6 million in 1992. Revenues for the year were $1.49 billion compared with $1.38 billion for the prior year. Individual insurance revenues increased 13% to $634.5 million from $582.3 million in 1992. Employee benefits revenues rose 10% to $608.0 million from $551.1 million in 1992. For the quarter ended 12/31/93, income, before extraordinary charges, was $22.1 million, compared with net income of $17.6 million for the same quarter last year. Revenues for the quarter increased 9.1% to $385.4 million from $353.1 million for the year-ago quarter.

BUSINESS

THE NWNL COMPANIES, INC., is a holding company whose subsidiaries specialize in life insurance and related financial services businesses. Through its subsidiaries the Company issues and distributes individual life insurance and annuities; group life and health insurance; life and health reinsurance; and markets and manages mutual funds. NWNL operates in four business segments: Individual Insurance, Employee Benefits, Life and Health Reinsurance and Pension. Subsidiaries owned by the Company are: Northwestern National Life Insurance Company; Northern Life Insurance Company of Seattle, Washington; The North Atlantic Life Insurance Company of America of Jericho, New York; NWNL Benefits Corporation, Washington Square Capital, Inc. and Washington Square Securities, Inc. of Minneapolis, Minnesota; Washington Square Mortgage Company of West Des Moines, Iowa; and NWNL Northstar of Greenwich, Connecticut.

BUSINESS LINE ANALYSIS

(12/31/93)	Rev(%)	Inc(%)
Individual	42.6	69.4
Employee Benefits	40.8	31.6
Pension	6.3	(11.2)
Life & Health Reinsurance	8.9	22.4
Other	1.4	(12.2)
Total	100.0	100.0

ANNUAL EARNINGS AND DIVIDENDS PER SHARE

	1993	1992	1991	1990	1989	1988	1987
Earnings Per Share	**2.63**	**[2] 2.07**	**[3] 1.72**	**[3] 2.45**	**2.07**	**[4] 2.01**	**1.85**
Dividends Per Share	**[1] 1.17**	**0.73**	**0.69**	**0.645**	**0.59**	**0.54**	**0.468**
Dividend Payout %	**44.5**	**35.3**	**40.2**	**26.3**	**28.5**	**26.9**	**25.3**

[1] 2-for-1 stk split,05/24/93 [2] Before extraord. item [3] Before disc. oper. [4] Before realized invest gains

ANNUAL FINANCIAL DATA

RECORD OF EARNINGS (IN MILLIONS):							
Premiums	659.6	589.9	548.0	535.9	583.4	1,806.5	1,646.0
Net Investment Income	635.0	606.7	616.1	651.2	660.8	420.4	382.6
Total Revenues	1,490.4	1,378.0	1,339.8	1,331.7	1,393.2	2,270.6	2,052.5
Benefits to Policyholders	1,006.3	950.1	928.8	922.4	958.7	682.3	596.4
Income Bef Income Taxes	128.6	89.6	70.8	69.2	86.3	65.7	53.9
Income Tax Exp (benefit)	46.1	29.0	23.1	7.4	27.9	20.4	8.1
Realized Invest Secur Gains	...	...	...	...	...	d14.5	5.1
Net Income	65.3	59.3	[1] 47.2	[2] 61.2	53.5	33.0	38.0
Aver. Shs. Outstg. (000)	28,151	24,800	24,092	25,010	25,814	21,912	22,360

[1] Before disc. op. dr$350,000. [2] Before disc. op. dr$11,585,000.

BALANCE SHEET (IN MILLIONS):							
Cash	34.0	37.6	29.6	32.7	20.9	18.7	9.7
Fixed Maturity Secur, At Cost	5,359.4	4,662.9	3,954.0	3,606.9	3,450.5	2,119.9	1,760.7
Equity Securities	44.9	30.3	45.3	28.7	32.1	68.0	92.4
Policy Loans	257.4	217.9	179.0	140.7	117.5	169.1	160.3
Mtge Loans on Real Estate	1,781.1	1,859.8	2,010.7	2,340.9	2,510.9	1,623.5	1,518.4
Total Assets	9,912.9	9,014.4	8,770.3	8,473.7	8,270.7	7,593.9	6,819.4
Benefits and Claims	7,809.9	7,251.6	7,099.2	6,879.0	6,602.3	4,292.4	3,808.6
Net Stockholders' Equity	800.6	679.8	594.1	513.4	500.1	409.1	391.8
Year End Shs Outstg (000)	29,446	26,910	24,528	24,528	25,848	21,816	22,360

STATISTICAL RECORD:							
Book Value Per Share	24.04	21.80	20.42	20.93	19.35	18.75	17.52
Return on Equity %	10.3	8.9	8.0	11.9	10.7	8.1	9.7
Return on Assets %	0.8	0.7	0.5	0.7	0.7	0.4	0.6
Average Yield %	3.7	3.6	5.1	4.8	3.3	3.8	3.5
P/E Ratio	14.7-9.3	12.4-7.2	10.9-4.9	8.6-2.4	10.7-6.5	8.6-5.7	8.8-5.6
Price Range	38¾-24⅜	25⅝-14⅞	18⅝-8⅜	21-5⅞	22⅛-13½	17¼-11⅜	16¼-10⅜

Statistics are as originally reported.

OFFICERS:
J.G. Turner, Chmn., C.E.O. & Pres.
R.N. Sanner, Sr. V.P., Sec. & Couns.
R.C. Salipante, Sr. V.P. & C.F.O.
W.R. Huneke, V.P., Treas. & Chief Acctg. Off.

INCORPORATED: MN, Jan., 1989

PRINCIPAL OFFICE: 20 Washington Avenue South, Minneapolis, MN 55401

TELEPHONE NUMBER: (612) 372-5432

FAX: (612) 372-1192

NO. OF EMPLOYEES: 2,562

ANNUAL MEETING: In May

SHAREHOLDERS: 716 (pfd.); 31,234 (com.)

INSTITUTIONAL HOLDINGS:
No. of Institutions: 3
Shares Held: 32,500

REGISTRAR(S):

TRANSFER AGENT(S): Norwest Bank Minnesota, N.A., St. Paul, MN

NASDAQ SYMBOL OCAS
Rec. Pr. 63⅝ (Marginable)

OHIO CASUALTY CORP.

YIELD ...%
P/E RATIO 13.2

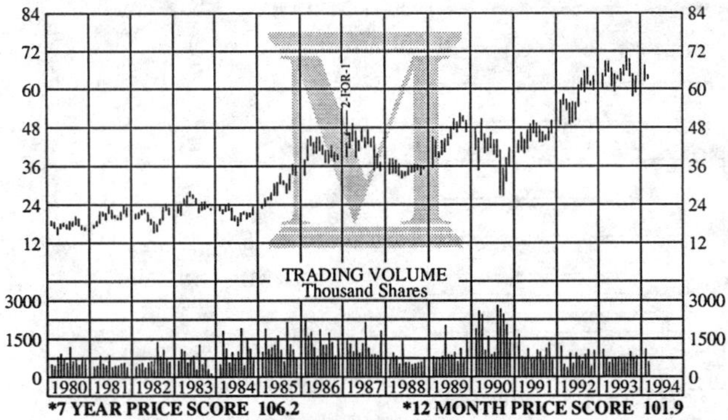

***7 YEAR PRICE SCORE 106.2** ***12 MONTH PRICE SCORE 101.9**

*NYSE COMPOSITE INDEX=100

INTERIM EARNINGS (Per Share):

Qtr.	Mar.	June	Sept.	Dec.
1990	0.80	1.14	1.62	0.82
1991	1.00	1.50	2.08	1.44
1992	1.33	1.35	1.02	1.79
1993	1.10	1.73	1.01	0.99

INTERIM DIVIDENDS (Per Share):

Amt.	Decl.	Ex.	Rec.	Pay.
0.71Q	5/20/93	5/25/93	6/1/93	6/10/93
0.71Q	8/20	8/26	9/1	9/10
0.71Q	11/18	11/24	12/1	12/10
0.73Q	2/17/94	2/23/94	3/1/94	3/10/94
2-for-1	2/17	4/25	4/1	4/22

CAPITALIZATION (12/31/93):

	($000)	(%)
Total Debt	103,000	10.7
Common & Surplus	862,338	89.3
Total	965,338	100.0

DIVIDEND ACHIEVER STATUS:
Rank: 205 1983-93 Growth Rate: 8.5%
Total Years of Dividend Growth: 48

RECENT DEVELOPMENTS: For the year ended 12/31/93, net income was $87.0 million, or $4.83 per share, compared with $97.1 million, or $5.40 per share, before an accounting change, last year, a decline of 10.4%. For the quarter ended 12/31/93, net income was $17.8 million, or $0.99 per share, which includes the after-tax charge of $0.62 per share for OCAS's portion of the New Jersey Market Transition Facility, compared with $32.1 million, or $1.79 per share, last year. Gross written premiums and finance charges earned were $335.2 million compared with $383.5 million last year, due to OCAS's decision in 1992 to withdraw from the California market, with the withdrawal having been completed in December 1993. Net investment income totaled $52.6 million compared with $55.8 million a year ago. Written premiums for property-casualty operations declined 11% to $305.1 million. Premium income from life operations totaled $4.8 million versus $5.3 million in 1992.

BUSINESS

OHIO CASUALTY CORPORATION operates primarily as a holding company and is principally engaged, through its direct and indirect subsidiaries, in the business of property and casualty insurance, life insurance and insurance premium finance. The Corporation conducts its property and casualty insurance business through The Ohio Casualty Insurance and its three property and casualty insurance subsidiaries: West American Insurance Company; Ohio Security Insurance Company; and American Fire and Casualty Company. This group of companies presently underwrites most forms of property and casualty insurance. The Corporation conducts its life insurance business through The Ohio Life Insurance Company, and its insurance premium finance business through Ocasco Budget, Inc. Ohio Life and Ocasco are direct subsidiaries of Ohio Casualty Insurance Company.

BUSINESS LINE ANALYSIS

(12/31/93)	Rev(%)	Inc(%)
Property & Casualty	96.7	93.3
Life Insurance	3.0	9.6
Premium Finance & Other	0.3	(2.9)
Total	100.0	100.0

ANNUAL EARNINGS AND DIVIDENDS PER SHARE

	1993	1992	1991	1990	1989	1988	1987
Earnings Per Share	**4.83**	**[1] 5.40**	**6.02**	**4.38**	**4.74**	**6.53**	**4.31**
Dividends Per Share	**2.84**	**[2] 2.68**	**2.48**	**2.32**	**2.08**	**1.88**	**[3] 1.68**
Dividend Payout %	**58.8**	**49.6**	**41.2**	**53.0**	**43.9**	**28.8**	**39.0**

Note: 2-for-1stk.split,4/22/94. [1] Before acctg. chg. [2] Bef acctg chge [3] 2-for-1 stk split, 1/87

ANNUAL FINANCIAL DATA

	1993	1992	1991	1990	1989	1988	1987
RECORD OF EARNINGS (IN MILLIONS):							
Prem & Fin Chrgs Earned	1,400.6	1,538.4	1,488.6	1,455.9	1,381.2	1,384.6	1,401.0
Invest Income Less Exps	219.4	221.0	218.1	204.1	216.4	191.5	174.2
Total Income	1,669.8	1,812.1	1,714.2	1,637.5	1,577.1	1,576.1	1,575.2
Losses & Bens for Policyholders	919.8	992.6	914.4	909.0	821.3	785.1	812.9
Income Bef Income Taxes	96.2	117.7	124.3	83.3	116.4	165.9	128.8
Total Income Taxes	9.2	20.7	16.4	cr0.8	14.9	23.8	31.6
Gain on Sale Of Securities	...	...	...	...	...	d14.1	d18.7
Net Income	87.0	[1] 97.1	107.9	84.1	101.5	128.0	78.6
Aver. Shs. Outstg. (000)	18,008	17,976	17,924	19,218	21,429	21,778	22,533
[1] Before acctg. change cr$1,471,000.							
BALANCE SHEET (IN MILLIONS):							
Cash	14.3	20.0	14.3	9.4	3.1	13.9	8.5
Fixed Matur, At Amort Cost	2,629.2	2,664.7	2,411.9	1,960.4	1,996.9	1,758.9	1,737.0
Equity Securities, At Mkt	492.2	438.2	423.0	354.6	432.4	376.3	306.0
Total Assets	3,816.8	3,760.7	3,531.3	3,252.9	3,145.7	2,922.0	2,682.4
Benefits and Claims	2,617.9	2,552.4	2,443.9	2,322.3	2,159.9	1,966.5	1,836.4
Net Stockholders' Equity	862.3	825.2	774.5	651.2	775.0	718.5	615.7
Year End Shs Outstg (000)	18,015	17,994	17,944	17,899	20,983	21,573	22,101
STATISTICAL RECORD:							
Return on Equity %	10.1	11.8	13.9	12.9	13.1	17.8	12.8
Book Value Per Share	47.87	45.86	43.16	36.38	36.94	33.30	27.86
Average Yield %	4.4	4.6	5.5	6.0	4.7	5.3	4.0
P/E Ratio	22.9-18.4	19.2-14.0	8.3-6.6	11.6-6.1	11.1-7.5	5.9-4.9	11.4-8.0
Price Range	72-57⅝	66⅝-48¾	50¼-40	50¾-26¾	52½-35½	38¼-32¼	49¼-34½

Statistics are as originally reported.

OFFICERS:
J.L. Marcum, Chairman
L.N. Patch, Pres. & C.E.O.
H.L. Sloneker, III, V.P. & Sec.
B.S. Porter, C.F.O. & Treas.

INCORPORATED: OH, Aug., 1969

PRINCIPAL OFFICE: 136 North Third Street, Hamilton, OH 45025

TELEPHONE NUMBER: (513) 867-3000

FAX: (513) 867-3215

NO. OF EMPLOYEES: 3,973

ANNUAL MEETING: In April

SHAREHOLDERS: 7,200

INSTITUTIONAL HOLDINGS:
No. of Institutions: 131
Shares Held: 9,125,734

REGISTRAR(S): Mellon Bank, N.A., Pittsburgh, PA

TRANSFER AGENT(S): Mellon Bank, N.A., Pittsburgh, PA

NASDAQ SYMBOL OKEN
Rec. Pr. 33⅝ (Marginable)

OLD KENT FINANCIAL CORP.

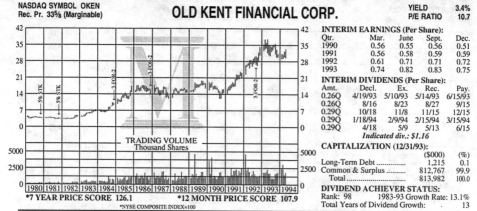

YIELD 3.4%
P/E RATIO 10.7

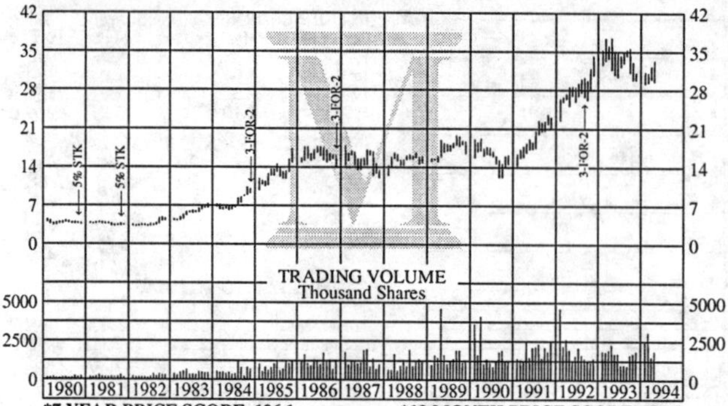

42
35
28
21
14
7
0
5% STK
5% STK
3-FOR-2
3-FOR-2
3-FOR-2
TRADING VOLUME
Thousand Shares
5000
2500
0
1980 1981 1982 1983 1984 1985 1986 1987 1988 1989 1990 1991 1992 1993 1994

***7 YEAR PRICE SCORE 126.1** ***12 MONTH PRICE SCORE 107.9**

*NYSE COMPOSITE INDEX=100

INTERIM EARNINGS (Per Share):

Qtr.	Mar.	June	Sept.	Dec.
1990	0.56	0.55	0.56	0.51
1991	0.56	0.58	0.59	0.59
1992	0.61	0.71	0.71	0.72
1993	0.74	0.82	0.83	0.75

INTERIM DIVIDENDS (Per Share):

Amt.	Decl.	Ex.	Rec.	Pay.
0.26Q	4/19/93	5/10/93	5/14/93	6/15/93
0.26Q	8/16	8/23	8/27	9/15
0.29Q	10/18	11/8	11/15	12/15
0.29Q	1/18/94	2/9/94	2/15/94	3/15/94
0.29Q	4/18	5/9	5/13	6/15

Indicated div.: $1.16

CAPITALIZATION (12/31/93):

	($000)	(%)
Long-Term Debt	1,215	0.1
Common & Surplus	812,767	99.9
Total	813,982	100.0

DIVIDEND ACHIEVER STATUS:
Rank: 98 1983-93 Growth Rate: 13.1%
Total Years of Dividend Growth: 13

RECENT DEVELOPMENTS: For the year ended 12/31/93 net income increased to $127.9 million from $111.1 million for 1992. The Company cited balance sheet growth, improved credit quality and increased fee-based income as primary reasons for results. The provision for loan losses was reduced 41% from 1992 to $34.0 million. Other income rose 15% to $146.8 million. Assets increased 13% to $9.86 billion as deposits moved up 10% to $7.97 billion. Loans totaled $5.49 billion compared with $4.91 billion in the prior year. Commercial loans accounted for 26% of the total loan portfolio; real estate-residential mortgages, 22%; real-estate-commercial, 21%; consumer loans, 21%; real estate-consumer home equity, 8%; and real estate construction, 2%. The return on average assets improved to 1.38% from 1.27%. OKEN agreed to acquire Edgemark Financial Corp. of Chicago.

BUSINESS

OLD KENT FINANCIAL CORP. is a bank holding company headquartered in Grand Rapids, Michigan with assets of $9.9 billion. The Company provides commercial banking and related services through its 16 banking subsidiaries and five non-banking subsidiaries. The Company offers a full range of banking and fiduciary services, including commercial, mortgage and retail loans, business and personal checking accounts, savings and individual retirement accounts, time deposit instruments, automated teller machines and electronically accessed banking services, credit and debit cards, money transfer services, safe deposit facilities, cash management, real estate and lease financing, international banking services, credit life insurance, personal investment and brokerage services, and corporate and personal trust services. The principal markets for the financial services are communities within Michigan and Illinois. The Company and its subsidiaries serve these markets through 213 banking offices. Old Kent Bank and Trust Company, the largest subsidiary and lead bank accounted for 42% of total deposits and 45% of total loans of the Company and its subsidiaries on a consolidated basis in 1993. The principal sources of revenues for the Company are interest and fees on loans, which accounted for 51.9% of the total revenues in 1993, and interest on investment securities, which accounted for 28.9%.

ANNUAL EARNINGS AND DIVIDENDS PER SHARE

	1993	1992	1991	1990	1989	1988	1987
Earnings Per Share	**3.14**	**[1] 2.75**	**2.31**	**2.19**	**2.15**	**1.97**	**1.87**
Dividends Per Share	**1.07**	**[2] 0.903**	**0.787**	**0.723**	**0.637**	**0.583**	**0.543**
Dividend Payout %	**34.1**	**32.8**	**34.0**	**33.0**	**29.6**	**29.7**	**29.0**

[1] Primary [2] 3-for-2 stk split, 9/16/92

ANNUAL FINANCIAL DATA

	1993	1992	1991	1990	1989	1988	1987
RECORD OF EARNINGS (IN MILLIONS):							
Total Revenues	806.8	815.2	862.5	870.3	863.1	725.8	536.2
Costs and Expenses	613.3	651.3	729.1	747.1	745.1	622.1	450.9
Operating Income	193.6	164.0	133.4	123.2	118.0	103.7	85.3
Income Bef Income Taxes	193.6	164.0	133.4	123.2	118.0	103.7	85.3
Income Taxes	65.7	52.9	40.4	35.7	32.6	26.5	21.9
Net Income	127.9	111.1	93.0	87.5	85.4	77.1	63.4
Aver. Shs. Outstg. (000)	40,748	40,357	40,245	39,647	37,875	36,989	31,481
BALANCE SHEET (IN MILLIONS):							
Cash and Cash Equivalents	4,103.5	3,566.2	3,495.6	2,648.7	2,818.4	2,906.5	2,412.4
Gross Property	133.9	117.1	112.4	114.3	102.1	99.1	89.6
Long-Term Debt	1.2	16.2	74.7	80.9	87.6	93.4	63.4
Net Stockholders' Equity	812.8	726.3	672.6	607.6	600.1	540.8	437.6
Total Assets	9,855.7	8,698.6	8,826.1	8,205.0	8,127.2	7,854.1	6,455.1
Total Current Assets	4,103.5	3,566.2	3,495.6	2,648.7	2,818.4	2,906.5	2,412.4
Total Current Liabilities	8,929.4	7,880.7	8,009.4	7,442.3	7,343.6	7,128.5	5,870.3
Net Working Capital	d4,826.0	d4,314.5	d4,513.8	d4,793.5	d4,525.2	d4,222.0	d3,457.8
Year End Shs Outstg (000)	40,539	40,442	40,156	39,920	38,156	37,142	31,484
STATISTICAL RECORD:							
Book Value Per Share	20.05	17.96	16.75	15.22	15.08	13.76	12.90
Return on Equity %	15.7	15.3	13.8	14.4	14.2	14.3	14.5
Return on Assets %	1.3	1.3	1.1	1.1	1.1	1.0	1.0
Average Yield %	3.2	3.2	4.2	4.6	3.7	4.0	3.6
P/E Ratio	11.9-9.5	12.5-8.2	10.2-6.2	8.8-5.5	9.2-6.9	8.5-6.3	9.7-6.5
Price Range	37½-29¾	34¼-22½	23⅝-14¼	19¼-12⅛	19¾-14⅞	16¾-12⅜	17⅞-12

Statistics are as originally reported.

OFFICERS:
J.C. Canepa, Chmn., Pres. & C.E.O.
R.L. Sadler, Vice-Chmn.
B.P. Sherwood, III, Vice-Chmn. & Treas.
R.W. Wroten, Exec. V.P. & C.F.O.
M.J. Allen, Jr., Sr. V.P. & Sec.

INCORPORATED: DE, Oct., 1971

PRINCIPAL OFFICE: One Vandenberg Center, Grand Rapids, MI 49503

TELEPHONE NUMBER: (616) 771-5000

NO. OF EMPLOYEES: 4,745

ANNUAL MEETING: In April

SHAREHOLDERS: 12,700 (approx.)

INSTITUTIONAL HOLDINGS:
No. of Institutions: 139
Shares Held: 15,595,876

REGISTRAR(S):

TRANSFER AGENT(S): At Company's Office

NYS SYMBOL ORI
Rec. Pr. 22½

OLD REPUBLIC INTERNATIONAL CORP.

YIELD 2.1%
P/E RATIO 8.6

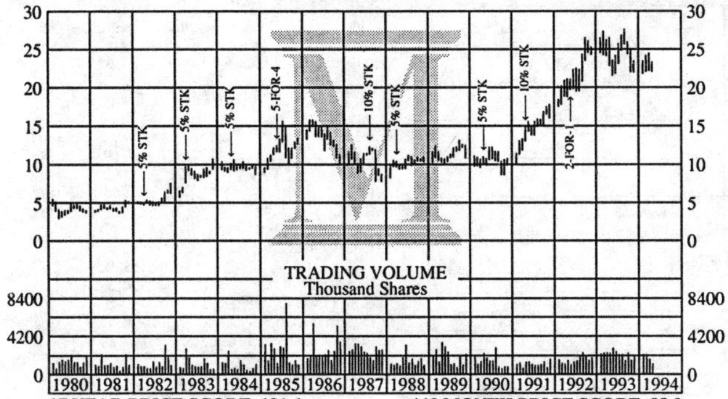

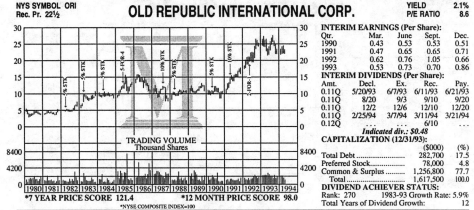

*7 YEAR PRICE SCORE 121.4 *12 MONTH PRICE SCORE 98.0

•NYSE COMPOSITE INDEX=100

INTERIM EARNINGS (Per Share):

Qtr.	Mar.	June	Sept.	Dec.
1990	0.43	0.53	0.53	0.51
1991	0.47	0.65	0.65	0.71
1992	0.62	0.76	1.05	0.66
1993	0.53	0.73	0.70	0.86

INTERIM DIVIDENDS (Per Share):

Amt.	Decl.	Ex.	Rec.	Pay.
0.11Q	5/20/93	6/7/93	6/11/93	6/21/93
0.11Q	8/20	9/3	9/10	9/20
0.11Q	12/2	12/6	12/10	12/20
0.11Q	2/25/94	3/7/94	3/11/94	3/21/94
0.12Q	...	...	6/10	...

Indicated div.: $0.48

CAPITALIZATION (12/31/93):

	($000)	(%)
Total Debt	282,700	17.5
Preferred Stock	78,000	4.8
Common & Surplus	1,256,800	77.7
Total	1,617,500	100.0

DIVIDEND ACHIEVER STATUS:
Rank: 270 1983-93 Growth Rate: 5.9%
Total Years of Dividend Growth: 12

RECENT DEVELOPMENTS: For the three months ended 12/31/93, net income rose 32% from the prior-year period to $50.4 million. Revenues increased 16% to $486.0 million. Title insurance pre-tax operating income soared 102% to $11.7 million while mortgage guaranty pre-tax operating income rose 39% to $17.7 million. Results were adversely affected by exsisting soft pricing in the property and liability market. Revenues totaled $1.74 billion compared with $1.62 billion in the prior-year.

PROSPECTS: Mortgage guaranty and title insurance businesses are turning in strong performances as a result of low mortgage rates, increased refinancings and improved home sales. The Company anticipates more price firming in the soft property and liability market this year and has planned accordingly. The general insurance unit is benefiting from greater premium volume stemming from its new Texas and Minnehoma businesses.

BUSINESS

OLD REPUBLIC INTERNATIONAL CORP. is a multiple lines insurance holding company. Its subsidiaries market, underwrite, and manage a wide range of specialty and general insurance programs in the property & liability, life & disability, title, and mortgage guaranty insurance fields. The Company primarily serves the insurance and related needs of major financial services and industrial corporations, with an emphasis on the coal and mineral mining, energy, forest products, transportation and housing industries.

BUSINESS LINE ANALYSIS

(12/31/93)	Rev(%)	Inc(%)
General Insurance Group	61.0	51.2
Title Isurance Group	26.9	13.2
Mortgage Guaranty Group	6.8	25.2
Life Insurance Group	2.9	2.7
Other	0.1	(8.8)
Realized Gains	2.3	16.5
Total	100.0	100.0

ANNUAL EARNINGS AND DIVIDENDS PER SHARE

	1993	1992	1991	1990	1989	1988	1987
Earnings Per Share	**2.83**	**3.09**	**2.48**	**2.02**	**1.93**	**[5] 0.87**	**1.81**
Dividends Per Share	**0.43**	**[1] 0.392**	**[2] 0.363**	**[3] 0.339**	**[4] 0.316**	**[6] 0.301**	**[7] 0.286**
Dividend Payout %	**15.2**	**12.7**	**14.7**	**16.8**	**16.4**	**34.7**	**15.8**

[1] 2-for-1 stk split, 5/1/92 [2] 10% stk div, 4/2/91 [3] Adj for 5% stk div, 5/15/90 [4] Adj for 5% stk div, 3/10/89 [5] Before realized gains [6] Adj for 5% stk div, 5/06/88 [7] Adj for 10% stk, div, 9/87

ANNUAL FINANCIAL DATA

RECORD OF EARNINGS (IN MILLIONS):	1993	1992	1991	1990	1989	1988	1987
Net Premiums Earned	1,246.0	1,103.5	972.0	886.4	812.5	804.7	819.3
Net Investment Income	220.7	221.5	219.3	206.6	198.3	173.2	152.2
Total Revenues	1,736.3	1,617.0	1,374.5	1,242.7	1,181.9	1,102.1	1,094.5
Income Bef Income Taxes	243.3	250.7	175.2	132.8	119.4	33.5	89.0
Total Income Taxes	78.0	75.0	45.2	28.9	21.2	cr11.6	cr3.6
Realized Gains, Net Of Taxes	...	...	...	...	...	3.7	9.5
Net Income	[1] 166.4	174.7	131.0	104.6	98.9	50.9	102.8
Aver. Shs. Outstg. (000)	57,078	54,517	52,408	51,206	50,481	48,475	48,807

[1] Before acctg. change cr$8,600,000.

BALANCE SHEET (IN MILLIONS):	1993	1992	1991	1990	1989	1988	1987
Cash	43.9	42.4	...	20.9	27.2	36.1	29.2
Fixed Maturities	3,152.2	2,846.3	2,518.6	2,210.1	2,008.1	1,736.0	1,775.9
Equity Securities (at Mkt)	191.9	125.9	51.4	40.1	11.5	29.1	29.8
Total Assets	6,098.3	4,141.6	3,713.2	3,328.5	3,123.5	3,005.5	2,797.7
Benefits and Claims	4,097.8	2,403.5	2,285.3	2,143.1	2,023.5	1,919.4	1,760.5
Net Stockholders' Equity	1,334.8	1,165.5	962.3	789.1	696.2	591.8	591.3
Year End Shs Outstg (000)	51,871	50,693	46,896	46,221	44,406	41,978	41,554

STATISTICAL RECORD:	1993	1992	1991	1990	1989	1988	1987
Book Value Per Share	24.23	21.40	18.80	16.54	14.93	13.29	12.45
Return on Equity %	12.6	15.2	13.9	13.5	14.7	8.9	17.9
Return on Assets %	2.7	4.2	3.5	3.1	3.2	1.7	3.7
Average Yield %	1.8	1.8	2.6	3.2	2.7	3.1	2.8
P/E Ratio	9.8-7.6	8.6-5.7	7.2-4.0	6.1-4.3	6.8-5.3	12.4-9.1	6.7-4.1
Price Range	27⅝-21½	26½-17½	17⅞-10	12¼-8⅝	13⅛-10⅛	11¼-8¼	12⅝-7¾

Statistics are as originally reported.

OFFICERS:
A.C. Zucaro, Chmn., Pres. & C.E.O.
P.D. Adams, Sr. V.P., C.F.O. & Treas.
S. LeRoy, III, Sr. V.P., Sec. & Gen. Couns.

INCORPORATED: DE, 1969

PRINCIPAL OFFICE: 307 North Michigan Avenue, Chicago, IL 60601

TELEPHONE NUMBER: (312) 346-8100

NO. OF EMPLOYEES: 6,100 (approx.)

ANNUAL MEETING: In May

SHAREHOLDERS: 3,973

INSTITUTIONAL HOLDINGS:
No. of Institutions: 164
Shares Held: 37,462,569

REGISTRAR(S):

TRANSFER AGENT(S):

NYS SYMBOL ORU
Rec. Pr. 33⅜

ORANGE & ROCKLAND UTILITIES, INC.

YIELD 7.6%
P/E RATIO 10.9

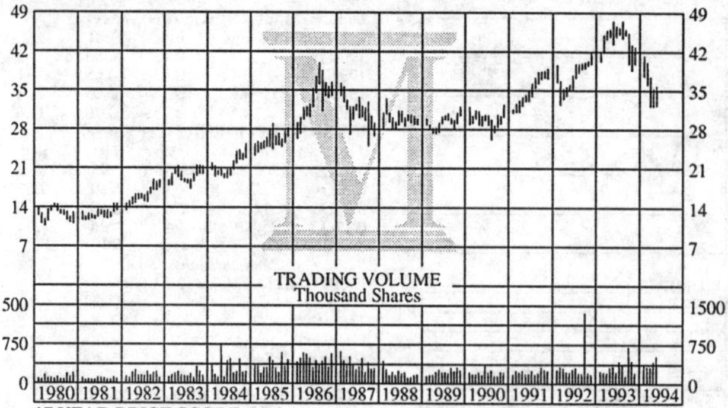

***7 YEAR PRICE SCORE 95.6** ***12 MONTH PRICE SCORE 83.5**

*NYSE COMPOSITE INDEX=100

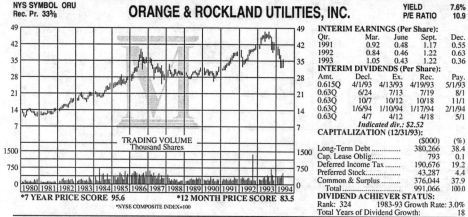

INTERIM EARNINGS (Per Share):

Qtr.	Mar.	June	Sept.	Dec.
1991	0.92	0.48	1.17	0.55
1992	0.84	0.46	1.22	0.63
1993	1.05	0.43	1.22	0.36

INTERIM DIVIDENDS (Per Share):

Amt.	Decl.	Ex.	Rec.	Pay.
0.615Q	4/1/93	4/13/93	4/19/93	5/1/93
0.63Q	6/24	7/13	7/19	8/1
0.63Q	10/7	10/12	10/18	11/1
0.63Q	1/6/94	1/10/94	1/17/94	2/1/94
0.63Q	4/7	4/12	4/18	5/1

Indicated div.: $2.52

CAPITALIZATION (12/31/93):

	($000)	(%)
Long-Term Debt	380,266	38.4
Cap. Lease Oblig.	793	0.1
Deferred Income Tax	190,676	19.2
Preferred Stock	43,287	4.4
Common & Surplus	376,044	37.9
Total	991,066	100.0

DIVIDEND ACHIEVER STATUS:

Rank: 324 1983-93 Growth Rate: 3.0%
Total Years of Dividend Growth: 18

RECENT DEVELOPMENTS: For the year ended 12/31/93, net income was $44.8 million compared with $45.8 million last year. Revenues were $971.4 million, up 15.1%. Results were negatively affected by $6.1 million of investigatory and litigation expenses associated with the criminal wrongdoing of former employees. Retail electric sales totaled 4,357,528 megawatthours, up 3.5%. Gas sales to firm customers totaled 20,556 million cubic feet.

PROSPECTS: Three former ORU employees have pleaded guilty to misappropriating company funds. The New York District Attorney is investigating ORU for any other possible wrongdoings. The Company filed with the New York Public Service Commission for a $17.1 million rate increase. Due to the above issues, the Public Service Commission has put off its decision concerning the rate case until its own investigation is complete.

BUSINESS

ORANGE & ROCKLAND UTILITIES INC. is an investor-owned utility serving 254,200 electric customers and 108,200 natural gas customers in a 1,350 square-mile territory in southeastern New York as well as in adjacent sections of northern New Jersey and northeastern Pennsylvania. ORU has two wholly owned utility subsidiaries - Rockland Electric Company and Pike County Light and Power Company. The Company also has three wholly owned non-utility subsidiaries: Clove Development Corporation, a real estate operation, O & R Energy Development, Inc., a gas and oil exploration company and O & R Development Inc., an industrial and corporate development company.

BUSINESS LINE ANALYSIS

(12/31/93)	Rev(%)	Inc(%)
Electric	75.3	82.3
Gas	24.7	17.7
Total	100.0	100.0

ANNUAL EARNINGS AND DIVIDENDS PER SHARE

	1993	1992	1991	1990	1989	1988	1987
Earnings Per Share	**3.06**	**3.15**	**3.12**	**[1] 2.99**	**3.14**	**3.18**	**2.93**
Dividends Per Share	**2.49**	**2.43**	**2.37**	**2.32**	**2.28**	**2.24**	**2.20**
Dividend Payout %	**N.M.**	**77.1**	**76.0**	**77.6**	**72.6**	**70.4**	**75.1**

[1] Before extraord. item

ANNUAL FINANCIAL DATA

	1993	1992	1991	1990	1989	1988	1987
RECORD OF EARNINGS (IN MILLIONS):							
Total Operating Revenues	971.4	844.2	732.0	559.2	536.2	486.7	451.3
Depreciation & Amort	34.5	34.5	32.1	24.2	27.8	26.9	...
Maintenance	42.9	42.5	40.3	36.7	32.1	32.6	32.4
Income Taxes	25.9	22.2	19.7	15.4	20.2	25.2	26.3
Income From Operations	82.5	79.2	77.3	74.4	75.3	74.6	60.2
Total Interest Charges	34.1	35.4	34.1	33.4	31.2	28.8	25.9
Net Income	44.8	45.8	44.9	[1] 42.6	44.1	44.2	40.9
Aver. Shs. Outstg. (000)	13,532	13,438	13,238	13,040	12,840	12,659	12,630
[1] Before extra. item cr$7,205,000.							
BALANCE SHEET (IN MILLIONS):							
Gross Plant	1,239.3	1,197.2	1,151.6	1,091.4	1,037.3	992.7	942.4
Accumulated Depreciation	385.3	360.4	336.8	311.7	300.6	285.0	262.8
Prop, Plant & Equip, Net	854.0	836.8	814.8	779.7	736.7	707.7	679.6
Long-term Debt	381.1	381.5	378.6	373.8	292.7	290.4	288.8
Net Stockholders' Equity	419.3	411.6	394.3	386.0	369.7	354.5	344.0
Total Assets	1,281.0	1,127.5	1,087.8	1,036.9	978.3	922.2	886.7
Year End Shs Outstg (000)	13,532	13,531	13,328	13,132	12,932	12,728	12,631
STATISTICAL RECORD:							
Book Value Per Share	27.79	27.22	26.33	25.46	24.17	23.23	22.45
Op. Inc/Net Pl %	9.7	9.5	9.5	9.5	10.2	10.5	8.9
Dep/Gr. Pl %	2.8	2.9	2.8	2.2	2.7	2.7	2.5
Accum. Dep/Gr. Pl %	31.1	30.1	29.2	28.6	29.0	28.7	28.4
Return on Equity %	10.7	11.1	11.4	11.3	12.4	13.0	12.5
Average Yield %	5.8	6.5	6.8	7.9	7.7	7.3	7.2
P/E Ratio	15.5-12.6	13.3-10.3	12.5-9.9	10.8-8.7	10.2-8.7	10.5-8.8	12.4-8.5
Price Range	47½-38⅝	41⅞-32⅜	39-30⅞	32⅜-26⅛	32-27¼	33½-27⅞	36¼-25

Statistics are as originally reported.

OFFICERS:
J.F. Smith, Chmn. & C.E.O.
V.J. Blanchet, Jr., Pres. & C.O.O.
P.J. Chambers, Jr., Sr. V.P. & C.F.O.
V.A. Roque, V.P., Gen. Couns. & Sec.

INCORPORATED: NY, May, 1926

PRINCIPAL OFFICE: One Blue Hill Plaza, Pearl River, NY 10965

TELEPHONE NUMBER: (914) 352-6000
FAX: (914) 577-2730
NO. OF EMPLOYEES: 1,700
ANNUAL MEETING: In May
SHAREHOLDERS: 24,328 common; 570, pfd.; 1,038, prefer.
INSTITUTIONAL HOLDINGS:
No. of Institutions: 75
Shares Held: 1,622,794

REGISTRAR(S): Chemical Bank, New York, NY

TRANSFER AGENT(S): Chemical Bank, New York, NY

SYMBOL OSH A
Rec. Pr. 23¾

OSHAWA GROUP LTD.

YIELD 2.1%
P/E RATIO 95.0

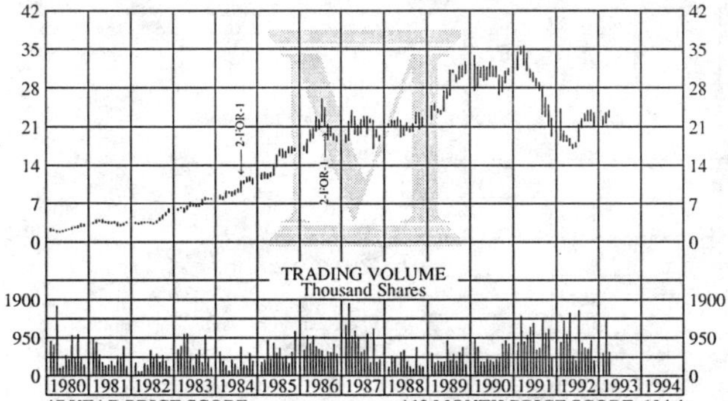

***7 YEAR PRICE SCORE ... *12 MONTH PRICE SCORE 104.4**

*NYSE COMPOSITE INDEX=100

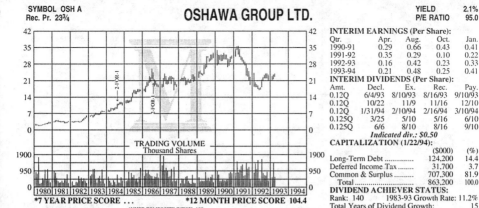

INTERIM EARNINGS (Per Share):

Qtr.	Apr.	Aug.	Oct.	Jan.
1990-91	0.29	0.66	0.43	0.41
1991-92	0.35	0.29	0.10	0.22
1992-93	0.16	0.42	0.23	0.33
1993-94	0.21	0.48	0.25	0.41

INTERIM DIVIDENDS (Per Share):

Amt.	Decl.	Ex.	Rec.	Pay.
0.12Q	6/4/93	8/10/93	8/16/93	9/10/93
0.12Q	10/22	11/9	11/16	12/10
0.12Q	1/31/94	2/10/94	2/16/94	3/10/94
0.125Q	3/25	5/10	5/16	6/10
0.125Q	6/6	8/10	8/16	9/10

Indicated div.: $0.50

CAPITALIZATION (1/22/94):

	($000)	(%)
Long-Term Debt	124,200	14.4
Deferred Income Tax	31,700	3.7
Common & Surplus	707,300	81.9
Total	863,200	100.0

DIVIDEND ACHIEVER STATUS:
Rank: 140 1983-93 Growth Rate: 11.2%
Total Years of Dividend Growth: 15

RECENT DEVELOPMENTS: For the year ended 1/22/94, net income rose 20.1% to $50.2 million, or $1.35 per share, from $41.8 million, or $1.14 per share, for the prior year. Included in earnings were charges of $8.4 million for the cost to reconfigure stores and warehouses, settlement of the final landlord claim related to the 11/90 disposal of Towers, the Company's former department store division, and other expenses not typical of current operations. Consolidated sales and other revenue increased 14.3% to $5.73 billion from $5.01 billion a year ago. Revenue was enhanced by the full-year results of wholesale and retail food businesses purchased last year. Growth was moderated, however, by the low rate of food price inflation and declining tobacco volume. Food distribution revenue totaled $5.29 million, or 92.4% of total revenue, up 15.6% over $4.58 billion reported in the prior year.

BUSINESS

OSHAWA GROUP LTD. is a Canadian company operating in nine provinces. The Company services 716 "IGA" food stores as well as 808 additional independent grocers trading under the names "Knechtel," "Food Town," "Bonichoix" and others. Oshawa manages 110 corporate stores including 45 "IGA," 37 "Food City" and 16 "Price Chopper" supermarkets. Through its foodservice operation, the Company wholesales to restaurants, hotels and institutions such as hospitals, schools and company cafeterias. Oshawa also has 146 pharmacies operating in Ontario and Manitoba under the name "Pharma Plus." Other divisions include produce packaging and wholesaling facilities, public cold storage warehouses, a dairy, a uniform rental company and revenue-producing real estate. Oshawa's Class A shares are listed on both the Toronto Stock Exchange and the Montreal Exchange.

BUSINESS LINE ANALYSIS

(1/22/94)	Rev(%)	Inc(%)
Food..........................	92.4	83.8
Drug Stores...............	7.3	5.2
Real Estate................	0.3	11.0
Total	100.0	100.0

ANNUAL EARNINGS AND DIVIDENDS PER SHARE

	1/22/94	1/23/93	1/25/92	1/26/91	1/27/90	1/28/89	1/23/88
Earnings Per Share	**1.35**	**1.14**	**0.96**	**[1] 1.95**	**2.11**	**1.78**	**1.56**
Dividends Per Share	**0.475**	**0.46**	**0.455**	**0.43**	**0.39**	**0.35**	**0.31**
Dividend Payout %	**35.2**	**40.4**	**47.4**	**22.1**	**18.5**	**19.7**	**19.9**

[1] Before disc. oper.

ANNUAL FINANCIAL DATA

	1/22/94	1/23/93	1/25/92	1/26/91	1/27/90	1/28/89	1/23/88
RECORD OF EARNINGS (IN MILLIONS):							
Sales and Other Revenue	5,727.8	5,011.4	4,613.8	4,598.8	4,948.2	4,274.5	3,804.0
Costs and Expenses	5,590.2	4,904.1	4,531.9	4,456.7	4,793.2	4,144.4	3,685.3
Depreciation & Amort	53.1	43.3	38.2	33.8	35.5	29.0	25.2
Operating Income	84.5	64.0	38.6	102.0	107.0	94.6	88.5
Earn Bef Income Taxes	77.9	64.2	54.5	112.7	114.0	99.4	94.2
Income Taxes	27.7	22.4	19.4	42.4	44.4	42.5	44.3
Net Income	50.2	41.8	35.1	[1] 70.3	69.6	56.9	49.9
Aver. Shs. Outstg. (000)	37,235	36,800	36,499	36,029	32,915	32,037	31,940
[1] Before disc. op. dr$9,948,000.							
BALANCE SHEET (IN MILLIONS):							
Cash & Short-term Invests	35.1	5.2	94.8	112.4	37.7	3.1	46.9
Receivables, Net	260.0	237.0	198.2	198.1	161.5	136.6	115.9
Inventories	318.1	313.4	285.5	286.5	365.8	324.8	246.8
Gross Property	760.3	712.3	564.9	536.8	530.3	452.0	367.0
Accumulated Depreciation	286.4	245.8	214.7	190.2	186.8	161.0	139.3
Long-Term Debt	124.2	23.7	23.2	25.3	30.5	38.2	38.2
Net Stockholders' Equity	707.3	664.9	633.2	607.0	552.9	389.6	341.4
Total Assets	1,259.7	1,158.1	1,006.4	994.0	953.8	795.2	672.9
Total Current Assets	627.3	566.1	588.2	605.7	579.2	479.4	420.0
Total Current Liabilities	371.1	411.0	290.8	303.2	348.8	345.8	272.4
Net Working Capital	256.2	155.1	297.4	302.5	230.4	133.6	147.6
Year End Shs Outstg (000)	36,825	36,301	36,618	36,346	35,844	32,114	32,114
STATISTICAL RECORD:							
Operating Profit Margin %	1.5	1.3	0.8	2.2	2.2	2.2	2.3
Book Value Per Share	17.07	16.47	17.29	16.70	15.42	12.13	10.63
Return on Equity %	7.1	6.3	5.5	11.6	12.6	14.6	14.6
Return on Assets %	4.0	3.6	3.5	7.1	7.3	7.2	7.4
Average Yield %	2.1	2.2	1.6	1.4	1.4	1.6	1.5
P/E Ratio	18.7-14.9	21.2-14.9	37.1-21.7	17.4-13.7	15.5-10.5	13.3-10.7	15.4-10.9
Price Range	25¼-20⅛	24⅛-17	35⅝-20⅞	33⅞-26¾	32¾-22¼	23⅝-19⅛	24-17

Statistics are as originally reported.
All figures are in Canadian dollars.

OFFICERS:
A.P. Graham, Chmn. & C.E.O.
J.A. Wolfe, Pres. & C.O.O.
R.E. Boyd, Exec. V.P.-Fin. & C.F.O.
L. Eisen, Treas.
H.J. Wolfe, Sec.

PRINCIPAL OFFICE: 302 The East Mall, Etobicoke, Ontario, Canada M9B 6B8

TELEPHONE NUMBER: (416) 236-1971

FAX: (416) 236-2071

NO. OF EMPLOYEES: 17,041

ANNUAL MEETING: In June

SHAREHOLDERS:

INSTITUTIONAL HOLDINGS:
No. of Institutions: 46
Shares Held: 3,842,550

REGISTRAR(S): Montreal Trust Co., Montreal, Vancouver, Calgary, Regina, Winnipeg, Toronto, Canada

TRANSFER AGENT(S): Montreal Trust Co., Montreal, Vancouver, Calgary, Regina, Winnipeg, Toronto, Canada

NASDAQ SYMBOL OTTR
Rec. Pr. 31¼ (Marginable)

OTTER TAIL POWER CO.

YIELD 5.5%
P/E RATIO 14.1

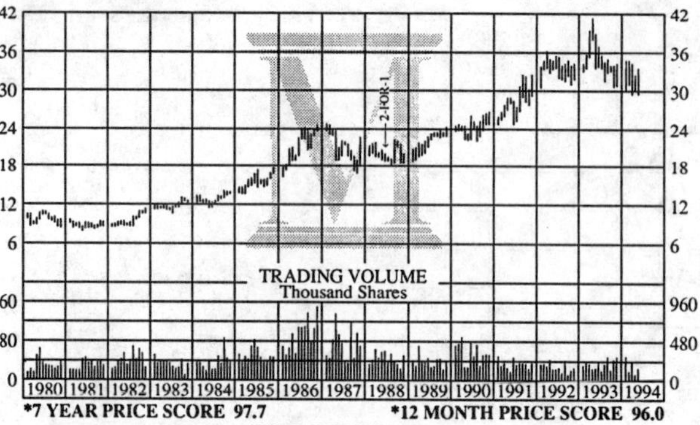

*7 YEAR PRICE SCORE 97.7 *12 MONTH PRICE SCORE 96.0
*NYSE COMPOSITE INDEX=100

INTERIM EARNINGS (Per Share):

Qtr.	Mar.	June	Sept.	Dec.
1990	0.70	0.43	0.42	0.44
1991	0.80	0.44	0.43	0.47
1992	0.75	0.53	0.36	0.53
1993	0.77	0.46	0.45	0.54

INTERIM DIVIDENDS (Per Share):

Amt.	Decl.	Ex.	Rec.	Pay.
0.42Q	4/13/93	5/10/93	5/14/93	6/10/93
0.42Q	7/19	8/9	8/13	9/10
0.42Q	10/19	11/8	11/15	12/10
0.43Q	1/31/94	2/9/94	2/15/94	3/10/94
0.43Q	4/12	5/9	5/13	6/10

Indicated div.: $1.72

CAPITALIZATION (12/31/93):

	($000)	(%)
Long-Term Debt	166,563	51.7
Deferred Income Tax	116,458	36.2
Preferred Stock	38,831	12.1
Common & Surplus	. . .	0.0
Total	321,852	100.0
Current Debt	9,356	

DIVIDEND ACHIEVER STATUS:
Rank: 319 1983-93 Growth Rate: 3.3%
Total Years of Dividend Growth: 18

RECENT DEVELOPMENTS: For the twelve months ended 12/31/93, earnings per share were $2.23, an increase of $0.06 over the $2.17 recorded in 1992. Net income of $27.4 million for 1993 is up from the $26.5 million attained by the Company in 1992. Total revenues were up to $265.2 million in 1993, above the $209.5 million reported in 1992. Electric revenues advanced 8.6% to $192.3 million from $177.1 million in 1992. Revenues reported from diversified operations in 1993 were $40.9 million compared with $32.4 million last year. For the fourth quarter ended 12/31/93, earnings per share were $0.54 compared with $$0.53 posted in the fourth quarter of 1992. Net income for the fourth quarter was $6.7 million versus $6.6 million in the comparable period of 1992. Total revenues for the quarter were $67.4 million compared with $58.8 million in the prior year.

BUSINESS

OTTER TAIL POWER COMPANY is an operating electric utility engaged in the production, transmission and distribution and sale of electric energy in western Minnesota, eastern North Dakota and northeastern South Dakota. OTTR, through its subsidiaries, is also engaged in telephone and other nonutility operations. The aggregate population of OTTR's retail service area is approximately 230,000. The territory served by OTTR is predominately agricultural, including part of the Red River Valley. In this service area of 423 communities, the only communities served that have a population in excess of 10,000 are Jamestown, North Dakota; Fergus Falls, Minnesota; and Bemidji, Minnesota. The total number of electric customers is 121,997. Quadrant Co. operates a municipal building facility. Mid-States Development, Inc. owns six nonutility businesses in such industries as manufacturing (fabricated metal parts and agricultural equipment), radio broadcasting, and utility contracting for overhead and underground systems. North Central Utilities, Inc. owns RD Communications, Inc., an independent telephone company.

ANNUAL EARNINGS AND DIVIDENDS PER SHARE

	1993	1992	1991	1990	1989	1988	1987
Earnings Per Share	**2.22**	**2.17**	**2.15**	**1.99**	**1.94**	**1.92**	**1.61**
Dividends Per Share	**1.68**	**1.64**	**1.60**	**1.56**	**1.52**	**1 1.48**	**1.46**
Dividend Payout %	**75.7**	**75.6**	**74.4**	**78.4**	**78.4**	**77.1**	**90.7**

1 100% stk. div., 6/88.

ANNUAL FINANCIAL DATA

	1993	1992	1991	1990	1989	1988	1987
RECORD OF EARNINGS (IN THOUSANDS):							
Total Operating Revenues	265,227	209,538	179,660	172,541	172,840	178,221	167,002
Depreciation & Amort	20,512	18,697	17,816	17,431	17,849	18,944	17,768
Electric Maintenance	12,914	10,927	11,866	10,760	10,638	9,622	10,076
Prov for Fed Inc Taxes	14,331	14,024	14,328	13,850	12,948	17,361	17,083
Operating Income	39,655	38,362	36,121	34,072	34,561	35,853	34,742
Interest Charges, Net	13,825	13,165	11,462	9,965	10,337	10,371	11,865
Net Income	27,369	26,538	26,096	24,852	25,266	25,317	21,566
Aver. Shs. Outstg.	11,180	11,185	11,196	11,455	11,917	11,968	11,962
BALANCE SHEET (IN THOUSANDS):							
Gross Plant	722,249	691,567	654,835	638,274	616,298	605,593	596,486
Accumulated Depreciation	270,385	252,663	236,506	225,539	212,004	198,183	183,868
Net Plant	451,864	438,904	418,329	412,735	404,294	407,410	412,618
Long-term Debt	166,563	159,295	146,103	134,929	118,959	121,815	124,485
Net Stockholders' Equity	18,000	18,000	13,150	13,705	14,815	15,925	17,035
Total Assets	563,905	530,456	487,663	474,356	467,233	482,570	467,082
Year End Shares Outstg	11,180	11,180	11,185	11,223	11,795	11,968	11,968
STATISTICAL RECORD:							
Op. Inc/Net Pl %	8.8	8.7	8.6	8.3	8.5	8.8	8.4
Dep/Gr. Pl %	. . .	2.5	2.7	2.7	2.9	3.1	3.0
Accum. Dep/Gr. Pl %	. . .	36.5	36.1	35.3	34.4	32.7	30.8
Average Yield %	4.7	4.9	5.6	6.4	7.0	7.3	7.0
P/E Ratio	18.5-13.7	16.7-14.1	15.1-11.5	13.4-11.1	12.6-9.7	11.6-9.5	15.5-10.5
Price Range	41¼-30⅝	36¼-30½	32½-24¾	26¾-22	24⅜-18¾	22¼-18¼	24⅞-16¾

Statistics are as originally reported.

OFFICERS:
J.C. MacFarlane, Chmn., Pres. & C.E.O.
D.R. Emmen, Sr. V.P.-Fin., Treas. & C.F.O.
J.D. Myster, V.P.-Gov. & Legal & Sec.

INCORPORATED: MN, Jul., 1907

PRINCIPAL OFFICE: 215 South Cascade Street, Box 496, Fergus Falls, MN 56538-0496

TELEPHONE NUMBER: (218) 739-8200
FAX: (218) 739-8218
NO. OF EMPLOYEES: 108
ANNUAL MEETING: In April
SHAREHOLDERS: 9,530
INSTITUTIONAL HOLDINGS:
No. of Institutions: 51
Shares Held: 1,170,809

REGISTRAR(S): Community First National Bank, Fergus Falls, MN

TRANSFER AGENT(S): Shareholder Services, Fergus Falls, MN 56537
Norwest Bank Minnesota, N.A., St. Paul, MN

PACIFIC TELECOM, INC.

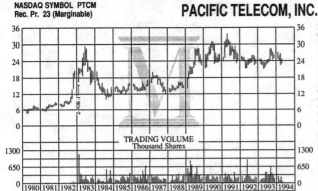

*7 YEAR PRICE SCORE 85.5   *12 MONTH PRICE SCORE 98.8
*NYSE COMPOSITE INDEX=100

INTERIM EARNINGS (Per Share):

Qtr.	Mar.	June	Sept.	Dec.
1990	0.75	0.49	0.51	0.71
1991	0.46	0.46	0.72	0.63
1992	0.53	0.30	0.37	0.50
1993	0.36	0.35	0.35	0.43

INTERIM DIVIDENDS (Per Share):

Amt.	Decl.	Ex.	Rec.	Pay.
0.33Q	4/29/93	5/17/93	5/21/93	6/7/93
0.33Q	7/23	8/16	8/20	9/6
0.33Q	10/29	11/5	11/12	12/6
0.33Q	2/4/94	2/14/94	2/18/94	3/7/94
0.33Q	4/28	5/16	5/20	6/6

Indicated div.: $1.32

CAPITALIZATION (12/31/93):

	($000)	(%)
Long-Term Debt	426,669	34.0
Deferred Income Tax	171,781	13.7
Minority Interest	16,770	1.4
Common & Surplus	638,711	50.9
Total	1,253,931	100.0

DIVIDEND ACHIEVER STATUS:
Rank: 263   1983-93 Growth Rate: 6.2%
Total Years of Dividend Growth: 17

RECENT DEVELOPMENTS: For the year ended 12/31/93, income from continuing operations was $59.1 million, compared with $67.2 million in 1992. PTCM recorded a $60.4 million after-tax gain from discontinued operations in 1993 as a result of the sale of its international operations to IDB Communication Group, Inc. Operating revenues for the year increased slightly to $709.1 million from $704.5 million in 1992. For the quarter, net income was $16.8 million, compared with income from continuing operations of $19.6 million for the same period in 1992. Operating revenues decreased to $178.8 million from $186.3 million in 1992. Revenues increased from continued access line growth in local exchange operations and out-of-period revenues, partially offset by the revenue effect of rate base reductions and lower private line revenues in long distance operations, and reduced sales on PTCM's trans-Pacific fiber optic cable.

BUSINESS

PACIFIC TELECOM, INC., operates local exchange systems across an eleven-state service territory, a state-wide long-distance network in Alaska and a cellular telelphone business based in the Upper Midwest. PTCM is also one of the founding companies in the North Pacific Cable, the first direct undersea fiber optic cable between the U.S. and Japan. PTI Communications is PTCM's local exchange business and serves more than 400 communities in the Pacific Northwest, the Midwest and Alaska. Over the last five years, the Company's total customer access lines have increased 66 percent to 398,700. PTCM's long distance subsidiary, Alascom, serves Alaska through more than 220 earth stations connected by the Aurora II satellite, 3,300 miles of microwave radio systems and an undersea fiber optic connection to the lower 48 states. PTCM's cellular telephone business has ownership interests in 29 rural and metropolitan cellular markets. These markets are largely concentrated in Wisconsin, but PTCM also has ownership positions in Michigan, Minnesota, South Dakota, Alaska, Oregon and Washington.

ANNUAL EARNINGS AND DIVIDENDS PER SHARE

	1993	1992	1991	1990	1989	1988	1987
Earnings Per Share	1.49	① 1.70	② 2.27	③ 2.46	1.91	1.52	1.16
Dividends Per Share	1.32	1.305	1.235	1.13	1.02	0.96	0.88
Dividend Payout %	88.6	76.8	54.4	45.9	53.4	63.2	75.9

① Before disc. oper.

ANNUAL FINANCIAL DATA

RECORD OF EARNINGS (IN MILLIONS):

	1993	1992	1991	1990	1989	1988	1987
Total Operating Revenues	709.1	704.5	724.4	638.0	657.0	552.1	525.0
Costs and Expenses	461.4	454.4	449.7	383.7	406.6	337.3	288.8
Depreciation & Amort	106.8	111.5	115.2	100.2	112.7	97.0	105.6
Operating Income	140.8	138.6	159.6	154.1	137.7	117.8	130.6
Income Bef Income Taxes	82.9	99.8	120.4	137.5	102.9	69.3	95.7
Income Taxes	23.8	32.5	30.9	42.1	29.4	10.9	51.0
Net Income	① 59.1	② 67.2	③ 89.5	④ 95.4	73.5	58.4	44.6
Aver. Shs. Outstg. (000)	39,584	39,526	39,477	38,768	38,395	38,395	38,318

① Before disc. op. cr$60,444,000. ② Before disc. op. dr$45,741,000. ③ Before disc. op. dr$8,431,000. ④ Before disc. op. dr$5,186,000.

BALANCE SHEET (IN MILLIONS):

	1993	1992	1991	1990	1989	1988	1987
Cash & Temp Cash Invests	4.9	9.7	10.4	16.3	22.8	12.9	5.2
Receivables, Net	...	...	105.3	136.3	161.9	147.5	132.2
Inventories	81.7	102.2	111.3	126.6	33.8	26.1	24.7
Gross Property	1,664.4	1,631.9	1,688.5	1,672.7	1,562.4	1,456.1	1,280.5
Accumulated Depreciation	741.1	696.0	661.3	680.2	662.8	583.9	477.1
Long-Term Debt	426.7	571.6	528.4	480.9	294.0	302.4	323.2
Net Stockholders' Equity	638.7	569.8	598.5	563.9	491.7	456.6	434.2
Total Assets	1,486.3	1,607.3	1,685.7	1,725.0	1,229.1	1,242.4	1,165.8
Total Current Assets	224.3	238.4	385.7	438.4	221.0	192.0	167.7
Total Current Liabilities	163.4	220.0	383.7	486.6	245.0	289.2	188.0
Net Working Capital	60.8	18.4	1.9	d48.3	d24.0	d97.3	d20.4
Year End Shs Outstg (000)	39,609	39,545	39,487	39,408	38,395	38,395	38,328

STATISTICAL RECORD:

	1993	1992	1991	1990	1989	1988	1987
Book Value Per Share	10.82	9.12	11.05	10.06	11.20	9.77	9.22
Return on Equity %	9.2	11.8	15.0	16.9	15.0	12.8	10.3
Average Yield %	5.3	5.5	4.3	4.3	4.7	6.6	5.5
P/E Ratio	19.3-14.1	15.3-12.5	14.9-10.2	12.6-8.6	15.2-7.3	10.9-8.4	17.2-10.6
Price Range	28¾-21	26-21¼	33¾-23¼	31-21¼		29-14	16½-12¾	20-12¼

Statistics are as originally reported.

OFFICERS:
C.E. Robinson, Chmn., Pres. & C.E.O.
J.H. Huesgen, Exec. V.P. & C.F.O.
B.M. Wirkkala, V.P. & Treas.
D.T. Wonnell, V.P. & Corp. Sec.

INCORPORATED: WA, Jul., 1955

PRINCIPAL OFFICE: 805 Broadway, P.O. Box 9901, Vancouver, WA 98668-8701

TELEPHONE NUMBER: (206) 696-0983

NO. OF EMPLOYEES: 2,834

ANNUAL MEETING: In April

SHAREHOLDERS: 4,435

INSTITUTIONAL HOLDINGS:
No. of Institutions: 48
Shares Held: 2,236,768

REGISTRAR(S): First Interstate Bank of California, Calabasas, CA 91302

TRANSFER AGENT(S): First Interstate Bank of California, Calabasas, CA 91302

PALL CORP.

YIELD 2.6%
P/E RATIO 16.5

*7 YEAR PRICE SCORE 100.4 *12 MONTH PRICE SCORE 93.1
*NYSE COMPOSITE INDEX=100

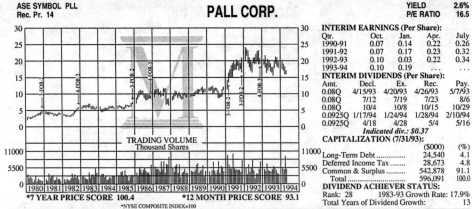

TRADING VOLUME
Thousand Shares

INTERIM EARNINGS (Per Share):

Qtr.	Oct.	Jan.	Apr.	July
1990-91	0.07	0.14	0.22	0.26
1991-92	0.07	0.17	0.23	0.32
1992-93	0.10	0.03	0.22	0.34
1993-94	0.10	0.19	...	...

INTERIM DIVIDENDS (Per Share):

Amt.	Decl.	Ex.	Rec.	Pay.
0.08Q	4/15/93	4/20/93	4/26/93	5/7/93
0.08Q	7/12	7/19	7/23	8/6
0.08Q	10/4	10/8	10/15	10/29
0.0925Q	1/17/94	1/24/94	1/28/94	2/10/94
0.0925Q	4/18	4/28	5/4	5/16

Indicated div.: $0.37

CAPITALIZATION (7/31/93):

	($000)	(%)
Long-Term Debt	24,540	4.1
Deferred Income Tax	28,673	4.8
Common & Surplus	542,878	91.1
Total	596,091	100.0

DIVIDEND ACHIEVER STATUS:

Rank: 28 1983-93 Growth Rate: 17.9%
Total Years of Dividend Growth: 13

RECENT DEVELOPMENTS: For the three months ended 1/29/94, net income jumped to $22.0 million from $3.3 million, including a pretax charge of $26.7 million for restructuring, in the prior-year period. Sales improved slightly to $169.7 million from $167.5 million. Foreign currency exchange rates reduced sales by $2.3 million. A 9% reduction in Military Aerospace sales was offset by sales growth of 10% in the Industrial Hydraulics Division, while overall Aeropower sales remained flat.

PROSPECTS: Pall's earnings, of which a sizeable amount are derived outside the United States, continue to be affected by the sluggish European economy. However, orders are increasing in many of Pall's business segments as the U.S. economy recovers. The Company's entry into the high end of the industrial separations market is exposing PLL to industrial markets with a sales potential approaching that of its traditional filtration products.

BUSINESS

PALL CORP. is a leading supplier of fine filters primarily produced by the Company using its proprietary filter media, and other fluid clarification equipment for the removal of solid, liquid and gaseous contaminants from a variety of liquids and gases. The Company serves its diversified customer base through integrated businesses in the U.S. and Europe. Sales (and operating profits) in 1993 were derived as follows: fluid processing 23% (12%), aeropower 26% (21%), and health care 51% (67%). Sales (operating profit) in the Western Hemisphere accounted for 44% (43%) of the total, with Europe and the Pacific Basin accounting for 42% (50%) and 14% (7%), respectively.

ANNUAL EARNINGS AND DIVIDENDS PER SHARE

	7/31/93	8/1/92	8/3/91	7/28/90	7/29/89	7/30/88	8/1/87
Earnings Per Share	0.68	① 0.77	0.69	0.57	0.50	0.52	0.44
Dividends Per Share	0.33	② 0.27	0.22	0.187	0.16	0.134	③ 0.113
Dividend Payout %	48.5	35.1	31.8	32.6	31.8	25.8	26.0

① Before acctg. chg. ② 3-for-2 stk split, 12/30/91 ③ 33.333% stk. div., 12/86.

ANNUAL FINANCIAL DATA

RECORD OF EARNINGS (IN THOUSANDS):

Total Revenues	691,935	690,464	663,094	575,582	505,888	435,482	389,669
Costs and Expenses	543,785	519,223	499,643	429,515	375,936	327,450	289,277
Depreciation	35,188	34,360	31,854	26,803	24,673	21,895	18,033
Operating Income	112,962	136,881	131,597	119,264	105,279	86,137	82,359
Earn Bef Income Taxes	104,279	126,201	115,825	97,403	84,069	84,862	67,774
Income Taxes	25,967	35,968	35,904	31,168	26,388	27,458	19,688
Net Income	78,312	① 90,233	79,921	66,235	57,681	57,404	48,086
Aver. Shs. Outstg.	115,856	116,928	116,193	115,735	114,873	111,095	110,360

① Before acctg. change cr$2,475,000.

BALANCE SHEET (IN THOUSANDS):

Cash and Cash Equivalents	107,052	101,329	59,069	81,401	128,743	91,636	85,975
Receivables, Net	216,662	220,074	168,306	173,669	155,262	131,891	123,404
Inventories	127,525	144,947	140,923	142,931	130,035	101,354	96,430
Gross Property	544,002	561,104	489,449	454,704	366,767	306,732	273,616
Accumulated Depreciation	186,382	195,041	157,616	135,735	110,943	89,339	77,772
Long-Term Debt	24,540	59,003	51,663	56,343	40,419	39,508	39,957
Net Stockholders' Equity	542,878	545,595	487,998	441,439	373,692	321,353	267,182
Total Assets	902,273	912,876	774,459	786,364	707,274	570,444	521,524
Total Current Assets	470,288	482,724	385,065	414,721	433,339	339,260	317,962
Total Current Liabilities	277,760	259,391	202,753	261,306	268,928	185,540	188,083
Net Working Capital	192,528	223,333	182,312	153,415	164,411	153,720	129,879
Year End Shares Outstg	116,063	86,718	116,181	115,915	115,639	111,452	110,780

STATISTICAL RECORD:

Operating Profit Margin %	16.3	19.8	19.8	20.7	20.8	19.8	21.1
Book Value Per Share	4.68	6.29	4.18	3.81	3.23	2.88	2.41
Return on Equity %	14.4	16.5	16.4	15.0	15.4	17.9	18.0
Return on Assets %	8.7	9.9	10.3	8.4	8.2	10.1	9.2
Average Yield %	1.8	1.3	1.4	1.8	1.5	1.4	1.2
P/E Ratio	31.8-23.0	31.3-21.4	30.3-16.3	21.9-15.4	24.3-18.0	21.2-15.4	26.7-14.8
Price Range	21⅝-15⅝	24⅛-16½	20⅞-11¼	12½-8¾	12⅛-9	11-8	11¾-6½

Statistics are as originally reported.

OFFICERS:
M.G. Hardy, Chmn. & C.E.O.
E. Krasnoff, Pres. & C.O.O.
J. Hayward-Surry, Exec. V.P., Treas. & C.F.O.

INCORPORATED: NY, Jul., 1946

PRINCIPAL OFFICE: 2200 Northern Blvd., East Hills, NY 11548

TELEPHONE NUMBER: (516) 484-5400
FAX: (516) 484-5228
NO. OF EMPLOYEES: 454
ANNUAL MEETING: In November
SHAREHOLDERS: 2,270
INSTITUTIONAL HOLDINGS:
No. of Institutions: 346
Shares Held: 75,821,839 (adj.)

REGISTRAR(S): Wachovia Bank & Trust Co., N.A., Winston-Salem, NC 27102

TRANSFER AGENT(S): Wachovia Bank & Trust Co., N.A., Winston-Salem, NC 27102

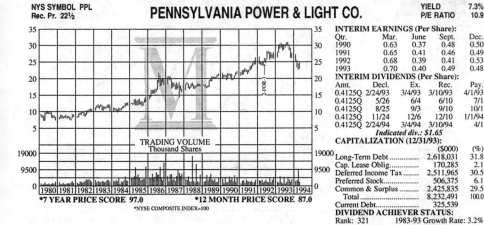

PENNSYLVANIA POWER & LIGHT CO.

YIELD 7.3%
P/E RATIO 10.9

INTERIM EARNINGS (Per Share):

Qtr.	Mar.	June	Sept.	Dec.
1990	0.63	0.37	0.48	0.50
1991	0.65	0.41	0.46	0.49
1992	0.68	0.39	0.41	0.53
1993	0.70	0.40	0.49	0.48

INTERIM DIVIDENDS (Per Share):

Amt.	Decl.	Ex.	Rec.	Pay.
0.4125Q	2/24/93	3/4/93	3/10/93	4/1/93
0.4125Q	5/26	6/4	6/10	7/1
0.4125Q	8/25	9/3	9/10	10/1
0.4125Q	11/24	12/6	12/10	1/1/94
0.4125Q	2/24/94	3/4/94	3/10/94	4/1

Indicated div.: $1.65

CAPITALIZATION (12/31/93):

	($000)	(%)
Long-Term Debt	2,618,031	31.8
Cap. Lease Oblig.	170,285	2.1
Deferred Income Tax	2,511,965	30.5
Preferred Stock	506,375	6.1
Common & Surplus	2,425,835	29.5
Total	8,232,491	100.0
Current Debt	325,539	

DIVIDEND ACHIEVER STATUS:
Rank: 321   1983-93 Growth Rate: 3.2%
Total Years of Dividend Growth: 17

TRADING VOLUME
Thousand Shares

*7 YEAR PRICE SCORE 97.0   ***12 MONTH PRICE SCORE 87.0**

*NYSE COMPOSITE INDEX=100

RECENT DEVELOPMENTS: For the year ended 12/31/93, net income was $348.1 million versus $346.7 million in 1992. Revenues were down slightly to $2.73 billion. The improvement in earnings was primarily due to increasing economic activity in Pennsylvania and the effects of hot weather on sales. Residential and commercial electric sales were up 4.1% and 3.7%, respectively. Net income for the fourth quarter was $80.7 million, down 11.3%.

PROSPECTS: The Company has been successful in marketing and selling its available capacity to other capacity-short, investor-owned utilities. This successful marketing has bolstered earnings and returns, despite the absence of base rate increases since 1985. Construction expenditures will be higher over the next five years, but will not include any baseload plant construction.

BUSINESS

PENNSYLVANIA POWER & LIGHT CO. derives almost all of its revenues from electric service. It serves a 10,000 sq. mile territory in 29 counties in central eastern Pennsylvania. The area has a high percentage of open land as well as 116 communities with populations of over 5,000, the largest of which are Allentown, Bethlehem, Harrisburg, Hazelton, Lancaster, Scranton, Williamsport and Wilkes-Barre.

ELECTRIC REVENUES

(12/31/93)	($000)	(%)
Residential	905,650	33.2
Commercial	735,192	27.0
Industrial	524,160	19.2
Other Energy Sales	91,205	3.4
Sales to Other		
Utilities	313,578	11.5
Other	155,954	5.7
Total	2,725,739	100.0

ANNUAL EARNINGS AND DIVIDENDS PER SHARE

	1993	1992	1991	1990	1989	1988	1987
Earnings Per Share	2.07	2.02	2.01	1.98	2.03	1.87	1.66
Dividends Per Share	1.637	☐ 1.587	1.535	1.475	1.418	1.37	1.33
Dividend Payout %	79.1	78.6	76.7	74.7	70.0	73.5	80.1

☐ 2-for-1 stk split, 5/12/92

ANNUAL FINANCIAL DATA

RECORD OF EARNINGS (IN MILLIONS):

	1993	1992	1991	1990	1989	1988	1987
Operating Revenues	2,727.0	2,744.1	2,559.7	2,388.7	2,356.4	2,213.9	2,088.8
Depreciation & Amort	289.1	270.0	246.2	234.3	222.5	234.3	...
Maintenance	193.2	201.3	206.9	223.5	234.1	224.4	...
Income Taxes	235.2	228.3	217.4	196.3	207.2	191.2	237.8
Operating Income	562.8	573.4	582.3	590.4	618.9	605.1	584.6
Total Interest Charges	232.6	245.5	245.4	258.0	275.9	283.7	285.0
Net Income	348.1	346.7	348.4	343.9	353.4	332.0	302.5
Aver. Shs. Outstg. (000)	151,904	151,676	151,382	150,924	150,628	150,142	149,288

BALANCE SHEET (IN MILLIONS):

	1993	1992	1991	1990	1989	1988	1987
Gross Plant	9,550.4	9,219.2	8,934.0	8,749.0	8,553.1	8,374.9	7,921.4
Accumulated Depreciation	2,404.9	2,199.7	2,004.4	1,854.8	1,686.4	1,533.4	1,392.7
Prop Plant & Equipment	7,145.6	7,019.5	6,929.6	6,894.2	6,866.6	6,841.6	6,528.7
Long-term Debt	2,788.3	2,784.9	2,767.3	2,648.4	2,878.1	2,898.4	2,839.9
Net Stockholders' Equity	2,932.2	2,916.2	2,894.0	2,836.8	2,780.7	2,719.5	2,696.9
Total Assets	9,454.1	8,191.8	7,934.6	7,735.4	7,599.0	7,524.6	7,194.6
Year End Shs Outstg (000)	152,132	151,885	151,655	151,298	150,846	150,496	149,944

STATISTICAL RECORD:

	1993	1992	1991	1990	1989	1988	1987
Book Value Per Share	15.95	15.58	15.15	14.68	14.18	13.62	13.14
Op. Inc/Net Pl %	7.9	8.2	8.4	8.6	9.0	8.8	9.0
Dep/Gr. Pl %	3.0	2.8	2.7	2.5	2.3	2.2	2.1
Accum. Dep/Gr. Pl %	25.2	23.9	22.4	21.2	19.7	18.3	17.6
Return on Equity %	11.9	11.9	12.0	12.1	12.7	12.2	11.2
Average Yield %	5.7	6.1	6.5	7.1	7.3	7.7	7.6
P/E Ratio	15.0-12.6	14.0-11.8	13.1-10.4	11.3-9.9	10.6-8.4	10.2-8.9	12.5-8.7
Price Range	31-26⅛	28¼-23⅞	26⅜-20⅞	22¼-19½	21½-17⅛	19-16⅝	20¾-14⅜

Statistics are as originally reported.

OFFICERS:
W.F. Hecht, Chmn., Pres. & C.E.O.
G.D. Caliendo, Sr. V.P., Gen. Couns. & Sec.
R.E. Hill, C.F.O., V.P.-Fin. & Compt.

INCORPORATED: PA, Jun., 1920

PRINCIPAL OFFICE: Two North Ninth Street, Allentown, PA 18101-1179

TELEPHONE NUMBER: (215) 774-5151
FAX: (215) 774-4198
NO. OF EMPLOYEES: 7,981
ANNUAL MEETING: In April
SHAREHOLDERS: 129,394 (common)
INSTITUTIONAL HOLDINGS:
No. of Institutions: 243
Shares Held: 40,569,940

REGISTRAR(S): First Chicago Trust Co. of New York, New York, NY 10008
At Company's Office

TRANSFER AGENT(S): First Chicago Trust Co. of New York, New York, NY 10008
At Company's Office

PENTAIR, INC.

YIELD 2.1%
P/E RATIO 15.3

*7 YEAR PRICE SCORE 118.6   *12 MONTH PRICE SCORE 101.8
*NYSE COMPOSITE INDEX=100

INTERIM EARNINGS (Per Share):

Qtr.	Mar.	June	Sept.	Dec.
1991	0.37	0.47	0.61	0.76
1992	0.39	0.36	0.59	0.80
1993	0.45	0.46	0.66	0.69

INTERIM DIVIDENDS (Per Share):

Amt.	Decl.	Ex.	Rec.	Pay.
3-for-2	4/21/93	6/14/93	5/14/93	6/11/93
0.17Q	7/9	7/19	7/23	8/12
0.17Q	10/8	10/18	10/22	11/12
0.18Q	1/19/94	1/25/94	1/31/94	2/14/94
0.18Q	4/8	4/18	4/22	5/13

Indicated div.: $0.72

CAPITALIZATION (12/31/93):

	($000)	(%)
Long-Term Debt	238,856	38.7
Deferred Income Tax	7,518	1.2
Preferred Stock	69,380	11.2
Common & Surplus	301,469	48.9
Total	617,223	100.0

DIVIDEND ACHIEVER STATUS:
Rank: 206   1983-93 Growth Rate: 8.5%
Total Years of Dividend Growth: 17

RECENT DEVELOPMENTS: For the year ended 12/31/93, net income advanced 9% to $46.6 million from income before the cumulative effects of accounting changes of $42.8 million in 1992. Net sales for the year were $1.33 billion, an increase of 7% over 1992 net sales of $1.24 billion. Pentair's improved earnings in 1993 were driven primarily by the Company's domestic industrial businesses. Positive results by the domestic industrial businesses were partially offset by the effects of a weak European economy and an over-sup- plied paper market. Earnings of the Specialty Product Group, excluding the Brazilian operations sold in 1992, increased 8% over 1992, while the General Industrial Group contrib- uted a 9.3% earnings gain. Lincoln Industrial's North Ameri- can operation built both sales and earnings in 1993, only to have them offset by weakness in the Company's recession- plagued European markets. Paper Group earnings were down 6.3%.

BUSINESS

PENTAIR INC. is comprised of 10 businesses which manufacture wood- working equipment, electric power tools, sporting ammunition, electrical enclosures, automotive service equip- ment, industrial lubrication systems, material dispensing equipment, pumps and paper. Paper manufacturing is the largest business segment. Niagara of Wisconsin Paper Corporation, Niag- ara, Wisconsin, makes coated papers for magazines, catalogs and commer- cial printing. Miami Paper Corpora- tion, West Carrollton, Ohio offers book papers as well as printing and specialty grades. Flambeau Paper Corp., Par Falls, Wisconsin, produces business and commercial printing papers. Industrial manufacturing is an expanding segment of the company. Porter-Cable Corporation, Jackson, Tennessee, makes portable power tools for professional and industrial markets. Delta International Machin- ery Corporation, Pittsburgh, Penn- sylvania, produces woodworking machinery for construction trades and industry. Delta has plant in Tupelo, Mississippi, and subsidiaries in Guelph, Ontario and in Brazil.

ANNUAL EARNINGS AND DIVIDENDS PER SHARE

	1993	1992	1991	1990	1989	1988	1987
Earnings Per Share	2.26	② 2.15	2.20	1.69	1.99	2.47	1.36
Dividends Per Share	① 0.68	③ 0.653	0.613	0.587	0.533	④ 0.445	0.418
Dividend Payout %	30.1	30.4	27.9	34.8	26.8	18.0	30.7

① 3-for-2 stk split,06/14/93   ② Before acctg. chg.   ③ Bef acctg chge   ④ 10% stk. div., 6/88.

ANNUAL FINANCIAL DATA

RECORD OF EARNINGS (IN MILLIONS):

	1993	1992	1991	1990	1989	1988	1987
Total Revenues	1,328.2	1,238.7	1,169.1	1,175.9	1,163.6	823.3	789.2
Costs and Expenses	1,177.9	1,098.5	1,034.4	1,056.3	1,042.5	718.7	718.5
Depreciation & Amort	50.1	47.9	47.2	43.8	40.4	27.4	28.1
Operating Income	98.2	94.0	95.1	80.6	87.1	78.7	42.6
Income Bef Income Taxes	77.4	72.7	74.1	57.4	62.4	68.3	34.0
Income Taxes	30.8	29.9	33.0	24.4	26.0	28.5	12.1
Net Income	46.6	① 42.8	41.1	33.0	36.4	39.8	21.9
Aver. Shs. Outstg. (000)	17,891	15,936	15,775	15,779	16,070	16,212	14,954	14,360

① Before acctg. change dr$41,625,000.

BALANCE SHEET (IN MILLIONS):

	1993	1992	1991	1990	1989	1988	1987
Cash & Cash Equivalents	10.3	8.4	6.1	8.8	8.7	9.9	4.7
Receivables, Net	222.0	201.1	198.6	184.4	178.5	177.6	109.7
Inventories	198.8	182.9	158.6	155.4	166.7	181.1	122.1
Gross Property	621.6	551.9	491.1	457.8	448.3	373.9	268.1
Accumulated Depreciation	305.8	262.1	232.8	194.2	165.6	130.0	107.5
Long-Term Debt	238.9	211.5	198.4	224.7	251.1	252.1	90.7
Net Stockholders' Equity	370.8	337.4	349.8	316.2	306.9	281.7	208.6
Total Assets	958.8	869.4	790.6	768.9	781.4	744.7	440.4
Total Current Assets	438.8	398.6	372.6	356.6	360.2	374.9	260.4
Total Current Liabilities	218.5	209.5	185.2	172.2	167.7	167.4	118.8
Net Working Capital	220.3	189.2	187.4	184.4	192.5	207.5	141.7
Year End Shs Outstg (000)	18,135	10,548	15,685	15,551	16,223	16,046	13,032

STATISTICAL RECORD:

	1993	1992	1991	1990	1989	1988	1987
Operating Profit Margin %	7.4	7.6	8.1	6.9	7.5	9.6	5.4
Book Value Per Share	11.72	11.92	8.60	6.31	8.74	7.37	12.17
Return on Equity %	12.6	12.7	11.8	10.4	11.9	14.1	10.5
Return on Assets %	4.9	4.9	5.2	4.3	4.7	5.4	5.0
Average Yield %	2.0	2.4	2.7	3.3	2.6	2.4	2.8
P/E Ratio	18.3-11.5	14.9-10.6	13.1-7.2	12.9-8.3	11.7-8.5	9.7-5.2	14.2-7.5
Price Range	41¼-26	32-22⅞	28⅞-15⅞	21⅞-14	23⅜-17	23⅞-12⅞	19½-10¼

Statistics are as originally reported.

OFFICERS:
W.H. Buxton, Chmn., Pres. & C.E.O.
D.D. Harrison, Sr. V.P. & C.F.O.
R.T. Rueb, V.P. & Treas.

INCORPORATED: MN, Aug., 1966

PRINCIPAL OFFICE: 1500 County Road B2 West, St. Paul, MN 55113-3105

TELEPHONE NUMBER: (612) 636-7920
FAX: (612) 639-5251
NO. OF EMPLOYEES: 1,129 (approx.)
ANNUAL MEETING: In April
SHAREHOLDERS: 2,267
INSTITUTIONAL HOLDINGS:
No. of Institutions: 102
Shares Held: 7,413,763

REGISTRAR(S): Norwest Bank Minnesota, N.A., St. Paul, MN

TRANSFER AGENT(S): Norwest Bank Minnesota, N.A., St. Paul, MN

PEOPLES ENERGY CORP.

YIELD 6.6%
P/E RATIO 13.0

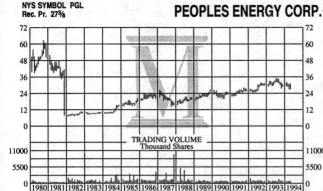

TRADING VOLUME
Thousand Shares

7 YEAR PRICE SCORE 99.2   **12 MONTH PRICE SCORE 94.0**
NYSE COMPOSITE INDEX=100

INTERIM EARNINGS (Per Share):

Qtr.	Dec.	Mar.	June	Sept.
1989-90	1.18	1.22	0.26	d0.59
1990-91	0.83	1.50	0.07	d0.35
1991-92	0.94	1.29	0.30	d0.43
1992-93	0.89	1.45	0.14	d0.38

INTERIM DIVIDENDS (Per Share):

Amt.	Decl.	Ex.	Rec.	Pay.
0.445Q	5/5/93	6/14/93	6/18/93	7/15/93
0.445Q	8/4	9/13	9/17	10/15
0.445Q	12/1	12/13	12/17	1/14/94
0.45Q	2/2/94	3/14/94	3/18/94	4/15
0.45Q	5/4	6/13	6/17	7/15

Indicated div.: $1.80

CAPITALIZATION (9/30/93):

	($000)	(%)
Long-Term Debt	528,075	37.9
Deferred Income Tax	236,340	17.0
Common & Surplus	628,451	45.1
Total	1,392,866	100.0
Current Debt	76,000	

DIVIDEND ACHIEVER STATUS:
Rank: 271   1983-93 Growth Rate: 5.9%
Total Years of Dividend Growth: 10

RECENT DEVELOPMENTS: For the year ended 12/31/93, net income advanced 15.1% to $81.3 million from $70.7 million last year. Revenues increased 12% to $1.26 billion. Results benefitted from a federal tax settlement and a rate increase by its Peoples Gas subsidiary and from weather that was nearly 5% colder compared with last year. Results were adversly affected by higher operating expenses. Net income for the quarter ended 12/31/93 was $39.0 million compared with $31.1 million last year.

PROSPECTS: Peoples Energy has implemented a hiring freeze, scaled back capital outlays for fiscal 1994 and refinanced debt at lower interest rates. Peoples Energy has reached a settlement with the IRS covering the Company's past income tax returns for fiscal years 1978 through 1990. Under the settlement, the IRS will pay the Company about $28 million, including principal and interest, to resolve disputed issues for the years in question.

BUSINESS

PEOPLES ENERGY CORP. is the holding company of two natural gas utilites that are engaged in the distribution of natural gas. Peoples Gas Light and Coke Co. distributes natural and synthetic gas to about 850,000 customers in Chicago. Another subsidiary, North Shore Gas Company, is engaged in the sale of gas at retail to 124,000 customers in Northeastern Illinois. On December 31, 1981, Peoples Energy implemented its corporate restructuring plan and spun-off its gas transmission contract drilling, oil and gas exploration and coal mining operations to shareholders in the form of a new holding company MidCon Corp.

REVENUES

(09/30/93)	($000)	(%)
Residential	929,407	73.8
Commercial	156,377	12.4
Industrial	41,354	3.3
Transportation	117,949	9.4
Other	13,854	1.1
Total	1,258,941	100.0

ANNUAL EARNINGS AND DIVIDENDS PER SHARE

	9/30/93	9/30/92	9/30/91	9/30/90	9/30/89	9/30/88	9/30/87
Earnings Per Share	2.11	2.06	2.05	2.07	⊡ 2.39	2.31	1.66
Dividends Per Share	1.775	1.75	1.705	1.645	1.58	1.50	1.41
Dividend Payout %	84.1	85.0	83.2	79.2	66.1	64.9	84.9

⊡ Before acctg. chg.

ANNUAL FINANCIAL DATA

RECORD OF EARNINGS (IN MILLIONS):

	9/30/93	9/30/92	9/30/91	9/30/90	9/30/89	9/30/88	9/30/87
Total Operating Revenues	1,258.9	1,096.8	1,103.7	1,165.2	1,188.0	1,116.8	1,174.6
Depreciation	60.8	57.3	55.4	54.8	49.8	46.8	45.1
Maintenance Expense	35.7	36.8	36.7	34.1	33.7	33.2	30.3
Prov for Fed Inc Taxes	37.6	33.6	35.0	37.3	41.4	46.8	47.9
Operating Income	113.0	107.3	105.0	102.1	103.0	105.5	84.3
Interest Expense	45.2	46.5	48.2	45.8	42.6	43.9	41.0
Net Income	73.4	70.4	67.0	67.5	⊡78.0	75.3	53.8
Aver. Shs. Outstg. (000)	34,809	34,151	32,741	32,672	32,596	32,549	32,479

⊡ Before acctg. change cr$9,663,000.

BALANCE SHEET (IN MILLIONS):

Gross Plant	1,951.0	1,843.6	1,746.9	1,667.8	1,593.0	1,472.2	1,400.0
Accumulated Depreciation	633.0	600.0	565.6	533.8	508.0	472.2	439.8
Prop, Plant & Equip, Net	1,318.0	1,243.6	1,181.2	1,134.0	1,085.1	1,000.0	960.2
Total Long-term Debt	528.1	489.6	493.0	502.2	452.8	459.8	409.7
Net Stockholders' Equity	628.5	629.1	571.9	563.9	554.1	521.1	497.0
Total Assets	1,765.9	1,615.8	1,541.4	1,534.2	1,470.6	1,407.9	1,379.8
Year End Shs Outstg (000)	34,823	34,774	32,762	32,701	32,614	32,569	32,510

STATISTICAL RECORD:

Book Value Per Share	18.05	17.72	16.95	16.61	16.20	15.09	14.27
Op. Inc/Net Pl %	8.6	8.6	8.9	9.0	9.5	10.5	8.8
Dep/Gr. Pl %	3.1	3.1	3.2	3.3	3.1	3.2	3.2
Accum. Dep/Gr. Pl %	32.4	32.5	32.4	32.0	31.9	32.1	31.4
Return on Equity %	11.7	11.4	12.1	12.4	14.8	15.3	11.6
Average Yield %	5.7	6.3	6.8	7.1	6.9	8.1	6.9
P/E Ratio	16.6-13.0	15.4-11.8	13.8-10.6	12.8-9.7	11.2-7.9	9.3-6.7	16.1-8.6
Price Range	35-27½	31⅝-24⅜	28¼-21¾	26½-20	26¾-18⅞	21½-15⅜	26¾-14¼

Statistics are as originally reported.

OFFICERS:
R.E. Terry, Chmn. & C.E.O.
J.B. Hasch, Pres. & C.O.O.
E.P. Cassidy, Sec. & Treas.

PRINCIPAL OFFICE: 122 South Michigan Avenue, Chicago, IL 60603-9942

TELEPHONE NUMBER: (312) 431-4000
FAX: (312) 431-4082
NO. OF EMPLOYEES: 465
ANNUAL MEETING: In February
SHAREHOLDERS: 21,051
INSTITUTIONAL HOLDINGS:
No. of Institutions: 186
Shares Held: 14,658,613

REGISTRAR(S):

TRANSFER AGENT(S):

PEP BOYS-MANNY, MOE & JACK

YIELD 0.6%
P/E RATIO 28.9

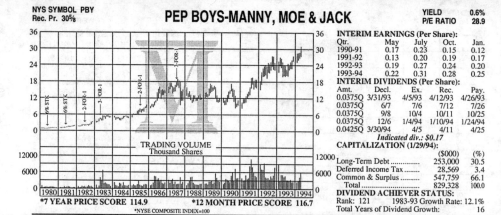

INTERIM EARNINGS (Per Share):

Qtr.	May	July	Oct.	Jan.
1990-91	0.17	0.23	0.15	0.12
1991-92	0.13	0.20	0.19	0.17
1992-93	0.19	0.27	0.24	0.20
1993-94	0.22	0.31	0.28	0.25

INTERIM DIVIDENDS (Per Share):

Amt.	Decl.	Ex.	Rec.	Pay.
0.0375Q	3/31/93	4/5/93	4/12/93	4/26/93
0.0375Q	6/7	7/6	7/12	7/26
0.0375Q	9/8	10/4	10/11	10/25
0.0375Q	12/6	1/4/94	1/10/94	1/24/94
0.0425Q	3/30/94	4/5	4/11	4/25

Indicated div.: $0.17

CAPITALIZATION (1/29/94):

	($000)	(%)
Long-Term Debt	253,000	30.5
Deferred Income Tax	28,569	3.4
Common & Surplus	547,759	66.1
Total	829,328	100.0

DIVIDEND ACHIEVER STATUS:
Rank: 121   1983-93 Growth Rate: 12.1%
Total Years of Dividend Growth: 16

TRADING VOLUME
Thousand Shares

*7 YEAR PRICE SCORE 114.9   *12 MONTH PRICE SCORE 116.7
*NYSE COMPOSITE INDEX=100

RECENT DEVELOPMENTS: In February, the Company opened eight automotive supercenters, including its first unit in the state of Kentucky. For the thirteen weeks ended 10/30/93, net income was $17.4 million compared with $14.8 million in 1992. Sales rose 6% to $316.0 million. Comparable store sales decreased 1%. Although operations were hurt by weak tire sales and lower freon sales, PBY posted improved results due to higher gross margins as a result of an improved sales mix, as well as solid expense controls.

PROSPECTS: Margins should continue to improve with the aid of an ongoing expense control program. Also a new inventory system that keeps supercenters stocked at optimum levels should cut costs by producing more accurate orders in shorter periods of time. In response to weak tire sales, PBY will likely increase advertising of a new program that features three national brands and its own private-label brand. Growth should come from PBY's store expansion program.

BUSINESS

PEP BOYS operates a chain of specialty retail stores which sell a full range of brand name and private label automotive parts and accessories at discount prices. Most Pep Boys stores contain service centers for automobile maintenance and service, as well as for installation of automotive parts and accessories sold by PBY. The Company has 362 stores, including both full-service and satellite stores, in operation. The stores are located in 22 states, mostly in middle Atlantic, west Southwest and Southeast regions of the U.S. PBY operates about 23,000 gross square feet per store.

REVENUES

(1/29/94)	($000)	(%)
Merchandise Sales	1,076,543	86.7
Service Revenue	164,590	13.3
Total	1,241,133	100.0

ANNUAL EARNINGS AND DIVIDENDS PER SHARE

	1/29/94	1/30/93	2/1/92	2/2/91	2/3/90	1/28/89	1/30/88
Earnings Per Share	1.06	0.90	0.69	0.67	0.63	①0.68	0.62
Dividends Per Share	0.147	0.135	0.125	0.115	0.105	0.09	②0.076
Dividend Payout %	13.9	15.0	18.1	17.2	16.7	13.2	12.3

① Before acctg. chg.   ② 3-for-1 stk split, 7/87

ANNUAL FINANCIAL DATA

RECORD OF EARNINGS (IN MILLIONS):

	1/29/94	1/30/93	2/1/92	2/2/91	2/3/90	1/28/89	1/30/88
Total Revenues	1,241.1	1,155.6	1,001.5	884.7	798.7	656.0	553.8
Costs and Expenses	1,081.4	1,016.1	884.4	779.4	706.7	573.0	133.9
Depreciation & Amort	39.1	36.7	33.4	27.8	22.9	17.0	13.2
Operating Profit	120.6	102.8	83.7	77.4	69.1	65.9	58.1
Earn Bef Income Taxes	104.5	85.6	60.5	58.8	55.1	60.2	59.8
Income Taxes	39.0	31.0	21.6	21.2	20.1	22.5	25.5
Net Income	65.5	54.6	38.9	37.5	35.1	①37.7	34.3
Aver. Shs. Outstg. (000)	61,891	60,636	56,494	56,109	55,890	55,431	55,513

① Before acctg. change cr$4,688,000.

BALANCE SHEET (IN MILLIONS):

	1/29/94	1/30/93	2/1/92	2/2/91	2/3/90	1/28/89	1/30/88
Cash and Cash Equivalents	12.1	11.6	14.4	15.1	14.3	20.0	19.2
Receivables, Net	10.6	10.2	2.1	2.5	1.7	2.6	3.3
Inventories	305.9	295.2	230.9	234.7	163.8	117.2	96.4
Gross Property	923.2	796.9	728.4	665.8	566.4	488.6	367.6
Accumulated Depreciation	199.7	168.0	139.8	108.8	85.8	72.4	56.8
Long-Term Debt	253.0	209.3	279.3	285.9	227.6	187.0	138.1
Net Stockholders' Equity	547.8	509.8	378.5	344.6	311.8	275.7	237.7
Total Assets	1,078.5	967.8	856.9	819.4	676.0	581.8	469.8
Total Current Assets	341.7	327.1	258.8	258.2	189.6	146.5	122.6
Total Current Liabilities	249.2	222.5	176.9	168.1	116.8	101.3	76.0
Net Working Capital	92.5	104.6	81.9	91.8	70.2	45.2	46.6
Year End Shs Outstg (000)	60,112	60,669	55,774	55,606	55,436	54,603	54,519

STATISTICAL RECORD:

	1/29/94	1/30/93	2/1/92	2/2/91	2/3/90	1/28/89	1/30/88
Operating Profit Margin %	9.7	8.9	8.4	8.8	8.6	10.0	. . .
Book Value Per Share	9.11	8.40	6.79	6.20	5.62	5.05	4.36
Return on Equity %	12.0	10.7	10.3	10.9	11.2	13.7	14.4
Return on Assets %	6.1	5.6	4.5	4.6	5.2	6.5	7.3
Average Yield %	0.6	0.6	0.9	0.9	0.8	0.7	0.5
P/E Ratio	25.8-18.8	30.4-16.8	28.3-12.1	25.7-12.7	27.4-16.7	23.3-15.3	30.4-15.3
Price Range	27⅜-19⅞	27⅜-15⅛	19½-8⅜	17¼-8½	17¼-10½	15⅞-10⅜	18⅞-9½

Statistics are as originally reported.

OFFICERS:
M.G. Leibovitz, Chmn., C.E.O. & Pres.
M.J. Holden, Sr. V.P., C.F.O. & Treas.
F.A. Stampone, Sr. V.P., Chief Admin. Off. & Sec.

INCORPORATED: PA, Jan., 1925

PRINCIPAL OFFICE: 3111 West Allegheny Ave., Philadelphia, PA 19132

TELEPHONE NUMBER: (215) 229-9000
FAX: (215) 227-4067
NO. OF EMPLOYEES: 13,391
ANNUAL MEETING: In June
SHAREHOLDERS: 3,675
INSTITUTIONAL HOLDINGS:
No. of Institutions: 251
Shares Held: 36,023,234

REGISTRAR(S): American Stock Transfer & Trust Co., 40 Wall Street, New York, NY 10005

TRANSFER AGENT(S): American Stock Transfer & Trust Co., 40 Wall Street, New York, NY 10005

PEPSICO INC.

YIELD		1.9%
P/E RATIO		18.9

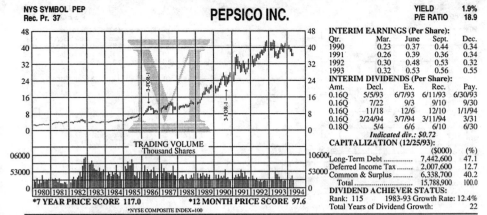

INTERIM EARNINGS (Per Share):

Qtr.	Mar.	June	Sept.	Dec.
1990	0.23	0.37	0.44	0.34
1991	0.26	0.39	0.36	0.34
1992	0.30	0.48	0.53	0.32
1993	0.32	0.53	0.56	0.55

INTERIM DIVIDENDS (Per Share):

Amt.	Decl.	Ex.	Rec.	Pay.
0.16Q	5/5/93	6/7/93	6/11/93	6/30/93
0.16Q	7/22	9/3	9/10	9/30
0.16Q	11/18	12/6	12/10	1/1/94
0.16Q	2/24/94	3/7/94	3/11/94	3/31
0.18Q	5/4	6/6	6/10	6/30

Indicated div.: $0.72

CAPITALIZATION (12/25/93):

	($000)	(%)
Long-Term Debt	7,442,600	47.1
Deferred Income Tax	2,007,600	12.7
Common & Surplus	6,338,700	40.2
Total	15,788,900	100.0

DIVIDEND ACHIEVER STATUS:
Rank: 115   1983-93 Growth Rate: 12.4%
Total Years of Dividend Growth: 22

TRADING VOLUME
Thousand Shares

*7 YEAR PRICE SCORE 117.0   *12 MONTH PRICE SCORE 97.6
*NYSE COMPOSITE INDEX=100

RECENT DEVELOPMENTS: For the year ended 12/25/93, net income was $1.59 billion compared with $1.30 billion last year. Sales rose 13.9% to $25.02 billion. Worldwide snack food sales increased 15% to $7.03 billion and operating profits rose 21%. International profits increased 16% to $288.9 million. Worldwide beverage sales rose 14% to $8.64 billion, and operating profits rose 18%. Restaurant profits advanced 8%, led by an 18% increase in profits at Taco Bell.

PROSPECTS: The Company's restaurant segment will continue to benefit from expansions in the near term. Although profits at KFC are being affected by soft international results, profits at Pizza Hut and Taco Bell will continue to grow. In the domestic beverage market, contributions from the new line of Lipton products should boost sales and earnings. Market share gains should aid results at Frito-Lay.

BUSINESS

PEPSICO, INC. operates on a world-wide basis within three distinct business segments: soft drinks, snack-foods and restaurants. The soft drinks segment manufactures concentrates, and markets Pepsi-Cola, Diet Pepsi, Mountain Dew, Slice and allied brands worldwide, and 7-up internationally. This segment also operates soft drink bottling businesses principally in the United States. Snack Foods manufactures and markets snack chips through Frito-Lay Inc. Well known brands include: Doritos, Ruffles and Lays. Restaurants consists of Pizza Hut, Taco Bell and Kentucky Fried Chicken.

BUSINESS LINE ANALYSIS

(12/25/93)	Rev(%)	Inc(%)
Beverages	34.5	36.0
Snack Foods	28.1	38.7
Restaurants	37.4	25.3
Total	100.0	100.0

ANNUAL EARNINGS AND DIVIDENDS PER SHARE

	12/25/93	12/26/92	12/28/91	12/29/90	12/30/89	12/31/88	12/28/87
Earnings Per Share	1.96	1.61	1.35	1.37	1.13	0.97	①0.77
Dividends Per Share	0.58	0.50	0.44	0.367	0.31	0.25	0.22
Dividend Payout %	29.6	31.1	32.6	26.8	27.1	26.2	28.7

① Before disc. oper.

ANNUAL FINANCIAL DATA

RECORD OF EARNINGS (IN MILLIONS):

Total Revenues	25,020.7	21,970.0	19,607.9	17,802.7	15,242.4	13,007.0	11,485.2
Costs and Expenses	21,810.5	19,332.9	17,276.3	15,558.0	13,309.1	11,017.7	9,778.9
Depreciation & Amort	1,444.2	1,214.9	1,034.5	884.0	772.0	629.3	563.0
Operating Income	2,906.5	2,371.2	2,122.9	2,055.6	1,782.9	1,360.0	1,143.3
Income Bef Income Taxes	2,422.5	1,898.8	1,670.3	1,667.4	1,350.5	1,137.6	960.4
Provision for Inc Taxes	834.6	597.1	590.1	576.8	449.1	375.4	355.3
Net Income	1,587.9	374.3	1,080.2	①1,090.6	901.4	762.2	②605.1
Aver. Shs. Outstg. (000)	810,100	806,700	802,500	798,700	795,900	790,500	789,300

① Before disc. op. dr$13,700,000. ② Before disc. op. dr$10,300,000.

BALANCE SHEET (IN MILLIONS):

Tot Cash & Sh-tm Invests	1,856.2	2,058.4	2,036.0	1,815.7	1,533.9	1,617.8	1,352.6
Receivables, Net	1,883.4	1,588.5	1,481.7	1,414.7	1,239.7	979.3	885.6
Inventories	924.7	768.8	661.5	585.8	546.1	442.4	433.0
Gross Property	14,250.0	12,095.2	10,501.7	8,977.7	7,818.4	6,658.4	6,000.6
Accumulated Depreciation	5,394.4	4,653.2	3,907.0	3,266.8	2,688.2	2,195.9	1,883.2
Long-Term Debt	7,442.6	7,964.8	7,806.2	5,600.1	5,777.1	2,356.6	2,150.6
Net Stockholders' Equity	6,338.7	5,355.7	5,545.4	4,904.2	3,891.1	3,161.0	2,508.6
Total Assets	23,705.8	20,951.2	18,775.1	17,143.4	15,126.7	11,135.3	9,022.7
Total Current Assets	5,164.1	4,842.3	4,566.1	4,081.4	3,550.8	3,264.7	2,939.6
Total Current Liabilities	6,574.9	4,324.4	3,722.1	4,770.5	3,691.8	3,873.6	2,722.8
Net Working Capital	d1,410.8	517.9	844.0	d689.1	d141.0	d608.9	216.8
Year End Shs Outstg (000)	798,800	798,800	789,101	788,389	791,057	863,100	781,239

STATISTICAL RECORD:

Operating Profit Margin %	11.6	10.8	10.8	11.5	11.7	10.5	10.0
Return on Equity %	25.1	24.3	19.5	22.2	23.2	24.1	24.1
Return on Assets %	6.7	6.2	5.8	6.4	6.0	6.8	6.7
Average Yield %	1.5	1.4	1.5	1.6	1.8	2.0	1.9
P/E Ratio	22.3-13.6	26.9-18.9	27.0-17.4	20.3-13.1	19.5-11.2	14.9-10.3	18.3-11.0
Price Range	43⅝-34½	43⅜-30½	36½-23½	27⅞-18	22-12⅝	14½-10	14⅛-8½

Statistics are as originally reported.

OFFICERS:
D.W. Calloway, Chmn. & C.E.O.
R.G. Dettmer, Exec. V.P. & C.F.O.
E.V. Lahey, Jr., Sr. V.P., Couns. & Sec.
R.C. Barnes, Sr. V.P. & Treas.

INCORPORATED: NC, Dec., 1986

PRINCIPAL OFFICE: Purchase, NY 10577

TELEPHONE NUMBER: (914) 253-2000

FAX: (914) 253-2070

NO. OF EMPLOYEES: 118,296

ANNUAL MEETING: In May

SHAREHOLDERS: 67,210

INSTITUTIONAL HOLDINGS:
No. of Institutions: 1,077
Shares Held: 470,494,447

REGISTRAR(S): Chemical Bank, New York, NY

TRANSFER AGENT(S): Chemical Bank, New York, NY

NYS SYMBOL PFE
Rec. Pr. 63¼

PFIZER INC.

YIELD 3.0%
P/E RATIO 30.9

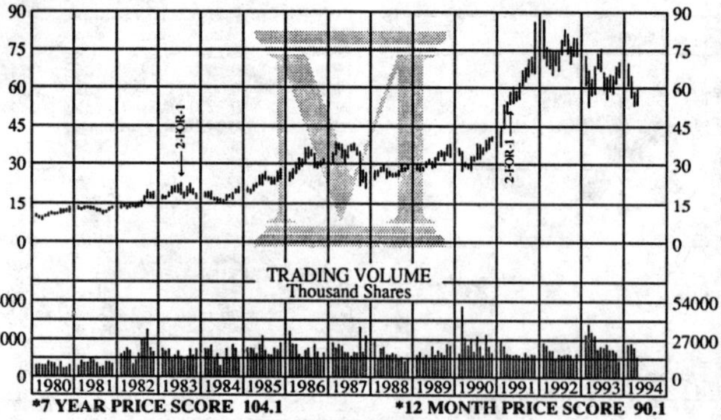

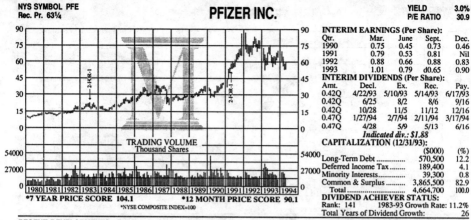

***7 YEAR PRICE SCORE 104.1** ***12 MONTH PRICE SCORE 90.1**

*NYSE COMPOSITE INDEX=100

INTERIM EARNINGS (Per Share):

Qtr.	Mar.	June	Sept.	Dec.
1990	0.75	0.45	0.73	0.46
1991	0.79	0.53	0.81	Nil
1992	0.88	0.66	0.88	0.83
1993	1.01	0.79	d0.65	0.90

INTERIM DIVIDENDS (Per Share):

Amt.	Decl.	Ex.	Rec.	Pay.
0.42Q	4/22/93	5/10/93	5/14/93	6/17/93
0.42Q	6/25	8/2	8/6	9/16
0.42Q	10/28	11/5	11/12	12/16
0.47Q	1/27/94	2/7/94	2/11/94	3/17/94
0.47Q	4/28	5/9	5/13	6/16

Indicated div.: $1.88

CAPITALIZATION (12/31/93):

	($000)	(%)
Long-Term Debt	570,500	12.2
Deferred Income Tax	189,400	4.1
Minority Interests	39,300	0.8
Common & Surplus	3,865,500	82.9
Total	4,664,700	100.0

DIVIDEND ACHIEVER STATUS:
Rank: 141 1983-93 Growth Rate: 11.2%
Total Years of Dividend Growth: 26

RECENT DEVELOPMENTS: For the year ended 12/31/93, net income declined 39.9% to $657.5 million compared with $1.09 billion, before an accounting adjustment the previous year. Earnings in 1993 included non-recurring pre-tax charges of $752 million. Sales were up 3.4% to $7.48 billion from $7.23 billion. Sales growth was driven by the Company's newer products, which include Norvasc, Cardura, Zoloft and Zithromax.

PROSPECTS: Operating results will continue to benefit from strong sales of Diflucan, the world's leading antifungal, and Pfizer's cardiovascular products. Competitive conditions in the U.S. healthcare market will minimize price inflation. PFE has filed several new drug applications with U.S. and international regulatory agencies including one for Enable, a once-a-day treatment for arthritis.

BUSINESS

PFIZER INC. is a research-based, diversified health care company with global operations. Health care products consist of pharmaceutical products and medical devices. Animal Health includes animal health products. Food Science consists of bulk antibiotics, food grade chemicals, vitamins, industrial chemicals and specialty products. Consumer Health Care products include proprietary health items such as Visine, Ben-Gay, Plax, and Unisom. U.S. sales represented 54% of total sales; Europe 24%; Asia 14%; Canada/Latin America 6%; and Africa/Middle East 2%.

BUSINESS LINE ANALYSIS

(12/31/93)	Rev(%)	Inc($000)
Health Care	83.1	1,129,900
Consumer Health Care	5.0	(102,300)
Food Science	4.2	16,100
Animal Health	7.7	(5,800)
Total	100.0	1,037,900

ANNUAL EARNINGS AND DIVIDENDS PER SHARE

	1993	1992	1991	1990	1989	1988	1987
Earnings Per Share	2.05	[1] 3.25	2.13	2.39	2.02	2.35	2.04
Dividends Per Share	1.68	[2] 1.48	[3] 1.32	1.20	1.10	1.00	0.90
Dividend Payout %	82.0	45.5	62.0	50.3	54.5	42.6	44.1

[1] Before acctg. chg. [2] Bef acctg chge [3] 2-for-1 stk split, 4/1/91

ANNUAL FINANCIAL DATA

	1993	1992	1991	1990	1989	1988	1987
RECORD OF EARNINGS (IN MILLIONS):							
Total Revenues	7,477.7	7,230.2	6,950.0	6,406.0	5,671.5	5,385.4	4,919.8
Costs and Expenses	6,306.2	5,412.4	5,752.4	5,127.4	4,496.2	4,179.0	3,806.8
Depreciation & Amort	258.2	263.9	244.1	224.8	207.1	194.5	172.2
Income From Operations	913.3	1,553.9	953.5	1,053.8	968.2	1,011.9	940.8
Inc Bef Taxes on Income	851.4	1,534.8	943.7	1,103.3	916.5	1,103.8	1,010.8
Provision for Taxes on Inc	191.3	438.6	218.4	297.9	231.3	309.4	317.3
Minority Interests	2.6	2.7	3.2	4.2	4.1	3.1	3.3
Net Income	657.5	810.9	722.1	801.2	681.1	791.3	690.2
Aver. Shs. Outstg. (000)	320,400	336,500	339,343	337,152	339,392	338,800	341,200
BALANCE SHEET (IN MILLIONS):							
Cash and Cash Equivalents	1,176.5	1,703.7	1,548.1	1,068.2	1,057.7	807.5	1,031.1
Receivables, Net	1,925.6	2,020.6	1,756.5	1,962.1	2,064.9	2,015.6	1,861.5
Total Inventories	1,093.5	1,067.8	1,171.5	1,142.6	1,080.5	1,089.4	1,028.2
Gross Property	4,300.7	3,816.4	4,007.5	3,616.3	3,252.5	3,153.6	2,875.9
Accumulated Depreciation	1,668.2	1,511.3	1,626.5	1,506.5	1,468.4	1,498.5	1,370.0
Long-Term Debt	570.5	571.3	396.6	193.3	190.6	226.9	248.9
Net Stockholders' Equity	3,865.5	4,718.6	5,026.3	5,092.0	4,535.8	4,301.1	3,882.4
Total Assets	9,330.9	9,590.1	9,634.6	9,052.0	8,324.8	7,637.6	6,922.6
Total Current Assets	4,733.2	5,384.8	4,808.2	4,435.9	4,504.8	4,094.8	4,100.7
Total Current Liabilities	3,443.6	3,217.4	3,420.5	3,116.9	2,911.6	2,344.3	1,956.6
Net Working Capital	1,289.6	2,167.4	1,387.7	1,319.0	1,593.2	1,750.5	2,144.1
Year End Shs Outstg (000)	320,922	325,141	329,647	330,244	330,626	330,792	328,978
STATISTICAL RECORD:							
Operating Profit Margin %	12.2	21.5	13.7	16.5	17.1	18.8	19.1
Book Value Per Share	11.32	13.38	14.08	13.91	12.42	11.73	11.08
Return on Equity %	17.0	23.2	14.4	15.7	15.0	18.4	17.8
Return on Assets %	7.0	11.4	7.5	8.9	8.2	10.4	10.0
Average Yield %	2.6	1.9	2.1	3.5	3.4	3.7	3.0
P/E Ratio	36.9-25.6	26.8-20.0	40.4-17.3	17.2-11.4	18.8-13.4	12.8-10.1	16.0-8.6
Price Range	75⅝-52½	87-65⅛	86⅛-36¾	40⅞-27¼	37⅞-27	30⅛-23¾	38½-20⅝

Statistics are as originally reported.

OFFICERS:
W.C. Steere, Jr., Chmn. & C.E.O.
H.A. McKinnell, Exec. V.P. & C.F.O.
W.E. Harvey, V.P. & Treas.
D.L. Shedlarz, V.P.-Finance

INCORPORATED: DE, 1942

PRINCIPAL OFFICE: 235 East 42nd St., New York, NY 10017-5755

TELEPHONE NUMBER: (212) 573-2323

FAX: (212) 573-2641

NO. OF EMPLOYEES: 40,500 (approx.)

ANNUAL MEETING: In April

SHAREHOLDERS: 61,500 (approx.)

INSTITUTIONAL HOLDINGS:
No. of Institutions: 970
Shares Held: 203,294,309

REGISTRAR(S): Mellon Securities Trust Co., New York, NY

TRANSFER AGENT(S): At Company's Office

NYS SYMBOL MO
Rec. Pr. 55¼

PHILIP MORRIS COS., INC.

YIELD 5.0%
P/E RATIO 13.6

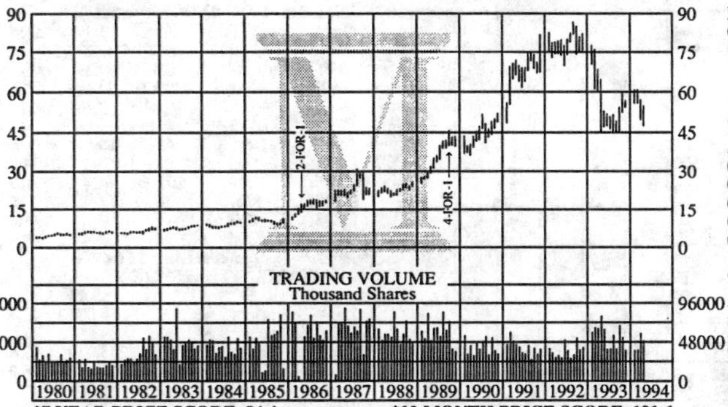

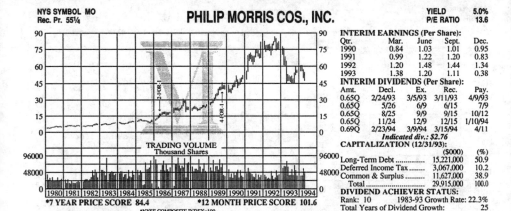

***7 YEAR PRICE SCORE 84.4** ***12 MONTH PRICE SCORE 101.6**

*NYSE COMPOSITE INDEX=100

INTERIM EARNINGS (Per Share):

Qtr.	Mar.	June	Sept.	Dec.
1990	0.84	1.03	1.01	0.95
1991	0.99	1.22	1.20	0.83
1992	1.20	1.48	1.44	1.34
1993	1.38	1.20	1.11	0.38

INTERIM DIVIDENDS (Per Share):

Amt.	Decl.	Ex.	Rec.	Pay.
0.65Q	2/24/93	3/5/93	3/11/93	4/9/93
0.65Q	5/26	6/9	6/15	7/9
0.65Q	8/25	9/9	9/15	10/12
0.65Q	11/24	12/9	12/15	1/10/94
0.69Q	2/23/94	3/9/94	3/15/94	4/11

Indicated div.: $2.76

CAPITALIZATION (12/31/93):

	($000)	(%)
Long-Term Debt	15,221,000	50.9
Deferred Income Tax	3,067,000	10.2
Common & Surplus	11,627,000	38.9
Total	29,915,000	100.0

DIVIDEND ACHIEVER STATUS:
Rank: 10 1983-93 Growth Rate: 22.3%
Total Years of Dividend Growth: 25

RECENT DEVELOPMENTS: For the year ended 12/31/93, net income declined 27.8% to $3.57 billion. Revenues increased 3.0% to $60.90 billion. Domestic tobacco posted a 46.0% decrease in income to $2.81 billion due to price reductions and reduced cigarette shipments. International tobacco income increased 17.0% to $2.4 billion on a 15.2% increase in revenues. North American food operations posted a 10.5% increase in income to $2.40 billion. International food income increased 4.1% to $1.11 billion.

PROSPECTS: Although international tobacco, worldwide food, and beer operations are performing well, lower U.S. cigarette pricing and continued volatile and competitive market conditions will hurt near-term earnings. International tobacco results should benefit from higher cigarette volumes as a result of several acquisitions. The Company's food operations will benefit from higher market share in its confectionery and coffee businesses.

BUSINESS

PHILIP MORRIS INC. is the world's largest consumer products company with major operations in tobacco, food, and beer. Tobacco operates through Philip Morris U.S.A. and Philip Morris International Inc. Food consists of the Kraft General Foods Group which operates seven divisions domestically and internationally. Miller Brewing Co. produces Miller/Miller Lite, Lowenbrau and Miller Genuine Draft beers. MO also has interests in financial services and real estate. In May 1993, Kraft General Foods acquired Freia Marabou a.s., a Norwegian confectionary and snack food company.

BUSINESS LINE ANALYSIS

(12/31/93)	Rev(%)	Inc(%)
Tobacco	42.6	61.5
Food	49.9	32.7
Beer	6.8	2.7
Finan Servs & Real Estate	0.7	3.1
Total	100.0	100.0

ANNUAL EARNINGS AND DIVIDENDS PER SHARE

	1993	1992	1991	1990	1989	1988	1987
Earnings Per Share	**4.06**	**5.45**	**① 4.24**	**3.83**	**3.18**	**① 2.21**	**1.94**
Dividends Per Share	**2.60**	**2.225**	**1.815**	**1.461**	**② 1.188**	**0.956**	**0.75**
Dividend Payout %	**64.0**	**40.8**	**42.8**	**38.1**	**37.4**	**10.8**	**38.7**

① Before acctg. chg. ② 4-for-1 stk split, 10/10/89

ANNUAL FINANCIAL DATA

	1993	1992	1991	1990	1989	1988	1987
RECORD OF EARNINGS (IN MILLIONS):							
Operating Revenues	60,901.0	59,131.0	56,458.0	51,169.0	44,759.0	31,742.0	27,695.0
Costs and Expenses	52,745.0	48,551.0	47,337.0	42,775.0	37,585.0	27,220.0	23,524.0
Depreciation & Amort	1,619.0	1,542.0	1,497.0	1,367.0	1,194.0	0.8	0.7
Operating Income	7,587.0	10,059.0	8,622.0	7,946.0	6,789.0	4,397.0	4,193.0
Earn Bef Income Taxes	6,196.0	8,608.0	6,971.0	6,311.0	5,058.0	3,727.0	3,348.0
Provision for Inc Taxes	2,628.0	3,669.0	3,044.0	2,771.0	2,112.0	1,663.0	1,506.0
Net Income	① 3,568.0	4,939.0	② 3,927.0	3,540.0	2,946.0	2,337.0	1,842.0
Aver. Shs. Outstg. (000)	878,121	906,178	925,123	925,191	926,521	932,000	951,284

① Before acctg. change dr$477,000,000. ② Before acctg. change dr$921,000,000.

	1993	1992	1991	1990	1989	1988	1987
BALANCE SHEET (IN MILLIONS):							
Cash & Cash Equivalents	182.0	1,021.0	126.0	146.0	118.0	168.0	189.0
Receivables, Net	3,982.0	4,147.0	4,121.0	4,101.0	2,956.0	2,222.0	2,083.0
Inventories	7,358.0	7,785.0	7,445.0	7,153.0	5,751.0	5,384.0	4,154.0
Gross Property	16,930.0	16,512.0	15,281.0	14,281.0	12,357.0	11,932.0	9,398.0
Accumulated Depreciation	6,467.0	5,982.0	5,335.0	4,677.0	3,900.0	3,284.0	2,816.0
Long-Term Debt	15,221.0	14,583.0	14,213.0	16,121.0	14,861.0	17,122.0	5,222.0
Net Stockholders' Equity	11,627.0	12,563.0	12,512.0	11,947.0	9,571.0	7,679.0	6,823.0
Total Assets	51,205.0	50,014.0	47,384.0	46,569.0	38,528.0	36,960.0	19,145.0
Total Current Assets	12,808.0	13,906.0	12,594.0	12,367.0	9,380.0	8,151.0	6,572.0
Total Current Liabilities	14,468.0	14,021.0	12,642.0	12,084.0	9,266.0	8,233.0	5,176.0
Net Working Capital	d1,660.0	d115.0	d48.0	283.0	114.0	d82.0	1,396.0
Year End Shs Outstg (000)	877,091	892,757	919,851	926,219	928,530	924,000	946,504
STATISTICAL RECORD:							
Operating Profit Margin %	12.5	17.0	15.3	15.5	15.2	13.9	15.1
Return on Equity %	30.7	39.3	31.4	29.6	30.8	26.9	27.0
Return on Assets %	7.0	9.9	8.3	7.6	7.6	5.6	9.6
Average Yield %	4.2	2.9	2.8	3.3	3.4	4.2	3.0
P/E Ratio	19.1-11.1	15.9-12.8	19.3-11.4	13.6-9.4	14.4-7.9	11.5-9.1	16.0-9.3
Price Range	77⅝-45	86⅝-69½	81¾-48¼	52-36	45¾-25	25½-20⅛	31⅛-18⅛

Statistics are as originally reported.

OFFICERS:
M.A. Miles, Chmn. & C.E.O.
W. Murray, Pres. & C.O.O.
H.G. Storr, Exec. V.P. & C.F.O.
D.T. Bartlett, V.P. & Sec.

INCORPORATED: VA, Mar., 1985

PRINCIPAL OFFICE: 120 Park Ave., New York, NY 10017

TELEPHONE NUMBER: (212) 880-5000

NO. OF EMPLOYEES: 51,198

ANNUAL MEETING: In April

SHAREHOLDERS: 61,899 (approx.)

INSTITUTIONAL HOLDINGS:
No. of Institutions: 1,313
Shares Held: 471,842,697

REGISTRAR(S): First Chicago Trust Co. of New York, New York, NY 10008

TRANSFER AGENT(S): First Chicago Trust Co. of New York, New York, NY 10008

PIEDMONT NATURAL GAS CO., INC.

YIELD 5.3%
P/E RATIO 13.5

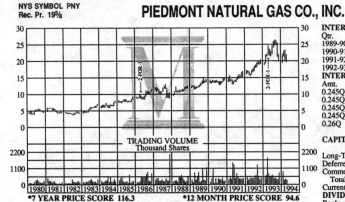

TRADING VOLUME
Thousand Shares

*7 YEAR PRICE SCORE 116.3 *12 MONTH PRICE SCORE 94.6
*NYSE COMPOSITE INDEX=100

INTERIM EARNINGS (Per Share):

Qtr.	Jan.	Apr.	July	Oct.
1989-90	1.12	0.70	d0.27	d0.32
1990-91	0.80	0.68	d0.29	d0.19
1991-92	0.99	0.79	d0.15	d0.21
1992-93	1.06	0.87	d0.20	d0.28

INTERIM DIVIDENDS (Per Share):

Amt.	Decl.	Ex.	Rec.	Pay.
0.245Q	3/1/93	3/4/93	3/10/93	4/15/93
0.245Q	5/28	6/18	6/24	7/15
0.245Q	8/27	9/20	9/24	10/15
0.245Q	12/3	12/16	12/22	1/14/94
0.26Q	2/25/94	3/21/94	3/25/94	4/15

Indicated div.: $1.04

CAPITALIZATION (10/31/93):

	($000)	(%)
Long-Term Debt	278,000	42.6
Deferred Income Tax	89,857	13.8
Common & Surplus	285,020	43.6
Total	652,877	100.0
Current Debt	5,000	

DIVIDEND ACHIEVER STATUS:
Rank: 244   1983-93 Growth Rate: 7.2%
Total Years of Dividend Growth: 14

RECENT DEVELOPMENTS: For the quarter ended 1/31/94, net income was $27.7 million compared with $27.2 million last year. Revenues were $233.1 million, up 15%. Customer growth and favorable weather conditions were the primary factors for the improved results. Gas deliveries advanced 12.9% to 44,858,000 dekatherms. For the twelve-month period ended 1/31/94, net income edged up 0.1% to $38.1 million. Revenues advanced 19.1% to $583.2 million in the prior-year.

PROSPECTS: Growth continues to be strong in PNY's service territory. Earnings should stabilize as a result of weather normalization clauses in the utility's various jurisdictions. External funding for planned capital expenditures will be substantial. PNY has some unregulated propane operations, whose earnings are potentially more volatile than the natural gas utility's. However, current returns are positive. Earnings may lag permitted returns as a result of the Company's rapidly growing rate base.

BUSINESS

PIEDMONT NATURAL GAS CO. is engaged in the purchase, distribution and sale of natural gas to residential, commercial and industrial customers in North Carolina, South Carolina and Tennessee. Non-utility subsidiaries and divisions are involved in the exploration, development, marketing and transportation of natural gas, oil, and propane. PNY's utility operations are subject to regulation by the North Carolina Utilities Commission, the Tennessee Public Service Commission and the Public Service Commission of South Carolina. PNY also owns Tennessee Natural Resources, Inc., and its subsidiaries. PNY serves 40,000 propane customers in a three-state area.

REVENUES

(10/31/93)	($000)	(%)
Residential	217,545	39.4
Commercial	154,894	28.0
Industrial	173,943	31.5
Public Housing	4,087	0.7
For Resale	1	0.0001
Miscellaneous	2,290	0.4
Total	552,760	100.0

ANNUAL EARNINGS AND DIVIDENDS PER SHARE

	10/31/93	10/31/92	10/31/91	10/31/90	10/31/89	10/31/88	10/31/87
Earnings Per Share	1.45	1.39	0.88	1.22	1.21	1.18	1.10
Dividends Per Share	① 0.965	0.91	0.87	0.83	0.785	0.72	0.645
Dividend Payout %	66.6	65.2	98.3	68.0	64.9	60.8	58.9

① 2-for-1 stk split,04/01/93

ANNUAL FINANCIAL DATA

RECORD OF EARNINGS (IN THOUSANDS):

Operating Revenues	552,760	459,902	411,548	403,815	420,824	399,005	411,715
Depreciation & Amort	...	23,056	20,893	18,474	14,928	13,078	11,674
Maintenance	14,969	13,326	13,059	11,641	10,084	8,945	8,069
Income Taxes	21,572	19,055	9,756	12,773	12,913	11,646	14,041
Operating Income	56,575	53,358	40,078	43,936	41,217	34,766	30,913
Total Utility Int Charges	21,907	21,511	22,463	21,565	19,445	15,102	13,255
Net Income	37,534	35,310	20,552	25,733	24,875	22,412	19,330
Aver. Shs. Outstg.	25,960	25,346	23,282	21,130	20,528	18,948	17,642

BALANCE SHEET (IN THOUSANDS):

Gross Plant	900,333	818,232	744,275	677,763	609,687	549,155	475,162
Accumulated Depreciation	222,423	202,741	185,012	169,873	157,338	146,041	135,467
Prop, Plant & Equip, Net	677,910	615,491	559,263	507,890	452,349	403,114	339,695
Long-term Debt	278,000	231,300	220,525	173,654	186,261	141,887	110,295
Net Stockholders' Equity	285,020	264,890	238,718	196,177	181,441	167,829	133,864
Total Assets	796,453	723,955	665,853	617,082	560,340	512,292	432,882
Year End Shares Outstg	26,152	25,796	24,728	21,433	20,783	20,335	17,868

STATISTICAL RECORD:

Book Value Per Share	10.90	10.27	9.65	9.15	8.73	8.25	7.49
Op. Inc/Net Pl %	8.3	8.7	7.2	8.7	9.1	8.6	9.1
Dep/Gr. Pl %	2.5	2.5	2.4	2.3	2.4	2.4	2.5
Accum. Dep/Gr. Pl %	24.7	24.8	24.9	25.1	25.8	26.6	28.5
Return on Equity %	13.2	13.3	8.6	13.1	13.7	13.4	14.4
Average Yield %	4.3	5.1	5.8	6.0	6.0	6.5	5.9
P/E Ratio	18.2-13.0	14.7-11.2	19.2-14.8	12.2-10.5	12.3-9.5	10.7-8.2	11.9-8.0
Price Range	26⅜-18⅞	20½-15½	16⅞-13	14⅞-12¾	14⅞-11½	12⅝-9⅝	13⅛-8¾

Statistics are as originally reported.

OFFICERS:
J.H. Maxheim, Chmn., Pres. & C.E.O.
E.C. Hinson, Sr. V.P.-Fin.
T.C. Coble, V.P., Treas. & Asst. Sec.

INCORPORATED: NY, May, 1950

PRINCIPAL OFFICE: 1915 Rexford Road, Charlotte, NC 28211

TELEPHONE NUMBER: (704) 364-3120
FAX: (704) 365-3849
NO. OF EMPLOYEES: 265
ANNUAL MEETING: In February
SHAREHOLDERS: 8,305 common
INSTITUTIONAL HOLDINGS:
No. of Institutions: 110
Shares Held: 6,090,319

REGISTRAR(S): Wachovia Bank & Trust Co., N.A., Winston-Salem, NC 27102

TRANSFER AGENT(S): Wachovia Bank & Trust Co., N.A., Winston-Salem, NC 27102

PITNEY BOWES, INC.

YIELD 2.8%
P/E RATIO 16.9

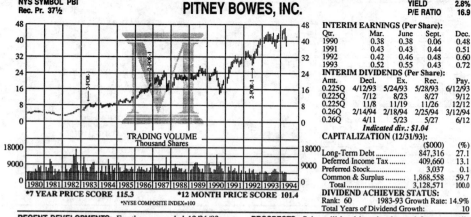

*7 YEAR PRICE SCORE 115.3
*12 MONTH PRICE SCORE 101.4
*NYSE COMPOSITE INDEX=100

TRADING VOLUME
Thousand Shares

INTERIM EARNINGS (Per Share):

Qtr.	Mar.	June	Sept.	Dec.
1990	0.38	0.38	0.06	0.48
1991	0.43	0.43	0.44	0.51
1992	0.42	0.46	0.48	0.60
1993	0.52	0.55	0.43	0.72

INTERIM DIVIDENDS (Per Share):

Amt.	Decl.	Ex.	Rec.	Pay.
0.225Q	4/12/93	5/24/93	5/28/93	6/12/93
0.225Q	7/12	8/23	8/27	9/12
0.225Q	11/8	11/19	11/26	12/12
0.26Q	2/14/94	2/18/94	2/25/94	3/12/94
0.26Q	4/11	5/23	5/27	6/12

Indicated div.: $1.04

CAPITALIZATION (12/31/93):

	($000)	(%)
Long-Term Debt	847,316	27.1
Deferred Income Tax	409,660	13.1
Preferred Stock	3,037	0.1
Common & Surplus	1,868,558	59.7
Total	3,128,571	100.0

DIVIDEND ACHIEVER STATUS:

Rank: 60   1983-93 Growth Rate: 14.9%
Total Years of Dividend Growth: 10

RECENT DEVELOPMENTS: For the year ended 12/31/93, net income increased 13.1% to $353.2 million compared with $312.2 million a year ago. Revenues were up 3.2% to $3.54 billion. Sales growth was primarily attributable to strong acceptance of new mailing, shipping and office-system products late in the year. Fourth quarter revenues increased 5% to $973.9 million and net income rose 21% to $114.8 million. PBI also experienced a significant increase in its lease/sales ratio.

PROSPECTS: Sales will be driven by demand for new mailing and shipping products, such as the PARAGON, the SPECTRUM, and the 9 Series Inserting System for production mailers. New office system products such as the Digital Express 4000 advanced dictation system and the Smart Image line of copiers will also contribute to revenue growth. Monarch Marking Systems will introduce a new line of portable bar-code printer products. New products are generating interest worldwide.

BUSINESS

PITNEY BOWES INC. is a multinational manufacturing and marketing company that provides mailing, shipping, copying, dictating, facsimile and retail systems; business supplies and services; and product financing. Products and services include postage meters; mailing machines; scales; folding and inserting machines; manifest shipping systems; copiers and copier supplies; hand-held, desk top and central dictation systems; communications recording loggers; facsimile equipment and supplies; item identification and price marketing equipment and supplies; mailroom and reprographics facilities management; and leasing services.

BUSINESS LINE ANALYSIS

(12/31/93)	Rev(%)	Inc(%)
Business Equipment	70.6	63.9
Supplies & Services	12.1	4.1
Financial Services	17.3	32.0
Total	100.0	100.0

ANNUAL EARNINGS AND DIVIDENDS PER SHARE

	1993	1992	1991	1990	1989	1988	1987
Earnings Per Share	2.22	① ②1.96	①1.80	①1.30	① ②1.13	1.50	1.27
Dividends Per Share	0.90	③0.78	0.68	0.60	0.52	0.46	0.38
Dividend Payout %	40.5	39.4	37.8	46.2	45.8	30.8	30.0

① Before disc. oper. ② Before acctg. chg. ③ 2-for-1 stk split, 6/3/92

ANNUAL FINANCIAL DATA

RECORD OF EARNINGS (IN MILLIONS):

	1993	1992	1991	1990	1989	1988	1987
Total Revenue	3,542.9	3,434.1	3,332.5	3,195.6	2,875.7	2,649.9	2,250.5
Costs and Expenses	2,529.1	2,472.8	2,389.0	2,308.0	2,081.3	1,958.9	①2,001.5
Depreciation & Amort	263.0	250.8	238.1	220.6	194.5	166.2	...
Operating Income	750.8	710.5	705.4	667.0	599.9	524.8	249.0
Income Bef Income Taxes	574.8	495.4	461.6	327.6	261.1	364.2	228.7
Provision for Inc Taxes	221.6	183.2	173.7	121.0	80.9	127.2	95.7
Net Income	353.2	②312.2	③287.9	④206.6	⑤180.1	⑥237.0	199.4
Aver. Shs. Outstg. (000)	159,369	159,235	159,955	159,250	158,646	158,000	157,858

① Incl. Dep. ② Before disc. op. ③ Before disc. op. cr$2,700,000. ③ Before disc. op. cr$7,440,000. ④ Before disc. op. cr$6,646,000. ⑤ Before disc. op. cr$6,609,000. ⑥ Before disc. op. cr$6,315,000.

BALANCE SHEET (IN MILLIONS):

	1993	1992	1991	1990	1989	1988	1987
Cash and Cash Equivalents	55.8	73.1	118.5	79.9	61.1	45.7	94.4
Receivables, Net	1,406.8	1,362.4	1,387.8	1,280.4	1,156.6	1,061.3	465.0
Inventories	394.7	344.4	342.1	381.4	440.2	372.6	381.2
Gross Property	2,612.0	2,446.8	2,416.8	2,286.2	2,057.9	1,816.6	1,612.8
Accumulated Depreciation	1,400.0	1,277.6	1,205.9	1,092.4	927.5	798.8	722.5
Long-Term Debt	847.3	1,015.4	1,058.8	1,099.4	1,369.3	1,059.2	240.6
Capital Lease Obligations	...	...	...	...	...	...	47.2
Net Stockholders' Equity	1,871.6	1,652.9	1,800.7	1,589.4	1,428.3	1,269.2	1,038.2
Total Assets	6,793.8	6,498.8	6,380.6	6,060.5	5,611.1	4,788.4	2,431.7
Total Current Assets	1,936.7	1,838.7	1,935.5	1,799.1	1,698.6	1,519.3	963.1
Total Current Liabilities	3,273.4	3,096.5	2,995.4	2,888.9	2,270.9	1,853.1	791.5
Net Working Capital	d1,336.6	d1,257.8	d1,059.9	d1,089.8	d572.3	d333.8	171.7
Year End Shs Outstg (000)	158,174	157,175	158,764	157,377	156,730	156,250	152,728

STATISTICAL RECORD:

	1993	1992	1991	1990	1989	1988	1987
Operating Profit Margin %	21.2	20.7	21.2	20.9	20.9	19.8	11.1
Book Value Per Share	10.35	9.59	10.34	9.06	8.11	7.62	6.35
Return on Equity %	18.9	18.9	16.0	13.0	12.6	18.7	19.2
Return on Assets %	5.2	4.8	4.5	3.4	3.2	5.0	8.2
Average Yield %	2.2	2.3	2.6	3.0	2.2	2.3	1.9
P/E Ratio	20.0-16.3	20.9-14.3	18.2-10.6	20.6-10.4	24.2-18.1	15.8-11.3	19.9-11.8
Price Range	44½-36¼	41-28	32¾-19	26¾-13½	27⅜-20½	23¾-16⅞	25⅛-14⅞

Statistics are as originally reported.

OFFICERS:
G.B. Harvey, Chmn., Pres. & C.E.O.
C.F. Adimando, V.P.-Fin. & Admin. & Treas.

PRINCIPAL OFFICE: 1 Elmcroft Rd., Stamford, CT 06926-0700

TELEPHONE NUMBER: (203) 356-5000
NO. OF EMPLOYEES: 1,252
ANNUAL MEETING: In May
SHAREHOLDERS: 9,997
INSTITUTIONAL HOLDINGS:
No. of Institutions: 429
Shares Held: 59,784,437

REGISTRAR(S):

TRANSFER AGENT(S):

NYS SYMBOL PCH
Rec. Pr. 40⅛

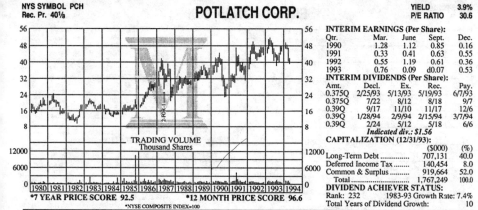

POTLATCH CORP.

YIELD 3.9%
P/E RATIO 30.6

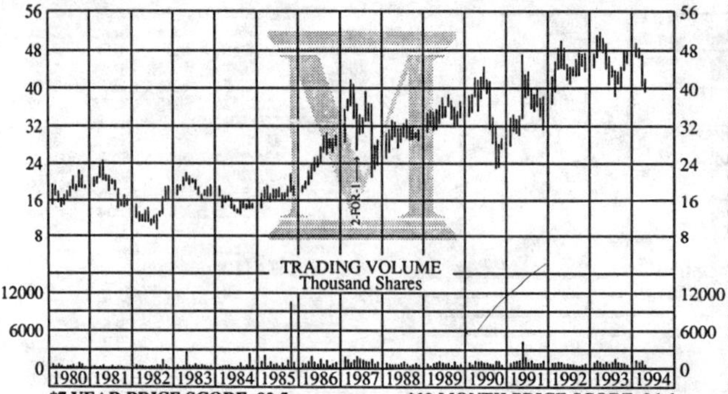
56
48
40
32
24
16
8
2-FOR-1
TRADING VOLUME
Thousand Shares
12000
6000
0
1980 1981 1982 1983 1984 1985 1986 1987 1988 1989 1990 1991 1992 1993 1994

*7 YEAR PRICE SCORE 92.5 *12 MONTH PRICE SCORE 96.6

*NYSE COMPOSITE INDEX=100

INTERIM EARNINGS (Per Share):

Qtr.	Mar.	June	Sept.	Dec.
1990	1.28	1.12	0.85	0.16
1991	0.33	0.41	0.63	0.55
1992	0.55	1.19	0.61	0.36
1993	0.76	0.09	d0.07	0.53

INTERIM DIVIDENDS (Per Share):

Amt.	Decl.	Ex.	Rec.	Pay.
0.375Q	2/25/93	5/13/93	5/19/93	6/7/93
0.375Q	7/22	8/12	8/18	9/7
0.39Q	9/17	11/10	11/17	12/6
0.39Q	1/28/94	2/9/94	2/15/94	3/7/94
0.39Q	2/24	5/12	5/18	6/6

Indicated div.: $1.56

CAPITALIZATION (12/31/93):

	($000)	(%)
Long-Term Debt	707,131	40.0
Deferred Income Tax	140,454	8.0
Common & Surplus	919,664	52.0
Total	1,767,249	100.0

DIVIDEND ACHIEVER STATUS:
Rank: 232 1983-93 Growth Rate: 7.4%
Total Years of Dividend Growth: 10

RECENT DEVELOPMENTS: Net income for the year ended 12/31/93, before charges of $31.7 million for accounting changes, decreased 51.4% to $38.3 million from $78.9 million in 1992. Revenue for the year increased 3.2% to $1.37 billion from $1.33 billion the previous year. The decrease in earnings reflected weak pricing for pulp-based products. The Wood Products Group and the Northwest Paper Division finished the year strong with improved earnings.

PROSPECTS: Wood products continue to be the Company's most profitable line of business as the market remains strong. Operating difficulties at the Lewiston, Idaho pulp mill are now taken care of and the modernization and expansion project can proceed in order to accomplish production goals. PCH has withdrawn from outside sales of market pulp until significant price increases are possible.

BUSINESS

POTLATCH CORP. is an integrated forest products company with 1.5 million acres of timberland in Arkansas, Idaho and Minnesota, supplying about 80% of the Company's total fiber needs. PCH's manufacturing facilities convert wood fiber into two main lines of products: wood items (lumber, plywood, oriented strand board, particleboard and wood specialties) and bleached fiber products (bleached kraft pulp, paperboard and packaging, printing papers and consumer tissue).

BUSINESS LINE ANALYSIS

(12/31/93)	Rev(%)	Inc($000)
Wood Products	36.8	160,220
Printing Papers	27.0	15,796
Other Pulp-Based Products	36.2	(40,944)
Total	100.0	135,072

ANNUAL EARNINGS AND DIVIDENDS PER SHARE

	1993	1992	1991	1990	1989	1988	1987
Earnings Per Share	**1.32**	**2.71**	**1.92**	**3.41**	**4.79**	**4.04**	**3.13**
Dividends Per Share	**1.515**	**1.425**	**1.34**	**1.23**	**1.08**	**0.95**	**[1] 0.86**
Dividend Payout %	**N.M.**	**52.6**	**69.8**	**36.1**	**22.5**	**23.5**	**27.5**

[1] 2-for-1 stk. split, 5/87 & 1/77.

ANNUAL FINANCIAL DATA

	1993	1992	1991	1990	1989	1988	1987
RECORD OF EARNINGS (IN MILLIONS):							
Total Revenues	1,368.9	1,326.6	1,237.0	1,252.9	1,227.6	1,084.1	992.1
Costs and Expenses	1,148.2	1,090.3	1,020.9	991.3	923.3	817.9	767.6
Depreciation & Amort	123.5	107.2	96.9	86.2	77.3	72.4	65.1
Earnings From Operations	97.1	129.2	119.2	175.5	227.0	193.8	159.5
Earn Bef Taxes on Income	65.0	124.6	85.2	152.3	208.6	175.6	134.6
Provision for Taxes on Inc	26.7	45.7	29.4	53.7	71.8	63.3	47.0
Net Income	[1] 38.3	78.9	55.8	98.6	136.7	112.4	87.6
Aver. Shs. Outstg. (000)	29,184	29,110	29,012	28,935	28,513	26,884	26,837
[1] Before acctg. change dr$31,704,000.							
BALANCE SHEET (IN MILLIONS):							
Cash and Cash Equivalents	8.3	13.4	22.0	1.7	221.1	84.6	57.4
Receivables, Net	118.6	115.0	100.7	96.6	117.3	103.3	92.1
Inventories	155.6	151.6	147.7	148.9	132.9	123.1	99.2
Gross Property	2,618.2	2,424.7	2,292.0	2,047.6	1,759.1	1,646.6	1,550.1
Accumulated Depreciation	926.0	825.3	765.8	693.4	642.9	596.0	544.1
Long-Term Debt	707.1	634.2	563.0	391.9	458.5	367.5	364.8
Net Stockholders' Equity	919.7	955.6	914.8	896.1	829.5	722.0	638.0
Total Assets	2,066.8	1,998.8	1,891.8	1,707.8	1,686.0	1,417.7	1,306.6
Total Current Assets	308.3	324.0	310.4	292.4	516.2	344.9	279.4
Total Current Liabilities	179.1	183.7	196.0	205.7	190.5	145.9	133.2
Net Working Capital	129.1	140.3	114.5	86.7	325.7	199.1	146.2
Year End Shs Outstg (000)	29,199	29,144	29,033	28,972	28,859	26,908	26,854
STATISTICAL RECORD:							
Operating Profit Margin %	7.1	9.7	9.6	14.0	18.5	17.9	16.1
Book Value Per Share	31.50	32.79	31.51	30.93	28.74	24.98	21.90
Return on Equity %	4.2	8.3	6.1	11.0	16.5	15.6	13.7
Return on Assets %	1.9	3.9	2.9	5.8	8.1	7.9	6.7
Average Yield %	3.4	3.3	3.6	3.6	3.1	3.3	2.7
P/E Ratio	39.6-29.2	18.5-13.6	24.5-14.5	13.0-6.7	8.1-6.4	8.3-6.2	13.4-6.7
Price Range	51⅞-38¼	50-36¾	47-27¾	44½-23	38⅝-30¾	33⅜-25	41⅞-21

Statistics are as originally reported.

OFFICERS:
J.M. Richards, Chmn. & C.E.O.
G.F. Jewett, Jr., Vice-Chmn.
G.E. Pfautsch, Sr. V.P.-Fin. & Treas.
S.T. Powell, V.P.-Fin. Svcs. & Sec.

INCORPORATED: ME, 1931; reincorp., DE, Aug., 1955

PRINCIPAL OFFICE: One Maritime Plaza, San Francisco, CA 94111

TELEPHONE NUMBER: (415) 576-8800

NO. OF EMPLOYEES: 7,000 (approx.)

ANNUAL MEETING: In May

SHAREHOLDERS: 3,600 (approx.)

INSTITUTIONAL HOLDINGS:
No. of Institutions: 184
Shares Held: 11,871,257

REGISTRAR(S):

TRANSFER AGENT(S):

POTOMAC ELECTRIC POWER CO.

YIELD 8.6%
P/E RATIO 10.0

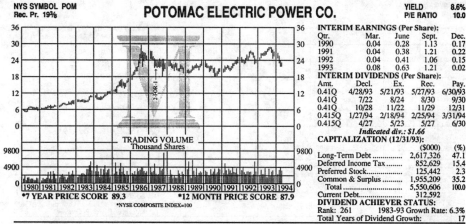

*7 YEAR PRICE SCORE 89.3   *12 MONTH PRICE SCORE 87.9
*NYSE COMPOSITE INDEX=100

TRADING VOLUME
Thousand Shares

INTERIM EARNINGS (Per Share):

Qtr.	Mar.	June	Sept.	Dec.
1990	0.04	0.28	1.13	0.17
1991	0.04	0.38	1.21	0.22
1992	0.04	0.41	1.06	0.15
1993	0.08	0.63	1.21	0.02

INTERIM DIVIDENDS (Per Share):

Amt.	Decl.	Ex.	Rec.	Pay.
0.41Q	4/28/93	5/21/93	5/27/93	6/30/93
0.41Q	7/22	8/24	8/30	9/30
0.41Q	10/28	11/22	11/29	12/31
0.415Q	1/27/94	2/18/94	2/25/94	3/31/94
0.415Q	4/27	5/23	5/27	6/30

Indicated div.: $1.66

CAPITALIZATION (12/31/93):

	($000)	(%)
Long-Term Debt	2,617,326	47.1
Deferred Income Tax	852,629	15.4
Preferred Stock	125,442	2.3
Common & Surplus	1,955,209	35.2
Total	5,550,606	100.0
Current Debt	312,592	

DIVIDEND ACHIEVER STATUS:
Rank: 261   1983-93 Growth Rate: 6.3%
Total Years of Dividend Growth: 17

RECENT DEVELOPMENTS: For the year ended 12/31/93, net income was $241.6 million compared with $200.7 million in 1992. Revenues were $1.73 billion, up 7.7%. The improved results reflect increased electricity sales due to last summer's hotter than average weather. Net income for the fourth quarter was $6.8 million compared with $20.7 million in the prior year. Revenues were $351.8 million, up 6.1%.

PROSPECTS: Potomac Electric benefits from adequate regulatory treatment, a stable service territory, a manageable construction program, and competitive electric rates. Potomac Electric received a rate increase of $27 million in Maryland, effective November 1, 1993. Potomac Electric's request for an increase in revenues of $78 million in the District of Columbia is pending approval.

BUSINESS

POTOMAC ELECTRIC POWER CO. (PEPCO) furnishes electricity to the District of Columbia and adjoining sections of Maryland and Virginia, an area containing only 640 square miles. PEPCO also sells electricity at wholesale to the Southern Maryland Electric Cooperative, Inc. PEPCO's service area has a stable government work force and a growing number of high technology and private sector businesses.

REVENUES

(12/31/93)	($000)	(%)
Residential	505,173	29.7
Commercial	791,357	46.5
US Government	238,192	13.9
DC Government	53,551	3.1
Wholesale	108,162	6.4
Other	6,007	0.4
Total	1,702,442	100.0

ANNUAL EARNINGS AND DIVIDENDS PER SHARE

	1993	1992	1991	1990	1989	1988	1987
Earnings Per Share	1.95	1.66	1.87	1.62	2.16	2.14	2.11
Dividends Per Share	1.64	① 1.60	1.56	1.52	1.46	1.38	② 1.30
Dividend Payout %	84.1	96.4	83.4	93.8	67.6	64.5	61.6

① Bef acctg chge ② 2-for-1 stk. split, 5/87.

ANNUAL FINANCIAL DATA

RECORD OF EARNINGS (IN MILLIONS):

	1993	1992	1991	1990	1989	1988	1987
Total Revenue	1,725.2	1,601.6	1,552.1	1,411.7	1,394.9	1,349.8	1,332.1
Depreciation & Amort	163.6	149.8	134.3	123.8	119.8	120.8	115.9
Maintenance	93.7	90.8	90.4	90.6	93.3	92.9	99.6
Prov for Fed Inc Taxes	110.2	75.3	82.7	74.1	89.2	92.8	127.2
Operating Income	324.7	279.5	290.2	256.1	274.5	273.0	262.2
Net Utility Interest Charges	131.6	124.4	119.1	109.6	100.2	92.2	86.3
Net Income	241.6	① 200.8	210.2	170.2	214.6	211.1	208.2
Aver. Shs. Outstg. (000)	115,640	112,390	105,911	98,621	95,203	94,450	94,438

① Before acctg. change cr$16,022,000.

BALANCE SHEET (IN MILLIONS):

	1993	1992	1991	1990	1989	1988	1987
Gross Plant	5,665.1	5,367.6	5,048.1	4,659.3	4,270.7	3,945.7	3,700.0
Accumulated Depreciation	1,534.0	1,436.4	1,341.3	1,261.3	1,173.2	1,088.7	1,021.0
Net Property & Plant	4,131.1	3,931.3	3,706.9	3,398.0	3,097.5	2,857.0	2,678.9
Long-term Debt	2,617.3	2,467.6	2,483.0	2,117.5	1,638.9	1,531.0	1,104.4
Net Stockholders' Equity	2,080.7	1,948.4	1,842.1	1,561.1	1,469.5	1,324.6	1,334.4
Total Assets	6,665.5	6,142.3	5,853.8	5,239.7	4,642.7	4,146.5	3,345.0
Year End Shs Outstg (000)	117,798	114,296	111,106	99,715	97,910	94,453	94,447

STATISTICAL RECORD:

	1993	1992	1991	1990	1989	1988	1987
Book Value Per Share	16.60	15.95	15.45	14.40	14.24	13.22	12.61
Op. Inc/Net Pl %	0.1	0.1	0.1	0.1	0.1	0.1	0.1
Accum. Dep/Gr. Pl %	0.3	0.3	0.3	0.3	0.3	0.3	0.3
Return on Equity %	11.6	10.3	11.4	10.9	14.6	15.9	16.4
Average Yield %	6.2	6.4	7.0	7.2	6.7	6.4	5.7
P/E Ratio	14.8-12.2	16.6-13.6	13.4-10.5	14.8-11.1	11.2-8.9	11.2-9.0	13.0-8.5
Price Range	28⅞-23⅞	27½-22⅝	25⅛-19⅝	24-18	24¼-19¼	24-19¼	27⅜-18

Statistics are as originally reported.

OFFICERS:
E.F. Mitchell, Chmn. & C.E.O.
H.L. Davis, Vice-Chmn. & C.F.O.
J.M. Derrick, Jr., Pres. & C.O.O.
B.K. Cauley, Secretary

INCORPORATED: DC, Dec., 1896

PRINCIPAL OFFICE: 1900 Pennsylvania Ave. NW, Washington, DC 20068

TELEPHONE NUMBER: (202) 872-2000
FAX: (202) 331-6874
NO. OF EMPLOYEES: 5,035
ANNUAL MEETING: In April
SHAREHOLDERS: 100,780 com.; 3,449, pfd.
INSTITUTIONAL HOLDINGS:
No. of Institutions: 245
Shares Held: 19,699,663

REGISTRAR(S): Chemical Bank, New York, NY
Riggs National Bank of Washington, D.C., Washington, DC

TRANSFER AGENT(S): Chemical Bank, New York, NY
Riggs National Bank of Washington, D.C., Washington, DC

NYS SYMBOL PPG
Rec. Pr. 75⅜

PPG INDUSTRIES, INC.

YIELD ...%
P/E RATIO 27.1

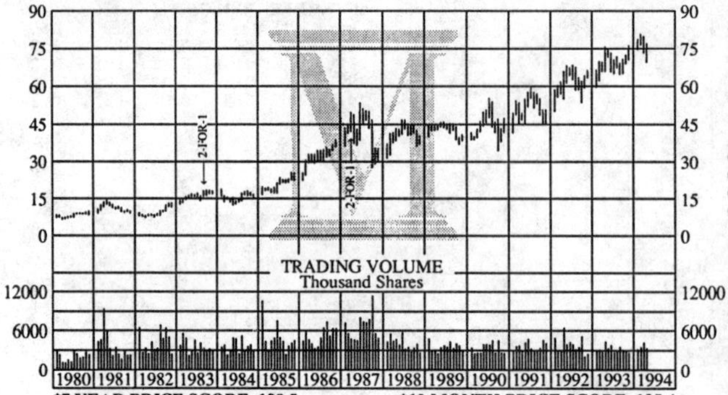

***7 YEAR PRICE SCORE 108.5** ***12 MONTH PRICE SCORE 105.4**

*NYSE COMPOSITE INDEX=100

INTERIM EARNINGS (Per Share):

Qtr.	Mar.	June	Sept.	Dec.
1990	1.16	1.31	1.00	0.96
1991	0.21	0.75	0.65	0.29
1992	0.74	1.01	0.62	0.64
1993	1.04	1.00	0.23	0.51

INTERIM DIVIDENDS (Per Share):

Amt.	Decl.	Ex.	Rec.	Pay.
0.54Q	7/15/93	8/4/93	8/10/93	9/10/93
0.54Q	10/14	11/4	11/10	12/10
0.54Q	1/20/94	2/15/94	2/22/94	3/11/94
0.56Q	4/21	5/4	5/10	6/10
100%	4/21	6/13	5/10	6/10

CAPITALIZATION (12/31/93):

	($000)	(%)
Long-Term Debt	743,900	20.9
Cap. Lease Oblig.	30,100	0.8
Deferred Income Tax	268,600	7.5
Minority Interest	51,900	1.5
Common & Surplus	2,473,100	69.3
Total	3,567,600	100.0

DIVIDEND ACHIEVER STATUS:
Rank: 99 1983-93 Growth Rate: 13.0%
Total Years of Dividend Growth: 22

RECENT DEVELOPMENTS: For the three months ended 12/31/93, net income was $53.9 million compared with $67.9 million in the comparable period of 1992. Results included a $38 million divestiture-related charge for the pending sale of a significant part of the medical electronics operation. Sales declined to $1.38 billion from $1.41 billion. Gains achieved in the North American businesses were offset by foreign currency translation and lower European volumes.

PROSPECTS: Despite increased results from North American businesses, plans to streamline operations continue with write-downs of assets of inactive plants and the closing of two glass plants. Sale of the commercial construction-fabrication unit is pending. The sale of a significant part of the medical electronics business, which has accumulated $200 million in sales, is also pending.

BUSINESS

PPG INDUSTRIES, INC. is a leading supplier of products for manufacturing, building, processing and numerous other industries. This diversified global manufacturer makes flat glass and fabricated glass products, continuous-strand fiberglass, original and refinish coatings, and industrial and specialty chemicals. PPG operates 73 major manufacturing facilities in countries including Canada, France, Italy, Mexico, Spain, Taiwan, the U.K., the U.S. and Germany.

BUSINESS LINE ANALYSIS

(12/31/93)	Rev(%)	Inc(%)
Coatings & Resins	40.2	56.2
Glass	37.6	26.8
Chemicals	20.0	18.5
Other	2.2	(1.5)
Total	100.0	100.0

ANNUAL EARNINGS AND DIVIDENDS PER SHARE

	1993	1992	1991	1990	1989	1988	1987
Earnings Per Share	**2.78**	**3.01**	**[1] 1.90**	**4.43**	**4.18**	**4.26**	**3.19**
Dividends Per Share	**2.08**	**1.88**	**1.72**	**1.64**	**1.48**	**1.33**	**[2] 1.11**
Dividend Payout %	**74.8**	**62.5**	**90.5**	**37.0**	**35.4**	**31.2**	**34.8**

Note: 100%stk.div.6/10/94. [1] Before acctg. chg. [2] 100% stk div, 3/87

ANNUAL FINANCIAL DATA

RECORD OF EARNINGS (IN MILLIONS):	1993	1992	1991	1990	1989	1988	1987
Total Revenues	5,753.9	5,813.9	5,672.6	6,021.4	5,734.1	5,616.7	5,182.6
Costs and Expenses	4,706.2	4,777.6	4,755.0	4,793.5	4,605.5	4,444.3	4,225.5
Depreciation	331.1	351.5	351.2	323.5	292.3	292.6	282.5
Operating Profit	917.8	887.8	786.8	1,122.3	1,068.9	1,125.3	918.4
Income Bef Income Taxes	544.1	541.8	353.5	778.7	756.7	788.3	642.3
Income Taxes	236.2	218.4	146.7	292.1	283.5	311.4	259.8
Minority Interest	12.9	4.0	5.4	11.8	8.0	9.3	5.4
Net Income	[1] 295.0	319.4	[2] 201.4	474.8	465.2	467.6	377.1
Aver. Shs. Outstg. (000)	212,600	212,200	212,400	214,400	222,600	219,600	236,400

[1] Before acctg. change dr$272,800,000. [2] Before acctg. change cr$74,800,000.

BALANCE SHEET (IN MILLIONS):	1993	1992	1991	1990	1989	1988	1987
Cash and Cash Equivalents	111.9	61.4	37.6	59.3	64.6	103.4	82.1
Receivables, Net	1,144.1	1,073.3	1,057.9	1,069.3	1,107.9	1,010.0	1,037.3
Inventories	683.3	742.3	875.3	945.1	753.7	683.1	650.7
Gross Property	6,041.9	6,157.7	6,212.4	5,995.0	5,447.5	5,005.6	4,754.4
Accumulated Depreciation	3,254.6	3,186.2	3,029.2	2,739.9	2,440.7	2,247.9	2,069.4
Long-Term Debt	743.9	837.6	1,124.2	1,148.6	1,139.0	838.0	863.0
Obligs Under Cap Lses	30.1	34.7	39.0	37.6	38.5	38.9	40.3
Net Stockholders' Equity	2,473.1	2,698.9	2,654.5	2,546.5	2,282.3	2,243.4	2,043.5
Total Assets	5,651.5	5,661.7	6,056.2	6,108.2	5,645.4	5,154.1	4,987.9
Total Current Assets	2,025.9	1,950.8	2,173.3	2,216.9	2,056.3	1,899.0	1,835.6
Total Current Liabilities	1,281.0	1,253.0	1,340.5	1,470.5	1,337.7	1,264.5	1,274.8
Net Working Capital	744.9	697.8	832.8	746.4	718.6	634.5	560.8
Year End Shs Outstg (000)	213,682	212,270	212,340	212,082	217,612	219,120	221,742

STATISTICAL RECORD:	1993	1992	1991	1990	1989	1988	1987
Operating Profit Margin %	12.5	11.8	10.0	15.0	14.6	16.0	13.3
Book Value Per Share	11.57	12.71	12.50	12.01	10.49	10.24	9.22
Return on Equity %	11.9	11.8	7.6	18.6	20.4	20.8	18.5
Return on Assets %	5.2	5.6	3.3	7.8	8.2	9.1	7.6
Average Yield %	3.1	3.2	3.4	3.7	3.6	3.4	2.7
P/E Ratio	54.9-42.7	45.4-33.2	62.5-43.7	24.9-15.6	22.0-17.7	22.0-14.7	33.5-17.2
Price Range	76¼-59⅜	68⅜-50	59⅜-41½	55¼-34½	46-37	46⅞-31¼	53½-27½

Statistics are as originally reported.

OFFICERS:
J.E. Dempsey, Chmn. & C.E.O.
E.J. Mazeski, Jr., V.P. & Sec.
H.K. Linge, Treas.

INCORPORATED: PA, Aug., 1883; reincorp., PA, Nov., 1920

PRINCIPAL OFFICE: One PPG Place, Pittsburgh, PA 15272

TELEPHONE NUMBER: (412) 434-3131

NO. OF EMPLOYEES: 31,400 (avg.)

ANNUAL MEETING: In April

SHAREHOLDERS: 33,909

INSTITUTIONAL HOLDINGS:
No. of Institutions: 447
Shares Held: 50,940,669

REGISTRAR(S): Chemical Bank, New York, NY

TRANSFER AGENT(S): Chemical Bank, New York, NY

PRATT & LAMBERT, INC.

YIELD 3.8%
P/E RATIO 15.6

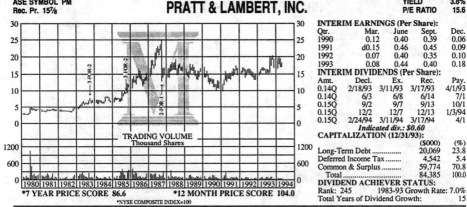

*7 YEAR PRICE SCORE 86.6   *12 MONTH PRICE SCORE 104.0
*NYSE COMPOSITE INDEX=100

INTERIM EARNINGS (Per Share):

Qtr.	Mar.	June	Sept.	Dec.
1990	0.12	0.40	0.39	0.06
1991	d0.15	0.46	0.45	0.09
1992	0.07	0.40	0.35	0.10
1993	0.08	0.44	0.40	0.18

INTERIM DIVIDENDS (Per Share):

Amt.	Decl.	Ex.	Rec.	Pay.
0.14Q	2/18/93	3/11/93	3/17/93	4/1/93
0.14Q	6/3	6/8	6/14	7/1
0.15Q	9/2	9/7	9/13	10/1
0.15Q	12/2	12/7	12/13	1/3/94
0.15Q	2/24/94	3/11/94	3/17/94	4/1

Indicated div.: $0.60

CAPITALIZATION (12/31/93):

	($000)	(%)
Long-Term Debt	20,069	23.8
Deferred Income Tax	4,542	5.4
Common & Surplus	59,774	70.8
Total	84,385	100.0

DIVIDEND ACHIEVER STATUS:
Rank: 245   1983-93 Growth Rate: 7.0%
Total Years of Dividend Growth: 15

RECENT DEVELOPMENTS: For the year ended 12/31/93, net income increased 20.3% to $6.2 million from $5.2 million in 1992. Net sales for the year rose 2.6% to $241.8 million from $235.6 million a year ago. Sales of architectural finishes declined slightly during the year while sales of construction adhesives continued to advance as a result in the upturn in building activity and additional market penetration. Demand

for the Company's packaging and graphic arts products combined with an increase in purchases by the U.S. General Services Administration contributed to the increase in sales of industrial products. For the quarter, net income nearly doubled to $1.0 million from $576,000 for the 1992 quarter. Net sales for the quarter increased 10% to $59.4 million from $54.0 million for the year-ago quarter.

BUSINESS

PRATT & LAMBERT, INC. develops, produces and sells of architectural finishes and chemical specialties, including industrial coatings and adhesives. Architectural finishes include paints and allied products distributed largely through independent dealers for application by consumers, contractors and maintenance users. Specialty products consist of coatings and adhesives marketed through specialized intermediaries for construction, remodeling and do-it-yourself applications.

QUARTERLY DATA

(12/31/93)($000)	Rev	Inc
1st Quarter	54,294	466
2nd Quarter	64,040	2,480
3rd Quarter	63,990	2,254
4th Quarter	59,437	1,011

ANNUAL EARNINGS AND DIVIDENDS PER SHARE

	1993	1992	1991	1990	1989	1988	1987
Earnings Per Share	1.10	0.92	0.85	0.98	1.06	1.18	1.42
Dividends Per Share	0.57	0.56	0.53	0.52	0.46	0.44	① 0.40
Dividend Payout %	51.8	60.9	62.4	53.1	43.4	37.3	28.2

① 2-for-1 stk. split, 10/87.

ANNUAL FINANCIAL DATA

RECORD OF EARNINGS (IN THOUSANDS):

	1993	1992	1991	1990	1989	1988	1987
Total Revenues	241,761	235,628	238,953	243,098	245,536	232,939	226,016
Costs and Expenses	225,861	220,637	224,049	226,739	228,154	216,099	205,406
Depreciation	4,735	4,669	4,602	4,257	3,956	3,449	3,389
Income From Operations	11,165	10,322	10,302	12,102	13,426	13,391	17,221
Inc Bef Taxes on Income	10,206	8,823	7,947	9,321	10,557	11,923	15,437
Taxes on Income	3,995	3,660	3,191	3,702	4,112	4,680	6,815
Net Income	6,211	5,163	4,756	5,619	6,445	7,243	8,622
Aver. Shs. Outstg.	5,553	5,534	5,520	5,687	6,005	6,010	5,816

BALANCE SHEET (IN THOUSANDS):

	1993	1992	1991	1990	1989	1988	1987
Cash and Cash Equivalents	2,443	4,349	2,381	2,176	2,015	2,020	1,511
Receivables, Net	39,950	36,000	36,367	35,396	36,254	34,133	34,133
Inventories	38,401	32,897	41,592	38,625	38,329	38,222	31,513
Gross Property	78,679	72,053	67,232	64,751	61,450	57,263	51,275
Accumulated Depreciation	43,872	38,926	35,720	33,057	29,729	26,545	23,839
Long-Term Debt	20,069	21,363	21,427	22,236	21,582	19,182	18,297
Net Stockholders' Equity	59,774	57,331	55,866	53,937	55,223	56,336	48,697
Total Assets	128,278	118,744	124,032	119,939	119,632	116,497	103,924
Total Current Assets	86,623	78,724	85,835	80,782	80,654	78,799	72,049
Total Current Liabilities	43,893	36,624	43,296	40,288	39,075	37,466	33,623
Net Working Capital	42,730	42,100	42,539	40,494	41,579	41,333	38,426
Year End Shares Outstg	5,585	5,539	5,531	5,519	5,833	6,120	5,824

STATISTICAL RECORD:

	1993	1992	1991	1990	1989	1988	1987
Operating Profit Margin %	4.6	4.4	4.3	5.0	5.5	5.7	7.6
Book Value Per Share	10.70	10.35	10.10	9.77	9.47	9.21	8.36
Return on Equity %	10.4	9.0	8.5	10.4	11.7	12.9	17.7
Return on Assets %	4.8	4.3	3.8	4.7	5.4	6.2	8.3
P/E Ratio	18.5-13.3	18.3-14.4	20.6-11.5	17.5-10.3	17.0-12.5	16.4-11.9	17.5-9.0
Price Range	20⅜-14⅝	16⅞-13¼	17½-9¾	17⅛-10⅛	18-13¼	19⅜-14	24⅞-12¾

Statistics are as originally reported.

OFFICERS:
R.D. Stevens, Jr., Chairman
J.J. Castiglia, Pres. & C.E.O.
J.R. Boldt, V.P.-Fin., Sec. & C.F.O.
J.M. Culligan, Treasurer

INCORPORATED: NY, 1885

PRINCIPAL OFFICE: 75 Tonawanda St., Buffalo, NY 14207

TELEPHONE NUMBER: (716) 873-6000

FAX: (716) 877-9646

NO. OF EMPLOYEES: 1,425

ANNUAL MEETING: In May

SHAREHOLDERS: 2,098

INSTITUTIONAL HOLDINGS:
No. of Institutions: 43
Shares Held: 2,159,585

REGISTRAR(S): Mellon Securities Trust Co., New York, NY

TRANSFER AGENT(S): Mellon Securities Trust Co., New York, NY

PREMIER INDUSTRIAL CORP.

YIELD 1.8%
P/E RATIO 20.6

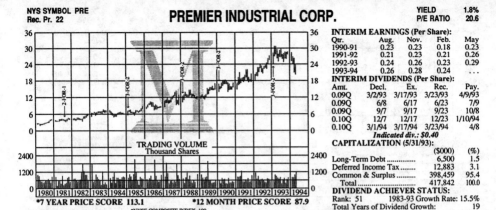

*7 YEAR PRICE SCORE 113.1 *12 MONTH PRICE SCORE 87.9
*NYSE COMPOSITE INDEX=100

TRADING VOLUME
Thousand Shares

INTERIM EARNINGS (Per Share):

Qtr.	Aug.	Nov.	Feb.	May
1990-91	0.23	0.23	0.18	0.23
1991-92	0.21	0.23	0.21	0.26
1992-93	0.24	0.26	0.23	0.29
1993-94	0.26	0.28	0.24	...

INTERIM DIVIDENDS (Per Share):

Amt.	Decl.	Ex.	Rec.	Pay.
0.09Q	3/2/93	3/17/93	3/23/93	4/9/93
0.09Q	6/8	6/17	6/23	7/9
0.09Q	9/7	9/17	9/23	10/8
0.10Q	12/7	12/17	12/23	1/10/94
0.10Q	3/1/94	3/17/94	3/23/94	4/8

Indicated div.: $0.40

CAPITALIZATION (5/31/93):

	($000)	(%)
Long-Term Debt	6,500	1.5
Deferred Income Tax	12,883	3.1
Common & Surplus	398,459	95.4
Total	417,842	100.0

DIVIDEND ACHIEVER STATUS:
Rank: 51   1983-93 Growth Rate: 15.5%
Total Years of Dividend Growth: 19

RECENT DEVELOPMENTS: For the quarter ended 11/30/93, net income rose 7% to $24.0 million compared with $22.5 million for the same period in 1992. Revenues climbed 7% to $183.2 million versus $171.7 million a year ago. Manufacturers' emphasis on cutting costs through repairing old machinery instead of buying new machinery also contributed to earnings through higher sales in maintenance products.

PROSPECTS: PRE's Electronics Segment continues to produce strong earnings growth for the Company, and prospects for further growth are good as the segment rapidly expands throughout Europe. Additionally, near-term sales will remain strong due to demand by manufacturers for replacement parts. The Company's diverse customer base along with its comprehensive product offerings will also support long-term results.

BUSINESS

PREMIER INDUSTRIAL CORPORATION is a broad line distributor of electronic components used in the production and maintenance of equipment, a supplier of maintenance products for industrial, commercial and institutional applications, and a manufacturer of high-performance firefighting accessories. PRE's business is broken down into two categories: Electronics Distribution supplies communications, research, and maintenance and repair applications; General Products manufacturers equipment, vehicle and building maintenance products.

BUSINESS LINE ANALYSIS

(5/31/93)	Rev(%)	Inc(%)
Electronics		
Distribution	70.2	71.8
General Products	29.8	28.2
Total	100.0	100.0

ANNUAL EARNINGS AND DIVIDENDS PER SHARE

	5/31/93	5/31/92	5/31/91	5/31/90	5/31/89	5/31/88	5/31/87
Earnings Per Share	1.02	0.91	0.86	0.86	0.75	0.65	0.49
Dividends Per Share	①0.48	0.307	0.273	②0.267	0.18	③0.13	0.119
Dividend Payout %	47.1	33.6	31.5	31.0	23.5	19.9	24.5

① 3-for-2 stk split,01/11/93 ② 3-for-2 stk split, 1/10/90 ③ 50% stk split, 1/88

ANNUAL FINANCIAL DATA

RECORD OF EARNINGS (IN THOUSANDS):

	5/31/93	5/31/92	5/31/91	5/31/90	5/31/89	5/31/88	5/31/87
Total Revenues	695,012	646,087	641,122	629,255	602,341	535,936	464,688
Costs and Expenses	548,586	513,018	521,376	509,652	490,137	432,130	377,208
Depreciation & Amort	7,845	7,873	7,368	6,738	7,169	5,712	5,775
Operating Income	138,581	125,196	112,378	112,865	105,035	98,094	81,705
Earn Bef Income Taxes	138,229	124,753	111,766	112,495	104,787	97,938	81,421
Income Taxes	50,005	45,918	37,048	37,780	35,083	33,909	33,141
Net Income	88,224	78,835	74,718	74,715	69,704	64,029	48,280
Aver. Shs. Outstg	86,868	86,569	86,413	87,149	92,501	98,222	100,107

BALANCE SHEET (IN THOUSANDS):

Cash and Cash Equivalents	144,583	107,477	77,990	48,767	33,230	130,188	117,272
Receivables, Net	102,888	95,470	90,392	90,869	85,961	78,309	71,252
Inventories	131,484	128,292	104,984	106,743	89,276	79,000	70,197
Gross Property	111,668	103,467	100,240	95,793	85,480	74,446	71,259
Accumulated Depreciation	63,673	58,453	52,327	46,587	43,896	39,073	36,819
Long-Term Debt	6,500	6,500	6,500	6,500	6,503	6,561	6,662
Net Stockholders' Equity	398,459	344,947	292,078	251,319	212,434	289,026	266,888
Total Assets	466,060	407,417	348,666	320,807	277,833	354,817	325,569
Total Current Assets	384,307	336,518	277,587	250,220	214,625	292,700	263,972
Total Current Liabilities	48,218	44,284	38,599	51,049	45,626	42,519	35,199
Net Working Capital	336,089	292,234	238,988	199,171	168,999	250,181	228,773
Year End Shares Outstg	85,887	86,293	86,118	86,564	87,402	98,388	99,135

STATISTICAL RECORD:

Operating Profit Margin %	19.9	19.4	17.5	17.9	17.4	18.3	17.6
Book Value Per Share	4.64	4.00	3.39	2.90	2.43	2.94	2.69
Return on Equity %	22.1	22.9	25.6	29.7	32.8	22.2	18.1
Return on Assets %	18.9	19.3	21.4	23.3	25.1	18.0	14.8
Average Yield %	2.1	1.7	1.7	1.9	1.4	1.1	1.3
P/E Ratio	26.5-18.0	24.3-16.3	21.1-16.1	19.8-13.1	19.7-13.8	22.3-13.1	21.4-15.3
Price Range	27-18⅜	22⅛-14⅞	18⅜-14	17-11¼	14¾-10⅜	14½-8½	10½-7½

Statistics are as originally reported.

OFFICERS:
M.L. Mandel, Chmn.
B.W. Johnson, Pres.
S.D. Neidus, V.P. & Treas.
G.C. Grinnell, V.P. & Sec.

INCORPORATED: OH, Jun., 1946

PRINCIPAL OFFICE: 4500 Euclid Ave., Cleveland, OH 44103

TELEPHONE NUMBER: (216) 391-8300

NO. OF EMPLOYEES: 2,332 (approx.)

ANNUAL MEETING: In October

SHAREHOLDERS: 3,384 (approx.)

INSTITUTIONAL HOLDINGS:
No. of Institutions: 135
Shares Held: 18,051,427

REGISTRAR(S): National City Bank, Cleveland, OH 44114

TRANSFER AGENT(S): National City Bank, Cleveland, OH 44114

PROCTER & GAMBLE CO.

YIELD 2.2%
P/E RATIO 76.9

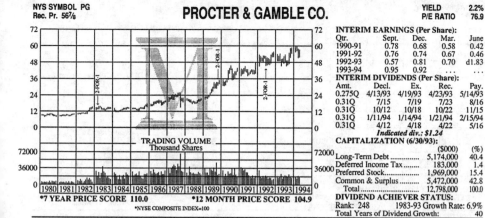

*7 YEAR PRICE SCORE 110.0   *12 MONTH PRICE SCORE 104.9

*NYSE COMPOSITE INDEX=100

INTERIM EARNINGS (Per Share):

Qtr.	Sept.	Dec.	Mar.	June
1990-91	0.78	0.68	0.58	0.42
1991-92	0.76	0.74	0.67	0.46
1992-93	0.57	0.81	0.70	d1.83
1993-94	0.95	0.92	...	...

INTERIM DIVIDENDS (Per Share):

Amt.	Decl.	Ex.	Rec.	Pay.
0.275Q	4/13/93	4/19/93	4/23/93	5/14/93
0.31Q	7/15	7/19	7/23	8/16
0.31Q	10/12	10/18	10/22	11/15
0.31Q	1/11/94	1/14/94	1/21/94	2/15/94
0.31Q	4/12	4/18	4/22	5/16

Indicated div.: $1.24

CAPITALIZATION (6/30/93):

	($000)	(%)
Long-Term Debt	5,174,000	40.4
Deferred Income Tax	183,000	1.4
Preferred Stock	1,969,000	15.4
Common & Surplus	5,472,000	42.8
Total	12,798,000	100.0

DIVIDEND ACHIEVER STATUS:
Rank: 248   1983-93 Growth Rate: 6.9%
Total Years of Dividend Growth: 40

RECENT DEVELOPMENTS: Net income for the quarter ended 12/31/93 was $653 million compared with $576 million a year ago, an increase of 13%. Sales fell by 1% to $7.79 billion. Lower costs and strong unit volume growth in the U.S. and abroad, particularly in the Far East, Latin America and Eastern Europe, boosted earnings. However, adverse foreign exchange rates limited earnings growth.

PROSPECTS: PG's restructuring will enable the Company to better compete with lower-priced rivals. PG will improve manufacturing efficiencies and reduce operating costs, as well as lower prices on most of its products that have lost market share to competitors, primarily in the soap, hardsurface cleaner, food and diaper categories. This strategy will help expand margins and boost market share.

BUSINESS

PROCTER & GAMBLE CO. manufactures and markets laundry, cleaning and personal care products, pharmaceuticals, foods and beverages, and business and industrial products. Leading brands are: Cheer, Spic & Span and Tide cleansing compounds; Crisco shortenings, Crest toothpastes, Ivory soaps, and Prell and Head and Shoulders shampoos. Other products include Vick's cough and cold remedies, Charmin toilet tissue, Pampers diapers, Oil of Olay skin products, Old Spice deodorants and fragrances, Folger's coffee and Hawaiian Punch fruit drinks. In the fiscal year ending 6/30/93, 52% of sales originated overseas. Citrus Hill was discontinued in 1992.

REVENUES

(6/30/93)	($000)	(%)
Laundry & Cleaning	10,061	32.7
Personal Care	16,238	52.8
Food & Beverage	3,271	10.7
Pulp & Chemicals	1,172	3.8
Total	30,742	100.0

ANNUAL EARNINGS AND DIVIDENDS PER SHARE

	6/30/93	6/30/92	6/30/91	6/30/90	6/30/89	6/30/88	6/30/87
Earnings Per Share	① 0.25	② 2.62	2.46	2.25	1.78	1.49	0.47
Dividends Per Share	1.17	② 1.075	1.00	③ 0.925	1.20	0.70	0.675
Dividend Payout %	N.M.	41.0	40.7	41.2	67.4	47.0	N.M.

① Before acctg. chg. ② 2-for-1 stk split,06/15/92 ③ 2-for-1 stk split, 11/89

ANNUAL FINANCIAL DATA

RECORD OF EARNINGS (IN MILLIONS):

Total Revenues	30,433.0	29,890.0	27,406.0	24,642.0	21,689.0	19,491.0	17,163.0
Costs and Expenses	28,837.0	25,444.0	23,368.0	20,920.0	18,592.0	16,843.0	15,564.0
Deprec, Depl & Amort	1,140.0	1,051.0	956.0	859.0	767.0	697.0	629.0
Operating Income	456.0	3,395.0	3,082.0	2,863.0	2,330.0	1,951.0	970.0
Earn Bef Income Taxes	349.0	2,885.0	2,687.0	2,421.0	1,939.0	1,630.0	617.0
Income Taxes	80.0	1,013.0	914.0	819.0	733.0	610.0	290.0
Net Income	① 269.0	1,872.0	1,773.0	1,602.0	1,206.0	1,020.0	327.0
Aver. Shs. Outstg. (000)	680,000	677,000	690,000	690,000	692,000	669,000	674,000

① Before acctg. change dr$925,000,000.

BALANCE SHEET (IN MILLIONS):

Cash & Cash Equivalents	2,322.0	1,776.0	1,384.0	1,407.0	1,587.0	1,065.0	741.0
Receivables, Net	3,851.0	3,699.0	3,024.0	2,647.0	2,090.0	1,759.0	1,557.0
Inventories	2,903.0	3,311.0	3,190.0	2,865.0	2,337.0	2,292.0	2,164.0
Gross Property	14,877.0	15,184.0	13,034.0	11,789.0	10,546.0	10,170.0	9,521.0
Accumulated Depreciation	5,392.0	5,488.0	4,761.0	4,353.0	3,753.0	3,392.0	2,990.0
Long-Term Debt	5,174.0	5,223.0	4,111.0	3,588.0	3,698.0	2,462.0	2,524.0
Net Stockholders' Equity	7,441.0	9,071.0	7,736.0	7,518.0	6,215.0	6,337.0	5,990.0
Total Assets	24,935.0	24,025.0	20,468.0	18,487.0	16,351.0	14,820.0	13,715.0
Total Current Assets	9,975.0	9,366.0	8,435.0	7,644.0	6,578.0	5,593.0	4,981.0
Total Current Liabilities	8,287.0	7,642.0	6,733.0	5,417.0	4,656.0	4,224.0	3,458.0
Net Working Capital	1,688.0	1,724.0	1,702.0	2,227.0	1,922.0	1,369.0	1,523.0
Year End Shs Outstg (000)	682,000	679,000	676,000	693,000	648,000	677,000	676,000

STATISTICAL RECORD:

Operating Profit Margin %	1.5	11.4	11.2	11.6	10.7	10.0	5.7
Book Value Per Share	2.51	4.75	4.23	5.66	4.49	6.49	6.00
Return on Equity %	3.6	20.6	22.9	21.3	19.4	16.1	5.5
Return on Assets %	1.1	7.8	8.7	8.7	7.4	6.9	2.4
Average Yield %	2.2	2.1	2.3	2.4	4.3	3.5	3.3
P/E Ratio	N.M	21.3-17.2	19.4-15.4	20.3-13.7	19.8-11.9	14.8-11.9	55.1-31.9
Price Range	58⅞-45¼	55¾-45⅛	47¾-38	45⅝-30⅞	35¼-21⅛	22-17¾	25⅞-15

Statistics are as originally reported.

OFFICERS:
E.L. Artzt, Chmn. & C.E.O.
J.E. Pepper, Pres.
E.G. Nelson, Sr. V.P. & C.F.O.
T.L. Overbey, Sec.

INCORPORATED: OH, May, 1905

PRINCIPAL OFFICE: One Procter & Gamble Plaza, Cincinnati, OH 45202

TELEPHONE NUMBER: (513) 983-1100

NO. OF EMPLOYEES: 103,500 (approx.)

ANNUAL MEETING: In October

SHAREHOLDERS: 201,990

INSTITUTIONAL HOLDINGS:
No. of Institutions: 807
Shares Held: 159,332,101

REGISTRAR(S): The Central Trust Comapny, N.A., Cincinnati, OH 45202

TRANSFER AGENT(S): At Company's Office

PROGRESSIVE CORP.

YIELD 0.6%
P/E RATIO 8.9

*7 YEAR PRICE SCORE 156.9   *12 MONTH PRICE SCORE 86.9
*NYSE COMPOSITE INDEX=100

INTERIM EARNINGS (Per Share):

Qtr.	Mar.	June	Sept.	Dec.
1990	0.36	0.50	0.25	0.16
1991	0.34	0.13	0.13	d0.25
1992	0.31	0.60	0.70	0.50
1993	0.71	1.11	1.10	0.68

INTERIM DIVIDENDS (Per Share):

Amt.	Decl.	Ex.	Rec.	Pay.
0.05Q	4/23/93	6/7/93	6/11/93	6/30/93
0.05Q	7/30	9/3	9/10	9/30
0.05Q	10/22	12/6	12/10	12/30
0.05Q	2/7/94	3/7/94	3/11/94	3/31/94
0.05Q	4/22	6/6	6/10	6/30

Indicated div.: $0.20

CAPITALIZATION (12/31/93):

	($000)	(%)
Total Debt	477,100	32.3
Preferred Shares	87,900	6.0
Common & Surplus	910,000	61.7
Total	1,475,000	100.0

DIVIDEND ACHIEVER STATUS:
Rank: 4   1983-93 Growth Rate: 29.6%
Total Years of Dividend Growth: 24

RECENT DEVELOPMENTS: For the three months ended 12/31/93, net income increased 62% from the prior-year period to $53.4 million. Revenues were up 18% from the comparable 1992 period to $509.7 million. Net premiums written were $462.0 million to $371.8 million a year ago. For 1993, net income was $267.3 million compared with $139.6 million for 1992. Revenues were $1.95 billion or 12% above 1992's level. Premiums written totaled $1.97 billion.

PROSPECTS: The Company's core business of writing non-standard private passenger automobile and small fleet commercial vehicle insurance for individuals whose insurance has been cancelled or rejected by another company is responsible for nine out of ten premiums written. The strength of core business operations is should fuel earnings growth throughout 1994. PGR's diversified businesses are reporting solid growth patterns, providing a jolt to earnings.

BUSINESS

PROGRESSIVE CORP. is an insurance holding company which writes specialty property-casualty and credit-related insurance. Personal insurance lines include nonstandard automobile, recreational vehicle and mobile home coverage. Nonstandard automobile programs provide insurance for private passenger auto risks that are rejected or cancelled by other companies. Recreational vehicle programs provide insurance for motor homes, travel trailers, recreational vans and motorcycles. Mobile home programs offer insurance for factory-built housing. Commercial insurance lines include both nonstandard and standard vehicle coverages for commercial and industrial activities. Credit related-insurance lines provide collateral protection. P.B. Lewis holds about 14% of PGR stock.

ANNUAL EARNINGS AND DIVIDENDS PER SHARE

	1993	1992	1991	1990	1989	1988	1987
Earnings Per Share	3.59	① 2.09	0.41	1.28	0.98	1.29	① 1.05
Dividends Per Share	0.20	② 0.19	0.173	0.16	0.147	0.133	0.077
Dividend Payout %	5.6	9.1	42.6	12.5	15.0	10.4	7.3

① Before acctg. chg.   ② 3-for-1 stk split,12/09/92

ANNUAL FINANCIAL DATA

RECORD OF EARNINGS (IN MILLIONS):

	1993	1992	1991	1990	1989	1988	1987
Premiums Earned	1,668.7	1,426.1	1,286.9	1,191.2	1,196.5	1,215.4	994.4
Investment Income	134.5	139.0	144.8	139.7	168.1	...	...
Total Revenues	1,954.8	1,738.9	1,493.1	1,376.2	1,392.7	1,227.3	999.9
Losses & Loss Adj Exps	1,028.0	930.9	858.0	762.9	799.3	752.0	571.9
Income Bef Income Taxes	373.1	178.7	32.9	88.1	86.1	132.0	107.5
Income Taxes	105.8	39.1	...	cr5.3	8.1	23.9	16.2
Gain on Sale Of Securities	...	...	...	...	...	117.4	59.1
Net Income	267.3	153.8	32.9	93.4	78.0	108.1	93.5
Aver. Shs. Outstg. (000)	71,800	62,300	66,600	72,900	79,800	80,700	86,700

BALANCE SHEET (IN MILLIONS):

	1993	1992	1991	1990	1989	1988	1987
Cash	8.7	22.9	19.2	18.7	21.7	17.7	18.9
Fixed Maturities	2,101.7	1,687.5	1,466.9	1,190.5	1,091.1	...	...
Eq Secur- Available for Sale, At Mkt	453.9	398.6	349.4	184.4	243.3	...	...
Total Assets	4,011.3	3,440.9	2,979.1	2,694.5	2,646.8	2,307.1	1,785.7
Benefits and Claims	2,180.7	1,941.1	1,440.7	1,336.4	1,298.1	1,223.0	964.5
Net Stockholders' Equity	997.9	629.0	465.7	408.5	435.2	417.2	395.0
Year End Shs Outstg (000)	72,100	67,100	63,300	69,300	76,200	80,700	86,220

STATISTICAL RECORD:

	1993	1992	1991	1990	1989	1988	1987
Book Value Per Share	12.62	7.94	5.83	5.89	5.71	5.17	4.58
Return on Equity %	26.8	22.2	7.1	22.9	17.9	25.9	22.7
Return on Assets %	6.7	4.1	1.1	3.5	3.0	4.7	5.0
Average Yield %	0.5	0.9	1.0	1.1	1.1	1.3	0.8
P/E Ratio	12.8-7.7	14.1-7.1	50.3-36.6	14.6-8.6	14.8-7.7	8.3-5.6	11.3-8.1
Price Range	46⅛-27½	29⅜-14¾	20⅝-15	18¾-11	14½-7½	10¾-7¼	11⅞-8½

Statistics are as originally reported.

BUSINESS LINE ANALYSIS

(12/31/93)	Rev(%)	Inc(%)
Insurance Operations.	85.4	41.6
Services Operations...	2.2	1.6
Investment Income	12.4	56.8
Total	100.0	100.0

OFFICERS:
P.B. Lewis, Chmn., Pres. & C.E.O.
D.R. Lewis, Treasurer
D.M. Schneider, Secretary

INCORPORATED: OH, Feb., 1965

PRINCIPAL OFFICE: 6300 Wilson Mills Road, Mayfield Village, OH 44143

TELEPHONE NUMBER: (216) 461-5000
FAX: (216) 446-7168
NO. OF EMPLOYEES: 6,101
ANNUAL MEETING: In April
SHAREHOLDERS: 4,859 (common; 356 preferred)
INSTITUTIONAL HOLDINGS:
No. of Institutions: 173
Shares Held: 38,606,275

REGISTRAR(S): National City Bank, Cleveland, OH 44114

TRANSFER AGENT(S): National City Bank, Cleveland, OH 44114

NYS SYMBOL PVN
Rec. Pr. 32⅜

PROVIDIAN CORP.

YIELD 2.5%
P/E RATIO 5.2

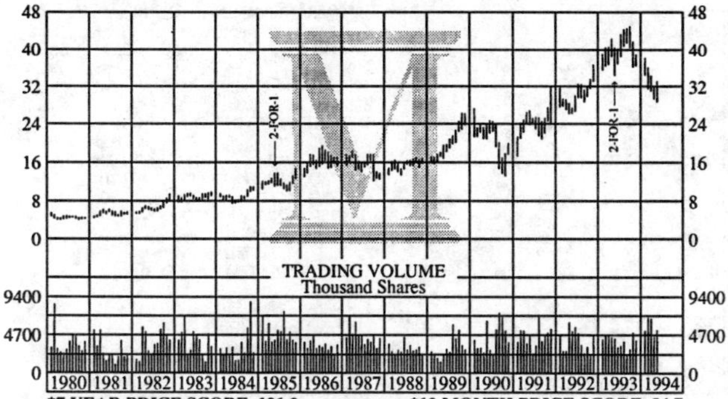

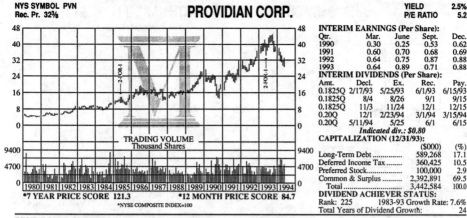

***7 YEAR PRICE SCORE 121.3** ***12 MONTH PRICE SCORE 84.7**

*NYSE COMPOSITE INDEX=100

INTERIM EARNINGS (Per Share):

Qtr.	Mar.	June	Sept.	Dec.
1990	0.30	0.25	0.53	0.62
1991	0.60	0.70	0.68	0.69
1992	0.64	0.75	0.87	0.88
1993	0.64	0.89	0.71	0.88

INTERIM DIVIDENDS (Per Share):

Amt.	Decl.	Ex.	Rec.	Pay.
0.1825Q	2/17/93	5/25/93	6/1/93	6/15/93
0.1825Q	8/4	8/26	9/1	9/15
0.1825Q	11/3	11/24	12/1	12/15
0.20Q	12/1	2/23/94	3/1/94	3/15/94
0.20Q	5/11/94	5/25	6/1	6/15

Indicated div.: $0.80

CAPITALIZATION (12/31/93):

	($000)	(%)
Long-Term Debt	589,268	17.1
Deferred Income Tax	360,425	10.5
Preferred Stock	100,000	2.9
Common & Surplus	2,392,891	69.5
Total	3,442,584	100.0

DIVIDEND ACHIEVER STATUS:

Rank: 225 1983-93 Growth Rate: 7.6%

Total Years of Dividend Growth: 24

RECENT DEVELOPMENTS: For the year ended 12/31/93, net income totaled $322.7 million. Agency Group results were adversely affected by unfavorable mortality rates and narrowing interest rate spreads although pretax income was up 1.8%. Direct Response Group results benefited from the acquisition of Academy Insurance Group as pretax income was up 15.8%. The Banking Group benefitted from higher fee income, a surge in customer accounts and lower credit-related costs as pretax income jumped 31.3%.

PROSPECTS: Agency Group's growth is modest but improvement in policy termination rates continues. Life and health insurance product sales are down, reflecting consolidation with the recently aqcuired Durham Life Corp., a home service insurance company. Direct Response Group sales are benefitting from the Academy Insurance Group acquisition. First Deposit's First Gold credit card and Select Equity, the home equity line, are adding impressive gains to revenue. Fee income is also on the rise.

BUSINESS

PROVIDIAN CORP. is a consumer-oriented insurance company. Agency Group markets a full range of life and health insurance products through home service representatives. Direct Response Group markets life and health insurance products through National Liberty Corp., media, direct mail, telephone and third-party programs. Banking Group consists of First Deposit Corp. and its subsidiaries, which offer consumer lending and desposit products nationwide. Accumulation and Investment Group is responsible for the management of investment products.

BUSINESS LINE ANALYSIS

(12/31/93)	Rev(%)	Inc(%)
Agency Group	19.3	21.7
Direct Response Group	6.5	23.5
Accumul & Invest Group	49.5	9.0
Other	24.7	45.8
Total	100.0	100.0

ANNUAL EARNINGS AND DIVIDENDS PER SHARE

	1993	1992	1991	1990	1989	1988	1987
Earnings Per Share	**3.12**	**3.14**	**2.67**	**[1] 1.7**	**[1] 2.93**	**2.00**	**1.67**
Dividends Per Share	**[2] 0.91**	**0.91**	**0.66**	**0.60**	**0.50**	**0.47**	**0.44**
Dividend Payout %	**29.2**	**21.0**	**22.5**	**31.9**	**17.1**	**23.5**	**26.4**

[1] Before acctg. chg. [2] 2-for-1 split, 4/30/93

ANNUAL FINANCIAL DATA

	1993	1992	1991	1990	1989	1988	1987
RECORD OF EARNINGS (IN MILLIONS):							
Total Revenues	2,884.2	2,853.3	2,670.7	2,577.3	2,500.1	2,045.9	3,351.1
Costs and Expenses	2,010.3	2,091.0	2,013.2	2,103.5	1,848.9	1,571.6	2,939.8
Operating Profit	558.4	529.5	432.8	286.0	433.1	308.0	272.8
Income Before Income Tax	487.1	452.0	345.9	224.7	384.5	259.2	229.1
Income Taxes	164.4	129.5	95.7	58.5	108.8	69.3	58.4
Net Income	322.7	322.5	250.2	166.2	[1] 275.7	189.9	172.1
Aver. Shs. Outstg. (000)	115,325	100,532	90,700	91,820	90,594	91,272	98,410
[1] Before acctg. change dr$56,021,000.							
BALANCE SHEET (IN MILLIONS):							
Cash and Cash Equivalents	412.3	728.8	611.8	584.6	779.4	392.4	186.2
Receivables, Net	324.2	351.4	339.0	306.5	241.4	180.7	137.9
Gross Property	167.3	161.6	131.2	117.6	121.3	137.3	111.3
Long-Term Debt	589.3	589.3	611.2	386.2	330.3	262.6	287.6
Net Stockholders' Equity	2,492.9	2,185.9	1,930.9	1,552.5	1,516.3	1,257.5	1,243.3
Total Assets	22,929.0	20,588.3	18,873.0	16,668.5	14,970.0	12,963.3	10,385.6
Total Current Assets	736.6	1,080.3	950.8	891.1	1,020.8	573.1	324.0
Total Current Liabilities	2,767.1	2,623.9	2,583.0	2,059.9	2,080.4	2,008.9	1,462.6
Net Working Capital	d2,030.5	d1,543.7	d1,632.2	d1,168.8	d1,059.7	d1,435.8	d1,138.6
Year End Shs Outstg (000)	101,426	94,802	92,706	89,566	92,284	89,790	94,384
STATISTICAL RECORD:							
Book Value Per Share	23.59	20.55	17.86	15.66	14.81	12.89	12.11
Return on Equity %	12.9	14.8	13.0	10.7	18.2	15.1	13.8
Return on Assets %	1.4	1.6	1.3	1.0	1.8	1.5	1.7
Average Yield %	2.3	4.2	4.9	5.4	4.8	6.2	5.7
P/E Ratio	14.4-11.1	11.7-8.3	12.0-6.5	16.0-7.7	8.9-5.3	8.5-6.7	11.1-7.3
Price Range	44⅞-34½	36¾-26	31⅞-17¼	27⅛-13⅛	26⅛-15⅝	17-13⅜	18½-12⅛

Statistics are as originally reported.

OFFICERS:
I.W. Bailey, II, Chmn., Pres. & C.E.O.
R.L. Walker, Sr. V.P. & C.F.O.
E.J. Robinson, V.P. & Treas.

INCORPORATED: DE, Mar., 1969

PRINCIPAL OFFICE: Capital Holding Center 400 West Market Street Post Office Box 32830, Louisville, KY 40232

TELEPHONE NUMBER: (502) 560-2000
FAX: (502) 560-2550
NO. OF EMPLOYEES: 9,300
ANNUAL MEETING: In May
SHAREHOLDERS: 16,200
INSTITUTIONAL HOLDINGS:
No. of Institutions: 412
Shares Held: 71,349,365 223

REGISTRAR(S):

TRANSFER AGENT(S):

NASDAQ SYMBOL PSNC
Rec. Pr. 14 (Marginable)

PUBLIC SERVICE COMPANY OF NORTH CAROLINA, INC.

YIELD 5.9%
P/E RATIO 15.1

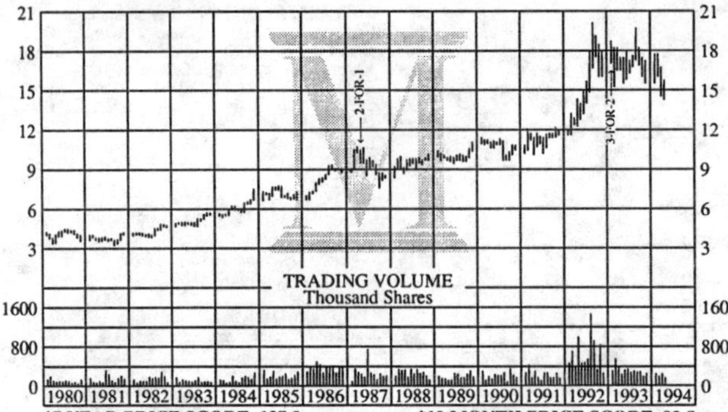

21
18
15
12
9
6
3
2-FOR-1
3-FOR-2
TRADING VOLUME
Thousand Shares
1600
800
0
1980 1981 1982 1983 1984 1985 1986 1987 1988 1989 1990 1991 1992 1993 1994

***7 YEAR PRICE SCORE 107.8** ***12 MONTH PRICE SCORE 92.8**

*NYSE COMPOSITE INDEX=100

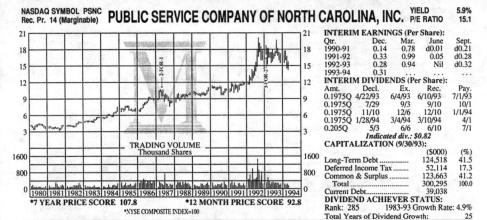

INTERIM EARNINGS (Per Share):

Qtr.	Dec.	Mar.	June	Sept.
1990-91	0.14	0.78	d0.01	d0.21
1991-92	0.33	0.99	0.05	d0.28
1992-93	0.28	0.94	Nil	d0.32
1993-94	0.31	...	...	...

INTERIM DIVIDENDS (Per Share):

Amt.	Decl.	Ex.	Rec.	Pay.
0.1975Q	4/22/93	6/4/93	6/10/93	7/1/93
0.1975Q	7/29	9/3	9/10	10/1
0.1975Q	11/10	12/6	12/10	1/1/94
0.1975Q	1/28/94	3/4/94	3/10/94	4/1
0.205Q	5/3	6/6	6/10	7/1

Indicated div.: $0.82

CAPITALIZATION (9/30/93):

	($000)	(%)
Long-Term Debt	124,518	41.5
Deferred Income Tax	52,114	17.3
Common & Surplus	123,663	41.2
Total	300,295	100.0
Current Debt	39,038	

DIVIDEND ACHIEVER STATUS:

Rank: 285 1983-93 Growth Rate: 4.9%

Total Years of Dividend Growth: 25

RECENT DEVELOPMENTS: For the quarter ended 12/31/93, net income was $5.0 million, up 12.2% from $4.5 million in 1992. Operating revenues were down 7.2% to $71.4 million compared with $77.0 million last year. Gross margin for the quarter was $29.9 million compared with $29.4 million last year. The improvement in gross margin was due primarily to a 3% increase in natural gas throughput to lower-margin industrial and large commercial customers. Quantities sold to the higher-margin residential customers fell 3% and quantities sold to higher-margin small commercial customers were relatively flat. Residential and small commercial customer bases increased 5% and 4%, respectively, while the industrial and large commercial customer base increased 2%. For the twelve month period ended 12/31/93, net income was $14.8 million versus $16.2 million in the prior year. Operating revenues for the twelve month period were $274.5 million, up 10.2%.

BUSINESS

PUBLIC SERVICE COMPANY OF NORTH CAROLINA, INC. is engaged primarily in the business of distributing natural gas to over 246,000 customers at regulated rates in 87 cities, towns and villages in North Carolina. The Company's 26-county service area has a population in excess of 2.5 million and includes the Raleigh-Durham area, with the Research Triangle Park, sections of the Piedmont and western parts of the State. Industrial activities in the service area are diverse, including the manufacture of textiles, chemicals, ceramics and clay products, glass, automotive products, minerals, pharmaceuticals, plastics, fabricated metals, electronic equipment, furniture, as well as the processing of tobacco and food. The Company, through its subsidiaries, participates in oil and gas exploration and development activities and sells propane at retail in and around its natural gas service area. In connection with its gas distribution business, the Company promotes, sells and installs both new and replacement cooking, water heating, laundry and space heating gas appliances.

ANNUAL EARNINGS AND DIVIDENDS PER SHARE

	9/30/93	9/30/92	9/30/91	9/30/90	9/30/89	9/30/88	9/30/87
Earnings Per Share	**0.90**	**1.09**	**0.70**	**0.84**	**0.93**	**1.03**	**[2] 0.93**
Dividends Per Share	**0.775**	**[1] 0.747**	**0.733**	**0.723**	**0.693**	**0.667**	**[3] 0.607**
Dividend Payout %	**86.1**	**68.5**	**N.M.**	**86.1**	**74.3**	**64.5**	**65.0**

[1] 3-for-2 stk split,01/05/93 [2] Co. changed to fiscal yr. end 9/30 from 12/31 in 1987 [3] 100% stk div, 4/87

ANNUAL FINANCIAL DATA

	9/30/93	9/30/92	9/30/91	9/30/90	9/30/89	9/30/88	9/30/87
RECORD OF EARNINGS (IN THOUSANDS):							
Operating Revenues	279,989	240,403	193,239	201,940	213,712	200,717	221,112
Depreciation	...	14,710	13,792	12,335	11,180	8,781	7,977
Maintenance	4,868	5,216	4,333	4,365	3,894	3,479	3,113
Prov for Fed Inc Taxes	5,917	8,072	4,756	5,277	5,938	6,497	7,887
Operating Income	28,376	30,647	24,159	23,240	22,919	21,684	19,582
Total Interest Deductions	13,891	13,510	13,453	13,036	10,084	7,889	8,511
Net Income	14,219	16,750	10,590	12,305	13,310	14,382	11,711
Aver. Shs. Outstg.	15,812	15,373	14,928	14,502	14,099	13,725	12,226
BALANCE SHEET (IN THOUSANDS):							
Gross Plant	477,652	445,010	416,677	382,321	352,590	312,398	277,780
Accumulated Depreciation	140,146	134,722	123,186	111,581	102,094	93,199	85,748
Net Gas Utility Plant	337,506	310,288	293,491	270,740	250,496	219,199	192,032
Long-term Debt	124,518	130,056	104,094	108,511	85,436	89,360	67,297
Net Stockholders' Equity	123,663	115,069	106,118	102,592	97,046	90,945	84,047
Total Assets	400,946	380,541	352,126	317,821	290,720	257,261	227,673
Year End Shares Outstg	15,992	10,368	15,081	14,651	14,243	13,851	13,539
STATISTICAL RECORD:							
Book Value Per Share	7.73	11.10	6.92	6.87	6.66	6.34	5.91
Op. Inc/Net Pl %	8.4	9.9	8.2	8.6	9.1	9.9	10.2
Dep/Gr. Pl %	3.0	3.0	2.9	2.9	2.8	2.8	2.9
Accum. Dep/Gr. Pl %	29.3	30.5	29.8	29.3	29.1	29.9	31.0
Return on Equity %	11.5	14.6	10.1	12.2	14.0	16.4	14.6
Average Yield %	4.4	7.1	6.6	6.9	6.8	7.2	6.6
P/E Ratio	21.9-16.9	18.6-10.8	17.3-14.5	13.5-11.5	12.0-10.1	9.8-8.1	11.6-8.2
Price Range	19¾-15¼	20⅛-11⅝	12⅛-10⅛	11⅜-9⅝	11⅛-9⅜	10⅛-8⅜	10¾-7⅝

Statistics are as originally reported.

OFFICERS:
C.E. Zeigler, Jr., Chmn., Pres. & C.E.O.
R.D. Voigt, Sr. V.P.-Fin. & Treas.

INCORPORATED: NC, Sep., 1938

PRINCIPAL OFFICE: 400 Cox Road, Gastonia, NC 28054

TELEPHONE NUMBER: (704) 864-6731

NO. OF EMPLOYEES: 1,186 (full-time)

ANNUAL MEETING: In January

SHAREHOLDERS: 10,900

INSTITUTIONAL HOLDINGS:
No. of Institutions: 39
Shares Held: 2,441,699

REGISTRAR(S): First Union National Bank of N.C., Charlotte, NC

TRANSFER AGENT(S): First Union National Bank of N.C., Charlotte, NC

QUAKER CHEMICAL CORP.

YIELD 3.4%
P/E RATIO ...

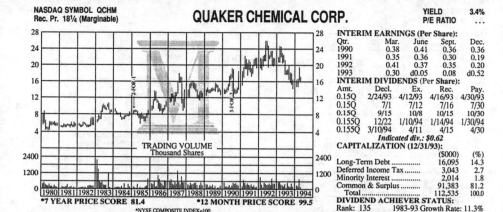

INTERIM EARNINGS (Per Share):

Qtr.	Mar.	June	Sept.	Dec.
1990	0.38	0.41	0.36	0.36
1991	0.35	0.36	0.30	0.19
1992	0.41	0.37	0.35	0.20
1993	0.30	d0.05	0.08	d0.52

INTERIM DIVIDENDS (Per Share):

Amt.	Decl.	Ex.	Rec.	Pay.
0.15Q	2/24/93	4/12/93	4/16/93	4/30/93
0.15Q	7/1	7/12	7/16	7/30
0.15Q	9/15	10/8	10/15	10/30
0.155Q	12/22	1/10/94	1/14/94	1/30/94
0.155Q	3/10/94	4/11	4/15	4/30

Indicated div.: $0.62

CAPITALIZATION (12/31/93):

	($000)	(%)
Long-Term Debt	16,095	14.3
Deferred Income Tax	3,043	2.7
Minority Interest	2,014	1.8
Common & Surplus	91,383	81.2
Total	112,535	100.0

DIVIDEND ACHIEVER STATUS:
Rank: 135   1983-93 Growth Rate: 11.3%
Total Years of Dividend Growth: 22

RECENT DEVELOPMENTS: For the quarter ended 12/31/93, the Company incurred a net loss of $4.8 million compared with net income of $1.9 million last year. Net sales declined 1.7% to $46.9 million from $47.7 million in the comparable period of 1992. North American operations showed a slight improvement over last year, while European results continued to suffer from the continuing recession and weaker exchange rates versus the U.S. dollar. The implementation of the previously announced repositioning program, which includes a broad scope of changes focused on bringing the Company's operating costs in line with current and projected operating revenues, resulted in pre-tax charges of $8.4 million in the fourth quarter and $11.9 million for the year. For the twelve months ended 12/31/93, QCHM reported a net loss of $1.8 million compared with net income of $12.1 million in 1992. Net sales for the year were $195.0 million compared with $212.5 million last year.

BUSINESS

QUAKER CHEMICAL CORPORATION develops, produces and markets a wide range of high performance products and services used in industrial institutional and manufacturing to protect, make more efficient and extend the life of manufacturing equipment. The Corporation also provided specially engineered products and specialty engineering services to industry. Certain resin products are used in industrial, institutional and marine markets for specialty deckings and floorings. For the steel industry, the Company produces lubricants for the hot and cold reduction of flat-rolled steel, aluminum and other metals; cleaners for processing steel, metal parts and industrial maintenance; and additives to prolong life of rolling solutions. For the pulp and paper industry, the Company makes agents to improve absorbency; agents to increase the utilization of recycled fibers; dispersants to prevent the build-up of scale in manufacturing systems; drainage acids and cleaners for use on wires, felts and for cleaning paper machines. For the metals industry, the Company produces machinery and grinding coolants for producing all types of metal parts; corrosion preventatives.

ANNUAL EARNINGS AND DIVIDENDS PER SHARE

	1993	1992	1991	1990	1989	1988	1987
Earnings Per Share	d0.19	☐1.33	☐1.20	1.51	1.35	1.21	1.05
Dividends Per Share	0.60	0.56	0.52	0.497	0.40	0.36	0.33
Dividend Payout %	...	42.1	43.3	32.9	29.7	29.7	31.6

☐ Before acctg. chg.

ANNUAL FINANCIAL DATA

RECORD OF EARNINGS (IN THOUSANDS):

	1993	1992	1991	1990	1989	1988	1987
Total Revenues	196,425	214,970	194,150	205,155	184,874	170,196	150,377
Costs and Expenses	190,945	189,011	172,016	177,656	161,767	☑152,836	☑133,602
Depreciation & Amort	7,566	7,812	6,742	5,945	4,785	...	...
Income From Operations	d2,086	18,147	15,392	21,554	18,322	17,360	16,775
Income Before Taxes	d2,177	...	...	...	...	...	...
Taxes on Income	234	6,947	6,098	8,474	6,807	7,208	7,088
Eq In Net Inc Of Assoc Cos	1,001	1,328	1,898	1,476	1,790	1,951	1,005
Minor Int In Net Inc Of Subs	348	430	402	450	465	372	269
Net Income	d1,758	12,098	☑10,790	14,106	12,840	11,731	10,423

☐ Incl. Dep. ☑ Before acctg. change dr$5,675,000.

BALANCE SHEET (IN THOUSANDS):

	1993	1992	1991	1990	1989	1988	1987
Cash and Cash Equivalents	20,293	24,508	23,808	26,371	22,562	20,474	22,563
Receivables, Net	39,965	37,970	35,064	36,268	33,292	30,014	27,817
Inventories	17,547	17,736	17,135	18,694	16,626	15,742	...
Gross Property	107,076	97,698	89,004	83,697	68,093	62,026	59,771
Accumulated Depreciation	50,525	45,519	40,343	37,382	32,454	29,205	27,149
Long-Term Debt	16,095	18,604	5,219	5,453	5,665	5,000	5,000
Net Stockholders' Equity	91,383	101,642	89,898	99,113	90,440	82,884	78,079
Total Assets	170,985	166,613	155,593	152,408	131,430	121,125	118,367
Total Current Assets	84,387	85,567	82,725	84,833	75,427	69,326	66,633
Total Current Liabilities	42,642	28,126	36,592	40,342	27,848	26,924	29,447
Net Working Capital	41,745	57,441	46,133	44,491	47,579	42,402	37,186
Year End Shares Outstg	9,242	9,188	9,028	8,921	9,473	9,669	9,644

STATISTICAL RECORD:

	1993	1992	1991	1990	1989	1988	1987
Operating Profit Margin %	...	8.4	7.9	10.5	9.9	10.2	11.2
Book Value Per Share	8.32	10.03	10.05	10.14	8.64	7.66	7.15
Return on Equity %	...	11.9	10.9	14.2	14.2	14.2	13.3
Return on Assets %	...	7.3	6.9	9.3	9.8	9.7	8.8
Average Yield %	3.1	2.5	2.8	3.2	2.8	2.6	2.4
P/E Ratio	...	19.5-14.1	18.5-12.5	12.7-7.9	11.6-9.3	13.3-9.4	17.1-8.6
Price Range	24⅝-14¼	26-18¾	22¼-15	19¼-12	15⅝-12½	16⅛-11⅜	18-9

Statistics are as originally reported.

OFFICERS:
P.A. Benoliel, Chairman
S.W. Lubsen, Pres. & C.E.O.
K.H. Spaeth, V.P. & Corp. Sec.
W.G. Hamilton, Corp. Treas.

INCORPORATED: PA, 1930

PRINCIPAL OFFICE: Elm & Lee Streets, Conshohocken, PA 19428

TELEPHONE NUMBER: (215) 832-4000
FAX: (215) 832-4494
NO. OF EMPLOYEES: 137
ANNUAL MEETING: In May
SHAREHOLDERS: 720
INSTITUTIONAL HOLDINGS:
No. of Institutions: 58
Shares Held: 4,870,500

REGISTRAR(S): American Stock Transfer & Trust Co., 40 Wall Street, New York, NY 10005

TRANSFER AGENT(S): American Stock Transfer & Trust Co., 40 Wall Street, New York, NY 10005

NYS SYMBOL OAT
Rec. Pr. 65⅞

QUAKER OATS CO.

YIELD 3.2%
P/E RATIO 15.2

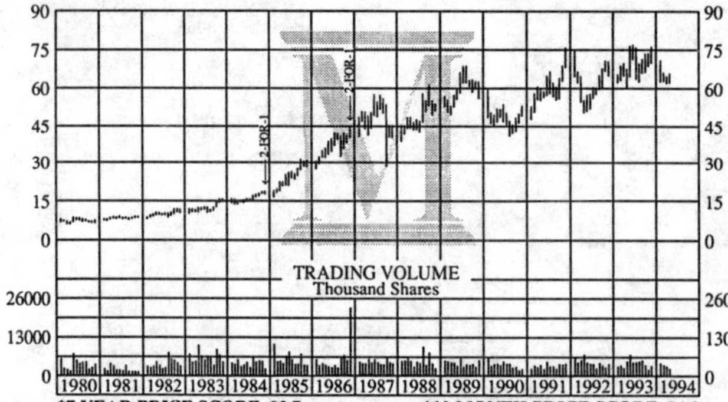

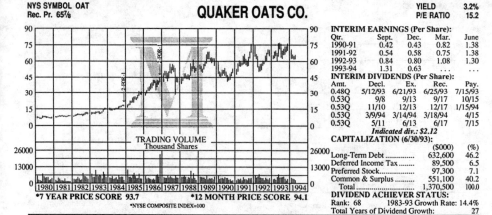

*7 YEAR PRICE SCORE 93.7 *12 MONTH PRICE SCORE 94.1

*NYSE COMPOSITE INDEX=100

INTERIM EARNINGS (Per Share):

Qtr.	Sept.	Dec.	Mar.	June
1990-91	0.42	0.43	0.82	1.38
1991-92	0.54	0.58	0.75	1.38
1992-93	0.84	0.80	1.08	1.30
1993-94	1.31	0.63	...	...

INTERIM DIVIDENDS (Per Share):

Amt.	Decl.	Ex.	Rec.	Pay.
0.48Q	5/12/93	6/21/93	6/25/93	7/15/93
0.53Q	9/8	9/13	9/17	10/15
0.53Q	11/10	12/13	12/17	1/15/94
0.53Q	3/9/94	3/14/94	3/18/94	4/15
0.53Q	5/11	6/13	6/17	7/15

Indicated div.: $2.12

CAPITALIZATION (6/30/93):

	($000)	(%)
Long-Term Debt	632,600	46.2
Deferred Income Tax	89,500	6.5
Preferred Stock	97,300	7.1
Common & Surplus	551,100	40.2
Total	1,370,500	100.0

DIVIDEND ACHIEVER STATUS:
Rank: 68 1983-93 Growth Rate: 14.4%
Total Years of Dividend Growth: 27

RECENT DEVELOPMENTS: For the quarter ended 12/30/93, net income totaled $42.8 million compared with $56.2 million last year. Sales increased 1.6% to $1.35 billion. Comparisons were made with restated prior-year figures. U.S. and Canadian Grocery Products reported income of $84.6 million, up 10% on sales of $925.3 million due to volume gains from Gatorade and ready-to-eat cereals. International Grocery Products posted a 37% decrease in income to $25.1 million, while sales fell 7% to $428.6 million.

PROSPECTS: The Company should benefit from a differentiated product mix and a balanced price/value relationship. In addition, new product introductions in the ready-to-eat cereal market will help volume growth, while efforts to improve manufacturing, distribution, and marketing activities should help increase margins. The international expansion of Gatorade, especially in Latin America, should help earnings growth in the future.

BUSINESS

QUAKER OATS CO. is a major international producer of foods, beverages and pet foods. U.S. & Canadian Grocery products accounted for 69% of sales (78% of operating income) in the year ended 6/30/93. The Company produces ready-to-eat cereals, hot cereals, grain-based snacks, fresh breakfast products, beverages, rice, pasta, pet food and institutional and food service products. Brandname products include: Quaker cereals, Gatorade thirst quencher and Aunt Jemima breakfast products. International Grocery products, which accounted for 31% of sales (22% of operating income) produce and market food and pet food products in Europe, Latin America and the Pacific region.

BUSINESS LINE ANALYSIS

(6/30/93)	Rev(%)	Inc(%)
United States	64.7	74.4
Canada	3.9	3.3
Europe	23.3	9.1
Latin America & Pacific	8.1	13.2
Total	100.0	100.0

ANNUAL EARNINGS AND DIVIDENDS PER SHARE

	6/30/93	6/30/92	6/30/91	6/30/90	6/30/89	
Earnings Per Share	**[1] 3.93**	**3.25**	**[2] 3.05**	**[2] 2.93**	**2.56**	...
Dividends Per Share	**1.97**	**1.77**	**1.60**	**1.44**	**1.25**	...
Dividend Payout %	**50.1**	**54.5**	**52.5**	**49.1**	**48.8**	...

[1] Before acctg. chg. [2] Before disc. oper. [3] 2-for-1 stk split, 12/86

ANNUAL FINANCIAL DATA

RECORD OF EARNINGS (IN MILLIONS):						
Total Revenues	5,730.6	5,576.4	5,491.2	5,030.6	5,724.2	...
Costs and Expenses	4,980.9	4,874.8	4,783.2	4,367.5	5,049.4	...
Depreciation & Amort	156.9	155.9	177.7	162.5	135.5	...
Operating Profit	592.8	545.7	530.3	500.6	539.3	...
Income Bef Income Taxes	467.6	421.5	411.5	382.4	328.7	...
Income Taxes	180.8	173.9	175.7	153.5	125.7	...
Net Income	[1] 286.8	247.6	[2] 235.8	[3] 228.9	203.0	...
Aver. Shs. Outstg. (000)	71,974	74,881	75,904	76,537	79,307	...

[1] Before acctg. change dr$115,500,000. [2] Before disc. op. dr$30,000,000. [3] Before disc. op. dr$59,900,000.

BALANCE SHEET (IN MILLIONS):						
Cash and Cash Equivalents	61.0	95.2	30.2	18.3	23.7	91.2
Trade Accts Receiv-net	478.9	575.3	691.1	629.9	872.1	826.0
Total Inventories	354.0	435.3	422.3	473.9	589.4	539.8
Gross Property	2,059.2	2,066.1	1,914.6	1,745.6	1,725.2	1,628.6
Accumulated Depreciation	831.0	792.8	681.9	591.5	633.3	600.2
Long-Term Debt	632.6	688.7	701.2	740.3	766.8	299.1
Net Stockholders' Equity	648.4	940.5	1,000.3	1,117.5	1,237.1	1,251.1
Total Assets	2,815.9	3,039.9	3,016.1	3,326.1	3,221.9	2,974.6
Total Current Assets	1,067.6	1,256.2	1,258.1	1,481.3	1,598.2	1,490.3
Total Current Liabilities	1,105.1	1,054.6	926.9	1,138.5	902.4	1,072.8
Net Working Capital	d37.5	201.6	331.2	342.8	695.8	417.5
Year End Shs Outstg (000)	69,456	73,403	76,329	75,587	78,767	...
STATISTICAL RECORD:						
Operating Profit Margin %	10.3	9.8	9.7	10.0	9.4	...
Book Value Per Share	1.72	5.65	5.96	7.29	8.02	...
Return on Equity %	44.2	26.3	23.6	20.5	16.4	...
Return on Assets %	10.2	8.1	7.8	6.9	6.3	...
Average Yield %	2.9	2.8	2.6	2.9	2.1	2.1
P/E Ratio	19.6-15.4	22.9-15.5	24.8-15.7	20.3-14.0	26.9-19.4	...
Price Range	77-60⅜	74⅜-50¼	75¾-47¾	59½-41	68⅞-49⅝	61½-38½

Statistics are as originally reported.

OFFICERS:
W.D. Smithburg, Chmn. & C.E.O.
P.A. Marineau, Pres. & C.O.O.
L.C. McKinney, Sr. V.P. & Sec.
T.G. Westbrook, Sr. V.P. & C.F.O.

INCORPORATED: NJ, Sep., 1901

PRINCIPAL OFFICE: Quaker Tower 321 North Clark St., Chicago, IL 60610-4714

TELEPHONE NUMBER: (312) 222-7111

NO. OF EMPLOYEES: 20,200

ANNUAL MEETING: In November

SHAREHOLDERS: 33,154 common; 4,841 pfd.

INSTITUTIONAL HOLDINGS:
No. of Institutions: 427
Shares Held: 39,168,142

REGISTRAR(S): Harris Trust & Savings Bank, Chicago, IL

TRANSFER AGENT(S): Harris Trust & Savings Bank, Chicago, IL

NYS SYMBOL STR
Rec. Pr. 32

QUESTAR CORP.

YIELD 3.6%
P/E RATIO 14.9

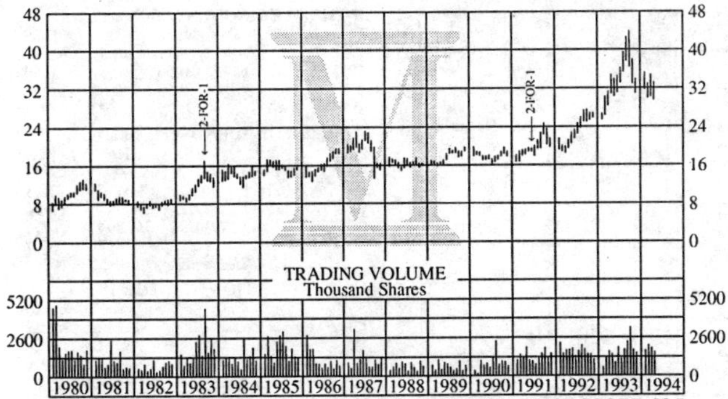
48
40
32
24
16
8
0
2-FOR-1
2-FOR-1
TRADING VOLUME
Thousand Shares
5200
2600
0
1980 1981 1982 1983 1984 1985 1986 1987 1988 1989 1990 1991 1992 1993 1994

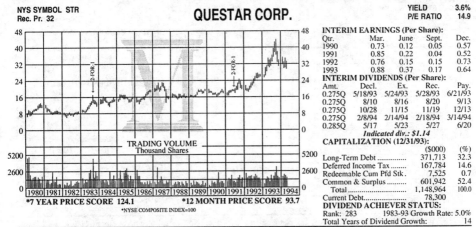

***7 YEAR PRICE SCORE 124.1** ***12 MONTH PRICE SCORE 93.7**

*NYSE COMPOSITE INDEX=100

INTERIM EARNINGS (Per Share):

Qtr.	Mar.	June	Sept.	Dec.
1990	0.73	0.12	0.05	0.57
1991	0.85	0.22	0.04	0.52
1992	0.76	0.15	0.15	0.73
1993	0.88	0.37	0.17	0.64

INTERIM DIVIDENDS (Per Share):

Amt.	Decl.	Ex.	Rec.	Pay.
0.275Q	5/18/93	5/24/93	5/28/93	6/21/93
0.275Q	8/10	8/16	8/20	9/13
0.275Q	10/28	11/15	11/19	12/13
0.275Q	2/8/94	2/14/94	2/18/94	3/14/94
0.285Q	5/17	5/23	5/27	6/20

Indicated div.: $1.14

CAPITALIZATION (12/31/93):

	($000)	(%)
Long-Term Debt	371,713	32.3
Deferred Income Tax	167,784	14.6
Redeemable Cum Pfd Stk.	7,525	0.7
Common & Surplus	601,942	52.4
Total	1,148,964	100.0
Current Debt	78,300	

DIVIDEND ACHIEVER STATUS:

Rank: 283 1983-93 Growth Rate: 5.0%
Total Years of Dividend Growth: 14

RECENT DEVELOPMENTS: For the year ended 12/31/93, income from continuing operations was $84.7 million compared with $73.8 million in 1992. Revenues were $660.4 million, up 11.7%. Questar's exploration and production companies reported operating income of $36.3 million compared with $27.8 million last year. Questar Pipeline increased operating income to $23.3 million from $22.5 million last year. Mountain Fuel reported operating income of $25.1 million, up 7.2%.

PROSPECTS: The Public Service Commission of Utah issued two rate orders concerning Mountain Fuel Supply Co. The net effect of the two orders is a $6.5 million rate decrease. The utility had orginally sought a $10.3 million rate increase. The Company will ask the commission for a rehearing on the order. Under an agreement with Nextel Communications, Nextel will acquire Questar Telecom in exchange for 3.9 million shares of Nextel common stock.

BUSINESS

QUESTAR CORP. is a diversified energy company that, through its affilites, conducts oil and gas exploration and production, interstate natural gas transmission, retail gas distribution and telecommunications. Celsius Energy Company conducts oil and gas exploration activities primarily in the Rocky Mountain region. Questar Pipeline Co. operates a 2,400 mile system in Colorado, Wyoming and Utah. The utility operations transport gas to market areas in southwestern Wyoming and northern and central Utah through two major pipeline systems. Other operations include Questar Service Corp., which conducts microwave communications and data processing; Questar Telecom Inc., involves mobile radio-telephone and business communications; and Questar Development Corp.

BUSINESS LINE ANALYSIS

(12/31/93)	Rev(%)	Inc(%)
Explor & Production	41.9	33.3
Natl Gas Transmission	26.0	33.2
Natl Gas Distribution	60.9	31.4
Other Operations	4.3	2.1
Intercompany Transactions	(33.0)	0.0
Total	100.0	100.0

ANNUAL EARNINGS AND DIVIDENDS PER SHARE

	1993	1992	1991	1990	1989	1988	1987
Earnings Per Share	**2.10**	**[1] 1.79**	**1.63**	**1.45**	**1.28**	**0.64**	**0.66**
Dividends Per Share	**1.09**	**1.04**	**[2] 1.01**	**0.97**	**0.945**	**0.94**	**0.91**
Dividend Payout %	**51.9**	**58.1**	**62.0**	**66.7**	**74.1**	**N.M.**	**N.M.**

[1] Before acctg. chg. [2] 2-for-1 stk split,06/18/91

ANNUAL FINANCIAL DATA

	1993	1992	1991	1990	1989	1988	1987
RECORD OF EARNINGS (IN MILLIONS):							
Revenues	660.4	604.8	632.3	536.3	509.4	486.0	492.6
Depreciation & Amort	86.8	77.2	67.9	63.3	60.0	...	...
Prov for Fed Inc Taxes	28.8	29.3	34.3	30.1	27.1	...	...
Operating Income	148.3	133.9	129.7	116.0	105.3	64.3	70.4
Debt Expense	34.0	35.8	36.1	35.6	32.2	29.6	29.5
Net Income	81.7	[1] 71.3	64.0	57.5	50.8	25.9	25.9
Aver. Shs. Outstg. (000)	39,995	39,492	38,715	38,898	38,928	38,466	37,016
[1] Before acctg. change cr$9,303,000.							
BALANCE SHEET (IN MILLIONS):							
Gross Plant	2,024.4	1,898.2	1,749.5	1,637.3	1,546.0	1,479.4	1,432.2
Accumulated Depreciation	871.7	800.5	728.9	675.9	651.9	610.2	542.5
Net Prop, Plant & Equip	1,152.7	1,097.7	1,020.6	961.3	894.1	869.2	889.8
Lg tm Debt, Less Curr Port	371.7	364.6	354.4	328.2	275.6	249.3	254.7
Net Stockholders' Equity	609.5	562.5	511.9	471.6	468.2	464.8	488.3
Total Assets	1,417.7	1,323.7	1,219.6	1,151.0	1,075.0	1,026.1	1,046.7
Year End Shs Outstg (000)	40,169	39,795	39,277	38,515	39,512	37,976	38,580
STATISTICAL RECORD:							
Book Value Per Share	14.99	13.55	12.49	11.76	11.54	11.88	12.24
Op. Inc/Net Pl %	12.9	12.2	12.7	12.1	11.8	7.4	7.9
Dep/Gr. Pl %	4.3	4.1	3.9	3.9	3.9	4.3	4.5
Accum. Dep/Gr. Pl %	43.1	42.2	41.7	41.3	42.2	41.2	37.9
Return on Equity %	13.6	12.9	12.8	12.5	10.8	5.6	5.3
Average Yield %	3.1	4.5	4.9	5.4	5.3	5.7	5.0
P/E Ratio	21.0-12.1	15.4-10.3	15.2-10.2	13.7-11.3	15.5-12.3	27.9-23.4	35.2-20.1
Price Range	44-25 3/8	27 1/2-18 1/2	24 3/4-16 5/8	19 7/8-16 3/8	19 7/8-15 3/4	17 7/8-15	23 1/4-13 1/4

Statistics are as originally reported.

OFFICERS:
R.D. Cash, Chmn., Pres. & C.E.O.
W.F. Edwards, Sr. V.P. & C.F.O.
C.C. Holbrook, V.P. & Corp. Sec.

INCORPORATED: UT, Oct., 1984

PRINCIPAL OFFICE: 180 East First South
P.O. Box 11150, Salt Lake City, UT 84147

TELEPHONE NUMBER: (801) 534-5000
NO. OF EMPLOYEES: 362
ANNUAL MEETING: In May
SHAREHOLDERS: 7,799
INSTITUTIONAL HOLDINGS:
No. of Institutions: 215
Shares Held: 31,498,701

REGISTRAR(S): Zions First National Bank, Salt Lake City, UT 84111
Mellon Bank, N.A., Pittsburgh, PA

TRANSFER AGENT(S): At Company's Office
First Chicago Trust Co. of New York, New York, NY 10008

NASDAQ SYMBOL RGBK
Rec. Pr. 34¼ (Marginable)

REGIONS FINANCIAL CORP.

YIELD 3.5%
P/E RATIO 15.2

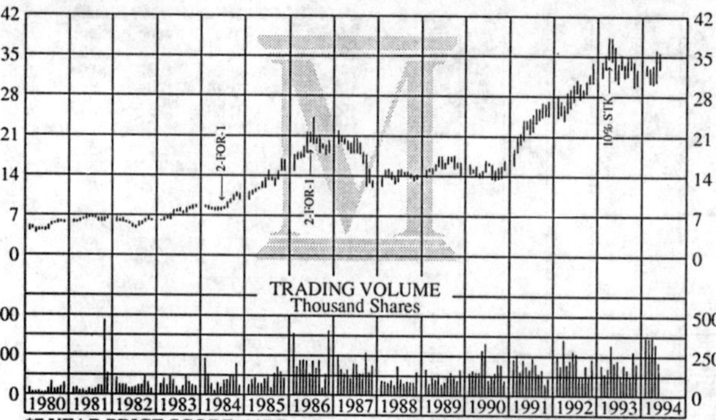

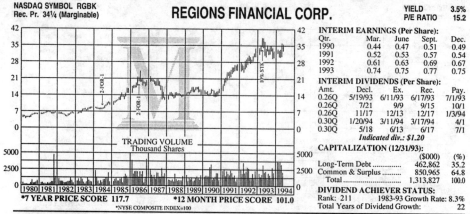

***7 YEAR PRICE SCORE 117.7** ***12 MONTH PRICE SCORE 101.0**

*NYSE COMPOSITE INDEX=100

INTERIM EARNINGS (Per Share):

Qtr.	Mar.	June	Sept.	Dec.
1990	0.44	0.47	0.51	0.49
1991	0.52	0.53	0.57	0.54
1992	0.61	0.63	0.69	0.67
1993	0.74	0.75	0.77	0.75

INTERIM DIVIDENDS (Per Share):

Amt.	Decl.	Ex.	Rec.	Pay.
0.26Q	5/19/93	6/11/93	6/17/93	7/1/93
0.26Q	7/21	9/9	9/15	10/1
0.26Q	11/17	12/13	12/17	1/3/94
0.30Q	1/20/94	3/11/94	3/17/94	4/1
0.30Q	5/18	6/13	6/17	7/1

Indicated div.: $1.20

CAPITALIZATION (12/31/93):

	($000)	(%)
Long-Term Debt	462,862	35.2
Common & Surplus	850,965	64.8
Total	1,313,827	100.0

DIVIDEND ACHIEVER STATUS:
Rank: 211 1983-93 Growth Rate: 8.3%
Total Years of Dividend Growth: 22

RECENT DEVELOPMENTS: The Company has changed its name from First Alabama Bancshares, Inc. As a part of the name change, the bank subsidiaries in Florida, Georgia, Tennessee and Louisiana will also change their names to Region during 1994. For the year ended 12/31/93, net income increased 18% from the prior year to $112.0 million. Interest income totaled $555.7 million compared with $536.7 million in 1992. Noninterest income advanced 11% to $132.0 million, paced by a 19% gain in mortgage servicing and origination fees to $44.1 million. The provision for loan losses declined to $21.5 million from $27.1 million in 1992. RGBK also announced plans to acquire Guaranty Bancorp of Baton Rouge, Louisiana and First Bank of Fayette, Alabama.

BUSINESS

REGIONS FINANCIAL CORP. is a $10.5 billion bank holding company. The Company operates 231 full-service banking offices in Alabama, Tennessee, Florida, Louisiana and Georgia. RGBK offers commercial banking services and trust services in several locations. First Alabama Bank, the Company's principal banking subsidiary, operates 166 full-service banking offices throughout Alabama. Regions Bank of Florida, the Company's Florida banking affiliate, operates 15 full-service banking offices in northwest Florida. Supplementing the Company's banking operations are a mortgage banking company, credit-life insurance related companies and a registered broker/dealer firm. First Alabama has no foreign operations, although it has an International Department to assist with their foreign transactions. The Company also has real estate loan origination offices in Georgia, Tennessee, Mississippi and South Carolina.

LOANS DISTRIBUTION

(12/31/93)	($000)	(%)
Commercial	1,497,502	21.8
Real Estate-Construction	262,918	3.8
Real Estate-Mortgage	3,315,843	48.3
Consumer	1,793,234	26.1
Total	6,869,497	100.0

ANNUAL EARNINGS AND DIVIDENDS PER SHARE

	12/31/93	12/31/92	12/31/91	12/31/90	12/31/89	12/31/88	12/30/87
Earnings Per Share	**3.01**	**2.60**	**2.16**	**1.91**	**1.73**	**1.61**	**1.55**
Dividends Per Share	**0.984**	**[1] 0.90**	**0.864**	**0.818**	**0.755**	**0.718**	**0.664**
Dividend Payout %	**32.7**	**34.6**	**39.9**	**42.9**	**43.7**	**44.6**	**42.7**

[1] 10% stk div,03/01/93

ANNUAL FINANCIAL DATA

	12/31/93	12/31/92	12/31/91	12/31/90	12/31/89	12/31/88	12/30/87
RECORD OF EARNINGS (IN MILLIONS):							
Total Revenues	687.7	655.8	658.3	613.5	567.6	473.9	414.7
Costs and Expenses	522.2	515.8	546.4	517.4	483.9	398.1	341.4
Operating Income	165.5	140.0	111.9	96.1	83.7	75.8	73.3
Income Bef Income Taxes	165.5	140.0	111.9	96.1	83.7	75.8	73.3
Applicable Income Taxes	53.5	45.0	33.7	27.2	21.0	17.6	17.1
Net Income	112.0	95.0	78.3	68.9	62.6	58.2	56.2
Aver. Shs. Outstg. (000)	37,205	36,532	36,191	36,097	36,331	36,281	36,243
BALANCE SHEET (IN MILLIONS):							
Cash and Cash Equivalents	2,968.6	2,251.4	2,059.8	1,887.8	1,639.6	1,794.3	1,484.6
Receivables, Net	143.4	80.3	79.8	70.7	60.5	58.2	52.1
Gross Property	140.2	115.9	111.7	110.2	104.2	106.8	99.0
Long-Term Debt	462.9	137.0	18.8	19.7	45.3	20.6	68.5
Net Stockholders' Equity	851.0	656.7	573.0	524.1	489.4	455.6	417.8
Total Assets	10,476.3	7,881.0	6,745.1	6,344.4	5,549.6	5,173.6	4,390.9
Total Current Assets	3,112.0	2,331.7	2,139.6	1,958.5	1,700.0	1,852.4	1,536.6
Total Current Liabilities	9,050.4	6,981.5	6,073.3	5,723.5	4,941.4	4,625.8	3,846.7
Net Working Capital	d5,938.4	d4,649.7	d3,933.7	d3,765.0	d3,241.4	d2,773.4	d2,310.1
Year End Shs Outstg (000)	41,049	37,272	36,352	36,048	36,299	37,348	35,896
STATISTICAL RECORD:							
Book Value Per Share	20.73	17.62	15.76	14.54	13.48	12.20	11.64
Return on Equity %	13.2	14.5	13.7	13.1	12.8	12.8	13.5
Return on Assets %	1.1	1.2	1.2	1.1	1.1	1.1	1.3
Average Yield %	2.9	3.1	4.0	5.4	4.8	5.2	3.9
P/E Ratio	12.7-9.8	13.0-9.1	12.6-7.3	8.8-6.9	10.2-7.9	9.5-7.5	14.1-7.7
Price Range	38⅜-29⅝	33⅞-23¾	27⅛-15⅞	16⅞-13¼	17⅝-13¾	15¼-12⅛	21⅞-12

Statistics are as originally reported.

OFFICERS:
J.S. Mackin, Chmn. & C.E.O.
R.D. Horsley, Vice-Chmn. & Exec. Fin. Off.
L.B. Barnes, III, Gen. Counsel & Sec.

INCORPORATED: DE, Jun., 1970

PRINCIPAL OFFICE: 417 North 20th St. P.O. Box 10247, Birmingham, AL 35202-0247

TELEPHONE NUMBER: (205) 326-7100

FAX: (205) 240-2840

NO. OF EMPLOYEES: 5,439

ANNUAL MEETING: In April

SHAREHOLDERS: 16,532

INSTITUTIONAL HOLDINGS:
No. of Institutions: 163
Shares Held: 15,702,174

REGISTRAR(S): First Alabama Bank, Montgomery, AL 36103

TRANSFER AGENT(S): First Alabama Bank, Montgomery, AL 36103

REPUBLIC NEW YORK CORP.

YIELD 2.8%
P/E RATIO 9.2

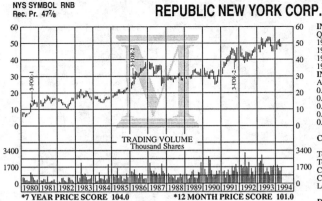

7 YEAR PRICE SCORE 104.0   *12 MONTH PRICE SCORE 101.0*

*NYSE COMPOSITE INDEX=100

TRADING VOLUME
Thousand Shares

INTERIM EARNINGS (Per Share):

Qtr.	Mar.	June	Sept.	Dec.
1990	0.87	0.95	0.95	0.85
1991	0.97	0.99	0.99	1.00
1992	1.04	1.08	1.16	1.14
1993	1.18	1.30	1.34	1.38

INTERIM DIVIDENDS (Per Share):

Amt.	Decl.	Ex.	Rec.	Pay.
0.27Q	4/22/93	6/9/93	6/15/93	7/1/93
0.27Q	7/21	9/9	9/15	10/1
0.27Q	10/20	12/9	12/15	1/1/94
0.33Q	1/19/94	3/9/94	3/15/94	4/1
0.33Q	4/20	6/9	6/15	7/1

Indicated div.: $1.32

CAPITALIZATION (12/31/93):

	($000)	(%)
Total Deposits	22,801,250	65.2
Total Debt	9,130,254	26.1
Cum Preferred Stock	556,425	1.6
Common & Surplus	2,190,797	6.2
Loan Valuation Reserve	311,855	0.9
Total	34,990,581	100.0

DIVIDEND ACHIEVER STATUS:
Rank: 288   1983-93 Growth Rate: 4.8%
Total Years of Dividend Growth: 18

RECENT DEVELOPMENTS: For the quarter ended 12/31/93, net income was $79.9 million, up 19.6% from the corresponding 1992 quarter. The provision for loan losses declined 57% to $15 million. During the quarter the Company purchased Mase Westpac Ltd., an authorized United Kingdom gold bullion bank, and also acquired Citibank's World Banknote Services business which ships US dollars to and from financial institutions in nearly 40 countries. For 1993, net income was $301.2 million.

PROSPECTS: The acquisition of SafraBank, now known as Republic Bank California, with 3 offices in Los Angeles County, introduces RNB to California's domestic private banking and mortgage banking markets. The acqusition of Bank Leumi, a Canadian bank with deposits of $179 million, marks RNB's entry into the Toronto market. The Company has been approved by the Federal Reserve System to deal in all forms of debt and equity securities through Republic New York Securities Corp., a wholly-owned subsidiary.

BUSINESS

REPUBLIC NEW YORK CORP. is a bank holding company, the principal subsidiaries of which are Republic National Bank of New York and The Manhattan Savings Bank. The Company provides a variety of commercial banking services, with primary emphasis on international banking. With assets of $39.5 billion, Republic New York is one of the largest bank holding companies in the nation. RNB owns 49% of Safra Republic Holdings.

ANNUAL EARNINGS AND DIVIDENDS PER SHARE

	1993	1992	1991	1990	1989	1988	1987
Earnings Per Share	5.20	4.42	3.95	3.62	0.03	3.34	☑ 0.43
Dividends Per Share	1.06	1.00	☐ 0.92	0.873	0.84	0.793	0.767
Dividend Payout %	20.4	22.6	23.3	24.1	N.M.	23.8	N.M.

☐ 3-for-2 stk split,10/22/91   ☑ Before extraord. item

ANNUAL FINANCIAL DATA

RECORD OF EARNINGS (IN MILLIONS):

	1993	1992	1991	1990	1989	1988	1987
Total Interest Income	1,932.9	2,038.6	2,263.9	2,501.6	2,347.5	1,927.5	1,532.9
Total Interest Expense	1,157.1	1,318.2	1,682.7	2,044.2	1,990.6	1,499.3	1,147.2
Net Interest Income	775.9	720.4	581.2	457.3	356.9	428.2	385.7
Provision for Loan Losses	85.0	120.0	62.0	40.0	209.0	41.5	140.0
Net Income	301.2	258.9	227.4	201.2	24.0	169.7	☐ 33.0
Aver. Shs. Outstg. (000)	52,466	52,204	51,852	49,726	45,223	44,942	44,438

☐ Before extra. item dr$15,869,000.

BALANCE SHEET (IN MILLIONS):

	1993	1992	1991	1990	1989	1988	1987
Cash & Due From Banks	636.6	490.7	412.0	424.9	397.9	375.3	428.1
Loans, Net	9,196.7	7,766.4	8,341.5	8,768.2	6,292.9	5,544.0	5,342.7
Total Domestic Deposits	10,152.3	10,401.2	9,925.1	10,532.2	8,291.4	8,434.9	7,340.1
Total Foreign Deposits	12,648.9	10,701.0	10,457.6	9,454.6	8,233.4	7,911.4	7,498.4
Long-term Debt	4,854.8	4,633.4	3,120.4	2,416.2	2,521.3	2,272.4	1,717.3
Net Stockholders' Equity	2,747.2	2,263.4	1,997.6	1,683.0	1,372.0	1,426.3	1,325.4
Total Assets	39,493.5	37,146.4	31,220.8	29,597.0	25,467.0	24,519.0	22,387.6
Year End Shs Outstg (000)	52,703	52,190	52,045	51,608	45,332	45,060	44,790

STATISTICAL RECORD:

	1993	1992	1991	1990	1989	1988	1987
Return on Assets %	0.76	0.70	0.73	0.68	0.09	0.69	0.15
Return on Equity %	11.00	11.40	11.40	12.00	1.70	11.90	2.50
Book Value Per Share	41.57	32.71	29.60	26.61	23.44	24.79	22.51
Average Yield %	2.2	2.3	2.3	2.9	2.7	2.7	2.4
P/E Ratio	10.3-8.5	10.9-8.6	12.0-7.9	9.6-6.9	N.M	9.6-7.9	89.5-56.1
Price Range	53¾-44⅜	48¼-38	47¼-31⅜	34⅞-24⅞	34⅜-28⅜	32⅛-26⅜	38½-24⅛

Statistics are as originally reported.

LOAN DISTRIBUTION

(12/31/93)	($000)	(%)
Real Estate- Residential	1,310,718	13.7
Real Estate- Commercial	1,854,377	19.3
Banks, Brokers & Others	685,874	7.1
Commercial & Industrial	2,152,691	22.4
Individuals	90,218	0.9
All Other	16,915	0.2
Foreign	3,492,590	36.4
Total	9,603,383	100.0

OFFICERS:
W.H. Weiner, Chmn. & C.E.O.
E. Ginsberg, Vice-Chmn. & Gen. Couns.

INCORPORATED: MD, Sep., 1973

PRINCIPAL OFFICE: 452 Fifth Avenue, New York, NY 10018

TELEPHONE NUMBER: (212) 525-6100
NO. OF EMPLOYEES: 5,262 (approx.)
ANNUAL MEETING: In April
SHAREHOLDERS: 2,713
INSTITUTIONAL HOLDINGS:
No. of Institutions: 181
Shares Held: 27,825,294

REGISTRAR(S): Manufacturers Hanover Trust Co., New York, NY

TRANSFER AGENT(S): Manufacturers Hanover Trust Co., New York, NY

RITE AID CORP.

YIELD 3.1%
P/E RATIO 50.3

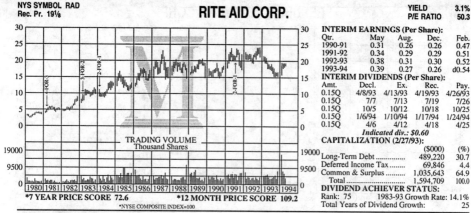

*7 YEAR PRICE SCORE 72.6   *12 MONTH PRICE SCORE 109.2
*NYSE COMPOSITE INDEX=100

INTERIM EARNINGS (Per Share):

Qtr.	May	Aug.	Dec.	Feb.
1990-91	0.31	0.26	0.26	0.47
1991-92	0.34	0.29	0.29	0.51
1992-93	0.38	0.31	0.30	0.52
1993-94	0.39	0.27	0.26	d0.54

INTERIM DIVIDENDS (Per Share):

Amt.	Decl.	Ex.	Rec.	Pay.
0.15Q	4/8/93	4/13/93	4/19/93	4/26/93
0.15Q	7/7	7/13	7/19	7/26
0.15Q	10/5	10/12	10/18	10/25
0.15Q	1/6/94	1/10/94	1/17/94	1/24/94
0.15Q	4/6	4/12	4/18	4/25

Indicated div.: $0.60

CAPITALIZATION (2/27/93):

	($000)	(%)
Long-Term Debt	489,220	30.7
Deferred Income Tax	69,846	4.4
Common & Surplus	1,035,643	64.9
Total	1,594,709	100.0

DIVIDEND ACHIEVER STATUS:
Rank: 75   1983-93 Growth Rate: 14.1%
Total Years of Dividend Growth: 25

RECENT DEVELOPMENTS: Net income for the 13 weeks ended 11/27/93 declined to $23.0 million from $26.4 million. Revenues grew 6.8% to $1.08 billion. Drugstore earnings fell 15.6% to $20.7 million on revenues of $1.01 billion. Comparable drugstore sales increased 2.8%. At ADAP Auto Parts, earnings increased 14.8% to $1.0 million on sales of $27.5 million, up 6.3%. Sales at Encore Books increased 19.4% to $18.1 million. Encore posted a loss of $499,000 versus a loss of $455,000 in 1992.

PROSPECTS: The Company announced plans to sell four of its noncore units, repurchase 25% of its common shares, and close 200 unprofitable stores. This strategy will enable RAD to focus on its core drugstore business along with future expansion into the managed-care end of the pharmacy business. Additionally, a new point-of-sale scanning system will improve inventory control by tracking sales information to make more efficient purchasing decisions.

BUSINESS

RITE AID CORP. operates the largest retail drug chain in the United States with 2,663 drugstores in 23 eastern states. The Company also operates a specialty retailing division which includes 94 ADAP Auto parts stores in six New England states, 103 Encore bookstores in six mid-Atlantic states, and 171 Concord Custom Cleaners outlets in 11 midwestern and southwestern states. Rite Aid's medical services division comprises 33 Sera-Tec Biologicals centers which provides plasma for use in therapeutic and diagnostic products.

BUSINESS LINE ANALYSIS

(2/27/93)	Rev(%)	Inc(%)
Retail Drug	93.8	92.9
Special Retailing	4.7	3.9
Medical Services	1.5	3.2
Total	100.0	100.0

ANNUAL EARNINGS AND DIVIDENDS PER SHARE

	2/27/93	2/29/92	3/3/91	3/3/90	3/4/89	2/27/88	2/28/87
Earnings Per Share	1.51	1.43	1.30	①0.99	1.15	①②1.13	0.95
Dividends Per Share	0.55	0.50	0.45	0.41	0.37	0.34	0.29
Dividend Payout %	36.4	35.0	34.7	41.4	32.2	30.0	30.7

① Before disc. oper. ② Before acctg. chg.

ANNUAL FINANCIAL DATA

RECORD OF EARNINGS (IN MILLIONS):

	2/27/93	2/29/92	3/3/91	3/3/90	3/4/89	2/27/88	2/28/87
Total Revenues	4,085.1	3,748.4	3,447.5	3,172.8	2,868.3	2,486.3	1,756.7
Costs and Expenses	3,739.3	3,412.1	3,127.1	2,877.9	2,596.9	2,236.6	1,556.5
Depreciation & Amort	98.3	93.5	93.3	84.4	76.8	61.0	44.3
Operating Income	247.5	242.8	227.1	210.5	194.6	188.7	155.9
Income Bef Income Taxes	214.6	202.0	174.7	133.8	151.3	154.2	133.0
Income Taxes	82.2	78.0	67.4	51.9	59.1	62.8	59.8
Net Income	132.4	124.0	107.3	①81.9	②92.1	③93.8	78.0
Aver. Shs. Outstg. (000)	87,933	86,917	82,996	82,958	82,904	82,660	82,562

① Before disc. op. cr$20,165,000. ② Before disc. op. cr$3,094,000. ③ Before disc. op. cr$47,059,000; and acctg. chg cr$3,712,000.

BALANCE SHEET (IN MILLIONS):

	2/27/93	2/29/92	3/3/91	3/3/90	3/4/89	2/27/88	2/28/87
Cash and Cash Equivalents	5.4	27.4	25.9	14.5	15.3	19.8	23.7
Receivables, Net	196.1	185.6	192.0	175.1	151.7	116.9	82.2
Inventories	863.0	771.3	707.0	643.6	596.5	514.9	433.4
Gross Property	1,131.9	1,010.9	931.8	837.5	730.3	612.6	479.8
Accumulated Depreciation	532.5	465.4	397.0	326.9	267.2	211.0	165.0
Long-Term Debt	489.2	427.5	585.4	542.1	228.3	227.2	153.4
Net Stockholders' Equity	1,035.6	950.6	773.9	704.4	636.2	571.0	452.5
Total Assets	1,875.2	1,734.5	1,667.0	1,539.3	1,417.5	1,224.2	964.3
Total Current Assets	1,092.2	1,013.1	944.6	849.2	776.4	666.6	549.7
Total Current Liabilities	280.5	289.9	237.1	215.9	479.0	357.5	315.3
Net Working Capital	811.6	723.2	707.5	633.3	297.3	309.1	234.4
Year End Shs Outstg (000)	90,240	87,814	83,051	82,987	82,896	82,702	82,578

STATISTICAL RECORD:

	2/27/93	2/29/92	3/3/91	3/3/90	3/4/89	2/27/88	2/28/87
Operating Profit Margin %	6.1	6.5	6.6	6.6	6.8	7.6	8.9
Book Value Per Share	9.86	9.17	7.43	6.57	6.03	5.43	4.79
Return on Equity %	12.8	13.0	13.9	11.6	14.5	16.4	17.2
Return on Assets %	7.1	7.2	6.4	5.3	6.5	7.7	8.1
Average Yield %	2.5	2.4	2.6	2.5	2.1	1.8	1.9
P/E Ratio	16.0-12.7	16.7-12.1	15.0-11.4	20.8-14.9	18.5-13.2	20.5-12.6	18.7-12.8
Price Range	24⅛-19¼	23⅞-17¼	19⅜-14¾	20⅝-14¾	20½-14⅝	23⅛-14¼	17¾-12⅛

Statistics are as originally reported.

OFFICERS:
A. Grass, Chmn. & C.E.O.
M.L. Grass, Pres. & C.O.O.
F.M. Bergonzi, Sr. V.P.-Fin.
T. Coogan, V.P. & Treas.

INCORPORATED: PA, Apr., 1968

PRINCIPAL OFFICE: 30 Hunter Lane, Camp Hill, PA 17011

TELEPHONE NUMBER: (717) 761-2633

NO. OF EMPLOYEES: 31,128

ANNUAL MEETING: In July

SHAREHOLDERS: 9,000 (approx.)

INSTITUTIONAL HOLDINGS:
No. of Institutions: 310
Shares Held: 60,699,118

REGISTRAR(S): Harris Trust Co. of N.Y., New York, NY 10005

TRANSFER AGENT(S): Harris Trust Co. of N.Y., New York, NY 10005

RLI CORP.

YIELD 2.5%
P/E RATIO 9.1

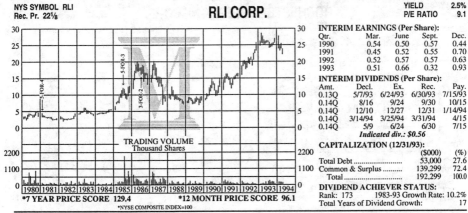

*7 YEAR PRICE SCORE 129.4   *12 MONTH PRICE SCORE 96.1
*NYSE COMPOSITE INDEX=100

INTERIM EARNINGS (Per Share):

Qtr.	Mar.	June	Sept.	Dec.
1990	0.54	0.50	0.57	0.44
1991	0.45	0.52	0.55	0.70
1992	0.52	0.57	0.57	0.63
1993	0.51	0.66	0.32	0.93

INTERIM DIVIDENDS (Per Share):

Amt.	Decl.	Ex.	Rec.	Pay.
0.13Q	5/7/93	6/24/93	6/30/93	7/15/93
0.14Q	8/16	9/24	9/30	10/15
0.14Q	12/10	12/27	12/31	1/14/94
0.14Q	3/14/94	3/25/94	3/31/94	4/15
0.14Q	5/9	6/24	6/30	7/15

Indicated div.: $0.56

CAPITALIZATION (12/31/93):

	($000)	(%)
Total Debt	53,000	27.6
Common & Surplus	139,299	72.4
Total	192,299	100.0

DIVIDEND ACHIEVER STATUS:
Rank: 173   1983-93 Growth Rate: 10.2%
Total Years of Dividend Growth: 17

RECENT DEVELOPMENTS: For the year ended 12/31/91, net income rose 8% to $12.6 million from $12.6 million a year earlier. Net investment income was $12.1 million, up 9%. Total assets grew 14% to $303.6 million. The specialty property and casualty segment combined ratio was 91.8% versus 92.9% last year. The loss ratio increased to 58.4% from 51.6% a year ago while the expense ratio declined to 33.4% from 41.3% last year. Gross sales declined 19% to $124.8 million from $180.5 million. For the quarter net income soared 57% to $4.0 million from $2.5 million a year earlier. Net premiums written were $21.0 million, up 6.5%. Gross sales climbed 15.5% to $52.9 million from $45.8 million a year earlier. Gross insurance premiums written expanded 12.1% to $46.0 million from $41.1 million a year ago.

BUSINESS

RLI CORP. is a holding company which, through its insurance subsidiaries, underwrites contact lens insurance and specialty property and casualty insurance. In addition, RLI administers extended service programs and develops and markets a comprehensive computerized office automation system to practitioners in the ophthalmic industry. The Company believes it is the world's largest provider of contact lens insurance and ophthalmic extended service programs. RLI also markets a computerized office automation system for eye care professionals which uses proprietary software called the RLI Practice Automation System and IBM personal computers. The principal specialty insurance coverages currently written by the Company are commercial property, general liability and aviation. Smaller programs include commercial umbrella, directors' and officers' liability for not-for-profit organizations, miscellaneous professional liability, commercial multiperil, personal umbrella, fidelity and surety and accident and health insurance.

ANNUAL EARNINGS AND DIVIDENDS PER SHARE

	1993	1992	1991	1990	1989	1988	1987
Earnings Per Share	2.42	2.29	2.22	2.05	1.43	1.21	2.11
Dividends Per Share	0.53	0.49	0.45	0.41	0.38	0.34	0.30
Dividend Payout %	21.9	21.4	20.3	20.0	26.6	28.1	14.2

ANNUAL FINANCIAL DATA

RECORD OF EARNINGS (IN THOUSANDS):

	1993	1992	1991	1990	1989	1988	1987
Premiums Earned	125,989	103,177	76,763	72,610	70,389	85,701	88,178
Net Investment Income	16,857	13,483	12,742	11,065	9,558	7,811	6,916
Total Revenues	155,125	129,757	102,343	92,221	88,995	103,135	104,361
Losses & Settlement Exps	79,737	62,187	46,493	37,688	39,436	49,898	44,496
Inc Fr Cont Opers Bef Income Taxes	18,149	21,226	22,706	14,729	9,886	9,193	19,737
Income Tax Exp (benefit)	4,017	5,019	5,906	3,108	1,376	1,425	5,378
Realized Gains on Invests	...	...	...	...	...	...	985
Net Income	⊡ 14,132	16,207	16,800	11,621	8,200	7,254	13,965
Aver. Shs. Outstg.	5,829	2,727	5,659	5,659	5,751	5,980	6,164

⊡ Before acctg. change cr$1,665,000.

BALANCE SHEET (IN THOUSANDS):

	1993	1992	1991	1990	1989	1988	1987
Cash	9,247	4,394	7,964	3,038	9,467	2,801	1,975
Fixed Matur, At Amortized Cost	242,052	172,831	146,182	141,081	108,723	107,220	99,561
Eq Secur, At Mkt Value	116,529	75,934	63,323	39,914	35,870	25,048	23,467
Total Assets	668,921	529,660	303,553	266,787	243,346	227,824	220,199
Benefits and Claims	416,799	358,786	157,789	142,823	129,120	126,973	110,557
Net Stockholders' Equity	139,299	117,393	92,816	77,205	70,276	64,026	57,764
Year End Shares Outstg	5,918	5,761	5,659	5,659	5,659	5,980	5,980

STATISTICAL RECORD:

	1993	1992	1991	1990	1989	1988	1987
Return on Equity %	10.1	13.8	18.1	15.1	11.7	11.3	24.2
Book Value Per Share	23.54	20.38	16.40	13.64	12.42	10.71	9.66
Average Yield %	2.0	2.3	3.2	3.5	4.6	3.5	2.2
P/E Ratio	11.8-10.0	9.1-5.7	5.6-3.8	7.3-4.1	6.6-4.8	10.3-5.9	9.6-3.3
Price Range	28⅝-24⅛	25¾-16	16½-11⅜	14⅞-8⅜	9½-6⅞	12½-7⅛	20¼-7

Statistics are as originally reported.

OFFICERS:
G.D. Stephens, Pres. & C.E.O.
J.E. Dondanville, V.P. & C.F.O.
J.E. Zogby, Treasurer
K.J. Hensey, Corp. Sec.

INCORPORATED: DE, May, 1984

PRINCIPAL OFFICE: 9025 N. Lindbergh Drive, Peoria, IL 61615

TELEPHONE NUMBER: (309) 692-1000
FAX: (309) 692-1068
NO. OF EMPLOYEES: 404
ANNUAL MEETING: In May
SHAREHOLDERS: 701
INSTITUTIONAL HOLDINGS:
No. of Institutions: 41
Shares Held: 1,960,172

REGISTRAR(S): Harris Trust & Savings Bank, Chicago, IL

TRANSFER AGENT(S): Harris Trust & Savings Bank, Chicago, IL

ROCHESTER TELEPHONE CORP.

YIELD 3.6%
P/E RATIO 9.3

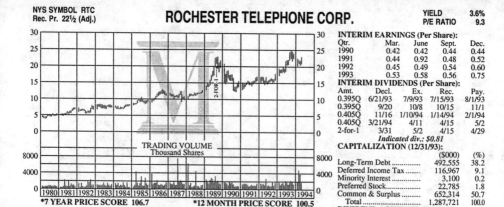

7 YEAR PRICE SCORE 106.7   **12 MONTH PRICE SCORE 100.5**
*NYSE COMPOSITE INDEX=100

TRADING VOLUME
Thousand Shares

INTERIM EARNINGS (Per Share):

Qtr.	Mar.	June	Sept.	Dec.
1990	0.42	0.42	0.44	0.44
1991	0.44	0.92	0.48	0.52
1992	0.45	0.49	0.54	0.60
1993	0.53	0.58	0.56	0.75

INTERIM DIVIDENDS (Per Share):

Amt.	Decl.	Ex.	Rec.	Pay.
0.395Q	6/21/93	7/9/93	7/15/93	8/1/93
0.395Q	9/20	10/8	10/15	11/1
0.405Q	11/16	1/10/94	1/14/94	2/1/94
0.405Q	3/21/94	4/11	4/15	5/2
2-for-1	3/31	5/2	4/15	4/29

Indicated div.: $0.81

CAPITALIZATION (12/31/93):

	($000)	(%)
Long-Term Debt	492,555	38.2
Deferred Income Tax	116,967	9.1
Minority Interest	3,100	0.2
Preferred Stock	22,785	1.8
Common & Surplus	652,314	50.7
Total	1,287,721	100.0

DIVIDEND ACHIEVER STATUS:
Rank: 309   1983-93 Growth Rate: 3.9%
Total Years of Dividend Growth: 34

RECENT DEVELOPMENTS: For the year ended 12/31/93, net income was $82.7 million compared with $70.5 million in 1992. Revenues advanced 12.7% to $906.5 million. The Telecommunication Services group reported sales of $312.6 million, up 32%. Telephone Operation's revenues advanced 4.7% to $593.9 million. For the quarter ended 12/31/93, net income was $25.6 million compared with $20.2 million in the comparable period last year.

PROSPECTS: RTC has grown by offering long-distance services to small businesses at lower cost while still bringing in a profit. RTC has substantial room for growth in the market for long-distance service to small businesses. Also, RTC's rural subsidiaries, acquired since the late 1980s, have favorable growth prospects. RTC plans to expand its cellular coverage in upstate New York in a joint venture with Nynex Corp.

BUSINESS

ROCHESTER TELEPHONE CORP. is one of the nation's leading telecommunications companies, providing a full range of services and products. It's the parent company of 37 local exchange telephone companies and seven communications-related subsidiaries. The Telephone Group provides local exchange services to more than 800,000 customers in New York State, Pennsylvania, Michigan, Indiana, Wisconsin, and Illinois. The Telecommunications Group provides competitive services and products throughout the Northeast and Mid-Atlantic region. Rochester Tel Mobile Communications provides cellular and paging services. Rotelcom designs, installs and maintains integrated business communications systems.

BUSINESS LINE ANALYSIS

(12/31/93)	Rev(%)	Inc(%)
Telephone	65.5	84.3
Telecommunication	34.5	15.7
Total	100.0	100.0

ANNUAL EARNINGS AND DIVIDENDS PER SHARE

	1993	1992	1991	1990	1989	1988	1987
Earnings Per Share	2.42	① 2.08	③ 2.36	1.72	② 2.00	2.17	⑤ 1.60
Dividends Per Share	1.58	② 1.54	1.50	1.46	① 1.42	1.36	1.32
Dividend Payout %	65.3	74.0	63.6	84.9	71.0	62.7	82.5

Note: 2-for-1stk.split,4/29/94. ① Before extraord. item ② Bef extraord item ③ Before extraod item ④ Before extraord. credit ⑤ 2-for-1 stk split, 09/05/89 ⑥ Before acctg. chg.

ANNUAL FINANCIAL DATA

RECORD OF EARNINGS (IN MILLIONS):

Total Revenues & Sales	906.5	804.0	703.2	600.0	562.0	478.7	439.2
Costs and Expenses	596.7	514.9	460.9	404.1	389.2	① 316.3	① 295.6
Depreciation	114.8	114.0	97.1	79.8	65.4	...	...
Operating Income	194.9	175.1	145.2	116.1	107.5	100.2	86.5
Income Before Taxes	133.0	112.0	119.3	79.3	76.3	76.9	66.1
Income Taxes	50.2	41.5	46.0	29.6	24.8	26.0	29.9
Net Income	82.7	② 70.5	③ 73.3	49.7	④ 51.5	50.9	41.9
Aver. Shs. Outstg. (000)	33,727	33,319	30,622	28,194	25,135	22,948	21,834

① Incl. Dep. ② Before extra. item dr$1,072,000. ③ Before extra. item cr$3,757,000. ④ Before extra. item cr$20,645,000.

BALANCE SHEET (IN MILLIONS):

Cash and Cash Equivalents	31.6	70.0	45.0	27.9	60.4	9.0	23.4
Accounts Receivable	157.3	134.0	119.6	105.0	92.0	75.8	79.7
Inventories	11.2	15.9	18.6	19.3	21.5	19.2	15.6
Gross Property	1,748.0	1,755.1	1,651.8	1,315.6	1,124.0	994.3	891.6
Accumulated Depreciation	720.8	715.4	635.0	460.2	367.3	306.3	259.6
Long-Term Debt	492.6	525.6	591.2	363.0	338.1	241.1	254.6
Net Stockholders' Equity	675.1	621.6	587.3	471.7	417.3	356.0	332.9
Total Assets	1,510.2	1,513.9	1,475.7	1,179.9	1,052.6	884.7	830.8
Total Current Assets	221.7	241.7	205.8	175.5	192.3	122.6	133.9
Total Current Liabilities	206.4	245.1	185.3	198.4	154.2	151.1	121.1
Net Working Capital	15.4	d5.3	20.5	d23.0	38.1	d28.4	12.8
Year End Shs Outstg (000)	33,968	33,319	31,843	28,861	25,242	22,948	21,734

STATISTICAL RECORD:

Book Value Per Share	14.31	13.89	13.16	13.51	15.63	14.52	14.27
Return on Equity %	12.3	11.3	12.5	10.5	12.3	14.3	10.9
Average Yield %	7.4	9.5	10.0	8.8	7.9	11.8	12.1
P/E Ratio	10.4-7.2	8.6-7.0	7.2-5.5	12.1-7.2	11.4-6.4	6.0-4.7	7.8-5.8
Price Range	25⅛-17⅞	17⅜-14⅝	17-13	20⅜-12⅜	22⅞-12⅞	12⅞-10⅛	12½-9¼

Statistics are as originally reported.

OFFICERS:
A.C. Hasselwander, Chairman
R.L. Bittner, Pres. & C.E.O.

INCORPORATED: NY, Feb., 1920

PRINCIPAL OFFICE: 180 South Clinton Avenue, Rochester, NY 14646-0700

TELEPHONE NUMBER: (716) 777-1000
FAX: (716) 325-4624
NO. OF EMPLOYEES: 4,701
ANNUAL MEETING: In April
SHAREHOLDERS: 20,011 com.; 995 pfd.
INSTITUTIONAL HOLDINGS:
No. of Institutions: 171
Shares Held: 9,427,991

REGISTRAR(S): First Chicago Trust Co. of New York, New York, NY 10008

TRANSFER AGENT(S): First Chicago Trust Co. of New York, New York, NY 10008

ROCKWELL INTERNATIONAL CORP.

YIELD 2.8%
P/E RATIO 13.3

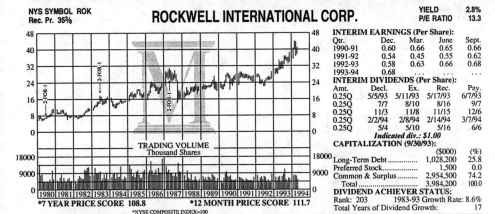

*7 YEAR PRICE SCORE 108.8   *12 MONTH PRICE SCORE 111.7

*NYSE COMPOSITE INDEX=100

INTERIM EARNINGS (Per Share):

Qtr.	Dec.	Mar.	June	Sept.
1990-91	0.60	0.66	0.65	0.66
1991-92	0.54	0.45	0.55	0.62
1992-93	0.58	0.63	0.66	0.68
1993-94	0.68	...	...	...

INTERIM DIVIDENDS (Per Share):

Amt.	Decl.	Ex.	Rec.	Pay.
0.25Q	5/5/93	5/11/93	5/17/93	6/7/93
0.25Q	7/7	8/10	8/16	9/7
0.25Q	11/3	11/8	11/15	12/6
0.25Q	2/2/94	2/8/94	2/14/94	3/7/94
0.25Q	5/4	5/10	5/16	6/6

Indicated div.: $1.00

CAPITALIZATION (9/30/93):

	($000)	(%)
Long-Term Debt	1,028,200	25.8
Preferred Stock	1,500	0.0
Common & Surplus	2,954,500	74.2
Total	3,984,200	100.0

DIVIDEND ACHIEVER STATUS:

Rank: 203   1983-93 Growth Rate: 8.6%
Total Years of Dividend Growth: 17

RECENT DEVELOPMENTS: For the quarter ended 12/31/93, net income increased 17.0% to $149.5 million. Sales increased 4.5% to $2.60 billion. Electronics posted a 20.7% increase in earnings to $168.9 million as a result of strengthening markets and customer acceptance of new products in the Industrial Automation and Telecommunications businesses. Automotive earnings rose 33.6% to $35.0 million due to strong North American truck markets. Aerospace earnings increased 5.2% to $81.7 million.

PROSPECTS: The Automotive segment will continue to benefit from a restructuring program and a strengthening truck market. Aggressive cost reductions and significant investments in new products will help results in the near term. However, several businesses continue to be hurt by the weak European economy. Despite lower government spending, Aerospace should benefit from cost containment initiatives. New product introductions will continue to increase earnings at the Electronic segment.

BUSINESS

ROCKWELL INTERNATIONAL CORP. is a multi-industry company applying advanced technology to products in the electronics, aerospace, automotive and graphics industries. Aerospace is a leader in spacecraft and rocket propulsion systems, and a designer and producer of military and commercial aircraft. Electronics includes industrial automation controls, avionics, telecommunications and defense electronics products and systems. Automotive manufactures components for trucks, buses, trailers, heavy-duty, off-highway vehicles, and passenger cars. Graphics manufactures high-speed printing presses and related graphic arts equipment. Government contracts accounted for 39% of sales in 1993.

BUSINESS LINE ANALYSIS

(9/30/93)	Rev(%)	Inc(%)
Electronics	43.1	54.9
Aerospace	27.7	33.9
Automotive	23.4	11.6
Graphics	5.8	(0.4)
Total	100.0	100.0

ANNUAL EARNINGS AND DIVIDENDS PER SHARE

	9/30/93	9/30/92	9/30/91	9/30/90	9/30/89	9/30/88	9/30/87
Earnings Per Share	2.55	☐ 2.16	2.57	2.56	2.87	3.04	2.27
Dividends Per Share	0.98	0.92	0.875	0.82	0.765	0.72	☐ 0.66
Dividend Payout %	38.4	42.6	34.1	32.0	26.7	23.7	29.1

☐ Before acctg. chg. ☐ 2-for-1 stk split, 4/87

ANNUAL FINANCIAL DATA

RECORD OF EARNINGS (IN MILLIONS):

	9/30/93	9/30/92	9/30/91	9/30/90	9/30/89	9/30/88	9/30/87
Total Revenues	10,920.9	11,027.1	12,359.2	12,462.5	12,797.4	12,098.6	12,200.0
Costs and Expenses	9,421.8	9,583.2	10,599.2	10,765.9	10,962.5	10,450.3	10,432.1
Depreciation & Amort	490.9	558.1	601.4	500.3	496.5	493.9	491.3
Operating Income	1,008.2	885.8	1,158.6	1,196.3	1,338.4	1,154.4	1,276.6
Income Bef Income Taxes	904.1	778.4	1,023.5	1,052.0	1,205.7	1,053.0	1,186.7
Provision for Inc Taxes	342.2	295.4	423.0	427.7	470.8	241.1	551.6
Net Income	561.9	☐ 483.0	600.5	624.3	734.9	811.9	635.1
Aver. Shs. Outstg. (000)	219,800	223,600	233,700	244,100	255,605	266,605	280,035

☐ Before acctg. change dr$1,519,000,000.

BALANCE SHEET (IN MILLIONS):

Cash	772.8	602.6	503.8	411.2	332.4	899.7	1,103.4
Receivables	2,209.1	2,316.9	2,486.4	2,425.7	2,137.2	2,209.0	1,990.1
Inventories	1,430.8	1,445.9	1,387.1	1,619.6	1,574.1	1,526.7	1,451.6
Gross Property	6,018.1	5,988.7	5,887.7	6,006.1	5,575.0	5,527.0	5,229.9
Accumulated Depreciation	3,692.3	3,613.9	3,426.5	3,337.9	2,980.8	2,886.6	2,560.8
Long-Term Debt	1,028.2	1,035.4	740.3	552.9	552.1	745.3	762.6
Net Stockholders' Equity	2,956.0	2,778.0	4,223.7	4,185.9	3,977.6	3,693.0	3,314.2
Total Assets	9,885.1	9,731.0	9,375.5	9,738.1	8,938.8	9,208.5	8,739.2
Total Current Assets	4,946.4	4,889.0	4,823.1	4,775.3	4,366.8	4,924.8	4,622.0
Total Current Liabilities	2,990.9	3,112.2	3,322.0	3,843.4	3,482.2	3,795.9	3,992.4
Net Working Capital	1,955.5	1,776.8	1,501.1	931.9	884.6	1,128.9	629.6
Year End Shs Outstg (000)	221,000	220,300	228,200	238,900	249,800	261,100	275,000

STATISTICAL RECORD:

Operating Profit Margin %	9.2	8.0	9.4	9.6	10.5	9.5	10.5
Book Value Per Share	9.71	8.83	14.46	12.61	11.53	10.10	8.05
Return on Equity %	19.0	17.4	14.2	14.9	18.5	22.0	19.2
Return on Assets %	5.7	5.0	6.4	6.4	8.2	8.8	7.3
Average Yield %	3.0	3.6	3.4	3.3	3.3	3.6	2.9
P/E Ratio	15.1-10.9	13.6-10.3	11.4-8.9	11.2-8.0	9.5-6.9	7.7-5.3	13.7-6.3
Price Range	38½-27⅞	29⅜-22¼	29¼-22¾	28¾-20½	27⅛-19¾	23½-16⅛	31-14¼

Statistics are as originally reported.

OFFICERS:

D.R. Beall, Chmn. & C.E.O.
W.M. Barnes, Sr. V.P.-Fin. & C.F.O.
C.H. Harff, Sr. V.P., Couns. & Sec.
L.H. Cramer, V.P. & Treas.

INCORPORATED: DE, Dec., 1928

PRINCIPAL OFFICE: 2201 Seal Beach Blvd., Seal Beach, CA 90740-8250

TELEPHONE NUMBER: (310) 797-3311
NO. OF EMPLOYEES: 77,028
ANNUAL MEETING: In February
SHAREHOLDERS: 79,332 common; 62,281, class A common

INSTITUTIONAL HOLDINGS:
No. of Institutions: 328
Shares Held: 113,335,886

REGISTRAR(S): Mellon Bank, N.A., Pittsburgh, PA

TRANSFER AGENT(S): Mellon Bank, N.A., Pittsburgh, PA

NYS SYMBOL ROH
Rec. Pr. 58⅛

ROHM & HAAS CO.

YIELD 2.4%
P/E RATIO 33.2

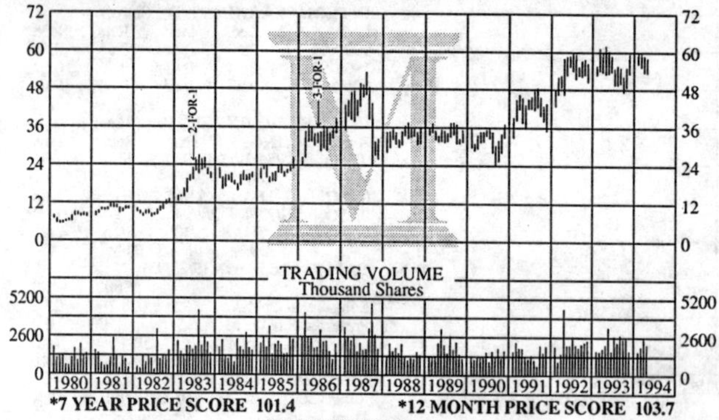

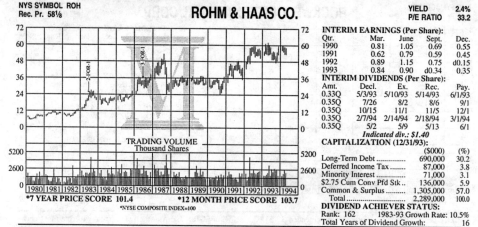

*7 YEAR PRICE SCORE 101.4 *12 MONTH PRICE SCORE 103.7

*NYSE COMPOSITE INDEX=100

INTERIM EARNINGS (Per Share):

Qtr.	Mar.	June	Sept.	Dec.
1990	0.81	1.05	0.69	0.55
1991	0.62	0.79	0.59	0.45
1992	0.89	1.15	0.75	d0.15
1993	0.84	0.90	d0.34	0.35

INTERIM DIVIDENDS (Per Share):

Amt.	Decl.	Ex.	Rec.	Pay.
0.33Q	5/3/93	5/10/93	5/14/93	6/1/93
0.35Q	7/26	8/2	8/6	9/1
0.35Q	10/15	11/1	11/5	12/1
0.35Q	2/7/94	2/14/94	2/18/94	3/1/94
0.35Q	5/2	5/9	5/13	6/1

Indicated div.: $1.40

CAPITALIZATION (12/31/93):

	($000)	(%)
Long-Term Debt	690,000	30.2
Deferred Income Tax	87,000	3.8
Minority Interest	71,000	3.1
$2.75 Cum Conv Pfd Stk	136,000	5.9
Common & Surplus	1,305,000	57.0
Total	2,289,000	100.0

DIVIDEND ACHIEVER STATUS:
Rank: 162 1983-93 Growth Rate: 10.5%
Total Years of Dividend Growth: 16

RECENT DEVELOPMENTS: For the three months ended 12/31/93, net income was $26 million compared with an $8 million loss in the comparable 1992 period. Sales were $760 million to last year's $756 million. The polymers, resins and monomers and plastics businesses in North America and Europe reported good growth. Soft markets and costs related to the start-up of a new facility in Japan adversely affected results in the Pacific.

PROSPECTS: The European and Japanese economies are providing particularly difficult profit environments. While shipping volumes in all regions and for most of the Company's businesses are up, the pressure on selling prices continues to force prices downward. Manufacturing facilities maintain smooth operations and expenses are controlled. Latin American operations have delivered satisfactory results.

BUSINESS

ROHM & HAAS CO. is a multinational producer of specialty polymers and biologically active compounds. Products range from basic petrochemicals such as propylene, acetone and styrene to differentiated specialty products. It has developed acrylic plastics, a field which it pioneered with its development of Plexiglas (used in outdoor signs, industrial lighting, skylights, and boat windshields). Other products include polymers, resins and monomers which are geared toward a wide variety of industrial applications. The Company also manufactures agricultural and industrial chemicals.

BUSINESS LINE ANALYSIS

(12/31/93)	Rev(%)	Inc(%)
Polymers, Resins & Monomers	46.5	57.3
Plastics	17.7	6.0
Performance Chemicals	23.3	12.7
Agricultural Chemicals	12.5	24.0
Total	100.0	100.0

ANNUAL EARNINGS AND DIVIDENDS PER SHARE

	1993	1992	1991	1990	1989	1988	1987
Earnings Per Share	**1.74**	**2.53**	**2.45**	**3.10**	**2.65**	**3.46**	**2.85**
Dividends Per Share	**1.36**	**[1] 1.28**	**1.24**	**1.22**	**1.16**	**1.02**	**0.86**
Dividend Payout %	**78.2**	**50.6**	**50.6**	**39.4**	**43.8**	**29.5**	**30.2**

[1] Bef acctg chge

ANNUAL FINANCIAL DATA

	1993	1992	1991	1990	1989	1988	1987
RECORD OF EARNINGS (IN MILLIONS):							
Total Revenues	3,269.0	3,063.0	2,763.0	2,824.0	2,661.0	2,535.0	2,203.0
Costs and Expenses	2,743.0	2,559.0	2,331.0	2,367.0	2,246.0	2,055.0	1,787.0
Depreciation	226.0	203.0	183.0	159.0	150.0	128.0	120.0
Operating Income	300.0	301.0	249.0	298.0	265.0	352.0	296.0
Earn Bef Income Taxes	194.0	261.0	240.0	313.0	251.0	346.0	303.0
Income Taxes	68.0	87.0	77.0	106.0	75.0	116.0	108.0
Net Income	[1] 126.0	[2] 174.0	163.0	207.0	176.0	230.0	195.0
Aver. Shs. Outstg. (000)	67,619	66,396	64,103	66,218	66,593	66,561	68,578
[1] Before acctg. change dr$19,000,000. [2] Before acctg. change dr$179,000,000.							
BALANCE SHEET (IN MILLIONS):							
Cash and Cash Equivalents	35.0	91.0	208.0	65.0	150.0	223.0	220.0
Accounts Receivable, Net	604.0	549.0	473.0	458.0	420.0	394.0	356.0
Inventories	394.0	437.0	343.0	386.0	347.0	340.0	309.0
Gross Property	3,696.0	3,470.0	3,015.0	2,770.0	2,396.0	2,062.0	1,754.0
Accumulated Depreciation	1,827.0	1,702.0	1,545.0	1,380.0	1,248.0	1,127.0	1,024.0
Long-Term Debt	690.0	699.0	718.0	598.0	359.0	288.0	258.0
Net Stockholders' Equity	1,441.0	1,428.0	1,231.0	1,233.0	1,311.0	1,207.0	1,053.0
Total Assets	3,524.0	3,445.0	2,897.0	2,702.0	2,455.0	2,242.0	1,954.0
Total Current Assets	1,200.0	1,257.0	1,141.0	1,009.0	1,011.0	1,032.0	962.0
Total Current Liabilities	701.0	713.0	535.0	585.0	577.0	547.0	476.0
Net Working Capital	499.0	544.0	606.0	424.0	434.0	485.0	486.0
Year End Shs Outstg (000)	67,645	67,564	64,156	63,981	66,618	66,541	66,735
STATISTICAL RECORD:							
Operating Profit Margin %	9.2	9.8	9.0	10.6	10.0	13.9	13.4
Book Value Per Share	19.29	19.12	19.19	19.27	19.68	18.14	15.78
Return on Equity %	8.7	12.2	13.2	16.8	13.4	19.1	18.5
Return on Assets %	3.6	5.1	5.6	7.7	7.2	10.3	10.0
Average Yield %	2.5	2.5	3.1	4.0	3.4	3.1	2.2
P/E Ratio	35.6-27.2	23.6-16.9	19.8-13.4	11.9-7.8	14.2-11.7	10.8-8.1	18.7-8.4
Price Range	62-47¼	59⅝-42¾	48½-32¾	37-24¼	37½-31	37½-28	53¼-24

Statistics are as originally reported.

OFFICERS:
J.L. Wilson, Chmn. & C.E.O.
J.P. Mulroney, Pres. & C.O.O.
F.W. Shaffer, V.P. & C.F.O.
G.P. Granoff, Secretary

INCORPORATED: DE, Apr., 1917

PRINCIPAL OFFICE: Independence Mall West, Philadelphia, PA 19105

TELEPHONE NUMBER: (215) 592-3000

NO. OF EMPLOYEES: 4,397

ANNUAL MEETING: In May

SHAREHOLDERS: 2,657

INSTITUTIONAL HOLDINGS:
No. of Institutions: 275
Shares Held: 46,654,437

REGISTRAR(S): First Chicago Trust Co. of New York, New York, NY 10008

TRANSFER AGENT(S): First Chicago Trust Co. of New York, New York, NY 10008

RPM, INC.

YIELD 2.8%
P/E RATIO 21.1

TRADING VOLUME
Thousand Shares

*7 YEAR PRICE SCORE 112.7   *12 MONTH PRICE SCORE 103.1
*NYSE COMPOSITE INDEX=100

INTERIM EARNINGS (Per Share):

Qtr.	Aug.	Nov.	Feb.	May
1990-91	0.25	0.22	0.07	0.15
1991-92	0.22	0.21	0.09	0.21
1992-93	0.25	0.23	0.10	0.25
1993-94	0.27	0.25	...	...

INTERIM DIVIDENDS (Per Share):

Amt.	Decl.	Ex.	Rec.	Pay.
0.12Q	4/5/93	4/12/93	4/16/93	4/30/93
0.12Q	7/8	7/13	7/19	7/30
0.13Q	10/8	10/12	10/18	10/29
0.13Q	1/7/94	1/10/94	1/17/94	1/31/94
0.13Q	4/4	4/11	4/15	4/29

Indicated div.: $0.52

CAPITALIZATION (5/31/93):

	($000)	(%)
Long-Term Debt	220,942	48.0
Common & Surplus	239,079	52.0
Total	460,021	100.0

DIVIDEND ACHIEVER STATUS:
Rank: 69   1983-93 Growth Rate: 14.4%
Total Years of Dividend Growth: 20

RECENT DEVELOPMENTS: For the six months ended 11/30/93, sales were $411.6 million, a 6% increase from $387.6 million in 1992. Earnings increased 32% to $29.2 million from $22.1 million last year. Earnings per share increased 24% to $0.52 per share from $0.42 per share in 1992. These results reflect strong gains in sales and earnings of RPOW's core operations and the impact of two recent acquisitions. The 1992 results were restated to reflect the June 1993 acquisition of Dynatron/Bondo Corp., and the October 1993 acquisition of Stonhard, Inc. Also, sales were negatively impacted in the amount of $6 million as a result of change in foreign currency exchange rates. For the quarter, sales were $202.2 million, a 9% increase from $184.7 million last year. Earnings increased 45% to $13.9 million from $9.6 million in 1992. Earnings per share totaled $0.25, a 39% increase over earnings per share of $0.18 in 1992.

BUSINESS

RPM, INC. is a widely-diversified manufacturer of protective coatings, marketing products to more than 110 countries and operating 39 plants in the United States, Belgium, Canada and Luxembourg. The Company participates in five broad market categories worldwide: (1) industrial waterproofing and general maintenance; (2) industrial corrosion-control; (3) specialty chemicals; (4) consumer do-it-yourself (D-I-Y); and (5) consumer hobby and leisure. More than 60% of the Company's sales is derived from the three industrial market sectors, with the remainder in consumer products. The vast majority of RPM's specialty coatings, both consumer and industrial, protect existing goods or structures and are generally not affected by cyclical movements in the economy.

BUSINESS LINE ANALYSIS

(5/31/93)	Rev(%)	Inc(%)
United States	88.0	94.7
European Operations.	10.6	5.4
Other Foreign Operations	1.4	(0.1)
Total	100.0	100.0

ANNUAL EARNINGS AND DIVIDENDS PER SHARE

	5/31/93	5/31/92	5/31/91	5/31/90	5/31/89	5/31/88	5/31/87
Earnings Per Share	0.83	0.73	0.69	0.65	0.57	0.51	0.41
Dividends Per Share	① 0.46	0.423	② 0.373	0.339	0.307	0.267	0.229
Dividend Payout %	55.4	57.7	54.4	51.6	53.2	52.6	56.1

① 3-for-2 stk split,12/07/92   ② 5-for-4 stk split, 12/7/90

ANNUAL FINANCIAL DATA

RECORD OF EARNINGS (IN THOUSANDS):

Total Revenues	625,680	552,092	500,258	444,824	376,117	341,966	290,525
Costs and Expenses	546,118	460,941	427,431	378,197	318,884	289,542	246,962
Depreciation & Amort	21	19,422	14,400	12,199	10,144	9,588	8,292
Operating Income	79,541	71,729	58,427	54,427	47,089	42,835	35,271
Income Bef Income Taxes	66,100	57,280	51,681	45,006	39,128	35,295	29,434
Provision for Inc Taxes	26,724	22,769	19,849	17,228	14,790	13,955	13,422
Minor Int In Consol Subsids	...	45	cr17	68	95	cr27	150
Net Income	39,376	34,466	31,849	27,710	24,243	21,368	15,863
Aver. Shs. Outstg.	47,589	47,112	46,541	43,392	42,283	42,243	42,092

BALANCE SHEET (IN THOUSANDS):

Cash and Cash Equivalents	24,750	27,324	18,604	2,522	4,968	6,449	3,033
Receivables, Net	127,155	116,455	93,838	90,787	68,321	60,636	54,566
Inventories	115,482	110,916	85,741	87,399	71,645	62,932	47,693
Gross Property	221,652	202,065	134,597	129,735	107,127	93,908	86,695
Accumulated Depreciation	87,433	75,779	52,059	48,158	41,008	33,365	25,043
Long-Term Debt	220,942	238,882	114,479	145,170	76,946	75,401	76,143
Net Stockholders' Equity	239,079	221,781	206,281	161,032	147,045	136,436	118,181
Total Assets	584,609	558,934	401,221	375,300	286,188	260,785	242,260
Total Current Assets	280,673	263,032	205,393	185,618	150,128	133,307	110,332
Total Current Liabilities	117,929	90,058	75,679	63,211	56,836	44,399	43,086
Net Working Capital	162,744	172,974	129,713	122,408	93,292	88,908	67,246
Year End Shares Outstg	47,322	47,177	46,562	43,318	42,167	42,041	41,880

STATISTICAL RECORD:

Operating Profit Margin %	12.7	13.0	11.7	12.2	12.5	12.5	12.1
Book Value Per Share	2.12	1.69	2.44	1.41	2.08	1.97	1.49
Return on Equity %	16.5	15.5	15.4	17.2	16.5	15.7	13.4
Return on Assets %	6.7	6.2	7.9	7.4	8.5	8.2	6.5
Average Yield %	3.0	3.2	3.7	3.6	3.6	3.6	3.1
P/E Ratio	22.3-15.2	21.2-14.9	17.6-12.0	16.3-12.7	16.9-12.7	17.9-11.3	20.7-15.2
Price Range	18½-12⅝	15½-10⅞	12⅛-8¼	10⅝-8¼	9⅝-7¼	9⅛-5¾	8½-6¼

Statistics are as originally reported.

OFFICERS:
T.C. Sullivan, Chmn. & C.E.O.
J.A. Karman, Pres. & C.O.O.
P.A. Granzier, V.P., Sec. & Couns.
R.E. Klar, V.P. & Treas.
F.C. Sullivan, C.F.O.

INCORPORATED: OH, May, 1947

PRINCIPAL OFFICE: 2628 Pearl Road, Medina, OH 44258

TELEPHONE NUMBER: (216) 273-5090
FAX: (216) 225-8743
NO. OF EMPLOYEES: 3,500 (approx.)
ANNUAL MEETING: In October
SHAREHOLDERS: 19,250
INSTITUTIONAL HOLDINGS:
No. of Institutions: 124
Shares Held: 13,164,831

REGISTRAR(S): Society National Bank, Cleveland, OH

TRANSFER AGENT(S): Society National Bank, Cleveland, OH

RUBBERMAID, INC.

YIELD 1.6%
P/E RATIO 21.2

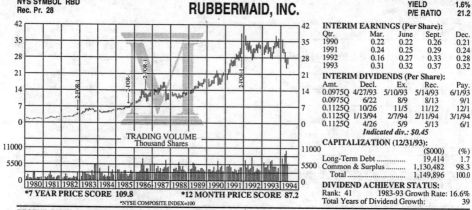

*7 YEAR PRICE SCORE 109.8   *12 MONTH PRICE SCORE 87.2
*NYSE COMPOSITE INDEX=100

INTERIM EARNINGS (Per Share):

Qtr.	Mar.	June	Sept.	Dec.
1990	0.22	0.22	0.26	0.21
1991	0.24	0.25	0.29	0.24
1992	0.16	0.27	0.33	0.28
1993	0.31	0.32	0.37	0.32

INTERIM DIVIDENDS (Per Share):

Amt.	Decl.	Ex.	Rec.	Pay.
0.0975Q	4/27/93	5/10/93	5/14/93	6/1/93
0.0975Q	6/22	8/9	8/13	9/1
0.1125Q	10/26	11/5	11/12	12/1
0.1125Q	1/13/94	2/7/94	2/11/94	3/1/94
0.1125Q	4/26	5/9	5/13	6/1

Indicated div.: $0.45

CAPITALIZATION (12/31/93):

	($000)	(%)
Long-Term Debt	19,414	1.7
Common & Surplus	1,130,482	98.3
Total	1,149,896	100.0

DIVIDEND ACHIEVER STATUS:

Rank: 41   1983-93 Growth Rate: 16.6%
Total Years of Dividend Growth: 39

RECENT DEVELOPMENTS: For the quarter ended 12/31/93, net income rose 15% to $50.8 million compared with $44.1 million for the comparable period in 1992. Meanwhile, revenues increased 9% to $472.9 million, which reflected strong unit volume increases as products continued to sell well. Earnings were favorably affected by RBD's focus on distinct and creative marketing programs throughout the entire corporation as well as by the successful performance of several new market entries.

PROSPECTS: Continued emphasis on cost reduction alongside aggressive use of technology and new marketing campaigns should help results both in the U.S. and internationally. In addition, RBD's strategy of frequent product introductions will support sales growth as new entries are generally met with positive consumer response. Due to the inexpensive and basic nature of RBD's products, future sales should remain strong through any stagnation or downturn in the economy.

BUSINESS

RUBBERMAID, INC. operates in a single line of business, the manufacture and sale of plastic and rubber products for the consumer and institutional markets. The Housewares Products Division manufactures sinkware, home organizers and food storage products. Seasonal products such as outdoor casual furniture, insulated products, and home horticulture are assimilated under the Specialty Products division. The Little Tikes Co. manufactures pre-school toys and furniture. Commercial Products Division designs and manufactures goods for the institutional and industrial markets. The Office Products group develops a wide range of office accessory products.

BUSINESS LINE ANALYSIS

(12/31/93)	Rev(%)	Inc(%)
United States	89.5	94.1
Foreign	10.5	5.9
Total	100.0	100.0

ANNUAL EARNINGS AND DIVIDENDS PER SHARE

	1993	1992	1991	1990	1989	1988	1987
Earnings Per Share	1.32	① 1.04	1.02	0.90	0.79	0.67	0.58
Dividends Per Share	0.405	0.352	② 0.31	0.27	0.23	0.19	0.16
Dividend Payout %	30.7	33.8	30.4	30.0	29.1	28.1	27.8

① Before acctg. chg. ② 2-for-1 stk split,12/02/91

ANNUAL FINANCIAL DATA

RECORD OF EARNINGS (IN MILLIONS):

	1993	1992	1991	1990	1989	1988	1987
Net Sales	1,960.2	1,805.3	1,667.3	1,534.0	1,343.9	1,193.5	1,015.0
Costs and Expenses	1,205.1	1,130.7	1,040.0	959.2	844.5	785.2	635.5
Depreciation	80.9	69.9	62.7	55.3	62.7	47.4	47.5
Operating Profit	345.5	294.3	256.8	232.8	202.6	171.0	159.3
Earn Bef Income Taxes	341.9	266.8	262.6	231.3	190.6	159.5	148.2
Income Taxes	130.5	99.9	99.9	87.7	74.1	60.3	63.6
Net Income	211.4	① 166.9	162.7	143.5	116.4	99.3	84.5
Aver. Shs. Outstg. (000)	160,318	160,207	160,126	159,688	147,324	147,080	146,768

① Before acctg. change dr$2,831,000.

BALANCE SHEET (IN MILLIONS):

	1993	1992	1991	1990	1989	1988	1987
Cash and Cash Equivalents	194.1	122.5	153.3	77.5	97.2	33.7	48.7
Receivables, Net	322.3	295.0	277.0	302.3	238.4	212.1	178.8
Inventories	303.4	271.9	225.2	216.8	176.5	159.0	140.6
Gross Property	1,081.1	960.2	855.5	746.9	670.0	594.0	520.7
Accumulated Depreciation	508.9	443.1	394.1	341.3	303.6	257.8	221.2
Long-Term Debt	19.4	20.3	27.8	39.2	50.3	39.0	40.0
Net Stockholders' Equity	1,130.5	987.6	885.7	768.2	598.4	511.4	435.9
Total Assets	1,513.1	1,326.6	1,244.5	1,114.3	915.4	781.7	716.0
Total Current Assets	829.7	699.7	664.0	602.7	515.7	407.5	375.3
Total Current Liabilities	259.3	223.2	245.5	235.3	202.4	186.0	194.2
Net Working Capital	570.4	476.4	418.5	367.4	313.2	221.5	181.2
Year End Shs Outstg (000)	160,357	160,239	160,189	159,985	147,328	147,124	146,860

STATISTICAL RECORD:

	1993	1992	1991	1990	1989	1988	1987
Operating Profit Margin %	34.4	33.5	33.9	33.9	15.1	14.3	15.7
Book Value Per Share	7.05	6.16	5.53	4.80	4.06	3.48	2.97
Return on Equity %	18.7	16.9	18.4	18.7	19.5	19.4	19.4
Return on Assets %	14.0	12.6	13.1	12.9	12.7	12.7	11.8
Average Yield %	1.2	1.1	1.1	1.4	1.4	1.5	1.2
P/E Ratio	28.3-20.9	35.9-26.0	37.5-18.1	25.0-17.2	23.9-15.8	20.1-15.7	30.7-16.7
Price Range	37⅜-27⅝	37⅜-27	38¼-18½	22½-15½	18⅞-12½	13½-10½	17½-9½

Statistics are as originally reported.

OFFICERS:
W.R. Schmitt, Chmn. & C.E.O.
C.A. Carroll, Pres. & C.O.O.
G.C. Weigand, Sr. V.P. & C.F.O.
J.W. Dean III, V.P. & Treas.

INCORPORATED: OH, Apr., 1920

PRINCIPAL OFFICE: 1147 Akron Rd., Wooster, OH 44691-6000

TELEPHONE NUMBER: (216) 264-6464
FAX: (216) 287-2864
NO. OF EMPLOYEES: 11,978
ANNUAL MEETING: In April
SHAREHOLDERS: 22,508
INSTITUTIONAL HOLDINGS:
No. of Institutions: 439
Shares Held: 68,603,263

REGISTRAR(S): Society National Bank, Cleveland, OH

TRANSFER AGENT(S): Society National Bank, Cleveland, OH

NASDAQ SYMBOL SAFC
Rec. Pr. 53⅞ (Marginable)

SAFECO CORP.

YIELD 3.3%
P/E RATIO 8.0

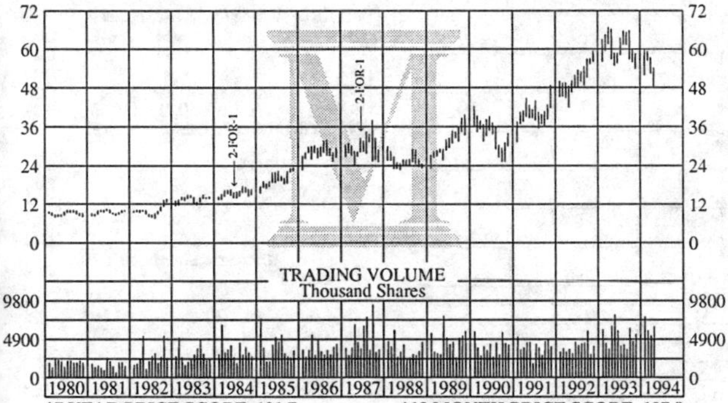

***7 YEAR PRICE SCORE 121.7** ***12 MONTH PRICE SCORE 107.9**

*NYSE COMPOSITE INDEX=100

INTERIM EARNINGS (Per Share):

Qtr.	Mar.	June	Sept.	Dec.
1990	0.89	1.20	0.84	1.48
1991	0.88	0.82	1.09	1.35
1992	1.35	0.67	1.28	1.66
1993	1.15	2.06	1.49	2.07

INTERIM DIVIDENDS (Per Share):

Amt.	Decl.	Ex.	Rec.	Pay.
0.41Q	2/3/93	4/2/93	4/9/93	4/26/93
0.45Q	5/6	7/2	7/9	7/26
0.45Q	8/4	10/4	10/8	10/25
0.45Q	11/3	1/3/94	1/7/94	1/24/94
0.45Q	2/2/94	4/4	4/8	4/25

Indicated div.: $1.80

CAPITALIZATION (12/31/93):

	($000)	(%)
Total Debt	918,435	24.1
Deferred Income Tax	117,927	3.1
Common & Surplus	2,774,391	72.8
Total	3,810,753	100.0

DIVIDEND ACHIEVER STATUS:

Rank: 144 1983-93 Growth Rate: 11.1%

Total Years of Dividend Growth: 18

RECENT DEVELOPMENTS: For the year ended 12/31/93, income before accounting changes was $307.0 million compared with $271.5 million last year. Total revenues rose 3.4% to $3.54 billion from $3.42 billion in 1992. SAFC ended the yer with a $9.8 million underwriting profit, compared with a $72 million loss the year before. For the quarter, net income was $130.3 million versus $104.0 million in the same period last year. Total revenues increased 7.7% to $889.6 million from $826.1 million in 1992's fourth quarter. SAFC's property and casualty companies produced a $19.2 million underwriting profit, compared with a $14.7 million profit a year ago. All lines of SAFC's property/casualty business showed improvement. Life and health insurance operations posted a $125.3 million pre-tax profit compared with $123.6 million in 1992. Claims from the Los Angeles earthquake will be recorded in the first quarter of 1994.

BUSINESS

SAFECO CORPORATION is one of the 25 largest diversified financial corporations, with more than 100 offices across the United States and Canada. Its insurance operations include property, casualty, life, health, title and surety. The Property and Casualty group underwrites personal and commercial lines of insurance covering automobiles, homes, business and related insurance risks. The Surety segment provides bonding services. The Life and Health group provides individual and group coverage, including medical/dental plans, IRA products, Keogh tax-favored universal life, and traditional life insurance products.

REVENUES

(12/31/93)	($000)	(%)
Insurance	2,235,677	63.6
Real Estate	78,252	2.2
Finance	50,061	1.4
Asset Management	13,250	0.4
Net Investment Income	951,795	27.1
Realized Investment Gain	187,649	5.3
Total	3,516,684	100.0

ANNUAL EARNINGS AND DIVIDENDS PER SHARE

	1993	1992	1991	1990	1989	1988	1987
Earnings Per Share	6.77	4.96	4.14	4.41	4.75	3.59	3.12
Dividends Per Share	1.72	1.56	1.42	1.28	1.14	1.02	[1] 0.905
Dividend Payout %	25.4	31.5	34.3	29.0	24.0	28.4	29.0

[1] 2-for-1 stk. split, 6/87

ANNUAL FINANCIAL DATA

	1993	1992	1991	1990	1989	1988	1987
RECORD OF EARNINGS (IN MILLIONS):							
Total Insurance	2,235.7	2,083.0	1,969.4	1,976.2	1,850.2	2,079.6	1,928.2
Total Interest Income	951.8	903.0	846.8	764.8	670.0	537.0	436.2
Total Revenues	3,516.7	3,294.7	3,148.3	3,043.5	2,807.6	2,872.9	2,592.5
Inc Fr Cont Opers Bef Income Taxes	576.9	403.3	317.3	304.0	375.4	310.4	253.9
Tot Prov for Fed & Canadian Inc Tax	151.0	92.0	57.7	25.6	75.1	41.8	0.9
Gain on Sale Of Securities	...	...	35.1	10.7	52.8	36.1	44.0
Net Income	428.8	311.3	259.6	278.4	300.2	268.6	253.0
Aver. Shs. Outstg. (000)	62,879	62,792	62,739	63,119	63,192	65,450	67,465
BALANCE SHEET (IN MILLIONS):							
Cash	67.8	73.1	60.3	41.4	37.3	28.4	32.0
Mktable Eq Secur, At Market Value	910.3	919.2	864.1	724.5	772.5	674.6	624.4
Policy Loans	50.5	50.5	45.4	41.1	37.9	34.1	31.7
Mortgage Loans	402.1	391.1	369.4	349.0	273.2	239.9	207.6
Total Assets	14,807.3	13,391.1	11,907.2	10,552.9	9,278.7	7,732.1	6,615.3
Benefits and Claims	10,328.7	9,366.5	8,217.6	7,185.7	6,028.4	4,856.9	3,895.4
Net Stockholders' Equity	2,774.4	2,448.1	2,221.1	1,975.7	1,850.7	1,570.4	1,435.4
Year End Shs Outstg (000)	62,932	62,815	62,748	62,722	63,232	63,137	67,119
STATISTICAL RECORD:							
Book Value Per Share	44.09	38.97	35.40	31.50	29.27	24.87	21.39
Return on Equity %	15.4	12.7	11.7	14.1	16.2	17.1	17.6
Return on Assets %	2.9	2.3	2.2	2.6	3.2	3.5	3.8
Average Yield %	2.9	3.1	3.6	3.8	3.6	3.9	2.9
P/E Ratio	9.9-8.0	12.0-8.5	11.8-7.5	9.6-5.7	8.4-4.9	7.3-5.5	10.1-6.5
Price Range	66¾-53⅞	59⅜-42	48¾-31¼	42⅜-25⅛	39¾-23⅛	30-22¾	38-24⅜

Statistics are as originally reported.

OFFICERS:
R.H. Eigsti, Chmn., Pres. & C.E.O.
B.A. Dickey, Exec. V.P. & C.F.O.
R.W. Hubbard, Sr. V.P. & Treas.
R.A. Pierson, Sr. V.P., Contr. & Sec.

INCORPORATED: WA, Jul., 1929

PRINCIPAL OFFICE: SAFECO Plaza, Seattle, WA 98185

TELEPHONE NUMBER: (206) 545-5000

FAX: (206) 543-5363

NO. OF EMPLOYEES: 7,004 (approx.)

ANNUAL MEETING: In May

SHAREHOLDERS: 5,100 (approx.)

INSTITUTIONAL HOLDINGS:
No. of Institutions: 321
Shares Held: 42,664,443

REGISTRAR(S):

TRANSFER AGENT(S): First Chicago Trust Co. of New York, New York, NY 10008

NYS SYMBOL SAJ
Rec. Pr. 28⅛

ST. JOSEPH LIGHT & POWER CO.

YIELD 6.4%
P/E RATIO 14.2

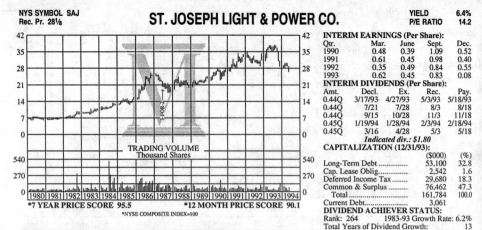

***7 YEAR PRICE SCORE 95.5** ***12 MONTH PRICE SCORE 90.1**

*NYSE COMPOSITE INDEX=100

INTERIM EARNINGS (Per Share):

Qtr.	Mar.	June	Sept.	Dec.
1990	0.48	0.39	1.09	0.52
1991	0.61	0.45	0.98	0.40
1992	0.35	0.49	0.84	0.55
1993	0.62	0.45	0.83	0.08

INTERIM DIVIDENDS (Per Share):

Amt.	Decl.	Ex.	Rec.	Pay.
0.44Q	3/17/93	4/27/93	5/3/93	5/18/93
0.44Q	7/21	7/28	8/3	8/18
0.44Q	9/15	10/28	11/3	11/18
0.45Q	1/19/94	1/28/94	2/3/94	2/18/94
0.45Q	3/16	4/28	5/3	5/18

Indicated div.: $1.80

CAPITALIZATION (12/31/93):

	($000)	(%)
Long-Term Debt	53,100	32.8
Cap. Lease Oblig.	2,542	1.6
Deferred Income Tax	29,680	18.3
Common & Surplus	76,462	47.3
Total	161,784	100.0
Current Debt	3,061	

DIVIDEND ACHIEVER STATUS:
Rank: 264 1983-93 Growth Rate: 6.2%
Total Years of Dividend Growth: 13

RECENT DEVELOPMENTS: For the year ended 12/31/93, net income fell 12.2% to $7.9 million from $9.0 million last year. Revenues were $88.5 million, up 7.1%. Results were negatively affected by increased fuel and purchased power expenses, and increased pension and other post-employment benefit expenses. Net income for the fourth quarter plunged 85% to $326,000, primarily due to the Iatan power plant outage in November and December.

PROSPECTS: Earnings growth will be very difficult to achieve in 1994. The Company has filed for increases of 7.9% in electric prices and 12.2% in industrial stem prices. The Missouri Public Service Commission has until late 1994 to decide the cases. The outcome of these rate cases will be critical to the Company's growth prospects. The economy in SJI's service territory has been hit hard by the 1993 flood and the effects of high unemployment.

BUSINESS

ST. JOSEPH LIGHT & POWER CO. is engaged primarily in the generation, transmission and distribution of electric energy to customers in its ten-county service territory in northwest Missouri. It supplies this service in St. Joseph and 52 other incorporated communities and the intervening rural territory. The service area contains 3,300 square miles. Electric revenues account for 85.9% of total operating revenues. The remaining 14.1% of total revenues is derived from industrial stem sales and natural gas sales. Natural gas for residential, commercial and industrial purposes is provided to customers in Maryville, a town of nearly 10,000, and 14 other smaller communities in northwest Missouri.

BUSINESS LINE ANALYSIS

(12/31/93)	Rev(%)	Inc(%)
Electric	85.5	98.2
Other	14.5	1.8
Total	100.0	100.0

ANNUAL EARNINGS AND DIVIDENDS PER SHARE

	1993	1992	1991	1990	1989	1988	1987
Earnings Per Share	**1.98**	**2.23**	**2.44**	**2.48**	**2.45**	**2.34**	**2.31**
Dividends Per Share	**1.76**	**1.72**	**1.66**	**1.60**	**1.52**	**1.40**	**[1] 1.30**
Dividend Payout %	**88.9**	**77.1**	**68.0**	**64.5**	**62.0**	**59.8**	**56.3**

[1] 3-for-2 stk. split, 6/87.

ANNUAL FINANCIAL DATA

	1993	1992	1991	1990	1989	1988	1987
RECORD OF EARNINGS (IN THOUSANDS):							
Total Operating Revenues	88,539	82,555	89,580	79,752	79,082	76,858	76,106
Depreciation	9,514	9,134	8,735	8,307	7,783	7,361	7,317
Maintenance	8,186	8,170	8,319	8,342	7,807	7,708	7,906
Prov for Fed Inc Taxes	cr1,562	4,358	5,205	5,394	5,426	5,058	6,553
Operating Income	12,248	13,405	14,692	14,201	14,620	14,855	14,792
Interest Charges, Net	4,457	4,681	4,856	4,133	4,409	4,756	5,011
Net Income	7,922	8,958	9,790	10,215	10,678	10,712	10,693
Aver. Shs. Outstg.	4,008	4,019	4,019	4,126	4,351	4,585	4,627
BALANCE SHEET (IN THOUSANDS):							
Gross Plant	276,444	267,153	257,030	245,929	235,021	221,680	216,120
Accumulated Depreciation	131,107	123,729	115,341	106,735	99,293	91,066	84,272
Utility Plant, Net	145,337	143,424	141,689	139,194	135,728	130,614	131,848
Long-term Debt	55,642	53,779	53,038	41,261	45,295	48,205	52,252
Net Stockholders' Equity	76,462	75,458	73,819	70,995	72,631	74,129	72,816
Total Assets	180,985	178,743	170,893	165,223	162,743	165,624	167,344
Year End Shares Outstg	4,009	4,005	4,019	4,030	4,241	4,490	4,626
STATISTICAL RECORD:							
Book Value Per Share	19.07	18.84	18.37	17.62	17.13	16.51	15.74
Op. Inc/Net Pl %	8.4	9.3	10.4	10.2	10.8	11.4	11.2
Dep/Gr. Pl %	3.4	3.4	3.4	3.4	3.3	3.3	3.4
Accum. Dep/Gr. Pl %	47.4	46.3	44.9	43.4	42.2	41.1	39.0
Return on Equity %	10.4	11.9	13.3	14.4	14.7	14.5	14.7
Average Yield %	5.3	5.4	5.5	6.3	6.8	6.4	6.0
P/E Ratio	19.1-14.5	15.6-12.9	14.0-10.9	11.4-9.2	10.1-8.2	10.5-8.1	11.1-7.6
Price Range	37⅞-28¾	34¾-28⅞	34¼-26⅝	28¼-22¾	24⅝-20	24½-19	25¾-17⅝

Statistics are as originally reported.

OFFICERS:
T.F. Steinbecker, Pres. & C.E.O.
L.J. Stoll, V.P.-Fin., Treas. & Asst. Sec.
G.L. Myers, Gen. Couns. & Sec.

INCORPORATED: MO, Nov., 1895

PRINCIPAL OFFICE: 520 Francis St., St. Joseph, MO 64502

TELEPHONE NUMBER: (816) 233-8888
FAX: (816) 233-7915
NO. OF EMPLOYEES: 48
ANNUAL MEETING: In May
SHAREHOLDERS: 4,207
INSTITUTIONAL HOLDINGS:
No. of Institutions: 43
Shares Held: 655,903

REGISTRAR(S): Harris Trust & Savings Bank, Chicago, IL
Manufacturers Hanover Trust Co., New York, NY

TRANSFER AGENT(S): Harris Trust & Savings Bank, Chicago, IL
Manufacturers Hanover Trust Co., New York, NY

NYS SYMBOL SDO
Rec. Pr. 19⅜

SAN DIEGO GAS & ELECTRIC CO.

YIELD 7.8%
P/E RATIO 10.7

TRADING VOLUME
Thousand Shares
2-FOR-1

***7 YEAR PRICE SCORE 93.3** ***12 MONTH PRICE SCORE 90.6**

•NYSE COMPOSITE INDEX=100

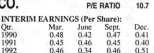

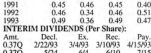

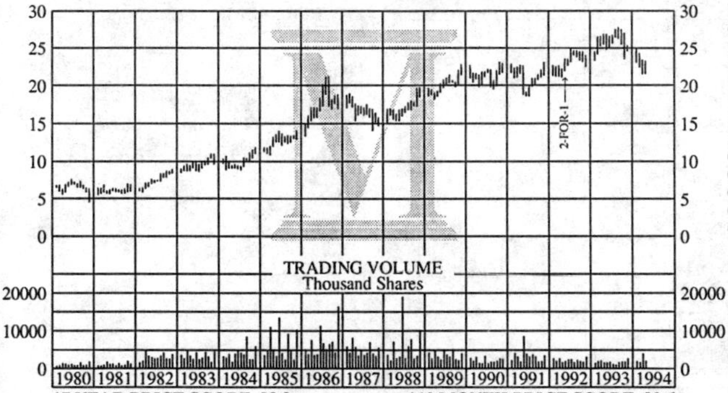

INTERIM EARNINGS (Per Share):

Qtr.	Mar.	June	Sept.	Dec.
1990	0.48	0.42	0.47	0.41
1991	0.45	0.46	0.45	0.40
1992	0.46	0.34	0.46	0.51
1993	0.49	0.36	0.49	0.47

INTERIM DIVIDENDS (Per Share):

Amt.	Decl.	Ex.	Rec.	Pay.
0.37Q	2/22/93	3/4/93	3/10/93	4/15/93
0.37Q	5/24	6/4	6/10	7/15
0.37Q	8/23	9/3	9/10	10/15
0.37Q	11/23	12/6	12/10	1/15/94
0.38Q	3/1/94	3/4/94	3/10/94	4/15

Indicated div.: $1.52

CAPITALIZATION (12/31/93):

	($000)	(%)
Long-Term Debt	1,411,948	38.4
Deferred Income Tax	634,235	17.2
Preferred Stock	118,493	3.2
Common & Surplus	1,516,240	41.2
Total	3,680,916	100.0

DIVIDEND ACHIEVER STATUS:
Rank: 294 1983-93 Growth Rate: 4.5%
Total Years of Dividend Growth: 17

RECENT DEVELOPMENTS: For the year ended 12/31/93, net income rose 3.8% to $218.7 million from $210.7 million last year. Revenues were $1.98 billion, up 5.8%. Utility earnings were down in 1993 due to rate recovery in 1992 of some abandoned projects and the receipt in 1992 of a judgment from the U.S. District Court. Earnings for the year benefited from improved subsidiary results. Additional investments in Enova/Califia increased earnings and cash flow.

PROSPECTS: The Company is benefiting from improved results at its non-utility subsidiaries. The Company's aggressive use of purchased power diminishes financial flexibility. Results will be negatively affected by poor economic conditions in its service territory, competitive pressures, and the Company's sizable construction program. The utility's service area has slowed due to defense cutbacks. Favorable regulatory support is critical to future results.

BUSINESS

SAN DIEGO GAS & ELECTRIC CO. distributes electricity and gas in San Diego County and the southwestern section of Orange County. The Company services a population of about 2.7 million and an electric and gas customer base of 1,100,000 and 680,000 customers, respectively. Major economic factors in the area are education, tourism, manufacturing, and a large concentration of Navy facilities. More than 90% of the Company's revenues come from electric and natural gas sales. The remainder flow primarily from Wahlco Environmental Systems, a subsidiary that markets air pollution controls world wide. SDO also has two other active subsidiaries, Pacific Diversified Capital, an independently operated holding company, and Califia Company.

BUSINESS LINE ANALYSIS

(12/31/93)	Rev(%)	Inc(%)
Electric	76.5	89.7
Gas	17.5	8.4
Diversified		
Operations	6.0	1.9
Total	100.0	100.0

ANNUAL EARNINGS AND DIVIDENDS PER SHARE

	1993	1992	1991	1990	1989	1988	1987
Earnings Per Share	**1.81**	**1.77**	**1.76**	**1.76**	**1.58**	**1.59**	**[2] 1.64**
Dividends Per Share	**1.47**	**[1] 1.43**	**1.375**	**1.35**	**1.338**	**1.287**	**1.235**
Dividend Payout %	**81.2**	**80.8**	**77.9**	**76.7**	**84.9**	**81.0**	**75.3**

[1] 2-for-1 stk split, 5/28/92 [2] Before acctg. chg.

ANNUAL FINANCIAL DATA

	1993	1992	1991	1990	1989	1988	1987
RECORD OF EARNINGS (IN MILLIONS):							
Total Operating Revenues	1,980.1	1,870.9	1,789.0	1,771.9	2,082.5	2,076.1	1,904.2
Deprec & Decommising	250.6	213.7	195.4	185.9	177.1	172.8	151.7
Maintenance	81.8	73.0	68.1	62.9	67.6	66.5	66.0
Income Taxes	148.5	149.3	130.6	146.4	141.8	118.4	151.0
Operating Income	293.7	296.3	315.5	301.1	280.0	272.2	261.8
Net Interest Charges	101.3	106.3	106.3	108.7	101.5	102.1	102.7
Net Income	218.7	210.7	208.1	207.8	187.1	189.4	[1] 179.1
Aver. Shs. Outstg. (000)	116,049	113,806	111,988	111,842	111,790	111,750	111,698
[1] Before acctg. change cr$17,673,000.							
BALANCE SHEET (IN MILLIONS):							
Gross Plant	5,134.3	4,818.9	4,823.2	4,594.3	4,383.8	4,159.2	4,051.5
Accumulated Depreciation	2,016.6	1,840.2	1,791.4	1,606.4	1,433.8	1,221.0	1,134.6
Utility Plant - Net	3,117.6	2,978.7	3,031.8	2,987.8	2,950.0	2,938.2	2,916.9
Long-term Debt	1,411.9	1,495.7	1,164.2	1,167.1	1,112.7	1,179.5	1,204.6
Net Stockholders' Equity	1,634.7	1,579.8	1,497.2	1,445.8	1,403.1	1,379.9	1,399.7
Total Assets	4,702.2	4,199.8	3,747.6	3,656.6	3,546.5	3,532.7	3,601.2
Year End Shs Outstg (000)	116,515	115,034	112,496	111,898	111,844	111,796	111,746
STATISTICAL RECORD:							
Book Value Per Share	12.55	12.11	11.55	11.22	10.86	10.65	10.78
Op. Inc/Net Pl %	9.4	9.9	10.4	10.1	9.5	9.3	9.0
Dep/Gr. Pl %	4.9	4.4	4.1	4.0	4.0	4.2	3.7
Accum. Dep/Gr. Pl %	39.3	38.2	37.1	35.0	32.7	29.4	28.0
Return on Equity %	13.6	13.9	14.4	14.9	13.9	14.4	13.5
Average Yield %	5.8	6.2	6.6	6.3	6.5	7.4	7.5
P/E Ratio	15.3-12.8	14.1-11.9	13.1-10.6	13.1-11.1	14.5-11.6	12.4-9.4	12.8-9.5
Price Range	27¾-23¼	25-21⅛	23⅛-18⅝	23⅛-19½	22⅞-18¼	19¾-15	19-14⅛

Statistics are as originally reported.

OFFICERS:
T.A. Page, Chmn., C.E.O. & Pres.
M.K. Malquist, V.P.-Fin. & Treas.

INCORPORATED: CA, Apr., 1905

PRINCIPAL OFFICE: 101 Ash Street, San Diego, CA 92101

TELEPHONE NUMBER: (619) 696-2000
FAX: (619) 233-6875
NO. OF EMPLOYEES: 4,166 full-time; 63 part-time
ANNUAL MEETING: In April
SHAREHOLDERS: 70,389 com.; 2,003 pfd.
INSTITUTIONAL HOLDINGS:
No. of Institutions: 160
Shares Held: 19,543,208

REGISTRAR(S): First Interstate Bank of California, Los Angeles, CA

TRANSFER AGENT(S): First Interstate Bank of California, Los Angeles, CA

SARA LEE CORP.

YIELD 2.8%
P/E RATIO 15.5

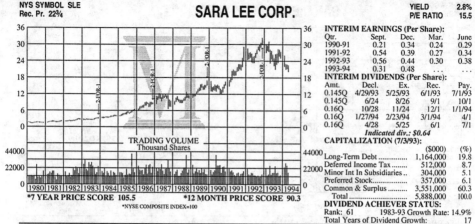

*7 YEAR PRICE SCORE 105.5   ***12 MONTH PRICE SCORE 90.3**
*NYSE COMPOSITE INDEX=100

INTERIM EARNINGS (Per Share):

Qtr.	Sept.	Dec.	Mar.	June
1990-91	0.21	0.34	0.24	0.29
1991-92	0.54	0.39	0.27	0.34
1992-93	0.56	0.44	0.30	0.38
1993-94	0.31	0.48	...	...

INTERIM DIVIDENDS (Per Share):

Amt.	Decl.	Ex.	Rec.	Pay.
0.145Q	4/29/93	5/25/93	6/1/93	7/1/93
0.145Q	6/24	8/26	9/1	10/1
0.16Q	10/28	11/24	12/1	1/1/94
0.16Q	1/27/94	2/23/94	3/1/94	4/1
0.16Q	4/28	5/25	6/1	7/1

Indicated div.: $0.64

CAPITALIZATION (7/3/93):

	($000)	(%)
Long-Term Debt	1,164,000	19.8
Deferred Income Tax	512,000	8.7
Minor Int In Subsidiaries	304,000	5.1
Preferred Stock	357,000	6.1
Common & Surplus	3,551,000	60.3
Total	5,888,000	100.0

DIVIDEND ACHIEVER STATUS:
Rank: 61   1983-93 Growth Rate: 14.9%
Total Years of Dividend Growth: 17

RECENT DEVELOPMENTS: Net income for the 13 weeks was $236.0 million compared with $220 million a year ago. Sales advanced 4.4% to $4.01 billion. Packaged Meats and Bakery posted a 28.1% increase in profits on a 11.8% increase in sales. Coffee and Grocery reported a 3.9% decrease in operating income on a 8.9% increase in sales. Margins widened due to improved operating efficiencies. Personal Products posted a 1.2% decrease in sales and an 8.4% decrease in profits.

PROSPECTS: Despite competitive market conditions, SLE's businesses should enjoy improved volume growth in selected product categories. However, continued softness in the U.S. and European hosiery and knit products operations will keep earnings flat in the Personal Products segment. The acquisition of several bath and body-care brands from SmithKline Beecham should contribute positively to the Household and Personal Care segment.

BUSINESS

SARA LEE CORP. is a global brand-name foods and consumer products company. Packaged Foods manufactures and markets brand-name food products which includes Hillshire Farm packaged meats, and Sara Lee baked goods in North America, Europe and Australia. This segment comprises two lines of business: Packaged Meats and Bakery, and Coffee and Grocery. Packaged Consumer Products includes brand-name products such as Hanes, L'eggs, Champion, Kiwi and Playtex. The segment comprises two lines of business: Personal Products and Household and Personal Care.

BUSINESS LINE ANALYSIS

(07/3/93)	Rev(%)	Inc($000)
Packaged Meats & Bakery	35.3	287,000
Coffee & Grocery	14.1	292,000
Personal Products	41.8	602,000
Household & Personal Care	8.8	126,000
Total	100.0	1,307,000

ANNUAL EARNINGS AND DIVIDENDS PER SHARE

	7/3/93	6/27/92	6/29/91	6/30/90	7/1/89	7/2/88	6/27/87
Earnings Per Share	1.40	1.54	1.08	0.96	0.88	0.71	0.59
Dividends Per Share	0.58	① 0.62	0.47	0.42	0.36	0.30	② 0.25
Dividend Payout %	41.4	40.3	43.7	44.0	41.1	42.4	42.6

① 2-for-1 stk split,12/22/92; includes $0.12 special dividend. ② 2-for-1 stk. split, 12/86.

ANNUAL FINANCIAL DATA

RECORD OF EARNINGS (IN MILLIONS):

Total Revenues	14,580.0	13,243.0	12,381.5	11,605.9	11,717.7	10,423.8	9,154.6
Costs and Expenses	12,894.0	11,725.0	11,037.5	10,395.6	10,696.7	9,563.3	8,436.7
Depreciation & Amort	522.0	472.0	393.8	351.4	279.9	250.9	201.6
Operating Income	1,164.0	1,046.0	950.2	858.9	741.1	609.6	516.3
Income Bef Income Taxes	1,082.0	1,174.0	829.5	713.4	639.5	513.3	447.8
Income Taxes	378.0	413.0	294.5	243.1	229.0	188.3	180.8
Net Income	704.0	761.0	535.0	470.3	410.5	325.1	267.1
Aver. Shs. Outstg. (000)	485,000	476,000	464,324	460,088	453,580	446,680	447,484

BALANCE SHEET (IN MILLIONS):

Cash and Cash Equivalents	325.0	198.0	124.9	169.4	117.5	178.6	302.9
Receivables, Net	1,171.0	1,180.0	946.0	922.2	813.7	717.5	610.0
Inventories	2,280.0	2,160.0	1,706.9	1,653.7	1,452.0	1,127.5	1,011.7
Gross Property	4,842.0	4,409.0	3,948.3	3,611.4	2,887.2	2,484.6	2,267.0
Accumulated Depreciation	1,964.0	1,836.0	1,559.2	1,407.2	1,114.2	1,067.9	1,026.4
Long-Term Debt	1,164.0	1,389.0	1,399.1	1,523.9	1,488.2	877.0	617.4
Lg tm Obligs Under Cap Lses	...	...	...	...	...	16.4	15.2
Net Stockholders' Equity	3,908.0	3,733.0	2,894.7	2,629.5	2,097.4	1,800.1	1,491.0
Total Assets	10,862.0	9,989.0	8,122.0	7,636.4	6,522.7	5,012.1	4,191.7
Total Current Assets	3,976.0	3,695.0	2,919.9	2,868.3	2,499.7	2,088.9	1,960.4
Total Current Liabilities	4,269.0	3,300.0	2,526.4	2,482.7	2,275.4	1,806.2	1,595.3
Net Working Capital	d293.0	395.0	393.5	385.5	224.3	282.7	365.1
Year End Shs Outstg (000)	485,378	479,725	465,368	460,678	454,669	444,234	442,896

STATISTICAL RECORD:

Operating Profit Margin %	8.0	7.9	7.7	7.4	6.3	5.8	5.6
Book Value Per Share	0.55	0.89	0.44	0.32	0.26	0.94	1.74
Return on Equity %	19.7	22.4	20.9	20.5	21.4	20.6	18.9
Return on Assets %	6.5	7.6	6.6	6.2	6.3	6.5	6.4
Average Yield %	2.2	2.2	2.1	2.9	2.6	2.8	2.6
P/E Ratio	22.2-15.0	21.1-15.2	27.0-13.8	17.4-12.6	19.2-12.2	18.1-11.6	20.8-11.2
Price Range	31⅛-21	32½-23⅜	29⅛-14⅞	16¾-12⅛	16⅞-10¾	12⅞-8¼	12¼-6⅝

Statistics are as originally reported.

OFFICERS:
J.H. Bryan, Chmn. & C.E.O.
M.E. Murphy, Vice-Chmn. & C.F.O.
G.H. Newman, Sr. V.P., Sec. & Couns.
INCORPORATED: MD, Sep., 1941
PRINCIPAL OFFICE: Three First National Plaza, Chicago, IL 60602-4260

TELEPHONE NUMBER: (312) 726-2600
NO. OF EMPLOYEES: 9,947 (approx.)
ANNUAL MEETING: In October
SHAREHOLDERS: 28,571
INSTITUTIONAL HOLDINGS:
No. of Institutions: 646
Shares Held: 226,300,526

REGISTRAR(S): At Company's Office

TRANSFER AGENT(S): At Company's Office

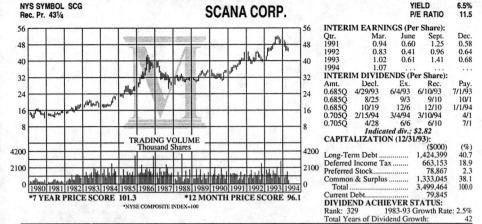

NYS SYMBOL SCG			
Rec. Pr. 43¼			

SCANA CORP.

YIELD	6.5%
P/E RATIO	11.5

INTERIM EARNINGS (Per Share):

Qtr.	Mar.	June	Sept.	Dec.
1991	0.94	0.60	1.25	0.58
1992	0.83	0.41	0.96	0.64
1993	1.02	0.61	1.41	0.68
1994	1.07	...	...	...

INTERIM DIVIDENDS (Per Share):

Amt.	Decl.	Ex.	Rec.	Pay.
0.685Q	4/29/93	6/4/93	6/10/93	7/1/93
0.685Q	8/25	9/3	9/10	10/1
0.685Q	10/19	12/6	12/10	1/1/94
0.705Q	2/15/94	3/4/94	3/10/94	4/1
0.705Q	4/28	6/6	6/10	7/1

Indicated div.: $2.82

CAPITALIZATION (12/31/93):

	($000)	(%)
Long-Term Debt	1,424,399	40.7
Deferred Income Tax	663,153	18.9
Preferred Stock	78,867	2.3
Common & Surplus	1,333,045	38.1
Total	3,499,464	100.0
Current Debt	79,845	

DIVIDEND ACHIEVER STATUS:
Rank: 329   1983-93 Growth Rate: 2.5%
Total Years of Dividend Growth: 42

TRADING VOLUME
Thousand Shares

*7 YEAR PRICE SCORE 101.3   *12 MONTH PRICE SCORE 96.1

*NYSE COMPOSITE INDEX=100

RECENT DEVELOPMENTS: For the year ended 12/31/93, net income advanced 43% to $168.0 million from $117.6 million last year. Revenues were $1.26 billion, up 11.1%. Total kilowatthour sales of electricity by South Carolina Electric & Gas (SCE&G) were up 7.6% due to a colder winter, a warmer summer and a 1.5% annual growth in SCE&G's customer base. Results also benefited from the 5.1% increase in SCE&G's retail electric rates.

PROSPECTS: The Public Service Commission of South Carolina approved a two-phase increase in retail electric base rates for South Carolina Electric & Gas Co. totaling $60.5 million, or 7.4% on an annual basis. Earnings are benefiting from SCE's non-regulated activities. SCANA Petroleum Resources acquired NICOR Exploration and Production Co. from a subsidiary of NICOR, Inc. The $123 million purchase nearly doubled SCG's proven reserves of natural gas.

BUSINESS

SCANA CORP. is a holding company for South Carolina Electric & Gas (SCE&G) which provides electricity and natural gas in central and southern South Carolina. SCANA has 11 other direct subsidiaries and 1 indirect subsidiary. Natural gas pipeline operations fall under South Carolina Pipeline Corp., another subsidiary of SCANA Corp. SCG's natural gas service area covers more than 80% of South Carolina. Electric generating capacity is over 3,900 megawatts with the fuel mix comprised of 68% coal, 21% nuclear, and 11% hydro and other. Other subsidiaries are engaged in oil and natural gas production, propane operations, real estate, digital telecommunications services, power plant operations maintenance and natural gas marketing.

BUSINESS LINE ANALYSIS

(12/31/93)	Rev($)	Rev(%)
Electric	940,121	74.4
Gas	320,195	25.3
Transit	3,851	.3
Total	1,264,167	100.0

ANNUAL EARNINGS AND DIVIDENDS PER SHARE

	1993	1992	1991	1990	1989	1988	1987
Earnings Per Share	3.72	2.84	3.37	4.44	3.04	3.00	3.20
Dividends Per Share	2.725	2.665	2.595	2.505	2.445	2.38	2.30
Dividend Payout %	73.3	93.8	77.0	56.4	80.4	79.3	71.9

ANNUAL FINANCIAL DATA

RECORD OF EARNINGS (IN MILLIONS):

	1993	1992	1991	1990	1989	1988	1987
Total Operating Revenues	1,264.2	1,138.4	1,147.8	1,133.2	1,123.3	1,083.3	1,116.0
Depreciation & Amort	112.8	108.3	102.7	97.1	102.3	97.4	92.6
Maintenance	67.7	65.4	61.6	67.5	69.3	54.1	58.0
Prov for Fed Inc Taxes	90.0	60.9	77.6	77.4	65.5	69.0	95.1
Operating Income	245.3	209.8	222.4	226.0	213.2	204.7	204.4
Total Int Chrgs (crs), Net	101.2	97.6	91.5	92.3	90.4	80.1	71.5
Net Income	168.0	117.6	135.9	181.6	122.6	120.7	128.9
Aver. Shs. Outstg. (000)	45,203	41,475	40,361	40,882	40,296	40,296	40,296

BALANCE SHEET (IN MILLIONS):

	1993	1992	1991	1990	1989	1988	1987
Gross Plant	4,263.8	4,003.2	3,788.9	3,586.9	3,400.4	3,257.7	3,099.9
Accumulated Depreciation	1,259.7	1,192.9	1,124.3	1,037.1	956.1	873.1	797.8
Utility Plant, Net	3,004.1	2,810.3	2,664.7	2,549.8	2,444.3	2,384.6	2,302.1
Long-term Debt, Net	1,424.4	1,204.8	1,122.4	938.9	1,004.0	885.7	887.0
Net Stockholders' Equity	1,411.9	1,244.1	1,116.9	1,094.4	1,012.3	999.0	982.3
Total Assets	4,040.5	3,557.7	3,305.9	3,144.9	2,984.5	2,887.3	2,702.4
Year End Shs Outstg (000)	46,619	43,911	40,784	40,882	40,296	40,296	40,296

STATISTICAL RECORD:

	1993	1992	1991	1990	1989	1988	1987
Book Value Per Share	28.59	26.46	25.23	24.56	22.79	22.23	21.63
Op. Inc/Net Pl %	8.2	7.5	8.3	8.9	8.7	8.6	8.9
Dep/Gr. Pl %	2.6	2.7	2.7	2.7	3.0	3.0	3.0
Accum. Dep/Gr. Pl %	29.5	29.8	29.7	28.9	28.1	26.8	25.7
Return on Equity %	12.4	9.9	12.9	17.6	13.0	13.1	14.4
Average Yield %	5.9	6.4	6.7	7.6	7.5	7.6	6.9
P/E Ratio	14.0-10.8	15.8-13.6	13.1-9.9	8.1-6.8	11.8-9.7	11.3-9.5	12.5-8.3
Price Range	52¼-40⅛	44¾-38⅝	44¼-33½	35⅞-30¼	35¾-29⅝	33¾-28½	40-26½

Statistics are as originally reported.

OFFICERS:
L.M. Gressette, Jr., Chmn., Pres. & C.E.O.
W.B. Timmerman, Sr. V.P., Contr., C.F.O. & Asst. Sec.
K.B. Marsh, V.P.-Fin., Treas. & Sec.

INCORPORATED: SC, Oct., 1984

PRINCIPAL OFFICE: Palmetto Center 1426 Main Street, Columbia, SC 29201

TELEPHONE NUMBER: (803) 748-3000
FAX: (803) 733-2825
NO. OF EMPLOYEES: 4,849
ANNUAL MEETING: In April
SHAREHOLDERS: 41,564
INSTITUTIONAL HOLDINGS:
No. of Institutions: 215
Shares Held: 22,366,422

REGISTRAR(S):

TRANSFER AGENT(S): South Carolina National Bank, Columbia, SC 29226
Manufacturers Hanover Trust Co., New York, NY

SCECORP

YIELD 10.1%
P/E RATIO 9.7

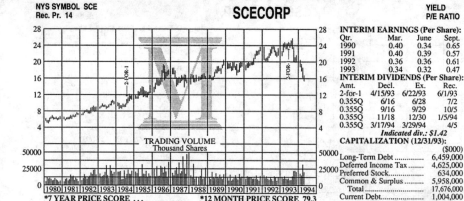

*7 YEAR PRICE SCORE ... *12 MONTH PRICE SCORE 79.3
*NYSE COMPOSITE INDEX=100

INTERIM EARNINGS (Per Share):

Qtr.	Mar.	June	Sept.	Dec.
1990	0.40	0.34	0.65	0.42
1991	0.40	0.39	0.57	0.26
1992	0.36	0.36	0.61	0.34
1993	0.34	0.32	0.47	0.31

INTERIM DIVIDENDS (Per Share):

Amt.	Decl.	Ex.	Rec.	Pay.
2-for-1	4/15/93	6/22/93	6/1/93	6/21/93
0.355Q	6/16	6/28	7/2	7/31
0.355Q	9/16	9/29	10/5	10/31
0.355Q	11/18	12/30	1/5/94	1/31/94
0.355Q	3/17/94	3/29/94	4/5	4/30

Indicated div.: $1.42

CAPITALIZATION (12/31/93):

	($000)	(%)
Long-Term Debt	6,459,000	36.5
Deferred Income Tax	4,625,000	26.2
Preferred Stock	634,000	3.6
Common & Surplus	5,958,000	33.7
Total	17,676,000	100.0
Current Debt	1,004,000	

DIVIDEND ACHIEVER STATUS:
Rank: 292   1983-93 Growth Rate: 4.6%
Total Years of Dividend Growth: 17

RECENT DEVELOPMENTS: For the year ended 12/31/93, net income fell 13.5% to $639.0 million from $738.7 million last year. Revenues were $7.82 billion, down 2%. Results were negatively affected by a lower return on common equity authorized for 1993. Partially offsetting the lower authorized return was SEC's aggressive debt refinancing program and cost-control measures. Net income for the quarter ended 12/31/93 was $137.8 million versus $151.7 million last year.

PROSPECTS: The agreement under which SCE subsidiary Mission Energy and partners would have acquired a generating plant from the Mexican government was ended by mutual agreement. The CPUC adopted an agreement which settles disputes regarding Edison's purchases of power from 13 projects partly owned by Mission Energy. Under its terms, Edison will refund $250 million to its customers over a two-year period beginnning 1/1/94.

BUSINESS

SCECORP, through its subsidiary Southern California Edison, provides electric service in a 50,000 square-mile area of Central and Southern California, which includes some 800 cities and communities, serving a population of nearly 11.0 million people. SCE serves 4.1 million customers, and sold 74.2 billion kilowatt-hours. The generation mix was 24% oil and gas; 14% coal; 22% nuclear; 3% hydro; and 37% purchased power. Sources of revenue were: 36% commercial; 35% residential; 13% industrial; 8% public authorities; 5% other electric and 3% diversified operations. The Mission Companies control non-utility subsidiaries that provide energy-related services.

BUSINESS LINE ANALYSIS

(12/31/93)	Rev($)	Rev(%)
Electric	7,397,000	94.6
Diversified		
Operations	424,000	5.4
Total	7,821,000	100.0

ANNUAL EARNINGS AND DIVIDENDS PER SHARE

	1993	1992	1991	1990	1989	1988	1987
Earnings Per Share	1.43	1.66	1.61	1.80	1.78	1.75	② 1.54
Dividends Per Share	① 1.40	1.38	1.34	1.30	1.26	1.215	1.215
Dividend Payout %	97.9	83.1	83.5	72.0	70.8	69.6	78.9

① 2-for-1 stk split,06/22/93 ② Before acctg. chg.

ANNUAL FINANCIAL DATA

RECORD OF EARNINGS (IN MILLIONS):

	1993	1992	1991	1990	1989	1988	1987
Total Operating Revenue	7,821.0	7,984.0	7,502.5	7,198.5	6,904.4	6,252.7	5,492.7
Depreciation	922.0	807.0	763.6	715.7	689.6	646.6	688.6
Maintenance	363.0	362.0	382.0	375.3	377.9	375.4	361.2
Income Taxes	465.0	544.0	447.5	489.8	497.8	446.4	545.8
Operating Income	1,217.0	1,343.0	1,231.1	1,251.1	1,167.8	1,096.4	999.9
Interest Expense	507.0	528.0	555.5	570.2	574.0	518.8	414.1
Net Income	639.0	739.0	702.6	786.4	778.2	761.8	① 720.6
Aver. Shs. Outstg. (000)	448,000	446,000	437,320	436,948	436,926	436,664	435,932

① Before acctg. change cr$68,044,000.

BALANCE SHEET (IN MILLIONS):

	1993	1992	1991	1990	1989	1988	1987
Gross Plant	19,441.0	18,652.0	17,523.1	16,916.0	16,375.8	15,925.3	15,656.5
Accumulated Depreciation	7,138.0	6,715.0	6,339.1	5,696.1	5,095.1	4,529.9	4,024.5
Total Utility Plant	12,303.0	11,937.0	11,184.0	11,219.9	11,280.7	11,395.3	11,632.0
Long-term Debt	6,459.0	6,320.0	5,745.3	5,291.4	5,282.8	5,421.7	5,028.7
Net Stockholders' Equity	6,592.0	6,591.0	6,238.4	6,071.9	5,871.2	5,662.6	5,665.7
Total Assets	21,379.0	19,140.0	16,828.2	16,312.2	15,443.1	14,866.3	14,218.6
Year End Shs Outstg (000)	447,799	447,736	439,906	436,949	436,948	436,924	434,254

STATISTICAL RECORD:

	1993	1992	1991	1990	1989	1988	1987
Book Value Per Share	13.31	13.30	12.91	12.59	12.10	11.59	11.57
Op. Inc/Net Pl %	9.9	11.3	11.0	11.2	10.4	9.6	8.6
Dep/Gr. Pl %	4.7	4.3	4.4	4.2	4.2	4.1	3.5
Accum. Dep/Gr. Pl %	36.7	36.0	36.2	33.7	31.1	28.4	25.7
Return on Equity %	10.1	11.7	11.6	13.4	13.8	14.0	13.4
Average Yield %	6.1	6.3	6.4	7.1	7.0	7.6	7.5
P/E Ratio	18.0-13.9	14.4-12.1	14.8-11.2	11.2-9.3	11.5-8.7	9.9-8.4	12.0-9.0
Price Range	25¾-19⅞	23⅞-20⅛	23¾-18	20⅛-16¾	20½-15½	17¼-14⅝	18½-13⅞

Statistics are as originally reported.

OFFICERS:
J.E. Bryson, Chmn. & C.E.O.
A.J. Fohner, Sr. V.P., C.F.O. & Treas.
K.S. Stewart, Sec. & Asst. Gen. Couns.

INCORPORATED: CA, Apr., 1987

PRINCIPAL OFFICE: 2244 Walnut Grove Ave., Rosemead, CA 91770

TELEPHONE NUMBER: (818) 302-2222
FAX: (818) 302-4815
NO. OF EMPLOYEES: 16,487
ANNUAL MEETING: In April
SHAREHOLDERS: 140,600
INSTITUTIONAL HOLDINGS:
No. of Institutions: 496
Shares Held: 150,186,022

REGISTRAR(S): At Company's Office

TRANSFER AGENT(S): At Company's Office

NASDAQ SYMBOL SIGI
Rec. Pr. 25¾ (Marginable)

SELECTIVE INSURANCE GROUP INC.

YIELD 4.3%
P/E RATIO 15.5

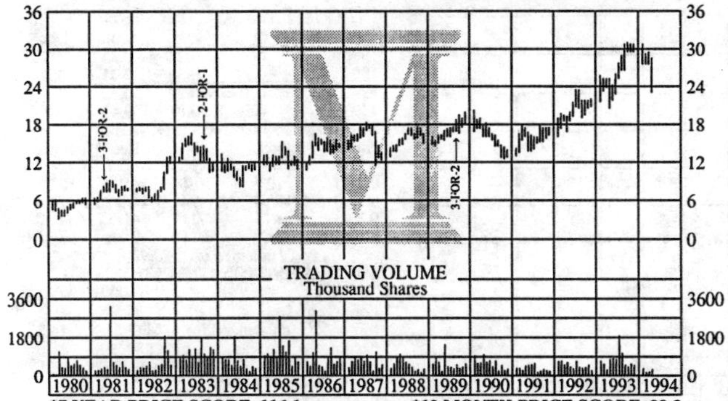

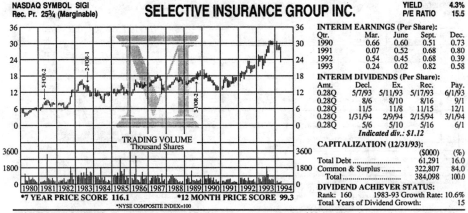

*7 YEAR PRICE SCORE 116.1 *12 MONTH PRICE SCORE 99.3

*NYSE COMPOSITE INDEX=100

INTERIM EARNINGS (Per Share):

Qtr.	Mar.	June	Sept.	Dec.
1990	0.66	0.60	0.51	0.73
1991	0.07	0.52	0.68	0.80
1992	0.54	0.45	0.68	0.39
1993	0.24	0.02	0.82	0.58

INTERIM DIVIDENDS (Per Share):

Amt.	Decl.	Ex.	Rec.	Pay.
0.28Q	5/7/93	5/11/93	5/17/93	6/1/93
0.28Q	8/6	8/10	8/16	9/1
0.28Q	11/5	11/8	11/15	12/1
0.28Q	1/31/94	2/9/94	2/15/94	3/1/94
0.28Q	5/6	5/10	5/16	6/1

Indicated div.: $1.12

CAPITALIZATION (12/31/93):

	($000)	(%)
Total Debt	61,291	16.0
Common & Surplus	322,807	84.0
Total	384,098	100.0

DIVIDEND ACHIEVER STATUS:
Rank: 160 1983-93 Growth Rate: 10.6%
Total Years of Dividend Growth: 15

RECENT DEVELOPMENTS: For the year ended 12/31/91, net income declined 16% to $27.3 million from $32.4 million the year before. Revenues rose 6% to $571.2 million from $540.0 million a year earlier. Net premiums written increased 4% and net premiums earned grew 7%. Net investment income rose 6% to $68.5 million from $64.5 million last year. The underwriting loss for the year was $38.1 million compared with $38.4 million in the prior year. The underwriting loss reflects a $9.7 million increase in the loss generated from business assigned from the National Workers Compensation Reinsurance Pool. For the quarter, net income increased 9% to $10.5 million from $9.6 million last year. Revenues grew 12% to $158.9 million from $141.7 million a year ago.

BUSINESS

SELECTIVE INSURANCE GROUP INC. is a holding company comprised of four multi-line property/casualty insurance companies, a premium finance company and a real estate holding company. The Company maintains offices throughout the northeastern and southeatern United States including Delaware, Georgia, Maryland, New Jersey, New York, North Carolina, Pennsylvania, South Carolina and Virginia. The insurance products, which include personal and commercial coverages, are marketed through a distribution force of approximately 800 independent insurance agents.

BUSINESS LINE ANALYSIS

(12/31/93)	Rev(%)	Inc(%)
Commercial Lines	66.7	(51.5)
Personal Lines	33.0	(47.0)
Other	0.3	(1.5)
Total	100.0	(100.0)

ANNUAL EARNINGS AND DIVIDENDS PER SHARE

	1993	1992	1991	1990	1989	1988	1987
Earnings Per Share	**1.66**	**[1] 2.06**	**2.07**	**[2] 2.50**	**3.05**	**[4] 2.99**	**[5] 2.73**
Dividends Per Share	**1.12**	**1.10**	**1.04**	**1.02**	**[3] 0.92**	**0.80**	**0.67**
Dividend Payout %	**67.5**	**53.4**	**50.2**	**40.8**	**30.2**	**26.8**	**24.4**

[1] Before acctg. chg. [2] Per primary share [3] 3-for-2 stk split, 9/01/89 [4] Before realized invest gains [5] Before extraord. item

ANNUAL FINANCIAL DATA

	1993	1992	1991	1990	1989	1988	1987
RECORD OF EARNINGS (IN MILLIONS):							
Net Premiums Earned	594.9	536.3	497.0	463.5	450.0	425.8	375.4
Total Interest Income	77.3	73.5	68.5	64.5	59.8	52.8	46.0
Total Revenues	679.6	616.1	571.2	540.0	516.1	...	...
Losses Incurred	358.8	312.8	282.0	268.9	263.3	251.7	221.8
Inc Bef Fed Income Tax	21.4	31.5	31.6	35.4	46.1	...	...
Income Taxes	cr1.3	4.0	4.3	3.0	5.5	4.8	2.2
Net Income	22.7	[1] 27.4	27.3	32.4	40.6	41.5	[2] 45.5

[1] Before acctg. change cr$26,468,000. [2] Before extra. item cr$1,825,000.

	1993	1992	1991	1990	1989	1988	1987
BALANCE SHEET (IN MILLIONS):							
Fixed Matur-at Amortized Cost	1,052.9	967.8	849.9	751.7	711.8	646.2	568.5
Equity Securs-at Market	88.2	86.3	70.2	72.8	91.1	76.1	70.7
Mtge Loans on Real Estate	...	...	...	...	3.0	3.4	3.2
Total Assets	1,739.2	1,634.3	1,210.6	1,138.8	1,074.3	962.4	855.4
Benefits and Claims	1,229.1	1,141.1	853.9	806.5	740.4	657.9	577.9
Net Stockholders' Equity	322.8	311.7	270.0	248.3	230.4	213.7	179.5
Year End Shs Outstg (000)	13,753	13,444	13,274	13,131	12,550	13,596	13,581
STATISTICAL RECORD:							
Return on Equity %	7.0	8.8	10.1	13.1	17.6	19.4	25.4
Book Value Per Share	23.47	23.19	20.34	18.91	18.36	15.72	13.22
Average Yield %	4.3	5.6	6.7	6.2	5.3	5.2	4.5
P/E Ratio	18.7-12.3	11.4-7.8	8.7-6.3	8.1-5.0	6.6-4.8	5.9-4.3	6.7-4.2
Price Range	31-20½	23½-16	18-13	20¼-12½	20-14½	17⅝-12⅞	18⅜-11½

Statistics are as originally reported.

OFFICERS:
F.H. Jarvis, Chmn. & C.E.O.
J.W. Entringer, Pres. & C.O.O.
D.J. Addesso, Exec. V.P. & C.F.O.
T.R. Land, Sr. V.P., Couns. & Sec.
C.L. Tice, Sr. V.P. & Treas.

INCORPORATED: NJ, Aug., 1977

PRINCIPAL OFFICE: 40 Wantage Ave., Branchville, NJ 07890-0001

TELEPHONE NUMBER: (201) 948-3000

NO. OF EMPLOYEES: 2,103 (approx.)

ANNUAL MEETING: In May

SHAREHOLDERS: 2,908

INSTITUTIONAL HOLDINGS:
No. of Institutions: 71
Shares Held: 6,001,370

REGISTRAR(S): Midlantic National Bank, Edison, NJ 08818

TRANSFER AGENT(S): Midlantic National Bank, Edison, NJ 08818

NYS SYMBOL SVM
Rec. Pr. 24⅜

SERVICEMASTER L.P.

YIELD 3.8%
P/E RATIO 12.8

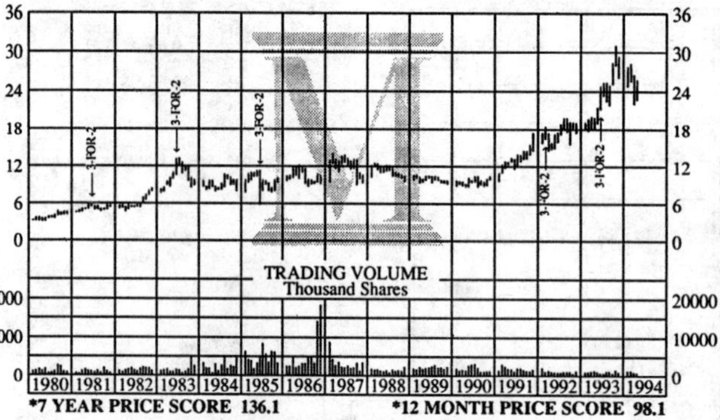

*7 YEAR PRICE SCORE 136.1 *12 MONTH PRICE SCORE 98.1

*NYSE COMPOSITE INDEX=100

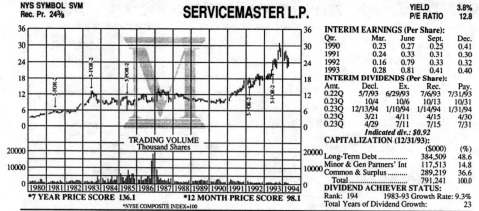

INTERIM EARNINGS (Per Share):

Qtr.	Mar.	June	Sept.	Dec.
1990	0.23	0.27	0.25	0.41
1991	0.24	0.33	0.31	0.30
1992	0.16	0.79	0.33	0.32
1993	0.28	0.81	0.41	0.40

INTERIM DIVIDENDS (Per Share):

Amt.	Decl.	Ex.	Rec.	Pay.
0.22Q	5/7/93	6/29/93	7/6/93	7/31/93
0.23Q	10/4	10/6	10/13	10/31
0.23Q	12/13/94	1/10/94	1/14/94	1/31/94
0.23Q	3/21	4/11	4/15	4/30
0.23Q	4/29	7/11	7/15	7/31

Indicated div.: $0.92

CAPITALIZATION (12/31/93):

	($000)	(%)
Long-Term Debt	384,509	48.6
Minor & Gen Partners' Int	117,513	14.8
Common & Surplus	289,219	36.6
Total	791,241	100.0

DIVIDEND ACHIEVER STATUS:

Rank: 194 1983-93 Growth Rate: 9.3%

Total Years of Dividend Growth: 23

RECENT DEVELOPMENTS: For the three months ended 12/31/93 net income increased 27% from the comparable 1992 period to $31.0 million. Operating revenues were $695.3 million versus $633.9 million last year. For 1993, net income was $145.9 million compared with $122.1 million for 1992. Operating revenues advanced 11% to $2.76 billion. The Consumer Service segment posted revenues of $940 million and net income of $70.5 million. Management Services revenues were $1.76 billion and net income was $61 million.

PROSPECTS: Management Services continues to benefit from strong demand for outsourcing non-core functions. A new sales and marketing program increased sales significantly within the industrial/commercial market. Consumer Services should maintain the accelerated growth pattern as a result of the faster than expected assimilation of recently acquired ChemLawn, and the continued reduction of operating costs and interest expenses. The Company has a strong cash position to fund internal growth and strategic acquisitions.

BUSINESS

SERVICEMASTER LIMITED PARTNERSHIP, the parent for The ServiceMaster Company, Terminix, TruGreen-ChemLawn, Merry Maids, and American Home Shield, consists of two major segments. ServiceMaster Management Services provides facility management services for 2,300 healthcare, education, industrial and commercial customers. These services include: housekeeping, maintenance, food service, laundry and linen care, grounds and landscaping. ServiceMaster Consumer Services includes 5 market-leading companies operating a network of more than 5,700 company-owned and independent franchises worldwide. Services include carpet and upholstery cleaning, janitorial, termite and pest control services, lawn care, maid service, radon testing and warranty plans.

BUSINESS LINE ANALYSIS

(12/31/93)	Rev(%)	Inc(%)
Management Services	63.9	39.4
Consumer Services....	34.1	53.7
Intl & New Bus & Parent.....................	2.0	6.9
Total	100.0	100.0

ANNUAL EARNINGS AND DIVIDENDS PER SHARE

	1993	1992	1991	1990	1989	1988	1987
Earnings Per Share	**1.90**	**1.61**	**1.19**	**1.17**	**0.93**	**0.90**	**0.85**
Dividends Per Share	**[1] 0.89**	**[2] 0.867**	**0.845**	**0.822**	**0.782**	**0.747**	**0.675**
Dividend Payout %	**46.8**	**53.7**	**71.2**	**70.6**	**83.8**	**83.2**	**80.0**

[1] 3-for-2 stk split,06/23/93 [2] 3-for-2 stk split, 2/3/92

ANNUAL FINANCIAL DATA

	1993	1992	1991	1990	1989	1988	1987
RECORD OF EARNINGS (IN MILLIONS):							
Operating Revenue	2,758.9	2,488.9	2,109.9	1,825.8	1,609.3	1,531.3	1,425.3
Costs and Expenses	2,137.9	1,979.9	1,724.5	1,515.7	1,492.9	1,424.1	1,326.0
Depreciation & Amort	50.0	46.3	38.2	29.9	23.6	21.7	19.9
Operating Income	173.0	62.4	121.4	95.8	92.8	85.5	79.5
Income Bef Income Taxes	148.1	130.8	87.4	85.4	68.8	67.4	63.0
Provision for Inc Taxes	2.1	1.2	1.4	2.3	0.7	...	...
Net Income	145.9	[1] 129.6	86.0	83.1	68.0	64.6	60.0
Aver. Shs. Outstg. (000)	76,415	75,670	72,557	71,206	72,957	71,858	70,882
[1] Before acctg. change dr$7,500,000.							
BALANCE SHEET (IN MILLIONS):							
Tot Cash & Mktable Secur	32.7	41.6	43.1	68.5	73.3	76.4	20.4
Receivables, Net	173.3	140.9	115.4	114.6	105.9	...	...
Inventories	37.9	36.3	26.3	23.4	19.3	18.8	16.7
Gross Property	226.5	204.5	158.3	151.6	111.7	96.0	78.5
Accumulated Depreciation	110.7	93.2	75.2	62.5	54.9	44.6	35.1
Long-Term Debt	384.5	426.9	334.7	341.8	389.2	280.0	183.6
Net Stockholders' Equity	289.2	209.7	122.0	96.0	39.1	51.4	42.2
Total Assets	1,122.5	1,000.1	843.7	796.9	593.7	483.8	371.1
Total Current Assets	291.3	254.4	217.5	237.3	231.3	202.2	128.8
Total Current Liabilities	239.6	203.7	157.5	158.0	138.1	81.2	64.5
Net Working Capital	51.7	50.8	60.1	79.2	93.2	121.0	64.3
Year End Shs Outstg (000)	76,426	75,774	72,717	72,475	72,401	74,426	70,542
STATISTICAL RECORD:							
Operating Profit Margin %	6.3	2.5	5.8	5.2	5.8	5.6	5.6
Return on Equity %	50.5	61.8	70.5	86.5	N.M.	N.M.	N.M.
Return on Assets %	13.0	13.0	10.2	10.4	11.5	13.4	16.2
Average Yield %	3.7	5.0	6.2	8.5	7.8	6.7	5.8
P/E Ratio	16.3-9.3	12.3-9.1	14.6-8.2	9.0-7.5	11.6-9.9	14.0-10.8	16.8-10.7
Price Range	31-17⅝	19⅞-14⅝	17⅜-9¾	10½-8¾	10¾-9¼	12⅝-9¾	14¼-9⅛

Statistics are as originally reported.

OFFICERS:
C.W. Pollard, Chmn. & C.E.O.
E.J. Mrozek, V.P., Treas. & C.F.O.

INCORPORATED: DE, Oct., 1986

PRINCIPAL OFFICE: One ServiceMaster Way, Downers Grove, IL 60515

TELEPHONE NUMBER: (708) 964-1300
FAX: (708) 719-6878
NO. OF EMPLOYEES: 8,809 (approx.)
ANNUAL MEETING: In May
SHAREHOLDERS: 10,810 (approx.)
INSTITUTIONAL HOLDINGS:
No. of Institutions: 135
Shares Held: 11,820,992

REGISTRAR(S): Harris Trust & Savings Bank, Chicago, IL

TRANSFER AGENT(S): Harris Trust & Savings Bank, Chicago, IL

NYS SYMBOL SHW
Rec. Pr. 30⅛

SHERWIN-WILLIAMS CO.

YIELD 1.9%
P/E RATIO 16.3

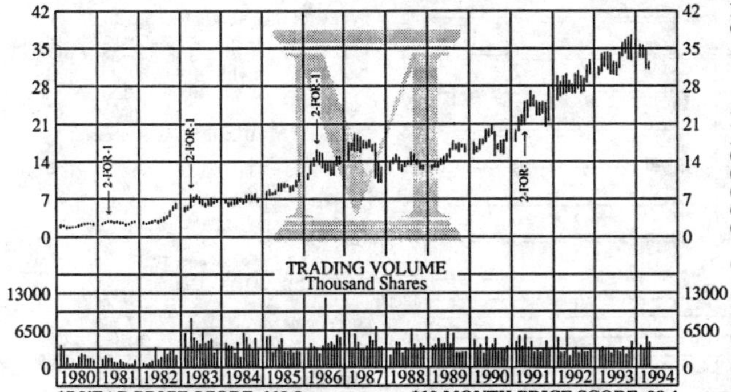

***7 YEAR PRICE SCORE 119.8** ***12 MONTH PRICE SCORE 98.4**

*NYSE COMPOSITE INDEX=100

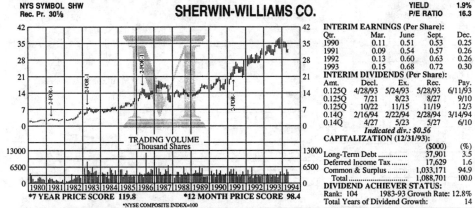

INTERIM EARNINGS (Per Share):

Qtr.	Mar.	June	Sept.	Dec.
1990	0.11	0.51	0.53	0.25
1991	0.09	0.54	0.57	0.26
1992	0.13	0.60	0.63	0.26
1993	0.15	0.68	0.72	0.30

INTERIM DIVIDENDS (Per Share):

Amt.	Decl.	Ex.	Rec.	Pay.
0.125Q	4/28/93	5/24/93	5/28/93	6/11/93
0.125Q	7/21	8/23	8/27	9/10
0.125Q	10/22	11/15	11/19	12/3
0.14Q	2/16/94	2/22/94	2/28/94	3/14/94
0.14Q	4/27	5/23	5/27	6/10

Indicated div.: $0.56

CAPITALIZATION (12/31/93):

	($000)	(%)
Long-Term Debt	37,901	3.5
Deferred Income Tax	17,629	1.6
Common & Surplus	1,033,171	94.9
Total	1,088,701	100.0

DIVIDEND ACHIEVER STATUS:

Rank: 104 1983-93 Growth Rate: 12.8%

Total Years of Dividend Growth: 14

RECENT DEVELOPMENTS: For the year ended 12/31/93, net income increased 14.2% to $165.2 million compared with $144.6 million, before the cumulative effect of accounting changes, in 1992. Sales were up 7.3% to $2.95 billion from $2.75 billion the previous year. The Paint Stores segment posted an 8.8% increase in sales with comparable-store sales improving 8.5%. Operating profit for this segment increased 28.5% due to a significant increase in paint gallons sold.

PROSPECTS: Sherwin-Williams will see margin improvement as a result of continued cost containment efforts. SHW is poised to take advantage of any opportunities that may arise due to its strong cash position and reduced debt. Results in the automotive division will be enhanced by booming industry demand. Demand for consumer brands and aerosol products is likely to pick up as the economy continues to improve.

BUSINESS

SHERWIN-WILLIAMS COMPANY is engaged in the manufacture and distribution of coatings and related products. SHW sells Sherwin-Williams labeled architectural coatings, industrial finishes, and other associated products and tools through 2,012 company-operated paint and wall covering stores in 48 states and Canada. SHW also manufactures and sells coatings such as Dutch Boy, Martin-Senour, Kem-Tone, Dupli-Color, and Krylon, plus private label brands to independent dealers, mass merchandisers, and home improvement centers.

BUSINESS LINE ANALYSIS

(12/31/93)	Rev(%)	Inc(%)
Paint Stores	62.1	37.0
Coatings	37.5	61.4
Other	0.4	1.6
Total	100.0	100.0

ANNUAL EARNINGS AND DIVIDENDS PER SHARE

	1993	1992	1991	1990	1989	1988	1987
Earnings Per Share	**1.85**	**1 1.63**	**1.45**	**1.41**	**1.26**	**1.15**	**3 1.05**
Dividends Per Share	**0.50**	**0.44**	**2 0.42**	**0.38**	**0.35**	**0.32**	**0.28**
Dividend Payout %	**27.0**	**27.0**	**29.0**	**27.0**	**27.8**	**27.8**	**26.8**

1 Before acctg. chg. 2 2-for-1 stk split, 4/1/91 3 Before disc. oper.

ANNUAL FINANCIAL DATA

	1993	1992	1991	1990	1989	1988	1987
RECORD OF EARNINGS (IN MILLIONS):							
Total Revenues	2,949.3	2,747.8	2,541.4	2,266.7	2,123.5	1,950.5	1,792.7
Costs and Expenses	2,609.4	2,437.8	2,278.3	2,039.1	1,918.8	1,778.6	1,613.6
Depreciation & Amort	68.8	66.3	47.9	44.5	42.0	36.9	28.9
Operating Income	271.1	243.8	215.3	183.1	162.7	135.1	150.2
Income Bef Income Taxes	264.4	226.0	198.8	187.3	170.2	163.0	161.7
Income Taxes	99.1	81.4	70.6	64.6	61.3	62.0	67.9
Net Income	165.2	62.9	128.2	122.7	108.9	101.1	1 93.8
Aver. Shs. Outstg. (000)	89,436	88,905	88,182	87,056	86,326	87,830	89,676
1 Before disc. op. cr$2,772,000.							
BALANCE SHEET (IN MILLIONS):							
Cash and Cash Equivalents	269.8	167.7	100.8	99.0	202.1	154.2	208.5
Accts Receiv, Less Allow	297.5	277.3	246.5	229.9	205.7	195.7	177.7
Inventories	428.9	407.8	421.8	373.3	326.5	323.0	281.4
Gross Property	838.8	786.9	734.9	687.9	646.7	599.5	438.8
Accumulated Depreciation	444.7	399.0	357.8	314.5	287.9	266.9	225.6
Long-Term Debt	37.9	60.1	71.8	138.0	105.0	129.6	89.2
Net Stockholders' Equity	1,033.2	905.8	868.0	763.7	667.6	601.3	549.7
Total Assets	1,914.7	1,729.9	1,611.9	1,504.4	1,375.0	1,258.7	1,140.0
Total Current Assets	1,151.1	988.2	887.1	824.3	845.9	766.1	757.2
Total Current Liabilities	567.5	505.8	488.4	432.2	433.3	378.0	370.2
Net Working Capital	583.6	482.3	398.7	392.1	412.5	388.1	387.1
Year End Shs Outstg (000)	88,506	88,381	87,643	86,739	86,254	86,082	87,446
STATISTICAL RECORD:							
Operating Profit Margin %	9.2	8.9	8.5	8.1	7.7	6.9	8.4
Book Value Per Share	11.67	10.25	9.90	8.80	7.74	6.98	6.29
Return on Equity %	16.0	16.0	14.8	16.1	16.3	16.8	17.1
Return on Assets %	8.6	8.4	8.0	8.2	7.9	8.0	8.2
Average Yield %	1.5	1.5	1.9	2.1	2.3	2.3	1.9
P/E Ratio	20.3-16.1	20.2-15.6	19.1-12.2	15.0-10.7	14.2-9.9	13.8-10.4	18.5-9.7
Price Range	37½-29⅞	32⅞-25⅜	27¾-17⅝	21⅛-15⅛	17⅞-12½	15⅞-12	19¼-10⅛

Statistics are as originally reported.

OFFICERS:
J.G. Breen, Chmn. & C.E.O.
T.A. Commes, Pres. & C.O.O.
L.J. Pitorak, Sr. V.P.-Fin., Treas. & C.F.O.
L.E. Stellato, V.P., Gen. Couns. & Sec.

INCORPORATED: OH, Jul., 1884

PRINCIPAL OFFICE: 101 Prospect Ave. N.W., Cleveland. OH 44115-1075

TELEPHONE NUMBER: (216) 566-2000

FAX: (216) 566-3310

NO. OF EMPLOYEES: 17,200 (approx.)

ANNUAL MEETING: In April

SHAREHOLDERS: 11,853

INSTITUTIONAL HOLDINGS:
No. of Institutions: 359
Shares Held: 55,214,201

REGISTRAR(S): Society National Bank, Cleveland, OH

TRANSFER AGENT(S): Society National Bank, Cleveland, OH

NASDAQ SYMBOL SIAL
Rec. Pr. 41½ (Marginable)

SIGMA-ALDRICH CORP.

YIELD 0.8%
P/E RATIO 19.3

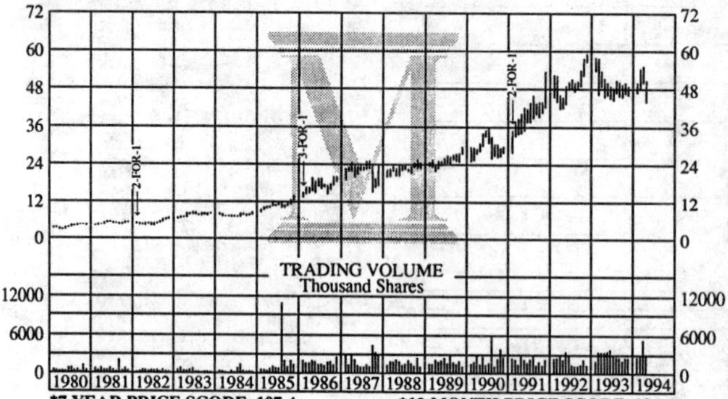

72
60
48
36
24
12
0
2-FOR-1
3-FOR-1
2-FOR-1
TRADING VOLUME
Thousand Shares
12000
6000
0
1980 1981 1982 1983 1984 1985 1986 1987 1988 1989 1990 1991 1992 1993 1994

***7 YEAR PRICE SCORE 107.4** ***12 MONTH PRICE SCORE 104.6**

*NYSE COMPOSITE INDEX=100

INTERIM EARNINGS (Per Share):

Qtr.	Mar.	June	Sept.	Dec.
1990	0.37	0.36	0.36	0.35
1991	0.41	0.40	0.40	0.39
1992	0.48	0.48	0.50	0.46
1993	0.54	0.54	0.54	0.53

INTERIM DIVIDENDS (Per Share):

Amt.	Decl.	Ex.	Rec.	Pay.
0.0725Q	5/4/93	5/25/93	6/1/93	6/15/93
0.0725Q	8/10	8/26	9/1	9/15
0.0825Q	11/9	12/9	12/15	1/3/94
0.0825Q	2/15/94	2/23/94	3/1/94	3/15
0.0825Q	5/3	5/25	6/1	6/15

Indicated div.: $0.33

CAPITALIZATION (12/31/93):

	($000)	(%)
Long-Term Debt	17,266	2.8
Common & Surplus	591,140	97.2
Total	608,406	100.0

DIVIDEND ACHIEVER STATUS:
Rank: 66 1983-93 Growth Rate: 14.6%
Total Years of Dividend Growth: 12

RECENT DEVELOPMENTS: For the year ended 12/31/93, net income before the cumulative effect of accounting changes grew by 12.3% to $107.2 from $95.5 million in 1992. Net sales increased 13.0% to $739.4 million compared with $654.4 million last year. For the quarter, net income rose 17.8% to $26.6 million from $22.6 million in the fourth quarter of 1992. Sales rose 17.1% to $184.8 million compared with sales of $157.7 million last year. Chemical sales increased almost 11% for 1993. Growth in both U.S. and overseas markets was supplemented by the acquisitiion of Supelco, Inc., in May 1993. Sales growth was affected by economic slowdowns in several markets and by adverse translation effects of a stronger U.S. dollar which reduced chemical sales growth by 3% for the fourth quarter and 4% for the year. Metals sales increased nearly 25% for the year due to the June 1993 acquisition of Circle AW, increased volume from improved construction demand, and modest price increases.

BUSINESS

SIGMA-ALDRICH CORP. is in two lines of business. The Company and its subsidiary, Fluka Chemie AG, develop, manufacture and distribute a broad range of biochemicals, organic and inorganic chemicals, diagnostic reagents and related products. These are used primarily in research and development, in the diagnosis of disease, and as specialty chemicals for manufacturing purposes. B-Line Systems, Inc., a subsidiary, manufactures and sells metal components for strut, cable tray, pipe support and telecommunications systems. These components are used in routing electrical and mechanical services in industrial installations and supporting telecommunications applications.

BUSINESS LINE ANALYSIS

(12/31/93)	Rev(%)	Inc(%)
Chemical	82.9	88.8
Metal	17.1	11.2
Total	100.0	100.0

ANNUAL EARNINGS AND DIVIDENDS PER SHARE

	1993	1992	1991	1990	1989	1988	1987
Earnings Per Share	2.15	1.92	1.60	1.44	1.29	1.14	0.85
Dividends Per Share	0.29	0.25	[1] 0.22	0.20	0.18	0.16	0.14
Dividend Payout %	13.5	13.0	13.8	13.9	13.9	14.0	16.5

[1] 2-for-1 stk split, 1/3/91

ANNUAL FINANCIAL DATA

	1993	1992	1991	1990	1989	1988	1987
RECORD OF EARNINGS (IN THOUSANDS):							
Total Revenues	739,435	654,406	589,371	529,103	441,099	375,282	304,858
Costs and Expenses	541,313	478,231	438,667	394,719	324,800	274,185	221,585
Depreciation & Amort	32,505	28,863	26,826	24,356	16,427	12,575	11,051
Operating Income	165,617	147,312	123,878	110,028	99,872	88,522	72,222
Inc Bef Inc Tax & Cumul Effect Of Acct Chg	165,617	147,312	123,878	110,028	99,872	88,522	72,222
Income Taxes	58,463	51,854	44,085	38,780	35,914	32,045	30,333
Net Income	[1] 107,154	95,458	79,793	71,248	63,958	56,477	41,889
Aver. Shs. Outstg.	49,802	49,770	49,716	49,618	49,472	49,324	49,234
[1] Before acctg. change dr$10,806,000.							
BALANCE SHEET (IN THOUSANDS):							
Cash and Cash Equivalents	10,252	44,932	28,119	6,578	9,675	5,722	3,406
Accounts Receivable, Net	113,439	91,927	83,737	79,386	64,812	49,206	43,005
Inventories	305,487	260,145	261,738	232,981	194,994	166,348	128,042
Gross Property	425,536	329,402	311,579	290,725	247,530	174,276	141,163
Accumulated Depreciation	168,214	141,099	119,888	98,353	71,099	54,758	44,188
Long-Term Debt	17,266	18,737	69,275	70,804	61,465	15,694	15,513
Net Stockholders' Equity	591,140	511,777	440,953	368,468	298,851	243,906	196,012
Total Assets	753,431	615,790	596,513	546,190	472,424	359,671	285,343
Total Current Assets	450,807	415,776	391,013	340,606	284,046	233,426	185,547
Total Current Liabilities	111,357	66,159	70,906	92,868	98,626	88,155	60,608
Net Working Capital	339,450	349,617	320,107	247,738	185,420	145,271	124,939
Year End Shares Outstg	49,805	49,776	49,746	49,658	49,538	49,356	49,270
STATISTICAL RECORD:							
Operating Profit Margin %	22.4	22.5	21.0	20.8	22.6	23.6	23.7
Book Value Per Share	11.87	10.28	8.86	7.42	6.03	4.94	3.98
Return on Equity %	18.1	18.7	18.1	19.3	21.4	23.2	21.4
Return on Assets %	14.2	15.5	13.4	13.0	13.5	15.7	14.7
Average Yield %	0.6	0.5	0.5	0.7	0.7	0.7	0.7
P/E Ratio	27.0-20.7	30.9-21.7	33.4-17.3	24.9-17.4	23.1-17.0	22.3-17.3	29.9-17.8
Price Range	58-44½	59¼-41¾	53½-27¾	35⅞-25	29¾-21⅞	25⅝-19⅞	25⅝-15⅛

Statistics are as originally reported.

OFFICERS:
T. Cori, Chmn., Pres. & C.E.O.
P.A. Gleich, V.P. & Sec.
T.M. Tallarico, V.P. & Treas.

INCORPORATED: DE, Jul., 1975

PRINCIPAL OFFICE: 3050 Spruce St., St. Louis, MO 63103

TELEPHONE NUMBER: (314) 771-5765

NO. OF EMPLOYEES: 5,110

ANNUAL MEETING: In May

SHAREHOLDERS: 2,234

INSTITUTIONAL HOLDINGS:
No. of Institutions: 241
Shares Held: 31,657,515

REGISTRAR(S): Boatmen's Trust Co., St.Louis, MO 63101

TRANSFER AGENT(S): Boatmen's Trust Co., St. Louis, MO 63101

ASE SYMBOL SJW
Rec. Pr. 36¾

SJW CORP.

YIELD 5.7%
P/E RATIO 10.1

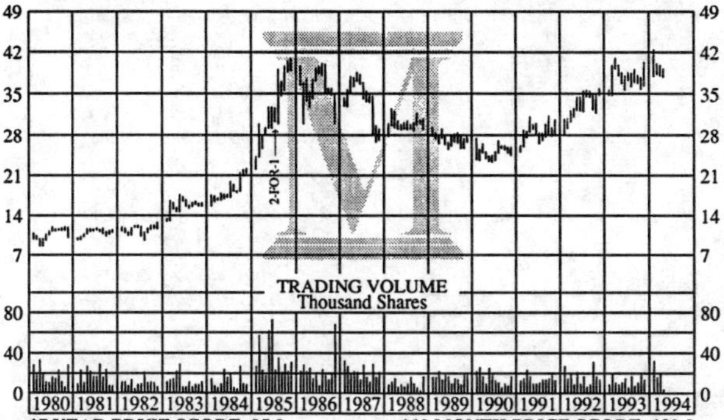

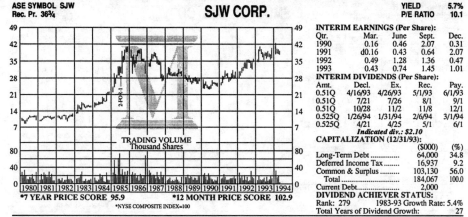

*7 YEAR PRICE SCORE 95.9 *12 MONTH PRICE SCORE 102.9

*NYSE COMPOSITE INDEX=100

INTERIM EARNINGS (Per Share):

Qtr.	Mar.	June	Sept.	Dec.
1990	0.16	0.46	2.07	0.31
1991	d0.16	0.43	0.64	2.07
1992	0.49	1.28	1.36	0.47
1993	0.43	0.74	1.45	1.01

INTERIM DIVIDENDS (Per Share):

Amt.	Decl.	Ex.	Rec.	Pay.
0.51Q	4/16/93	4/26/93	5/1/93	6/1/93
0.51Q	7/21	7/26	8/1	9/1
0.51Q	10/28	11/2	11/8	12/1
0.525Q	1/26/94	1/31/94	2/6/94	3/1/94
0.525Q	4/21	4/25	5/1	6/1

Indicated div.: $2.10

CAPITALIZATION (12/31/93):

	($000)	(%)
Long-Term Debt	64,000	34.8
Deferred Income Tax	16,937	9.2
Common & Surplus	103,130	56.0
Total	184,067	100.0
Current Debt	2,000	

DIVIDEND ACHIEVER STATUS:
Rank: 279 1983-93 Growth Rate: 5.4%
Total Years of Dividend Growth: 27

RECENT DEVELOPMENTS: For the year ended 12/31/93, net income increased 21% to $10.2 million from $8.4 million in 1992. Operating revenue for the year was up 17% to $89.1 million from $76.3 million in the prior year. The revenue increase was due to the inclusion of Western Precision, Inc. operating revenue, decreased rates and revenue adjustments, increased usage, increased customers and SJW Land Company increased parking revenue. Total water delivered in 1993 was 43 billion gallons, up 3 billion gallons, or 7%, from 1992. For the quarter ended 12/31/93, net income was $3.3 million, compared with $1.4 million for the same quarter last year. Operating revenue for the quarter increased 13.4% to $22.6 million from $19.9 million for the corresponding 1992 quarter.

BUSINESS

SJW CORP. is a holding company with three wholly-owned subsidiaries, San Jose Water Company, SJW Land Company and Western Precision, Inc. The Company's primary business is the production, storage, purification, distribution and retail sales of water. San Jose Water Company provides water service to a population of approximately 913,000 in an area comprising about 134 square miles in the metropolitan San Jose, California area. Western Precision, Inc. holds a 9.7% interest in California Water Service Company and also operates a precision parts manufacturing facility located in Sunnyvale, California and Austin, Texas. Utilization of rates, service and other matters affecting business are subject to regulation by the Public Utilities Commission of the state of California.

QUARTERLY DATA

(12/31/93)($000)	Rev	Inc
1st Quarter	17,176	1,391
2nd Quarter	23,847	2,397
3rd Quarter	31,469	4,695
4th Quarter	22,553	3,284

ANNUAL EARNINGS AND DIVIDENDS PER SHARE

	1993	1992	1991	1990	1989	1988	1987
Earnings Per Share	**3.64**	**3.60**	**2.98**	**3.00**	**1.50**	**2.50**	**3.08**
Dividends Per Share	**2.04**	**2.13**	**1.92**	**1.86**	**1.82**	**1.76**	**1.68**
Dividend Payout %	**56.0**	**59.2**	**64.4**	**62.0**	**N.M.**	**70.4**	**54.5**

ANNUAL FINANCIAL DATA

RECORD OF EARNINGS (IN THOUSANDS):							
Operating Revenues	95,045	89,109	76,281	70,458	56,044	62,627	65,655
Depreciation	6,823	6,153	5,773	5,249	5,019	4,797	4,652
Maintenance	5,417	4,397	3,778	3,963	3,098	3,151	2,885
Prov for Fed Inc Taxes	8,071	7,619	6,123	5,660	3,057	4,818	6,859
Operating Income	14,960	14,123	12,152	11,587	6,774	10,038	12,229
Interest Expense	4,489	4,002	3,865	3,504	2,467	3,794	3,089
Net Income	11,767	10,227	8,448	8,539	4,307	7,190	8,888
Aver. Shs. Outstg.	3,237	2,838	2,838	2,838	2,831	2,819	2,807
BALANCE SHEET (IN THOUSANDS):							
Gross Plant	293,683	272,999	255,325	244,068	233,010	222,288	213,424
Accumulated Depreciation	90,030	84,158	78,675	73,405	69,118	64,548	60,135
Net Utility Plant	203,653	188,841	176,650	170,663	163,892	157,740	153,289
Lg tm Debt, Less Curr Matur	64,000	58,503	41,248	35,193	38,138	42,583	41,528
Net Stockholders' Equity	103,130	96,155	77,374	74,374	72,444	73,019	72,265
Total Assets	256,851	230,198	197,095	188,313	185,905	187,856	182,318
Year End Shares Outstg	3,251	3,256	2,838	2,838	2,838	2,825	2,813
STATISTICAL RECORD:							
Book Value Per Share	31.14	29.07	27.27	26.21	25.08	25.39	24.66
Op. Inc/Net Pl %	7.3	7.5	6.9	6.8	4.1	6.4	8.0
Dep/Gr. Pl %	2.3	2.3	2.3	2.2	2.2	2.2	2.2
Accum. Dep/Gr. Pl %	30.7	30.8	30.8	30.1	29.7	29.0	28.2
Return on Equity %	11.4	10.6	10.9	11.5	6.0	9.9	12.7
Average Yield %	5.4	6.6	6.8	7.3	6.6	5.8	5.1
P/E Ratio	11.3-9.5	10.0-7.8	10.5-8.4	9.1-7.8	19.7-17.1	13.0-11.1	12.5-8.7
Price Range	41-34¾	36-28¼	31¼-25⅛	27⅞-23⅜	29½-25⅝	32½-27¾	38½-26¾

Statistics are as originally reported.

OFFICERS:
J.W. Weinhardt, Pres. & C.E.O.
W.R. Roth, V.P.-Fin., C.F.O. & Treas.
B.Y. Nilsen, Secretary

INCORPORATED: CA, Apr., 1985

PRINCIPAL OFFICE: 374 West Santa Clara St., San Jose, CA 95196

TELEPHONE NUMBER: (408) 279-7810

FAX: (408) 279-7934

NO. OF EMPLOYEES: 274

ANNUAL MEETING: In April

SHAREHOLDERS: 1,663

INSTITUTIONAL HOLDINGS:
No. of Institutions: 22
Shares Held: 351,520

REGISTRAR(S): First National Bank of Boston, Boston, MA

TRANSFER AGENT(S): First National Bank of Boston, Boston, MA

NYS SYMBOL SJM A
Rec. Pr. 23½

SMUCKER (J.M.) CO.

YIELD 2.1%
P/E RATIO 18.5

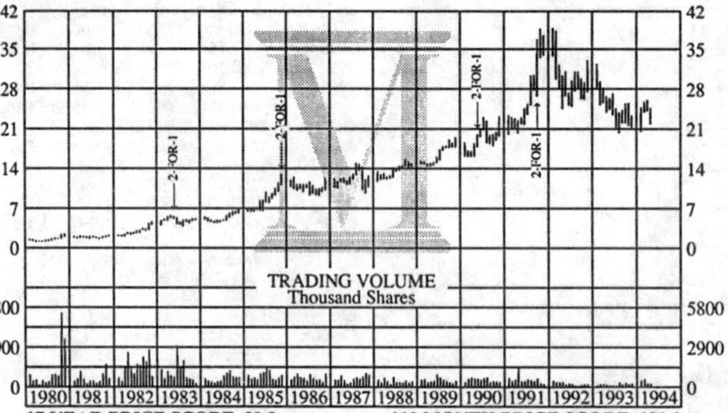

42
35
28
21
14
7
0
2-FOR-1
2-FOR-1
2-FOR-1
2-FOR-1
TRADING VOLUME
Thousand Shares
5800
2900
0
1980 1981 1982 1983 1984 1985 1986 1987 1988 1989 1990 1991 1992 1993 1994

*7 YEAR PRICE SCORE 88.5 *12 MONTH PRICE SCORE 103.3
*NYSE COMPOSITE INDEX=100

INTERIM EARNINGS (Per Share):

Qtr.	July	Oct.	Jan.	Apr.
1990-91	0.29	0.30	0.21	0.29
1991-92	0.30	0.32	0.23	0.31
1992-93	0.32	0.35	0.25	0.35
1993-94	0.31	0.35	0.26	...

INTERIM DIVIDENDS (Per Share):

Amt.	Decl.	Ex.	Rec.	Pay.
0.115Q	4/16/93	5/12/93	5/18/93	6/1/93
0.115Q	7/21	8/12	8/18	9/1
0.115Q	10/26	11/10	11/17	12/1
0.115Q	1/21/94	2/9/94	2/15/94	3/1/94
0.125Q	4/15	5/12	5/18	6/1

Indicated div.: $0.50

CAPITALIZATION (4/30/93):

	($000)	(%)
Deferred Income Tax	3,308	1.5
Common & Surplus	220,469	98.5
Total	223,777	100.0

DIVIDEND ACHIEVER STATUS:
Rank: 42 1983-93 Growth Rate: 16.6%
Total Years of Dividend Growth: 18

RECENT DEVELOPMENTS: For the quarter ended 1/31/92, net income rose 7% to $6.73 million from $6.27 million last year. Sales increased 10% to $112.0 million from $102.0 million in the prior year. Volume growth in the consumer and industrial business areas accounted for the majority of the sales increase. In the consumer area, traditional fruit spreads recorded the largest unit growth. Industrial sales of fruit based ingredients increased significantly.

PROSPECTS: The rising need for increased marketing and merchandising programs for current and new products will probably affect future results, but the Company's favorable mix of products in an otherwise traditional line of name brands should help maintain growth. The Foodservice area will benefit from increased sales and ongoing cost reductions efforts. The acquisition of Henry Jones Foods has increased the percentage of international sales to approximately 10%.

BUSINESS

THE J.M. SMUCKER COMPANY manufactures and markets a wide variety of jams, jellies, preserves and marmalades. The Company also produces ice cream toppings, spreads, pancake syrups, ketchup, mustard, fruit butter, puree, syrups, low sugar items, and juices. Well-recognized brand names include: Smucker's, Dickinson's, Magic Shell and Goober Jelly. The Company also provides industrial fruit products such as baker and dairy fillings. Products are sold primarily through brokers to various grocery accounts, plus food service distributors and chains. SJM's distribution outside of the U.S. is principally in Canada and the U.K., although products are exported to other countries.

BUSINESS LINE ANALYSIS

(4/30/93)	Rev(%)	Inc(%)
United States	92.2	99.1
Foreign	7.8	0.9
Total	100.0	100.0

ANNUAL EARNINGS AND DIVIDENDS PER SHARE

	4/30/93	4/30/92	4/30/91	4/30/90	4/30/89	4/30/88	4/30/87
Earnings Per Share	**[1] 1.27**	**1.16**	**1.07**	**1.03**	**0.94**	**0.78**	**0.61**
Dividends Per Share	**0.41**	**0.39**	**[2] 0.32**	**0.25**	**0.21**	**0.173**	**0.15**
Dividend Payout %	**32.3**	**33.6**	**29.8**	**24.4**	**22.4**	**22.1**	**24.9**

[1] Before acctg. chg. [2] 2-for-1 stk split, 5/30/90

ANNUAL FINANCIAL DATA

	4/30/93	4/30/92	4/30/91	4/30/90	4/30/89	4/30/88	4/30/87
RECORD OF EARNINGS (IN THOUSANDS):							
Total Revenues	491,309	483,472	454,976	422,357	366,855	314,245	288,263
Costs and Expenses	418,519	416,213	391,660	362,906	314,455	268,655	247,522
Depreciation & Amort	13,052	12,808	11,771	10,452	9,679	8,018	6,679
Operating Income	59,738	54,451	51,545	48,999	42,721	37,572	34,062
Income Bef Income Taxes	61,470	56,083	52,581	49,944	44,582	38,592	34,730
Income Taxes	24,071	21,965	20,837	19,767	17,027	15,722	17,051
Net Income	[1] 37,399	34,118	31,744	30,177	27,555	22,870	17,679
[1] Before acctg. change dr$4,454,000.							
BALANCE SHEET (IN THOUSANDS):							
Cash and Cash Equivalents	50,445	36,268	24,513	18,402	36,652	27,111	25,227
Receivables, Net	40,354	41,565	42,328	35,591	29,640	24,799	26,192
Inventories	71,863	77,777	66,531	61,495	47,180	47,000	42,946
Gross Property	166,904	150,879	136,722	122,168	102,484	88,036	74,913
Accumulated Depreciation	70,578	62,556	53,813	46,750	40,570	34,053	28,597
Long-Term Debt	...	...	4,267	4,277	4,954	3,081	4,150
Net Stockholders' Equity	220,469	212,215	190,223	167,125	144,536	125,322	107,546
Total Assets	294,811	277,768	252,429	224,840	198,457	170,025	152,872
Total Current Assets	168,399	161,571	141,036	119,947	118,129	101,847	96,461
Total Current Liabilities	56,543	53,560	50,029	45,742	41,856	35,624	35,613
Net Working Capital	111,856	108,011	91,007	74,205	76,273	66,223	60,848
Year End Shares Outstg	29,199	29,538	29,535	29,540	29,428	29,452	29,400
STATISTICAL RECORD:							
Operating Profit Margin %	12.2	11.3	11.3	11.6	11.6	12.0	11.8
Book Value Per Share	6.76	6.47	5.68	4.86	4.44	3.86	3.38
Return on Equity %	17.0	16.1	16.7	18.1	19.1	18.2	16.4
Return on Assets %	12.7	12.3	12.6	13.4	13.9	13.5	11.6
Average Yield %	1.3	1.3	1.6	1.5	1.5	1.4	1.4
P/E Ratio	30.7-19.3	33.5-17.2	21.6-15.0	18.9-14.0	16.6-12.4	19.2-12.5	20.5-15.2
Price Range	39-24½	38⅞-20	23⅛-16	19½-14⅜	15⅝-11⅝	15-9¾	12½-9¼

Statistics are as originally reported.

OFFICERS:
T. Smucker, Chmn.
R.K. Smucker, Pres.
P.P. Yuschak, Treas.
S.J. Ellcessor, Sec. & Gen. Couns.

INCORPORATED: OH, Sep., 1921

PRINCIPAL OFFICE: Strawberry Lane, Orrville, OH 44667

TELEPHONE NUMBER: (216) 682-3000

NO. OF EMPLOYEES: 1,950

ANNUAL MEETING: In August

SHAREHOLDERS: 6,805 (cl. A); 5,355 (cl. B.)

INSTITUTIONAL HOLDINGS:
No. of Institutions: 102
Shares Held: 6,866,401

REGISTRAR(S): National City Bank, Cleveland, OH 44114

TRANSFER AGENT(S): National City Bank, Cleveland, OH 44114

SONOCO PRODUCTS CO.

YIELD 2.7%
P/E RATIO 15.2

TRADING VOLUME
Thousand Shares

*7 YEAR PRICE SCORE 98.3   *12 MONTH PRICE SCORE 102.5
*NYSE COMPOSITE INDEX=100

INTERIM EARNINGS (Per Share):

Qtr.	Mar.	June	Sept.	Dec.
1990	0.29	0.32	d0.33	0.31
1991	0.27	0.26	0.29	0.29
1992	0.26	0.33	0.32	0.03
1993	0.31	0.36	0.33	0.35

INTERIM DIVIDENDS (Per Share):

Amt.	Decl.	Ex.	Rec.	Pay.
2-for-1	4/21/93	6/11/93	5/21/93	6/10/93
0.135Q	7/21	8/16	8/20	9/10
0.135Q	10/20	11/15	11/19	12/10
0.135Q	2/2/94	2/14/94	2/18/94	3/10/94
0.14Q	4/20	5/16	5/20	6/10

Indicated div.: $0.56

CAPITALIZATION (12/31/93):

	($000)	(%)
Long-Term Debt	455,262	36.6
Preferred Stock	172,500	13.9
Common & Surplus	615,864	49.5
Total	1,243,626	100.0

DIVIDEND ACHIEVER STATUS:
Rank: 57   1983-93 Growth Rate: 15.1%
Total Years of Dividend Growth: 10

RECENT DEVELOPMENTS: For the year ended 12/31/93, net income was $118.8 million compared with income before accounting changes of $81.3 million in 1992. Consolidated net sales for 1993 were $1.95 billion, an increase of 5.9% over the $1.84 billion recorded in 1992. For the quarter, net sales were $539.5 million, an 11.4% increase over the $484.1 million reported in 1992. Net income for the fourth quarter of 1993 was $31.6 million compared with 1992's fourth quarter

earnings from ongoing operations of $3.1 million. The results included the consolidation of Engraph for the first time. In addition, SONO added an injection molding business with the acquisition of Crellin Holdings, Inc., and significant new tube business in Europe with the acquisition of OPV/Durener Group in Germany. Along with some smaller tactical acquisitions, these businesses add $400.0 million in annual sales.

BUSINESS

SONOCO PRODUCTS CO. is a major packaging manufacturer serving a wide variety of consumer and industrial markets with containers and carriers made from paper, plastic, metal and wood. Sonoco has a high degree of vertical integration, producing most of its adhesives, paperboard and paper converting machinery. The Converted Products Segment manufactures fiber and plastic tubes, cores and cones, used primarily as industrial carriers; composite canisters, used to package a variety of products from frozen concentrates and snack foods to coffee, paints and cleansers; caulking cartridges, used for packaging adhesives and sealants; fiber drums, plastic drums, intermediate bulk containers, used for packaging a wide variety of products for bulk packaging; protective packging products like solid fiber partitions, edgeboard and Sonopost corner posts. The Paper Segment consists of 21 U.S. cylinder board machines, one Fourdrinier paper machine and Paper Stock Dealers, Inc., a recovered paper collection and processing subsidiary. The Miscellaneous Segment includes High Density Film Products, producers of plastic sacks for the grocery and retail industries, agricultural mulch film and other products. Also included is Baker Reels, a national manufacturer of nailed wood and metal reels for the wire and cable industries.

ANNUAL EARNINGS AND DIVIDENDS PER SHARE

	1993	1992	1991	1990	1989	1988	1987
Earnings Per Share	1.35	[2]0.94	1.10	0.58	1.18	1.10	0.70
Dividends Per Share	[1]0.53	[3]0.49	0.46	0.45	0.405	0.32	[4]0.25
Dividend Payout %	39.3	52.4	41.8	77.6	34.3	29.1	35.7

[1] 2-for-1 stk split,06/11/93 [2] Before acctg. chg. [3] Bef acctg chge [4] 2-for-1 stk split, 6/87

ANNUAL FINANCIAL DATA

RECORD OF EARNINGS (IN MILLIONS):

	1993	1992	1991	1990	1989	1988	1987
Total Revenues	1,947.2	1,838.0	1,697.1	1,669.1	1,655.8	1,599.8	1,312.1
Costs and Expenses	1,633.4	1,599.8	1,452.0	1,484.1	1,401.0	1,343.3	1,116.6
Deprec, Depl & Amort	95.7	83.3	76.6	72.2	67.3	69.1	57.1
Operating Income	218.0	155.0	168.5	112.9	187.5	187.4	138.3
Inc Fr Opers Bef Income Taxes	192.9	131.0	155.7	87.0	158.1	162.2	109.7
Taxes on Income	75.2	51.8	63.6	43.9	60.9	67.0	48.7
Net Income	118.8	[1]81.3	94.8	50.4	103.6	96.3	61.5
Aver. Shs. Outstg. (000)	87,316	86,732	86,304	87,109	87,794	87,632	87,730

[1] Before acctg. change dr$37,892,000.

BALANCE SHEET (IN MILLIONS):

Cash and Cash Equivalents	25.9	38.1	28.6	39.9	25.7	20.4	14.4
Receivables, Net	270.4	238.6	198.8	201.6	164.8	164.3	140.0
Inventories	186.1	159.6	156.0	157.1	151.6	163.7	134.4
Gross Property	1,315.7	1,135.0	1,052.1	986.1	856.7	877.6	772.8
Accumulated Depreciation	578.5	521.0	471.3	423.5	362.4	344.1	290.5
Long-Term Debt	455.3	241.0	227.5	279.1	226.2	275.5	263.5
Net Stockholders' Equity	788.4	561.9	562.3	512.8	511.6	454.5	379.9
Total Assets	1,707.1	1,246.5	1,135.9	1,113.6	995.1	977.5	877.6
Total Current Assets	513.1	464.9	420.7	431.7	376.2	377.8	321.5
Total Current Liabilities	303.2	312.5	256.9	247.6	183.1	189.8	177.5
Net Working Capital	209.9	152.5	163.9	184.1	193.0	188.1	144.0
Year End Shs Outstg (000)	87,447	87,144	86,490	86,100	87,453	87,722	87,532

STATISTICAL RECORD:

Operating Profit Margin %	11.2	8.4	9.9	6.8	11.3	11.7	10.5
Book Value Per Share	3.16	5.77	5.80	5.30	5.03	4.66	3.85
Return on Equity %	15.1	14.5	16.9	9.8	20.2	21.2	16.2
Return on Assets %	7.0	6.5	8.3	4.5	10.4	9.8	7.0
Average Yield %	2.4	2.3	2.7	2.8	2.3	2.3	2.1
P/E Ratio	18.4-14.6	26.9-18.0	17.6-13.0	33.0-21.8	16.5-13.8	15.9-8.9	22.0-12.9
Price Range	24⅞-19¾	25¼-16⅞	19⅜-14¼	19⅛-12⅝	19½-16¼	17½-9¾	15⅜-9

Statistics are as originally reported.

OFFICERS:
C.W. Coker, Chmn. & C.E.O.
R.C. King, Jr., Pres. & C.O.O.
C.T. Tsang, V.P.-Fin.
C.J. Hupfer, Treas.
J.L. Coker, Corp. Sec.

INCORPORATED: SC, May, 1899

PRINCIPAL OFFICE: North Second Street, Hartsville, SC 29550

TELEPHONE NUMBER: (803) 383-7000

FAX: (803) 339-6098

NO. OF EMPLOYEES: 692

ANNUAL MEETING: In April

SHAREHOLDERS: 9,997 (approx.)

INSTITUTIONAL HOLDINGS:
No. of Institutions: 189
Shares Held: 29,379,725

REGISTRAR(S):

TRANSFER AGENT(S): Wachovia Bank & Trust Co., N.A., Winston-Salem, NC 27102

NYS SYMBOL SCW
Rec. Pr. 18¾

SOUTHERN CALIFORNIA WATER CO.

YIELD 6.4%
P/E RATIO 11.4

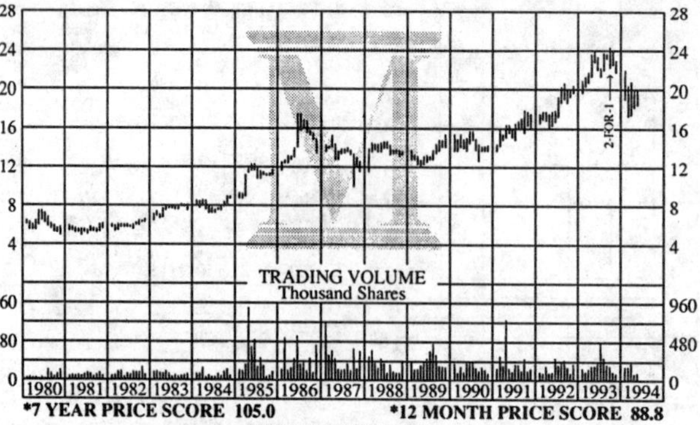

***7 YEAR PRICE SCORE 105.0** ***12 MONTH PRICE SCORE 88.8**

*NYSE COMPOSITE INDEX=100

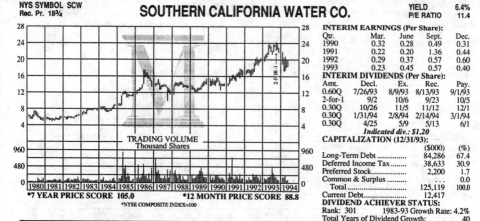

INTERIM EARNINGS (Per Share):

Qtr.	Mar.	June	Sept.	Dec.
1990	0.32	0.28	0.49	0.31
1991	0.22	0.20	1.36	0.44
1992	0.29	0.37	0.57	0.60
1993	0.23	0.45	0.57	0.40

INTERIM DIVIDENDS (Per Share):

Amt.	Decl.	Ex.	Rec.	Pay.
0.60Q	7/26/93	8/9/93	8/13/93	9/1/93
2-for-1	9/2	10/6	9/23	10/5
0.30Q	10/26	11/5	11/12	12/1
0.30Q	1/31/94	2/8/94	2/14/94	3/1/94
0.30Q	4/25	5/9	5/13	6/1

Indicated div.: $1.20

CAPITALIZATION (12/31/93):

	($000)	(%)
Long-Term Debt	84,286	67.4
Deferred Income Tax	38,633	30.9
Preferred Stock	2,200	1.7
Common & Surplus	...	0.0
Total	125,119	100.0
Current Debt	12,417	

DIVIDEND ACHIEVER STATUS:

Rank: 301 1983-93 Growth Rate: 4.2%

Total Years of Dividend Growth: 40

RECENT DEVELOPMENTS: For the year ended 12/31/93, net income was $12.0 million, or $1.66 per share, compared with $12.1 million, or $1.82 per share, in 1992. Operating revenues for the year increased 7.8% to $108.5 million from $100.7 million for the prior year. Water operating revenues of $98.2 million increased 8.3% from $90.6 million in 1992. The increase is attributable to a 1.2% increase in the volume of water sold, and increase in the average number of customers and increased water rates associated with general rate case decisions and other supply and rate base offset decisions. Electric operating revenues increased 3.2% to $10.4 million from $10.0 million in 1992. This resulted from a 0.8% increase in kilowatt-hour sales and a change in the mix of those sales from industrial to commercial.

BUSINESS

SOUTHERN CALIFORNIA WATER CO. is engaged principally in the purchase, production, distribution and sale of water. The Company also distributes electricity in one community. The Company provides service in 17 separate operating districts, 16 of which are water districts and one an electric district, located in 75 communities in ten counties throughout the state of California. The Company serves a total of 257,116 customers, 236,985 of which receive water services and 20,131 of which receive electric services.

REVENUES

(12/31/93)	($000)	(%)
Water	98,155	90.5
Electric	10,351	9.5
Total	108,506	100.0

ANNUAL EARNINGS AND DIVIDENDS PER SHARE

	1993	1992	1991	1990	1989	1988	1987
Earnings Per Share	**1.66**	**1.82**	**2.34**	**1.40**	**1.38**	**0.97**	**[2] 1.33**
Dividends Per Share	**[1] 1.188**	**1.15**	**1.10**	**1.07**	**1.035**	**1.01**	**0.965**
Dividend Payout %	**71.6**	**63.4**	**47.0**	**76.2**	**75.0**	**N.M.**	**72.6**

[1] 2-for-1 stk split,10/06/93 [2] Before acctg. chg.

ANNUAL FINANCIAL DATA

	1993	1992	1991	1990	1989	1988	1987
RECORD OF EARNINGS (IN THOUSANDS):							
Total Operating Revenues	108,506	100,660	90,660	90,398	85,564	80,175	77,730
Depreciation	7,398	6,526	6,027	...	...	...	...
Maintenance	6,450	5,091	5,147	4,982	4,610	5,006	4,578
Prov for Fed Inc Taxes	5,491	7,791	5,340	6,034	4,233	3,902	5,373
Operating Income	20,050	19,098	16,825	14,733	14,814	12,191	12,687
Interest Expense	8,378	7,890	7,583	6,421	7,673	6,230	5,500
Net Income	12,026	12,142	15,363	8,907	8,730	6,127	[1] 8,370
Aver. Shs. Outstg.	7,186	6,628	6,518	6,272	6,242	6,218	6,194
[1] Before acctg. change cr$1,575,000.							
BALANCE SHEET (IN THOUSANDS):							
Gross Plant	379,798	355,399	330,514	299,925	275,399	275,043	252,348
Accumulated Depreciation	84,808	77,874	71,956	64,212	60,934	60,380	56,694
Prop, Plant & Equip, Net	294,990	277,525	258,558	235,713	214,465	214,663	195,654
Long-term Debt	84,286	84,195	82,634	67,246	67,767	73,532	57,153
Net Stockholders' Equity	600	640	680	720	760	800	840
Total Assets	358,533	312,491	293,444	268,028	254,346	237,450	222,106
Year End Shs Outstg	7,805	6,643	6,607	6,272	6,258	6,230	6,206
STATISTICAL RECORD:							
Op. Inc/Net Pl %	6.8	6.9	6.5	6.3	6.9	5.7	6.5
Dep/Gr. Pl %	1.9	1.8	1.8	1.7	1.7	1.6	1.6
Accum. Dep/Gr. Pl %	22.3	21.9	21.8	21.4	22.1	22.0	22.5
Average Yield %	5.4	6.3	7.0	7.5	7.5	7.7	7.6
P/E Ratio	14.7-11.8	11.3-8.8	7.6-5.8	11.3-9.0	11.1-8.8	15.1-11.9	11.5-7.5
Price Range	24⅜-19⅝	20⅝-16	17⅞-13⅝	15¾-12⅝	15⅜-12⅛	14⅝-11½	15¼-10

Statistics are as originally reported.

OFFICERS:
W.V. Caveney, Chairman
F.E. Wicks, Pres. & C.E.O.
J.B. Gallagher, Sec., Treas. & C.F.O.

INCORPORATED: CA, Dec., 1929

PRINCIPAL OFFICE: 630 East Foothill Blvd., San Dimas, CA 91773

TELEPHONE NUMBER: (909) 394-3600
FAX: (909) 394-0711
NO. OF EMPLOYEES: 57
ANNUAL MEETING: In April
SHAREHOLDERS: 2,866 com.; 21 pfd.
INSTITUTIONAL HOLDINGS:
No. of Institutions: 41
Shares Held: 810,284

REGISTRAR(S):

TRANSFER AGENT(S): First National Bank of Omaha, Omaha, NE 68102
First Interstate Bank, Ltd., Los Angeles, CA

SOUTHERN INDIANA GAS & ELECTRIC CO.

YIELD 5.9%
P/E RATIO 11.4

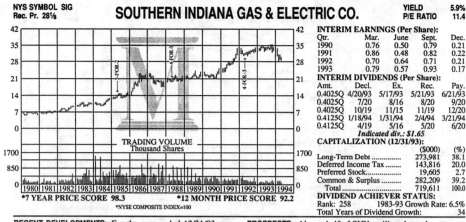

7 YEAR PRICE SCORE 98.3   **12 MONTH PRICE SCORE 92.2**
*NYSE COMPOSITE INDEX=100

INTERIM EARNINGS (Per Share):

Qtr.	Mar.	June	Sept.	Dec.
1990	0.76	0.50	0.79	0.21
1991	0.86	0.48	0.82	0.22
1992	0.70	0.64	0.71	0.21
1993	0.79	0.57	0.93	0.17

INTERIM DIVIDENDS (Per Share):

Amt.	Decl.	Ex.	Rec.	Pay.
0.4025Q	4/20/93	5/17/93	5/21/93	6/21/93
0.4025Q	7/20	8/16	8/20	9/20
0.4025Q	10/19	11/15	11/19	12/20
0.4125Q	1/18/94	1/31/94	2/4/94	3/21/94
0.4125Q	4/19	5/16	5/20	6/20

Indicated div.: $1.65

CAPITALIZATION (12/31/93):

	($000)	(%)
Long-Term Debt	273,981	38.1
Deferred Income Tax	143,816	20.0
Preferred Stock	19,605	2.7
Common & Surplus	282,209	39.2
Total	719,611	100.0

DIVIDEND ACHIEVER STATUS:
Rank: 258   1983-93 Growth Rate: 6.5%
Total Years of Dividend Growth: 34

RECENT DEVELOPMENTS: For the year ended 12/31/93, net income increased 7.8% to $39.7 million from $36.8 million last year. Revenues were $328.5 million, up 7.4%. Electric revenues for the year advanced 6.3% and gas revenues increased 11.5%. Hot summer weather contributed to increased electricity sales to residential and commercial customers. For the quarter ended 12/31/93, net income was $2.9 million compared with $3.6 million in the prior year. Revenues for the quarter were $76.6 million, up 1.3%.

PROSPECTS: Almost half of SIG's utility plants do not meet the standards of the Clean Air Act. SIG estimates that construction expenditures for the five year period 1993-1997 will total approximately $305 million. Included in that amount is $90-110 million to comply with the Clean Air Act Amendments of 1990. SIG's construction budget will require substantial external financing. The absence of major capital expenditures during the second half of the 1990's will allow SIG's capital structure to recover.

BUSINESS

SOUTHERN INDIANA GAS & ELECTRIC CO. is an operating public utility engaged in the generation, transmission, distribution and sale of electricity and the purchase of natural gas and its transportation, distribution, and sale in a service area which covers ten counties in Southwestern Indiana. SIG's electric business services approximately 116,887 customers in Evansville and 74 cities, towns, communities and adjacent areas. Additionally, wholesale electric service is supplied to another nine communities. The Company's gas business services approximately 98,996 customers in the Evansville area and 63 cities, towns and nearby communities and their environs.

ANNUAL EARNINGS AND DIVIDENDS PER SHARE

	1993	1992	1991	1990	1989	1988	1987
Earnings Per Share	2.45	2.26	2.37	2.27	2.11	2.22	1.93
Dividends Per Share	1.61	☐ 1.56	1.50	1.425	1.35	☐ 1.275	1.193
Dividend Payout %	65.7	69.0	63.3	62.9	64.1	57.4	62.0

☐ 33.3% stk div, 4/20/92   ☐ 4-for-3 stk split, 3/11/88

ANNUAL FINANCIAL DATA

RECORD OF EARNINGS (IN MILLIONS):

	1993	1992	1991	1990	1989	1988	1987
Total Operating Revenues	328.5	305.9	322.6	322.5	311.5	312.8	276.9
Depreciation & Amort	36.9	36.2	36.8	34.5	33.5	32.7	31.0
Maintenance	26.7	21.9	27.1	29.3	26.6	22.5	25.3
Operating Income	51.6	50.9	53.2	51.9	51.6	56.2	47.9
Total Interest Charges	18.5	18.2	19.2	18.9	20.8	20.0	17.8
Net Income	39.7	36.8	38.5	37.7	36.2	38.2	33.3
Aver. Shs. Outstg. (000)	15,705	15,705	15,705	16,092	16,584	16,550	16,507

BALANCE SHEET (IN MILLIONS):

Gross Plant	1,059.2	988.7	942.9	911.3	858.4	834.5	795.7
Accumulated Depreciation	423.7	391.5	358.9	327.9	302.5	276.6	243.6
Net Utility Plant	635.5	597.1	584.0	583.4	555.9	557.9	552.1
Long-term Debt	274.0	212.0	235.7	255.5	218.6	228.6	213.0
Net Stockholders' Equity	301.8	288.6	278.1	264.5	270.6	258.1	232.5
Total Assets	860.0	761.3	747.4	738.8	721.1	698.9	652.3
Year End Shs Outstg (000)	15,705	15,705	15,705	15,705	16,584	16,584	16,775

STATISTICAL RECORD:

Book Value Per Share	17.97	17.12	16.46	15.59	15.13	14.37	12.75
Op. Inc/Net Pl %	8.1	8.5	9.1	8.9	9.3	10.1	8.7
Dep/Gr. Pl %	3.5	3.7	3.9	3.8	3.9	3.9	3.9
Accum. Dep/Gr. Pl %	40.0	39.6	38.1	36.0	35.2	33.1	30.6
Return on Equity %	13.5	13.1	13.8	14.3	13.4	14.8	14.3
Average Yield %	4.8	4.8	5.2	6.2	6.0	6.1	5.9
P/E Ratio	14.5-13.0	15.1-13.4	14.3-9.9	11.1-8.2	11.4-9.8	10.2-8.7	12.0-9.1
Price Range	35½-31⅞	34⅛-30⅜	33⅞-23½	25-20⅞	24⅛-20⅝	22⅝-19⅜	23¼-17½

Statistics are as originally reported.

BUSINESS LINE ANALYSIS

(12/31/93)	Rev(%)	Inc(%)
Electric	78.7	99.4
Gas	21.3	0.6
Total	100.0	100.0

OFFICERS:
R.G. Reherman, Chmn., Pres. & C.E.O.
A.E. Goebel, Sr. V.P., C.F.O., Sec. & Treas.

INCORPORATED: IN, Jun., 1912

PRINCIPAL OFFICE: 20 Northwest Fourth Street, Evansville, IN 47741-0001

TELEPHONE NUMBER: (812) 464-4554
FAX: (812) 464-4554
NO. OF EMPLOYEES: 964 (Consol.)
ANNUAL MEETING: In March
SHAREHOLDERS: 9,468 com.; 875 pfd.
INSTITUTIONAL HOLDINGS:
No. of Institutions: 95
Shares Held: 3,835,528

REGISTRAR(S): Continental Stock Transfer & Trust Co., New York, NY
The National City Bank of Evansville, Evansville, IN 47705

TRANSFER AGENT(S): Continental Stock Transfer & Trust Co., New York, NY
The National City Bank of Evansville, Evansville, IN 47705

SOUTHERN NATIONAL CORP.

YIELD 3.4%
P/E RATIO 8.8

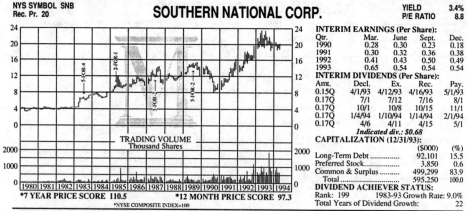

INTERIM EARNINGS (Per Share):

Qtr.	Mar.	June	Sept.	Dec.
1990	0.28	0.30	0.23	0.18
1991	0.30	0.32	0.36	0.38
1992	0.41	0.43	0.50	0.49
1993	0.65	0.54	0.54	0.54

INTERIM DIVIDENDS (Per Share):

Amt.	Decl.	Ex.	Rec.	Pay.
0.15Q	4/1/93	4/12/93	4/16/93	5/1/93
0.17Q	7/1	7/12	7/16	8/1
0.17Q	10/1	10/8	10/15	11/1
0.17Q	1/4/94	1/10/94	1/14/94	2/1/94
0.17Q	4/6	4/11	4/15	5/1

Indicated div.: $0.68

CAPITALIZATION (12/31/93):

	($000)	(%)
Long-Term Debt	92.101	15.5
Preferred Stock	3,850	0.6
Common & Surplus	499,299	83.9
Total	595.250	100.0

TRADING VOLUME
Thousand Shares

*7 YEAR PRICE SCORE 110.5
*12 MONTH PRICE SCORE 97.3
*NYSE COMPOSITE INDEX=100

DIVIDEND ACHIEVER STATUS:
Rank: 199   1983-93 Growth Rate: 9.0%
Total Years of Dividend Growth: 22

RECENT DEVELOPMENTS: For the three months ended 12/31/93 net income was $18.6 million compared with $7.1 million in the corresponding 1992 period. Interest income was up 8% to $59.7 million and noninterest income increased 29% to $14.4 million. The provision for loan losses was $1.3 million, down significantly from $3.1 million the year before. The return on average assets improved to 1.30% from 0.58%. Comparisons were made with restated 1992 results.

PROSPECTS: The Company completed its acquisition of East Coast Savings Bank, S.S.B. in October of 1993. East Coast's assets totaled $275 million and net income for the first six months of 1993, was $3.6 million. The pending acquisitions of The First Savings Bank, FSB, with assets of $2 billion; Regency Bancshares, Inc., with assets of $277 million; and Home Federal Savings Bank of Statesville, with assets of $100 million are scheduled for closing early this year.

BUSINESS

SOUTHERN NATIONAL CORP., with $5.9 billion in assets, is one of the largest bank holding companies in North Carolina and South Carolina. Its principal subsidiaries form a network of 170 banking and thrift offices in 88 cities and communities. Subsidiaries offer a wide range of personal and commercial banking and related financial services. Insurance services are offered through Unified Investors Life Insurance Co. Other subsidiaries include Southern National Leasing Corp. and two savings and loans.

ANNUAL EARNINGS AND DIVIDENDS PER SHARE

	1993	1992	1991	1990	1989	1988	1987
Earnings Per Share	2.28	1.84	1.36	1.01	1.19	1.13	0.95
Dividends Per Share	0.64	0.50	0.46	0.42	① 0.387	0.36	② 0.342
Dividend Payout %	28.1	27.2	33.8	41.6	32.5	31.9	36.2

① 3-for-2 stk split, 6/30/89 ② 3-for-2 stk split, 6/22/87

ANNUAL FINANCIAL DATA

RECORD OF EARNINGS (IN MILLIONS):

	1993	1992	1991	1990	1989	1988	1987
Total Revenues	437.9	381.6	362.6	357.4	310.4	248.6	202.2
Costs and Expenses	324.4	305.8	317.5	325.6	277.2	219.3	177.8
Operating Income	113.5	75.8	45.0	31.8	33.3	29.2	24.4
Income Bef Income Taxes	113.5	75.8	45.0	31.8	33.3	29.2	24.4
Provision for Inc Taxes	37.9	25.6	14.2	9.0	9.5	7.7	6.5
Net Income	① 75.6	50.1	30.8	22.9	23.8	21.6	18.0
Aver. Shs. Outstg. (000)	30,958	24,801	22,669	22,674	20,027	19,043	19,031

① Before acctg. change dr$3,571,000.

BALANCE SHEET (IN MILLIONS):

	1993	1992	1991	1990	1989	1988	1987
Cash and Cash Equivalents	2,230.0	1,420.1	2,220.7	1,715.3	1,661.8	1,387.7	1,062.7
Gross Property	107.3	83.7	73.9	71.6	65.5	57.3	53.2
Long-Term Debt	92.1	33.2	24.2	29.4	35.3	35.8	36.9
Net Stockholders' Equity	503.1	377.2	235.3	214.8	170.6	147.8	133.1
Total Assets	5,898.4	4,598.4	3,729.7	3,342.2	2,924.4	2,601.1	2,268.8
Total Current Assets	2,230.0	1,420.1	2,220.7	1,715.3	1,661.8	1,387.7	1,062.7
Total Current Liabilities	5,303.1	4,188.0	3,470.2	3,098.1	2,718.5	2,417.4	2,098.8
Net Working Capital	d3,073.1	d2,767.9	d1,249.5	d1,382.8	d1,056.7	d1,029.7	d1,036.1
Year End Shs Outstg (000)	31,845	25,228	22,669	22,662	20,085	19,043	19,041

STATISTICAL RECORD:

	1993	1992	1991	1990	1989	1988	1987
Book Value Per Share	15.68	14.80	10.38	9.48	8.49	7.76	6.99
Return on Equity %	15.0	13.3	13.1	10.6	13.9	14.6	13.5
Return on Assets %	1.3	1.1	0.8	0.7	0.8	0.8	0.8
Average Yield %	3.0	3.1	3.7	3.7	2.8	3.0	2.8
P/E Ratio	10.3-8.1	10.7-7.1	11.9-6.4	14.4-7.9	13.0-10.1	11.5-9.6	15.1-10.5
Price Range	23½-18½	19¾-13	16¼-8¾	14½-8	15½-12	13-10⅞	14⅛-10

Statistics are as originally reported.

LOAN DISTRIBUTION

(12/31/93)	($000)	(%)
Comm. Financial & Agric.	553,118	16.6
Real Estate-Construction	151,009	4.5
Real Estate-Mortgage	2,198,871	66.2
Consumer	370,860	11.2
Loans Held For Sale	49,692	1.5
Total	3,323,550	100.0

OFFICERS:
L.G. Orr, Jr., Chmn., Pres. & C.E.O.
J.R. Spruill, Exec. V.P. & C.F.O.
M.D. Marley, Exec. V.P. & Treas.
D.L. Craven, Sr. V.P. & Sec.

INCORPORATED: NC, 1968

PRINCIPAL OFFICE: 500 North Chestnut Street, Lumberton, NC 28358

TELEPHONE NUMBER: (919) 671-2000

NO. OF EMPLOYEES: 2,549 (approx.)

ANNUAL MEETING: In April

SHAREHOLDERS: 20,058

INSTITUTIONAL HOLDINGS:
No. of Institutions: 62
Shares Held: 3,568,117

REGISTRAR(S):

TRANSFER AGENT(S):

SOUTHTRUST CORP.

YIELD	3.5%
P/E RATIO	9.9

*7 YEAR PRICE SCORE 124.0   *12 MONTH PRICE SCORE 110.4
•NYSE COMPOSITE INDEX=100

INTERIM EARNINGS (Per Share):

Qtr.	Mar.	June	Sept.	Dec.
1990	0.21	0.31	0.31	0.31
1991	0.33	0.37	0.37	0.36
1992	0.39	0.41	0.42	0.44
1993	0.46	0.48	0.50	0.50

INTERIM DIVIDENDS (Per Share):

Amt.	Decl.	Ex.	Rec.	Pay.
50%	4/14/93	5/20/93	4/23/93	5/19/93
0.15Q	4/14	5/24	5/28	7/1
0.15Q	7/21	8/23	8/27	10/1
0.15Q	10/20	11/19	11/26	1/1/94
0.17Q	1/19/94	2/18/94	2/25/94	4/1

Indicated div.: $0.68

CAPITALIZATION (12/31/93):

	($000)	(%)
Total Deposits	11,515,311	78.7
Total Debt	1,926,445	13.2
Common & Surplus	1,051,766	7.2
Loan Valuation Reserve	135,233	0.9
Total	14,628,755	100.0

DIVIDEND ACHIEVER STATUS:
Rank: 142   1983-93 Growth Rate: 11.2%
Total Years of Dividend Growth: 24

RECENT DEVELOPMENTS: For the year ended 12/31/93 net income was $150.5 million compared with $114.2 million for 1992. Increased results were attributed to market expansion and a continued focus on cost management and credit quality. The provision for loan losses was $45.0 million versus $43.3 million in the prior year; however, nonperforming assets declined 12% to $113.1 million. Noninterest income rose to $174.7 million from $136.7 million paced by 48%

gain on mortgage origination and servicing fees to $33.8 million. Income from trust fees increased 28% to $15.2 million. The net interest margin narrowed to 4.35% from 4.61%. During 1993, the Company completed 14 acquisitions adding $1.3 billion in assets, $1.05 billion in deposits and $699.9 million in loans. The acquisitions were comprised of nine Florida-based banks, two Georgia-based banks, two Alabama-based banks, and one in South Carolina.

BUSINESS

SOUTHTRUST CORPORATION, a multibank holding company with headquarters in Birmingham, Alabama, owns 39 banks and several bank-related affiliates in Alabama (198 offices), Florida (99), Georgia (88), North Carolina (18), South Carolina (9) and Tennessee (4). Consolidated total assets of $14.7 billion rank the Company as one of the major bank holding companies in the Southeast. The banks serve their customers from 396 offices located throughout the six-state area. The lead bank of the Company is the $4.8 billion South-Trust Bank of Alabama in Birmingham. Bank-related subsidiaries include SouthTrust Securities, Inc., an investment subsidiary; SouthTrust Mortgage Insurance Agency; South-Trust Data Services, a bank data processing company; SouthTrust Insurance Agency Inc.; SouthTrust Life Insurance Company, a credit life insurance company; SouthTrust Leasing, Inc., SouthTrust Estate and Trust Company of Florida; and SouthTrust Estate and Trust Company of Georgia.

ANNUAL EARNINGS AND DIVIDENDS PER SHARE

	1993	1992	1991	1990	1989	1988	1987
Earnings Per Share	1.94	1.66	1.42	1.14	1.21	1.14	1.04
Dividends Per Share	[1] 0.577	[2] 0.51	0.475	0.453	0.414	0.369	0.329
Dividend Payout %	29.7	30.7	33.4	39.7	34.1	32.4	31.6

[1] 3-for-2 stk split,05/20/93 [2] 3-for-2 stk split, 1/27/92

ANNUAL FINANCIAL DATA

RECORD OF EARNINGS (IN MILLIONS):

	1993	1992	1991	1990	1989	1988	1987
Total Interest Income	927.6	832.2	827.2	780.4	688.0	560.8	447.0
Total Interest Expense	397.7	382.9	474.5	498.3	450.1	345.3	264.7
Net Interest Income	529.8	449.3	352.8	282.1	237.8	215.5	182.3
Provision for Loan Losses	45.0	43.3	38.0	44.6	21.2	19.1	18.1
Net Income	150.5	114.2	90.0	69.7	72.8	67.6	60.4
Aver. Shs. Outstg. (000)	77,772	68,948	63,255	61,148	60,077	59,333	58,043

BALANCE SHEET (IN MILLIONS):

	1993	1992	1991	1990	1989	1988	1987
Cash and Due From Banks	607.8	540.5	431.2	403.9	375.1	333.3	331.6
Loans & Lse Financing, Net	9,313.1	7,442.8	5,884.6	5,460.6	4,630.8	4,024.8	3,533.7
Total Domestic Deposits	9,732.5	8,484.5	7,171.6	6,175.4	5,125.5	4,269.6	3,860.0
Long-term Debt	470.0	258.2	140.2	148.8	144.8	147.0	139.0
Net Stockholders' Equity	1,051.8	860.4	662.0	549.6	507.1	445.8	395.6
Total Assets	14,708.0	12,714.4	10,158.1	9,005.9	7,763.2	6,645.3	5,924.0
Year End Shs Outstg (000)	79,401	74,477	65,836	61,167	61,013	59,522	58,275

STATISTICAL RECORD:

	1993	1992	1991	1990	1989	1988	1987
Return on Assets %	1.02	0.90	0.89	0.77	0.94	1.02	1.02
Return on Equity %	14.30	13.30	13.60	12.70	14.40	15.20	15.30
Book Value Per Share	13.25	11.55	10.06	8.98	8.31	7.49	6.79
Average Yield %	3.0	3.2	4.0	5.6	4.1	4.4	3.8
P/E Ratio	11.4-8.6	10.9-8.5	12.1-4.7	9.1-5.0	9.3-7.2	8.3-6.5	10.2-6.6
Price Range	22⅛-16⅝	18⅛-14⅛	17¼-6⅝	10⅜-5¾	11¼-8¾	9½-7⅜	10⅝-6⅞

Statistics are as originally reported.

OFFICERS:
W.D. Malone, Jr., Chmn. & C.E.O.
R.W. Gilbert, Jr., Pres. & C.O.O.
A.D. Barnard, Sec., Treas. & Contr. & Contr.

INCORPORATED: DE, 1968

PRINCIPAL OFFICE: 420 North 20th Street, Birmingham, AL 35203

TELEPHONE NUMBER: (205) 254-5509

FAX: (205) 254-5404

NO. OF EMPLOYEES: 7,000 (approx.)

ANNUAL MEETING: In April

SHAREHOLDERS: 10,632 (approx.)

INSTITUTIONAL HOLDINGS:
No. of Institutions: 159
Shares Held: 32,950,886

REGISTRAR(S):

TRANSFER AGENT(S): Mellon Securities Trust Company, New York, NY

NYS SYMBOL STH
Rec. Pr. 33⅞

STANHOME, INC.

YIELD 3.0%
P/E RATIO 20.2

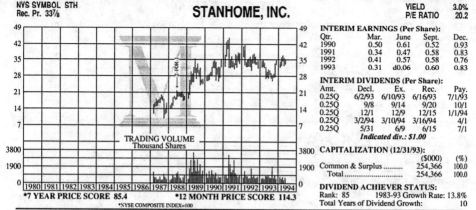

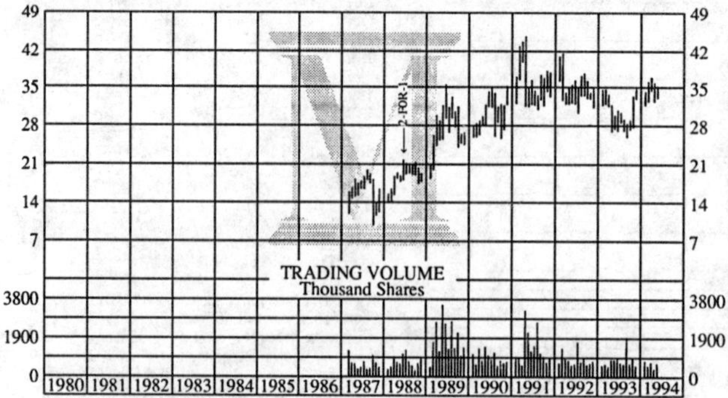
49
42
35
28
21
14
7
2-FOR-1
TRADING VOLUME
Thousand Shares
3800
1900
0
1980 1981 1982 1983 1984 1985 1986 1987 1988 1989 1990 1991 1992 1993 1994

***7 YEAR PRICE SCORE 85.4** ***12 MONTH PRICE SCORE 114.3**

*NYSE COMPOSITE INDEX=100

INTERIM EARNINGS (Per Share):

Qtr.	Mar.	June	Sept.	Dec.
1990	0.50	0.61	0.52	0.93
1991	0.34	0.47	0.58	0.83
1992	0.41	0.57	0.58	0.76
1993	0.31	d0.06	0.60	0.83

INTERIM DIVIDENDS (Per Share):

Amt.	Decl.	Ex.	Rec.	Pay.
0.25Q	6/2/93	6/10/93	6/16/93	7/1/93
0.25Q	9/8	9/14	9/20	10/1
0.25Q	12/1	12/9	12/15	1/1/94
0.25Q	3/2/94	3/10/94	3/16/94	4/1
0.25Q	5/31	6/9	6/15	7/1

Indicated div.: $1.00

CAPITALIZATION (12/31/93):

	($000)	(%)
Common & Surplus..........	254,366	100.0
Total..............................	254,366	100.0

DIVIDEND ACHIEVER STATUS:
Rank: 85 1983-93 Growth Rate: 13.8%
Total Years of Dividend Growth: 10

RECENT DEVELOPMENTS: For the year ended 12/31/93, net income declined 29.1% to $33.1 million compared with $46.7 million the previous year. Sales increased slightly to $750.7 million from $744.1 million. Results include a one-time restructuring charge of $17 million pretax, $11.5 million after-tax or $0.58 per share. Sales from Enesco Giftware were up 5% to $367.5 million and Hamilton Direct Response sales gained 35% to $129.4 million. The Direct Selling Group's sales fell 15% to $255.1 million.

PROSPECTS: Near-term operating results will be affected by soft markets in many European countries. The Company will continue to restructure the Direct Selling Group and expects to begin realizing the benefits of these actions in 1994. Higher levels of consumer confidence and spending should boost sales in the United States. However, higher taxes and the ongoing downsizing in corporate America will constrain further gains in consumer spending.

BUSINESS

STANHOME INC. is a worldwide marketer of consumer products. The Company's key product segments include quality designed giftware and collectibles sold to retailers; collectible dolls, plates and figurines sold through direct response; and home care, personal care and giftware items sold through direct selling. The Enesco Giftware Group is a leader in creatively designed giftware including licensed lines and collectibles. The group encompasses the businesses of Enesco Corp., Tomorrow-Today Corp, Sports Impressions, Inc., Hamilton Gifts Ltd., and Via Vermont Ltd., with a global network of sales organizations to support the distribution of its quality designed giftware and collectibles to retail outlets. The Hamilton Group is a leader in direct response selling. Stanhome's direct selling Group markets a broad line of home care, personal care and giftware items in the U.S., Europe, and Latin America.

BUSINESS LINE ANALYSIS

(12/31/93)	Rev(%)	Inc(%)
Giftware.....................	48.9	71.9
Direct Response.........	17.2	14.2
Direct Selling.............	33.9	13.9
Total	100.0	100.0

ANNUAL EARNINGS AND DIVIDENDS PER SHARE

	1993	1992	1991	1990	1989	1988	1987
Earnings Per Share	**1.00**	**2.32**	**2.22**	**2.55**	**2.23**	**[1] 1.96**	**1.58**
Dividends Per Share	**1.00**	**0.94**	**0.92**	**0.80**	**0.68**	**[2] 0.56**	**0.45**
Dividend Payout %	**100**	**40.5**	**51.6**	**31.5**	**30.5**	**28.6**	**28.5**

[1] Primary [2] 2-for-1 stock split, 6/88.

ANNUAL FINANCIAL DATA

RECORD OF EARNINGS (IN THOUSANDS):							
Total Revenues	750,663	744,072	710,208	675,665	571,380	480,374	433,154
Costs and Expenses	676,757	652,243	623,131	580,506	484,365	399,529	362,648
Depreciation & Amort	8,354	8,396	7,940	7,649	6,725	6,660	5,771
Operating Profit	65,552	83,433	79,136	87,509	80,290	74,185	64,735
Income Bef Income Taxes	66,140	86,992	81,139	90,258	79,650	71,799	62,436
Income Taxes	33,007	40,276	36,086	39,191	35,027	31,159	29,726
Net Income	33,133	46,716	45,053	51,067	44,624	40,640	32,711
Aver. Shs. Outstg.	19,749	20,152	20,295	20,040	20,024	20,664	20,625
BALANCE SHEET (IN THOUSANDS):							
Cash and Cash Equivalents	60,726	42,270	52,221	51,827	43,790	65,632	44,712
Notes & Accts Receiv, Net	123,018	107,366	105,713	88,600	75,453	53,154	47,863
Inventories	94,877	119,971	114,926	111,560	83,928	62,550	55,284
Gross Property	107,852	109,466	121,903	116,883	108,486	101.607	100,187
Accumulated Depreciation	63,177	59,388	63,144	56,960	52,948	45,494	40,017
Long-Term Debt	...	911	1,173	1,421	1,438	1,598	1,996
Net Stockholders' Equity	254,366	256,956	241,074	211,457	170,399	158,169	130,755
Total Assets	429,731	415,618	419,319	391,822	335,154	275,525	244,267
Total Current Assets	314,352	298,246	293,651	271,390	218,582	182,327	148,762
Total Current Liabilities	155,052	143,072	159,452	162,234	150,162	104,439	99,773
Net Working Capital	159,299	155,174	134,199	109,156	68,420	77,888	48,989
Year End Shares Outstg	19,392	19,774	19,791	19,550	19,365	19,953	19,585
STATISTICAL RECORD:							
Operating Profit Margin %	8.7	11.2	11.1	13.0	14.1	15.4	14.9
Book Value Per Share	9.93	10.00	9.19	8.08	5.96	6.12	6.68
Return on Equity %	13.0	18.2	18.7	24.2	26.2	25.7	25.0
Return on Assets %	7.7	11.2	10.7	13.0	13.3	14.8	13.4
Average Yield %	3.3	2.6	2.4	2.6	2.5	3.1	3.0
P/E Ratio	20.7-15.4	17.9-13.0	20.2-13.9	13.8-10.0	15.9-8.2	11.0-7.0	12.5-6.1
Price Range	34¾-25⅞	41⅝-30⅛	44¾-30¾	35¼-25⅝	35½-18⅜	21¾-13⅞	19⅞-9¾

Statistics are as originally reported.

OFFICERS:
H.L. Tower, Chmn.
G.W. Seawright, Pres. & C.E.O.
A.G. Keirstead, Exec. V.P., Chief. Admin. Off. & C.F.O.
B.H. Wyatt, V.P., Gen. Couns. & Sec.

INCORPORATED: MA, Jul., 1931

PRINCIPAL OFFICE: 333 Western Ave., Westfield, MA 01085

TELEPHONE NUMBER: (413) 562-3631

FAX: (413) 568-2820

NO. OF EMPLOYEES: 4,159

ANNUAL MEETING: In April

SHAREHOLDERS: 3,723

INSTITUTIONAL HOLDINGS:
No. of Institutions: 142
Shares Held: 12,440,972

REGISTRAR(S):

TRANSFER AGENT(S):

NYS SYMBOL SWK
Rec. Pr. 37⅞

STANLEY WORKS

YIELD 3.6%
P/E RATIO 18.4

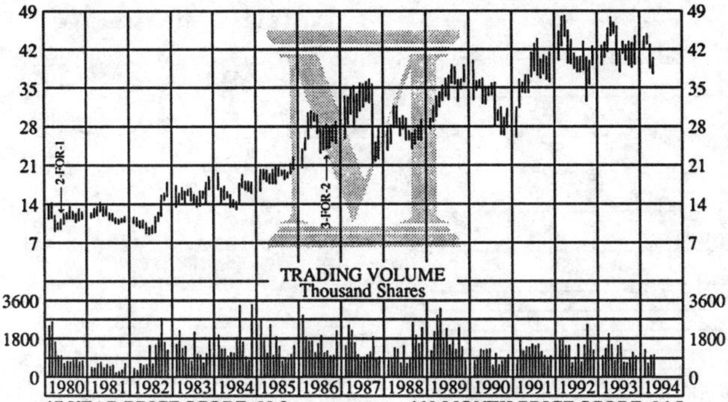

49
42
35
28
21
14
7
2-FOR-1
3-FOR-2
TRADING VOLUME
Thousand Shares
3600
1800
0
1980
1981
1982
1983
1984
1985
1986
1987
1988
1989
1990
1991
1992
1993
1994

***7 YEAR PRICE SCORE 92.0** ***12 MONTH PRICE SCORE 96.5**

*NYSE COMPOSITE INDEX=100

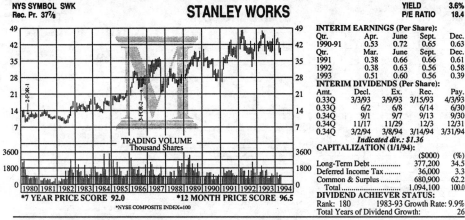

INTERIM EARNINGS (Per Share):

Qtr.	Apr.	June	Sept.	Dec.
1990-91	0.53	0.72	0.65	0.63
Qtr.	Mar.	June	Sept.	Dec.
1991	0.38	0.66	0.66	0.61
1992	0.38	0.63	0.56	0.58
1993	0.51	0.60	0.56	0.39

INTERIM DIVIDENDS (Per Share):

Amt.	Decl.	Ex.	Rec.	Pay.
0.33Q	3/3/93	3/9/93	3/15/93	4/3/93
0.33Q	6/2	6/8	6/14	6/30
0.34Q	9/1	9/7	9/13	9/30
0.34Q	11/17	11/29	12/3	12/31
0.34Q	3/2/94	3/8/94	3/14/94	3/31/94

Indicated div.: $1.36

CAPITALIZATION (1/1/94):

	($000)	(%)
Long-Term Debt	377,200	34.5
Deferred Income Tax	36,000	3.3
Common & Surplus	680,900	62.2
Total	1,094,100	100.0

DIVIDEND ACHIEVER STATUS:
Rank: 180 1983-93 Growth Rate: 9.9%
Total Years of Dividend Growth: 26

RECENT DEVELOPMENTS: Net income for the year ended 12/31/93, before the cumulative effect of $8.5 million for accounting changes, was down 5.6% to $92.6 million from $98.1 million in 1992. Net sales increased 3.5% to a record $2.27 billion from $2.20 billion the previous year. A gain of $29 million on the sale of an investment was offset by charges of $5 million for a fine and contingency reserves of $23 million for litigation, restructuring activities and environmental clean-up.

PROSPECTS: Stanley's sales are being affected by a weak European economy. However, U.S. demand for SWK's products is improving as consumer confidence builds. Operating results will benefit from growth in housing starts and existing home sales as interest rates remain low. Stanley's commitment to increase manufacturing efficiencies through technology and process improvements has positioned the Company to take advantage of sustained growth in factory activity.

BUSINESS

STANLEY WORKS is a worldwide manufacturer and marketer of tools, hardware and specialty hardware products for consumer home improvement, professional and industrial use. The Tools segment includes Stanley Tools, Stanley Fastening Systems, National Hand Tool, Taylor Rental, Mac Tools, Stanley Air Tools and Hydraulic Tools, Stanley-Vidmar and Stanley-Proto. Hardware includes Stanley Hardware, Acmetrack and Industrial Hardware. Specialty Hardware includes Stanley Door Systems and Magic-Door. Overseas business accounted for 29% of sales (31% of operating profits).

BUSINESS LINE ANALYSIS

(01/01/94)	Rev(%)	Inc(%)
Tools	75.0	77.4
Hardware	13.2	16.1
Specialty Hardware	11.8	6.5
Total	100.0	100.0

ANNUAL EARNINGS AND DIVIDENDS PER SHARE

	1/1/94	1/2/93	12/28/91	12/29/90	12/30/89	12/31/88	1/2/88
Earnings Per Share	**2.06**	**2.15**	**[1] 2.31**	**2.53**	**2.71**	**2.40**	**[2] 2.22**
Dividends Per Share	**1.34**	**1.28**	**1.19**	**1.14**	**1.02**	**0.92**	**0.82**
Dividend Payout %	**65.1**	**59.5**	**51.5**	**45.1**	**37.6**	**38.3**	**36.9**

[1] Before acctg. chg. [2] Before disc. oper.

ANNUAL FINANCIAL DATA

	1/1/94	1/2/93	12/28/91	12/29/90	12/30/89	12/31/88	1/2/88
RECORD OF EARNINGS (IN MILLIONS):							
Total Revenues	2,273.1	2,217.7	1,962.2	1,976.7	1,971.5	1,909.0	1,763.1
Costs and Expenses	1,986.8	1,931.2	1,681.3	1,681.0	1,657.7	1,626.0	1,487.1
Depreciation & Amort	78.5	78.5	74.9	74.3	69.8	64.0	64.8
Operating Profit	720.1	735.8	668.4	684.4	693.2	656.3	620.2
Earn Bef Income Taxes	148.0	158.1	156.5	172.0	193.9	172.5	165.2
Income Taxes	55.4	60.0	61.4	65.4	76.2	69.0	68.9
Net Income	[1] 92.6	98.1	[2] 95.1	106.6	117.7	103.5	[3] 96.3
Aver. Shs. Outstg. (000)	44,935	45,703	43,266	42,192	43,378	43,109	43,357

[1] Before acctg. change dr$8,500,000. [2] Before acctg. change dr$12,500,000. [3] Before disc. op. dr$9,698,000.

	1/1/94	1/2/93	12/28/91	12/29/90	12/30/89	12/31/88	1/2/88
BALANCE SHEET (IN MILLIONS):							
Cash and Cash Equivalents	43.7	81.1	58.3	94.7	55.4	36.6	46.5
Receivables, Net	371.2	354.9	352.6	330.6	360.1	336.6	333.1
Inventories	308.1	302.0	299.6	291.8	313.2	308.0	318.1
Gross Property	1,119.0	1,088.8	1,045.5	979.4	918.8	849.0	768.2
Accumulated Depreciation	552.5	522.2	483.8	441.1	399.2	358.2	319.8
Long-Term Debt	377.2	438.0	396.7	398.1	416.4	339.4	354.1
Net Stockholders' Equity	680.9	696.3	705.5	696.5	674.1	697.9	625.6
Total Assets	1,576.9	1,607.6	1,547.9	1,493.8	1,491.2	1,405.2	1,387.5
Total Current Assets	758.6	778.7	743.9	744.2	759.7	710.5	744.6
Total Current Liabilities	357.1	329.9	308.9	282.4	283.7	266.5	311.7
Net Working Capital	401.5	448.8	435.0	461.8	476.0	443.9	432.8
Year End Shs Outstg (000)	44,696	45,439	45,241	41,176	43,017	42,790	42,872
STATISTICAL RECORD:							
Operating Profit Margin %	9.1	9.4	10.5	11.2	12.4	11.5	12.0
Book Value Per Share	11.40	11.47	12.55	14.38	13.15	14.01	12.16
Return on Equity %	13.6	14.1	13.5	15.3	17.5	14.8	15.4
Return on Assets %	5.9	6.1	6.1	7.1	7.9	7.4	6.9
Average Yield %	3.1	3.2	3.4	3.4	3.1	3.3	2.8
P/E Ratio	23.2-18.4	22.4-15.1	19.0-11.3	15.8-10.4	14.5-10.1	13.2-9.8	16.5-9.6
Price Range	47⅞-37⅞	48⅛-32½	44-26	40-26⅜	39¼-27½	31¾-23⅝	36⅝-21¼

Statistics are as originally reported.

OFFICERS:
R.H. Ayers, Chmn. & C.E.O.
R.A. Hunter, Pres. & C.O.O.
R. Huck, V.P.-Fin. & C.F.O.
S.S. Weddle, V.P., Couns. & Sec.

INCORPORATED: CT, Jul., 1852

PRINCIPAL OFFICE: 1000 Stanley Drive, New Britain, CT 06053

TELEPHONE NUMBER: (203) 225-5111
FAX: (203) 827-3911
NO. OF EMPLOYEES: 9,885 (avg.)
ANNUAL MEETING: In April
SHAREHOLDERS: 9,711
INSTITUTIONAL HOLDINGS:
No. of Institutions: 268
Shares Held: 23,290,062

REGISTRAR(S): Mellon Securities Trust Co., Hartford, CT

TRANSFER AGENT(S): Mellon Securities Trust Co., Hartford, CT

STAR BANC CORP.

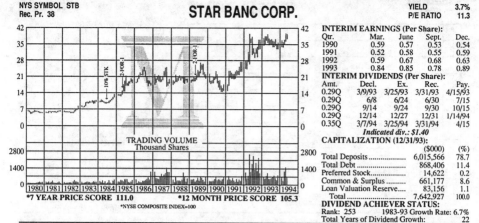

*7 YEAR PRICE SCORE 111.0 ***12 MONTH PRICE SCORE 105.3**
*NYSE COMPOSITE INDEX=100

INTERIM EARNINGS (Per Share):

Qtr.	Mar.	June	Sept.	Dec.
1990	0.59	0.57	0.53	0.54
1991	0.52	0.58	0.55	0.59
1992	0.59	0.67	0.68	0.63
1993	0.84	0.85	0.78	0.89

INTERIM DIVIDENDS (Per Share):

Amt.	Decl.	Ex.	Rec.	Pay.
0.29Q	3/9/93	3/25/93	3/31/93	4/15/93
0.29Q	6/8	6/24	6/30	7/15
0.29Q	9/14	9/24	9/30	10/15
0.29Q	12/14	12/27	12/31	1/14/94
0.35Q	3/7/94	3/25/94	3/31/94	4/15

Indicated div.: $1.40

CAPITALIZATION (12/31/93):

	($000)	(%)
Total Deposits	6,015,566	78.7
Total Debt	868,406	11.4
Preferred Stock	14,622	0.2
Common & Surplus	661,177	8.6
Loan Valuation Reserve	83,156	1.1
Total	7,642,927	100.0

DIVIDEND ACHIEVER STATUS:
Rank: 253   1983-93 Growth Rate: 6.7%
Total Years of Dividend Growth: 22

RECENT DEVELOPMENTS: For the year ended 12/31/93, net income rose 31.7% to $100.3 million from $76.1 million in 1992. The return on average assets was 1.33%, up from 1.06% in 1992. Net interest income increased 4.9% due to an increase in interest-earning assets, which resulted from increased loan volume and a full year's effect of the Ameritrust branch purchase. Noninterest income continued to improve and now represents 25.7% of STB's tax-equivalent net revenues in 1993, compared to 24.2% in 1992. Growth in noninterest income was led by trust income, services charges on deposits and fees from other banking services. In 1993, STB lowered its loan loss provision by 19.3% to reflect a 21.1% reduction in the level of net charge-offs and a 23.6% reduction in nonaccrual loans and other real estate owned.

BUSINESS

STAR BANC CORPORATION is a multi-bank holding company. Headquartered in Cincinnati, the Company is the parent of 9 Star Bank subsidiaries which currently operate 199 banking offices in Ohio, Kentucky and Indiana. Of the 9 bank subsidiaries, seven banks, including Star Bank, N.A., are national banks and two are state-chartered non-member institutions. Through its banking subsidiaries, the Company is engaged in general commercial banking and trust business. The Miami Valley Insurance Company, a wholly-owned subsidiary, is engaged solely in the business of issuing credit life and accident and health insurance in connection with the lending activities of the Company's Ohio bank subsidiaries. First National Cincinnati Corporation, a wholly-owned subsidiary, holds a 75.5% ownership in the Company's headquarters building. The Company owns the remaining 24.5% interest in the building.

ANNUAL EARNINGS AND DIVIDENDS PER SHARE

	1993	1992	1991	1990	1989	1988	1987
Earnings Per Share	3.36	2.57	2.24	2.23	2.01	1.92	1.86
Dividends Per Share	1.13	1.03	0.99	0.94	[1] 0.865	0.81	0.77
Dividend Payout %	33.6	40.1	44.2	42.2	43.0	42.2	41.4

[1] 2-for-1 stk split, 4/14/89

ANNUAL FINANCIAL DATA

RECORD OF EARNINGS (IN MILLIONS):

Total Interest Income	518.2	541.4	576.8	586.8	563.9	467.1	350.5
Total Interest Expense	194.7	233.0	307.3	340.2	336.3	261.5	194.4
Net Interest Income	323.5	308.4	269.4	246.6	227.6	205.6	156.2
Provision for Loan Losses	33.0	40.9	39.9	40.4	35.4	25.9	21.8
Net Income	100.3	76.1	65.8	64.9	58.0	58.5	45.8
Aver. Shs. Outstg. (000)	29,549	29,227	29,064	29,064	28,885	28,884	24,596

BALANCE SHEET (IN MILLIONS):

Cash & Due From Banks	387.8	434.8	326.9	395.3	399.4	326.9	304.2
U.S. Treasury & Agencies	...	...	...	716.2	705.4	747.8	544.0
States & Political Subdivis Obligs	...	...	...	83.4	91.7	90.9	94.5
Net Loans	5,211.3	4,914.1	4,784.6	4,493.8	4,210.3	3,834.2	3,011.1
Total Domestic Deposits	6.015.6	6,402.8	5,428.5	5,129.8	4,973.1	4,723.1	3,664.5
Long-term Debt	51.7	56.8	62.9	31.9	35.4	36.9	34.5
Net Stockholders' Equity	675.8	602.3	555.0	500.0	462.5	429.6	348.7
Total Assets	7,636.8	7,715.4	6,645.9	6,295.4	5,949.4	5,656.6	4,533.5
Year End Shs Outstg (000)	29,607	29,217	28,903	28,888	28,715	28,736	24,462

STATISTICAL RECORD:

Return on Assets %	1.31	0.99	0.99	1.03	0.97	0.98	0.92
Return on Equity %	14.80	12.60	11.90	13.00	12.50	12.90	11.90
Book Value Per Share	22.33	20.09	18.58	17.31	16.11	14.95	14.26
Average Yield %	3.1	3.2	4.7	5.0	3.8	4.1	3.7
P/E Ratio	11.7-9.8	15.4-9.4	12.3-6.7	10.5-6.5	13.4-9.2	11.3-9.1	14.8-9.9
Price Range	39⅜-33	39½-24¼	27½-15	23⅜-14½	27-18½	21¾-17½	25-16¼

Statistics are as originally reported.

OFFICERS:
J.A. Grundhofer, Chmn., Pres. & C.E.O.
D.M. Moffett, Exec. V.P. & C.F.O.
F.K. Koepcke, V.P., Gen. Couns. & Sec.

INCORPORATED: DE, Sep., 1973; reincorp., OH, 1988

PRINCIPAL OFFICE: Star Bank Center 425 Walnut St., Cincinnati, OH 45202

TELEPHONE NUMBER: (513) 632-4008
FAX: (513) 632-5512
NO. OF EMPLOYEES: 3,540
ANNUAL MEETING: In April
SHAREHOLDERS: 7,901 com.; 98 pfd.
INSTITUTIONAL HOLDINGS:
No. of Institutions: 111
Shares Held: 11,125,251

REGISTRAR(S):

TRANSFER AGENT(S): At Company's Office

STATE STREET BOSTON CORP.

YIELD 1.5%
P/E RATIO 15.6

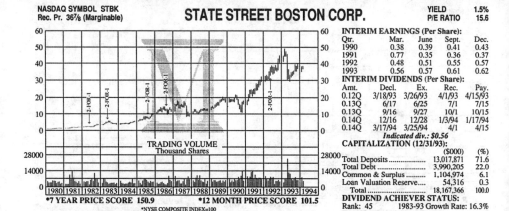

INTERIM EARNINGS (Per Share):

Qtr.	Mar.	June	Sept.	Dec.
1990	0.38	0.39	0.41	0.43
1991	0.77	0.35	0.36	0.37
1992	0.48	0.51	0.55	0.57
1993	0.56	0.57	0.61	0.62

INTERIM DIVIDENDS (Per Share):

Amt.	Decl.	Ex.	Rec.	Pay.
0.12Q	3/18/93	3/26/93	4/1/93	4/15/93
0.13Q	6/17	6/25	7/1	7/15
0.13Q	9/16	9/27	10/1	10/15
0.14Q	12/16	12/28	1/3/94	1/17/94
0.14Q	3/17/94	3/25/94	4/1	4/15

Indicated div.: $0.56

CAPITALIZATION (12/31/93):

	($000)	(%)
Total Deposits	13,017,871	71.6
Total Debt	3,990,205	22.0
Common & Surplus	1,104,974	6.1
Loan Valuation Reserve	54,316	0.3
Total	18,167,366	100.0

DIVIDEND ACHIEVER STATUS:
Rank: 45   1983-93 Growth Rate: 16.3%
Total Years of Dividend Growth: 13

RECENT DEVELOPMENTS: For the year ended 12/31/93, net income was $179.8 million, or $2.36 per share, compared with $160.4 million, or $2.10 per share, in 1992. Total revenue grew $173.4 million to $1.2 billion, driven primarily by a $130.5 million, or 19%, increase in fee revenue. For the quarter, net income was $47.7 million, up from $43.6 million a year ago. Total revenue increased 18% to $302.7 million from $256.1 million in fourth quarter 1992. Growth occurred across the product line and around the world, with the largest

increase in dollars of revenue from mutual fund services and institutional money management. Revenue growth was partially offset by increased operating expenses to support growth and the higher level of investment spending. At 12/31/93, STBK's total risk-based capital ratio was 12.7%, which compares to a regulatory requirement of 8.0%. Total assets were $18.7 million. Loans were $2.7 billion, 14% of total assets.

BUSINESS

STATE STREET BOSTON CORP. is a bank holding company that carries on its business principally through its subsidiary, State Street Bank and Trust Company. The Company is a leading servicer of financial assets worldwide. State Street is the leading U.S. mutual fund custodian and the largest U.S. master trust/master custody bank. The Company is the leader in global custody for U.S. pension plans and the largest global custodian in Australia. State Street is the third largest money management firm in the U.S. and the largest international index firm in the world. The Company also provides a full range of commercial banking and capital markets services, as well as corporate trust, corporate stock transfer, defined contribution plan, planned gift management and personal trust services. Services are provided from offices in the United States, Canada, Grand Cayman, Netherlands Antilles, United Kingdom, France, Belgium, Luxembourg, Germany, United Arab Emirates, Hong Kong, Taiwan, Japan, Australia and New Zealand.

ANNUAL EARNINGS AND DIVIDENDS PER SHARE

	1993	1992	1991	1990	1989	1988	1987
Earnings Per Share	2.36	2.10	1.86	1.59	1.42	1.26	1.12
Dividends Per Share	0.50	① 0.43	0.37	0.33	0.29	0.25	0.21
Dividend Payout %	21.2	20.5	19.9	20.8	20.4	19.9	18.8

① 2-for-1 stk split, 5/14/92

ANNUAL FINANCIAL DATA

RECORD OF EARNINGS (IN MILLIONS):

	1993	1992	1991	1990	1989	1988	1987
Total Interest Revenue	698.9	714.4	737.8	817.5	648.3	499.3	427.9
Total Interest Expense	381.3	432.1	464.2	546.7	431.3	299.7	230.6
Net Interest Income	317.6	282.3	273.6	270.8	217.0	199.6	197.3
Provision for Loan Losses	11.3	12.2	60.0	45.7	19.4	15.6	22.6
Net Income	179.8	160.4	139.3	117.3	104.0	92.3	83.1
Aver. Shs. Outstg. (000)	76,193	76,225	74,969	73,888	73,314	73,686	74,526

BALANCE SHEET (IN MILLIONS):

	1993	1992	1991	1990	1989	1988	1987
Cash & Due From Banks	1,469.4	1,284.5	1,016.8	1,403.1	1,225.1	781.0	574.4
Net Loans	2,625.9	1,945.8	1,839.4	2,054.1	2,414.7	2,128.8	2,096.5
Total Domestic Deposits	7,590.6	6,642.5	6,074.3	5,241.1	4,692.9	4,259.4	3,824.6
Total Foreign Deposits	5,427.2	4,417.6	2,657.1	2,416.6	1,485.2	1,129.0	713.3
Long-term Debt	128.9	145.8	147.0	112.4	114.6	123.2	125.4
Net Stockholders' Equity	1,105.0	953.1	816.6	695.1	597.2	505.6	471.4
Total Assets	18,720.1	16,489.8	15,046.3	11,650.9	9,983.0	8,372.0	6,955.2
Year End Shs Outstg (000)	75,874	75,061	74,440	73,098	72,054	70,048	73,052

STATISTICAL RECORD:

	1993	1992	1991	1990	1989	1988	1987
Return on Assets %	0.96	0.97	0.93	1.01	1.04	1.10	1.20
Return on Equity %	16.30	16.80	17.10	16.90	17.40	18.30	17.60
Book Value Per Share	14.56	12.70	10.97	9.51	8.29	7.22	6.45
Average Yield %	1.3	1.2	1.6	2.0	1.7	2.1	1.6
P/E Ratio	20.8-12.4	21.4-13.9	17.3-8.3	13.6-6.9	14.4-9.0	11.0-7.8	16.2-7.4
Price Range	49⅛-29¼	44⅞-29¼	32⅛-15½	21⅝-11	20½-12¾	13¾-9¾	18⅛-8¼

Statistics are as originally reported.

OFFICERS:
M.N. Carter, Chmn. & C.E.O.
D.A. Spina, Vice-Chmn.
G.J. Fesus, Exec. V.P., C.F.O. & Treas.

INCORPORATED: MA, Oct., 1969

PRINCIPAL OFFICE: 225 Franklin Street, Boston, MA 02110

TELEPHONE NUMBER: (617) 786-3000

NO. OF EMPLOYEES: 10,117

ANNUAL MEETING: In April

SHAREHOLDERS: 5,926

INSTITUTIONAL HOLDINGS:
No. of Institutions: 327
Shares Held: 53,057,747

REGISTRAR(S):

TRANSFER AGENT(S): State Street Bank & Trust Co., Boston, MA 02266

ASE SYMBOL SCL
Rec. Pr. 27 7/8

STEPAN CO.

YIELD 3.0%
P/E RATIO 15.3

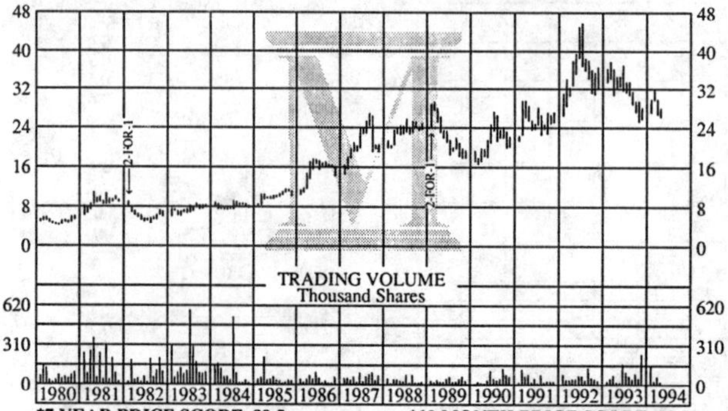

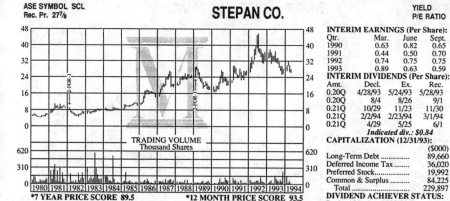

***7 YEAR PRICE SCORE 89.5** ***12 MONTH PRICE SCORE 93.5**

*NYSE COMPOSITE INDEX=100

INTERIM EARNINGS (Per Share):

Qtr.	Mar.	June	Sept.	Dec.
1990	0.63	0.82	0.65	0.53
1991	0.44	0.50	0.70	0.67
1992	0.74	0.75	0.75	d0.29
1993	0.89	0.63	0.59	d0.15

INTERIM DIVIDENDS (Per Share):

Amt.	Decl.	Ex.	Rec.	Pay.
0.20Q	4/28/93	5/24/93	5/28/93	6/15/93
0.20Q	8/4	8/26	9/1	9/15
0.21Q	10/29	11/23	11/30	12/15
0.21Q	2/2/94	2/23/94	3/1/94	3/15/94
0.21Q	4/29	5/25	6/1	6/15

Indicated div.: $0.84

CAPITALIZATION (12/31/93):

	($000)	(%)
Long-Term Debt	89,660	39.0
Deferred Income Tax	36,020	15.7
Preferred Stock	19,992	8.7
Common & Surplus	84,225	36.6
Total	229,897	100.0

DIVIDEND ACHIEVER STATUS:
Rank: 154 1983-93 Growth Rate: 10.8%
Total Years of Dividend Growth: 27

RECENT DEVELOPMENTS: For the year ended 12/31/93, net sales increased slightly to $438.8 million from $435.8 million in 1992. Operating income, pre-tax income before net interest expense, was $27.3 million in 1993, a 13.8% increase from 1992. Net income for the year was $10.8 million, or $1.96 per share, compared with income, before cumulative effect of accounting changes, of $10.4 million, or $1.91 per share, a year ago. For the quarter ended 12/31/93, net sales declined slightly to $102.5 million from $104.6 million for the same period in 1992. SCL incurred a net loss for the quarter of $449,000, or $0.15 per share, compared with a net loss of $1.2 million, or $0.29 per share, for the year-ago quarter.

BUSINESS

STEPAN COMPANY is a major manufacturer of basic and intermediate chemicals used in a broad range of industries. The Company is a leading merchant producer of surfactants, which are the key ingredient in consumer and industrial cleaning compounds. Stepan produces other specialty products which are often custom-made to meet individual needs. These include emulsifiers which facilitate spreading of insecticides and herbicides, and lubricant and cutting-oil ingredients. The Company is also a principal supplier of phthalic anhydride, a commodity chemical intermediate which is used in polyester resins, alkyd resins and plasticizers. Polyurethane foam systems sold by the Company are used in the expanding thermal insulation market primarily by the construction and refrigeration industries.

BUSINESS LINE ANALYSIS

(12/31/93)	Rev(%)	Inc(%)
United States	84.0	81.2
Other	16.0	18.8
Total	100.0	100.0

ANNUAL EARNINGS AND DIVIDENDS PER SHARE

	1993	1992	1991	1990	1989	1988	1987
Earnings Per Share	**1.96**	**[1] 1.91**	**2.30**	**2.64**	**1.42**	**2.39**	**1.83**
Dividends Per Share	**0.81**	**0.74**	**0.66**	**0.58**	**0.53**	**[2] 0.475**	**0.415**
Dividend Payout %	**41.3**	**38.7**	**28.7**	**22.0**	**37.3**	**19.9**	**22.7**

[1] Before acctg. chg. [2] 2-for-1 stk split, 12/88

ANNUAL FINANCIAL DATA

	1993	1992	1991	1990	1989	1988	1987
RECORD OF EARNINGS (IN THOUSANDS):							
Total Revenues	438,825	435,764	414,069	389,612	346,350	333,033	288,935
Costs and Expenses	383,896	381,341	367,611	342,976	311,620	292,575	251,919
Depreciation & Amort	27,679	23,914	21,108	19,391	17,061	15,393	13,815
Operating Profit	44,919	45,643	40,681	40,670	30,520	38,121	34,491
Income Bef Income Taxes	19,624	17,365	18,866	22,294	11,701	20,554	19,230
Income Taxes	8,848	6,942	6,319	7,803	3,861	7,126	8,271
Net Income	10,776	[1] 10,423	12,547	14,491	7,840	13,428	10,959
Aver. Shs. Outstg.	4,947	5,286	5,458	5,496	5,517	5,608	5,976
[1] Before acctg. change cr$5,406,000.							
BALANCE SHEET (IN THOUSANDS):							
Cash and Cash Equivalents	1,515	2,915	2,275	1,631	1,607	929	1,714
Receivables, Net	57,250	57,030	55,118	51,772	48,479	43,286	38,590
Inventories	48,918	47,778	43,955	39,894	29,724	26,278	22,897
Gross Property	377,439	353,999	322,260	288,764	251,526	218,372	200,210
Accumulated Depreciation	208,558	186,069	165,197	145,422	129,017	113,675	101,216
Long-Term Debt	89,660	90,505	89,759	77,326	68,568	45,369	44,399
Net Stockholders' Equity	104,217	99,506	90,866	82,698	70,741	66,790	59,936
Total Assets	300,488	297,080	271,442	246,992	215,351	185,601	172,726
Total Current Assets	119,160	118,625	104,005	95,976	83,091	72,743	66,463
Total Current Liabilities	70,591	74,360	62,033	57,033	46,139	44,245	39,826
Net Working Capital	48,569	44,265	41,972	38,943	36,952	28,498	26,637
Year End Shares Outstg	4,948	4,936	5,438	5,464	5,483	5,504	5,626
STATISTICAL RECORD:							
Operating Profit Margin %	6.2	7.0	6.1	7.0	5.1	7.5	8.0
Book Value Per Share	17.02	16.11	16.71	15.14	12.90	12.13	10.65
Return on Equity %	10.3	10.5	13.8	17.5	11.1	20.1	18.3
Return on Assets %	3.6	3.5	4.6	5.9	3.6	7.2	6.3
Average Yield %	2.6	2.1	2.6	2.6	2.2	2.1	2.0
P/E Ratio	19.3-12.8	24.0-13.7	12.9-9.2	10.3-6.3	20.8-12.5	10.7-8.3	14.6-7.9
Price Range	37 7/8-25 1/8	45 3/4-26 1/4	29 3/4-21 1/4	27 1/4-16 5/8	29 1/2-17 3/4	25 5/8-19 3/4	26 3/4-14 1/2

Statistics are as originally reported.

OFFICERS:
F.Q. Stepan, Chmn., Pres. & C.E.O.
J.W. Bartlett, V.P., Gen. Couns. & Sec.
W.J. Klein, V.P.-Fin.

INCORPORATED: IL, Jan., 1940; reincorp., DE, 1959

PRINCIPAL OFFICE: Edens & Winnetka Rds., Northfield, IL 60093

TELEPHONE NUMBER: (708) 446-7500

FAX: (708) 501-2443

NO. OF EMPLOYEES: 1,302

ANNUAL MEETING: In April

SHAREHOLDERS: 1,230

INSTITUTIONAL HOLDINGS:
No. of Institutions: 29
Shares Held: 899,760

REGISTRAR(S): First Chicago Trust Co. of New York, New York, NY 10008

TRANSFER AGENT(S): First Chicago Trust Co. of New York, New York, NY 10008

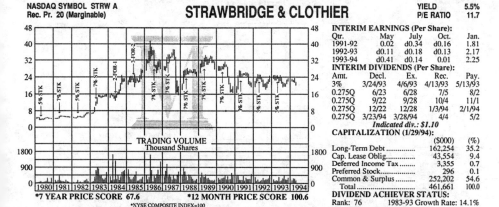

STRAWBRIDGE & CLOTHIER

NASDAQ SYMBOL STRW A
Rec. Pr. 20 (Marginable)

YIELD 5.5%
P/E RATIO 11.7

INTERIM EARNINGS (Per Share):

Qtr.	May	July	Oct.	Jan.
1991-92	0.02	d0.34	d0.16	1.81
1992-93	d0.11	d0.18	d0.13	2.17
1993-94	d0.41	d0.14	0.01	2.25

INTERIM DIVIDENDS (Per Share):

Amt.	Decl.	Ex.	Rec.	Pay.
3%	3/24/93	4/6/93	4/13/93	5/13/93
0.275Q	6/23	6/28	7/5	8/2
0.275Q	9/22	9/28	10/4	11/1
0.275Q	12/22	12/28	1/3/94	2/1/94
0.275Q	3/23/94	3/28/94	4/4	5/2

Indicated div.: $1.10

CAPITALIZATION (1/29/94):

	($000)	(%)
Long-Term Debt	162,254	35.2
Cap. Lease Oblig.	43,554	9.4
Deferred Income Tax	3,355	0.7
Preferred Stock	296	0.1
Common & Surplus	252,202	54.6
Total	461,661	100.0

DIVIDEND ACHIEVER STATUS:
Rank: 76   1983-93 Growth Rate: 14.1%
Total Years of Dividend Growth: 10

*7 YEAR PRICE SCORE 67.6   *12 MONTH PRICE SCORE 100.6
*NYSE COMPOSITE INDEX=100

RECENT DEVELOPMENTS: For the year ended 1/29/94, net income slid 2% to $17.7 million compared with income before accounting changes of $18.0 million for the previous fiscal year. Sales rose 2% to $984.6 million from last year's levels. For the quarter, earnings increased by 5% to $23.3 million, while sales rose 2% to $338.8 million compared with the same period in the prior year. The Company was encouraged by strong sales during the Christmas season, but sales for the full quarter were negatively affected by severe weather conditions during most of January. The increase in quarterly earnings resulted from the improvement in sales and continued expense control. During the last six months of 1993, the Company completed the renovation of several stores which significantly enhanced sales volume. For the quarter ended 10/30/93, net sales increased 3.7% to $223.6 million from $215.7 million last year.

BUSINESS

STRAWBRIDGE & CLOTHIER operates 38 retail stores, including 13 department and 25 self-service Clover stores, which sell general merchandise in Philadelphia and the surrounding Delaware Valley area of Southeastern Pennsylvania, Southern New Jersey, and Northern Delaware. The Company grants credit to customers, substantially all of whom are residents of its trading area.

QUARTERLY DATA

(1/29/94)($000)	Rev	Inc
1st Quarter	197,151	(4,255)
2nd Quarter	225,018	(1,425)
3rd Quarter	223,639	69
4th Quarter	338,807	23,338

ANNUAL EARNINGS AND DIVIDENDS PER SHARE

	1/29/94	1/30/93	2/1/92	2/2/91	2/3/90	1/28/89	1/30/88
Earnings Per Share	1.71	①1.76	1.34	1.72	3.12	2.76	2.75
Dividends Per Share	1.084	②1.084	1.022	0.974	③0.91	④0.818	⑤0.673
Dividend Payout %	63.4	61.6	76.3	56.6	29.2	29.7	24.4

① Before acctg. chg. ② 3% stk div, 4/8/92 ③ 7% stk div, 5/11/89 ④ 7% stk div, 5/12/88 ⑤ 7% stk div, 5/87

ANNUAL FINANCIAL DATA

RECORD OF EARNINGS (IN THOUSANDS):

Gross Operating Revenues	987,027	968,855	968,628	982,403	950,960	904,787	815,165
Costs and Expenses	905,736	885,260	888,824	895,291	844,887	810,589	722,808
Depreciation	28,829	28,322	28,710	27,910	24,565	22,112	18,812
Operating Profit	52,462	55,273	51,094	59,202	81,508	72,294	73,545
Earn Bef Income Taxes	26,829	27,189	20,714	28,606	51,726	45,026	48,739
Income Taxes	9,102	9,169	7,146	11,385	20,567	17,756	21,725
Net Income	17,727	①18,020	13,568	17,221	31,159	27,270	27,014
Aver. Shs. Outstg.	10,324	10,216	10,099	9,988	9,965	9,836	9,780

① Before acctg. change dr$16,850,000.

BALANCE SHEET (IN THOUSANDS):

Cash & Equivalents	2,860	5,372	2,813	1,318	1,932	3,444	1,883
Receivables, Net	202,830	184,059	173,208	162,647	159,822	165,093	153,278
Inventories	143,132	144,961	133,271	138,832	139,149	130,434	115,022
Gross Property	588,949	569,582	547,539	532,239	485,380	442,584	387,340
Accumulated Depreciation	288,581	262,424	234,663	210,180	184,152	163,247	153,832
Long-Term Debt	162,254	171,617	156,237	158,880	167,188	154,267	128,685
Capital Lease Obligations	43,554	52,030	55,481	59,370	59,179	63,773	63,351
Net Stockholders' Equity	252,498	243,313	251,203	244,967	235,799	211,960	191,434
Total Assets	663,052	653,939	631,987	645,603	618,546	593,278	518,289
Total Current Assets	356,201	342,464	314,309	312,270	307,535	305,429	276,902
Total Current Liabilities	146,620	129,950	129,668	140,766	119,124	126,523	90,874
Net Working Capital	209,581	212,514	184,641	171,504	188,411	178,906	186,028
Year End Shares Outstg	10,386	9,958	10,256	9,618	9,171	9,100	9,746

STATISTICAL RECORD:

Operating Profit Margin %	5.3	5.7	5.3	6.0	8.6	8.0	9.0
Book Value Per Share	24.28	24.39	24.43	25.39	25.60	23.16	19.50
Return on Equity %	7.0	7.4	5.4	7.1	13.3	12.9	14.2
Return on Assets %	2.7	2.8	2.1	2.7	5.0	4.6	5.2
Average Yield %	4.9	4.8	4.7	4.0	3.0	3.6	2.5
P/E Ratio	14.5-11.3	14.3-10.4	20.1-12.5	18.2-9.7	11.0-8.3	10.2-6.5	13.6-5.6
Price Range	24¾-19¼	25¼-18¼	27-16¾	31⅜-16¾	34⅜-26	28⅛-17⅞	37⅜-15½

Statistics are as originally reported.

OFFICERS:
F.R. Strawbridge, III, Chmn.
P.S. Strawbridge, Pres.
S.L. Strawbridge, V.P., Treas. & Sec.

INCORPORATED: PA, Feb., 1922

PRINCIPAL OFFICE: 801 Market St., Philadelphia, PA 19107-3199

TELEPHONE NUMBER: (215) 629-6000
FAX: (215) 629-7947
NO. OF EMPLOYEES: 695 full time; 2,094, part time
ANNUAL MEETING: In May
SHAREHOLDERS: 3,747 Ser. A; 251 Ser. B;
INSTITUTIONAL HOLDINGS:
No. of Institutions: 58
Shares Held: 3,303,578 (adj.)

REGISTRAR(S):

TRANSFER AGENT(S): Mellon Bank, N.A., Pittsburgh, PA

SUPERVALU INC.

YIELD 2.8%
P/E RATIO 12.5

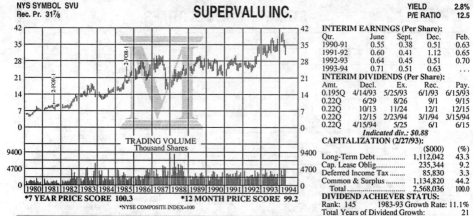

7 YEAR PRICE SCORE 100.3   **12 MONTH PRICE SCORE 99.2**
*NYSE COMPOSITE INDEX=100

INTERIM EARNINGS (Per Share):

Qtr.	June	Sept.	Dec.	Feb.
1990-91	0.55	0.38	0.51	0.63
1991-92	0.60	0.41	1.12	0.65
1992-93	0.64	0.45	0.51	0.70
1993-94	0.71	0.51	0.63	...

INTERIM DIVIDENDS (Per Share):

Amt.	Decl.	Ex.	Rec.	Pay.
0.195Q	4/14/93	5/25/93	6/1/93	6/15/93
0.22Q	6/29	8/26	9/1	9/15
0.22Q	10/13	11/24	12/1	12/15
0.22Q	12/15	2/23/94	3/1/94	3/15/94
0.22Q	4/15/94	5/25	6/1	6/15

Indicated div.: $0.88

CAPITALIZATION (2/27/93):

	($000)	(%)
Long-Term Debt	1,112,042	43.3
Cap. Lease Oblig.	235,344	9.2
Deferred Income Tax	85,830	3.3
Common & Surplus	1,134,820	44.2
Total	2,568,036	100.0

DIVIDEND ACHIEVER STATUS:
Rank: 145   1983-93 Growth Rate: 11.1%
Total Years of Dividend Growth: 21

RECENT DEVELOPMENTS: For the twelve weeks ended 12/4/93, net income increased 23.2% to $45.2 million compared with $36.7 million a year ago. Sales were up 24% to $3.67 billion from $2.96 billion. Sales in the food distribution segment rose 23% to $3.37 billion from $2.74 billion. The improved food distribution revenues were largely attributable to the acquisition of Wetterau Incorporated. Sales in the retail food segment increased 38% to $851 million from $616 million.

PROSPECTS: A competitive wholesale industry will continue to exert pressure on sales growth. Operations will be enhanced by the recent opening of a second MAX CLUB in Sierra Vista, Arizona. In addition, SUPERVALUE should benefit from an agreement in principle to acquire all the outstanding stock of Suffield, CT-based Sweet Life Foods, Inc. Sweet Life supplies 280 independent food retailers throughout New England and New York.

BUSINESS

SUPERVALU STORES, INC. is the nation's leading distributor to independently owned retail food stores and a major food retailer. The Company services over 4,350 retail food stores through 28 food distribution divisions located in 47 states, principally in the Midwest, Northwest, and Southwest regions of the U.S. SVU's retail support operation includes sales to corporate-owned stores and independent owned food stores and the operations of several allied service operations. The U.S. Retail Food operation, 8%, include company-owned and franchised Cub Food Stores. SVU owns approximately 252 retail food stores under the names of Cub Food, Shop 'n Save, Laneco, and Scott's Foods.

BUSINESS LINE ANALYSIS

(2/27/93)	Rev(%)	Inc(%)
Retail Support	80.9	92.0
Retail Food	19.1	8.0
Total	100.0	100.0

ANNUAL EARNINGS AND DIVIDENDS PER SHARE

	2/27/93	2/29/92	2/23/91	2/24/90	2/25/89	2/27/88	2/28/87
Earnings Per Share	2.31	2.78	2.06	1.97	1.81	1.50	1.20
Dividends Per Share	0.75	0.705	0.63	0.56	0.47	0.43	0.40
Dividend Payout %	32.5	25.4	30.6	28.4	26.0	28.7	33.3

ANNUAL FINANCIAL DATA

RECORD OF EARNINGS (IN MILLIONS):

	2/27/93	2/29/92	2/23/91	2/24/90	2/25/89	2/27/88	2/28/87
Total Revenues	12,568.0	10,632.3	11,612.4	11,136.0	10,296.3	9,371.7	9,065.8
Costs and Expenses	12,137.5	10,279.9	11,161.2	10,716.2	9,911.3	9,027.4	8,754.7
Depreciation & Amort	140.8	111.5	144.9	123.2	110.1	103.3	86.2
Operating Income	289.7	240.9	306.3	296.7	274.9	241.0	224.9
Earn Bef Income Taxes	258.6	322.8	254.1	243.5	224.4	198.3	188.9
Income Taxes	94.1	115.2	99.0	95.7	86.9	86.5	99.6
Net Income	164.5	① 207.7	155.1	147.7	137.5	111.8	89.3
Aver. Shs. Outstg. (000)	71,341	74,700	75,165	75,085	74,972	74,785	74,387

① Before acctg. change dr$13,288,000.

BALANCE SHEET (IN MILLIONS):

	2/27/93	2/29/92	2/23/91	2/24/90	2/25/89	2/27/88	2/28/87
Cash and Cash Equivalents	1.8	1.5	2.7	2.2	2.2	2.2	3.4
Receivables, Net	357.7	379.3	209.5	216.6	238.7	206.9	177.7
Inventories	1,134.1	745.1	745.4	901.4	833.2	779.0	698.4	650.7
Gross Property	2,061.1	1,471.0	1,931.0	1,725.4	1,549.4	1,340.4	1,161.5
Accumulated Depreciation	676.9	591.8	709.5	612.0	513.7	437.3	364.2
Long-Term Debt	1,112.0	396.2	382.4	387.9	399.7	389.5	295.1
Lg tm Obligs Under Cap Lses	235.3	212.1	195.0	173.3	171.5	155.6	134.0
Net Stockholders' Equity	1,134.8	1,031.0	978.7	869.9	778.3	677.4	596.2
Total Assets	4,064.2	2,484.3	2,615.1	2,428.9	2,305.1	2,016.2	1,797.9
Total Current Assets	1,573.6	1,163.3	1,144.1	1,080.9	1,045.2	931.8	854.6
Total Current Liabilities	1,325.8	745.2	997.6	951.1	906.3	757.1	742.2
Net Working Capital	247.8	418.1	146.5	129.9	138.9	174.7	112.4
Year End Shs Outstg (000)	71,655	75,335	75,225	75,085	74,822	74,724	74,548

STATISTICAL RECORD:

	2/27/93	2/29/92	2/23/91	2/24/90	2/25/89	2/27/88	2/28/87
Operating Profit Margin %	2.3	2.3	2.6	2.7	2.7	2.6	2.5
Book Value Per Share	9.75	13.58	13.01	11.59	10.40	9.07	8.00
Return on Equity %	14.5	20.1	15.9	17.0	17.7	16.5	15.0
Return on Assets %	4.0	8.4	5.9	6.1	6.0	5.5	5.0
Average Yield %	2.6	2.7	2.5	2.1	2.2	1.9	1.7
P/E Ratio	15.1-10.1	10.9-7.8	14.1-10.6	15.3-11.5	14.6-9.4	20.3-10.7	23.2-16.5
Price Range	34⅞-23⅜	30¼-21⅝	29-21¾	30⅛-22⅝	26⅜-17	30⅜-16	27⅞-19¾

Statistics are as originally reported.

OFFICERS:
M.W. Wright, Chmn., Pres. & C.E.O.
J.C. Girard, Exec. V.P. & C.F.O.
D.A. Cairns, V.P. & Treas.
T.H. Johnson, Sec.
INCORPORATED: DE, Dec., 1925
PRINCIPAL OFFICE: 11840 Valley View Road, Eden Prairie, MN 55344

TELEPHONE NUMBER: (612) 828-4000
FAX: (612) 828-8998
NO. OF EMPLOYEES: 42,000 (approx.)
ANNUAL MEETING: In June
SHAREHOLDERS: 8,427 (approx.)
INSTITUTIONAL HOLDINGS:
No. of Institutions: 315
Shares Held: 49,584,464

REGISTRAR(S):

TRANSFER AGENT(S):

SUPERIOR SURGICAL MANUFACTURING CO., INC.

YIELD 2.5%
P/E RATIO 14.5

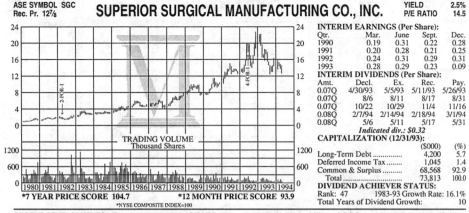

*7 YEAR PRICE SCORE 104.7   *12 MONTH PRICE SCORE 93.9
*NYSE COMPOSITE INDEX=100

TRADING VOLUME
Thousand Shares

INTERIM EARNINGS (Per Share):

Qtr.	Mar.	June	Sept.	Dec.
1990	0.19	0.31	0.22	0.28
1991	0.20	0.28	0.21	0.25
1992	0.24	0.31	0.29	0.31
1993	0.28	0.29	0.23	0.09

INTERIM DIVIDENDS (Per Share):

Amt.	Decl.	Ex.	Rec.	Pay.
0.07Q	4/30/93	5/5/93	5/11/93	5/26/93
0.07Q	8/6	8/11	8/17	8/31
0.07Q	10/22	10/29	11/4	11/16
0.08Q	2/7/94	2/14/94	2/18/94	3/1/94
0.08Q	5/6	5/11	5/17	5/31

Indicated div.: $0.32

CAPITALIZATION (12/31/93):

	($000)	(%)
Long-Term Debt	4,200	5.7
Deferred Income Tax	1,045	1.4
Common & Surplus	68,568	92.9
Total	73,813	100.0

DIVIDEND ACHIEVER STATUS:
Rank: 47   1983-93 Growth Rate: 16.1%
Total Years of Dividend Growth: 10

RECENT DEVELOPMENTS: For the year ended 12/31/93, net sales increased 1% to $130.1 million from $128.7 million in 1992, due to the continuation of new uniform programs and the targeting of new customers from non-healthcare marketplaces, but offset by the uncertainty and generally sluggish healthcare marketplace. Cost of goods as a percent of sales increased to 67.1% from 66.3% in 1992, due to increased costs and the inability of SGC to raise sales prices. Selling and administrative expenses increased 3% to $27.8 million from $27.0 million in 1992. The increase was attributable to normal cost pressures. Interest expense as a percentage of sales was 0.5% compared with 0.4% in 1992. Net income was $7.7 million, or 5.9% of sales compared with $9.9 million, or 7.7% of sales, last year.

BUSINESS

SUPERIOR SURGICAL MANUFACTURING COMPANY, INC. mnufactures and sells a wide range of uniforms, career apparel and accessories for the hospital and healthcare fields; hotels; fast food and other restaurants; and public safety, industrial, transportation and commercial markets.

QUARTERLY DATA

(12/31/93)($000)	Rev	Inc
1st Quarter..............	31,578	2,465
2nd Quarter..............	33,752	2,507
3rd Quarter..............	32,382	1,993
4th Quarter..............	32,414	739

ANNUAL EARNINGS AND DIVIDENDS PER SHARE

	1993	1992	1991	1990	1989	1988	1987
Earnings Per Share	0.89	1.15	0.94	1.00	0.79	0.72	0.50
Dividends Per Share	0.28	☐0.25	0.22	0.18	0.15	0.125	0.11
Dividend Payout %	31.5	21.7	23.2	18.0	19.0	17.4	22.0

☐ 4-for-1 stk split, 6/23/92

ANNUAL FINANCIAL DATA

RECORD OF EARNINGS (IN THOUSANDS):

	1993	1992	1991	1990	1989	1988	1987
Total Revenues	130,127	128,666	117,503	123,002	113,754	112,389	103,755
Costs and Expenses	114,862	110,046	101,736	106,272	99,687	98,832	93,252
Depreciation & Amort	2,504	2,169	2,103	1,900	1,650	1,657	1,309
Operating Income	12,761	16,451	13,664	14,830	12,417	11,900	9,194
Earn Bef Taxes on Income	12,119	15,864	12,840	13,755	11,360	11,190	8,560
Taxes on Income	4,415	5,950	4,815	5,090	4,200	4,140	3,640
Net Income	7,704	9,914	8,025	8,665	7,160	7,050	4,920
Aver. Shs. Outstg.	8,693	8,648	8,500	8,644	9,072	9,807	9,849
BALANCE SHEET (IN THOUSANDS):							
Cash and Cash Equivalents	3,030	2,624	6,360	892	396	708	487
Accounts Receivable, Net	20,850	20,317	18,239	19,295	18,501	18,560	16,046
Inventories	39,633	38,860	33,914	33,861	32,488	30,617	28,988
Gross Property	38,497	32,424	28,000	26,557	26,243	23,590	21,220
Accumulated Depreciation	17,625	15,780	14,496	13,478	12,603	11,100	9,702
Long-Term Debt	4,200	4,955	7,110	8,946	9,416	10,382	4,124
Net Stockholders' Equity	68,568	63,082	54,659	47,686	44,327	40,319	40,643
Total Assets	87,168	80,585	74,471	69,193	66,968	64,498	58,851
Total Current Assets	64,201	62,231	59,250	54,504	51,779	50,451	45,874
Total Current Liabilities	11,105	10,878	11,376	11,262	11,825	12,397	12,484
Net Working Capital	53,097	51,353	47,874	43,242	39,953	38,054	33,390
Year End Shares Outstg	8,703	8,678	8,579	8,450	8,847	9,068	9,859
STATISTICAL RECORD:							
Operating Profit Margin %	9.8	12.8	11.6	12.1	10.9	10.6	8.9
Book Value Per Share	7.78	7.17	6.27	5.54	4.91	4.35	4.03
Return on Equity %	11.2	15.7	14.7	18.2	16.2	17.5	12.1
Return on Assets %	8.8	12.3	10.8	12.5	10.7	10.9	8.4
Average Yield %	1.6	1.4	1.7	1.9	1.7	2.0	2.1
P/E Ratio	25.0-13.9	19.8-11.1	16.1-10.8	11.5-7.4	12.7-9.3	11.1-6.6	12.5-8.0
Price Range	22¼-12⅜	22¾-12¾	15⅛-10⅛	11½-7⅜	10-7⅜	8-4¾	6¼-4

Statistics are as originally reported.

OFFICERS:
G.M. Benstock, Chmn. & C.E.O.
A.D. Schwartz, Co-Pres.
M. Benstock, Co-Pres.
J.W. Johansen, Sr. V.P., C.F.O., Treas. & Sec.

INCORPORATED: NY, 1922

PRINCIPAL OFFICE: 10099 Seminole Blvd.
P.O. Box 4002, Seminole, FL 34642-0002

TELEPHONE NUMBER: (813) 397-9611

FAX: (813) 391-5401

NO. OF EMPLOYEES: 272

ANNUAL MEETING: In May

SHAREHOLDERS: 460

INSTITUTIONAL HOLDINGS:
No. of Institutions: 29
Shares Held: 1,084,485

REGISTRAR(S): Chemical Bank, New York, NY

TRANSFER AGENT(S): Chemical Bank, New York, NY

NYS SYMBOL SYN
Rec. Pr. 23

SYNTEX CORP.

YIELD 4.5%
P/E RATIO 12.9

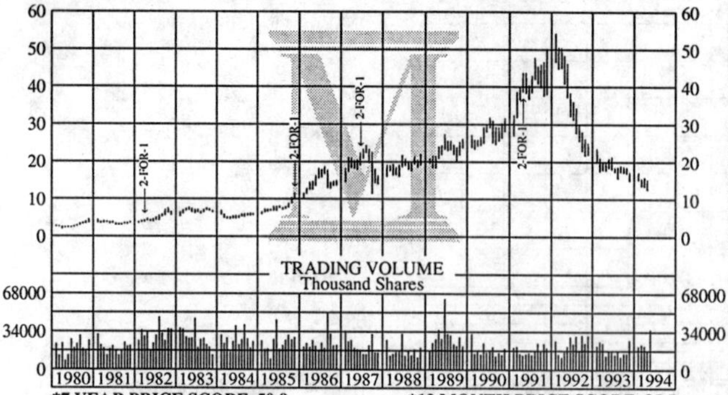

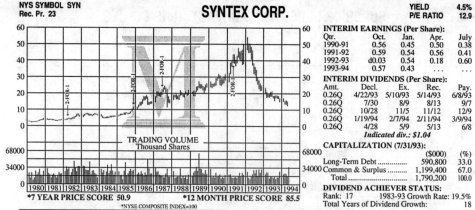

***7 YEAR PRICE SCORE 50.9** ***12 MONTH PRICE SCORE 85.5**

*NYSE COMPOSITE INDEX=100

INTERIM EARNINGS (Per Share):

Qtr.	Oct.	Jan.	Apr.	July
1990-91	0.56	0.45	0.50	0.38
1991-92	0.59	0.54	0.56	0.41
1992-93	d0.03	0.54	0.18	0.60
1993-94	0.57	0.43	...	...

INTERIM DIVIDENDS (Per Share):

Amt.	Decl.	Ex.	Rec.	Pay.
0.26Q	4/22/93	5/10/93	5/14/93	6/8/93
0.26Q	7/30	8/9	8/13	9/7
0.26Q	10/28	11/5	11/12	12/9
0.26Q	1/19/94	2/7/94	2/11/94	3/9/94
0.26Q	4/28	5/9	5/13	6/8

Indicated div.: $1.04

CAPITALIZATION (7/31/93):

	($000)	(%)
Long-Term Debt	590,800	33.0
Common & Surplus	1,199,400	67.0
Total	1,790,200	100.0

DIVIDEND ACHIEVER STATUS:
Rank: 17 1983-93 Growth Rate: 19.5%
Total Years of Dividend Growth: 18

RECENT DEVELOPMENTS: For the quarter ended 1/31/94, net income declined 19.6% to $95.8 million compared with $119.1 million a year ago. Sales fell 3.2% to $489.1 million. The decreased earnings were due primarily to the loss in U.S. market share of Naprosyn and Anaprox branded products to lower-priced generic naproxen and naproxen sodium products, including those sold by Syntex's subsidiary Hamilton Pharma, Inc.

PROSPECTS: The expiration of U.S. patents for the Company's leading products, Naprosyn (naproxen) and Anaprox (naproxen sodium) will adversely affect sales and earnings in 1994. Syntex will continue to implement strategies to reduce costs and improve the research and development pipeline. SYN expects to submit a New Drug Application in early 1994 for an oral formulation of Cytovene, prescribed to treat cytomegalovirus infections in patients with suppressed immune systems.

BUSINESS

SYNTEX CORPORATION is involved in the manufacture of human and animal pharmaceutical products and medical diagnostic systems. The pharmaceuticals segment consists of human pharmaceuticals and animal health products. Human pharmaceuticals are primarily ethical pharmaceuticals available to patients upon a prescription by a physician. Animal health products include growth-promoting agents for food-producing animals and nutritional products for the animal feed industry. The diagnostic segment (Syva) consists of systems to measure the levels of therapeutic drugs, abusive substances, naturally occuring substances, and detection of separating transmissible and infectious diseases.

BUSINESS LINE ANALYSIS

(7/31/93)	Rev(%)	Inc(%)
Pharmaceuticals	90.0	95.8
Diagnostics	10.0	4.2
Total	100.0	100.0

ANNUAL EARNINGS AND DIVIDENDS PER SHARE

	7/31/93	7/31/92	7/31/91	7/31/90	7/31/89	7/31/88	7/31/87
Earnings Per Share	**1.29**	**2.10**	**1.89**	**1.53**	**1.34**	**1.26**	**1.04**
Dividends Per Share	**1.04**	**1.01**	**[1] 0.89**	**0.587**	**0.725**	**0.612**	**[2] 0.475**
Dividend Payout %	**80.6**	**48.1**	**47.1**	**38.5**	**54.3**	**48.8**	**45.9**

[1] 2-for-1 stk split, 4/19/91 [2] 100% stk div, 6/87

ANNUAL FINANCIAL DATA

	7/31/93	7/31/92	7/31/91	7/31/90	7/31/89	7/31/88	7/31/87
RECORD OF EARNINGS (IN MILLIONS):							
Total Revenues	2,123.0	2,085.0	1,816.9	1,521.0	1,349.4	1,271.5	1,129.2
Costs and Expenses	1,806.0	1,466.0	1,249.1	1,063.3	959.0	883.9	787.3
Depreciation & Amort	118.7	100.5	80.9	65.8	54.4	50.6	46.3
Operating Income	198.3	518.5	486.9	391.9	336.0	337.0	295.6
Inc Bef Taxes on Income	132.7	542.9	476.2	379.4	336.9	340.9	290.9
Income Taxes	d155.4	70.6	52.4	37.9	33.7	44.3	42.1
Net Income	287.2	472.3	423.8	341.5	303.2	296.6	248.8
Aver. Shs. Outstg. (000)	222,400	225,400	224,700	223,800	227,400	236,800	240,400
BALANCE SHEET (IN MILLIONS):							
Cash and Cash Equivalents	609.6	701.7	722.7	558.1	381.4	490.1	283.9
Receivables, Net	264.2	278.0	212.0	193.0	163.3	166.3	151.8
Inventories	362.1	351.6	257.0	200.0	155.6	139.5	143.5
Gross Property	1,643.5	1,529.9	1,208.8	998.5	866.8	739.5	639.2
Accumulated Depreciation	558.3	496.7	423.8	372.9	321.4	281.8	247.8
Long-Term Debt	590.8	231.2	273.1	225.0	219.6	131.7	129.5
Net Stockholders' Equity	1,199.4	1,283.7	1,004.5	771.7	587.2	753.8	604.8
Total Assets	2,960.7	2,809.1	2,272.8	1,786.5	1,440.2	1,443.7	1,144.6
Total Current Assets	1,389.7	1,465.2	1,293.9	1,036.4	766.4	854.8	619.3
Total Current Liabilities	792.5	1,177.0	874.7	705.3	557.1	558.2	410.3
Net Working Capital	597.2	288.2	419.2	331.1	209.3	296.6	209.0
Year End Shs Outstg (000)	221,000	225,700	225,100	224,500	223,400	236,200	236,600
STATISTICAL RECORD:							
Operating Profit Margin %	9.3	24.9	26.8	25.8	24.9	26.5	26.2
Book Value Per Share	5.43	5.69	4.46	3.44	2.63	3.19	2.55
Return on Equity %	23.9	36.8	42.2	44.3	51.6	39.4	41.2
Return on Assets %	9.7	16.8	18.6	19.1	21.1	20.5	21.7
Average Yield %	4.0	2.6	2.3	2.1	3.2	3.2	2.6
P/E Ratio	26.5-13.6	25.8-11.0	26.6-14.2	20.8-15.3	20.5-13.7	17.7-12.9	23.7-11.2
Price Range	34 1/8-17 1/2	54 1/4-23	50 1/4-26 7/8	31 7/8-23 3/8	27 1/4-18 1/4	22 1/8-16 1/8	24 3/8-11 1/2

Statistics are as originally reported.

OFFICERS:
P.E. Freiman, Chmn. & C.E.O.
J.N. Wilson, Pres. & C.O.O.
R.P. Powers, Sr. V.P. & C.F.O.
C.J. Gillespie, Vice-Pres. & Sec.
A.B. Stevenson, Vice-Pres. & Treas.

PRINCIPAL OFFICE: 3401 Hillview Ave., Palo Alto, CA 94304-1397

TELEPHONE NUMBER: (415) 855-5050

NO. OF EMPLOYEES: 10,300

ANNUAL MEETING:

SHAREHOLDERS: 36,700

INSTITUTIONAL HOLDINGS:
No. of Institutions: Not Available
Shares Held: Not Available

REGISTRAR(S): Chase Manhattan Bank, N.A., New York, NY 10031

TRANSFER AGENT(S): Chase Manhattan Bank, N.A., New York, NY 10031

NYS SYMBOL SYY
Rec. Pr. 25½

SYSCO CORP.

YIELD 1.4%
P/E RATIO 22.4

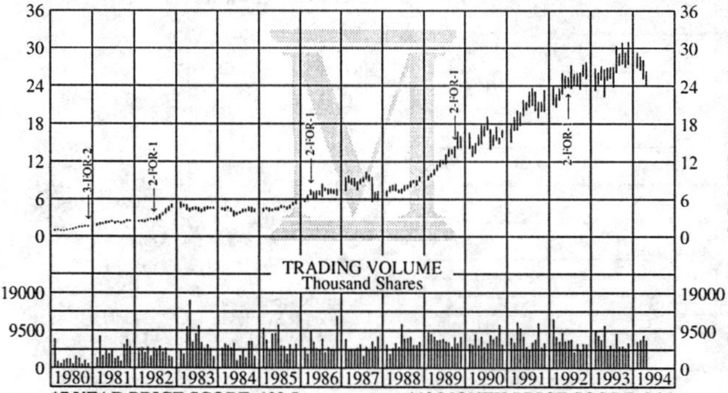
36
30
24
18
12
6
0
3-FOR-2
2-FOR-1
2-FOR-1
2-FOR-1
2-FOR-
TRADING VOLUME
Thousand Shares
19000
9500
0
1980 1981 1982 1983 1984 1985 1986 1987 1988 1989 1990 1991 1992 1993 1994

***7 YEAR PRICE SCORE 122.5** ***12 MONTH PRICE SCORE 96.2**

*NYSE COMPOSITE INDEX=100

INTERIM EARNINGS (Per Share):

Qtr.	Sept.	Dec.	Mar.	June
1990-91	0.21	0.22	0.17	0.24
1991-92	0.23	0.24	0.20	0.27
1992-93	0.24	0.26	0.23	0.35
1993-94	0.26	0.30	...	...

INTERIM DIVIDENDS (Per Share):

Amt.	Decl.	Ex.	Rec.	Pay.
0.07Q	5/12/93	7/26/93	7/30/93	8/13/93
0.07Q	9/3	10/25	10/29	11/12
0.09Q	11/5	1/24/94	1/28/94	2/18/94
0.09Q	2/9/94	4/25	4/29	5/13
0.09Q	5/11	7/25	7/29	8/12

Indicated div.: $0.36

CAPITALIZATION (7/3/93):

	($000)	(%)
Long-Term Debt	494,062	27.7
Deferred Income Tax	152,292	8.5
Common & Surplus	1,137,216	63.8
Total	1,783,570	100.0

DIVIDEND ACHIEVER STATUS:
Rank: 13 1983-93 Growth Rate: 21.5%
Total Years of Dividend Growth: 17

RECENT DEVELOPMENTS: For the quarter ended 1/1/94, net income increased 14.9% to $55.6 million compared with $48.4 million a year ago. Sales were up 11.4% to $2.67 billion. Sales growth excluding acquisitions and inflation was about 6%. The improved earnings reflected efficiency and productivity gains that were the result of significant investments in new fleet and facilities over the past several years. Sysco continued to benefit from growth in away-from-home-dining.

PROSPECTS: Revenue growth will be driven by expansion, acquisitions, and unit volume gains. Earnings will continue to grow as a result of improved operating efficiencies and increased sales. Investments in new facilities and efforts to expand storage capacity are anticipated in the current fiscal year. The Company has entered the market for providing medical supply and dietary products to long-term healthcare customers.

BUSINESS

SYSCO CORP. is the largest marketer and distributor of foodservice products in America. Included among its customers are more than 245,000 restaurants, hotels, hospitals, schools and other institutions. The Company distributes entree items, dry and canned foods, fresh produce, beverages, dairy products and certain nonfood products. Through its SYGMA subsidiary, the Company serves pizza and hamburgers to fast-food chains and other limited menu chain restaurants. In fiscal 1993, the foodservice sales breakdown was: 60% restaurants; 13% hospitals and nursing homes; 7% schools; 6% hotels; 14% other.

QUARTERLY DATA

(07/03/93)($000)	Rev	Inc
1st Quarter	2,415,827	44,859
2nd Quarter	2,392,345	48,354
3rd Quarter	2,399,326	42,779
4th Quarter	2,814,015	65,815

ANNUAL EARNINGS AND DIVIDENDS PER SHARE

	7/3/93	6/27/92	6/29/91	6/30/90	7/1/89	7/2/88	6/27/87
Earnings Per Share	**1.08**	**0.93**	**0.84**	**0.73**	**0.60**	**[2] 0.45**	**0.35**
Dividends Per Share	**0.28**	**[1] 0.22**	**0.14**	**0.10**	**0.093**	**0.08**	**0.07**
Dividend Payout %	**25.9**	**23.7**	**16.7**	**13.8**	**15.5**	**17.8**	**20.0**

[1] 2-for-1 stk split, 6/22/92 [2] 100% stk dividend, payable 10/17/89

ANNUAL FINANCIAL DATA

RECORD OF EARNINGS (IN MILLIONS):							
Total Revenues	10,021.5	8,892.8	8,149.7	7,590.6	6,851.3	4,384.7	3,655.9
Costs and Expenses	9,545.0	8,474.8	7,765.1	7,240.8	6,545.1	4,195.8	3,495.8
Depreciation & Amort	107.7	99.5	92.2	84.4	76.8	45.0	38.4
Operating Income	368.8	318.5	292.4	265.4	229.4	143.9	121.8
Earn Bef Income Taxes	332.0	281.7	250.9	216.1	176.9	129.4	122.3
Income Taxes	130.2	109.4	97.0	83.6	69.0	49.2	60.5
Net Income	201.8	172.2	153.8	132.5	107.9	[1] 80.2	61.8
Aver. Shs. Outstg. (000)	186,746	186,001	184,440	182,674	180,740	179,544	177,164

[1] Before acctg. change cr$6,743,000.

BALANCE SHEET (IN MILLIONS):							
Cash and Cash Equivalents	68.8	74.4	70.2	56.0	55.5	35.6	37.7
Receivables, Net	799.4	660.3	600.6	548.3	518.1	336.7	263.5
Inventories	534.2	491.6	460.3	431.9	436.8	285.4	247.7
Gross Property	1,255.6	1,159.0	1,058.0	939.4	795.4	527.6	434.2
Accumulated Depreciation	495.7	424.6	358.9	303.5	253.4	194.4	164.7
Long-Term Debt	494.1	488.8	543.2	583.5	620.2	93.3	98.5
Net Stockholders' Equity	1,137.2	1,056.8	918.6	770.8	642.7	543.6	456.0
Total Assets	2,530.0	2,301.6	2,160.1	1,992.1	1,869.4	1,020.9	860.3
Total Current Assets	1,419.7	1,240.4	1,143.9	1,047.3	1,021.7	666.6	556.7
Total Current Liabilities	746.5	655.4	611.8	573.7	566.3	356.3	274.8
Net Working Capital	673.3	585.0	532.1	473.7	455.5	310.2	281.9
Year End Shs Outstg (000)	184,457	185,776	185,200	183,508	181,762	180,484	178,828

STATISTICAL RECORD:							
Operating Profit Margin %	3.7	3.6	3.6	3.5	3.3	3.3	3.3
Book Value Per Share	4.72	4.25	3.48	2.73	2.01	3.01	2.55
Return on Equity %	17.7	16.3	16.7	17.2	16.8	14.7	13.6
Return on Assets %	8.0	7.5	7.1	6.6	5.8	7.9	7.2
Average Yield %	1.1	0.9	0.7	0.6	0.7	1.0	0.9
P/E Ratio	28.7-20.6	29.8-22.2	28.6-18.1	26.4-17.6	27.9-15.2	21.7-14.4	29.6-16.1
Price Range	31-22¼	27¾-20⅝	23¾-15	19¼-12⅞	16¾-9⅛	9¾-6½	10⅜-5⅝

Statistics are as originally reported.

OFFICERS:
J.F. Baugh, Sen. Chmn. & Chmn. Exec. Comm.
J.F. Woodhouse, Chmn. & C.E.O.
B.M. Lindig, Pres. & C.O.O.
L.G. Riker, V.P. & Sec.

INCORPORATED: DE, May, 1969

PRINCIPAL OFFICE: 1390 Enclave Parkway, Houston, TX 77077-2099

TELEPHONE NUMBER: (713) 584-1390
FAX: (713) 584-1245
NO. OF EMPLOYEES: 1,744 (approx.)
ANNUAL MEETING: First Friday of November
SHAREHOLDERS: 5,773 (approx.)
INSTITUTIONAL HOLDINGS:
No. of Institutions: 408
Shares Held: 110,853,879

REGISTRAR(S): First National Bank of Boston, Shareholder Services Division, Boston, MA

TRANSFER AGENT(S): First National Bank of Boston, Shareholder Services Division, Boston, MA

TAMBRANDS, INC.

YIELD 4.7%
P/E RATIO 18.9

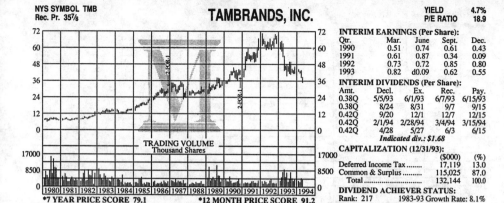

*7 YEAR PRICE SCORE 79.1   *12 MONTH PRICE SCORE 91.2
*NYSE COMPOSITE INDEX=100

TRADING VOLUME
Thousand Shares

INTERIM EARNINGS (Per Share):

Qtr.	Mar.	June	Sept.	Dec.
1990	0.51	0.74	0.61	0.43
1991	0.61	0.87	0.34	0.09
1992	0.73	0.72	0.85	0.80
1993	0.82	d0.09	0.62	0.55

INTERIM DIVIDENDS (Per Share):

Amt.	Decl.	Ex.	Rec.	Pay.
0.38Q	5/5/93	6/1/93	6/7/93	6/15/93
0.38Q	8/24	8/31	9/7	9/15
0.42Q	9/20	12/1	12/7	12/15
0.42Q	2/1/94	2/28/94	3/4/94	3/15/94
0.42Q	4/28	5/27	6/3	6/15

Indicated div.: $1.68

CAPITALIZATION (12/31/93):

	($000)	(%)
Deferred Income Tax	17,119	13.0
Common & Surplus	115,025	87.0
Total	132,144	100.0

DIVIDEND ACHIEVER STATUS:

Rank: 217   1983-93 Growth Rate: 8.1%
Total Years of Dividend Growth: 42

RECENT DEVELOPMENTS: For the year ended 12/31/93, net income before an accounting adjustment fell 39.8% to $73.7 million compared with $122.4 million a year ago. Sales declined 10.6% to $611.5 million from $684.1 million. Results included $20.3 million of restructuring charges and other costs. Sales were adversely affected by the negative impact of a strong U.S. dollar on foreign currency exchange rates. Sales were also affected by lower volumes.

PROSPECTS: International operations will continue to fuel growth along with increased volume levels and market share. Tampax Comfort Shape should lift sales and shipments throughout the U.S. and Europe. An inventory reduction program along with strong market share and continued cost control measures will boost margins. In addition, results will benefit from higher prices as well as staff reductions. The Company has authorized the purchase of up to 2 million shares of its common stock.

BUSINESS

TAMPBRANDS, INC. is a leading manufacturer and marketer of feminine protection products, home diagnostics, cosmetics and other personal care products in various countries around the world. Brand names include Tampax, Maxithins and First Response. It has principal operating subsidiaries in Canada, Mexico, Switzerland, the United Kingdom, Ireland, Russia, Ukraine, South Africa and France, and a joint venture company operating in the People's Republic of China. The sales organization is made up of Tambrands employees, agents, brokers and distributors who create a unique distribution network covering over 150 countries.

BUSINESS LINE ANALYSIS

(12/31/93)	Rev(%)	Inc(%)
United States	59.4	90.6
Europe	29.9	15.3
Other International	10.7	(5.9)
Total	100.0	100.0

ANNUAL EARNINGS AND DIVIDENDS PER SHARE

	1993	1992	1991	1990	1989	1988	1987
Earnings Per Share	1.91	3.09	1.92	2.30	0.04	1.91	1.73
Dividends Per Share	1.56	1.40	1.24	①1.11	1.035	0.975	0.915
Dividend Payout %	81.7	45.3	64.6	48.3	N.M.	50.9	53.0

① 2-for-1 stk split,12/17/90

ANNUAL FINANCIAL DATA

RECORD OF EARNINGS (IN THOUSANDS):

Total Revenues	611,465	684,113	660,722	631,511	583,408	563,347	538,861
Costs and Expenses	476,785	472,066	515,082	468,399	537,407	413,081	400,033
Depreciation & Amort	18,372	17,315	15,506	13,186	12,960	13,903	12,893
Operating Income	116,308	194,732	130,134	149,926	33,041	136,363	125,935
Earn Bef Income Taxes	118,652	191,863	131,825	154,696	30,859	134,017	126,076
Income Taxes	44,950	69,454	52,790	56,928	29,140	48,741	49,475
Net Income	①73,702	②122,409	79,035	97,768	1,719	85,276	76,601
Aver. Shs. Outstg.	38,632	39,640	41,216	42,524	44,571	44,580	44,470

① Before acctg. change dr$10,252,000. ② Before acctg. change dr$1,009,000.

BALANCE SHEET (IN THOUSANDS):

Cash and Cash Equivalents	15,937	23,785	72,712	100,297	115,401	87,525	56,548
Accounts Receivable, Net	75,592	98,639	99,963	92,474	82,778	101,922	82,924
Inventories	38,000	38,578	38,231	39,430	42,252	42,938	41,938
Gross Property	275,349	244,988	239,728	205,583	213,525	206,797	197,859
Accumulated Depreciation	94,953	86,801	104,051	95,884	95,894	76,381	68,055
Capital Lease Obligations	...	...	2,072	2,377	...	...	...
Net Stockholders' Equity	115,025	168,206	222,873	249,175	284,456	352,930	313,914
Total Assets	362,398	372,981	390,266	381,029	411,002	465,306	408,236
Total Current Assets	173,762	197,202	234,396	250,212	249,456	238,689	188,816
Total Current Liabilities	186,381	184,310	152,865	116,900	112,819	83,265	61,652
Net Working Capital	d12,619	12,892	81,531	133,312	136,637	155,424	127,164
Year End Shares Outstg	38,293	39,163	40,648	41,538	44,100	44,634	44,510

STATISTICAL RECORD:

Operating Profit Margin %	19.0	28.5	19.7	23.7	5.7	24.2	23.4
Book Value Per Share	3.00	4.30	5.48	6.00	6.45	7.91	7.05
Return on Equity %	64.1	72.8	35.5	39.2	0.6	24.2	24.4
Return on Assets %	20.3	32.8	20.3	25.7	0.4	18.3	18.8
Average Yield %	3.0	2.2	2.4	2.8	3.2	3.4	3.2
P/E Ratio	34.0-20.7	22.8-19.0	34.8-20.1	19.8-14.7	N.M	16.6-13.2	20.7-13.0
Price Range	65-39½	70½-58⅜	66⅞-38⅝	45½-33¾	38⅛-26⅜	31⅝-25¼	35⅜-22⅜

Statistics are as originally reported.

OFFICERS:

H.B. Wentz, Jr., Chmn.
E.T. Fogerty, Pres. & C.E.O.
R.F. Wright, Sr. V.P. & C.F.O.
M.B. Lindsay, Treas.

INCORPORATED: DE, Mar., 1936

PRINCIPAL OFFICE: 777 Westchester Ave., White Plains, NY 10604

TELEPHONE NUMBER: (914) 696-6000

NO. OF EMPLOYEES: 3,600

ANNUAL MEETING: In April

SHAREHOLDERS: 7,001

INSTITUTIONAL HOLDINGS:
No. of Institutions: 288
Shares Held: 30,765,202

REGISTRAR(S): First Chicago Trust Co. of New York, New York, NY 10008

TRANSFER AGENT(S): First Chicago Trust Co. of New York, New York, NY 10008

TCA CABLE TV, INC.

YIELD 2.1%
P/E RATIO 24.7

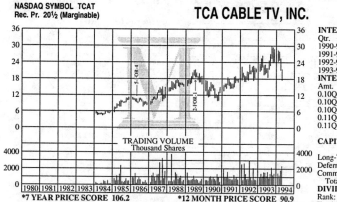

*7 YEAR PRICE SCORE 106.2   *12 MONTH PRICE SCORE 90.9
*NYSE COMPOSITE INDEX=100

TRADING VOLUME
Thousand Shares

INTERIM EARNINGS (Per Share):

Qtr.	Jan.	Apr.	July	Oct.
1990-91	0.08	0.08	0.09	0.10
1991-92	0.14	0.16	0.16	0.15
1992-93	0.19	0.21	0.20	0.23
1993-94	0.23	...	...	...

INTERIM DIVIDENDS (Per Share):

Amt.	Decl.	Ex.	Rec.	Pay.
0.10Q	3/30/93	4/7/93	4/14/93	4/28/93
0.10Q	6/30	7/9	7/15	7/29
0.10Q	9/7	9/16	9/22	10/6
0.11Q	12/17	1/5/94	1/11/94	1/25/94
0.11Q	3/31/94	4/8	4/14	4/28

Indicated div.: $0.44

CAPITALIZATION (10/31/93):

	($000)	(%)
Long-Term Debt	143,253	53.4
Deferred Income Tax	35,013	13.0
Common & Surplus	90,251	33.6
Total	268,517	100.0

DIVIDEND ACHIEVER STATUS:
Rank: 5   1983-93 Growth Rate: 26.9%
Total Years of Dividend Growth: 11

RECENT DEVELOPMENTS: For the quarter ended 1/31/94, income before accounting changes was $5.8 million, $0.23 per share, compared with $4.8 million, or $0.19 per share, in the same period last year. Revenues increased 7.2% to $39.3 million from $36.7 million a year ago, mostly attributable to internal growth. Operating income was $11.2 million, up 5.6% from $10.6 million in the corresponding period of the previous year. Interest expense decreased by $395,000 or appproximately 14% due to a reduction in debt. The com-

pany's basic accounts increased from 442,356 at 1/31/93 to 457,061 at 1/31/94 or approximately 3%. Average revenue per account increased from $27.76 to $28.72 or approxmately 3%. For the year ended 10/31/93, revenues were $152.3 million, up 10% over 1992 revenues of $138.8 million and operating income before depreciation was $77.7 million was up 10% over the 1992 operating income before depreciation of $70.4 million.

BUSINESS

TCA CABLE TV, INC. is the nation's 25th largest multiple system cable television operator. The Company owns and operates 53 cable television systems and manages two additional systems owned by affiliated corporations. Formed in 1981 from the consolidation of corporations led by founder Robert M. Rogers since 1954, the Company serves 458,000 customers in Arkansas, Idaho, Louisiana, Mississippi, New Mexico and Texas. Its "classic" systems with an average size of 8,600 customer accounts are located in mostly rural markets, whose residents rely on cable to provide quality reception and service.

REVENUES

(10/31/93)	($000)	(%)
Basic Subscriptions	108,888	71.5
Premium Subscriptions	27,412	18.0
Advertising	9,899	6.5
Other Sources	6,092	4.0
Total	152,291	100.0

ANNUAL EARNINGS AND DIVIDENDS PER SHARE

	10/31/93	10/31/92	10/31/91	10/31/90	10/31/89	10/31/88	10/31/87
Earnings Per Share	0.83	0.61	0.35	0.20	0.45	0.40	0.23
Dividends Per Share	0.40	0.34	0.28	0.24	① 0.20	0.16	0.12
Dividend Payout %	48.2	55.7	80.0	N.M.	44.4	40.5	52.2

① 2-for-1 stk split, 7/11/89

ANNUAL FINANCIAL DATA

RECORD OF EARNINGS (IN THOUSANDS):

	10/31/93	10/31/92	10/31/91	10/31/90	10/31/89	10/31/88	10/31/87
Total Revenues	152,292	138,839	127,090	113,738	79,088	68,938	60,397
Costs and Expenses	74,622	68,439	61,708	53,055	37,987	33,979	30,021
Depreciation & Amort	33,330	32,805	34,007	32,110	18,050	15,611	13,930
Operating Income	44,340	37,594	31,374	28,574	23,052	19,347	16,445
Income Bef Income Taxes	33,690	24,671	13,868	8,219	18,022	15,669	10,205
Income Taxes	13,241	9,682	5,375	3,464	7,209	6,096	5,135
Net Income	20,449	14,989	8,493	4,755	10,813	9,573	5,070
Aver. Shs. Outstg.	24,638	24,563	24,426	24,222	24,236	24,197	22,225

BALANCE SHEET (IN THOUSANDS):

Cash and Cash Equivalents	1,450	819	987	727	1,013	813	685
Total Receivables	5,185	3,805	3,440	3,404	2,543	1,655	1,368
Gross Property	254,420	236,756	229,279	217,747	197,882	153,124	141,843
Accumulated Depreciation	147,999	132,075	119,649	97,373	76,733	66,397	53,146
Long-Term Debt	143,253	163,319	189,252	218,541	227,416	48,285	58,215
Net Stockholders' Equity	90,251	70,762	70,762	64,940	65,787	59,450	53,713
Total Assets	288,077	289,889	305,700	324,826	327,637	135,432	138,223
Total Current Assets	7,259	5,292	4,875	4,595	3,798	2,817	2,053
Total Current Liabilities	19,560	15,649	15,793	14,608	10,953	7,382	9,420
Net Working Capital	d12,301	d10,357	d10,918	d10,013	d7,155	d4,565	d7,367
Year End Shares Outstg	24,657	24,559	24,511	24,220	24,201	24,149	24,143

STATISTICAL RECORD:

Operating Profit Margin %	29.1	27.1	24.7	25.1	29.1	28.1	27.2
Book Value Per Share	...	...	...	...	...	0.56	2.22
Return on Equity %	22.7	19.2	12.0	7.3	16.4	16.1	9.4
Return on Assets %	7.1	5.2	2.8	1.5	3.3	7.1	3.7
Average Yield %	1.6	1.7	1.7	1.8	1.1	1.0	1.0
P/E Ratio	36.3-22.3	38.1-27.9	54.3-38.6	87.5-49.4	47.5-34.2	44.4-33.1	65.8-36.4
Price Range	30⅛-18½	23¼-17	19-13½	17½-9⅞	21⅜-15⅜	17¾-13¼	15⅛-8⅜

Statistics are as originally reported.

OFFICERS:
R.M. Rogers, Chmn. & C.E.O.
F.R. Nichols, Pres. & C.O.O.
J.F. Taylor, V.P., C.F.O. & Treas.
M.S. Hensley, Sec.

INCORPORATED: TX, Dec., 1981

PRINCIPAL OFFICE: 3015 SSE Loop 323
P.O. Box 130489, Tyler, TX 75713-0489

TELEPHONE NUMBER: (903) 595-3701

NO. OF EMPLOYEES: 126

ANNUAL MEETING: In March

SHAREHOLDERS: 1,518 (approx.)

INSTITUTIONAL HOLDINGS:
No. of Institutions: 75
Shares Held: 10,387,183

REGISTRAR(S): First Chicago Trust Co. of New York, New York, NY 10008

TRANSFER AGENT(S): First Chicago Trust Co. of New York, New York, NY 10008

TECO ENERGY, INC.

YIELD 5.1%
P/E RATIO 15.0

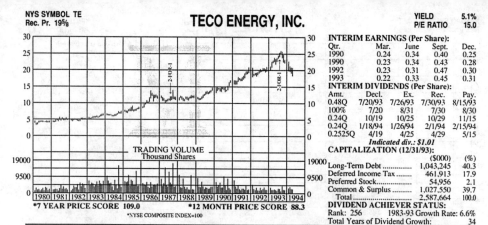

7 YEAR PRICE SCORE 109.0 *12 MONTH PRICE SCORE 88.3*
*NYSE COMPOSITE INDEX=100

INTERIM EARNINGS (Per Share):

Qtr.	Mar.	June	Sept.	Dec.
1990	0.24	0.34	0.40	0.25
1990	0.23	0.34	0.43	0.28
1992	0.23	0.31	0.47	0.30
1993	0.22	0.33	0.45	0.31

INTERIM DIVIDENDS (Per Share):

Amt.	Decl.	Ex.	Rec.	Pay.
0.48Q	7/20/93	7/26/93	7/30/93	8/15/93
100%	7/20	8/31	7/30	8/30
0.24Q	10/19	10/25	10/29	11/15
0.24Q	1/18/94	1/26/94	2/1/94	2/15/94
0.2525Q	4/19	4/25	4/29	5/15

Indicated div.: $1.01

CAPITALIZATION (12/31/93):

	($000)	(%)
Long-Term Debt	1,043,245	40.3
Deferred Income Tax	461,913	17.9
Preferred Stock.............	54,956	2.1
Common & Surplus	1,027,550	39.7
Total....................	2,587,664	100.0

DIVIDEND ACHIEVER STATUS:
Rank: 256   1983-93 Growth Rate: 6.6%
Total Years of Dividend Growth: 34

RECENT DEVELOPMENTS: For the year ended 12/31/93, net income before the cumulative effect of an accounting change was $150.3 million compared with $149.0 million in 1992. Revenues were $1.28 billion, up 8.5%. Operating income from diversified businesses rose 23% to $75.9 million. The Company's diversified businesses benefited from the on-time, on-budget start-up of Hardee Power Station. Natural gas earnings were up 50% due to increased production and improved gas prices.

PROSPECTS: Starting in 1994, the allowed return on common equity will be lowered to 11.35% from 12%. This is in addition to the $10 million refund plus interest awarded to customers by the Florida Office of Public Counsel. The Public Counsel will also seek to reduce the return on common equity even more. Earnings growth will be heavily dependent on strong results from TE's diversified companies. The completed Hardee Power Project should boost earnings.

BUSINESS

TECO ENERGY, INC. is a diversified energy holding company. Tampa Electric, which accounted for 85% of net income, generates, purchases, transmits, distributes and sells electric energy to more than 474,693 customers in a 2,000-square-mile area in West Central Florida. TECO Diversified, Inc. provides direction for several diversified activities of TE. TECO Power Services is a wholesale power supply. TECO Investments, Inc. invests capital in short- and long-term investments. TECO Finance, Inc. acts as the financing arm for all of TECO Energy's activities. TECO Coal produces and sells 3.5 million tons of coal annually. Electric retail sales were derived: 41.0% residential, 19.4% industrial, 32.0% commercial, and 7.6% other.

BUSINESS LINE ANALYSIS

(12/31/93)	Rev(%)	Inc(%)
Regulated Electric	68.9	74.0
Other Energy		
Services	31.1	26.0
Total	100.0	100.0

ANNUAL EARNINGS AND DIVIDENDS PER SHARE

	1993	1992	1991	1990	1989	1988	1987
Earnings Per Share	1.30	1.30	1.28	1.22	1.18	1.07	0.98
Dividends Per Share	[1] 1.655	0.898	0.847	0.798	0.748	0.70	[2] 0.66
Dividend Payout %	N.M.	69.0	66.5	65.1	63.6	65.7	67.7

[1] 2-for-1 stk split,08/31/93 [2] 2-for-1 stk. split, 8/87.

ANNUAL FINANCIAL DATA

RECORD OF EARNINGS (IN MILLIONS):

Revenues	1,283.9	1,183.2	1,154.1	1,097.1	1,060.0	1,034.0	970.4
Depreciation	165.3	142.5	132.7	...	...	...	...
Maintenance	98.9	94.3	89.4	79.2	78.6	81.8	71.2
Prov for Fed Inc Taxes	55.0	56.5	53.3	63.1	70.5	60.0	77.5
Operating Income	290.5	269.0	262.3	258.0	254.0	233.7	251.2
Interest Expense	76.1	64.5	65.0	59.5	57.0	60.3	58.0
Net Income	[1] 150.3	149.0	145.3	139.4	133.8	[2] 120.6	110.7
Aver. Shs. Outstg. (000)	115,340	114,611	113,922	113,664	113,549	113,413	113,290

[1] Before acctg. change cr$11,228,000. [2] Before extra. item dr$6,293,000.

BALANCE SHEET (IN MILLIONS):

Gross Plant	3,846.1	3,638.7	3,286.2	2,881.1	2,668.9	2,557.6	2,458.7
Accumulated Depreciation	1,363.1	1,256.8	1,067.2	936.6	853.5	784.7	698.8
Prop, Plant & Equip, Net	2,483.0	2,381.9	2,219.0	1,944.6	1,815.4	1,772.8	1,759.9
Lg tm Debt. Less Amount Due Within 1 Yr	1,043.2	1,048.5	907.9	762.9	674.8	684.0	659.8
Net Stockholders' Equity	1,082.5	1,010.7	946.3	885.5	938.4	900.6	876.9
Total Assets	3,127.8	3,024.3	2,833.6	2,513.0	2,386.8	2,314.6	2,270.1
Year End Shs Outstg (000)	115,621	114,966	114,219	113,697	113,597	113,496	113,336

STATISTICAL RECORD:

Book Value Per Share	8.89	8.31	7.80	7.30	7.72	7.29	6.99
Op. Inc/Net Pl %	11.7	11.3	11.8	13.3	14.0	13.2	14.3
Dep/Gr. Pl %	4.3	3.9	4.0	4.2	4.2	4.2	4.1
Accum. Dep/Gr. Pl %	35.4	34.5	32.5	32.5	32.0	30.7	28.4
Return on Equity %	13.9	14.7	15.4	15.7	14.4	13.7	13.1
Average Yield %	7.2	4.6	4.6	5.3	5.8	6.1	5.5
P/E Ratio	19.9-15.6	16.3-13.8	16.4-12.4	13.9-10.8	12.5-9.3	11.7-9.9	14.3-10.3
Price Range	25⅞-20¼	21⅛-18	20⅞-15¾	17-13⅛	14¾-11	12½-10⅝	14-10⅛

Statistics are as originally reported.

OFFICERS:
T.L. Guzzle, Chmn., Pres. & C.E.O.
A.D. Oak, Sr. V.P.-Fin., Treas. & C.F.O.
R.H. Kessel, V.P., Sec. & Couns.

INCORPORATED: FL, Jan., 1981

PRINCIPAL OFFICE: TECO Plaza 702 N. Franklin Street, Tampa, FL 33602

TELEPHONE NUMBER: (813) 228-4111
FAX: (813) 228-1670
NO. OF EMPLOYEES: 4,744
ANNUAL MEETING: In April
SHAREHOLDERS: 29,757
INSTITUTIONAL HOLDINGS:
No. of Institutions: 235
Shares Held: 45,860,950

REGISTRAR(S): First National Bank of Boston, Shareholder Services Division, Boston, MA

TRANSFER AGENT(S): First National Bank of Boston, Shareholder Services Division, Boston, MA

TELEFLEX, INC.

YIELD 1.6%
P/E RATIO 17.8

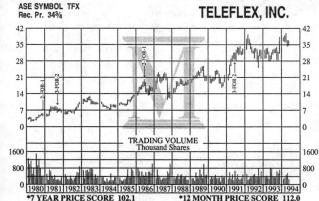

7 YEAR PRICE SCORE 102.1   **12 MONTH PRICE SCORE 112.0**
*NYSE COMPOSITE INDEX=100

TRADING VOLUME
Thousand Shares

INTERIM EARNINGS (Per Share):

Qtr.	Mar.	June	Sept.	Dec.
1990	0.44	0.46	0.35	0.48
1991	0.45	0.47	0.35	0.50
1992	0.47	0.50	0.36	0.54
1993	0.50	0.54	0.34	0.57

INTERIM DIVIDENDS (Per Share):

Amt.	Decl.	Ex.	Rec.	Pay.
0.115Q	4/30/93	5/19/93	5/25/93	6/15/93
0.115Q	8/3	8/19	8/25	9/15
0.115Q	11/2	11/18	11/24	12/15
0.115Q	2/8/94	2/18/94	2/25/94	3/15/94
0.135Q	4/29	5/19	5/25	6/15

Indicated div.: $0.54

CAPITALIZATION (12/26/93):

	($000)	(%)
Long-Term Debt	183,504	37.5
Deferred Income Tax	36,429	7.4
Common & Surplus	269,790	55.1
Total	489,723	100.0

DIVIDEND ACHIEVER STATUS:
Rank: 86   1983-93 Growth Rate: 13.8%
Total Years of Dividend Growth: 16

RECENT DEVELOPMENTS: For the quarter ended 12/26/93, net income rose 7% to $10.0 million compared with $9.3 million for the same period in 1992. Revenues climbed 18% to $177.4 million versus $150.7 million last year. The Commercial Products segment remained the primary contributor to earnings, as sales for the unit increased 30% due to improved market conditions for all three product lines. Meanwhile, sales for the Aerospace segment rose 14%.

PROSPECTS: Continued healthy demand for marine, industrial and automotive products along with increased applications for the commercial segment will continue to be the main contributors to earnings, although sluggish returns for the Medical segment will constrain profits. Emphasis on the commercial aviation market where demand for repairs of gas turbine engines are increasing brightens the outlook for the aerospace sector. The acquisition of The Engineering Group will offset lower demand for defense products.

BUSINESS

TELEFLEX, INC. designs, develops and manufactures a broad range of proprietary products for the automotive, aerospace, defense and medical markets. Aerospace Products and Services include the design and manufacture of precision mechanical electromechanical controls and systems; corrosion resistant coatings and repairs for gas turbine engines. Medical Products manufactures a broad range of disposable products for medical markets. Commercial Products develops mechanical, electrical and hydraulic controls for the automotive, pleasure marine and power equipment market.

BUSINESS LINE ANALYSIS

(12/27/93)	Rev(%)	Inc(%)
Commercial Products	42.6	50.9
Medical Products	27.1	29.0
Aerospace Prod & Services	30.3	20.1
Total	100.0	100.0

ANNUAL EARNINGS AND DIVIDENDS PER SHARE

	12/26/93	12/27/92	12/29/91	12/30/90	12/31/89	12/25/88	12/27/87
Earnings Per Share	1.95	1.87	1.77	1.73	1.63	1.48	1.19
Dividends Per Share	0.45	0.415	① 0.343	0.35	0.307	0.257	0.217
Dividend Payout %	23.1	22.2	19.4	20.2	18.8	17.3	18.2

① 5% stk div, 6/17/91

ANNUAL FINANCIAL DATA

RECORD OF EARNINGS (IN THOUSANDS):

	12/26/93	12/27/92	12/29/91	12/30/90	12/31/89	12/25/88	12/27/87
Revenues	666,796	570,338	483,009	444,213	360,066	328,223	271,766
Costs and Expenses	571,949	484,650	405,506	371,750	301,034	274,573	225,464
Depreciation & Amort	28,071	21,556	18,404	17,154	12,908	11,046	9,755
Operating Profit	66,776	64,132	59,099	55,308	46,123	42,604	36,547
Income Before Taxes	52,310	48,650	45,334	42,907	39,237	36,379	31,661
Estimated Taxes on Inc	18,624	16,638	15,527	14,340	12,440	12,370	11,990
Net Income	33,686	① 32,012	29,807	28,567	26,797	24,009	19,671
Aver. Shs. Outstg.	17,267	17,132	16,850	16,476	16,403	16,244	16,460

① Before acctg. change cr$860,000.

BALANCE SHEET (IN THOUSANDS):

Cash & Cash Equivalents	11,255	36,331	24,503	44,267	18,383	33,173	26,221
Accounts Receivable, Net	143,489	116,818	105,081	87,841	82,034	67,046	58,004
Inventories	159,287	128,970	117,414	98,530	88,594	57,661	53,124
Gross Property	382,809	300,897	268,986	235,715	205,661	142,948	121,241
Accumulated Depreciation	121,389	101,305	90,187	76,129	59,543	48,120	41,457
Long-Term Debt	183,504	134,600	119,370	112,941	106,128	57,104	55,013
Net Stockholders' Equity	269,790	240,467	211,702	187,875	160,038	136,328	115,517
Total Assets	640,576	534,931	477,693	425,100	366,662	264,116	225,907
Total Current Assets	322,249	289,821	255,012	236,930	194,274	160,549	139,789
Total Current Liabilities	150,853	123,018	123,424	103,090	81,949	62,332	49,519
Net Working Capital	171,397	166,803	131,589	133,840	112,325	98,217	90,270
Year End Shares Outstg	17,084	16,876	16,630	16,417	16,213	16,051	15,940

STATISTICAL RECORD:

Operating Profit Margin %	10.0	11.2	12.2	12.5	12.8	13.0	13.4
Book Value Per Share	15.79	14.25	12.73	11.44	9.87	8.49	7.25
Return on Equity %	12.5	13.3	14.1	15.2	16.7	17.6	17.0
Return on Assets %	5.3	6.0	6.2	6.7	7.3	9.1	8.7
Average Yield %	1.4	1.3	1.3	1.7	1.4	1.5	1.2
P/E Ratio	19.6-14.2	21.1-13.4	19.4-11.1	13.9-9.6	15.9-11.5	13.8-9.6	19.5-9.8
Price Range	38¼-27¾	39½-25	34⅜-19⅝	24⅛-16⅝	25⅞-18¾	20⅜-14¼	23¼-11⅝

Statistics are as originally reported.

OFFICERS:
L.K. Black, Chmn. & C.E.O.
D.S. Boyer, Pres.
H.L. Zuber, Jr., V.P. & C.F.O.

INCORPORATED: DE, 1943

PRINCIPAL OFFICE: 630 West Germantown Pike, Suite 450, Plymouth Meeting, PA 19462

TELEPHONE NUMBER: (215) 834-6301
FAX: (215) 834-8228
NO. OF EMPLOYEES: 8,000 (approx.)
ANNUAL MEETING: In April
SHAREHOLDERS: 1,600 (approx.)
INSTITUTIONAL HOLDINGS:
No. of Institutions: 131
Shares Held: 8,668,752

REGISTRAR(S): Mellon Securities Trust Company, Ridgefield Park, NJ

TRANSFER AGENT(S): Mellon Securities Trust Company, Ridgefield Park, NJ

TELEPHONE & DATA SYSTEMS, INC.

YIELD 0.9%
P/E RATIO 58.4

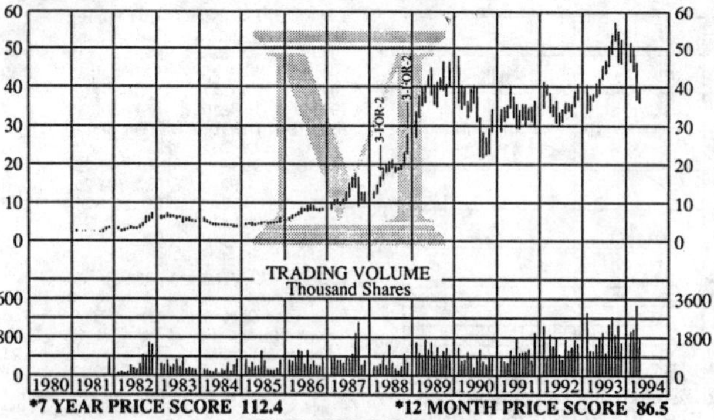

TRADING VOLUME
Thousand Shares

*7 YEAR PRICE SCORE 112.4 *12 MONTH PRICE SCORE 86.5
*NYSE COMPOSITE INDEX=100

INTERIM EARNINGS (Per Share):

Qtr.	Mar.	June	Sept.	Dec.
1991	0.18	0.17	0.17	0.07
1992	0.35	0.16	0.15	0.26
1993	0.14	0.18	0.24	0.11

INTERIM DIVIDENDS (Per Share):

Amt.	Decl.	Ex.	Rec.	Pay.
0.085Q	3/2/93	3/11/93	3/17/93	3/31/93
0.085Q	6/8	6/14	6/18	6/30
0.085Q	9/7	9/13	9/17	9/30
0.085Q	12/6	12/13	12/17	12/31
0.09Q	3/7/94	3/11/94	3/17/94	3/31/94

Indicated div.: $0.36

CAPITALIZATION (12/31/93):

	($000)	(%)
Long-Term Debt	514,442	24.8
Deferred Income Tax	66,127	3.2
Minor Int In Subsidiaries ..	223,480	10.8
Preferred Stock..............	42,465	2.1
Common & Surplus	1,224,285	59.1
Total	2,070,799	100.0

DIVIDEND ACHIEVER STATUS:
Rank: 215   1983-93 Growth Rate: 8.2%
Total Years of Dividend Growth: 19

RECENT DEVELOPMENTS: For the year ended 12/31/93, net income was $33.9 million, compared with income, before extraordinary item and accounting changes, of $38.5 million in 1992. Operating revenues for the year increased 29.3% to $590.7 million from $456.9 million for the prior year. The growth in revenues was led by a 50.7% increase in cellular telephone revenues to $247.3 million from $164.1 million in 1992. Operating results for 1993 also reflect steady growth in telephone operations, increases in paging units in service, improving economies of scale in cellular and paging operations, continuing improvements in business processes and systems, the impact of acquisitions and trades and the costs of financing these activities. For the quarter ended 12/31/93, net income was $6.2 million, compared with income, before extraordinary item and accounting changes, of $11.7 million for the 1992 quarter. Operating revenues for the quarter rose 27.1% to $160.0 million from $126.4 million in 1992.

BUSINESS

TELEPHONE AND DATA SYSTEMS, INC. is a diversified telecommunications company providing telecommunications services to more than one million consolidated telephone, cellular telephone and radio paging customers in 37 states and the District of Columbia. TELEPHONE—TDS Telecommunications Corporation operates 94 telephone companies that serve 356,200 access lines in 29 states. CELLULAR TELEPHONE—United States Cellular Corporation (USM) is TDS's 81.5%-owned cellular telephone subsidiary. USM's owned and managed systems have 261,000 cellular telephones in service. RADIO PAGING—American Paging, Inc., (API), TDS's 85.2%-owned subsidiary, provides radio paging and related services through 17 customer operations centers and has 460,900 pagers in service. ASSOCIATED SERVICE COMPANIES—TDS also operates several service subsidiaries which provide engineering, data processing, custom printing, telephone answering and other products and services.

ANNUAL EARNINGS AND DIVIDENDS PER SHARE

	1993	1992	1991	1990	1989	1988	1987
Earnings Per Share	0.67	① 0.91	② 0.59	0.86	③ 0.35	④ 0.40	0.46
Dividends Per Share	0.34	0.32	0.30	0.28	0.26	④ 0.24	0.229
Dividend Payout %	50.8	35.2	50.8	32.6	74.3	60.0	49.1

① Before acctg. chg. & extraord. item ② Before extraord. item ③ Before acctg. chg. ④ Before disc. oper. ⑤ 50% stk div, 3/17/88

ANNUAL FINANCIAL DATA

RECORD OF EARNINGS (IN MILLIONS):

	1993	1992	1991	1990	1989	1988	1987
Total Operating Revenues	590.7	456.1	354.0	294.6	239.7	196.3	174.6
Costs and Expenses	393.5	303.1	236.7	184.6	158.3	122.2	105.3
Depreciation & Amort	127.5	99.0	76.8	62.9	53.3	44.1	38.6
Operating Income	69.7	54.1	40.5	47.1	28.2	30.0	30.7
Income Bef Income Taxes	60.4	68.3	36.1	...	...	...	...
Income Tax Expense	26.5	29.8	14.9	16.4	7.9	7.3	8.2
Net Income	33.9	① 38.5	16.1	27.2	11.1	② 10.6	③ 11.3
Aver. Shs. Outstg. (000)	47,266	39,074	33,036	30,415	27,543	24,417	22,456

① Before extra. item dr$769,000. ② Before disc. op. cr$731,000. ③ Before disc. op. cr$1,182,000.

BALANCE SHEET (IN MILLIONS):

Cash and Cash Equivalents	74.9	58.9	54.8	73.6	64.0	53.9	51.0
Receivables, Net	...	...	51.3	36.6	37.8	29.5	27.4
Inventories	13.9	9.7	9.3	7.5	6.4	6.4	6.1
Gross Property	2,225.4	1,668.0	1,324.1	891.4	757.2	626.2	531.0
Accumulated Depreciation	487.1	392.5	326.9	266.7	243.1	205.0	175.9
Long-Term Debt	514.4	405.0	381.1	255.5	255.8	234.9	217.4
Net Stockholders' Equity	1,266.8	918.8	686.8	449.6	368.9	212.1	147.6
Total Assets	2,259.2	1,696.5	1,368.1	940.3	771.2	597.6	500.8
Total Current Assets	179.6	143.4	121.5	121.8	114.0	94.0	87.0
Total Current Liabilities	163.5	164.2	129.3	145.9	72.7	90.9	96.2
Net Working Capital	16.0	d20.9	d7.8	d24.0	41.3	3.1	d9.2
Year End Shs Outstg (000)	50,689	41,247	34,964	30,317	29,566	24,794	23,154

STATISTICAL RECORD:

Book Value Per Share	24.15	21.27	18.46	14.17	12.00	7.81	5.89
Return on Equity %	2.7	4.3	3.2	6.1	3.1	5.3	8.1
Average Yield %	0.8	0.9	0.9	0.8	0.7	1.2	1.8
P/E Ratio	85.1-49.6	45.3-33.1	68.4-48.3	55.8-25.3	N.M	69.4-28.1	38.0-17.7
Price Range	57-33¼	41¼-30⅛	40⅜-28½	48-21¾	46½-26⅞	27¾-11¼	17½-8⅛

Statistics are as originally reported.

OFFICERS:
L.T. Carlson, Chairman
L.T. Carlson, Jr., Pres. & C.E.O.
M.L. Swanson, Exec. V.P.-Fin.
R.D. Webster, V.P. & Treas.

INCORPORATED: IA, Mar., 1968

PRINCIPAL OFFICE: 30 N. LaSalle St., Suite 4000, Chicago, IL 60602

TELEPHONE NUMBER: (312) 630-1900
NO. OF EMPLOYEES: 4,343
ANNUAL MEETING: In May
SHAREHOLDERS: 2,555 com., ser. A com., 113.
INSTITUTIONAL HOLDINGS:
No. of Institutions: 190
Shares Held: 32,003,902

REGISTRAR(S): Harris Trust & Savings Bank, Chicago, IL

TRANSFER AGENT(S): Harris Trust & Savings Bank, Chicago IL

NASDAQ SYMBOL TANT
Rec. Pr. 43⅜ (Marginable)

TENNANT CO.

YIELD 3.0%
P/E RATIO 23.3

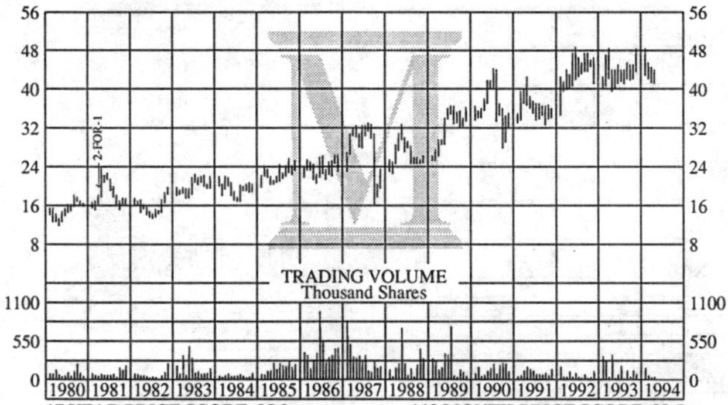

*7 YEAR PRICE SCORE 95.0 *12 MONTH PRICE SCORE 99.5

*NYSE COMPOSITE INDEX=100

INTERIM EARNINGS (Per Share):

Qtr.	Mar.	June	Sept.	Dec.
1990	0.39	0.94	0.85	0.99
1991	0.37	0.62	0.69	0.74
1992	0.50	0.66	0.65	0.93
1993	0.10	0.62	0.65	0.49

INTERIM DIVIDENDS (Per Share):

Amt.	Decl.	Ex.	Rec.	Pay.
0.32Q	5/6/93	5/25/93	6/1/93	6/14/93
0.32Q	8/5	8/25	8/31	9/14
0.32Q	12/10	12/15	12/21	12/31
0.32Q	2/17/94	3/1/94	3/7/94	3/14/94
0.32Q	5/5	5/24	5/31	6/14

Indicated div.: $1.28

CAPITALIZATION (12/31/93):

	($000)	(%)
Long-Term Debt	1,103	1.3
Common & Surplus	84,093	98.7
Total	85,196	100.0

DIVIDEND ACHIEVER STATUS:
Rank: 302 1983-93 Growth Rate: 4.2%
Total Years of Dividend Growth: 21

RECENT DEVELOPMENTS: For the quarter ended 12/31/93, net sales increased 7% to $65.0 million from $60.7 million for the same period last year. Net earnings declined 48% to $2.4 million from $4.6 million for the corresponding 1992 quarter. For the year ended 12/31/93, net sales increased 3% to $221.0 million from $214.9 million in 1992. Net earnings were $9.1 million, compared with earnings, before extraordinary gain and cumulative effect of accounting change, of $13.2 million a year ago. The 1993 results include a restructuring charge of $4.1 million related primarily to the integration of Tennant Trend into the newly acquired Castex Industries, Inc. The acquisition of Castex was completed on 2/1/94 for an aggregate consideration of approximately $28 million. Castex, a manufacturer of commercial floor maintenance equipment located in Holland, Michigan, had sales of approximately $32 million in 1993.

BUSINESS

TENNANT COMPANY is engaged in the manufacture and design of specialized industrial and commercial surface maintenance equipment and related products. The Company also markets replacement component parts for its equipment. The equipment manufactured includes gas, diesel or battery-powered sweepers, scrubbers and scarifiers. Accessories and floor-treating materials are also sold by the Company. Products are sold in more than 60 countries throughout the world. The equipment manufactured by the Company is generally used to clean and maintain commercial and industrial floors, roadways, parking areas and the like. Domestic manufacturing operations are carried on in a plant facility in Minneapolis, Minnesota. Operations overseas include Tennant N.V., a wholly-owned subsidiary in the Netherlands selling to customers throughout Europe; Equipamentos Tennant Limitada, a sale and manufacturing facility in Brazil; and Fuji-Tennant Ltd. a 50%-owned affiliate in Japan.

BUSINESS LINE ANALYSIS

(12/31/93)	Rev(%)	Inc(%)
North American	74.0	74.9
International	26.0	25.1
Total	100.0	100.0

ANNUAL EARNINGS AND DIVIDENDS PER SHARE

	1993	1992	1991	1990	1989	1988	1987
Earnings Per Share	**1.86**	**[1] 2.68**	**2.42**	**[1] 3.17**	**2.87**	**[2] 2.18**	**1.85**
Dividends Per Share	**1.28**	**1.22**	**1.20**	**1.18**	**1.10**	**0.98**	**0.96**
Dividend Payout %	**68.8**	**45.5**	**49.6**	**37.2**	**38.3**	**45.0**	**51.9**

[1] Before extraord. item & acctg. chg. [2] Before extraord. item

ANNUAL FINANCIAL DATA

RECORD OF EARNINGS (IN THOUSANDS):

	1993	1992	1991	1990	1989	1988	1987
Total Revenues	221,002	214,863	198,575	211,503	197,078	183,888	166,924
Costs and Expenses	194,592	188,493	173,124	183,347	169,002	157,737	143,205
Depreciation & Amort	10,987	10,241	8,730	8,652	8,027	7,900	7,162
Profit From Operations	11,333	16,129	16,721	19,504	20,049	18,251	16,557
Profit Bef Income Taxes	12,928	17,993	18,521	19,878	23,804	19,700	17,510
Income Tax Expense	3,802	4,803	6,529	4,257	9,052	8,126	7,692
Net Income	9,126	[1] 13,190	11,992	[2] 15,621	14,752	[3] 11,574	9,818
Aver. Shs. Outstg.	4,918	4,916	4,946	4,921	5,134	5,296	5,320

[1] Before extra. item cr$395,000. [2] Before extra. item cr$590,000. [3] Before extra. item cr$1,689,000.

BALANCE SHEET (IN THOUSANDS):

	1993	1992	1991	1990	1989	1988	1987
Cash & Cash Equivalents	2,675	3,512	2,349	1,412	3,175	7,016	3,564
Inventories	22,893	25,805	22,533	24,440	22,668	20,865	20,074
Gross Property	111,131	104,874	94,131	91,242	84,397	74,233	72,036
Accumulated Depreciation	64,509	59,444	53,401	48,654	43,448	38,617	36,453
Long-Term Debt	1,103	3,107	1,853	1,995	2,568	2,401	2,480
Net Stockholders' Equity	84,093	84,850	76,613	73,164	74,050	77,998	69,516
Total Assets	128,634	128,988	111,644	116,234	117,627	117,813	106,098
Total Current Assets	73,752	74,741	66,028	67,065	70,325	79,222	68,661
Total Current Liabilities	30,847	30,340	32,864	40,386	36,987	33,657	30,972
Net Working Capital	42,905	44,401	33,164	26,679	33,338	45,565	37,689
Year End Shares Outstg	4,913	4,912	4,867	4,927	4,923	5,294	5,268

STATISTICAL RECORD:

	1993	1992	1991	1990	1989	1988	1987
Operating Profit Margin %	5.1	7.5	8.4	9.2	10.2	9.9	9.9
Book Value Per Share	17.12	17.27	15.74	14.85	15.04	14.73	13.20
Return on Equity %	10.9	15.5	15.7	21.4	19.9	14.8	14.1
Return on Assets %	7.1	10.2	10.7	13.4	12.5	9.8	9.3
Average Yield %	2.9	2.9	3.2	3.3	3.6	3.5	3.9
P/E Ratio	26.1-21.2	18.2-12.9	17.6-13.4	14.0-8.8	12.7-8.8	15.0-10.3	17.8-8.6
Price Range	48½-39½	48¾-34½	42½-32½	44¼-27¾	36½-25¼	32¾-22½	33-16

Statistics are as originally reported.

OFFICERS:
R.L. Hale, Pres. & C.E.O.
R.A. Snyder, V.P., Treas. & C.F.O.
J.M. Dolan, V.P., Gen. Couns. & Sec.

INCORPORATED: MN, Jan., 1909

PRINCIPAL OFFICE: 701 N. Lilac Dr. P.O. Box 1452, Minneapolis, MN 55440

TELEPHONE NUMBER: (612) 540-1200

FAX: (612) 540-1437

NO. OF EMPLOYEES: 1,750

ANNUAL MEETING: In May

SHAREHOLDERS: 3,000

INSTITUTIONAL HOLDINGS:
No. of Institutions: 43
Shares Held: 3,247,981

REGISTRAR(S): Norwest Bank Minnesota, N.A., St. Paul, MN

TRANSFER AGENT(S): Norwest Bank Minnesota, N.A., St. Paul, MN

TEXAS UTILITIES CO.

YIELD 9.4%
P/E RATIO 19.4

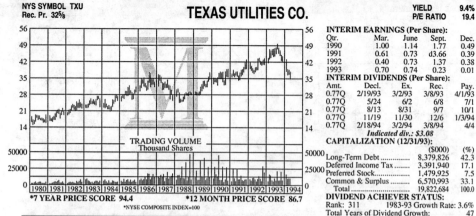

*7 YEAR PRICE SCORE 94.4   *12 MONTH PRICE SCORE 86.7
*NYSE COMPOSITE INDEX=100

INTERIM EARNINGS (Per Share):

Qtr.	Mar.	June	Sept.	Dec.
1990	1.00	1.14	1.77	0.49
1991	0.61	0.73	d3.66	0.39
1992	0.40	0.73	1.37	0.38
1993	0.70	0.74	0.23	0.01

INTERIM DIVIDENDS (Per Share):

Amt.	Decl.	Ex.	Rec.	Pay.
0.77Q	2/19/93	3/2/93	3/8/93	4/1/93
0.77Q	5/24	6/2	6/8	7/1
0.77Q	8/13	8/31	9/7	10/1
0.77Q	11/19	11/30	12/6	1/3/94
0.77Q	2/18/94	3/2/94	3/8/94	4/4

Indicated div.: $3.08

CAPITALIZATION (12/31/93):

	($000)	(%)
Long-Term Debt	8,379,826	42.3
Deferred Income Tax	3,391,940	17.1
Preferred Stock	1,479,925	7.5
Common & Surplus	6,570,993	33.1
Total	19,822,684	100.0

DIVIDEND ACHIEVER STATUS:
Rank: 311   1983-93 Growth Rate: 3.6%
Total Years of Dividend Growth: 47

RECENT DEVELOPMENTS: For the year ended 12/31/93, net income was $368.7 million versus $619.2 million in 1992. Income for 1993 reflects charges of $359.6 million, primarily related to the resolution of all remaining Comanche Peak design, construction and cost issues. Revenues were $5.43 billion, up 10.7%. Construction expenditures for 1994 are expected to be $400 million, a reduction from the privious forecast of $650 million. Fourth quarter net income was $1.2 million versus $82.1 million last year.

PROSPECTS: Beginning in August 1993, Texas Utilities Company had been reflecting a rate increase of about 12% in its operating revenues. A rate increase of approximately 8.7% was granted by the Public Utility Commission of Texas. An adjustment was made to reflect the lower amount of rate relief. The Company expects to require additional power early in the next decade as a result of increasing customer demand and the expiration of purchased power contracts.

BUSINESS

TEXAS UTILITIES CO. is the holding company of an electric system located entirely within the state of Texas. Its electric utility subsidiary, Texas Utilities Electric Co. generates and distributes in the north central, eastern and western parts of Texas, with a population estimated at 5,500,000 about one-third of the population of Texas. The territory includes the petroleum industry, banking, agriculture, and other commercial and industrial businesses. Other subsidiaries include: Texas Utilities Fuel Company (a natural gas pipeline system), Texas Utilities Mining Co., Texas Utilities Service (financial services), Basic Resources Inc., and Chaco Energy Co.

REVENUES

(12/31/93)	($000)	(%)
Residential	2,254,832	41.5
Commercial	1,499,266	27.6
Industrial	864,452	15.9
Government & Municipal	342,639	6.3
Other Electric	215,625	4.0
Other Operating	257,698	4.7
Total	5,434,512	100.0

ANNUAL EARNINGS AND DIVIDENDS PER SHARE

	1993	1992	1991	1990	1989	1988	1987
Earnings Per Share	1.66	① 2.88	d1.98	4.40	4.44	4.00	4.55
Dividends Per Share	3.07	3.03	2.99	2.95	2.91	2.86	2.77
Dividend Payout %	N.M.	N.M.	...	67.1	65.5	71.5	60.9

① Before acctg. chg.

ANNUAL FINANCIAL DATA

RECORD OF EARNINGS (IN MILLIONS):

	1993	1992	1991	1990	1989	1988	1987
Operating Revenues	5,434.5	4,907.9	4,893.2	4,542.6	4,320.5	4,153.7	4,082.9
Depreciation & Amort.	439.5	421.3	436.9	327.6	251.4	242.3	234.1
Maintenance	350.0	301.3	309.4	296.6	265.1	294.8	300.5
Income Taxes	322.1	171.1	120.1	113.9	144.1	129.1	194.5
Operating Income	1,186.9	1,163.3	1,135.7	1,083.5	1,032.8	953.3	848.9
Total Interest Charges	639.7	644.6	702.7	533.6	475.8	480.9	377.1
Net Income	368.7	① 619.2	d410.0	850.8	779.1	642.7	680.0
Aver. Shs. Outstg. (000)	221,555	214,850	207,358	193,461	175,567	160,561	149,449

① Before acctg. change cr$80,907,000.

BALANCE SHEET (IN MILLIONS):

	1993	1992	1991	1990	1989	1988	1987
Gross Plant	22,413.4	21,685.7	20,593.9	20,715.3	19,137.0	17,391.1	15,173.0
Accumulated Depreciation	4,595.5	4,201.4	3,825.9	3,435.5	3,148.4	2,931.6	2,718.3
Utility Plant, Net	17,817.9	17,484.3	16,768.0	17,279.8	15,988.6	14,459.5	12,454.7
Lg tm Debt, Less Amounts Due Curly	8,379.8	7,932.0	7,951.1	7,380.6	6,416.9	6,342.5	5,141.5
Net Stockholders' Equity	8,050.9	7,918.8	7,717.2	8,262.3	7,667.0	6,879.4	6,174.9
Total Assets	21,518.1	19,428.6	18,792.8	18,651.0	17,219.2	16,057.6	13,986.3
Year End Shs Outstg (000)	224,345	217,316	210,700	196,970	183,189	169,009	152,409

STATISTICAL RECORD:

	1993	1992	1991	1990	1989	1988	1987
Book Value Per Share	29.29	30.33	29.82	34.66	34.56	33.38	33.02
Op. Inc/Net Pl %	6.7	6.7	6.8	6.3	6.5	6.6	6.8
Dep/Gr. Pl %	...	1.9	2.1	1.6	1.3	1.4	1.5
Accum. Dep/Gr. Pl %	...	19.4	18.6	16.6	16.5	16.9	17.9
Return on Equity %	4.8	8.3	...	10.9	10.6	9.8	11.4
Average Yield %	6.7	7.5	7.8	8.3	8.9	10.4	8.9
P/E Ratio	30.0-25.1	15.2-12.8	...	8.9-7.3	8.4-6.3	7.7-6.2	8.0-5.6
Price Range	49¾-41⅝	43¾-37	43-34⅛	39-32	37½-27¾	30⅝-24⅝	36⅝-25½

Statistics are as originally reported.

OFFICERS:
J.S. Farrington, Chmn. & C.E.O.
E. Nye, President
C.C. Hulen, Treas. & Asst. Sec.
P.B. Tinkham, Sec. & Asst. Treas.

INCORPORATED: TX, Sep., 1945

PRINCIPAL OFFICE: 2001 Bryan Tower, Dallas, TX 75201

TELEPHONE NUMBER: (214) 812-4600

NO. OF EMPLOYEES: 10,687

ANNUAL MEETING: Third Friday in May.

SHAREHOLDERS: 111,599

INSTITUTIONAL HOLDINGS:
No. of Institutions: 576
Shares Held: 119,547,109

REGISTRAR(S): At Company's Office

TRANSFER AGENT(S): At Company's Office

NYS SYMBOL TR
Rec. Pr. 63

TOOTSIE ROLL INDUSTRIES, INC.

YIELD . . .%
P/E RATIO 18.6

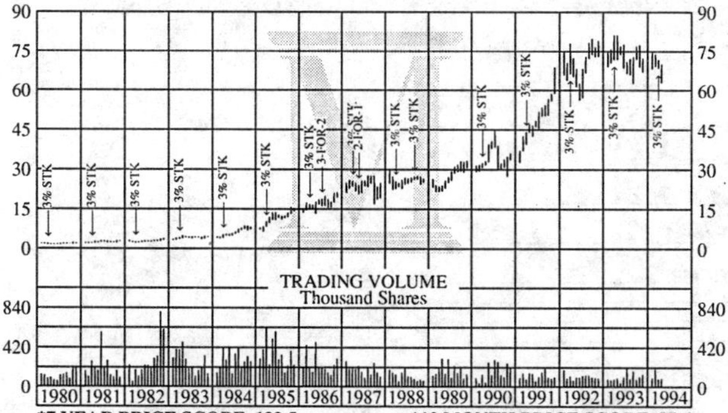

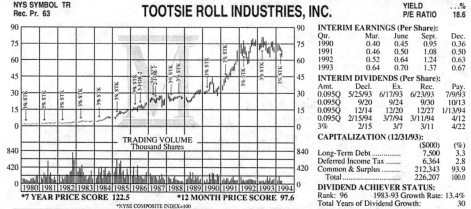

*7 YEAR PRICE SCORE 122.5 *12 MONTH PRICE SCORE 97.6

*NYSE COMPOSITE INDEX=100

INTERIM EARNINGS (Per Share):

Qtr.	Mar.	June	Sept.	Dec.
1990	0.40	0.45	0.95	0.36
1991	0.46	0.50	1.08	0.50
1992	0.52	0.64	1.24	0.63
1993	0.64	0.70	1.37	0.67

INTERIM DIVIDENDS (Per Share):

Amt.	Decl.	Ex.	Rec.	Pay.
0.095Q	5/25/93	6/17/93	6/23/93	7/9/93
0.095Q	9/20	9/24	9/30	10/13
0.095Q	12/14	12/20	12/27	1/13/94
0.095Q	2/15/94	3/7/94	3/11/94	4/12
3%	2/15	3/7	3/11	4/22

CAPITALIZATION (12/31/93):

	($000)	(%)
Long-Term Debt	7,500	3.3
Deferred Income Tax	6,364	2.8
Common & Surplus	212,343	93.9
Total	226,207	100.0

DIVIDEND ACHIEVER STATUS:
Rank: 96 1983-93 Growth Rate: 13.4%
Total Years of Dividend Growth: 30

RECENT DEVELOPMENTS: Net income for the year ended 12/31/93 was $35.4 million, up 10.6% from a year ago. Sales increased 5.8% to $259.6 million. Sales growth was achieved as a result of effective promotional programs. Net income for the quarter ended 12/31/93 was $7.0 million compared with $6.7 million last year. Sales decreased 3% to $62.4 million. During the quarter, the Company completed the purchase of certain assets of the chocolate and caramel confections business of Warner-Lambert.

PROSPECTS: The Company will continue its aggressive advertising and promotional programs in order to enhance demand in all markets. With plenty of cash on hand and a practically debt-free balance sheet, investments in new products will continue. TR's sales and earnings will continue to benefit from an established brand names and stable costs for raw materials. TR is now the leading producer of lollipops, which will help protect the Company from a highly competitive candy market.

BUSINESS

TOOTSIE ROLL INDUSTRIES, INC. is engaged in the manufacture and sale of candy. Major products include: Tootsie Roll, Tootsie Roll Pops, Tootsie Pop Drops, Tootsie Flavor Rolls, Charms, Blow-Pop lollipops. Other candy products include Tootsie Frooties, Cellas chocolate covered cherries, Mason Dots and Mason Crows. In September 1988, TR acquired Charms Co. for approximately $65.0 million. The Company has manufacturing facilities in Chicago, New York, Covington, Tennessee and Mexico City.

REVENUES

(12/31/93)	($000)	(%)
United States	234,460	90.3
Mexico & Canada	25,133	9.7
Total	259,593	100.0

ANNUAL EARNINGS AND DIVIDENDS PER SHARE

	1993	1992	1991	1990	1989	1988	1987
Earnings Per Share	**3.36**	**3.04**	**[2] 2.51**	**2.14**	**1.92**	**1.57**	**1.39**
Dividends Per Share	**0.336**	**[1] 0.268**	**[3] 0.228**	**[4] 0.208**	**[5] 0.202**	**[6] 0.196**	**[7] 0.175**
Dividend Payout %	**10.0**	**8.8**	**9.1**	**9.7**	**10.5**	**12.4**	**12.7**

Note: 3%stk.div.4/22/94. [1] 3% stk div, 3/12/92 [2] Before acctg. chg. [3] 3% stk div, 3/12/91 [4] 3% stk div 4/25/90. [5] 3% stk. div., 4/89. [6] 3% stk div, 4/88. [7] 2-for-1 stk. split, 5/87.

ANNUAL FINANCIAL DATA

	1993	1992	1991	1990	1989	1988	1987
RECORD OF EARNINGS (IN THOUSANDS):							
Total Revenues	259,593	245,424	207,875	194,299	179,294	128,598	114,803
Costs and Expenses	204,566	196,226	165,376	157,534	140,253	101,212	87,877
Depreciation & Amort	8,814	6,071	5,202	5,696	5,133	3,626	2,408
Earnings From Operations	53,517	47,933	41,235	35,509	33,908	23,760	24,518
Earn Bef Income Taxes	57,710	51,922	44,174	37,119	33,206	25,481	26,014
Provision for Inc Taxes	22,268	19,890	17,641	14,563	12,994	8,929	11,449
Net Income	35,442	32,032	[1] 26,533	22,556	20,212	16,552	14,565
Aver. Shs. Outstg.	10,850	10,850	10,854	10,856	10,858	10,860	10,863
[1] Before acctg. change dr$1,038,000.							
BALANCE SHEET (IN THOUSANDS):							
Cash and Cash Equivalents	56,203	88,942	65,313	36,758	18,492	16,820	50,749
Receivables, Net	22,750	12,889	13,035	16,207	12,061	11,381	9,971
Inventories	29,294	24,845	21,453	22,927	22,296	16,104	...
Gross Property	137,273	86,578	74,405	67,975	63,147	60,796	46,527
Accumulated Depreciation	50,574	44,766	40,386	35,876	32,240	29,240	26,412
Long-Term Debt	7,500	7,500	...	...	...	...	...
Net Stockholders' Equity	212,343	181,704	152,759	129,845	109,562	91,543	77,131
Total Assets	303,940	222,478	184,427	159,702	136,342	129,123	94,415
Total Current Assets	111,914	129,665	101,729	77,929	54,208	45,144	72,761
Total Current Liabilities	50,862	22,498	21,160	22,551	20,722	31,717	13,973
Net Working Capital	61,052	107,167	80,569	55,378	33,486	13,427	58,789
Year End Shares Outstg	10,850	10,536	10,853	10,856	10,858	10,860	10,863
STATISTICAL RECORD:							
Operating Profit Margin %	20.6	19.5	19.8	18.3	18.9	18.5	21.4
Book Value Per Share	10.23	12.96	9.79	7.56	5.55	3.77	7.10
Return on Equity %	16.7	17.6	17.4	17.4	18.4	18.1	18.9
Return on Assets %	11.7	14.4	14.4	14.1	14.8	12.8	15.4
Average Yield %	0.5	0.4	0.5	0.6	0.7	0.8	0.8
P/E Ratio	24.8-19.2	27.0-19.1	28.0-13.3	21.4-13.2	17.9-11.7	19.5-14.8	20.5-12.5
Price Range	81-62⅝	79⅝-56⅜	68⅝-32⅝	44⅜-27½	33¼-21⅝	29¾-22½	27⅝-16⅞

Statistics are as originally reported.

OFFICERS:
M.J. Gordon, Chmn. & C.E.O.
E.R. Gordon, Pres. & C.O.O.
G.H. Ember, Jr., V.P.-Fin. & Asst. Sec.
B.P. Bowen, Treas.

INCORPORATED: VA, Jun., 1919

PRINCIPAL OFFICE: 7401 South Cicero Ave., Chicago, IL 60629

TELEPHONE NUMBER: (312) 838-3400

NO. OF EMPLOYEES: 108 approx.

ANNUAL MEETING: In May

SHAREHOLDERS: 3,059

INSTITUTIONAL HOLDINGS:
No. of Institutions: 79
Shares Held: 2,397,051

REGISTRAR(S): Manufacturers Hanover Trust Co., New York, NY

TRANSFER AGENT(S): Manufacturers Hanover Trust Co., New York, NY

TORCHMARK CORP.

YIELD 2.8%
P/E RATIO 11.3

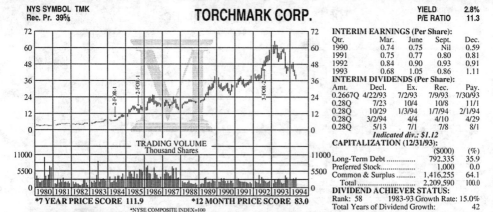

INTERIM EARNINGS (Per Share):

Qtr.	Mar.	June	Sept.	Dec.
1990	0.74	0.75	Nil	0.59
1991	0.75	0.77	0.80	0.81
1992	0.84	0.90	0.93	0.91
1993	0.68	1.05	0.86	1.11

INTERIM DIVIDENDS (Per Share):

Amt.	Decl.	Ex.	Rec.	Pay.
0.2667Q	4/22/93	7/2/93	7/9/93	7/30/93
0.28Q	7/23	10/4	10/8	11/1
0.28Q	10/29	1/3/94	1/7/94	2/1/94
0.28Q	3/2/94	4/4	4/10	4/29
0.28Q	5/13	7/1	7/8	8/1

Indicated div.: $1.12

CAPITALIZATION (12/31/93):

	($000)	(%)
Long-Term Debt	792,335	35.9
Preferred Stock	1,000	0.0
Common & Surplus	1,416,255	64.1
Total	2,209,590	100.0

DIVIDEND ACHIEVER STATUS:
Rank: 58   1983-93 Growth Rate: 15.0%
Total Years of Dividend Growth: 42

TRADING VOLUME
Thousand Shares

*7 YEAR PRICE SCORE 111.9   ***12 MONTH PRICE SCORE 83.0**
*NYSE COMPOSITE INDEX=100

RECENT DEVELOPMENTS: For the quarter ended 12/31/93 net income increased 22% from the corresponding 1992 quarter to $81.8 million. Results included a $30.9 million after-tax gain from the sale of 73% of Vesta Insurance Group and accounting adjustment charges of $4.0 million. Revenues totaled $577.1 million compared with $514.0 million last year. For 1993, net income was $298.0 million versus $265.5 million for 1992. Revenues grew 6% to $2.18 billion.

PROSPECTS: The financial services unit results continue to improve, profit margins for mutual fund operations particularly. Businesses with consistent revenue and satisfactory profit margins are the focal point of the earnings stream. Sales of Medicare supplement coverage has been adversely affected by uncertainty surrounding the Clinton administration's proposed health-care reform policy. The Company will acquire United Investors Management Co., and form a new subsidiary.

BUSINESS

TORCHMARK CORP. is a diversified insurance and financial services company. Through Liberty National Life Insurance Co., Globe Life & Accident Insurance Co., United American Insurance Co., Family Service Life Insurance Co., and other subsidiaries, TMK offers complete lines of individual life and health insurance products. Liberty National Fire offers domestic and foreign reinsurance through off-shore subsidiaries. Waddell & Reed, Inc. offers financial planning services. Non-insurance operations include energy, asset management, real estate, oil and gas and equipment leases.

REVENUES

(12/31/93)	($000)	(%)
Net Investment Income	8,705	19.2
Realized Investment Gains	9,301	20.4
Other Income	27,435	60.4
Total	45,441	100.0

ANNUAL EARNINGS AND DIVIDENDS PER SHARE

	1993	1992	1991	1990	1989	1988	1987
Earnings Per Share	4.01	3.58	3.13	2.85	2.59	2.13	② 1.99
Dividends Per Share	1.08	① 1.066	1.00	0.933	0.833	0.733	0.667
Dividend Payout %	26.9	29.8	31.9	32.7	32.2	34.4	33.6

① 3-for-2 stk split, 8/20/92 ② Before extraord. item

ANNUAL FINANCIAL DATA

RECORD OF EARNINGS (IN MILLIONS):

	1993	1992	1991	1990	1989	1988	1987
Total Revenue	2,176.8	2,045.8	1,932.0	1,796.1	1,633.6	1,669.8	1,590.5
Costs and Expenses	1,668.2	1,572.3	1,501.0	1,397.4	1,261.3	1,346.9	1,245.9
Operating Income	508.7	473.5	431.0	398.8	372.2	322.8	344.6
Inc Bef Income Tax & Eq In Subsids	441.4	417.9	380.8	352.5	324.1	282.0	312.3
Income Taxes	153.1	140.8	125.4	114.4	105.2	93.5	107.3
Eq In Earn Of Unconsol Subs	2.0	0.8	1.1	0.4	...	...	0.7
Minor Int In Consol Subs	10.7	12.4	10.0	9.3	7.6	3.4	5.2
Net Income	① 279.6	265.5	246.5	229.2	211.3	180.1	193.0
Aver. Shs. Outstg. (000)	73,502	73,237	76,728	77,949	78,635	83,070	98,636

① Before acctg. change cr$18,403,000.

BALANCE SHEET (IN MILLIONS):

	1993	1992	1991	1990	1989	1988	1987
Cash and Cash Equivalents	236.6	139.3	175.0	737.9	648.7	477.9	538.7
Receivables, Net	209.7	181.0	144.4	126.1	153.9	122.1	125.5
Gross Property	80.5	183.1	174.2	92.7	78.4	68.8	74.3
Long-Term Debt	792.3	497.9	667.1	529.3	498.2	497.5	300.1
Net Stockholders' Equity	1,417.3	1,115.7	1,079.3	943.8	894.5	807.9	923.5
Total Assets	7,646.2	6,770.1	6,160.7	5,535.9	4,921.4	4,427.6	4,241.2
Total Current Assets	446.3	320.4	319.4	864.0	802.6	600.0	664.2
Total Current Liabilities	524.5	656.6	413.1	386.6	469.1	327.3	423.7
Net Working Capital	d78.2	d336.3	d93.6	477.4	333.5	272.7	240.5
Year End Shs Outstg (000)	73,784	73,512	76,145	76,973	79,284	80,247	91,734

STATISTICAL RECORD:

	1993	1992	1991	1990	1989	1988	1987
Book Value Per Share	19.19	15.16	14.16	12.25	11.27	10.06	10.06
Return on Equity %	19.7	23.8	22.8	24.3	23.6	22.3	20.9
Return on Assets %	3.7	3.9	4.0	4.1	4.3	4.1	4.6
Average Yield %	2.0	2.3	2.8	2.9	2.8	3.8	3.4
P/E Ratio	17.2-10.9	16.3-10.1	12.6-9.9	13.4-8.9	15.1-7.7	10.5-7.5	12.3-7.3
Price Range	64¾-41⅛	58⅜-36	39½-30⅞	38¼-25⅜	39⅛-20	22⅜-15⅞	24½-14½

Statistics are as originally reported.

OFFICERS:
R.K. Richey, Chmn. & C.E.O.
K.A. Tucker, Vice-Chmn.
S.E. Upchurch, Jr., V.P., Gen. Couns. & Sec.

INCORPORATED: DE, Nov., 1979

PRINCIPAL OFFICE: 2001 Third Ave. South, Birmingham, AL 35233

TELEPHONE NUMBER: (205) 325-4200

NO. OF EMPLOYEES: 6,242

ANNUAL MEETING: In April

SHAREHOLDERS: 8,003

INSTITUTIONAL HOLDINGS:
No. of Institutions: 349
Shares Held: 39,378,543

REGISTRAR(S): First Chicago Trust Co. of New York, New York, NY 10008

TRANSFER AGENT(S): First Chicago Trust Co. of New York, New York, NY 10008

NASDAQ SYMBOL TRMK
Rec. Pr. 16¼ (Marginable)

TRUSTMARK CORP.

YIELD 2.5%
P/E RATIO 9.8

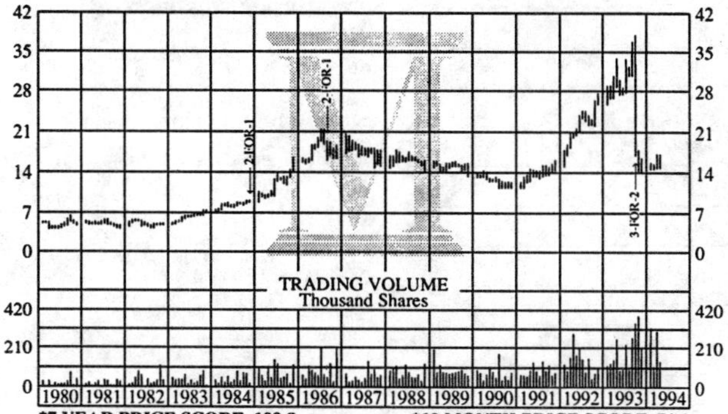

***7 YEAR PRICE SCORE 100.8** ***12 MONTH PRICE SCORE 71.1**

*NYSE COMPOSITE INDEX=100

INTERIM EARNINGS (Per Share):

Qtr.	Mar.	June	Sept.	Dec.
1990	0.24	0.26	0.22	0.28
1991	0.12	0.27	0.26	0.30
1992	0.29	0.30	0.34	0.38
1993	0.39	0.46	0.41	0.40

INTERIM DIVIDENDS (Per Share):

Amt.	Decl.	Ex.	Rec.	Pay.
0.28Q	5/12/93	5/25/93	6/1/93	6/15/93
0.28Q	7/13	9/16	9/1	9/15
3-for-1	9/14	10/12	9/30	10/8
0.10Q	11/10	11/24	12/1	12/15
0.10Q	2/24/94	2/28/94	3/1/94	3/15/94

Indicated div.: $0.40

CAPITALIZATION (12/31/93):

	($000)	(%)
Total Deposits	3,189,205	71.6
Total Debt	845,135	19.0
Common & Surplus	358,627	8.0
Loan Valuation Reserve	62,650	1.4
Total	4,455,617	100.0

DIVIDEND ACHIEVER STATUS:
Rank: 246 1983-93 Growth Rate: 7.0%
Total Years of Dividend Growth: 20

RECENT DEVELOPMENTS: For the year ended 12/31/93, net income increased 31.1% to $50.2 million, or $1.66 per share, from $38.3 million, or $1.30 per share, in 1992. The 1993 net income includes a $1.5 million credit for cumulative effect of a change in accounting principle. Net income increased primarily because of substantial improvement in net interest income combined with continued growth in noninterest income, effective management of noninterest expenses and a lower provision for loan losses. The return on average assets for 1993 was 1.17% compared with 0.97% in 1992. The return on average equity was 15.37% for 1993 compared with 13.57% in 1992. Net income for the quarter ended 12/31/93 was $12.5 million, or $0.40 per share, up 13.2% from the $11.0 million, or $0.37 per share, reported for the same quarter last year.

BUSINESS

TRUSTMARK CORP. is a one-bank holding company which, through its subsidiaries, engages in the banking, real estate and consumer finance fields. The Corporation's principal operating subsidiary is Trustmark National Bank, which is the second largest bank in the state of Mississippi. Trustmark provides a full range of consumer banking services including checking accounts, NOW accounts, savings programs, other interest-bearing time accounts, personal and business loans, money transfers and safe deposit facilities. Trustmark also offers its customers the MasterCard and VISA credit cards.

LOAN DISTRIBUTION

(12/31/93)	($000)	(%)
Real Estate Loans	996,757	47.8
To Finance Agric Product	29,248	1.4
Commerical & Industrial	471,942	22.6
To Individuals	521,119	25.0
Oblig of States & Politic	36,973	1.8
For Purch or Carry Secus	3,995	0.3
Lease Fin Receiv & Other	23,792	1.1
Total	2,083,826	100.0

ANNUAL EARNINGS AND DIVIDENDS PER SHARE

	1993	1992	1991	1990	1989	1988	1987
Earnings Per Share	**1.66**	**1.30**	**0.94**	**0.99**	**0.96**	**0.94**	**0.89**
Dividends Per Share	**[1] 0.38**	**0.359**	**0.346**	**0.336**	**0.319**	**0.299**	**0.274**
Dividend Payout %	**22.9**	**27.6**	**36.9**	**34.1**	**33.4**	**32.0**	**30.7**

[1] Adj for 3-for-1 stk split, 10/12/93

ANNUAL FINANCIAL DATA

	1993	1992	1991	1990	1989	1988	1987
RECORD OF EARNINGS (IN MILLIONS):							
Total Interest Income	290.6	288.7	309.7	304.8	277.2	240.4	213.0
Total Interest Expense	109.0	128.7	174.3	187.9	172.4	140.3	121.4
Net Interest Income	181.6	160.0	135.3	116.8	104.8	100.1	91.5
Provision for Loan Losses	17.6	24.1	25.2	15.1	11.5	9.4	8.5
Net Income	[1] 48.6	38.3	27.6	29.1	28.1	27.5	26.2
[1] Before acctg. change cr$1,519,000.							
BALANCE SHEET (IN MILLIONS):							
Cash & Due Fr Banks (non-int Bearing)	238.4	252.4	243.8	241.6	276.2	286.7	213.3
Net Loans	2,021.2	1,856.2	1,848.1	1,818.4	1,780.7	1,748.4	1,577.7
Total Domestic Deposits	3,189.2	3,196.9	3,160.7	3,065.6	2,570.3	2,421.8	2,330.2
Net Stockholders' Equity	358.6	295.4	267.7	250.3	231.2	212.5	193.8
Total Assets	4,432.0	4,085.1	3,878.4	3,700.0	3,108.4	2,894.6	2,767.4
Year End Shs Outstg (000)	31,173	29,476	29,476	29,476	29,476	29,476	29,476
STATISTICAL RECORD:							
Return on Assets %	1.10	0.94	0.71	0.79	0.90	0.95	0.95
Return on Equity %	13.60	13.00	10.30	11.60	12.10	13.00	13.50
Book Value Per Share	11.50	10.02	9.08	8.49	7.84	7.21	6.57
Average Yield %	1.5	1.7	2.5	2.6	2.2	1.8	1.6
P/E Ratio	23.6-8.7	21.3-11.6	17.2-12.2	14.6-11.5	16.8-14.0	19.3-15.4	23.2-16.4
Price Range	38-14	27⅝-15	16⅛-11⅜	14⅜-11⅜	16-13⅜	18-14⅜	20⅝-14⅝

Statistics are as originally reported.

OFFICERS:
F.R. Day, Chmn. & C.E.O.
A. Hunt, Vice-Chmn.
H.M. Walker, Pres. & C.O.O.
D.R. Carter, Exec. V.P. & C.F.O.

INCORPORATED: MS, Aug., 1968

PRINCIPAL OFFICE: 248 East Capitol Street
P.O. Box 291, Jackson, MS 39205-0291

TELEPHONE NUMBER: (601) 354-5863

FAX: (601) 949-2387

NO. OF EMPLOYEES: 2,000 (approx.)

ANNUAL MEETING: In March

SHAREHOLDERS: 4,200 (approx.)

INSTITUTIONAL HOLDINGS:
No. of Institutions: 34
Shares Held: 1,799,792

REGISTRAR(S): Trustmark National Bank, Jackson, MS

TRANSFER AGENT(S): Trustmark National Bank, Jackson, MS

TRW INC.

YIELD 3.0%
P/E RATIO 18.4

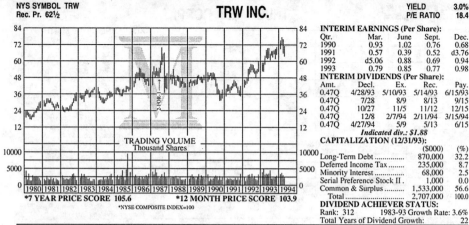

*7 YEAR PRICE SCORE 105.6   *12 MONTH PRICE SCORE 103.9
*NYSE COMPOSITE INDEX=100

INTERIM EARNINGS (Per Share):

Qtr.	Mar.	June	Sept.	Dec.
1990	0.93	1.02	0.76	0.68
1991	0.57	0.39	0.52	d3.76
1992	d5.06	0.88	0.69	0.94
1993	0.79	0.85	0.77	0.98

INTERIM DIVIDENDS (Per Share):

Amt.	Decl.	Ex.	Rec.	Pay.
0.47Q	4/28/93	5/10/93	5/14/93	6/15/93
0.47Q	7/28	8/9	8/13	9/15
0.47Q	10/27	11/5	11/12	12/15
0.47Q	12/8	2/7/94	2/11/94	3/15/94
0.47Q	4/27/94	5/9	5/13	6/15

Indicated div.: $1.88

CAPITALIZATION (12/31/93):

	($000)	(%)
Long-Term Debt	870,000	32.2
Deferred Income Tax	235,000	8.7
Minority Interest	68,000	2.5
Serial Preference Stock II	1,000	0.0
Common & Surplus	1,533,000	56.6
Total	2,707,000	100.0

DIVIDEND ACHIEVER STATUS:
Rank: 312   1983-93 Growth Rate: 3.6%
Total Years of Dividend Growth: 22

RECENT DEVELOPMENTS: Net income for the year ended 12/31/93, including a gain of $2.1 million from restructuring, was $220.1 million compared with $193.7 million in 1992. Sales fell 4.4% to $7.95 billion from $8.31 billion the previous year. Foreign currency exchange rates had an unfavorable impact of $160 million on Automotive sales. North American sales for this segment improved substantially, but were offset by weak sales in its European operations.

PROSPECTS: TRW will continue to benefit from sales and profit growth in its air bag business. The Company continues focusing on improving cost controls to offset the prolonged weakness of the European economy, which isn't expected to improve in the near term. Future results should benefit from increased vehicle production in North America. TRW will continue to streamline Space & Defense operations in an attempt to improve results in this price-competitive industry.

BUSINESS

TRW, INC. provides high technology products and services primarily to the automotive, space and defense and information markets. Automotive products include steering, suspension, and occupant restraint systems, engine valves and valve train parts, electro mechanical assemblies, fasteners, car and truck accessories and car care products. Space & Defense designs and manufactures spacecraft and related equipment as well as software and systems engineering support services. Information Systems & Services include consumer estate and commercial credit services, plus real estate information systems. In 1989, TRW acquired Chilton Corp., a major consumer credit reporting concern, and the automotive inflatable restraints business of Talley Industries.

BUSINESS LINE ANALYSIS

(12/31/93)	Rev(%)	Inc(%)
Automotive	57.1	54.3
Space & Defense	35.1	35.0
Info Systems & Services	7.7	13.0
Other	0.1	(2.3)
Total	100.0	100.0

ANNUAL EARNINGS AND DIVIDENDS PER SHARE

	1993	1992	1991	1990	1989	1988	1987
Earnings Per Share	3.39	① 3.09	d2.30	3.39	4.31	4.29	4.01
Dividends Per Share	1.88	1.82	1.80	1.74	1.77	1.63	② 1.60
Dividend Payout %	55.5	58.9	...	51.3	41.1	38.0	39.9

① Before acctg. chg.   ② 2-for-1 stk. split, 6/87.

ANNUAL FINANCIAL DATA

RECORD OF EARNINGS (IN MILLIONS):

Costs and Expenses	5,910.0	6,136.0	5,838.0	5,995.0	5,379.0	5,216.0	4,968.0
Depreciation & Amort	458.0	481.0	469.0	452.0	400.0	349.0	322.0
Operating Profit	d7,075.0	d7,443.0	d7,148.0	d7,309.0	d6,559.0	d6,345.0	d6,100.0
Earn Bef Income Taxes	359.0	348.0	d129.0	343.0	399.0	420.0	415.0
Income Taxes	139.0	154.0	11.0	135.0	136.0	159.0	172.0
Net Income	① 220.0	② 194.0	d140.0	208.0	263.0	261.0	243.0
Aver. Shs. Outstg. (000)	64,700	62,300	61,200	61,900	61,900	60,500	60,300

① Before acctg. change dr$25,000,000.   ② Before acctg. change dr$350,000,000.

BALANCE SHEET (IN MILLIONS):

Cash and Cash Equivalents	79.0	66.0	75.0	72.0	114.0	127.0	145.0
Receivables, Net	1,219.0	1,289.0	1,356.0	1,309.0	1,431.0	1,286.0	1,233.0
Total Inventories	410.0	422.0	512.0	530.0	480.0	419.0	487.0
Gross Property	5,120.0	5,052.0	5,010.0	4,734.0	4,127.0	3,733.0	3,674.0
Accumulated Depreciation	2,793.0	2,741.0	2,686.0	2,519.0	2,173.0	1,940.0	1,874.0
Long-Term Debt	870.0	941.0	1,213.0	1,042.0	1,063.0	863.0	870.0
Net Stockholders' Equity	1,534.0	1,416.0	1,685.0	1,907.0	1,749.0	1,566.0	1,417.0
Total Assets	5,336.0	5,458.0	5,635.0	5,555.0	5,259.0	4,442.0	4,378.0
Total Current Assets	1,994.0	2,116.0	2,262.0	2,237.0	2,295.0	2,105.0	1,986.0
Total Current Liabilities	1,826.0	2,012.0	1,982.0	1,947.0	1,794.0	1,396.0	1,496.0
Net Working Capital	168.0	104.0	280.0	290.0	501.0	709.0	490.0
Year End Shs Outstg (000)	64,100	62,900	61,600	60,800	60,600	60,200	59,700

STATISTICAL RECORD:

Book Value Per Share	13.35	11.10	15.73	18.52	16.32	20.07	23.72
Return on Equity %	14.3	13.7	...	10.9	15.0	16.7	17.1
Return on Assets %	4.1	3.6	...	3.7	5.0	5.9	5.6
Average Yield %	3.1	3.6	4.5	4.2	3.9	3.4	3.0
P/E Ratio	21.0-15.7	19.5-13.3	...	15.3-9.3	11.6-9.6	12.6-9.5	17.5-9.2
Price Range	70¼-52½	60¼-41	46¼-34½	51¾-34⅜	49⅞-41¼	54-40⅝	70-37

Statistics are as originally reported.

OFFICERS:
J.T. Gorman, Chmn. & C.E.O.
E.D. Dunford, Pres. & C.O.O.
P.S. Hellman, Exec. V.P. & C.F.O.
R.D. Sugar, Exec. V.P. & C.F.O.

PRINCIPAL OFFICE: 1900 Richmond Road, Cleveland, OH 44124-3760

TELEPHONE NUMBER: (216) 291-7000
FAX: (216) 291-7758
NO. OF EMPLOYEES: 61,200
ANNUAL MEETING: in April
SHAREHOLDERS: 30,100
INSTITUTIONAL HOLDINGS:
No. of Institutions: 379
Shares Held: 35,003,407

REGISTRAR(S): First Chicago Trust Co. of New York, New York, NY 10008
National City Bank, Cleveland, OH 44114

TRANSFER AGENT(S): At Company's Office
First Chicago Trust Co. of New York, New York, NY 10008

NYS SYMBOL UEP
Rec. Pr. 33⅜

UNION ELECTRIC CO.

YIELD 7.1%
P/E RATIO 12.0

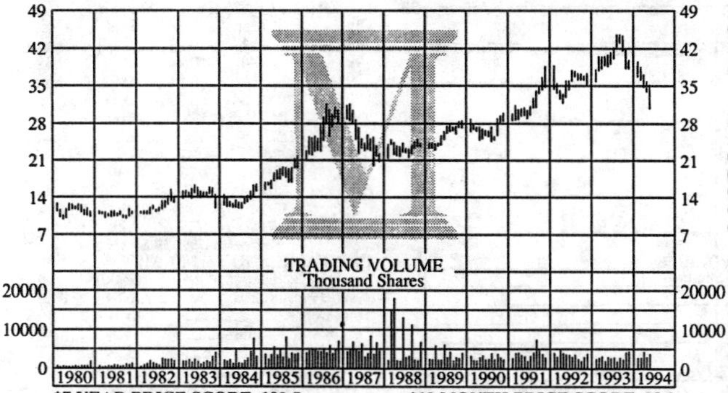

49
42
35
28
21
14
7
TRADING VOLUME
Thousand Shares
20000
10000
0
1980 1981 1982 1983 1984 1985 1986 1987 1988 1989 1990 1991 1992 1993 1994

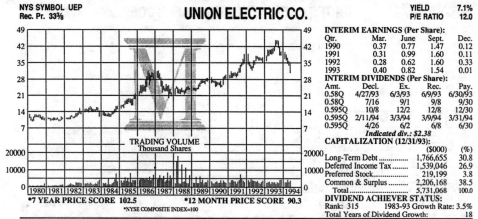

***7 YEAR PRICE SCORE 102.5** ***12 MONTH PRICE SCORE 90.3**

*NYSE COMPOSITE INDEX=100

INTERIM EARNINGS (Per Share):

Qtr.	Mar.	June	Sept.	Dec.
1990	0.37	0.77	1.47	0.12
1991	0.31	0.99	1.60	0.11
1992	0.28	0.62	1.60	0.33
1993	0.40	0.82	1.54	0.01

INTERIM DIVIDENDS (Per Share):

Amt.	Decl.	Ex.	Rec.	Pay.
0.58Q	4/27/93	6/3/93	6/9/93	6/30/93
0.58Q	7/16	9/1	9/8	9/30
0.595Q	10/8	12/2	12/8	12/30
0.595Q	2/11/94	3/3/94	3/9/94	3/31/94
0.595Q	4/26	6/2	6/8	6/30

Indicated div.: $2.38

CAPITALIZATION (12/31/93):

	($000)	(%)
Long-Term Debt	1,766,655	30.8
Deferred Income Tax	1,539,046	26.9
Preferred Stock	219,199	3.8
Common & Surplus	2,206,168	38.5
Total	5,731,068	100.0

DIVIDEND ACHIEVER STATUS:

Rank: 315 1983-93 Growth Rate: 3.5%

Total Years of Dividend Growth: 18

RECENT DEVELOPMENTS: For the year ended 12/31/93, net income was $297.2 million compared with $302.7 million in 1992. Revenues were $2.07 billion, up 2.5%. Net income for the year was negatively affected by increased expenses as a result of the Midwest floods. Residential and commercial sales increased 12% and 4%, respectively. Industrial sales fell 11%. Net income for the fourth quarter was $4.8 million versus $36.9 million last year. Results for 1992 include a gain of $18 million.

PROSPECTS: Continuing cost controls and modest capital requirements should enable UEP to strengthen its measurements of debt protection over the next several years, without reliance on additional rate increases. The Company benefits from efficient operations, strong cash flow and successful cost containment programs. UEP has adequate purchased power sources and transmission capability; therefore, no baseload plant additions are scheduled before the year 2000.

BUSINESS

UNION ELECTRIC CO. is engaged mainly in supplying electricity in and around St. Louis, East St. Louis, and Alton, Illinois and a small portion of southern Iowa. The Company also furnishes similar service in sections of central, northern and southeastern Missouri. In addition, UEP also provides gas, steam and water services. The 24,000-square mile service area, with a population of 2.7 million, is well diversified. Residential sales account for about 39.1% of electric revenue while 35.1% was from commercial, 21.3% from industrial and 4.5% other.

REVENUES

(12/31/93)	($000)	(%)
Residential	817,713	39.6
Commercial	684,446	33.1
Industrial	373,353	18.1
Other Electric Utilities	59,160	2.9
Miscellaneous	31,308	1.5
Gas	99,552	4.8
Other	472	----
Total	2,066,004	100.0

ANNUAL EARNINGS AND DIVIDENDS PER SHARE

	1993	1992	1991	1990	1989	1988	1987
Earnings Per Share	**2.77**	**2.83**	**3.01**	**2.74**	**2.61**	**2.56**	**2.91**
Dividends Per Share	**2.335**	**2.26**	**2.18**	**2.10**	**2.02**	**1.94**	**1.92**
Dividend Payout %	**84.3**	**79.9**	**72.4**	**76.6**	**77.4**	**75.8**	**66.0**

ANNUAL FINANCIAL DATA

	1993	1992	1991	1990	1989	1988	1987
RECORD OF EARNINGS (IN MILLIONS):							
Total Operating Revenues	2,066.0	2,015.1	2,096.9	2,023.0	2,010.3	2,029.1	1,946.4
Depreciation & Amort	219.6	246.3	236.6	232.9	230.3	235.4	181.0
Maintenance	190.1	187.3	170.5	176.4	156.2	163.0	158.9
Income Taxes	179.5	196.4	222.7	192.2	203.4	194.2	180.5
Operating Income	411.3	412.0	482.8	457.5	466.5	484.2	488.5
Net Interest Charges	124.5	130.4	160.8	175.6	161.3	186.4	214.5
Net Income	297.2	302.7	321.5	294.2	285.6	291.6	333.9
Aver. Shs. Outstg. (000)	102,124	102,124	102,124	102,124	102,124	102,124	102,124
BALANCE SHEET (IN MILLIONS):							
Gross Plant	8,344.5	8,062.1	7,752.7	7,512.2	7,310.0	7,126.3	6,936.8
Accumulated Depreciation	3,079.5	2,860.7	2,634.1	2,391.5	2,192.2	1,974.4	1,735.7
Total Property & Plant, Net	5,265.0	5,201.4	5,118.6	5,120.7	5,117.7	5,151.9	5,201.1
Long-term Debt	1,766.7	1,659.6	1,730.3	1,948.0	2,106.8	2,188.6	2,357.6
Net Stockholders' Equity	2,425.4	2,382.5	2,324.7	2,240.1	2,182.9	2,236.0	2,256.5
Total Assets	6,595.6	5,797.4	5,733.5	5,702.3	5,760.3	5,827.2	5,957.8
Year End Shs Outstg (000)	102,124	102,124	102,124	102,124	102,124	102,124	102,124
STATISTICAL RECORD:							
Book Value Per Share	21.60	21.19	20.62	19.79	19.14	18.56	17.97
Op. Inc/Net Pl %	7.8	7.9	9.4	8.9	9.1	9.4	9.4
Dep/Gr. Pl %	2.6	3.1	3.1	3.1	3.2	3.3	2.6
Accum. Dep/Gr. Pl %	36.9	35.5	34.0	31.8	30.0	27.7	25.0
Return on Equity %	12.3	12.7	13.8	13.1	13.1	13.4	15.2
Average Yield %	5.8	6.4	6.5	7.7	7.8	8.4	7.5
P/E Ratio	16.1-12.9	13.7-11.2	12.8-9.5	10.9-9.0	11.0-8.8	9.8-8.3	10.9-6.8
Price Range	44⅝-35¾	38¾-31¾	38⅝-28½	30-24⅝	28⅝-23	25-21⅜	31⅝-19⅞

Statistics are as originally reported.

OFFICERS:
W.E. Cornelius, Chmn. & C.E.O.
C.W. Mueller, President
D.E. Brandt, Sr. V.P.-Fin. & Corp. Svcs.
J.C. Thompson, Secretary

INCORPORATED: MO, Nov., 1922

PRINCIPAL OFFICE: 1901 Chouteau Ave., Saint Louis, MO 63103

TELEPHONE NUMBER: (314) 621-3222
FAX: (314) 554-4014
NO. OF EMPLOYEES: 6,594
ANNUAL MEETING: In April
SHAREHOLDERS: 123,723
INSTITUTIONAL HOLDINGS:
No. of Institutions: 299
Shares Held: 32,059,047

REGISTRAR(S): At Company's Office

TRANSFER AGENT(S): At Company's Office

UNITED CAROLINA BANCSHARES CORP.

YIELD 3.7%
P/E RATIO 9.6

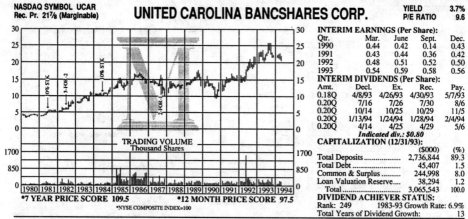

*7 YEAR PRICE SCORE 109.5   *12 MONTH PRICE SCORE 97.5

*NYSE COMPOSITE INDEX=100

TRADING VOLUME
Thousand Shares

INTERIM EARNINGS (Per Share):

Qtr.	Mar.	June	Sept.	Dec.
1990	0.44	0.42	0.14	0.43
1991	0.43	0.44	0.36	0.42
1992	0.48	0.51	0.52	0.50
1993	0.54	0.59	0.58	0.56

INTERIM DIVIDENDS (Per Share):

Amt.	Decl.	Ex.	Rec.	Pay.
0.18Q	4/8/93	4/26/93	4/30/93	5/7/93
0.20Q	7/16	7/26	7/30	8/6
0.20Q	10/14	10/25	10/29	11/5
0.20Q	1/13/94	1/24/94	1/28/94	2/4/94
0.20Q	4/14	4/25	4/29	5/6

Indicated div.: $0.80

CAPITALIZATION (12/31/93):

	($000)	(%)
Total Deposits	2,736,844	89.3
Total Debt	45,407	1.5
Common & Surplus	244,998	8.0
Loan Valuation Reserve	38,294	1.2
Total	3,065,543	100.0

DIVIDEND ACHIEVER STATUS:
Rank: 249   1983-93 Growth Rate: 6.9%
Total Years of Dividend Growth: 13

RECENT DEVELOPMENTS: For the year ended 12/31/93, income, before cumulative effect of a change in accounting method, was $31.7 million, or $2.27 per share, a 13.5% increase over net income of $28.0 million, or $2.01 per share, in 1992. The increase in income was primarily the result of higher levels of tax-equivalent net interest income and noninterest income and declines in the provisions for credit losses. For the quarter ended 12/31/93, net income increased 13.4% to $7.9 million, or $0.56 per share, from $6.9 million, or $0.50 per share, for the same period last year. Effective 11/12/93, the Company's North Carolina subsidiary bank acquired Home Federal Savings Bank headquartered in Greenville, NC for $20.6 million cash. The North Carolina subsidiary has also reached agreements to acquire Sanford Real Estate, Loan & Insurance Company, located in Sanford, NC, and the Bank of Iredell, headquartered in Statesville, NC.

BUSINESS

UNITED CAROLINA BANCSHARES CORP. is a bank holding company whose principal subsidiaries are United Carolina Bank and United Carolina Bank of South Carolina. The banks offer a wide variety of financial services to the retail and business sectors of North and South Carolina. UCB has 126 banking offices in 24 North Carolina counties and 14 banking offices in 14 South Carolina counties.

LOAN DISTRIBUTION

(12/31/93)	($000)	(%)
Real Estate	1,371,193	63.2
Commercial, Finl & Agric	230,955	10.7
Loans to Indiv	498,305	23.0
Other Loan & Lease Receiv	66,844	3.1
Total	2,167,297	100.0

ANNUAL EARNINGS AND DIVIDENDS PER SHARE

	1993	1992	1991	1990	1989	1988	1987
Earnings Per Share	2.27	2.01	1.65	1.43	1.74	1.65	1.46
Dividends Per Share	0.76	0.66	0.61	0.60	0.59	0.56	☐ 0.53
Dividend Payout %	33.5	32.8	37.0	42.0	33.9	33.9	36.3

☐ 2-for-1 stk. split, 9/87.

ANNUAL FINANCIAL DATA

RECORD OF EARNINGS (IN MILLIONS):

	1993	1992	1991	1990	1989	1988	1987
Total Interest Income	201.0	208.0	230.0	237.3	229.1	199.0	172.1
Total Interest Expense	76.8	89.8	120.0	134.5	130.7	104.1	86.4
Net Interest Income	124.2	118.2	110.0	102.8	98.4	94.9	85.7
Provision for Credit Losses	4.9	11.8	14.4	17.3	7.4	6.1	5.6
Net Income	☐ 31.7	28.0	23.0	19.9	24.2	22.9	20.3
Aver. Shs. Outstg. (000)	13,992	13,937	13,937	13,937	13,937	13,926	13,901

☐ Before acctg. change cr$867,000.

BALANCE SHEET (IN MILLIONS):

	1993	1992	1991	1990	1989	1988	1987
Cash & Due Fr Banks-nonint Bearing	144.8	138.1	142.7	268.3	176.4	159.9	146.4
United States Govt Secur	129.5	508.5	338.5	351.1	322.9	195.7	150.1
Obligs Of State & Political Subdiviss	77.8	102.2	94.1	77.3	88.9	106.7	130.0
Net Loans	2,127.8	1,819.0	1,748.5	1,648.8	1,556.4	1,495.7	1,399.2
Total Domestic Deposits	2,736.8	2,481.5	2,372.3	2,358.4	2,229.1	2,014.2	1,820.0
Long-term Debt	1.4	0.4	1.7	3.0	3.9	4.8	5.7
Net Stockholders' Equity	245.0	222.4	203.4	185.1	174.2	159.2	145.8
Total Assets	3,050.6	2,808.5	2,621.1	2,589.5	2,457.8	2,230.2	2,036.8
Year End Shs Outstg (000)	14,023	13,958	13,937	13,937	13,937	13,937	13,921

STATISTICAL RECORD:

	1993	1992	1991	1990	1989	1988	1987
Return on Assets %	1.04	1.00	0.88	0.77	0.99	1.03	0.99
Return on Equity %	12.90	12.60	11.30	10.70	13.90	14.40	13.90
Book Value Per Share	17.47	15.93	14.59	13.28	12.50	11.42	10.47
Average Yield %	3.3	3.7	4.3	4.8	3.8	4.4	4.0
P/E Ratio	11.3-8.7	10.8-7.1	10.2-7.0	11.2-6.5	10.2-7.5	8.8-6.7	11.1-6.8
Price Range	25¾-19¾	21¾-14¼	16¾-11½	16-9¼	17¾-13	14½-11	16¼-10

Statistics are as originally reported.

OFFICERS:
E.R. Sasser, Chmn., Pres. & C.E.O.
R.C. Monger, Exec. V.P. & C.F.O.
H.V. Hudson, Jr., Sec. & Gen. Couns.

PRINCIPAL OFFICE: 127 West Webster Street, Whiteville, NC 28472

TELEPHONE NUMBER: (919) 642-5131
FAX: (919) 642-1452
NO. OF EMPLOYEES: 1,991
ANNUAL MEETING: In April
SHAREHOLDERS: 8,100
INSTITUTIONAL HOLDINGS:
No. of Institutions: 31
Shares Held: 2,079,216

REGISTRAR(S): United Carolina Bank, Whiteville, NC 28472

TRANSFER AGENT(S): United Carolina Bank, Whiteville NC 28472

UNITED CITIES GAS CO.

YIELD 6.3%
P/E RATIO 13.3

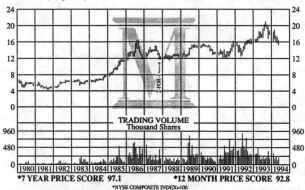

24 — 24
20 — 20
16 — 16
12 — 12
8 — 8
4 — 4
0 — 0

TRADING VOLUME
Thousand Shares

960 — 960
480 — 480
0 — 0

1980|1981|1982|1983|1984|1985|1986|1987|1988|1989|1990|1991|1992|1993|1994

*7 YEAR PRICE SCORE 97.1   *12 MONTH PRICE SCORE 92.8
*NYSE COMPOSITE INDEX=100

INTERIM EARNINGS (Per Share):

Qtr.	Mar.	June	Sept.	Dec.
1990	0.78	d0.34	d0.58	0.59
1991	1.24	d0.45	d0.40	0.65
1992	1.25	d0.29	d0.47	0.68
1993	1.32	d0.31	d0.50	0.69

INTERIM DIVIDENDS (Per Share):

Amt.	Decl.	Ex.	Rec.	Pay.
0.245Q	4/23/93	5/24/93	5/28/93	6/15/93
0.245Q	8/9	8/25	8/31	9/15
0.25Q	11/1	11/23	11/30	12/15
0.25Q	1/31/94	2/22/94	2/28/94	3/15/94
0.25Q	4/29	5/24	5/31	6/15

Indicated div.: $1.00

CAPITALIZATION (12/31/93):

	($000)	(%)
Long-Term Debt	151,843	84.4
Deferred Income Tax	28,157	15.6
Total	180,000	100.0
Current Debt	6,402	

DIVIDEND ACHIEVER STATUS:
Rank: 303   1983-93 Growth Rate: 4.2%
Total Years of Dividend Growth: 12

RECENT DEVELOPMENTS: For the year ended 12/31/93, net income was $12.2 million, or $1.19 per share, compared with $10.2 million, or $1.07 per share, last year. Operating revenues increased 8.3% to $287.5 million from $265.5 million a year ago. Natural gas sales resulted in an operating margin of $106.5 million in 1993, an increase of $7.2 million over the 1992 margin of $99.3 million. Subsidiary operations contrib-

uted 35% of the company's earnings for 1993, down from 42% last year. For the quarter, earnings were $7.1 million, or $0.69 per share, versus $6.8 million, or $0.68 per share, in the fourth quarter of 1992. Operating revenues were $90.3 million compared with $93.3 million in the corresponding period last year. Operating income was $10.5 million, up 14.9% from operating income of $9.1 million a year ago.

BUSINESS

UNITED CITIES GAS COMPANY is primarily a distributor of natural and propane gas, operating in ten states and serving approximately 303,000 customers (283,000 natural and 20,000 propane). UCIT's natural gas business is conducted in eight states: Tennessee, Georgia, Illinois, South Carolina, Missouri, Virginia, Iowa and Kansas. Propane is distributed through UCIT's wholly-owned subsidiary, UCG Energy Corporation. The propane division of UCG Energy serves customers in Tennessee, North Carolina and Virginia. The subsidiary is engaged in other activities complementing the natural gas business through its rental and utility services divisions. United Cities Gas Storage Company provides UCIT and others with supplemental natural gas supplies through company-owned natural gas storage fields in Kentucky and Kansas.

REVENUES

(12/31/93)	($000)	(%)
Residential	134,856	46.9
Commercial	74,361	25.9
Industrial	67,955	23.6
Other	3,411	1.2
Transportation	6,924	2.4
Total	287,507	100.0

ANNUAL EARNINGS AND DIVIDENDS PER SHARE

	1993	1992	1991	1990	1989	1988	1987
Earnings Per Share	1.19	1.07	0.97	0.44	1.52	1.24	1.06
Dividends Per Share	0.985	0.965	0.93	0.92	0.88	0.84	① 0.80
Dividend Payout %	83.2	90.2	95.9	N.M.	57.9	67.7	75.5

① 2-for-1 stk. split, 11/87.

ANNUAL FINANCIAL DATA

RECORD OF EARNINGS (IN THOUSANDS):

	1993	1992	1991	1990	1989	1988	1987
Total Revenues	326,416	297,943	266,252	247,051	215,979	189,306	179,127
Depreciation & Amort	13,104	15,111	15,782	15,007	11,090	9,477	8,212
Maintenance	6,070	6,989	3,169	3,796	3,192	2,606	2,390
Prov for Fed Inc Taxes	1,835	2,117	1,488	754	1,612	1,307	1,141
Interest Expense	16,097	13,581	14,457	14,336	8,658	7,174	5,337
Net Income	12,150	10,218	7,875	3,373	10,310	7,224	5,669
Aver. Shs. Outstg.	10,197	9,459	8,000	7,238	6,572	5,218	4,848

BALANCE SHEET (IN THOUSANDS):

Gross Plant	442,287	412,576	388,265	366,445	326,199	220,043	193,725
Accumulated Depreciation	147,699	135,925	124,241	114,699	103,309	69,270	60,804
Prop, Plant & Equip, Net	294,588	276,651	264,024	251,746	222,890	150,773	132,921
Long-term Debt	151,843	157,734	127,430	96,521	78,230	64,719	70,941
Total Assets	401,520	373,682	368,257	340,648	307,160	199,036	183,612
Year End Shares Outstg	10,314	10,052	8,517	7,292	7,197	5,274	4,821

STATISTICAL RECORD:

Dep/Gr. Pl %	3.7	3.7	4.0	4.0	3.4	4.3	4.2
Accum. Dep./Gr. Pl %	33.4	32.9	32.0	31.3	31.7	31.5	31.4
Average Yield %	5.3	6.6	6.6	6.5	6.3	6.8	6.0
P/E Ratio	17.6-13.4	15.7-11.7	16.8-12.4	35.5-29.3	10.2-8.1	10.6-9.3	14.3-11.1
Price Range	21-16	16¾-12½	16¼-12	15⅝-12⅞	15½-12¼	13⅛-11½	15⅛-11¾

Statistics are as originally reported.

OFFICERS:
G.C. Koonce, Pres. & C.E.O.
S.M. Hawkins, Sr. V.P. & Sec.
J.B. Ford, Sr. V.P. & Treas.
T.S. Hawkins, Jr., V.P.-Fin.

INCORPORATED: IL, Sep., 1929

PRINCIPAL OFFICE: 5300 Maryland Way, Brentwood, TN 37027

TELEPHONE NUMBER: (615) 373-0104
FAX: (615) 371-5053
NO. OF EMPLOYEES: 183
ANNUAL MEETING: In April
SHAREHOLDERS: 3,929
INSTITUTIONAL HOLDINGS:
No. of Institutions: 37
Shares Held: 1,560,903

REGISTRAR(S): Harris Trust & Savings Bank, Chicago, IL

TRANSFER AGENT(S): Harris Trust & Savings Bank, Chicago, IL

NASDAQ SYMBOL USBC
Rec. Pr. 24½ (Marginable)

U.S. BANCORP

YIELD 3.6%
P/E RATIO 10.0

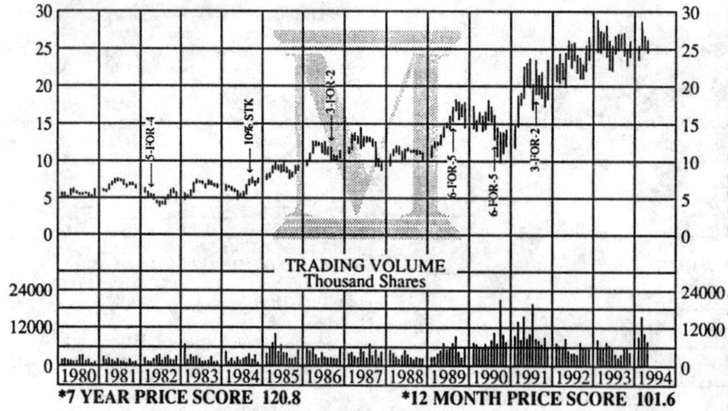

***7 YEAR PRICE SCORE 120.8** ***12 MONTH PRICE SCORE 101.6**

*NYSE COMPOSITE INDEX=100

INTERIM EARNINGS (Per Share):

Qtr.	Mar.	June	Sept.	Dec.
1990	0.46	0.52	0.52	0.49
1991	0.51	0.43	0.53	0.54
1992	0.48	0.54	0.40	0.63
1993	0.59	0.61	0.63	0.64

INTERIM DIVIDENDS (Per Share):

Amt.	Decl.	Ex.	Rec.	Pay.
0.22Q	5/14/93	6/7/93	6/11/93	7/1/93
0.22Q	8/19	8/30	9/3	10/1
0.22Q	11/18	12/6	12/10	1/3/94
0.22Q	2/18/94	3/7/94	3/11/94	4/1
0.22Q	4/20	6/6	6/10	7/1

Indicated div.: $0.88

CAPITALIZATION (12/31/93):

	($000)	(%)
Total Deposits	15,510,701	74.6
Total Debt	3,456,999	16.7
Series A Preferred Stock	150,000	0.7
Common & Surplus	1,668,195	8.0
Total	20,785,895	100.0

DIVIDEND ACHIEVER STATUS:
Rank: 136 1983-93 Growth Rate: 11.3%
Total Years of Dividend Growth: 34

RECENT DEVELOPMENTS: For the year ended 12/31/93, net income increased 24% to a record $257.9 million compared with the $208.1 million earned before accounting changes in 1992. Net interest income increased over 7%, resulting from increased loan growth over the last three quarters of the year, strong net interest margins and continued reductions in nonperforming assets. The net interest margin, primarily benefiting from lower funding costs, was 5.29%, up from 5.18% in 1992. Noninterest revenues rose 20% to $531.8 million due to strong gains in bank card revenues, brokerage commissions, equity investment income, mortgage banking revenues and service charges. For the quarter, net income totaled $67.1 million compared with $66.1 million in the same period in 1992. Net interest margin was 5.22%, unchanged from fourth quarter 1992. Nonperforming assets at year-end dropped 13% from prior year levels to $252.1 million, representing only 1.77% of total loans and foreclosed assets.

BUSINESS

U.S. BANCORP is a financial services holding company. Its banking subsidiaries include U.S. Bank of Oregon, U.S. Bank of Washington, U.S. Bank of California, U.S. Bank of Nevada, and U.S. Bank of Idaho. These full service retail commercial banks operate through 176 locations in Oregon, 159 locations in Washington and 67 locations in Northern California, 28 locations in Nevada and 8 locations in Idaho. Other financial service businesses include U.S. Bancorp Corporate Banking Group, U.S. Bancorp Leasing & Financial, U.S. Bancorp Merchant Banking, U.S. Bancorp Mortgage Company, U.S. Bancorp National Products Group, and U.S. Bancorp Securities & Trust Group.

LOAN DISTRIBUTION

(12/31/93)	($000)	(%)
Commercial	6,796,800	48.0
Real Estate-Construction	699,900	4.9
Real Estate-Mortgage	2,611,200	18.4
Consumer	3,198,400	22.6
Foreign	96,300	0.7
Lease Financing	765,900	5.4
Total	14,168,500	100.0

ANNUAL EARNINGS AND DIVIDENDS PER SHARE

	1993	1992	1991	1990	1989	1988	1987
Earnings Per Share	**2.47**	**[1] 2.05**	**2.01**	**2.04**	**1.69**	**1.40**	**1.13**
Dividends Per Share	**0.85**	**0.76**	**[2] 0.69**	**[3] 0.583**	**[4] 0.486**	**0.439**	**0.371**
Dividend Payout %	**34.4**	**37.1**	**34.3**	**28.6**	**28.7**	**31.4**	**32.9**

[1] Before acctg. chg. [2] Adj for 3-for-2 stk split, 8/13/91 [3] 20% stk div, 9/14/90 [4] 20% stk div, 9/15/89

ANNUAL FINANCIAL DATA

	1993	1992	1991	1990	1989	1988	1987
RECORD OF EARNINGS (IN MILLIONS):							
Total Interest Income	1,433.7	1,491.5	1,638.6	1,625.3	1,436.5	1,163.0	976.8
Total Interest Expense	505.6	631.1	869.3	966.3	832.9	635.5	529.4
Net Interest Income	928.1	860.4	769.3	659.1	603.6	527.5	447.4
Provision for Loan Losses	92.9	134.5	125.4	102.8	83.8	69.2	57.4
Net Income	257.9	148.2	196.4	182.7	150.8	123.9	108.5
Aver. Shs. Outstg. (000)	99,327	98,650	97,640	89,697	89,097	88,626	88,316
BALANCE SHEET (IN MILLIONS):							
Cash & Due From Banks	1,250.6	1,246.2	1,119.7	1,172.1	1,324.7	1,261.8	1,115.1
Loans & Lse Financing, Net	13,898.3	...	14,146.5	13,164.1	11,470.0	9,628.2	8,597.8
Total Domestic Deposits	15,510.7	15,425.3	13,316.4	12,533.9	11,432.2	10,167.7	9,521.5
Long-term Debt	1,051.6	1,329.2	1,214.1	666.3	603.0	624.8	475.5
Net Stockholders' Equity	1,818.2	1,631.3	1,411.9	1,196.5	1,053.7	943.8	857.5
Total Assets	21,415.5	20,741.1	18,875.1	17,613.1	16,975.4	14,383.4	13,352.7
Year End Shs Outstg (000)	99,476	99,068	98,194	90,498	89,310	88,797	88,424
STATISTICAL RECORD:							
Return on Assets %	1.20	1.00	1.04	1.04	0.89	0.86	0.75
Return on Equity %	14.20	12.80	13.90	15.30	14.30	13.10	11.60
Book Value Per Share	16.77	14.95	14.38	13.22	11.80	10.63	9.70
Average Yield %	3.3	3.3	3.9	4.2	3.4	4.1	3.2
P/E Ratio	11.7-8.9	13.0-9.7	11.8-5.8	8.9-4.8	10.8-6.2	8.6-6.7	12.8-7.7
Price Range	28⅞-22	26⅝-19⅞	23¾-11¾	18⅛-9⅞	18¼-10½	12-9⅜	14½-8¾

Statistics are as originally reported.

OFFICERS:
R.L. Breezley, Chairman
E.P. Jensen, Vice-Chmn. & C.E.O.
K.R. Kelly, President
P.M. Devore, Exec. V.P. & Treas.

INCORPORATED: OR, Sep., 1968

PRINCIPAL OFFICE: 111 S.W. Fifth Ave. P.O. Box 8837, Portland, OR 97208

TELEPHONE NUMBER: (503) 275-6111

NO. OF EMPLOYEES: 12,863

ANNUAL MEETING: In April

SHAREHOLDERS: 15,604

INSTITUTIONAL HOLDINGS:
No. of Institutions: 274
Shares Held: 53,928,079

REGISTRAR(S):

TRANSFER AGENT(S): First Chicago Trust Co. of New York, New York, NY 10008

UNIVERSAL CORP.

	YIELD	5.2%
	P/E RATIO	4.0

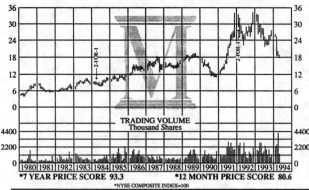

TRADING VOLUME
Thousand Shares

*7 YEAR PRICE SCORE 93.3   *12 MONTH PRICE SCORE 80.6
*NYSE COMPOSITE INDEX=100

INTERIM EARNINGS (Per Share):

Qtr.	Sept.	Dec.	Mar.	June
1991-92	0.62	0.89	0.57	Nil
1992-93	0.72	1.08	0.58	2.39
1993-94	0.52	0.57	...	...

INTERIM DIVIDENDS (Per Share):

Amt.	Decl.	Ex.	Rec.	Pay.
0.22Q	5/6/93	7/6/93	7/12/93	8/9/93
0.22Q	8/5	10/5	10/12	11/8
0.24Q	12/2	1/4/94	1/10/94	2/7/94
0.24Q	2/3/94	4/5	4/11	5/9
0.24Q	5/5	7/5	7/11	8/8

Indicated div.: $0.96

CAPITALIZATION (6/30/93):

	($000)	(%)
Long-Term Debt	281,807	38.3
Deferred Income Tax	32,827	4.5
Minority Interests	2,452	0.3
Common & Surplus	417,913	56.9
Total	734,999	100.0

DIVIDEND ACHIEVER STATUS:
Rank: 233   1983-93 Growth Rate: 7.4%
Total Years of Dividend Growth: 23

RECENT DEVELOPMENTS: For the quarter ended 12/31/93, net income was $20.2 million compared with $35.2 million in 1992. Revenues declined 2.8% to $863.7 million. International tobacco operations were hurt by lower margins as a result of a worldwide surplus, while domestic operations were hurt by weak demand and a poor quality tobacco crop. The core agri-products businesses reported lower results versus last year due to losses incurred on coffee trading.

PROSPECTS: Market conditions in the tobacco industry remain unfavorable due to a worldwide surplus which continues to restrain margins. However, international operations should benefit from strong sales and demand for tobacco in Brazil and Africa. Also, lumber and building products operations should benefit from an ongoing cost containment program. Meanwhile, UVV is making substantial investments to develop tobacco markets in Eastern Europe and China.

BUSINESS

UNIVERSAL CORP. has operations in tobacco, lumber and building products and agri-products. UVV's primary subsidiary, Universal Leaf, is the world's largest independent tobacco dealer, providing buying, processing, packing, storing and financing services for manufacturers of tobacco products. Lumber and building products operations involve distribution to the building and construction trade in Europe, and the manufacture of laminated wood products in the United States Agri-products operations primarily involve the buying and selling of physical products such as rubber, coffee, tea, peanuts, sunflower seeds and vegetable oils. Title insurance operations were spun off in 1991.

BUSINESS LINE ANALYSIS

(6/30/93)	Rev(%)	Inc(%)
Tobacco	74.9	84.2
Lumber & Building Prods	12.6	9.5
Agri-products	12.5	6.3
Total	100.0	100.0

ANNUAL EARNINGS AND DIVIDENDS PER SHARE

	6/30/93	6/30/92	6/30/91	6/30/90	6/30/89	6/30/88	6/30/87
Earnings Per Share	2.39	2.15	②1.72	③1.11	1.60	1.78	1.63
Dividends Per Share	0.88	①0.80	0.76	0.74	0.70	0.64	0.57
Dividend Payout %	36.8	37.2	44.2	66.7	43.9	36.0	35.1

① 2-for-1 stk split, 1/2/92 ② Before dicont oper. & extraord. item ③ Before acctg. chg.

ANNUAL FINANCIAL DATA

RECORD OF EARNINGS (IN MILLIONS):

Total Revenues	3,047.2	2,989.0	2,896.5	2,815.1	2,920.3	2,429.0	2,115.8
Costs and Expenses	2,850.1	2,809.0	2,736.3	2,708.1	2,789.4	2,299.5	①1,996.1
Depreciation	32.8	29.2	25.8	27.1	25.6	22.0	...
Operating Income	164.3	150.9	134.3	79.9	105.3	107.4	119.6
Inc Bef Income Taxes	118.2	101.1	76.3	46.2	75.7	74.9	88.5
Income Taxes	43.5	35.3	24.3	13.6	24.4	17.7	34.3
Eq In Net Inc Of Affils	4.7	4.6	4.4	4.1	3.4	3.3	1.6
Minority Interests	cr0.7	cr0.3	④0.1	cr0.1	0.6	cr0.1	cr0.1
Net Income	80.2	70.7	②56.4	③37.1	54.0	60.7	56.0
Aver. Shs. Outstg. (000)	33,599	32,822	32,792	33,522	33,872	34,118	34,406

① Incl. Dep. ② Before disc. op. dr$32,350,000; and extra. item dr$3,800,000. ③ Before acctg. change cr$7,984,000. ④ Equal to $62,000.

BALANCE SHEET (IN MILLIONS):

Cash and Cash Equivalents	119.7	82.7	59.5	50.8	68.4	53.1	42.7
Receivables, Net	369.5	323.9	395.4	7.6	0.9	259.3	234.3
Inventories	569.3	544.3	406.1	356.1	279.3	267.5	278.3
Gross Property	524.2	446.9	408.2	385.5	341.9	313.2	272.6
Accumulated Depreciation	246.5	219.4	197.9	199.2	175.5	154.2	135.5
Long-Term Debt	281.8	190.2	160.0	144.3	85.2	88.1	93.3
Net Stockholders' Equity	417.9	301.7	389.8	397.1	386.4	356.9	325.7
Total Assets	1,562.0	1,261.4	1,275.6	1,170.7	1,062.1	1,006.6	943.4
Total Current Assets	1,086.9	970.5	877.5	717.0	638.6	610.2	571.4
Total Current Liabilities	786.4	697.2	654.0	452.9	438.2	429.0	398.8
Net Working Capital	300.5	273.3	223.5	264.1	200.4	181.2	172.7
Year End Shs Outstg (000)	35,632	32,863	32,778	32,880	33,862	33,928	34,406

STATISTICAL RECORD:

Operating Profit Margin %	5.4	5.0	4.6	2.8	3.6	4.4	5.7
Book Value Per Share	7.81	8.83	11.49	11.16	10.57	9.67	8.60
Return on Equity %	19.2	23.4	14.5	9.3	14.0	17.0	17.2
Return on Assets %	5.1	5.6	4.4	3.2	5.1	6.0	5.9
Average Yield %	3.2	2.8	3.3	5.1	3.9	4.1	3.6
P/E Ratio	14.1-9.1	15.9-10.3	19.8-6.9	16.3-9.9	12.2-10.3	9.5-7.9	11.3-7.9
Price Range	33¾-21¾	34¼-22¼	34-11⅞	18⅛-11	19½-16½	16⅞-14	18⅜-12⅞

Statistics are as originally reported.

OFFICERS:
H.H. Harrell, Chmn. & C.E.O.
A.B. King, Pres. & C.O.O.

INCORPORATED: VA, Jan., 1918

PRINCIPAL OFFICE: Hamilton Street at Broad, Richmond, VA 23230

TELEPHONE NUMBER: (804) 359-9311
FAX: (804) 254-8594
NO. OF EMPLOYEES: 13,250 (approx.)
ANNUAL MEETING: In October
SHAREHOLDERS: 1,942 (com.)
INSTITUTIONAL HOLDINGS:
No. of Institutions: 176
Shares Held: 19,182,585

REGISTRAR(S): Sovran Bank, N.A., Richmond, VA 23219

TRANSFER AGENT(S): Sovran Bank, N.A., Richmond, VA 23219

NYS SYMBOL USH
Rec. Pr. 36⅜

USLIFE CORP.

YIELD 3.4%
P/E RATIO 10.0

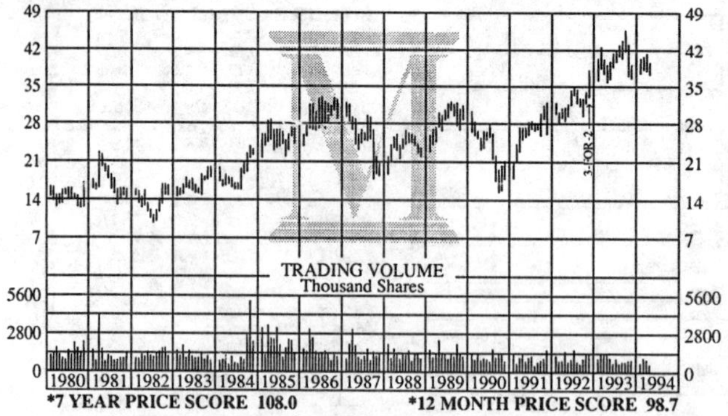

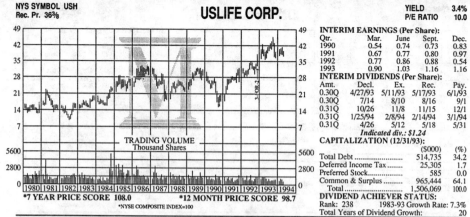

***7 YEAR PRICE SCORE 108.0** ***12 MONTH PRICE SCORE 98.7**

*NYSE COMPOSITE INDEX=100

INTERIM EARNINGS (Per Share):

Qtr.	Mar.	June	Sept.	Dec.
1990	0.54	0.74	0.73	0.83
1991	0.67	0.77	0.80	0.97
1992	0.77	0.86	0.88	0.54
1993	0.90	1.03	1.16	1.16

INTERIM DIVIDENDS (Per Share):

Amt.	Decl.	Ex.	Rec.	Pay.
0.30Q	4/27/93	5/11/93	5/17/93	6/1/93
0.30Q	7/14	8/10	8/16	9/1
0.31Q	10/26	11/8	11/15	12/1
0.31Q	1/25/94	2/8/94	2/14/94	3/1/94
0.31Q	4/26	5/12	5/18	5/31

Indicated div.: $1.24

CAPITALIZATION (12/31/93):

	($000)	(%)
Total Debt	514,735	34.2
Deferred Income Tax	25,305	1.7
Preferred Stock	585	0.0
Common & Surplus	965,444	64.1
Total	1,506,069	100.0

DIVIDEND ACHIEVER STATUS:

Rank: 238 1983-93 Growth Rate: 7.3%

Total Years of Dividend Growth: 20

RECENT DEVELOPMENTS: For the three months ended 12/31/93 net income soared to $26.4 million from $12.5 million in the corresponding 1992 period. Revenues increased to $412.7 million from $391.6 million a year earlier. For the twelve months ended 12/13/93 net income was $97.2 million compared with $69.6 million for 1992. Revenues increased to $1.60 billion from last yea's $1.52 billion. Total benefits and expenses were controlled amounting to $1.45 billion versus $1.43 billion in 1992.

PROSPECTS: The US Life Insurance Co., a wholly-owned subsidiary, has stopped selling new employer-employee medical insurance business in areas where insurance in force is minimal. Marketing efforts will emphasize areas where market presence is already significant. The employer/employee group life segment should continue to post healthy earnings. Increases in prices and stricter underwriting policies are benefiting results.

BUSINESS

USLIFE CORPORATION is a life insurance-based company. Growth has come through acquisitions and the forming of new operating units. With nationwide operations, USLIFE has three ordinary life insurance companies and a credit insurance group which provide individual and group life and health insurance. Other subsidiaries provide services to the life insurance companies. These subsidiaries are engaged in investment advisory, broker-dealer, real estate, data processing and administrative services.

PREMIUM INCOME

(12/31/93)	($000)	(%)
Life & Annuities	455,170	48.2
Accident & Health	489,136	51.8
Total	944,306	100.0

ANNUAL EARNINGS AND DIVIDENDS PER SHARE

	1993	1992	1991	1990	1989	1988	1987
Earnings Per Share	**4.25**	**[1] 3.05**	**3.22**	**2.85**	**3.09**	**2.54**	**[3] 2.63**
Dividends Per Share	**1.21**	**[2] 1.14**	**1.067**	**0.987**	**0.94**	**0.867**	**0.813**
Dividend Payout %	**28.5**	**37.4**	**33.1**	**34.7**	**30.5**	**34.1**	**31.0**

[1] Before acctg. chg. [2] 3-for-2 stk split,12/23/92 [3] Before disc. oper.

ANNUAL FINANCIAL DATA

	1993	1992	1991	1990	1989	1988	1987
RECORD OF EARNINGS (IN MILLIONS):							
Insurance Premiums	944.3	926.4	840.3	760.6	743.5	966.7	897.6
Net Investment Income	444.6	414.4	361.6	322.6	307.9	289.6	270.7
Total Income	1,600.0	1,529.5	1,382.9	1,235.6	1,200.2	1,279.1	1,189.0
Death & Other Benefits	737.3	740.9	686.9	622.0	595.6	606.2	574.2
Income Bef Income Taxes	151.6	104.3	111.0	103.5	120.5	94.8	112.0
Income Taxes	54.4	34.7	36.2	34.8	40.2	27.0	37.3
Gain on Sale Of Securities	...	...	...	...	...	3.1	5.6
Net Income	97.2	[1] 69.6	74.9	68.6	[2] 80.3	70.9	[3] 80.2
Aver. Shs. Outstg. (000)	22,582	22,723	23,136	23,979	25,833	26,463	...

[1] Before acctg. change dr$37,990,000. [2] Before extra. item dr$6,526,000. [3] Before disc. op. dr$479,000.

	1993	1992	1991	1990	1989	1988	1987
BALANCE SHEET (IN MILLIONS):							
Cash on Hand & In Demand Accts	60.3	74.6	76.5	76.5	72.7	70.5	43.5
Fixed Maturities	4,751.7	4,160.5	3,408.6	2,705.1	2,177.6	2,284.8	2,053.8
Equity Securities	9.2	19.5	23.8	25.3	25.9	29.4	32.3
Policy Loans	282.1	283.9	286.2	285.6	288.3	295.6	314.7
Mortgage Loans	361.1	388.4	434.1	442.1	449.2	416.6	428.7
Total Assets	6,740.2	6,095.3	5,329.3	4,573.3	4,336.4	4,145.3	3,880.3
Benefits and Claims	1,657.5	1,528.4	1,497.2	1,471.3	1,466.8	2,568.8	2,349.4
Net Stockholders' Equity	966.0	890.4	972.6	932.3	934.1	924.0	905.9
Year End Shs Outstg (000)	22,658	22,503	22,525	23,037	24,980	25,208	26,507
STATISTICAL RECORD:							
Book Value Per Share	42.61	39.54	43.02	40.27	37.17	36.23	33.73
Return on Equity %	10.1	7.8	7.7	7.4	8.6	7.7	8.9
Return on Assets %	1.4	1.1	1.4	1.5	1.9	1.7	2.1
Average Yield %	3.0	3.4	4.3	4.3	3.4	3.8	3.3
P/E Ratio	10.8-8.4	12.5-9.2	9.9-5.6	10.6-5.4	10.4-7.4	10.5-7.3	12.1-6.8
Price Range	45¾-35¾	38¼-28⅛	31⅞-17⅞	30⅛-15½	32⅛-22¾	26¾-18⅝	31⅞-17⅞

Statistics are as originally reported.

OFFICERS:
G.E. Crosby, Jr., Chmn. & C.E.O.
G.F. Henderson, Vice-Chmn. & C.F.O.
R.J. Casper, Pres. & C.O.O.
R.G. Hohn, Sr. V.P., Sec. & Couns.

INCORPORATED: NY, Nov., 1966

PRINCIPAL OFFICE: 125 Maiden Lane, New York, NY 10038

TELEPHONE NUMBER: (212) 709-6000
FAX: (212) 425-8010
NO. OF EMPLOYEES: 2,140 (approx.)
ANNUAL MEETING: In May
SHAREHOLDERS: 8,100 (approx.)
INSTITUTIONAL HOLDINGS:
No. of Institutions: 231
Shares Held: 15,547,320

REGISTRAR(S): Manufacturers Hanover Trust Co., New York, NY

TRANSFER AGENT(S): Manufacturers Hanover Trust Co., New York, NY

UST, INC.

	YIELD	4.1%
	P/E RATIO	15.9

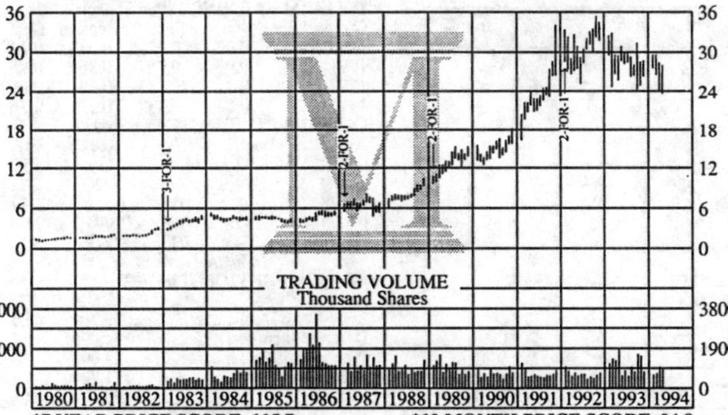

*7 YEAR PRICE SCORE 115.7   *12 MONTH PRICE SCORE 94.8*
NYSE COMPOSITE INDEX=100

TRADING VOLUME
Thousand Shares

INTERIM EARNINGS (Per Share):

Qtr.	Mar.	June	Sept.	Dec.
1990	0.23	0.25	0.26	0.24
1991	0.26	0.30	0.33	0.30
1992	0.31	0.35	0.38	0.36
1993	0.47	0.41	0.41	0.41

INTERIM DIVIDENDS (Per Share):

Amt.	Decl.	Ex.	Rec.	Pay.
0.24Q	5/4/93	5/28/93	6/4/93	6/15/93
0.24Q	7/22	8/30	9/3	9/15
0.24Q	10/28	11/29	12/3	12/15
0.28Q	12/16	2/28/94	3/4/94	3/15/94
0.28Q	5/3/94	5/27	6/3	6/15

Indicated div.: $1.12

CAPITALIZATION (12/31/93):

	($000)	(%)
Long-Term Debt	40,000	7.8
Deferred Income Tax	7,955	1.6
Common & Surplus	462,972	90.6
Total	510,927	100.0

DIVIDEND ACHIEVER STATUS:
Rank: 15   1983-93 Growth Rate: 20.8%
Total Years of Dividend Growth: 23

RECENT DEVELOPMENTS: For the year ended 12/31/93, net income was $368.9 million compared with $312.6 million a year ago. Results were before an accounting change of $19.8 million. Sales increased 6.8% to $1.11 billion. The Tobacco and Wine segments posted sales gains for the year, led by higher sales of moist smokeless tobacco. Domestic unit volume for moist smokeless tobacco increased to 611.6 million cans, up 2.3% from last year.

PROSPECTS: UST will continue to post improved results. Sales and unit volume figures for moist smokeless tobacco are strong, aided by UST's two flagship brands, Copenhagen and Skoal. However, UST will continue to face increased competition from private label manufacturers. Over the long-term, sales may be constrained by federal and state initiatives to tax tobacco products and limit tobacco advertising.

BUSINESS

UST INC. is a holding company, and through its subsidiaries is a leading manufacturer of moist smokeless tobacco products with Copenhagen, Skoal, Skoal Bandits and Skoal Long Cut as principal brands. Other consumer products made and marketed by UST subsidiaries include premium wines from Washington State and California's Napa Valley, sold nationally under the Chateau Ste. Michelle, Columbia Crest, Conn Creek, and Villa Mt. Eden labels. UST also makes and markets pipes and imported pipe tobaccos, imported cigars, and other tobacco-related products, and is involved in a diverse mix of small businesses in other industries.

BUSINESS LINE ANALYSIS

(12/31/93)	Rev(%)	Inc(%)
Tobacco	85.5	97.4
Wine	7.2	1.0
Other	7.3	1.6
Total	100.0	100.0

ANNUAL EARNINGS AND DIVIDENDS PER SHARE

	1993	1992	1991	1990	1989	1988	1987
Earnings Per Share	1.71	1.41	1.18	0.98	0.82	0.71	0.56
Dividends Per Share	0.96	0.80	①0.66	0.55	②0.46	0.37	③0.30
Dividend Payout %	56.1	56.7	66.0	56.0	56.4	52.5	53.1

① 2-for-1 stk split,01/28/92   ② 2-for-1 stk split, 1/27/89   ③ 100% stk. div. 1/87.

ANNUAL FINANCIAL DATA

RECORD OF EARNINGS (IN MILLIONS):

	1993	1992	1991	1990	1989	1988	1987
Total Revenues	1,110.4	1,044.4	907.3	764.7	682.5	618.5	576.1
Costs and Expenses	519.0	519.2	461.0	396.1	367.5	340.6	321.7
Depreciation & Amort	26.7	24.5	22.6	19.6	16.5	17.7	17.0
Operating Profit	564.8	789.5	680.8	572.9	497.0	444.0	407.2
Earn Bef Income Taxes	601.8	502.6	426.1	352.2	301.6	261.3	234.6
Income Taxes	232.9	190.1	160.2	128.9	111.1	99.1	103.8
Net Income	①368.9	312.6	265.9	223.3	190.5	162.2	130.9
Aver. Shs. Outstg. (000)	215,719	222,033	225,130	227,667	233,305	230,416	232,372

① Before acctg. change dr$19,846,000.

BALANCE SHEET (IN MILLIONS):

	1993	1992	1991	1990	1989	1988	1987
Cash & Cash Equivalents	25.3	36.4	41.5	46.6	54.6	72.7	50.4
Accounts Receivable	64.4	53.8	50.1	34.9	39.5	29.7	29.6
Inventories	215.6	213.5	193.7	169.9	168.8	174.8	162.2
Gross Property	472.9	423.9	406.1	380.7	347.6	327.8	311.8
Accumulated Depreciation	163.2	142.9	131.1	113.7	99.0	85.8	81.1
Long-Term Debt	40.0	...	...	3.1	6.8	21.8	37.1
Net Stockholders' Equity	463.0	516.6	482.9	473.9	482.3	453.3	401.1
Total Assets	706.2	674.0	656.5	622.6	636.3	598.0	549.0
Total Current Assets	335.0	330.2	305.4	265.9	279.6	291.0	260.5
Total Current Liabilities	106.6	81.2	95.5	68.7	92.1	69.9	63.2
Net Working Capital	228.4	249.0	210.0	197.2	187.5	221.1	197.3
Year End Shs Outstg (000)	196,290	211,037	210,980	212,983	218,204	219,960	220,364

STATISTICAL RECORD:

	1993	1992	1991	1990	1989	1988	1987
Operating Profit Margin %	50.9	47.9	46.7	45.6	43.7	42.1	41.2
Book Value Per Share	2.36	2.45	2.29	2.22	2.21	2.06	1.82
Return on Equity %	79.7	60.5	55.1	47.1	39.5	35.8	32.6
Return on Assets %	52.2	46.4	40.5	35.9	29.9	27.1	23.8
Average Yield %	3.4	2.6	2.6	3.6	3.7	4.5	4.6
P/E Ratio	19.2-14.3	25.1-17.9	28.8-13.9	18.6-12.6	19.0-12.0	14.8-8.6	14.5-8.7
Price Range	32¾-24⅜	35⅜-25¼	34-16⅜	18¼-12⅜	15⅜-9¾	10½-6⅛	8⅛-4⅞

Statistics are as originally reported.

OFFICERS:
V.A. Gierer, Jr., Chmn. & C.E.O.
J.J. Bucchignano, Exec. V.P. & C.F.O.
J.P. Nelson, Sr. V.P. & Sec.
J.D. Harris, Treas.

INCORPORATED: DE, Dec., 1986

PRINCIPAL OFFICE: 100 West Putnam Ave., Greenwich, CT 06830

TELEPHONE NUMBER: (203) 661-1100

NO. OF EMPLOYEES: 3,724 (avg.)

ANNUAL MEETING: In May

SHAREHOLDERS: 13,621

INSTITUTIONAL HOLDINGS:
No. of Institutions: 441
Shares Held: 109,248,053

REGISTRAR(S): First National Bank of Boston, Shareholder Services Division, Boston, MA

TRANSFER AGENT(S): First National Bank of Boston, Shareholder Services Division, Boston, MA

UTILICORP UNITED INC.

YIELD 5.9%
P/E RATIO 14.4

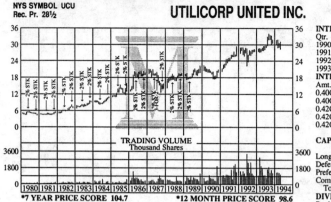

TRADING VOLUME
Thousand Shares

*7 YEAR PRICE SCORE 104.7   *12 MONTH PRICE SCORE 98.6
*NYSE COMPOSITE INDEX=100

INTERIM EARNINGS (Per Share):

Qtr.	Mar.	June	Sept.	Dec.
1990	0.92	0.12	0.35	0.74
1991	0.95	0.15	0.36	0.75
1992	0.77	d0.23	0.10	0.68
1993	0.87	0.13	0.22	0.76

INTERIM DIVIDENDS (Per Share):

Amt.	Decl.	Ex.	Rec.	Pay.
0.40Q	5/5/93	5/14/93	5/20/93	6/12/93
0.40Q	8/4	8/16	8/20	9/12
0.42Q	11/3	11/15	11/19	12/12
0.42Q	2/2/94	2/14/94	2/18/94	3/12/94
0.42Q	5/4	5/13	5/19	6/12

Indicated div.: $1.68

CAPITALIZATION (12/31/93):

	($000)	(%)
Long-Term Debt	1,009,700	45.9
Deferred Income Tax	254,000	11.6
Preferred Stock	83,900	3.8
Common & Surplus	851,700	38.7
Total	2,199,300	100.0

DIVIDEND ACHIEVER STATUS:
Rank: 166   1983-93 Growth Rate: 10.4%
Total Years of Dividend Growth: 36

RECENT DEVELOPMENTS: For the year ended 12/31/93, net income was $86.4 million compared with $52.9 million in 1992. Revenues were $1.60 billion, up 23%. Revenues benefited from increased sales due to more normal weather and rate relief at two of the Company's electric utility divisions. Net income for the quarter ended 12/31/93 was $33.3 million versus $25.6 million in the prior year. Fourth quarter results include a one-time gain of $48 million, mostly offset by an after-tax charge of approximately $45 million.

PROSPECTS: UCU completed its initial public offering of common shares of Aquila Gas Pipeline Corp. Proceeds from the offering totaled approximately $75.6 million and were used to retire short-term debt. To improve margins, Aquila has terminated unfavorably priced gas sales contracts and written off certain offshore assets. UCU will continue to pursue its long-term growth and diversification strategy in regulated and non-regulated businesses.

BUSINESS

UTILICORP UNITED INC. provides electric and gas utility service to nearly 1 million customers in eight states and one Canadian province. Utility divisions include: Missouri Public Service; Kansas Public Service; Peoples Natural Gas; Northern Minnesota Utilities; West Virginia Power; Michigan Gas Utilities, WestPlains Energy; and its Canadian subsidiary West Kootenay Power, B.C. Virtually all of UCU's U.S. electric power generation is coal or gas-fired, and all of its Canadian generation is hydroelectric. The Company does not operate nuclear power plants. Aquila Energy, a wholly owned subsidiary is one of the nations largest independent marketers of natural gas. Utilco Group, another wholly-owned subsidiary, owns and operates independent electric generating projects.

BUSINESS LINE ANALYSIS

(12/31/93)	Rev(%)	Inc(%)
Electric Opers	34.8	53.8
Gas Opers	43.7	29.6
Energy Related Business	21.5	16.6
Total	100.0	100.0

ANNUAL EARNINGS AND DIVIDENDS PER SHARE

	1993	1992	1991	1990	1989	1988	1987
Earnings Per Share	1.95	1.32	2.23	2.13	2.04	1.98	⑤ 1.79
Dividends Per Share	1.62	1.60	1.54	1.46	① 1.413	② 1.028	④ 0.942
Dividend Payout %	83.1	N.M.	69.1	68.5	69.3	51.9	52.6

① 2% stk div, 3/89 ② 2% stk div, 12/88 & 6/88 ③ Before acctg. chg. ④ 3-for-2 stk split, 7/87

ANNUAL FINANCIAL DATA

RECORD OF EARNINGS (IN MILLIONS):

	1993	1992	1991	1990	1989	1988	1987
Total Revenues	1,571.6	1,298.9	1,075.2	894.4	731.9	672.8	594.9
Depreciation & Amort	74.5	66.1	53.9	49.2	44.2	38.9	34.2
Maintenance	47.2	40.5	37.1	29.2	31.7	29.8	21.2
Prov for Fed Inc Taxes	...	...	...	...	21.7	18.5	19.7
Income From Operations	152.2	169.0	188.8	145.0	86.9	77.2	61.6
Interest Expense	100.1	99.1	81.7	58.9	49.4	38.9	32.9
Net Income	86.4	52.9	73.5	58.9	48.3	40.9	① 33.2
Aver. Shs. Outstg. (000)	40,740	34,930	29,390	29,390	23,968	20,863	19,420	16,664

① Before acctg. change dr$2,702,000.

BALANCE SHEET (IN MILLIONS):

Gross Plant	2,445.2	2,220.7	2,087.8	1,590.5	1,479.2	1,199.0	1,112.9
Accumulated Depreciation	865.0	767.2	721.8	506.5	475.7	386.2	356.3
Total Utility Plant (net)	1,580.2	1,453.5	1,366.0	1,084.0	1,003.5	812.9	756.6
Long-term Debt	1,009.7	890.8	928.1	667.6	437.6	358.0	317.7
Net Stockholders' Equity	935.6	756.2	767.4	588.4	474.9	357.1	289.4
Tot Util Plt & Other Assets	2,850.5	2,552.8	2,402.2	1,844.6	1,466.9	1,124.9	966.1
Year End Shs Outstg (000)	42,021	35,422	34,456	28,088	22,763	20,723	18,631

STATISTICAL RECORD:

Book Value Per Share	20.27	18.66	19.45	17.49	16.58	15.54	14.19
Op. Inc/Net Pl %	9.6	11.6	13.8	13.4	8.7	9.5	8.1
Dep/Gr. Pl %	3.0	3.0	2.6	3.1	3.0	3.2	3.1
Accum. Dep/Gr. Pl %	35.4	34.5	34.6	31.8	32.2	32.2	32.0
Return on Equity %	9.2	7.0	9.6	10.0	10.2	11.4	11.5
Average Yield %	5.3	6.3	6.2	7.3	7.2	6.1	5.6
P/E Ratio	17.4-13.9	22.0-16.8	13.2-9.0	10.5-8.2	10.9-8.4	9.9-7.1	11.7-7.0
Price Range	34-27⅛	29-22⅛	29⅜-20⅛	22⅜-17⅜	22¼-17⅛	19⅝-14⅛	21-12⅝

Statistics are as originally reported.

OFFICERS:
R.C. Green, Jr., Chmn., Pres. & C.E.O.
J.R. Baker, Vice-Chmn.
D.J. Wolf, V.P.-Fin. & Sec.
INCORPORATED: MO, Apr., 1950; reincorp., DE, Apr., 1987
PRINCIPAL OFFICE: 3000 Commerce Tower 911 Main, Kansas City, MO 64105

TELEPHONE NUMBER: (816) 421-6600
FAX: (816) 691-3591
NO. OF EMPLOYEES: 4,737
ANNUAL MEETING: In May
SHAREHOLDERS: 33,902
INSTITUTIONAL HOLDINGS:
No. of Institutions: 135
Shares Held: 8,127,315

REGISTRAR(S): First Chicago Trust Co. of New York, New York, NY 10008
First National Bank of Chicago, Chicago, IL 60670

TRANSFER AGENT(S): First Chicago Trust Co. of New York, New York, NY 10008
United Missouri Bank, N.A., Kansas City, MO 64141-0064

NASDAQ SYMBOL VYBN
Rec. Pr. 37 (Marginable)

VALLEY BANCORPORATION

YIELD 2.6%
P/E RATIO 16.6

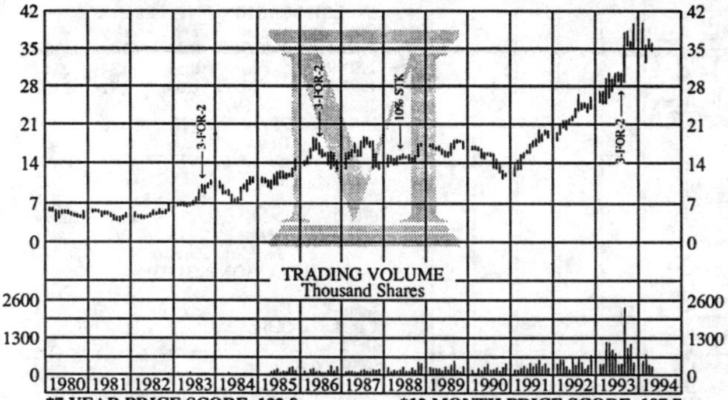

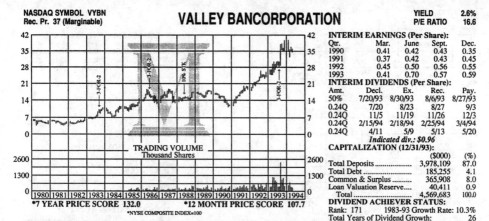

***7 YEAR PRICE SCORE 132.0** ***12 MONTH PRICE SCORE 107.7**

*NYSE COMPOSITE INDEX=100

INTERIM EARNINGS (Per Share):

Qtr.	Mar.	June	Sept.	Dec.
1990	0.41	0.42	0.43	0.35
1991	0.37	0.42	0.43	0.45
1992	0.45	0.50	0.56	0.55
1993	0.41	0.70	0.57	0.59

INTERIM DIVIDENDS (Per Share):

Amt.	Decl.	Ex.	Rec.	Pay.
50%	7/20/93	8/30/93	8/6/93	8/27/93
0.24Q	7/20	8/23	8/27	9/3
0.24Q	11/5	11/19	11/26	12/3
0.24Q	2/15/94	2/18/94	2/25/94	3/4/94
0.24Q	4/11	5/9	5/13	5/20

Indicated div.: $0.96

CAPITALIZATION (12/31/93):

	($000)	(%)
Total Deposits	3,978,109	87.0
Total Debt	185,255	4.1
Common & Surplus	365,908	8.0
Loan Valuation Reserve	40,411	0.9
Total	4,569,683	100.0

DIVIDEND ACHIEVER STATUS:
Rank: 171 1983-93 Growth Rate: 10.3%
Total Years of Dividend Growth: 26

RECENT DEVELOPMENTS: As of 6/1/94, the Company had been acquired by Marshall & Ilsley Corp. for stock valued at more than $760 million. For the year ended 12/31/93, net income was $45.9, or $2.26 per share, million compared with $39.8 million, or $2.07 per share, in 1992. Earnings for 1993 benefited from an increase in fully tax equivalent (FTE) net interest income of $7.6 million over 1992, resulting from growth in average earning assets between years of 7.46%, or $280.2 million. External growth accounted for approximately $150 million of this increase. VYBN's margin continued to show pressure with a reduction to 4.46% this quarter compared with 4.60% in the fourth quarter of 1992. For the quarter, net income amounted to $11.9 million, up 8% from $11.0 million in the same period a year ago. Earnings per share for the quarter were $0.58 versus $0.55 last year. At year-end 1993, VYBN had total assets of $4.59 billion, an increase of 4.74% over the $4.38 billion at year-end 1992.

BUSINESS

VALLEY BANCORPORATION is a diversified financial services company headquartered in Appleton, Wisconsin. The Company has 18 banking subsidiaries serving customers from a total of 160 locations in Wisconsin. The four largest Valley Banks, in Madison, Appleton, Green Bay and Janesville represent more than half of Valley's total assets. Through certain subsidiaries Valley makes available to its customers a variety of trust and fiduciary services, credit cards, insurance sales and securities brokerage services. Other subsidiaries offer credit life reinsurance for loans originated by Valley Banks and extensive data processing, which are utilized primarily by Valley Banks. The Company also offers equipment leasing services through one of its subsidiary banks.

LOAN DISTRIBUTION

(12/31/93)	($000)	(%)
Commercial	723,941	22.7
Real Est Construct	119,240	3.7
Real Est Mortgage	1,696,927	53.2
Installment	650,377	20.4
Total	3,190,486	100.0

ANNUAL EARNINGS AND DIVIDENDS PER SHARE

	1993	1992	1991	1990	1989	1988	1987
Earnings Per Share	**2.26**	**2.07**	**1.67**	**1.61**	**1.67**	**1.51**	**1.24**
Dividends Per Share	**[1] 1.16**	**0.853**	**0.80**	**0.747**	**0.693**	**0.587**	**0.497**
Dividend Payout %	**51.3**	**41.3**	**47.8**	**46.3**	**41.6**	**38.8**	**40.0**

[1] 3-for-2 stk split,08/30/93

ANNUAL FINANCIAL DATA

	1993	1992	1991	1990	1989	1988	1987
RECORD OF EARNINGS (IN MILLIONS):							
Total Interest Income	311.3	321.6	331.8	306.6	279.1	242.6	218.2
Total Interest Expense	135.8	155.1	190.2	179.5	164.5	136.2	123.3
Net Interest Income	175.4	166.5	141.6	127.1	114.7	106.4	94.9
Provision for Loan Losses	9.0	8.4	8.4	7.9	6.8	5.2	5.9
Net Income	45.9	39.8	30.7	29.0	29.7	26.5	20.3
Aver. Shs. Outstg. (000)	20,326	19,244	18,336	18,015	17,800	17,535	17,321
BALANCE SHEET (IN MILLIONS):							
Cash & Due From Banks	202.4	230.9	213.9	247.9	191.3	180.1	172.2
Total Loans, Net	3,150.1	2,979.4	2,581.3	2,288.8	1,999.2	1,842.9	1,564.4
Total Domestic Deposits	3,978.1	3,832.6	3,441.2	3,056.6	2,757.1	2,575.9	2,311.5
Long-term Borrowings	53.3	68.3	75.8	81.3	29.8	45.2	45.3
Net Stockholders' Equity	365.9	326.8	269.8	252.4	234.6	215.3	187.3
Total Assets	4,592.2	4,384.3	3,975.9	3,550.8	3,153.8	2,957.8	2,652.8
Year End Shs Outstg (000)	20,726	20,122	18,368	18,101	17,880	17,678	16,377
STATISTICAL RECORD:							
Return on Assets %	1.00	0.91	0.77	0.82	0.94	0.90	0.77
Return on Equity %	12.50	12.20	11.40	11.50	12.70	12.30	10.90
Book Value Per Share	17.65	16.24	14.69	13.94	13.12	12.18	11.44
Average Yield %	3.6	3.8	5.0	5.3	4.2	3.8	3.1
P/E Ratio	17.5-11.0	12.8-8.7	12.0-7.1	10.6-7.1	10.9-9.0	11.6-8.9	15.1-10.4
Price Range	39⅝-24⅞	26½-18	20-11⅞	17-11⅜	18⅛-15	17½-13⅜	18¾-12⅞

Statistics are as originally reported.

OFFICERS:
G.A. Zuehlke, Chairman
P.M. Platten, III, Pres. & C.E.O.
G.A. Lichtenberg, Sr. V.P., C.F.O. & Sec.

INCORPORATED: WI, 1962

PRINCIPAL OFFICE: 100 West Lawrence St. P.O. Box 1061, Appleton, WI 54911

TELEPHONE NUMBER: (414) 738-3830
FAX: (414) 738-5120
NO. OF EMPLOYEES: 3,162
ANNUAL MEETING: In April
SHAREHOLDERS: 7,630
INSTITUTIONAL HOLDINGS:
No. of Institutions: 68
Shares Held: 6,719,717

REGISTRAR(S):

TRANSFER AGENT(S): First National Bank of Boston, Shareholder Services Division, Boston, MA

VALLEY RESOURCES, INC.

YIELD 6.0%
P/E RATIO 13.4

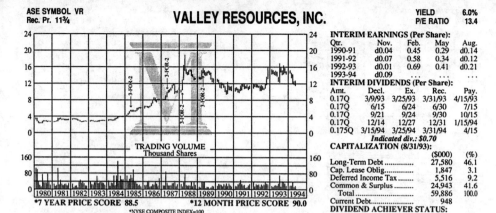

*7 YEAR PRICE SCORE 88.5   *12 MONTH PRICE SCORE 90.0

*NYSE COMPOSITE INDEX=100

INTERIM EARNINGS (Per Share):

Qtr.	Nov.	Feb.	May	Aug.
1990-91	d0.04	0.45	0.29	d0.14
1991-92	d0.07	0.58	0.34	d0.12
1992-93	d0.01	0.69	0.41	d0.21
1993-94	d0.09	...	...	...

INTERIM DIVIDENDS (Per Share):

Amt.	Decl.	Ex.	Rec.	Pay.
0.17Q	3/9/93	3/25/93	3/31/93	4/15/93
0.17Q	6/15	6/24	6/30	7/15
0.17Q	9/21	9/24	9/30	10/15
0.17Q	12/14	12/27	12/31	1/15/94
0.175Q	3/15/94	3/25/94	3/31/94	4/15

Indicated div.: $0.70

CAPITALIZATION (8/31/93):

	($000)	(%)
Long-Term Debt	27,580	46.1
Cap. Lease Oblig.	1,847	3.1
Deferred Income Tax	5,516	9.2
Common & Surplus	24,943	41.6
Total	59,886	100.0
Current Debt	948	

DIVIDEND ACHIEVER STATUS:
Rank: 218   1983-93 Growth Rate: 8.1%
Total Years of Dividend Growth: 13

RECENT DEVELOPMENTS: For the three months ended 11/30/93, the Company incurred a net loss of $377,000, or $0.09 per share, compared with a net loss of $28,000, or $0.01 per share, for the corresponding 1992 quarter. Operating revenues for the three months increased 7.7% to $15.8 million from $14.6 million for the year-ago quarter. Revenues from firm customers were $10.0 million, an increase of 10% over the same period in 1992. Firm revenues increased as a result of increased PGPA revenues and the inclusion of rate relief for the full fiscal quarter. Nonutility revenues for the quarter increased 5% to $4.7 million. Merchandise, service contract, and rental revenues increased 10% while wholesale revenues increased 3%. The improvement in service contract and rental revenues are the result of rate increases.

BUSINESS

VALLEY RESOURCES, INC. is a holding company that has seven wholly-owned subsidiaries. Valley Gas Company is a regulated natural gas distribution company. Valley Appliance and Merchandising Company is a merchandising and appliance rental company. Valley Propane, Inc. is a retail propane company. Morris Merchants, Inc. is a wholesale distributor of franchised lines in plumbing and heating contractor supply and other energy related business. Bristol & Warren Gas Company is a regulated natural gas distribution company. New England Gas Company is a retail propane company. Rhode Island Development and Exploration Company is an inactive company.

BUSINESS LINE ANALYSIS

(8/31/93)	Rev(%)	Inc(%)
Gas Operations	76.7	81.5
Appliance & Contr Sales	21.0	14.4
Other Operations	2.3	4.1
Total	100.0	100.0

ANNUAL EARNINGS AND DIVIDENDS PER SHARE

	8/31/93	8/31/92	8/31/91	8/31/90	8/31/89	8/31/88	8/31/87
Earnings Per Share	0.89	0.74	0.56	0.80	0.78	0.72	0.68
Dividends Per Share	0.67	0.635	0.615	0.59	①0.553	②0.533	②0.498
Dividend Payout %	75.3	85.8	N.M.	73.8	70.9	75.1	74.3

① 3-for-2 stk split, 4/15/89 ② 3-for-2 stk. split, 1/88 & 4/87.

ANNUAL FINANCIAL DATA

RECORD OF EARNINGS (IN THOUSANDS):

Total Revenues	77,286	67,144	59,990	61,408	59,686	56,440	59,412
Depreciation	2,304	1,770	1,594	1,506	1,385	1,265	1,152
Maintenance	1,497	1,369	1,260	1,237	1,202	1,495	1,102
Prov for Fed Inc Taxes	1,400	955	652	1,202	1,223	896	1,486
Operating Income	6,084	4,898	3,791	4,718	4,431	4,050	3,965
Total Interest Charges	2,610	2,051	1,813	1,743	1,695	1,631	1,558
Net Income	3,727	3,115	2,358	3,209	2,982	2,711	2,538
Aver. Shs. Outstg.	4,203	4,201	4,200	4,036	3,823	3,778	3,720

BALANCE SHEET (IN THOUSANDS):

Gross Plant	69,219	63,881	52,521	48,843	46,153	42,626	38,692
Accumulated Depreciation	21,177	19,520	15,948	14,832	13,831	13,549	12,570
Prop, Plant & Equip, Net	48,042	44,361	36,573	34,011	32,322	29,077	26,122
Long-term Debt	29,427	17,585	15,509	15,046	15,620	14,792	13,303
Net Stockholders' Equity	24,943	24,018	23,600	23,648	18,280	18,091	19,542
Total Assets	80,795	75,863	60,165	54,444	49,673	46,032	45,924
Year End Shares Outstg	4,213	4,213	4,213	4,213	3,843	3,800	3,752

STATISTICAL RECORD:

Book Value Per Share	5.92	5.70	5.60	5.61	4.76	4.73	5.18
Op. Inc/Net Pl %	12.7	11.0	10.4	13.9	13.7	13.9	15.2
Dep/Gr. Pl %	3.3	2.8	3.0	3.1	3.0	3.0	3.0
Accum. Dep/Gr. Pl %	30.6	30.6	30.4	30.4	30.0	31.8	32.5
Return on Equity %	14.9	13.0	10.0	13.6	16.3	15.1	13.1
Average Yield %	4.6	4.9	5.6	5.2	4.0	3.7	5.0
P/E Ratio	19.0-13.8	21.5-13.9	21.7-17.4	16.4-11.7	20.2-15.7	26.2-13.7	17.6-11.8
Price Range	16⅞-12¼	15⅞-10¼	12⅛-9¾	13⅛-9⅜	15¾-12¼	18⅞-9⅞	12-8

Statistics are as originally reported.

OFFICERS:
C.H. Goss, Chmn., Pres. & C.E.O.
K.W. Hogan, V.P., Treas. & Sec.

PRINCIPAL OFFICE: 1595 Mendon Road, Cumberland, RI 02864

TELEPHONE NUMBER: (401) 333-1595
FAX: (401) 333-3527
NO. OF EMPLOYEES: 252
ANNUAL MEETING: In December
SHAREHOLDERS: 2,834
INSTITUTIONAL HOLDINGS:
No. of Institutions: 15
Shares Held: 562,433

REGISTRAR(S):

TRANSFER AGENT(S):

ASE SYMBOL VAL
Rec. Pr. 35

VALSPAR CORP.

YIELD 1.5%
P/E RATIO 18.5

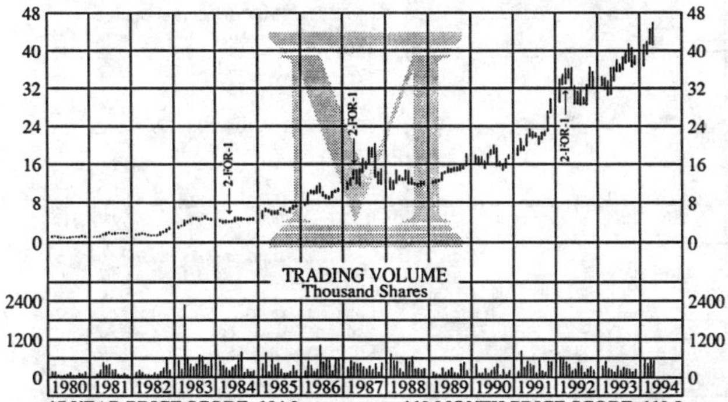

*7 YEAR PRICE SCORE 134.2 *12 MONTH PRICE SCORE 112.8
*NYSE COMPOSITE INDEX=100

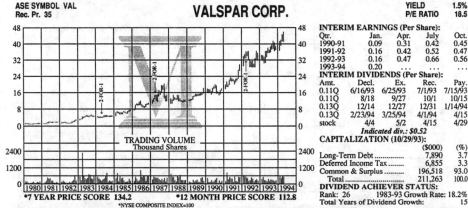

INTERIM EARNINGS (Per Share):

Qtr.	Jan.	Apr.	July	Oct.
1990-91	0.09	0.31	0.42	0.45
1991-92	0.16	0.42	0.52	0.47
1992-93	0.16	0.47	0.66	0.56
1993-94	0.20	...	...	...

INTERIM DIVIDENDS (Per Share):

Amt.	Decl.	Ex.	Rec.	Pay.
0.11Q	6/16/93	6/25/93	7/1/93	7/15/93
0.11Q	8/18	9/27	10/1	10/15
0.13Q	12/14	12/27	12/31	1/14/94
0.13Q	2/23/94	3/25/94	4/1/94	4/15
stock	4/4	5/2	4/15	4/29

Indicated div.: $0.52

CAPITALIZATION (10/29/93):

	($000)	(%)
Long-Term Debt	7,890	3.7
Deferred Income Tax	6,855	3.3
Common & Surplus	196,518	93.0
Total	211,263	100.0

DIVIDEND ACHIEVER STATUS:
Rank: 26 1983-93 Growth Rate: 18.2%
Total Years of Dividend Growth: 15

RECENT DEVELOPMENTS: Net income for the quarter ended 1/28/94, including a pretax charge of $2.5 million for the writedown of a plant, increased 25.7% to $4.3 million compared with $3.4 million a year ago. Sales were up 7.9% to $148.0 million from $137.2 million in the same period last year. The Industrial Group, McWhorter Resins, and Color Corporation contributed the most to the sales increase. McWhorter completed the acquisition of the Cargill Resin Products Division on Feb. 18, 1994 for $90 million.

PROSPECTS: Continued efforts to improve manufacturing efficiencies and cut costs will reduce operating expenses and benefit earnings. A recently completed restructuring program designed to consolidate plants and research facilities will improve operations at the Industrial Coatings Group. Once the transfer to VAL of technology associated with the Cargill Division is completed, the common stock of McWhorter will be distributed to VAL's stockholders.

BUSINESS

VALSPAR CORP. is a major domestic manufacturer of paints and related coatings. Products include industrial and protective coatings sold directly to manufacturers; latex and oil-based paints, stains, and varnishes sold through dealers primarily to the do-it-yourself market; and specialty products, including resins, emulsions, colorants, floor coatings and industrial maintenance coatings. Operations are carried out through four divisions: Consumer Coatings, Industrial Coatings, Packaging Coatings, and Special Products Division. Valspar operates 21 manufacturing plants in North America and licenses its technology worldwide.

REVENUES

(10/29/93)	($000)	(%)
Consumer Coatings	208,103	30.0
Industrial Coatings	187,293	27.0
Packaging Coatings	159,546	23.0
Special Products	138,736	20.0
Total	693,678	100.0

ANNUAL EARNINGS AND DIVIDENDS PER SHARE

	10/29/93	10/30/92	10/25/91	10/26/90	10/27/89	10/28/88	10/30/87
Earnings Per Share	**1.85**	**1.57**	**1.27**	**1.22**	**1.04**	**0.82**	**0.81**
Dividends Per Share	**0.44**	**[1] 0.36**	**0.30**	**0.26**	**0.22**	**0.20**	**[2] 0.16**
Dividend Payout %	**23.8**	**22.9**	**23.7**	**21.2**	**21.2**	**24.5**	**19.9**

[1] 2-for-1 stk split, 3/30/92 [2] 2-for-1 stk. split, 4/84 & 3/87

ANNUAL FINANCIAL DATA

	10/29/93	10/30/92	10/25/91	10/26/90	10/27/89	10/28/88	10/30/87
RECORD OF EARNINGS (IN THOUSANDS):							
Total Revenues	693,678	683,485	632,562	568,108	528,447	482,350	449,423
Costs and Expenses	603,742	603,531	560,700	504,181	470,209	433,837	399,433
Depreciation & Amort	20,621	19,793	18,896	15,119	13,975	12,759	11,687
Operating Income	69,315	60,161	52,966	48,808	44,263	35,754	38,303
Income Bef Income Taxes	65,632	56,869	45,776	44,104	38,425	29,384	32,076
Income Taxes	25,450	22,451	18,100	17,373	15,191	11,089	14,024
Net Income	40,182	34,418	27,676	26,731	23,234	18,295	18,052
Aver. Shs. Outstg.	21,691	21,973	21,862	21,854	22,330	22,488	22,490
BALANCE SHEET (IN THOUSANDS):							
Cash and Cash Equivalents	1,637	1,780	1,211	1,503	1,323	1,921	1,325
Receivables, Net	105,505	92,198	88,048	75,102	77,987	64,540	61,106
Inventories	68,390	70,726	72,355	77,370	68,338	64,900	68,569
Gross Property	207,168	190,097	179,742	179,369	143,454	126,085	117,357
Accumulated Depreciation	104,029	89,092	80,924	72,748	60,767	52,433	42,609
Long-Term Debt	7,890	10,684	27,299	45,888	36,475	38,539	54,299
Obligs Under Cap Lses-less Curr Port	...	...	3,398	3,568	3,726	3,873	4,262
Net Stockholders' Equity	196,518	169,377	147,896	128,707	112,698	99,895	85,807
Total Assets	336,798	321,618	319,367	302,806	261,103	232,974	236,099
Total Current Assets	197,480	184,711	182,173	167,094	159,607	139,782	140,265
Total Current Liabilities	113,481	127,211	124,107	110,895	96,088	79,088	83,117
Net Working Capital	83,999	57,500	58,066	56,199	63,519	60,694	57,148
Year End Shares Outstg	21,506	21,612	21,769	21,748	22,044	22,394	22,282
STATISTICAL RECORD:							
Operating Profit Margin %	10.0	8.8	8.4	8.6	8.4	7.4	8.5
Book Value Per Share	9.14	7.84	6.79	5.92	5.11	4.46	3.85
Return on Equity %	20.4	20.3	18.7	20.8	20.6	18.3	21.0
Return on Assets %	11.9	10.7	8.7	8.8	8.9	7.9	7.6
Average Yield %	1.2	1.1	1.3	1.5	1.5	1.6	1.0
P/E Ratio	22.4-16.4	23.2-18.1	23.4-14.1	16.4-12.1	17.5-11.4	18.2-13.1	25.3-13.4
Price Range	41½-30⅜	36½-28⅜	29¾-17⅞	20-14¾	18¼-11⅞	14¾-10⅝	20¼-10¾

Statistics are as originally reported.

OFFICERS:
C.A. Wurtele, Chmn. & C.E.O.
R.M. Rompala, Pres.
P.C. Reyelts, V.P.-Fin.
R. Engh, Gen. Couns. & Sec.

INCORPORATED: DE, Dec., 1934

PRINCIPAL OFFICE: 1101 Third St. South, Minneapolis, MN 55415

TELEPHONE NUMBER: (612) 332-7371
FAX: (612) 375-7723
NO. OF EMPLOYEES: 2,513
ANNUAL MEETING: In February
SHAREHOLDERS: 1,866
INSTITUTIONAL HOLDINGS:
No. of Institutions: 91
Shares Held: 13,467,767

REGISTRAR(S): Mellon Securities Trust Co., New York, NY

TRANSFER AGENT(S): Mellon Financial Securities, New York, NY

NYS SYMBOL VFC
Rec. Pr. 47⅞

VF CORP.

YIELD 2.7%
P/E RATIO 11.9

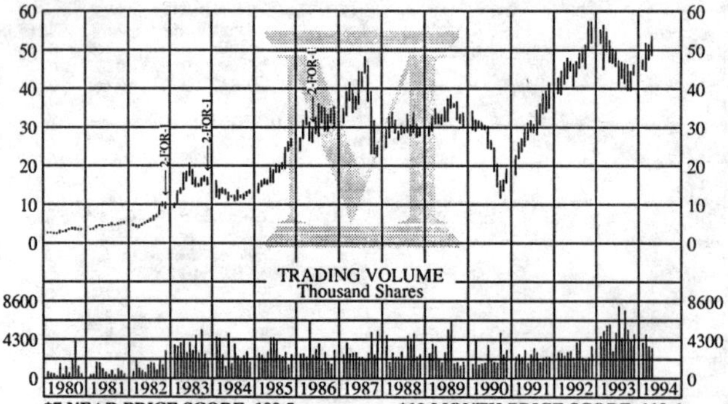

***7 YEAR PRICE SCORE 100.5** ***12 MONTH PRICE SCORE 110.6**

*NYSE COMPOSITE INDEX=100

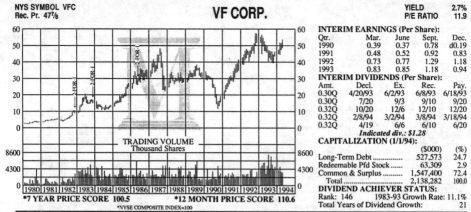

INTERIM EARNINGS (Per Share):

Qtr.	Mar.	June	Sept.	Dec.
1990	0.39	0.37	0.78	d0.19
1991	0.48	0.52	0.92	0.83
1992	0.73	0.77	1.29	1.18
1993	0.83	0.85	1.18	0.94

INTERIM DIVIDENDS (Per Share):

Amt.	Decl.	Ex.	Rec.	Pay.
0.30Q	4/20/93	6/2/93	6/8/93	6/18/93
0.30Q	7/20	9/3	9/10	9/20
0.32Q	10/20	12/6	12/10	12/20
0.32Q	2/8/94	3/2/94	3/8/94	3/18/94
0.32Q	4/19	6/6	6/10	6/20

Indicated div.: $1.28

CAPITALIZATION (1/1/94):

	($000)	(%)
Long-Term Debt	527,573	24.7
Redeemable Pfd Stock	63,309	2.9
Common & Surplus	1,547,400	72.4
Total	2,138,282	100.0

DIVIDEND ACHIEVER STATUS:

Rank: 146 1983-93 Growth Rate: 11.1%

Total Years of Dividend Growth: 21

RECENT DEVELOPMENTS: For the year ended 12/31/93, net income increased 4% to $246.4 million from $237.0 million in 1992. Sales were up 13% to $4.32 billion from $3.82 billion the previous year. Although there was improvement for the year, several business segments showed signs of weakness in the latter half of 1993. The fall-off in performance was attributed to reduced volume in fleecewear, manufacturing inefficiencies at Vanity Fair and poor results at Girbaud.

PROSPECTS: Vanity Fair should begin to realize the benefits of a product mix and sourcing shift. Meanwhile, at Girbaud, management is aggressively attacking cost and manufacturing inefficiency problems. The acquisition of Nutmeg, a leading designer and producer of licensed adult sports apparel, will complement the acquisition of H.H. Cutler and position VFC to gain a big share of the fast-growing licensed sports apparel market.

BUSINESS

VF CORP. is one of the world's largest publicly held apparel companies, competing primarily in the jeanswear, activewear, intimate apparel and occupational apparel categories. Apparel is manufactured and marketed principally under the following brands: jeanswear-Lee, Wrangler, Rustler, Riders and Marithe & Francois Girbaud; casual/sportswear-Lee, Jantzen and JanSport; intimate apparel-Vanity Fair, Vassarette and Barbizon; and other product groups such as Red Kap and WorkWear in occupational apparel and Healthtex in children's apparel. In international markets, jeanswear is manufactured and marketed under the Lee and Wrangler brands, and intimate apparel is marketed under various labels.

BUSINESS LINE ANALYSIS

(01/01/94)	Rev(%)	Inc(%)
Jeanswear	48.5	56.8
Casual/Sportswear	14.8	5.2
Intimate Apparel	10.1	8.6
International	14.9	15.0
Other Apparel	11.7	14.4
Total	100.0	100.0

ANNUAL EARNINGS AND DIVIDENDS PER SHARE

	1/1/94	1/2/93	1/4/92	12/29/90	12/30/89	12/31/88	1/2/88
Earnings Per Share	**3.80**	**3.97**	**2.75**	**1.35**	**2.72**	**2.55**	**2.65**
Dividends Per Share	**1.22**	**1.11**	**1.02**	**1.00**	**0.91**	**0.85**	**0.75**
Dividend Payout %	**32.1**	**27.5**	**37.1**	**74.1**	**33.5**	**33.3**	**28.3**

ANNUAL FINANCIAL DATA

	1/1/94	1/2/93	1/4/92	12/29/90	12/30/89	12/31/88	1/2/88
RECORD OF EARNINGS (IN MILLIONS):							
Costs and Expenses	3,781.9	3,304.2	2,572.1	2,324.4	2,146.9	2,141.2	2,144.6
Depreciation	106.7	90.9	76.3	80.9	72.9	70.3	70.6
Operating Income	431.8	429.4	304.1	207.3	312.9	304.6	358.6
Income Bef Income Taxes	400.0	375.8	263.2	143.1	283.7	274.9	313.7
Income Taxes	153.6	138.7	101.9	62.0	107.7	101.3	134.1
Net Income	246.4	237.0	161.3	81.1	176.0	173.7	179.7
Aver. Shs. Outstg. (000)	64,011	58,608	57,152	57,122	64,803	68,165	67,793
BALANCE SHEET (IN MILLIONS):							
Cash and Cash Equivalents	151.6	86.3	162.3	62.0	36.2	86.7	112.1
Receivables, Net	550.0	514.8	353.3	314.0	320.0	266.4	285.4
Inventories	778.8	742.5	537.0	436.7	507.5	422.8	493.0
Gross Property	1,250.0	1,241.6	1,041.1	954.3	877.3	792.5	769.9
Accumulated Depreciation	537.3	530.5	464.1	417.1	363.4	310.2	262.8
Long-Term Debt	527.6	767.6	583.2	585.1	637.5	302.3	322.9
Net Stockholders' Equity	1,610.7	1,217.9	1,002.6	888.1	819.8	1,095.4	980.6
Total Assets	2,877.3	2,712.4	2,126.9	1,852.8	1,889.8	1,759.9	1,925.7
Total Current Assets	1,500.2	1,365.6	1,071.1	824.2	873.5	786.5	912.0
Total Current Liabilities	659.8	684.0	510.8	351.5	325.1	231.0	464.0
Net Working Capital	840.3	681.6	560.3	472.8	548.5	555.4	448.0
Year-end Shs Outstg (000)	64,489	59,519	57,700	57,013	57,986	68,255	67,940
STATISTICAL RECORD:							
Book Value Per Share	15.07	10.07	8.94	6.94	6.69	9.46	14.43
Return on Equity %	15.9	20.5	17.2	9.9	21.5	15.9	18.3
Return on Assets %	8.6	8.7	7.6	4.4	9.3	9.9	9.3
Average Yield %	2.5	2.3	3.5	4.4	2.8	2.9	2.1
P/E Ratio	14.9-10.4	14.5-9.7	15.1-6.4	25.4-8.6	14.1-10.2	13.3-9.7	18.2-8.5
Price Range	56½-39½	57½-38½	41½-17⅝	34¼-11⅝	38⅜-27¾	33⅞-24¾	48¼-22½

Statistics are as originally reported.

OFFICERS:
L.R. Pugh, Chmn. & C.E.O.
M.J. McDonald, Pres. & C.O.O.
G.G. Johnson, V.P.-Fin. & C.F.O.
L.M. Tarnoski, V.P. & Sec.

INCORPORATED: PA, Dec., 1889

PRINCIPAL OFFICE: 1047 No. Park Rd., Wyomissing, PA 19610

TELEPHONE NUMBER: (215) 378-1151

FAX: (215) 375-9371

NO. OF EMPLOYEES: 7,752

ANNUAL MEETING: In April

SHAREHOLDERS: 5,643

INSTITUTIONAL HOLDINGS:
No. of Institutions: 316
Shares Held: 48,537,079

REGISTRAR(S): First Chicago Trust Co. of New York, New York, NY 10008

TRANSFER AGENT(S): First Chicago Trust Co. of New York, New York, NY 10008

WACHOVIA CORP.

YIELD 3.6%
P/E RATIO 11.9

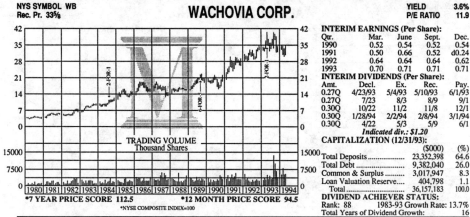

*7 YEAR PRICE SCORE 112.5   *12 MONTH PRICE SCORE 94.5
*NYSE COMPOSITE INDEX=100

TRADING VOLUME
Thousand Shares

INTERIM EARNINGS (Per Share):

Qtr.	Mar.	June	Sept.	Dec.
1990	0.52	0.54	0.52	0.54
1991	0.50	0.66	0.52	d0.24
1992	0.64	0.64	0.64	0.62
1993	0.70	0.71	0.71	0.71

INTERIM DIVIDENDS (Per Share):

Amt.	Decl.	Ex.	Rec.	Pay.
0.27Q	4/23/93	5/4/93	5/10/93	6/1/93
0.27Q	7/23	8/3	8/9	9/1
0.30Q	10/22	11/2	11/8	12/1
0.30Q	1/28/94	2/2/94	2/8/94	3/1/94
0.30Q	4/22	5/3	5/9	6/1

Indicated div.: $1.20

CAPITALIZATION (12/31/93):

	($000)	(%)
Total Deposits	23,352,398	64.6
Total Debt	9,382,040	26.0
Common & Surplus	3,017,947	8.3
Loan Valuation Reserve	404,798	1.1
Total	36,157,183	100.0

DIVIDEND ACHIEVER STATUS:
Rank: 88   1983-93 Growth Rate: 13.7%
Total Years of Dividend Growth: 16

RECENT DEVELOPMENTS: For the three months ended 12/31/93 net income rose 12% from the corresponding 1992 period to $123.0 million. The provision for credit losses was reduced 37% to $18.0 million. For 1993, net income increased 14% to $492.1 million. Results benefited from increased net interest income, growth in other service revenues, reduced credit loss provisions and effective cost-management. The provision for credit losses was lowered by 22% to $92.7 million.

PROSPECTS: Credit card fees, trading profits and deposit account service charges are providing non-interest income with a solid boost. The new additions to WB's Biltmore Funds family will provide new opportunities for income growth in trust services. Cost cutting measures such as the consolidation of 17 North Carolina sales finance offices into one new facility will reflect favorably on results. Loan demand remains soft despite the low interest rate environment.

BUSINESS

WACHOVIA CORPORATION is one of the leading interstate bank holding companies in the Southeast. Its principal banking subsidiaries are Wachovia Bank of Georgia, N.A., Wachovia Bank of North Carolina, N.A., and the South Carolina National Bank. The company operates 514 full service banking offices in 219 cities throughout Georgia, North Carolina and South Carolina. In addition to full-service banking, Wachovia offers investment banking, mortgage banking and a line of several other businesses to customers.

LOAN DISTRIBUTION

(12/31/93)	($000)	(%)
Commercial	8,686,473	37.8
Retail	6,601,052	28.7
Real Estate	7,460,182	32.5
Lease Financing - net	156,726	0.7
Foreign	73,055	0.3
Total	22,977,488	100.0

ANNUAL EARNINGS AND DIVIDENDS PER SHARE

	1993	1992	1991	1990	1989	1988	1987
Earnings Per Share	2.83	2.51	1.34	2.14	1.94	1.80	1.34
Dividends Per Share	1.11	① 1.00	0.92	0.82	② 0.698	0.584	0.50
Dividend Payout %	39.2	39.8	68.7	38.6	36.0	32.3	37.0

① Adj for 2-for-1 stk split, 3/1/93   ② 20% stk div, 8/31/89

ANNUAL FINANCIAL DATA

RECORD OF EARNINGS (IN MILLIONS):

	1993	1992	1991	1990	1989	1988	1987
Total Interest Income	2,122.8	2,222.1	2,637.0	2,137.2	2,092.1	1,718.4	1,499.6
Total Interest Expense	839.0	967.0	1,467.8	1,320.4	1,321.5	982.5	816.7
Net Interest Income	1,283.8	1,255.1	1,169.2	816.8	770.6	735.9	682.9
Provision for Loan Losses	92.7	119.4	293.0	86.5	62.2	61.3	149.6
Net Income	492.1	433.2	229.5	297.2	269.0	244.3	176.6
Aver. Shs. Outstg. (000)	173,941	172,641	171,481	139,910	139,024	134,944	130,590

BALANCE SHEET (IN MILLIONS):

	1993	1992	1991	1990	1989	1988	1987
Cash & Due From Banks	2,529.5	2,627.9	2,475.6	3,080.1	2,737.3	2,749.2	2,104.2
State & Municipal	655.2	748.0	851.2	737.6	788.6	817.8	844.6
Net Loans	22,572.7	20,706.1	20,257.4	16,432.9	15,102.0	13,561.7	12,119.4
Tot Deps In Domestic Offices	22,545.3	22,856.7	22,602.0	17,713.3	16,911.1	15,915.8	13,877.6
Total Deps In Fgn Offices	807.1	518.8	404.3	499.1	475.5	576.2	464.3
Long-term Debt	2,960.5	1,196.9	170.8	113.1	171.0	178.7	284.2
Net Stockholders' Equity	3,017.9	2,774.8	2,484.4	1,928.7	1,739.9	1,557.3	1,297.8
Total Assets	36,525.8	33,366.5	33,158.3	26,270.8	24,049.5	21,815.2	19,342.2
Year End Shs Outstg (000)	171,376	171,471	170,646	139,357	128,803	137,618	130,120

STATISTICAL RECORD:

	1993	1992	1991	1990	1989	1988	1987
Return on Assets %	1.35	1.30	0.69	1.13	1.12	1.12	0.91
Return on Equity %	16.30	15.60	9.20	15.40	15.50	15.70	13.60
Book Value Per Share	17.61	16.18	14.56	13.84	13.51	11.32	9.97
Average Yield %	3.1	3.2	3.7	4.3	3.6	3.8	3.1
P/E Ratio	14.3-11.3	13.8-11.3	22.4-15.1	10.4-7.6	11.7-8.0	9.4-7.7	14.5-9.5
Price Range	40½-31⅞	34¾-28¼	30-20¼	22¼-16¼	22¾-15½	17-13⅞	19⅜-12¾

Statistics are as originally reported.

OFFICERS:
J.G. Medlin, Jr., Chmn.
L.M. Baker, Jr., Pres. & C.E.O.
R.S. McCoy, Jr., Exec. V.P. & C.F.O.
R.B. Roberts, Exec. V.P. & Treas.

INCORPORATED: NC, Jul., 1985

PRINCIPAL OFFICE: 301 N. Main Street, Winston-Salem, NC 2710

TELEPHONE NUMBER: (919) 770-5000

NO. OF EMPLOYEES: 16,164

ANNUAL MEETING: In April

SHAREHOLDERS: 26,706

INSTITUTIONAL HOLDINGS:
No. of Institutions: 345
Shares Held: 79,893,105

REGISTRAR(S): Wachovia Bank & Trust Co., N.A., Winston-Salem, NC 27102

TRANSFER AGENT(S): Wachovia Bank & Trust Co., N.A., Winston-Salem, NC 27102

NYS SYMBOL WMT
Rec. Pr. 23¾

WAL-MART STORES, INC.

YIELD 0.7%
P/E RATIO 24.2

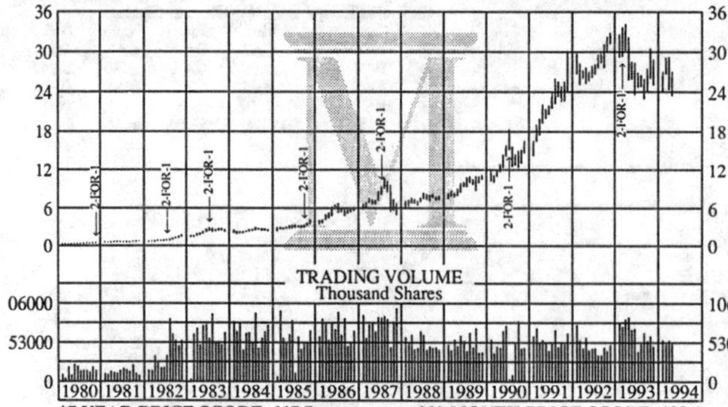

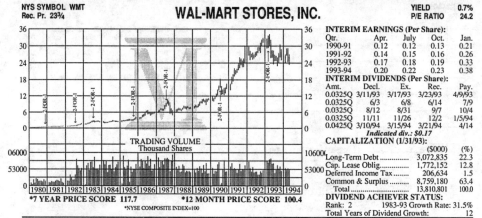

***7 YEAR PRICE SCORE 117.7** ***12 MONTH PRICE SCORE 100.4**

*NYSE COMPOSITE INDEX=100

INTERIM EARNINGS (Per Share):

Qtr.	Apr.	July	Oct.	Jan.
1990-91	0.12	0.12	0.13	0.21
1991-92	0.14	0.15	0.16	0.26
1992-93	0.17	0.18	0.19	0.33
1993-94	0.20	0.22	0.23	0.38

INTERIM DIVIDENDS (Per Share):

Amt.	Decl.	Ex.	Rec.	Pay.
0.0325Q	3/11/93	3/17/93	3/23/93	4/9/93
0.0325Q	6/3	6/8	6/14	7/9
0.0325Q	8/12	8/31	9/7	10/4
0.0325Q	11/11	11/26	12/2	1/5/94
0.0425Q	3/10/94	3/15/94	3/21/94	4/14

Indicated div.: $0.17

CAPITALIZATION (1/31/93):

	($000)	(%)
Long-Term Debt	3,072,835	22.3
Cap. Lease Oblig.	1,772,152	12.8
Deferred Income Tax	206,634	1.5
Common & Surplus	8,759,180	63.4
Total	13,810,801	100.0

DIVIDEND ACHIEVER STATUS:
Rank: 2 1983-93 Growth Rate: 31.5%
Total Years of Dividend Growth: 12

RECENT DEVELOPMENTS: For the year ended 1/31/94, net income was $2.33 billion compared with $1.99 billion in 1993. Sales increased 21.4% to $67.34 billion. Results were aided by continued expansion in the U.S. and Mexico, and growth in the wholesale club business. As a percentage of sales, operating expenses increased to 15.3% from 15.0%. During the year, the Company opened 143 new Wal-Mart stores and 164 Sam's Clubs (99 acquired from Pace).

PROSPECTS: WMT is facing intense competition in the warehouse club business and the grocery store business, especially in the Northeast where operating costs are higher. In order to boost its underperforming warehouse clubs, WMT plans to offer credit, purchase-order tracking and billing services to big corporate and institutional customers to make buying from its stores easier. An agreement to buy 120 Canadian Woolco stores from Woolworth will provide WMT with a solid presence in Canada.

BUSINESS

WAL-MART STORES, INC. operates 2,021 discount department stores (including 68 Supercenter stores) and 419 Sam's Wholesale Clubs in a 49-state trade territory and Puerto Rico. Stores are located primarily in small towns, although an increasing number of stores are being opened in and around the metropolitan areas within the chain's regional trade territory. WMT also operates McLane and Western, a specialty distribution subsidiary, serving over 30,000 convenience stores and independent grocers. Wal-Mart stores are designed to be one-stop shopping centers which provide a wide assortment of merchandise to satisfy most of the clothing, home recreational and convenience needs of the family. Stores range in size from 30,000 square feet to 126,000 square feet.

QUARTERLY DATA

(1/31/93)($000)	Rev	Inc
1st Quarter	11,649,430	386,955
2nd Quarter	13,028,445	420,448
3rd Quarter	13,683,824	437,804
4th Quarter	17,122,072	749,587

ANNUAL EARNINGS AND DIVIDENDS PER SHARE

	1/31/93	1/31/92	1/31/91	1/31/90	1/31/89	1/31/88	1/31/87
Earnings Per Share	**0.87**	**0.70**	**0.57**	**0.48**	**0.37**	**0.28**	**0.20**
Dividends Per Share	**[1] 0.10**	**0.081**	**[2] 0.066**	**0.052**	**0.04**	**0.028**	**[3] 0.021**
Dividend Payout %	**11.5**	**11.6**	**11.7**	**10.8**	**10.1**	**10.1**	**10.3**

Note: k100%stk.div.2/25/93. [1] 2-for-1 stk split,02/26/93 [2] 2-for-1 stk split; 7/90 [3] 2-for-1 stk. split, 7/87.

ANNUAL FINANCIAL DATA

RECORD OF EARNINGS (IN MILLIONS):							
Total Revenues	55,984.6	44,289.4	32,863.4	25,985.3	20,785.9	16,064.0	11,993.7
Costs and Expenses	51,846.4	40,995.1	30,305.4	23,870.3	19,111.1	14,715.1	[1] 11,060.9
Depreciation & Amort	649.1	475.4	346.6	269.4	213.6	166.0	...
Operating Income	3,489.0	2,819.0	2,211.4	1,845.6	1,461.1	1,182.9	932.8
Inc Fr Cont Opers Bef Income Taxes	3,166.3	2,553.1	2,042.8	1,707.5	1,325.5	1,068.7	846.0
Prov for Fed & State Inc Taxes	1,171.5	944.7	751.7	631.6	488.2	441.0	395.9
Net Income	1,994.8	1,608.5	1,291.0	1,075.9	837.2	627.6	450.1

[1] Incl. Dep.

BALANCE SHEET (IN MILLIONS):							
Cash and Cash Equivalents	12.4	30.6	13.0	12.8	12.6	11.3	165.5
Receivables, Net	836.6	1,100.3	544.9	234.5	241.3	222.8	137.5
LIFO Inventories	9,268.3	7,384.3	5,808.4	4,428.1	3,351.4	2,651.8	2,031.0
Gross Property	11,848.0	8,140.8	5,996.7	4,401.8	3,391.4	2,684.8	2,070.1
Accumulated Depreciation	2,055.1	1,707.0	1,284.6	971.7	729.5	539.9	393.9
Long-Term Debt	3,072.8	1,722.0	740.3	185.2	184.4	185.7	179.2
Lg tm Obligs Under Cap Lses	1,772.2	1,555.9	1,158.6	1,087.4	1,009.0	867.0	764.1
Net Stockholders' Equity	8,759.2	6,989.7	5,365.5	3,965.6	3,007.9	2,257.3	1,690.5
Total Assets	20,565.1	15,443.4	11,388.9	8,198.5	6,359.7	5,131.8	4,049.1
Total Current Assets	10,197.6	8,575.4	6,414.8	4,712.6	3,631.0	2,905.1	2,353.3
Total Current Liabilities	6,754.3	5,003.8	3,990.4	2,845.3	2,065.9	1,743.8	1,340.3
Net Working Capital	3,443.3	3,571.6	2,424.4	1,867.3	1,565.1	1,161.4	1,013.0
Year End Shs Outstg (000)	2,299,638	2,298,056	2,284,564	2,264,540	2,262,364	2,260,448	2,257,456

STATISTICAL RECORD:							
Operating Profit Margin %	6.2	6.4	6.7	7.1	7.0	7.4	7.8
Book Value Per Share	3.81	3.04	2.35	1.75	1.31	0.98	0.75
Return on Equity %	22.8	23.0	24.1	27.1	27.8	27.8	26.6
Return on Assets %	9.7	10.4	11.3	13.1	13.2	12.2	11.1
Average Yield %	0.3	0.4	0.5	0.6	0.5	0.4	0.4
P/E Ratio	37.9-28.9	42.9-20.4	32.2-17.8	23.4-15.6	23.0-16.6	38.4-17.9	33.8-18.1
Price Range	33-25⅛	30-14¼	18⅜-10⅛	11¼-7½	8½-6⅛	10¾-5	6¾-3⅝

Statistics are as originally reported.

OFFICERS:
S.R. Walton, Chmn.
D.D. Glass, Pres. & C.E.O.
P.R. Carter, Exec. V.P. & C.F.O.
R.K. Rhoads, Sr. V.P., Couns. & Sec.

INCORPORATED: DE, Oct., 1969

PRINCIPAL OFFICE: P.O. Box 116, Bentonville, AR 72716

TELEPHONE NUMBER: (501) 273-4000

NO. OF EMPLOYEES: 434,000

ANNUAL MEETING: In June

SHAREHOLDERS: 180,584

INSTITUTIONAL HOLDINGS:
No. of Institutions: 738
Shares Held: 345,463,181

REGISTRAR(S):

TRANSFER AGENT(S):

NYS SYMBOL WAG
Rec. Pr. 40¾

WALGREEN CO.

YIELD 1.7%
P/E RATIO 19.0

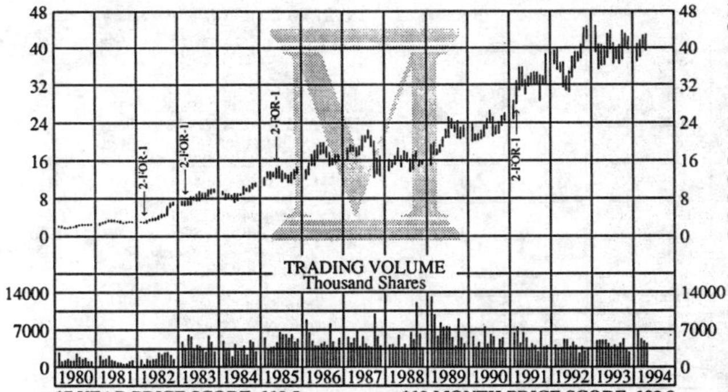

48
40
32
24
16
8
0
2-FOR-1
2-FOR-1
2-FOR-1
2-FOR-1
TRADING VOLUME
Thousand Shares
14000
7000
0
1980 1981 1982 1983 1984 1985 1986 1987 1988 1989 1990 1991 1992 1993 1994

*7 YEAR PRICE SCORE 112.8 *12 MONTH PRICE SCORE 103.9
*NYSE COMPOSITE INDEX=100

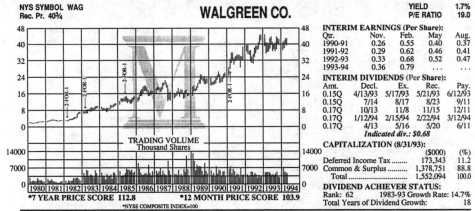

INTERIM EARNINGS (Per Share):

Qtr.	Nov.	Feb.	May	Aug.
1990-91	0.26	0.55	0.40	0.37
1991-92	0.29	0.62	0.46	0.41
1992-93	0.33	0.68	0.52	0.47
1993-94	0.36	0.79	...	...

INTERIM DIVIDENDS (Per Share):

Amt.	Decl.	Ex.	Rec.	Pay.
0.15Q	4/13/93	5/17/93	5/21/93	6/12/93
0.15Q	7/14	8/17	8/23	9/11
0.17Q	10/13	11/8	11/15	12/11
0.17Q	1/12/94	2/15/94	2/22/94	3/12/94
0.17Q	4/13	5/16	5/20	6/11

Indicated div.: $0.68

CAPITALIZATION (8/31/93):

	($000)	(%)
Deferred Income Tax........	173,343	11.2
Common & Surplus..........	1,378,751	88.8
Total..............................	1,552,094	100.0

DIVIDEND ACHIEVER STATUS:
Rank: 62 1983-93 Growth Rate: 14.7%
Total Years of Dividend Growth: 18

RECENT DEVELOPMENTS: For the quarter ended 11/30/93, net income was $44.2 million compared with $39.6 million last year. Results were before a $23.6 million accounting change. Sales increased 10.6% to $2.12 billion. Earnings per share rose to $0.36 from $0.32. Pharmacy sales, which comprise over 40% of overall sales, rose 19.4%. Comparable store sales rose 5.3% despite lower inflation in pharmaceuticals and general merchandise. During the quarter, the Company opened 63 new stores, 43 of them in November.

PROSPECTS: Growth will continue to come from new store openings and growing demand for prescriptions. POS registers have been installed in all stores, providing better inventory management and lowering costs. Capital spending is expected to reach $300 million in 1994 with most of this targeted for new stores and high technology systems. WAG's expansion program in fiscal 1994 calls for the opening of 175 full service drugstores, including new market entries into Cleveland and Buffalo.

BUSINESS

WALGREEN CO. is the largest retail drugstore chain in the United States. The Company operates 1,892 drugstores located in 30 states and Puerto Rico. Forty-five percent of stores are located in Florida, Illinois and Texas. These stores serve more than 1.8 million customers a day and average over $4.1 million in annual sales per unit, or $425 per square foot. Walgreen drugstores are served by eight major distribution centers and five photoprocessing plants. Pharmacy comprises 38% of fiscal 1993 total sales; general merchandise, 25%; nonprescription drugs, 14%; liquor and beverages, 10%; cosmetics and toiletries, 9%; and tobacco, 4%.

QUARTERLY DATA

(8/31/93)($000)	Rev	Inc
1st Quarter.................	1,914,630	16,005
2nd Quarter................	2,257,921	83,583
3rd Quarter................	2,085,255	63,765
4th Quarter.................	2,037,034	58,313

ANNUAL EARNINGS AND DIVIDENDS PER SHARE

	8/31/93	8/31/92	8/31/91	8/31/90	8/31/89	8/31/88	8/31/87
Earnings Per Share	**[1] 1.98**	**1.78**	**1.58**	**1.41**	**1.25**	**1.05**	**0.84**
Dividends Per Share	**0.62**	**0.54**	**[2] 0.475**	**0.415**	**0.355**	**0.31**	**0.278**
Dividend Payout %	**31.3**	**30.3**	**30.1**	**29.3**	**28.4**	**29.5**	**33.0**

[1] Before acctg. chg. [2] 2-for-1 stk split,02/04/91

ANNUAL FINANCIAL DATA

	8/31/93	8/31/92	8/31/91	8/31/90	8/31/89	8/31/88	8/31/87
RECORD OF EARNINGS (IN MILLIONS):							
Total Revenues	8,294.8	7,475.0	6,733.0	6,047.5	5,380.1	4,883.5	4,281.6
Costs and Expenses	7,784.0	7,024.4	6,327.6	5,692.9	5,062.9	4,599.9	4,017.1
Depreciation & Amort	104.7	92.1	84.3	70.4	63.8	59.4	53.7
Operating Income	406.2	358.5	321.1	284.2	253.5	224.3	210.8
Earn Bef Inc Tax Provision	399.7	353.0	311.9	280.9	243.8	209.0	194.2
Income Tax Provision	154.4	132.4	117.0	106.3	89.6	79.9	90.6
Net Income	221.7	220.6	195.0	174.6	154.2	129.1	103.5
Aver. Shs. Outstg. (000)	123,770	123,671	123,582	123,393	123,287	123,162	123,196
BALANCE SHEET (IN MILLIONS):							
Cash and Cash Equivalents	121.3	225.6	135.1	213.9	225.5	209.7	41.2
Receivables, Net	139.3	136.1	132.4	97.6	93.4	76.1	65.1
Inventories	1,094.0	994.2	912.0	828.0	728.5	655.4	694.1
Gross Property	1,380.5	1,258.3	1,154.6	993.0	831.0	757.6	743.0
Accumulated Depreciation	453.2	402.0	345.3	295.9	252.1	220.7	205.5
Long-Term Debt	...	18.7	123.0	146.7	150.1	172.1	141.4
Oblig Under Cap Lses, Less Curr Maturs	...	...	...	...	...	19.1	25.2
Net Stockholders' Equity	1,378.8	1,233.3	1,081.2	947.2	823.4	712.6	622.3
Total Assets	2,535.2	2,373.6	2,094.6	1,913.6	1,681.1	1,511.9	1,361.9
Total Current Assets	1,463.1	1,438.8	1,247.4	1,187.0	1,083.0	974.3	823.6
Total Current Liabilities	883.5	889.3	683.8	632.3	544.9	488.6	465.5
Net Working Capital	579.6	549.6	563.6	554.8	538.1	485.7	358.1
Year End Shs Outstg (000)	123,071	123,071	123,071	123,048	123,033	123,028	123,008
STATISTICAL RECORD:							
Operating Profit Margin %	4.9	4.8	4.8	4.7	4.7	4.6	4.9
Book Value Per Share	11.20	10.02	8.78	7.70	6.69	5.79	5.06
Return on Equity %	17.8	17.9	18.0	18.4	18.7	18.1	16.6
Return on Assets %	9.7	9.3	9.3	9.1	9.2	8.5	7.6
Average Yield %	1.6	1.4	1.5	1.8	1.8	1.9	1.6
P/E Ratio	22.5-17.9	25.0-17.1	24.4-15.7	18.9-14.2	20.1-12.0	17.9-13.0	26.8-14.7
Price Range	44⅝-35⅜	44½-30⅜	38⅝-24¾	26⅝-20	25⅛-15	18¾-13⅝	22½-12⅜

Statistics are as originally reported.

OFFICERS:
C.R. Walgreen, III, Chmn. & C.E.O.
C.D. Hunter, Vice-Chmn. & C.F.O.
L.D. Jorndt, Pres. & C.O.O.
J.A. Oettinger, V.P., Couns. & Sec.

INCORPORATED: IL, Feb., 1909

PRINCIPAL OFFICE: 200 Wilmot Rd., Deerfield, IL 60015

TELEPHONE NUMBER: (708) 940-2500

NO. OF EMPLOYEES: 58,000

ANNUAL MEETING: In January

SHAREHOLDERS: 28,000

INSTITUTIONAL HOLDINGS:
No. of Institutions: 409
Shares Held: 59,450,683

REGISTRAR(S): Harris Trust & Savings Bank, Chicago, IL

TRANSFER AGENT(S): Harris Trust & Savings Bank, Chicago, IL

WALLACE COMPUTER SERVICES, INC.

YIELD 2.0%
P/E RATIO 17.2

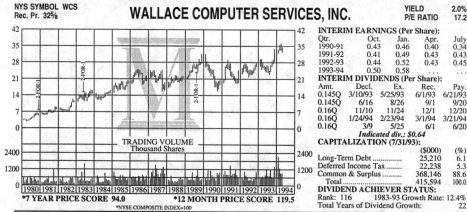

7 YEAR PRICE SCORE 94.0   **12 MONTH PRICE SCORE 119.5**
*NYSE COMPOSITE INDEX=100

INTERIM EARNINGS (Per Share):

Qtr.	Oct.	Jan.	Apr.	July
1990-91	0.43	0.46	0.40	0.34
1991-92	0.41	0.49	0.43	0.43
1992-93	0.44	0.52	0.43	0.45
1993-94	0.50	0.58	...	...

INTERIM DIVIDENDS (Per Share):

Amt.	Decl.	Ex.	Rec.	Pay.
0.145Q	3/10/93	5/25/93	6/1/93	6/21/93
0.145Q	6/16	8/26	9/1	9/20
0.16Q	11/10	11/24	12/1	12/20
0.16Q	1/24/94	2/23/94	3/1/94	3/21/94
0.16Q	3/9	5/25	6/1	6/20

Indicated div.: $0.64

CAPITALIZATION (7/31/93):

	($000)	(%)
Long-Term Debt	25,210	6.1
Deferred Income Tax	22,238	5.3
Common & Surplus	368,146	88.6
Total	415,594	100.0

DIVIDEND ACHIEVER STATUS:
Rank: 116   1983-93 Growth Rate: 12.4%
Total Years of Dividend Growth: 22

RECENT DEVELOPMENTS: For the quarter ended 1/31/94, net income increased 10.3% to $12.8 million compared with $11.6 million a year ago. Sales were up 10.9% to $153.1 million from $138.1 million. The improved results reflected strong customer demand for the Wallace Information Network (W.I.N.) and the new electronic forms products, PLAT-FORMS. Colorforms experienced a strong recovery due to improved economic conditions, cost controls, investments in technologies, and changes in the marketing program.

PROSPECTS: Wallace will continue to actively pursue expansion and acquisition opportunities. The Company expects further growth in its W.I.N. system. The system allows customers greater control in managing their inventory levels, faster delivery of materials, and lower internal operating-costs. W.I.N.'s strong menu of products should prove beneficial as companies are reducing the number of vendors they use. An improved retail environment will boost sales.

BUSINESS

WALLACE COMPUTER SER-VICES, INC. is engaged primarily in the computer services and supply industry. The Company provides its customers with a full line of products and services in the business forms, commercial printing, computer labels, machine ribbons, computer hardware and software, and computer accessory supplies market. Principal products supplied by the Company include the design, manufacture and sale of business forms, industrial and consumer catalogues, directories and price lists, pressure sensitive labels, and one-time carbon paper and carbon inks. The Company also markets accessory supplies, computer software, tax and utility billing forms and computer and business machine ribbons.

ANNUAL EARNINGS AND DIVIDENDS PER SHARE

	7/31/93	7/31/92	7/31/91	7/31/90	7/31/89	7/31/88	7/31/87
Earnings Per Share	1.84	1.76	1.63	1.86	1.76	1.53	1.27
Dividends Per Share	0.57	0.55	0.51	①0.47	0.415	②0.348	0.307
Dividend Payout %	31.0	31.3	31.3	25.3	23.6	22.8	24.2

① 2-for-1 stk split, 8/1/89 ② 2-for-1 stk split; 8/89.

ANNUAL FINANCIAL DATA

RECORD OF EARNINGS (IN THOUSANDS):

	7/31/93	7/31/92	7/31/91	7/31/90	7/31/89	7/31/88	7/31/87
Total Revenues	545,315	511,572	458,840	448,700	429,008	383,045	340,504
Costs and Expenses	454,129	428,155	387,226	374,851	358,746	321,218	282,868
Depreciation & Amort	30,299	28,580	22,454	18,403	16,953	14,390	10,805
Operating Income	60,887	54,837	49,160	55,446	53,309	47,437	46,831
Income Bef Income Taxes	62,379	59,780	53,860	60,854	56,542	48,631	48,198
Total Income Taxes	21,209	20,325	18,851	21,299	19,675	17,021	22,171
Net Income	41,170	39,455	35,009	39,555	36,867	31,610	26,027
Aver. Shs. Outstg.	22,348	22,418	21,526	21,278	21,007	20,748	20,486

BALANCE SHEET (IN THOUSANDS):

Cash and Cash Equivalents	46,930	55,119	52,325	54,402	60,922	39,412	24,435
Accounts Receivable, Net	92,775	89,193	75,630	69,085	64,604	59,762	61,962
Inventories	68,690	56,038	53,534	59,327	50,613	52,072	44,746
Gross Property	398,846	371,035	315,810	277,790	230,911	205,089	181,673
Accumulated Depreciation	170,975	145,691	123,459	105,360	91,278	78,034	66,093
Long-Term Debt	25,210	25,959	19,790	20,155	20,465	20,830	21,180
Net Stockholders' Equity	368,146	355,564	308,809	279,446	244,080	211,001	182,124
Total Assets	480,722	467,142	399,093	375,203	331,830	291,764	260,004
Total Current Assets	213,104	205,200	184,331	186,556	179,164	153,874	134,568
Total Current Liabilities	55,167	52,954	42,941	48,958	40,946	36,735	34,440
Net Working Capital	157,937	152,246	141,390	137,598	138,218	117,139	100,128
Year End Shares Outstg	22,061	22,606	21,722	21,433	21,169	20,912	20,632

STATISTICAL RECORD:

Operating Profit Margin %	11.2	10.7	10.7	12.4	12.4	12.4	13.8
Book Value Per Share	15.95	15.00	14.15	12.97	11.46	10.02	8.76
Return on Equity %	11.2	11.1	11.3	14.2	15.1	15.0	14.3
Return on Assets %	8.6	8.4	8.8	10.5	11.1	10.8	10.0
Average Yield %	2.2	2.2	2.1	2.0	1.6	1.8	1.5
P/E Ratio	16.0-12.4	15.9-12.4	17.9-11.7	16.9-8.5	17.9-11.9	14.7-11.3	19.5-12.3
Price Range	29½-22⅞	28-21¾	29⅛-19	31½-15⅞	31½-21	22½-17¼	24¾-15⅝

Statistics are as originally reported.

OFFICERS:
T. Dimitriou, Chmn.
R.J. Cronin, Pres. & C.E.O.
M.J. Halloran, V.P., C.F.O. & Sec.

INCORPORATED: DE, Jun., 1963

PRINCIPAL OFFICE: 4600 W. Roosevelt Rd., Hillside, IL 60162

TELEPHONE NUMBER: (312) 626-2000

NO. OF EMPLOYEES: 456

ANNUAL MEETING: In November

SHAREHOLDERS: 2,850

INSTITUTIONAL HOLDINGS:
No. of Institutions: 161
Shares Held: 15,688,807

REGISTRAR(S): Harris Trust & Savings Bank, Chicago, IL

TRANSFER AGENT(S): Harris Trust & Savings Bank, Chicago, IL

NYS SYMBOL WLA
Rec. Pr. 69⅜

WARNER-LAMBERT CO.

YIELD 3.5%
P/E RATIO 28.3

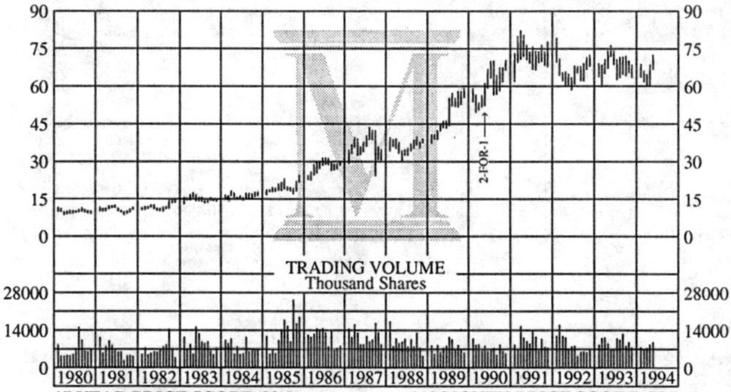

*7 YEAR PRICE SCORE 92.5 *12 MONTH PRICE SCORE 95.7

*NYSE COMPOSITE INDEX=100

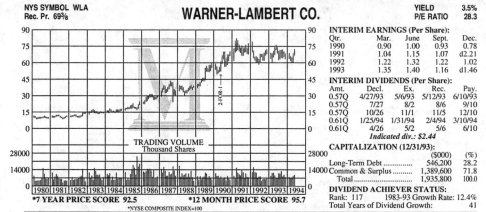

INTERIM EARNINGS (Per Share):

Qtr.	Mar.	June	Sept.	Dec.
1990	0.90	1.00	0.93	0.78
1991	1.04	1.15	1.07	d2.21
1992	1.22	1.32	1.22	1.02
1993	1.35	1.40	1.16	d1.46

INTERIM DIVIDENDS (Per Share):

Amt.	Decl.	Ex.	Rec.	Pay.
0.57Q	4/27/93	5/6/93	5/12/93	6/10/93
0.57Q	7/27	8/2	8/6	9/10
0.57Q	10/26	11/1	11/5	12/10
0.61Q	1/25/94	1/31/94	2/4/94	3/10/94
0.61Q	4/26	5/2	5/6	6/10

Indicated div.: $2.44

CAPITALIZATION (12/31/93):

	($000)	(%)
Long-Term Debt	546,200	28.2
Common & Surplus	1,389,600	71.8
Total	1,935,800	100.0

DIVIDEND ACHIEVER STATUS:
Rank: 117 1983-93 Growth Rate: 12.4%
Total Years of Dividend Growth: 41

RECENT DEVELOPMENTS: For the year ended 12/31/93, net income before an accounting adjustment fell 55.7% to $285.0 million compared with $643.7 million the previous year. Sales were up 3.5% to $5.79 billion from $5.60 billion. Earnings included a $525.2 million ($360.4 million after-tax) restructuring charge for the disposition of Novon Products Group, the October sale of the chocolate/caramel business, and the charge for organizational restructuring and plant rationalization.

PROSPECTS: Sales growth will be driven by the widening acceptance of the cardiovascular drug Accupril and the launch of two new products: Cognex for Alzheimer's disease and the anticonvulsant Neurontin. Sales will be adversely affected by the patent-expiration for Lopid. Revenues will also benefit from a joint-venture with Wellcome plc, Warner Wellcome, which will be the third largest OTC drug operation in the world. Sales are expected to exceed $1.60 billion.

BUSINESS

WARNER-LAMBERT CO. develops, manufactures and markets ethical pharmaceuticals and non-prescription health care products. Non-prescription health care products include Benadryl anti-allergy medication, Lubriderm skin lotion, Rolaids antacid, Efferdent denture cleanser, Halls cough tablets, and Listerine. Other products include Schick razors and blades, Tetra pet care products and empty gelatin capsules for pharmaceutical use.

BUSINESS LINE ANALYSIS

(12/31/93)	Rev(%)	Inc(%)
Pharmaceutical	36.5	37.5
Consumer Health Care	41.0	42.9
Confectionery	22.5	19.6
Total	100.0	100.0

ANNUAL EARNINGS AND DIVIDENDS PER SHARE

	1993	1992	1991	1990	1989	1988	1987
Earnings Per Share	**2.11**	**4.78**	**[1] 1.05**	**3.61**	**3.05**	**2.50**	**2.08**
Dividends Per Share	**2.28**	**2.04**	**1.76**	**[2] 1.52**	**1.28**	**1.08**	**0.89**
Dividend Payout %	**N.M.**	**42.7**	**N.M.**	**42.1**	**42.0**	**43.2**	**42.7**

[1] Bef. acctg. chge. [2] 2-for-1 stk split, 5/90

ANNUAL FINANCIAL DATA

	1993	1992	1991	1990	1989	1988	1987
RECORD OF EARNINGS (IN MILLIONS):							
Total Revenues	5,790.0	5,597.6	5,166.6	4,773.8	4,272.0	3,970.3	3,543.2
Costs and Expenses	5,333.9	4,608.7	4,751.4	3,904.7	3,520.0	3,267.4	2,910.1
Depreciation & Amort	170.4	155.6	135.5	119.7	104.8	96.4	79.4
Operating Profit	d4,514.2	d4,290.8	1,246.9	1,128.7	956.0	865.9	785.5
Income Bef Income Taxes	318.5	858.2	221.5	680.7	591.6	538.3	492.8
Provision for Inc Taxes	33.5	214.5	80.7	195.8	178.9	198.0	197.0
Net Income	[1] 285.0	643.7	[2] 140.8	484.9	412.7	340.3	295.8
Aver. Shs. Outstg. (000)	135,000	134,717	134,441	134,330	135,336	136,070	142,600
[1] Before acctg. change cr$46,000,000. [2] Before acctg. change dr$106,000,000.							
BALANCE SHEET (IN MILLIONS):							
Cash & Cash Equivalents	440.5	718.4	535.7	306.1	252.5	176.6	220.8
Receivables, Net	890.8	752.8	650.5	634.4	532.8	525.2	469.9
Inventories	476.5	424.6	418.5	412.8	374.3	381.4	379.0
Gross Property	2,834.2	2,546.1	2,323.5	2,127.9	1,884.2	1,761.6	1,615.7
Accumulated Depreciation	1,234.9	1,039.0	973.5	826.5	751.7	708.6	655.9
Long-Term Debt	546.2	564.6	447.9	306.8	303.4	318.2	293.8
Net Stockholders' Equity	1,389.6	1,528.5	1,170.7	1,402.3	1,129.8	998.6	874.4
Total Assets	4,828.1	4,077.4	3,602.0	3,261.3	2,859.8	2,702.8	2,475.9
Total Current Assets	2,218.7	2,176.3	1,843.7	1,558.6	1,366.5	1,264.5	1,252.6
Total Current Liabilities	2,015.9	1,333.3	1,249.9	1,100.7	1,031.3	1,025.2	974.3
Net Working Capital	202.8	843.0	593.8	457.9	335.2	239.3	278.3
Year End Shs Outstg (000)	134,140	135,340	134,594	134,341	134,842	160,330	137,174
STATISTICAL RECORD:							
Operating Profit Margin %	...	...	5.4	15.7	15.1	15.3	15.6
Book Value Per Share	8.02	10.14	7.52	9.24	7.34	5.30	5.80
Return on Equity %	20.5	42.1	12.0	34.6	36.5	34.1	33.8
Return on Assets %	5.9	15.8	3.9	14.9	14.4	12.6	11.9
Average Yield %	3.3	3.0	2.4	2.5	2.6	3.1	2.6
P/E Ratio	36.2-28.3	16.6-12.2	78.3-58.8	19.5-13.7	19.5-12.2	15.9-12.0	21.0-11.6
Price Range	76⅜-59¾	79¼-58⅜	82¼-61¾	70⅜-49⅝	59⅜-37¼	39¾-30	43¾-24⅛

Statistics are as originally reported.

OFFICERS:
M.R. Goodes, Chmn. & C.E.O.
L.J. De Vink, Pres. & C.O.O.
E.J. Larini, V.P. & C.F.O.
R.G. Paltiel, Sec.

INCORPORATED: DE, Nov., 1920

PRINCIPAL OFFICE: 201 Tabor Rd., Morris Plains, NJ 07950

TELEPHONE NUMBER: (201) 540-2000

NO. OF EMPLOYEES: 34,000

ANNUAL MEETING: In April

SHAREHOLDERS: 47,300

INSTITUTIONAL HOLDINGS:
No. of Institutions: 702
Shares Held: 85,947,022

REGISTRAR(S): First Chicago Trust Co. of New York, New York, NY 10008

TRANSFER AGENT(S): First Chicago Trust Co. of New York, New York, NY 10008

NYS SYMBOL WGL
Rec. Pr. 39

WASHINGTON GAS LIGHT CO.

YIELD 5.7%
P/E RATIO 14.3

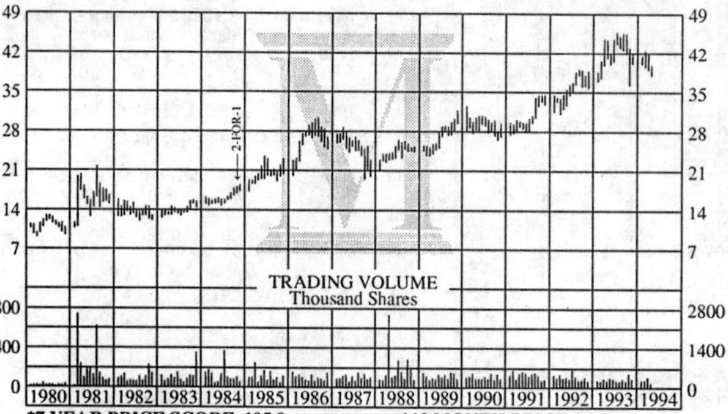

***7 YEAR PRICE SCORE 105.0** ***12 MONTH PRICE SCORE 96.3**

*NYSE COMPOSITE INDEX=100

INTERIM EARNINGS (Per Share):

Qtr.	Dec.	Mar.	June	Sept.
1990-91	1.22	1.95	d0.29	d0.59
1991-92	1.24	2.14	d0.15	d0.69
1992-93	1.36	2.39	d0.31	d0.79
1993-94	1.44	...	...	...

INTERIM DIVIDENDS (Per Share):

Amt.	Decl.	Ex.	Rec.	Pay.
0.545Q	3/31/93	4/5/93	4/12/93	5/1/93
0.545Q	6/30	7/6	7/12	8/1
0.545Q	9/29	10/5	10/12	11/1
0.545Q	12/15	1/4/94	1/10/94	2/1/94
0.555Q	3/30/94	4/5	4/11	5/1

Indicated div.: $2.22

CAPITALIZATION (9/30/93):

	($000)	(%)
Long-Term Debt	347,701	37.4
Deferred Income Tax	96,082	10.3
Preferred Stock	28,521	3.1
Common & Surplus	458,044	49.2
Total	930,348	100.0

DIVIDEND ACHIEVER STATUS:
Rank: 299 1983-93 Growth Rate: 4.3%
Total Years of Dividend Growth: 17

RECENT DEVELOPMENTS: For the quarter ended 12/31/93, net income was $30.3 million compared with $28.0 million last year. Revenues decreased slightly to $271.2 million. Therm sales to firm customers rose by 3.2% which included the effect of a 3.3% rise in the number of customer meters. Excluding sales for electric generation, therms delivered to interruptible customers declined 1.9%. However, margin sharing arrangements minimized the effect on income of volumetric changes in sales to the interruptible class.

PROSPECTS: The Company will benefit from District of Columbia metropolitan area population growth of 13% by the year 2000. The Company is experiencing higher conversion rates and an increase in its construction market share. A construction survey in WGL's service territory shows that all 1,500 single family detached residential homes planned for construction and 91% of the 1,600 townhouse units planned for construction are scheduled to have gas heating.

BUSINESS

WASHINGTON GAS LIGHT CO. distributes natural gas to Washington D.C. and adjoining areas through three divisions: District of Columbia Natural Gas, Maryland Natural Gas, and Northern Virginia Natural Gas. WGL also has five active subsidiaries: Shenandoah Gas, Frederick Gas and Hampshire Gas, which provide gas service to areas in Virginia and West Virginia, Crab Run Gas, that is involved in the exploration and development of natural gas prospects, and Washington Resources Group that conducts the Company's non-gas investments including real estate, energy-related services and equity holdings in emerging growth companies. Consolidated gas sales for 1993 were: 55% residential, 31% commercial and industrial, 13% interruptible and 1% interruptible-electric generation.

QUARTERLY DATA

(9/30/93)($000)	Rev	Inc
1st Quarter	273,120	27,975
2nd Quarter	383,844	49,279
3rd Quarter	139,806	-6,110
4th Quarter	97,530	16,065

ANNUAL EARNINGS AND DIVIDENDS PER SHARE

	9/30/93	9/30/92	9/30/91	9/30/90	9/30/89	9/30/88	12/31/87
Earnings Per Share	**2.62**	**2.53**	**2.28**	**2.51**	**2.43**	**2.52**	**2.27**
Dividends Per Share	**2.17**	**2.13**	**2.085**	**2.02**	**1.94**	**1.86**	**1.79**
Dividend Payout %	**82.8**	**84.2**	**91.4**	**80.5**	**79.8**	**73.8**	**78.9**

ANNUAL FINANCIAL DATA

	9/30/93	9/30/92	9/30/91	9/30/90	9/30/89	9/30/88	12/31/87
RECORD OF EARNINGS (IN MILLIONS):							
Operating Revenues	894.3	746.2	697.9	735.5	755.6	698.0	683.8
Depreciation & Amort	39.8	37.2	36.1	36.1	32.8	29.4	34.4
Maintenance	33.5	31.4	30.9	32.3	31.4	30.0	30.1
Prov for Fed Inc Taxes	34.6	31.5	26.9	29.3	26.8	25.3	27.3
Operating Income	86.0	82.2	70.8	75.7	68.7	65.6	59.0
Interest Expense	29.1	28.0	27.4	28.3	25.1	22.8	20.1
Net Income	55.1	52.2	46.4	50.2	47.3	45.1	39.4
Aver. Shs. Outstg. (000)	20,522	20,122	19,777	19,478	18,907	17,021	16,817
BALANCE SHEET (IN MILLIONS):							
Gross Plant	1,405.3	1,313.5	1,240.4	1,186.1	1,108.7	1,037.6	954.1
Accumulated Depreciation	484.2	449.0	419.3	402.8	379.7	361.3	353.9
Prop, Plant & Equip, Net	921.1	864.5	821.1	783.3	729.0	676.2	600.2
Long-term Debt	347.7	294.5	263.0	279.6	296.8	252.5	227.0
Net Stockholders' Equity	486.6	461.7	441.0	427.5	410.1	411.2	347.4
Total Assets	1,194.7	1,065.7	1,013.9	967.5	924.0	922.5	826.7
Year End Shs Outstg (000)	20,752	20,308	19,944	19,614	19,352	17,148	16,956
STATISTICAL RECORD:							
Book Value Per Share	22.07	21.33	20.68	20.33	19.71	22.30	18.80
Op. Inc/Net Pl %	9.3	9.5	8.6	9.7	9.4	9.7	9.8
Dep/Gr. Pl %	2.8	2.8	2.9	3.0	3.0	2.8	3.2
Accum. Dep/Gr. Pl %	34.5	34.2	33.8	34.0	34.2	34.8	37.1
Return on Equity %	11.3	11.3	10.5	11.7	11.5	11.0	11.4
Average Yield %	5.3	6.1	6.7	6.8	7.0	7.8	7.4
P/E Ratio	17.5-13.8	15.5-12.3	15.1-12.0	12.9-10.6	13.1-9.7	10.5-8.4	12.7-8.6
Price Range	45¾-36¼	39⅛-31⅛	34½-27⅞	32½-26½	31¾-23⅝	26½-21⅛	28¾-19½

Statistics are as originally reported.

OFFICERS:
P.J. Maher, Chmn. & C.E.O.
J.K. Hughitt, Pres. & C.O.O.
E.W. Smallwood, Sr. V.P. & C.F.O.
D.V. Pope, Secretary

INCORPORATED: DC, Mar., 1957

PRINCIPAL OFFICE: 1100 H Street, N.W., Washington, DC 20080

TELEPHONE NUMBER: (703) 750-4440
FAX: (202) 624-6196
NO. OF EMPLOYEES: 2,670
ANNUAL MEETING: In February
SHAREHOLDERS: 22,607
INSTITUTIONAL HOLDINGS:
No. of Institutions: 128
Shares Held: 4,695,020

REGISTRAR(S): Riggs National Bank of Washington, D.C., 808 17th Street, N.W., Suite 240, Washington, DC 20006-3950

TRANSFER AGENT(S): Riggs National Bank of Washington, D.C., 808 17th Street, N.W., Suite 240, Washington, DC 20006-3950

ASE SYMBOL WRE
Rec. Pr. 19½

WASHINGTON REAL ESTATE INVESTMENT TRUST

YIELD 4.7%
P/E RATIO 24.1

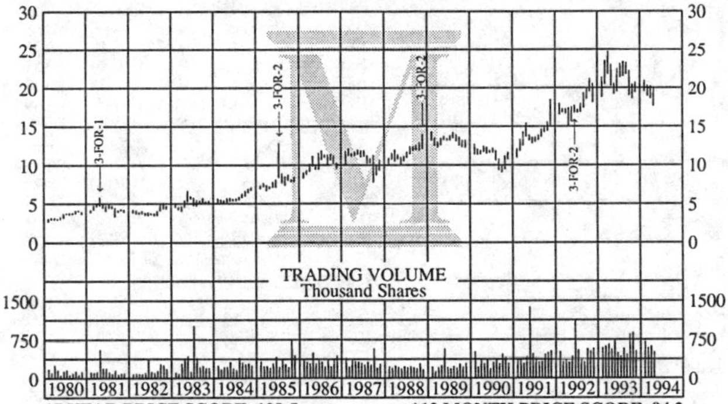

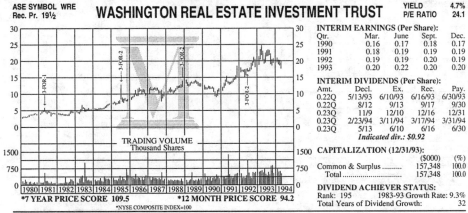

30
25
20
15
10
5
0
3-FOR-1
3-FOR-2
3-FOR-2
3-FOR-2
TRADING VOLUME
Thousand Shares
1500
750
0
1980 1981 1982 1983 1984 1985 1986 1987 1988 1989 1990 1991 1992 1993 1994

***7 YEAR PRICE SCORE 109.5** ***12 MONTH PRICE SCORE 94.2**

*NYSE COMPOSITE INDEX=100

INTERIM EARNINGS (Per Share):

Qtr.	Mar.	June	Sept.	Dec.
1990	0.16	0.17	0.18	0.17
1991	0.18	0.19	0.19	0.19
1992	0.19	0.19	0.20	0.19
1993	0.20	0.22	0.20	0.20

INTERIM DIVIDENDS (Per Share):

Amt.	Decl.	Ex.	Rec.	Pay.
0.22Q	5/13/93	6/10/93	6/16/93	6/30/93
0.22Q	8/12	9/13	9/17	9/30
0.23Q	11/9	12/10	12/16	12/31
0.23Q	2/23/94	3/11/94	3/17/94	3/31/94
0.23Q	5/13	6/10	6/16	6/30

Indicated div.: $0.92

CAPITALIZATION (12/31/93):

	($000)	(%)
Common & Surplus	157,348	100.0
Total	157,348	100.0

DIVIDEND ACHIEVER STATUS:
Rank: 195 1983-93 Growth Rate: 9.3%
Total Years of Dividend Growth: 32

RECENT DEVELOPMENTS: For the year ended 12/31/93, income, before gain on sale of real estate, was $22.5 million, or $0.80 per share, compared with net income of $20.4 million, or $0.76 per share, in 1992. Real estate rental revenue for the year rose 15.4% to $39.4 million from $34.1 million for the prior year. The office building and shopping center groups contributed most of the increase in revenue in 1993 due, in part, to the acquisition of three office buildings in November. In the rental market, the Company improved its average occupancy from 93% in 1992 to 95% in 1993. For the quarter ended 12/31/93, net income was $5.6 million, or $0.20 per share, compared with $5.2 million, or $0.19 per share, for the same quarter last year. Real estate rental revenue for the quarter was $10.0 million, compared with $8.6 million for the year-ago quarter.

BUSINESS

WASHINGTON R.E. INVESTMENT TRUST is a self-administered qualified equity real estate investment trust. The Trust's business consists of the ownership of income-producing real estate properties principally in the Washington, D.C. metropolitan area. Upon the purchase of a property, WRE begins a program of improving real estate to increase the value and to improve the operations with the goals of generating higher rental income and reducing expenses. The Trust currently owns a diversified portfolio consisting of ten shopping centers, eight office buildings, five high-rise apartment buildings and nine business centers. WRE's principal objective is to invest in high-quality real estate in prime locations and to monitor closely the management of these properties, which includes active leasing and ongoing capital improvement programs.

ANNUAL EARNINGS AND DIVIDENDS PER SHARE

	1993	1992	1991	1990	1989	1988	1987
Earnings Per Share	**0.80**	**0.76**	**0.75**	**0.69**	**0.64**	**0.56**	**0.51**
Dividends Per Share	**0.89**	**① 0.836**	**0.787**	**0.733**	**0.68**	**② 0.633**	**0.582**
Dividend Payout %	**N.M.**	**N.M.**	**N.M.**	**N.M.**	**N.M.**	**N.M.**	**N.M.**

① 3-for-2 stk split, 6/1/92 ② 3-for-2 stk split, 12/88.

ANNUAL FINANCIAL DATA

	1993	1992	1991	1990	1989	1988	1987
RECORD OF EARNINGS (IN THOUSANDS):							
Costs and Expenses	14,648	13,138	12,850	12,165	11,526	10,876	10,117
Depreciation	3,656	3,422	3,321	3,108	3,015	2,753	2,451
Operating Profit	d18,304	d16,559	d16,171	d15,272	d14,541	d13,629	d12,568
Net Income	23,247	20,429	18,386	16,122	14,266	11,573	10,525
Aver. Shs. Outstg.	28,223	26,910	24,708	23,223	22,269	20,664	20,660
BALANCE SHEET (IN THOUSANDS):							
Cash & Temporary Invests	...	...	...	14,173	...	...	7,195
Receivables, Net	2,473	1,498	1,562	1,121	933	998	1,317
Long-Term Debt	...	1,115	11,329	12,379	12,012	12,463	12,877
Net Stockholders' Equity	157,348	159,027	119,944	90,621	91,479	61,564	63,043
Total Assets	162,011	185,673	135,741	106,955	106,518	76,511	78,074
Total Current Assets	24,005	60,369	45,524	18,066	30,500	7,203	10,467
Total Current Liabilities	4,663	25,532	4,467	3,955	3,027	2,484	2,153
Net Working Capital	19,342	34,837	41,057	14,112	27,473	4,719	8,314
Year End Shares Outstg	...	28,211	25,594	23,765	23,217	20,667	20,660
STATISTICAL RECORD:							
Return on Equity %	14.8	12.8	15.3	17.8	15.6	18.8	16.7
Return on Assets %	14.4	11.0	13.6	15.1	13.4	15.1	13.5
Book Value Per Share	...	5.64	4.69	3.81	3.94	2.98	3.05
Average Yield %	4.1	4.6	5.4	6.7	5.1	5.3	5.9
P/E Ratio	30.9-23.3	28.0-19.6	24.7-14.5	18.5-13.2	22.5-19.1	25.0-17.9	23.8-15.2
Price Range	24¾-18⅝	21¼-14⅞	18½-10⅞	12¾-9⅛	14⅜-12¼	14-10	12⅛-7¾

Statistics are as originally reported.

QUARTERLY DATA

(12/31/93)($000)	Rev	Inc
1st Quarter................	9,758	5,771
2nd Quarter................	9,714	5,581
3rd Quarter................	9,905	5,535
4th Quarter................	9,998	5,619

OFFICERS:
B.F. Kahn, Chmn. & Pres.
H.E. Cochran, V.P.-Fin. & C.F.O.
B.H. Dorsey, Sec. & Gen. Couns.

INCORPORATED: DC, Nov., 1960

PRINCIPAL OFFICE: 10400 Connecticut Avenue Concourse Level, Kensington, MD 20895

TELEPHONE NUMBER: (301) 929-5900

NO. OF EMPLOYEES: 15

ANNUAL MEETING: In June

SHAREHOLDERS: 25,000 (approx.)

INSTITUTIONAL HOLDINGS:
No. of Institutions: 77
Shares Held: 4,392,229

REGISTRAR(S): American Stock Transfer & Trust Co., 40 Wall Street, New York, NY 10005

TRANSFER AGENT(S): American Stock Transfer & Trust Co., 40 Wall Street, New York, NY 10005

WEIS MARKETS, INC.

YIELD 2.9%
P/E RATIO 14.7

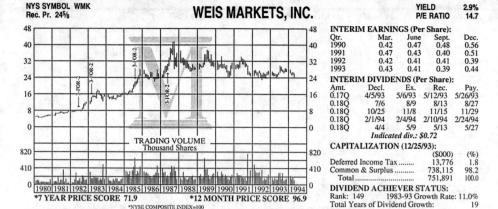

INTERIM EARNINGS (Per Share):

Qtr.	Mar.	June	Sept.	Dec.
1990	0.42	0.47	0.48	0.56
1991	0.47	0.43	0.40	0.51
1992	0.42	0.41	0.41	0.39
1993	0.43	0.41	0.39	0.44

INTERIM DIVIDENDS (Per Share):

Amt.	Decl.	Ex.	Rec.	Pay.
0.17Q	4/5/93	5/6/93	5/12/93	5/26/93
0.18Q	7/6	8/9	8/13	8/27
0.18Q	10/25	11/8	11/15	11/29
0.18Q	2/1/94	2/4/94	2/10/94	2/24/94
0.18Q	4/4	5/9	5/13	5/27

Indicated div.: $0.72

CAPITALIZATION (12/25/93):

	($000)	(%)
Deferred Income Tax	13,776	1.8
Common & Surplus	738,115	98.2
Total	751,891	100.0

DIVIDEND ACHIEVER STATUS:
Rank: 149   1983-93 Growth Rate: 11.0%
Total Years of Dividend Growth: 19

RECENT DEVELOPMENTS: For the year ended 12/25/93, net income was $73.0 million compared with $71.7 million last year. Prior-year's results were before an accounting credit of $1.0 million. Sales advanced 11.8% to $1.44 billion. Earnings per share increased to $1.66 from $1.63. The Company closed the year with 141 stores in operation. For the thirteen weeks ended 12/25/93, net income was $19.5 million compared with $17.1 million last year. Sales advanced to $371.8 million from $328.2 million.

PROSPECTS: As a result of price competition, WMK will likely focus on offering everyday low prices and lowering promotional expenses. Meanwhile, Weis plans to continue with its store expansion program, remodeling about 10 existing stores and opening about four new supermarkets. A healthy financial position, with no long term debt, will support possible acquisitions and will allow expansions to be financed from internally generated funds.

BUSINESS

WEIS MARKETS INC. operates 141 supermarkets in Pennsylvania, New Jersey, New York, Maryland, Virginia and West Virginia. Many of WMK's 1,800 different private label products are supplied by the Company's ice cream manufacturing plant, fresh meat processing plant, milk processing plant, and delicatessen kitchen. Distribution centers located in Sunbury and Milton, PA are served by a Company-owned fleet of tractor trailers. WMK conducts food service operations through its wholly-owned Weis Food Service subsidiary which distributes frozen foods and grocery items to restaurants and institutions. Full-service pharmacy departments are located in 66 WMK markets. The Company also operates one Amity House restaurant. Management owns approximately 79% of the stock.

QUARTERLY DATA

(12/25/93)($000)	Rev	Inc
1st Quarter	356,579	18,687
2nd Quarter	357,868	17,754
3nd Quarter	354,884	17,044
4rd Quarter	371,759	19,468

ANNUAL EARNINGS AND DIVIDENDS PER SHARE

	12/25/93	12/26/92	12/28/91	12/29/90	12/30/89	12/31/88	12/26/87
Earnings Per Share	1.66	1.63	1.81	1.93	1.91	1.82	1.66
Dividends Per Share	0.70	0.68	0.64	0.60	0.56	0.61	① 0.414
Dividend Payout %	42.2	41.7	35.4	31.1	29.3	33.5	24.9

① 3-for-2 stk. split, 5/87, 8/85, 2/83, 5/82 & 5/79.

ANNUAL FINANCIAL DATA

RECORD OF EARNINGS (IN MILLIONS):

	12/25/93	12/26/92	12/28/91	12/29/90	12/30/89	12/31/88	12/26/87
Total Revenues	1,441.1	1,289.2	1,294.3	1,271.8	1,239.3	1,189.2	1,128.3
Costs and Expenses	1,332.5	1,187.4	1,181.7	1,151.9	1,117.2	1,069.0	1,007.3
Depreciation & Amort	29.0	26.4	25.1	23.2	22.0	19.6	17.0
Income From Operations	79.7	75.4	87.5	96.7	100.1	100.6	104.1
Income Bef Income Taxes	113.7	110.2	124.2	132.3	134.0	129.9	130.8
Provision for Inc Taxes	40.7	38.6	43.6	45.5	47.6	47.3	54.9
Net Income	73.0	① 71.7	80.6	86.8	86.4	82.6	76.0
Aver. Shs. Outstg. (000)	43,827	43,979	44,503	45,050	45,338	45,514	45,722

① Before acctg. change cr$1,046,000.

BALANCE SHEET (IN MILLIONS):

	12/25/93	12/26/92	12/28/91	12/29/90	12/30/89	12/31/88	12/26/87
Cash and Cash Equivalents	467.2	420.6	408.6	391.4	356.1	318.1	294.2
Receivables, Net	20.4	25.9	21.1	13.8	12.1	10.5	10.9
Inventories	111.8	97.7	92.3	87.7	85.3	81.7	76.3
Gross Property	496.5	450.3	422.1	388.1	369.6	336.3	293.4
Accumulated Depreciation	271.2	245.8	223.0	201.0	182.4	163.1	148.6
Net Stockholders' Equity	738.1	680.3	647.4	610.1	567.3	509.8	454.0
Total Assets	844.5	761.5	734.5	693.9	655.6	595.7	536.7
Total Current Assets	605.8	552.4	530.2	503.3	464.7	418.7	388.1
Total Current Liabilities	92.6	68.8	73.8	71.6	77.1	76.6	74.2
Net Working Capital	513.2	483.6	456.5	431.7	387.6	342.2	313.9
Year End Shs Outstg (000)	43,796	43,832	44,216	44,730	45,307	45,418	45,558

STATISTICAL RECORD:

	12/25/93	12/26/92	12/28/91	12/29/90	12/30/89	12/31/88	12/26/87
Operating Profit Margin %	5.5	5.9	6.8	7.6	8.1	8.5	9.2
Book Value Per Share	16.55	15.41	14.53	13.56	12.44	11.14	9.88
Return on Equity %	9.9	10.5	12.4	14.2	15.2	16.2	16.7
Return on Assets %	8.6	9.4	11.0	12.5	13.2	13.9	14.2
Average Yield %	2.6	2.7	2.2	2.0	1.7	1.9	1.3
P/E Ratio	18.0-14.5	17.1-14.1	18.9-13.7	17.8-12.6	19.6-14.7	20.3-14.8	25.1-14.4
Price Range	29⅞-24	27⅞-23	34¼-24¾	34⅜-24¼	37½-28⅛		37-27 41⅝-23⅞

Statistics are as originally reported.

OFFICERS:
S. Weis, Pres.
N.S. Rich, V.P. & Sec.
R.F. Weis, V.P. & Treas.
W.R. Mills, V.P.-Fin.

INCORPORATED: PA, Dec., 1924

PRINCIPAL OFFICE: 1000 S. 2nd St., Sunbury, PA 17801

TELEPHONE NUMBER: (717) 286-4571

NO. OF EMPLOYEES: 4,452 (approx.)

ANNUAL MEETING: In April

SHAREHOLDERS: 2,115

INSTITUTIONAL HOLDINGS:
No. of Institutions: 67
Shares Held: 20,736,365

REGISTRAR(S):

TRANSFER AGENT(S):

WESCO FINANCIAL CORP.

YIELD 0.8%
P/E RATIO N.M

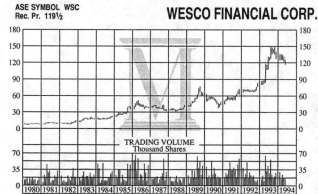

*7 YEAR PRICE SCORE 157.4   *12 MONTH PRICE SCORE 98.7
*NYSE COMPOSITE INDEX=100

TRADING VOLUME
Thousand Shares

INTERIM EARNINGS (Per Share):

Qtr.	Mar.	June	Sept.	Dec.
1990	0.95	0.91	0.86	0.85
1991	0.90	1.52	0.96	0.77
1992	0.75	0.84	0.73	d1.62
1993	0.90	0.51	0.43	0.79

INTERIM DIVIDENDS (Per Share):

Amt.	Decl.	Ex.	Rec.	Pay.
0.235Q	3/26/93	5/7/93	5/13/93	6/3/93
0.235Q	7/23	7/30	8/5	9/2
0.235Q	11/2	11/5	11/13	12/2
0.245Q	1/27/94	2/3/94	2/9/94	3/9/94
0.245Q	3/25	5/5	5/11	6/8

Indicated div.: $0.98

CAPITALIZATION (12/31/93):

	($000)	(%)
Total Debt	37,896	5.7
Common & Surplus	626,087	94.3
Total	663,983	100.0

DIVIDEND ACHIEVER STATUS:
Rank: 273   1983-93 Growth Rate: 5.7%
Total Years of Dividend Growth: 22

RECENT DEVELOPMENTS: For the year ended 12/31/93, income, before cumulative effect of change in accounting principle, was $18.7 million, or $2.63 per share, compared with net income of $5.0 million, or $0.70 per share, in 1992. Revenues for the year declined 11% to $117.4 million from $131.8 million in the prior year. Revenues include significant amounts of substantially tax-exempt dividend income from preferred and common stocks as well as fully tax-exempt interest on state and municipal bonds. For the quarter ended 12/31/93, income, before unusual items and cumulative effect of accounting change, was $4.7 million, or $0.66 per share, compared with income, before unusual items, of $5.9 million, or $0.83 per share, for the corresponding 1992 quarter. Revenues for the quarter declined 13% to $25.8 million from $29.6 million for the year-ago quarter.

BUSINESS

WESCO FINANCIAL CORPORATION was incorporated in Delaware on March 19, 1959. The principal businesses of the Company, conducted by wholly-owned subsidiaries, are the savings and loan business, through Mutual Savings and Loan Association; the property and casualty insurance business, through Wesco-Financial Insurance Company; and the steel service center business, through Precision Steel Warehouse, Inc. The Company's operations also include the manufacture of electrical equipment through New America Electrical Corporation, which is 80%-owned by the Company. In addition, Wesco has investments in real estate and securities held for investment, and owns a small insurance agency. The Company's activities fall into three business segments—financial, insurance and industrial.

ANNUAL EARNINGS AND DIVIDENDS PER SHARE

	1993	1992	1991	1990	1989	1988	1987
Earnings Per Share	① 2.63	0.70	4.15	3.57	4.26	4.22	2.14
Dividends Per Share	0.94	0.90	0.86	0.82	0.78	0.74	0.70
Dividend Payout %	35.7	N.M.	20.7	23.0	18.3	17.5	32.7

① Bef. acctg. chge.

ANNUAL FINANCIAL DATA

RECORD OF EARNINGS (IN THOUSANDS):

	1993	1992	1991	1990	1989	1988	1987
Total Interest Income	36,104	44,874	49,673	53,191	50,436	49,425	41,927
Total Interest Expense	5,792	11,986	18,311	21,975	21,261	20,579	20,903
Net Interest Income	30,312	32,888	31,362	31,216	29,175	28,846	21,024
Income Bef Income Taxes	23,741	25,874	34,629	25,790	33,185	34,938	12,688
Income Taxes	5,046	20,873	5,107	361	2,851	4,849	cr2,525
Net Income	① 18,695	5,001	29,522	25,429	30,334	30,089	15,213
Aver. Shs. Outstg.	7,120	7,120	7,120	7,120	7,120	7,120	7,120

① Before acctg. change cr$1,023,000.

BALANCE SHEET (IN THOUSANDS):

	1993	1992	1991	1990	1989	1988	1987
Cash & Sec. Etc.	...	...	...	...	...	...	112,132
Investments and Advances	872,019	591,442	684,845	513,735	479,308	460,746	341,182
Real Estate Loans Receiv	1,848	101,891	100,876	107,382	153,763	137,007	139,468
Long-term Debt	37,896	55,119	55,429	55,726	56,011	31,786	31,017
Net Stockholders' Equity	626,087	411,714	406,363	308,978	281,496	238,588	212,820
Total Assets	915,155	864,959	871,129	744,081	737,505	706,264	647,396
Year End Shares Outstg	7,120	7,120	7,120	7,120	7,120	7,120	7,120

STATISTICAL RECORD:

	1993	1992	1991	1990	1989	1988	1987
Return on Equity %	3.0	1.2	7.3	8.2	10.8	12.6	7.1
Return on Assets %	2.0	0.6	3.4	3.4	4.1	4.3	2.4
Book Value Per Share	87.93	57.83	57.07	43.40	39.54	33.51	29.89
Average Yield %	0.8	1.2	1.5	1.6	1.3	2.0	1.8
P/E Ratio	56.9-30.4	N.M	17.4-10.8	17.8-10.6	18.1-9.4	10.2-7.5	20.4-15.0
Price Range	149¾-80	83⅞-66⅜	72⅜-45	63½-38	77¼-40⅛	42⅞-31⅝	43⅝-32⅛

Statistics are as originally reported.

BUSINESS LINE ANALYSIS

(12/31/93)	Rev(%)	Inc(%)
Financial	20.7	31.2
Insurance	24.8	56.2
Industrial	54.5	12.6
Total	100.0	100.0

OFFICERS:
C.T. Munger, Chairman
R.H. Bird, President
J.L. Jacobsen, V.P. & C.F.O.
M. Patrick, Secretary

INCORPORATED: DE, Mar., 1959

PRINCIPAL OFFICE: 315 East Colorado Boulevard, Pasadena, CA 91101-1954

TELEPHONE NUMBER: (818) 449-2345

NO. OF EMPLOYEES: 360 (approx.)

ANNUAL MEETING: In April

SHAREHOLDERS: 900 (approx.)

INSTITUTIONAL HOLDINGS:
No. of Institutions: 36
Shares Held: 6,233,358

REGISTRAR(S): Security Pacific National Bank, Los Angeles, CA 90060

TRANSFER AGENT(S): Security Pacific National Bank, Los Angeles, CA 90060

WESTERN RESOURCES, INC.

YIELD 7.0%
P/E RATIO 10.2

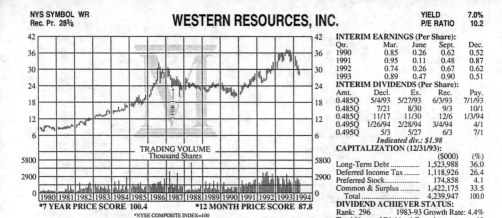

*7 YEAR PRICE SCORE 100.4   *12 MONTH PRICE SCORE 87.8
•NYSE COMPOSITE INDEX=100

INTERIM EARNINGS (Per Share):

Qtr.	Mar.	June	Sept.	Dec.
1990	0.85	0.26	0.62	0.52
1991	0.95	0.11	0.48	0.87
1992	0.74	0.26	0.67	0.62
1993	0.89	0.47	0.90	0.51

INTERIM DIVIDENDS (Per Share):

Amt.	Decl.	Ex.	Rec.	Pay.
0.485Q	5/4/93	5/27/93	6/3/93	7/1/93
0.485Q	7/21	8/30	9/3	10/1
0.485Q	11/17	11/30	12/6	1/3/94
0.495Q	1/26/94	2/28/94	3/4/94	4/1
0.495Q	5/3	5/27	6/3	7/1

Indicated div.: $1.98

CAPITALIZATION (12/31/93):

	($000)	(%)
Long-Term Debt	1,523,988	36.0
Deferred Income Tax	1,118,926	26.4
Preferred Stock	174,858	4.1
Common & Surplus	1,422,175	33.5
Total	4,239,947	100.0

DIVIDEND ACHIEVER STATUS:

Rank: 296   1983-93 Growth Rate: 4.4%
Total Years of Dividend Growth: 19

RECENT DEVELOPMENTS: For the year ended 12/31/93, net income was $177.4 million compared with $127.9 million in 1992. Revenues were $1.91 billion, up 23%. Results benefited from a return to near normal weather, reduced interest costs, and the full 12-month effect of the merger with Kansas Gas and Electric Company (KG&E). Total kilowatthour sales of electricity in 1993 were up 26% to 20 billion kilowattours.

PROSPECTS: Cash flow has improved significantly due to the merger with Kansas Gas and Electric Company. External debt financing in the foreseeable future will be limited to redemptions of high-cost issues with less expensive securities. WR has an agreement with Southern Union to sell its gas properties in Missouri for about $360 million in cash. The agreement is subject to regulatory approval. Proceeds from the sale will be used for debt reduction.

BUSINESS

WESTERN RESOURCES, INC. (formerly The Kansas Power and Light Company) is a combination electric and natural gas public utility engaged in the generation, transmission, distribution and sale of electric energy in Kansas and the purchase transmission, distribution, transportation and sale of natural gas in Kansas, Missouri and Oklahoma. In March 1992, the Company acquired The Kansas Gas and Electric Company under a merger agreement for approximately $1 billion in which KG&E is to become a wholly-owned subsidiary of WR. KG&E provides electric service to over 250,000 retail customers in the Southeast quarter of Kansas.

BUSINESS LINE ANALYSIS

(12/31/93)	Rev(%)	Inc(%)
Natural Gas	42.2	18.0
Electric	57.8	82.0
Total	100.0	100.0

ANNUAL EARNINGS AND DIVIDENDS PER SHARE

	1993	1992	1991	1990	1989	1988	1987
Earnings Per Share	2.76	2.20	[1] 1.91	2.25	2.05	2.25	2.46
Dividends Per Share	1.93	1.89	2.025	1.79	1.75	1.703	[2] 1.634
Dividend Payout %	69.9	85.9	N.M.	79.6	85.4	75.7	66.4

[1] Before acctg. chg.   [2] 2-for-1 stk. split, 5/87.

ANNUAL FINANCIAL DATA

RECORD OF EARNINGS (IN MILLIONS)

	1993	1992	1991	1990	1989	1988	1987
Total Operating Revenues	1,909.4	1,556.2	1,162.2	1,149.8	1,127.6	1,166.1	1,166.5
Depreciation & Amort	164.4	144.0	85.7	76.8	73.3	70.4	67.8
Maintenance	117.8	101.6	60.5	57.8	58.4	55.1	49.6
Prov for Fed Inc Taxes	62.4	34.9	24.5	24.6	27.3	36.4	50.6
Operating Income	292.1	239.2	129.6	132.0	125.5	130.4	138.3
Total Interest Charges	140.2	135.5	60.7	61.4	53.6	50.2	51.2
Net Income	177.4	127.9	[1] 72.3	79.6	72.8	79.8	88.7
Aver. Shs. Outstg. (000)	59,294	52,272	34,566	34,566	34,566	34,566	34,566

[1] Before acctg. change cr$17,360,000.

BALANCE SHEET (IN MILLIONS)

	1993	1992	1991	1990	1989	1988	1987
Gross Plant	6,331.9	6,125.6	2,552.6	2,441.8	2,324.9	2,187.2	2,085.4
Accumulated Depreciation	1,821.7	1,682.8	826.1	761.6	701.0	642.3	585.2
Net Utility Plant	4,510.2	4,442.8	1,726.4	1,680.2	1,623.8	1,544.9	1,500.2
Long-term Debt	1,524.0	1,926.0	586.6	590.2	545.9	548.5	486.5
Net Stockholders' Equity	1,597.0	1,424.7	771.3	661.0	646.7	637.9	621.0
Total Assets	5,412.0	5,523.6	2,120.1	2,016.0	1,959.0	1,777.5	1,729.6
Year End Shs Outstg (000)	61,618	58,046	34,566	34,566	34,566	34,566	34,566

STATISTICAL RECORD:

	1993	1992	1991	1990	1989	1988	1987
Book Value Per Share	23.08	21.51	18.59	18.25	17.80	17.51	16.98
Op. Inc/Net Pl %	6.5	5.4	7.5	7.9	7.7	8.4	9.2
Dep/Gr. Pl %	2.9	2.6	3.4	3.1	3.2	3.2	3.3
Accum. Dep/Gr. Pl %	28.8	27.5	32.4	31.2	30.2	29.4	28.1
Return on Equity %	12.3	10.0	10.8	12.1	11.4	12.7	14.5
Average Yield %	5.7	6.5	8.2	8.0	7.4	6.9	6.4
P/E Ratio	13.5-11.0	14.8-11.4	14.9-10.9	11.2-8.8	12.4-10.5	12.0-9.9	12.5-8.1
Price Range	37¼-30⅜	32⅝-25⅛	28½-20¾	25⅛-19¾	25⅜-21⅝	27-22¼	30¾-20

Statistics are as originally reported.

OFFICERS:
J.E. Hayes, Jr., Chmn., Pres. & C.E.O.
S.L. Kitchen, Exec. V.P. & C.F.O.

INCORPORATED: KS, Mar., 1924

PRINCIPAL OFFICE: 818 Kansas Ave., Topeka, KS 66612-1217

TELEPHONE NUMBER: (913) 575-6300
FAX: (913) 575-6596
NO. OF EMPLOYEES: 5,192
ANNUAL MEETING: In May
SHAREHOLDERS: 32,040 (common); pfd., 2,164
INSTITUTIONAL HOLDINGS:
No. of Institutions: 215
Shares Held: 20,720,814

REGISTRAR(S): Chemical Bank, New York, NY
Merchants National Bank, Topeka, KS 66601

TRANSFER AGENT(S): Chemical Bank, New York, NY
Bank IV Topeka N.A. Trust Department, Topeka, KS 66601

WEYCO GROUP, INC.

YIELD 2.3%
P/E RATIO 10.8

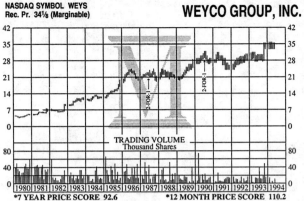

TRADING VOLUME
Thousand Shares

INTERIM EARNINGS (Per Share):

Qtr.	Mar.	June	Sept.	Dec.
1990	0.66	0.69	0.78	0.89
1991	0.18	0.29	0.67	1.23
1992	0.61	0.47	0.70	1.32
1993	0.54	0.61	0.59	1.00

INTERIM DIVIDENDS (Per Share):

Amt.	Decl.	Ex.	Rec.	Pay.
0.20Q	4/27/93	5/25/93	6/1/93	7/1/93
0.20Q	8/12	8/26	9/1	10/1
0.20Q	11/8	11/24	12/1	1/1/94
0.20Q	1/17/94	3/1/94	3/7/94	4/1
0.20Q	5/18	5/25	6/1	7/1

Indicated div.: $0.80

CAPITALIZATION (12/31/93):

	($000)	(%)
Common & Surplus	62,335	100.0
Total	62,335	100.0

DIVIDEND ACHIEVER STATUS:
Rank: 186   1983-93 Growth Rate: 9.7%
Total Years of Dividend Growth: 13

RECENT DEVELOPMENTS: For the year ended 12/31/93, net sales declined 12.4% to $122.1 million from $139.5 million in 1992. Earnings, before cumulative effect of accounting change, were $4.9 million, or $2.32 per share, compared with net earnings of $6.6 million, or $3.10 per share, a year ago. For the quarter, net sales declined 11.8% to $32.5 million from $36.8 million for the same period last year. Net earnings for the quarter were $1.2 million, or $0.58 per share, compared with $2.8 million, or $1.32 per share, for the year-ago quarter. The decrease in earnings is primarily due to a 39% drop in sales by WEYS's retail division caused by the closing of 71 leased departments. On 2/9/94, WEYS announced that it had signed a definitive merger agreement to be acquired by a management group, including the principal shareholders of the Company, for $34.00 per share, in cash.

BUSINESS

WEYCO GROUP, INC. and its subsidiaries engage in the manufacture, purchase and distribution of men's footwear. The Company distributes a broad line of quality men's dress and casual shoes. These shoes are sold under various brand names, the better known ones being "Nunn-Bush," "Brass Boot," "Stacy Adams," and "Weyenberg." The Company and a subsidiary, Nunn-Bush Shoe Company, market their footwear through more than 8,000 shoe stores, clothing stores and department stores throughout the United States. In addition, Nunn-Bush Shoe Company operates 40 retail shoe stores in principal cities in the United States and 135 leased departments in men's clothing and department stores throughout the country.

ANNUAL EARNINGS AND DIVIDENDS PER SHARE

	1993	1992	1991	1990	1989	1988	1987
Earnings Per Share	2.74	3.10	2.37	3.02	2.95	2.32	2.08
Dividends Per Share	0.76	0.68	0.62	① 0.55	0.45	0.38	② 0.36
Dividend Payout %	27.7	21.9	26.2	18.2	15.3	16.4	17.3

① 2-for-1 stk split; 7/1990 ② 2-for-1 stk. split, 6/87.

ANNUAL FINANCIAL DATA

RECORD OF EARNINGS (IN THOUSANDS):

Total Revenues	122,144	139,462	140,940	148,495	138,868	126,295	117,856
Costs and Expenses	113,809	128,282	132,292	137,202	128,232	117,505	109,779
Depreciation	1,203	1,325	1,184	1,171	944	1,172	1,029
Earnings From Operations	7,131	9,855	7,464	10,122	9,692	7,618	7,049
Earn Bef Prov for Inc Taxes	7,716	10,493	8,368	10,584	10,237	8,138	7,762
Income Taxes	2,808	3,924	3,258	4,035	3,852	3,044	3,189
Net Income	① 4,908	6,569	5,110	6,549	6,385	5,094	4,573
Aver. Shs. Outstg.	2,117	2,120	2,158	2,166	2,167	2,197	2,206

① Before acctg. change cr$880,000.

BALANCE SHEET (IN THOUSANDS):

Cash and Cash Equivalents	26,536	25,659	20,021	8,843	6,604	8,740	7,446
Receivables, Net	20,853	20,633	22,313	20,796	24,183	20,055	18,629
Total Inventories	17,050	16,496	22,654	26,827	24,985	18,226	19,831
Gross Property	8,966	9,402	8,784	9,047	9,766	9,357	10,167
Accumulated Depreciation	4,106	4,821	5,213	5,072	5,489	5,662	5,869
Net Stockholders' Equity	62,335	57,745	52,986	50,235	44,969	39,799	36,522
Total Assets	74,915	71,848	71,660	63,147	62,142	52,130	51,136
Total Current Assets	64,996	62,808	64,988	56,466	55,772	47,021	45,906
Total Current Liabilities	9,132	11,094	15,132	9,524	14,066	10,345	10,169
Net Working Capital	55,864	51,714	49,856	46,942	41,705	36,675	35,737
Year End Shares Outstg	2,132	2,114	2,125	2,166	2,176	2,176	2,211

STATISTICAL RECORD:

Operating Profit Margin %	5.8	7.1	5.3	6.8	7.0	6.0	6.0
Book Value Per Share	29.24	27.32	24.93	23.19	20.67	18.29	16.52
Return on Equity %	7.9	11.4	9.6	13.0	14.2	12.8	12.5
Return on Assets %	6.6	9.1	7.1	10.4	10.3	9.8	8.9
Average Yield %	2.4	2.5	2.2	1.9	1.9	1.7	1.7
P/E Ratio	13.0-10.0	9.9-7.7	13.3-10.1	10.6-8.8	9.7-6.6	10.6-8.6	11.8-9.1
Price Range	35½-27½	30¾-24	31½-24	32-26½	28½-19½	24½-20	24½-19

Statistics are as originally reported.

OFFICERS:
T.W. Florsheim, Chmn. & C.E.O.
R. Feitler, Pres. & C.O.O.
R. Keuler, V.P.-Fin.
J. Wittkowske, Treas. & Sec.

INCORPORATED: WI, Jun., 1906

PRINCIPAL OFFICE: 234 E. Reservoir Ave.
P.O. Box 1188, Milwaukee, WI 53201

TELEPHONE NUMBER: (414) 263-8800

FAX: (414) 263-8808

NO. OF EMPLOYEES: 800 (approx.)

ANNUAL MEETING: In April

SHAREHOLDERS: 547 com.; 224 Cl. B com.

INSTITUTIONAL HOLDINGS:
No. of Institutions: 19
Shares Held: 478,872

REGISTRAR(S): American Stock Transfer & Trust Co., 40 Wall Street, New York, NY 10005

TRANSFER AGENT(S): American Stock Transfer & Trust Co., 40 Wall Street, New York, NY 10005

WICOR, INC.

YIELD 5.4%
P/E RATIO 16.0

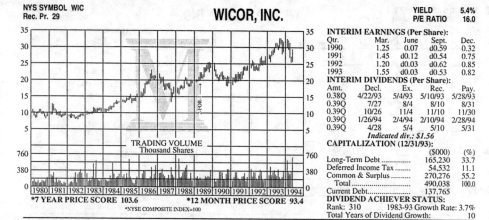

*7 YEAR PRICE SCORE 103.6   *12 MONTH PRICE SCORE 93.4

*NYSE COMPOSITE INDEX=100

INTERIM EARNINGS (Per Share):

Qtr.	Mar.	June	Sept.	Dec.
1990	1.25	0.07	d0.59	0.32
1991	1.45	d0.12	d0.54	0.75
1992	1.20	d0.03	d0.62	0.85
1993	1.55	d0.03	d0.53	0.82

INTERIM DIVIDENDS (Per Share):

Amt.	Decl.	Ex.	Rec.	Pay.
0.38Q	4/22/93	5/4/93	5/10/93	5/28/93
0.39Q	7/27	8/4	8/10	8/31
0.39Q	10/26	11/4	11/10	11/30
0.39Q	1/26/94	2/4/94	2/10/94	2/28/94
0.39Q	4/28	5/4	5/10	5/31

Indicated div.: $1.56

CAPITALIZATION (12/31/93):

	($000)	(%)
Long-Term Debt	165,230	33.7
Deferred Income Tax	54,532	11.1
Common & Surplus	270,276	55.2
Total	490,038	100.0
Current Debt	137,765	

DIVIDEND ACHIEVER STATUS:
Rank: 310   1983-93 Growth Rate: 3.7%
Total Years of Dividend Growth: 10

RECENT DEVELOPMENTS: For the year ended 12/31/93, net income was $29.3 million compared with $22.8 million last year. Revenues were $849.5 million, up 13.7%. Operating income reported by the gas distribution segment advanced 6.7% to $46.2 million from $43.3 million last year. Gas operations benefited from the addition of nearly 14,000 new natural gas customers and cost controls. Operating income from manufacturing operations increased 77% to $17.8 million.

PROSPECTS: Improving economic conditions have increased demand for many Sta-Rite and Shurflo products. The natural gas segment is benefiting from reduced operating expenses and a new rate increase at Wisconsin Gas. Wisconsin Gas received approval for a $12.3 million rate increase effective November 1993. Wisconsin Gas has asked the Public Service Commission of Wisconsin for permission to change to a productivity-based ratemaking process.

BUSINESS

WICOR INC. is a holding company for Wisconsin Gas Company, the state's largest distributor of natural gas, and Sta-Rite Industries, a worldwide manufacturer of pumps and filters. Wisconsin Gas serves 460,000 customers in 416 communities throughout the state. Sta-Rite Industries, Inc. is a leading manufacturer of pumps and other water processing equipment. Sta-Rite markets its products through the United States and worldwide on six continents.

BUSINESS LINE ANALYSIS

(12/31/93)	Rev(%)	Inc(%)
Gas Distribution	67.7	73.2
Manufacturing	32.3	27.8
Total	100.0	100.0

ANNUAL EARNINGS AND DIVIDENDS PER SHARE

	1993	1992	1991	1990	1989	1988	1987
Earnings Per Share	1.82	0.86	1.54	[2] 1.04	2.40	2.46	1.43
Dividends Per Share	1.54	[1] 1.50	1.46	1.42	[3] 1.37	1.32	1.30
Dividend Payout %	84.6	N.M.	94.8	N.M.	57.1	53.7	91.2

[1] Bef acctg chge   [2] Before extraord. item   [3] 2-for-1 stk split, 4/89.

ANNUAL FINANCIAL DATA

RECORD OF EARNINGS (IN THOUSANDS):

	1993	1992	1991	1990	1989	1988	1987
Total Operating Revenues	849,528	704,905	681,708	659,779	710,601	754,187	677,602
Deprec, Depl & Amort	28,044	26,650	24,759	34,790	22,030	20,612	21,842
Oper Inc Fr Contin Opers	63,951	49,393	49,022	41,455	69,680	67,424	50,833
Interest Expense	17,428	17,980	16,554	18,064	17,419	16,537	15,516
Net Income	29,313	[1] 20,469	21,527	[2] 14,323	32,657	33,750	20,533
Aver. Shs. Outstg.	16,096	14,589	13,988	13,755	13,615	13,452	13,298

[1] Before acctg. change dr$7,965,000.   [2] Before disc. op. dr$5,524,000.

BALANCE SHEET (IN THOUSANDS):

Gross Plant	777,704	757,364	690,087	654,850	653,984	623,839	587,089
Accumulated Depreciation	377,004	369,162	342,316	318,614	347,440	322,717	302,120
Prop, Plant & Equip, Net	400,700	388,202	347,771	336,236	306,544	301,122	284,969
Long-term Debt	165,230	164,001	168,154	127,683	122,453	132,137	126,488
Net Stockholders' Equity	270,276	235,762	235,486	230,169	238,028	221,341	210,485
Total Assets	933,726	809,896	668,691	637,856	607,956	553,452	525,446
Year End Shares Outstg	16,407	14,821	14,464	13,829	13,686	13,542	13,242

STATISTICAL RECORD:

Book Value Per Share	16.47	15.91	16.28	16.64	17.39	16.34	15.29
Op. Inc/Net Pl %	16.0	12.7	14.1	12.3	22.7	22.4	17.8
Dep/Gr. Pl %	4.1	4.1	4.2	4.3	4.1	4.0	3.7
Accum. Dep/Gr. Pl %	55.4	57.4	58.5	57.4	65.3	63.1	51.5
Return on Equity %	10.8	8.7	9.1	6.2	13.7	15.2	10.1
Average Yield %	5.3	6.0	6.8	6.5	6.1	7.2	7.4
P/E Ratio	18.1-14.1	19.6-16.3	15.9-12.1	24.3-17.5	10.6-8.1	8.5-6.4	15.3-9.4
Price Range	32⅞-25⅝	27⅜-22⅞	24½-18⅝	25¼-18¼	25½-19⅜	20⅞-15⅝	21⅞-13⅜

Statistics are as originally reported.

OFFICERS:
G.E. Wardeberg, Pres., C.E.O. & Chmn.
J.P. Wenzler, V.P., C.F.O. & Treas.
R.A. Nuernberg, Secretary

PRINCIPAL OFFICE: 626 East Wisconsin Avenue, P.O. Box 344, Milwaukee, WI 53201-0344

TELEPHONE NUMBER: (414) 291-7026
FAX: (414) 291-7025
NO. OF EMPLOYEES: 2,804
ANNUAL MEETING: In April
SHAREHOLDERS: 17,780
INSTITUTIONAL HOLDINGS:
No. of Institutions: 86
Shares Held: 5,441,192

REGISTRAR(S):

TRANSFER AGENT(S):

NASDAQ SYMBOL WILM
Rec. Pr. 25½ (Marginable)

WILMINGTON TRUST CORP.

YIELD 3.9%
P/E RATIO 11.4

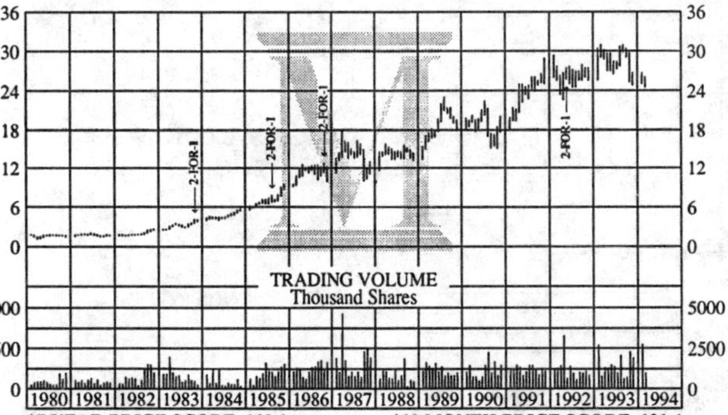

36
30
24
18
12
6
0
2-FOR-1
2-FOR-1
2-FOR-1
2-FOR-1
TRADING VOLUME
Thousand Shares
5000
2500
0
1980 1981 1982 1983 1984 1985 1986 1987 1988 1989 1990 1991 1992 1993 1994

*7 YEAR PRICE SCORE 112.1 *12 MONTH PRICE SCORE 101.4

*NYSE COMPOSITE INDEX=100

INTERIM EARNINGS (Per Share):

Qtr.	Mar.	June	Sept.	Dec.
1990	0.41	0.46	0.50	0.53
1991	0.46	0.50	0.53	0.54
1992	0.47	0.51	0.56	0.56
1993	0.53	0.55	0.59	0.57

INTERIM DIVIDENDS (Per Share):

Amt.	Decl.	Ex.	Rec.	Pay.
0.225Q	1/21/93	1/26/93	2/1/93	2/15/93
0.25Q	4/15	4/27	5/3	5/17
0.25Q	7/15	7/27	8/2	8/16
0.25Q	10/21	10/26	11/1	11/15
0.25Q	1/20/94	1/26/94	2/1/94	2/15/94

Indicated div.: $1.00

CAPITALIZATION (12/31/93):

	($000)	(%)
Total Deposits	3,391,446	73.5
Total Debt	777,058	16.8
Common & Surplus	395,175	8.6
Loan Valuation Reserve	51,363	1.1
Total	4,615,042	100.0

DIVIDEND ACHIEVER STATUS:
Rank: 31 1983-93 Growth Rate: 17.5%
Total Years of Dividend Growth: 12

RECENT DEVELOPMENTS: For the year ended 12/31/93, income before the cumulative effect of accounting changes was $82.8 million compared with $78.8 million in 1992. For the quarter, income before the cumulative effect of accounting changes was $20.8 million versus $20.7 million for the fourth quarter a year ago. As of 12/31/93, total loans outstanding reached $3.0 billion. The net interest margin improved to 4.76% in 1993 from 4.62% in 1992. The reserve for loan losses at year-end totaled $51.4 million or 1.69% of total loans. This compares to a reserve of $47.0 million, or 1.57% of loans outstanding, a year ago. On 12/31/93, total assets were $4.64 billion, total deposits were $3.4 billion, and stockholders' equity reached $395.2 million. The results for the year produced return on average assets of 1.96% and return on average stockholder's equity of 21.12%, which compare with 1.90% and 20.62%, respectively, for 1992 before the accounting adjustments.

BUSINESS

WILMINGTON TRUST CORP. and its subsidiaries provide a full range of banking and related services to individual and corporate customers in the Delaware region. A general and commercial and retail banking business with normal banking services including acceptance of demand, savings and time deposits and the making of various types of loans. The Company operates 60 branches in Wilmington, New Castle County, Kent County and Sussex County, Delaware, one branch in West Chester, Pennsylvania and three trust offices in Florida. It offers a full range of trust, custody and investment services to institutions and individuals, including a family of mutual funds, portfolio management and precious metals storage. The bank also provides discount brokerage, insurance and travel services.

LOAN DISTRIBUTION

(12/31/93)	($000)	(%)
Commercial, Finan & Agri	922,499	30.3
Real Estate-Construction	122,329	4.0
Mortgage-Commercial	651,011	21.4
Mortgage-Residential	609,031	20.0
Install To Individuals	734,916	24.3
Total	3,039,786	100.0

ANNUAL EARNINGS AND DIVIDENDS PER SHARE

	1993	1992	1991	1990	1989	1988	1987
Earnings Per Share	**2.24**	**2.09**	**2.04**	**1.90**	**1.70**	**1.49**	**1.23**
Dividends Per Share	**0.975**	**[1] 0.88**	**0.795**	**0.72**	**0.59**	**0.46**	**0.39**
Dividend Payout %	**43.8**	**42.1**	**39.0**	**37.9**	**34.7**	**30.9**	**31.7**

[1] 2-for-1 stk split, 5/18/92

ANNUAL FINANCIAL DATA

	1993	1992	1991	1990	1989	1988	1987
RECORD OF EARNINGS (IN MILLIONS):							
Total Interest Income	291.0	315.5	333.1	337.5	301.1	239.5	213.3
Total Interest Expense	116.1	150.3	191.4	212.0	186.7	140.6	127.5
Net Interest Income	174.8	165.2	141.7	125.5	114.5	99.0	85.9
Provision for Loan Losses	9.5	13.0	13.3	10.5	10.3	10.3	10.7
Net Income	82.8	[1] 78.8	71.9	67.0	59.4	51.8	43.4
Aver. Shs. Outstg. (000)	37,029	37,765	35,352	35,302	35,904	34,820	35,236
[1] Before acctg. change dr$14,749,000.							
BALANCE SHEET (IN MILLIONS):							
Cash & Due From Banks	186.3	210.1	203.4	195.6	224.9	194.5	161.7
Obligs Of State & Political Subdiviss	69.3	93.2	93.1	89.2	83.4	84.5	258.4
Net Loans	2,986.2	2,950.2	2,723.2	2,567.5	2,337.3	2,014.4	1,745.4
Total Domestic Deposits	3,391.4	3,274.2	3,046.2	2,853.0	2,613.3	2,291.1	2,394.7
Net Stockholders' Equity	395.2	377.2	345.7	296.0	257.6	228.0	193.0
Total Assets	4,637.8	4,284.6	4,061.3	3,834.3	3,702.7	2,982.1	2,890.8
Year End Shs Outstg (000)	...	...	35,582	35,194	34,598	34,960	34,728
STATISTICAL RECORD:							
Return on Assets %	1.78	1.84	1.77	1.75	1.60	1.74	1.50
Return on Equity %	20.90	20.90	20.80	22.60	23.10	22.70	22.50
Book Value Per Share	...	...	9.72	8.41	7.44	6.52	5.56
Average Yield %	3.5	3.4	3.4	3.8	3.2	3.4	2.8
P/E Ratio	13.8-11.0	14.1-10.8	14.2-8.8	11.8-8.0	13.6-7.8	10.6-7.7	14.6-8.1
Price Range	31-24¾	29⅜-22⅝	29-18	22½-15⅛	23⅛-13¼	15¾-11½	18-10

Statistics are as originally reported.

OFFICERS:
L.W. Quill, Chmn., Pres. & C.E.O.
T.T. Cecala, Exec. V.P. & C.F.O.
T.P. Collins, V.P. & Sec.

INCORPORATED: DE, Mar., 1901

PRINCIPAL OFFICE: Wilmington Trust Center Rodney Square North 1100 North Market St., Wilmington, DE 19890-0001

TELEPHONE NUMBER: (800) 441-7120

FAX: (302) 651-8010

NO. OF EMPLOYEES: 2,254

ANNUAL MEETING: In April

SHAREHOLDERS: 8,880

INSTITUTIONAL HOLDINGS:
No. of Institutions: 146
Shares Held: 15,177,254

REGISTRAR(S): At Company's Office

TRANSFER AGENT(S): At Company's Office

NYS SYMBOL WIN
Rec. Pr. 46⅛

WINN-DIXIE STORES, INC.

YIELD 3.1%
P/E RATIO 14.5

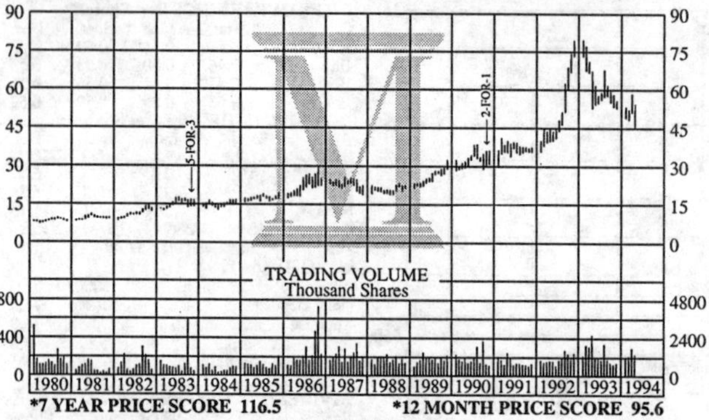

5-FOR-3
2-FOR-1
TRADING VOLUME
Thousand Shares
1980 1981 1982 1983 1984 1985 1986 1987 1988 1989 1990 1991 1992 1993 1994

***7 YEAR PRICE SCORE 116.5** ***12 MONTH PRICE SCORE 95.6**

*NYSE COMPOSITE INDEX=100

INTERIM EARNINGS (Per Share):

Qtr.	Sept.	Jan.	Mar.	June
1990-91	0.31	0.63	0.62	0.64
1991-92	0.35	0.70	0.70	1.07
1992-93	0.44	0.82	0.75	1.10
1993-94	0.48	0.85	...	...

INTERIM DIVIDENDS (Per Share):

Amt.	Decl.	Ex.	Rec.	Pay.
0.12M	1/3/94	2/9/94	2/15/94	3/1/94
0.12M	1/3	3/9	3/15	4/4
0.12M	4/4	4/11	4/15	5/2
0.12M	4/4	5/10	5/16	6/1
0.12M	4/4	6/9	6/15	7/1

Indicated div.: $1.44

CAPITALIZATION (6/30/93):

	($000)	(%)
Cap. Lease Oblig.	87,153	8.1
Common & Surplus	984,965	91.9
Total	1,072,118	100.0

DIVIDEND ACHIEVER STATUS:
Rank: 265 — 1983-93 Growth Rate: 6.2%
Total Years of Dividend Growth: 50

RECENT DEVELOPMENTS: For the 16 weeks ended 1/12/94, net income increased 1.3% to $63.8 million. Sales increased 4.2% to $3.38 billion. Identical store sales increased 1.9% and average store sales increased 4.8%. Results were attributed to controlled expenses and increased sales in the Company's larger stores. As a percentage of sales, operating profit increased to 2.1% from 1.8%, while gross profit fell slightly to 22.7% from 22.4%.

PROSPECTS: Winn-Dixie's everyday low price format, with reduced prices on more than 5,000 grocery items and 1,000 health and beauty care products, should continue to increase sales. Also, larger store formats with expanded specialty departments and continued cost control measures will aid near-term earnings and sales growth. With a capital expenditure budget of $600 million, Winn-Dixie is committed to expanding the average size of its stores.

BUSINESS

WINN-DIXIE STORES INC., with stores in thirteen southeastern and southwestern states, is the largest food retailer in the Sunbelt. The Company operates 1,172 stores, totaling 39.0 million square feet, of which 581 stores are larger than 35,000 square feet. Winn-Dixie also operates support facilities, including 16 distribution centers, 27 processing and manufactring plants, and a truck delivery fleet. The Davis family owns about 40% of the Company's common stock.

QUARTERLY DATA

(6/30/93)($000)	Rev	Inc
1st Quarter	2,392,129	33,377
2nd Quarter	3,244,672	63,031
3rd Quarter	2,504,214	57,199
4th Quarter	2,690,520	82,778

ANNUAL EARNINGS AND DIVIDENDS PER SHARE

	6/30/93	6/24/92	6/26/91	6/27/90	6/28/89	6/29/88	6/24/87
Earnings Per Share	**3.11**	**[1] 2.82**	**2.20**	**1.93**	**1.68**	**1.44**	**1.36**
Dividends Per Share	**1.37**	**1.20**	**[2] 1.13**	**1.028**	**0.973**	**0.943**	**0.913**
Dividend Payout %	**44.1**	**42.6**	**51.4**	**53.3**	**57.9**	**65.7**	**67.1**

[1] Before acctg. chg. [2] 2-for-1 stk split, 10/31/90

ANNUAL FINANCIAL DATA

RECORD OF EARNINGS (IN MILLIONS):							
Total Revenues	10,831.5	10,337.3	10,074.3	9,744.5	9,151.1	9,007.7	8,803.9
Costs and Expenses	10,441.0	9,976.7	9,792.8	9,497.5	8,909.6	8,760.7	8,545.6
Depreciation & Amort	141.1	126.9	113.4	118.1	136.0	161.9	163.7
Operating Income	249.4	233.8	168.2	128.9	105.5	85.2	94.6
Earn Bef Income Taxes	363.7	328.0	259.0	224.2	197.9	168.8	174.2
Income Taxes	127.3	111.6	88.1	71.7	63.3	52.1	61.9
Net Income	236.4	[1] 216.4	170.9	152.5	134.5	116.7	112.3
Aver. Shs. Outstg. (000)	74,956	76,805	77,826	79,037	80,064	81,344	82,556
[1] Before acctg. change dr$20,485,000.							
BALANCE SHEET (IN MILLIONS):							
Tot Cash & Sh-tm Invests	107.8	203.7	102.5	198.1	128.2	132.4	120.2
Receivables, Net	162.6	124.0	98.8	69.7	65.4	57.8	65.6
Inventories	1,041.5	948.3	924.3	848.4	784.7	753.3	632.1
Gross Property	1,892.4	1,789.5	1,691.9	1,589.0	1,514.5	1,476.9	1,461.0
Accumulated Depreciation	1,305.8	1,260.4	1,198.2	1,152.6	1,087.8	1,048.0	973.5
Long-Term Debt	...	...	...	...	...	24.2	24.6
Obligs Under Cap Lses	87.2	90.3	96.9	83.4	72.4	63.1	78.0
Net Stockholders' Equity	985.0	952.2	860.0	813.2	783.2	726.3	739.4
Total Assets	2,062.6	1,977.4	1,817.5	1,732.7	1,575.1	1,514.0	1,417.7
Total Current Assets	1,413.2	1,363.5	1,202.6	1,168.7	1,031.0	988.9	851.1
Total Current Liabilities	868.5	812.7	766.8	742.3	634.8	631.2	516.8
Net Working Capital	544.7	550.8	435.8	426.4	396.2	357.7	334.3
Year End Shs Outstg (000)	74,956	76,851	77,129	78,314	79,862	79,814	82,464
STATISTICAL RECORD:							
Operating Profit Margin %	2.3	2.3	1.7	1.3	1.2	0.9	1.1
Book Value Per Share	13.14	12.39	11.15	10.38	9.81	9.10	8.97
Return on Equity %	24.0	22.7	19.9	18.8	17.2	16.1	15.2
Return on Assets %	11.5	10.9	9.4	8.8	8.5	7.7	7.9
Average Yield %	2.1	2.1	3.2	3.1	3.6	4.5	4.1
P/E Ratio	25.6-17.0	28.2-12.7	18.8-13.5	20.0-14.7	19.3-12.8	16.3-13.0	19.1-13.8
Price Range	79¾-52¾	79½-35¾	41¼-29¾	38⅝-28⅜	32½-21½	23½-18¾	26-18¾

Statistics are as originally reported.

OFFICERS:
A.D. Davis, Chmn. & C.E.O.
J. Kufeldt, Pres.
W.E. Ripley, Jr., V.P., Gen. Couns. & Sec.
D.H. Bragin, Treas. & Chief Acct. Off.

INCORPORATED: FL, Dec., 1928

PRINCIPAL OFFICE: 5050 Edgewood Court, Jacksonville, FL 32254

TELEPHONE NUMBER: (904) 783-5000

NO. OF EMPLOYEES: 19,080 (full-time); 69,000 (part-time).

ANNUAL MEETING: In October

SHAREHOLDERS: 19,365

INSTITUTIONAL HOLDINGS:
No. of Institutions: 201
Shares Held: 14,143,669

REGISTRAR(S): American Transtech, Inc., Jacksonville, FL

TRANSFER AGENT(S): American Transtech, Inc., Jacksonville, FL

NYS SYMBOL WEC
Rec. Pr. 25

WISCONSIN ENERGY CORP.

YIELD 5.6%
P/E RATIO 13.7

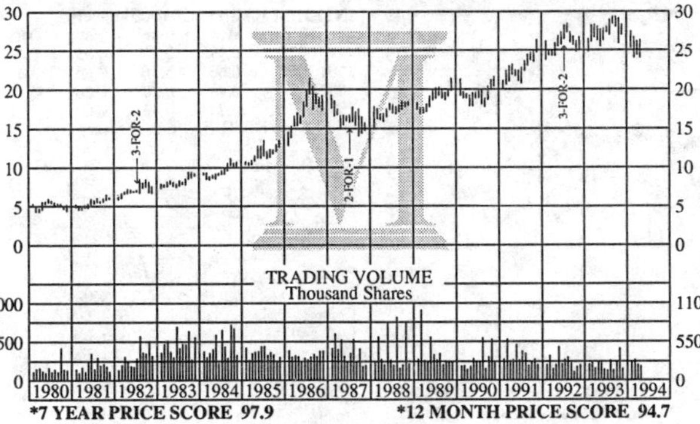

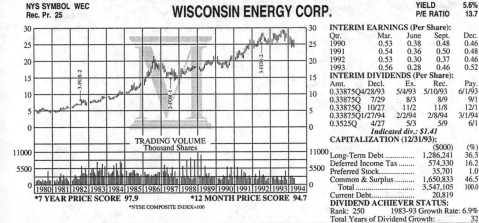

***7 YEAR PRICE SCORE 97.9** ***12 MONTH PRICE SCORE 94.7**

*NYSE COMPOSITE INDEX=100

INTERIM EARNINGS (Per Share):

Qtr.	Mar.	June	Sept.	Dec.
1990	0.53	0.38	0.48	0.46
1991	0.54	0.36	0.50	0.48
1992	0.53	0.30	0.37	0.46
1993	0.56	0.28	0.46	0.52

INTERIM DIVIDENDS (Per Share):

Amt.	Decl.	Ex.	Rec.	Pay.
0.33875Q	4/28/93	5/4/93	5/10/93	6/1/93
0.33875Q	7/29	8/3	8/9	9/1
0.33875Q	10/27	11/2	11/8	12/1
0.33875Q	1/27/94	2/2/94	2/8/94	3/1/94
0.3525Q	4/27	5/3	5/9	6/1

Indicated div.: $1.41

CAPITALIZATION (12/31/93):

	($000)	(%)
Long-Term Debt	1,286,241	36.3
Deferred Income Tax	574,330	16.2
Preferred Stock	35,701	1.0
Common & Surplus	1,650,833	46.5
Total	3,547,105	100.0
Current Debt	20,819	

DIVIDEND ACHIEVER STATUS:
Rank: 250 1983-93 Growth Rate: 6.9%
Total Years of Dividend Growth: 32

RECENT DEVELOPMENTS: For the year ended 12/31/93, net income was $188.5 million compared with $169.7 million in 1992. Revenues were $1.64 billion, up 5.9%. The improved results are primarily due to higher electric kilowatthour sales at Wisconsin Electric Power Co. Total electric sales increased 3.8% mainly because of significantly warmer weather during the summer. Results also benefited from a 2.3% electric rate increase.

PROSPECTS: A new organizational structure will be centered around five operational groups. The five groups are customer operations, fossil operations, nuclear power, bulk power and a corporate support center. The goal of the revitalization effort is to give WEC a stronger competitive position by lowering costs. Wisconsin Southern Gas Co., Inc. was acquired by Wisconsin Energy through a merger of Wisconsin Southern into Wisconsin Natural Gas Co.

BUSINESS

WISCONSIN ENERGY CORP. is the holding company for Wisconsin Electric Power Co. and Wisconsin Natural Gas Co. and five non-utility subsidiaries. Wisconsin Electric is an electric utility operating in southeastern, east central and northern Wisconsin and in the Upper Peninsula of Michigan. Wisconsin Natural distributes and sells natural gas within the service territory of Wisconsin Electric. About 84% of revenues are derived from the sale of electricity.

BUSINESS LINE ANALYSIS

(12/31/93)	Rev(%)	Inc(%)
Electric	82.0	91.6
Gas	17.1	7.5
Steam	0.9	0.9
Total	100.0	100.0

ANNUAL EARNINGS AND DIVIDENDS PER SHARE

	1993	1992	1991	1990	1989	1988	1987
Earnings Per Share	**1.81**	**1.67**	**1.87**	**1.85**	**1.92**	**1.82**	**1.70**
Dividends Per Share	**1.341**	**[1] 1.285**	**1.223**	**1.157**	**1.087**	**1.01**	**[2] 0.943**
Dividend Payout %	**74.1**	**76.9**	**65.3**	**62.6**	**56.6**	**55.5**	**55.5**

[1] 3-for-2 stk split, 7/1/92 [2] 2-for-1 stk. split, 6/87.

ANNUAL FINANCIAL DATA

	1993	1992	1991	1990	1989	1988	1987
RECORD OF EARNINGS (IN MILLIONS):							
Total Operating Revenues	1,643.7	1,551.8	1,538.9	1,442.5	1,493.4	1,540.7	1,364.6
Depreciation	165.3	162.7	146.7	144.7	141.8	129.8	...
Maintenance	155.2	149.6	142.2	133.7	150.4	171.3	138.8
Income Taxes	102.7	94.4	104.8	99.5	111.6	106.2	117.8
Operating Income	262.6	238.9	251.3	241.2	264.0	260.2	252.6
Total Interest Charges	101.8	89.4	84.9	82.6	85.2	85.0	85.6
Net Income	188.5	169.7	189.3	186.7	194.0	183.2	169.5
Aver. Shs. Outstg. (000)	104,240	101,744	101,037	101,037	101,037	100,530	99,869
BALANCE SHEET (IN MILLIONS):							
Gross Plant	4,773.4	4,462.9	4,169.5	3,977.0	3,805.3	3,676.1	3,597.9
Accumulated Depreciation	1,964.3	1,834.2	1,703.5	1,603.4	1,745.5	1,650.7	1,558.0
Prop, Plant & Equip, Net	2,809.1	2,628.7	2,466.0	2,373.6	2,059.8	2,025.4	2,039.9
Long Term Debt	1,286.2	1,210.4	1,093.6	990.4	1,003.7	1,044.3	849.5
Net Stockholders' Equity	1,686.5	1,641.8	1,550.4	1,484.7	1,414.8	1,330.7	1,228.9
Total Assets	4,223.1	3,744.6	3,496.0	3,361.0	2,994.0	2,849.2	2,741.8
Year End Shs Outstg (000)	105,320	103,093	101,037	101,037	101,037	101,037	99,869
STATISTICAL RECORD:							
Book Value Per Share	15.67	14.97	14.35	13.70	13.01	12.18	11.30
Op. Inc/Net Pl %	9.3	9.1	10.2	10.2	12.8	12.8	12.4
Dep/Gr. Pl %	3.5	3.6	3.5	3.6	3.7	3.5	3.9
Accum. Dep/Gr. Pl %	41.2	41.1	40.9	40.3	45.9	44.9	43.3
Return on Equity %	11.2	10.8	12.8	13.2	14.4	14.5	14.6
Average Yield %	5.0	4.9	5.3	5.9	5.7	6.0	5.7
P/E Ratio	16.2-13.7	17.1-14.2	14.1-10.7	11.7-9.6	11.1-8.7	10.2-8.2	11.3-8.2
Price Range	$29\frac{3}{8}$-$24\frac{3}{4}$	$28\frac{1}{2}$-$23\frac{3}{4}$	$26\frac{3}{8}$-20	$21\frac{5}{8}$-$17\frac{3}{4}$	$21\frac{3}{8}$-$16\frac{3}{4}$	$18\frac{5}{8}$-15	$19\frac{1}{4}$-14

Statistics are as originally reported.

OFFICERS:
R.A. Abdoo, Chmn., Pres. & C.E.O.
J.H. Goetsch, V.P. & Sec.
J.G. Remmel, V.P., Treas. & C.F.O.

INCORPORATED: WI, Jun., 1981

PRINCIPAL OFFICE: 231 West Michigan Street P.O. Box 2949, Milwaukee, WI 53201

TELEPHONE NUMBER: (414) 221-2100

NO. OF EMPLOYEES: 5,849

ANNUAL MEETING: In May

SHAREHOLDERS: 84,058

INSTITUTIONAL HOLDINGS:
No. of Institutions: 280
Shares Held: 32,528,729

REGISTRAR(S): First Chicago Trust Co. of New York, New York, NY 10008

TRANSFER AGENT(S): First Chicago Trust Co. of New York, New York, NY 10008
At Company's Office

NYS SYMBOL WPS
Rec. Pr. 28⅝

WISCONSIN PUBLIC SERVICE CORP.

YIELD 6.2%
P/E RATIO 11.6

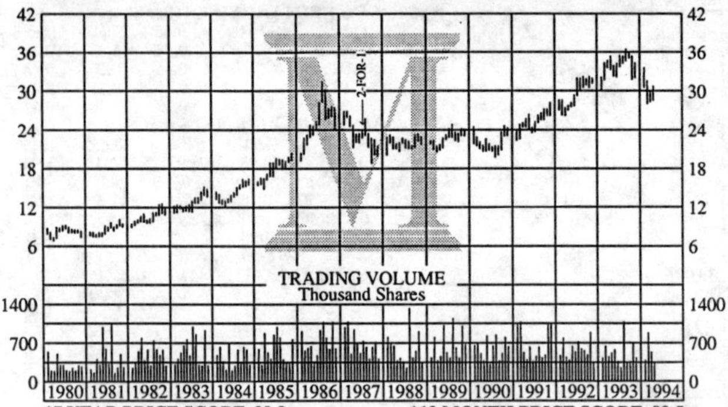

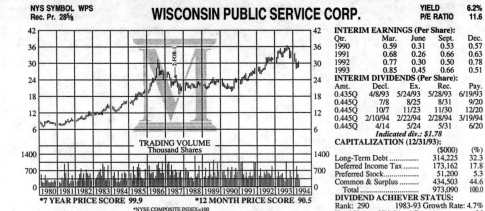

***7 YEAR PRICE SCORE 99.9** ***12 MONTH PRICE SCORE 90.5**

*NYSE COMPOSITE INDEX=100

INTERIM EARNINGS (Per Share):

Qtr.	Mar.	June	Sept.	Dec.
1990	0.59	0.31	0.53	0.57
1991	0.68	0.26	0.66	0.63
1992	0.77	0.30	0.50	0.78
1993	0.85	0.45	0.66	0.51

INTERIM DIVIDENDS (Per Share):

Amt.	Decl.	Ex.	Rec.	Pay.
0.435Q	4/8/93	5/24/93	5/28/93	6/19/93
0.445Q	7/8	8/25	8/31	9/20
0.445Q	10/7	11/23	11/30	12/20
0.445Q	2/10/94	2/22/94	2/28/94	3/19/94
0.445Q	4/14	5/24	5/31	6/20

Indicated div.: $1.78

CAPITALIZATION (12/31/93):

	($000)	(%)
Long-Term Debt	314,225	32.3
Deferred Income Tax	173,162	17.8
Preferred Stock	51,200	5.3
Common & Surplus	434,503	44.6
Total	973,090	100.0

DIVIDEND ACHIEVER STATUS:
Rank: 290 1983-93 Growth Rate: 4.7%
Total Years of Dividend Growth: 35

RECENT DEVELOPMENTS: For the year ended 12/31/93, net income was $62.2 million, up 7.2% from $58.0 million in 1992. Revenues were $680.6 million, up 7.2%. Earnings for the year were up due to increased sales of electricity and natural gas coupled with decreases in fuel and purchased power costs. Kilowatthour sales of electricity rose 4.1%. Sales of natural gas totaled 347.8 million therms, up 11.2%.

PROSPECTS: The Wisconsin commission ordered a $16.1 million rate reduction for the Company, effective January 1, 1994. The reduction is based on a 11.30% return on equity compared with a 12.30% return that had been awarded a year earlier. WPS is waiting for the Wisconsin commission to decide on its proposal to build a 116-megawatt cogeneration plant that can burn coal and paper mill waste.

BUSINESS

WISCONSIN PUBLIC SERVICE CORP. supplies electricity and gas services in north-central and northeastern Wisconsin and an adjacent part of upper Michigan. Included in the service area are the cities of Green Bay, Sheboygan, Oshkosh and Wausau. The area is balanced between industry, agriculture, dairying and recreation. About 33% of electric revenues come from residential customers, 53% from commercial & industrial and 15% other. The Company purchases most of its supply of natural gas from ANR Pipeline Company and makes spot markets purchases for the remainder. WPS' primary generation mix was; 65.5% steam, 15.6% nuclear, 3.2% hydro, and 15.7% purchased and other.

BUSINESS LINE ANALYSIS

(12/31/93)	Rev(%)	Inc(%)
Electric	72.5	90.2
Gas	27.5	9.8
Total	100.0	100.0

ANNUAL EARNINGS AND DIVIDENDS PER SHARE

	1993	1992	1991	1990	1989	1988	1987
Earnings Per Share	**2.47**	**2.35**	**2.23**	**2.00**	**1.98**	**2.28**	**2.11**
Dividends Per Share	**1.76**	**1.72**	**1.68**	**1.64**	**1.60**	**1.56**	**[1] 1.52**
Dividend Payout %	**71.3**	**73.2**	**75.3**	**82.0**	**80.8**	**68.4**	**72.0**

[1] 2-for-1 stk. split, 7/87.

ANNUAL FINANCIAL DATA

	1993	1992	1991	1990	1989	1988	1987
RECORD OF EARNINGS (IN MILLIONS):							
Total Operating Revenues	680.6	634.8	623.5	589.0	585.8	604.3	580.5
Depreciation	60.6	58.6	55.7	55.4	53.1	50.5	...
Maintenance	51.6	46.4	48.2	44.3	43.4	43.4	35.1
Income Taxes	27.7	23.1	22.0	20.8	21.0	26.6	28.6
Operating Income	83.7	79.1	75.0	70.8	70.3	77.2	73.9
Total Interest Expense	25.8	26.6	24.8	24.9	23.8	23.0	20.7
Net Income	62.2	58.0	54.2	49.0	49.1	56.4	52.8
Aver. Shs. Outstg. (000)	23,888	23,350	22,889	22,889	23,087	23,201	23,201
BALANCE SHEET (IN MILLIONS):							
Gross Plant	1,644.9	1,595.5	1,506.2	1,568.7	1,513.0	1,448.0	1,381.0
Accumulated Depreciation	801.1	748.4	695.6	759.2	834.8	779.8	724.6
Net Utility Plant	843.9	847.1	810.6	809.5	678.3	668.3	656.5
Long-term Debt	314.2	321.5	332.9	273.3	255.3	256.3	254.9
Net Stockholders' Equity	485.7	464.4	420.5	423.3	425.0	424.5	414.9
Total Assets	1,198.8	1,145.6	1,073.5	1,009.2	877.0	843.4	824.6
Year End Shs Outstg (000)	23,897	23,846	22,889	22,889	22,889	23,201	23,201
STATISTICAL RECORD:							
Book Value Per Share	18.18	17.33	16.13	16.26	16.30	16.00	15.52
Op. Inc/Net Pl %	9.9	9.3	9.3	8.7	10.4	11.6	11.3
Dep/Gr. Pl %	3.7	3.7	3.7	3.5	3.5	3.5	4.1
Accum. Dep/Gr. Pl %	48.7	46.9	46.2	47.8	55.2	53.8	51.8
Return on Equity %	12.8	12.5	12.9	11.6	11.6	13.4	12.8
Average Yield %	5.3	5.9	6.7	7.4	7.1	7.2	6.6
P/E Ratio	14.8-12.2	13.7-11.1	12.7-10.0	12.3-9.9	12.6-10.4	10.3-8.8	12.7-8.9
Price Range	36½-30⅛	32¼-26⅛	28¼-22¼	24⅝-19¾	24⅞-20½	23⅜-20	26⅞-18⅞

Statistics are as originally reported.

OFFICERS:
D.A. Bollom, Pres. & C.E.O.
D.P. Bittner, Sr. V.P.-Fin.
R.H. Knuth, Asst. V.P. & Sec.
R.G. Baeten, Treasurer

INCORPORATED: WI, Jul., 1883

PRINCIPAL OFFICE: 700 N. Adams St. P.O. Box 19001, Green Bay, WI 54307-9001

TELEPHONE NUMBER: (414) 433-1445
FAX: (414) 433-1526
NO. OF EMPLOYEES: 2,603
ANNUAL MEETING: In May
SHAREHOLDERS: 25,240 common; 3,577, pfd.
INSTITUTIONAL HOLDINGS:
No. of Institutions: 139
Shares Held: 6,112,499

REGISTRAR(S): First Wisconsin Trust Co., Milwaukee, WI

TRANSFER AGENT(S): First Wisconsin Trust Co., Milwaukee, WI

NYS SYMBOL WIT
Rec. Pr. 28⅛

WITCO CORP.

YIELD 3.6%
P/E RATIO 58.6

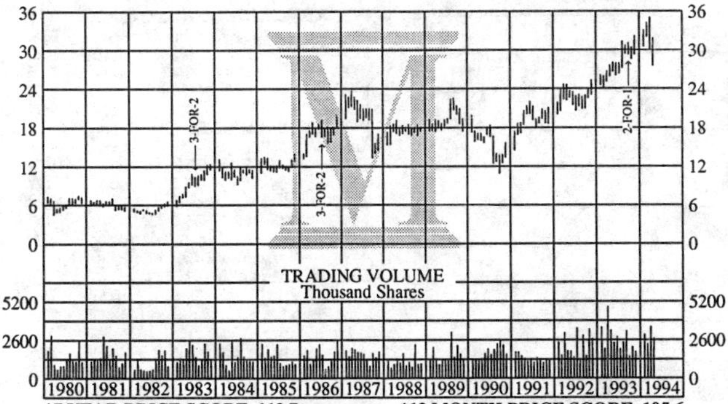

***7 YEAR PRICE SCORE 112.7** ***12 MONTH PRICE SCORE 105.6**

*NYSE COMPOSITE INDEX=100

INTERIM EARNINGS (Per Share):

Qtr.	Mar.	June	Sept.	Dec.
1990	0.32	0.49	0.43	0.25
1991	0.37	0.35	0.46	0.43
1992	0.41	0.39	0.41	d0.02
1993	0.39	0.29	0.27	d0.47

INTERIM DIVIDENDS (Per Share):

Amt.	Decl.	Ex.	Rec.	Pay.
0.46Q	6/9/93	6/14/93	6/18/93	7/1/93
0.50Q	9/2	9/10	9/16	10/5
100%	9/2	10/6	9/16	10/5
0.25Q	12/2	12/10	12/16	1/4/94
0.25Q	3/1/94	3/4/94	3/10/94	4/5

Indicated div.: $1.00

CAPITALIZATION (12/31/93):

	($000)	(%)
Long-Term Debt	496,266	41.0
Preferred Stock	9	0.0
Common & Surplus	713,406	59.0
Total	1,209,681	100.0

DIVIDEND ACHIEVER STATUS:
Rank: 208 1983-93 Growth Rate: 8.4%
Total Years of Dividend Growth: 21

RECENT DEVELOPMENTS: For the quarter ended 12/31/93 a net loss of $27.7 million was recorded compared with a net loss of $1.9 million in the corresponding 1992 quarter. Results included $60.1 million in charges for provisions for environmental remediation and compliance, disposition of certain assets, workforce reduction and other matters. Results also included a $5.7 million gain from the sale of assets. For 1993, net income was $19.8 million versus $53.9 million in 1992.

PROSPECTS: The consolidation and restructuring of some operations including relocating key management to New York has improved the focus of The Company. Improved efficiencies and tight control over costs should continue to result in better performance for engineered materials. The chemical segment is taking advantage of its enhanced and expanded product lines and economies of scale afforded by the acquisition of the natural substances and industrial chemicals divisions of Schering AG Germany.

BUSINESS

WITCO CORP. is a manufacturer of specialty chemical and petroleum products and engineered materials with 65 plant sites around the world. Specialty chemicals include organic chemicals, epoxy plasticizers and stabilizers, all raw materials for the plastics industry, detergent products, and mining and distribution of diatomaceous earth. Specialty petroleum products include white oils, petrolatums and petroleum sulfonates. Two refineries primarily produce lubricating oils sold under private label brands as well as under the Kendall and Amalie names.

BUSINESS LINE ANALYSIS

(12/31/93)	Rev(%)	Inc(%)
Chemical	57.1	94.5
Petroleum	34.6	13.2
Diversified products	8.3	(7.7)
Total	100.0	100.0

ANNUAL EARNINGS AND DIVIDENDS PER SHARE

	1993	1992	1991	1990	1989	1988	1987
Earnings Per Share	**0.46**	**1.19**	**1.61**	**1.48**	**0.80**	**[3] 1.53**	**1.36**
Dividends Per Share	**[1] 0.94**	**[2] 0.92**	**0.89**	**0.86**	**0.805**	**0.695**	**0.58**
Dividend Payout %	**N.M.**	**77.3**	**55.5**	**58.3**	**N.M.**	**45.6**	**42.6**

[1] 2-for-1 stk split,10/06/93 [2] Bef acctg chge [3] Before acctg. chg.

ANNUAL FINANCIAL DATA

	1993	1992	1991	1990	1989	1988	1987
RECORD OF EARNINGS (IN MILLIONS):							
Total Revenues	2,151.2	1,738.2	1,641.1	1,650.9	1,609.0	1,590.9	1,440.6
Costs and Expenses	1,879.9	1,545.8	1,449.5	1,477.6	1,433.3	1,410.2	1,274.8
Depreciation & Amort	102.5	76.2	67.6	60.1	52.7	48.8	53.7
Operating Profit	168.9	116.2	123.9	113.2	123.1	131.9	115.9
Inc Bef Fed & Fgn Income Taxes	33.3	82.1	109.8	105.8	53.4	115.5	100.2
Fed & Foreign Inc Taxes	13.6	28.2	36.3	37.9	18.4	43.9	36.9
Net Income	19.8	[1] 53.9	73.5	68.0	35.0	[2] 71.6	63.3
Aver. Shs. Outstg. (000)	54,866	49,801	49,212	49,702	50,674	50,498	49,478
[1] Before acctg. change dr$14,690,000. [2] Before acctg. change cr$20,289,000.							
BALANCE SHEET (IN MILLIONS):							
Cash and Cash Equivalents	183.1	134.4	139.3	116.4	213.4	194.4	227.2
Accts & Notes Receiv, Net	340.9	329.2	250.2	261.4	245.4	251.2	228.6
Inventories	227.5	249.7	162.8	166.5	155.0	156.4	151.3
Gross Property	1,318.1	1,287.9	991.9	964.9	864.2	823.3	758.4
Accumulated Depreciation	621.7	566.7	517.2	493.8	447.0	422.3	383.7
Long-Term Debt	496.3	173.1	179.1	230.2	235.5	240.7	242.6
Net Stockholders' Equity	713.4	614.3	625.7	587.5	571.6	578.3	513.6
Total Assets	1,839.0	1,811.8	1,198.3	1,178.9	1,139.3	1,114.6	1,056.3
Total Current Assets	792.6	747.3	576.8	562.9	635.9	635.0	620.2
Total Current Liabilities	341.3	769.0	255.9	203.8	179.7	195.8	202.9
Net Working Capital	451.2	d21.6	320.9	359.1	456.2	439.3	417.3
Year End Shs Outstg (000)	50,500	44,456	43,554	43,304	45,054	44,812	44,692
STATISTICAL RECORD:							
Operating Profit Margin %	7.8	6.7	7.6	6.9	7.6	8.3	8.0
Book Value Per Share	9.83	8.20	12.77	11.88	12.29	12.50	11.07
Return on Equity %	2.8	8.8	11.7	11.6	6.1	12.4	12.3
Return on Assets %	1.1	3.0	6.1	5.8	3.1	6.4	6.0
Average Yield %	3.3	4.1	4.9	5.6	4.0	4.0	3.1
P/E Ratio	70.1-52.2	21.3-16.8	13.7-9.0	13.6-7.4	28.3-21.7	12.7-10.1	17.5-9.8
Price Range	32¼-24	25⅜-20	22-14½	20-10⅞	22⅝-17⅜	19¼-15⅝	23¾-13⅜

Statistics are as originally reported.

OFFICERS:
W.R. Toller, Chmn. & C.E.O.
M.D. Fullwood, Exec. V.P. & C.F.O.
D. McCoy, V.P., Sec. & Couns.
J.M. Rutledge, V.P. & Treas.

INCORPORATED: DE, Jun., 1958

PRINCIPAL OFFICE: 520 Madison Ave., New York, NY 10022-4236

TELEPHONE NUMBER: (212) 605-3800

FAX: (212) 605-3660

NO. OF EMPLOYEES: 1,110

ANNUAL MEETING: In April

SHAREHOLDERS: 109 pfd.; 5,097 com.

INSTITUTIONAL HOLDINGS:
No. of Institutions: 169
Shares Held: 15,516,087

REGISTRAR(S): First Chicago Trust Co. of New York, New York, NY 10008

TRANSFER AGENT(S): First Chicago Trust Co. of New York, New York, NY 10008

NYS SYMBOL WMX
Rec. Pr. 29

WMX TECHNOLOGIES INC.

YIELD 2.1%
P/E RATIO 30.9

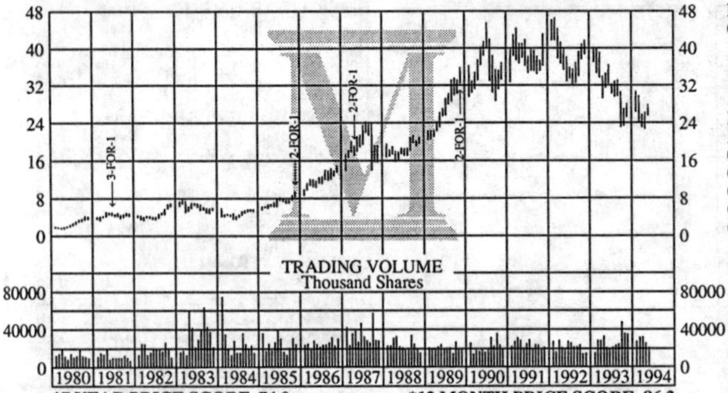
48
40
32
24
16
8
0
3-FOR-1
2-FOR-1
2-FOR-1
2-FOR-1
TRADING VOLUME
Thousand Shares
80000
40000
0
1980 1981 1982 1983 1984 1985 1986 1987 1988 1989 1990 1991 1992 1993 1994

*7 YEAR PRICE SCORE 74.0 *12 MONTH PRICE SCORE 86.3

*NYSE COMPOSITE INDEX=100

INTERIM EARNINGS (Per Share):

Qtr.	Mar.	June	Sept.	Dec.
1990	0.31	0.38	0.40	0.40
1991	0.34	0.42	0.42	0.05
1992	0.39	0.66	0.44	0.37
1993	0.41	0.45	d0.26	0.34

INTERIM DIVIDENDS (Per Share):

Amt.	Decl.	Ex.	Rec.	Pay.
0.15Q	5/14/93	6/10/93	6/16/93	7/1/93
0.15Q	8/10	9/16	9/22	10/7
0.15Q	11/9	12/16	12/22	1/6/94
0.15Q	1/28/94	3/17/94	3/23/94	4/7
0.15Q	5/13	6/16	6/22	7/7

Indicated div.: $0.60

CAPITALIZATION (12/31/93):

	($000)	(%)
Long-Term Debt	6,145,584	50.7
Deferred Income Tax	475,712	3.9
Minor Int In Subsidiaries	1,348,559	11.1
Common & Surplus	4,159,452	34.3
Total	12,129,307	100.0

DIVIDEND ACHIEVER STATUS:
Rank: 11 1983-93 Growth Rate: 22.3%
Total Years of Dividend Growth: 17

RECENT DEVELOPMENTS: For the year ended 12/31/93, net income was $452.8 million, or $0.93 per share, compared with income, before cumulative effect of accounting changes, of $921.2 million, or $1.86 per share, in 1992. Revenue for the year rose 5.5% to $9.14 billion from $8.66 billion a year ago. For the quarter ended 12/31/93, net income was $162.9 million, or $0.34 per share, compared with $182.8 million, or $0.37 per share, for the same period last year. During the quarter, a new corporate management team was formed at Waste Management, Inc. and the organization was returned to its nine-group management structure. The reorganization is intended to focus the senior management on division-level operations and profitability, operating cost reductions, improved returns on capital and business growth.

BUSINESS

WMX TECHNOLOGIES, INC. provides comprehensive environmental, engineering and construction, industrial and related services through five principal subsidiaries, each of which operates in a relatively discrete portion of the environmental services industry or geographic area. Waste Management, Inc. provides integrated solid waste services and Chemical Waste Management provides hazardous waste collection, transportation, treatment and disposal services in North America. Waste Management International provides these services, as well as trash-to energy services, outside North America. Wheelabrator Technologies is involved in trash-to-energy and independent power projects, water and wastewater treatment, including biosolids management, and air quality control, primarily in North America. Rust International serves the engineering, construction, environmental and infrastructure consulting, hazardous substance remediation and on-site industrial and related services markets in the United States and a number of foreign countries.

ANNUAL EARNINGS AND DIVIDENDS PER SHARE

	1993	1992	1991	1990	1989	1988	1987
Earnings Per Share	**0.93**	**[1] 1.86**	**1.23**	**[2] 1.49**	**1.22**	**1.02**	**0.73**
Dividends Per Share	**0.56**	**0.48**	**0.40**	**0.34**	**[3] 0.27**	**0.21**	**[4] 0.17**
Dividend Payout %	**60.2**	**25.8**	**32.5**	**22.8**	**22.1**	**20.5**	**23.3**

[1] Before acctg. chges [2] Before extraord. item [3] 2-for-1 stk split, 12/89 [4] 2-for-1 stk. split, 4/87 & 12/85.

ANNUAL FINANCIAL DATA

	1993	1992	1991	1990	1989	1988	1987
RECORD OF EARNINGS (IN MILLIONS):							
Revenue	9,135.6	8,661.0	7,550.9	6,034.4	4,458.9	3,565.6	2,757.6
Costs and Expenses	8,025.1	7,213.7	6,372.3	4,818.9	3,208.4	2,455.7	1,881.3
Depreciation & Amort	796.7	714.1	592.8	501.3	394.8	301.7	232.0
Operating Income	1,016.1	1,370.2	1,117.0	1,168.0	855.7	808.3	644.4
Income Bef Income Taxes	809.2	1,398.4	1,027.9	1,173.2	850.7	746.3	584.1
Income Taxes	356.4	477.2	421.6	463.9	288.5	282.1	257.0
Net Income	452.8	850.0	606.3	[1] 709.3	562.1	464.2	327.1
Aver. Shs. Outstg. (000)	485,374	493,948	493,167	476,580	459,727	453,710	449,146
[1] Before extraord. item dr$24,547,000.							
BALANCE SHEET (IN MILLIONS):							
Cash and Cash Equivalents	126.4	68.1	222.1	232.7	106.8	54.1	20.3
Receivables, Net	2,111.1	1,971.0	1,558.7	1,249.6	745.9	587.9	424.4
Inventories	148.0	126.6	114.5	105.9	58.4	54.5	56.0
Gross Property	11,804.9	10,382.7	8,846.7	7,454.4	4,931.1	3,685.9	2,731.2
Accumulated Depreciation	3,035.4	2,624.5	2,147.2	1,737.4	1,272.0	991.2	767.6
Long-Term Debt	6,145.6	4,312.5	3,783.0	3,139.6	1,503.8	1,270.3	467.5
Net Stockholders' Equity	4,159.5	4,319.6	4,133.1	3,673.0	2,738.0	2,179.2	1,885.3
Total Assets	16,264.5	14,114.2	12,572.3	10,518.2	6,405.2	4,878.5	3,351.2
Total Current Assets	2,777.5	2,508.4	2,144.6	1,904.8	1,086.1	826.5	598.5
Total Current Liabilities	2,677.6	2,379.6	2,114.0	1,916.0	1,242.2	744.6	590.3
Net Working Capital	100.0	128.8	30.6	d11.1	d156.1	81.9	8.2
Year End Shs Outstg (000)	483,453	490,177	493,621	488,665	465,782	453,200	426,344
STATISTICAL RECORD:							
Operating Profit Margin %	11.1	15.8	14.8	19.4	19.2	22.7	23.4
Book Value Per Share	1.44	3.14	3.30	3.70	3.72	2.96	2.91
Return on Equity %	10.9	21.3	14.7	19.3	20.5	21.3	17.3
Return on Assets %	2.3	6.5	4.8	6.7	8.8	9.5	9.8
Average Yield %	1.8	1.2	1.0	0.9	1.0	1.1	0.9
P/E Ratio	43.5-24.7	25.1-17.2	36.1-26.5	30.5-19.2	29.4-16.7	21.0-15.4	33.2-19.0
Price Range	40½-23	46⅝-32	44⅜-32⅝	45½-28⅝	35⅞-20⅜	21⅜-15¾	24¼-13⅞

Statistics are as originally reported.

OFFICERS:
D.L. Buntrock, Chmn. & C.E.O.
P.B. Rooney, Pres. & C.O.O.
J.E. Koenig, Sr. V.P., C.F.O. & Treas.
H.A. Getz, V.P., Sec. & Gen. Couns.

INCORPORATED: DE, Sep., 1968

PRINCIPAL OFFICE: 3003 Butterfield Rd., Oak Brook, IL 60521

TELEPHONE NUMBER: (708) 572-8800

FAX: (708) 572-3094

NO. OF EMPLOYEES: 33,411 (approx.)

ANNUAL MEETING: In May

SHAREHOLDERS: 71,200 (approx.)

INSTITUTIONAL HOLDINGS:
No. of Institutions: 959
Shares Held: 262,308,363

REGISTRAR(S): Harris Trust and Savings Bank, Chicago, IL 60606

TRANSFER AGENT(S): Harris Trust and Savings Bank, Chicago, IL 60606

WPL HOLDINGS, INC.

YIELD 6.7%
P/E RATIO 13.6

7 YEAR PRICE SCORE 95.6   **12 MONTH PRICE SCORE 91.6**
*NYSE COMPOSITE INDEX=100

INTERIM EARNINGS (Per Share):

Qtr.	Mar.	June	Sept.	Dec.
1990	0.74	0.34	0.67	0.48
1991	0.71	0.39	0.67	0.67
1992	0.69	0.26	0.45	0.71
1993	0.71	0.24	0.44	0.73

INTERIM DIVIDENDS (Per Share):

Amt.	Decl.	Ex.	Rec.	Pay.
0.475Q	4/14/93	4/26/93	4/30/93	5/15/93
0.475Q	7/15	7/26	7/30	8/14
0.475Q	10/13	10/25	10/29	11/15
0.48Q	1/19/94	1/25/94	1/31/94	2/15/94
0.48Q	4/15	4/25	4/29	5/14

Indicated div.: $1.92

CAPITALIZATION (12/31/93):

	($000)	(%)
Long-Term Debt	425,105	32.1
Deferred Income Tax	255,528	19.3
Pfd Stk Without Mand Redemption	59,963	4.5
Common & Surplus	582,966	44.1
Total	1,323,562	100.0

DIVIDEND ACHIEVER STATUS:

Rank: 286   1983-93 Growth Rate: 4.9%
Total Years of Dividend Growth: 21

RECENT DEVELOPMENTS:

For the year ended 12/31/93, net income increased 7.8% to $62.5 million from $58.0 million in 1992. Revenues were $773.1 million, up 14.8%. Results benefited from warmer summer weather and lower electric fuel costs. The warmer summer weather resulted in a 5% increase in residential kilowatthour sales. Colder winter weather increased gas sales 5% for both residential and commercial customers.

PROSPECTS:

The Public Service Commission of Wisconsin approved overall rate increases for all customer classes of $15.6 million for electric; $1.8 million for natural gas; $20,000 for Ripon, WI, water; and $240,000 for Beloit water. The PSC rejected WPL's rate-freeze proposal and ordered a reduction in the Company's return on equity to 11.6% from 12.4%. The new retail rates will remain effective until year-end 1994.

BUSINESS

WPL HOLDINGS is a diversified holding company for Wisconsin Power and Light, an electric energy utility, and Heartland Development, a non-utility business dealing with telecommunications and real estate development. Wisconsin Power and Light provides electric energy, natural gas and water to 376,600 customers in a 16,000-square-mile area in south-central Wisconsin. WP&L's generating mix at its major power plants include coal, nuclear and hydroelectric power. Heartland Development is an unregulated, non-utility business engaged in three major areas: environmental consulting and engineering, affordable housing and energy technology.

REVENUES

(12/31/93)	($000)	(%)
Electric	503,187	65.1
Gas	138,384	17.9
Other	131,486	17.0
Total	773,057	100.0

ANNUAL EARNINGS AND DIVIDENDS PER SHARE

	1993	1992	1991	1990	1989	1988	1987
Earnings Per Share	2.11	2.11	2.43	2.23	1.93	2.18	2.08
Dividends Per Share	1.90	1.86	1.80	1.74	1.68	① 1.62	1.54
Dividend Payout %	90.1	88.2	74.1	78.0	87.0	74.3	74.2

① 2-for-1 stk split, 9/88.

ANNUAL FINANCIAL DATA

RECORD OF EARNINGS (IN MILLIONS):

Total Operating Revenues	773.1	651.7	648.8	618.5	604.8	600.9	549.4
Depreciation	69.1	59.5	53.0	55.3	54.6	52.3	...
Maintenance	44.8	45.1	42.9	41.7	40.6	39.8	36.3
Income Taxes	25.1	22.6	31.8	28.5	26.9	31.2	24.6
Operating Income	126.2	116.2	131.0	126.3	116.2	120.9	88.0
Total Interest Expense	37.0	37.6	34.8	32.1	29.3	29.3	29.1
Net Income	62.5	57.0	64.9	59.5	51.5	57.9	58.8
Aver. Shs. Outstg. (000)	29,681	27,043	26,730	26,663	26,663	26,528	26,474

BALANCE SHEET (IN MILLIONS):

Gross Plant	2,119.0	1,968.3	1,819.6	1,694.3	1,633.1	1,553.1	1,465.5
Accumulated Depreciation	779.8	728.4	681.0	640.5	739.6	695.7	644.3
Prop, Plant & Equip, Net	1,339.1	1,239.9	1,138.5	1,053.8	893.5	857.4	821.2
Long-term Debt	425.1	417.8	367.5	360.2	321.2	323.2	322.8
Net Stockholders' Equity	642.9	540.9	517.7	497.0	483.9	477.3	458.1
Total Assets	1,761.9	1,556.9	1,376.3	1,251.7	1,047.4	1,026.2	996.0
Year End Shs Outstg (000)	30,439	27,313	26,785	26,663	26,663	26,663	26,474

STATISTICAL RECORD:

Book Value Per Share	19.15	17.61	17.09	16.39	15.90	15.65	15.04
Op. Inc/Net Pl %	9.4	9.4	11.5	12.0	13.0	14.1	10.7
Dep/Gr. Pl %	3.3	3.0	2.9	3.3	3.3	3.4	4.0
Accum. Dep/Gr. Pl %	36.8	37.0	37.4	37.8	45.3	44.8	44.0
Return on Equity %	9.7	10.5	12.5	12.0	10.6	12.1	12.8
Average Yield %	5.6	5.6	6.5	7.7	7.2	7.2	6.3
P/E Ratio	17.4-14.8	17.2-14.0	13.5-9.3	11.3-9.0	12.7-11.3	11.0-9.7	13.2-10.2
Price Range	36¾-31¼	36⅜-29⅝	32¾-22⅝	25¼-20	24½-21⅞	23⅞-21¼	27⅜-21¼

Statistics are as originally reported.

OFFICERS:

E.B. Davis, Jr., Pres. & C.E.O.
E.M. Gleason, V.P., Treas. & Sec.

INCORPORATED: WI, Apr., 1981

PRINCIPAL OFFICE: 222 West Washington Ave., Madison, WI 53703

TELEPHONE NUMBER: (608) 252-3311

NO. OF EMPLOYEES: 4,064

ANNUAL MEETING: In May

SHAREHOLDERS: 38,626 (approx.)

INSTITUTIONAL HOLDINGS:
No. of Institutions: 108
Shares Held: 4,763,972

REGISTRAR(S): At Company's Office

TRANSFER AGENT(S): At Company's Office

WRIGLEY (WM.) JR. CO.

YIELD 1.0%
P/E RATIO 33.3

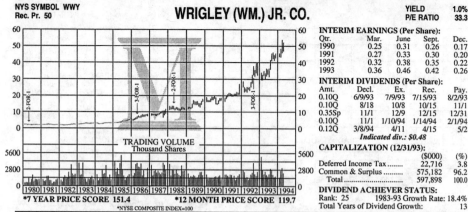

TRADING VOLUME
Thousand Shares

| | 1980 | 1981 | 1982 | 1983 | 1984 | 1985 | 1986 | 1987 | 1988 | 1989 | 1990 | 1991 | 1992 | 1993 | 1994 |

*7 YEAR PRICE SCORE 151.4   *12 MONTH PRICE SCORE 119.7
*NYSE COMPOSITE INDEX=100

INTERIM EARNINGS (Per Share):

Qtr.	Mar.	June	Sept.	Dec.
1990	0.25	0.31	0.26	0.17
1991	0.27	0.33	0.30	0.20
1992	0.32	0.38	0.35	0.22
1993	0.36	0.46	0.42	0.26

INTERIM DIVIDENDS (Per Share):

Amt.	Decl.	Ex.	Rec.	Pay.
0.10Q	6/9/93	7/9/93	7/15/93	8/2/93
0.10Q	8/18	10/8	10/15	11/1
0.35Sp	11/1	12/9	12/15	12/31
0.10Q	11/1	1/10/94	1/14/94	2/1/94
0.12Q	3/8/94	4/11	4/15	5/2

Indicated div.: $0.48

CAPITALIZATION (12/31/93):

	($000)	(%)
Deferred Income Tax	22,716	3.8
Common & Surplus	575,182	96.2
Total	597,898	100.0

DIVIDEND ACHIEVER STATUS:
Rank: 25   1983-93 Growth Rate: 18.4%
Total Years of Dividend Growth: 13

RECENT DEVELOPMENTS: Net income for the year ended 12/31/93 was $174.9 million, up 17.7% last year. Earnings per share increased to $1.50 from $1.27. Prior-year's results were before a $7.3 million accounting change. Total sales increased 11.0% to $1.43 billion as a result of selected price increases and higher worldwide volume. As a percentage of sales, SG&A expenses declined to 38.0% from 38.5%. For the fourth quarter, net income was $29.9 million and sales increased to $349.5 million.

PROSPECTS: WWY will continue its aggressive marketing and brand support programs. The Company is continuing promoting chewing gum as an alternative to cigarettes. In Europe, sugarfree brands should add momentum to volume growth in France and England. The opening of markets in the former East Germany offers potential for sales growth. In the Pacific Rim, the Company will seek to build businesses in China when a new facility there opens in the near term.

BUSINESS

WM. WRIGLEY JR. CO. is the world's largest chewing gum producer. Wrigley brands are produced in 12 factories around the world and sold in over 100 countries. Main brands are Wrigley's Spearmint, Doublemint, Juicy Fruit, Big Red, Extra, and Freedent plus Hubba Bubba bubble gum. All other businesses account for less than 10% of combined revenues, operating profit and assets. Wrigley operates plants in Chicago, Ill., Santa Cruz, Calif. and Gainesville, Ga., plus others in Europe, Asia, Africa and Australia. U.S. wholly-owned subsidiaries are Amurol Products Co., Four-Ten Corp., L.A. Dreyfus Co. and Northwestern Flavors, Inc. Wrigley has also expanded distribution into Hungary, and Yugoslavia, where it also has wholly-owned subsidiaries.

BUSINESS LINE ANALYSIS

(12/31/93)	Rev(%)	Inc(%)
United States	55.6	55.8
Europe	30.8	33.1
Other	13.6	11.1
Total	100.0	100.0

ANNUAL EARNINGS AND DIVIDENDS PER SHARE

	1993	1992	1991	1990	1989	1988	1987
Earnings Per Share	1.50	① 0.42	1.09	1.00	0.90	0.73	0.56
Dividends Per Share	0.75	② 0.62	0.55	0.493	0.453	③ 0.363	0.283
Dividend Payout %	50.0	N.M.	50.3	49.5	50.0	50.0	50.4

① Before acctg. chg.   ② 3-for-1 stk split,09/16/92   ③ 2-for-1 stk. split, 4/88 & 4/86.

ANNUAL FINANCIAL DATA

RECORD OF EARNINGS (IN MILLIONS):

	1993	1992	1991	1990	1989	1988	1987
Total Revenues	1,440.4	1,301.3	1,159.8	1,123.5	1,010.7	902.0	788.9
Costs and Expenses	1,125.5	1,038.0	921.7	907.3	814.8	737.5	644.3
Depreciation	34.6	29.8	28.7	26.9	24.6	23.2	21.0
Operating Profit	823.3	728.8	652.0	614.6	558.9	509.5	450.8
Earn Bef Income Taxes	278.8	232.3	208.0	188.3	170.4	140.7	123.0
Income Taxes	103.9	83.7	79.4	70.9	64.3	53.5	52.9
Net Income	174.9	① 148.6	128.7	117.4	106.1	87.2	70.1
Aver. Shs. Outstg. (000)	116,511	117,055	117,517	117,743	118,035	120,309	125,004

① Before acctg. change dr$7,278,000.

BALANCE SHEET (IN MILLIONS):

Cash and Cash Equivalents	189.8	182.5	144.9	114.2	108.7	114.7	99.5
Accounts Receivable	118.2	95.9	92.5	85.9	76.8	60.7	60.7
Inventories	176.8	155.8	155.5	147.8	122.4	93.4	81.8
Gross Property	550.9	513.4	486.5	457.1	416.8	387.8	370.7
Accumulated Depreciation	311.0	291.3	285.1	268.2	244.9	232.6	219.2
Net Stockholders' Equity	575.2	498.9	463.4	401.4	343.0	308.5	289.0
Total Assets	815.3	711.4	625.1	563.7	498.6	440.4	407.4
Total Current Assets	502.3	448.6	403.4	357.0	307.9	268.8	242.0
Total Current Liabilities	159.2	149.5	127.3	127.3	147.9	125.2	111.2
Net Working Capital	343.1	299.1	276.0	229.7	160.0	143.7	130.8
Year End Shs Outstg (000)	116,400	116,834	117,418	117,507	117,876	119,196	120,792

STATISTICAL RECORD:

Operating Profit Margin %	19.5	17.9	18.1	16.9	16.9	15.7	15.7
Book Value Per Share	4.94	4.27	3.95	3.42	2.91	2.59	2.39
Return on Equity %	30.4	29.8	27.8	29.2	30.9	28.3	24.3
Return on Assets %	21.5	20.9	20.6	20.8	21.3	19.8	17.2
Average Yield %	2.0	2.0	2.5	2.9	3.0	3.0	3.1
P/E Ratio	30.8-19.7	31.4-17.4	24.8-15.0	19.8-14.6	19.9-13.2	18.7-14.6	21.2-11.6
Price Range	46⅛-29½	39⅞-22⅛	27-16⅜	19¾-14⅝	17⅞-11⅞	13⅝-10⅝	11⅞-6½

Statistics are as originally reported.

OFFICERS:
W. Wrigley, Pres. & C.E.O.
W.M. Piet, V.P.-Corp. Affairs & Sec.
D. Petrovich, V.P. & Treas.

INCORPORATED: DE, Oct., 1927

PRINCIPAL OFFICE: Wrigley Building 410 N. Michigan Ave., Chicago, IL 60611

TELEPHONE NUMBER: (312) 644-2121
FAX: (312) 644-7879
NO. OF EMPLOYEES: 870
ANNUAL MEETING: In March
SHAREHOLDERS: 10,037
INSTITUTIONAL HOLDINGS:
No. of Institutions: 232
Shares Held: 11,083,317

REGISTRAR(S): First Chicago Trust Co. of New York, New York, NY 10008

TRANSFER AGENT(S): First Chicago Trust Co. of New York, New York, NY 10008